# CISSP® Practice

# CISSP® Practice

## 2,250 QUESTIONS, ANSWERS, AND EXPLANATIONS FOR PASSING THE TEST

S. Rao Vallabhaneni

WILEY

John Wiley & Sons, Inc.

CISSP® Practice: 2,250 Questions, Answers, and Explanations for Passing the Test

Published by
John Wiley & Sons, Inc.
10475 Crosspoint Boulevard
Indianapolis, IN 46256
www.wiley.com

Copyright © 2011 by S. Rao Vallabhaneni

Published simultaneously in Canada

ISBN: 978-1-118-10594-8
ISBN: 978-1-118-17612-2 (ebk)
ISBN: 978-1-118-17613-9 (ebk)
ISBN: 978-1-118-17614-6 (ebk)

Manufactured in the United States of America

10 9 8 7 6 5 4 3 2 1

For general information on our other products and services please contact our Customer Care Department within the United States at (877) 762-2974, outside the United States at (317) 572-3993 or fax (317) 572-4002.

Wiley also publishes its books in a variety of electronic formats. Some content that appears in print may not be available in electronic books.

Library of Congress Control Number: 2011936911

*This book is dedicated to my parents who taught me from the beginning that education is the only thing that endures.*

# ABOUT THE AUTHOR

**S. RAO VALLABHANENI** is an educator, author, publisher, consultant, and practitioner in the business field, with more than 30 years of management and teaching experience in manufacturing, finance, accounting, auditing, and information technology. He has authored more than 60 books, mostly study guides to help students prepare for for several professional certification exams, in various business functions. He earned four master's degrees in management, accounting, industrial engineering, and chemical engineering, and holds 24 professional certifications in various business disciplines. He is a graduate of the Advanced Management Development Program at the University of Chicago's Graduate School of Business.

He is the recipient of the 2004 Joseph J. Wasserman Memorial Award for the distinguished contribution to the Information Systems Audit field, conferred by the New York Chapter of the Information Systems Audit and Control Association (ISACA). He is the first independent author and publisher in the CISSP Exam market to develop a comprehensive two-volume (Practice and Theory) reviewing products to help students prepare for the CISSP Exam in 2000. In addition to teaching undergraduate and graduate courses in business schools, he taught the Certified Information Systems Auditor (CISA) Exam and the Certified Internal Auditor (CIA) Exam review courses to prepare for these exams.

# ABOUT THE TECHNICAL EDITOR

**RONALD L. KRUTZ** is a senior information system security consultant. He has over 30 years of experience in distributed computing systems, computer architectures, real-time systems, information assurance methodologies, and information security training. He holds B.S., M.S., and Ph.D. degrees in Electrical and Computer Engineering and is the author of best-selling texts in the area of information system security. Dr. Krutz is a Certified Information Systems Security Professional (CISSP) and Information Systems Security Engineering Professional (ISSEP).

He coauthored the *CISSP Prep Guide* for John Wiley & Sons and is coauthor of the Wiley *Advanced CISSP Prep Guide*; *CISSP Prep Guide, Gold Edition*; *Security +Certification Guide*; *CISM Prep Guide*; *CISSP Prep Guide, 2nd Edition: Mastering CISSP and ISSEP*; *Network Security Bible, CISSP and CAP Prep Guide, Platinum Edition: Mastering CISSP and CAP*; *Certified Ethical Hacker (CEH) Prep Guide*; *Certified Secure Software Lifecycle Prep Guide*, *Cloud Security*, and *Web Commerce Security*.

He is also the author of *Securing SCADA Systems* and of three textbooks in the areas of microcomputer system design, computer interfacing, and computer architecture. Dr. Krutz has seven patents in the area of digital systems and has published over 40 technical papers. Dr. Krutz is a Registered Professional Engineer in Pennsylvania.

# CREDITS

# ACKNOWLEDGMENTS

**I WANT TO THANK** the following organizations and institutions for enabling me to use their publications and reports. They were valuable and authoritative resources for developing the practice questions, answers, and explanations.

➤ ISC2, Inc., for the use of its Common Body of Knowledge described in the "CISSP Candidate Information Bulletin," January 1, 2012.

➤ National Institute of Standards and Technology (NIST), U.S. Department of Commerce, Gaithersburg, Maryland, for the use of various IT-related publications (FIPS, NISTIR, SP 500 series, SP 800 series).

➤ National Communications System (NCS) and the U.S. Department of Defense (DOD) for their selected IT-related publications.

➤ U.S. Government Accountability Office (GAO), formerly known as General Accounting Office, Washington, DC, for various IT-related reports and staff studies.

➤ Office of Technology Assessment (OTA), U.S. Congress, Washington, DC, for various publications in IT security and privacy in network technology.

➤ Office of Management and Budget (OMB), Washington, DC, for selected publications in IT security and privacy.

➤ Federal Trade Commission (FTC), Washington, DC, at www.ftc.gov.

➤ Chief Information Officer (CIO) council, Washington, DC at www.cio.gov.

➤ Information Assurance Technical Framework (IATF), Release 3.1, National Security Agency (NSA), Fort Meade, Maryland, September 2002.

➤ Security Technical Implementation Guides (STIGs) by Defense Information Systems Agency (DISA) developed for the U.S. Department of Defense (DOD).

I want to thank the following individuals for helping me to improve the content, quality, and completeness of this book:

➤ Dean Bushmiller, of Austin, Texas, for grouping the author's questions and making them into scenario-based questions and answers. Dean teaches the CISSP Exam and CISM Exam review classes to prepare for the exams.

➤ Carol A. Long, executive acquisitions editor at Wiley Publishing, Inc., for publishing this book.

➤ Ronald Krutz (technical editor), Apostrophe Editing Services (copy editor) and all the people at Wiley who made this book possible.

# CISSP PRACTICE

# PREFACE

The purpose of *CISSP Practice: 2,250 Questions, Answers, and Explanations for Passing the Test* is to help the Certified Information Systems Security Professional (CISSP) examination candidates prepare for the exam by studying and practicing the sample test questions with the goal to succeed on the exam.

A total of 2,250 traditional multiple-choice (M/C) questions, answers, and explanations are presented in this book. In addition, a total of 82 scenario-based M/C questions, answers, and explanations are taken from the traditional 2,250 questions and grouped into the scenario-based format to give a flavor to the scenario questions. Traditional questions contain one stem followed by one question set with four choices of a., b., c., and d., and scenario questions contain one stem followed by several question sets with four choices of a., b., c., and d. The scenario-based questions can focus on more than one domain to test the comprehensive application of the subject matter in an integrated manner whereas the traditional questions focus on a single domain.

These 2,250 sample test practice questions are not duplicate questions and are not taken from the ISC2 or from anywhere else. The author developed these unique M/C questions for each domain based on the current CISSP Exam content specifications (see the "Description of the CISSP Examination" later in this preface). Each unique and insightful question focuses on a specific and necessary depth and breadth of the subject matter covered in the CISSP Exam.

The author sincerely believes that the more questions you practice, the better prepared you are to take the CISSP Exam with greater confidence because the real exam includes 250 questions. The total number of 2,250 questions represents nine times the number of questions tested on the exam, thus providing a great value to the CISSP Exam candidate. This value is in the form of increasing the chances to pass the CISSP Exam.

Because ISC2 did not publish the percentage-weights for ten domains, the author has assigned the following percentage-weights for each domain (for example, Domain 1 = 15%) based on what he thinks is important to the CISSP Exam candidate. These assigned weights are based on the author's assumption that all the ten domains cannot receive equal weight in the exam due to the differences in relative importance of these domains. These weights are assigned as a systematic way to distribute the 2,250 questions among the ten domains, as follows:

- ➤ Domain 1: Access Control (**15%**)
- ➤ Domain 2: Telecommunications and Network Security (**15%**)
- ➤ Domain 3: Information Security Governance and Risk Management (**10%**)
- ➤ Domain 4: Software Development Security (**10%**)
- ➤ Domain 5: Cryptography (**10%**)
- ➤ Domain 6: Security Architecture and Design (**10%**)
- ➤ Domain 7: Security Operations (**10%**)

➤ Domain 8: Business Continuity and Disaster Recovery Planning (**5%**)

➤ Domain 9: Legal, Regulations, Investigations, and Compliance (**10%**)

➤ Domain 10: Physical and Environmental Security (**5%**)

The following table presents the number of traditional questions and scenario questions for each of the ten domains.

| DOMAIN | TRADITIONAL QUESTIONS | SCENARIO QUESTIONS |
|---|---|---|
| 1 | 338 (2,250 x 15%) | 9 |
| 2 | 338 | 7 |
| 3 | 225 | 9 |
| 4 | 225 | 11 |
| 5 | 225 | 7 |
| 6 | 225 | 12 |
| 7 | 225 | 8 |
| 8 | 112 | 7 |
| 9 | 225 | 5 |
| 10 | 112 | 7 |
| **Totals** | **2,250** | **82** |

The real CISSP Exam consists of 250 M/C questions with four choices of a., b., c., and d. for each question. There can be some scenario-based questions in addition to most of traditional questions. Regardless of the type of questions on the exam, there is only one correct answer (choice). You must complete the entire CISSP Exam in one six-hour session. The scope of the CISSP Exam consists of the subject matter covered in ten domains of this book, which is in accordance with the description of the CISSP Exam (content specifications) as defined in the ISC2's "CISSP Candidate Information Bulletin" with an **effective date of January 1, 2012.** Note that these practice questions are also good for the CISSP Exam with an effective date of January 1, 2009 because we accommodated both effective dates (January 2009 and January 2012) due to their minor differences in the content specifications.

With no bias intended and for the sake of simplicity, the pronoun "he" has been used throughout the book rather than "he/she" or "she."

—S. Rao Vallabhaneni
*Chicago, Illinois*
*August 2011*

# HOW TO STUDY FOR THE CISSP EXAM

To study for the CISSP Exam, follow these guidelines:

➤ Read the official description of the CISSP Exam at the end of this section.

➤ Read the glossary terms and acronyms found in Appendixes A and B at the back of this book to become familiar with the technical terms and acronyms.

➤ Take the sample practice tests for each of the ten domains.

➤ If you score less than 75 percent for each domain, study the glossary terms again until you master the subject matter or score higher than 75 percent.

➤ Complete the scenario-based practice questions to integrate your learning and thought processes.

The types of questions a candidate can expect to see on the CISSP Exam are mostly objective and traditional multiple-choice questions and some scenario-based multiple-choice questions with only one choice as the correct answer. Answering these multiple-choice questions requires a significant amount of practice and effort.

The following tips and techniques are helpful for answering the multiple-choice questions:

➤ Stay with your first impression of the correct choice.

➤ Know the subject area or topic. Don't read too much into the question.

➤ Remember that all questions are independent of specific countries, products, practices, vendors, hardware, software, or industries.

➤ Read the last sentence of the question first, followed by all the choicesthen read the body of the question. Underline or circle the key words.

➤ Read the question twice (or read the underlined or circled key words twice) and watch for tip-off words such as *not, except, all, every, always, never, least,* or *most* that denote absolute conditions.

➤ Don't project the question into your own organizational environment, practices, policies, procedures, standards, and guidelines.

➤ Try to eliminate wrong choices quickly by striking or drawing a line through the choices or by using other ways convenient to you.

➤ When you are left with two probable choices after the process of elimination, take a big picture approach. For example, if choices a. and d. remain and choice d. could be a part of choice a., then select choice a. However, if choice d. could be a more complete answer, then select choice d.

➤ Don't spend too much time on one question. If you are not sure of an answer, move on and come back to it if time permits. The last resort is to guess the answer. There is no penalty for guessing a wrong answer.

➤ Transfer all questions to the answer sheet either after each question is answered individually or in small groups of 10 or 15 questions. Allocate sufficient time for this task because it is important. Mark the right answer in the correct circle on the answer sheet.

Remember that success on the exam depends on your education and experience, time-management skills, preparation effort and time, memory recall of the subject matter, state of mind, and decision-making skills.

# DESCRIPTION OF THE CISSP EXAMINATION

The following is the official description of the Certified Information System Security Professional (CISSP) Examination content specifications as defined in the ISC2's "CISSP Candidate Information Bulletin" with an **effective date of January 1, 2012.** The scope of the CISSP Exam consists of the following subject matter (content specifications) covered in the ten domains.

# DOMAIN 1: ACCESS CONTROL

## Overview

Access control domain covers any mechanism by which a system grants or revokes the right to access data or perform some action. The access control mechanism controls various operations a user may or may not perform.

Access controls systems include

➤ File permissions such as create, read, edit, or delete on a file server

➤ Program permissions such as the right to execute a program on an application server

➤ Data rights such as the right to retrieve or update information in a database

The candidate should fully understand access control concepts, methodologies, and implementation within centralized and decentralized environments across the enterprise's computer systems. Access control techniques and detective and corrective measures should be studied to understand the potential risks, vulnerabilities, and exposures.

## Key Areas of Knowledge

➤ Control access by applying the following concepts/methodologies/techniques.

1. Policies

2. Types of controls such as preventive, detective, and corrective

3. Techniques such as nondiscretionary, discretionary, and mandatory

4. Identification and authentication

5. Decentralized/distributed access control techniques

**6.** Authorization mechanisms

**7.** Logging and monitoring

➤ Understand access control attacks.

**1.** Threat modeling

**2.** Asset valuation

**3.** Vulnerability analysis

**4.** Access aggregation

➤ Assess effectiveness of access controls.

**1.** User entitlement

**2.** Access review and audit

➤ Identity and access provisioning life cycle such as provisioning, review, and revocation.

# DOMAIN 2: TELECOMMUNICATIONS AND NETWORK SECURITY

## Overview

The telecommunications and network security domain encompasses the structures, techniques, transport protocols, and security measures used to provide integrity, availability, confidentiality, and authentication for transmissions over private and public communications networks and media.

The candidate is expected to demonstrate an understanding of communications and network security as it relates to data communications in local-area and wide-area networks, remote access; Internet/intranet/extranet configurations, and other network equipment (such as switches, bridges, and routers), protocols (such as TCP/IP); VPNs and, techniques (such as the correct use and placement of firewalls and IDS) for preventing and detecting network based attacks.

## Key Areas of Knowledge

➤ Understand secure network architecture and design such as IP and non-IP protocols, and segmentation.

**1.** OSI and TCP/IP models

**2.** IP networking

**3.** Implications of multi-layer protocols

➤ Secure network components.

**1.** Hardware such as modems, switches, routers, and wireless access points

**2.** Transmission media such as wired, wireless, and fiber

**3.** Network access control devices such as firewalls and proxies

**4.** End-point security

➤ Establish secure communication channels such as VPN, TLS/SSL, and VLAN.

**1.** Voice such as POTS, PBX, and VoIP

**2.** Multimedia collaboration such as remote meeting technology and instant messaging

**3.** Remote access such as screen scraper, virtual application/desktop, and telecommuting

**4.** Data communications

➤ Understand network attacks such as DDoS and spoofing.

# DOMAIN 3: INFORMATION SECURITY GOVERNANCE AND RISK MANAGEMENT

## Overview

Information security governance and risk management domain entails the identification of an organization's information assets and the development, documentation, implementation, and updating of policies, standards, procedures, and guidelines that ensure confidentiality, integrity, and availability. Management tools such as data classification, risk assessment, and risk analysis are used to identify threats, classify assets, and to rate their vulnerabilities so that effective security measures and controls can be implemented.

The candidate is expected to understand the planning, organization, and roles and responsibilities of individuals in identifying and securing an organization's information assets; the development and use of policies stating management's views and position on particular topics, and the use of guidelines, standards, and procedures to support the policies; security training to make employees aware of the importance of information security, its significance, and the specific security-related requirements relative to their position; the importance of confidentiality, proprietary, and private information; third party management and service level agreements related to information security; employment agreements; employee hiring and termination practices; and risk management practices and tools to identify, rate, and reduce the risk to specific resources.

## Key Areas of Knowledge

➤ Understand and align security function to goals, mission, and objectives of the organization.

➤ Understand and apply security governance.

**1.** Organizational processes such as acquisitions, divestitures, and governance committees

**2.** Security roles and responsibilities

**3.** Legislative and regulatory compliance

**4.** Privacy requirements compliance

**5.** Control frameworks

**6.** Due care

**7.** Due diligence

➤ Understand and apply concepts of confidentiality, integrity, and availability.

➤ Develop and implement security policy.

**1.** Security policies

**2.** Standards/baselines

**3.** Procedures

**4.** Guidelines

**5.** Documentation

➤ Manage the information life cycle such as classification, categorization, and ownership.

➤ Manage third-party governance such as onsite assessment, document exchange and review, and process/poly review.

➤ Understand and apply risk management concepts.

**1.** Identify threats and vulnerabilities

**2.** Risk assessments/analysis such as qualitative, quantitative, and hybrid

**3.** Risk assignment/acceptance

**4.** Countermeasure selection

**5.** Tangible and intangible asset valuation

➤ Manage personnel security.

**1.** Employment candidate screening such as reference checks, education, and verification

**2.** Employment agreements and policies

**3.** Employee termination processes

**4.** Vendor, consultant, and contractor controls

➤ Develop and manage security education, training, and awareness.

➤ Manage the security function.

**1.** Budget

**2.** Metrics

**3.** Resources

**4.** Develop and implement information security strategies

**5.** Assess the completeness and effectiveness of the security program

# DOMAIN 4: SOFTWARE DEVELOPMENT SECURITY

## Overview

Software development security domain refers to the controls that are included within systems and applications software and the steps used in their development. Software refers to system software (operating systems) and application programs (agents, applets, software, databases, data warehouses, and knowledge-based systems). These applications may be used in distributed or centralized environments.

The candidate should fully understand the security and controls of the systems development process, system life cycle, application controls, change controls, data warehousing, data mining, knowledge-based systems, program interfaces, and concepts used to ensure data and application integrity, security, and availability.

## Key Areas of Knowledge

➤ Understand and apply security in the software development life cycle.

   **1.** Development life cycle

   **2.** Maturity models

   **3.** Operation and maintenance

   **4.** Change management

➤ Understand the environment and security controls.

   **1.** Security of the software environment

   **2.** Security issues of programming languages

   **3.** Security issues in source code such as buffer overflow, escalation of privilege, and backdoor

   **4.** Configuration management

➤ Assess the effectiveness of software security.

   **1.** Certification and accreditation such as system authorization

   **2.** Auditing and logging

   **3.** Risk analysis and mitigation

# DOMAIN 5: CRYPTOGRAPHY

## Overview

The cryptography domain addresses the principles, means, and methods of disguising information to ensure its integrity, confidentiality, and authenticity.

Procedures and protocols that meet some or all of the above criteria are known as cryptosystems. Cryptosystems are often thought to refer only to mathematical procedures and computer programs; however, they also include the regulation of human behavior, such as choosing hard-to-guess passwords, logging off unused systems, and not discussing sensitive procedures with outsiders.

The candidate is expected to know the basic concepts within cryptography; public and private key algorithms in terms of their applications and uses; algorithm construction, key distribution and management, and methods of attack; the applications, construction, use of digital signatures to provide authenticity of electronic transactions, and nonrepudiation of the parties involved; and the organization and management of the public key infrastructures (PKIs) and digital certificates distribution and management.

## Key Areas of Knowledge

➤ Understand the application and use of cryptography:

  **1.** Data at rest (e.g., Hard drive)

  **2.** Data in transit (e.g., On the wire)

➤ Understand the cryptographic life cycle such as cryptographic limitations, algorithm/protocol governance.

➤ Understand encryption concepts.

  **1.** Foundational concepts

  **2.** Symmetric cryptography

  **3.** Asymmetric cryptography

  **4.** Hybrid cryptography

  **5.** Message digests

  **6.** Hashing

➤ Understand key management processes.

   **1.** Creation/distribution

   **2.** Storage/destruction

   **3.** Recovery

   **4.** Key escrow

➤ Understand digital signatures.

➤ Understand nonrepudiation.

➤ Understand methods of cryptanalytic attacks.

   **1.** Chosen plaintext

   **2.** Social engineering for key discovery

   **3.** Brute force such as rainbow tables, specialized/scalable architecture

   **4.** Ciphertext only

   **5.** Known plaintext

   **6.** Frequency analysis

   **7.** Chosen ciphertext

   **8.** Implementation attacks

➤ Use cryptography to maintain network security.

➤ Use cryptography to maintain application security.

➤ Understand public key infrastructure (PKI).

➤ Understand certificate-related issues.

➤ Understand information-hiding alternatives such as steganography and watermarking.

# DOMAIN 6: SECURITY ARCHITECTURE AND DESIGN

## Overview

The security architecture and design domain contains the concepts, principles, structures, and standards used to design, implement, monitor, and secure operating systems, equipment, networks, applications, and those controls used to enforce various levels of confidentiality, integrity, and availability.

Information security architecture and design covers the practice of applying a comprehensive and rigorous method for describing a current and/or future structure and behavior for an organization's security processes, information security systems, personnel and organizational sub-units, so that these practices and processes align with the organization's core goals and strategic direction.

The candidate is expected to understand security models in terms of confidentiality, integrity, information flow; system models in terms of the Common Criteria (CC); technical platforms in terms of hardware, firmware, and software; and system security techniques in terms of preventative, detective, and corrective controls.

## Key Areas of Knowledge

➤ Understand the fundamental concepts of security models (e.g., confidentiality, integrity, and multilevel models).

➤ Understand the components of information systems security evaluation models.

   **1.** Product evaluation models such as Common Criteria

   **2.** Industry and international security implementation guidelines such as PCI-DSS and ISO

➤ Understand security capabilities of information systems (e.g., memory protection, virtualization, and trusted platform module).

➤ Understand the vulnerabilities of security architectures.

   **1.** Systems such as covert channels, state attacks, and emanations

   **2.** Technology and process integration such as single point of failure and service-oriented architecture (SOA)

➤ Understand software and system vulnerabilities and threats.

   **1.** Web-based vulnerabilities/threats such as XML, SAML, and OWASP

   **2.** Client-based vulnerabilities/threats such as applets

   **3.** Server-based vulnerabilities/threats such as data flow control

   **4.** Database security such as inference, aggregation, data mining, and data warehousing

   **5.** Distributed systems such as cloud computing, grid computing, and peer-to-peer computing

➤ Understand countermeasure principles such as defense-in-depth.

# DOMAIN 7: SECURITY OPERATIONS

## Overview

Security operations domain is used to identify critical information and the execution of selected measures that eliminate or reduce adversary exploitation of critical information. It includes the definition of the controls over hardware, media, and **the** operators with access privileges to any of these resources. Auditing and monitoring are the mechanisms, tools, and facilities that permit the identification of security events and subsequent actions to identify the key elements and report the pertinent information to the appropriate individual, group, or process.

The candidate is expected to know the resources that must be protected, the privileges that must be restricted, the control mechanisms available, the potential for abuse of access, the appropriate controls, and the principles of good practice.

## Key Areas of Knowledge

➤ Understand security operations concepts.

   **1.** Need-to-know/least privilege

   **2.** Separation of duties and responsibilities

   **3.** Monitor special privileges (e.g., operators and administrators)

   **4.** Job rotation

   **5.** Marking, handling, storing, and destroying of sensitive information

   **6.** Record retention

➤ Employ resource protection.

   **1.** Media management

   **2.** Asset management (e.g., equipment life cycle and software licensing)

➤ Manage incident response.

   **1.** Detection

   **2.** Response

   **3.** Reporting

   **4.** Recovery

   **5.** Remediation and review (e.g., root cause analysis)

➤ Implement preventative measures against attacks (e.g., malicious code, zero-day exploit, and denial-of-service).

➤ Implement and support patch and vulnerability management.

➤ Understand change and configuration management (e.g., versioning and base lining).

➤ Understand system resilience and fault tolerance requirements.

# DOMAIN 8: BUSINESS CONTINUITY AND DISASTER RECOVERY PLANNING

## Overview

The business continuity planning (BCP) and disaster recovery planning (DRP) domain addresses the preservation of the business in the face of major disruptions to normal business operations. BCP and

DRP involve the preparation, testing, and updating of specific actions to protect critical business processes from the effect of major systems and network failures.

Business continuity planning (BCP) helps to identify the organization's exposure to internal and external threats; synthesize hard and soft assets to provide effective prevention and recovery for the organization, and maintains competitive advantage and value system integrity. BCP counteracts interruptions to business activities and should be available to protect critical business processes from the effects of major failures or disasters. It deals with the natural and man-made events and the consequences, if not dealt with promptly and effectively.

Business impact analysis (BIA) determines the proportion of impact an individual business unit would sustain subsequent to a significant interruption of computing or telecommunication services. These impacts may be financial, in terms of monetary loss, or operational, in terms of inability to deliver.

Disaster recovery plans (DRP) contain procedures for emergency response, extended backup operation, and post-disaster recovery, should a computer installation experience a partial or total loss of computer resources and physical facilities. The primary objective of the DRP is to provide the capability to process mission-essential applications, in a degraded mode, and return to normal mode of operation within a reasonable amount of time.

The candidate is expected to know the difference between BCP and DRP; BCP in terms of project scope and planning, business impact analysis, recovery strategies, recovery plan development, and implementation. Moreover, the candidate should understand disaster recovery in terms of recovery plan development, implementation, and restoration.

## Key Areas of Knowledge

- ➤ Understand business continuity requirements by developing and documenting project scope and plan.
- ➤ Conduct business impact analysis.
  1. Identify and prioritize critical business functions
  2. Determine maximum tolerable downtime (MTD) and other criteria
  3. Assess exposure to outages such as local, regional, and global
  4. Define recovery objectives such as RTO and RPO
- ➤ Develop a recovery strategy.
  1. Implement a backup storage strategy such as offsite storage, electronic vaulting, and tape rotation
  2. Recovery site strategies such as cold site, warm site, or hot site
- ➤ Understand disaster recovery process.
  1. Response
  2. Personnel

    **3.** Communications

    **4.** Assessment

    **5.** Restoration

    **6.** Training

➤ Exercise, assess, and maintain the plan (e.g., version control and distribution).

# DOMAIN 9: LEGAL, REGULATIONS, INVESTIGATIONS, AND COMPLIANCE

## Overview

The legal, regulations, investigations, and compliance domain addresses computer crime laws and regulations. This domain includes the investigative measures and techniques used to determine if a crime has been committed, and methods to gather evidence.

A computer crime is any illegal action where the data on a computer is accessed without permission. This includes unauthorized access or alteration of data, or unlawful use of computers and services.

Incident handling provides the ability to react quickly and efficiently to malicious technical threats or incidents.

The candidate is expected to know the methods for determining whether a computer crime has been committed; the laws that would be applicable for the crime; laws prohibiting specific types of computer crime; methods to gather and preserve evidence of a computer crime; investigative methods and techniques; and ways to address compliance.

## Key Areas of Knowledge

➤ Understand legal issues that pertain to information security internationally.

    **1.** Computer crime

    **2.** Licensing and intellectual property such as copyright and trademark

    **3.** Import/export controls

    **4.** Trans-border data flow

    **5.** Privacy

➤ Understand professional ethics.

    **1.** ISC2 Code of Professional Ethics

    **2.** Support organization's Code of Ethics

➤ Understand and support investigations.

   **1.** Policy, roles, and responsibilities (e.g., rules of engagement, authorization, and scope)

   **2.** Incident handling and response

   **3.** Evidence collection and handling such as chain of custody and interviewing

   **4.** Reporting and documenting

➤ Understand forensic procedures.

   **1.** Media analysis

   **2.** Network analysis

   **3.** Software analysis

   **4.** Hardware/embedded device analysis

➤ Understand compliance requirements and procedures.

   **1.** Regulatory environment

   **2.** Audits

   **3.** Reporting

➤ Ensure security in contractual agreements and procurement processes (e.g., cloud computing, outsourcing, and vendor governance).

# DOMAIN 10: PHYSICAL AND ENVIRONMENTAL SECURITY

## Overview

The physical and environmental security domain addresses the threats, vulnerabilities, and countermeasures that can be utilized to physically protect an enterprise's resources and sensitive information. These resources include people, the facility in which they work, and the data, equipment, support systems, media, and supplies they utilize.

Physical security describes measures that are designed to deny access to unauthorized personnel (including attackers) from physically accessing a building, facility, resource, or stored information; and guidance on how to design structures to resist potentially hostile acts.

The candidate is e expected to know the elements involved in choosing a secure site, its design and configuration, and the methods for securing the facility against unauthorized access, theft of equipment and information, and the environmental and safety measures needed to protect people, the facility, and its resources.

## Key Areas of Knowledge

➤ Understand site and facility design considerations.

➤ Support the implementation and operation of perimeter security (e.g., physical access control and monitoring and audit trails/access logs).

➤ Support the implementation and operation of internal security (e.g., escort requirements/visitor control and keys and locks).

➤ Support the implementation and operation of facilities security such as technology convergence.

   **1.** Communications and server rooms

   **2.** Restricted and work area security

   **3.** Data center security

   **4.** Utilities and heating, ventilation, and air conditioning (HVAC) considerations

   **5.** Water issues such as leakage and flooding

   **6.** Fire prevention, detection, and suppression

➤ Support the protection and securing of equipment.

➤ Understand personnel privacy and safety (e.g., duress, travel, and monitoring).

# DOMAIN 1

## Access Control

1.  **For intrusion detection and prevention system capabilities, stateful protocol analysis uses which of the following?**

    1.  Blacklists
    2.  Whitelists
    3.  Threshold
    4.  Program code viewing
        a.  1 and 2
        b.  1, 2, and 3
        c.  3 only
        d.  1, 2, 3, and 4

    ***1. d.*** Stateful protocol analysis (also known as deep packet inspection) is the process of comparing predetermined profiles of generally accepted definitions of benign protocol activity for each protocol state against observed events to identify deviations. Stateful protocol analysis uses blacklists, whitelists, thresholds, and program code viewing to provide various security capabilities.

    A blacklist is a list of discrete entities, such as hosts or applications that have been previously determined to be associated with malicious activity. A whitelist is a list of discrete entities, such as hosts or applications known to be benign. Thresholds set the limits between normal and abnormal behavior of the intrusion detection and prevention systems (IDPS). Program code viewing and editing features are established to see the detection-related programming code in the IDPS.

2.  **Electronic authentication begins with which of the following?**

    a.  Token
    b.  Credential

    c.    Subscriber

    d.    Credential service provider

***2. c.*** An applicant applies to a registration authority (RA) to become a subscriber of a credential service provider (CSP) and, as a subscriber, is issued or registers a secret, called a token, and a credential (public key certificate) that binds the token to a name and other attributes that the RA has verified. The token and credential may be used in subsequent authentication events.

**3.** **In the electronic authentication process, who performs the identity proofing?**

    a.    Subscriber

    b.    Registration authority

    c.    Applicant

    d.    Credential service provider

***3. b.*** The RA performs the identity proofing after registering the applicant with the CSP. An applicant becomes a subscriber of the CSP.

**4.** **In electronic authentication, which of the following provides the authenticated information to the relying party for making access control decisions?**

    a.    Claimant/subscriber

    b.    Applicant/subscriber

    c.    Verifier/claimant

    d.    Verifier/credential service provider

***4. d.*** The relying party can use the authenticated information provided by the verifier/CSP to make access control decisions or authorization decisions. The verifier verifies that the claimant is the subscriber/applicant through an authentication protocol. The verifier passes on an assertion about the identity of the subscriber to the relying party. The verifier and the CSP may or may not belong to the same identity.

**5.** **In electronic authentication, an authenticated session is established between which of the following?**

    a.    Claimant and the relying party

    b.    Applicant and the registration authority

    c.    Subscriber and the credential service provider

    d.    Certifying authority and the registration authority

***5. a.*** An authenticated session is established between the claimant and the relying party. Sometimes the verifier is also the relying party. The other three choices are incorrect because the correct answer is based on facts.

**6.** **Under which of the following electronic authentication circumstances does the verifier need to directly communicate with the CSP to complete the authentication activity?**

    a. Use of a digital certificate

    b. A physical link between the verifier and the CSP

    c. Distributed functions for the verifier, relying party, and the CSP

    d. A logical link between the verifier and the CSP

*6. b.* The use of digital certificates represents a logical link between the verifier and the CSP rather than a physical link. In some implementations, the verifier, relying party, and the CSP functions may be distributed and separated. The verifier needs to directly communicate with the CSP only when there is a physical link between them. In other words, the verifier does not need to directly communicate with the CSP for the other three choices.

**7.** **In electronic authentication, who maintains the registration records to allow recovery of registration records?**

    a. Credential service provider

    b. Subscriber

    c. Relying party

    d. Registration authority

*7. a.* The CSP maintains registration records for each subscriber to allow recovery of registration records. Other responsibilities of the CSP include the following:

The CSP is responsible for establishing suitable policies for renewal and reissuance of tokens and credentials. During renewal, the usage or validity period of the token and credential is extended without changing the subscriber's identity or token. During reissuance, a new credential is created for a subscriber with a new identity and/or a new token.

The CSP is responsible for maintaining the revocation status of credentials and destroying the credential at the end of its life. For example, public key certificates are revoked using *certificate revocation lists* (CRLs) after the certificates are distributed. The verifier and the CSP may or may not belong to the same entity.

The CSP is responsible for mitigating threats to tokens and credentials and managing their operations. Examples of threats include disclosure, tampering, unavailability, unauthorized renewal or reissuance, delayed revocation or destruction of credentials, and token use after decommissioning.

The other three choices are incorrect because the (i) subscriber is a party who has received a credential or token from a CSP, (ii) relying party is an entity that relies upon the subscriber's credentials or verifier's assertion of an identity, and (iii) registration authority (RA) is a trusted entity that establishes and vouches for the identity of a subscriber to a CSP. The RA may be an integral part of a CSP, or it may be independent of a CSP, but it has a relationship to the CSP(s).

**8.** **Which of the following is used in the unique identification of employees and contractors?**

    a.   Personal identity verification card token

    b.   Passwords

    c.   PKI certificates

    d.   Biometrics

**8. a.** It is suggested that a *personal identity verification* (PIV) card token is used in the unique identification of employees and contractors. The PIV is a physical artifact (e.g., identity card or smart card) issued to an individual that contains stored identity credentials (e.g., photograph, cryptographic keys, or digitized fingerprint).

The other three choices are used in user authenticator management, not in user identifier management. Examples of user authenticators include passwords, tokens, cryptographic keys, *personal identification numbers* (PINs), biometrics, *public key infrastructure* (PKI) certificates, and key cards. Examples of user identifiers include internal users, external users, contractors, guests, PIV cards, passwords, tokens, and biometrics.

**9.** **In electronic authentication, which of the following produces an authenticator used in the authentication process?**

    a.   Encrypted key and password

    b.   Token and cryptographic key

    c.   Public key and verifier

    d.   Private key and claimant

**9. b.** The token may be a piece of hardware that contains a cryptographic key that produces the authenticator used in the authentication process to authenticate the claimant. The key is protected by encrypting it with a password.

The other three choices cannot produce an authenticator. A public key is the public part of an asymmetric key pair typically used to verify signatures or encrypt data. A verifier is an entity that verifies a claimant's identity. A private key is the secret part of an asymmetric key pair typically used to digitally sign or decrypt data. A claimant is a party whose identity is to be verified using an authentication protocol.

**10.** **In electronic authentication, shared secrets are based on which of the following?**

    1.   Asymmetric keys

    2.   Symmetric keys

    3.   Passwords

    4.   Public key pairs

        a.   1 only

        b.   1 or 4

    c.    2 or 3

    d.    3 or 4

**10. c.**  Shared secrets are based on either symmetric keys or passwords. The asymmetric keys are used in public key pairs. In a protocol sense, all shared secrets are similar and can be used in similar authentication protocols.

**11.**    **For electronic authentication, which of the following is *not* an example of assertions?**

    a.    Cookies

    b.    Security assertions markup language

    c.    X.509 certificates

    d.    Kerberos tickets

**11. c.**  An assertion is a statement from a verifier to a relying party that contains identity information about a subscriber. Assertions may be digitally signed objects, or they may be obtained from a trusted source by a secure protocol. X.509 certificates are examples of electronic credentials, not assertions. Cookies, *security assertions markup language* (SAML), and Kerberos tickets are examples of assertions.

**12.**    **In electronic authentication, electronic credentials are stored as data in a directory or database. Which of the following refers to when the directory or database is trusted?**

    a.    Signed credentials are stored as signed data.

    b.    Unsigned credentials are stored as unsigned data.

    c.    Signed credentials are stored as unsigned data.

    d.    Unsigned credentials are stored as signed data.

**12. b.**  Electronic credentials are digitally signed objects, in which case their integrity is verified. When the directory or database server is trusted, unsigned credentials may be stored as unsigned data.

**13.**    **In electronic authentication, electronic credentials are stored as data in a directory or database. Which of the following refers to when the directory or database is untrusted?**

    a.    Self-authenticating

    b.    Authentication to the relying party

    c.    Authentication to the verifier

    d.    Authentication to the credential service provider

**13. a.**  When electronic credentials are stored in a directory or database server, the directory or database may be an untrusted entity because the data it supplies is self-authenticated. Alternatively, the directory or database server may be a trusted entity that authenticates itself to the relying party or verifier, but not to the CSP.

**14.** **The correct flows and proper interactions between parties involved in electronic authentication include:**

    a.    Applicant ⇨ Registration Authority ⇨ Subscriber ⇨ Claimant

    b.    Registration Authority ⇨ Applicant ⇨ Claimant ⇨ Subscriber

    c.    Subscriber ⇨ Applicant ⇨ Registration Authority ⇨ Claimant

    d.    Claimant ⇨ Subscriber ⇨ Registration Authority ⇨ Applicant

*14. a.* The correct flows and proper interactions between the various parties involved in electronic authentication include the following:

➤ An individual applicant applies to a registration authority (RA) through a registration process to become a subscriber of a credential service provider (CSP)

➤ The RA identity proofs that applicant

➤ On successful identity proofing, the RA sends the CSP a registration confirmation message

➤ A secret token and a corresponding credential are established between the CSP and the new subscriber for use in subsequent authentication events

➤ The party to be authenticated is called a claimant (subscriber) and the party verifying that identity is called a verifier

The other three choices are incorrect because they do not represent the correct flows and proper interactions.

**15.** **In electronic authentication, which of the following represents the correct order of passing information about assertions?**

    a.    Subscriber ⇨ Credential Service Provider ⇨ Registration Authority

    b.    Verifier ⇨ Claimant ⇨ Relying Party

    c.    Relying Party ⇨ Claimant ⇨ Registration Authority

    d.    Verifier ⇨ Credential Service Provider ⇨ Relying Party

*15. b.* An assertion is a statement from a verifier to a relying party that contains identity information about a subscriber (i.e., claimant). These assertions are used to pass information about the claimant from the verifier to a relying party. Assertions may be digitally signed objects or they may be obtained from a trusted source by a secure protocol. When the verifier and the relying parties are separate entities, the verifier conveys the result of the authentication protocol to the relying party. The object created by the verifier to convey the result of the authentication protocol is called an assertion. The credential service provider and the registration authority are not part of the assertion process.

**16.** **From an access control viewpoint, which of the following are restricted access control models?**

1. Identity-based access control policy

2. Attribute-based access control policy

3. Bell-LaPadula access control model

4. Domain type enforcement access control model

    a. 1 and 2

    b. 2 and 3

    c. 3 and 4

    d. 1, 2, 3, and 4

*16. c.* Both the Bell-LaPadula model and domain type enforcement model uses restricted access control models because they are employed in safety-critical systems, such as military and airline systems. In a restricted model, the access control policies are expressed only once by a trusted principal and fixed for the life of the system. The identity-based and attribute-based access control policies are not based on restricted access control models but based on identities and attributes respectively.

**17.** **Regarding password guessing and cracking threats, which of the following can help mitigate such threats?**

    a. Passwords with low entropy, larger salts, and smaller stretching

    b. Passwords with high entropy, smaller salts, and smaller stretching

    c. Passwords with high entropy, larger salts, and larger stretching

    d. Passwords with low entropy, smaller salts, and larger stretching

*17. c.* Entropy in an information system is the measure of the disorder or randomness in the system. Passwords need high entropy because low entropy is more likely to be recovered through brute force attacks.

Salting is the inclusion of a random value in the password hashing process that greatly decreases the likelihood of identical passwords returning the same hash. Larger salts effectively make the use of Rainbow Tables (lookup tables) by attackers infeasible. Many operating systems implement salted password hashing mechanisms to reduce the effectiveness of password cracking.

Stretching, which is another technique to mitigate the use of rainbow tables, involves hashing each password and its salt thousands of times. Larger stretching makes the creation of rainbow tables more time-consuming, which is not good for the attacker, but good for the attacked organization. Rainbow tables are lookup tables that contain precomputed password hashes. Therefore, passwords with high entropy, larger salts, and larger stretching can mitigate password guessing and cracking attempts by attackers.

**18.** In electronic authentication using tokens, the authenticator in the general case is a function of which of the following?

    a. Token secret and salt or challenge

    b. Token secret and seed or challenge

    c. Token secret and nonce or challenge

    d. Token secret and shim or challenge

**18. c.** The authenticator is generated through the use of a token. In the trivial case, the authenticator may be the token secret itself where the token is a password. In the general case, an authenticator is generated by performing a mathematical function using the token secret and one or more optional token input values such as a nonce or challenge.

A salt is a nonsecret value used in a cryptographic process, usually to ensure that the results of computations for one instance cannot be reused by an attacker.

A seed is a starting value to generate initialization vectors. A nonce is an identifier, a value, or a number used only once. Using a nonce as a challenge is a different requirement than a random-challenging because a nonce is predictable.

A shim is a layer of host-based intrusion detection and prevention code placed between existing layers of code on a host that intercepts data and analyzes it.

**19.** In electronic authentication, using one token to gain access to a second token is called a:

    a. Single-token, multifactor scheme

    b. Single-token, single-factor scheme

    c. Multitoken, multifactor scheme

    d. Multistage authentication scheme

**19. b.** Using one token to gain access to a second token is considered a single token and a single factor scheme because all that is needed to gain access is the initial token. Therefore, when this scheme is used, the compound solution is only as strong as the token with the lowest assurance level. The other choices are incorrect because they are not applicable to the situation here.

**20.** As a part of centralized password management solutions, which of the following statements are true about password synchronization?

    1. No centralized directory

    2. No authentication server

    3. Easier to implement than single sign-on technology

    4. Less expensive than single sign-on technology

        a. 1 and 3

        b. 2 and 4

        c. 3 and 4

        d. 1, 2, 3, and 4

**20. d.** A password synchronization solution takes a password from a user and changes the passwords on other resources to be the same as that password. The user then authenticates directly to each resource using that password. There is no centralized directory or no authentication server performing authentication on behalf of the resources. The primary benefit of password synchronization is that it reduces the number of passwords that users need to remember; this may permit users to select stronger passwords and remember them more easily. Unlike *single sign-on* (SSO) technology, password synchronization does not reduce the number of times that users need to authenticate. Password synchronization solutions are typically easier, less expensive, and less secure to implement than SSO technologies.

**21.** As a part of centralized password management solutions, password synchronization becomes a single point-of-failure due to which of the following?

    a. It uses the same password for many resources.

    b. It can enable an attacker to compromise a low-security resource to gain access to a high-security resource.

    c. It uses the lowest common denominator approach to password strength.

    d. It can lead passwords to become unsynchronized.

**21. a.** All four choices are problems with password synchronization solution. Because the same password is used for many resources, the compromise of any one instance of the password compromises all the instances, therefore becoming a single point-of-failure. Password synchronization forces the use of the lowest common denominator approach to password strength, resulting in weaker passwords due to character and length constraints. Passwords can become unsynchronized when a user changes a resource password directly with that resource instead of going through the password synchronization user interface. A password could also be changed due to a resource failure that requires restoration of a backup.

**22.** RuBAC is rule-based access control; RAdAC is risk adaptive access control; UDAC is user-directed access control; MAC is mandatory access control; ABAC is attribute-based access control; RBAC is role-based access control; IBAC is identity-based access control; and PBAC is policy-based access control. From an access control viewpoint, separation of domains is achieved through which of the following?

    a. RuBAC or RAdAC

    b. UDAC or MAC

    c. ABAC or RBAC

    d. IBAC or PBAC

**22. c.** Access control policy may benefit from separating Web services into various domains or compartments. This separation can be implemented in ABAC using resource attributes or through additional roles defined in RBAC. The other three choices cannot handle separation of domains.

23. **Regarding local administrator password selection, which of the following can become a single point-of-failure?**

    a.   Using the same local root account password across systems

    b.   Using built-in root accounts

    c.   Storing local passwords on the local system

    d.   Authenticating local passwords on the local system

*23. a.* Having a common password shared among all local administrator or root accounts on all machines within a network simplifies system maintenance, but it is a widespread security weakness, becoming a single point-of-failure. If a single machine is compromised, an attacker may recover the password and use it to gain access to all other machines that use the shared password. Therefore, it is good to avoid using the same local administrator or root account passwords across many systems. The other three choices, although risky in their own way, do not yield a single point-of-failure.

24. **In electronic authentication, which of the following statements is *not* true about a multistage token scheme?**

    a.   An additional token is used for electronic transaction receipt.

    b.   Multistage scheme assurance is higher than the multitoken scheme assurance using the same set of tokens.

    c.   An additional token is used as a confirmation mechanism.

    d.   Two tokens are used in two stages to raise the assurance level.

*24. b.* In a multistage token scheme, two tokens are used in two stages, and additional tokens are used for transaction receipt and confirmation mechanism to achieve the required assurance level. The level of assurance of the combination of the two stages can be no higher than that possible through a multitoken authentication scheme using the same set of tokens.

25. **Online guessing is a threat to the tokens used for electronic authentication. Which of the following is a countermeasure to mitigate the online guessing threat?**

    a.   Use tokens that generate high entropy authenticators.

    b.   Use hardware cryptographic tokens.

    c.   Use tokens with dynamic authenticators.

    d.   Use multifactor tokens.

*25. a.* Entropy is the uncertainty of a random variable. Tokens that generate high entropy authenticators prevent online guessing of secret tokens registered to a legitimate claimant and offline cracking of tokens. The other three choices cannot prevent online guessing of tokens or passwords.

**26.** Token duplication is a threat to the tokens used for electronic authentication. Which of the following is a countermeasure to mitigate the token duplication threat?

    a.    Use tokens that generate high entropy authenticators.

    b.    Use hardware cryptographic tokens.

    c.    Use tokens with dynamic authenticators.

    d.    Use multifactor tokens.

*26. b.* In token duplication, the subscriber's token has been copied with or without the subscriber's knowledge. A countermeasure is to use hardware cryptographic tokens that are difficult to duplicate. Physical security mechanisms can also be used to protect a stolen token from duplication because they provide tamper evidence, detection, and response capabilities. The other three choices cannot handle a duplicate tokens problem.

**27.** Eavesdropping is a threat to the tokens used for electronic authentication. Which of the following is a countermeasure to mitigate the eavesdropping threat?

    a.    Use tokens that generate high entropy authenticators.

    b.    Use hardware cryptographic tokens.

    c.    Use tokens with dynamic authenticators.

    d.    Use multifactor tokens.

*27. c.* A countermeasure to mitigate the eavesdropping threat is to use tokens with dynamic authenticators where knowledge of one authenticator does not assist in deriving a subsequent authenticator. The other choices are incorrect because they cannot provide dynamic authentication.

**28.** Identifier management is applicable to which of the following accounts?

    a.    Group accounts

    b.    Local user accounts

    c.    Guest accounts

    d.    Anonymous accounts

*28. b.* All users accessing an organization's information systems must be uniquely identified and authenticated. Identifier management is applicable to local user accounts where the account is valid only on a local computer, and its identity can be traced to an individual. Identifier management is not applicable to shared information system accounts, such as group, guest, default, blank, anonymous, and nonspecific user accounts.

**29.** **Phishing or pharming is a threat to the tokens used for electronic authentication. Which of the following is a countermeasure to mitigate the phishing or pharming threat?**

    a.    Use tokens that generate high entropy authenticators.

    b.    Use hardware cryptographic tokens.

    c.    Use tokens with dynamic authenticators.

    d.    Use multifactor tokens.

*29. c.* A countermeasure to mitigate the phishing or pharming threat is to use tokens with dynamic authenticators where knowledge of one authenticator does not assist in deriving a subsequent authenticator. The other choices are incorrect because they cannot provide dynamic authentication.

Phishing is tricking individuals into disclosing sensitive personal information through deceptive computer-based means. Phishing attacks use social engineering and technical subterfuge to steal consumers' personal identity data and financial account credentials. It involves Internet fraudsters who send spam or pop-up messages to lure personal information (e.g., credit card numbers, bank account information, social security numbers, passwords, or other sensitive information) from unsuspecting victims. Pharming is misdirecting users to fraudulent websites or proxy servers, typically through DNS hijacking or poisoning.

**30.** **Theft is a threat to the tokens used for electronic authentication. Which of the following is a countermeasure to mitigate the theft threat?**

    a.    Use tokens that generate high entropy authenticators.

    b.    Use hardware cryptographic tokens.

    c.    Use tokens with dynamic authenticators.

    d.    Use multifactor tokens.

*30. d.* A countermeasure to mitigate the threat of token theft is to use multifactor tokens that need to be activated through a PIN or biometric. The other choices are incorrect because they cannot provide multifactor tokens.

**31.** **Social engineering is a threat to the tokens used for electronic authentication. Which of the following is a countermeasure to mitigate the social engineering threat?**

    a.    Use tokens that generate high entropy authenticators.

    b.    Use hardware cryptographic tokens.

    c.    Use tokens with dynamic authenticators.

    d.    Use multifactor tokens.

*31. c.* A countermeasure to mitigate the social engineering threat is to use tokens with dynamic authenticators where knowledge of one authenticator does not assist in deriving a subsequent authenticator. The other choices are incorrect because they cannot provide dynamic authentication.

**32.** **In electronic authentication, which of the following is used to verify proof-of-possession of registered devices or identifiers?**

    a.    Lookup secret token

    b.    Out-of-band token

    c.    Token lock-up feature

    d.    Physical security mechanism

*32. b.* Out-of-band tokens can be used to verify proof-of-possession of registered devices (e.g., cell phones) or identifiers (e.g., e-mail IDs). The other three choices cannot verify proof-of-possession. Lookup secret tokens can be copied. Some tokens can lock up after a number of repeated failed activation attempts. Physical security mechanisms can be used to protect a stolen token from duplication because they provide tamper evidence, detection, and response capabilities.

**33.** **In electronic authentication, which of the following are examples of weakly bound credentials?**

    1.    Unencrypted password files

    2.    Signed password files

    3.    Unsigned public key certificates

    4.    Signed public key certificates

    a.    1 only

    b.    1 and 3

    c.    1 and 4

    d.    2 and 4

*33. b.* Unencrypted password files and unsigned public key certificates are examples of weakly bound credentials. The association between the identity and the token within a weakly bound credential can be readily undone, and a new association can be readily created. For example, a password file is a weakly-bound credential because anyone who has "write" access to the password file can potentially update the association contained within the file.

**34.** **In electronic authentication, which of the following are examples of strongly bound credentials?**

    1.    Unencrypted password files

    2.    Signed password files

    3.    Unsigned public key certificates

    4.    Signed public key certificates

    a.    1 only

    b.    1 and 3

c. 1 and 4

d. 2 and 4

***34. d.*** Signed password files and signed public key certificates are examples of strongly bound credentials. The association between the identity and the token within a strongly bound credential cannot be easily undone. For example a digital signature binds the identity to the public key in a public key certificate; tampering of this signature can be easily detected through signature verification.

**35.** **In electronic authentication, which of the following can be used to derive, guess, or crack the value of the token secret or spoof the possession of the token?**

a. Private credentials

b. Public credentials

c. Paper credentials

d. Electronic credentials

***35. a.*** A private credential object links a user's identity to a representation of the token in a way that the exposure of the credential to unauthorized parties can lead to any exposure of the token secret. A private credential can be used to derive, guess, or crack the value of the token secret or spoof the possession of the token. Therefore, it is important that the contents of the private credential be kept confidential (e.g., a hashed password values).

Public credentials are shared widely, do not lead to an exposure of the token secret, and have little or no confidentiality requirements. Paper credentials are documents that attest to the identity of an individual (e.g., passports, birth certificates, and employee identity cards) and are based on written signatures, seals, special papers, and special inks. Electronic credentials bind an individual's name to a token with the use of X.509 certificates and Kerberos tickets.

**36.** **Authorization controls are a part of which of the following?**

a. Directive controls

b. Preventive controls

c. Detective controls

d. Corrective controls

***36. b.*** Authorization controls such as access control matrices and capability tests are a part of preventive controls because they block unauthorized access. Preventive controls deter security incidents from happening in the first place.

Directive controls are broad-based controls to handle security incidents, and they include management's policies, procedures, and directives. Detective controls enhance security by monitoring the effectiveness of preventive controls and by detecting security incidents where preventive controls were circumvented. Corrective controls are procedures to react to security incidents and to take remedial actions on a timely basis. Corrective controls require proper planning and preparation as they rely more on human judgment.

**37.** In electronic authentication, after a credential has been created, which of the following is responsible for maintaining the credential in storage?

    a.   Verifier

    b.   Relying party

    c.   Credential service provider

    d.   Registration authority

***37. c.*** The credential service provider (CSP) is the only one responsible for maintaining the credential in storage. The verifier and the CSP may or may not belong to the same entity. The other three choices are incorrect because they are not applicable to the situation here.

**38.** Which of the following is the correct definition of privilege management?

    a.   Privilege management = Entity attributes + Entity policies

    b.   Privilege management = Attribute management + Policy management

    c.   Privilege management = Resource attributes + Resource policies

    d.   Privilege management = Environment attributes + Environment policies

***38. b*** Privilege management is defined as a process that creates, manages, and stores the attributes and policies needed to establish criteria that can be used to decide whether an authenticated entity's request for access to some resource should be granted. Privilege management is conceptually split into two parts: attribute management and policy management. The attribute management is further defined in terms of entity attributes, resource attributes, and environment attributes. Similarly, the policy management is further defined in terms of entity policies, resource policies, and environment policies.

**39.** The extensible access control markup language (XACML) does *not* define or support which of the following?

    a.   Trust management

    b.   Privilege management

    c.   Policy language

    d.   Query language

***39. a.*** The extensible access control markup language (XACML) is a standard for managing access control policy and supports the enterprise-level privilege management. It includes a policy language and a query language. However, XACML does not define authority delegation and trust management.

**40.** For intrusion detection and prevention system (IDPS) security capabilities, which of the following prevention actions should be performed first to reduce the risk of inadvertently blocking benign activity?

    1.   Alert enabling capability.

    2.   Alert disabling capability.

3.  Sensor learning mode ability.

4.  Sensor simulation mode ability.

    a.    1 and 2

    b.    1 and 3

    c.    2 and 4

    d.    3 and 4

***40. d.*** Some intrusion detection and prevention system (IDPS) sensors have a learning mode or simulation mode that suppresses all prevention actions and instead indicates when a prevention action should have been performed. This ability enables administrators to monitor and fine-tune the configuration of the prevention capabilities before enabling prevention actions, which reduces the risk of inadvertently blocking benign activity. Alerts can be enabled or disabled later.

**41.** **In the electronic authentication process, which of the following is weakly resistant to man-in-the-middle (MitM) attacks?**

    a.    Account lockout mechanism

    b.    Random data

    c.    Sending a password over server authenticated TLS

    d.    Nonce

***41. c.*** A protocol is said to have weak resistance to MitM attacks if it provides a mechanism for the claimant to determine whether he is interacting with the real verifier, but still leaves the opportunity for the nonvigilant claimant to reveal a token authenticator to an unauthorized party that can be used to masquerade as the claimant to the real verifier. For example, sending a password over server authenticated transport layer security (TLS) is weakly resistant to MitM attacks. The browser enables the claimant to verify the identity of the verifier; however, if the claimant is not sufficiently vigilant, the password will be revealed to an unauthorized party who can abuse the information. The other three choices do not deal with MitM attacks, but they can enhance the overall electronic authentication process.

An account lockout mechanism is implemented on the verifier to prevent online guessing of passwords by an attacker who tries to authenticate as a legitimate claimant. Random data and nonce can be used to disguise the real data.

**42.** **In the electronic authentication process, which of the following is strongly resistant to man-in-the-middle (MitM) attacks?**

    a.    Encrypted key exchange (EKE)

    b.    Simple password exponential key exchange (SPEKE)

    c.    Secure remote password protocol (SRP)

    d.    Client authenticated transport layer security (TLS)

**42. d.**   A protocol is said to be highly resistant to man-in-the-middle (MitM) attacks if it does not enable the claimant to reveal, to an attacker masquerading as the verifier, information (e.g., token secrets and authenticators) that can be used by the latter to masquerade as the true claimant to the real verifier. For example, in client authenticated transport layer security (TLS), the browser and the Web server authenticate one another using public key infrastructure (PKI) credentials, thus strongly resistant to MitM attacks. The other three choices are incorrect, because they are examples of being weakly resistant to MitM attacks and are examples of zero-knowledge password protocol where the claimant is authenticated to a verifier without disclosing the token secret.

**43.**  In electronic authentication, which of the following controls is effective against cross site scripting (XSS) vulnerabilities?

   a.   Sanitize inputs to make them nonexecutable.

   b.   Insert random data into any linked uniform resource locator.

   c.   Insert random data into a hidden field.

   d.   Use a per-session shared secret.

**43. a.**   In a cross site scripting (XSS) vulnerability, an attacker may use an extensible markup language (XML) injection to perform the equivalent of an XSS, in which requesters of a valid Web service have their requests transparently rerouted to an attacker-controlled Web service that performs malicious operations. To prevent XSS vulnerabilities, the relying party should sanitize inputs from claimants or subscribers to ensure they are not executable, or at the very least not malicious, before displaying them as content to the subscriber's browser. The other three choices are incorrect because they are not applicable to the situation here.

**44.**  In electronic authentication, which of the following controls is *not* effective against a cross site request forgery (CSRF) attack?

   a.   Sanitize inputs to make them nonexecutable.

   b.   Insert random data into any linked uniform resource locator.

   c.   Insert random data into a hidden field.

   d.   Generate a per-session shared secret.

**44. a.**   A cross site request forgery (CSRF) is a type of session hijacking attack where a malicious website contains a link to the URL of the legitimate relying party. Web applications, even those protected by secure sockets layer/transport layer security (SSL/TLS), can still be vulnerable to the CSRF attack. One control to protect the CSRF attack is by inserting random data, supplied by the relying party, into any linked uniform resource locator with side effects and into a hidden field within any form on the relying party's website. Generating a per-session shared secret is effective against a session hijacking problem. Sanitizing inputs to make them nonexecutable is effective against cross site scripting (XSS) attacks, not CSRF attacks.

**45.** In electronic authentication, which of the following can mitigate the threat of assertion manufacture and/or modification?

    a.   Digital signature and TLS/SSL

    b.   Timestamp and short lifetime of validity

    c.   Digital signature with a key supporting nonrepudiation

    d.   HTTP and TLS

**45. *a.*** An assertion is a statement from a verifier to a relying party that contains identity information about a subscriber. To mitigate the threat of assertion manufacture and/or modification, the assertion may be digitally signed by the verifier and the assertion sent over a protected channel such as TLS/SSL. The other three choices are incorrect because they are not applicable to the situation here.

**46.** In electronic authentication, which of the following can mitigate the threat of assertion reuse?

    a.   Digital signature and TLS/SSL

    b.   Timestamp and short lifetime of validity

    c.   Digital signature with a key supporting nonrepudiation

    d.   HTTP and TLS

**46. *b.*** An assertion is a statement from a verifier to a relying party that contains identity information about a subscriber. To mitigate the threat of assertion reuse, the assertion should include a timestamp and a short lifetime of validity. The other three choices are incorrect because they are not applicable to the situation here.

**47.** In electronic authentication, which of the following can mitigate the threat of assertion repudiation?

    a.   Digital signature and TLS/SSL

    b.   Timestamp and short lifetime of validity

    c.   Digital signature with a key supporting nonrepudiation

    d.   HTTP and TLS

**47. *c.*** An assertion is a statement from a verifier to a relying party that contains identity information about a subscriber. To mitigate the threat of assertion repudiation, the assertion may be digitally signed by the verifier using a key that supports nonrepudiation. The other three choices are incorrect because they are not applicable to the situation here.

**48.** In electronic authentication, which of the following can mitigate the threat of assertion substitution?

    a.   Digital signature and TLS/SSL

    b.   Timestamp and short lifetime of validity

     c.     Digital signature with a key supporting nonrepudiation

     d.     HTTP and TLS

**48. d.**    An assertion is a statement from a verifier to a relying party that contains identity information about a subscriber. To mitigate the threat of assertion substitution, the assertion may include a combination of HTTP to handle message order and TLS to detect and disallow malicious reordering of packets. The other three choices are incorrect because they are not applicable to the situation here.

**49.**    **Serious vulnerabilities exist when:**

     a.     An untrusted individual has been granted an unauthorized access.

     b.     A trusted individual has been granted an authorized access.

     c.     An untrusted individual has been granted an authorized access.

     d.     A trusted individual has been granted an unauthorized access.

**49. a.**    Vulnerabilities typically result when an untrusted individual is granted unauthorized access to a system. Granting unauthorized access is riskier than granting authorized access to an untrusted individual, and trusted individuals are better than untrusted individuals. Both trust and authorization are important to minimize vulnerabilities. The other three choices are incorrect because serious vulnerabilities may not exist with them.

**50.**    **In mobile device authentication, password and personal identification number (PIN) authentication is an example of which of the following?**

     a.     Proof-by-possession

     b.     Proof-by-knowledge

     c.     Proof-by-property

     d.     Proof-of-origin

**50. b.**    Proof-by-knowledge is where a claimant authenticates his identity to a verifier by the use of a password or PIN (i.e., something you know) that he has knowledge of.

Proof-by-possession and proof-by-property, along with proof-by-knowledge, are used in mobile device authentication and robust authentication. Proof-of-origin is the basis to prove an assertion. For example, a private signature key is used to generate digital signatures as a proof-of-origin.

**51.**    **In mobile device authentication, fingerprint authentication is an example of which of the following?**

     a.     Proof-by-possession

     b.     Proof-by-knowledge

     c.     Proof-by-property

     d.     Proof-of-origin

**51. c.** Proof-by-property is where a claimant authenticates his identity to a verifier by the use of a biometric sample such as fingerprints (i.e., something you are).

Proof-by-possession and proof-by-knowledge, along with proof-by-property, are used in mobile device authentication and robust authentication. Proof-of-origin is the basis to prove an assertion. For example, a private signature key is used to generate digital signatures as a proof-of-origin.

**52.** Which of the following actions is effective for reviewing guest/anonymous accounts, temporary accounts, inactive accounts, and emergency accounts?

    a. Disabling

    b. Auditing

    c. Notifying

    d. Terminating

**52. b.** All the accounts mentioned in the question can be disabled, notified, or terminated, but it is not effective. Auditing of account creation, modification, notification, disabling, and termination (i.e., the entire account cycle) is effective because it can identify anomalies in the account cycle process.

**53.** Regarding access enforcement, which of the following mechanisms should *not* be employed when an immediate response is necessary to ensure public and environmental safety?

    a. Dual cable

    b. Dual authorization

    c. Dual use certificate

    d. Dual backbone

**53. b.** Dual authorization mechanisms require two forms of approval to execute. The organization should not employ a dual authorization mechanism when an immediate response is necessary to ensure public and environmental safety because it could slow down the needed response. The other three choices are appropriate when an immediate response is necessary.

**54.** Which of the following is *not* an example of nondiscretionary access control?

    a. Identity-based access control

    b. Mandatory access control

    c. Role-based access control

    d. Temporal constraints

**54. a.** Nondiscretionary access control policies have rules that are not established at the discretion of the user. These controls can be changed only through administrative action and not by users. An identity-based access control (IBAC) decision grants or denies a request based on the presence of an entity on an access control list (ACL). IBAC and discretionary access control are considered equivalent and are not examples of nondiscretionary access controls.

The other three choices are examples of nondiscretionary access controls. Mandatory access control deals with rules, role-based access control deals with job titles and functions, and temporal constraints deal with time-based restrictions and control time-sensitive activities.

**55.** **Encryption is used to reduce the probability of unauthorized disclosure and changes to information when a system is in which of the following secure, non-operable system states?**

      a.    Troubleshooting

      b.    Offline for maintenance

      c.    Boot-up

      d.    Shutdown

*55. b.* Secure, non-operable system states are states in which the information system is not performing business-related processing. These states include offline for maintenance, troubleshooting, bootup, and shutdown. Offline data should be stored with encryption in a secure location. Removing information from online storage to offline storage eliminates the possibility of individuals gaining unauthorized access to that information via a network.

**56.** **Bitmap objects and textual objects are part of which of the following security policy filters?**

      a.    File type checking filters

      b.    Metadata content filters

      c.    Unstructured data filters

      d.    Hidden content filters

*56. c.* Unstructured data consists of two basic categories: bitmap objects (e.g., image, audio, and video files) and textual objects (e.g., e-mails and spreadsheets). Security policy filters include file type checking filters, dirty word filters, structured and unstructured data filters, metadata content filters, and hidden content filters.

**57.** **Information flow control enforcement employing rulesets to restrict information system services provides:**

1.    Structured data filters

2.    Metadata content filters

3.    Packet filters

4.    Message filters

      a.    1 and 2

      b.    2 and 3

      c.    3 and 4

      d.    1, 2, 3, and 4

*57. c.* Packet filters are based on header information whereas message filters are based on content using keyword searches. Both packet filters and message filters use rulesets. Structured data filters and metadata content filters do not use rulesets.

**58.** **For information flow enforcement, what are explicit security attributes used to control?**

    a.    Release of sensitive data

    b.    Data content

    c.    Data structure

    d.    Source objects

*58. a.* Information flow enforcement using explicit security attributes are used to control the release of certain types of information such as sensitive data. Data content, data structure, and source and destination objects are examples of implicit security attributes.

**59.** **What do policy enforcement mechanisms, used to transfer information between different security domains prior to transfer, include?**

    1.    Embedding rules

    2.    Release rules

    3.    Filtering rules

    4.    Sanitization rules

        a.    1 and 2

        b.    2 and 3

        c.    3 and 4

        d.    1, 2, 3, and 4

*59. c.* Policy enforcement mechanisms include the filtering and/or sanitization rules that are applied to information prior to transfer to a different security domain. Embedding rules and release rules do not handle information transfer.

**60.** **Which of the following is *not* an example of policy rules for cross domain transfers?**

    a.    Prohibiting more than two-levels of embedding

    b.    Facilitating policy decisions on source and destination

    c.    Prohibiting the transfer of archived information

    d.    Limiting embedded components within other components

*60. b.* Parsing transfer files facilitates policy decisions on source, destination, certificates, classification subject, or attachments. The other three choices are examples of policy rules for cross domain transfers.

**61.** **Which of the following are the ways to reduce the range of potential malicious content when transferring information between different security domains?**

1. Constrain file lengths

2. Constrain character sets

3. Constrain schemas

4. Constrain data structures

    a. 1 and 3

    b. 2 and 3

    c. 3 and 4

    d. 1, 2, 3, and 4

**61. d.** The information system, when transferring information between different security domains, implements security policy filters that constrain file lengths, character sets, schemas, data structures, and allowed enumerations to reduce the range of potential malicious and/or unsanctioned content.

**62.** **Which of the following *cannot* detect unsanctioned information and prohibit the transfer of such information between different security domains (i.e., domain-type enforcement)?**

    a. Implementing one-way flows

    b. Checking information for malware

    c. Implementing dirty word list searches

    d. Applying security attributes to metadata

**62. a.** One-way flows are implemented using hardware mechanisms for controlling the flow of information within a system and between interconnected systems. As such they cannot detect unsanctioned information.

The other three choices do detect unsanctioned information and prohibit the transfer with actions such as checking all transferred information for malware, implementing dirty word list searches on transferred information, and applying security attributes to metadata that are similar to information payloads.

**63.** **Which of the following binds security attributes to information to facilitate information flow policy enforcement?**

    a. Security labels

    b. Resolution labels

    c. Header labels

    d. File labels

**63. b.** Means to bind and enforce the information flow include resolution labels that distinguish between information systems and their specific components, and between individuals involved in preparing, sending, receiving, or disseminating information. The other three types of labels cannot bind security attributes to information.

64. **Which of the following access enforcement mechanisms provides increased information security for an organization?**

    a.    Access control lists

    b.    Business application system

    c.    Access control matrices

    d.    Cryptography

*64. b.* Normal access enforcement mechanisms include access control lists, access control matrices, and cryptography. Increased information security is provided at the application system level (i.e., accounting and marketing systems) due to the use of password and PIN.

65. **What do architectural security solutions to enforce security policies about information on interconnected systems include?**

    1.    Implementing access-only mechanisms

    2.    Implementing one-way transfer mechanisms

    3.    Employing hardware mechanisms to provide unitary flow directions

    4.    Implementing regrading mechanisms to reassign security attributes

        a.    1 only

        b.    2 only

        c.    3 only

        d.    1, 2, 3, and 4

*65. d.* Specific architectural security solutions can reduce the potential for undiscovered vulnerabilities. These solutions include all four items mentioned.

66. **From an access control point of view, separation of duty is of two types: static and dynamic. Which of the following are examples of static separation of duties?**

    1.    Role-based access control

    2.    Workflow policy

    3.    Rule-based access control

    4.    Chinese Wall policy

        a.    1 and 2

        b.    1 and 3

        c.    2 and 4

        d.    3 and 4

**66. b.** Separation of duty constraints require that two roles be mutually exclusive because no user should have the privileges from both roles. Both role-based and rule-based access controls are examples of static separation of duty.

Dynamic separation of duty is enforced at access time, and the decision to grant access refers to the past access history. Examples of dynamic separation of duty include workflow policy and the Chinese Wall policy.

**67.** **In biometrics-based identification and authentication techniques, which of the following statements are true about biometric errors?**

1. High false rejection rate is preferred.
2. Low false acceptance rate is preferred.
3. High crossover error rate represents low accuracy.
4. Low crossover error rate represents low accuracy.

    a. 1 and 3
    b. 1 and 4
    c. 2 and 3
    d. 2 and 4

**67. c.** The goal of biometrics-based identification and authentication techniques about biometric errors is to obtain low numbers for both false rejection rate and false acceptance rate errors. Another goal is to obtain a low crossover error rate because it represents high accuracy or a high crossover error rate because it represents low accuracy.

**68.** **For password management, user-selected passwords generally contain which of the following?**

1. Less entropy
2. Easier for users to remember
3. Weaker passwords
4. Easier for attackers to guess

    a. 2 only
    b. 2 and 3
    c. 2, 3, and 4
    d. 1, 2, 3, and 4

**68. d.** User-selected passwords generally contain less entropy, are easier for users to remember, use weaker passwords, and at the same time are easier for attackers to guess or crack.

**69.** As a part of centralized password management solution, which of the following architectures for single sign-on technology becomes a single point-of-failure?

    a.    Kerberos authentication service

    b.    Lightweight directory access protocol

    c.    Domain passwords

    d.    Centralized authentication server

**69. d.** A common architecture for single sign-on (SSO) is to have an authentication service, such as Kerberos, for authenticating SSO users, and a database or directory service such as lightweight directory access protocol (LDAP) that stores authentication information for the resources the SSO handles authentication for. By definition, the SSO technology uses a password, and an SSO solution usually includes one or more centralized servers containing authentication credentials for many users. Such a server becomes a single point-of-failure for authentication to many resources, so the availability of the server affects the availability of all the resources that rely on that server.

**70.** If proper mutual authentication is *not* performed, what is the single sign-on technology vulnerable to?

    a.    Man-in-the-middle attack

    b.    Replay attack

    c.    Social engineering attack

    d.    Phishing attack

**70. a.** User authentication to the single sign-on (SSO) technology is important. If proper mutual authentication is not performed, the SSO technology using passwords is vulnerable to a man-in-the-middle (MitM) attack. Social engineering and phishing attacks are based on passwords, and replay attacks do not use passwords.

**71.** From an access control point of view, separation of duty is of two types: static and dynamic. Which of the following are examples of dynamic separation of duties?

    1.    Two-person rule

    2.    History-based separation of duty

    3.    Design-time

    4.    Run-time

        a.    1 and 2

        b.    1 and 3

        c.    2 and 4

        d.    3 and 4

**71. a.** The two-person rule states that the first user can be any authorized user, but the second user can be any authorized user different from the first. History-based separation of duty regulates that the same subject (role or user) cannot access the same object (program or device) for a variable number of times. Design-time and run-time are used in the workflow policy.

**72.** From an access control point of view, the Chinese Wall policy focuses on which of the following?

      a.    Confidentiality

      b.    Integrity

      c.    Availability

      d.    Assurance

**72. a.** The Chinese Wall policy is used where company sensitive information (i.e., confidentiality) is divided into mutually disjointed conflict-of-interest categories. The Biba model focuses on integrity. Availability, assurance, and integrity are other components of security principles that are not relevant to the Chinese Wall policy.

**73.** From an access control point of view, which of the following maintains consistency between the internal data and users' expectations of that data?

      a.    Security policy

      b.    Workflow policy

      c.    Access control policy

      d.    Chinese Wall policy

**73. b.** The goal of workflow policy is to maintain consistency between the internal data and external (users') expectations of that data. This is because the workflow is a process, consisting of tasks, documents, and data. The Chinese Wall policy deals with dividing sensitive data into separate categories. The security policy and the access control policy are too general to be of any importance here.

**74.** From an access control point of view, separation of duty is *not* related to which of the following?

      a.    Safety

      b.    Reliability

      c.    Fraud

      d.    Security

**74. b.** Computer systems must be designed and developed with security and safety in mind because unsecure and unsafe systems can cause injury to people and damage to assets (e.g., military and airline systems). With separation of duty (SOD), fraud can be minimized when sensitive tasks are separated from each other (e.g., signing a check from requesting a check). Reliability is more of an engineering term in that a computer system is expected to perform with the required precision on a consistent basis. On the other hand, SOD deals with people and their work-related actions, which are not precise and consistent.

**75.** **Which of the following statements are true about access controls, safety, trust, and separation of duty?**

1. No leakage of access permissions are allowed to an unauthorized principal.

2. No access privileges can be escalated to an unauthorized principal.

3. No principals' trust means no safety.

4. No separation of duty means no safety.

    a. 1 only

    b. 2 only

    c. 1, 2, and 3

    d. 1, 2, 3, and 4

**75. d.** If complete trust by a principal is not practical, there is a possibility of a safety violation. The separation of duty concept is used to enforce safety and security in some access control models. In an event where there are many users (subjects), objects, and relations between subjects and objects, safety needs to be carefully considered.

**76.** **From a safety configuration viewpoint, the separation of duty concept is *not* enforced in which of the following?**

    a. Mandatory access control policy

    b. Bell-LaPadula access control model

    c. Access control matrix model

    d. Domain type enforcement access control model

**76. c.** The separation of duty concept is not enforced by the access control matrix model because it is not safety configured and is based on an arbitrary constraint. The other three choices use restricted access control models with access constraints that describe the safety requirements of any configuration.

**77.** **Which of the following statements are true about access controls and safety?**

1. More complex safety policies need more flexible access controls.

2. Adding flexibility to restricted access control models increases safety problems.

3. A trade-off exists between the expressive power of an access control model and the ease of safety enforcement.

4. In the implicit access constraints model, safety enforcement is relatively easier than in the arbitrary constraints model.

    a. 1 and 3

    b. 2 and 3

c. 3 and 4

d. 1, 2, 3, and 4

**77. d.** In general, access control policy expression models, such as role-based and access control matrix models, operate on arbitrary constraints and safety enforcement is difficult. In implicit (restricted) access constraints models (e.g., Bell-LaPadula), the safety enforcement is attainable.

**78.** **The purpose of static separation of duty is to address problems, such as static exclusivity and the assurance principle. Which of the following refers to the static exclusivity problem?**

1. To reduce the likelihood of fraud.

2. To prevent the loss of user objectivity.

3. One user is less likely to commit fraud when this user is a part of many users involved in a business transaction.

4. Few users are less likely to commit collusion when these users are a part of many users involved in a business transaction.

    a. 1 and 2

    b. 2 and 3

    c. 3 and 4

    d. 1, 2, 3, and 4

**78. a.** A static exclusivity problem is the condition for which it is considered dangerous for any user to gain authorization for a conflicting set of access capabilities. The motivation for exclusivity relations includes reducing the likelihood of fraud or preventing the loss of user objectivity. The assurance principle deals with committing fraud or collusion when many users are involved in handling a business transaction.

**79.** **Role-based access control and the least privilege principle do *not* enable which of the following?**

    a. Read access to a specified file

    b. Write access to a specified directory

    c. Connect access to a given host computer

    d. One administrator with super-user access permissions

**79. d.** The concept of limiting access or least privilege is simply to provide no more authorization than necessary to perform required functions. Best practice suggests it is better to have several administrators with limited access to security resources rather than one administrator with super-user access permissions. The principle of least privilege is connected to the role-based access control in that each role is assigned those access permissions needed to perform its functions, as mentioned in the other three choices.

**80.** Extensible access control markup language (XACML) framework incorporates the support of which of the following?

    a.   Rule-based access control (RuBAC)

    b.   Mandatory access control (MAC)

    c.   Role-based access control (RBAC)

    d.   Discretionary access control (DAC)

***80. c.*** The extensible access control markup language (XACML) framework does not provide support for representing the traditional access controls (e.g., RuBAC, MAC, and DAC), but it does incorporate the role-based access control (RBAC) support. The XACML specification describes building blocks from which an RBAC solution is developed.

**81.** From an access control viewpoint, which of the following requires an audit the most?

    a.   Public access accounts

    b.   Nonpublic accounts

    c.   Privileged accounts

    d.   Non-privileged accounts

***81. c.*** The goal is to limit exposure due to operating from within a privileged account or role. A change of role for a user or process should provide the same degree of assurance in the change of access authorizations for that user or process. The same degree of assurance is also needed when a change between a privileged account and non-privileged account takes place. Auditing of privileged accounts is required mostly to ensure that privileged account users use only the privileged accounts and that non-privileged account users use only the non-privileged accounts. An audit is not required for public access accounts due to little or no risk involved. Privileged accounts are riskier than nonpublic accounts.

**82.** From an information flow policy enforcement viewpoint, which of the following allows forensic reconstruction of events?

    1.   Security attributes

    2.   Security policies

    3.   Source points

    4.   Destination points

        a.   1 and 2

        b.   2 and 3

        c.   3 and 4

        d.   1, 2, 3, and 4

***82. c.*** The ability to identify source and destination points for information flowing in an information system allows for forensic reconstruction of events and increases compliance to security policies. Security attributes are critical components of the operations security concept.

**83.** From an access control policy enforcement viewpoint, which of the following should *not* be given a privileged user account to access security functions during the course of normal operations?

1.   Network administration department

2.   Security administration department

3.   End user department

4.   Internal audit department

    a.   1 and 2

    b.   3 only

    c.   4 only

    d.   3 and 4

*83. d.*   Privileged user accounts should be established and administered in accordance with a role-based access scheme to access security functions. Privileged roles include network administration, security administration, system administration, database administration, and Web administration, and should be given access to security functions. End users and internal auditors should not be given a privileged account to access security functions during the course of normal operations.

**84.** From an access control account management point of view, service-oriented architecture implementations rely on which of the following?

    a.   Dynamic user privileges

    b.   Static user privileges

    c.   Predefined user privileges

    d.   Dynamic user identities

*84. a.*   Service-oriented architecture (SOA) implementations rely on run-time access control decisions facilitated by dynamic privilege management. In contrast, conventional access control implementations employ static information accounts and predefined sets of user privileges. Although user identities remain relatively constant over time, user privileges may change more frequently based on the ongoing business requirements and operational needs of the organization.

**85.** For privilege management, which of the following is the correct order?

    a.   Access control ⇨ Access management ⇨ Authentication management ⇨ Privilege management

    b.   Access management ⇨ Access control ⇨ Privilege management ⇨ Authentication management

    c.   Authentication management ⇨ Privilege management ⇨ Access control ⇨ Access management

    d.   Privilege management ⇨ Access management ⇨ Access control ⇨ Authentication management

**85. c.** Privilege management is defined as a process that creates, manages, and stores the attributes and policies needed to establish criteria that can be used to decide whether an authenticated entity's request for access to some resource should be granted. Authentication management deals with identities, credentials, and any other authentication data needed to establish an identity. Access management, which includes privilege management and access control, encompasses the science and technology of creating, assigning, storing, and accessing attributes and policies. These attributes and policies are used to decide whether an entity's request for access should be allowed or denied. In other words, a typical access decision starts with authentication management and ends with access management, whereas privilege management falls in between.

**86.** From an access control viewpoint, which of the following are examples of super user accounts?

    a.    Root and guest accounts

    b.    Administrator and root accounts

    c.    Anonymous and root accounts

    d.    Temporary and end-user accounts

**86. b.** Super user accounts are typically described as administrator or root accounts. Access to super user accounts should be limited to designated security and system administration staff only, and not to the end-user accounts, guest accounts, anonymous accounts, or temporary accounts. Security and system administration staff use the super user accounts to access key security/system parameters and commands.

**87.** Responses to unsuccessful login attempts and session locks are implemented with which of the following?

    a.    Operating system and firmware

    b.    Application system and hardware

    c.    Operating system and application system

    d.    Hardware and firmware

**87.c.** Response to unsuccessful login attempts can be implemented at both the operating system and the application system levels. The session lock is implemented typically at the operating system level but may be at the application system level. Hardware and firmware are not used for unsuccessful login attempts and session lock.

**88.** Which of the following statements is *not* true about a session lock in access control?

    a.    A session lock is a substitute for logging out of the system.

    b.    A session lock can be activated on a device with a display screen.

    c.    A session lock places a publicly viewable pattern on to the device display screen.

    d.    A session lock hides what was previously visible on the device display screen.

**88. a.** A session lock prevents further access to an information system after a defined time period of inactivity. A session lock is not a substitute for logging out of the system as in logging out at the end of the workday. The other three choices are true statements about a session lock.

**89.** Which of the following user actions are permitted without identification or authentication?

1. Access to public websites

2. Emergency situations

3. Unsuccessful login attempts

4. Reestablishing a session lock

    a.    1 only

    b.    2 only

    c.    1 and 2

    d.    3 and 4

**89. c.** Access to public websites and emergency situations are examples of user permitted actions that don't require identification or authentication. Both unsuccessful login attempts and reestablishing a session lock require proper identification or authentication procedures. A session lock is retained until proper identification or authentication is submitted, accepted, and reestablished.

**90.** Which of the following circumstances require additional security protections for mobile devices after unsuccessful login attempts?

    a.    When a mobile device requires a login to itself, and not a user account on the device

    b.    When a mobile device is accessing a removable media without a login

    c.    When information on the mobile device is encrypted

    d.    When the login is made to any one account on the mobile device

**90. a.** Additional security protection is needed for a mobile device (e.g., PDA) requiring a login where the login is made to the mobile device itself, not to any one account on the device. Additional protection is not needed when removable media is accessed without a login and when the information on the mobile device is encrypted. A successful login to any account on the mobile device resets the unsuccessful login count to zero.

**91.** An information system dynamically reconfigures with which of the following as information is created and combined?

    a.    Security attributes and data structures

    b.    Security attributes and security policies

    c.    Security attributes and information objects

    d.    Security attributes and security labels

*91.b.* An information system dynamically reconfigures security attributes in accordance with an identified security policy as information is created and combined. The system supports and maintains the binding of security attributes to information in storage, in process, and in transmission. The term security label is often used to associate a set of security attributes with a specific information object as part of the data structures (e.g., records, buffers, and files) for that object.

92. **For identity management, international standards do *not* use which of the following access control policies for making access control decisions?**

   1. Discretionary access control (DAC)

   2. Mandatory access control (MAC)

   3. Identity-based access control (IBAC)

   4. Rule-based access control (RuBAC)

      a. 1 and 2

      b. 1 and 3

      c. 2 and 3

      d. 3 and 4

*92. a.* International standards for access control decisions do not use the U.S.-based discretionary or mandatory access control policies. Instead, they use identity-based and rule-based access control policies.

93. **Which of the following is an example of less than secure networking protocols for remote access sessions?**

      a. Secure shell-2

      b. Virtual private network with blocking mode enabled

      c. Bulk encryption

      d. Peer-to-peer networking protocols

*93. d.* An organization must ensure that remote access sessions for accessing security functions employ security measures and that they are audited. Bulk encryption, session layer encryption, secure shell-2 (SSH-2), and virtual private networking (VPN) with blocking enabled are standard security measures. Bluetooth and peer-to-peer (P2P) networking are examples of less than secure networking protocols.

94. **For wireless access, in which of the following ways does an organization confine wireless communications to organization-controlled boundaries?**

   1. Reducing the power of the wireless transmission and controlling wireless emanations

   2. Configuring the wireless access path such that it is point-to-point in nature

3.  Using mutual authentication protocols

4.  Scanning for unauthorized wireless access points and connections

    a.  1 only

    b.  3 only

    c.  2 and 4

    d.  1, 2, 3, and 4

***94. d.***  Actions that may be taken to confine wireless communication to organization-controlled boundaries include all the four items mentioned. Mutual authentication protocols include EAP/TLS and PEAP. Reducing the power of the wireless transmission means that the transmission cannot go beyond the physical perimeter of the organization. It also includes installing TEMPEST measures to control emanations.

**95.**  **For access control for mobile devices, which of the following assigns responsibility and accountability for addressing known vulnerabilities in the media?**

    a.  Use of writable, removable media

    b.  Use of personally owned removable media

    c.  Use of project-owned removable media

    d.  Use of nonowner removable media

***95. c.***  An identifiable owner (e.g., employee, organization, or project) for removable media helps to reduce the risk of using such technology by assigning responsibility and accountability for addressing known vulnerabilities in the media (e.g., malicious code insertion). Use of project-owned removable media is acceptable because the media is assigned to a project, and the other three choices are not acceptable because they have no accountability feature attached to them. Restricting the use of writable, removable media is a good security practice.

**96.**  **For access control for mobile devices, which of the following actions can *trigger* an incident response handling process?**

    a.  Use of external modems or wireless interfaces within the device

    b.  Connection of unclassified mobile devices to unclassified systems

    c.  Use of internal modems or wireless interfaces within the device

    d.  Connection of unclassified mobile devices to classified systems

***96. d.***  When unclassified mobile devices are connected to classified systems containing classified information, it is a risky situation because a security policy is violated. This action should trigger an incident response handling process. Connection of an unclassified mobile device to an unclassified system still requires an approval; although, it is less risky. Use of internal or external modems or wireless interfaces within the mobile device should be prohibited.

**97.** For least functionality, organizations utilize which of the following to identify and prevent the use of prohibited functions, ports, protocols, and services?

1. Network scanning tools
2. Intrusion detection and prevention systems
3. Firewalls
4. Host-based intrusion detection systems

    a. 1 and 3
    b. 2 and 4
    c. 3 and 4
    d. 1, 2, 3, and 4

*97. d.* Organizations can utilize network scanning tools, intrusion detection and prevention systems (IDPS), endpoint protections such as firewalls, and host-based intrusion detection systems to identify and prevent the use of prohibited functions, ports, protocols, and services.

**98.** An information system uses multifactor authentication mechanisms to minimize potential risks for which of the following situations?

1. Network access to privileged accounts
2. Local access to privileged accounts
3. Network access to non-privileged accounts
4. Local access to non-privileged accounts

    a. 1 and 2
    b. 1 and 3
    c. 3 and 4
    d. 1, 2, 3, and 4

*98. d.* An information system must use multifactor authentication mechanisms for both network access (privileged and non-privileged) and local access (privileged and non-privileged) because both situations are risky. System/network administrators have administrative (privileged) accounts, and these individuals have access to a set of "access rights" on a given system. Malicious non-privileged account users are as risky as privileged account users because they can cause damage to data and program files.

**99.** Which of the following statements is *not* true about identification and authentication requirements?

    a. Group authenticators should be used with an individual authenticator
    b. Group authenticators should be used with a unique authenticator

c.    Unique authenticators in group accounts need greater accountability

d.    Individual authenticators should be used at the same time as the group authenticators

***99. d.***   You need to require that individuals are authenticated with an individual authenticator prior to using a group authenticator. The other three choices are true statements.

**100.**   **Which of the following can prevent replay attacks in an authentication process for network access to privileged and non-privileged accounts?**

1.    Nonces

2.    Challenges

3.    Time synchronous authenticators

4.    Challenge-response one-time authenticators

    a.    1 and 2

    b.    2 and 3

    c.    3 and 4

    d.    1, 2, 3, and 4

***100. d.***   An authentication process resists replay attacks if it is impractical to achieve a successful authentication by recording and replaying a previous authentication message. Techniques used to address the replay attacks include protocols that use nonces or challenges (e.g., TLS) and time synchronous or challenge-response one-time authenticators.

**101.**   **For device identification and authentication, the authentication between devices and connections to networks is an example of a(n):**

    a.    Bidirectional authentication

    b.    Group authentication

    c.    Device-unique authentication

    d.    Individual authentication

***101. a.***   An information system authenticates devices before establishing remote and wireless network connections using bidirectional authentication between devices that are cryptographically-based. Examples of device identifiers include media access control (MAC) addresses, IP addresses, e-mail IDs, and device-unique token identifiers. Examples of device authenticators include digital/PKI certificates and passwords. The other three choices are not correct because they lack two-way authentication.

**102.**   **For device identification and authentication, dynamic address allocation process for devices is standardized with which of the following?**

    a.    Dynamic host configuration protocol

    b.    Dynamic authentication

    c.    Dynamic hypertext markup language

    d.    Dynamic binding

***102. a.*** For dynamic address allocation for devices, dynamic host configuration protocol (DHCP)-enabled clients obtain leases for Internet Protocol (IP) addresses from DHCP servers. Therefore, the dynamic address allocation process for devices is standardized with DHCP. The other three choices do not have the capability to obtain leases for IP addresses.

**103.** **For identifier management, service-oriented architecture implementations do not reply on which of the following?**

    a.    Dynamic identities

    b.    Dynamic attributes and privileges

    c.    Preregistered users

    d.    Pre-established trust relationships

***103. c.*** Conventional approaches to identifications and authentications employ static information system accounts for known preregistered users. Service-oriented architecture (SOA) implementations do not rely on static identities but do rely on establishing identities at run-time for entities (i.e., dynamic identities) that were previously unknown. Dynamic identities are associated with dynamic attributes and privileges as they rely on pre-established trust relationships.

**104.** **For authenticator management, which of the following presents a significant security risk?**

    a.    Stored authenticators

    b.    Default authenticators

    c.    Reused authenticators

    d.    Refreshed authenticators

***104. b.*** Organizations should change the default authenticators upon information system installation or require vendors and/or manufacturers to provide unique authenticators prior to delivery. This is because default authenticator credentials are often well known, easily discoverable, and present a significant security risk, and therefore, should be changed upon installation. A stored or embedded authenticator can be risky depending on whether it is encrypted or unencrypted. Both reused and refreshed authenticators are less risky compared to default and stored authenticators because they are under the control of the user organization.

**105.** **For authenticator management, use of which of the following is risky and leads to possible alternatives?**

    a.    A single sign-on mechanism

    b.    Same user identifier and different user authenticators on all systems

    c.    Same user identifier and same user authenticator on all systems

    d.    Different user identifiers and different user authenticators on each system

***105. c.*** Examples of user identifiers include internal users, contractors, external users, guests, passwords, tokens, and biometrics. Examples of user authenticators include passwords, PINs, tokens, biometrics, PKI/digital certificates, and key cards. When an individual has accounts on multiple information systems, there is the risk that if one account is compromised and the individual uses the same user identifier and authenticator, other accounts will be compromised as well. Possible alternatives include (i) having the same user identifier but different authenticators on all systems, (ii) having different user identifiers and different user authenticators on each system, (iii) employing a single sign-on mechanism, or (iv) having one-time passwords on all systems.

**106.** **For authenticator management, which of the following is the *least* risky situation when compared to the others?**

    a.   Authenticators embedded in an application system

    b.   Authenticators embedded in access scripts

    c.   Authenticators stored on function keys

    d.   Identifiers created at run-time

***106. d.*** It is less risky to dynamically manage identifiers, attributes, and access authorizations. Run-time identifiers are created on-the-fly for previously unknown entities. Information security management should ensure that unencrypted, static authenticators are not embedded in application systems or access scripts or not stored on function keys. This is because these approaches are risky. Here, the concern is to determine whether an embedded or stored authenticator is in the encrypted or unencrypted form.

**107.** **Which of the following access authorization policies applies to when an organization has a list of software *not* authorized to execute on an information system?**

    a.   Deny-all, permit-by-exception

    b.   Allow-all, deny-by-exception

    c.   Allow-all, deny-by-default

    d.   Deny-all, accept-by-permission

***107. a.*** An organization employs a deny-all, permit-by-exception authorization policy to identify software not allowed to execute on the system. The other three choices are incorrect because the correct answer is based on specific access authorization policy.

**108.** **Encryption is a part of which of the following?**

    a.   Directive controls

    b.   Preventive controls

    c.   Detective controls

    d.   Corrective controls

**108. b.** Encryption prevents unauthorized access and protects data and programs when they are in storage (at rest) or in transit. Preventive controls deter security incidents from happening in the first place.

Directive controls are broad-based controls to handle security incidents, and they include management's policies, procedures, and directives. Detective controls enhance security by monitoring the effectiveness of preventive controls and by detecting security incidents where preventive controls were circumvented. Corrective controls are procedures to react to security incidents and to take remedial actions on a timely basis. Corrective controls require proper planning and preparation as they rely more on human judgment.

**109.** Which of the following access authorization policies applies to external networks through managed interfaces employing boundary protection devices such as gateways or firewalls?

  a. Deny-all, permit-by-exception

  b. Allow-all, deny-by-exception

  c. Allow-all, deny-by-default

  d. Deny-all, accept-by-permission

**109. a.** Examples of managed interfaces employing boundary protection devices include proxies, gateways, routers, firewalls, hardware/software guards, and encrypted tunnels on a demilitarized zone (DMZ). This policy "deny-all, permit-by-exception" denies network traffic by default and enables network traffic by exception only.

The other three choices are incorrect because the correct answer is based on specific access authorization policy. Access control lists (ACL) can be applied to traffic entering the internal network from external sources.

**110.** Which of the following are needed when the enforcement of normal security policies, procedures, and rules are difficult to implement?

  1. Compensating controls

  2. Close supervision

  3. Team review of work

  4. Peer review of work

  a. 1 only

  b. 2 only

  c. 1 and 2

  d. 1, 2, 3, and 4

**110. d.** When the enforcement of normal security policies, procedures, and rules is difficult, it takes on a different dimension from that of requiring contracts, separation of duties, and system access controls. Under these situations, compensating controls in the form of close supervision, followed by peer and team review of quality of work are needed.

**111.** **Which of the following is critical to understanding an access control policy?**

    a.    Reachable-state

    b.    Protection-state

    c.    User-state

    d.    System-state

*111. b.*   A protection-state is that part of the system-state critical to understanding an access control policy. A system must be either in a protection-state or reachable-state. User-state is not critical because it is the least privileged mode.

**112.** **Which of the following should *not* be used in Kerberos authentication implementation?**

    a.    Data encryption standard (DES)

    b.    Advanced encryption standard (AES)

    c.    Rivest, Shamir, and Adelman (RSA)

    d.    Diffie-Hellman (DH)

*112. a.*   DES is weak and should not be used because of several documented security weaknesses. The other three choices can be used. AES can be used because it is strong. RSA is used in key transport where the authentication server generates the user symmetric key and sends the key to the client. DH is used in key agreement between the authentication server and the client.

**113.** **From an access control decision viewpoint, failures due to flaws in permission-based systems tend to do which of the following?**

    a.    Authorize permissible actions

    b.    Fail-safe with permission denied

    c.    Unauthorize prohibited actions

    d.    Grant unauthorized permissions

*113. b.*   When failures occur due to flaws in permission-based systems, they tend to fail-safe with permission denied. There are two types of access control decisions: permission-based and exclusion-based.

**114.** **Host and application system hardening procedures are a part of which of the following?**

    a.    Directive controls

    b.    Preventive controls

    c.    Detective controls

    d.    Corrective controls

*114. b.* Host and application system hardening procedures are a part of preventive controls, as they include antivirus software, firewalls, and user account management. Preventive controls deter security incidents from happening in the first place.

Directive controls are broad-based controls to handle security incidents, and they include management's policies, procedures, and directives. Detective controls enhance security by monitoring the effectiveness of preventive controls and by detecting security incidents where preventive controls were circumvented. Corrective controls are procedures to react to security incidents and to take remedial actions on a timely basis. Corrective controls require proper planning and preparation as they rely more on human judgment.

**115.** **From an access control decision viewpoint, fail-safe defaults operate on which of the following?**

1. Exclude and deny
2. Permit and allow
3. No access, yes default
4. Yes access, yes default

    a. 1 only

    b. 2 only

    c. 2 and 3

    d. 4 only

*115. c.* Fail-safe defaults mean that access control decisions should be based on permit and allow policy (i.e., permission rather than exclusion). This equates to the condition in which lack of access is the default (i.e., no access, yes default). "Allow all and deny-by-default" refers to yes-access, yes-default situations.

**116.** **For password management, automatically generated random passwords usually provide which of the following?**

1. Greater entropy
2. Passwords that are hard for attackers to guess
3. Stronger passwords
4. Passwords that are hard for users to remember

    a. 2 only

    b. 2 and 3

    c. 2, 3, and 4

    d. 1, 2, 3, and 4

*116. d.* Automatically generated random (or pseudo-random) passwords usually provide greater entropy, are hard for attackers to guess or crack, stronger passwords, but at the same time are hard for users to remember.

**117.** **In biometrics-based identification and authentication techniques, which of the following indicates that security is unacceptably weak?**

    a.    Low false acceptance rate

    b.    Low false rejection rate

    c.    High false acceptance rate

    d.    High false rejection rate

*117. c.* The trick is balancing the trade-off between the false acceptance rate (FAR) and false rejection rate (FRR). A high FAR means that security is unacceptably weak.

A FAR is the probability that a biometric system can incorrectly identify an individual or fail to reject an imposter. The FAR given normally assumes passive imposter attempts, and a low FAR is better. The FAR is stated as the ratio of the number of false acceptances divided by the number of identification attempts.

An FRR is the probability that a biometric system will fail to identify an individual or verify the legitimate claimed identity of an individual. A low FRR is better. The FRR is stated as the ratio of the number of false rejections divided by the number of identification attempts.

**118.** **In biometrics-based identification and authentication techniques, which of the following indicates that technology used in a biometric system is *not* viable?**

    a.    Low false acceptance rate

    b.    Low false rejection rate

    c.    High false acceptance rate

    d.    High false rejection rate

*118. d.* A high false rejection rate (FRR) means that the technology is creating a (PP) nuisance to falsely rejected users thereby undermining user acceptance and questioning the viability of the technology used. This could also mean that the technology is obsolete, inappropriate, and/or not meeting the user's changing needs.

A false acceptance rate (FAR) is the probability that a biometric system will incorrectly identify an individual or fail to reject an imposter. The FAR given normally assumes passive imposter attempts, and a low FAR is better and a high FAR is an indication of a poorly operating biometric system, not related to technology. The FAR is stated as the ratio of the number of false acceptances divided by the number of identification attempts.

A FRR is the probability that a biometric system will fail to identify an individual or verify the legitimate claimed identity of an individual. A low FRR is better. The FRR is stated as the ratio of the number of false rejections divided by the number of identification attempts.

**119.** **In biometrics-based identification and authentication techniques, what is a countermeasure to mitigate the threat of identity spoofing?**

    a.    Liveness detection

    b.    Digital signatures

c. Rejecting exact matches

d. Session lock

**119. a.** An adversary may present something other than his own biometric to trick the system into verifying someone else's identity, known as spoofing. One type of mitigation for an identity spoofing threat is liveness detection (e.g., pulse or lip reading). The other three choices cannot perform liveness detection.

**120.** In biometrics-based identification and authentication techniques, what is a countermeasure to mitigate the threat of impersonation?

a. Liveness detection

b. Digital signatures

c. Rejecting exact matches

d. Session lock

**120. b.** Attackers can use residual data on the biometric reader or in memory to impersonate someone who authenticated previously. Cryptographic methods such as digital signatures can prevent attackers from inserting or swapping biometric data without detection. The other three choices do not provide cryptographic measures to prevent impersonation attacks.

**121.** In biometrics-based identification and authentication techniques, what is a countermeasure to mitigate the threat of replay attack?

a. Liveness detection

b. Digital signatures

c. Rejecting exact matches

d. Session lock

**121. c.** A replay attack occurs when someone can capture a valid user's biometric data and use it at a later time for unauthorized access. A potential solution is to reject exact matches, thereby requiring the user to provide another biometric sample. The other three choices do not provide exact matches.

**122.** In biometrics-based identification and authentication techniques, what is a countermeasure to mitigate the threat of a security breach from unsuccessful authentication attempts?

a. Liveness detection

b. Digital signatures

c. Rejecting exact matches

d. Session lock

**122. d.**   It is good to limit the number of attempts any user can unsuccessfully attempt to authenticate. A session lock should be placed where the system locks the user out and logs a security event whenever a user exceeds a certain amount of failed logon attempts within a specified timeframe.

The other three choices cannot stop unsuccessful authentication attempts. For example, if an adversary can repeatedly submit fake biometric data hoping for an exact match, it creates a security breach without a session lock. In addition, rejecting exact matches creates ill will with the genuine user.

**123.**   **In the single sign-on technology, timestamps thwart which of the following?**

     a.    Man-in-the-middle attack

     b.    Replay attack

     c.    Social engineering attack

     d.    Phishing attack

**123. b.**   Timestamps or other mechanisms to thwart replay attacks should be included in the single sign-on (SSO) credential transmissions. Man-in-the-middle (MitM) attacks are based on authentication and social engineering, and phishing attacks are based on passwords.

**124.**   **Which of the following correctly represents the flow in the identity and authentication process involved in the electronic authentication?**

     a.    Claimant ⇨ Authentication Protocol ⇨ Verifier

     b.    Claimant ⇨ Authenticator ⇨ Verifier

     c.    Verifier ⇨ Claimant ⇨ Relying Party

     d.    Claimant ⇨ Verifier ⇨ Relying Party

**124. d.**   The party to be authenticated is called a claimant and the party verifying that identity is called a verifier. When a claimant successfully demonstrates possession and control of a token in an online authentication to a verifier through an authentication protocol, the verifier can verify that the claimant is the subscriber. The verifier passes on an assertion about the identity of the subscriber to the relying party. The verifier must verify that the claimant has possession and control of the token that verifies his identity. A claimant authenticates his identity to a verifier by the use of a token and an authentication protocol, called proof-of-possession protocol.

The other three choices are incorrect as follows:

➤   **The flow of authentication process involving Claimant ⇨ Authentication Protocol ⇨ Verifier:** The authentication process establishes the identity of the claimant to the verifier with a certain degree of assurance. It is implemented through an authentication protocol message exchange, as well as management mechanisms at each end that further constrain or secure the authentication activity. One or more of the messages of the authentication protocol may need to be carried on a protected channel.

> ➤ **The flow of tokens and credentials involving Claimant ⇨ Authenticator ⇨ Verifier:** Tokens generally are something the claimant possesses and controls that may be used to authenticate the claimant's identity. In E-authentication, the claimant authenticates to a system or application over a network by proving that he has possession of a token. The token produces an output called an authenticator and this output is used in the authentication process to prove that the claimant possesses and controls the token.

> ➤ **The flow of assertions involving Verifier ⇨ Claimant ⇨ Relying Party:** Assertions are statements from a verifier to a relying party that contain information about a subscriber (claimant). Assertions are used when the relying party and the verifier are not collocated (e.g., they are connected through a shared network). The relying party uses the information in the assertion to identify the claimant and make authorization decisions about his access to resources controlled by the relying party.

**125.** **Which of the following authentication techniques is appropriate for accessing nonsensitive IT assets with multiple uses of the same authentication factor?**

    a.   Single-factor authentication

    b.   Two-factor authentication

    c.   Three-factor authentication

    d.   Multifactor authentication

***125. a.*** Multiple uses of the same authentication factor (e.g., using the same password more than once) is appropriate for accessing nonsensitive IT assets and is known as a single-factor authentication. The other three factors are not needed for authentication of low security risk and nonsensitive assets.

**126.** **From an access control effectiveness viewpoint, which of the following represents biometric verification when a user submits a combination of a personal identification number (PIN) first and biometric sample next for authentication?**

    a.   One-to-one matching

    b.   One-to-many matching

    c.   Many-to-one matching

    d.   Many-to-many matching

***126. a.*** This combination of authentication represents something that you know (PIN) and something that you are (biometric). At the authentication system prompt, the user enters the PIN and then submits a biometric live-captured sample. The system compares the biometric sample to the biometric reference data associated with the PIN entered, which is a one-to-one matching of biometric verification. The other three choices are incorrect because the correct answer is based on its definition.

**127.** From an access control effectiveness viewpoint, which of the following represents biometric identification when a user submits a combination of a biometric sample first and a personal identification number (PIN) next for authentication?

    a. One-to-one matching

    b. One-to-many matching

    c. Many-to-one matching

    d. Many-to-many matching

*127. b.* This combination of authentication represents something that you know (PIN) and something that you are (biometric). The user presents a biometric sample first to the sensor, and the system conducts a one-to-many matching of biometric identification. The user is prompted to supply a PIN that provided the biometric reference data. The other three choices are incorrect because the correct answer is based on its definition.

**128.** During biometric identification, which of the following can result in slow system response times and increased expense?

    a. One-to-one matching

    b. One-to-many matching

    c. Many-to-one matching

    d. Many-to-many matching

*128. b.* The biometric identification with one-to-many matching can result in slow system response times and can be more expensive depending on the size of the biometric database. That is, the larger the database size, the slower the system response time. A personal identification number (PIN) is entered as a second authentication factor, and the matching is slow.

**129.** During biometric verification, which of the following can result in faster system response times and can be less expensive?

    a. One-to-one matching

    b. One-to-many matching

    c. Many-to-one matching

    d. Many-to-many matching

*129. a.* The biometric verification with one-to-one matching can result in faster system response times and can be less expensive because the personal identification number (PIN) is entered as a first authenticator and the matching is quick.

**130.** From an access control effectiveness viewpoint, which of the following is represented when a user submits a combination of hardware token and a personal identification number (PIN) for authentication?

    1. A weak form of two-factor authentication

    2. A strong form of two-factor authentication

    3.    Supports physical access

    4.    Supports logical access

        a.    1 only

        b.    2 only

        c.    1 and 3

        d.    2 and 4

*130. c.*   This combination represents something that you have (i.e., hardware token) and something that you know (i.e., PIN). The hardware token can be lost or stolen. Therefore, this is a weak form of two-factor authentication that can be used to support unattended access controls for physical access only. Logical access controls are software-based and as such do not support a hardware token.

**131.**   **From an access control effectiveness viewpoint, which of the following is represented when a user submits a combination of public key infrastructure (PKI) keys and a personal identification number (PIN) for authentication?**

    1.    A weak form of two-factor authentication

    2.    A strong form of two-factor authentication

    3.    Supports physical access

    4.    Supports logical access

        a.    1 only

        b.    2 only

        c.    1 and 3

        d.    2 and 4

*131. d.*   This combination represents something that you have (i.e., PKI keys) and something that you know (i.e., PIN). There is no hardware token to lose or steal. Therefore, this is a strong form of two-factor authentication that can be used to support logical access.

**132.**   **RuBAC is rule-based access control, ACL is access control list, IBAC is identity-based access control, DAC is discretionary access control, and MAC is mandatory access control. For identity management, which of the following equates the access control policies and decisions between the U.S. terminology and the international standards?**

    1.    RuBAC = ACL

    2.    IBAC = ACL

    3.    IBAC = DAC

    4.    RuBAC = MAC

        a. 1 only

        b. 2 only

c. 3 only

d. 3 and 4

***132. d.*** Identity-based access control (IBAC) and discretionary access control (DAC) are considered equivalent. The rule-based access control (RuBAC) and mandatory access control (MAC) are considered equivalent. IBAC uses access control lists (ACLs) whereas RuBAC does not.

**133.** **For identity management, most network operating systems are based on which of the following access control policy?**

  a. Rule-based access control (RuBAC)

  b. Identity-based access control (IBAC)

  c. Role-based access control (RBAC)

  d. Attribute-based access control (ABAC)

***133. b.*** Most network operating systems are implemented with an identity-based access control (IBAC) policy. Entities are granted access to resources based on any identity established during network logon, which is compared with one or more access control lists (ACLs). These lists may be individually administered, may be centrally administered and distributed to individual locations, or may reside on one or more central servers. Attribute-based access control (ABAC) deals with subjects and objects, rule-based (RuBAC) deals with rules, and role-based (RBAC) deals with roles or job functions.

**134.** **RBAC is role-based access control, MAC is mandatory access control, DAC is discretionary access control, ABAC is attribute-based access control, PBAC is policy-based access control, IBAC is identity-based access control, RuBAC is rule-based access control, RAdAC is risk adaptive access control, and UDAC is user-directed access control. For identity management, RBAC policy is defined as which of the following?**

  a. RBAC = MAC + DAC

  b. RBAC = ABAC + PBAC

  c. RBAC = IBAC + RuBAC

  d. RBAC = RAdAC + UDAC

***134. c.*** Role-based access control policy (RBAC) is a composite access control policy between identity-based access control (IBAC) policy and rule-based access control (RuBAC) policy and should be considered as a variant of both. In this case, an identity is assigned to a group that has been granted authorizations. Identities can be members of one or more groups.

**135.** **A combination of something you have (one time), something you have (second time), and something you know is used to represent which of the following personal authentication proofing scheme?**

  a. One-factor authentication

  b. Two-factor authentication

c.    Three-factor authentication

d.    Four-factor authentication

**135. b.**    This situation illustrates that multiple instances of the same factor (i.e., something you have is used two times) results in one-factor authentication. When this is combined with something you know, it results in a two-factor authentication scheme.

**136.**    **Remote access controls are a part of which of the following?**

a.    Directive controls

b.    Preventive controls

c.    Detective controls

d.    Corrective controls

**136. b.**    Remote access controls are a part of preventive controls, as they include Internet Protocol (IP) packet filtering by border routers and firewalls using access control lists. Preventive controls deter security incidents from happening in the first place.

Directive controls are broad-based controls to handle security incidents, and they include management's policies, procedures, and directives. Detective controls enhance security by monitoring the effectiveness of preventive controls and by detecting security incidents where preventive controls were circumvented. Corrective controls are procedures to react to security incidents and to take remedial actions on a timely basis. Corrective controls require proper planning and preparation as they rely more on human judgment.

**137.**    **What is using two different passwords for accessing two different systems in the same session called?**

a.    One-factor authentication

b.    Two-factor authentication

c.    Three-factor authentication

d.    Four-factor authentication

**137. b.**    Requiring two different passwords for accessing two different systems in the same session is more secure than requiring one password for two different systems. This equates to two-factor authentication. Requiring multiple proofs of authentication presents multiple barriers to entry access by intruders. On the other hand, using the same password (one-factor) for accessing multiple systems in the same session is a one-factor authentication, because only one type (and the same type) of proof is used. The key point is whether the type of proof presented is same or different.

**138.**    **What is using a personal identity card with attended access (e.g., a security guard) and a PIN called?**

a.    One-factor authentication

b.    Two-factor authentication

    c.    Three-factor authentication

    d.    Four-factor authentication

**138. *b.*** On the surface, this situation may seem a three-factor authentication, but in reality it is a two-factor authentication, because only a card (proof of one factor) and PIN (proof of second factor) are used, resulting in a two-factor authentication. Note that it is not the strongest two-factor authentication because of the attended access. A security guard is an example of attended access, who is checking for the validity of the card, and is counted as one-factor authentication. Other examples of attended access include peers, colleagues, and supervisors who will vouch for the identify of a visitor who is accessing physical facilities.

**139.** **A truck driver, who is an employee of a defense contractor, transports highly sensitive parts and components from a defense contractor's manufacturing plant to a military installation at a highly secure location. The military's receiving department tracks the driver's physical location to ensure that there are no security problems on the way to the installation. Upon arrival at the installation, the truck driver shows his employee badge with photo ID issued by the defense contractor, enters his password and PIN, and takes a biometric sample of his fingerprint prior to entering the installation and unloading the truck's content. What does this described scenario represents?**

    a.    One-factor authentication

    b.    Two-factor authentication

    c.    Three-factor authentication

    d.    Four-factor authentication

**139. *d.*** Tracking the driver's physical location (perhaps with GPS or wireless sensor network) is an example of somewhere you are (proof of first factor). Showing the employee a physical badge with photo ID is an example of something you have (proof of second factor). Entering a password and PIN is an example of something you know (proof of third factor). Taking a biometric sample of fingerprint is an example of something you are (proof of fourth factor). Therefore, this scenario represents a four-factor authentication. The key point is that it does not matter whether the proof presented is one item or more items in the same category (e.g, somewhere you are, something you have, something you know, and something you are).

**140.** **Which of the following is achieved when two authentication proofs of something that you have is implemented?**

    a.    Least assurance

    b.    Increased assurance

    c.    Maximum assurance

    d.    Equivalent assurance

**140. *a.*** Least assurance is achieved when two authentication proofs of something that you have (e.g., card, key, and mobile ID device) are implemented because the card and the key can be lost or stolen. Consequently, multiple uses of something that you have offer lesser access control assurance than using a combination of multifactor authentication techniques. Equivalent assurance is neutral and does not require any further action.

**141.** Which of the following is achieved when two authentication proofs of something that you know are implemented?

    a. Least assurance

    b. Increased assurance

    c. Maximum assurance

    d. Equivalent assurance

***141. b.*** Increased assurance is achieved when two authentication proofs of something that you know (e.g., using two different passwords with or without PINs) are implemented. Multiple proofs of something that you know offer greater assurance than does multiple proofs of something that you have. However, multiple uses of something that you know provide equivalent assurance to a combination of multifactor authentication techniques.

**142.** Which of the following is achieved when "two authentication proofs of something that you are" is implemented?

    a. Least assurance

    b. Increased assurance

    c. Maximum assurance

    d. Equivalent assurance

***142. c.*** Maximum assurance is achieved when two authentication proofs of something that you are (e.g., personal recognition by a colleague, user, or guard, and a biometric verification check) are implemented. Multiple proofs of something that you are offer the greatest assurance than does multiple proofs of something that you have or something that you know, used either alone or combined. Equivalent assurance is neutral and does not require any further action.

**143.** For key functions of intrusion detection and prevention system (IDPS) technologies, which of the following is referred to when an IDPS configuration is altered?

    a. Tuning

    b. Evasion

    c. Blocking

    d. Normalization

***143. a.*** Altering the configuration of an intrusion detection and prevention system (IDPS) to improve its detection accuracy is known as tuning. IDPS technologies cannot provide completely accurate detection at all times. Access to the targeted host is blocked from the offending user account or IP address.

Evasion is modifying the format or timing of malicious activity so that its appearance changes but its effect is the same. Attackers use evasion techniques to try to prevent intrusion detection and prevention system (IDPS) technologies from detecting their attacks. Most IDPS technologies can overcome common evasion techniques by duplicating special processing performed by the targeted host. If the IDPS configuration is same as the targeted host, then evasion techniques will be unsuccessful at hiding attacks.

Some intrusion prevention system (IPS) technologies can remove or replace malicious portions of an attack to make it benign. A complex example is an IPS that acts as a proxy and normalizes incoming requests, which means that the proxy repackages the payloads of the requests, discarding header information. This might cause certain attacks to be discarded as part of the normalization process.

**144.** **A reuse of a user's operating system password for preboot authentication should *not* be practiced in the deployment of which of the following storage encryption authentication products?**

      a.    Full-disk encryption

      b.    Volume encryption

      c.    Virtual disk encryption

      d.    File/folder encryption

***144. a.*** Reusing a user' operating system password for preboot authentication in a full (whole) disk encryption deployment would allow an attacker to learn only a single password to gain full access to the device's information. The password could be acquired through technical methods, such as infecting the device with malware, or through physical means, such as watching a user type in a password in a public location. The correct choice is risky compared to the incorrect choices because the latter do not deal with booting a computer or pre-boot authentication.

**145.** **All the following storage encryption authentication products may use the operating system's authentication for single sign-on *except*:**

      a.    Full-disk encryption

      b.    Volume encryption

      c.    Vi rtual disk encryption

      d.    File/folder encryption

***145. a.*** Products such as volume encryption, virtual disk encryption, or file/folder encryption may use the operating system's authentication for single sign-on (SSO). After a user authenticates to the operating system at login time, the user can access the encrypted file without further authentication, which is risky. You should not use the same single-factor authenticator for multiple purposes. A full-disk encryption provides better security than the other three choices because the entire disk is encrypted, as opposed to part of it.

**146.** **Which of the following security mechanisms for high-risk storage encryption authentication products provides protection against authentication-guessing attempts and favors security over functionality?**

      a.    Alert consecutive failed login attempts.

      b.    Lock the computer for a specified period of time.

    c.    Increase the delay between attempts.

    d.    Delete the protected data from the device.

*146. d.*   For high-security situations, storage encryption authentication products can be configured so that too many failed attempts cause the product to delete all the protected data from the device. This approach strongly favors security over functionality. The other three choices can be used for low-security situations.

**147.**   **Recovery mechanisms for storage encryption authentication solutions require which of the following?**

    a.    A trade-off between confidentiality and security

    b.    A trade-off between integrity and security

    c.    A trade-off between availability and security

    d.    A trade-off between accountability and security

*147. c.*   Recovery mechanisms increase the availability of the storage encryption authentication solutions for individual users, but they can also increase the likelihood that an attacker can gain unauthorized access to encrypted storage by abusing the recovery mechanism. Therefore, information security management should consider the trade-off between availability and security when selecting and planning recovery mechanisms. The other three choices do not provide recovery mechanisms.

**148.**   **For identity management, which of the following requires multifactor authentication?**

    a.    User-to-host architecture

    b.    Peer-to-peer architecture

    c.    Client host-to-server architecture

    d.    Trusted third-party architecture

*148. a.*   When a user logs onto a host computer or workstation, the user must be identified and authenticated before access to the host or network is granted. This process requires a mechanism to authenticate a real person to a machine. The best methods of doing this involve multiple forms of authentication with multiple factors, such as something you know (password), something you have (physical token), and something you are (biometric verification). The other three choices do not require multifactor authentication because they use different authentication methods.

Peer-to-peer architecture, sometimes referred to as mutual authentication protocol, involves the direct communication of authentication information between the communicating entities (e.g., peer-to-peer or client host-to-server).

The architecture for trusted third-party (TTP) authentication uses a third entity, trusted by all entities, to provide authentication information. The amount of trust given the third entity must be evaluated. Methods to establish and maintain a level of trust in a TTP include certification practice statements (CPS) that establishes rules, processes, and procedures that a certificate authority (CA) uses to ensure the integrity of the authentication process and use of secure protocols to interface with authentication servers. A TTP may provide authentication information in each instance of authentication, in real-time, or as a precursor to an exchange with a CA.

**149.** **For password management, which of the following ensures password strength?**

    a.    Passwords with maximum keyspace, shorter passphrases, low entropy, and simple passphrases

    b.    Passwords with balanced keyspace, longer passphrases, high entropy, and complex passphrases

    c.    Passwords with minimum keyspace, shorter passphrases, high entropy, and simple passphrases

    d.    Passwords with most likely keyspace, longer passphrases, low entropy, and complex passphrases

***149. b.***   Password strength is determined by a password's length and its complexity, which is determined by the unpredictability of its characters. Passwords based on patterns such as keyspace may meet password complexity and length requirement, but they significantly reduce the keyspace because attackers are aware of these patterns. The ideal keyspace is a balanced one between maximum, most likely, and minimum scenarios. Simple and short passphrases have low entropy because they consist of concatenated dictionary words, which are easy to guess and attack. Therefore, passphrases should be complex and longer to provide high entropy. Passwords with balanced keyspace, longer passphrases, high entropy, and complex passphrases ensure password strength.

**150.** **Regarding password management, which of the following enforces password strength requirements effectively?**

    a.    Educate users on password strength.

    b.    Run a password cracker program to identify weak passwords.

    c.    Perform a cracking operation offline.

    d.    Use a password filter utility program.

***150. d.***   One way to ensure password strength is to add a password filter utility program, which is specifically designed to verify that a password created by a user complies with the password policy. Adding a password filter is a more rigorous and proactive solution, whereas the other three choices are less rigorous and reactive solutions.

The password filter utility program is also referred to as a password complexity enforcement program.

**151.** **Which of the following controls over telecommuting use tokens and/or one-time passwords?**

    a.    Firewalls

    b.    Robust authentication

    c.    Port protection devices

    d.    Encryption

**151. *b.*** Robust authentication increases security in two significant ways. It can require the user to possess a token in addition to a password or personal identification number (PIN). Tokens, when used with PINs, provide significantly more security than passwords. For a hacker or other would-be impersonator to pretend to be someone else, the impersonator must have both a valid token and the corresponding PIN. This is much more difficult than obtaining a valid password and user ID combination. Robust authentication can also create one-time passwords. Electronic monitoring (eavesdropping or sniffing) or observing a user type in a password is not a threat with one-time passwords because each time a user is authenticated to the computer, a different "password" is used. (A hacker could learn the one-time password through electronic monitoring, but it would be of no value.)

The firewall is incorrect because it uses a secure gateway or series of gateways to block or filter access between two networks, often between a private network and a larger, more public network such as the Internet or public-switched network (e.g., the telephone system). Firewall does not use tokens and passwords as much as robust authentication.

A port protection device (PPD) is incorrect because it is fitted to a communications port of a host computer and authorizes access to the port itself, prior to and independent of the computer's own access control functions. A PPD can be a separate device in the communications stream or may be incorporated into a communications device (e.g. a modem). PPDs typically require a separate authenticator, such as a password, to access the communications port. One of the most common PPDs is the dial-back modem. PPD does not use tokens and passwords as much as robust authentication.

Encryption is incorrect because it is more expensive than robust authentication. It is most useful if highly confidential data needs to be transmitted or if moderately confidential data is transmitted in a high-threat area. Encryption is most widely used to protect the confidentiality of data and its integrity (it detects changes to files). Encryption does not use tokens and passwords as much as robust authentication.

**152.**    **Which of the following statements about an access control system is *not* true?**

    a.    It is typically enforced by a specific application.

    b.    It indicates what a specific user could have done.

    c.    It records failed attempts to perform sensitive actions.

    d.    It records failed attempts to access restricted data.

**152. *a.*** Some applications use access control (typically enforced by the operating system) to restrict access to certain types of information or application functions. This can be helpful to determine what a particular application user could have done. Some applications record information related to access control, such as failed attempts to perform sensitive actions or access restricted data.

**153.** **What occurs in a man-in-the-middle (MitM) attack on an electronic authentication protocol?**

1. An attacker poses as the verifier to the claimant.

2. An attacker poses as the claimant to the verifier.

3. An attacker poses as the CA to RA.

4. An attacker poses as the RA to CA.

    a. 1 only

    b. 3 only

    c. 4 only

    d. 1 and 2

*153. d.* In a man-in-the-middle (MitM) attack on an authentication protocol, the attacker interposes himself between the claimant and verifier, posing as the verifier to the claimant, and as the claimant to the verifier. The attacker thereby learns the value of the authentication token. Registration authority (RA) and certification authority (CA) has no roles in the MitM attack.

**154.** **Which of the following is not a preventive measure against network intrusion attacks?**

    a. Firewalls

    b. Auditing

    c. System configuration

    d. Intrusion detection system

*154. b.* Auditing is a detection activity, not a preventive measure. Examples of preventive measures to mitigate the risks of network intrusion attacks include firewalls, system configuration, and intrusion detection system.

**155.** **Smart card authentication is an example of which of the following?**

    a. Proof-by-knowledge

    b. Proof-by-property

    c. Proof-by-possession

    d. Proof-of-concept

*155. c.* Smart cards are credit card-size plastic cards that host an embedded computer chip containing an operating system, programs, and data. Smart card authentication is perhaps the best-known example of proof-by-possession (e.g., key, card, or token). Passwords are an example of proof-by-knowledge. Fingerprints are an example of proof-by-property. Proof-of-concept deals with testing a product prior to building an actual product.

**156.** For token threats in electronic authentication, countermeasures used for which one of the following threats are different from the other three threats?

  a. Online guessing

  b. Eavesdropping

  c. Phishing and pharming

  d. Social engineering

***156. a.*** In electronic authentication, a countermeasure against the token threat of online guessing uses tokens that generate high entropy authenticators. Common countermeasures against the threats listed in the other three choices are the same and they do not use high entropy authenticators. These common countermeasures include (i) use of tokens with dynamic authenticators where knowledge of one authenticator does not assist in deriving a subsequent authenticator and (ii) use of tokens that generate authenticators based on a token input value.

**157.** Which of the following is a component that provides a security service for a smart card application used in a mobile device authentication?

  a. Challenge-response protocol

  b. Service provider

  c. Resource manager

  d. Driver for the smart card reader

***157. a.*** The underlying mechanism used to authenticate users via smart cards relies on a challenge-response protocol between the device and the smart card. For example, a personal digital assistant (PDA) challenges the smart card for an appropriate and correct response that can be used to verify that the card is the one originally enrolled by the PDA device owner. The challenge-response protocol provides a security service. The three main software components that support a smart card application include the service provider, a resource manager, and a driver for the smart card reader.

**158.** Which of the following is *not* a sophisticated technical attack against smart cards?

  a. Reverse engineering

  b. Fault injection

  c. Signal leakage

  d. Impersonating

***158. d.*** For user authentication, the fundamental threat is an attacker impersonating a user and gaining control of the device and its contents. Of all the four choices, impersonating is a nonsophisticated technical attack. Smart cards are designed to resist tampering and monitoring of the card, including sophisticated technical attacks that involve reverse engineering, fault injection, and signal leakage.

**159.** **Which of the following is an example of nonpolled authentication?**

    a.    Smart card

    b.    Password

    c.    Memory token

    d.    Communications signal

***159. b.*** Nonpolled authentication is discrete; after the verdict is determined, it is inviolate until the next authentication attempt. Examples of nonpolled authentication include password, fingerprint, and voice verification. Polled authentication is continuous; the presence or absence of some token or signal determines the authentication status. Examples of polled authentication include smart card, memory token, and communications signal, whereby the absence of the device or signal triggers a nonauthenticated condition.

**160.** **Which of the following does *not* complement intrusion detection systems (IDS)?**

    a.    Honeypots

    b.    Inference cells

    c.    Padded cells

    d.    Vulnerability assessment tools

***160.b.*** Honeypot systems, padded cell systems, and vulnerability assessment tools complement IDS to enhance an organization's ability to detect intrusion. Inference cells do not complement IDS. A honeypot system is a host computer that is designed to collect data on suspicious activity and has no authorized users other than security administrators and attackers. Inference cells lead to an inference attack when a user or intruder is able to deduce privileged information from known information. In padded cell systems, an attacker is seamlessly transferred to a special padded cell host. Vulnerability assessment tools determine when a network or host is vulnerable to known attacks.

**161.** **Sniffing precedes which of the following?**

    a.    Phishing and pharming

    b.    Spoofing and hijacking

    c.    Snooping and scanning

    d.    Cracking and scamming

***161. b.*** Sniffing is observing and monitoring packets passing by on the network traffic using packet sniffers. Sniffing precedes either spoofing or hijacking. Spoofing, in part, is using various techniques to subvert IP-based access control by masquerading as another system by using their IP address. Spoofing is an attempt to gain access to a system by posing as an authorized user. Other examples of spoofing include spoofing packets to hide the origin of attack in a DoS, spoofing e-mail headers to hide spam, and spoofing phone numbers to fool caller-ID. Spoofing is synonymous with impersonating, masquerading, or mimicking, and is not synonymous with sniffing. Hijacking is an attack that occurs during an authenticated session with a database or system.

Snooping, scanning, and sniffing are all actions searching for required and valuable information. They involve looking around for vulnerabilities and planning to attack. These are preparatory actions prior to launching serious penetration attacks.

Phishing is tricking individuals into disclosing sensitive personal information through deceptive computer-based means. Phishing attacks use social engineering and technical subterfuge to steal consumers' personal identity data and financial account credentials. It involves Internet fraudsters who send spam or pop-up messages to lure personal information (e.g., credit card numbers, bank account information, social security number, passwords, or other sensitive information) from unsuspecting victims. Pharming is misdirecting users to fraudulent websites or proxy servers, typically through DNS hijacking or poisoning.

Cracking is breaking for passwords and bypassing software controls in an electronic authentication system such as user registration. Scamming is impersonating a legitimate business using the Internet. The buyer should check out the seller before buying goods or services. The seller should give out a physical address with a working telephone number.

**162.** **Passwords and personal identification numbers (PINs) are examples of which of the following?**

    a.   Procedural access controls

    b.   Physical access controls

    c.   Logical access controls

    d.   Administrative access controls

**162. C.** Logical, physical, and administrative controls are examples of access control mechanisms. Passwords, PINs, and encryption are examples of logical access controls.

**163.** **Which of the following statements is *not* true about honeypots' logs?**

    a.   Honeypots are deceptive measures.

    b.   Honeypots collect data on indications.

    c.   Honeypots are hosts that have no authorized users.

    d.   Honeypots are a supplement to properly securing networks, systems, and applications.

**163. b.** Honeypots are deceptive measures collecting better data on precursors, not on indications. A precursor is a sign that an incident may occur in the future. An indication is a sign that an incident may have occurred or may be occurring now.

Honeypots are hosts that have no authorized users other than the honeypot administrators because they serve no business function; all activity directed at them is considered suspicious. Attackers scan and attack honeypots, giving administrators data on new trends and attack/attacker tools, particularly malicious code. However, honeypots are a supplement to, not a replacement for, properly securing networks, systems, and applications.

**164.** Each user is granted the lowest clearance needed to perform authorized tasks. Which of the following principles is this?

    a.    The principle of least privilege

    b.    The principle of separation of duties

    c.    The principle of system clearance

    d.    The principle of system accreditation

**164. a.** The principle of least privilege requires that each subject (user) in a system be granted the most restrictive set of privileges (or lowest clearances) needed to perform authorized tasks. The application of this principle limits the damage that can result from accident, error, and/or unauthorized use. The principle of separation of duties states that no single person can have complete control over a business transaction or task.

The principle of system clearance states that users' access rights should be based on their job clearance status (i.e., sensitive or non-sensitive). The principle of system accreditation states that all systems should be approved by management prior to making them operational.

**165.** Which of the following intrusion detection and prevention system (IDPS) methodology is appropriate for analyzing both network-based and host-based activity?

    a.    Signature-based detection

    b.    Misuse detection

    c.    Anomaly-based detection

    d.    Stateful protocol analysis

**165. d.** IDPS technologies use many methodologies to detect incidents. The primary classes of detection methodologies include signature-based, anomaly-based, and stateful protocol analysis, where the latter is the only one that analyzes both network-based and host-based activity.

Signature-based detection is the process of comparing signatures against observed events to identify possible incidents. A signature is a pattern that corresponds to a known threat. It is sometimes incorrectly referred to as misuse detection or stateful protocol analysis. Misuse detection refers to attacks from within the organizations.

Anomaly-based detection is the process of comparing definitions of what activity is considered normal against observed events to identify significant deviations and abnormal behavior.

Stateful protocol analysis (also known as deep packet inspection) is the process of comparing predetermined profiles of generally accepted definitions of benign protocol activity for each protocol state against observed events to identify deviations. The stateful protocol is appropriate for analyzing both network-based and host-based activity, whereas deep packet inspection is appropriate for network-based activity only. One network-based IDPS can listen on a network segment or switch and can monitor the network traffic affecting multiple hosts that are connected to the network segment. One host-based IDPS operates on information collected from within an individual computer system and determines which processes and user accounts are involved in a particular attack.

**166.** The Clark-Wilson security model focuses on which of the following?

    a.    Confidentiality

    b.    Integrity

    c.    Availability

    d.    Accountability

***166. b.*** The Clark-Wilson security model is an approach that provides data integrity for common commercial activities. It is a specific model addressing "integrity," which is one of five security objectives. The five objectives are: confidentiality, integrity, availability, accountability, and assurance.

**167.** The Biba security model focuses on which of the following?

    a.    Confidentiality

    b.    Integrity

    c.    Availability

    d.    Accountability

***167. b.*** The Biba security model is an integrity model in which no subject may depend on a less trusted object, including another subject. It is a specific model addressing only one of the security objectives such as confidentiality, integrity, availability, and accountability.

**168.** The Take-Grant security model focuses on which of the following?

    a.    Confidentiality

    b.    Accountability

    c.    Availability

    d.    Access rights

***168. d.*** The Take-Grant security model uses a directed graph to specify the rights that a subject can transfer to an object or that a subject can take from another subject. It does not address the security objectives such as confidentiality, integrity, availability, and accountability. Access rights are a part of access control models.

**169.** Which of the following is based on precomputed password hashes?

    a.    Brute force attack

    b.    Dictionary attack

    c.    Rainbow attack

    d.    Hybrid attack

***169. c.*** Rainbow attacks are a form of a password cracking technique that employs rainbow tables, which are lookup tables that contain pre-computed password hashes. These tables enable an attacker to attempt to crack a password with minimal time on the victim system and without constantly having to regenerate hashes if the attacker attempts to crack multiple accounts. The other three choices are not based on pre-computed password hashes; although, they are all related to passwords.

A brute force attack is a form of a guessing attack in which the attacker uses all possible combinations of characters from a given character set and for passwords up to a given length.

A dictionary attack is a form of a guessing attack in which the attacker attempts to guess a password using a list of possible passwords that is not exhaustive.

A hybrid attack is a form of a guessing attack in which the attacker uses a dictionary that contains possible passwords and then uses variations through brute force methods of the original passwords in the dictionary to create new potential passwords.

**170.** **For intrusion detection and prevention system capabilities, anomaly-based detection uses which of the following?**

1. Blacklists
2. Whitelists
3. Threshold
4. Program code viewing

   a. 1 and 2
   b. 1, 2, and 3
   c. 3 only
   d. 1, 2, 3, and 4

*170. c.* Anomaly-based detection is the process of comparing definitions of what activity is considered normal against observed events to identify significant deviations. Thresholds are most often used for anomaly-based detection. A threshold is a value that sets the limit between normal and abnormal behavior.

An anomaly-based detection does not use blacklists, whitelists, and program code viewing. A blacklist is a list of discrete entities, such as hosts or applications that have been previously determined to be associated with malicious activity. A whitelist is a list of discrete entities, such as hosts or applications known to be benign. Program code viewing and editing features are established to see the detection-related programming code in the intrusion detection and prevention system (IDPS).

**171.** **Which of the following security models addresses "separation of duties" concept?**

   a. Biba model
   b. Clark-Wilson model
   c. Bell-LaPadula model
   d. Sutherland model

***171. b.*** The Clark and Wilson security model addresses the separation of duties concept along with well-formed transactions. Separation of duties attempts to ensure the external consistency of data objects. It also addresses the specific integrity goal of preventing authorized users from making improper modifications. The other three models do not address the separation of duties concept.

**172.** From a computer security viewpoint, the Chinese-Wall policy is related to which of the following?

    a.    Aggregation problem

    b.    Data classification problem

    c.    Access control problem

    d.    Inference problem

***172. c.*** As presented by Brewer and Nash, the Chinese-Wall policy is a mandatory access control policy for stock market analysts. According to the policy, a market analyst may do business with any company. However, every time the analyst receives sensitive "inside" information from a new company, the policy prevents him from doing business with any other company in the same industry because that would involve him in a conflict of interest situation. In other words, collaboration with one company places the Chinese-Wall between him and all other companies in the same industry.

The Chinese-Wall policy does not meet the definition of an aggregation problem; there is no notion of some information being sensitive with the aggregate being more sensitive. The Chinese-Wall policy is an access control policy in which the access control rule is not based just on the sensitivity of the information, but is based on the information already accessed. It is neither an inference nor a data classification problem.

**173.** Which of the following security models promotes security clearances and sensitivity classifications?

    a.    Biba model

    b.    Clark-Wilson model

    c.    Bell-LaPadula model

    d.    Sutherland model

***173. c.*** In a Bell-LaPadula model, the clearance/classification scheme is expressed in terms of a lattice. To determine whether a specific access model is allowed, the clearance of a subject is compared to the classification of the object, and a determination is made as to whether the subject is authorized for the specific access mode. The other three models do not deal with security clearances and sensitivity classifications.

**174.** Which of the following solutions to local account password management problem could an attacker exploit?

    a.    Use multifactor authentication to access the database.

    b.    Use a hash-based local password and a standard password.

    c.    Use randomly generated passwords.

    d.    Use a central password database.

**174. b.**   A local password could be based on a cryptographic hash of the media access control address and a standard password. However, if an attacker recovers one local password, the attacker could easily determine other local passwords. An attacker could not exploit the other three choices because they are secure. Other positive solutions include disabling built-in accounts, storing the passwords in the database in an encrypted form, and generating passwords based on a machine name or a media access control address.

**175.**   **Which of the following statements is true about intrusion detection systems (IDS) and firewalls?**

    a.    Firewalls are a substitution for an IDS.

    b.    Firewalls are an alternative to an IDS.

    c.    Firewalls are a complement to an IDS.

    d.    Firewalls are a replacement for an IDS.

**175. c.**   An IDS should be used as a complement to a firewall, not a substitute for it. Together, they provide a synergistic effect.

**176.**   **The Bell-LaPadula Model for a computer security policy deals with which of the following?**

    a.    $ -property

    b.    @ -property

    c.    Star (*) -property

    d.    # -property

**176. c.**   Star property (* -property) is a Bell-LaPadula security rule enabling a subject write access to an object only if the security level of the object dominates the security level of the subject.

**177.**   **Which of the following cannot prevent shoulder surfing?**

    a.    Promoting education and awareness

    b.    Preventing password guessing

    c.    Installing encryption techniques

    d.    Asking people not to watch while a password is typed

**177. c.**   The key thing in shoulder surfing is to make sure that no one watches the user while his password is typed. Encryption does not help here because it is applied after a password is entered, not before. Proper education and awareness and using difficult-to-guess passwords can eliminate this problem.

**178.** What does the Bell-LaPadula's star.property (* -property) mean?

    a.    No write-up is allowed.

    b.    No write-down is allowed.

    c.    No read-up is allowed.

    d.    No read-down is allowed.

***178. b.*** The star property means no write-down and yes to a write-up. A subject can write objects only at a security level that dominates the subject's level. This means, a subject of one higher label cannot write to any object of a lower security label. This is also known as the confinement property. A subject is prevented from copying data from one higher classification to a lower classification. In other words, a subject cannot write anything below that subject's level.

**179.** Which of the following security models covers integrity?

    a.    Bell-LaPadula model

    b.    Biba model

    c.    Information flow model

    d.    Take-Grant model

***179. b.*** The Biba model is an example of an integrity model. The Bell-LaPadula model is a formal state transition model of a computer security policy that describes a set of access control rules. Both the Bell-LaPadula and the Take-Grant models are a part of access control models.

**180.** Which of the following security models covers confidentiality?

    a.    Bell-LaPadula model

    b.    Biba model

    c.    Information flow model

    d.    Take-grant model

***180. a.*** The Bell-LaPadula model addresses confidentiality by describing different security levels of security classifications for documents. These classification levels, from least sensitive to most insensitive, include Unclassified, Confidential, Secret, and Top Secret.

**181.** Which one of the following is *not* an authentication mechanism?

    a.    What the user knows

    b.    What the user has

    c.    What the user can do

    d.    What the user is

***181. c.*** "What the user can do" is defined in access rules or user profiles, which come after a successful authentication. The other three choices are part of an authentication process. The authenticator factor "knows" means a password or PIN, "has" means key or card, and "is" means a biometric identity.

**182.** Which of the following models is used to protect the confidentiality of classified information?

    a.    Biba model and Bell-LaPadula model

    b.    Bell-LaPadula model and information flow model

    c.    Bell-LaPadula model and Clark-Wilson model

    d.    Clark-Wilson model and information flow model

*182. b.* The Bell-LaPadula model is used for protecting the confidentiality of classified information, based on multilevel security classifications. The information flow model, a basis for the Bell-LaPadula model, ensures that information at a given security level flows only to an equal or higher level. Each object has an associated security level. An object's level indicates the security level of the data it contains. These two models ensure the confidentiality of classified information.

The Biba model is similar to the Bell-LaPadula model but protects the integrity of information instead of its confidentiality. The Clark-Wilson model is a less formal model aimed at ensuring the integrity of information, not confidentiality. This model implements traditional accounting controls including segregation of duties, auditing, and well-formed transactions such as double entry bookkeeping. Both the Biba and Clark-Wilson models are examples of integrity models.

**183.** Which of the following is the *most* important part of intrusion detection and containment?

    a.    Prevent

    b.    Detect

    c.    Respond

    d.    Report

*183. c.* It is essential to detect insecure situations to respond in a timely manner. Also, it is of little use to detect a security breach if no effective response can be initiated. No set of prevention measures is perfect. Reporting is the last step in the intrusion detection and containment process.

**184.** Which of the following is the heart of intrusion detection systems?

    a.    Mutation engine

    b.    Processing engine

    c.    State machine

    d.    Virtual machine

*184. b.* The processing engine is the heart of the intrusion detection system (IDS). It consists of the instructions (language) for sorting information for relevance, identifying key intrusion evidence, mining databases for attack signatures, and decision making about thresholds for alerts and initiation of response activities.

For example, a mutation engine is used to obfuscate a virus, polymorphic or not, to aid the proliferation of the said virus. A state machine is the basis for all computer systems because it is a model of computations involving inputs, outputs, states, and state transition functions. A virtual machine is software that enables a single host computer to run using one or more guest operating systems.

**185.** **From an access control decision viewpoint, failures due to flaws in exclusion-based systems tend to do which of the following?**

    a.   Authorize permissible actions

    b.   Fail-safe with permission denied

    c.   Unauthorize prohibited actions

    d.   Grant unauthorized permissions

*185. d.* When failures occur due to flaws in exclusion-based systems, they tend to grant unauthorized permissions. The two types of access control decisions are permission-based and exclusion-based.

**186.** **Which of the following is a major issue with implementation of intrusion detection systems?**

    a.   False-negative notification

    b.   False-positive notification

    c.   True-negative notification

    d.   True-positive notification

*186. b.* One of the biggest single issues with intrusion detection system (IDS) implementation is the handling of false-positive notification. An anomaly-based IDS produces a large number of false alarms (false-positives) due to the unpredictable nature of users and networks. Automated systems are prone to mistakes, and human differentiation of possible attacks is resource-intensive.

**187.** **Which of the following provides strong authentication for centralized authentication servers when used with firewalls?**

    a.   User IDs

    b.   Passwords

    c.   Tokens

    d.   Account numbers

*187. c.* For basic authentication, user IDs, passwords, and account numbers are used for internal authentication. Centralized authentication servers such as RADIUS and TACACS/TACACS+ can be integrated with token-based authentication to enhance firewall administration security.

**188.** **How is authorization different from authentication?**

    a.   Authorization comes after authentication.

    b.   Authorization and authentication are the same.

    c.   Authorization is verifying the identity of a user.

    d.   Authorization comes before authentication.

**188. a.** Authorization comes after authentication because a user is granted access to a program (authorization) after he is fully authenticated. Authorization is permission to do something with information in a computer. Authorization and authentication are not the same, where the former is verifying the user's permission and the latter is verifying the identity of a user.

**189.** **Which of the following is required to thwart attacks against a Kerberos security server?**

    a.   Initial authentication

    b.   Pre-authentication

    c.   Post-authentication

    d.   Re-authentication

**189. b.** The simplest form of initial authentication uses a user ID and password, which occurs on the client. The server has no knowledge of whether the authentication was successful. The problem with this approach is that anyone can make a request to the server asserting any identity, allowing an attacker to collect replies from the server and successfully launching a real attack on those replies.

In pre-authentication, the user sends some proof of his identity to the server as part of the initial authentication process. The client must authenticate prior to the server issuing a credential (ticket) to the client. The proof of identity used in pre-authentication can be a smart card or token, which can be integrated into the Kerberos initial authentication process. Here, post-authentication and re-authentication processes do not apply because it is too late to be of any use.

**190.** **Which of the following statements is *not* true about discretionary access control?**

    a.   Access is based on the authorization granted to the user.

    b.   It uses access control lists.

    c.   It uses grant or revoke access to objects.

    d.   Users and owners are different.

**190. d.** Discretionary access control (DAC) permits the granting and revoking of access control privileges to be left to the discretion of individual users. A discretionary access control mechanism enables users to grant or revoke access to any of the objects under the control. As such, users are said to be the owners of the objects under their control. It uses access control lists.

**191.** **Which of the following does *not* provide robust authentication?**

    a.    Kerberos

    b.    Secure remote procedure calls

    c.    Reusable passwords

    d.    Digital certificates

*191. c.*    Robust authentication means strong authentication that should be required for accessing internal computer systems. Robust authentication is provided by Kerberos, one-time passwords, challenge-response exchanges, digital certificates, and secure remote procedure calls (Secure RPC). Reusable passwords provide weak authentication.

**192.** **Which of the following statements is *not* true about Kerberos protocol?**

    a.    Kerberos uses an asymmetric key cryptography.

    b.    Kerberos uses a trusted third party.

    c.    Kerberos is a credential based authentication system.

    d.    Kerberos uses a symmetric key cryptography.

*192. a.*    Kerberos uses symmetric key cryptography and a trusted third party. Kerberos users authenticate with one another using Kerberos credentials issued by a trusted third party. The bit size of Kerberos is the same as that of DES, which is 56 bits because Kerberos uses a symmetric key algorithm similar to DES.

**193.** **Which of the following authentication types is *most* effective?**

    a.    Static authentication

    b.    Robust authentication

    c.    Intermittent authentication

    d.    Continuous authentication

*193. d.*    Continuous authentication protects against impostors (active attacks) by applying a digital signature algorithm to every bit of data sent from the claimant to the verifier. Also, continuous authentication prevents session hijacking and provides integrity.

Static authentication uses reusable passwords, which can be compromised by replay attacks. Robust authentication includes one-time passwords and digital signatures, which can be compromised by session hijacking. Intermittent authentication is not useful because of gaps in user verification.

**194.** **For major functions of intrusion detection and prevention system technologies, which of the following statements are true?**

    1.    It is not possible to eliminate all false positives and false negatives.

    2.    Reducing false positives increases false negatives and vice versa.

3.  Decreasing false negatives is always preferred.

4.  More analysis is needed to differentiate false positives from false negatives.

    a.  1 only

    b.  2 only

    c.  3 only

    d.  1, 2, 3, and 4

**194. d.**   Intrusion detection and prevention system (IDPS) technologies cannot provide completely accurate detection at all times. All four items are true statements. When an IDPS incorrectly identifies benign activity as being malicious, a false positive has occurred. When an IDPS fails to identify malicious activity, a false negative has occurred.

**195.**   **Which of the following authentication techniques is impossible to forge?**

    a.  What the user knows

    b.  What the user has

    c.  What the user is

    d.  Where the user is

**195. d.**   Passwords and PINs are often vulnerable to guessing, interception, or brute force attack. Devices such as access tokens and crypto-cards can be stolen. Biometrics can be vulnerable to interception and replay attacks. A location cannot be different than what it is. The techniques used in the other three choices are not foolproof. However, "where the user is" based on a geodetic location is foolproof because it cannot be spoofed or hijacked.

Geodetic location, as calculated from a location signature, adds a fourth and new dimension to user authentication and access control mechanisms. The signature is derived from the user's location. It can be used to determine whether a user is attempting to log in from an approved location. If unauthorized activity is detected from an authorized location, it can facilitate finding the user responsible for that activity.

**196.**   **How does a rule-based access control mechanism work?**

    a.  It is based on filtering rules.

    b.  It is based on identity rules.

    c.  It is based on access rules.

    d.  It is based on business rules.

**196. c.**   A rule-based access control mechanism is based on specific rules relating to the nature of the subject and object. These specific rules are embedded in access rules. Filtering rules are specified in firewalls. Both identity and business rules are inapplicable here.

**197.** Which of the following is an example of a system integrity tool used in the technical security control category?

    a.    Auditing

    b.    Restore to secure state

    c.    Proof-of-wholeness

    d.    Intrusion detection tool

*197. c.*    The proof-of-wholeness control is a system integrity tool that analyzes system integrity and irregularities and identifies exposures and potential threats. The proof-of-wholeness principle detects violations of security policies.

Auditing is a detective control, which enables monitoring and tracking of system abnormalities. "Restore to secure state" is a recovery control that enables a system to return to a state that is known to be secure, after a security breach occurs. Intrusion detection tools detect security breaches.

**198.** Individual accountability does *not* include which of the following?

    a.    Unique identifiers

    b.    Access rules

    c.    Audit trails

    d.    Policies and procedures

*198. d.*    A basic tenet of IT security is that individuals must be accountable for their actions. If this is not followed and enforced, it is not possible to successfully prosecute those who intentionally damage or disrupt systems or to train those whose actions have unintended adverse effects.

The concept of individual accountability drives the need for many security safeguards, such as unique (user) identifiers, audit trails, and access authorization rules. Policies and procedures indicate what to accomplish and how to accomplish objectives. By themselves, they do not exact individual accountability.

**199.** From an access control viewpoint, which of the following is computed from a passphrase?

    a.    Access password

    b.    Personal password

    c.    Valid password

    d.    Virtual password

*199.d.*    A virtual password is a password computed from a passphrase that meets the requirements of password storage (e.g., 56 bits for DES). A passphrase is a sequence of characters, longer than the acceptable length of a regular password, which is transformed by a password system into a virtual password of acceptable length.

An access password is a password used to authorize access to data and is distributed to all those who are authorized to have similar access to that data. A personal password is a password known by only one person and is used to authenticate that person's identity. A valid password is a personal password that authenticates the identity of an individual when presented to a password system. It is also an access password that enables the requested access when presented to a password system.

**200.** Which of the following is an incompatible function for a database administrator?

    a.    Data administration

    b.    Information systems administration

    c.    Systems security

    d.    Information systems planning

***200. c.*** The database administrator (DBA) function is concerned with short-term development and use of databases, and is responsible for the data of one or several specific databases. The DBA function should be separate from the systems' security function due to possible conflict of interest for manipulation of access privileges and rules for personal gain. The DBA function can be mixed with data administration, information systems administration, or information systems planning because there is no harm to the organization.

**201.** Kerberos uses which of the following to protect against replay attacks?

    a.    Cards

    b.    Timestamps

    c.    Tokens

    d.    Keys

***201. b.*** A replay attack refers to the recording and retransmission of message packets in the network. Although a replay attack is frequently undetected, but it can be prevented by using packet timestamping. Kerberos uses the timestamps but not cards, tokens, and keys.

**202.** Which of the following user identification and authentication techniques depend on reference profiles or templates?

    a.    Memory tokens

    b.    Smart cards

    c.    Cryptography

    d.    Biometric systems

***202. d.*** Biometric systems require the creation and storage of profiles or templates of individuals wanting system access. This includes physiological attributes such as fingerprints, hand geometry, or retina patterns, or behavioral attributes such as voice patterns and handwritten signatures.

Memory tokens and smart cards involve the creation and distribution of a token device with a PIN, and data that tell the computer how to recognize valid tokens or PINs. Cryptography requires the generation, distribution, storage, entry, use, distribution, and archiving of cryptographic keys.

**203.** When security products *cannot* provide sufficient protection through encryption, system administrators should consider using which of the following to protect intrusion detection and prevention system management communications?

  1. Physically separated network
  2. Logically separated network
  3. Virtual private network
  4. Encrypted tunneling

    a. 1 and 4

    b. 2 and 3

    c. 3 and 4

    d. 1, 2, 3, and 4

*203. c.* System administrators should ensure that all intrusion detection and prevention system (IDPS) management communications are protected either through physical separation (management network) or logical separation (virtual network) or through encryption using transport layer security (TLS). However, for security products that do not provide sufficient protection through encryption, administrators should consider using a virtual private network (VPN) or other encrypted tunneling method to protect the network traffic.

**204.** What is the objective of separation of duties?

    a. No one person has complete control over a transaction or an activity.

    b. Employees from different departments do not work together well.

    c. Controls are available to protect all supplies.

    d. Controls are in place to operate all equipment.

*204. a.* The objective is to limit what people can do, especially in conflict situations or incompatible functions, in such a way that no one person has complete control over a transaction or an activity from start to finish. The goal is to limit the possibility of hiding irregularities or fraud. The other three choices are not related to separation of duties.

**205.** What names does an access control matrix place?

    a. Users in each row and the names of objects in each column

    b. Programs in each row and the names of users in each column

    c. Users in each column and the names of devices in each row

    d. Subjects in each column and the names of processes in each row

**205. a.**   Discretionary access control is a process to identify users and objects. An access control matrix can be used to implement a discretionary access control mechanism where it places the names of users (subject) in each row and the names of objects in each column of a matrix. A subject is an active entity, generally in the form of a person, process, or device that causes information to flow among objects or changes the system's state. An object is a passive entity that contains or receives information. Access to an object potentially implies access to the information it contains. Examples of objects include records, programs, pages, files, and directories. An access control matrix describes an association of objects and subjects for authentication of access rights.

**206.**   **Which situation is Kerberos not used in?**

  a. Managing distributed access rights

  b. Managing encryption keys

  c. Managing centralized access rights

  d. Managing access permissions

**206. a.**   Kerberos is a private key authentication system that uses a central database to keep a copy of all users' private keys. The entire system can be compromised due to the central database. Kerberos is used to manage centralized access rights, encryption keys, and access permissions.

**207.**   **Which of the following security control mechanisms is simplest to administer?**

  a. Discretionary access control

  b. Mandatory access control

  c. Access control list

  d. Logical access control

**207. b.**   Mandatory access controls are the simplest to use because they can be used to grant broad access to large sets of files and to broad categories of information.

Discretionary access controls are not simple to use due to their finer level of granularity in the access control process. Both the access control list and logical access control require a significant amount of administrative work because they are based on the details of each individual user.

**208.**   **What implementation is an example of an access control policy for a bank teller?**

  a. Role-based policy

  b. Identity-based policy

  c. User-directed policy

  d. Rule-based policy

**208. a.**   With role-based access control, access decisions are based on the roles that individual users have as part of an organization. Users take on assigned roles (such as doctor, nurse, bank teller, and manager). Access rights are grouped by role name, and the use of resources is restricted to individuals authorized to assume the associated role. The use of roles to control access can be an effective means for developing and enforcing enterprise-specific security policies and for streamlining the security management process.

Identity-based and user-directed policies are incorrect because they are examples of discretionary access control. Identity-based access control is based only on the identity of the subject and object. In user-directed access controls, a subject can alter the access rights with certain restrictions. Rule-based policy is incorrect because it is an example of a mandatory type of access control and is based on specific rules relating to the nature of the subject and object.

**209.** Which of the following access mechanisms creates a potential security problem?

    a.   Location-based access mechanism

    b.   IP address-based access mechanism

    c.   Token-based access mechanism

    d.   Web-based access mechanism

**209. b.** IP address-based access mechanisms use Internet Protocol (IP) source addresses, which are not secure and subject to IP address spoofing attacks. The IP address deals with identification only, not authentication.

Location-based access mechanism is incorrect because it deals with a physical address, not IP address. Token-based access mechanism is incorrect because it uses tokens as a means of identification and authentication. Web-based access mechanism is incorrect because it uses secure protocols to accomplish authentication. The other three choices accomplish both identification and authentication and do not create a security problem as does the IP address-based access mechanism.

**210.** Rank the following authentication mechanisms providing most to least protection against replay attacks?

    a.   Password only, password and PIN, challenge response, and one-time password

    b.   Password and PIN, challenge response, one-time password, and password only

    c.   Challenge response, one-time password, password and PIN, and password only

    d.   Challenge-response, password and PIN, one-time password, and password only

**210. c.** A challenge-response protocol is based on cryptography and works by having the computer generate a challenge, such as a random string of numbers. The smart token then generates a response based on the challenge. This is sent back to the computer, which authenticates the user based on the response. Smart tokens that use either challenge-response protocols or dynamic password generation can create one-time passwords that change periodically (e.g., every minute).

If the correct value is provided, the log-in is permitted, and the user is granted access to the computer system. Electronic monitoring is not a problem with one-time passwords because each time the user is authenticated to the computer, a different "password" is used. A hacker could learn the one-time password through electronic monitoring, but it would be of no value.

Passwords and personal identification numbers (PINs) have weaknesses such as disclosing and guessing. Passwords combined with PINs are better than passwords only. Both passwords and PINs are subject to electronic monitoring. Simple encryption of a password that will be used again does not solve the monitoring problem because encrypting the same password creates the same cipher-text; the cipher-text becomes the password.

**211.** **Some security authorities believe that re-authentication of every transaction provides stronger security procedures. Which of the following security mechanisms is *least* efficient and *least* effective for re-authentication?**

    a.   Recurring passwords

    b.   Nonrecurring passwords

    c.   Memory tokens

    d.   Smart tokens

*211. a.* Recurring passwords are static passwords with reuse and are considered to be a relatively weak security mechanism. Users tend to use easily guessed passwords. Other weaknesses include spoofing users, users stealing passwords through observing keystrokes, and users sharing passwords. The unauthorized use of passwords by outsiders (hackers) or insiders is a primary concern and is considered the least efficient and least effective security mechanism for re-authentication.

Nonrecurring passwords are incorrect because they provide a strong form of re-authentication. Examples include a challenge-response protocol or a dynamic password generator where a unique value is generated for each session. These values are not repeated and are good for that session only.

Tokens can help in re-authenticating a user or transaction. Memory tokens store but do not process information. Smart tokens expand the functionality of a memory token by incorporating one or more integrated circuits into the token itself. In other words, smart tokens store and process information. Except for passwords, all the other methods listed in the question are examples of advanced authentication methods that can be applied to re-authentication.

**212.** **Which of the following lists a pair of compatible functions within the IT organization?**

    a.   Computer operations and applications programming

    b.   Systems programming and data security administration

    c.   Quality assurance and data security administration

    d.   Production job scheduling and computer operations

*212. c.* Separation of duties is the first line of defense against the prevention, detection, and correction of errors, omissions, and irregularities. The objective is to ensure that no one person has complete control over a transaction throughout its initiation, authorization, recording, processing, and reporting. If the total risk is acceptable, then two different jobs can be combined. If the risk is unacceptable, the two jobs should not be combined. Both quality assurance and data security are staff functions and would not handle the day-to-day operations tasks.

The other three choices are incorrect because they are examples of incompatible functions. The rationale is to minimize such functions that are not conducive to good internal control structure. For example, if a computer operator is also responsible for production job scheduling, he could submit unauthorized production jobs.

**213.** **A security label, or access control mechanism, is supported by which of the following access control policies?**

    a. Role-based policy

    b. Identity-based policy

    c. User-directed policy

    d. Mandatory access control policy

**213. d.** Mandatory access control is a type of access control that cannot be made more permissive by subjects. They are based on information sensitivity such as security labels for clearance and data classification. Rule-based and administratively directed policies are examples of mandatory access control policy.

Role-based policy is an example of nondiscretionary access controls. Access control decisions are based on the roles individual users are taking in an organization. This includes the specification of duties, responsibilities, obligations, and qualifications (e.g., a teller or loan officer associated with a banking system).

Both identity-based and user-directed policies are examples of discretionary access control. It is a type of access control that permits subjects to specify the access controls with certain limitations. Identity-based access control is based only on the identity of the subject and object. User-directed control is a type of access control in which subjects can alter the access rights with certain restrictions.

**214.** **The principle of least privilege refers to the security objective of granting users only those accesses they need to perform their job duties. Which of the following actions is inconsistent with the principle of least privilege?**

    a. Authorization creep

    b. Re-authorization when employees change positions

    c. Users have little access to systems

    d. Users have significant access to systems

**214. a.** Authorization creep occurs when employees continue to maintain access rights for previously held positions within an organization. This practice is inconsistent with the principle of least privilege.

All the other three choices are incorrect because they are consistent with the principle of least privilege. Reauthorization can eliminate authorization creep, and it does not matter how many users have access to the system or how much access to the system as long as their access is based on need-to-know concept.

Permanent changes are necessary when employees change positions within an organization. In this case, the process of granting account authorizations occurs again. At this time, however, it is also important that access authorizations of the prior position be removed. Many instances of authorization-creep have occurred with employees continuing to maintain access rights for previously held positions within an organization. This practice is inconsistent with the principle of least privilege, and it is security vulnerability.

**215.** **Accountability is important to implementing security policies. Which of the following is *least* effective in exacting accountability from system users?**

    a.    Auditing requirements

    b.    Password and user ID requirements

    c.    Identification controls

    d.    Authentication controls

**215. b.** Accountability means holding individual users responsible for their actions. Due to several problems with passwords and user IDs, they are considered to be the least effective in exacting accountability. These problems include easy to guess passwords, easy to spoof users for passwords, easy to steal passwords, and easy to share passwords. The most effective controls for exacting accountability include a policy, authorization scheme, identification and authentication controls, access controls, audit trails, and auditing.

**216.** **Which of the following statement is *not* true in electronic authentication?**

    a.    The registration authority and the credential service provider may be the same entity

    b.    The verifier and the relying party may be the same entity

    c.    The verifier, credential service provider, and the relying party may be separate entities

    d.    The verifier and the relying party may be separate entities

**216. a.** The relationship between the registration authority (RA) and the credential service provider (CSP) is a complex one with ongoing relationship. In the simplest and perhaps the most common case, the RA and CSP are separate functions of the same entity. However, an RA might be part of a company or organization that registers subscribers with an independent CSP, or several different CSPs. Therefore a CSP may be an integral part of RA, or it may have relationships with multiple independent RAs, and an RA may have relationships with different CSPs as well.

The statements in the other three choices are true. The party to be authenticated is called a claimant (subscriber) and the party verifying that identity is called a verifier. When a subscriber needs to authenticate to perform a transaction, he becomes a claimant to a verifier. A relying party relies on results of an online authentication to establish the identity or attribute of a subscriber for the purpose of some transaction. Relying parties use a subscriber's authenticated identity and other factors to make access control or authorization decisions. The verifier and the relying party may be the same entity, or they may be separate entities.

In some cases the verifier does not need to directly communicate with the CSP to complete the authentication activity (e.g., the use of digital certificates), which represents a logical link between the two entities rather than a physical link. In some implementations, the verifier, the CSP functions, and the relying party may be distributed and separated.

**217.** **Location-based authentication techniques for transportation firms can be effectively used to provide which of the following?**

    a.   Static authentication

    b.   Intermittent authentication

    c.   Continuous authentication

    d.   Robust authentication

***217. c.*** Transportation firms can use location-based authentication techniques continuously, as there are no time and resource limits. It does not require any secret information to protect at either the host or user end. Continuous authentication is better than robust authentication, where the latter can be intermittent.

**218.** **System administrators pose a threat to computer security due to their access rights and privileges. Which of the following statements is true for an organization with one administrator?**

    a.   Masquerading by a system administrator can be prevented.

    b.   A system administrator's access to the system can be limited.

    c.   Actions by the system administrator can be detected.

    d.   A system administrator cannot compromise system integrity.

***218. c.*** Authentication data needs to be stored securely, and its value lies in the data's confidentiality, integrity, and availability. If confidentiality is compromised, someone may use the information to masquerade as a legitimate user. If system administrators can read the authentication file, they can masquerade as another user. Many systems use encryption to hide the authentication data from the system administrators.

Masquerading by system administrators cannot be entirely prevented. If integrity is compromised, authentication data can be added, or the system can be disrupted. If availability is compromised, the system cannot authenticate users, and the users may not be able to work. Because audit controls would be out of the control of the administrator, controls can be set up so that improper actions by the system administrators can be detected in audit records. Due to their broader responsibilities, the system administrators' access to the system cannot be limited. System administrators can compromise a system's integrity; again their actions can be detected in audit records.

It makes a big difference whether an organization has one or more than one system administrator for separation of duties or for "least privilege" principle to work. With several system administrators, a system administrator account could be set up for one person to have the capability to add accounts. Another administrator could have the authority to delete them. When there is only one system administrator employed, breaking up the duties is not possible.

**219.** Logical access controls provide a technical means of controlling access to computer systems. Which of the following is *not* a benefit of logical access controls?

    a.    Integrity

    b.    Availability

    c.    Reliability

    d.    Confidentiality

*219. c.* Computer-based access controls are called logical access controls. These controls can prescribe not only who or what is to have access to a specific system resource but also the type of access permitted, usually in software. Reliability is more of a hardware issue.

Logical access controls can help protect (i) operating systems and other systems software from unauthorized modification or manipulation (and thereby help ensure the system's integrity and availability); (ii) the integrity and availability of information by restricting the number of users and processes with access; and (iii) confidential information from being disclosed to unauthorized individuals.

**220.** Which of the following internal access control methods offers a strong form of access control and is a significant deterrent to its use?

    a.    Security labels

    b.    Passwords

    c.    Access control lists

    d.    Encryption

*220. a.* Security labels are a strong form of access control. Unlike access control lists, labels cannot ordinarily be changed. Because labels are permanently linked to specific information, data cannot be disclosed by a user copying information and changing the access to that file so that the information is more accessible than the original owner intended. Security labels are well suited for consistently and uniformly enforcing access restrictions, although their administration and inflexibility can be a significant deterrent to their use.

Passwords are a weak form of access control, although they are easy to use and administer. Although encryption is a strong form of access control, it is not a deterrent to its use when compared to labels. In reality, the complexity and difficulty of encryption can be a deterrent to its use.

**221.** It is vital that access controls protecting a computer system work together. Which of the following types of access controls should be *most* specific?

    a.    Physical

    b.    Application system

    c.    Operating system

    d.    Communication system

*221. b.*   At a minimum, four basic types of access controls should be considered: physical, operating system, communications, and application. In general, access controls within an application are the most specific. However, for application access controls to be fully effective, they need to be supported by operating system and communications system access controls. Otherwise, access can be made to application resources without going through the application. Operating system, communication, and application access controls need to be supported by physical access controls such as physical security and contingency planning.

**222.**   **Which of the following types of logical access control mechanisms does *not* rely on physical access controls?**

    a.   Encryption controls

    b.   Application system access controls

    c.   Operating system access controls

    d.   Utility programs

*222. a.*   Most systems can be compromised if someone can physically access the CPU machine or major components by, for example, restarting the system with different software. Logical access controls are, therefore, dependent on physical access controls (with the exception of encryption, which can depend solely on the strength of the algorithm and the secrecy of the key).

Application systems, operating systems, and utility programs are heavily dependent on logical access controls to protect against unauthorized use.

**223.**   **A system mechanism and audit trails assist business managers to hold individual users accountable for their actions. To utilize these audit trails, which of the following controls is a prerequisite for the mechanism to be effective?**

    a.   Physical

    b.   Environmental

    c.   Management

    d.   Logical access

*223. d.*   By advising users that they are personally accountable for their actions, which are tracked by an audit trail that logs user activities, managers can help promote proper user behavior. Users are less likely to attempt to circumvent security policy if they know that their actions will be recorded in an audit log. Audit trails work in concert with logical access controls, which restrict use of system resources. Because logical access controls are enforced through software, audit trails are used to maintain an individual's accountability. The other three choices collect some data in the form of an audit trail, and their use is limited due to the limitation of useful data collected.

**224.**   **Which of the following is the *best* place to put the Kerberos protocol?**

    a.   Application layer

    b.   Transport layer

c. Network layer

d. All layers of the network

**224. d.** Placing the Kerberos protocol below the application layer and at all layers of the network provides greatest security protection without the need to modify applications.

**225.** An inherent risk is associated with logical access that is difficult to prevent or mitigate but can be identified via a review of audit trails. Which of the following types of access is this risk most associated with?

a. Properly used authorized access

b. Misused authorized access

c. Unsuccessful unauthorized access

d. Successful unauthorized access

**225. b.** Properly authorized access, as well as misused authorized access, can use audit trail analysis but more so of the latter due to its high risk. Although users cannot be prevented from using resources to which they have legitimate access authorization, audit trail analysis is used to examine their actions. Similarly, unauthorized access attempts, whether successful or not, can be detected through the analysis of audit trails.

**226.** Many computer systems provide maintenance accounts for diagnostic and support services. Which of the following security techniques is *least* preferred to ensure reduced vulnerability when using these accounts?

a. Call-back confirmation

b. Encryption of communications

c. Smart tokens

d. Password and user ID

**226. d.** Many computer systems provide maintenance accounts. These special login accounts are normally preconfigured at the factory with preset, widely known weak passwords. It is critical to change these passwords or otherwise disable the accounts until they are needed. If the account is to be used remotely, authentication of the maintenance provider can be performed using callback confirmation. This helps ensure that remote diagnostic activities actually originate from an established phone number at the vendor's site. Other techniques can also help, including encryption and decryption of diagnostic communications, strong identification and authentication techniques, such as smart tokens, and remote disconnect verification.

**227.** Below is a list of pairs, which are related to one another. Which pair of items represents the integral reliance on the first item to enforce the second?

a. The separation of duties principle, the least privilege principle

b. The parity check, the limit check

    c.    The single-key system, the Rivest-Shamir-Adelman (RSA) algorithm

    d.    The two-key system, the Data Encryption Standard (DES) algorithm

**227. a.** The separation of duties principle is related to the "least privilege" principle; that is, users and processes in a system should have the least number of privileges and for the minimal period of time necessary to perform their assigned tasks. The authority and capacity to perform certain functions should be separated and delegated to different individuals. This principle is often applied to split the authority to write and approve monetary transactions between two people. It can also be applied to separate the authority to add users to a system and other system administrator duties from the authority to assign passwords, conduct audits, and perform other security administrator duties.

There is no relation between the parity check, which is hardware-based, and the limit check, which is a software-based application. The parity check is a check that tests whether the number of ones (1s) or zeros (0s) in an array of binary digits is odd or even. Odd parity is standard for synchronous transmission and even parity for asynchronous transmission. In the limit check, a program tests the specified data fields against defined high or low value limits for acceptability before further processing. The RSA algorithm is incorrect because it uses two keys: private and public. The DES is incorrect because it uses only one key for both encryption and decryption (secret or private key).

**228.** Which of the following is the *most* effective method for password creation?

    a.    Using password generators

    b.    Using password advisors

    c.    Assigning passwords to users

    d.    Implementing user selected passwords

**228. b.** Password advisors are computer programs that examine user choices for passwords and inform the users if the passwords are weak. Passwords produced by password generators are difficult to remember, whereas user selected passwords are easy to guess. Users write the password down on a paper when it is assigned to them.

**229.** Which one of the following items is a more reliable authentication device than the others?

    a.    Fixed callback system

    b.    Variable callback system

    c.    Fixed and variable callback system

    d.    Smart card system

**229. d.** Authentication is providing assurance about the identity of a subject or object; for example, ensuring that a particular user is who he claims to be. A smart card system uses cryptographic-based smart tokens that offer great flexibility and can solve many authentication problems such as forgery and masquerading. A smart token typically requires a user to provide something the user knows (i.e., a PIN or password), which provides a stronger control than the smart token alone. Smart cards do not require a callback because the codes used in the smart card change frequently, which cannot be repeated.

Callback systems are used to authenticate a person. A fixed callback system calls back to a known telephone associated with a known place. However, the called person may not be known, and it is a problem with masquerading. It is not only insecure but also inflexible because it is tied to a specific place. It is not applicable if the caller moves around. A variable callback system is more flexible than the fixed one but requires greater maintenance of the variable telephone numbers and locations. These phone numbers can be recorded or decoded by a hacker.

**230.** What does an example of a drawback of smart cards include?

    a.    A means of access control

    b.    A means of storing user data

    c.    A means of gaining unauthorized access

    d.    A means of access control and data storage

**230. c.** Because valuable data is stored on a smart card, the card is useless if lost, damaged, or forgotten. An unauthorized person can gain access to a computer system in the absence of other strong controls. A smart card is a credit card-sized device containing one or more integrated circuit chips, which performs the functions of a microprocessor, memory, and an input/output interface.

Smart cards can be used (i) as a means of access control, (ii) as a medium for storing and carrying the appropriate data, and (iii) a combination of (1) and (2).

**231.** Which of the following is a more simple and basic login control?

    a.    Validating username and password

    b.    Monitoring unsuccessful logins

    c.    Sending alerts to the system operators

    d.    Disabling accounts when a break-in occurs

**231. a.** Login controls specify the conditions users must meet for gaining access to a computer system. In most simple and basic cases, access will be permitted only when both a username and password are provided. More complex systems grant or deny access based on the type of computer login; that is, local, dialup, remote, network, batch, or subprocess. The security system can restrict access based on the type of the terminal, or the remote computer's access will be granted only when the user or program is located at a designated terminal or remote system. Also, access can be defined by the time of day and the day of the week. As a further precaution, the more complex and sophisticated systems monitor unsuccessful logins, send messages or alerts to the system operator, and disable accounts when a break-in occurs.

**232.** **There are trade-offs among controls. A security policy would be most useful in which of the following areas?**

1. System-generated passwords versus user-generated passwords

2. Access versus confidentiality

3. Technical controls versus procedural controls

4. Manual controls versus automated controls

    a. 1 and 2

    b. 3 and 4

    c. 2 and 3

    d. 2 and 4

*232. c.* A security policy is the framework within which an organization establishes needed levels of information security to achieve the desired confidentiality goals. A policy is a statement of information values, protection responsibilities, and organizational commitment for a computer system. It is a set of laws, rules, and practices that regulate how an organization manages, protects, and distributes sensitive information.

There are trade-offs among controls such as technical controls and procedural controls. If technical controls are not available, procedural controls might be used until a technical solution is found. Nevertheless, technical controls are useless without procedural controls and a robust security policy.

Similarly, there is a trade-off between access and confidentiality; that is, a system meeting standards for access allows authorized users access to information resources on an ongoing basis. The emphasis given to confidentiality, integrity, and access depends on the nature of the application. An individual system may sacrifice the level of one requirement to obtain a greater degree of another. For example, to allow for increased levels of availability of information, standards for confidentiality may be lowered. Thus, the specific requirements and controls for information security can vary.

Passwords and controls also involve trade-offs, but at a lower level. Passwords require deciding between system-generated passwords, which can offer more security than user-generated passwords because system-generated passwords are randomly generated pseudo words not found in the dictionary. However, system-generated passwords are harder to remember, forcing users to write them down, thus defeating the purpose. Controls require selecting between a manual and automated control or selecting a combination of manual and automated controls. One control can work as a compensating control for the other.

**233.** **Ensuring data and program integrity is important. Which of the following controls *best* applies the separation of duties principle in an automated computer operations environment?**

    a. File placement controls

    b. Data file naming conventions

c.   Program library controls

d.   Program and job naming conventions

**233. c.**   Program library controls enable only assigned programs to run in production and eliminate the problem of test programs accidentally entering the production environment. They also separate production and testing data to ensure that no test data are used in normal production. This practice is based on the "separation of duties" principle.

File placement controls ensure that files reside on the proper direct access storage device so that data sets do not go to a wrong device by accident. Data file, program, and job naming conventions implement the separation of duties principle by uniquely identifying each production and test data file names, program names, job names, and terminal usage.

**234.** **Which of the following pairs of high-level system services provide controlled access to networks?**

a.   Access control lists and access privileges

b.   Identification and authentication

c.   Certification and accreditation

d.   Accreditation and assurance

**234. b.**   Controlling access to the network is provided by the network's identification and authentication services, which go together. This service is pivotal in providing controlled access to the resources and services offered by the network and in verifying that the mechanisms provide proper protection. Identification is the process that enables recognition of an entity by a computer system, generally by the use of unique machine-readable usernames. Authentication is the verification of the entity's identification. That is when the host, to whom the entity must prove his identity, trusts (through an authentication process) that the entity is who he claims to be. The threat to the network that the identification and authentication service must protect against is impersonation.

Access control list (ACL) and access privileges do not provide controlled access to networks because ACL is a list of the subjects that are permitted to access an object and the access rights (privileges) of each subject. This service comes after initial identification and authentication service.

Certification and accreditation services do not provide controlled access to networks because certification is the administrative act of approving a computer system for use in a particular application. Accreditation is the management's formal acceptance of the adequacy of a computer system's security. Certification and accreditation are similar in concept. This service comes after initial identification and authentication service.

Accreditation and assurance services do not provide controlled access to networks because accreditation is the management's formal acceptance of the adequacy of a computer system's security. Assurance is confidence that a computer system design meets its requirements. Again, this service comes after initial identification and authentication service.

**235.** **Which of the following is not subjected to impersonation attacks?**

    a.    Packet replay

    b.    Forgery

    c.    Relay

    d.    Interception

*235. a.* Packet replay is one of the most common security threats to network systems, similar to impersonation and eavesdropping in terms of damage, but dissimilar in terms of functions. Packet replay refers to the recording and retransmission of message packets in the network. It is a significant threat for programs that require authentication-sequences because an intruder could replay legitimate authentication sequence messages to gain access to a system. Packet replay is frequently undetectable but can be prevented by using packet timestamping and packet-sequence counting.

Forgery is incorrect because it is one of the ways an impersonation attack is achieved. Forgery is attempting to guess or otherwise fabricate the evidence that the impersonator knows or possesses.

Relay is incorrect because it is one of the ways an impersonation attack is achieved. Relay is where one can eavesdrop upon another's authentication exchange and learn enough to impersonate a user.

Interception is incorrect because it is one of the ways an impersonation attack is achieved. Interception is where one can slip in between the communications and "hijack" the communications channel.

**236.** **Which of the following security features is *not* supported by the principle of least privilege?**

    a.    All or nothing privileges

    b.    The granularity of privilege

    c.    The time bounding of privilege

    d.    Privilege inheritance

*236. a.* The purpose of a privilege mechanism is to provide a means of granting specific users or processes the ability to perform security-relevant actions for a limited time and under a restrictive set of conditions, while still permitting tasks properly authorized by the system administrator. This is the underlying theme behind the security principle of least privilege. It does not imply an "all or nothing" privilege.

The granularity of privilege is incorrect because it is one of the security features supported by the principle of least privilege. A privilege mechanism that supports granularity of privilege can enable a process to override only those security-relevant functions needed to perform the task. For example, a backup program needs to override only read restrictions, not the write or execute restriction on files.

The time bounding of privilege is incorrect because it is one of the security features supported by the principle of least privilege. The time bounding of privilege is related in that privileges required by an application or a process can be enabled and disabled as the application or process needs them.

Privilege inheritance is incorrect because it is one of the security features supported by the principle of least privilege. Privilege inheritance enables a process image to request that all, some, or none of its privileges get passed on to the next process image. For example, application programs that execute other utility programs need not pass on any privileges if the utility program does not require them.

**237.** **Authentication is a protection against fraudulent transactions. Authentication process does *not* assume which of the following?**

    a.    Validity of message location being sent

    b.    Validity of the workstations that sent the message

    c.    Integrity of the message that is transmitted

    d.    Validity of the message originator

*237. c.*    Authentication assures that the data received comes from the supposed origin. It is not extended to include the integrity of the data or messages transmitted. However, authentication is a protection against fraudulent transactions by establishing the validity of messages sent, validity of the workstations that sent the message, and the validity of the message originators. Invalid messages can come from a valid origin, and authentication cannot prevent it.

**238.** **Passwords are used as a basic mechanism to identify and authenticate a system user. Which of the following password-related factors *cannot* be tested with automated vulnerability testing tools?**

    a.    Password length

    b.    Password lifetime

    c.    Password secrecy

    d.    Password storage

*238. c.*    No automated vulnerability-testing tool can ensure that system users have not disclosed their passwords; thus secrecy cannot be guaranteed.

Password length can be tested to ensure that short passwords are not selected. Password lifetime can be tested to ensure that they have a limited lifetime. Passwords should be changed regularly or whenever they may have been compromised. Password storage can be tested to ensure that they are protected to prevent disclosure or unauthorized modification.

**239.** **Use of login IDs and passwords is the *most* commonly used mechanism for which of the following?**

    a.    Providing dynamic verification of a user

    b.    Providing static verification of a user

c. Providing a strong user authentication

d. Batch and online computer systems alike

***239. b.*** By definition, a static verification takes place only once at the start of each login session. Passwords may or may not be reusable.

Dynamic verification of a user takes place when a person types on a keyboard and leaves an electronic signature in the form of keystroke latencies in the elapsed time between keystrokes. For well-known, regular type strings, this signature can be quite consistent. Here is how a dynamic verification mechanism works: When a person wants to access a computer resource, he is required to identify himself by typing his name. The latency vector of the keystrokes of this name is compared with the reference signature stored in the computer. If this claimant's latency vector and the reference signature are statistically similar, the user is granted access to the system. The user is asked to type his name a number of times to provide a vector of mean latencies to be used as a reference. This can be viewed as an electronic signature of the user.

Passwords do not provide a strong user authentication. If they did, there would not be a hacker problem today. Passwords provide the weakest user authentication due to their sharing and guessable nature. Only online systems require a user ID and password from a user due to their interactive nature. Only batch jobs and files require a user ID and password when submitting a job or modifying a file. Batch systems are not interactive.

**240.** **Which of the following password selection procedures would be the *most* difficult to remember?**

a. Reverse or rearrange the characters in the user's birthday

b. Reverse or rearrange the characters in the user's annual salary

c. Reverse or rearrange the characters in the user's spouse's name

d. Use randomly generated characters

***240. d.*** Password selection is a difficult task to balance between password effectiveness and its remembrance by the user. The selected password should be simple to remember for oneself and difficult for others to know. It is no advantage to have a scientifically generated password if the user cannot remember it. Using randomly generated characters as a password is not only difficult to remember but also easy to publicize. Users will be tempted to write them down in a conspicuous place if the password is difficult to remember.

The approaches in the other three choices would be relatively easy to remember due to the user familiarity with the password origin. A simple procedure is to use well-known personal information that is rearranged.

**241.** **How does a role-based access control mechanism work?**

a. Based on job enlargement concept

b. Based on job duties concept

c. Based on job enrichment concept

d. Based on job rotation concept

***241. b.*** Users take on assigned roles such as doctor, nurse, teller, and manager. With role-based access control mechanism, access decisions are based on the roles that individual users have as part of an organization, that is, job duties. Job enlargement means adding width to a job; job enrichment means adding depth to a job; and job rotation makes a person well rounded.

**242.** **What do the countermeasures against a rainbow attack resulting from a password cracking threat include?**

    a.    One-time password and one-way hash

    b.    Keyspace and passphrase

    c.    Salting and stretching

    d.    Entropy and user account lockout

***242. c.*** Salting is the inclusion of a random value in the password hashing process that greatly decreases the likelihood of identical passwords returning the same hash. If two users choose the same password, salting can make it highly unlikely that their hashes are the same. Larger salts effectively make the use of rainbow tables infeasible. Stretching involves hashing each password and its salt thousands of times. This makes the creation of the rainbow tables correspondingly more time-consuming, while having little effect on the amount of effort needed by the organization's systems to verify password authentication attempts.

Keyspace is the large number of possible key values (keys) created by the encryption algorithm to use when transforming the message. Passphrase is a sequence of characters transformed by a password system into a virtual password. Entropy is a measure of the amount of uncertainty that an attacker faces to determine the value of a secret.

**243.** **Passwords can be stored safely in which of the following places?**

    a.    Initialization file

    b.    Script file

    c.    Password file

    d.    Batch file

***243. c.*** Passwords should not be included in initialization files, script files, or batch files due to possible compromise. Instead, they should be stored in a password file, preferably encrypted.

**244.** **Which of the following is *not* a common method used to gain unauthorized access to computer systems?**

    a.    Password sharing

    b.    Password guessing

    c.    Password capturing

    d.    Password spoofing

*244. d.* Password spoofing is where intruders trick system security into permitting normally disallowed network connections. The gained passwords allow them to crack security or to steal valuable information. For example, the vast majority of Internet traffic is unencrypted and therefore easily readable. Consequently, e-mail, passwords, and file transfers can be obtained using readily available software. Password spoofing is not that common.

The other three choices are incorrect because they are the most commonly used methods to gain unauthorized access to computer systems. Password sharing allows an unauthorized user to have the system access and privileges of a legitimate user, with the legitimate user's knowledge and acceptance. Password guessing occurs when easy-to-use or easy-to-remember codes are used and when other users know about them (e.g., hobbies, sports, favorite stars, and social events). Password capturing is a process in which a legitimate user unknowingly reveals the user's login ID and password. This may be done through the use of a Trojan horse program that appears to the user as a legitimate login program; however, the Trojan horse program is designed to capture passwords.

**245.** What are the Bell-LaPadula access control model and mandatory access control policy examples of?

    a.    Identity-based access controls (IBAC)

    b.    Attribute-based access controls (ABAC)

    c.    Role-based access controls (RBAC)

    d.    Rule-based access controls (RuBAC)

*245. d.* The rule-based access control (RuBAC) is based on specific rules relating to the nature of the subject and object. A RuBAC decision requires authorization information and restriction information to compare before any access is granted. Both Bell-LaPadula access control model and mandatory access control policy deals with rules. The other three choices do not deal with rules.

**246.** Which of the following security solutions for access control is simple to use and easy to administer?

    a.    Passwords

    b.    Cryptographic tokens

    c.    Hardware keys

    d.    Encrypted data files

*246. c.* Hardware keys are devices that do not require a complicated process of administering user rights and access privileges. They are simple keys, similar to door keys that can be plugged into the personal computer before a person can successfully log on to access controlled data files and programs. Each user gets a set of keys for his personal use. Hardware keys are simple to use and easy to administer.

Passwords is an incorrect answer because they do require some amount of security administrative work such as setting up the account and helping users when they forget passwords. Passwords are simple to use but hard to administer.

Cryptographic tokens is an incorrect answer because they do require some amount of security administrative work. Tokens need to be assigned, programmed, tracked, and disposed of.

Encrypted data files is an incorrect answer because they do require some amount of security administrative work. Encryption keys need to be assigned to the owners for encryption and decryption purposes.

**247.** Cryptographic authentication systems must specify how the cryptographic algorithms will be used. Which of the following authentication systems would reduce the risk of impersonation in an environment of networked computer systems?

    a.    Kerberos-based authentication system

    b.    Password-based authentication system

    c.    Memory token-based authentication system

    d.    Smart token-based authentication system

***247. a.*** The primary goal of Kerberos is to prevent system users from claiming the identity of other users in a distributed computing environment. The Kerberos authentication system is based on secret key cryptography. The Kerberos protocol provides strong authentication of users and host computer systems. Further, Kerberos uses a trusted third party to manage the cryptographic keying relationships, which are critical to the authentication process. System users have a significant degree of control over the workstations used to access network services, and these workstations must therefore be considered not trusted.

Kerberos was developed to provide distributed network authentication services involving client/server systems. A primary threat in this type of client/server system is the possibility that one user claims the identity of another user (impersonation), thereby gaining access to system services without the proper authorization. To protect against this threat, Kerberos provides a trusted third party accessible to network entities, which supports the services required for authentication between these entities. This trusted third party is known as the Kerberos key distribution server, which shares secret cryptographic keys with each client and server within a particular realm. The Kerberos authentication model is based upon the presentation of cryptographic tickets to prove the identity of clients requesting services from a host system or server.

The other three choices are incorrect because they cannot reduce the risk of impersonation. For example: (i) passwords can be shared, guessed, or captured and (ii) memory tokens and smart tokens can be lost or stolen. Also, these three choices do not use a trusted third party to strengthen controls as Kerberos does.

**248.** What do the weaknesses of Kerberos include?

    1.    Subject to dictionary attacks.

    2.    Works with existing security systems software.

3. Intercepting and analyzing network traffic is difficult.

4. Every network application must be modified.

    a. 1 and 2

    b. 2 and 3

    c. 1 and 4

    d. 3 and 4

**248. c.** Kerberos is an authentication system with encryption mechanisms that make network traffic secure. Weaknesses of Kerberos include (i) it is subject to dictionary attacks where passwords can be stolen by an attacker and (ii) it requires modification of all network application source code, which is a problem with vendor developed applications with no source code provided to users. Kerberos strengths include that it can be added to an existing security system and that it makes intercepting and analyzing network traffic difficult. This is due to the use of encryption in Kerberos.

**249.** Less common ways to initiate impersonation attacks on the network include the use of which of the following?

    a. Firewalls and account names

    b. Passwords and account names

    c. Biometric checks and physical keys

    d. Passwords and digital certificates

**249. c.** Impersonation attacks involving the use of physical keys and biometric checks are less likely due to the need for the network attacker to be physically near the biometric equipment. Passwords and account names are incorrect because they are the most common way to initiate impersonation attacks on the network. A firewall is a mechanism to protect IT computing sites against Internet-borne attacks. Most digital certificates are password-protected and have an encrypted file that contains identification information about its holder.

**250.** Which of the following security services can Kerberos *best* provide?

    a. Authentication

    b. Confidentiality

    c. Integrity

    d. Availability

**250. a.** Kerberos is a de facto standard for an authentication protocol, providing a robust authentication method. Kerberos was developed to enable network applications to securely identify their peers and can be used for local/remote logins, remote execution, file transfer, transparent file access (i.e., access of remote files on the network as though they were local) and for client/server requests. The Kerberos system includes a Kerberos server, applications which use Kerberos authentication, and libraries for use in developing applications which use Kerberos authentication. In addition to secure remote procedure call (Secure RPC),

Kerberos prevents impersonation in a network environment and only provides authentication services. Other services such as confidentiality, integrity, and availability must be provided by other means. With Kerberos and secure RPC, passwords are not transmitted over the network in plaintext.

In Kerberos two items need to prove authentication. The first is the ticket and the second is the authenticator. The ticket consists of the requested server name, the client name, the address of the client, the time the ticket was issued, the lifetime of the ticket, the session key to be used between the client and the server, and some other fields. The ticket is encrypted using the server's secret key and thus cannot be correctly decrypted by the user. If the server can properly decrypt the ticket when the client presents it and if the client presents the authenticator encrypted using the session key contained in the ticket, the server can have confidence in the user's identity. The authenticator contains the client name, address, current time, and some other fields. The authenticator is encrypted by the client using the session key shared with the server. The authenticator provides a time-validation for the credential. If a user possesses both the proper credential and the authenticator encrypted with the correct session key and presents these items within the lifetime of the ticket, then the user's identity can be authenticated.

Confidentiality is incorrect because it ensures that data is disclosed to only authorized subjects. Integrity is incorrect because it is the property that an object is changed only in a specified and authorized manner. Availability is incorrect because it is the property that a given resource will be usable during a given time period.

**251.** **What is the *major* advantage of a single sign-on?**

    a.    It reduces management work.

    b.    It is a convenience for the end user.

    c.    It authenticates a user once.

    d.    It provides a centralized administration.

*251. b.*    Under a single sign-on (SSO), a user can authenticate once to gain access to multiple applications that have been previously defined in the security system. The SSO system is convenient for the end user in that it provides fewer areas to manage when compared to multiple sign-on systems, but SSO is risky. Many points of failure exist in multiple sign-on systems as they are inconvenient for the end user because of many areas to manage.

**252.** **Kerberos can prevent which one of the following attacks?**

    a.    Tunneling attack

    b.    Playback attack

    c.    Destructive attack

    d.    Process attack

*252. b.*    In a playback (replay) attack, messages received from something or from somewhere are replayed back to it. It is also called a reflection attack. Kerberos puts the time of day in the request to prevent an eavesdropper from intercepting the request for service and retransmitting it from the same host at a later time.

A tunneling attack attempts to exploit a weakness in a system that exists at a level of abstraction lower than that used by the developer to design the system. For example, an attacker might discover a way to modify the microcode of a processor used when encrypting some data, rather than attempting to break the system's encryption algorithm.

Destructive attacks damage information in a fashion that denies service. These attacks can be prevented by restricting access to critical data files and protecting them from unauthorized users.

In process attacks, one user makes a computer unusable for others that use the computer at the same time. These attacks are applicable to shared computers.

**253.** **From an access control point of view, which of the following are examples of history-based access control policies?**

1. Role-based access control

2. Workflow policy

3. Rule-based access control

4. Chinese Wall policy

    a. 1 and 2

    b. 1 and 3

    c. 2 and 4

    d. 3 and 4

*253.* **c.** History-based access control policies are defined in terms of subjects and events where the events of the system are specified as the object access operations associated with activity at a particular security level. This assumes that the security policy is defined in terms of the sequence of events over time, and that the security policy decides which events of the system are permitted to ensure that information does not flow in an unauthorized manner. History-based access control policies are not based on standard access control mechanism but based on practical applications. In the history-based access control policies, previous access events are used as one of the decision factors for the next access authorization. The workflow and the Chinese Wall policies are examples of history-based access control policies.

**254.** **Which of the following is *most* commonly used in the implementation of an access control matrix?**

    a. Discretionary access control

    b. Mandatory access control

    c. Access control list

    d. Logical access control

*254.* **c.** The access control list (ACL) is the most useful and flexible type of implementation of an access control matrix. The ACL permits any given user to be allowed or disallowed access to any object. The columns of an ACL show a list of users attached to protected objects. One can associate access rights for individuals and resources directly with each object. The other three choices require extensive administrative work and are useful but not that flexible.

**255.** **What is Kerberos?**

    a.    Access-oriented protection system

    b.    Ticket-oriented protection system

    c.    List-oriented protection system

    d.    Lock-and-key-oriented protection system

*255. b.* Kerberos was developed to enable network applications to securely identify their peers. It uses a ticket, which identifies the client, and an authenticator that serves to validate the use of that ticket and prevent an intruder from replaying the same ticket to the server in a future session. A ticket is valid only for a given time interval. When the interval ends, the ticket expires, and any later authentication exchanges require a new ticket.

An access-oriented protection system can be based on hardware or software or a combination of both to prevent and detect unauthorized access and to permit authorized access. In list-oriented protection systems, each protected object has a list of all subjects authorized to access it. A lock-and-key-oriented protection system involves matching a key or password with a specific access requirement. The other three choices do not provide a strong authentication protection, as does the Kerberos.

**256.** **For intrusion detection and prevention system capabilities using anomaly-based detection, administrators should check which of the following to determine whether they need to be adjusted to compensate for changes in the system and changes in threats?**

    a.    Whitelists

    b.    Thresholds

    c.    Program code viewing

    d.    Blacklists

*256. b.* Administrators should check the intrusion detection and prevention system (IDPS) thresholds and alert settings to determine whether they need to be adjusted periodically to compensate for changes in the system environment and changes in threats. The other three choices are incorrect because the anomaly-based detection does not use whitelists, blacklists, and program code viewing.

**257.** **Intrusion detection systems *cannot* do which of the following?**

    a.    Report alterations to data files

    b.    Trace user activity

    c.    Compensate for weak authentication

    d.    Interpret system logs

**257. c.** An intrusion detection system (IDS) cannot act as a "silver bullet," compensating for weak identification and authentication mechanisms, weaknesses in network protocols, or lack of a security policy. IDS can do the other three choices, such as recognizing and reporting alterations to data files, tracing user activity from the point of entry to the point of exit or impact, and interpreting the mass of information contained in operating system logs and audit trail logs.

**258.** **Intrusion detection systems can do which of the following?**

    a.   Analyze all the traffic on a busy network

    b.   Deal with problems involving packet-level attacks

    c.   Recognize a known type of attack

    d.   Deal with high-speed asynchronous transfer mode networks

**258. c.** Intrusion detection systems (IDS) can recognize when a known type of attack is perpetrated on a system. However, IDS cannot do the following: (i) analyze all the traffic on a busy network, (ii) compensate for receiving faulty information from system sources, (iii) always deal with problems involving packet-level attacks (e.g., an intruder using fabricated packets that elude detection to launch an attack or multiple packets to jam the IDS itself), and (iv) deal with high-speed asynchronous transfer mode networks that use packet fragmentation to optimize bandwidth.

**259.** **What is the *most* risky part of the primary nature of access control?**

    a.   Configured or misconfigured

    b.   Enabled or disabled

    c.   Privileged or unprivileged

    d.   Encrypted or decrypted

**259. b.** Access control software can be enabled or disabled, meaning security function can be turned on or off. When disabled, the logging function does not work. The other three choices are somewhat risky but not as much as enabled or disabled.

**260.** **Intrusion detection refers to the process of identifying attempts to penetrate a computer system and gain unauthorized access. Which of the following assists in intrusion detection?**

    a.   Audit records

    b.   Access control lists

    c.   Security clearances

    d.   Host-based authentication

**260. a.** If audit records showing trails have been designed and implemented to record appropriate information, they can assist in intrusion detection. Usually, audit records contain pertinent data (e.g., date, time, status of an action, user IDs, and event ID), which can help in intrusion detection.

Access control lists refer to a register of users who have been given permission to use a particular system resource and the types of access they have been permitted. Security clearances are associated with a subject (e.g., person and program) to access an object (e.g., files, libraries, directories, and devices). Host-based authentication grants access based upon the identity of the host originating the request, instead of the identity of the user making the request. The other three choices have no facilities to record access activity and therefore cannot assist in intrusion detection.

**261.** **Which of the following is the technique used in anomaly detection in intrusion detection systems where user and system behaviors are expressed in terms of counts?**

    a.    Parametric statistics

    b.    Threshold detection measures

    c.    Rule-based measures

    d.    Nonparametric statistics

*261. b.* Anomaly detectors identify abnormal, unusual behavior (anomalies) on a host or network. In threshold detection measures, certain attributes of user and system behavior are expressed in terms of counts, with some level established as permissible. Such behavior attributes can include the number of files accessed by a user in a given period of time.

Statistical measures include parametric and nonparametric. In parametric measures the distribution of the profiled attributes is assumed to fit a particular pattern. In the nonparametric measures the distribution of the profiled attributes is "learned" from a set of historical data values, observed over time.

Rule-based measures are similar to nonparametric statistical measures in that observed data defines acceptable usage patterns but differs in that those patterns are specified as rules, not numeric quantities.

**262.** **Which of the following is *best* to replace the use of personal identification numbers (PINs) in the world of automated teller machines (ATMs)?**

    a.    Iris-detection technology

    b.    Voice technology

    c.    Hand technology

    d.    Fingerprint technology

*262. a.* An ATM customer can stand within three feet of a camera that automatically locates and scans the iris in the eye. The scanned bar code is then compared against previously stored code in the bank's file. Iris-detection technology is far superior for accuracy compared to the accuracy of voice, face, hand, and fingerprint identification systems. Iris technology does not require a PIN.

**263.** **Which of the following is true about biometrics?**

    a.    Least expensive and least secure

    b.    Most expensive and least secure

    c.    Most expensive and most secure

    d.    Least expensive and most secure

***263. c.***    Biometrics tends to be the most expensive and most secure. In general, passwords are the least expensive authentication technique and generally the least secure. Memory tokens are less expensive than smart tokens but have less functionality. Smart tokens with a human interface do not require reading equipment but are more convenient to use.

**264.**    **Which of the following is preferable for environments at high risk of identity spoofing?**

    a.    Digital signature

    b.    One-time passwords

    c.    Digital certificate

    d.    Mutual authentication

***264. d.***    If a one-way method is used to authenticate the initiator (typically a road warrior) to the responder (typically an IPsec gateway), a digital signature is used to authenticate the responder to the initiator. One-way authentication, such as one-time passwords or digital certificates on tokens is well suited for road warrior usage, whereas mutual authentication is preferable for environments at high risk of identity spoofing, such as wireless networks.

**265.**    **Which of the following is *not* a substitute for logging out of the information system?**

    a.    Previous logon notification

    b.    Concurrent session control

    c.    Session lock

    d.    Session termination

***265. c.***    Both users and the system can initiate session lock mechanisms. However, a session lock is not a substitute for logging out of the information system because it is done at the end of the workday. Previous logon notification occurs at the time of login. Concurrent session control deals with either allowing or not allowing multiple sessions at the same time. Session termination can occur when there is a disconnection of the telecommunications link or other network operational problems.

**266.**    **Which of the following violates a user's privacy?**

    a.    Freeware

    b.    Firmware

    c.    Spyware

    d.    Crippleware

***266. c.***    Spyware is malicious software (i.e., malware) intended to violate a user's privacy because it is invading many computer systems to monitor personal activities and to conduct financial fraud.

Freeware is incorrect because it is software made available to the public at no cost, but the author retains the copyright and can place restrictions on how the program is used. Some freeware can be harmless whereas others are harmful. Not all freeware violates a user's privacy.

Firmware is incorrect because it is software that is permanently stored in a hardware device, which enables reading but not writing or modifying. The most common device for firmware is read-only-memory (ROM).

Crippleware is incorrect because it enables trial (limited) versions of vendor products that operate only for a limited period of time. Crippleware does not violate a user's privacy.

**267.** **Network-based intrusion prevention systems (IPS) are typically deployed:**

    a.    Inline

    b.    Outline

    c.    Online

    d.    Offline

**267. *a.*** Network-based IPS performs packet sniffing and analyzes network traffic to identify and stop suspicious activity. They are typically deployed inline, which means that the software acts like a network firewall. It receives packets, analyzes them, and decides whether they should be permitted, and allows acceptable packets to pass through. They detect some attacks on networks before they reach their intended targets. The other three choices are not relevant here.

**268.** **Identity thieves can get personal information through which of the following means?**

    1.    Dumpster diving

    2.    Skimming

    3.    Phishing

    4.    Pretexting

        a.    1 only

        b.    3 only

        c.    1 and 3

        d.    1, 2, 3, and 4

**268. *d.*** Identity thieves get personal information by stealing records or information while they are on the job, bribing an employee who has access to these records, hacking electronic records, and conning information out of employees. Sources of personal information include the following: Dumpster diving, which includes rummaging through personal trash, a business' trash, or public trash dumps.

Skimming includes stealing credit card or debit card numbers by capturing the information in a data storage device. Phishing and pretexting deal with stealing information through e-mail or phone by posing as legitimate companies and claiming that you have a problem with your account. This practice is known as phishing online or pretexting (social engineering) by phone respectively.

**269.** **Which of the following application-related authentication types is risky?**

    a.   External authentication

    b.   Proprietary authentication

    c.   Pass-through authentication

    d.   Host/user authentication

*269. c.* Pass-through authentication refers to passing operating system credentials (e.g., username and password) unencrypted from the operating system to the application system. This is risky due to unencrypted credentials. Note that pass-through authentications can be encrypted or unencrypted.

External authentication is incorrect because it uses a directory server, which is not risky. Proprietary authentication is incorrect because username and passwords are part of the application, not the operating system. This is less risky. Host/user authentication is incorrect because it is performed within a controlled environment (e.g., managed workstations and servers within an organization). Some applications may rely on previous authentication performed by the operating system. This is less risky.

**270.** **Inference attacks are based on which of the following?**

    a.   Hardware and software

    b.   Firmware and freeware

    c.   Data and information

    d.   Middleware and courseware

*270. c.* An inference attack is where a user or an intruder can deduce information to which he had no privilege from information to which he has privilege.

**271.** **Out-of-band attacks against electronic authentication protocols include which of the following?**

    1.   Password guessing attack

    2.   Replay attack

    3.   Verifier impersonation attack

    4.   Man-in-the-middle attack

    a.   1 only

    b.   3 only

    c.   1 and 2

    d.   3 and 4

**271. d.** In an out-of-band attack, the attack is against an authentication protocol run where the attacker assumes the role of a subscriber with a genuine verifier or relying party. The attacker obtains secret and sensitive information such as passwords and account numbers and amounts when a subscriber manually enters them into a one-time password device or confirmation code sent to the verifier or relying party.

In an out-of-band attack, the attacker alters the authentication protocol channel through session hijacking, verifier impersonation, or man-in-the-middle (MitM) attacks. In a verifier impersonation attack, the attacker impersonates the verifier and induces the claimant to reveal his secret token. The MitM attack is an attack on the authentication protocol run in which the attacker positions himself in between the claimant and verifier so that he can intercept and alter data traveling between them.

In a password guessing attack, an impostor attempts to guess a password in repeated logon trials and succeeds when he can log onto a system. In a replay attack, an attacker records and replays some part of a previous good protocol run to the verifier. Both password guessing and replay attacks are examples of in-band attacks. In an in-band attack, the attack is against an authentication protocol where the attacker assumes the role of a claimant with a genuine verifier or actively alters the authentication channel. The goal of the attack is to gain authenticated access or learn authentication secrets.

**272.** Which of the following information security control families requires a cross-cutting approach?

    a. Access control

    b. Audit and accountability

    c. Awareness and training

    d. Configuration management

**272. a.** Access control requires a cross-cutting approach because it is related to access control, incident response, audit and accountability, and configuration management control families (areas). Cross-cutting means a control in one area affects the controls in other-related areas. The other three choices require a control-specific approach.

**273.** Confidentiality controls include which of the following?

    a. Cryptography

    b. Passwords

    c. Tokens

    d. Biometrics

**273. a.** Cryptography, which is a part of technical control, ensures the confidentiality goal. The other three choices are part of user identification and authentication controls, which are also a part of technical control.

**274.** Which of the following is *not* an example of authorization and access controls?

    a.   Logical access controls

    b.   Role-based access controls

    c.   Reconstruction of transactions

    d.   System privileges

*274. c.* Reconstruction of transactions is a part of audit trail mechanisms. The other three choices are a part of authorization and access controls.

**275.** Which of the following is *not* an example of access control policy?

    a.   Performance-based policy

    b.   Identity-based policy

    c.   Role-based policy

    d.   Rule-based policy

*275. a.* Performance-based policy is used to evaluate an employee's performance annually or other times. The other three choices are examples of an access control policy where they control access between users and objects in the information system.

**276.** From security and safety viewpoints, which of the following does *not* support the static separation-of-duty constraints?

    a.   Mutually exclusive roles

    b.   Reduced chances of collusion

    c.   Conflict-of-interest in tasks

    d.   Implicit constraints

*276. d.* It is difficult to meet the security and safety requirements with flexible access control policies expressed in implicit constraints such as role-based access control (RBAC) and rule-based access control (RuBAC). Static separation-of-duty constraints require that two roles of an individual must be mutually exclusive, constraints must reduce the chances of collusion, and constraints must minimize the conflict-of-interest in task assignments to employees.

**277.** Which of the following are compatible with each other in the pair in performing similar functions in information security?

    a.   SSO and RSO

    b.   DES and DNS

    c.   ARP and PPP

    d.   SLIP and SKIP

***277. a.*** A single sign-on (SSO) technology allows a user to authenticate once and then access all the resources the user is authorized to use. A reduced sign-on (RSO) technology allows a user to authenticate once and then access many, but not all, of the resources the user is authorized to use. Hence, SSO and RSO perform similar functions.

The other three choices do not perform similar functions. Data encryption standard (DES) is a symmetric cipher encryption algorithm. Domain name system (DNS) provides an Internet translation service that resolves domain names to Internet Protocol (IP) addresses and vice versa. Address resolution protocol (ARP) is used to obtain a node's physical address. Point-to-point protocol (PPP) is a data-link framing protocol used to frame data packets on point-to-point lines. Serial line Internet protocol (SLIP) carries Internet Protocol (IP) over an asynchronous serial communication line. PPP replaced SLIP. Simple key management for Internet protocol (SKIP) is designed to work with the IPsec and operates at the network layer of the TCP/IP protocol, and works very well with sessionless datagram protocols.

**278.** **How is identification different from authentication?**

    a.    Identification comes after authentication.

    b.    Identification requires a password, and authentication requires a user ID.

    c.    Identification and authentication are the same.

    d.    Identification comes before authentication.

***278. d.*** Identification is the process used to recognize an entity such as a user, program, process, or device. It is performed first, and authentication is done next. Identification and authentication are not the same. Identification requires a user ID, and authentication requires a password.

**279.** **Accountability is *not* related to which of the following information security objectives?**

    a.    Identification

    b.    Availability

    c.    Authentication

    d.    Auditing

***279. b.*** Accountability is typically accomplished by identifying and authenticating system users and subsequently tracing their actions through audit trails (i.e., auditing).

**280.** **Which of the following statements is true about mandatory access control?**

    a.    It does not use sensitivity levels.

    b.    It uses tags.

    c.    It does not use security labels.

    d.    It reduces system performance.

***280. d.*** Mandatory access control is expensive and causes system overhead, resulting in reduced system performance of the database. Mandatory access control uses sensitivity levels and security labels. Discretionary access controls use tags.

**281.** **What control is referred to when an auditor reviews access controls and logs?**

    a.    Directive control

    b.    Preventive control

    c.    Corrective control

    d.    Detective control

***281. d.*** The purpose of auditors reviewing access controls and logs is to find out whether employees follow security policies and access rules, and to detect any violations and anomalies. The audit report helps management to improve access controls.

**282.** **Logical access controls are a technical means of implementing security policy decisions. It requires balancing the often-competing interests. Which of the following trade-offs should receive the highest interest?**

    a.    User-friendliness

    b.    Security principles

    c.    Operational requirements

    d.    Technical constraints

***282. a.*** A management official responsible for a particular application system, subsystem, or group of systems develops the security policy. The development of an access control policy may not be an easy endeavor. User-friendliness should receive the highest interest because the system is designed for users, and the system usage is determined by whether the system is user-friendly. The other three choices have a competing interest in a security policy, but they are not as important as the user-friendliness issue. An example of a security principle is "least privilege."

**283.** **Which of the following types of passwords is counterproductive?**

    a.    System-generated passwords

    b.    Encrypted passwords

    c.    Nonreusable passwords

    d.    Time-based passwords

***283. a.*** A password-generating program can produce passwords in a random fashion, rather than relying on user-selected ones. System-generated passwords are usually hard to remember, forcing users to write them down. This defeats the whole purpose of stronger passwords.

Encrypted passwords protect from unauthorized viewing or using. The encrypted password file is kept secure with access permission given to security administration for maintenance or to the passwords system itself. This approach is productive in keeping the passwords secure and secret.

Nonreusable passwords are used only once. A series of passwords are generated by a cryptographic secure algorithm and given to the user for use at the time of login. Each password expires after its initial use and is not repeated or stored anywhere. This approach is productive in keeping the passwords secure and secret.

In time-based passwords, the password changes every minute or so. A smart card displays some numbers that are a function of the current time and the user's secret key. To get access, the user must enter a number based on his own key and the current time. Each password is a unique one and therefore need not be written down or guessed. This approach is productive and effective in keeping the passwords secure and secret.

**284.** **Which of the following issues is closely related to logical access controls?**

    a.    Employee issues

    b.    Hardware issues

    c.    Operating systems software issues

    d.    Application software issues

*284. a.* The largest risk exposure remains with employees. Personnel security measures are aimed at hiring honest, competent, and capable employees. Job requirements need to be programmed into the logical access control software. Policy is also closely linked to personnel issues. A deterrent effect arises among employees when they are aware that their misconduct (intentional or unintentional) may be detected. Selecting the right type and access level for employees, informing which employees need access accounts and what type and level of access they require, and informing changes to access requirements are also important. Accounts and accesses should not be granted or maintained for employees who should not have them in the first place. The other three choices are distantly related to logical access controls when compared to employee issues.

**285.** **Which of the following password methods are based on fact or opinion?**

    a.    Static passwords

    b.    Dynamic passwords

    c.    Cognitive passwords

    d.    Conventional passwords

*285. c.* Cognitive passwords use fact-based and opinion-based cognitive data as a basis for user authentication. It uses interactive software routines that can handle initial user enrollment and subsequent cue response exchanges for system access. Cognitive passwords are based on a person's lifetime experiences and events where only that person, or his family, knows about them. Examples include the person's favorite high school teachers' names, colors, flowers, foods, and places. Cognitive password procedures do not depend on the "people memory" often associated with the conventional password dilemma. However, implementation of a cognitive password mechanism could cost money and take more time to authenticate a user. Cognitive passwords are easier to recall and difficult for others to guess.

Conventional (static) passwords are difficult to remember whether user-created or system-generated and are easy to guess by others. Dynamic passwords change each time a user signs on to the computer. Even in the dynamic password environment, a user needs to remember an initial code for the computer to recognize him. Conventional passwords are reusable whereas dynamic ones are not. Conventional passwords rely on memory.

**286.** Which of the security codes is the longest, thereby making it difficult to guess?

    a.   Passphrases

    b.   Passwords

    c.   Lockwords

    d.   Passcodes

*286. a.* Passphrases have the virtue of length (e.g., up to 80 characters), making them both difficult to guess and burdensome to discover by an exhaustive trial-and-error attack on a system. The number of characters used in the other three choices is smaller (e.g., four to eight characters) than passphrases. All four security codes are user identification mechanisms.

Passwords are uniquely associated with a single user. Lockwords are system-generated terminal passwords shared among users. Passcodes are a combination of password and ID card.

**287.** Anomaly detection approaches used in intrusion detection systems (IDS) require which of the following?

    a.   Tool sets

    b.   Skill sets

    c.   Training sets

    d.   Data sets

*287. c.* Anomaly detection approaches often require extensive training sets of system event records to characterize normal behavior patterns. Skill sets are also important for the IT security analyst. Tool sets and data sets are not relevant here because the tool sets may contain software or hardware, and the data sets may contain data files and databases.

**288.** What is a marking assigned to a computing resource called?

    a.   Security tag

    b.   Security label

    c.   Security level

    d.   Security attribute

***288. b.*** A security label is a marking bound to a resource (which may be a data unit) that names or designates the security attributes of that resource. A security tag is an information unit containing a representation of certain security-related information (e.g., a restrictive attribute bitmap).

A security level is a hierarchical indicator of the degree of sensitivity to a certain threat. It implies, according to the security policy enforced, a specific level of protection. A security attribute is a security-related quality of an object. Security attributes may be represented as hierarchical levels, bits in a bitmap, or numbers. Compartments, caveats, and release markings are examples of security attributes.

**289.** **Which of the following is *most* risky?**

    a.    Permanent access

    b.    Guest access

    c.    Temporary access

    d.    Contractor access

***289. c.*** The greatest problem with temporary access is that once temporary access is given to an employee, it is not reverted back to the previous status after the project has been completed. This can be due to forgetfulness on both sides of employee and employer or the lack of a formal system for change notification. There can be a formal system of change notification for permanent access, and guest or contractor accesses are removed after the project has been completed.

**290.** **Which of the following deals with access control by group?**

    a.    Discretionary access control

    b.    Mandatory access control

    c.    Access control list

    d.    Logical access control

***290. a.*** Discretionary access controls deal with the concept of control objectives, or control over individual aspects of an enterprise's processes or resources. They are based on the identity of the users and of the objects they want to access. Discretionary access controls are implemented by one user or the network/system administrator to specify what levels of access other users are allowed to have.

Mandatory access controls are implemented based on the user's security clearance or trust level and the particular sensitivity designation of each file. The owner of a file or object has no discretion as to who can access it.

An access control list is based on which user can access what objects. Logical access controls are based on a user-supplied identification number or code and password. Discretionary access control is by group association whereas mandatory access control is by sensitivity level.

**291.** Which of the following provides a finer level of granularity (i.e., more restrictive security) in the access control process?

    a.    Mandatory access control

    b.    Discretionary access control

    c.    Access control list

    d.    Logical access control

***291. b.*** Discretionary access control offers a finer level of granularity in the access control process. Mandatory access controls can provide access to broad categories of information, whereas discretionary access controls can be used to fine-tune those broad controls, override mandatory restrictions as needed, and accommodate special circumstances.

**292.** For identity management, which of the following is supporting the determination of an authentic identity?

    1.    X.509 authentication framework

    2.    Internet Engineering Task Force's PKI

    3.    Secure DNS initiatives

    4.    Simple public key infrastructure

    a.    1 only

    b.    2 only

    c.    3 only

    d.    1, 2, 3, and 4

***292. d.*** Several infrastructures are devoted to providing identities and the means of authenticating those identities. Examples of these infrastructures include the X.509 authentication framework, the Internet Engineering Task Force's PKI (IETF's PKI), the secure domain name system (DNS) initiatives, and the simple public key infrastructure (SPKI).

**293.** Which one of the following methodologies or techniques provides the *most* effective strategy for limiting access to individual sensitive files?

    a.    Access control list and both discretionary and mandatory access control

    b.    Mandatory access control and access control list

    c.    Discretionary access control and access control list

    d.    Physical access control to hardware and access control list with discretionary access control

***293. a.*** The best control for protecting sensitive files is using mandatory access controls supplemented by discretionary access controls and implemented through the use of an access control list. A complementary mandatory access control mechanism can prevent the Trojan horse attack that can be allowed by the discretionary access control. The mandatory access control prevents the system from giving sensitive information to any user who is not explicitly authorized to access a resource.

**294.** **Which of the following security control mechanisms is simplest to administer?**

    a.    Discretionary access control

    b.    Mandatory access control

    c.    Access control list

    d.    Logical access control

*294. b.* Mandatory access controls are the simplest to use because they can be used to grant broad access to large sets of files and to broad categories of information. Discretionary access controls are not simple to use due to their finer level of granularity in the access control process. Both the access control list and logical access control require a significant amount of administrative work because they are based on the details of each individual user.

**295.** **Which of the following use data by row to represent the access control matrix?**

    a.    Capabilities and profiles

    b.    Protection bits and access control list

    c.    Profiles and protection bits

    d.    Capabilities and access control list

*295. a.* Capabilities and profiles are used to represent the access control matrix data by row and connect accessible objects to the user. On the other hand, a protection bit-based system and access control list represents the data by column, connecting a list of users to an object.

**296.** **The process of identifying users and objects is important to which of the following?**

    a.    Discretionary access control

    b.    Mandatory access control

    c.    Access control

    d.    Security control

*296. a.* Discretionary access control is a means of restricting access to objects based on the identity of subjects and/or groups to which they belong. In a mandatory access control mechanism, the owner of a file or object has no discretion as to who can access it. Both security control and access control are too broad and vague to be meaningful here.

**297.** **Which of the following is a hidden file?**

    a.    Password aging file

    b.    Password validation file

    c.    Password reuse file

    d.    Shadow password file

**297. d.**    The shadow password file is a hidden file that stores all users' passwords and is readable only by the root user. The password validation file uses the shadow password file before allowing the user to log in. The password-aging file contains an expiration date, and the password reuse file prevents a user from reusing a previously used password. The files mentioned in the other three choices are not hidden.

**298.** From an access control point of view, which of the following are examples of task transactions and separation of conflicts-of-interests?

    1.    Role-based access control

    2.    Workflow policy

    3.    Rule-based access control

    4.    Chinese Wall policy

        a.    1 and 2

        b.    1 and 3

        c.    2 and 4

        d.    3 and 4

**298. c.**    Workflow policy is a process that operates on rules and procedures. A workflow is specified as a set of tasks and a set of dependencies among the tasks, and the sequencing of these tasks is important (i.e., task transactions). The various tasks in a workflow are usually carried out by several users in accordance with organizational rules represented by the workflow policy. The Chinese Wall policy addresses conflict-of-interest issues, with the objective of preventing illicit flows of information that can result in conflicts of interest. The Chinese Wall policy is simple and easy to describe but difficult to implement. Both role- and rule-based access control can create conflict-of-interest situations because of incompatibility between employee roles and management rules.

**299.** For identity management, which of the following qualifies as continuously authenticated?

        a.    Unique ID

        b.    Signed X.509 certificate

        c.    Password with access control list

        d.    Encryption

**299. d.**    A commonly used method to ensure that access to a communications session is controlled and authenticated continuously is the use of encryption mechanisms to prevent loss of control of the session through session stealing or hijacking. Other methods such as signed x.509 certificates and password files associated with access control lists (ACLs) can bind entities to unique IDs. Although these other methods are good, they do not prevent the loss of control of the session.

**300.** What is a control to prevent an unauthorized user from starting an alternative operating system?

    a. Shadow password

    b. Encryption password

    c. Power-on password

    d. Network password

***300. c.*** A computer system can be protected through a power-on password, which prevents an unauthorized user from starting an alternative operating system. The other three types of passwords mentioned do not have the preventive nature, as does the power-on password.

**301.** The concept of least privilege is based on which of the following?

    a. Risk assessment

    b. Information flow enforcement

    c. Access enforcement

    d. Account management

***301. a.*** An organization practices the concept of least privilege for specific job duties and information systems, including specific responsibilities, network ports, protocols, and services in accordance with risk assessments. These practices are necessary to adequately mitigate risk to organizations' operations, assets, and individuals. The other three choices are specific components of access controls.

**302.** Which of the following is the primary technique used by commercially available intrusion detection and prevention systems (IDPS) to analyze events to detect attacks?

    a. Signature-based IDPS

    b. Anomaly-based IDPS

    c. Behavior-based IDPS

    d. Statistical-based IDPS

***302. a.*** There are two primary approaches to analyzing events to detect attacks: signature detection and anomaly detection. Signature detection is the primary technique used by most commercial systems; however, anomaly detection is the subject of much research and is used in a limited form by a number of intrusion detection and prevention systems (IDPS). Behavior and statistical based IDPS are part of anomaly-based IDPS.

**303.** For electronic authentication, which of the following is an example of a passive attack?

    a. Eavesdropping

    b. Man-in-the-middle

    c. Impersonation

    d. Session hijacking

**303. a.** A passive attack is an attack against an authentication protocol where the attacker intercepts data traveling along the network between the claimant and verifier but does not alter the data. Eavesdropping is an example of a passive attack.

A man-in-the-middle (MitM) attack is incorrect because it is an active attack on the authentication protocol run in which the attacker positions himself between the claimant and verifier so that he can intercept and alter data traveling between them.

Impersonation is incorrect because it is an attempt to gain access to a computer system by posing as an authorized user. It is the same as masquerading, spoofing, and mimicking.

Session hijacking is incorrect because it is an attack that occurs during an authentication session within a database or system. The attacker disables a user's desktop system, intercepts responses from the application, and responds in ways that probe the session. Man-in-the-middle, impersonation, and session hijacking are examples of active attacks. Note that MitM attacks can be passive or active depending on the intent of the attacker because there are mild MitM or strong MitM attacks.

**304.** Which of the following complementary strategies to mitigate token threats raise the threshold for successful attacks?

    a. Physical security mechanisms

    b. Multiple security factors

    c. Complex passwords

    d. System and network security controls

**304. b.** Token threats include masquerading, off-line attacks, and guessing passwords. Multiple factors raise the threshold for successful attacks. If an attacker needs to steal the cryptographic token and guess a password, the work factor may be too high.

Physical security mechanisms are incorrect because they may be employed to protect a stolen token from duplication. Physical security mechanisms can provide tamper evidence, detection, and response.

Complex passwords are incorrect because they may reduce the likelihood of a successful guessing attack. By requiring the use of long passwords that do not appear in common dictionaries, attackers may be forced to try every possible password.

System and network security controls are incorrect because they may be employed to prevent an attacker from gaining access to a system or installing malicious software (malware).

**305.** Which of the following is the correct description of roles between a registration authority (RA) and a credential service provider (CSP) involved in identity proofing?

    a. The RA may be a part of the CSP.

    b. The RA may be a separate entity.

    c. The RA may be a trusted relationship.

    d. The RA may be an independent entity.

**305. c.**   The RA may be a part of the CSP, or it may be a separate and independent entity; however a trusted relationship always exists between the RA and CSP. Either the RA or CSP must maintain records of the registration. The RA and CSP may provide services on behalf of an organization or may provide services to the public.

**306.** **What is spoofing?**

    a.    Active attack

    b.    Passive attack

    c.    Surveillance attack

    d.    Exhaustive attack

**306. a.**   Spoofing is a tampering activity and is an active attack. Sniffing is a surveillance activity and is a passive attack. An exhaustive attack (i.e., brute force attack) consists of discovering secret data by trying all possibilities and checking for correctness. For a four-digit password, you might start with 0000 and move to 0001 and 0002 until 9999.

**307.** **Which of the following is an example of infrastructure threats related to the registration process required in identity proofing?**

    a.    Separation of duties

    b.    Record keeping

    c.    Impersonation

    d.    Independent audits

**307. c.**   There are two general categories of threats to the registration process: impersonation and either compromise or malfeasance of the infrastructure (RAs and CSPs). Infrastructure threats are addressed by normal computer security controls such as separation of duties, record keeping, and independent audits.

**308.** **In electronic authentication, which of the following is not trustworthy?**

    a.    Claimants

    b.    Registration authorities

    c.    Credentials services providers

    d.    Verifiers

**308. a.**   Registration authorities (RAs), credential service providers (CSPs), verifiers, and relying parties are ordinarily trustworthy in the sense of being correctly implemented and not deliberately malicious. However, claimants or their systems may not be trustworthy or else their identity claims could simply be trusted. Moreover, whereas RAs, CSPs, and verifiers are normally trustworthy, they are not invulnerable and could become corrupted. Therefore, protocols that expose long-term authentication secrets more than are absolutely required, even to trusted entities, should be avoided.

**309.** An organization is experiencing excessive turnover of employees. Which of the following is the *best* access control policy under these situations?

    a.    Rule-based access control (RuBAC)

    b.    Mandatory access control (MAC)

    c.    Role-based access control (RBAC)

    d.    Discretionary access control (DAC)

*309. c.*   Employees can come and go, but their roles do not change, such as a doctor or nurse in a hospital. With role-based access control, access decisions are based on the roles that individual users have as part of an organization. Employee names may change but the roles does not. This access control is the best for organizations experiencing excessive employee turnover.

Rule-based access control and mandatory access control are the same because they are based on specific rules relating to the nature of the subject and object. Discretionary access control is a means to restrict access to objects based on the identity of subjects and/or groups to which they belong.

**310.** The principle of *least* privilege supports which of the following?

    a.    All or nothing privileges

    b.    Super-user privileges

    c.    Appropriate privileges

    d.    Creeping privileges

*310. c.*   The principle of least privilege refers to granting users only those accesses required to perform their duties. Only the concept of "appropriate privilege" is supported by the principle of least privilege.

**311.** What is password management an example of?

    a.    Directive control

    b.    Preventive control

    c.    Detective control

    d.    Corrective control

*311. b.*   Password management is an example of preventive controls in that passwords deter unauthorized users from accessing a system unless they know the password through some other means.

**312.** Which one of the following access control policy uses an access control matrix for its implementation?

    a.    Discretionary access control (DAC)

    b.    Mandatory access control (MAC)

    c.    Role-based access control (RBAC)

    d.    Access control lists (ACLs)

*312. a.*   A discretionary access control (DAC) model uses access control matrix where it places the name of users (subjects) in each row and the names of objects (files or programs) in each column of a matrix. The other three choices do not use an access control matrix.

**313.**    **Access control mechanisms include which of the following?**

    a.    Directive, preventive, and detective controls

    b.    Corrective, recovery, and preventive controls

    c.    Logical, physical, and administrative controls

    d.    Management, operational, and technical controls

*313. c.*   Access control mechanisms include logical (passwords and encryption), physical (keys and tokens), and administrative (forms and procedures) controls. Directive, preventive, detective, corrective, and recovery controls are controls by action. Management, operational, and technical controls are controls by nature.

**314.**    **Which one of the following access control policy uses security labels?**

    a.    Discretionary access control (DAC)

    b.    Mandatory access control (MAC)

    c.    Role-based access control (RBAC)

    d.    Access control lists (ACLs)

*314. b.*   Security labels and interfaces are used to determine access based on the mandatory access control (MAC) policy. A security label is the means used to associate a set of security attributes with a specific information object as part of the data structure for that object. Labels could be designated as proprietary data or public data. The other three choices do not use security labels.

**315.**    **Intrusion detection and prevention systems serve as which of the following?**

    a.    Barrier mechanism

    b.    Monitoring mechanism

    c.    Accountability mechanism

    d.    Penetration mechanism

*315. b.*   Intrusion detection and prevention systems (IDPS) serve as monitoring mechanisms, watching activities, and making decisions about whether the observed events are suspicious. IDPS can spot attackers circumventing firewalls and report them to system administrators, who can take steps to prevent damage. Firewalls serve as barrier mechanisms, barring entry to some kinds of network traffic and allowing others, based on a firewall policy.

**316.** Which of the following can coexist in providing strong access control mechanisms?

    a. Kerberos authentication and single sign-on system

    b. Kerberos authentication and digital signature system

    c. Kerberos authentication and asymmetric key system

    d. Kerberos authentication and digital certificate system

*316. a.* When Kerberos authentication is combined with single sign-on systems, it requires establishment of and operating the privilege servers. Kerberos uses symmetric key cryptography, and the other three choices are examples of asymmetric key cryptography.

**317.** Uses of honeypots and padded cells have which of the following?

    a. Social implications

    b. Legal implications

    c. Technical implications

    d. Psychological implications

*317. b.* The legal implications of using honeypot and padded cell systems are not well defined. It is important to seek guidance from legal counsel before deciding to use either of these systems.

**318.** From security and safety viewpoints, safety enforcement is tied to which of the following?

    a. Job rotation

    b. Job description

    c. Job enlargement

    d. Job enrichment

*318. b.* Safety is fundamental to ensuring that the most basic of access control policies can be enforced. This enforcement is tied to the job description of an individual employee through access authorizations (e.g., permissions and privileges). Job description lists job tasks, duties, roles, and responsibilities expected of an employee, including safety and security requirements.

The other three choices do not provide safety enforcements. Job rotation makes an employee well-rounded because it broadens an employee's work experience, job enlargement adds width to a job, and job enrichment adds depth to a job.

**319.** Which of the following is the correct sequence of actions in access control mechanisms?

    a. Access profiles, authentication, authorization, and identification

    b. Security rules, identification, authorization, and authentication

    c. Identification, authentication, authorization, and accountability

    d. Audit trails, authorization, accountability, and identification

***319. c.*** Identification comes before authentication, and authorization comes after authentication. Accountability is last where user actions are recorded.

**320.** **The principle of least privilege is *most* closely linked to which of the following security objectives?**

    a.    Confidentiality

    b.    Integrity

    c.    Availability

    d.    Nonrepudiation

***320. b.*** The principle of least privilege deals with access control authorization mechanisms, and as such the principle ensures integrity of data and systems by limiting access to data/information and information systems.

**321.** **Which of the following is a *major* vulnerability with Kerberos model?**

    a.    User

    b.    Server

    c.    Client

    d.    Key-distribution-server

***321. d.*** A major vulnerability with the Kerberos model is that if the key distribution server is attacked, every secret key used on the network is compromised. The principals involved in the Kerberos model include the user, the client, the key-distribution-center, the ticket-granting-service, and the server providing the requested services.

**322.** **For electronic authentication, identity proofing involves which of the following?**

    a.    CSP

    b.    RA

    c.    CSP and RA

    d.    CA and CRL

***322. c.*** Identity proofing is the process by which a credential service provider (CSP) and a registration authority (RA) validate sufficient information to uniquely identify a person. A certification authority (CA) is not involved in identity proofing. A CA is a trusted entity that issues and revokes public key certificates. A certificate revocation list (CRL) is not involved in identity proofing. A CRL is a list of revoked public key certificates created and digitally signed by a CA.

**323.** **A lattice security model is an example of which of the following access control policies?**

    a.    Discretionary access control (DAC)

    b.    Non-DAC

    c.    Mandatory access control (MAC)

    d.    Non-MAC

***323. b.*** A lattice security model is based on a nondiscretionary access control (non-DAC) model. A lattice model is a partially ordered set for which every pair of elements (subjects and objects) has a greatest lower bound and a least upper bound. The subject has the greatest lower bound, and the object has the least upper bound.

**324.** **Which of the following is *not* a common type of electronic credential?**

    a.    SAML assertions

    b.    X.509 public-key identity certificates

    c.    X.509 attribute certificates

    d.    Kerberos tickets

***324. a.*** Electronic credentials are digital documents used in authentication that bind an identity or an attribute to a subscriber's token. Security assertion markup language (SAML) is a specification for encoding security assertions in the extensible markup language (XML). SAML assertions have nothing to do with electronic credential because they can be used by a verifier to make a statement to a relying party about the identity of a claimant.

An X.509 public-key identity certificate is incorrect because binding an identity to a public key is a common type of electronic credential. X.509 attribute certificate is incorrect because binding an identity or a public key with some attribute is a common type of electronic credential. Kerberos tickets are incorrect because encrypted messages binding the holder with some attribute or privilege is a common type of electronic credential.

**325.** **Registration fraud in electronic authentication can be deterred by making it more difficult to accomplish or by increasing the likelihood of which of the following?**

    a.    Direction

    b.    Prevention

    c.    Detection

    d.    Correction

***325. c.*** Making it more difficult to accomplish or increasing the likelihood of detection can deter registration fraud. The goal is to make impersonation more difficult.

**326.** **Which one of the following access control policies treats users and owners as the same?**

    a.    Discretionary access control (DAC)

    b.    Mandatory access control (MAC)

    c.    Role-based access control (RBAC)

    d.    Access control lists (ACLs)

***326. a.*** A discretionary access control (DAC) mechanism enables users to grant or revoke access to any of the objects under their control. As such, users are said to be the owners of the objects under their control. Users and owners are different in the other three choices.

**327.** For electronic authentication protocol threats, which of the following are assumed to be physically able to intercept authentication protocol runs?

    a.    Eavesdroppers

    b.    Subscriber impostors

    c.    Impostor verifiers

    d.    Hijackers

*327. a.*   Eavesdroppers are assumed to be physically able to intercept authentication protocol runs; however, the protocol may be designed to render the intercepted messages unintelligible, or to resist analysis that would allow the eavesdropper to obtain information useful to impersonate the claimant.

Subscriber impostors are incorrect because they need only normal communications access to verifiers or relying parties. Impostor verifiers are incorrect because they may have special network capabilities to divert, insert, or delete packets. But, in many cases, such attacks can be mounted simply by tricking subscribers with incorrect links or e-mails or on Web pages, or by using domain names similar to those of relying parties or verifiers. Therefore, the impostors do not necessarily need to have any unusual network capabilities. Hijackers are incorrect because they must divert communications sessions, but this capability may be comparatively easy to achieve today when many subscribers use wireless network access.

**328.** Which of the following is *not* commonly detected and reported by intrusion detection and prevention systems (IDPS)?

    a.    System scanning attacks

    b.    Denial-of-service attacks

    c.    System penetration attacks

    d.    IP address spoofing attacks

*328. d.*   An attacker can send attack packets using a fake source IP address but arrange to wiretap the victims reply to the fake address. The attacker can do this without having access to the computer at the fake address. This manipulation of IP addressing is called IP address spoofing.

A system scanning attack occurs when an attacker probes a target network or system by sending different kinds of packets. Denial-of-service attacks attempt to slow or shut down targeted network systems or services. System penetration attacks involve the unauthorized acquisition and/or alteration of system privileges, resources, or data.

**329.** In-band attacks against electronic authentication protocols include which of the following?

    a.    Password guessing

    b.    Impersonation

    c.    Password guessing and replay

    d.    Impersonation and man-in-the-middle

*329. c.* In an in-band attack, the attacker assumes the role of a claimant with a genuine verifier. These include a password guessing attack and a replay attack. In a password guessing attack, an impostor attempts to guess a password in repeated logon trials and succeeds when he can log onto a system. In a replay attack, an attacker records and replays some part of a previous good protocol run to the verifier. In the verifier impersonation attack, the attacker impersonates the verifier and induces the claimant to reveal his secret token. A man-in-the-middle attack is an attack on the authentication protocol run in which the attacker positions himself between the claimant and verifier so that he can intercept and alter data traveling between them.

**330.** Which of the following access control policies or models provides a straightforward way of granting or denying access for a specified user?

    a.    Role-based access control (RBAC)

    b.    Access control lists (ACLs)

    c.    Mandatory access control (MAC)

    d.    Discretionary access control (DAC)

*330. b.* An access control list (ACL) is an object associated with a file and containing entries specifying the access that individual users or groups of users have to the file. ACLs provide a straightforward way to grant or deny access for a specified user or groups of users. Other choices are not that straightforward in that they use labels, tags, and roles.

**331.** What is impersonating a user or system called?

    a.    Snooping attack

    b.    Spoofing attack

    c.    Sniffing attack

    d.    Spamming attack

*331. b.* Spoofing is an unauthorized use of legitimate identification and authentication data such as user IDs and passwords. Intercepted user names and passwords can be used to impersonate the user on the login or file transfer server host that the user accesses.

Snooping and sniffing attacks are the same in that sniffing is observing the packet's passing by on the network. Spamming is posting identical messages to multiple unrelated newsgroups on the Internet or sending unsolicited e-mail sent indiscriminately to multiple users.

**332.** Which one of the following access-control policy or model requires security clearances for subjects?

    a.    Discretionary access control (DAC)

    b.    Mandatory access control (MAC)

    c.    Role-based access control (RBAC)

    d.    Access control lists (ACLs)

***332. b.***   A mandatory access control (MAC) restricts access to objects based on the sensitivity of the information contained in the objects and the formal authorization (i.e., clearance) of subjects to access information of such sensitivity.

**333.**   **Which of the following is *not* an example of attacks on data and information?**

    a.    Hidden code

    b.    Inference

    c.    Spoofing

    d.    Traffic analysis

***333. c.***   Spoofing is using various techniques to subvert IP-based access control by masquerading as another system by using its IP address. Attacks such as hidden code, inference, and traffic analysis are based on data and information.

**334.**   **Honeypot systems do *not* contain which of the following?**

    a.    Event triggers

    b.    Sensitive monitors

    c.    Sensitive data

    d.    Event loggers

***334. c.***   The honeypot system is instrumented with sensitive monitors, event triggers, and event loggers that detect unauthorized accesses and collect information about the attacker's activities. These systems are filled with fabricated data designed to appear valuable.

**335.**   **Intrusion detection and prevention systems look at security policy violations:**

    a.    Statically

    b.    Dynamically

    c.    Linearly

    d.    Nonlinearly

***335. b.***   Intrusion detection and prevention systems (IDPS) look for specific symptoms of intrusions and security policy violations dynamically. IDPS are analogous to security monitoring cameras. Vulnerability analysis systems take a static view of symptoms. Linearly and nonlinearly are not applicable here because they are mathematical concepts.

**336.**   **For biometric accuracy, which of the following defines the point at which the false rejection rates and the false acceptance rates are equal?**

    a.    Type I error

    b.    Type II error

    c.    Crossover error rate

    d.    Type I and II error

**336. c.** In biometrics, crossover error rate is defined as the point at which the false rejection rates and the false acceptance rates are equal. Type I error, called false rejection rate, is incorrect because genuine users are rejected as imposters. Type II error, called false acceptance rate, is incorrect because imposters are accepted as genuine users.

337. Which one of the following does not help in preventing fraud?

    a.    Separation of duties

    b.    Job enlargement

    c.    Job rotation

    d.    Mandatory vacations

**337. b.** Separation of duties, job rotation, and mandatory vacations are management controls that can help in preventing fraud. Job enlargement and job enrichment do not prevent fraud because they are not controls; their purpose is to expand the scope of an employee's work for a better experience and promotion.

338. Access triples used in the implementation of Clark-Wilson security model include which of the following?

    a.    Policy, procedure, and object

    b.    Class, domain, and subject

    c.    Subject, program, and data

    d.    Level, label, and tag

**338. c.** The Clark-Wilson model partitions objects into programs and data for each subject forming a subject/program/data access triple. The generic model for the access triples is <subject, rights, object>.

# SCENARIO-BASED QUESTIONS, ANSWERS, AND EXPLANATIONS

Use the following information to answer questions 1 through 9.

The KPT Company is analyzing authentication alternatives. The company has 10,000 users in 10 locations with five different databases of users. The current authentication access controls are a mix of UNIX and Microsoft related tools. KPT priorities include security, cost, scalability, and transparency.

1. Symbolic link (symlink) attacks do *not* exist on which of the operating systems?

    a.    UNIX

    b.    Windows

    c.    LINUX

    d.    MINIX

**1. b.** Symbolic links are links on UNIX, MINIX, and LINUX systems that point from one file to another file. A symlink vulnerability is exploited by making a symbolic link from a file to which an attacker does have access to a file to which the attacker does not have access. Symlinks do not exist on Windows systems, so symlink attacks cannot be performed against programs or files on those systems. MINIX is a variation of UNIX and is small in size. A major difference between MINIX and UNIX is the editor where the former is faster and the latter is slower.

**2.** Which one of the following is *not* an authentication mechanism?

    a.    What the user knows

    b.    What the user has

    c.    What the user can do

    d.    What the user is

**2. c.** "What the user can do" is defined in access rules or user profiles, which come after a successful authentication. The other three choices are part of an authentication process.

**3.** Which of the following provides strong authentication for centralized authentication servers when used with firewalls?

    a.    User IDs

    b.    Passwords

    c.    Tokens

    d.    Account numbers

**3. c.** For basic authentication, user IDs, passwords, and account numbers are used for internal authentication. Centralized authentication servers such as RADIUS and TACACS/TACACS+ can be integrated with token-based authentication to enhance firewall administration security.

**4.** Which of the following does *not* provide robust authentication?

    a.    Kerberos

    b.    Secure RPC

    c.    Reusable passwords

    d.    Digital certificates

**4. c.** Robust authentication means strong authentication that should be required for accessing internal computer systems. Robust authentication is provided by Kerberos, one-time passwords, challenge-response exchanges, digital certificates, and secure RPC. Reusable passwords provide weak authentication.

**5.** **Which of the following authentication types is *most* effective?**

    a.    Static authentication

    b.    Robust authentication

    c.    Intermittent authentication

    d.    Continuous authentication

*5. d.* Continuous authentication protects against impostors (active attacks) by applying a digital signature algorithm to every bit of data sent from the claimant to the verifier. Also, continuous authentication prevents session hijacking. Static authentication uses reusable passwords, which can be compromised by replay attacks. Robust authentication includes one-time passwords and digital signatures, which can be compromised by session hijacking. Intermittent authentication is not useful because of gaps in user verification.

**6.** **What is the basis for a two-factor authentication mechanism?**

    a.    Something you know and a password

    b.    Something you are and a fingerprint

    c.    Something you have and a key

    d.    Something you have and something you know

*6. d.* A two-factor authentication uses two different kinds of evidence. For example, a challenge-response token card typically requires both physical possession of the card (something you have, one factor) and a PIN (something you know, another factor). The other three choices have only one factor to authenticate.

**7.** **Individual accountability does *not* include which of the following?**

    a.    Unique identifiers

    b.    Access rules

    c.    Audit trails

    d.    Policies and procedures

*7. d.* A basic tenet of IT security is that individuals must be accountable for their actions. If this is not followed and enforced, it is not possible to successfully prosecute those who intentionally damage or disrupt systems or to train those whose actions have unintended adverse effects. The concept of individual accountability drives the need for many security safeguards, such as unique (user) identifiers, audit trails, and access authorization rules. Policies and procedures indicate what to accomplish and how to accomplish objectives. By themselves, they do not exact individual accountability.

**8.** **Which of the following user identification and authentication techniques depend on reference profiles or templates?**

    a.    Memory tokens

    b.    Smart tokens

    c.    Cryptography

    d.    Biometric systems

***8. d.***   Biometric systems require the creation and storage of profiles or templates of individuals wanting system access. This includes physiological attributes such as fingerprints, hand geometry, or retina patterns, or behavioral attributes such as voice patterns and handwritten signatures. Memory tokens and smart tokens involve the creation and distribution of token/PINs and data that tell the computer how to recognize valid tokens or PINs. Cryptography requires the generation, distribution, storage, entry, use, distribution, and archiving of cryptographic keys.

**9.** **Some security authorities believe that re-authentication of every transaction provides stronger security procedures. Which of the following security mechanisms is *least* efficient and least effective for re-authentication?**

    a.    Recurring passwords

    b.    Nonrecurring passwords

    c.    Memory tokens

    d.    Smart tokens

***9. a.***   Recurring passwords are static passwords with reuse and are considered to be a relatively weak security mechanism. Users tend to use easily guessed passwords. Other weaknesses include spoofing users, users stealing passwords through observing keystrokes, and users sharing passwords. The unauthorized use of passwords by outsiders (hackers) or insiders is a primary concern and is considered the least efficient and least effective security mechanism for re-authentication.

Nonrecurring passwords is incorrect because they provide a strong form of re-authentication. Examples include a challenge-response protocol or a dynamic password generator where a unique value is generated for each session. These values are not repeated and are good for that session only. Tokens can help in re-authenticating a user or transaction. Memory tokens store but do not process information. Smart tokens expand the functionality of a memory token by incorporating one or more integrated circuits into the token itself. In other words, smart tokens store and process information. Except for passwords, all the other methods listed in the question are examples of advanced authentication methods that can be applied to re-authentication.

## SOURCES AND REFERENCES

"Access Control in Support of Information Systems, Security Technical Implementation Guide (DISA-STIG, Version 2 and Release 2)," Defense Information Systems Agency (DISA), U.S. Department of Defense (DOD), December 2008.

"Assessment of Access Control Systems (NISTIR 7316)," National Institute of Standards and Technology (NIST), U.S. Department of Commerce, Gaithersburg, Maryland, September 2006.

"Electronic Authentication Guideline (NIST SP800-63R1)," National Institute of Standards and Technology (NIST), U.S. Department of Commerce, Gaithersburg, Maryland, December 2008.

"Guide to Enterprise Password Management (NIST SP800-118 Draft)," National Institute of Standards and Technology (NIST), U.S. Department of Commerce, Gaithersburg, Maryland, April 2009.

"Guide to Intrusion Detection and Prevention Systems (NIST SP800-94)," National Institute of Standards and Technology (NIST), U.S. Department of Commerce, Gaithersburg, Maryland, February 2007.

"Guide to Storage Encryption Technologies (NIST SP 800-111)," National Institute of Standards and Technology (NIST), U.S. Department of Commerce, Gaithersburg, Maryland, November 2007.

"Interfaces for Personal Identity Verification (NIST SP 800-73R1)," National Institute of Standards and Technology (NIST), U.S. Department of Commerce, Gaithersburg, Maryland, March 2006.

"Privilege Management (NISTIR 7657 V0.4 Draft)," National Institute of Standards and Technology (NIST), U.S. Department of Commerce, Gaithersburg, Maryland, November 2009.

# DOMAIN 2

## Telecommunications and Network Security

### TRADITIONAL QUESTIONS, ANSWERS, AND EXPLANATIONS

1.  If QoS is quality of service, QoP is quality of protection, QA is quality assurance, QC is quality control, DoQ is denial of quality, and DoS is denial of service, which of the following affects a network system's performance?

    1.  QoS and QoP

    2.  QA and QC

    3.  DoQ

    4.  DoS

        a.  1 only

        b.  1 and 4

        c.  2 and 3

        d.  1, 2, 3, and 4

    *1. d.* All four items affect a network system performance. QoS parameters include reliability, delay, jitter, and bandwidth, where applications such as e-mail, file transfer, Web access, remote login, and audio/video require different levels of the parameters to operate at different quality levels (i.e., high, medium, or low levels).

    QoP requires that overall performance of a system should be improved by prioritizing traffic and considering the rate of failure or average latency at the lower layer protocols.

QA is the planned systematic activities necessary to ensure that a component, module, or system conforms to established technical requirements. QC is the prevention of defective components, modules, and systems. DoQ results from not implementing the required QA methods and QC techniques for delivering messages, packets, and services.

DoS is the prevention of authorized access to resources or the delaying of time-critical operations. DoS results from DoQ. QoS is related to QoP and DoS which, in turn, relates to DoQ. Therefore, QoS, QoP, QA, QC, DoQ, and DoS are related to each other.

2. **The first step toward securing the resources of a local-area network (LAN) is to verify the identities of system users. Organizations should consider which of the following prior to connecting their LANs to outside networks, particularly the Internet?**

    a.   Plan for implementing locking mechanisms.

    b.   Plan for protecting the modem pools.

    c.   Plan for considering all authentication options.

    d.   Plan for providing the user with his account usage information.

**2. c.** The best thing is to consider all authentication options, not just using the traditional method of passwords. Proper password selection (striking a balance between being easy to remember for the user but difficult to guess for everyone else) has always been an issue. Password-only mechanisms, especially those that transmit the password in the clear (in an unencrypted form) are susceptible to being monitored and captured. This can become a serious problem if the local-area network (LAN) has any uncontrolled connections to outside networks such as the Internet. Because of the vulnerabilities that still exist with the use of password-only mechanisms, more robust mechanisms such as token-based authentication and use of biometrics should be considered.

Locking mechanisms for LAN devices, workstations, or PCs that require user authentication to unlock can be useful to users who must frequently leave their work areas (for a short period of time). These locks enable users to remain logged into the LAN and leave their work areas without exposing an entry point into the LAN.

Modems that provide users with LAN access may require additional protection. An intruder that can access the modem may gain access by successfully guessing a user password. The availability of modem use to legitimate users may also become an issue if an intruder is allowed continual access to the modem. A modem pool is a group of modems acting as a pool instead of individual modems on each workstation. Modem pools provide greater security in denying access to unauthorized users. Modem pools should not be configured for outgoing connections unless access can be carefully controlled.

Security mechanisms that provide a user with his account usage information may alert the user that the account was used in an abnormal manner (e.g., multiple login failures). These mechanisms include notification such as date, time, and location of the last successful login and the number of previous login failures.

**3.** **Which of the following attacks take advantage of dynamic system actions and the ability to manipulate the timing of those actions?**

    a.    Active attacks

    b.    Passive attacks

    c.    Asynchronous attacks

    d.    Tunneling attacks

*3. c.*   Asynchronous attacks take advantage of dynamic system activity to get access. User requests are placed into a queue and are satisfied by a set of predetermined criteria. An attacker can penetrate the queue and modify the data that is waiting to be processed or printed. He might change a queue entry to replace someone else's name or data with his own or to subvert that user's data by replacing it. Here, the time variable is manipulated.

With an active attack, the intruder modifies the intercepted messages with the goal of message modification. An effective tool for protecting messages against both active and passive attacks is cryptography.

With a passive attack, an intruder intercepts messages to view the data. This intrusion is also known as eavesdropping.

Tunneling attacks use one data transfer method to carry data for another method. It may carry unauthorized data in legitimate data packets. It exploits a weakness in a system at a low level of abstraction.

**4.** **Routers, which are network connectivity devices, use which of the following?**

    a.    Sink tree and spanning tree

    b.    Finger table and routing table

    c.    Fault tree and decision tree

    d.    Decision table and truth table

*4. a.*   A sink tree shows the set of optimal routes from all sources to a given destination, rooted at the destination. A sink tree does not contain any loops, so each packet is delivered within a finite and bounded number of hops. The goal of all routing algorithms is to identify and use the sink trees for all routers. A spanning tree uses the sink tree for the router initiating the broadcast. A spanning tree is a subset of the subnet that includes all the routers but does not contain any loops.

A finger table is used for node lookup in peer-to-peer (P2P) networks. Routers use routing tables to route messages and packets. A fault tree is used in analyzing errors and problems in computer software. A decision tree is a graphical representation of the conditions, actions, and rules in making a decision with the use of probabilities in calculating outcomes. A decision table presents a tabular representation of the conditions, actions, and rules in making a decision. A truth table is used in specifying computer logic blocks by defining the values of the outputs for each possible set of input values.

**5.** Enforcing effective data communications security requires other types of security such as physical security. Which of the following can easily compromise such an objective?

    a.    Smart cards with PINs

    b.    Nonreusable passwords

    c.    Network cabling

    d.    Last login messages

**5. c.** Data communications security requires physical security and password controls. The network cables that carry data are vulnerable to intruders. It is a simple matter to tap into cabling and relatively easy to cut the wiring. Therefore, a basic physical security control such as locking up the wiring closet is important.

Smart cards with PINs are incorrect because they do not compromise data communications. They enhance security by using cryptographic keys. Nonreusable passwords are used only once. A series of passwords are generated by a cryptographic secure algorithm and given to the user for use at the time of login. Each password expires after its initial use and is not repeated or stored anywhere. Last login messages are incorrect because they alert unauthorized uses of a user's password and ID combination.

**6.** Which of the following refers to closed-loop control to handle network congestion problems?

    1.    Mid-course corrections are not made.

    2.    Current state of the network is ignored.

    3.    Feedback loop is provided.

    4.    Mid-course corrections are made.

    a.    1 only

    b.    1 and 2

    c.    4 only

    d.    3 and 4

**6. d.** With the open-loop control, when the system is up and running, mid-course corrections are not made, thus ignoring the current states of the network. On the other hand, the closed-loop control is based on the concept of feedback loop with mid-course corrections allowed.

**7.** Which of the following security threats is not applicable to wireless local-area networks (WLANs)?

    a.    Message interception

    b.    System unavailability

    c.    System unreliability

    d.    Theft of equipment

**7. c.**  Even with wireless local-area networks (WLANs), message interception is possible, the system can go down, thus making it unavailable, and equipment can be stolen. However, the wireless LAN is more reliable than the wired LAN due to lack of wiring problems. Cable cuts and wire jams are the most common problems with the wired LANs. Therefore, system unreliability is not a threat for wireless LANs. This is because of the overlapping coverage of wireless access points (APs) provides some level of network redundancy from an end user standpoint; that is, if one AP goes down, the other one's wireless coverage may make the reliability failure seem minimal.

**8.**  **Wireless local-area networks (LANs) have greater risks than wired LANs in which of the following areas?**

    a.    Masquerading and modification/substitution

    b.    Modification/substitution of messages and theft of equipment

    c.    Eavesdropping and masquerading

    d.    Eavesdropping and theft of equipment

**8. b.**  In wireless LANs, the stronger node could block the weaker one, substitute its own messages, and even acknowledge responses from other nodes. Similarly, theft of equipment is a major risk in wireless LANs due to their portability. When equipment moves around, things can easily become missing. Eavesdropping and masquerading are common to both the wired and wireless LANs. Eavesdropping is an unauthorized interception of information. Masquerading is an attempt to gain access to a computer system by posing as an authorized user.

**9.**  **The World Wide Web (WWW) can be protected against the risk of eavesdropping in an economical and convenient manner through the use of which of the following?**

    a.    Link and document encryption

    b.    Secure sockets layer and secure HTTP

    c.    Link encryption and secure socket layer

    d.    Document encryption and secure HTTP

**9. b.**  The risk of eavesdropping occurs on the Internet in at least two ways: traffic analysis and stealing of sensitive information such as credit card numbers. Secure sockets layer (SSL) provides an encrypted TCP/IP pathway between two hosts on the Internet. SSL can be used to encrypt any TCP/IP, such as HTTP, TELNET, or FTP. SSL can use a variety of public key and token-based systems for exchanging a session key. SHTTP (secure HTTP) is an encryption system designed for HTTP and works only with HTTP.

Link encryption provides encryption for all traffic, but it can be performed only with prior arrangement. It is expensive. Document encryption is cumbersome because it requires the documents to be encrypted before they are placed on the server, and they must be decrypted when they are received. Link and document encryption can use either TCP/IP or other protocols.

**10.** **An effective way to run a World Wide Web (WWW) service is *not* by:**

    a.    Disabling automatic directory listings

    b.    Placing the standalone WWW computer outside the firewall in the DMZ

    c.    Implementing encryption

    d.    Relying on third-party providers

*10. d.* Important security features of WWW include (i) disabling automatic directory listings for names and addresses, (ii) placing the standalone, stripped-down WWW computer outside the firewall in the demilitarized zone (DMZ), and (iii) providing encryption when sensitive or personal information is transmitted or stored. There is a potential risk posed by dependence on a limited number of third-party providers in terms of performance and availability of service.

**11.** **For Web services, which of the following uses binary tokens for authentication, digital signatures for integrity, and content-level encryption for confidentiality?**

    a.    Web service interoperability (WS-I)

    b.    Web services security (WS-Security)

    c.    Web services description languages (WSDL)

    d.    Web-Oriented architecture (WOA)

*11. b.* The Web service is a software component or system designed to support an interoperable machine or application-oriented interaction over a network. The Web service has an interface described in a machine-processable format (specifically WSDL). Other systems interact with the Web service in a manner prescribed by its description using simple object access protocol (SOAP) messages, typically conveyed using hypertext transfer protocol (HTTP) with an extensible markup language (XML) serialization with other Web-related standards. Web services security (WS-Security) is a mechanism for incorporating security information into SOAP messages. WS-Security uses binary tokens for authentication, digital signatures for integrity, and content-level encryption for confidentiality.

The other three choices do not provide the same security services as the WS-Security. The Web service interoperability (WS-I) basic profile is a set of standards and clarifications to standards that vendors must follow for basic interoperability with SOAP products. The Web services description language (WSDL) is an XML format for describing network services as a set of endpoints operating on messages containing either document-oriented or procedure-oriented information. WSDL complements the universal description, discovery, and integration (UDDI) standard by providing a uniform way of describing the abstract interface and protocol bindings and deployment details of arbitrary network services. The Web-oriented architecture (WOA) is a set of Web protocols (e.g., HTTP and plain XML) to provide dynamic, scalable, and interoperable Web services.

**12.** **Radio frequency identification technologies rely on which of the following to ensure security?**

    a.   Defense-in-depth strategy

    b.   Defense-in-breadth strategy

    c.   Defense-in-time strategy

    d.   Defense-in-technology strategy

*12. b.*   Radio frequency identification (RFID) technologies are used in supply chain systems which, in turn, use defense-in-breadth strategy for ensuring security. Defense-in-depth strategy considers layered defenses to make security stronger. Defense-in-time strategy considers different time zones in the world where information systems operate. Defense-in-technology strategy deals with making technology less complicated and more secure.

**13.** **Which of the following is *not* an example of race condition attacks?**

    a   Symbolic links

    b.   Object-oriented

    c.   Deadlock

    d.   Core-file manipulation

*13. c.*   Allowing exclusive access to a dedicated input/output device (e.g., printer, plotter, and disk) in response to a user request can lead to a deadlock situation in the absence of spooling. Deadlocks are not related to race condition attacks because the latter is called timing attacks. A symbolic link (symlink) is a file that points to another file. Often, there are programs that can change the permissions granted to a file. If these programs run with privileged permission, a user could strategically create symlinks to trick these programs into modifying or listing critical system files. Symlink attacks are often coupled with race condition attacks.

Symbolic links are links on UNIX, MINIX, and LINUX systems that point from one file to another file. A symlink vulnerability is exploited by making a symbolic link from a file an attacker does have access to a file to which the attacker does not have access. Symlinks do not exist on Windows systems, so symlink attacks cannot be performed against programs or files on those systems. MINIX is a variation of UNIX and is small in size. A major difference between MINIX and UNIX is the editor where the former is faster and the latter is slower.

In object-oriented programming, race conditions occur due to the sharing of common variables among object instances, which could be verified within the program code. For each file access, the program should be written to verify that the file is free before opening it and to check for object-in-use errors.

Core-file manipulation is another example of a race condition where a program or process enters into a privileged mode before the program or process has given up its privileged mode. If an attacker successfully manages to compromise the program or process during its privileged state, then the attacker has won the race.

**14.** What do most effective security controls over remote maintenance ports include?

    a.    Legal contracts and dial-back systems

    b.    Dial-back systems and modem pools

    c.    Legal contracts and modem pools

    d.    Dial-back systems and disconnecting unneeded connections

**14. c.** Remote maintenance ports enable the vendor to fix operating problems. The legal contract with the vendor should specify that there be no trap doors and that any maintenance ports should be approved by both parties. Modem pools consist of a group of modems connected to a server (e.g., host, communications, or terminal). This provides a single point of control. Attackers can target the modem pool, so protect it by installing an application gateway-based firewall control. Dial-back security controls over remote maintenance ports are not effective because they are actually authenticating a place, not a person. It is good practice to disconnect unneeded connections to the outside world, but this makes it difficult for a maintenance contractor to access certain ports when needed in an emergency.

**15.** Which of the following statements is *not* true about Internet firewalls?

    a.    A firewall can enforce security policy.

    b.    A firewall can log Internet activity.

    c.    A firewall can limit an organization's security exposure.

    d.    A firewall can protect against all computer viruses in PCs.

**15. d.** Firewalls (also known as secure gateways) cannot keep personal computer viruses out of a network. There are simply too many types of viruses and too many ways a virus can hide within data. The most practical way to address the virus problem is through host-based virus-protection software and user education concerning the dangers of viruses and precautions to take against them. A firewall enforces the site's security policy, enabling only "approved" services to pass through and those only within the rules set up for them. Because all traffic passes through the firewall, the firewall provides a good place to collect information about system and network use and misuse. As a single point of access, the firewall can record what occurs between the protected network and the external network. A firewall can be used to keep one section of the site's network separate from another section, which also keeps problems in one section isolated from other sections. This limits an organization's security exposure.

**16.** In a distributed computing environment, system security takes on an important role. Two types of network attacks exist: passive and active. Which of the following is an example of a passive attack?

    a.    Attempting to log in to someone else's account

    b.    Installing a wiretap on a network cable to generate false messages

    c.    Denying services to legitimate users

    d.    Sniffing a system password when the user types it

**16. d.**   A passive attack is an attack where the threat merely watches information move across the system. However, no attempt is made to introduce information to exploit vulnerability. Sniffing a system password when the system user types it is an example of a passive attack.

The other three choices are incorrect because they are examples of active attacks. Active attacks occur when the threat makes an overt change or modification to the system in an attempt to take advantage of vulnerability.

**17.**   **Use of preshared keys (PSKs) in a wireless local-area network (WLAN) configuration leads to which of the following?**

1.   Dictionary attack

2.   Rainbow attack

3.   Online attack

4.   Offline attack

     a.   1 and 2

     b.   1 and 3

     c.   2 and 3

     d.   2 and 4

**17. a.**   Dictionary attack is a form of guessing attack in which the attacker attempts to guess a password using a list of possible passwords that is not exhaustive. Rainbow attacks occur in two ways: utilizing rainbow tables, which are used in password cracking, and using preshared keys (PSKs) in a WLAN configuration.

The use of PSK should be avoided. In PSK environments, a secret passphrase is shared between stations and access points. The PSK is generated by combining the WLAN's name and service set identifier (SSID) with a passphrase and then hashing this multiple times. Keys derived from a passphrase shorter than approximately 20 characters provide relatively low levels of security and are subject to dictionary and rainbow attacks. Changing the WLAN name or SSID will not improve the strength of the 256-bit PSK.

An online attack is an attack against an authentication protocol where the attacker either assumes the role of a claimant with a genuine verifier or actively alters the authentication channel. An offline attack is an attack where the attacker obtains some data through eavesdropping that he can analyze in a system of his own choosing. The goal of these attacks may be to gain authenticated access or learn authentication secrets.

**18.**   **Which of the following extensible authentication protocols is *not* secure?**

     a.   EAP-TLS

     b.   EAP-TTLS

     c.   MD5-Challenge

     d.   PEAP

**18. c.** The MD5-Challenge is a legacy-based extensible authentication protocol (EAP) method along with a one-time password and generic token card, which are not secure. Although one-time passwords are generally considered secure by themselves, they are not that secure when they are used in conjunction with a generic token because the token could have been duplicated, fake, lost, or stolen.

The MD-5 Challenge is based on the challenge-handshake authentication protocol (CHAP), which is not a secure protocol. The other three choices are a part of the transport layer security-based (TLS-based) EAP methods, which are very secure.

**19.** Web content filtering software is related to which of the following?

     a.    Web bug

     b.    Blacklisting

     c.    RED

     d.    BLACK

**19. b.** Web content filtering software is a program that prevents access to undesirable web-sites, typically by comparing a requested website address to a list of known bad websites (i.e., blacklisting). Blacklisting is a hold placed against IP addresses to prevent inappropriate or unauthorized use of Internet resources.

The other three choices are not related to the Web content filtering software. Web bug is a tiny image, invisible to a user, placed on Web pages in such a way to enable third parties to track use of Web servers and collect information about the user, including IP addresses, host name, browser type and version, operating system name and version, and cookies. The Web bug may contain malicious code. RED refers to data/information or messages that contain sensitive or classified information that is not encrypted, whereas BLACK refers to information that is encrypted.

**20.** Which of the following identifies calls originating from nonexistent telephone extensions to detect voice-mail fraud?

     a.    Antihacker software

     b.    Call-accounting system

     c.    Antihacker hardware

     d.    Toll-fraud monitoring system

**20. b.** A call-accounting system can indicate calls originating from nonexistent "phantom" telephone extensions or trunks. Along with misconfigured voice-mail systems, unused telephone extensions and uncontrolled maintenance ports are key reasons for voice-mail fraud.

Call-accounting systems provide information about hacking patterns. Antihacker software and hardware can provide multilevel passwords and a self-destruct feature that enables users to delete all messages in their mailboxes if they forget their password. Toll-fraud monitoring systems enable you to catch the voice hacker's activities quickly as the fraud is taking place.

**21.** **Which of the following voice-mail fraud prevention controls can be counterproductive and at the same time counterbalancing?**

1. Turning off direct inward system access ports during nonworking hours

2. Separating internal and external call-forwarding privileges

3. Implementing call vectoring

4. Disconnecting dial-in maintenance ports

    a. 1 and 2

    b. 1 and 4

    c. 3 and 4

    d. 2 and 3

*21. b.* Direct inward system access (DISA) is used to enable an inward calling person access to an outbound line, which is a security weakness when not properly secured. Because hackers work during nonworking hours (evenings and weekends), turning off DISA appears to be a preventive control. However, employees who must make business phone calls during these hours cannot use these lines. They have to use their company/personal credit cards when the DISA is turned off. Similarly, disconnecting dial-in maintenance ports appears to be a preventive control; although, hackers can get into the system through these ports.

Emergency problems cannot be handled when the maintenance ports are disabled. Turning off direct inward system access (DISA) ports during nonworking hours and disconnecting dial-in maintenance ports are counterproductive and counterbalancing.

By separating internal and external call-forwarding privileges for internal lines, an inbound call cannot be forwarded to an outside line unless authorized. Call vectoring can be implemented by answering a call with a recorded message or nothing at all, which may frustrate an attacker. Separating internal and external call-forwarding privileges and implementing call vectoring are counterproductive and balancing.

**22.** **Regarding instant messaging (IM), which of the following is an effective countermeasure to ensure that the enclave users *cannot* connect to public messaging systems?**

    a. Disable file-sharing feature

    b. Restrict IM chat announcements

    c. Block ports at the enclave firewall

    d. Install antivirus software

*22. c.* Blocking ports at the enclave firewall ensures that enclave users cannot connect to public messaging systems. Although a firewall can be effective at blocking incoming connections and rogue outgoing connections, it can be difficult to stop all instant messaging (IM) traffic connected to commonly allowed destination ports (e.g., HTTP, Telnet, FTP, and SMTP), thus resulting in a bypass of firewalls. Therefore, domain names or IP addresses should be blocked in addition to port blocking at a firewall.

IM also provides file-sharing capabilities, which is used to access files on remote computers via a screen name which could be infected with a Trojan horse. To launch malware and file-sharing attacks, an attacker may use the open IM ports because he does not need new ports. Therefore, the file-sharing feature should be disabled on all IM clients.

Restricting IM chat announcements to only authorized users can limit attackers from connecting to computers on the network and sending malicious code. IM is a potential carrier for malware because it provides the ability to transfer text messages and files, thereby becoming an access point for a backdoor Trojan horse. Installing antivirus software with plug-ins to IM clients and scanning files as they are received can help control malware.

**23.** **What do terminating network connections with internal and external communication sessions include?**

1. De-allocating associated TCP/IP addresses and port pairs at the operating system level

2. Logically separating user functionality from system management functionality

3. De-allocating networking assignments at the application system level

4. Isolating security functions from nonsecurity functions at boundaries

    a. 1 and 2

    b. 1 and 3

    c. 2 and 4

    d. 1, 2, 3, and 4

*23. b.* An information system should terminate the internal and external network connection associated with a communications session at the end of the session or after a period of inactivity. This is achieved through de-allocating addresses and assignments at the operating system level and application system level.

**24.** **In a wireless local-area network (WLAN) environment, what is a technique used to ensure effective data security called?**

    a. Message authentication code and transponder

    b. Transmitting in different channels and message authentication code

    c. Transmitting on different channels and enabling encryption

    d. Encryption and transponder

*24. c.* In a wireless local-area network (WLAN) environment, transmitting in different channels at the same time or different times ensures that an intruder cannot predict the transmission patterns. Data can be compared from different channels for completeness and accuracy. In addition, data encryption techniques can be used for encrypting all wireless traffic and for highly secure applications. It is true that anyone with the appropriate receiver device can capture the signal transmitted from one unit to another.

A message authentication code is not applicable here because it is a process for detecting unauthorized changes made to data transmitted between users or machines or to data retrieved from storage. A transponder is not applicable here because it is used in satellites to receive a signal, to change its frequency, and to retransmit it.

**25.** Synchronization of file updates in a local-area network environment cannot be accomplished by using which of the following?

    a.   File locks

    b.   Record locks

    c.   Semaphores

    d.   Security labels

***25. d.*** Security labels deal with security and confidentiality of data, not with file updates. A security label is a designation assigned to a system resource such as a file, which cannot be changed except in emergency situations. File updates deal with the integrity of data. The unique concept of a local-area network (LAN) file is its capability to be shared among several users. However, security controls are needed to assure synchronization of file updates by more than one user.

File locks, record locks, and semaphores are needed to synchronize file updates. File locks provide a coarse security due to file-level locking. Record locking can be done through logical or physical locks. The PC operating system ensures that the protected records cannot be accessed on the hard disk. Logical locks work by assigning a lock name to a record or a group of records. A semaphore is a flag that can be named, set, tested, changed, and cleared. Semaphores can be applied to files, records, group of records, or any shareable network device, such as a printer or modem. Semaphores are similar to logical locks in concept and can be used for advanced network control functions.

**26.** Which of the following is a byproduct of administering the security policy for firewalls?

    a.   Protocol filtering policy

    b.   Connectivity policy

    c.   Firewall implementation

    d.   Protocol filtering rules

***26. c.*** The role of site security policy is important for firewall administration. A firewall should be viewed as an implementation of a policy; the policy should never be made by the firewall implementation. In other words, agreement on what protocols to filter, what application gateways to use, how network connectivity will be made, and what the protocol filtering rules are all need to be codified beforehand because ad hoc decisions will be difficult to defend and will eventually complicate firewall administration.

**27.** Which of the following reduces the need to secure every user endpoint?

1. Diskless nodes

2. Thin client technology

3. Client honeypots

4. Thick client technology

    a. 1 only

    b. 1 and 2

    c. 3 only

    d. 3 and 4

***27. b.*** A deployment of information system components with minimal functionality (e.g., diskless nodes and thin client technology) reduces the need to secure every user endpoint and may reduce the exposure of data/information, information systems, and services to a successful attack. Client honeypots are devices that actively seek out Web-based malicious code by posing as clients. Thick client technology is not recommended because it cannot protect the user endpoints, and it is less secure than the thin client technology in the way encryption keys are handled.

**28.** Communications between computers can take several approaches. Which of the following approaches is *most* secure?

    a. Public telephone network

    b. Fiber optic cables

    c. Direct wiring of lines between the computer and the user workstation

    d. Microwave transmission or satellites

***28. b.*** Due to their design, fiber optic cables are relatively safer and more secure than other types of computer links. A dial-up connection through a public telephone network is not secure unless a dial-back control is established. Direct wiring of lines between the computer and the user workstation is relatively secure when compared to the public telephone network. Microwave transmissions or satellites are subject to sabotage, electronic warfare, and wiretaps.

**29.** Which of the following is risky for transmission integrity and confidentiality when a network commercial service provider is engaged to provide transmission services?

    a. Commodity service

    b. Cryptographic mechanisms

    c. Dedicated service

    d. Physical measures

**29. a.** An information system should protect the integrity and confidentiality of transmitted information whether using a network service provider. If the provider transmits data as a commodity service rather than a fully dedicated service, it is risky. Cryptographic mechanisms that include use of encryption and physical measures include a protected distribution system.

**30.** Network security and integrity do *not* depend on which of the following controls?

    a.    Logical access controls

    b.    Business application system controls

    c.    Hardware controls

    d.    Procedural controls

**30. b.** Application system controls include data editing and validation routines to ensure integrity of the business-oriented application systems such as payroll and accounts payable. It has nothing to do with the network security and integrity.

Logical access controls prevent unauthorized users from connecting to network nodes or gaining access to applications through computer terminals.

Hardware controls include controls over modem usage, the dial-in connection, and the like. A public-switched network is used to dial into the internal network. Modems enable the user to link to a network from a remote site through a dial-in connection.

Procedural controls include (i) limiting the distribution of modem telephone numbers on a need to know basis, (ii) turning the modem off when not in use, and (iii) frequent changes of modem telephone numbers.

**31.** Which of the following questions must be answered *first* when planning for secure telecommuting?

    a.    What data is confidential?

    b.    What systems and data do employees need to access?

    c.    What type of access is needed?

    d.    What is the sensitivity of systems and data?

**31. c.** Telecommuting is the use of telecommunications to create a *virtual office* away from the established (physical) office. The telecommuting office can be in an employee's home, a hotel room or conference center, an employee's travel site, or a telecommuting center. In planning for secure telecommuting, management must first determine what type of access is needed (i.e., end user, IT user, system/security administrator, permanent/temporary access, guest/contractor access, global/local access, read, write, update add, delete, or change, view, print, or collaborate). The type of access drives most of access control decisions, including the other three choices.

The other three choices come later, although they are important in their own way and support the type of access. What systems and data do employees need? What is the sensitivity of these systems and data? Do they need system administrator privileges? Do they need to share files with other employees? Is the data confidential?

**32.** **The Internet uses which of the following?**

a. Mesh topology

b. Star topology

c. Bus topology

d. Ring topology

*32. a.* The Internet uses the mesh topology with a high degree of fault tolerance. Dial-up telephone services and PBX systems (switched networks) use the star topology, Ethernet mostly uses the bus topology, and FDDI uses the ring topology.

**33.** **Phishing attacks can occur using which of the following?**

1. Cell phones

2. Personal digital assistants

3. Traditional computers

4. Websites

    a. 3 only

    b. 4 only

    c. 1 and 2

    d. 1, 2, 3, and 4

*33. d.* Phishing attacks are not limited to traditional computers and websites; they may also target mobile computing devices, such as cell phones and personal digital assistants. To perform a phishing attack, an attacker creates a website or e-mail that looks as if it is from a well-known organization, such as an online business, credit card company, or financial institution in the case of cell phones; it is often the SMS/MMS attack vector or calls with spoofed caller-ID.

**34.** **A sender in a transmission control protocol (TCP) network plans to transmit message packets of sizes 1,024, 2,048, 4,096, and 8,192 bytes to a receiver. The receiver's granted window size is 16,384 bytes and the timeout size is set at 8,192 bytes. What should be the sender's congestion window size to avoid network bursts or congestion problems?**

    a. 2,048 bytes

    b. 4,096 bytes

    c. 8,192 bytes

    d. 16,384 bytes

*34. b.* As long as the congestion window size remains at 4,096, which is less than the timeout size, no bursts take place, regardless of the receiver's granted window size. Network bursts can occur at a transmission of 8,192 bytes or higher because 8,192 bytes are the timeout limit. To be safe, the optimum size of the sender's congestion window must be set at less than the receiver's granted window size or the timeout size, whichever is smaller.

**35.** Which of the following network architectures is designed to provide data services using physical networks that are more reliable and offer greater bandwidth?

a. Integrated services digital network (ISDN)

b. Transmission control protocol/Internet Protocol (TCP/IP)

c. File transfer protocol (FTP)

d. The open system interconnection (OSI) protocol

**35. *a.*** Integrated services digital network (ISDN) was designed to provide both voice and a wide variety of data services, initially using the existing phone network. Broadband ISDN was designed to provide a more sophisticated set of services using reliable high-speed networks that can be provided using optical fiber physical networks of higher bandwidth. Both the TCP/IP and OSI protocol suites are designed to provide communications between heterogeneous systems. These two platforms support applications, such as file transfer, e-mail, and virtual terminal protocols. Interoperability between TCP/IP and OSI cannot be accomplished without building special software, or gateways, to translate between protocols. However, these architectures were designed to provide data services using physical networks that were not always reliable and offered limited bandwidth.

**36.** Which of the following is the *most* important aspect of a remote access?

a. User authentication

b. Media authentication

c. Device authentication

d. Server authentication

**36. *d.*** Server authentication is the most important for remote access methods where a user is manually establishing the remote access connections, such as typing a URL into a Web browser. A server is a host computer that provides one or more services for other hosts over a network as a primary function. Hence, the server, especially if it is a central server, provides a major entry point into the network. If the authentication method to the server is weak, it can affect the performance and security of the entire network negatively, and can become a single point of failure, resulting in major security risks. In terms of sequence of actions, the server authentication comes first, user authentication comes next or at the same as the server, and media (e.g., disk) and device (e.g., Phone, PDA, or PC) authentication comes last. Although the other choices are important in their own way, they are not as important as the server authentication in terms of potential security risks at the server.

**37.** Possible security threats inherent in a local-area network (LAN) environment include passive and active threats. Which of the following is a passive threat?

a. Denial of message service

b. Masquerading

c. Traffic analysis

d. Modification of message service

**37. c.** Passive threats do not alter any data in a system. They simply read information for the purpose of gaining some knowledge. Because there is no alteration of data and consequently no audit trail exists, passive threats are difficult to detect. Examples of passive threats include traffic analysis. If an attacker can read the packet header, then the source and destination of the message is known, even when the message is encrypted. Through traffic analysis, the attacker knows the total volume in the network and the amount of traffic entering and leaving selected nodes. Although encryption can limit the reading of header information and messages, traffic padding is also needed to counteract the traffic analysis. Traffic padding requires generating a continuous stream of random data or cipher text and padding the communication link so that the attacker would find it difficult to differentiate the useful data from the useless data. Padded data in traffic is useless.

The other three choices are incorrect because they are examples of active threats. Active threats generate or alter the data or control signals rather than to simply read the contents of those signals. A denial of message service results when an attacker destroys or delays most or all messages. Masquerading is an attempt to gain access to a computer system by posing as an authorized client or host. An attacker poses as an authentic host, switch, router, or similar device to communicate with a peer to acquire data or services. Modification of message service occurs when an attacker modifies, deletes, delays, reorders existing real messages, and adds fake messages.

**38.** **In which of the following remote access methods is a pinholing scheme used to facilitate the network address translation (NAT) contact to occur with internal workstations?**

    a.    Tunneling

    b.    Application portals

    c.    Remote desktop access

    d.    Direct application access

**38. c.** There are two major styles of remote desktop access: (i) direct between the telework client device (e.g., a consumer device such as a smartphone and PDA or PC used for performing telework) and the internal workstation, and (ii) indirect through a trusted intermediate system. However, direct access is often not possible because it is prevented by many firewalls. For example, if the internal workstation is behind a firewall performing network address translation (NAT), the telework client device cannot initiate contact with the internal workstation unless either the NAT enables such contact or the internal workstation initiates communications with the external telework client device (e.g., periodically checking with the client device to see if it wants to connect). A "pinholing" scheme can be used to facilitate the NAT contact to occur where particular ports are allocated to each internal workstation. The other three choices do not deal with the NAT.

Tunneling, which uses IPsec tunnel, SSL tunnel, or SSH tunnel with thick remote access client software, provides more control over the remote access environment. On the other hand, application portals, remote desktop access, and direct application access use thin remote access client software providing less control over the remote access environment. Because the remote desktop access method is less secure, it should be used only for exceptional cases after a careful analysis of the security risk.

**39.** When constructing the communications infrastructure for moving data over a wide-area network, the *major* implementation choices involve decisions about all the following except which of the following?

    a.    Multiplexers

    b.    Network interface cards

    c.    Concentrators

    d.    Front-end processors

***39. b.*** A network interface card (NIC) is used in implementing local-area networks (LANs), not wide-area networks (WANs). It is a device used primarily within a LAN to enable a number of independent devices, with varying protocols, to communicate with each other. This communication is accomplished by converting each device protocol into a common transmission protocol.

A multiplexer is incorrect because it is a device that combines the functions of multiplexing and demultiplexing of digital signals. It combines two or more information channels onto a common transmission medium.

A concentrator is incorrect because it is a device that connects a number of circuits, which are not all used at once, to a smaller group of circuits for economy. It usually provides communication capability between many low-speed, usually asynchronous, channels and one or more high-speed, usually synchronous channels. Different speeds, codes, and protocols can be accommodated on the low-speed side. The low-speed channels operate in contention and require buffering. A concentrator permits a common path to handle more data sources than there are channels currently available within the path.

A front-end processor is incorrect because it is a programmed-logic or stored-program device that interfaces data communication equipment with the input/output bus or memory of a data processing computer.

**40.** Network-based firewalls should perform or implement which of the following?

    1.    Ingress filtering

    2.    Egress filtering

    3.    Deny-by-default rulesets for incoming traffic

    4.    Deny-by-default rulesets for outgoing traffic

    a.    1 and 2

    b.    1 and 3

    c.    2 and 4

    d.    1, 2, 3, and 4

***40. d.*** Because network-based firewalls can restrict both incoming and outgoing traffic, they can also be used to stop certain worm infections within the organization from spreading to external systems. To prevent malware incidents, organizations should implement deny-by-default rulesets, meaning that the firewalls deny all incoming and outgoing traffic that is not expressly permitted. Organizations should also ensure that their network firewalls perform egress and ingress filtering. Egress filtering is blocking outgoing packets that should not exit a network. Ingress filtering is blocking incoming packets that should not enter a network.

**41.** **A website has been vandalized. Which of the following should be monitored closely?**

    a.   Illegal logging

    b.   Illegal privilege usage

    c.   Illegal file access

    d.   Illegal Web server shutdown

**41. c.** Selecting the illegal file access addresses the vandalism issue because that is what the attacker can benefit from the most. Files have critical data useful to an attacker. The other three choices are incidental.

**42.** **The Voice over Internet Protocol (VoIP) technology can lead to which of the following?**

    a.   Converged network

    b.   Ad hoc network

    c.   Content delivery network

    d.   Wireless sensor network

**42. a.** The Voice over Internet Protocol (VoIP) technology can lead to a converged network, where the latter combines two different networks such as data and voice networks, similar to the VoIP. Ad hoc network is a network of nodes near each other. Content delivery network delivers the contents of music, movie, sports, and/or news from a content owner's website to end users. Wireless sensor network is used to provide security over buildings, machinery, vehicle operation, and environmental changes in a building (e.g., humidity, voltage, and temperature).

**43.** **Which of the following transmission media is unsuitable for handling intra-building data or voice communications?**

    a.   Twisted pair

    b.   Coaxial cable

    c.   Optical fiber

    d.   Microwave transmission

**43. d.** Microwave transmission is a point-to-point transmission using radio frequency spectrum signals and is commonly used as a substitution for copper or fiber cable. Because of this, it is not suitable for handling intra-building communications and is more appropriate for long-distance transmission. Twisted pair, made of copper wire, is best for low-cost, short-distance local networks linking microcomputers. Coaxial cable is rarely used medium for data transmission in local-area networking. Optical fiber uses light signals to carry a stream of data at extremely high modulation rates and is sturdy and secure.

**44.** **From a corporation viewpoint, which of the following design objectives is *most* important for a local-area network?**

    a.    Productivity

    b.    Availability

    c.    Throughput

    d.    Responsiveness

***44. b.*** Availability is the ratio of the total time a functional unit is capable of being used during a given interval to the length of the interval. It is the time during which a functional unit can be used. What good are productivity, throughput, and response time if the system is shut down and not available? Therefore, system availability is the most important objective for a local-area network (LAN) or any other network.

**45.** **Which of the following wiring schemes makes future network changes easier to implement?**

    a.    Post wiring

    b.    Wiring on demand

    c.    Buildings with high ceilings

    d.    Cable conduits

***45. d.*** Because the cost of wiring an existing building goes up with the height of the ceiling and rises even higher after the tenants have moved in, making the right decisions as early as possible can significantly reduce future costs. Dangling cables can be a safety hazard. Therefore, proactive thinking such as prewiring and cable conduits during building construction should be planned carefully to make future changes easier with less cost. Post-wiring and wiring on demand are reactive in nature, relatively expensive, and disruptive to work.

**46.** **Which of the following is a disadvantage of satellite communications versus a conventional communications method?**

    a.    User-owned stations

    b.    Cost

    c.    Frequency bands

    d.    Broadcast ability

***46. c.*** Frequency bands are of two types: low and high frequency. All the lower frequency bands have become increasingly crowded, and developing higher frequencies is difficult and expensive. Also, transmission problems typically worsen at higher frequencies. In satellite systems, power must be increased at both the original transmission site (uplink) on earth and on the satellite. Increased satellite power generally increases costs.

The other three choices are advantages. Users purchase their own sending and receiving equipment. Satellites have a low-cost, point-to-multipoint broadcast capability that is most expensive to duplicate with conventional techniques.

**47.** **Host-based firewalls can have a serious negative effect on system usability and user satisfaction with which of the following?**

    a.   Deny-by-default rulesets for incoming traffic

    b.   Deny-by-default rulesets for outgoing traffic

    c.   Deny-by-default rulesets for servers

    d.   Deny-by-default rulesets for desktops

**47. b.** To prevent malware incidents, organizations should configure host-based firewalls with deny-by-default rulesets for incoming traffic. Organizations should also use deny-by-default rulesets for outgoing traffic, if feasible; however, such rulesets can have a serious negative effect on system usability and user satisfaction. Servers, desktops, and laptops use similar rulesets as host-based firewalls do.

**48.** **Remote control programs have a number of disadvantages when they are used for remote local-area network (LAN) access. Which of the following disadvantages is *most* difficult to manage?**

    a.   Telephone connect time not minimized

    b.   Manually connect and disconnect operations

    c.   Compatibility with host applications

    d.   Network management time

**48. d.** Limited network management for most remote control programs is a major disadvantage. Managing a large number of host workstations is difficult; each station must be managed individually. The remote control program that LAN access method uses does not implicitly minimize telephone connect time; although, it is possible to automate many operations using batch files or other programming mechanisms. Manual connect and disconnect operations are often augmented by timeout options not always found with other remote LAN access methods. Compatibility between the remote control programs and host applications is not guaranteed; often, compatibility must be determined by trial and error.

**49.** **What is a data communication switch that enables many computer terminals to share a single modem and a line called?**

    a.   Bypass switch

    b.   Fallback switch

    c.   Crossover switch

    d.   Matrix switch

**49. a.** Data communications switches are useful for routing data, online monitoring, fault diagnosis, and digital/analog testing. A switch is a mechanical, electromechanical, or electronic device for making, breaking, or changing the connection in or among circuits. It is used to transfer a connection from one circuit to another.

There are four basic types of switches: bypass, fallback, crossover, and matrix. A bypass switch enables many terminals to share a single modem and line. A fallback switch turns network components from online to standby equipment when there is a problem in the circuit. A crossover switch provides an easy method of interchanging data flows between two pairs of communications components. With a matrix switch a user can interconnect any combination of a group of incoming interfaces to any combination of a group of outgoing interfaces.

**50.** **An intranet can be found in an organization's internal network or shared between organizations over the Internet. Which of the following controls is *least* suited to establish a secure intranet over the Internet?**

    a.    Use encrypted tunnels.

    b.    Install encrypted routers.

    c.    Install encrypted firewalls.

    d.    Implement password controls in the private Web server.

***50. d.*** Intranets are similar to the organization's own networks, providing internal interaction. You do not need to be connected to the Internet to create an intranet. The infrastructure includes placing policies, procedures, and standards documents on an internal server. The intranet could be connected to the Internet, or an intranet could be created by using a private Web server on the Internet. Effective controls include encryption and firewalls. Private tunnels can be created over the Internet through the use of encryption devices, encrypting firewalls, or encrypting routers. Implementing password controls to the private Web server for each user is a weak control because password administration would be a difficult if not an impossible task. Group passwords would not be effective either.

**51.** **Which of the following is an example of an asynchronous attack?**

    a.    Data diddling attack

    b.    Data leakage attack

    c.    TOC-TOU attack

    d.    Salami attack

***51. c.*** In a time-of-check to time-of-use (TOC-TOU) attack, a print job under one user's name is exchanged with a print job for another user. Asynchronous attacks take advantage of time differentials between two events.

A data diddling attack is changing data before or during input to computers or during output from a computer system (e.g., forging a document). A data leakage attack is the removal of data from a computer system by covert means. A salami attack is a theft of small amounts of money from a number of bank accounts and customers (e.g., stealing a few cents from each customer's bank account and spreading over many customers).

**52.** Security mechanisms implement security services. Which of the following security services is provided by a notarization security mechanism?

     a.   Confidentiality

     b.   Integrity

     c.   Authentication

     d.   Nonrepudiation

*52. d.* Nonrepudiation services prevent the parties to a communication from denying that they sent or received it, or disputing its contents. It may provide either proof of origin or proof of delivery.

Confidentiality is incorrect because it provides security mechanisms such as encryption, traffic padding, and routing control, not notarization. Confidentiality protects data from unauthorized disclosure. Integrity is incorrect because it provides security mechanisms such as encryption, digital signature, and data integrity, not notarization. Integrity protects against the modification, insertion, deletion, or replay of data. Authentication is incorrect because it provides security mechanisms such as encryption, digital signature, and authentication, not notarization. Authentication services basically provide a reliable answer to the question: With whom am I communicating?

**53.** Legacy IEEE 802.11 wireless local-area networks (WLANs) operate in which of the following layers of the ISO/OSI reference model?

     a.   Physical and data layers

     b.   Data and network link layers

     c.   Transport and presentation layers

     d.   Application and session layers

*53. a.* Legacy IEEE 802.11 wireless LANs (WLANs) operate in the physical layer and the data link layer of the ISO/OSI reference model because they define the physical characteristics and access rules for the network. The physical layer addresses areas such as frequencies used and modulation techniques employed. The data link layer deals with how the network is shared between nodes. It defines rules such as who can talk on the network and how much they can say.

**54.** Which of the following security practices is supported by most remote control program (RCP) products when accessing a host workstation on a local-area network (LAN)?

     a.   Matching user ID and name with password

     b.   Controlling reboot options

     c.   Limiting access to local drives and directories

     d.   Controlling file transfer rights

**54. a.** Some remote control products provide minimal security support, whereas others provide varying degrees of support. Matching a user ID and name with a password and callback modem support are handled by most products. Other security mechanisms, such as the ability to limit access to local drives and directories to limit the use of host hardware (such as printer ports) and to control reboot options and file transfer rights are not widely supported.

**55.** When a nonremote user connection is established with a remote device using a virtual private network (VPN), the configuration settings generally prevent which of the following?

- a. Split knowledge
- b. Split domain name service
- c. Split tunneling
- d. Split gateway

**55. c.** Split tunneling is a method that routes organization-specific traffic through the secure sockets layer (SSL) VPN tunnel, but other traffic uses the remote user's default gateway. Remote users normally use split tunneling to communicate with the information system as an extension of that system and to communicate with local resources such as a printer or file server. The remote device, when connected by a nonremote connection, becomes an extension of the information system, enabling a dual communications path (i.e., split tunneling), which, in effect, enables unauthorized external connections into the system. Here the use of VPN for nonremote connection generally prevents the split tunneling, depending on the configuration settings and traffic types.

**56.** Extrusion detection at the information system boundary does *not* include which of the following?

- a. Looking for internal threats
- b. Analyzing outgoing network traffic
- c. Looking for external threats
- d. Analyzing incoming network traffic

**56. c.** Detecting internal actions that may pose a security threat to external information systems is called extrusion detection. It is also referred to as data loss prevention. Its scope includes the analysis of incoming and outgoing network traffic looking for indications of an internal threat (not an external threat) to the security of external systems.

**57.** Which of the following *prevents* the unauthorized exfiltration of information across managed interfaces such as proxies and routers?

1. Strict adherence to protocol formats
2. Monitoring for indications of beaconing from the information system
3. Monitoring for use of steganography
4. Disassembling and reassembling packet headers

a. 1 only

b. 1 and 2

c. 2 and 4

d. 1, 2, 3, and 4

**57. d.** All the four items are measures to prevent unauthorized exfiltration of information from the information system. Other preventive measures against exfiltration include disconnecting external network interfaces except when explicitly needed and conducting traffic profile analysis to detect deviations from the volume or types of traffic expected within the organization.

58. Which of the following devices can enforce strict adherence to protocol formats to prevent unauthorized exfiltration of information across managed interfaces using boundary protection devices?

1. Deep packet inspection firewalls

2. XML gateways

3. Routers

4. Bridges

a. 1 only

b. 1 and 2

c. 1 and 3

d. 3 and 4

**58. b.** Examples of devices enforcing strict adherence to protocol formats are deep packet inspection firewalls (also known as stateful protocol analysis capability) and extensible markup language (XML) gateways. These devices verify adherence to the protocol specification at the application layer and serve to identify vulnerabilities that cannot be detected by devices operating at the network layer or transport layer. Routers operate at the network layer and bridges operate at the data link layer. In addition, XML gateways are used to prevent and detect XML-based denial-of-service (DoS) attacks. Managed interfaces using boundary protection devices include proxies, gateways, routers, firewalls, software/hardware guards, and encrypted tunnels.

59. Network management, operations, and user support for a large distributed system together represent a complex undertaking. Which of the following issues *most* increases the complexity of network management?

a. Multiple topologies

b. Multiple transmission media

c. Multiple protocols

d. Multiple accesses

**59. b.** A number of issues affect network management in a large distributed system. They result from multiple network topologies (i.e., structures), multiple transmission media (e.g., wiring), multiple protocols (i.e., rules that govern communications across a network), and multiple network owners. Increases in the number of transmission media increase the complexity of large distributed system network management. For example, each medium may require different protocols, equipment, and software, with additional expertise in a network administrator. An increased number of transmission media may complicate the standardization of management procedures across a large distributed system. Using different transmission media may result in different costs, system reliability, or performance. A number of network "owners" may support a large distributed system. The sense of ownership can result from a variety of factors, including different organizations involved, functionality included, and geographic areas covered. Increases in the number of owners increase the complexity of network management due to coordination and communication required.

The other three choices are incorrect. A topology is a pattern of interconnection between nodes (i.e., end points) in a network. A large distributed system may require the use of one or more topologies to support the varying needs of subsystems, organizations, and individual users or to accommodate existing network architectures. Factors to consider include applications supported, robustness required, network architecture supported, protocols required, and local and remote connections needed. Multiple protocols establish the rules that govern data transmission and generally cover the method to represent and code data; the method to transmit and receive data; and the method of nonstandard information exchange. Multiple access is a scheme that allows temporary access to the network by individual users, on a demand basis, for the purpose of transmitting information. Multiple topologies and protocols are a necessary part of the infrastructure and are dictated by multiple transmission media and network owners.

**60.** **What is determining what components to include in the network configuration called?**

    a.    Configuration identification

    b.    Configuration control

    c.    Configuration requirements tracing

    d.    Configuration status accounting

*60. a.* Configuration management provides a valuable baseline for controlling maintenance and enhancement activity. Configuration management typically has four major functions: identification, control, requirements tracing, and status accounting. Configuration identification determines what components to include in the configuration and develops unique identifiers for tracking individual components and adding new ones.

Configuration control imposes discipline on the change process to ensure that items changed or added to the configuration complete all the necessary testing and approval steps before inclusion.

Configuration requirements tracing ensures that the configuration changes are traceable back to user requirements either directly (e.g., a user-requested change) or indirectly (e.g., better user support through improved system performance).

Configuration status accounting reports the current status of components in the configuration and components undergoing change or about to be added.

**61.** **Which of the following are countermeasures against network weaving?**

1.  Traffic flow signal
2.  Traffic encryption key
3.  Tunneling
4.  Traffic padding

    a.  1 and 2
    b.  1 and 3
    c.  2 and 4
    d.  3 and 4

*61. d.* Network weaving is a penetration technique in which different communication networks are linked to access an information system to avoid detection and trace-back. Tunneling enables one network to send its data via another network's connections. It works by encapsulating a network protocol within packets carried by the second network. Traffic padding generates mock communications or data units to disguise the amount of real data units being sent. The other two items cannot control network weaving penetration. Traffic flow signal is used to conduct traffic flow analysis. Traffic encryption key is used to encrypt plaintext or to super-encrypt previously encrypted text and/or to decrypt cipher-text.

**62.** **Which of the following supports the cloud computing infrastructure *most*?**

    a.  Virtualization technology
    b.  Service-oriented architecture
    c.  Web 2.0 services
    d.  Utility computing

*62. a.* Cloud computing, an emerging form of distributed computing, is an amalgamation of technologies, including virtualization, service-oriented architecture, Web 2.0 services, and utility computing. Out of these technologies, virtualization has taken a prominent role due to use of multiple virtual machines and guest virtual machines.

Virtualization technology enables multiple operating systems (OSs) to coexist on a computing platform. In virtualization, special purpose software successfully replicates the behavior of hardware. Through such methods, a single physical host computer can run multiple virtual machines, each with a distinct guest OS and associated applications. Various virtualization products exist that can be used to provide an isolated virtual machine environment for systems and applications to execute. Risky functions, such as Web browsing, may be confined to a virtual system designated and configured exclusively for that purpose. Should the virtual system be compromised, it can easily be restored to a known-good state.

Service-oriented architecture is a collection of services, which communicate with each other. The communication can involve either simple data passing or it could involve two or more services coordinating some activity. Web 2.0 service is the second-generation of

Internet-based services that enables people to collaborate and create information online in new ways, such as social networking sites, wikis, and communication tools. Utility computing deals with on-demand network access and self-service facilities for subscribers.

**63.** **Which of the following is an operational issue in data communications networks?**

    a. Network modularity and adaptability

    b. Network performance and throughput

    c. Network availability and redundancy

    d. Network size and interoperability

*63. b.* Performance management consists of day-to-day system requirements and evaluation to assess current performance and to identify and implement system adjustments that can improve performance. To ensure efficiency, the performance management staff must know the workloads imposed by users, the levels of service required to satisfy workloads, and current capacity. The other three choices are incorrect because they are examples of network planning and design issues.

**64.** **Asynchronous transfer mode (ATM) is an example of a fast packet-switching network. Which of the following statements about ATM is *not* true?**

    a. ATM networks can carry data communications.

    b. ATM networks can carry video communications.

    c. ATM networks use long packets with varying sizes.

    d. ATM networks can carry voice communications.

*64. c.* There are two different kinds of fast packet-switching networks: ATM and PTM. Asynchronous transfer mode (ATM) networks use short packets called "cells" that are always the same length. Packet transfer mode (PTM) does not use short cells but more additional packets that can be longer if necessary. Most packet-switching networks use packets that can be long and vary in size depending on the data being carried. The ATM network can carry data communications where packets are broken into several ATM cells. After travelling through the network, the cells are reassembled into packets. It can also carry video communications where the digital video bits are put in cells and sent through the network. At the destination, the bits are removed from the cells. The ATM also carries voice communications, and the voice is handled in the same way as video.

**65.** **Which of the following effectively facilitates telecommuting?**

    a. Integrated services digital network

    b. Regular modems

    c. Facsimile/modems

    d. Intelligent modems

**65. a.** Telecommuting enables employees to work from a remote location. An integrated services digital network (ISDN) can be considered as an "intermediate" step between the current analog local loop and the use of fiber optics. Because of the cost of deploying fiber, it may take a long time before homes are connected. ISDN is cheaper than fiber, can be deployed sooner, and although its capacity is only a fraction of fiber, represents a significant improvement over the current analog local loop. To connect to the office computers, employees need a device called a modem, which enables them to send digital computer data over the analog local loop. ISDN provides higher bits-per-second channels than modems. This would enable videoconferencing of reasonable quality, faster transfer of graphics information, and better quality fax transmission. It would also permit much-improved access to the Internet for home users.

Regular modems, facsimile/modems, and intelligent modems do not have the bits-per-second-channel capacity as that of ISDN. A modem is a device that modulates and demodulates. Modems are primarily used for converting digital signals into quasi-analog signals for transmission over analog communication channels and reconverting the quasi-analog signals into digital signals.

Facsimile/modem combines the features of fax and modem. Intelligent modems are intelligent because they add random-access memory, read-only memory, and erasable programmable read-only memory. Some major functions of intelligent modems include automatic dialing, negotiation of the method of modulation used to communicate with a distant modem, error detection and correction operations to ensure data integrity, and responses to status requests. Regular modems do not have the intelligence so that they cannot perform fax operations.

**66.** **Which of the following information technologies is better equipped to deliver multimedia applications?**

  a. Integrated services digital network (ISDN) and broadband ISDN

  b. Narrowband ISDN, central office switches, and copper-based local loops

  c. Narrowband ISDN, fiber optics, and asynchronous transfer mode (ATM)

  d. Broadband ISDN, fiber optics, and ATM

**66. d.** Multimedia applications take advantage of the capability of high-bandwidth integrated services networks to deliver many different kinds of data such as video, image, audio, and text and numerical data. They also take advantage of the processing power of advanced workstations and other devices attached to the network, enabling users to edit, process, and select data arriving from a variety of sources over the network. The capacity of a network, measured as the number of bits it can transmit every second, is called bandwidth. Narrowband networks are low-bandwidth networks, and broadband networks are high-bandwidth networks.

ATM has been chosen as the foundation for the broadband ISDN where the latter is used to carry voice, video, and data traffic to support a range of applications. ATM networks are also suitable for carrying data, video, and voice communications. Fiber optics is an enabling technology for broadband networks. With increased bandwidth, the links can move data more quickly and support the transport of bandwidth-intensive traffic such as video.

Broadband ISDN uses different technology from narrowband (ordinary) ISDN. Narrowband ISDN is best viewed as a digital upgrade of the telephone network's copper local loop. Broadband ISDN, by contrast, requires fiber optics and ATM, a new approach to network design. ISDN and broadband ISDN have little in common other than their names.

ISDN is a telecommunications industry standard for upgrading local loops to digital service. It enables the existing copper local loops to be used for digital service. However, it requires users to buy new equipment for their end of line, which converts their data to the ISDN format. It also requires that the telephone company's equipment, such as the central office switches, be upgraded. The local loop uses low-capacity analog copper wires.

**67.** **What is a physical security control that uses a network configuration mechanism to minimize theft or damage to computer equipment?**

    a.    Web server

    b.    Terminal server

    c.    Server farm

    d.    Redundant server

***67. c.***   In a server farm, all servers are kept in a single, secure location, and the chances of theft or damage to computer equipment are lower. Only those individuals who require physical access should be given a key. A redundant server concept is used in contingency planning and disaster recovery, which is kept away from the server farm.

**68.** **Which of the following performs application content filtering?**

    a.    Sensors

    b.    Gateway

    c.    Proxy

    d.    Hardware/software guard

***68. c.***   A software proxy agent performs application content filtering to remove or quarantine viruses that may be contained in e-mail attachments, to block specific MIME types, or to filter other active content (e.g., Java, JavaScript, and ActiveX Controls). The proxy accepts certain types of traffic entering or leaving a network, processes it, and forwards it.

The other three choices are not related to application content filtering. Sensors are composed of network monitors and network scanners, where the former performs intrusion detection, and the latter performs vulnerability scanning. A gateway is an interface providing compatibility between networks by converting transmission speeds, protocols, codes, or security measures. A hardware/software guard enables users to exchange data between private and public networks, which is normally prohibited because of information confidentiality.

**69.** **Which of the following functions is similar to a host firewall?**

      a.    Authentication header

      b.    TCP wrappers

      c.    Encapsulating security payload

      d.    Security parameters index

**69. b.** Transmission control protocol (TCP) wrappers are a freely available application that functions similarly to a firewall. It can be used to restrict access and configured in such a way that only specified user IDs or nodes can execute specified server processes. An authentication header is one part of IPsec's two security headers: (i) the authentication header and (ii) the encapsulating security payload. The authentication header provides source authentication and integrity to the IP datagram, and the payload provides confidentiality. A security parameter index consists of cryptographic keys and algorithms, and the authentication header contains the index.

**70.** **A *major* risk involving the use of packet-switching networking is that:**

      a.    It is possible that some packets can arrive at their destinations out of sequence.

      b.    It is not possible to vary the routing of packets depending on network conditions.

      c.    Terminals attached to a public data network may not have enough intelligence.

      d.    Terminals attached to a public data network may not have enough storage capacity.

**70. a.** Most packet-switching networks can vary the routing of packets depending on network conditions. Because of this, it is possible that some packets can arrive at their destinations out of sequence while most packets can arrive at their destination in normal sequence because they are reassembled at the receiver end. The reason for some packets not reaching their destinations is that there is a potential security risk in that a smart attacker can change the packet sequence numbers in the middle of the stream and divert the packet to his own site for later attack and then change the sequence numbers back to the original condition or forget to do it in the right way thus breaking the sequence. Even worse yet, a malicious attacker can insert fake sequence numbers so the packet would not reach its destination point. Here, the attacker's goal is to steal valuable information from these packets for his own benefit.

Terminals attached directly to a public data network must have enough intelligence and storage capacity to break large messages into packets and to reassemble them into proper sequence. A packet assembly and disassembly (PAD) facility can help accommodate intelligence and storage problems.

**71.** **One of the goals of penetration testing security controls is to determine:**

      a.    The time between the flaw identification and the flaw remediation process

      b.    The time between the vulnerability identification and the vulnerability remediation process

      c.    The time between the vulnerability identification and the vulnerability exploitation

      d.    The time between the weaknesses is discovered and the time to eliminate the weaknesses

***71. c.*** One of the goals of penetration testing is to determine exploitability of identified vulnerability. It is called time-to-exploitation, where the penetration testers (i.e., red team and blue team) determine the time to exploit. The other three choices require a corrective action in terms of a plan of action and milestones.

**72.** The basic protocols would *not* address which of the following?

   a.   Message size, sequence, and format

   b.   Message routing instructions

   c.   Error detection and correction

   d.   Message authentication

***72. d.*** A basic protocol is a set of rules governing a specific time sequence of events. It defines the method of formatting bits of data and messages for transmission, routing, and identification of messages including error detection and correction. However, it does not address a message authentication, which is a security feature.

**73.** The *least* effective control in mitigating communication network failures would be which of the following?

   a.   Network contingency plans

   b.   Network capacity planning

   c.   Network application system

   d.   Network performance monitoring

***73. c.*** A network application system that collects traffic statistics and provides reports to alert the network management does not help in minimizing communication network failures.

The other three choices are important to minimize losses from a network failure. Network contingency plans deal with redundant switching equipment, parallel physical circuits, and standby power supplies to address network disasters. Network capacity plans assist in forecasting computer resource requirements to ensure that adequate capacity exists when needed. For example, the capacity studies may call for higher bandwidth to accommodate newer technologies such as multimedia and videoconferencing. Capacity planning activities use current system performance data as a starting point to predict future resource needs. Network performance monitoring involves analyzing the performance of a computer system to determine how resources are currently utilized and how such utilization can be improved.

**74.** Conducting a periodic network monitoring to verify proper operations does *not* normally include:

   a.   Detecting network layers

   b.   Detecting line errors

   c.   Detecting terminal errors

   d.   Detecting modem errors

**74. a.**   A network is composed of distinct layers, which is a network design issue, with each layer providing a specific function for the network. Periodic monitoring of the network does not normally include detection of the network layers where covert channels in ICMP or DNS can be found. For example, the ISO/OSI reference model has seven layers: application layer, presentation layer, session layer, transport layer, network layer, data link layer, and physical layer. Detecting line errors, terminal errors, and modem errors are routinely detected and monitored to ensure proper network operations.

**75.**   Which of the following actions is *not* true about prohibiting remote activation for collaborative computing devices?

    a.   Block inbound and outbound traffic between instant messaging clients configured by end users.

    b.   Block inbound and outbound traffic between instant messaging clients configured by external providers.

    c.   Disconnect all unneeded collaborative computing devices physically.

    d.   Block inbound and outbound traffic between instant messaging clients configured by the IT security.

**75. d.**   Collaborative computing devices are networked white boards and cameras. It is a good security practice to block the inbound and outbound network traffic configured by end users and external service providers, and not block the configurations established by the IT security function.

**76.**   For worldwide interoperability for microwave access (WiMAX) security, when an adversary drains a client node's battery by sending a constant series of management messages to the subscriber station/mobile subscriber (SS/MS), what is it called?

    a.   Man-in-the-middle attack

    b.   Water torture attack

    c.   Radio frequency jamming attack

    d.   Radio frequency scrambling attack

**76. b.**   Exploitation of unencrypted management messages can result in subtle denial-of-service (DoS), replay, or manipulation attacks that are difficult to detect. These attacks spoof management messages. A water torture attack is an example of subtle DoS attack in which an adversary drains a client node's battery by sending a constant series of management messages to the SS/MS. Radio frequency (RF) jamming is classified as a DoS attack. RF scrambling attacks are the precise injections of RF interference during the transmission of specific management messages. A man-in-the-middle (MitM) attack occurs when an adversary deceives an SS/MS to appear as a legitimate base station (BS) while simultaneously deceiving a BS to appear as a legitimate SS/MS.

**77.** Regarding worldwide interoperability for microwave access (WiMAX) security, which of the following is *not* a weakness of data encryption standard-cipher block chaining (DES-CBC) algorithm?

    a. Replay attack

    b. Denial-of-service attack

    c. Eavesdropping attack

    d. Man-in-the-middle attack

*77. a.* The weaknesses of data encryption standard-cipher block chaining (DES-CBC) are well documented, and include denial-of-service (DoS), eavesdropping, and man-in-the-middle (MitM) attacks. Replay attacks occur when adversaries reuse expired traffic encryption keys (TEKs). Replay attacks lead to unauthorized disclosure of information and compromise of the TEK.

**78.** For worldwide interoperability for microwave access (WiMAX) security, denial-of-service (DoS) attacks occur due to which of the following?

    1. Lack of mutual authentication

    2. Use of nonunicast messages

    3. Use of wireless technology as a communications medium

    4. Use of unencrypted management messages

        a. 1 and 2

        b. 1 and 3

        c. 2 and 3

        d. 1, 2, 3, and 4

*78. d.* Lack of mutual authentication occurs between subscriber's station (SS) and base station (BS). This may enable a rogue BS operator to degrade performance or steal information by conducting denial-of-service (DoS) or forgery attacks against client SSs. In unencrypted management messages, nonunicast messages open WiMAX systems to DoS attacks. In the use of wireless as a communications medium, a DoS attack can be executed by the introduction of a powerful radio frequency (RF) source intended to overwhelm system radio spectrum.

**79.** For worldwide interoperability for microwave access (WiMAX) security, replay attacks occur due to which of the following?

    1. Injection of reused traffic encryption key

    2. Insecure unicast messages

    3. Unencrypted management messages

    4. Insecure nonunicast messages

a. 1 and 2

b. 1 and 3

c. 2 and 3

d. 3 and 4

**79. b.** Replay attacks occur due to injection of reused traffic encryption key (TEK) and unencrypted management messages. Integrity checks are added to unicast messages to prevent replay attacks. Nonunicast messages are open to DoS attacks.

**80.** **For worldwide interoperability for microwave access (WiMAX) security, a countermeasure for man-in-the-middle (MitM) attack is:**

a. DES-CBC

b. AES-CCM

c. AES only

d. VPN only

**80. b.** If a WiMAX system is not using the advanced encryption standard Counter with CBC message authentication code (AES-CCM), it can open up the possibility of a MitM attack. Data encryption standard-cipher block chaining (DES-CBC) is a weak algorithm that cannot ensure confidentiality of data and may lead to MitM attack. Virtual private network (VPN) is a mature technology and cannot defend against the MitM attacks. The advanced encryption standard (AES) is not as strong as the AES-CCM.

**81.** **Which of the following worldwide interoperability for microwave access (WiMAX) operating topologies uses only the non-line-of-sight (NLOS) signal propagation?**

a. Point-to-point

b. Point-to-multipoint

c. Multihop relay

d. Mobile

**81. d.** A mobile topology is similar to a cellular network because multiple base stations (BSs) collaborate to provide seamless communications over a distributed network to both subscriber stations (SSs) and mobile subscribers (MSs). A non-line-of-sight (NLOS) signal propagation is electromagnetic signaling that uses advanced modulation techniques to compensate for signal obstacles and enables indirect communications between transmitting stations. Mobile WiMAX topology operates on NLOS signal propagation, whereas the other three topologies use either LOS or NLOS signal propagation. A line-of-sight (LOS) signal propagation is electromagnetic signaling that is highly sensitive to radio frequency obstacles requiring an unobstructed view between transmitting stations. The other three choices are also examples of WiMAX operating topologies.

A point-to-point topology consists of a dedicated long-range, high-capacity wireless link between two sites. This topology is used for high-bandwidth wireless backhaul services at maximum operating ranges using either LOS or NLOS signal propagation. It uses a backhaul as a high-capacity line from a remote site or network to a central site or network.

A point-to-multipoint topology is composed of a central BS supporting multiple SSs, providing network access from one location to many locations. It is commonly used for last-mile broadband access, private enterprise connectivity to remote offices, and long-range wireless backhaul services for multiple sites. Last-mile broadband access refers to communications technology that bridges the transmission distance between the broadband service provider and the customer premises equipment.

A multihop relay topology, also referred to as mesh networking, is used to extend a BS's coverage area by permitting SSs or MSs to replay traffic by acting as a relay station.

**82.** **Which of the following worldwide interoperability for microwave access (WiMAX) operating topologies uses a concept of security zone?**

    a.    Point-to-point

    b.    Point-to-multipoint

    c.    Multihop relay

    d.    Mobile

*82. c.*   A multihop relay topology, also referred to as mesh networking, is used to extend a base station's (BS) coverage area by permitting subscriber stations (SSs) or mobile subscribers (MSs) to replay traffic by acting as a relay station. A multihop uses a security zone concept where it is a set of trusted relationships between a BS and a group of relay stations (RSs). An RS can forward traffic to only RSs or SSs within its security zone. The other three choices, which are also examples of WiMAX operating topologies, do not use the concept of security zone.

A point-to-point topology consists of a dedicated long-range, high-capacity wireless link between two sites. This topology is used for high-bandwidth wireless backhaul services at maximum operating ranges using either line-of-sight (LOS) or no-line-of-sight (NLOS) signal propagation. It uses a backhaul as a high-capacity line from a remote site or network to a central site or network.

A point-to-multipoint topology is composed of a central BS supporting multiple SSs, providing network access from one location to many locations. It is commonly used for last-mile broadband access, private enterprise connectivity to remote offices, and long-range wireless backhaul services for multiple sites. Last-mile broadband access refers to communications technology that bridges the transmission distance between the broadband service provider and the customer premises equipment.

A mobile topology is similar to a cellular network because multiple BSs collaborate to provide seamless communications over a distributed network to both SSs and MSs.

**83.** **Which of the following is a detective control in a local-area network (LAN) environment?**

    a.   File backup

    b.   Contingency plan

    c.   Electronic surveillance

    d.   Locks and keys

**83. c.** Electronic surveillance is an example of detective controls. File backup is incorrect because it is an example of recovery controls. A contingency plan is incorrect because it is an example of recovery controls. Locks and keys are incorrect because they are examples of preventive controls.

**84.** **Which of the following establishes accountability in a local-area network environment?**

    a.   Network monitoring tools

    b.   Access logs

    c.   Lock and key systems

    d.   Card key systems

**84. b.** Access logs along with user IDs and passwords provide a reasonable amount of accountability in a local-area network (LAN) environment because user actions are recorded.

Network monitoring tools are an example of a detective control used by network management. As such they do not show any accountability of the user. They watch the network traffic and develop trends.

Lock and key systems and card key systems are examples of preventive controls as a part of physical security. Keys can be lost or stolen, and, therefore, accountability is difficult to prove and control.

**85.** **Attackers use which of the following to distribute their warez files?**

    a.   File transfer protocol server

    b.   SOCKS server

    c.   Web proxy server

    d.   E-mail server

**85. a.** A warez server is a file server used to distribute illegal content such as copies of copyrighted songs, movies, and pirated software. Attackers often exploit vulnerabilities in file transfer protocol (FTP) servers to gain unauthorized access so that they can use the server to distribute their warez files.

The socket security (SOCKS) server is a networking-proxy protocol that enables full access across the SOCKS server from one host to another without requiring direct IP reachability. Web proxy servers are used to access external websites. E-mail servers can be used to do proper things such as sending normal messages and sending malicious code.

**86.** **Which of the following networks provides for movement of employees within an organization without the associated cabling costs?**

   a.   Traditional local-area networks (LANs)

   b.   Metropolitan-area networks (MANs)

   c.   Virtual local-area networks (VLANs)

   d.   Value-added networks (VANs)

***86. c.***   Virtual LANs are a logical collection of individual LANs, because they link local- and wide-area networks using routers, switches, and backbone equipment and related software so that users at various locations have access to data residing on multiple systems and locations that they would not have otherwise. The virtual network is transparent to users. Virtual LANs reassign users without changing cables when users move from one location to another. Network maintenance costs are lower and equipment moves are done faster. Another benefit of virtual LANs is that all servers in a building can be physically protected in a data center instead of spreading them throughout the building in the user departments.

Traditional (wired) LANs are incorrect because they require a change of cabling when users and their equipment move around. Network maintenance costs are higher and moves are slower. MANs and VANs are incorrect because they do not employ cables as traditional LANs do.

**87.** **Frame relay and X.25 networks are part of which of the following?**

   a.   Circuit-switched services

   b.   Cell-switched services

   c.   Packet-switched services

   d.   Dedicated digital services

***87. c.***   Packet-switched services are better suited to handle bursts of traffic. In packet-switched services, connections do not need to be established before data transmission begins. Instead, each packet is transmitted separately, and each may take a separate path through the mesh of network. X.25 networks are slow and are not suitable for most LAN-to-LAN traffic because of the time and bandwidth required for error checking by X.25. Frame relays, which are similar to X.25, provide faster and more efficient services. Frame relay does not employ the extensive error checking of X.25.

Circuit-switched services are incorrect because they are better suited for delay-sensitive traffic. They establish a virtual connection before transmitting data. They do not use X.25 and frame relay protocols.

Cell-switched services are incorrect because they use a fixed-size cell rather than a variable-size packet (e.g., asynchronous transfer mode networks). This type of switching is faster and less expensive. They do not use X.25 and frame relay protocols either.

Dedicated digital services are incorrect because they handle voice, video, and data. The dedicated lines are usually leased and installed between two points to provide dedicated, full-time service. T1 and T3 are examples of dedicated digital lines.

88. **Which of the following statements is *not* true? Intranets differ from the GroupWare concept in that intranets**

   a.  Are platform-dependent.

   b.  Are platform-independent.

   c.  Use layered communication protocols.

   d.  Are easy to set up.

*88. a.* Groupware is an alternative to intranets, where the former is good for document sharing, mail exchange, and group discussion. On the other hand, intranets facilitate external and internal communications more efficiently. One major advantage of the intranet over GroupWare is the Internet's inherent platform independence. For example, Web pages written on a Macintosh computer look the same when viewed from a Sun workstation. In addition to being easy to set up, intranets use the concept of layered communication protocols. There are seven layers between the physical network media and the applications running on the host machines.

89. **Which of the following characterizes the operation of a Bluetooth device?**

   a.  Content delivery network

   b.  Local-area network

   c.  Ad-hoc network

   d.  Wide-area network

*89. c.* A Bluetooth device operates under the ad-hoc network standard because it has no fixed network infrastructure, such as base stations or access points as in the wired network or other wireless networks. Bluetooth devices maintain random network configurations formed on-the-fly, relying on mobile routers connected by wireless links that enable devices to communicate with each other. The other three choices have a fixed network infrastructure.

90. **All the following are examples of performance measures of quality-of-service (QoS) for a communications network *except*:**

   a.  Signal-to-noise ratio

   b.  Mean time between failures

   c.  Bit error ratio

   d.  Call blocking probability

*90. b.* Mean time between failures (MTBF) is an indicator of expected system reliability based on known failure rates, which are expressed in hours. MTBF is mostly applied to equipment whereas QoS is applied to services.

The other three choices, along with message throughput rate, are examples of channel or system performance parameters, measuring QoS. Signal-to-noise ratio is the ratio of the amplitude of the peak signal to the amplitude of peak noise signals at a given point in time in a telecommunications system. Bit error ratio is the number of erroneous bits divided by the total number of bits transmitted, received, or processed over some stipulated time period in a telecommunications system. Call blocking probability is the probability that an unwanted incoming call would be blocked from going forward.

**91.**  Which of the following is *not* a function of a Web server?

    a.    Handling requests

    b.    Supplying documents

    c.    Securing requests

    d.    Navigating information

*91. d.*  The Web browser is the most common user interface for accessing an intranet. A Web browser provides navigating information. At the heart of an intranet is the Web server. Because an intranet is based on a system of requests and responses, the server controls and administers that flow of information through TCP/IP. Web servers handle requests and return the information in the form of either Web pages or other media types such as pictures, sound, and video. In addition to supplying documents, the Web server is also responsible for ensuring the security of requests from outside the organization or within.

**92.**  What is the *most* important element of intranet security?

    a.    Monitoring

    b.    Encryption

    c.    Authentication

    d.    Filtering

*92. a.*  The basic elements of intranet security tools are encryption, authentication, and filtering. For example, encryption may use pretty good privacy (PGP) for encrypting e-mail, digital certificates for code signing, and site certificates for Secure Socket Layers securing of intranet servers. Authentication deals with user and group-specific access. Firewalls act as filtering devices. In addition to the use of these tools, vigilant monitoring of all network connections is required on a regular basis. Each time a new feature is added to a network, the security implications should be reviewed. These three security tools are highly technical and automated whereas monitoring is a human activity, which is better than automation most of the time.

**93.**  Security mechanisms implement security services. Which of the following security mechanisms do *not* implement the confidentiality security service?

    a.    Encryption

    b.    Access control

    c.    Traffic padding

    d.    Routing control

*93. b.*  An access control security mechanism provides access control security service only. This mechanism controls access to authenticated entities to resources. They may be based upon security labels (tags), the time of attempted access, the route of attempted access, and the duration of access.

Encryption is incorrect because it implements confidentiality security service. Encryption refers to cryptographic technology using keys. Two classes of encryption exist: symmetric (using secret key) and asymmetric (using public key).

Traffic padding is incorrect because it provides confidentiality services. It is the observation of traffic patterns, even when enciphered, which may yield information to an intruder. This mechanism may be used to confound the analysis of traffic patterns.

Routing control is incorrect because it provides confidentiality service. With routing control, routes can be chosen so as to use only secure links in the communication line.

**94.** Which of the following is *not* an example of information system entry and exit points to protect from malicious code?

    a.    Firewalls

    b.    Electronic mail servers

    c.    Workstations

    d.    Web servers

**94. c.** An organization employs malicious code protection mechanisms at critical information system entry and exit points such as firewalls, e-mail servers, Web servers, proxy servers, and remote access servers. Workstations are internal to an organization and do not provide direct entry and exit points.

**95.** Which of the following statements about data gateways is *not* correct?

    a.    Data gateways cannot standardize communication protocols.

    b.    Data gateways are devices to adapt heterogeneous clients to servers.

    c.    Data gateways absorb diversity in implementation details.

    d.    Data gateways provide access control and authentication mechanisms.

**95. a.** Gateways translate between incompatible protocols, such as between IBM's SNA and TCP/IP. Data gateways, then, are devices to adapt heterogeneous clients and servers. They may simply absorb diversity in implementation details and provide access control and authentication mechanisms. It is incorrect to say that data gateways cannot standardize communication protocols.

**96.** Which of the following is *not* used in creating dynamic Web documents?

    a.    Common gateway interface (CGI)

    b.    Extensible markup language (XML)

    c.    JavaServer page (JSP)

    d.    ActiveServer page (ASP)

**96. b.** Extensible markup language (XML) is used in creating a static Web document. Dynamic Web documents (pages) are written in CGI, JSP, and ASP.

**97.** Which of the following is *not* a server-side script used in dynamic hypertext markup language (HTML)?

    a.    Common gateway interface (CGI)

    b.    ActiveServer page (ASP)

    c.    JavaApplets

    d.    Perl

**97. c.** A JavaApplet is a client-side script. Dynamic hypertext markup language (dynamic HTML) is a collection of dynamic HTML technologies for generating Web page contents on-the-fly. It uses the server-side scripts (e.g., CGI, ASP, JSP, PHP, and Perl) and the client-side scripts (e.g., JavaScript, JavaApplets, and Active -X controls).

**98.** Which of the following can provide a false sense of security?

1.    Encryption protocols

2.    Digital signatures

3.    Firewalls

4.    Certified authorities

    a.    1 and 2

    b.    2 and 3

    c.    1 and 3

    d.    2 and 4

**98. c.** Both encryption protocols and firewalls can provide a false sense of security. Encryption is used to provide confidentiality of data from the point of leaving the end user's software client to the point of being decrypted on the server system. After the data is stored "in the clear" on the server, data confidentiality is no longer ensured. Data confidentiality aside, encryption cannot prevent malicious attackers from breaking into the server systems and destroying data and transaction records. Firewalls have been used to protect internal computer systems from outside attacks and unauthorized inside users. The effectiveness of a firewall is usually in providing a deterrent for would be attacks. However, the bigger issue with firewalls is misconfiguration.

Digital signatures and certified authorities provide a good sense of security because they work together to form a trusted relationship. A digital signature stamped by the certifying authority can certify that the client and the server can be trusted.

**99.** The normal client/server implementation uses which of the following?

    a.    One-tier architecture

    b.    Two-tier architecture

    c.    Three-tier architecture

    d.    Four-tier architecture

**99. b.** The normal client/server implementation is a two-tiered architecture for simple networks (i.e., one client and one server). Multitiered architectures use one client and several servers.

**100.** All the following are examples of media access control (MAC) sublayer protocols *except*:

    a.    Carrier sense multiple access (CSMA)

    b.    Ethernet

    c.    Advanced data communications control procedure (ADCCP)

    d.    Logical link control (LLC)

**100. c.** Advanced data communications control procedure (ADCCP) is an example of a sliding window protocol. The other three choices are examples of media access control protocols. ADCCP is a modified synchronous data link control (SDLC), which became high-level data link control (HDLC), and later became link access procedure B (LAPB) to make it more compatible with HDLC.

Carrier sense multiple access (CSMA) protocols listen to the channel for a transmitting carrier and act accordingly. If the channel is busy, the station waits until it becomes idle. When the station detects an idle channel, it transmits a frame. If collision occurs, the station waits a random amount of time and starts all over again. The goal is to avoid a collision or detect a collision (CSMA/CA and CSMA/CD). The CSMA/CD is used on LANs in the MAC sublayer and is the basis of Ethernet. Logical link control (LLC) protocol hides the differences between the various kinds of IEEE 802 networks by providing a single format and interface to the network layer. LLC forms the upper half of the data link layer with the MAC sublayer below it.

**101.** All the following are examples of sliding window protocols *except*:

    a.    Wavelength division multiple access (WDMA)

    b.    Synchronous data link control (SDLC)

    c.    High-level data link control (HDLC)

    d.    Link access procedure B (LAPB)

**101. a.** Sliding window protocols, which are used to integrate error control and flow, are classified in terms of the size of the sender's window and the size of the receiver's window. Sliding window protocols (e.g., SDLC, HDLC, and LAPB) are bit-oriented protocols and use flag bytes to delimit frames and bit stuffing to prevent flag bytes from occurring in the data. Wavelength division multiple access (WDMA) is an example of medium/media access control (MAC) sublayer protocol that contains two channels for each station. A narrow channel is provided as a control channel to signal the station, and a wide channel is provided so that the station can output data frames.

**102.** **Data link layer VPN protocols such as the Cisco Layer 2 Forwarding (L2F) do *not* provide which of the following services?**

    a.   RADIUS

    b.   TACACS+

    c.   Encryption

    d.   Protects the traffic between the ISP and the organization

***102. c.*** Unlike PPTP and L2TP, L2F is intended for use between network devices, such as an ISP's network access server and an organization's VPN gateway. Like L2TP, L2F can use authentication protocols such as RADIUS and TACACS+. However, L2F does not support encryption.

**103.** **The wireless local-area network (WLAN) using the IEEE 802.11i standard for a robust security network (RSN) does not support the protection of which of the following?**

    a.   Stations and access points

    b.   Access points and authentication servers

    c.   Extensible authentication protocol and transport layer security

    d.   Stations and authentication servers

***103. b.*** The WLAN IEEE 802.11 and its related standards explicitly state that protection of the communications between the access points and authentication server is not available. Therefore, it is important to ensure that communications between each access point and its corresponding authentication servers are protected sufficiently through cryptography. In addition, the authentication servers should be secured through operating system configuration, firewall rules, and other security controls. The data confidentiality and integrity protocol, such as the counter mode with cipher block chaining message authentication code protocol (CCMP), protects communications between stations and access points. The extensible authentication protocol (EAP) with transport layer security (TLS) is considered the most secure EAP method because it enables strong mutual cryptographic authentications of both stations and authentication servers using public key certificates.

**104.** **Storing and hosting data on which of the following instant messaging (IM) architectures increases the risk of information theft, unauthorized access, and data tampering?**

    1.   Private hosting

    2.   Public hosting

    3.   Client-to-client

    4.   Public-switched network

a. 1 and 2

b. 1 and 4

c. 2 and 3

d. 3 and 4

**104. c.** There are four possible architectural designs for IM systems: private hosting, public hosting, client-to-client, and public-switched network. The difference between the four architectures is the location of the session data.

In the private hosting design (i.e., client-to-server), the data is located behind a firewall for internal users, which is safe and secure.

In public hosting design, the data is placed on public servers out on the Internet, which is vulnerable to attacks.

Two types of client-to-client (peer-to-peer) designs include pure and hybrid, which should be prohibited because they bypass the security and auditing policies within the enclave.

Because the data in public-switched network is not stored on a server, store and forward is not a security issue. However, data in transit is vulnerable to man-in-the-middle (MitM) attacks between the source and destination. The Internet has private global switched networks that deliver IM communications where data is not persistently stored on servers. In other words, the public-switched network is secure in terms of data storage on its servers. It is the data stored on public servers and client-to-client that increases the risk of information theft, unauthorized access, and data tampering. To protect the IM data, IM systems should implement client-to-server architecture (i.e., private hosting).

**105.** **For instant messaging (IM) systems, a virtual (remote) meeting moderator should configure which of the following properly to prevent potential exploits?**

a. Grant access based on need-to-know principle.

b. Implement role-based access controls.

c. Use application sharing capability.

d. Require a password to attend the meeting.

**105. c.** Some instant messaging (IM) systems enable two or more online users to communicate immediately over a network using shared applications (virtual meetings), presentations, white boards, and text messaging. Virtual meetings must have user access controls and virtual data classifications, and be restricted to authorized users only. Virtual users will be granted access based on the need-to-know principle established by the information owner and enforced by role-based access controls, and required by a password to participate in the meeting. Application sharing allows the virtual meeting participants to simultaneously run the same application with the same capability as remote control software. To limit this capability of application sharing and to prevent potential exploits, the meeting moderator should configure the application identifying so that users can use the application sharing feature.

**106.** The extensible authentication protocol (EAP) method with tunneled transport layer security (EAP-TTLS) used in a robust security network (RSN) such as wireless local-area network (WLAN) using the IEEE 802.11i standard does *not* prevent which of the following?

    a.    Eavesdropping attack

    b.    Man-in-the-middle attack

    c.    Replay attack

    d.    Dictionary attack

*106. b.* The root certificate may not be delivered securely to every client to prevent man-in-the-middle (MitM) attacks, thus not providing strong assurance against MitM attacks. Because passwords sent to the Web server are encrypted, EAP-TTLS protects the eavesdropping attack. The TLS tunnel protects the inner applications from replay attacks and dictionary attacks.

**107.** Which of the following classes of attacks focus on breaking security protection features?

    a.    Passive

    b.    Active

    c.    Close-in

    d.    Insider

*107. b.* With an active attack, an intruder modifies the intercepted messages. Breaking security protection features is an example of active attack. With a passive attack, an intruder intercepts messages to view the data. It includes traffic and packet analysis to disclose personal information such as credit card numbers and medical files. A close-in attack is where an unauthorized individual is in physical close proximity to networks and systems, or facilities for the purpose of modifying, gathering, or denying access to information. Insider attacks can be malicious or nonmalicious. Using information in a fraudulent manner is an example of a malicious insider attack.

**108.** In a legacy wireless local-area network (WLAN) environment using the IEEE 802.11 standard, which of the following provides a defense-in-depth strategy?

    1.    Wi-Fi protected access 2 (WPA2)

    2.    Wired equivalent privacy (WEP)

    3.    IPsec VPNs and SSL VPNs

    4.    Dedicated wired network or a VLAN

        a.    1 only

        b.    1 and 2

        c.    3 only

        d.    3 and 4

*108. d.* Both WPA2 and WEP do not provide a defense-in-depth strategy because they are weak in security. An alternative method for WPA2 and WEP for achieving confidentiality and integrity protection is to use virtual private network (VPN) technologies such as Internet Protocol security (IPsec) VPNs and secure sockets layer (SSL) VPNs. Because VPNs do not eliminate all risk from wireless networking, it is good to place the WLAN traffic on a dedicated wired network or a virtual local-area network (VLAN) as an option to VPN technologies. VLAN can also protect against denial-of-service (DoS) attacks. Therefore, IPsec VPNs, SSL VPNs, dedicated wired network, or a VLAN provides a defense-in-depth strategy.

**109.** **Information systems security testing is a part of which of the following?**

    a.   Directive controls

    b.   Preventive controls

    c.   Detective controls

    d.   Corrective controls

*109. c.* Information systems security testing is a part of detective controls because it includes vulnerability scanners, penetration tests, and war dialing. Detective controls enhance security by monitoring the effectiveness of preventive controls and by detecting security incidents where preventive controls were circumvented.

Directive controls are broad-based controls to handle security incidents, and they include management's policies, procedures, and directives. Preventive controls deter security incidents from happening in the first place. Corrective controls are procedures to react to security incidents and to take remedial actions on a timely basis. Corrective controls require proper planning and preparation because they rely more on human judgment.

**110.** **In a public cloud computing environment, which of the following is mostly needed to establish a level of trust among cloud service providers and subscribers?**

    a.   Compensating controls

    b.   Third-party audits

    c.   Threshold for alerts

    d.   Service contracts

*110. b.* Establishing a level of trust about a cloud service is dependent on the degree of control an organization can exert on the service provider to protect the organization's data and applications. Evidence is needed about the effectiveness of security controls over such data and applications. Third-party audits may be used to establish a level of trust and evidence if it is not feasible to verify through normal means. If the level of trust in the service falls below expectations and the organization cannot employ compensating controls, it must either reject the service or accept a greater degree of risk. Threshold for alerts and notification is needed to keep visibility on the cloud service provider.

**111.** **Which of the following is an example of a personal firewall?**

    a.    Network-based firewalls

    b.    Host-based firewalls

    c.    Source-based IP address

    d.    Destination-based IP address

***111. b.***   Host-based firewalls, also known as personal firewalls, can be effective at preventing unauthorized access to endpoints if configured to block unwanted activity. Host-based firewalls might need to be reconfigured from their typical settings to permit legitimate activity, such as enabling an IPsec endpoint. Accordingly, organizations should consider providing information to external endpoint administrators and users on which services, protocols, or port numbers the host-based firewalls should permit for necessary services. The other three choices are not related to personal firewalls.

**112.** **Which of the following is *not* used by an individual or a specialized computer program to read an online advertisement displayed by the Internet search engine without the intention of buying a product or service?**

    a.    Honeynets

    b.    Pay-per-click feature

    c.    Botnets

    d.    Third parties

***112. a.***   This question relates to click fraud. Honeynets are networks of honeypots, which are used to create fake production systems to attract attackers to study their behaviors and actions with an information system. Honeynets are not used in click fraud.

The other three choices are used to create a click fraud, which is a major problem at Internet service providers (ISPs) and other websites. The click fraud is perpetrated by a combination of individuals, specialized computer programs, bot networks (botnets), and third parties who are hired for a fee to click because they are paid on a per-click basis. (For example, the more clicks they do the more money they make.) In all these situations, fraudulent clicks are made on an online advertisement with no intention of learning further about a product or purchasing the product. The advertiser pays the website owners based on the number of clicks made on its advertisement. Unethical website owners are creating a click fraud to make easy money. Specialized computer programs are written to do the automatic clicking.

**113.** **The purpose of the packet filter is *not* based on which of the following?**

    a.    IP addresses

    b.    Protocols

    c.    Port numbers

    d.    Applications

***113. d.*** The purpose of the packet filter is to specify how each type of incoming and outgoing traffic should be handled—whether the traffic should be permitted or denied (usually based on IP addresses, protocols, and port numbers), and how permitted traffic should be protected. The type of application does not matter for the packet filter.

**114.** As the packet filtering rules become more complex, they can lead to which of the following?

    a.    Authentication errors

    b.    Cryptographic errors

    c.    Configuration errors

    d.    Performance errors

***114. c.*** One caveat in the packet filter is that the more complex the packet filtering rules become, the more likely it is that a configuration error may occur, which could permit traffic to traverse networks without sufficient controls.

**115.** The Internet Protocol security (IPsec) implementation typically supports which of the following authentication methods?

    1.    Preshared keys

    2.    Digital signatures

    3.    Kerberos

    4.    TACACS and RADIUS

        a.    1 and 2

        b.    2 and 3

        c.    3 and 4

        d.    1, 2, 3, and 4

***115. d.*** The endpoints of an IPsec connection use the same authentication method to validate each other. IPsec implementations typically support preshared keys and digital signatures, and in some implementations external authentication services, such as Kerberos. Some IPsec implementations also support the use of legacy asymmetric authentication servers such as terminal access controller access control system (TACACS) and remote authentication dial-in user service (RADIUS).

**116.** Which of the following does *not* require redundancy and fail-over capabilities to provide a robust Internet Protocol security (IPsec) solution?

    a.    IPsec client software in a managed environment

    b.    IPsec gateways

    c.    Authentication servers

    d.    Directory servers

**116. a.** Redundancy and fail-over capabilities should be considered not only for the core IPsec components, but also for supporting systems. IPsec client software may be broken by a new operating system update. This issue can be handled rather easily in a managed environment, but it can pose a major problem in a nonmanaged environment. Therefore, the IPsec client software does not require redundancy and fail-over capabilities.

IPsec gateways are incorrect because two IPsec gateways can be configured so that when one gateway fails, users automatically fail over to the other gateway. Authentication servers and directory servers are incorrect because they also need redundancy due to their support role.

**117.** All the following can be disallowed at the voice gateway in Voice over Internet Protocol (VoIP) *except*:

    a.    Application level gateway

    b.    H.323 gateway protocol

    c.    Session initiation protocol (SIP)

    d.    Media gateway control protocol (MGCP)

**117. a.** The application level gateway or firewall control proxy is designed for VoIP traffic to deny packets that are not part of a properly originated call or track the state of connections, which should be allowed to function. The protocols such as H.323, SIP, and MGCP, which are connections from the data network, should be disallowed at the voice gateway of the VoIP that interfaces with the public-switched telephone network (PSTN) because they are not secure.

H.323 gateway is a gateway protocol used in the Internet telephone systems, and it speaks the H.323 protocol on the Internet side and the PSTN protocols on the telephone side. The session initiation protocol (SIP) just handles setup, management, and session termination. The media gateway control protocol (MGCP) is used in large deployment for gateway decomposition.

**118.** Which of the following factors should be considered during the placement of an Internet Protocol security (IPsec) gateway?

1.    Device performance

2.    Traffic examination

3.    Gateway outages

4.    Network address translation

    a.    2 only

    b.    3 only

    c.    4 only

    d.    1, 2, 3, and 4

***118. d.*** The placement of an IPsec gateway has potential security, functionality, and performance implications. Specific factors to consider include device performance, traffic examination, gateway outages, and network address translation.

**119.** Which of the following establishes rules of engagement (ROE) prior to the start of penetration testing?

  a. White team

  b. Red team

  c. Tiger team

  d. Blue team

***119. a.*** The white team establishes the rules of engagement (ROE) prior to the start of penetration testing. ROE describes tools, techniques, and procedures that both the red team and blue team should follow. The tiger team is same as the red team, which is an old name for the red team. Outsiders (i.e., contractors and consultants) conduct both red team and blue team testing whereas white team members are employees of the testing organization. The white team does not conduct any testing.

**120.** Which of the following is difficult to achieve during the Internet Protocol security (IPsec) implementation?

  a. Control over all entry points into networks

  b. Control over all exit points from networks

  c. Security of all IPsec endpoints

  d. Incorporating IPsec considerations into organizational policies

***120. d.*** Organizations should implement technical, operational, and management controls that support and complement IPsec implementations. Examples include having control over all entry and exit points for the protected networks, ensuring the security of all IPsec endpoints, and incorporating IPsec considerations into organizational policies. Incorporating IPsec considerations into organizational policies is incorrect because it is difficult to achieve due to an organization's culture, work habits, and politics.

**121.** Virtual private network (VPN) protocols provide a viable option for protecting networks running with non-IP protocols in which of the following TCP/IP layers?

  a. Applications layer

  b. Transport layer

  c. Network layer

  d. Data link layer

***121. d.*** Data link layer VPN protocols function below the network layer in the TCP/IP model. This means that various network protocols, such as IP, IPX, and NetBEUI, can usually be used with a data link layer VPN. Most VPN protocols including IPsec support only IP, so data link layer VPN protocols may provide a viable option for protecting networks running non-IP protocols. As the name implies, IPsec is designed to provide security for IP traffic only.

**122.** Data link layer VPN protocols, such as Layer 2 Tunneling Protocols (L2TP), provide which of the following services?

1. RADIUS

2. TACACS+

3. Encryption

4. Key management services

    a. 1 and 2

    b. 3 only

    c. 4 only

    d. 1, 2, 3, and 4

**122. d.**  Like PPTP, L2TP protects communications between an L2TP-enabled client and an L2TP-enabled server, and it requires L2TP client software to be installed and configured on each user system. L2TP can use RADIUS and TACACS+ protocols for authentication, and often uses IPsec to provide encryption and key management services.

**123.** A virtual private network (VPN) *cannot* provide or improve which of the following security services?

    a. Availability

    b. Confidentiality

    c. Integrity

    d. Replay protection

**123. a.**  VPNs cannot provide or improve availability, which is the ability for authorized users to access systems as needed. Many VPN implementations tend to decrease availability somewhat because they add more components and services to the existing network infrastructure. A VPN can provide several types of data protection, including confidentiality, integrity, data origin authentication, replay protection, and access control.

**124.** What is the best way to handle bot attacks in an organization?

    a. Install antivirus software.

    b. Install antispyware software.

    c. Update software with patches.

    d. Develop and train a white team.

**124. d.** A white team is an internal team that initiates action to respond to security incidents on an emergency basis. The scope of a white team's work includes diagnosing attacks, profiling attacks, notifying law enforcement authorities and the Internet service provider (ISP), measuring the impact of the attack on customer service, and developing application systems to filter the bogus incoming data packets. There is no single preventive solution to handle the bot attack problems because new bots are created all the time. The best method is to respond on an after-the-fact basis with a white team supplemented by installing antivirus and spyware software and updating software with patches and fixes.

**125.** Which of the following models is used for formally specifying and verifying protocols?

    a.    Markov model

    b.    Finite state machine model

    c.    Protocol stack

    d.    Protocol data unit

**125. b.** The finite state machine (FSM) model is used for formally specifying and verifying protocols. In the FSM model, mathematical techniques are used in specifying and verifying the protocol correctness because it defines or implements the control structure of a system.

The other three choices do not deal with formally specifying and verifying protocols. The Markov model is used to model a system regarding its failure states to evaluate the reliability, safety, and availability of the system. A protocol stack is a list of protocols used by a system (e.g., TCP/IP suite). A protocol data unit is a unit of data specified in a protocol and includes user data and other information.

**126.** Which of the following *cannot* provide effective security at the endpoints of a network?

    a.    Antimalware software

    b.    Personal firewalls

    c.    Strong password policies

    d.    Host-based intrusion detection and prevention system

**126. c.** Password policies, even if they are strong, are difficult to implement and enforce at the personal computer and workstation levels due to unpredictable behavior of end users. If password policies are implemented incorrectly or used poorly, an attacker can undermine the best security configuration. The other three choices provide effective security at the endpoints of a network because they are technical security controls and do not deal with end users.

**127.** Both Internet Protocol security (IPsec) and a virtual private network (VPN) can be implemented with which of the following?

    1.    Using the symmetric cryptography

    2.    Protecting the data

    3.    Using the asymmetric cryptography

    4.    Authenticating the parties

a. 1 and 2

b. 1 and 3

c. 3 and 4

d. 1, 2, 3, and 4

**127. d.** VPNs can use both symmetric and asymmetric forms of cryptography. Symmetric cryptography uses the same key for both encryption and decryption, whereas asymmetric cryptography uses separate keys for encryption and decryption, or to digitally sign and verify a signature. Most IPsec implementations use both symmetric and asymmetric cryptography. Asymmetric cryptography is used to authenticate the identities of both parties, whereas symmetric encryption is used for protecting the actual data because of its relative efficiency.

**128.** **Which of the following is used to encrypt the bulk of the data being sent over a virtual private network (VPN)?**

1. Symmetric cryptography

2. Private key cryptography

3. Asymmetric cryptography

4. Public key cryptography

a. 1 only

b. 3 only

c. 4 only

d. 1 and 2

**128. d.** Symmetric cryptography (also known as private key cryptography) is generally more efficient and requires less processing power than asymmetric cryptography, which is why it is typically used to encrypt the bulk of the data being sent over a VPN. One problem with symmetric cryptography is with the key exchange process; keys must be exchanged out-of-band to ensure confidentiality. Out-of-band refers to using a separate communications mechanism to transfer information. For example, the VPN cannot be used to exchange the keys securely because the keys are required to provide the necessary protection. Asymmetric cryptography (also known as public key cryptography) uses two separate keys to exchange data.

**129.** **In sliding window protocols, a protocol is said to be in the stop-and-wait mode under which of the following conditions?**

a. When the sequence number for a sender's window is greater than 1, a receiver can discard all data frames.

b. When the sequence number for a sender's window and a receiver's window is equal to 1.

c. When the sequence number for a sender's window is greater than 1, a receiver can buffer out-of-order data frames.

d. When two separate physical circuits are used for forward channel and reverse channel.

**129. b.** Sliding window protocols are bit-oriented and bidirectional protocols that use the same physical circuit for data frame transmission in both directions. When the sequence number for a sender's window and a receiver's window is equal to 1, the protocol is said to be in the stop-and-wait mode.

The other three choices do not operate in a stop-and-wait mode. When the sequence number for a sender's window is greater than 1, the receiver can either discard all data frames or buffer out-of-order data frames. When two separate physical circuits are used for forward channel and reverse channel, it represents a full-duplex data transmission, which is inefficient because only once circuit is used for the forward channel and the circuit for the reverse channel is not used. The full-duplex transmission uses two circuits and wastes resources whereas the sliding window protocol uses only one circuit.

**130.** Which of the following is *not* a solution to the network congestion problems in terms of increasing the system resources?

   a.  Splitting traffic over multiple routes

   b.  Having spare routers available online

   c.  Having users schedule their work at nonpeak times

   d.  Increasing the transmission power for satellite systems

**130. c.** The presence of network congestion problems means that the network load is temporarily greater than the system resources can handle. Solutions include either increasing the system resources or decreasing the network load. Having users schedule their work at nonpeak times is a solution to decrease the network load, which may not go well with the good principles of customer service. The other three choices are solutions to increase the system resources.

**131.** Which of the following does *not* cause false positives and false negatives?

   a.  Antivirus software

   b.  Spyware detection and removal utility software

   c.  Host-based intrusion detection systems

   d.  Firewalls

**131. d.** False positives occur when a tool reports a security weakness when no weakness is present. False negatives occur when a tool does not report a security weakness when one is present. Firewalls do not cause false positives and false negatives due to use of rulesets and the practice of deny-by-default privileges.

Antivirus software is incorrect because it has the capability to cause false positives and false negatives due to use of heuristic techniques to detect new malware. Spyware detection and removal utility software is incorrect because it can cause false positives and false negatives. Host-based intrusion detection systems are incorrect because they can cause false positives and false negatives (false warnings and alerts in the form of alarms) due to malfunctioning sensors and that network activity is not visible to host-based sensors.

**132.** **Which of the following are the primary security goals of a domain name system (DNS)?**

1. Source authentication
2. Confidentiality
3. Integrity
4. Availability

    a. 1 and 2

    b. 2 and 3

    c. 1 and 3

    d. 3 and 4

*132. c.* Ensuring information authenticity and maintaining information integrity in transit is critical for efficient functioning of the Internet, for which DNS provides the name resolution service. Hence, integrity and source authentication are the primary DNS security goals. Confidentiality is not one of the security goals of DNS, and availability is a secondary security goal.

**133.** **Transmission control protocol (TCP) packet is associated with which of the following when sending domain name system (DNS) queries?**

1. Truncation
2. Little or no truncation
3. Higher overhead
4. Lower overhead

    a. 1 only

    b. 4 only

    c. 1 and 4

    d. 2 and 3

*133. d.* TCP is used when DNS queries result in little or no truncation, but it is subjected to higher overhead of resources. On the other hand, DNS requests using UDP result in truncation and utilizes a lower overhead of resources.

**134.** **A peer-to-peer (P2P) networking is similar to which of the following?**

    a. Content delivery network

    b. Value-added network

    c. Ad-hoc network

    d. Wide-area network

***134. c.*** Ad-hoc networks are similar to peer-to-peer (P2P) networking in that they both use decentralized networking, in which the information is maintained at the end user location rather than in a centralized database. The networks mentioned in the other three choices use centralized networking with centralized databases.

**135.** Which of the following is *not* a function of host-based scanners?

    a.   Identify outdated software versions

    b.   Identify outdated patches

    c.   Identify outdated system upgrades

    d.   Identify open ports

***135. d.*** Network-based scanners identify open ports. The other three choices are incorrect because they are functions of host-based scanners. Another tool is a port scanner, which is a program that attempts to determine remotely which ports on systems are open (i.e., whether systems enable connections through those ports). Port scanners help attackers to identify potential targets.

**136.** Which of the following system security testing and information gathering tools can produce false positives?

    a.   Information scanning tool

    b.   Vulnerability scanning tool

    c.   Network scanning tool

    d.   Penetration testing tool

***136. b.*** False positives occur when a tool reports a security weakness when no weakness is present. A vulnerability scanner is a program that looks for vulnerabilities on either the local system or on remote systems. Vulnerability scanners help attackers to find hosts that they can exploit successfully. The automated vulnerability scanning tools is used to scan a group of hosts or a network for known vulnerable services such as use of file transfer protocol (FTP) and sendmail relaying. Some of the vulnerabilities flagged by the automated scanning tool may actually not be vulnerable for a particular site based on its configuration. Thus, this scanning tool can produce false positives, which are warning and alerts that incorrectly indicate that malicious activity is occurring.

The automated information scanning tool does not produce false positives because it is used to collect system information efficiently to build individual profiles of the target IT system. The network scanning tool, which does not produce false positives, lists all active hosts and services operating in the address space scanned by the port-scanning tool. The penetration testing tool is a specific tool for information systems testing and does not produce false positives.

**137.** From a network data analysis perspective, what do many Web-based applications use?

    a.   Two-tiered client/server model

    b.   Three-tiered client/server model

   c.    Four-tiered client/server model

   d.    Five-tiered client/server model

*137. c.*   A client/server application is designed to split among multiple systems. Examples of typical client/server applications are medical records systems, e-commerce applications, and inventory systems. Many Web-based applications use four-tier client/server models: Web browser, Web server, application server, and database server. Each tier interacts only with the adjacent tiers, so in three- and four-tier models, the client does not directly interact with the database server.

A two-tiered client/server model is incorrect because the application stores its code, configuration settings, and supporting files on each user's workstation, and its data on one or more central servers accessed by all users. Programs are stored on a workstation, and data is stored on a central server. Logs are most likely stored on the workstations only. This model includes client workstations and a central server.

A three-tiered client/server model is incorrect because the application separates the user interface from the rest of the application, and also separates the data from the other components. The classic three-tier model places the user interface code on the client workstation, the rest of the application code on an application server, and the data on a database server. This model includes client workstations, application server, and database server. A five-tiered client/server model is incorrect because it is complex to configure, operate, and manage.

**138.**   **Which of the following enhances an instant messaging (IM) authentication process?**

   a.    Active directory service

   b.    Lightweight directory access protocol

   c.    Two-factor authentication

   d.    Role-based access permissions

*138. c.*   Instant messaging (IM) systems authenticate users for communication by linking user accounts to directory services (i.e., Active Directory and Lightweight Directory Access Protocol, LDAP) to associate with valid accounts and provide role-based access permissions. IM authentication could be enhanced using two-factor authentication because it is more secure. Two-factor authentication identifies users using two distinctive factors such as something they have (e.g., token or smart card), something they know (e.g., password or PIN), or something they are (e.g., a biometric sample). Requiring two forms of electronic identification reduces the risk of fraud.

**139.**   **Which of the following extensible authentication protocol (EAP) methods does *not* fully satisfy the security requirements for a robust security network (RSN) such as wireless local-area network (WLAN) using the IEEE 802.11i standard?**

   a.    EAP transport layer security (EAP-TLS)

   b.    EAP tunneled TLS (EAP-TTLS)

   c.    EAP flexible authentication via secure tunneling (EAP-FAST)

   d.    Protected EAP (PEAP)

**139. c.** The extensible authentication protocol (EAP) provides the authentication framework for IEEE 802.11 RSNs that use IEEE 802.11X port-based access control. The EAP provides mutual authentication between an access point (AP), a station (STA), and an authentication server (AS). EAP-FAST is especially suitable for unsophisticated devices (e.g., household appliances, vending machines, and other small devices not connected to WLANs) that might not have the computing power to perform TLS handshakes, and as such its security is limited for robust WLANs. The other three EAP methods are secure. It is important that organizations should select the EAP methods based on a risk assessment of the target environment.

**140.** Which of the following is a part of transport layer security policies and is not a part of data link layer security policies to prevent network congestion problems?

    a.    Retransmission policy

    b.    Timeout determination policy

    c.    Out-of-order caching policy

    d.    Flow control policy

**140. b.** The timeout determination policy is a part of the transport layer security policies but not a part of the data link layer security policies. The other three choices are the same between these two layer's policies.

**141.** Which of the following protects the confidentiality of data in transit in a file-sharing environment?

    a.    Network file sharing (NFS)

    b.    Apple filing protocol (AFP)

    c.    Server message block (SMB)

    d.    Secure file transfer protocol (SFTP)

**141. d.** Secure FTP (SFTP) and Secure Copy (SCP) encrypt their network communications to protect the confidentiality of data in transit. Examples of commonly used client/server file sharing services are file transfer protocol (FTP), network file sharing, Apple filing protocol, and server message block. These are standardized protocols without encryption that do not protect the confidentiality of the data in transit, including any supplied authentication credentials such as passwords.

**142.** Countermeasures against time-of-check to time-of-use (TOC-TOU) attacks include which of the following?

    1.    Use traffic padding techniques.

    2.    Apply task sequence rules.

    3.    Apply encryption tools.

    4.    Implement strong access controls.

    a.    1 and 2

    b.    2 and 3

    c.    3 and 4

    d.    1 and 3

***142. b.*** Time-of-check to time-of-use (TOC-TOU) attack is an example of asynchronous attacks where it takes advantage of timing differences between two events. Applying task sequence rules combined with encryption tools are effective against such attacks. Traffic padding technique is effective against traffic analysis attacks, and access controls are good against data inference attacks.

**143.** **In a legacy wireless local-area network (WLAN) environment using wired equivalent privacy (WEP) protocol (IEEE 802.11), a bit-flipping attack results in which of the following?**

    a.    Loss of confidentiality

    b.    Loss of integrity

    c.    Loss of availability

    d.    Loss of accountability

***143. b.*** A bit-flipping attack occurs when an attacker knows which cyclic redundancy check-32-bits (CRC-32 bits) can change when message bits are altered, resulting in loss of integrity. A proposed countermeasure is encrypting the CRC-32 to produce an integrity check value (ICV), but it did not work because of use of stream ciphers (WEP's RC4), meaning that the same bits flip whether encryption is used. Therefore, WEP ICV offers no additional protection against bit flipping. Eavesdropping attacks using sniffers result in loss of confidentiality. Packet flooding attacks and radio frequency signal jams result in loss of availability. Loss of accountability is not applicable here because it deals with an individual's actions.

**144.** **Which of the following factors contribute to network congestion problems?**

1.    Low-speed CPU and low memory for computers

2.    Low-bandwidth lines for communications

3.    More memory for routers

4.    Long queues of packets

    a.    1 only

    b.    2 only

    c.    4 only

    d.    1, 2, 3, and 4

***144. d.*** Network congestion problems occur when too many packets are present in the subnet (i.e., too much traffic), thus degrading the network performance in terms of some lost packets or all packets undelivered. When a queue is built up for packets and the CPU memory for computers is insufficient to hold all of them, some packets will be lost. When there is an imbalance between the routers with more memory and computers with less memory, duplicate packets are sent due to the timeout feature. Also, routers with slow CPU processors and low bandwidth lines can cause congestion problems.

**145.** Which of the following techniques to improve network quality-of-service (QoS) provides an easy and expensive solution?

    a.   Buffering

    b.   Over-provisioning

    c.   Traffic shaping

    d.   Packet scheduling

***145. b.*** Over-provisioning is providing higher levels of router capacity, buffer space, and bandwidth for the network packets to flow from source to destination. Because of this, an over-provisioning technique is an easy but an expensive solution.

The other three choices do not incur costs the way over-provisioning does. Network flows can be buffered on the receiving side before being delivered. Buffering the flow does not affect the reliability, delay, or bandwidth, but it does smooth out the jitter often found in audio and video on demand applications. Traffic shaping, also called traffic policing, is achieved through the use of a leaky bucket algorithm or token bucket algorithm to smooth traffic between routers and to regulate the host output. Packet scheduling algorithms such as fair queuing and weighted fair queuing are available to schedule the flow of packets through the router so that one flow does not dominate the other.

**146.** Which of the following might be unsuccessful at identifying infected hosts running personal firewalls?

    a.   Network login scripts

    b.   Packet sniffers

    c.   Host scans

    d.   File scans

***146. c.*** Personal firewalls can block the host scans, therefore making it unsuccessful in identifying the infected hosts. The other three choices are incorrect because they all can help to identify the possible infection on those hosts.

**147.** Which of the following is a mitigation technique to handle Internet relay chat (IRC) vulnerability for lack of confidentiality due to messages sent in plaintext throughout the IRC network?

    a.   Install operating system-level VPNs or application-level SSL/TLS.

    b.   Implement timers.

    c.   Put the system in a lockdown mode.

    d.   Block filtering requests based on filename extensions.

*147. a.* The Internet relay chat (IRC) communication is inherently insecure because it is a plaintext open protocol that uses transmission control protocol (TCP) that is susceptible to sniffing and interception. The original IRC protocol does not provide for any confidentiality, meaning that standard chat, nickname passwords, channel passwords, and private messaging are sent in plaintext throughout the IRC network. Confidentiality may be achieved by applying operating system level VPNs or SSL/TLS within the IRC network. The IRC clients and servers use encryption to protect information from unauthorized users. Furthermore, IPsec VPNs with PKI certificates or tunneled through Secure Shell should be used to provide further security for identification and authentication.

Timers are implemented to mitigate the IRC vulnerability of netsplits. A system lockdown mode is implemented to combat denial-of-service (DoS) attacks on the IRC network. The security administrator should block outright filtering requests based on filename extensions to prevent direct client connection (DCC) vulnerability within IRC networks. DCCs are performed directly from one client application to another, thus bypassing the IRC servers to form a client-to-client connection. DCC vulnerabilities, if not controlled properly, lead to unauthorized file transfers between IRC clients, allow users to bypass server-based security, shorten the communication path, allow social engineering attacks, and compromise the user's application system.

**148.** **Which of the following is the long-term solution as a core cryptographic algorithm for the wireless local-area network (WLAN) using the IEEE 802.11i standard to ensure a robust security network (RSN)?**

     a.    Wired equivalent privacy (WEP)

     b.    Temporal key integrity protocol (TKIP)

     c.    Counter mode with cipher block chaining message authentication code protocol (CCMP)

     d.    Wi-Fi protected access 2 (WPA2)

*148. c.* The counter mode with cipher block chaining message authentication code protocol (CCMP) is considered the long-term solution for IEEE 802.11 WLANs because it requires hardware updates and replaces pre-RSN equipment. Of all the four choices, only CCMP uses the advanced encryption standard (AES) as the core cryptographic algorithm. For legacy IEEE 802.11 equipment that does not provide CCMP, IPsec VPN can be used as auxiliary security protection. WEP is an original standard as a data confidentiality and integrity protocol with several security problems. Later, WPA2 was designed as the interim solution as an upgrade to existing WEP-enabled equipment to provide a higher level of security, primarily through the use of TKIP and MIC (message integrity code). TKIP is intended as an interim solution along with WEP and WPA2. TKIP can be implemented through software updates and does not require hardware replacement of access points and stations.

**149.** Which of the following provides stronger security in managing access point (AP) configuration in a legacy wireless local-area network (WLAN) environment?

    a.   Simple network management protocol (SNMP)

    b.   SNMP version 1

    c.   SNMP version 2

    d.   SNMP version 3

**149. d.**  Simple network management protocol (SNMP) version 3 provides strong security feature enhancements to basic SNMP, including encryption and message authentication, and therefore should be used.

The earlier versions of SNMP, SNMPv1, and SNMPv2 should not be used because they are fundamentally insecure as they support only trivial authentication based on default plaintext community strings. The default SNMP community string that SNMPv1 and SNMPv2 agents commonly use is the word "public" with assigned "read" or "read and write" privileges; using this string leaves devices vulnerable to attack. If an unauthorized user were to gain access and had read/write privileges, that user could write data to the AP, compromising its original configuration. Organizations using SNMPv1 or SNMPv2 should change the community string as often as needed, taking into consideration that the string is transmitted in plaintext. For all versions of SNMP, privileges should be set to the least required (e.g., read only).

**150.** Which of the following *cannot* defend the enclave boundary?

    a.   Firewalls

    b.   Switches and routers

    c.   Virtual private networks

    d.   Software/hardware guards

**150. b.**  Switches and routers defend the networks and their infrastructures such as LANs, campus area networks (CANs), MANs, and WANs. The other three choices defend the enclave boundary, which defines a clear separation between inside and outside of a network where local computing environment (LAN) is inside the enclave and connection to external networks and remote users (e.g., dial-up access, ISP connection, and dedicated line) is outside the enclave. Boundary protection is provided by software/hardware guards, firewalls, and other devices, which control access into the local computing environment (LAN). Remote access protection is provided by communications server, encryption, VPN, and others.

A single enclave may span a number of geographically separate locations with connectivity via commercially purchased point-to-point communications (e.g., T-1, T-3, and ISDN) along with WAN connectivity such as the Internet. An enclave is a collection of information systems connected by one or more internal networks under the control of a single organization and security policy. These systems may be structured by physical proximity or by function, independent of location. An enclave boundary is a point at which an enclave's internal network service layer connects to an external network's service layer (i.e., to another enclave or to a wide-area network).

**151.** **Which of the following virtual private network (VPN) architectures often replaces costly private wide-area network (WAN) circuits?**

    a.    Gateway-to-gateway

    b.    Host-to-gateway

    c.    Contractor-to-company

    d.    Host-to-host

**151. *a.*** The gateway-to-gateway virtual private network (VPN) architecture often replaces more costly private wide-area network (WAN) circuits.

The host-to-gateway VPN architecture often replaces dial-up modem pools, is somewhat complex to implement and maintain for user and host management, and is most often used to provide secure remote access.

The contractor-to-company architecture is an exclusive connection between the VPN client and the VPN network device; all other connectivity is blocked after the establishment of the VPN session, so there is no chance of IP packets being forwarded between the Internet and the company's private network.

The host-to-host VPN architecture is most often used when a small number of trusted users need to use or administer a remote system that requires the use of insecure protocols (e.g., a legacy system), that requires a secure remote access solution, and that can be updated to provide VPN services. System administrators performing remote management of a single server can use the host-to-host VPN architecture. The host-to-host VPN architecture is resource-intensive to implement and maintain for user and host management.

**152.** **Which of the following provides stronger security in administering the network devices, such as routers or switches?**

    a.    Simple network management protocol (SNMP)

    b.    SNMP version 1

    c.    SNMP version 2

    d.    SNMP version 3

**152. *d.*** Simple network management protocol (SNMP) version 3 provides security feature enhancements to basic SNMP, including encryption and message authentication. SNMP, SNMP version 1, and SNMP version 2 rely on default clear-text community strings (e.g., public and private) across the network without cryptographic protection. Therefore, SNMP, SNMP version 1, and SNMP version 2 should not be used to configure network devices over untrusted networks. The default community strings should be removed before real community strings are put into place. If both of these string types are present on the device at any time, an attacker could retrieve real community strings from the device using the default community strings. Hence, SNMP version 3 provides stronger security than the other three choices for administering the network devices such as routers or switches.

**153.** Which of the following models is used for formally specifying and verifying protocols?

    a.    Protocol converter

    b.    Protocol tunneling

    c.    Petri net model

    d.    Seeding model

*153. c.* Petri net model is used for formally specifying and verifying protocols. Petri nets are a graphical technique used to model relevant aspects of the system behavior and to assess and improve safety and operational requirements through analysis and redesign.

The other three choices do not deal with formally specifying and verifying protocols. A protocol converter is a device that changes one type of coded data to another type of coded data for computer processing. Protocol tunneling is a method to ensure confidentiality and integrity of data transmitted over the Internet. A seeding model is used to indicate software reliability in terms of error detection power of a set of test cases.

**154.** The penetration testing of security controls does *not* focus on which of the following?

    a.    Technical controls

    b.    Physical controls

    c.    Management controls

    d.    Procedural controls

*154. c.* Security controls are of three types: management, technical, and operational. Physical controls and procedural controls are part of operational controls. Penetration testing does not focus on management controls, such as policies and directives. Instead, it focuses on technical and operational controls dealing with ports, protocols, system services, and devices.

**155.** Which of the following is *not* used in creating static Web documents?

    a.    Hypertext markup language (HTML)

    b.    Joint photographic experts group (JPEG)

    c.    Hypertext preprocessor (PHP)

    d.    Extensible style language (XSL)

*155. c.* Hypertext preprocessor (PHP) is used in creating a dynamic Web document along with JavaScript and Active X controls. Static Web documents (pages) are written in HTML, XHTML, ASCII, JPEG, XML, and XSL.

**156.** All the following are work elements of penetration testing of security controls *except*:

    a.    Pretest analysis of the target system

    b.    Pretest identification of potential vulnerabilities

    c.    Independent verification and validation of vulnerabilities

    d.    Systematic determination of exploitability of identified vulnerabilities

**156. c.**   Independent verification and validation of vulnerabilities is a form of security assurance testing, not the work element of security penetration testing. The other three choices are work elements of the penetration testing.

**157.**   **Which of the following refers to open-loop control to handle network congestion problems?**

1.   Good design principles

2.   Preventive actions

3.   Detective actions

4.   Corrective actions

    a.   2 only

    b.   1 and 2

    c.   2 and 3

    d.   3 and 4

**157. b.**   Open-loop control includes good design principles and preventive actions whereas closed-loop control includes detective actions and corrective actions. Tools for open-loop controls include deciding when to accept new traffic, deciding when to discard packets and which ones, and making scheduling decisions at various points in the network.

**158.**   **Which of the following configurations for private servers hosting instant messaging (IM) data can lead to man-in-the middle (MitM) attack when it is not installed, installed incorrectly, or implemented improperly?**

    a.   Enclave perimeter

    b.   Demilitarized zone

    c.   Encrypted communication channel

    d.   Server services

**158. c.**   Client-to-server architecture protects data by storing it on private servers as opposed to client computers or public servers. Private servers hosting instant messaging (IM) data will be configured with a network infrastructure that protects the servers from unauthorized access using an enclave perimeter with a firewall, a demilitarized zone (DMZ) for a gateway server, encryption for communication channel, and server services. Using protocols that do not encrypt network traffic can easily be hijacked, resulting in the man-in-the-middle (MitM) attack. The IM server services provide activities such as user registration, authentication, account management, logging, and software downloads for users. Those services not required for operation should be disabled to prevent the potential risk of attack on those services.

**159.** Which of the following virtual private network (VPN) architectures is transparent to users and to users' systems?

    a.    Gateway-to-gateway

    b.    Host-to-gateway

    c.    Contractor-to-company

    d.    Host-to-host

***159. a.*** Gateway-to-gateway virtual private networks (VPNs) are typically transparent to users who do not need to perform separate authentication just to use the VPN. Also, the users' systems and the target hosts (e.g., servers) do not need to have any VPN client software installed, nor should they require any reconfiguration, to use the VPN.

A host-to-gateway VPN is incorrect because it is not transparent to users because they must be authenticated before using the VPN. Also, the user's hosts need to have VPN client software configured. A contractor-to-company is incorrect because it is not transparent to users and needs to have VPN client software configured. A host-to-host VPN model is not transparent to users because they must be authenticated before using the VPN.

**160.** Which of the following is *not* a primary component of an Internet Protocol security (IPsec)?

    a.    IPComp

    b.    AH

    c.    ESP

    d.    IKE protocol

***160. a.*** The IP payload compression protocol (IPComp) is a part of an Internet Protocol security (IPsec) implementation, not a primary component. Authentication header (AH), encapsulating security payload (ESP), and Internet key exchange (IKE) protocol are incorrect because they are primary components of IPsec.

**161.** The transport mode of an authentication header (AH) of Internet Protocol security (IPsec) is used in which of the following virtual private network (VPN) architectures?

    a.    Gateway-to-gateway

    b.    Host-to-gateway

    c.    Contractor-to-company

    d.    Host-to-host

***161. d.*** Authentication header (AH) has two modes: tunnel and transport. In tunnel mode, AH creates a new IP header for each packet. In transport mode, AH does not create a new IP header. This is because transport mode cannot alter the original IP header or create a new IP header. Transport mode is generally used in host-to-host architectures. AH is not used in the other three choices.

**162.** The encapsulating security payload (ESP) mode of Internet Protocol security (IPsec) *cannot* be used to provide which of the following?

    a.    Only encryption

    b.    Integrity protection at the outermost IP header

    c.    Encryption and integrity protection

    d.    Only integrity protection

*162. b.* Encapsulating security payload (ESP) can be used to provide only encryption, encryption and integrity protection, or only integrity protection. In the second version of IPsec, ESP became more flexible. It can perform authentication to provide integrity protection, although not for the outermost IP header. Also, ESP's encryption can be disabled through the Null Encryption Algorithm.

**163.** Which of the following is *not* an example of block cipher encryption algorithms used by the encapsulating security payload (ESP) mode of Internet Protocol security (IPsec)?

    a.    AES-Cipher block chaining (AES-CBC)

    b.    Hash message authentication code (HMAC)

    c.    AES Counter mode (AES-CTR)

    d.    Tripe DES (3DES)

*163. b.* The authentication header (AH) of IPsec uses HMAC. ESP uses symmetric cryptography to provide encryption for IPsec packets. When an endpoint encrypts data, it divides the data into small blocks and then performs multiple sets of cryptographic operations (known as rounds) using the data blocks and key. Encryption algorithms that work in this way are known as block cipher algorithms. Examples of encryption algorithms used by ESP are AES-CBC, AES-CTR, and 3DES.

**164.** Which of the following is the *most* important feature when evaluating Internet Protocol security (IPsec) client software for hosts?

    a.    Encryption

    b.    Authentication

    c.    Split tunneling

    d.    Compression

*164. c.* The most important Internet Protocol security (IPsec) client software feature is the capability to prevent split tunneling. Split tunneling occurs when an IPsec client on an external network is not configured to send all its traffic to the organization's IPsec gateway. Requests with a destination on the organization's network are sent to the IPsec gateway, and all other requests are sent directly to their destination without going through the IPsec tunnel. Prohibiting split tunneling can limit the potential impact of a compromise by preventing the attacker from taking advantage of the IPsec connection to enter the organization's network; the attacker could connect only to the compromised system when it is not using IPsec. Hosts should be configured so that only the network interface used for IPsec is enabled when IPsec is in use. Encryption, authentication, and compression are important features but not as important as the split tunneling, due to the risk it poses.

**165.** Which of the following Internet Protocol security (IPsec) components is compatible with network address translation (NAT) implementations?

a. AH tunnel mode

b. ESP transport mode

c. ESP tunnel mode

d. AH transport mode

**165. c.** There are known incompatibilities between IPsec and NAT because NAT modifies the IP addresses in the packet, which directly violates the packet integrity-assurance provided by IPsec. In tunnel mode, ESP can provide encryption and integrity protection for an encapsulated IP packet and authentication of the ESP header. Therefore, ESP tunnel mode can be compatible with NAT. However, protocols with embedded addresses (e.g., FTP, IRC, and SIP) can present additional complications.

The AH tunnel mode and the AH transport mode are incorrect because AH is not compatible with NAT implementations. This is because AH includes source and destination IP addresses in its integrity protection calculations. The ESP transport mode is incorrect because it is not compatible with NAT. In transport mode, ESP can provide encryption and integrity protection for the payload of an IP packet and integrity protection for the ESP header.

**166.** Which of the following is *not* a recommended solution to make network address translation (NAT) compatible with Internet Protocol security (IPsec)?

a. Perform NAT after applying IPsec.

b. Use UDP encapsulation of ESP packets.

c. Configure cable and DSL routers properly at small offices.

d. Configure cable and DSL routers properly at home offices.

**166. a.** Because network address translation (NAT) hides the network-addressing schema present behind a firewall environment and that NAT converts the limited number of Internet IP addresses into a large number of legal addresses, NAT should be performed before applying IPsec, not after. For example, the gateway can perform NAT first and then IPsec for outbound packets. The other three choices are incorrect because they are recommended solutions.

**167.** Which of the following is a viable option for providing confidentiality and integrity for dial-up communications?

    a. L2TP only

    b. L2TP with IPsec

    c. PPTP only

    d. L2F only

**167. b.** Layer 2 tunneling protocol (L2TP) with Internet Protocol security (IPsec) is a viable option for providing confidentiality and integrity for dial-up communications, particularly for organizations that contract virtual private network (VPN) services to an Internet service provider (ISP). L2TP and IPsec together provide stronger security, and the IPsec makes up for the L2TP weaknesses. Point-to-point tunneling protocol (PPTP) hides information in IP packets. Layer 2 forwarding (L2F) protocol protects communications between two network devices, such as an ISP network access server and VPN gateways. IPsec supersedes PPTP, whereas L2TP supersedes L2F.

**168.** Virtual private network (VPN) protocols are used in environments requiring high physical security in which of the following TCP/IP layers?

    a. Application layer

    b. Transport layer

    c. Network layer

    d. Data link layer

**168. d.** Data link layer virtual private network (VPN) protocols are used in high security environments to secure particular physical links, such as a dedicated circuit between two buildings, when there is concern for unauthorized physical access to the link's components. However, network performance should be considered.

**169.** Which of the following items are *not* synergistic in nature?

    a. Single sign-on system and Kerberos authentication technique

    b. Telecommuting and software piracy policies

    c. Firewalls and intrusion detection systems

    d. Architectural security design and layered protections

**169. b.** A synergistic control is a complementary control where two or more individual controls are combined to provide an additive or multiplicative (magnifying) effect. The other three choices are examples of synergistic controls. Telecommuting and software piracy policies are not synergistic as they are an example of contradictory control, where a company policy encouraging telecommuting work on one hand and another policy restricting employees to carry software home from work conflict with each other. In addition to accomplishing work from home, these policies target the software piracy issue, so there is no legal problem for the company.

Note that these software policies vary much in practice: (i) some companies allow the employee to carry software home and some do not, (ii) some companies allow the employee only to use the licensed software either by preloading the work/home PC or download the software to the work/home PC from a central computer, and (iii) some companies permit the employee to buy the approved and licensed software and the employee get reimbursed or the company may buy the software and give it to the employee. Regardless, an implicit and potential risk is that a noncompliant telecommuting employee or a family member could load unlicensed, unauthorized, and personal software on the work/home PC without the knowledge of the company. This action could infect the work/home PC with computer viruses and worms, thus risking the work-related data, programs, and systems.

**170.** **Which of the following makes the transport layer security (TLS) proxy server architecture fully compatible with network address translation (NAT)?**

    a.   HTTPS

    b.   PGP

    c.   GPG

    d.   SSH

***170. a.*** The transport layer security (TLS) proxy server provides transport layer VPN services. The use of HTTPS makes the proxy server architecture fully compatible with NAT. HTTPS usage is permitted by firewall rulesets. The other three choices are incorrect because PGP, GPG, and SSH are application layer VPN protocols. Pretty good privacy (PGP) provides security for e-mail encryption, disk encryption, and digital signatures for home and office use. GNU privacy guard (GPG) is the software for safe and encrypted e-mail communication, which is a free software alternative to the PGP.

**171.** **Which one of the following items replaces the other three items?**

    a.   telnet

    b.   SSH

    c.   rcp and rsh

    d.   FTP

***171. b.*** A commonly used application layer protocol suite is secure shell (SSH), which contains secure replacements for several unencrypted application protocols, including telnet, rcp, rsh, and FTP. SSH tunnel-based VPNs are resource-intensive to set up and are most commonly used by small groups of IT administrators.

**172.** **Which of the following *cannot* protect non-IP protocols?**

    a.   IPsec

    b.   PPTP

    c.   L2TP

    d.   L2F

**172. *a.*** The Internet Protocol security (IPsec) can protect only IP-based communications and protocols, which is one of its weaknesses. The other three choices are incorrect because PPTP, L2TP, and L2F can protect non-IP protocols. Point-to-point tunneling protocol (PPTP) hides information in IP packets. Layer 2 tunneling protocol (L2TP) protects communications between an L2TP-enabled client and a server. Layer 2 forwarding (L2F) protocol protects communications between two network devices, such as an ISP network access server and VPN gateways.

**173.** **Internet Protocol security (IPsec) protocols uses which of the following modes?**

a. Main mode and agressive mode

b. Quick mode and informational mode

c. State mode and user mode

d. Transport mode and tunnel mode

**173. *d.*** The Internet Key Exchange (IKE) of IPsec protocol consists of two phases: Phase 1 exchange includes main mode and aggressive mode. Phase 2 exchange includes quick mode and information exchange mode. If Authentication Header (AH) or Encapsulating Security Payload (ESP) is added to an IP packet following the existing IP header, it is referred to as a transport mode. A tunnel mode requires inserting an additional IP header to the packet but offers increased inflexibility. State mode and user mode are not relevant here.

**174.** **From a security configuration viewpoint, what is a managed or enterprise operational IT environment referred to as?**

a. Inward-facing

b. Inward-dialing

c. Outward-facing

d. Outward-dialing

**174. *a.*** The managed environment is an inward-facing environment typically structured and centrally managed. When a system connects on the interior of a network behind a firewall, it is called inward facing. When a high-risk system or network directly connects to the Internet, it is called outward facing (e.g., public Web server, e-mail server, and DNS server). Inward dialing is incorrect because it refers to calling into a system and is not a meaningful term here. Outward dialing is incorrect because it refers to calling from a system and is not a meaningful term here.

**175.** **What is a client/server application that requires nothing more than a browser and runs on only a user's computer called?**

a. Thick client

b. Thin client

c. Internet client

d. Web server

**175. b.**   A thin client is a software application that requires nothing more than a browser and can be run only on the user's computer (e.g., Microsoft Word). A thick client is a software application that requires programs other than just the browser on a user's computer, that is, it requires code on both a client and server computers (e.g., Microsoft Outlook).

The terms "thin" and "thick" refer to the amount of code that must be run on the client computer. Thin clients are generally more secure than thick clients in the way encryption keys are handled. The Internet client and Web server are incorrect because they are not needed for the thin client to work but are needed for the thick client to work.

**176.**   **Ethernet is a part of which of the following TCP/IP layers?**

    a.    Application layer

    b.    Transport layer

    c.    Network layer

    d.    Data link layer

**176. d.**   Ethernet is a part of the data link layer, along with address resolution protocol (ARP), network interface card (NIC), and media/medium access control (MAC). The data link layer handles communications on the physical network components.

The application layer is incorrect because it sends and receives data for particular applications. The transport layer is incorrect because it provides connection-oriented or connectionless services for transporting application layer services between networks. The network layer is incorrect because it routes packets across networks.

**177.**   **Most electronic commerce server applications use which of the following?**

    a.    One-tier architecture

    b.    Two-tier architecture

    c.    Three-tier architecture

    d.    Four-tier architecture

**177. c.**   Most electronic commerce applications use the three-tier architecture, representing three different classes of computers. The user tier consists of computers that have browsers that request and process Web pages. The server tier consists of computers that run Web servers and process application programs. The database tier consists of computers that run a database management system (DBMS) that process structured query language (SQL) requests to retrieve and store data.

**178.**   **Which of the following network connectivity hardware and software devices do *not* perform similar functions?**

    a.    Guards, firewalls, and routers

    b.    Connectors, concentrators, and sockets

    c.    Switches, hubs, and bridges

    d.    Bridges, routers, and brouters

**178. b.** Connectors, concentrators, and sockets do not perform similar functions. A connector is an electromechanical device on both ends of cables that permits them to be connected with and disconnected from other cables. A concentrator gathers several lines in one central location as in the fiber distributed data interface (FDDI). Sockets are endpoints created in a transmission control protocol (TCP) service by both the sender and the receiver.

The other three choices perform similar functions. The hardware/software guard system is composed of a server, workstations, malicious code detection, a firewall, and/or filtering routers all configured to allow transfer of information among communities of users operating at different security levels. Bridges are similar to switches in that both route on frame addresses. Switches are similar to hubs in that they enable communications between hosts. Bridges are routers that can also bridge; they route one or more protocols and bridge all other network traffic.

**179.** Which of the following uses spanning tree algorithm?

    a.    Firewalls, sensors, and instant messaging (IM) servers

    b.    Routers, bridges, and Internet relay chat (IRC) servers

    c.    Switches, guards, and instant messaging (IM) servers

    d.    Gateways, proxies, and Internet relay chat (IRC) servers

**179. b.** Multicast and broadcast routing is performed using spanning tree algorithm, which makes excellent use of bandwidth where each router knows which of its lines belong to the tree. The spanning tree algorithm is used to build plug-and-play bridges and Internet relay chat (IRC) servers. Each IRC server must have exactly one path to any other server. Therefore, routers, bridges, and IRC servers use the spanning tree algorithm and the other three choices do not deal with the spanning tree algorithm.

**180.** The Internet Control Message Protocol (ICMP) does not do or does not have which of the following?

    1.    Respond

    2.    Ports

    3.    Message types

    4.    Message codes

        a.    1 only

        b.    2 only

        c.    1 and 2

        d.    3 and 4

**180. c.** The Internet Control Message Protocol (ICMP) does not have ports and most ICMP messages are not intended to elicit a response. ICMP has message types, which indicate the purpose of each ICMP message. Some message types also have message codes, which can be thought of as subtypes.

**181.** Most hardware/software guard implementations use which of the following approaches?

    a.   Private network

    b.   Dual network

    c.   Public network

    d.   Backbone network

*181. b.* Most hardware/software guard implementations use a dual network approach, which physically separates the private and public sides from each other. A backbone network is a central network to which other networks connect.

Hardware and/or software guards enable users to exchange data between private and public networks, which is normally prohibited because of information confidentiality. A combination of hardware and/or software guards is used to allow secure local-area network (LAN) connectivity between enclave boundaries operating at different security classification levels (i.e., one private and the other public).

**182.** For active attacks on hardware/software guards, which of the following are countermeasures against manipulation of data on the private network?

    1.   Encryption algorithms

    2.   Key management processes

    3.   Cryptographic authentication

    4.   Data-separation methods

        a.   1 and 2

        b.   1 and 3

        c.   3 and 4

        d.   1, 2, 3, and 4

*182. c.* The appropriate countermeasure against manipulation of data on the private network is to permit only authorized users to access the data, through file transfers, on the private network using cryptographic authentication and data separation techniques. Encryption algorithms and key management processes are countermeasures against active attacks such as decrypting weakly encrypted traffic.

**183.** Which of the following is *not* an attack targeted at the Transmission Control Protocol (TCP) and Internet Protocol (IP)?

    a.   Session hijacking

    b.   Invalidated input

    c.   Ping of death

    d.   SYN flood

**183. *b.*** Invalidated input is an attack targeted at the application layer of the TCP/IP suite. Weaknesses in TCP and IP enable attacks, such as session hijacking, ping of death, synchronization (SYN) floods, and address impersonation. TCP operates at the transport layer whereas IP operates at the network layer of the TCP/IP suite.

**184.** For active attacks on hardware/software guards, which of the following are countermeasures against modification of data in transit?

1. Timestamps

2. Sequence numbers

3. Digital signatures

4. Keyed hash integrity checks

    a. 1 and 2

    b. 1 and 3

    c. 3 and 4

    d. 1, 2, 3, and 4

**184. *c.*** Countermeasures against modification of data in transit include the use of digital signatures or keyed hash integrity checks to detect unauthorized modification to the data in transit. E-mail, real-time messaging, and file transfers are all susceptible to interception and modification while in transit. Timestamps and sequence numbers are examples of countermeasures against active attacks such as the insertion of data or reinsertion of previous messages.

**185.** Most attacks are targeted at which of the following Transmission Control Protocol/ Internet Protocol (TCP/IP) layers?

    a. Application layer

    b. Transport layer

    c. Network layer

    d. Data link layer

**185. *a.*** In most cases, the application layer contains the actual activity of interest—most attacks are against vulnerabilities in applications, and nearly all misuse involves misuse of applications. The transport layer, the network layer, and the data link layer have fewer attacks compared to the application layer.

Hypertext transfer protocol (HTTP) is a function of the application layer, along with DNS, SMTP, FTP, and SNMP. This layer sends and receives data for particular applications. The transport layer provides connection-oriented or connectionless services for transporting application layer services between networks. The network layer routes packets across networks. The data link layer handles communications on the physical network components.

**186.** Which of the following statements about media access control/medium access control (MAC) address are true?

1.  Each frame contains two MAC addresses.

2.  Each frame contains either IP or ARP.

3.  A MAC address does not uniquely identify an IP address.

4.  NICs can be made with duplicate MAC addresses.

    a.    1 and 2

    b.    2 and 3

    c.    1 and 4

    d.    1, 2, 3, and 4

***186. d.*** Each frame of media access control/medium access control (MAC) contains two MAC addresses, which indicate the MAC address of the NIC that just routed the frame and the MAC address of the next NIC that the frame is being sent to. Besides the MAC addresses, each frame's payload contains either Internet protocol (IP) or address resolution protocol (ARP). When IP is used, each IP address maps to a particular MAC address. Multiple IP addresses can map to a single MAC address, so a MAC address does not uniquely identify an IP address. There have been cases in which manufacturers have accidentally created network interface cards (NICs) with duplicate MAC addresses, leading to networking problems and spoofing attacks.

**187.** For network data analysis, a host computer can be identified by which of the following?

    a.    Analyzing physical components

    b.    Reviewing logical aspects

    c.    Mapping an IP address to the MAC address of a NIC

    d.    Mapping multiple IP addresses

***187. c.*** For events within a network, an analyst can map an Internet protocol (IP) address (i.e., logical identifiers at the IP layer) to the media access control/medium access control (MAC) address of a particular network interface card (NIC) (i.e., physical identifier at the physical layer), thereby identifying a host of interest. Analyzing physical components and reviewing logical aspects are a partial approach. Mapping multiple IP addresses does not identify a host.

**188.** Regarding network data analysis, which of the following can tell a security analyst which application was most likely used or targeted?

    a.    IP number and port numbers

    b.    Network interface card

    c.    NIC and MAC address

    d.    IP and ARP

**188. a.** The combination of the Internet protocol (IP) number (IP layer field) and port numbers (transport layer fields) can tell an analyst which application was most likely used or targeted.

Network interface card (NIC) is incorrect because it is a physical device and a part of the data link layer; it cannot tell a security analyst which application was most likely used or targeted.

Media access control/medium access control (MAC) address is incorrect because it is a part of the data link layer and cannot tell a security analyst which application was most likely used or targeted.

Address resolution protocol (ARP) is incorrect because it is a part of the hardware layer (data link layer) and cannot tell a security analyst which application was most likely used or targeted.

**189.** For network traffic data sources, firewalls and routers do *not* typically record which of the following?

      a.    Date and time the packet was processed

      b.    Source IP address

      c.    Destination IP address

      d.    Packet contents

**189. d.** Firewalls and routers do not record the contents of packets. Instead, they are usually configured to log basic information for most or all denied connection attempts and connectionless packets; some log every packet. Information logged typically includes the date and time the packet was processed, the source and destination IP addresses, and the transport layer protocol (e.g., TCP, UDP, and ICMP) and basic protocol information (e.g., TCP or UDP port numbers and ICMP type and code).

**190.** Packet sniffers are commonly used to capture network traffic data for which of the following purposes?

      1.    Troubleshooting purposes

      2.    Investigative purposes

      3.    Marketing purposes

      4.    Strategic purposes

          a.    1 only

          b.    2 only

          c.    1 and 2

          d.    3 and 4

**190. c.** Packet sniffers are designed to monitor network traffic on wired or wireless networks and capture packets. Packet sniffers are commonly used to capture a particular type of traffic for troubleshooting (operational) or investigative (legal) purposes, which are technical purposes. For example, if IDS alerts indicate unusual network activity between two hosts, a packet sniffer could record all the packets between the hosts, potentially providing additional information for analysts. The marketing and strategic purposes are not relevant here because the question refers to the operational and legal purposes.

**191.** **A network-based intrusion detection system (IDS) does *not* do or contain which of the following?**

    a.   Perform packet sniffing

    b.   Analyze network traffic

    c.   Possess correction capabilities

    d.   Possess prevention capabilities

*191. c.*   Network-based intrusion detection systems (IDS) perform packet filtering and analyze network traffic to identify suspicious activity and record relevant information such as type of attack (e.g., buffer overflow), the targeted vulnerability, the apparent success or failure of the attack, and the pointers to more information on the attack. Some IDSs also have intrusion prevention capabilities, not correction capabilities.

**192.** **For network data analysis, remote access servers (RAS) do *not* do which of the following?**

    a.   Connect external systems to internal systems

    b.   Connect internal systems to external systems

    c.   Record application-specific data

    d.   Provide packet-filtering functions

*192. c.*   Because the remote access servers (RASs) have no understanding of the application's functions, they usually do not record any application-specific data.

The other three choices are proper functions of RAS. The RASs are devices such as VPN gateways and modem servers that facilitate connections between networks. This often involves external systems connecting to internal systems through the RAS but could also include internal systems connecting to external or internal systems. Some RASs also provide packet-filtering functions; this typically involves logging similar to that for firewalls and routers.

**193.** **Secure gateways block or filter access between two networks. Which of the following benefits resulting from the use of secure gateways is *not* true?**

    a.   Secure gateways prevent the spread of computer viruses.

    b.   Secure gateways reduce risks from malicious hackers.

    c.   Secure gateways reduce internal system security overhead.

    d.   Secure gateways can centralize management services.

*193. a.*   Questions frequently arise as to whether secure gateways (also known as firewalls) prevent the spread of viruses. In general, having a gateway scan transmitted files for viruses requires more system overhead than is practical, especially because the scanning would have to handle many different file formats. Secure gateways enable internal users to connect to external networks and at the same time prevent malicious hackers from compromising the internal systems. In addition to reducing the risks from malicious hackers, secure gateways have several other benefits. They can reduce internal system security overhead, because they enable an organization to concentrate security efforts on a limited number of machines. Another benefit is the centralization of services. A secure gateway can be used to provide a central management point for various services, such as advanced authentication, e-mail, or public dissemination of information. Having a central management point can reduce system overhead and improve service.

**194.** **For network data analysis, managed switches collect which of the following statistical data?**

    a.    Bandwidth usage

    b.    Payload size

    c.    Source and destination IP addresses

    d.    Ports for each packet

**194. a.**   Some managed switches and other network devices offer basic network monitoring capabilities, such as collecting statistics on bandwidth usage.

The other three choices are functions of network monitoring software, which collects information such as the payload size and the source and destination IP addresses and ports for each packet. Network monitoring software is designed to observe network traffic and gather statistics on it. Packet sniffers, protocol analyzers, and intrusion detection system (IDS) software may also perform basic network monitoring functions.

**195.** **Which of the following is *not* an example of alternative access points to an organization's IT resources?**

    a.    Internet gateway

    b.    Workstations

    c.    Modems

    d.    Wireless access points

**195. a.**   An organization's major access point is the Internet gateway. Attackers often enter networks from alternative access points to avoid detection by security controls monitoring major access points. A classic example of an alternative access point is a modem in a user's workstation. If an attacker can dial into the workstation and gain access, then attacks can be launched from that workstation against other hosts. In such cases, little or no information about the network activity may be logged because the activity does not pass through firewalls, intrusion detection system (IDS)-monitored network segments, and other common data collection points. Organizations typically address this by limiting alternative access points, such as modems and wireless access points, and ensuring that each is monitored and restricted through firewalls, IDS sensors, or other controls.

**196.** When monitoring failures occur, redundant equipment should be used for which of the following?

    a.   IDS sensors

    b.   Network-based firewalls

    c.   Host-based firewalls

    d.   System logs

*196. a.*   In most organizations, the cost of redundant monitoring makes it feasible only for the highest risk areas. In the case of dedicated monitoring systems, such as intrusion detection system (IDS) sensors, using redundant equipment (e.g., two sensors monitoring the same activity) can lessen the impact of monitoring failures. Another strategy is to perform multiple levels of monitoring, such as configuring network-based and host-based firewalls to log connections.

**197.** Which of the following is *not* a primary component or aspect of firewall systems?

    a.   Protocol filtering

    b.   Application gateways

    c.   Extended logging capability

    d.   Packet switching

*197. d.*   Packet switching is not related to a firewall system. It is a message delivery technique in which small units of information (packets) are relayed through stations in a computer network along the best route currently available between the source and the destination. A packet-switching network handles information in small units, breaking long messages into multiple packets before routing. Although each packet may travel along a different path, and the packets composing a message may arrive at different times or out of sequence, the receiving computer reassembles the original message. Packet-switching networks are considered to be fast and efficient. To manage the tasks of routing traffic and assembling or disassembling packets, such networks require some "intelligence" from the computers and software that control delivery.

Protocol filtering is incorrect because it is one of the primary components or aspects of firewall systems. A firewall filters protocols and services that are either not necessary or that cannot be adequately secured from exploitation. Application gateways are incorrect because they are one of the primary components or aspects of firewall systems. A firewall requires inside or outside users to connect first to the firewall before connecting further, thereby filtering the protocol. Extending logging capability is incorrect because it is one of the primary components or aspects of firewall systems. A firewall can concentrate extended logging of network traffic on one system.

**198.** Which of the following is a *major* risk in network traffic involving services running on unexpected port numbers?

    a.   Capturing

    b.   Monitoring

c. Analyzing

d. Detecting

***198. d.*** Applications such as intrusion detection systems and protocol analyzers often rely on port numbers to identify which service is in use for a given connection. Unfortunately, most services can be run on any port number. Traffic involving services running on unexpected port numbers may not be captured, monitored, or analyzed properly, causing unauthorized services usage (e.g., providing Web services on an atypical port) to be undetected. Another motivation is to slip traffic through perimeter devices that filter based on port numbers. Many Trojans create services on atypical ports for sending SPAM.

**199.** **For sources of network traffic data, which of the following provides the starting point for examining suspicious activity?**

a. Firewalls

b. IDS software

c. Proxy servers

d. Remote access servers

***199. b.*** Organizations typically have many different sources of network traffic data. Intrusion detection system (IDS) data is often the starting point for examining suspicious activity. Unfortunately, IDS software produces false positives, so IDS alerts need to be validated. By itself, data from these sources (e.g., firewalls, routers, proxy servers, and remote access servers) is usually of little value. Examining data over time may indicate overall trends, such as an increase in blocked connection attempts. However, because these sources typically record little information about each event, the data provides little insight as to the nature of the events.

**200.** **Intrusion detection system (IDS) software attempts to identify malicious network traffic at which of the following Transmission Control Protocol/Internet Protocol (TCP/IP) layers?**

1. Application layer

2. Transport layer

3. Network layer

4. Data link layer

a. 1 only

b. 2 only

c. 3 only

d. 1, 2, 3, and 4

***200. d.*** Not only does the intrusion detection system (IDS) software typically attempt to identify malicious network traffic at all TCP/IP layers, but it also logs many data fields (and sometimes raw packets) that can be useful in validating events and correlating them with other data sources.

**201.** Which of the following protocols are the *most* likely to be spoofed?

1. ICMP

2. UDP

3. TCP

4. Ethernet

    a. 1 only

    b. 2 only

    c. 1 and 2

    d. 3 and 4

*201. c.* Internet control message protocol (ICMP) and user datagram protocol (UDP) are connectionless protocols, thus most likely to be spoofed. Transmission control protocol (TCP) and Ethernet are incorrect because they are connection-oriented protocols, thus least likely to be spoofed. Many attacks use spoofed IP addresses. Spoofing is far more difficult to perform successfully for attacks that require connections to be established because the attacker needs an insight into sequence numbers and connection status.

**202.** Which of the following applications are used on local-area networks (LANs) with user datagram protocol (UDP)?

1. X.25

2. SMDS

3. DHCP

4. SNMP

    a. 1 only

    b. 2 only

    c. 1 and 2

    d. 3 and 4

*202. d.* User datagram protocol (UDP) is used for applications that are willing to take responsibility for ensuring reliable delivery of data, such as DNS, and applications that are intended for use only on LANs, such as Dynamic Host Configuration Protocol (DHCP) and Simple Network Management Protocol (SNMP). Like TCP, each UDP packet contains a source port and a destination port. X.25 and SMDS are incorrect because they are protocols used in a wide-area network (WAN).

X.25 is an international standard that defines the interface between a computing device and a packet-switched data network. Switched multi-megabit data service (SMDS) provides an effective vehicle for connecting LANs in a metropolitan or larger area.

**203.** **Spoofing in a local-area network (LAN) occurs with which of the following?**

1. Internet Protocol (IP) addresses

2. Media access control (MAC) addresses

3. Network address translation (NAT)

4. Dynamic host configuration protocol (DHCP) servers

   a. 1 or 2

   b. 2 or 3

   c. 1 or 4

   d. 3 or 4

***203. a.*** Dynamic host configuration protocol (DHCP) servers typically are configured to log each Internet Protocol (IP) address assignment and the associated media access control (MAC) address, along with a timestamp. This information can be helpful to analysts in identifying which host-performed activity uses a particular IP address. However, information security analysts should be mindful of the possibility that attackers on an organization's internal networks have falsified their IP addresses or MAC addresses to create spoofing. This is possible in light of manufacturers accidentally creating network interface cards (NICs) with duplicate MAC addresses. Network address translation (NAT) modifies the IP addresses in a packet, which directly violates the packet integrity assurance provided by IPsec. Spoofing MACs on a LAN can also occur by a malicious user trying to bypass authentication or by a malicious program modifying the device MAC.

**204.** **For network data analysis, which of the following is difficult when trying to identify and validate the identity of a suspicious host involving the Internet Protocol (IP) address spoofing?**

   a. Contact the IP address owner.

   b. Research the history of the IP address.

   c. Seek the assistance of Internet service provider.

   d. Look for clues in application content.

***204. c.*** The Internet service provider's (ISP's) assistance is needed when traffic passes through several ISPs. ISPs generally require a court order before providing any information to an organization on suspicious network activity.

The other three choices are incorrect because they are examples of other possible ways of attempting to validate the identity of a suspicious host. A WHOIS query mechanism can identify the organization or person that owns a particular IP address. Multiple IP addresses generating suspicious activity could have been registered to the same owner. Analysts can look for previous suspicious activity associated with the same IP address or IP address block. Internet search engines and online incident databases can be useful. Application data packets related to an attack may contain clues to the attacker's identity. Besides IP addresses, other valuable information could include an e-mail address or an Internet relay chat (IRC) nickname.

**205.** An information systems security analyst attempts to validate the identity of a suspicious host. Which of the following is *not* an acceptable approach?

    a.    Contact the IP address owner directly.

    b.    Contact management of his organization.

    c.    Contact legal advisors of his organization.

    d.    Seek Internet service provider assistance.

**205. a.** The information systems security analyst should not contact the owner directly. This is due primarily to concerns involving sharing information with external organizations; also, the owner of an Internet Protocol (IP) address could be the person attacking the organization.

The other three choices are incorrect because they are acceptable approaches. The analyst should provide information on the owner to the management and legal advisors for the analyst's organization. Seeking the Internet service provider (ISP) assistance is generally only an option during the most serious external network-based attacks; particularly those that involve IP address spoofing. Some ISPs may have the ability to trace ongoing attacks back to their source, whether the IP addresses are spoofed.

**206.** For network data acquisition, which of the following is the major downside to the victim organization of a network attack?

    a.    ISPs requiring a court order

    b.    Preserves privacy of the ISPs

    c.    Slows down the investigative process

    d.    Reduces the liability of the ISPs

**206. c.** As privacy becomes a greater concern to organizations, many have become less willing to share information with each other, including network data. For example, most Internet service providers (ISPs) now require a court order before providing any information related to suspicious network activity that might have passed through their network infrastructures. Although this preserves privacy of the ISPs and reduces the burden and liability of the ISPs, it also slows down the investigative process. This is a major downside to the victim organization because it wants a speedy investigative process with a clear and quick resolution to the attack.

**207.** Some attackers use anonymizers to validate the Internet Protocol (IP) address, which are:

    a.    DHCP servers

    b.    Remote access servers

    c.    Directory servers

    d.    Intermediary servers

**207. d.** Some attackers use anonymizers to validate the Internet Protocol (IP) address, which are intermediary servers that perform activity on a user's behalf to preserve the user's privacy.

DHCP servers are incorrect because they typically can be configured to log each IP address assignment and the associated MAC address, along with a timestamp. Remote access servers (RAS) are incorrect because they are devices such as VPN gateway and modem servers that facilitate connections between networks. Directory servers are incorrect because they are used for external authentication services.

**208.** **Commonly used protocols for audio and video communications include which of the following?**

1. H.323 protocols

2. Session Initiation Protocol (SIP)

3. Internet relay chat (IRC) protocol

4. Wired Equivalent Privacy (WEP) protocol

   a. 1 only

   b. 2 only

   c. 1 and 2

   d. 3 and 4

*208. c.* Commonly used protocols for audio and video communications include H.323 and SIP. H.323 is a suite of different protocols. Technologies such as voice over IP (VoIP) permit people to conduct telephone conversations over networks such as the Internet. Video technologies can be used to hold teleconferences or have "video phone" communications between two individuals. The most popular group chat protocol, IRC is a standard protocol that uses relatively simple text-based communications. IRC also provides a mechanism for users to send and receive files. WEP is a security protocol that encrypts data sent to and from wireless devices within a network. WEP is not as strong as Wi-Fi protected access (WPA) protocol.

**209.** **Which of the following are the primary software components of a domain name system (DNS)?**

1. Operating system

2. File system

3. Name server

4. Resolver

   a. 1 and 2

   b. 1 and 3

   c. 2 and 3

   d. 3 and 4

*209. d.* The domain name system (DNS) software primary components include the name server and the resolver. The operating system, file system, and communication stack are part of a DNS hosting environment.

**210.** Which of the following is the primary type of domain name system (DNS) data?

    a.    Configuration file

    b.    Zone file

    c.    File system

    d.    Zone transfer

***210. b.*** The primary type of domain name system (DNS) data is zone file, which contains information about various resources in that zone. The information about each resource is represented in a record called a Resource Record (RR). Logically, a zone file is made up of several RR sets.

Configuration file is incorrect because it is a secondary type of DNS data. File system is incorrect because it is a part of the DNS hosting environment. Zone transfer is incorrect because it is a part of DNS transactions.

**211.** Which of the following configurations is *not* a good security practice for a single domain name system (DNS) name server to perform?

    a.    Both authoritative name server and recursive name server

    b.    Both caching name server and local name server

    c.    Both primary name server and secondary name server

    d.    Both master name server and slave name server

***211. a.*** A specific name server can be configured to be both an authoritative and a recursive name server. In this configuration, the same name server provides authoritative information for queries pertaining to authoritative zones while it performs the resolving functions for queries pertaining to other zones. To perform the resolving function, it has to support recursive queries. Any server that supports recursive queries is more vulnerable to attack than a server that does not support such queries. As a result, authoritative information might be compromised. Therefore, it is not a good security practice to configure a single name server to perform both authoritative and recursive functions.

Caching name and local name server are incorrect because a caching name server generally is the local name server in the enterprise that performs the name resolution function on behalf of the various enterprise clients. A caching name server, also called a resolving/recursive name server, provides responses either through a series of queries to authoritative name servers in the hierarchy of domains found in the name resolution query or from a cache of responses built by using previous queries.

Primary, secondary, master, and slave name servers are incorrect because a master (or primary) name server contains zone files created and edited manually by the zone administrator. A slave (or secondary) name server also contains authoritative information for a zone, but its zone file is a replication of the one in the associated master name server. The replication is enabled through a transaction called "zone transfer" that transfers all Resource Records (RRs) from the zone file of a master name server to the slave name server.

**212.** **Which of the following is the *most* common transaction in a domain name system (DNS)?**

    a.    DNS query/response

    b.    Zone transfer

    c.    Dynamic updates

    d.    DNS NOTIFY message

*212. a.* Domain name system (DNS) query/response is the most common transaction in DNS. The most common query is a search for a Resource Record (RR), based on its owner name or RR type. The response may consist of a single RR, an RRset, or an appropriate error message.

A zone transfer is incorrect because it refers to the way a secondary (slave) server refreshes the entire contents of its zone file from the primary (master) name servers. The dynamic update facility is incorrect because it provides operations for addition and deletion of RRs in the zone file. The DNS NOTIFY message is incorrect because it signals a secondary DNS server to initiate a zone transfer.

**213.** **What does a domain name system (DNS) query originate from?**

    a.    Authoritative name server

    b.    Resolver

    c.    Caching name server

    d.    Recursive name server

*213. b.* A resolver, a component of DNS, accesses the services provided by a DNS name server on behalf of user programs. A DNS query originates from a resolver; the destination is an authoritative or caching name server.

An authoritative name server for a zone is incorrect because it provides responses to name resolution queries for resources for that zone, using the Resource Records (RRs) in its own zone file. Caching and recursive name servers are incorrect because two primary categories of resolver include (i) caching, recursive, resolving name server and (ii) stub resolver, distinguished by functionality.

**214.** **A user datagram protocol (UDP) packet is associated with which of the following when sending domain name system (DNS) queries?**

    1.    Truncation

    2.    Little or no truncation

    3.    Higher overhead

    4.    Lower overhead

        a.    1 only

        b.    4 only

        c.    1 and 4

        d.    2 and 3

*214. c.* Domain name system (DNS) queries are sent in a single UDP packet. The response usually is a single UDP packet as well, but data size may result in truncation. UDP consumes lower overhead of resources. On the other hand, TCP packet results in little or no truncation but consumes higher overhead of resources.

**215.** Which of the following is *not* an example of domain name system (DNS) host platform threats?

    a.    Buffer overflow attack

    b.    Zone drift error

    c.    Packet flooding attack

    d.    Address resolution protocol spoofing attack

*215. b.* Zone drift error is a threat due to domain name system (DNS) data contents, not from DNS host platform threats. Zone drift error results in incorrect zone data at the secondary name servers when there is a mismatch of data between the primary and secondary name servers. A buffer overflow attack, a packet flooding attack, and an Address Resolution Protocol (ARP) spoofing attack are examples of DNS host platform threats.

**216.** All the following are best practice protection approaches for domain name system (DNS) software *except*:

    a.    Running name server software with restricted privileges

    b.    Isolating name server software

    c.    Developing the zone file integrity checker software

    d.    Removing name server software from nondesignated hosts

*216. c.* Developing the zone file integrity checker software is a DNS data content control protection approach, not a DNS software protection approach. The other three choices are incorrect because they are examples of DNS software protection approaches.

**217.** In domain name system (DNS) transactions, which of the following is *not* a threat against DNS query/response transactions?

    a.    Forged response

    b.    Removal of resource records in responses

    c.    Incorrect application of wildcard expansion rules

    d.    Denial-of-service

*217. d.* Denial-of-service (DoS) is a threat against zone transfer transaction. The other three choices are incorrect because they are examples of threats in a DNS query/response transaction.

**218.** In domain name system (DNS) transactions, which of the following is *not* a threat against dynamic update transaction?

    a.    Unauthorized updates

    b.    Tampering of messages

    c.    Spurious notifications

    d.    Replay attacks

*218. c.*    Spurious notifications are a threat against a DNS NOTIFY message transaction. The other three choices are incorrect because they are examples of threats against dynamic update transactions.

**219.** Transaction signature (TSIG) is used in which of the following types of domain name system (DNS) transactions?

    1.    DNS query/response

    2.    DNS NOTIFY message

    3.    Zone transfer

    4.    Dynamic update

    a.    1 only

    b.    2 only

    c.    1 and 2

    d.    3 and 4

*219. d.*    Both zone transfer and dynamic update transactions use transaction signature (TSIG). In TSIG, mutual identification of servers is based on a shared secret key.

A DNS query/response is incorrect because IETF's DNSSEC standard is used in a DNS query/response transaction. A DNS NOTIFY message is incorrect because IETF specifies hosts from which messages can be received for DNS NOTIFY message transactions.

**220.** Which of the following statements about red teams are *not* true?

    1.    They can be effective when insider work is suspected.

    2.    They represent another independent attack on the system.

    3.    They prove that a computer system is secure.

    4.    They are a substitute for methodical testing.

    a.    1 and 2

    b.    1 and 3

    c.    3 and 4

    d.    2 and 4

*220. c.* A red team is a team of independent experts hired to attempt to breach a system's security. The red team cannot prove that a system is secure. Also, the red team's approach is not a substitute for methodical security testing. What it can do is be effective when insider work is suspected because it can show the areas of vulnerability. Also, the red team approach should be viewed as another independent attack on the system's integrity and security. If the system has not been thoroughly tested prior to red team testing, it is a waste of effort and money because the approach will be ineffective.

**221.** **Which of the following firewalls is *most* secure?**

    a.    Packet filtering firewall

    b.    Screened subnet firewall

    c.    Screened host firewall

    d.    Dual-homed gateway firewall

*221. b.* The screened subnet firewall adds an extra layer of security by creating a network where the bastion host resides. Often called a perimeter network, the screened subnet firewall separates the internal network from the external. This leads to stronger security.

**222.** **Who should *not* be given access to firewalls?**

    a.    Primary firewall administrator

    b.    Functional users

    c.    Backup firewall administrator

    d.    Network service manager

*222. b.* Firewalls should not be used as general-purpose servers. The only access accounts on the firewalls should be those of the primary and backup firewall administrators and the network service manager, where the latter manages both administrators. Functional users should not be given access to firewalls because they do not contain business-related application systems.

**223.** **Most common attacks against wireless technologies include which of the following?**

    a.    Spamming and loss of availability

    b.    Spoofing and loss of integrity

    c.    Eavesdropping and loss of confidentiality

    d.    Cracking and loss of authenticity

*223. c.* Wireless technologies invite privacy and fraud violations more easily than wired technologies due to their broadcast nature. The privacy implications of widespread use of mobile wireless technologies are potentially serious for both individuals and businesses. There will be a continuing need to guard against eavesdropping and breaches of confidentiality, as hackers and scanners develop ways to listen in and track wireless communications devices. For example, wired equivalent privacy (WEP) protocol can be attacked, and Wi-Fi protected access (WPA) and its version 2 (WPA2) can be attacked using rainbow tables. Attacks mentioned in the other three choices are not that common, but they do happen.

**224.** **Which of the following merits _most_ protection in the use of wireless technologies?**

1. Privacy of location
2. Privacy of equipment
3. Privacy of transmission contents
4. Privacy of third parties

    a. 1 and 2

    b. 1 and 3

    c. 3 and 4

    d. 2 and 3

_224. b._ There are two main types of information that merit most protection in the wireless context: the contents of a call or transmission and the location of the sender or recipient. Privacy of equipment and third parties are not relevant here.

**225.** **Which of the following involves a complicated technique that combines the public-key encryption method with a hashing algorithm that prevents reconstructing the original message?**

    a. Digital signature

    b. Voice over Internet Protocol

    c. Electronic signature

    d. Firewalls

_225. a._ Two steps are involved in creating a digital signature. First, the encryption software uses a hashing algorithm to create a message digest from the file being transmitted. Second, the software uses a sender's private (secret) key to encrypt the message digest. The result is a digital signature for that specific file.

Voice over Internet Protocol (VoIP) is incorrect because it is a technology that enables network managers to route phone calls and facsimile transmissions over the same network they use for data. Electronic signature is incorrect because it is an electronic sound, symbol, or process attached to or logically associated with a contract or other record and executed or adopted by a person with the intent to sign the record. Firewalls are incorrect because a firewall is software whose purpose is to block access to computing resources.

**226.** **Which of the following are more efficient and secure for use in wireless technologies?**

    a.   Spread spectrum

    b.   Radio spectrum

    c.   Radio signals

    d.   Radio carriers

***226. a.*** New digital communications systems such as time division multiple access (TDMA) or code division multiple access (CDMA) use spread spectrum much more efficiently than analog cellular and other traditional radio systems. The spread spectrum technology uses a wide band of frequencies to send radio signals. The other three choices are not relevant here.

**227.** **Which of the following is inherently efficient and difficult to intercept in the use of wireless technologies?**

    a.   Code division multiple access (CDMA)

    b.   Time division multiple access (TDMA)

    c.   Public-switched telephone network (PSTN)

    d.   Very small aperture terminal (VSAT)

***227. a.*** Code division multiple access (CDMA) is more efficient and secure than time division multiple access (TDMA) because it uses spread spectrum technology more efficiently. Instead of assigning a time slot on a single channel, CDMA uses many different channels simultaneously. CDMA is also inherently more difficult to crack because the coding scheme changes with each conversation and is given only once at the beginning of the transmission.

**228.** **Voice encryption in cell/mobile phones uses which of the following algorithms?**

    a.   RSA

    b.   3DES

    c.   IDEA

    d.   DES

***228. a.*** Voice encryption schemes are based on Rivest, Shamir, and Adelman (RSA) algorithm to provide privacy protection over mobile or cellular phones. The main constraints with encryption are the slow speed of processing and the lag that occurs if signals take too long to pass through the system. The other three choices (i.e., 3DES, IDEA, and DES) are not used in voice encryption because they are used in transaction encryption.

**229.** **Which of the following network connectivity devices require in-band and out-of-band management services such as administrative access to distributed local-area networks (LANs)?**

    a.   Firewalls and gateways

    b.   Switches and routers

  c. Sensors and bridges

  d. Repeaters and modems

**229. *b.*** Switches and routers require in-band and out-of-band management services. In in-band management, a secure shell (SSH) session is established with the connectivity device (e.g., switches and routers) in a distributed local-area network (LAN). This method is fast and convenient but less secure due to use of Telnet, line sniffing, and interception of privileged passwords.

In out-of-band management, the communications device is accessed via a dial-up circuit with a modem, directly connected terminal device, or LANs dedicated to managing traffic. Whether in-band or out-of-band, network paths and sessions used to access the device should be protected. The other three choices do not require in-band and out-of-band management services such as administrative access because they have their own access methods.

**230.** **For information system monitoring, which of the following anomaly within an information system is *most* risky?**

  a. Large file transfers

  b. Unusual protocols and ports in use

  c. Attempted communications with suspected external addresses

  d. Long-time persistent connections

**230. *c.*** Anomalies at selected interior points within a system (e.g., subnets and subsystems) include large file transfers, unusual protocols and ports in use, long-time persistent connections, and attempted communications with suspected external addresses. Of these, the attempted communications with suspected (malicious) external addresses is most risky. The other three choices are less risky.

**231.** **Which of the following are especially needed to provide a trustworthy cloud computing infrastructure?**

 1. ISO/IEC 27001 certification

 2. AICPA/SAS 70 attestation

 3. Security training

 4. Risk management

  a. 1 and 2

  b. 1 and 3

  c. 3 and 4

  d. 1, 2, 3, and 4

**231. *d.*** Microsoft, for example, has achieved a trustworthy cloud computing infrastructure by earning the International Organization for Standardization/International Society of Electrochemistry 27001:2005 (ISO/IEC 27001:2005) certification and American Institute of Certified Public Accountants/Statement on Auditing Standards (AICPA/SAS)70 Type I and Type II attestation. The Type I attestation report states that information systems at the service organizations for processing user transactions are suitably designed with internal controls to achieve the related control objectives. The Type II attestation report states that internal controls at the service organizations are properly designed and operating effectively. These two accomplishments of certification and attestation were combined with security training, adequate and effective security controls, continuous review and management of risks, and rapid response to security incidents and legal requests.

**232.** **Which of the following is the *true* purpose of "ping" in cellular wireless technologies?**

    a. The pinging tells the filters on the network.

    b. The pinging tells the frequencies of the network.

    c. The pinging tells the location of a phone user.

    d. The pinging tells the troubles on the network.

*232. c.* To monitor the state of the network and to respond quickly when calls are made, the main cellular controlling switch periodically "pings" all cellular telephones. This pinging lets the switch know which users are in the area and where in the network the telephone is located. This information can be used to give a rough idea of the location of the phone user to help catch the fraud perpetrator. Vehicle location service is an application of the ping technology. The other three choices are not true.

**233.** **Telecommuting from home requires special considerations to ensure integrity and confidentiality of data stored and used at home. Which of the following is *not* an effective control?**

    a. Employee accountability

    b. Removable hard drives

    c. Storage encryption

    d. Communications encryption

*233. a.* In addition to risks to internal corporate systems and data in transit, telecommuting from home raises other concerns related to whether employees are using their own computers or using computers supplied to them by the organization. Other members of the employee's household may want to use the computer used for telecommuting. Children, spouses, or other household members may inadvertently corrupt files, introduce viruses, or snoop. Therefore, employee accountability is difficult to monitor or enforce.

The other three choices provide effective controls. Removable hard drives are incorrect because they reduce the risk if corporate data is stored on them due to their removability, which can be safely stored away. Storage encryption and communications encryption are incorrect because they both provide confidentiality of data during its storage as well as in transit.

**234.** **Secure remote procedure call (RPC) uses which of the following algorithms?**

    a. DES

    b. DH

    c.    3DES

    d.    IDEA

***234. b.***   Secure remote procedure call (RPC) uses the Diffie-Hellman (DH) key generation method. Under this method, each user has a private/public key pair. Secure RPC does not use the other three choices.

**235.**   **In secure remote procedure call (RPC), which of the following provides the public and private keys to servers and clients?**

    a.    Users

    b.    Clients

    c.    Servers

    d.    Authentication servers

***235. d.***   The principals involved in the secure remote procedure call (RPC) authentication systems are the users, clients, servers, and authentication server. The authentication server provides the public and private keys to servers and clients.

**236.**   **The screened subnet firewall acts as which of the following?**

    a.    Fast packet network

    b.    Digital network

    c.    Perimeter network

    d.    Broadband network

***236. c.***   The screened subnet firewall acts as a perimeter network. If there is an attack on the firewall, the attacker is restricted to the perimeter (external) network and therefore is not attacking the internal network.

**237.**   **Which of the following are examples of security boundary access controls?**

    a.    Patches and probes

    b.    Fences and firewalls

    c.    Tags and labels

    d.    Encryption and smart cards

***237. b.***   A firewall is an example of logical access control whereas fences provide a physical security and perimeter access control. When these two controls are combined, they provide a total boundary control. By limiting access to host systems and services, firewalls provide a necessary line of perimeter defense against attacks, thus providing logical security boundary control. Similarly, perimeter fences provide a physical security boundary control for a facility or building.

A patch is a modification to software that fixes an error in an operational application system on a computer. Generally, the software vendor supplies the patch. A probe is a device programmed to gather information about a system or its users. Tags and labels are used in access controls. Encryption and smart cards are used in user identification and authentication mechanisms.

**238.** **Which of the following *cannot* prevent login spoofing?**

    a.    Providing a secure channel between the user and the system

    b.    Installing hardware-reset button for passwords

    c.    Implementing cryptographic authentication techniques

    d.    Installing input overflow checks

***238. d.*** Input overflow checks ensure that input is not lost during data entry or processing and are good against input overflow attacks. These attacks can be avoided by proper program design. Providing a secure channel between the user and the system can defend login spoofing. A hardware-reset button on a personal computer can be effective in removing password-based spoofing attacks. Cryptographic authentication techniques can increase security but only for complex systems.

**239.** **Which of the following can prevent both session hijacking and eavesdropping attacks?**

    a.    SET

    b.    PPP

    c.    FTP

    d.    SSL

***239. d.*** The secure sockets layer (SSL) protocol is the technology used in most Web-based applications. When both the Web client and the Web server are authenticated with SSL, the entire session is encrypted providing protection against session hijacking and eavesdropping attacks.

The other three choices are incorrect because SET is a secure electronic transaction protocol, PPP is a point-to-point protocol, and FTP is a file transfer protocol, and as such they cannot prevent session hijacking and eavesdropping attacks.

**240.** **Which of the following provides a security service in authenticating a remote network access?**

    a.    Remote access server

    b.    Windows NT server

    c.    An exchange server

    d.    A DNS server

***240. a.*** The remote access server (RAS) provides the following services: When a remote user dials in through a modem connection, the server hangs up and calls the remote user back at the known phone number. The other three servers mentioned do not have this kind of dial-in and callback dual control mechanism.

**241.** **Which one of the following firewalls is simple, inexpensive, and quick to implement?**

    a.    Static packet filter firewall

    b.    Dynamic packet filter firewall

    c.    Application gateway firewall

    d.    Stateful inspection gateway firewall

*241. a.* A static packet filtering firewall is the simplest and least expensive way to stop messages with inappropriate network addresses. It does not take much time to implement when compared to other types of firewalls.

**242.** **Which of the following can prevent e-mail spoofing?**

    a.    Pretty good privacy

    b.    Point-to-point protocol

    c.    Microcom networking protocol

    d.    Password authentication protocol

*242. a.* Pretty good privacy (PGP) is a cryptographic software application for the protection of computer files and e-mail. PGP provides a good authentication mechanism, confidentiality protection, and nonrepudiation protection.

Point-to-point protocol (PPP) connects two TCP/IP devices over a standard serial line, such as a common telephone link. Microcom networking protocol (MNP) defines various levels of error correction and compression for modems. Password authentication protocol (PAP) is a handshaking protocol.

**243.** **Security problems associated with network device passwords, network devices (e.g., routers and switches), and managing access points (APs) configuration in a legacy wireless local-area network (WLAN) environment require which of the following security controls to solve *all* these security problems?**

    a.    Switch Telnet to SSH

    b.    Switch HTTP to HTTPS

    c.    Switch SNMP to SNMPv3

    d.    Switch FTP to SFTP

*243. c.* The basic simple network management protocol (SNMP) should be switched to SNMP version 3 (SNMPv3) because the latter provides strong security feature enhancements to basic SNMP, including encryption and message authentication and therefore should be used. The earlier versions of SNMP, SNMPv1, and SNMPv2 should not be used because they are fundamentally insecure because they support only trivial authentication based on default plaintext community strings. SNMP version 3 handles all the security problems listed in the question. The other three choices mostly solve the password-related security problem after the protocol switch is made but do not solve all the other security problems listed. That is, Telnet should be switched to secure shell (SSH), HTTP should be switched to HTTPS using TLS, and FTP should be switched to secure FTP (SFTP).

**244.** A stronger barrier control around insecure application software is which of the following?

    a.    Firewalls

    b.    Intrusion detection systems

    c.    Virus checkers

    d.    Operating system's security features

***244. d.*** Application software often contains numerous vulnerabilities. Many security systems (e.g., firewalls, intrusion detection systems, and virus checkers) attempt to protect these insecure applications by monitoring and filtering the application's interactions with users. Ultimately, however, these barrier techniques are inadequate because users must be allowed to interface directly with the vulnerable applications software. The best defense is to install ever-stronger barriers around the applications software. The operating system is the best place for such a barrier.

**245.** Which of the following is an example of a boundary access control?

    a.    Gateway

    b.    Bridge

    c.    Modem

    d.    Firewall

***245. d.*** Firewalls monitor network traffic that enters and leaves a network. A firewall controls broad access to all networks and resources that lie "inside" it. By limiting access to host systems and services, firewalls provide a necessary line of perimeter defense against attack; that is, they form a boundary control.

A gateway is incorrect because it is an interface between two networks. A bridge is incorrect because it is a device used to link two or more homogeneous local-area networks (LANs). A modem is incorrect because it is a device that converts analog signals to digital signals and vice versa. The devices mentioned in the three incorrect choices do not have the ability to perform as a boundary access control.

**246.** Which of the following is used for high-speed remote access with virtual private networks (VPNs)?

    a.    Calling cards with ISDN

    b.    Cable modems with ADSL

    c.    Modem pools with ADSL

    d.    Toll-free lines with ISDN

***246. b.*** Modem pools, calling cards, and toll-free arrangements can be an expensive alternative to cable modems and asymmetric digital subscriber line (ADSL). An ISDN line is limited to 128 bits and is slow. Cable modems and ADSL technologies take advantage of the Internet and IPsec functioning at the network layer. These technologies provide high-speed remote access.

**247.** **Which of the following is suitable for a low-risk computing environment?**

    a.    Static packet filter firewall

    b.    Hybrid gateway firewall

    c.    Stateful inspection gateway firewall

    d.    Dynamic packet firewall

***247. a.*** The static packet filter firewall offers minimum-security provisions suitable for a low-risk computing environment. The hybrid gateway firewall is good for medium- to high-risk computing environment. Both stateful and dynamic packet firewalls are appropriate for high-risk computing environments.

**248.** **The Internet Protocol security (IPsec) is usually implemented in which of the following?**

    a.    Bridge

    b.    Gateway

    c.    Firewall

    d.    Backbone

***248. c.*** Usually, Internet Protocol security (IPsec) is implemented on a firewall for VPNs. The IPsec in tunnel mode, not in transport mode, encrypts and encapsulates IP packets, so outsiders cannot observe the true source and destinations. VPNs enable a trusted network to communicate with another network over untrusted networks such as the Internet. A policy is needed for use of firewalls with VPNs. Any connection between firewalls over public networks should use encrypted VPNs to ensure the privacy and integrity of the data passing over the public network. Bridges, gateways, and backbones do not have the access control mechanism as the firewall.

**249.** **Which of the following is an example of connectionless data communications?**

    a.    X.25

    b.    TCP

    c.    Ethernet

    d.    WAN

***249. c.*** Connectionless data communications does not require that a connection be established before data can be sent or exchanged. X.25, TCP, and WAN are examples of connection-oriented data communications that requires that a connection first be established.

**250.** Which of the following protocols provides cellular/mobile wireless security?

    a.   WSP

    b.   WTP

    c.   WTLS

    d.   WDP

**250. c.** Wireless transport layer security (WTLS) is a communications protocol that enables cellular/mobile phones to send and receive encrypted information over the Internet, thus providing wireless security. Wireless session protocol (WSP), wireless transaction protocol (WTP), WTLS, and wireless datagram protocol (WDP) are part of wireless access protocol (WAP). WAP is an Internet protocol that defines the way in which cell phones and similar devices can access the Internet.

**251.** In border gateway protocol (BGP), prefix filters help to limit the damage to the routes in which of the following ways?

    a.   The egress filters of an autonomous system (AS) is matched with the ingress filters of BGP peers.

    b.   The ingress filters of BGP peers is matched with the ingress filters of an autonomous system (AS).

    c.   The ingress filters of an autonomous system (AS) is matched with the ingress filters of BGP peers.

    d.   The egress filters of BGP peers is matched with egress filters of an autonomous system (AS).

**251. a.** Normally, border gateway protocol (BGP) peers should have matching prefix filters with the autonomous system (AS). This means, the egress filters of an AS should be matched by the ingress filters of BGP peers with which it communicates. This matching approach helps to reduce the risk from attackers that seek to inject false routes by pretending to send updates from the AS to its peers. Attackers can of course still send faulty routes, but filtering limits the damage to these routes.

**252.** Which of the following border gateway protocol (BGP) attacks does *not* use Time To Live (TTL) hack as a countermeasure?

    a.   Peer spoofing and TCP resets

    b.   Denial-of-service via resource exhaustion

    c.   Route flapping

    d.   Session hijacking

**252. c.** Because border gateway protocol (BGP) runs on transmission control protocol/Internet protocol (TCP/IP), any TCP/IP attack can be applied to BGP. Route flapping is a situation in which BGP sessions are repeatedly dropped and restarted, normally as a result of router problems. Examples of countermeasures for route flapping attacks include graceful restart and BGP route-flap damping method, not TTL hack.

Route-flap damping is a method of reducing route flaps by implementing an algorithm that ignores the router sending flapping updates for a configurable period of time. Each time a flapping event occurs, peer routers add a penalty value to a total for the flapping router. As time passes, the penalty value decays gradually; if no further flaps are seen, it reaches a reuse threshold, at which time the peer resumes receiving routes from the previously flapping router.

The other three choices use TTL hack. The Time To Live (TTL) or hop count is an 8-bit field in each IP packet that prevents packets from circulating endlessly in the Internet. TTL is based on the generalized TTL security mechanism (RFC 3682), often referred to as the TTL hack, which is a simple but effective defense that takes advantage of TTL processing. At each network node, the TTL is decremented by one and is discarded when it is reduced to zero without reaching its destination point.

In peer spoofing attack, the goal is to insert false information into a BGP peer's routing tables. A special case of peer spoofing, called a reset attack, involves inserting TCP RESET messages into an ongoing session between two BGP peers. Examples of countermeasures against peer spoofing and TCP resets include using strong sequence number randomization and TTL hack.

In a denial-of-service attack via resource exhaustion, routers use a large amount of storage for path prefixes. These resources are exhausted if updates are received too rapidly or if there are too many path prefixes to store due to malicious prefixes. Examples of countermeasures against denial-of-service via resource exhaustion attacks include using rate limit synchronization processing, increasing queue length, route filtering, and TTL hack.

In a session hijacking attack, the attack is designed to achieve more than simply bringing down a session between BGP peers. The objective is to change routes used by the peer, to facilitate eavesdropping, blackholing, or traffic analysis. Examples of countermeasures against session hijacking attacks include using strong sequence number randomization, IPsec authentication, and TTL hack.

**253.** **Which of the following is *not* one of the actions taken by a firewall on a packet?**

    a.   Accept

    b.   Deny

    c.   Discard

    d.   Destroy

***253. d.***   The firewall examines a packet's source and destination addresses and ports, and determines what protocol is in use. From there, it starts at the top of the rule base and works down through the rules until it finds a rule that permits or denies the packet. It takes one of the three actions: (i) The firewall passes the packet through the firewall as requested (accept), (ii) the firewall drops the packets, without passing it through the firewall (deny) or (iii) the firewall not only drops the packet, but it does not return an error message to the source system (discard). Destroy is not one of the actions taken by a firewall.

**254.** Network address translation (NAT) protocol operates at what layer of the ISO/OSI reference model?

    a.    Presentation Layer 6

    b.    Network Layer 3

    c.    Transport Layer 4

    d.    Session Layer 5

*254. b.*    The network address translation (NAT) protocol operates at the Layer 3 (network) of the ISO/OSI reference model.

**255.** All the following are countermeasures against software distribution attacks on software guards *except*:

    a.    Conducting third-party testing and evaluations

    b.    Complying with Common Criteria Guidelines

    c.    Reviewing audit logs

    d.    Implementing high-assurance configuration controls

*255. c.*    Distribution attacks can occur anytime during the transfer of a guard's software or hardware. The software or hardware could be modified during development or before production. The software is also susceptible to malicious modification during production or distribution.

Audit log is a countermeasure against insider attacks on hardware/software guards such as modification of data by insiders. Audit logs need to be generated and diligent reviews must be conducted in a timely manner.

Countermeasures protecting the software guards include implementing strong software development processes, performing continuous risk management, conducting third-party testing and evaluation of software, following trusted product evaluation program and Common Criteria guidelines, high-assurance configuration control, cryptographic signatures over tested software products, use of tamper detection technologies during packaging, use of authorized couriers and approved carriers, and use of blind-buy techniques.

**256.** Which of the following is *not* used to accomplish network address translation (NAT)?

    a.    Static network address translation

    b.    Hiding network address translation

    c.    Dynamic network address translation

    d.    Port address translation

*256. c.*    Network address translation (NAT) is accomplished in three schemes: (i) In a static network address translation, each internal system on the private network has a corresponding external, routable IP address associated with it. (ii) With hiding network address translation, all systems behind a firewall share the same external, routable IP address.

(iii) In a port address translation (PAT) schema, the implementation is similar to hiding network address translation, with two primary differences. First, port address translation is not required to use the IP address of the external firewall interface for all network traffic. Second, with port address translation, it is possible to place resources behind a firewall system and still make them selectively accessible to external users.

**257.** Which of the following ensures that all Web network traffic dealing with a firewall system is secured from an administration viewpoint?

    a.    DES

    b.    SSL

    c.    HTTP

    d.    SSH

*257. b.* There should be a policy stating that all firewall management functions take place over secure links. For Web-based interfaces, the security should be implemented through secure sockets layer (SSL) encryption, along with a user ID and password. If neither internal encryption nor SSL are available, tunneling solutions such as the Secure Shell (SSH) are usually appropriate. HTTP and DES are not appropriate here as they do not provide strong security.

**258.** All the following are applications of spanning tree concept *except*:

    a.    Multicast routing

    b.    Spanning port

    c.    Risk analysis

    d.    Bridges

*258. b.* A spanning port is a switch port that can see all network traffic going through the switch. The spanning port has nothing to do with the spanning tree whereas the other three choices are applications of the spanning tree concept. The spanning tree has several applications such as (i) multicast routing which makes excellent use of bandwidth where each router knows which of its lines belong to the tree, (ii) conducting risk analysis, and (iii) building plug-and-play bridges.

**259.** Which of the following does *not* perform "prefix filtering" services?

    a.    Border gateway protocol

    b.    Sensors

    c.    Routers

    d.    Firewalls

*259. b.* Sensors (intrusion detection systems) are composed of monitors and scanners, and they do not perform prefix filtering services. Sensors identify and stop unauthorized use, misuse, and abuse of computer systems by both internal network users and external attackers in near real time. Sensors do not perform permit and deny actions as do the border gateway protocol (BGP), routers, and firewalls. Prefix filtering services are provided by BGP, routers, and firewalls in that they perform permit and deny actions. Prefix filtering is the most basic mechanism for protecting BGP routers from accidental or malicious disruption, thus limiting the damage to the routes. Filtering of both incoming prefixes (ingress filtering) and outgoing prefixes (egress filtering) is needed. Router filters are specified using syntax similar to that for firewalls. Two options exist. One option is to list ranges of IP prefixes that are to be denied and then permit all others. The other option is to specify a range of permitted prefixes, and the rest are denied. The option of listing a range of permitted prefixes provides greater security.

**260.** **Local-area networks (LANs) operate at what layer of the ISO/OSI reference model?**

    a.    Physical Layer 1

    b.    Data link Layer 2

    c.    Network Layer 3

    d.    Transport Layer 4

***260. b.***   Layer 2 (data link) of the ISO/OSI reference model represents the layer at which network traffic delivery on local-area networks (LANs) occurs.

**261.** **Which of the following are examples of *major* problems associated with network address translation (NAT)?**

    1.    Cannot abide by the IP architecture model

    2.    Cannot locate the TCP source port correctly

    3.    Cannot work with the file transfer protocol

    4.    Cannot work with the H.323 Internet Telephony Protocol

        a.    1 and 2

        b.    1 and 3

        c.    2 and 4

        d.    1, 2, 3, and 4

***261. d.***   Major problems associated with network address translation (NAT) include (i) it violates the architectural model of IP, which states that every IP address must uniquely identify a single computer worldwide, (ii) it will not locate the TCP source port correctly, (iii) it violates the rules of protocol layering in that a lower-level layer should not make any assumptions about the next higher-level layer put into the payload field, and (iv) it needs to be patched every time a new application is introduced because it cannot work with file transfer protocol (FTP) or H.323 Internet Telephony Protocol. The FTP and H.323 protocols will fail because NAT does not know the IP addresses and cannot replace them.

**262.** **Hardware/software guards provide which of the following functions and properties?**

    1.    Data-filtering

    2.    Data-blocking

3. Data-sanitization

4. Data-regrading

    a. 1 and 2

    b. 2 and 3

    c. 1 and 4

    d. 1, 2, 3, and 4

*262. d.* Hardware/software guard technology can bridge across security boundaries by providing some of the interconnectivity required between systems operating at different security levels. Several types of guard exist. These protection approaches employ various data processing, data filtering, and data-blocking techniques in an attempt to provide data sanitization (e.g., downgrade) or separation between networks. Some approaches involve human review of the data flow and support data flow in one or both directions. Guards can be used to counteract attacks made on the enclave.

Information flowing from public to private networks is considered as a data upgrade. This type of transfer may not require a review cycle but should always require a verification of the integrity of the information originating from the public source system and network.

Information flowing from private to public networks is considered as data regrade and requires a careful review.

**263.** In a fully networked topology, if there are five nodes, how many direct paths does it result in?

    a. 2

    b. 3

    c. 5

    d. 10

*263. d.* The equation for the number of direct paths in a fully connected network is $n(n-1)/2$, where "n" is the number of nodes. Applying the equation results in 10 (i.e., $5(5-1)/2$). The answer 2 is obtained by using the equation as $(n-1)/2$. The answer 3 is obtained by using the equation as $(n+1)/2$.

**264.** Which of the following networks is used to distribute music, games, movies, and news using client caching, server replication, client's request redirection, and a proxy server?

    a. Asynchronous transfer mode (ATM) network

    b. Content delivery network (CDN)

    c. Voice over Internet Protocol (VoIP) network

    d. Integrated services digital network (ISDN)

***264. b.*** Content delivery networks are used to deliver the contents of music, games, movies, and news from content owner's website to end users quickly with the use of tools and techniques such as client caching, server replication, client's request redirection, and a proxy content server to enhance the Web performance in terms of optimizing the disk space and preload time.

ATMs are good for voice traffic only. VoIP is the transmission of voice over packet-switched IP networks and it takes a wide variety of forms, including traditional telephone handsets, conferencing units, and mobile units. ISDN is an international communications standard for sending voice, video, and data over digital or standard telephone wires. The ISDN security must begin with the user (i.e., may be a person, an organizational entity, or a computer process).

**265.** **Firewalls are the perfect complement to which of the following?**

    a.   Bridges

    b.   Routers

    c.   Brouters

    d.   Gateways

***265. b.*** Given that all routers support some type of access control functionality, routers are the perfect complement to firewalls. The generally accepted design philosophy is that boundary routers should protect firewall devices before the firewall devices ever have to protect themselves. This principle ensures that the boundary router can compensate for any operating system or platform-specific vulnerabilities that might be present on the firewall platform. Brouters combine the functionality of bridges and routers.

**266.** **Which of the following is the best backup strategy for firewalls?**

    a.   Incremental backup

    b.   Centralized backup

    c.   Day Zero backup

    d.   Differential backup

***266. c.*** The conduct and maintenance of backups are key points to any firewall administration policy. It is critical that all firewalls are subject to a Day Zero backup (full backup), i.e., all firewalls should be backed up immediately prior to production release. As a general principle, all firewall backups should be full backups, and there is no need for incremental, centralized, or differential backups because the latter are less than full backups.

**267.** **Which of the following needs to be protected for a failsafe performance?**

    a.   Virus scanners

    b.   Firewalls

    c.   Blocking filters

    d.   Network ports

**267. b.** Network firewalls are devices or systems that control the flow of network traffic between networks employing differing security postures. A failsafe is the automatic termination and protection of programs when a hardware or software failure is detected. Because firewalls provide a critical access control security service, multiple firewalls should be employed for failsafe performance. Depending on a person's viewpoint, firewalls provide either the first line of defense or the last line of defense in accessing a network.

Virus scanners look for common viruses and macro viruses. Blocking filters can block Active-X and Java applets. Network ports provide access points to a network. These are not that important when compared to the firewall to have a failsafe performance.

**268.** Which of the following does *not* require network address translation services?

    a.    Internet Protocol (IP) version 2

    b.    Internet Protocol (IP) version 3

    c.    Internet Protocol (IP) version 4

    d.    Internet Protocol (IP) version 6

**268. d.** The network address translation (NAT) services are not needed in the Internet Protocol (IP) version 6 but are needed in the IPv2, IPv3, and IPv4. IP addresses are in a limited supply. NAT is the process of converting between IP addresses used within an intranet or other private network (called a stub domain) and the Internet IP addresses. This approach makes it possible to use a large number of addresses within the stub domain without depleting the limited number of available numeric Internet IP addresses. In the IP version 6, the NAT services are not needed because this version takes care of the problem of insufficient IP addresses with automatically assigning the IP addresses to hosts.

**269.** Which of the following fills the gap left by firewalls in terms of not monitoring authorized users' actions and not addressing internal threats?

    a.    Sensors

    b.    Switches

    c.    Bridges

    d.    Routers

**269. a.** Firewalls do not monitor authorized users' actions of both internal and external users, and do not address internal (insider) threats, leaving a gap. Sensors fill the gap left by firewalls with the use of monitors and scanners. A sensor is an intrusion detection and prevention system (IDPS) component that monitors, scans, and analyzes network activity.

The other three choices cannot fill the gap left by firewalls. A switch is a mechanical, electromechanical, or electronic device for making, breaking, or changing the connections in or among circuits. A bridge is a device that connects similar or dissimilar two or more LANs together to form an extended LAN. A router converts between different data link protocols and resegments transport level protocol data units (PDUs) as necessary to accomplish this conversion and re-segmentation.

**270.** In a domain name system (DNS) environment, which of the following is referred to when indicating security status among parent and child domains?

    a.    Chain of trust

    b.    Chain of custody

    c.    Chain of evidence

    d.    Chain of documents

*270. a.* The information system, when operating as part of a distributed, hierarchical namespace, provides the means to indicate the security status of child subspaces and (if the child supports secure resolution services) enable verification of a chain of trust among parent and child domains. An example means to indicate the security status of child subspaces is through the use of delegation signer (DS) resource records in the DNS.

The other three choices are not related to the chain of trust but they are related to each other. Chain of custody refers to tracking the movement of evidence, chain of evidence shows the sequencing of evidence, and chain of documents supports the chain of custody and the chain of evidence, and all are required in a court of law.

**271.** Which of the following is *not* an example of centralized authentication protocols?

    a.    RADIUS

    b.    TACACS

    c.    SSO

    d.    DIAMETER

*271. c.* RADIUS, TACACS, and DIAMETER are examples of centralized authentication protocols to improve remote access security. Centralized authentication servers are flexible, inexpensive, and easy to implement. Single sign-on (SSO) is an example of decentralized or distributed access control methodologies along with Kerberos, SESAME, security domains, and thin-client systems. SSO means the user is not prompted to enter additional authentication information for the session after the initial log-on is successfully completed.

**272.** Which of the following is *not* part of the Internet Engineering Task Force (IETF) AAA Working Group dealing with the remote access security?

    a.    Assurance

    b.    Authentication

    c.    Authorization

    d.    Accounting

*272. a.* Assurance includes techniques to achieve integrity, availability, confidentiality, and accountability, and metrics to measure them. The IETF's AAA Working Group remote access security services are labeled as authentication, authorization, and accounting (AAA) services.

**273.** **Analyzing data protection requirements for installing a local-area network (LAN) does *not* include:**

    a.    Uninterruptible power source

    b.    Backups

    c.    Fault tolerance

    d.    Operating systems

***273. d.*** Identifying information or data protection requirements involves reviewing the need for an uninterruptible power source, backups, and fault tolerance. Selection of an operating system is a part of operational constraints, not data protection requirements.

**274.** **What is the *most* frequent source of local-area network (LAN) hardware failures?**

    a.    Repeater

    b.    Server disk drives

    c.    Network cabling

    d.    Server software

***274. c.*** Hardware failures are grouped as follows: network cabling (60 to 80 percent), repeater (10 to 20 percent), and server disk drive (10 to 20 percent). Cables should be tested before their first use, rather than after a problem surfaces. Testing an installed cable is a tedious job, particularly when there are many network connections (drops) and the organization is large. Failures result when electrical conductors either break open, short together, or are exposed to electromagnetic forces. Failures are also caused when cables are poorly routed. Cabling, unlike other computer equipment, is not protected from heat, electrical charges, physical abuse, or damage.

Repeaters, server disk drives, and server software are incorrect. A repeater repeats data packets or electrical signals between cable segments. It receives a message and then retransmits it, regenerating the signal at its original strength. Server disk drives and server software are comparatively safe and trouble-free devices compared with cabling.

**275.** **Which of the following internetworking devices sends traffic addressed to a remote location from a local-area network (LAN) over the wide-area network (WAN) to the remote destination?**

    a.    Bridge

    b.    Router

    c.    Brouter

    d.    Backbone

***275. b.*** A router sends traffic addressed to a remote location from the local network over the wide area connection to the remote destination. The router connects to either an analog line or a digital line. Routers connect to analog lines via modems or to digital lines via a channel-service unit or data-service units.

Bridge is incorrect because it is a device that connects similar or dissimilar LANs to form an extended LAN. Brouters are incorrect because they are routers that can also bridge; they route one or more protocols and bridge all other network traffic. Backbone is incorrect because it is the high-traffic-density connectivity portion of any communications network.

**276.** Which of the following protocols use *many* network ports?

    a.   SNMP and SMTP

    b.   TCP and UDP

    c.   ICMP and IGMP

    d.   ARP and RARP

***276. b.*** TCP and UDP protocols are part of the TCP/IP suite operating at the transport layer of the ISO/OSI model. Network ports are used by TCP and UDP, each having 65,535 ports. Attackers can reconfigure these ports and listen in for valuable information about network systems and services prior to attack. SNMP and SMTP are application layer protocols, which use few ports. ICMP and IGMP are network layer protocols, which do not use any ports. ARP and RARP are data link layer protocols, which do not use any ports.

Network ports 0 through 1,023 are assigned for service contact used by server processes. The contact ports are sometimes called "well-known" ports. These service contact ports are used by system (or root) processes or by programs executed by privileged users. Ports from 1,024 through 65,535 are called registered ports. All incoming packets that communicate via ports higher than 1,023 are replies to connections initiated by internal requests. For example, Telnet service operates at port #23 with TCP and X Windows operate at port #6,000 with TCP.

**277.** Which of the following is *not* compatible with the Internet Protocol (IP) version 6?

    a.   IP version 4

    b.   TCP

    c.   UDP

    d.   BGP

***277. a.*** The Internet Protocol version 6 (IPv6) is not backward compatible with IPv4 but is compatible with TCP, UDP, ICMP, IGMP, OSPF, BGP, and DNS. The IPsec services are provided at the IP layer (network layer), offering protection for IP and/or upper-layer protocols such as TCP, UDP, ICMP, IGMP, OSPF, BGP, and DNS.

**278.** Which of the following network connectivity devices use rules that could have a substantial negative impact on the device's performance?

    a.   Sensors and switches

    b.   Routers and firewalls

    c.   Guards and gateways

    d.   Connectors and concentrators

**278. b.** Rules or rulesets are used in routers and firewalls. Adding new rules to a router or firewall could have a substantial negative impact on the device's performance, causing network slowdowns or even a denial-of-service (DoS). The information security management should carefully consider where filtering should be implemented (e.g., border router, boundary router, and firewall). A boundary router is located at the organization's boundary to an external network.

The other three choices do not use rules or rulesets. A sensor is an intrusion detection and prevention system (IDPS) component that monitors and analyzes network activity. A switch is a mechanical, electromechanical, or electronic device for making, breaking, or changing the connections in or among circuits. A hardware/software guard is designed to provide a secure information path for sharing data between multiple system networks operating at different security levels. A gateway transfers information and converts it to a form compatible with the receiving network's protocols. A connector is an electromechanical device on the ends of cables that permit them to be connected with, and disconnected from, other cables. A concentrator gathers together several lines in one central location.

**279.** Countermeasures against sniffers do *not* include which of the following?

a. Using recent version of secure shell protocol.

b. Applying end-to-end encryption.

c. Using packet filters.

d. Implementing robust authentication techniques.

**279. c.** Packet filters are good against flooding attacks. Using either recent version of secure shell (e.g., SSHv2) or IPsec protocol, using end-to-end encryption, and implementing robust authentication techniques are effective against sniffing attacks.

**280.** Secure remote procedure call (RPC) provides which one of the following security services?

a. Authentication

b. Confidentiality

c. Integrity

d. Availability

**280. a.** Secure remote procedure call (RPC) provides authentication services only. Confidentiality, integrity, and availability services must be provided by other means.

**281.** Which of the following does *not* provide confidentiality protection for Web services?

a. Extensible markup language (XML) encryption

b. Web services security (WS-Security)

c. Advanced encryption standard (AES)

d. Hypertext transfer protocol secure (HTTPS)

**281. c.** The advanced encryption standard (AES) does not provide confidentiality protection for Web services. However, the AES is used for securing sensitive but unclassified information.

The other three choices provide confidentiality protection for Web services because most Web service data is stored in the form of extensible markup language (XML). Using XML encryption before storing data should provide confidentiality protection while maintaining compatibility. Web services security (WS-Security) and HTTPS are generally used to protect confidentiality of simple object access protocol (SOAP) messages in transit, leaving data at rest vulnerable to attacks.

**282.** Firewalls cannot provide a "line of perimeter defense" against attacks from which of the following?

    a.    Traffic entering a network

    b.    Traffic to and from the Internet

    c.    Traffic to host systems

    d.    Traffic leaving a network

**282. b.** Firewalls police network traffic that enters and leaves a network. Firewalls can stop many penetrating attacks by disallowing many protocols that an attacker could use to penetrate a network. By limiting access to host systems and services, firewalls provide a necessary line of perimeter defense against attack. The new paradigm of transaction-based Internet services makes these "perimeter" defenses less effective as their boundaries between friendly and unfriendly environments blur.

**283.** Sources of legal rights and obligations for privacy over electronic mail do *not* include which of the following?

    a.    Law of the country

    b.    Employer practices

    c.    Employee practices

    d.    Employer policies

**283. c.** E-mail networks function as decentralized systems. Independent, unconnected systems at multiple locations are decentralized. An electronic message flows through the system, going from one machine to another. Eventually the message reaches the correct machine and is placed in the targeted person's e-mail box. Because e-mail crosses many state and national boundaries and even continents, it is advised to review the principal sources of legal rights and obligations. These sources include the law of the country and employer policies and practices. Employee practices have no effect on the legal rights and obligations.

**284.** In the ISO/OSI reference model, which of the following relates to end system-level security?

    a.    Transport layer or network layer

    b.    Application layer or presentation layer

   c.    Session layer or transport layer

   d.    Data link layer or physical layer

***284. a.***   The ISO/OSI standards give a choice where either a transport layer or network layer can be used to provide end system-level security. An assumption is made that the end systems are trusted and that all underlying communication networks are not trusted.

**285.**   **A primary firewall has been compromised. What is the correct sequence of action steps to be followed by a firewall administrator?**

1.   Deploy the secondary firewall.

2.   Bring down the primary firewall.

3.   Restore the primary firewall.

4.   Reconfigure the primary firewall.

   a.    1, 2, 3, and 4

   b.    2, 3, 4, and 1

   c.    2, 1, 4, and 3

   d.    4, 1, 2, and 3

***285. c.***   Internal computer systems should not be connected to the Internet without a firewall. There should be at least two firewalls in place: primary and secondary. First, the attacked (primary) firewall should be brought down to contain the damage (i.e., damage control), and the backup (secondary) firewall should be deployed immediately. After the primary firewall is reconfigured, it must be brought back or restored to an operational state.

You should not deploy the secondary firewall first until the primary firewall is completely brought down to contain the risk due to its compromised state and to reduce the further damage. The elapsed time between these two actions can be very small.

**286.**   **Which of the following functions of Internet Control Message Protocol (ICMP) of TCP/IP model is used to trick routers and hosts?**

   a.    Detecting unreachable destinations

   b.    Redirecting messages

   c.    Checking remote hosts

   d.    Controlling traffic flow

***286. b.***   Internet Control Message Protocol (ICMP) redirect messages can be used to trick routers and hosts acting as routers into using "false" routes; these false routes aid in directing traffic to an attacker's system instead of a legitimate, trusted system.

**287.** Which of the following functions of the Internet Control Message Protocol (ICMP) of TCP/IP model cause a buffer overflow on the target machine?

      a.   Detecting unreachable destinations

      b.   Redirecting messages

      c.   Checking remote hosts

      d.   Controlling traffic flow

*287. c.* The ping command is used to send an Internet Control Message Protocol (ICMP) echo message for checking the status of a remote host. When large amounts of these messages are received from an intruder, they can cause a buffer overflow on the target host machine, resulting in a system reboot or total system crash. This is because the recipient host cannot handle the unexpected data and size in the packet, thereby possibly triggering a buffer overflow condition. The other three choices do not cause a buffer overflow on the target machine.

**288.** The basic causes of a majority of security-related problems in Web servers are due to which of the following?

      a.   Hardware design and protocols

      b.   Software design and configurations

      c.   Hardware specifications and testing

      d.   Software acquisition and implementation

*288. b.* A Web server is like a window to the world, and therefore it must be protected to provide a controlled network access to both authorized and unauthorized individuals. Web servers contain large and complex programs that can contain security weaknesses. These weaknesses are due to poor software design and configuration of the Web server. Hardware design and protocols provide better security than software design.

**289.** In electronic auctions, which of the following auction models has a minimal security mechanism that can lead to security breaches and fraud?

      a.   Business-to-business (B2B)

      b.   Government-to-business (G2B)

      c.   Consumer-to-consumer (C2C)

      d.   Consumer-to-business (C2B)

*289. c.* In the consumer-to-consumer (C2C) electronic auction model, consumers buy and sell goods with other consumers through auction sites. The C2C auction model has minimal security mechanism (i.e., no encryption and possibility of fraud in shipping defective products). The B2B, G2B, and C2B auction models are reasonably secure due to the use of private telephone lines (leased lines) and encryption.

**290.** Which of the following causes an increase in the attack surface of a public cloud computing environment?

    a.    Paging

    b.    Hypervisor

    c.    Checkpointing

    d.    Migration of virtual machines

***290. b.***   The hypervisor or virtual machine monitor is an additional layer of software between an operating system and hardware platform used to operate multitenant virtual machines. Compared with a traditional nonvirtualized implementation, the addition of a hypervisor causes an increase in the attack surface.

Paging, checkpointing, and migration of virtual machines can leak sensitive data to persistent storage, subverting protection mechanisms in the hosted operating system intended to prevent such occurrences.

**291.** Mobile computing is where remote users' access host computers for their computing needs. Remote access software controls the access to host computers. Which of the following technologies is behind the performance improvement to permit users to work offline on network tasks?

    a.    Agent-based technology

    b.    Windows-based technology

    c.    Hardware-based technology

    d.    Network-based technology

***291. a.***   Agent-based technology can boost the performance of remote access software capability. It gives the users the ability to work offline on network tasks, such as e-mail, and complete the task when the network connection is made. Agent-based technology is software-driven. It can work with the Windows operating system.

**292.** From a security viewpoint, which of the following should be the goal for a virtual private network (VPN)?

    a.    Make only one exit point from a company's network to the Internet.

    b.    Make only one entry point to a company's network from the Internet.

    c.    Make only one destination point from a company's network to the Internet.

    d.    Make only one transmission point from the Internet to a company's network.

***292. b.***   The goal for a virtual private network (VPN) should be to make it the only entry point to an organization's network from the Internet. This requires blocking all the organization's systems or making them inaccessible from the Internet unless outside users connect to the organization's network via its VPN.

**293.** In border gateway protocol (BGP), which of the following is physically present?

 a. Routing/forwarding table

 b. Adj-Routing Information Base (RIB)-In table

 c. Loc-RIB table

 d. Adj-RIB-Out table

***293. a.*** Only the routing/forwarding table is physically present, whereas, the tables mentioned in the other three choices are conceptually based tables, not physically present. However, system developers can decide whether to implement the routing information base (RIB) tables either in the physical form or in the conceptual form.

BGP is used in updating routing tables, which are essential in assuring the correct operation of networks, as it is a dynamic routing scheme. Routing information received from other BGP routers is accumulated in a routing table. These routes are then installed in the router's forwarding table.

An eavesdropper could easily mount an attack by changing routing tables to redirect traffic through nodes that can be monitored. The attacker could thus monitor the contents or source and destination of the redirected traffic or modify it maliciously.

The adj-RIB-In table routes after learning from the inbound update messages from BGP peers. The loc-RIB table routes after selecting from the adj-RIB-In table. The adj-RIB-Out table routes to its peers that the BGP router will advertise based on its local policy.

**294.** In Web services, which of the following can lead to a flooding-based denial-of-service (DoS) attack?

 a. Source IP address

 b. Network packet behavior

 c. SOAP/XML messages

 d. Business behavior

***294. d.*** Flooding attacks most often involve copying valid service requests and re-sending them to a provider. The attacker may issue repetitive SOAP/XML messages in an attempt to overload the Web service. The user behavior (business behavior) in using the Web service transactions may not be legitimate and is detected, thus constituting a DoS attack. The other three choices may not be detected because they are legitimate where the source IP address is valid, the network packet behavior is valid, and the SOAP/XML message is well formed.

**295.** It has been said that no system is completely secure and can handle all disasters. Which one of the following items is needed *most*, even when all the other three items are working properly, to ensure online operation and security?

 a. Intrusion detection systems (IDSs)

 b. Firewalls

 c. Antivirus software

 d. File backups

**295. d.** Intrusion detection systems (IDSs), firewalls, and antivirus software are critical to online security. But no system is completely secure and can handle all disasters. Important files stored on a computer must be copied onto a removable disc and kept in a safe and secure place (i.e., file backups). IDS has detection features, but this is not enough in case of a disaster. Firewalls have protection features, but this is not enough in case of a disaster. Antivirus software has dis-infection features, but this is not enough in case of a disaster.

**296.** **Which of the following technologies enables phone calls and facsimile transmissions to be routed over the same network used for data?**

    a. File transfer protocol

    b. Content streaming

    c. Voice over Internet Protocol

    d. Instant messaging

**296. c.** In a Voice over Internet Protocol (VoIP) technology, voice and data are combined in the same network. The other three choices cannot combine voice and data. File transfer protocol (FTP) is used to copy files from one computer to another. Content streaming is a method for playing continuous pictures and voice from multimedia files over the Internet. It enables users to browse large files in real time. Instant messaging (IM) technology provides a way to send quick notes or text messages from PC to PC over the Internet, so two people who are online at the same time can communicate instantly.

**297.** **The network address translation (NAT) changes which of the following from a connectionless network to a connection-oriented network?**

    a. Internet

    b. Transmission control protocol (TCP)

    c. Internet Protocol (IP)

    d. Switched multimegabit data services (SMDS)

**297. a.** The network address translation (NAT) changes the Internet from a connectionless network to a connection-oriented network through its converting, mapping, and hiding of the Internet IP addresses. By design, the TCP is a connection-oriented network and both IP and SMDS are connectionless networks, which are not changed by the NAT.

**298.** **Which of the following would be inherently in conflict with a traffic padding security mechanism?**

    a. Security labels and data splitting

    b. Packet-switching network and local-area network

    c. Packet-switching network and security labels

    d. Local-area network and data splitting

**298. b.**  A traffic-padding security mechanism provides security services such as traffic flow confidentiality. It involves collecting and transmitting spurious cases of communication and data and is used with encryption so that "dummy" data is separated from the real data.

A packet-switching network is in conflict with the traffic-padding security mechanism because it divides the data traffic into blocks, called packets. These packets, a group of binary digits, are delivered to the destination address in a data envelope. Because of a routing function used in packet switching, it is possible that packets can reach their destination out of sequence. The intended traffic-padding security mechanism will not be achieved with the use of a packet-switching network.

A local-area network refers to a network that interconnects systems located in a small geographic area, such as a building or a complex of buildings (campus). Traffic padding operates a network up to its full capacity thereby curtailing the resource sharing potential of the LAN.

Security label is a designation assigned to a system resource, such as a file, which cannot be changed except in emergency situations. Security labels protect the confidentiality of data. Similarly, data splitting increases the confidentiality of data where the file is broken up into two or more separate files so that an intruder cannot make any sense out of them. The separate files are then transferred independently via different routes and/or at different times.

**299.**  The Internet Protocol version 6 (IPv6) is *not* related to which of the following?

    a.   Session-less protocols

    b.   Datagram-based protocols

    c.   Session initiation protocol (SIP)

    d.   Simple Internet Protocol Plus (SIPP)

**299. c.**  Session initiation protocol (SIP) is a text-based protocol, like simple mail transfer protocol (SMTP) and hypertext transfer protocol (HTTP), for initiating interactive communication sessions between users. Such sessions include voice, video, data, instant messaging, chat, interactive games, and virtual reality. SIP is the protocol used to set up conferencing, telephony, multimedia, and other types of communication sessions on the Internet. SIP has nothing to do with and is not related to the Internet Protocol version 6 (IPv6).

Both the IPv4 and IPv6 are session-less and datagram-based protocols. The IPv6 security features include encryption, user authentication, end-to-end secure transmission, privacy, and automatic network configuration (automatically assigning IP addresses to hosts). IPv6 also handles real-time and delay-sensitive traffic. IPv6 runs on high-speed networks, those using asynchronous transfer mode (ATM) and wireless networks. Simple Internet Protocol Plus (SIPP) is used in IPv6.

**300.**  Which of the following border gateway protocol (BGP) attacks does *not* use message digest 5 (MD5) authentication signature option as a countermeasure?

    a.   Peer spoofing

    b.   Link cutting attack

  c. Malicious route injection

  d. Unallocated route injection

**300. b.** An inherent vulnerability in routing protocols is their potential for manipulation by cutting links in the network. By removing links, either through denial-of-service or physical attacks, an attacker can divert traffic to allow for eavesdropping, blackholing, or traffic analysis. Because routing protocols are designed to find paths around broken links, these attacks are hard to defend against. Examples of countermeasures against link cutting attacks include using encryption, intrusion detection systems, and redundant backup paths, not an MD5 authentication signature option.

The other three choices use a message digest 5 (MD5) authentication signature option. The MD5 hash algorithm can be used to protect BGP sessions by creating a keyed hash for TCP message authentication. Because MD5 is a cryptographic algorithm using a 128-bit cryptographic hash (checksum), rather than a simple checksum such as CRC-32 bit, it is computationally difficult to determine the MD5 key from the hash value.

In a peer spoofing attack, the goal is to insert false information into a BGP peer's routing tables. Examples of countermeasures against peer spoofing include using strong sequence number randomization and an MD5 authentication signature option.

In a malicious route injection attack, a malicious party could begin sending out updates with incorrect routing information. Examples of countermeasures against malicious route injection include using route filtering and an MD5 authentication signature option.

In an unallocated route injection attack, which is a variation of malicious route injection attack, routes are transmitted to unallocated prefixes. These prefixes contain a set of IP addresses that have not been assigned yet, so no traffic should be routed to them. Examples of countermeasures against unallocated route injection include dropping unallocated prefixes and using route filtering and an MD5 authentication signature option.

**301.** **Domain name system (DNS) is a part of which of the following TCP/IP layers?**

  a. Applications layer

  b. Transport layer

  c. Network layer

  d. Data link layer

**301. a.** DNS is a function of the application layer, along with HTTP, SMTP, FTP, and SNMP. This layer sends and receives data for particular applications.

The transport layer is incorrect because it provides connection-oriented or connectionless services for transporting application layer services between networks. The network layer is incorrect because it routes packets across networks. The data link layer is incorrect because it handles communications on the physical network components.

**302.** **Regarding Voice over Internet Protocol (VoIP), packets loss is *not* resulting from which of the following?**

    a.   Latency

    b.   Jitter

    c.   Speed

    d.   Bandwidth congestion

*302. c.*   Every facet of network traversal must be completed quickly in VoIP, so speed is not an issue. The other three choices can cause packet loss. The latency often associated with tasks in data networks will not be tolerated. Jitters are caused by low-bandwidth situations, leading to bandwidth congestion.

**303.** **A system administrator for an entertainment company is estimating the storage capacity of a video server to distribute movies on-demand for its customers. Which of the following law applies to the video servers?**

    a.   Moore's law

    b.   Zipf's law

    c.   Brooke's law

    d.   Pareto's law

*303. b.*   The Zipf's law states that the most popular movie is seven times as popular as the number seven movie. It is assumed that most customers will order the most popular movie more frequently. The other three choices are not related to video servers.

The Moore's law states that the number of transistors per square inch on an integrated circuit chip doubles every 18 months or the performance of a computer doubles every 18 months. The Brooke's law states that adding more people to a late system development project (or to any project) makes the project even later. The Pareto's law, as it applied to IT, states that 80 percent of IT-related problems are the result of 20 percent of IT-related causes.

**304.** **Which of the following is *not* a security goal of a domain name system (DNS)?**

    a.   Source authentication

    b.   Confidentiality

    c.   Integrity

    d.   Availability

*304. b.*   The DNS data provided by public DNS name servers is not deemed confidential. Therefore, confidentiality is not one of the security goals of DNS. Ensuring authenticity of information and maintaining the integrity of information in transit is critical for efficient functioning of the Internet, for which DNS provides the name resolution service. The DNS is expected to provide name resolution information for any publicly available Internet resource.

**305.** **Which of the following provides a dynamic mapping of an Internet Protocol (IP) address to a physical hardware address?**

    a.   PPP

    b.   ARP

    c.   SLIP

    d.   SKIP

**305. *b.*** The address resolution protocol (ARP) provides a dynamic mapping of a 32-bit IP address to a 48-bit physical hardware address. Other protocols such as point-to-point protocol (PPP), serial line interface protocol (SLIP), and simple key management for Internet protocol (SKIP) do not fit the description.

**306.** **Which of the following local-area network (LAN) topologies uses a central hub?**

    a.   Star

    b.   Bus

    c.   Token ring

    d.   Token bus

**306. *a.*** The star topology uses a central hub connecting workstations and servers. The bus topology uses a single cable running from one end of the network to the other. The ring topology interconnects nodes in a circular fashion.

**307.** **Which of the following is *not* susceptible to electronic interferences?**

    a.   Twisted-pair wire

    b.   Coaxial cable

    c.   Fiber-optical cable

    d.   Copper-based cable wire

**307. *c.*** Optical fiber is relatively secured, expensive, and is not susceptible to electronic interferences. The other three choices are subject to such interferences with varying degrees.

**308.** **Which of the following can be either an internal network or an external network?**

    a.   Internet

    b.   Local-area network

    c.   Virtual private network

    d.   Wide-area network

**308. *c.*** The Internet is an example of external network. Local-area network (LAN), campus-area network (CAN), wide-area network (WAN), intranet, and extranet are examples of internal networks. The virtual private network (VPN) can be either an internal network or external network. The VPN is considered an internal network only if the end user organization establishes the VPN connection between organization-controlled endpoints and does not depend on any external network to protect the confidentiality and integrity of information transmitted across the network. In other words, the VPN is considered an internal network only when it is adequately equipped with appropriate security controls by the end user organization, and no external organization exercises control over the VPN.

**309.** Which of the following permits Internet Protocol security (IPsec) to use external authentication services such as Kerberos and RADIUS?

    a.   EAP

    b.   PPP

    c.   CHAP

    d.   PAP

*309. a.* The Internet Key Exchange (IKE) Version 2 of IPsec supports the extensible authentication protocol (EAP), which permits IPsec to use external authentication services such as Kerberos and RADIUS.

The point-to-point protocol (PPP) standard specifies that password authentication protocol (PAP) and challenge handshake authentication protocol (CHAP) may be negotiated as authentication methods, but other methods can be added to the negotiation and used as well.

**310.** Which of the following supports the secure sockets layer (SSL) to perform client-to-server authentication process?

    a.   Application layer security protocol

    b.   Session layer security protocol

    c.   Transport layer security protocol

    d.   Presentation layer security protocol

*310. c.* Transport layer security (TLS) protocol supports the SSL to perform client-to-server authentication process. The TLS protocol enables client/server application to communicate in a way that is designed to prevent eavesdropping, tampering, or message forgery. The TLS protocol provides communication privacy and data integrity over the Internet.

**311.** Challenge handshake authentication protocol (CHAP) requires which of the following for remote users?

    a.   Initial authentication

    b.   Pre-authentication

    c.   Post-authentication

    d.   Re-authentication

*311. d.* CHAP supports re-authentication to make sure the users are still who they were at the beginning of the session. The other authentication methods mentioned would not achieve this goal.

**312.** **A *major* problem with Serial Line Internet Protocol (SLIP) is which of the following?**

    a.    The protocol does not contain address information.

    b.    The protocol is used on point-to-point connections.

    c.    The protocol is used to attach non-IP devices to an IP network.

    d.    The protocol does not provide error detection or correction mechanism.

*312. d.* SLIP is a protocol for sending IP packets over a serial line connection. Because SLIP is used over slow lines (56kb), this makes error detection or correction at that layer more expensive. Errors can be detected at a higher layer. The addresses are implicitly defined, which is not a major problem. Point-to-point connections make it less vulnerable to eavesdropping, which is strength. SLIP is a mechanism for attaching non-IP devices to an IP network, which is an advantage.

**313.** **A serious and strong attack on a network is just initiated. The *best* approach against this type of attack is to:**

    a.    Prevent and detect

    b.    Detect and recover

    c.    Prevent and correct

    d.    Prevent and intervene

*313. d.* On any attack, preventing network attacks from occurring is the first priority. For serious and strong attacks, prevention should be combined with intervening techniques to minimize or eliminate negative consequences of attacks that may occur. Intervening actions start right after full prevention and right before full detection, correction, and recovery actions by installing decoy systems (e.g., honeypot), vigilant network administrators, and alerts/triggers from central network monitoring centers. In other words, intervening actions face the attacker head on right after the initial signs and symptoms of attack detection but do not wait until the full detection to take place as in a normal case of detection, thus halting the attacker to proceed further. These intervening actions stop the attack right at the beginning by diverting or stalling the attacker.

For serious and strong attacks, normal detection alone is not enough, correction alone or combined with detection is not enough, recovery alone or combined with detection and correction is not enough because they may not contain the serious and strong attacks quickly as they are too late to be of any significant use. However, they are very useful in normal attacks. Intervening is pro-active and action-oriented, whereas detecting, correcting, and recovering are re-active and passive-oriented.

**314.** **Major vulnerabilities stemming from the use of the World Wide Web (WWW) are associated with which of the following?**

    a.    External websites and hypertext markup language (HTML)

    b.    Web browser software and Web server software

c. External websites and hypertext transfer protocol (HTTP)

d. Internal websites and Web pages

***314. b.*** Vulnerabilities stemming from the use of the Web are associated with browser software and server software. Although browser software can introduce vulnerabilities to an organization, these vulnerabilities are generally less severe than the threat posed by servers. Many organizations now support an external website describing their products and services. For security reasons, these servers are usually posted outside the organization's firewall, thus creating more exposure. Web clients, also called Web browsers, enable a user to navigate through information by pointing and clicking. Web servers deliver hypertext markup language (HTML) and other media to browsers through the hypertext transfer protocol (HTTP). The browsers interpret, format, and present the documents to users. The end result is a multimedia view of the Internet.

**315.** **Which of the following is an inappropriate control over telecommunication hardware?**

a. Logical access controls

b. Security over wiring closets

c. Contingency plans

d. Restricted access to test equipment

***315. a.*** Logical access control is a software-based control, not a hardware-based control. Security over wiring-closets circuits, transmission media, and hardware devices, and restricting access to test equipment are appropriate to protect hardware. Contingency plans to minimize losses from equipment failure or damage are important and appropriate. The other choices are physical security controls over telecommunications hardware. They minimize risks such as physical damage or unauthorized access to telecommunications hardware.

**316.** **Which of the following guarantees network quality-of-service (QoS) and quality-of-protection (QoP)?**

a. Memorandum of agreement (MOA)

b. Service-level agreement (SLA)

c. Memorandum of understanding (MOU)

d. Rules of network connection

***316. b.*** Either MOA or MOU are initial documents prior to finalizing the SLA document. The rules of network connection can be informal and not binding. The SLA document is between a user (customer) organization and a service provider, so as to satisfy specific customer application system requirements. The SLA should address performance properties such as throughput (bandwidth), transit delay (latency), error rates, packet priority, network security, packet loss, and packet jitter.

**317.** **For network security threats, which of the following steals or makes an unauthorized use of a service?**

    a.    Denial-of-service

    b.    Misappropriation

    c.    Message replay

    d.    Message modification

***317. b.***   Misappropriation is a threat in which an attacker steals or makes unauthorized use of a service. A denial-of-service (DoS) threat prevents or limits the normal use or management of networks or network devices. Message replay is a threat that passively monitors transmissions and retransmits messages, acting as if the attacker were a legitimate user. Message modification is a threat that alters a legitimate message by deleting, adding to, changing, or reordering it.

**318.** **Which of the following statements is *not* true about wireless local-area networks (WLANs)?**

    a.    Wireless LANs will not replace wired LANs.

    b.    Wireless LANs will augment the wired LANs.

    c.    Wireless LANs will substantially eliminate cabling.

    d.    Wireless LANs will serve as a direct replacement for the wired LANs.

***318. c.***   Wireless LANs augment and do not replace wired LANs. In some cases, wireless LANs serve as a direct replacement for the wired LANs when starting from scratch. In most cases, a wireless LAN complements a wired LAN and does not replace it. Due to poor performance and high-cost reasons, wireless LANs do not take over the wired LANs. Wireless LANs do not substantially eliminate cabling because bridges rely on cabling for interconnection. Wireless LANs provide unique advantages such as fast and easy installation, a high degree of user mobility, and equipment portability.

**319.** **Which of the following ISO/OSI layers does *not* provide confidentiality services?**

    a.    Presentation layer

    b.    Transport layer

    c.    Network layer

    d.    Session layer

***319. d.***   The session layer does not provide confidentiality service. It establishes, manages, and terminates connections between applications and provides checkpoint recovery services. It helps users interact with the system and other users.

The presentation layer is incorrect because it provides authentication and confidentiality services. It defines and transforms the format of data to make it useful to the receiving application. It provides a common means of representing a data structure in transit from one end system to another.

The transport layer is incorrect because it provides confidentiality, authentication, data integrity, and access control services. It ensures an error-free, in-sequence exchange of data between end points. It is responsible for transmitting a message between one network user and another.

The network layer is incorrect because it provides confidentiality, authentication, data integrity, and access control services. It is responsible for transmitting a message from its source to the destination. It provides routing (path control) services to establish connections across communications networks.

**320.** **User datagram protocol (UDP) is a part of which of the following TCP/IP layers?**

    a.   Applications layer

    b.   Transport layer

    c.   Network layer

    d.   Data link layer

***320. b.***   User datagram protocol (UDP) is a part of the transport layer, along with TCP. This layer provides connection-oriented or connectionless services for transporting application layer services between networks.

The application layer is incorrect because it sends and receives data for particular applications. The network layer is incorrect because it routes packets across networks. The data link layer is incorrect because it handles communications on the physical network components.

**321.** **Internet control message protocol (ICMP) is a part of which of the following TCP/IP layers?**

    a.   Applications layer

    b.   Transport layer

    c.   Network layer

    d.   Data link layer

***321. c.***   Internet control message protocol (ICMP) is a part of the network layer, along with IP, RAS, and IGMP. The network layer routes packets across networks.

The application layer is incorrect because it sends and receives data for particular applications. The transport layer is incorrect because it provides connection-oriented or connectionless services for transporting application layer services between networks. The data link layer is incorrect because it handles communications on the physical network components.

**322.** **Which of the following *cannot* log the details of encryption-protected hypertext transfer protocol (HTTP) requests?**

    a.   Web proxy servers

    b.   Routers

    c.   Nonproxying firewalls

    d.   Web browsers

***322. a.***   Hypertext transfer protocol (HTTP) is the mechanism for transferring data between the Web browsers and Web servers. Through Web browsers, people access Web servers that contain nearly any type of data imaginable. The richest source of information for Web usage is the hosts running the Web browsers. Another good source of Web usage information is Web servers, which keep logs of the requests that they receive. Besides Web browser and servers, several other types of devices and software might also log related information. For example, Web proxy servers and application proxying firewalls might perform detailed logging of HTTP activity, with a similar level of detail to Web server logs. However, Web proxy servers cannot log the details of SSL or TLS-protected HTTP requests because the requests and the corresponding responses pass through the proxy encrypted, which conceals their contents.

Routers, nonproxying firewalls, and other network devices might log the basic aspects of HTTP network connections, such as source and destination IP addresses and ports.

**323.**   **In a domain name system (DNS) environment, who is responsible for the configuration and operation of the name servers?**

    a.   Security administrators

    b.   System administrators

    c.   Zone administrators

    d.   Database administrators

***323. c.***   Zone administrators are also called DNS administrators, and they are responsible for the configuration and operation of the name servers.

**324.**   **All the following services and application traffic should always be blocked inbound by a firewall *except*:**

    a.   RPC

    b.   NFS

    c.   FTP

    d.   SNMP

***324. c.***   File transfer protocol (FTP) should be restricted to specific systems using strong authentication. Services such as remote procedure call (RPC), network file sharing (NFS), and simple network management protocol (SNMP) should always be blocked.

**325.**   **Packet-switching networks use which of the following protocol standards?**

    a.   X9.63

    b.   X9.44

    c.   X9.17

    d.   X.25

**325. d.**  X.25 protocol standard is used in packet-switching networks. It operates at the network and data link levels of a communications network.

X9.63 is used for key establishment schemes that employ asymmetric techniques. X9.44 is the transport of symmetric algorithm keys using reversible public key cryptography. X9.17 is used for cryptographic key management, especially for financial institution key management.

**326.** **Countermeasures against Internet Protocol (IP) address spoofing attacks do not include which of the following?**

    a.    Using firewalls

    b.    Disabling active-content

    c.    Using smart tokens

    d.    Using timestamps

**326. c.**  Smart tokens are part of robust authentication techniques to authenticate a user accessing a computer system. IP address spoofing is using various techniques to subvert IP-based access control by masquerading as another system by using their IP address. Countermeasures include (i) using firewalls, (ii) disabling active-content code (e.g., Active-X and JavaScript) from the Web browser, and (iii) using timestamps. Access control lists (ACLs) can also be used to block inbound traffic with source addresses matching the internal addresses of the target network.

**327.** **Which of the following can provide a seamless failover option for firewalls?**

    a.    Heartbeat solution

    b.    Network switches

    c.    Back-end system

    d.    Custom network interface

**327. b.**  Network switches that provide load-balancing and failover capabilities are the newest and most advanced solution currently available. In a failover configuration, these switches monitor the responsiveness of the production firewall and shift all traffic over to a backup firewall if a failure on the production system occurs. The primary advantage to this type of solution is that the switch masquerades both firewalls behind the same media access control (ISO/OSI Layer 2) address. This functionality enables seamless failover; that is, established sessions through the firewall are not impacted by a production system failure.

The heartbeat-based solutions typically involve a backend or custom network interface that exists to notify the backup system in the event of a primary system failure. These systems rely on established, reliable technology to handle failover. The primary drawback with this approach is that established sessions traversing the production firewalls are almost always lost in the transition from production to backup resources. The decision on which failover method to implement is often reduced to cost and the network switch-based failover solution is generally more expensive than a heartbeat-based system.

**328.** **A limitation of point-to-point tunneling Protocol (PPTP) is which of the following?**

    a.   End-to-end secure virtual networks

    b.   Lack of authentication at end nodes

    c.   Hiding information in IP packets

    d.   In-band management

***328. b.***   A limitation of the point-to-point tunneling protocol (PPTP), when compared to secure sockets layer (SSL), is that it does not provide authentication of the endpoints. PPTP is useful in implementing end-to-end secure virtual networks, hiding information in IP packets, and providing in-band management.

**329.** **Which of the following is the *most* important step to be followed by a firewall administrator when upgrading the firewall system?**

    a.   Analyze and upgrade

    b.   Evaluate and upgrade

    c.   Monitor and upgrade

    d.   Upgrade and test

***329. d.***   The firewall administrator must analyze and evaluate each new release of the firewall software to determine whether an upgrade is required. Prior to upgrade, the firewall administrator must verify with the vendor that an upgrade is required. The most important step occurs after an upgrade; the firewall must be tested to ensure proper functioning prior to making it fully operational.

**330.** **A virtual private network (VPN) creates a secure, private network over the Internet through all the following *except*:**

    a.   Authentication

    b.   Encryption

    c.   Packet tunneling

    d.   Firewalls

***330. a.***   VPNs enable an organization to create a secure, private network over a public network such as the Internet. They can be created using software, hardware, or a combination to create a secure link between peers over a public network. The secure link is built through encryption, firewalls, and packet tunneling. Authentication is done outside the network.

**331.** **What is an attack that attempts to exploit a weakness in a system at a level below the developers' design level (such as through operating system code versus application code) called?**

    a.   Technical attack

    b.   Tunneling attack

    c.    NAK attack

    d.    Active attack

**331. b.** A tunneling attack attempts to exploit a weakness in a system that exists at a level of abstraction lower than that used by the developer to design the system. For example, an attacker might discover a way to modify the microcode of a processor that is used when encrypting data, rather than attempting to break the system's encryption algorithm. Preventing a tunneling attack can be costly.

A technical attack is perpetrated by circumventing or nullifying hardware and software protection mechanisms, rather than by subverting system personnel or other users.

A NAK attack capitalizes on a potential weakness in an operating system that does not handle asynchronous interrupts properly and thus leaves the system in an unprotected state during such interrupts. An active attack alters data by bypassing security controls on a computer system.

**332.** In a distributed computing environment, system security takes on an important role. Two types of network attacks exist: passive and active attacks. Which of the following is the best definition of active attack?

    1.    Nonpreventable

    2.    Preventable

    3.    Detectable

    4.    Correctable

        a.    1 only

        b.    3 only

        c.    1 and 3

        d.    2, 3, and 4

**332. c.** Data communication channels are often insecure, subjecting messages transmitted over the channels to passive and active threats or attacks. An active attack is where the threat makes an overt change or modification to the system in an attempt to take advantage of vulnerability. Active attacks are nonpreventable and detectable.

A passive attack occurs when the threat merely watches information move across the system and when information is siphoned off the network. Passive attacks are preventable but difficult to detect because no modification is done to the information, and audit trails do not exist. All attacks are correctable with varying degrees of effort and cost.

**333.** What is an attacker connecting a covert computer terminal to a data communication line between the authorized terminal and the computer called?

        a.    Tunneling attack

        b.    Salami attack

   c.    Session hijacking attack

   d.    Asynchronous attack

***333. c.***   The attacker waits until the authorized terminal is online but not in use and then switches control to the covert terminal. The computer thinks it is still connected to the authorized user, and the attacker has access to the same files as the authorized user. Because a session was hijacked in the middle, it is called a session hijacking attack.

A tunneling attack is incorrect because it uses one data transfer method to carry data for another method. A salami attack is incorrect because it is an automated form of abuse using the Trojan horse method or secretly executing an unauthorized program that causes the unnoticed or immaterial debiting of small amounts of financial assets from a large number of sources or accounts. An asynchronous attack is incorrect because it takes advantage of the asynchronous functioning of a computer operating system. This may include a programmer (i) penetrating the job queue and modifying the data waiting to be processed or printed or (ii) disrupting the entire system by changing commands so that data is lost or programs crash.

**334.**  **Which of the following ISO/OSI layers provide both confidentiality and data integrity services?**

   a.    Data link layer

   b.    Physical layer

   c.    Application layer

   d.    Presentation layer

***334. c.***   The application layer is the only layer listed in the question that proves both confidentiality and data integrity services. The application layer provides services directly to users such as file transfer protocols. It consists of query software where a person could request a piece of information and the system display the answer.

The data link layer and physical layer are incorrect because they provide confidentiality service only, not data integrity. The data link layer provides a reliable transfer of data across physical links, error flow control, link-level encryption and decryption, and synchronization. It handles the physical transmission of frames over a single data link. The physical layer provides for the transmission of unstructured bit streams over the communications channel.

The presentation layer is incorrect because it provides authentication and confidentiality services but not data integrity and confidentiality. The presentation layer defines and transforms the format of data to make it useful to the receiving application.

**335.**  **Wireless local-area networks (WLANs) are connected to wired local-area networks (LANs) through the use of which of the following?**

   a.    Repeaters

   b.    Bridges

   c.    Brouters

   d.    Routers

**335. b.** Wireless LANs are often connected to wired LANs through a bridge, or they depend on a central hub to pass messages between nodes. These devices make good targets to alter traffic passing between wireless nodes.

A repeater is incorrect because it simply extends the range of one LAN. It rebuilds all the signals it hears on one LAN segment and passes them on to the other. A router connects LANs of different hardware types. They examine network addresses for forwarding packets on to another LAN. A brouter is incorrect because it is a combination of bridge and router that operates without protocol restrictions, routes data using a protocol it supports, and bridges data it cannot route.

**336.** What is an effective security control over an intranet?

    a. Callback

    b. Static passwords

    c. Firewalls

    d. Dynamic passwords

**336. c.** Because intranets connect between customers, suppliers, and the organization, access to information is a vital concern. Firewalls and routers keep intruders out of the intranets.

A callback is incorrect because it is a security mechanism used mostly on mainframe and mid-range computers. The static passwords are incorrect because they are not changed often, and as such, they are ineffective security controls. The dynamic passwords are not correct because they change each time a user is logged on to the system and are most effective security controls. All the other three choices are incorrect because they are most widely used in a mainframe computer environment. They are not used for intranets.

**337.** Which of the following ISO/OSI layers provide confidentiality, authentication, and data integrity services?

    a. Network layer

    b. Presentation layer

    c. Session layer

    d. Physical layer

**337. a.** The network layer is responsible for transmitting a message from the source to the destination. It provides routing (path control) services to establish connections across communications networks. Therefore, it requires confidentiality, authentication, and data integrity services to achieve this goal.

The presentation layer is incorrect because it provides authentication and confidentiality services but not data integrity. The presentation layer defines and transforms the format of data to make it useful to the receiving application.

Session layer is incorrect because it does not provide any security-related services. It establishes, manages, and terminates connections between applications and provides checkpoint recovery services. It helps users interact with the system and other users.

The physical layer is incorrect because it provides confidentiality service only. The physical layer provides for the transmission of unstructured bit streams over the communications channel. It is the innermost software that handles the electrical interface between a terminal and a modem.

**338.** **Which of the following ISO/OSI layers provide nonrepudiation services?**

    a.    Presentation layer

    b.    Application layer

    c.    Transport layer

    d.    Data link layer

*338. b.* The application layer provides nonrepudiation services, meaning that entities involved in a communication cannot deny having participated. It is a technique that assures genuine communication and that cannot subsequently be refuted.

The presentation layer is incorrect because it provides authentication and confidentiality services but not nonrepudiation. The presentation layer defines and transforms the format of data to make it useful to the receiving application. It provides a common means of representing a data structure in transit from one end system to another.

The transport layer is incorrect because it provides confidentiality, authentication, data integrity, and access control services but not nonrepudiation. It ensures an error-free, in-sequence exchange of data between end points. It is responsible for transmitting a message between one network user and another.

The data link layer is incorrect because it provides confidentiality service but not nonrepudiation. The data link layer provides a reliable transfer of data across physical links, an error flow control, a link-level encryption and decryption, and synchronization. It handles the physical transmission of frames over a single data link.

# SCENARIO-BASED QUESTIONS, ANSWERS, AND EXPLANATIONS

Use the following information to answer questions 1 through 7.

The RKG Company is reviewing its virtual private network (VPN) strategy. Its current vendor has a proprietary encryption protocol in place based on the Data Encryption Standard (DES). The one main office has a 1.5Mb connection to the Internet. It has 200 remote users on a variety of operating systems platforms. The primary uses for the remote users are order entry, timesheet reporting, and online meetings. The company has 1,000 clients that connect to the intranet for a custom order entry solution. Clients use the HTTPS protocol and a fixed password per account. They are willing to replace the current solution if a cost-effective alternative is available. The RKG priorities are security of remote connections and client connectivity.

**1.** **Which of the following is used to implement end-to-end VPNs?**

    a.    PPP

    b.    SSH

    c.    PPTP

    d.    SKIP

*1. c.* In the past, protocols such as PPP, SSH, and SKIP were used in a VPN. Later, point-to-point tunneling protocol (PPTP) became popular due to its hiding capabilities and is useful to implement end-to-end secure VPNs.

**2.** **Which of the following supersedes the point-to-point tunneling protocols (PPTP) used in VPNs?**

    a.    L2TP

    b.    L2F

    c.    IPsec

    d.    PPP

*2. c.* Internet protocol security (IPsec) supersedes PPTP. IPsec is a suite of authentication and encryption protocols that create VPNs so that data can be securely sent between the two end stations or networks. L2TP is Layer 2 tunneling protocol, L2F is Layer 2 forwarding, and PPP is point-to-point protocol. L2TP supersedes L2F.

**3.** **Which of the following is used for high-speed remote access with VPNs?**

    a.    Calling cards with ISDN

    b.    Cable modems with ADSL

    c.    Modem pools with ADSL

    d.    Toll-free lines with ISDN

*3. b.* Modem pools, calling cards, and toll-free arrangements can be an expensive alternative to cable modems and an asynchronous digital subscriber line (ADSL). An ISDN line is limited to 128 bits and is slow. Cable modems and ADSL technologies take advantage of the Internet and IPsec functioning at the network layer. These technologies provide high-speed remote access.

**4.** **The Internet Protocol security (IPsec) is usually implemented in which of the following?**

    a.    Bridge

    b.    Gateway

    c.    Firewall

    d.    Backbone

**4. c.**   Usually, IPsec is implemented on a firewall for VPNs. IPsec encrypts and encapsulates IP packets, so outsiders cannot observe the true source and destinations. VPNs enable a trusted network to communicate with another network over untrusted networks such as the Internet. A policy is needed for use of firewalls with VPNs. Any connection between firewalls over public networks should use encrypted VPNs to ensure the privacy and integrity of the data passing over the public network. Bridges, gateways, and backbones do not have the access control mechanism as the firewall.

**5.**   Which of the following permits IPsec to use external authentication services such as Kerberos and RADIUS?

   a.   EAP

   b.   PPP

   c.   CHAP

   d.   PAP

**5. a.**   The Internet Key Exchange (IKE) Version 2 of IPsec supports the extensible authentication protocol (EAP), which permits IPsec to use external authentication services such as Kerberos and RADIUS. The point-to-point protocol (PPP) standard specifies that password authentication protocol (PAP) and challenge handshake authentication protocol (CHAP) may be negotiated as authentication methods, but other methods can be added to the negotiation and used as well.

**6.**   A VPN creates a secure, private network over the Internet through all the following *except*:

   a.   Authentication

   b.   Encryption

   c.   Packet tunneling

   d.   Firewalls

**6. a.**   VPNs enable an organization to create a secure, private network over a public network such as the Internet. They can be created using software, hardware, or a combination to create a secure link between peers over a public network. The secure link is built through encryption, firewalls, and packet tunneling. Authentication is done outside the network.

**7.**   From a security viewpoint, which of the following should be the goal for a VPN?

   a.   Make only one exit point from a company's network to the Internet.

   b.   Make only one entry point to a company's network from the Internet.

   c.   Make only one destination point from a company's network to the Internet.

   d.   Make only one transmission point from the Internet to a company's network.

**7. b.**   The goal for a VPN should be to make it the only entry point to an organization's network from the Internet. This requires blocking all the organization's systems or making them inaccessible from the Internet unless outside users connect to the organization's network via its VPN.

# SOURCES AND REFERENCES

"Border Gateway Protocol Security (NIST SP 800-54)," National Institute of Standards and Technology (NIST), U.S. Department of Commerce, Gaithersburg, Maryland, June 2007.

"Establishing Wireless Robust Security Networks: A Guide to IEEE 802.11i (NIST SP800-97)," National Institute of Standards and Technology (NIST), U.S. Department of Commerce, Gaithersburg, Maryland, February 2007.

"Guide to Enterprise Telework and Remote Access Security (NIST SP800-46 Revision 1)," National Institute of Standards and Technology (NIST), U.S. Department of Commerce, Gaithersburg, Maryland, June 2009.

"Guidelines on Firewalls and Firewall Policy (NIST SP800-41 Revision 1)," National Institute of Standards and Technology (NIST), U.S. Department of Commerce, Gaithersburg, Maryland, September 2009.

"Guide to General Server Security (NIST SP800-123)," National Institute of Standards and Technology (NIST), U.S. Department of Commerce, Gaithersburg, Maryland, July 2008.

"Guide to IPsec VPNs (NIST SP800-77)," National Institute of Standards and Technology (NIST), U.S. Department of Commerce, Gaithersburg, Maryland, January 2005.

"Guide to Securing Legacy IEEE 802.11 Wireless Networks (NIST SP800-48R1)," National Institute of Standards and Technology (NIST), U.S. Department of Commerce, Gaithersburg, Maryland, July 2008.

"Guidelines on Securing Public Web Servers (NIST SP800-44 Version 2)," National Institute of Standards and Technology (NIST), U.S. Department of Commerce, Gaithersburg, Maryland, September 2007.

"Guide to Secure Web Services (NIST SP800-95)," National Institute of Standards and Technology (NIST), U.S. Department of Commerce, Gaithersburg, Maryland, August 2007.

"Guide to SSL VPNs, (NIST SP800-113 Draft)," National Institute of Standards and Technology (NIST), U.S. Department of Commerce, Gaithersburg, Maryland, August 2007.

"Guidelines for Securing Radio Frequency Identification (RFID) Systems (NIST SP800-98)," National Institute of Standards and Technology (NIST), The U.S. Department of Commerce, Gaithersburg, Maryland, April 2007.

"Guidelines on Cell Phone and PDA Security (NIST SP800-124)," National Institute of Standards and Technology (NIST), U.S. Department of Commerce, Gaithersburg, Maryland, October 2008.

"Guidelines on Electronic Mail Security (NIST SP800-45V2)," National Institute of Standards and Technology (NIST), U.S. Department of Commerce, Gaithersburg, Maryland, February 2007.

"Guideline on Network Security Testing (NIST SP800-42)," National Institute of Standards and Technology (NIST), U.S. Department of Commerce, Gaithersburg, Maryland, October 2003.

"Guidelines on Security and Privacy in Public Cloud Computing (NIST SP 800-144 Draft)," National Institute of Standards and Technology (NIST), U.S. Department of Commerce, Gaithersburg, Maryland, January 2011.

"Information Assurance Technical Framework (IATF), Release 3.1," National Security Agency (NSA), Fort Meade, Maryland, September 2002.

"Internet-Based Threats," Federal Deposit Insurance Corporation (FDIC), Washington, DC, www.fdic.gov.

"Instant Messaging, Security Technical Implementation Guide (STIG), Version 1, Release 2," Developed by Defense Information Systems Agency (DISA) for the Department of Defense (DOD), February 2008.

"Network Infrastructure, Security Technical Implementation Guide (STIG), Version 6, Release 2.1," Developed by Defense Information Systems Agency (DISA) for the Department of Defense (DOD), May 2005.

"P2P File-Sharing Technology," Federal Trade Commission (FTC), June 2005 (www.ftc.gov/reports/index.shtm).

"Peripheral, Security Technical Implementation Guide (STIG), Version 1, Release 0 (Draft)," Developed by Defense Information Systems Agency (DISA) for the Department of Defense (DOD), October 2004.

"Security Considerations for Voice Over IP systems (NIST SP800-58)," National Institute of Standards and Technology (NIST), U.S. Department of Commerce, Gaithersburg, Maryland, January 2005.

"Secure Domain Name System Deployment (NIST SP800-81)," National Institute of Standards and Technology (NIST), U.S. Department of Commerce, Gaithersburg, Maryland, May 2006.

Spyware Workshop, Federal Trade Commission (FTC), March 2005 (www.ftc.gov/reports/index.shtm).

"Technical Guide to Information Security Testing (NIST SP800-115 Draft)," National Institute of Standards and Technology (NIST), U.S. Department of Commerce, Gaithersburg, Maryland, November 2007.

"Security Architecture for Internet Protocol (IETF RFC 2401)," Kent & Atkinson, Internet Engineering Task Force (IETF), November 1998.

"Securing Microsoft's Cloud Infrastructure," a white paper published May 2009 by Microsoft Global Foundation Services.

Tanenbaum, Andrew S. 2003. *Computer Networks*, Fourth Edition, Chapter 5: Upper Saddle River, New Jersey: Prentice Hall PTR.

# DOMAIN 3

## Information Security Governance and Risk Management

### TRADITIONAL QUESTIONS, ANSWERS, AND EXPLANATIONS

1. **For information systems security, a penetration is defined as which of the following combinations?**

   a. Attack plus breach

   b. Attack plus threat

   c. Threat plus breach

   d. Threat plus countermeasure

   *1. a.* A penetration is the successful act of bypassing the security mechanisms of a computer system. An attack is an attempt to violate data security. A breach is the successful circumvention or disablement of a security control, with or without detection, which if carried to completion could result in penetration of the system. A threat is any circumstance or event with the potential to cause harm to a system in the form of destruction or modification of data, or denial-of-service. A countermeasure is any action, control, device, procedure, technique, or other measure that reduces the vulnerability of a threat to a system.

2. **Which of the following is *not* a basic objective of computer-based information systems security?**

   a. Protection of system assets from loss, damage, and misuse

   b. Accuracy of data and reliability of application processes

   c. Availability of information and application processes

   d. Control of data analysis

*2. d.* The control of information protection, accuracy, availability, and dissemination, not the control of data analysis, is one of the basic objectives of computer-based information systems security. Data analysis determines whether security objectives were achieved.

3. **Which of the following is the primary purpose of plan of action and milestones document?**

   a.   To reduce or eliminate known vulnerabilities

   b.   To use findings from security control assessments

   c.   To apply findings from security impact analyses

   d.   To implement findings from continuous monitoring activities

*3. a.* The primary purpose of a plan of action and milestones (POA&M) document is to correct deficiencies and to reduce or eliminate known vulnerabilities. The POA&M document updates are based on findings from security control assessment, security impact analyses, and continuous monitoring activities.

4. **For information systems security, an exposure is defined as which of the following combinations?**

   a.   Attack plus breach

   b.   Threat plus vulnerability

   c.   Threat plus attack

   d.   Attack plus vulnerability

*4. d.* An exposure is an instance of vulnerability in which losses may result from the occurrence of one or more attacks (i.e., attack plus vulnerability). An attack is an attempt to violate data security. Vulnerability is a weakness in security policy, procedure, personnel, management, administration, hardware, software, or facilities affecting security that may allow harm to an information system. The presence of vulnerability does not in itself cause harm. It is a condition that may allow the information system to be harmed by an attack. A threat is any circumstance or event with the potential to cause harm to a system in the form of destruction or modification of data or denial-of-service. A breach is the successful circumvention or disablement of a security control, with or without detection, which if carried to completion, could result in a penetration of the system. Note that vulnerability comes first and breach comes next.

5. **The benefits of good information security include which of the following?**

   1.   Reduces risks

   2.   Improves reputation

   3.   Increases confidence

   4.   Enhances trust from others

   a.   1 and 2

   b.   2 and 3

    c.    1, 2, and 3

    d.    1, 2, 3, and 4

**5. d.** All four items are benefits of good information security. It can even improve efficiency by avoiding wasted time and effort in recovering from a computer security incident.

**6.** **For risk mitigation, which of the following technical security controls are pervasive and interrelated with other controls?**

    a.    Supporting controls

    b.    Prevention controls

    c.    Detection controls

    d.    Recovery controls

**6. a.** From a risk mitigation viewpoint, technical security controls are divided into two categories: supporting controls and other controls (i.e., prevention, detection, and recovery controls). Supporting controls are, by their nature, pervasive and interrelated with many other controls such as prevention, detection, and recovery controls. Supporting controls must be in place to implement other controls, and they include identification, cryptographic key management, security administration, and system protection.

Preventive controls focus on preventing security breaches from occurring in the first place. Detection and recovery controls focus on detecting and recovering from a security breach.

**7.** **Information security must follow which of the following?**

    a.    Top-down process

    b.    Bottom-up process

    c.    Top-down and bottom-up

    d.    Bottom-up first, top-down next

**7. a.** Information security must be a top-down process requiring a comprehensive security strategy explicitly linked to the organization's business processes and strategy. Getting direction, support, and buy-in from top management sets the right stage or right tone for the entire organization.

**8.** **Information security baselines for information assets vary depending on which of the following?**

    a.    Availability and reliability

    b.    Sensitivity and criticality

    c.    Integrity and accountability

    d.    Assurance and nonrepudiation

**8. b.** Information security baselines vary depending on the sensitivity and criticality of the information asset, which is part of the confidentiality goal. The other three choices are not related to the confidentiality goal.

**9.** **Which of the following characteristics of information security are critical for electronic transactions?**

    a.    Trust and accountability

    b.    Trust and usefulness

    c.    Usefulness and possession

    d.    Accountability and possession

*9. a.* Trust and accountability are critical and needed in electronic transactions to make the customer comfortable with transactions, whereas usefulness and possession are needed to address theft, deception, and fraud.

**10.** **From a corporate viewpoint, information integrity is most needed in which of the following?**

    a.    Financial reporting

    b.    Inventory information

    c.    Trade secrets

    d.    Intellectual property

*10. a.* Corporate financial reporting requires integrity of information so that it is protected against unauthorized modification. The scope of financial reporting includes presenting balance sheet, income statement, cash flows, and the annual report with footnotes and disclosures.

Confidentiality is required to protect personnel (employees) data such as medical records, trade secrets, or intellectual property rights (e.g., copyrights) and business data such as shipping, billing, and inventory information.

**11.** **The relative priority given to confidentiality, integrity, and availability goals varies according to which of the following?**

    1.    Type of information system

    2.    Cost of information system

    3.    Data within the information system

    4.    Business context of use

        a.    1 and 2

        b.    2 and 3

        c.    1 and 4

        d.    3 and 4

*11. d.* The relative priority and significance given to confidentiality, integrity, and availability goals vary according to the data within the information system and the business context in which they are used. Cost and the type of information systems used are important but not that relevant to these goals.

**12.** **Effective information security governance requires which of the following?**

1. Corporate executive management endorsement

2. IT executive management endorsement

3. Board member endorsement

4. IT security officer endorsement

    a. 1 and 2

    b. 1 and 3

    c. 2 and 4

    d. 3 and 4

*12. b.* Corporate executive management must be conducive to effective information security governance. When corporate senior management follows the policies, it sends a positive signal to the rest of the organization. All the board members should endorse the information security governance policies. Note that the corporate executive management and the board members approve and endorse the security policies while the IT executive management and the IT security officer implements such policies.

**13.** **Which of the following is the major purpose of self-assessment of information security for improving the security?**

    a. Establish future targets

    b. Understand the current status

    c. Find out the industry average

    d. Analyze the current target

*13. a.* Information security self-assessment results can be used to establish targets for future development, based on where the organization wants to reach (major purpose) and how to improve security. The other three choices (minor purposes) can help in establishing future targets.

**14.** **What does risk analysis in the contingency planning process *not* include?**

    a. Prioritization of applications

    b. Development of test procedures

    c. Assessment of threat impact on the organization

    d. Development of recovery scenarios

*14. b.* Test procedures are detailed instructions that usually are not considered during a risk analysis exercise. Risk analysis is the initial phase of the contingency planning process, whereas testing comes after developing and documenting the plan. Application prioritization, assessment of impact on the organization (exposures and implications), and recovery scenarios are part of the risk analysis exercise. Risk analysis is a prerequisite to a complete and meaningful disaster recovery–planning program. It is the assessment of threats to resources and the determination of the amount of protection necessary to adequately safeguard them.

**15.** **Which of the following is *not* a key activity that facilitates the integration of information security governance components?**

    a.   Operational planning

    b.   Organizational structure

    c.   Roles and responsibilities

    d.   Enterprise architecture

*15. a.* The key activities that facilitate integration of information security governance components include strategic planning, organizational structure (design and development), roles and responsibilities, enterprise architecture, and security objectives. Operational planning is derived from strategic planning.

**16.** **Which of the following is *not* an example of protected communications controls that are part of technical preventive controls?**

    a.   Cryptographic technologies

    b.   Data encryption methods

    c.   Discretionary access controls

    d.   Escrowed encryption algorithms

*16. c.* Discretionary access controls (DAC) define access control security policy. The other choices are examples of protected communications controls, which ensure the integrity, availability, and confidentiality of sensitive information while it is in transit.

Cryptographic technologies include data encryption standard (DES), Triple DES (3DES), and secure hash standard. Data encryption methods include virtual private networks (VPNs) and Internet Protocol security (IPsec). Escrowed encryption algorithms include Clipper.

**17.** **For risk mitigation strategies, which of the following is *not* a proper and effective action to take when a determined attacker's potential or actual cost is too great?**

    a.   Apply security design principles.

    b.   Decrease an attacker's motivation.

    c.   Implement security architectural design.

    d.   Establish nontechnical security controls.

*17. b.* Usually, protection mechanisms to deter a normal and casual attacker are applied to decrease an attacker's motivation by increasing the attacker's cost when the attacker's cost is less than the potential gain for the attacker. However, these protection mechanisms may not prevent a determined attacker because the attacker's potential gain could be more than the cost or the attacker is seeking for a strategic and competitive advantage with the attack.

The other three choices are proper and effective actions to take when the potential or actual cost for an attacker is too great, whether the attacker is a normal, casual, or determined, because they are stronger protection mechanisms. Both technical and nontechnical security controls can be used to limit the extent of the attack.

**18.** **Which of the following actions are required to manage residual risk when new or enhanced security controls are implemented?**

1. Eliminate some of the system's vulnerabilities.

2. Reduce the number of possible threat-source/vulnerability pairs.

3. Add a targeted security control.

4. Reduce the magnitude of the adverse impact.

    a. 1 and 2

    b. 1 and 3

    c. 2 and 4

    d. 1, 2, 3, and 4

*18. d.* Implementation of new or enhanced security controls can mitigate risk by (i) eliminating some of the system's vulnerabilities (flaws and weaknesses) thereby reducing the number of possible threat-source/vulnerability pairs, (ii) adding a targeted control to reduce the capacity and motivation of a threat-source, and (iii) reducing the magnitude of the adverse impact by limiting the extent of a vulnerability.

**19.** **Which of the following ongoing security monitoring activities are more valuable in determining the effectiveness of security policies and procedures implementation?**

    a. Plans of action and milestones

    b. Configuration management

    c. Incident statistics

    d. Network monitoring

*19. c.* All four choices are examples of ongoing security monitoring activities. Incident and event statistics are more valuable in determining the effectiveness of security policies and procedures implementation. These statistics provide security managers with further insight into the status of security programs under their control and responsibility.

**20.** **Which of the following pairs of security objectives, rules, principles, and laws are in conflict with each other?**

    a. All-or-nothing access principle and the security perimeter rule

    b. Least privilege principle and employee empowerment

    c. File protection rules and access granularity principle

    d. Trans-border data flows and data privacy laws

*20. b.* Least privilege is a security principle that requires that each subject be granted the most restrictive set of privileges needed for the performance of authorized tasks. The application of this principle limits the damage resulting from an accident, error, or unauthorized use. This is in great conflict with employee empowerment in which employees are given freedom to do a wide variety of tasks in a given time period. Much discretion is left to each employee to achieve the stated goals.

The all-or-nothing access principle means access is either to all objects or none at all. The security perimeter rule uses increasingly strong defenses as one approach the core information or resources sought. Both strengthen the security practices.

File protection rules are designed to inhibit unauthorized access, modification, and deletion of a file. The access granularity principle states that protection at the data file level is considered coarse granularity, whereas protection at the data field level is considered to be of a finer granularity. Both strengthen the security practices.

The objectives of trans-border data flows and data privacy laws are to protect personal data from unauthorized disclosure, modification, and destruction. Trans-border data flow is the transfer of data across national borders. Privacy refers to the social balance between an individual's right to keep information confidential and the societal benefit derived from sharing information. Both strengthen the security practices.

**21.** Which of the following is *not* the major purpose of information system security plans?

    a.    Describe major application systems.

    b.    Define the security requirements.

    c.    Describe the security controls.

    d.    Delineate the roles and responsibilities.

*21. a.* The information security plan should reflect inputs from various managers with responsibilities concerning the system. Major applications are described when defining security boundaries of a system, meaning boundaries are established within and around application systems.

The major purposes of the information system security plan are to (i) provide an overview of the security requirements of the system, (ii) describe the security controls in place or planned for meeting those requirements, (iii) delineate the roles and responsibilities, and (iv) define the expected behavior of all individuals who access the system.

**22.** The information system security plan is an important deliverable in which of the following processes?

    a.    Configuration management

    b.    System development life cycle

    c.    Network monitoring

    d.    Continuous assessment

**22. b.** The information system security plan is an important deliverable in the system development life cycle (SDLC) process. Those responsible for implementing and managing information systems must participate in addressing security controls to be applied to their systems. The other three choices are examples of ongoing information security program monitoring activities.

23. Which of the following approves the system security plan prior to the security certification and accreditation process?

    a.    Information system owner

    b.    Program manager

    c.    Information system security officer

    d.    Business owner

**23. c.** Prior to the security certification and accreditation process, the information system security officer (the authorizing official, independent from the system owner) typically approves the security plan. In addition, some systems may contain sensitive information after the storage media is removed. If there is a doubt whether sensitive information remains on a system, the information system security officer should be consulted before disposing of the system because the officer deals with technical aspects of a system. The information system owner is also referred to as the program manager and business owner.

24. Which of the following is the key factor in the development of the security assessment and authorization policy?

    a.    Risk management

    b.    Continuous monitoring

    c.    Testing the system

    d.    Evaluating the system

**24. a.** An organization's risk management strategy is the key factor in the development of the security assessment and authorization policy. The other three choices are part of the purpose of assessing the security controls in an information system.

25. Which of the following is a prerequisite for developing an information system security plan?

    1.    Security categorization of a system

    2.    Analysis of impacts

    3.    Grouping of general support systems

    4.    Labeling of major application systems

        a.    1 and 4

        b.    2 and 3

        c.    1 and 2

        d.    3 and 4

**25. c.** Before the information system security plan can be developed, the information system and the data/information resident within that system must be categorized based on impact analysis (i.e., low, medium, or high impact). Then a determination can be made as to which systems in the inventory can be logically grouped into general support systems or major application systems.

26. Which of the following defines security boundaries for an information system?

1. Information

2. Personnel

3. Equipment

4. Funds

    a. 1 only

    b. 1 and 2

    c. 1 and 3

    d. 1, 2, 3, and 4

**26. d.** The process of uniquely assigning information resources (e.g., information, personnel, equipment, funds, and IT infrastructure) to an information system defines the security boundary for that system.

27. For new information systems, which of the following can be interpreted as having budgetary authority and responsibility for developing and deploying the information systems?

    a. Security control

    b. Management control

    c. Operational control

    d. Technical control

**27. b.** For new information systems, management control can be interpreted as having budgetary or programmatic authority and responsibility for developing and deploying the information systems. For current systems in the inventory, management control can be interpreted as having budgetary or operational authority for the day-to-day operation and maintenance of the information systems.

28. Which of the following actions should be implemented when a security function is unable to execute automated self-tests for verification?

1. Compensating controls

2. System-specific controls

3. Common controls

4. Accept the risk

a.   1 only

b.   2 and 3

c.   1, 2, and 3

d.   1, 2, 3, and 4

**28. d.**   For those security functions that are unable to execute automated self-tests, organizations should either implement compensating controls (i.e., management, technical, and operational controls), system-specific controls, common controls, or a combination of these controls. Otherwise, organization's management explicitly accepts the risk of not performing the verification process.

**29.**   **Compensating security controls for an information system should be used by an organization only under which of the following conditions?**

1.   Selecting compensating controls from the security control catalog

2.   Providing justification for the use of compensating controls

3.   Performing a formal risk assessment

4.   Accepting the risk associated with the use of compensating controls

    a.   1 only

    b.   3 only

    c.   1 and 3

    d.   1, 2, 3, and 4

**29. d.**   Compensating security controls for an information system should be used by an organization only under the following conditions: (i) the organization selects the compensating controls from the security control catalog, (ii) the organization provides a complete and convincing rationale and justification for how the compensating controls provide an equivalent security capability or level of protection for the information system, and (iii) the organization assesses and formally accepts the risk associated with using the compensating controls in the information system.

**30.**   **Common security controls can be applied to which of the following?**

1.   All of an organization's information systems

2.   A group of systems at a specific site

3.   Common systems at multiple sites

4.   Common subsystems at multiple sites

    a.   1 only

    b.   2 only

    c.   1 and 2

    d.   1, 2, 3, and 4

**30. d.** Common security controls can apply to (i) all of an organization's information systems, (ii) a group of information systems at a specific site, or (iii) common information systems, subsystems, or applications, including hardware, software, and firmware, deployed at multiple operational sites.

31. Which of the following should form the basis for management authorization to process information in a system or to operate an information system?

    a.    A plan of actions

    b.    Milestones

    c.    System security plan

    d.    Assessment report

**31. c.** Management authorization to process information in a system or to operate a system should be based on the assessment of management, operational, and technical controls. Because the system security plan establishes and documents the security controls, it should form the basis for the authorization, supplemented by the assessment report and the plan of actions and milestones.

32. Periodic assessment of the system security plan requires a review of changes occurring in which of the following areas?

    1.    System status

    2.    System scope

    3.    System architecture

    4.    System interconnections

        a.    1 and 2

        b.    3 and 4

        c.    1, 2, and 3

        d.    1, 2, 3, and 4

**32. d.** After the information system security plan is accredited, it is important to periodically assess the plan and review any change in system status, system scope, system architecture, and system interconnections.

33. The effectiveness of security controls depends on which of the following?

    1.    System management

    2.    Legal issues

    3.    Quality assurance

    4.    Management controls

a. 1 only

b. 3 only

c. 4 only

d. 1, 2, 3, and 4

**33. d.** The effectiveness of security controls depends on such factors as system management, legal issues, quality assurance, internal controls, and management controls. Information security needs to work with traditional security disciplines, including physical and personnel security.

**34.** **For information risk assessment, which of the following can improve the ability to realistically assess threats?**

a. Intrusion detection tools

b. Natural threat sources

c. Human threat sources

d. Environmental threat sources

**34. a.** Common threat sources collect data on security threats, which include natural threats, human threat sources, and environmental threat sources. In addition, intrusion detection tools collect data on security events, thereby improving the ability to realistically assess threats to information.

**35.** **Which of the following provides a 360-degree inspection of the system during the vulnerability identification of a system in the risk assessment process?**

a. Automated vulnerability scanning tools

b. Security requirement checklist

c. Security advisories

d. Security test and evaluation

**35. b.** Developing a security requirements checklist, based on the security requirements specified for the system during the conceptual, design, and implementation phases of the system development life cycle (SDLC), can be used to provide a 360-degree inspection of the system.

Automated vulnerability scanning tools and security test and evaluation augment the basic vulnerability reviews. Security advisories are typically provided by the vendor and give the organization up-to-date information on system vulnerabilities and remediation strategies

**36.** **During the risk assessment process of a system, what is the level of risk to the system derived by?**

a. Multiplying the threat likelihood rating with the impact level

b. Subtracting the threat likelihood rating from the impact level

c. Adding the threat likelihood rating to the impact level

d. Dividing the threat likelihood rating by the impact level

*36. a.* When the ratings for threat likelihood (i.e., high, moderate, or low) and impact levels (i.e., high, moderate, or low) have been determined through appropriate analysis, the level of risk to the system and the organization can be derived by multiplying the ratings assigned for threat likelihood (e.g., probability) and threat impact level.

**37.** **The effectiveness of recommended security controls is primarily related to which of the following?**

    a.   System safety

    b.   System reliability

    c.   System complexity

    d.   System regulations

*37. c.* The effectiveness of recommended security controls is primarily related to system complexity and compatibility. The level and type of security controls should fit with the system complexity, meaning more controls are needed for complex systems and fewer controls are needed for simple systems. At the same time, security controls should match the system compatibility, meaning application-oriented controls are needed for application systems, and operating system–oriented controls are needed for operating systems. Other factors that should be considered include legislation and regulations, the organization's policy, system impact, system safety, and system reliability.

**38.** **Risk mitigation does *not* strive to do which of the following?**

    a.   Control identification

    b.   Control prioritization

    c.   Control evaluation

    d.   Control implementation

*38. a.* Risk mitigation strives to prioritize, evaluate, and implement the appropriate risk-reducing controls recommended from the risk assessment process. Control identification is performed in the risk assessment process, which comes before risk mitigation.

**39.** **Which one of the following items can be a part of other items?**

    a.   Management controls

    b.   Operational controls

    c.   Technical controls

    d.   Preventive controls

*39. d.* System security controls selected are grouped into one of the three categories of management, operational, or technical controls. Each one of these controls can be preventive in nature.

**40.** **Risk management activities are performed for periodic system re-authorization in which of the following system development life cycle (SDLC) phases?**

    a.   Initiation

    b.   Development/acquisition

    c.   Implementation

    d.   Operation/maintenance

*40. d.*   In the operation/maintenance phase of the SDLC, risk management activities are performed for periodic system re-authorization or re-accreditation.

**41.** **Which of the following are the fundamental reasons why organizations implement a risk management process for their IT systems?**

    1.   Need for minimizing negative impact on an organization

    2.   Need for sound basis in decision making

    3.   Need for inventing a new risk management methodology for each SDLC phase

    4.   Need for noniterative process used in risk management

        a.   1 and 2

        b.   1 and 3

        c.   2 and 4

        d.   3 and 4

*41. a.*   Minimizing a negative impact on an organization and need a for sound basis in decision making are the fundamental reasons why organizations implement a risk management process for their IT systems. The risk management methodology is the same regardless of the system development life cycle (SDLC) phase and it is an iterative process that can be performed during each major phase of the SDLC.

**42.** **From a risk management viewpoint, system migration is conducted in which of the following system development life cycle (SDLC) phases?**

    a.   Development/acquisition

    b.   Implementation

    c.   Operation/maintenance

    d.   Disposal

*42. d.*   In the disposal phase of the SDLC process, system migration is conducted in a secure and systematic manner.

**43.** For gathering information in the risk assessment process, proactive technical methods include which of the following?

    a.   Questionnaires

    b.   Onsite interviews

    c.   Document review

    d.   Network mapping tool

**43. d.**  A network mapping tool, which is an automated information scanning tool, can identify the services that run on a large group of hosts and provide a quick way of building individual profiles of the target IT system(s). The other three choices are not examples of technical methods, whether proactive.

**44.** Which of the following is *not* a recommended approach for identifying system vulnerabilities?

    a.   Using vulnerability sources

    b.   Using threat sources

    c.   Conducting system security testing

    d.   Using security requirements checklist

**44. b.**  Vulnerabilities (flaws and weaknesses) are exploited by the potential threat sources such as employees, hackers, computer criminals, and terrorists. Threat source is a method targeted at the intentional exploitation of a vulnerability or a situation that may accidentally exploit a vulnerability.

Recommended approaches for identifying system vulnerabilities include the use of vulnerability sources, the performance of system security testing, and the development of a security-requirements checklist.

**45.** From a risk mitigation viewpoint, which of the following is *not* an example of system protection controls that are part of supporting technical security controls?

    a.   Modularity

    b.   Layering

    c.   Need-to-know

    d.   Access controls

**45. d.**  From a risk mitigation viewpoint, technical security controls are divided into two categories: supporting controls and other controls (i.e., prevention, detection, and recovery controls). Supporting controls must be in place in order to implement other controls. Access controls are a part of preventive technical security controls, whereas system protections are an example of supporting technical security controls.

Some examples of system protections include modularity, layering, need-to-know, and trust minimization (i.e., minimization of what needs to be trusted).

**46.** **Which of the following controls is typically and primarily applied at the point of transmission or reception of information?**

    a.    Nonrepudiation services

    b.    Access controls

    c.    Authorization controls

    d.    Authentication controls

*46. a.* All these controls are examples of preventive technical security controls. Nonrepudiation control ensures that senders cannot deny sending information and that receivers cannot deny receiving it. As a result, nonrepudiation control is typically applied at the point of transmission or reception of information. Access controls, authorization controls, and authentication controls support nonrepudiation services.

**47.** **Setting performance targets for which of the following information security metrics is relatively easier than the others?**

    a.    Implementation metrics

    b.    Effectiveness metrics

    c.    Efficiency metrics

    d.    Impact metrics

*47. a.* Setting performance targets for effectiveness, efficiency, and impact metrics is much more complex than the implementation metrics because these aspects of security operations do not assume a specific level of performance. Managers need to apply both qualitative and subjective reasoning to set effectiveness, efficiency, and impact performance targets.

Implementation metrics measure the results of implementation of security policies, procedures, and controls (i.e., demonstrates progress in implementation efforts). Effectiveness/efficiency metrics measure the results of security services delivery (i.e., monitors the results of security controls implementation).

Impact metrics measure the results of business or mission impact of security activities and events (i.e., provides the most direct insight into the value of security to the firm).

**48.** **Which of the following is *not* an example of detective controls in information systems?**

    a.    Audit trails

    b.    Encryption

    c.    Intrusion detection

    d.    Checksums

*48. b.* Encryption is an example of preventive controls, which inhibit attempts to violate security policy. Detective controls warn of violations or attempted violation of security policies and include audit trails, intrusion detection methods, and checksums.

**49.** Loss of system or data integrity reduces which of the following?

    a.    Assurance

    b.    Authorization

    c.    Authentication

    d.    Nonrepudiation

**49. a.** Loss of system or data integrity reduces the assurance of an IT system because assurance provides the highest level of confidence in a system. The other three choices cannot provide such assurance.

**50.** Which of the following should be performed first?

    a.    Threat-source analysis

    b.    Vulnerability analysis

    c.    Threat analysis

    d.    Risk analysis

**50. b.** Threat analysis cannot be performed until after vulnerability analysis has been conducted because vulnerabilities lead to threats which, in turn, lead to risks. Threat-source analysis is a part of threat analysis. Therefore, vulnerability analysis should be performed first.

**51.** Which of the following risk mitigation options prioritizes, implements, and maintains security controls?

    a.    Risk assumption

    b.    Risk avoidance

    c.    Risk limitation

    d.    Risk planning

**51. d.** The purpose of a risk planning option is to manage risk by developing a risk mitigation plan that prioritizes, implements, and maintains security controls. The purpose of the risk assumption option is to accept the potential risk and continue operating the IT system. The goal of risk avoidance is to eliminate the risk cause and/or consequence. (For example, forgo certain functions of the system or shut down the system when risks are identified.) The goal of risk limitation is to authorize system operation for a limited time during which additional risk mitigation controls are being put into place.

**52.** All the following are access agreements for employees prior to granting access to a computer system *except*:

    a.    Rules of engagement

    b.    Rules of behavior

    c.    Non-disclosure agreement

    d.    Acceptable use agreement

**52. a.**   Rules of engagement applies to outside individuals (e.g., vendors, contractors, and consultants) when conducting penetration testing of a computer system. Employees do not have rules of engagement, and they are bound by the access agreements. Examples of access agreements include rules of behavior, non-disclosure agreements (i.e., conflict-of-interest statements), and acceptable use agreement (or policy).

**53.** In general, which of the following is *not* a cost-effective or practical procedure required of vendors, consultants, and contractors who are hired for a short period of time to assist with computer hardware and software related work?

      a.    Service-level agreement

      b.    Rules of engagement

      c.    Background checks

      d.    Conflict-of-interest clauses

**53. c.**   Due to higher turnover among vendors, consultants, and contractors and due to short timeframe work (e.g., a month or two), it is not cost effective or practical to conduct background checks because they are applicable to regular full-time employees. Vendors, consultants, and contractors must meet all the requirements mentioned in the other three choices. Background checks include contacting previous employers, verifying education with schools, and contacting friends and neighbors. However, for consultants and other non-employees, security clearance cheeks (e.g., police, court, and criminal records) are made when they handle sensitive information at work.

**54.** For risk mitigation strategies, which of the following is *not* a proper action to take when there is a likelihood that a vulnerability can be exploited?

      a.    Implement assurance techniques

      b.    Apply layered protections

      c.    Apply administrative controls

      d.    Implement architectural design

**54. a.**   Assurance is the grounds for confidence that the set of intended security controls in an information system are effective in their application. Assurance techniques include trustworthiness and predictable execution, which may not be effective or timely.

The other three choices reflect proper actions to take when there is likelihood that a vulnerability can be exploited.

**55.** Residual risk results from which of the following steps taken in the approach to control implementation, which is done as part of the risk mitigation strategy?

      a.    Conduct cost-benefit analysis

      b.    Select controls

      c.    Implement the selected controls

      d.    Develop a control implementation plan

**55. c.** Implementing the selected controls is the first step in the control implementation approach. The other three choices precede the implementation of the selected controls. The risk remaining after the implementation of new or enhanced security controls is the residual risk.

**56.** **As part of security control assessment, which of the following must be in place prior to the start of penetration testing work by outsiders?**

    a. Rules of behavior

    b. Rules of negotiation

    c. Rules of engagement

    d. Rules of employment

**56. c.** Detailed rules of engagement must be agreed upon by all parties before the commencement of any penetration testing scenario by outsiders. These rules of engagement contain tools, techniques, and procedures that are anticipated to be used by threat-sources in carrying out attacks.

Rules of behavior and rules of employment apply to internal employees. Rules of negotiation apply to both insiders and outsiders as a matter of work ethics.

**57.** **Which of the following is *not* an example of supporting technical security controls used in mitigating risk?**

    a. Identification

    b. Authentication

    c. Cryptographic key management

    d. Security administration

**57. b.** From a risk mitigation viewpoint, technical security controls are divided into two categories: supporting controls and other controls (i.e., prevention, detection, and recovery controls). This means supporting controls must be in place to implement other controls. Authentication is an example of preventive technical controls.

The other three choices (i.e., identification, cryptographic key management, and security administration) are examples of supporting technical security controls.

**58.** **Which of the following is *not* an example of system protections?**

    a. Least privilege

    b. Process separation

    c. Authorization

    d. Object reuse

**58. c.** Authorization is a part of preventive technical security controls, whereas system protections are an example of supporting technical security controls. Some examples of system protections include least privilege, process separation, and object reuse.

**59.** Which of the following is the best way to ensure an acceptable level of trustworthiness of an information system?

    a.    Component-by-component

    b.    Subsystem-by-subsystem

    c.    Function-by-function

    d.    System-by-system

**59. d.** Typically, components, subsystems, and functions are highly interrelated, making separation by trustworthiness problematic with unpredictable results. Hence, system-by-system trustworthiness is best because it is wholesome and inclusive of system components, subsystems, and functions.

**60.** Which of the following is an example of detective (detection) personnel security controls?

    a.    Separation of duties

    b.    Least privilege

    c.    User computer access registration

    d.    Rotation of duties

**60. d.** Rotation of duties is an example of detective (detection) personnel security controls, which are part of management security controls. The other three choices are examples of preventive personnel security controls.

**61.** Which of the following is *not* an example of preventive management security controls?

    a.    Conducting periodic review of security controls

    b.    Assigning security responsibilities

    c.    Developing system security plans

    d.    Conducting security awareness and training

**61. a.** Conducting periodic review of security controls to ensure that the controls are effective is an example of detection management security controls. The other three choices are examples of preventive management security controls.

**62.** Which of the following characterizes information domains?

    1.    Partitioning information

    2.    Access control needs

    3.    Levels of protection required

    4.    Classifying information

a.    1 and 2

b.    2 and 3

c.    3 and 4

d.    1, 2, 3, and 4

**62. d.**    The partitioning of information according to access control needs and levels of protection required yields categories of information. These categories are often called information domains. Classifying information as secret, top-secret, and sensitive is also called information domains where information is compartmentalized.

**63.**    **A failure of common security controls can increase which of the following?**

a.    System-specific risks

b.    Site-specific risks

c.    Subsystem-specific risks

d.    Organization-wide risks

**63. d.**    Common security controls are identified during a collaborative organization-wide process involving many parties. Because of the potential dependence on common security controls by many of an organization's information systems, a failure of such common controls may result in a significant increase in organization-wide risks (i.e., risk that arises from operating the system that depends on these security controls).

**64.**    **Which of the following is the first step in the risk management process?**

a.    Selecting security controls

b.    Accomplishing security categorization

c.    Satisfying minimum security requirements

d.    Defining security control baselines

**64. b.**    Security categorization of data/information and information systems is the first step in the risk assessment process. Subsequent to the security categorization process, an organization must select an appropriate set of security controls for their information systems that satisfy the minimum-security requirements. The selected set of security controls (i.e., limited, serious, or catastrophic) must be one of three security control baselines (i.e., low, moderate, or high) that are associated with the designated impact levels of the information systems.

**65.**    **A periodic assessment of the system security plan requires a review of changes occurring in which of the following areas?**

1.    System functionality

2.    System design

3.    Information system owner

4.    System authorizing official

a.   1 and 2

b.   3 and 4

c.   1, 2, and 3

d.   1, 2, 3, and 4

**65. d.**   After the information system security plan is accredited, it is important to periodically assess the plan; review any change in system functionality, system design, information system owner, and system authorizing official.

**66.**   **Disciplinary actions are part of which of the following components of an information security program policy?**

a.   Purpose

b.   Scope

c.   Compliance

d.   Responsibilities

**66. c.**   Components of an information security program policy include purpose, scope, responsibilities, and compliance. The compliance component defines penalties and disciplinary actions.

**67.**   **Which of the following are required to enforce system-specific policies?**

1.   Logical access controls

2.   Physical security measures

3.   Management controls

4.   Technical controls

a.   1 and 2

b.   2 and 3

c.   3 and 4

d.   1, 2, 3, and 4

**67. d.**   Both technology-based and nontechnology-based controls are required to enforce system-specific policies. This covers all the four items listed in the question.

**68.**   **Benefits of central computer security programs include which of the following?**

1.   Sharing information

2.   Installing technical controls

3.   Controlling virus infections

4.   Administering day-to-day computer security

    a.    1 and 2

    b.    1 and 3

    c.    2 and 3

    d.    2 and 4

**68. b.** Organizations can develop expertise centrally and then share it, reducing the need to contract out repeatedly for similar services. The central computer security program can help facilitate information sharing. Similarly, controlling virus infections from central location is efficient and economical. Options 2 and 4 are examples of benefits of a system-level computer security program.

**69.** **Which of the following are essential to improving IT security performance through metrics?**

    1.    Quantifying performance gaps

    2.    Providing insights into root causes

    3.    Submitting reports to internal management

    4.    Collecting meaningful data for analysis

        a.    1 and 2

        b.    2 and 3

        c.    3 and 4

        d.    1, 2, 3, and 4

**69. a.** Performance metrics are essential to performance improvement because they quantify performance gaps and provide insights into root causes of inadequate performance. Submitting reports to internal management and collecting meaningful data for analysis support quantifying performance gaps and providing insights into root causes.

**70.** **The concept of least privilege is primarily based on which of the following?**

    a.    Risk assessment

    b.    Information flow enforcement

    c.    Access enforcement

    d.    Account management

**70. a.** An organization employs the concept of least privilege primarily for specific duties and information systems, including specific ports, protocols, and services in accordance with risk assessments as necessary to adequately mitigate risk to the organization's operations, assets, and individuals. The other three choices are specific components of access controls.

**71.** **Results-based training does *not* focus on which of the following?**

    a.    Roles and responsibilities

    b.    Understanding levels

    c.    Job titles

    d.    Backgrounds

***71. c.*** The results-based training focuses on job functions or roles and responsibilities, not job titles, and recognizes that individuals have unique backgrounds, and therefore, different levels of understanding.

**72.** **Which of the following are essential to reach a higher rate of success in protecting information?**

    1.    Proven security tools and techniques

    2.    Encouraging professional certification

    3.    Training employees in security policies

    4.    Role-based security responsibilities

    a.    1 and 2

    b.    2 and 3

    c.    1 and 4

    d.    3 and 4

***72. d.*** Organizations that continually train their workforce in organizational security policy and role-based security responsibilities have a higher rate of success in protecting information.

Proven security tools and techniques and encouraging professional certification indirectly support training employees in security policies and role-based security responsibilities.

**73.** **Which of the following is the ultimate purpose of information security performance metrics?**

    a.    To pinpoint problems

    b.    To scope resources for remediation

    c.    To track ownership of data

    d.    To improve information security

***73. d.*** The ultimate purpose of information security performance metrics is to support the organizational requirements and to assist in internal efforts to improve information security.

Intermediate benefits of performance measurement, leading to the ultimate purpose, include assisting with pinpointing problems, scoping the resources for remediation, tracking the status of remediation, and quantifying successes. Measurement also creates accountability for results by tracking ownership of data and its related activities.

**74.** What should the information security manager do when the residual risk has *not* been reduced to an acceptable level?

    a.    Repeat the risk management cycle.

    b.    Develop new policies and procedures.

    c.    Implement new security technologies.

    d.    Establish a specific schedule for assessing risk.

*74. a.* If the residual risk has not been reduced to an acceptable level, the information security manager must repeat the risk management cycle to identify a way of lowering the residual risk to an acceptable level. The other three choices are not strong enough actions to reduce the residual risk to an acceptable level.

**75.** The level of protection for an IT system is determined by an evaluation of which of the following elements?

    1.    Availability

    2.    Integrity

    3.    Sensitivity

    4.    Criticality

        a.    1 and 2

        b.    2 and 3

        c.    3 and 4

        d.    1, 2, 3, and 4

*75. c.* All IT systems and applications require some level of protection to ensure confidentiality, integrity, and availability, which is determined by an evaluation of the sensitivity and criticality of the information processed, the relation of the system to the organization mission, and the economic value of the system components. Sensitivity and criticality are a part of the confidentiality goal.

**76.** Which of the following IT metrics types measure the results of security services delivery?

    1.    Implementation metrics

    2.    Effectiveness metrics

    3.    Efficiency metrics

    4.    Impact metrics

a.   1 and 2

b.   2 and 3

c.   1 and 4

d.   3 and 4

**76. b.**   Implementation metrics measures the implementation of security policy. Effectiveness and efficiency metrics measures the results of security services delivery. Impact metrics measures the business or mission impact of security events.

**77.**   **Which of the following factors affects the trustworthiness of an information system?**

1.   Security functionality

2.   Security categorization

3.   Security certification

4.   Security assurance

   a.   1 and 2

   b.   1 and 4

   c.   3 and 4

   d.   1, 2, 3, and 4

**77. b.**   Two factors affecting the trustworthiness of an information system include security functionality (i.e., security features employed within the system) and security assurance (i.e., the grounds for confidence that the security functionality is effective in its application).

Security categorization and security certification are not relevant here because security categorization classifies systems according to security levels, and security certification deals with approving a new system prior to its operation.

**78.**   **When engaging information system services from an external service provider, which of the following is needed to mitigate security risk?**

   a.   Chain-of-custody

   b.   Chain-of-command

   c.   Chain-of-documents

   d.   Chain-of-trust

**78. d.**   A chain-of-trust requires that an internal organization establish and retain a level of confidence that each external service provider consider adequate security protection for the services rendered to the internal organization.

Chain-of-custody refers to preserving evidence, and it may include chain-of-documents. Chain-of-command is a management principle, which follows job hierarchy in giving orders to subordinate employees by a supervising employee.

**79.** **From a security viewpoint, which of the following is the most important document prepared by an external information system service provider?**

    a.    Service provider security role

    b.    End user security role

    c.    Memorandum of agreement

    d.    Service-level agreement

*79. d.*   The external information system services documentation must include the service provider security role, end user security role, signed contract, memorandum of agreement before the signed contract, and service-level agreement (most important). The service-level agreement (SLA) defines the expectations of performance for each required security control, describes measurable outcomes, and identifies remedies and response requirements for any identified instance of noncompliance.

**80.** **The results of information-security program assessment reviews can be used to do which of the following?**

    1.    To support the certification and accreditation process

    2.    To support the continuing monitoring requirement

    3.    To prepare for audits

    4.    To improve the system's security posture

        a.    1 and 2

        b.    2 and 3

        c.    3 and 4

        d.    1, 2, 3, and 4

*80. d.*   The results of information-security program assessment reviews can provide a much more reliable measure of security effectiveness. These results may be used to (i) fulfill the organization's internal reporting requirements, (ii) support the certification and accreditation process for the system, (iii) support the continuing monitoring requirements, (iv) prepare for audits, and (v) identify resource needs to improve the system's security posture.

**81.** **Which of the following should *not* be contained in the Rules of Behavior document?**

    a.    Copy of the security policy

    b.    Controls for working at home

    c.    Controls for dial-in access

    d.    Use of copyrighted work

*81. a.*   The rules of behavior should not be a complete copy of the security policy or procedures guide, but rather cover controls at a high level. Examples of controls contained in rules of behavior include controls for working at home and controls for dial-in access, use of copyrighted work, password usage, connections to the Internet, searching databases, and divulging information. The security policy may contain an acceptable use policy.

82. Which of the following represents the best definition and equation for a comprehensive and generic risk model?

    a.    Breach x Threat x Vulnerability

    b.    Attack + Threat + Impact

    c.    Threat x Vulnerability x Impact

    d.    Attack + Vulnerability + Impact

*82. c.* Risk is the potential for an unwanted outcome resulting from internal or external factors, as determined from the likelihood of occurrence and the associated consequences. In other words, risk is the product of interactions among threats, vulnerabilities, and impacts. Threats deal with events and actions with potential to harm, vulnerabilities are weaknesses, and impacts are consequences.

The other three choices are incorrect because they do not have the required components in the correct equation for the risk.

83. Which of the following has been determined to be a reasonable level of risk?

    a.    Minimum risk

    b.    Acceptable risk

    c.    Residual risk

    d.    Total risk

*83. b.* Acceptable risk is the level of residual risk that has been determined to be a reasonable level of potential loss or disruption for a specific computer system.

Minimum risk is incorrect because it is the reduction in the total risk that results from the impact of in-place safeguards or controls. Residual risk is incorrect because it results from the occurrence of an adverse event after adjusting for the impact of all safeguards in-place. Total risk is incorrect because it is the potential for the occurrence of an adverse event if no mitigating action is taken (i.e., the potential for any applicable threat to exploit system vulnerability).

84. When a contractor representing an organization uses an internal system to connect with an external organization's system for data exchange, the contractor should comply with which of the following agreed-upon trust relationships?

    1.    Conflict of interest statements

    2.    Rules of behavior

    3.    Remote session rules

    4.    Rules of operation

a. 1 only

b. 3 only

c. 2 and 4

d. 1, 2, 3, and 4

**84. d.** To comply with established trust relationships, employees and contractors have the same responsibility (principal and agent relationship) because the contractor is working on behalf of the internal organization. Hence, all the terms and conditions that apply to employees equally apply to contractors. These conditions include rules of behavior, remote session rules, rules of operation, and signed conflict of interest statements.

**85.** **The aim of risk analysis is to strike a(n):**

a. Technical balance between the impact of risks and the cost of protective measures

b. Operational balance between the impact of risks and the cost of protective measures

c. Economic balance between the impact of risks and the cost of protective measures

d. Legal balance between the impact of risks and the cost of protective measures

**85. c.** The aim of a risk analysis is to help systems management strike an economic balance between the impact of risks and the cost of protective measures. It lists risks first and protective measures second.

**86.** **To estimate the losses likely to occur when a threat is realized or a vulnerability is exploited, which of the following loss categories allow management the best means to estimate their potential losses?**

a. Single occurrence loss, actual loss

b. Expected loss, catastrophic loss

c. Catastrophic loss, actual loss

d. Expected loss, single occurrence loss

**86. d.** Two loss categories are usually identified, including (i) losses caused by threats with reasonably predictable occurrence rates, referred to as expected losses expressed as dollars per year and are computed as the product of occurrence rate, loss potential, and vulnerability factor, and (ii) losses caused by threats with a very low rate of occurrence (low-probability) that is difficult to estimate but the threat would cause a very high loss if it were to occur (high-consequence risk), referred to as a single occurrence loss and is expressed as the product of loss potential, vulnerability factor, and asset value. A catastrophic loss is referred to as a loss greater than its equity. An actual loss is the amount of assets or lives lost. Both catastrophic loss and actual loss do not enter into risk assessment because they are not estimable.

**87.** **From a security accountability viewpoint, which of the following pose a security risk?**

a. Executives and contractors

b. Full-time employees and contingent workers

    c.    Executives and full-time employees

    d.    Vendors and consultants

**87. b.** Most executives have an employment contract listing security policies, practices, procedures, and penalties for noncompliance of such policies and practices. Contractors, vendors, and consultants are bound by formal rules of engagement. Full-time employees operate under an employment-at-will arrangement; employees have no formal contract and can leave the company or the employer can terminate employment at any time. Contingent workers are part-time and short-time workers (temporary) and have no formal contract. In the absence of a formal contract or rules of engagement, it is difficult for the company to enforce or punish the full-time employees and contingent workers if they violate security policies and practices. Therefore, full-time employees and contingent workers are not truly accountable for the security in the absence of a formal contract (i.e., not legally bound and not enforceable), thus posing a security risk to the company.

**88.** What is the last thing to do upon friendly termination of an employee?

    a.    Conduct an exit interview.

    b.    Disable computer access immediately.

    c.    Take possession of keys and cards.

    d.    Send the employee to a career counselor.

**88. d.** The safest and first thing to do is to (i) disable computer access immediately, which should be a standard procedure, (ii) conduct an exit interview, and (iii) take possession of access keys and cards. The employee can be sent to a career counselor afterward (last thing).

**89.** Which of the following statements is true about data classification and application categorization for sensitivity?

    a.    Data classification and application categorization is the same.

    b.    There are clear-cut views on data classification and application categorization.

    c.    Data classification and application categorization must be organization-specific.

    d.    It is easy to use simple data classification and application categorization schemes.

**89. c.** No two organizations are the same, and it is especially true in cross-industries. For example, what works for a governmental organization may not work for a commercial organization. An example of data classification is critically sensitive, highly sensitive, sensitive, and nonsensitive.

**90.** What is the *least* effective technique for continually educating users in information systems security?

    a.    Presenting security awareness video programs

    b.    Posting policies on the intranet websites

    c.    Presenting one-size-fits-all security briefings

    d.    Declaring security awareness days

**90. c.** It is good to avoid a one-size-fits-all type of security briefing. It is important to relate security concerns to the specific risks faced by users in individual business units or groups and to ensure that security is an everyday consideration. Lax security can cost money and time. Security awareness is inexpensive and less time-consuming compared to installing security countermeasures.

**91. Trustworthy information systems are defined as:**

1. Operating within defined levels of risk

2. Handling environmental disruptions

3. Handling human errors

4. Handling purposeful attacks

    a. 1 only

    b. 3 only

    c. 4 only

    d. 1, 2, 3, and 4

**91. d.** Trustworthy information systems are those systems capable of being trusted to operate within defined levels of risk despite the environmental disruptions, human errors, and purposeful attacks expected to occur in the specified environments of operation.

**92. Which of the following combinations of conditions can put the IT assets at the most risk of loss?**

    a. System interconnectivity and poor security management

    b. System interconnectivity and poor controls over data sensitivity

    c. System interconnectivity and lack of system backups

    d. System interconnectivity and inadequate physical security

**92. a.** Poor security management does not proactively and systematically assess risks, monitor the effectiveness of security controls, and respond to identified problems. This situation can become much weaker with interconnected systems where the risk is the greatest. The other three choices are the result of poor security management.

**93. An IT security training program is a part of which of the following control categories?**

    a. Application controls

    b. General controls

    c. Administrative controls

    d. Technical controls

**93. c.** The security-training program is a part of administrative controls, which in turn, can be a part of management controls. Application controls relate to a specific application system, whereas general controls relate to a computer center. Technical controls can be useful in both application and general areas.

**94.** **What is the last step when an insider violates a security policy?**

    a.    Verbal warning

    b.    Dismissal

    c.    Legal action

    d.    Written warning

*94. c.* When an insider violates security policy, the first step is a verbal warning, followed by a written warning, dismissal, and the final step of legal action.

**95.** **Which of the following is referred to when data is transferred from high network users to low network users?**

    a.    Data downgrade

    b.    Data regrade

    c.    Data upgrade

    d.    Data release

*95. b.* Data regrade is the term used when data is transferred from high network users to low network users and from low network users to high network users.

Data downgrade is the change of a classification label to a lower label without the changing the contents of the data. Data upgrade is the change of a classification label to a higher label without the changing the contents of the data. Data release is the process of returning all unused disk space to the system when a dataset is closed at the end of processing.

**96.** **Which of the following must be done first to protect computer systems?**

    a.    Battling information abusers

    b.    Fighting hackers

    c.    Reducing vulnerabilities

    d.    Catching crackers

*96. c.* Reducing vulnerabilities decreases potential exposures and risks. The other three choices follow the vulnerabilities.

**97.** **Which of the following are major benefits of security awareness, training, and education programs accruing to an organization?**

    a.    Reducing fraud

    b.    Reducing unauthorized actions

    c.    Improving employee behavior

    d.    Reducing errors and omissions

**97. c.** Making computer system users aware of their security responsibilities and teaching them correct practices help users change their behavior. It also supports individual accountability, which is one of the most important ways to improve computer security. Without knowing the necessary security measures and knowing how to use them, users cannot be truly accountable for their actions. The other three choices are examples of major purposes of security awareness.

98. In developing a data security program for an organization, who should be responsible for defining security levels and access profiles for each data element stored in the computer system?

    a.    Database administrator

    b.    Systems programmer

    c.    Data owner

    d.    Applications programmer

**98. c.** Usually, the data owner defines security levels such as confidential or highly confidential and access profiles defining who can do what, such as add, change, or delete the data elements. It is the data owner who paid or sponsored the system for his department.

The database administrator is incorrect because he is concerned with creating and controlling the logical and physical database. The systems programmer is incorrect because he is responsible for installing new releases of systems software and monitoring the performance of systems software products. The applications programmer is incorrect because he is responsible for developing, testing, and maintaining computer-based application programs in the selected programming languages.

99. Which of the following is *not* a true statement about data collection efforts during IT security metrics development process?

    a.    Data collection process must be as nonintrusive as possible.

    b.    Collected data must have maximum usefulness.

    c.    Collected data must be valid.

    d.    More resources are needed to collect more data.

**99. d.** The data collection effort during the IT security metrics development process must be as nonintrusive as possible and of maximum usefulness to ensure that available resources are primarily used to correct problems, not simply to collect data for the sake of collecting. The collection of valid data is more important than collecting more data.

100. System or network administrators will be interested in which of the following IT security metrics?

    a.    Implementation

    b.    Effectiveness

c.    Efficiency

d.    Impact

**100. a.**  The four measurable aspects of IT security metrics speak to different stakeholders. System or network administrators want to know what went wrong during IT security implementation activities. Information security and program managers are interested in effectiveness and efficiency during IT security activities. The agency head or chief executive officer (CEO) is interested in the business and mission impact of IT security activities. As the primary stakeholders, the chief information officer (CIO) and information systems security officer are interested in the results of IT security metrics. As the secondary stakeholders, the chief financial officer (CFO), Inspector General (IG), or Chief Audit Executive (CAE) of Internal Audit are interested in the development and funding of IT security metrics.

**101.** **The prudent man concept is related to which of the following?**

    a.    Due care and due permissions

    b.    Due care and due rights

    c.    Due care and due diligence

    d.    Due care and due privileges

**101. c.**  The prudent man concept is related to due care and due diligence. Due care is maintaining reasonable care, whereas due diligence requires organizations to be vigilant and diligent. Good housekeeping in a data center is an example of due diligence. The prudent man concept states that reasonable people always act reasonably under the same conditions. Because people are infallible, courts and law require that people use reasonable care all the time.

Courts will find computer owners responsible for their insecure systems. Courts will not find liability every time a computer is hijacked. Rather, courts expect organizations to become reasonably prudent computer owners taking due care (reasonable care) to ensure adequate security. Due care means having the right policies and procedures, access controls, firewalls, and other reasonable security measures in place. Computer owners need not take super care, great care, or extraordinary care.

**102.** **What is the purpose of a system security plan?**

    1.    Document the security requirements of a system.

    2.    Describe the controls in place or planned.

    3.    Delineate roles and responsibilities.

    4.    Document the security protection of a system.

        a.    1 only

        b.    1 and 2

        c.    4 only

        d.    1, 2, 3, and 4

***102. d.*** The purpose of a system security plan is to provide an overview of the security requirements of the system and describe the controls in place or planned for meeting those requirements. The system security plan also delineates roles and responsibilities and expected behavior of all individuals who access the system. The system security plan should be viewed as documentation of the structured process of planning adequate, cost-effective security protection for a system.

**103.** **What does management authorization of a system to process information provide?**

1. Important quality control
2. Assessment of management controls
3. Assessment of operational controls
4. Assessment of technical controls

    a. 2 only

    b. 3 only

    c. 4 only

    d. 1, 2, 3, and 4

***103. d.*** Management authorization of a system to process information provides an important quality control. By authorizing processing in a system, the manager accepts its associated risk. Management authorization should be based on an assessment of management, operational, and technical controls.

**104.** **Which of the following should be performed prior to proceeding with the security certification and accreditation process for a system?**

    a. System security plan be developed

    b. System security plan be analyzed

    c. System security plan be updated

    d. System security plan be accepted

***104. a.*** Procedures should be in place outlining who reviews the security plan, keeps the plan current, and follows up on planned security controls. In addition, procedures should require that system security plans be developed and reviewed prior to proceeding with the security certification and accreditation process for the system.

**105.** **Which of the following individuals establishes the rules for appropriate use and protection of a system's data and information?**

    a. Chief information officer

    b. Information system security officer

    c. Information system owner

    d. Information owner

***105. d.*** The information owner is responsible for establishing the rules for appropriate uses and protection of a system's data and information. He establishes controls in terms of generation, collection, processing, dissemination, and disposal. The chief information officer (CIO) is incorrect because the CIO is responsible for developing and maintaining an organization-wide information security program. The information system security officer is incorrect because he is responsible for ensuring that the appropriate operational security posture is maintained for an information system. The information system owner (also known as program manager or business owner) is incorrect because he is responsible for the overall procurement, development, integration, modification, or operation and maintenance of the information system.

**106.** Which of the following states that every user should be *notified* prior to receiving authorization for access to a system and understand the consequences of noncompliance?

    a.    Rules-of-behavior

    b.    Rules-of-access

    c.    Rules-of-use

    d.    Rules-of-information

***106. a.*** The rules-of-behavior is a security control clearly delineating the responsibilities and expected behavior of all individuals with access to the system. The rules should state the consequences of inconsistent behavior or noncompliance and be made available to every user prior to receiving authorization for access to the system. Electronic signatures are acceptable for use in acknowledging the rules of behavior.

**107.** The baseline security controls can be tailored using the results from:

    1.    Assessment of risk

    2.    Specific threat information

    3.    Cost-benefit analyses

    4.    Availability of compensating controls

        a.    1 only

        b.    1 and 2

        c.    1, 2, and 3

        d.    1, 2, 3, and 4

***107. d.*** The baseline security controls can be tailored based on an assessment of risk and local conditions including organization-specific security requirements, specific threat information, cost-benefit analyses, the availability of compensating controls, or special circumstances.

**108.** For system security scoping guidance, which of the following addresses the breadth and depth of security control implementation?

    a.    Technology-related considerations

    b.    Physical infrastructure-related considerations

   c.    Scalability-related considerations

   d.    Public access–related considerations

***108. c.*** Scoping guidance provides an organization with specific terms and conditions on the applicability and implementation of individual security controls.

Scalability-related consideration addresses the breadth and depth of security control implementation. Technology-related considerations deal with specific technologies such as wireless, cryptography, and public key infrastructure. Physical infrastructure-related considerations include locks and guards, and environmental controls for temperature, humidity, lighting, fire, and power. Public access-related considerations address whether identification and authentication, and personnel security controls, are applicable to public access.

**109.** **The major reason for using compensating security controls for an information system is in lieu of which of the following?**

   a.    Prescribed controls

   b.    Management controls

   c.    Operational controls

   d.    Technical controls

***109. a.*** Compensating security controls are the management, operational, or technical controls used by an organization, which are implemented in lieu of prescribed controls in the low, moderate, or high security control baselines. All these controls provide equivalent or comparable protection for an information system.

**110.** **Which of the following is *not* a part of operational controls as they relate to system security controls?**

   a.    Access controls

   b.    Contingency planning controls

   c.    Incident response controls

   d.    Physical security controls

***110. a.*** Access control, along with identification and authentication and audit and accountability, is a part of technical control. Contingency planning controls are incorrect because they are a part of operational controls. Incident response controls are incorrect because they are a part of operational controls. Physical security controls are incorrect because they are a part of operational controls.

**111.** **The process of selecting the appropriate security controls and applying the system security scoping guidance is to achieve which of the following?**

   a.    Reasonable security

   b.    Adequate security

  c.  Normal security

  d.  Advanced security

***111. b.*** Adequate security is defined as security commensurate with the risk and the magnitude of harm resulting from the loss, misuse, or unauthorized access to or modification of information. The process of selecting the appropriate security controls and applying the scoping guidelines to achieve adequate security is a multifaceted, risk-based activity involving management and operational personnel within the organization. Note that the adequate security is more than the reasonable security and the normal security and less than the advanced security.

**112.** **Which of the following is *not* an example of a common security control?**

  a.  Access control

  b.  Management control

  c.  Operational control

  d.  Hybrid control

***112. a.*** Security controls not designated as common controls are considered system-specific controls and are the responsibility of the information system owner. For example, access control is a part of technical control and is a system-specific control. Many of the management and operational controls needed to protect an information system may be excellent candidates for common security control status. Common security controls reduce security costs when they are centrally managed in terms of development, implementation, and assessment. Hybrid controls contain both common and system-specific controls.

**113.** **Which of the following determines the adequacy of security in a software product?**

  1.  How a product is tested?

  2.  How a product is evaluated?

  3.  How a product is applied related to other systems?

  4.  How a product is developed related to other systems?

    a.  1 only

    b.  2 only

    c.  3 and 4

    d.  1, 2, 3, and 4

***113. c.*** The way in which a software product is developed, integrated, and applied to other system components affects the adequacy of its security.

Even when a product successfully completes a formal security evaluation, it may contain vulnerabilities (e.g., buffer overflow problems). Using a tested and evaluated software product does not necessarily ensure a secure and adequate operational environment.

**114.** Which of the following items is *not* a replacement for the other three items?

    a.    Enabling system logs

    b.    Conducting formal audits

    c.    Reviewing system logs manually

    d.    Reviewing system logs automatically

*114. b.* Although conducted periodically, formal audits are useful, but are not a replacement for day-to-day management of the security status of a system. Enabling system logs and reviewing their contents manually or through automated report summaries can sometimes be the best means of uncovering unauthorized behavior of people and systems and detecting security problems. The critical point here is that day-to-day management is more timely and effective than periodic audits, which could be too late.

**115.** Minimal functionality in an application system relates to which of the following security principles?

    a.    Security is relative to each organization.

    b.    Security is inversely related to complexity.

    c.    Security should be layered and have diverse defenses.

    d.    Security should be based on minimal privileges.

*115. b.* Security is inversely related to complexity; the more complex a system, the more difficult it is to secure. This is the focus of the safeguard titled "minimal functionality." Security should be relative to each organization and must take into account an organization's specific needs, budget, and culture. Security is not absolute. This is the focus of the safeguard titled "risk analysis and management." Defending an information system requires safeguards to be applied not only at points of entry, but also throughout. This is the focus of the safeguard titled "layered and diverse defenses." The principle of least (minimum) privilege states that programs should operate only with the privileges needed to accomplish their functions. This is the focus of the safeguard titled "least privilege."

**116.** Residual risk is calculated as which of the following?

    a.    Known risks minus unknown risks

    b.    Actual risks minus probable risks

    c.    Probable risks minus possible risks

    d.    Potential risks minus covered risks

*116. d.* Potential risks include all possible and probable risks. Countermeasures cover some, but not all risks. Therefore, the residual risk is potential risks minus covered risks.

**117.** Which of the following is the correct equation in risk management?

    a.    Risk management = Risk research + Risk analysis + Risk evaluation

    b.    Risk management = Risk analysis + Risk avoidance + Risk evaluation

    c.    Risk management = Risk assessment + Risk mitigation + Risk evaluation

    d.    Risk management = Risk transfer + Risk acceptance + Risk evaluation

**117. c.** Risk management includes risk assessment, risk mitigation, and risk evaluation. Risk assessment is also called risk analysis. Risk mitigation includes risk transfer (risk assignment), risk reduction, risk avoidance, risk sharing, risk limitation, and risk acceptance. Risk research is a part of risk analysis. Risk evaluation focuses on ongoing risk assessment.

**118.**    **What can be done with the residual risk?**

    a.    It can be either assigned or accepted.

    b.    It can be either identified or evaluated.

    c.    It can be either reduced or calculated.

    d.    It can be either exposed or assessed.

**118. a.** Residual risk is the remaining risk after countermeasures (controls) cover the risk population. The residual risk is either assigned to a third party (e.g., insurance company) or accepted by management as part of doing business. It may not be cost-effective to further reduce residual risk.

**119.**    **Which of the following is *not* part of risk analysis?**

    a.    Assets

    b.    Threats

    c.    Vulnerabilities

    d.    Countermeasures

**119. d.** Actual implementation of countermeasures and safeguards takes place after performing risk analysis. Risk analysis identifies the risks to system security and determines the probability of occurrence, the resulting impact, and the additional safeguards that could mitigate this impact. Assets, threats, and vulnerabilities are part of the risk analysis exercise.

**120.**    **Unacceptable risk is which of the following?**

1.    Attacker's cost < gain

2.    Loss anticipated > threshold

3.    Attacker's cost > gain

4.    Loss anticipated < threshold

    a.    1 and 2

    b.    2 and 3

    c.    1 and 4

    d.    3 and 4

*120. a.* Unacceptable risk is a situation where an attacker's cost is less than gain and where loss anticipated by an organization is greater than its threshold level. The organization's goals should be to increase an attacker's cost and to reduce an organization's loss.

**121.** **Security safeguards and controls cannot do which of the following?**

    a.   Risk reduction

    b.   Risk avoidance

    c.   Risk transfer

    d.   Risk analysis

*121. d.* Risk analysis identifies the risks to system security and determines the probability of occurrence, the resulting impact, and the additional safeguards that mitigate this impact. Risk analysis is a management exercise performed before deciding on specific safeguards and controls. The other three choices are a part of risk mitigation, which results from applying the selected safeguards and controls. Risk avoidance includes risk reduction and risk transfer is assigning risk to a third party.

**122.** **Selection and implementation of security controls refer to which of the following?**

    a.   Risk analysis

    b.   Risk mitigation

    c.   Risk assessment

    d.   Risk management

*122. b.* Risk mitigation involves the selection and implementation of security controls to reduce risks to an acceptable level. Risk analysis is the same as risk assessment. Risk management includes both risk analysis and risk mitigation.

**123.** **Which of the following is closely linked to risk acceptance?**

    a.   Risk detection

    b.   Risk prevention

    c.   Risk tolerance

    d.   Risk correction

*123. c.* Risk tolerance is the level of risk an entity or a manager is willing to assume or accept to achieve a potential desired result. Some managers accept more risk than others do because of their personal affinity toward risk.

**124.** **The amount of risk an organization can handle should be based on which of the following:**

    a.   Technological level

    b.   Acceptable level

    c.   Affordable level

    d.   Measurable level

***124. b.*** Often, losses cannot be measured in monetary terms alone, such as loss of customer confidence and loyalty. Risk should be handled at an acceptable level for an organization. Both affordable and technological levels vary with the type of organization (e.g., small, medium, or large size and technology dependent or not).

**125.** **In terms of information systems security, a risk is defined as which of the following combinations?**

    a.    Attack plus vulnerability

    b.    Threat plus attack

    c.    Threat plus vulnerability

    d.    Threat plus breach

***125. c.*** Vulnerability is a weakness in security policy, procedure, personnel, management, administration, hardware, software, or facilities affecting security that may allow harm to an information system. The presence of vulnerability does not in itself cause harm. It is a condition that may allow the information system to be harmed by an attack. A threat is any circumstance or event with the potential to cause harm to a system in the form of destruction or modification of data or denial-of-service. An attack is an attempt to violate data security. A risk is the probability that a particular threat can exploit a particular vulnerability of a system. An exposure is an instance of vulnerability in which losses may result from the occurrence of one or more attacks. A countermeasure is any action, control, device, procedure, technique, or other measure that reduces the vulnerability of a threat to a system. A breach is the successful circumvention or disablement of a security control, with or without detection, which if carried to completion, could result in a penetration of the system.

**126.** **Risk management is made up of primary and secondary activities. Which of the following is an example of a secondary activity?**

    a.    Risk analysis data

    b.    Risk assessment

    c.    Risk mitigation

    d.    Risk methodology

***126. a.*** Risk management must often rely on speculation, best guesses, incomplete data, and many unproven assumptions. The risk-based data are another source of uncertainty and are an example of a secondary activity. Data for risk analysis normally come from two sources: statistical data and expert analysis. Both have shortcomings; for example, the sample may be too small, or expert analysis may be subjective based on assumptions made.

Risk assessment, the process of analyzing and interpreting risk, is composed of three basic activities: (i) determining the assessment's scope and methodology, (ii) collecting and synthesizing data, and (iii) interpreting the risk. A risk assessment methodology should be a relatively simple process that could be adapted to various organizational units and involves a mix of individuals with knowledge of the business operations and technical aspects of the organization's systems and security controls.

Risk mitigation involves the selection and implementation of cost-effective security controls to reduce risk to a level acceptable to management, within applicable constraints. Risk methodology is a part of risk assessment. It can be formal or informal, detailed or simplified, high or low level, quantitative (computationally based) or qualitative (based on descriptions or rankings), or a combination of these. No single method is best for all users and all environments. The other three choices are examples of primary activities.

**127.** From a risk management viewpoint, which of the following options is *not* acceptable?

    a. Accept the risk

    b. Assign the risk

    c. Avoid the risk

    d. Defer the risk

***127. d.*** "Deferring risk" means either ignoring the risk at hand or postponing the issue until further consideration. If the decision to defer the risk is a calculated one, it is hoped that management had the necessary data.

"Accept the risk" is satisfactory when the exposure is small and the protection cost is high. "Assign the risk" is used when it costs less to assign the risk to someone else than to directly protect against it. "Avoid the risk" means placing necessary measures so that a security incident will not occur at all or so that a security event becomes less likely or costly.

**128.** What is an attacker repeatedly using multiple different attack vectors repeatedly to generate opportunities called?

    a. Adverse action

    b. Advanced threat

    c. Threat agent

    d. Threat source

***128. b.*** An advanced (persistent) threat is conducted by an adversary with sophisticated levels of expertise and significant resources, allowing it through the use of multiple different attack vectors (e.g., cyber, physical, and deception), to generate opportunities to achieve its objectives. The advanced threat pursues its objectives repeatedly over an extended period of time, adapting to a defender's efforts to resist it, and with determination to maintain the level of interaction needed to execute its objectives.

Adverse actions are actions performed by a threat agent on an asset. These actions influence one or more properties of an asset from which that asset derives its value. A threat consists of a threat agent, a targeted asset, and an adverse action of that threat agent on that asset. Threat agents are entities that can adversely act on assets. Examples of threat agents include hackers, users, computer processes, software development staff, and accidental/intentional errors. Threat agents and threat sources are the same in that their intents and methods are targeted at the intentional exploitation of vulnerability or a situation and the methods that may accidentally trigger vulnerability.

**129.** **What does a "deviation from an organization-wide approved security policy" mean?**

    a.    Risk acceptance

    b.    Risk assignment

    c.    Risk reduction

    d.    Risk containment

***129. a.***   To deviate from an organization-wide approved security policy, the business unit management needs to prepare a letter explaining the reason for the deviation and recognizing and accepting the related risk. Risk assignment is transferring risk to a third party. Risk reduction and risk containment deal with limiting risk by implementing controls.

**130.** **When performing risk analysis, annual loss exposure is calculated as which of the following?**

    a.    Impact multiplied by frequency of occurrence

    b.    Impact minus frequency of occurrence

    c.    Impact plus frequency of occurrence

    d.    Impact divided by frequency of occurrence

***130. a.***   Quantitative means of expressing both potential impact and estimated frequency of occurrence are necessary to perform a risk analysis. The essential elements of a risk analysis are an assessment of the damage that can be caused by an unfavorable event and an estimate of how often such an event may happen in a period of time. Because the exact impact and frequency cannot be specified accurately, it is only possible to approximate the loss with an annual loss exposure, which is the product of the estimated impact in dollars and the estimated frequency of occurrence per year. The product of the impact and the frequency of occurrence would be the statement of loss.

**131.** **A risk analysis provides management of all the following *except*:**

    a.    Accepting the occurrence of a harmful event

    b.    Reducing the impact of occurrence of a harmful event

    c.    Ranking critical applications

    d.    Recognizing that a potential for loss exists

***131. c.***   A risk analysis provides senior management with information to base decisions on, such as whether it is best to accept or prevent the occurrence of a harmful event, to reduce the impact of such occurrences, or to simply recognize that a potential for loss exists.

The risk analysis should help managers compare the cost of the probable consequences to the cost of effective safeguards. Ranking critical applications comes after the risk analysis is completed. Critical applications are those without which the organization could not function. Proper attention should be given to ensure that critical applications and software are sufficiently protected against loss.

**132.** Which of the following methods for handling risk involves a third party?

    a. Accepting risk

    b. Eliminating risk

    c. Reducing risk

    d. Transferring risk

*132. d.* An insurance company or a third party is involved in transferring risk. All the other three choices do not involve a third party because they are handled within an organization.

**133.** Which of the following security risk assessment techniques uses a group of experts as the basis for making decisions or judgments?

    a. Risk assessment audits

    b. Delphi method

    c. Expert systems

    d. Scenario-based threats

*133. b.* The Delphi method uses a group decision-making technique. The rationale for using this technique is that it is sometimes difficult to get a consensus on the cost or loss value and the probabilities of loss occurrence. Group members do not meet face-to-face. Rather, each group member independently and anonymously writes down suggestions and submits comments that are then centrally compiled. This process of centrally compiling the results and comments is repeated until full consensus is obtained.

Risk assessment audits are incorrect because these audits do not provide the same consensus as the one reached by a group of experts in the Delphi method. Usually, one or two individuals perform audits, not groups. Expert systems are incorrect because they are computer-based systems developed with the knowledge of human experts. These systems do not reach a consensus as a group of people. Scenario-based threats are incorrect because possible threats are identified based on scenarios by a group of people. However, this system does not have the same consensus reached as in the Delphi method. The process of submitting results and comments makes the Delphi method more useful than the other methods.

**134.** The costs and benefits of security techniques should be measured in monetary terms where possible. Which of the following is the most effective means to measure the cost of addressing relatively frequent threats?

    a. Single-occurrence losses

    b. Annualized loss expectancy

    c. Fatal losses

    d. Catastrophic losses

*134. b.* The annualized loss expectancy (ALE) is the estimated loss expressed in monetary terms at an annual rate, for example, dollars per year. The ALE for a given threat with respect to a given function or asset is equal to the product of the estimates of occurrence rate, loss potential, and vulnerability factor.

Single-occurrence loss (SOL) is incorrect because it is the loss expected to result from a single occurrence of a threat. It is determined for a given threat by first calculating the product of the loss potential and vulnerability factor for each function and asset for the threat being analyzed. Then the products are summed to generate the SOL for the threat. Because the SOL does not depend on an estimate of the threat's occurrence rate, it is particularly useful for evaluating rare but damaging threats. If a threat's SOL estimate is unacceptably high; it is prudent risk management to take security actions to reduce the SOL to an acceptable level.

Both fatal losses and catastrophic losses are big and rare. Fatal losses involve loss of human life, and catastrophic loss incurs great financial loss. In short, the ALE is useful for addressing relatively frequent threats, whereas SOL and fatal or catastrophic losses address rare threats.

**135.** **Surveys and statistics indicate that the greatest threat to any computer system is:**

    a.    Untrained or negligent users

    b.    Vendors and contractors

    c.    Hackers and crackers

    d.    Employees

*135. d.* Employees of all categories are the greatest threat to any computer system because they are trusted the most. They have access to the computer system, they know the physical layout of the area, and they could misuse the power and authority. Most trusted employees have an opportunity to perpetrate fraud if the controls in the system are weak. The consequence of untrained or negligent users is the creation of errors and other minor inconveniences.

Although vendors and contractors are a threat, they are not as great a threat as employees are. With proper security controls, threats arising from hackers and crackers can be minimized, if not completely eliminated. Hackers and crackers are the same, and they access computer systems for fun and/or damage.

**136.** **Risk management consists of risk assessment and risk mitigation. Which of the following is *not* an element of risk mitigation?**

    a.    Measuring risk

    b.    Selecting appropriate safeguards

    c.    Implementing and test safeguards

    d.    Accepting residual risk

**136. a.** The term risk management is commonly used to define the process of determining risk, applying controls to reduce the risk, and then determining if the residual risk is acceptable. Risk management supports two goals: measuring risk (risk assessment) and selecting appropriate controls that can reduce risk to an acceptable level (risk mitigation). Therefore, measuring risk is part of risk assessment.

The other three choices are incorrect because they are elements of risk mitigation. Risk mitigation involves three steps: determining those areas where risk is unacceptable; selecting effective safeguards and evaluating the controls; and determining if the residual risk is acceptable.

**137.** The value of information is measured by its:

    a.    Negative value

    b.    Value to the owner

    c.    Value to others

    d.    Value of immediate access

**137. c.** The value of information is measured by what others want from the owner. Negative value comes into play when there is a safety, security, or quality problem with a product. For example, the negative value of a product affects customers, manufacturers, vendors, and hackers, where the latter party can exploit an unsafe or unsecure product. Value of immediate access is situational and personal.

**138.** Risk is the possibility of something adverse happening to an organization. Which of the following steps is the most difficult one to accomplish in a risk management process?

    a.    Risk profile

    b.    Risk assessment

    c.    Risk mitigation

    d.    Risk maintenance

**138. b.** Risk management is the process of assessing risk, taking steps to reduce risk to an acceptable level, and maintaining that level of risk. Risk management includes two primary and one underlying activities. Risk assessment and risk mitigation are the primary activities, and uncertainty analysis is the underlying one.

Risk assessment, the process of analyzing and interpreting risk, is composed of three basic activities: (i) determining the assessment's scope and methodology, (ii) collecting and synthesizing data, and (iii) interpreting the risk. A risk assessment can focus on many different areas of controls (including management, technical, and operational). These controls can designed into a new application and incorporated into all areas of an organization's functions and operations (including telecommunication data centers, and business units). Because of the nature of the scope and the extent of risk assessment, it is the most difficult one to accomplish.

Risk profile and risk maintenance are not the most difficult to accomplish because they are the by-products of the risk assessment process. Risk profile for a computer system or facility involves identifying threats and developing controls and policies in order to manage risks.

Risk mitigation involves the selection and implementation of cost-effective security controls to reduce risk to a level acceptable to management, within applicable constraints. Again, risk mitigation comes after the completion of the risk assessment process.

**139.** **The focus of risk management is that risk must be:**

    a.    Eliminated

    b.    Prevented

    c.    Avoided

    d.    Managed

*139. d.* Risk must be managed because it cannot be completely eliminated or avoided. Some risks cannot be prevented in a cost-effective manner.

**140.** **What is a risk event that is an identifiable uncertainty called?**

    a.    Known-unknown

    b.    Unknown-unknown

    c.    Known-known

    d.    Unknown-known

*140. a.* Known-unknown is an identifiable uncertainty. Unknown-unknown is a risk event whose existence cannot be imagined. There is no risk in known-known because there is no uncertainty. Unknown-known is not relevant here.

**141.** **Which of the following is an optional requirement for organizations?**

    a.    Policies

    b.    Procedures

    c.    Standards

    d.    Guidelines

*141. d.* Guidelines assist users, systems personnel, and others in effectively securing their systems. Guidelines are suggestive and are not compulsory within an organization.

**142.** **Which of the following is the *least* sensitive data classification scheme?**

    a.    Unclassified

    b.    Unclassified but sensitive

    c.    Secret

    d.    Confidential

*142. a.* Data that is not sensitive or classified is unclassified. This is the least sensitive category, whereas secret is the most sensitive category.

**143.** Which of the following is *not* an example of a trade secret?

    a. Customer lists

    b. Supplier names

    c. Technical specifications

    d. Employee names

*143. d.* To qualify as a trade secret, information must be of competitive value or advantage to the owner or his business. Trade secrets can include technical information and customer and supplier lists. Employee names do not come under the trade secret category because they are somewhat public information, requiring protection from recruiters.

**144.** Which of the following covers system-specific policies and procedures?

    a. Technical controls

    b. Operational controls

    c. Management controls

    d. Development controls

*144. c.* Management controls are actions taken to manage the development, maintenance, and use of the system, including system-specific policies, procedures, and rules of behavior, individual roles and responsibilities, individual accountability, and personnel security decisions.

Technical controls include hardware and software controls used to provide automated protection to the computer system or applications. Technical controls operate within the technical systems and applications.

Operational controls are the day-to-day procedures and mechanisms used to protect operational systems and applications. Operational controls affect the system and application environment.

Development controls include the process of assuring that adequate controls are considered, evaluated, selected, designed, and built into the system during its early planning and development stages, and that an ongoing process is established to ensure continued operation at an acceptable level of risk during the installation, implementation, and operation stages.

**145.** Organizational electronic-mail policy is an example of which of the following?

    a. Advisory policy

    b. Regulatory policy

    c. Specific policy

    d. Informative policy

*145. c.* Advisory, regulatory, and informative policies are broad in nature and cover many topics and areas of interest. E-mail policy is an example of specific policy dealing with communication between and among individuals.

**146.** **What should be done when an employee leaves an organization?**

    a.     Review of recent performance evaluation

    b.     Review of human resource policies

    c.     Review of nondisclosure agreements

    d.     Review of organizational policies

**146. c.** When an employee leaves an organization, he should be reminded of nondisclosure agreements that he signed upon his hiring. This agreement includes measures to protect confidential and proprietary information such as trade secrets and inventions.

**147.** **For computer security, integrity does *not* mean which of the following?**

    a.     Accuracy

    b.     Authenticity

    c.     Completeness

    d.     Timeliness

**147. d.** Timeliness is a part of the availability goal, whereas accuracy, authenticity, and completeness are part of the integrity goal.

**148.** **For computer security, confidentiality does *not* mean which of the following?**

    a.     Nonrepudiation

    b.     Secrecy

    c.     Privacy

    d.     Sensitivity

**148. a.** Nonrepudiation is a part of the integrity goal, whereas secrecy, privacy, sensitivity, and criticality are part of the confidentiality goal.

**149.** **Which of the following security goals is meant for intended uses only?**

    a.     Confidentiality

    b.     Integrity

    c.     Availability

    d.     Accountability

**149. c.** Availability is for intended uses only and not for any other uses. Another definition of availability is ensuring timely and reliable access to and use of system-related information by authorized entities. Confidentiality (C), integrity (I), and availability (A) are security goals and are often called the CIA triad. Confidentiality is preserving authorized restrictions on information access and disclosure. Integrity is the property that protected and sensitive data has not been modified or deleted in an unauthorized and undetected manner. Accountability is tracing actions of an entity uniquely to that entity.

**150.** **The advanced encryption standard (AES) is useful for securing which of the following?**

    a.    Confidential but classified material

    b.    Secret but classified material

    c.    Top secret but unclassified material

    d.    Sensitive but unclassified material

*150. d.*   The advanced encryption standard (AES) is an encryption algorithm used for securing sensitive but unclassified material. The loss, misuse, or unauthorized access to or modification of sensitive but unclassified material might adversely affect an organization's security interests.

AES is not useful for securing confidential but classified material. AES is not useful for securing secret but classified material. AES is not useful for securing top secret but unclassified material. Top secret cannot be unclassified.

**151.** **Business data classification schemes usually do *not* include which of the following?**

    a.    Private

    b.    Public

    c.    For internal use only

    d.    Secret

*151. d.*   The data classification terms such as secret and top secret are mostly used by government. The terms used in the other choices usually belong to business data classification scheme.

**152.** **Data containing trade secrets is an example of which of the following data classification schemes?**

    a.    Classified

    b.    Unclassified

    c.    Unclassified but sensitive

    d.    Confidential

*152. c.*   A classified category includes sensitive, confidential, secret, and top secret. An unclassified category is public information, whereas an unclassified but sensitive category requires some protection as in the case of trade secrets.

**153.** **Which of the following assists in complying with others?**

    a.    Policy

    b.    Procedure

    c.    Standard

    d.    Guideline

*153. b.*   Procedures normally assist in complying with applicable policies, standards, and guidelines because they deal with specific steps to carry out a specific task.

**154.** Which of the following is referred to when at least one security objective (i.e., confidentiality, integrity, or availability) is assigned a moderate impact value and no security objective is assigned a high impact value for an information system?

    a.    Low-impact system

    b.    Moderate-impact system

    c.    High-impact system

    d.    No-impact system

*154. b.* A low-impact system is defined as an information system in which all three security objectives (i.e., confidentiality, integrity, and availability) are assigned a potential impact value of low. In a moderate-impact system, at least one objective is assigned as moderate and no objective is assigned as high. In a high-impact system, at least one objective is assigned as high. No-impact system is incorrect because every system will have some impact, whether low, moderate, or high.

**155.** Which of the following security controls are needed when data is transferred from low network users to high network users?

    1.    Software/hardware guards

    2.    Automated processing

    3.    Automated blocking

    4.    Automated filtering

        a.    1 and 2

        b.    1 and 3

        c.    2 and 3

        d.    3 and 4

*155. b.* Data should be sanitized or separated between high network data/users and low network data/users. When data is transferred from low network users to high network users (i.e., data is regraded), automated data-blocking techniques with firewalls and software/hardware guards are needed to regulate the transfer.

When data is transferred from high network users to low network users (i.e., data is regraded), software/hardware guards, automated processing, and automated filtering techniques are needed to regulate the transfer. The goal of automated processing, blocking, and filtering techniques is an attempt to eliminate or identify viruses and other malicious code transfers. The goal of software/hardware guard is to facilitate transfer of data between private and public networks.

**156.** Which of the following is a prerequisite to IT security training?

    a.    Certification

    b.    Education

c.  Awareness

d.  Training

***156. c.*** Awareness, training, and education are important processes for helping staff members carry out their roles and responsibilities for information technology security, but they are not the same. Awareness programs are a prerequisite to IT security training. Training is more formal and more active than awareness activities and is directed toward building knowledge and skills to facilitate job performance.

Education integrates all the security skills and competencies of the various functional specialists and adds a multidisciplinary study of concepts, issues, and principles. Normally, organizations seldom require evidence of qualification or certification as a condition of appointment.

**157.** **When developing information systems security policies, organizations should pay particular attention to which of the following?**

a.  User education

b.  User awareness

c.  User behavior

d.  User training

***157. c.*** A relatively new risk receiving particular attention in organizational policies is user behavior. Some users may feel no compunction against browsing sensitive organizational computer files or inappropriate Internet sites if there is no clear guidance on what types of user behaviors are acceptable. These risks did not exist before the extensive use of networks, electronic mail, and the Internet.

**158.** **A common technique for making an organization's information systems security policies more useful is to distinguish between:**

a.  Policies and procedures

b.  Policies and guidelines

c.  Principles and practices

d.  Policies and standards

***158. b.*** Policies generally outline fundamental requirements that top management consider imperative, whereas guidelines provide more detailed rules for implementing the broader policies. Guidelines, while encouraged, are not considered to be mandatory.

**159.** **Who must bear the primary responsibility for determining the level of protection needed for IT resources?**

a.  Information systems security analysts

b.  Business managers

c.  Information systems security managers

d.  Information systems auditors

*159. b.*   Business managers (functional managers) should bear the primary responsibility for determining the level of protection needed for information systems resources that support business operations. Therefore, business managers should be held accountable for managing the information security risks associated with their operations, much as they would for any other type of business risk. Both the information systems security analysts and managers can assist the business manager, whereas the systems auditor can evaluate the level of protection available in an information system.

The level of protection starts at the chief executive officer (CEO) level. This means having a policy on managing threats, responsibilities, and obligations, which will be reflected in employee conduct, ethics, and procurement policies and practices. Information security must be fully integrated into all relevant organizational policies, which can occur only when security consciousness exists at all levels.

**160.**   **Which of the following is a better method to ensure that information systems security issues have received appropriate attention by senior management of an organization?**

a.   Establish a technical-level committee

b.   Establish a policy-level committee

c.   Establish a control-level committee

d.   Establish a senior-level committee

*160. d.*   Some organizations have established senior-level committees consisting of senior managers to ensure that information technology issues, including information security, receive appropriate attention and support. The other committees collect data on specific issues that each committee deals with and recommend actions to senior-level committees for their approval.

**161.**   **What is a key characteristic that should be common to all information systems security central groups?**

a.   Organizational reporting relationships

b.   Information systems security responsibilities

c.   Information systems security technical assistance

d.   Support received from other organizational units

*161. b.*   The two key characteristics that a security central group should include (i) clearly defined information security responsibilities and (ii) dedicated staff resources to carry out these responsibilities.

**162.**   **To ensure that information systems security policies serve as the foundation of information systems security programs, organizations should link:**

a.   Policies to standards

b.   Policies to business risks

c.   Policies to procedures

d.   Policies to controls

**162. *b.*** Developing a comprehensive set of policies is the first step in establishing an orga-nization-wide security program. The policy should be linked to business risks and adjusted on a continuing basis to respond to newly identified risks or areas of misunderstanding.

**163.** Which of the following is a useful technique for impressing the users about the impor-tance of organization-wide information systems security policies?

a.   Making policies available through the Internet

b.   Ensuring policies are available through physical bulletin boards

c.   Requiring a signed statement from all users that they will abide by the policies

d.   Ensuring policies are available through electronic bulletin boards

**163. *c.*** A statement is required from new users at the time access to information system resources was first provided and from all users periodically, usually once a year. Requiring a signed statement can serve as a useful technique for impressing on the users the importance of understanding organizational policies. In addition, if the user was later involved in a security violation, the statement can serve as evidence that he had been informed of organi-zational policies.

**164.** Which of the following considers the loss of security objectives (i.e., confidentiality, integrity, and availability) that could be expected to have a limited, serious, or severe adverse effect on an organization's operations, assets, systems, or individuals and on other organizations?

a.   Low-impact

b.   Moderate-impact

c.   Potential impact

d.   High-impact

**164. *c.*** Potential impact considers all three levels of impact such as (i) a limited adverse effect representing a low impact, (ii) a serious adverse effect representing a moderate impact, and (iii) a severe or catastrophic adverse effect representing a high impact.

**165.** Effective information systems security measures cannot be maintained due to which of the following reasons?

a.   Lack of awareness

b.   Lack of a policy

c.   Lack of a procedure

d.   Lack of enforcement

**165. *d.*** If employees see that management is not serious about security policy enforcement, they will not pay attention to security, thus minimizing its effectiveness. In addition to the lack of enforcement, inconsistent enforcement is a problem.

**166.** Sensitivity criteria for a computer-based information system are *not* defined in terms of which of the following?

    a. The value of having an application system

    b. The cost of developing and maintaining an application system

    c. The value of having the needed information

    d. The cost of not having an application system

*166. b.* Sensitivity criteria are largely defined in terms of the value of having, or the cost of not having, an application system or needed information.

**167.** What is the first thing to do upon unfriendly termination of an employee?

    a. Complete a sign-out form immediately.

    b. Send employee to the accounting department for the last paycheck.

    c. Remove the system access quickly.

    d. Send employee to the human resource department for benefits status.

*167. c.* Whether the termination is friendly or unfriendly, the best security practice is to disable the system access quickly, including login to systems. Out-processing often involves a sign-out form initialed by each functional manager with an interest in the separation of the employee. The sign-out form is a type of checklist. Sending the employee to the accounting and human resource departments may be done later.

**168.** Which of the following have similar structures and complementary objectives?

    a. Training and awareness

    b. Hackers and users

    c. Compliance and common sense

    d. Need-to-know and threats

*168. a.* Training makes people learn new things and be aware of new issues and procedures. They have similar objectives—that is, to learn a new skill or knowledge. Hence, they complement each other.

A hacker is a person who attempts to compromise the security of an IT system, especially whose intention is to cause disruption or obtain unauthorized access to data. On the other hand, a user has the opposite objective, to use the system to fulfill his job duties. Hence, they conflict with each other.

Compliance means following the standards, rules, or regulations with no deviations allowed. On the other hand, common sense tells people to deviate when conditions are not practical. Hence, they conflict with each other.

Need-to-know means a need for access to information to do a job. Threats are actions or events that, if realized, can result in waste, fraud, abuse, or disruption of operations. Hence, they conflict with each other.

**169.** Establishing a data ownership program should be the responsibility of:

    a. Functional users

    b. Internal auditors

    c. Data processors

    d. External auditors

***169. a.*** Functional users (business users) own the data in computer systems. Therefore, they have an undivided interest and responsibility in establishing a data ownership program.

Internal/external auditors are incorrect because they have no responsibility in establishing a data ownership program even though they recommend one. Data processors are incorrect because they are custodians of the users' data.

**170.** When can the effectiveness of an information systems security policy be compromised?

    a. When a policy is published

    b. When a policy is reexamined

    c. When a policy is tested

    d. When policy enforcement is predictable

***170. d.*** Information systems security policies should be made public, but the actual enforcement procedures should be kept private. This is to prevent policies from being compromised when enforcement is predictable. The surprise element makes unpredictable enforcements more effective than predictable ones. Policies should be published so that all affected parties are informed. Policies should be routinely reexamined for their workability. Policies should be tested to ensure the accuracy of assumptions.

**171.** There are many different ways to identify individuals or groups who need specialized or advanced training. Which of the following methods is *least* important to consider when planning for such training?

    a. Job categories

    b. Job functions

    c. Specific systems

    d. Specific vendors

***171. d.*** One method is to look at job categories, such as executives, functional managers, or technology providers. Another method is to look at job functions, such as system design, system operation, or system user. A third method is to look at the specific technology and products used, especially for advanced training for user groups and training for a new system. Specific vendors are least important during planning but important in implementation.

**172.** Which of the following information systems security objective is most important in an IT security program?

    a.    The objective must be specific.

    b.    The objective must be clear.

    c.    The objective must be achievable.

    d.    The objective must be well defined.

*172. c.* The first step in the management process is to define information systems security objectives for the specific system. A security objective needs to be more specific; it should be concrete and well defined. It also should be stated so that it is clear and achievable. An example of an information systems security objective is one in which only individuals in the accounting and personnel departments are authorized to provide or modify information used in payroll processing. What good is a security objective if it is not achievable although it is specific, clear, and well defined?

**173.** In which of the following planning techniques are the information needs of the organization defined?

    a.    Strategic planning

    b.    Tactical planning

    c.    Operational planning

    d.    Information systems planning

*173. d.* Four types of planning help organizations identify and manage IT resources: strategic, tactical, operational, and information systems planning. IS planning is a special planning structure designed to focus organizational computing resource plans on its business needs. IS planning provides a three-phased structured approach for an organization to systematically define, develop, and implement all aspects of its near- and long-term information needs.

Strategic planning defines the organization's mission, goals, and objectives. It also identifies the major computing resource activities the organization will undertake to accomplish these plans.

Tactical planning identifies schedules, manages, and controls the tasks necessary to accomplish individual computing resource activities, using a shorter planning horizon than strategic planning. It involves planning projects, acquisitions, and staffing.

Operational planning integrates tactical plans and support activities and defines the short-term tasks that must be accomplished to achieve the desired results.

**174.** Which of the following is a somewhat stable document?

    a.    Information technology strategic plan

    b.    Information technology operational plan

    c.    Information technology security plan

    d.    Information technology training plan

**174. a.** The IT strategic plan sets the broad direction and goals for managing information within the organization and supporting the delivery of services to customers. It should be derived from and relate to the organization's strategic plan. The plan typically contains an IT mission statement, a vision describing the target IT environment of the future, an assessment of the current environment, and broad strategies for moving into the future. The IT strategic plan is a somewhat stable document. It does not require annual updates. However, an organization should periodically review and update the IT strategic plan as necessary to reflect significant changes in the IT mission or direction. The strategies presented in the IT strategic plan provide the basis for the IT operational plan, which includes security and training plans.

The IT operational plan describes how the organization will implement the strategic plan. The operational plan identifies logical steps for achieving the IT strategic vision. It may present an implementation schedule, identify key milestones, define project initiatives, and include resources (e.g., funding and personnel) estimates. The operational plan should identify dependencies among the IT strategies and present a logical sequence of project initiatives to assure smooth implementation.

The IT security plans and training plans are incorrect because they are components of the IT operational plan. Security plans should be developed for an organization or an individual system. These plans document the controls and safeguards for maintaining information integrity and preventing malicious/accidental use, destruction, or modification of information resources within the organization. Training plans document the types of training the IT staff will require to effectively perform their duties. The IT operational plans, security plans, and training plans are in a constant state of flux.

**175.** An information technology operational plan answers all the following questions *except*:

    a.    How do we get there?

    b.    When will it be done?

    c.    What is our goal?

    d.    Who will do it?

**175. c.** The IT operational plan describes how the organization will implement the strategic plan. Usually, the operational plan answers the following questions: How do we get there? When will it be done? Who will do it? The strategic plan answers the question: What is our goal?

**176.** Which of the following meets the criteria for an IT strategic plan?

    a.    Developing enterprise information technology models

    b.    Initiating work process redesign

    c.    Conducting business systems planning

    d.    Assessing internal and external environment

**176. d.**   The IT strategic planning is long-range thinking. Planners apply analytic techniques, creativity, and sound judgment to anticipate the requirements of the future. The strategic planning approach provides a framework for bounding the scope and presenting the results of long-range thinking. A strategic planning approach should foster strategic thinking and innovation, assess the organization's mission, vision, and strategies, define the IT mission, vision, and goals, and assess the internal and external environment. Internal influences are those that have implications for managing the organization such as customers, competitors, contractors, vendors, and user organizations (i.e., internal environment). External influences are broad in scope, often imposed from the outside environment, and uncontrollable by the organization. An organization derives its challenges and opportunities from external influences such as financial community, governments, and industry (i.e., external environment).

The other three choices are examples of IT approaches to augment the development of strategic plans and include enterprise IT models, work process redesign, and business systems planning. Enterprise models provide a means for examining the current environment. They do not foster the development of an organizational direction (i.e., mission and vision). Hence, they do not meet the criteria for strategic planning.

Work process redesign is synonymous with the following concepts: business re-engineering, business process improvement, and business process design. This approach helps managers to define relationships and activities within the organization. Business systems–planning is used to identify information requirements but does not consider strategic methodologies. Information planning approaches do not study organizational cultural issues or provide a strategic work focus.

**177.**   **Which of the following is *not* an example of IT mission statements?**

      a.    Streamlining work processes through automation

      b.    Maintaining reliability and timeliness of information

      c.    Anticipating technological advances and problems

      d.    Minimizing the cost to the organization by using information technology efficiently

**177. b.**   Maintaining reliability and timeliness of information is a goal statement. Goals specify objectives that support the organization's mission. The IT mission supports the organization's mission provided in its strategic plan. The IT mission statement identifies the basic concept of IT, the reason IT exists, and how IT supports the organization's mission. The IT mission statement may be examined three times during the planning process: at the beginning, after analyzing the current environment, and at the end. The IT organization collects, manages, controls, disseminates, and protects the information used by the organization.

IT supports the organization's mission by streamlining work processes through automation, anticipating technological advances and problems, and minimizing the cost to the organization by using IT efficiently.

**178.** **An information technology operational plan does *not* include:**

    a.    Risk assessment

    b.    Project descriptions

    c.    Project resource estimates

    d.    Project implementation schedules

**178. *a*.**   Risk assessment is part of the IT strategic plan along with mission, vision, goals, environmental analysis, strategies, and critical success factors. Typically a strategic plan covers a 5-year time span and is updated annually. IT operational planning begins when strategic planning ends. During operational planning, an organization develops a realistic implementation approach for achieving its vision based on its available resources.

The IT operational plan consists of three main parts: project descriptions, project resource estimates, and project implementation schedules. Depending upon its size and the complexity of its projects, an organization may also include the following types of documents as part of its operational plan: security plan summary, information plans, and information technology plans.

**179.** **The scope of the information technology tactical plan does *not* include:**

    a.    Budget plans

    b.    Application system development and maintenance plans

    c.    Technical support plans

    d.    Service objectives

**179. *d*.**   The scope of an IT tactical plan includes budget plans, application system development and maintenance plans, and technical support plans, but not service objectives. This is because service objectives are part of the IT operational plan along with performance objectives. Operational plans are based on the tactical plan but are more specific, providing a framework for daily activity. The focus of operational plans is on achieving service objectives.

Effective plans focus attention on objectives, help anticipate change and potential problems, serve as the basis for decision making, and facilitate control. IT plans are based on the overall organization's plans. The IT strategic, tactical, and operational plans provide direction and coordination of activities necessary to support mission objectives, ensure that the IT meets user requirements, and enable IT management to cope effectively with current and future changing requirements. Detailed plans move from abstract terms to closely controlled implementation schedules.

Tactical plans span approximately 1 year's time. Tactical plans address a detailed view of IT activities and focus on how to achieve IT objectives. Tactical plans include budgetary information detailing the allocation of resources or funds assigned to IT components. Often, the budget is the basis for developing tactical plans.

**180.** **An important measure of success for any IT project is whether the:**

    a.    Project was completed on time

    b.    Project was completed within budget

    c.    Project manager has conserved organizational resources

    d.    Project has achieved its projected benefits

*180. d.* One of the critical attributes for successful IT investments requires that organizations should use projected benefits, not project completion on time and within budget as important measures of success for any IT project. Business goals should be translated into objectives, results-oriented measures of performance, both quantitative and qualitative, which can form the basis for measuring the impact of IT investments. Management regularly monitors the progress of ongoing IT projects against projected cost, schedule, performance, and delivered benefits. It does not matter whether the project manager has conserved organizational resources as long as the project has achieved its projected benefits. Achievement of the (remaining two) choices does not automatically achieve the project's projected benefits.

**181.** **Staffing decisions and hiring procedures are critical in solving computer-related security issues and problems. Which of the following is the correct sequence of steps involved in the staffing process?**

    1.    Determining the sensitivity of the position

    2.    Defining the job duties

    3.    Filling the position

    4.    Determining the computer access levels

        a.    1, 2, 3, and 4

        b.    2, 4, 3, and 1

        c.    2, 4, 1, and 3

        d.    1, 4, 2, and 3

*181. c.* Personnel issues are closely linked to logical access security controls. Early in the process of defining a position, security issues should be identified and dealt with. After a job position and duties have been broadly defined, the responsible supervisor should determine the type of computer access levels (e.g., add, modify, and delete) needed for that position or job.

Knowledge of the job duties and access levels that a particular position requires is necessary for determining the sensitivity of the position (whether a security clearance is required). The responsible supervisor should correctly identify position sensitivity levels and computer access levels so that appropriate, cost-effective background checks and screening methods can be completed.

When a position's sensitivity has been determined, the position is ready to be staffed. Background checks and screening methods help determine whether a particular individual is suitable for a given position. Computer access levels and position sensitivity can also be determined in parallel.

**182.** **Establishing an information system security function program within an organization should be the responsibility of:**

    a.    Information systems management

    b.    Internal auditors

    c.    Compliance officers

    d.    External auditors

*182. a.*    Both information systems management and functional user management have a joint and shared responsibility in establishing an information systems security function within an organization. It is because the functional user is the data owner and information systems management is the data custodian. Internal/external auditors and compliance officers have no responsibility in actually establishing such a function; although, they make recommendations to management to establish such a function.

**183.** **Risk management is an aggregation of which of the following?**

1.    Risk assessment

2.    Risk mitigation

3.    Ongoing risk evaluation

4.    Risk profile

    a.    1 and 2

    b.    2 and 3

    c.    1 and 4

    d.    1, 2, and 3

*183. d.*    Risk management is an aggregation of risk assessment, risk mitigation, and ongoing evaluation of risk. Risk profile for a computer system or facility involves identifying threats and developing controls and policies in order to manage risks.

**184.** **Which of the following is *not* the major reason for conducting risk assessment?**

    a.    It is required by law or regulation.

    b.    It is integrated into the system development life-cycle process.

    c.    It is a good security practice.

    d.    It supports the business objectives.

**184. a.** Risk assessment should be conducted and integrated into the system/software development life cycle (SDLC) process for information systems, not because it is required by law or regulation, but because it is a good security practice and supports the organization's business objectives or mission.

**185.** **Which of the following is the first step in the risk assessment process?**

    a.    Threat identification

    b.    Vulnerability identification

    c.    System characterization

    d.    Risk analysis

**185. c.** System characterization is the first step in the risk assessment process. When characterizing the system, the mission criticality and sensitivity are described in sufficient terms to form a basis for the scope of the risk assessment. Characterizing an information system establishes the scope of the risk assessment effort, delineates the operational authorization or accreditation boundaries, and provides information (e.g., hardware, software, system connectivity, and associated personnel). This step begins with identifying the system boundaries, resources, and information.

**186.** **A low-impact system does *not* require which of the following to fully characterize the system?**

    a.    Questionnaires

    b.    Hands-on security testing and evaluation

    c.    Interviews

    d.    Automated scanning tools

**186. b.** A system's impact can be defined in terms of low, moderate, or high. For example, a system determined to be of low impact may not require hands-on security testing and evaluation. Various techniques, such as questionnaires, interviews, documentation reviews, and automated scanning tools can be used to collect the information needed to fully characterize the system.

**187.** **The level of effort and granularity of the risk assessment are based on which of the following?**

    a.    Threat identification

    b.    Vulnerability identification

    c.    Risk analysis

    d.    Security categorization

**187. d.** The level of effort and the granularity (i.e., the level of depth at which the assessment investigates the security of the system) of the risk assessment are based on security categorization.

**188.** Which of the following can be used to augment the vulnerability source reviews in the risk assessment process of identifying vulnerabilities?

    a.    Penetration testing

    b.    Previous risk assessments

    c.    Previous audit reports

    d.    Vulnerability lists

**188. *a.*** Penetration testing and system security testing methods (e.g., use of automated vulnerability scanning tools and security, test, and evaluation methods) can be used to augment the vulnerability source reviews and identify vulnerabilities that may not have been previously identified in other sources.

**189.** The risk analysis steps performed during the risk assessment process do *not* include which of the following?

    a.    Control analysis

    b.    Likelihood determination

    c.    Vulnerability identification

    d.    Risk determination

**189. *c.*** Risk analysis includes four substeps: control analysis, likelihood determination, impact analysis, and risk determination. Vulnerability identification is performed prior to risk analysis. The control analysis results are used to strengthen the determination of the likelihood that a specific threat might successfully exploit a particular vulnerability. Checklists and questionnaires are used in the control analysis exercise.

**190.** Regarding external service providers operating in external system environments, which one of the following items is required when the other three items are *not* present to provide sufficient confidence?

    a.    Level of trust

    b.    Compensating controls

    c.    Level of control

    d.    Chain of trust

**190. *b.*** Where a sufficient level of trust, level of control, or chain of trust cannot be established in the external system and/or by the external service provider through a service-level agreement (SLA), an internal organization employs compensating controls or accepts a greater degree of risk. Compensating controls include management, operational, and technical controls in lieu of the recommended controls that provide equivalent or comparable protection. An external service provider operating and controlling an external information system can provide a service that is used by an internal organization in a consumer-producer relationship. Examples of these relationships include joint ventures, partnerships, outsourcing, licensing, and supply chain arrangements.

**191.** **Security control recommendations made during the risk assessment process provide input for which of the following?**

    a.    Impact analysis

    b.    Risk mitigation

    c.    Risk analysis

    d.    Control analysis

*191. b.* Risk analysis, impact analysis, and control analysis are done prior to security control recommendations. Therefore, security control recommendations are essential input for the risk mitigation process.

**192.** **Which of the following should reflect the results of the risk assessment process?**

    1.    Control recommendations

    2.    Risk determinations

    3.    Plans of action and milestones

    4.    System security plans

        a.    1 and 2

        b.    1 and 3

        c.    2 and 4

        d.    3 and 4

*192. d.* Organizations should ensure that the risk assessment results are appropriately reflected in the system's plan of action and milestones and system security plans. Control recommendations and risk determinations are done prior to documenting the results of the risk assessment.

**193.** **System security categorization is used in which of the following ways?**

    1.    To determine minimum baseline security controls

    2.    To aid in the estimating the level of threat and vulnerability pair

    3.    To reduce the residual risk to an acceptable level

    4.    To repeat the risk management cycle for better results

        a.    1 and 2

        b.    1 and 3

        c.    2 and 4

        d.    3 and 4

**193. *a.*** The security categorization is used in two ways: (i) to determine which baseline security controls are selected and (ii) to aid in estimating the level of risk posed by a threat and vulnerability pair identified during the risk assessment step. Items 3 and 4 are part of the risk mitigation step.

**194.** From an economies of scale viewpoint, the assessment, implementation, and monitoring activities of common security controls are *not* conducted at which of the following levels?

    a. Organizational level

    b. Individual system level

    c. Multiple systems level

    d. Functional level

**194. *b.*** Common security controls do not benefit at the individual system level because they benefit many systems and the principle of economies of scale is applicable here. Organizations can leverage controls used among multiple systems by designating them as common controls where assessment, implementation, and monitoring activities are conducted at an organizational level or by functional level or areas of specific expertise (e.g., human resources and physical security).

**195.** Which of the following is *not* a goal of the risk management evaluation and assessment process in ensuring that the system continues to operate in a safe and secure manner?

    a. Implement a strong configuration management program.

    b. Monitor the system security on a continuous basis.

    c. Eliminate all potential threats, vulnerabilities, and risks to the system.

    d. Track findings from the security control assessment process.

**195. *c.*** Because it is not practical or cost-effective to eliminate all potential threats, vulnerabilities, and risks to the system, management should consider only the possible threats, vulnerabilities, and risks to the system so that management can better prepare the system to operate in its intended environment securely, safely, and effectively.

**196.** Which of the following statements is *not* true? Risk management is the process that allows IT security managers to:

    a. Balance the operational and economic cost of protective measures

    b. Achieve gains in mission-essential security capabilities

    c. Protect IT systems and data that support the organization's mission

    d. Request funding to protect all systems, assets, and data in a comprehensive manner

**196. d.** Most organizations have a tight budget for IT security; therefore, IT security spending must be reviewed as thoroughly as other management decisions. It is not wise to protect all systems, assets, and data in a comprehensive manner. Risk management is the process that allows IT security managers to balance the operational and economic costs of protective measures to achieve mission-essential security capabilities and to protect the IT systems and data that support the organization's mission.

**197.** A plan of action and milestones document used in the security assessment and authorization process is *not* based on which of the following?

    a.    Security impact analysis

    b.    Security controls assessment

    c.    Business impact analysis

    d.    Continuous monitoring activities

**197. c.** A business impact analysis (BIA) is a part of business continuity planning (BCP) process, not security assessment and authorization process.

The other three choices are part of the security assessment and authorization process. The plan of action and milestone (POA&M) document is developed to show the remedial actions to correct the weaknesses noted during the assessment of the security controls and the results from security impact analysis to reduce the weaknesses in the system. The POA&M document also contains continuous monitoring activities.

**198.** If an IT system has *not* yet been designed, the search for vulnerabilities should *not* focus on which of the following?

    a.    Security policies

    b.    Security procedures

    c.    Planned security features

    d.    White papers

**198. c.** The planned security features are described in the security design documentation, which occurs after identifying vulnerabilities. If the IT system has not yet been designed, the search for vulnerabilities should focus on the organization's security policies, security procedures, the system requirements definitions, and the vendor's or developers' security product analyses (e.g., white papers).

**199.** Which of the following proactive technical methods is used to complement the security controls review?

    a.    Information scanning tool

    b.    Vulnerability scanning tool

    c.    Network scanning tool

    d.    Penetration testing tool

**199. d.** Penetration testing tool can be used to complement the security controls review and to ensure that different facets of the IT system are secured. The penetration testing occurs after the review of security controls, which includes the use of the automated information scanning tool, automated vulnerability scanning tool, and automated network scanning tool, and security test and evaluation. The penetration testing uses the results obtained from the security controls review.

**200.** When an employee of an organization uses an internal system to connect with an external organization's system for data exchange, the employee should comply with which of the following agreed upon trust relationships?

1. Conflict of interest statements
2. Rules of behavior
3. Remote session rules
4. Rules of operation

    a. 1 and 2

    b. 2 and 3

    c. 1, 3, and 4

    d. 1, 2, 3, and 4

**200. d.** Employees of an organization should be bound by the terms and conditions consistent with any agreed upon trust relationships between internal system owner and external system owner. These conditions include rules of behavior, remote session rules, rules of operation, and signed conflict of interest statements.

**201.** The security objective or principle of confidentiality does *not* deal with which of the following?

    a. Authenticity

    b. Sensitivity

    c. Secrecy

    d. Criticality

**201. a.** Authentication is a part of the integrity security objective or principle, whereas the other three choices are part of a confidentiality objective or principle.

**202.** Which of the following is *not* a goal of IT security?

    a. Confidentiality

    b. Integrity

    c. Aggregation

    d. Availability

**202. c.** Aggregation is an element of sensitivity where data is summarized to mask the details of a subject matter. The other three choices are the goals of IT security.

**203.** **Which of the following is *not* an outcome of information security governance?**

    a.    Strategic alignment

    b.    Information asset

    c.    Risk management

    d.    Resource management

**203. b.** Information asset is a business-critical asset, without which most organizations would not function properly. It is a business enabler, not an outcome. The other three choices are examples of outcome of information security governance.

**204.** **Which of the following is *not* an input to the risk management and information security strategy?**

    a.    Business strategy

    b.    Security requirements

    c.    Business processes

    d.    Risk assessments

**204. b.** Security requirements are the outputs of the risk management activity. Inputs to the risk management and information security strategy include business strategy, business processes, risk assessments, business input analysis, information resources, and regulatory requirements.

**205.** **Which of the following is *not* a correct method of expressing information security baselines?**

    a.    Technical standards

    b.    Procedural standards

    c.    Vendor standards

    d.    Personnel standards

**205. c.** Information security baselines can be expressed as technical, procedural, and personnel standards because they are internal to an organization. In addition to the above standards, the baseline should consider laws, regulations, policies, directives, and organizational mission/business/operational requirements, which could identify security requirements.

Vendors are external to an organization and it would be difficult to accommodate their standards into the baseline due to many vendors. In addition, vendor standards could be unpredictable and unstable.

**206.** Regarding information security governance, which of the following does *not* change, unlike others?

    a.    Programs

    b.    Assets

    c.    Mission

    d.    Practices

*206. c.* An organization's basic mission does not change because it is the guiding principle to follow at all times. However, the organization may change its security practices and protection mechanisms over IT assets and computer programs. Yet, these changes must be made within the boundaries of the mission requirements and guidelines. Note that the information security governance must follow the IT governance and the corporate governance principles.

**207.** What is the most important objective of system security planning?

    a.    To improve the protection of information system resources

    b.    To protect highly sensitive systems

    c.    To protect highly critical systems

    d.    To focus on accredited systems

*207. a.* The most important objective of system security planning is to improve the protection of information system resources (e.g., systems, programs, people, data, and equipment). All information systems have some level of sensitivity and criticality and some systems may be accredited. The sensitive, critical, and accredited systems are part of the information system resources and they need protection as part of good management practices.

**208.** Which of the following policy types is usually broad in scope and function?

    a.    Program policies

    b.    Issue-specific policies

    c.    System-specific policies

    d.    Network policies

*208. a.* Program policy is usually broad in scope in that it does not require much modification over time, whereas other types of policies are likely to require more frequent revisions as changes in technology take place.

**209.** Which of the following is *not* a part of access agreements?

    a.    Nondisclosure agreements

    b.    Rules-of-behavior agreements

    c.    Employment agreements

    d.    Conflict-of-interest agreements

***209. c.*** Employment agreements come before the access agreements. Access agreements include nondisclosure, acceptable use, rules-of-behavior, and conflict-of-interest for individuals requiring access to information and information system resources before authorizing access to such resources.

**210.** **Which of the following linkages provide a high-level focus?**

    a.    Link information security metrics to the organization strategic goals

    b.    Link information security metrics to the organization strategic objectives

    c.    Link information security activities to the organization-level strategic planning

    d.    Link information security metrics to the information security program performance

***210. c.*** Information security metrics provides a low-level focus whereas security activities, which are part of the security program, provide a high-level focus. Security metrics monitors and measures implementation and effectiveness of security controls within the context of the security program.

**211.** **Which of the following IT security metrics focuses on implementation?**

    a.    Percentage of system users that have received basic awareness training

    b.    Percentage of operational systems that have completed certification and accreditation following major changes

    c.    Percentage of new systems that completed certification and accreditation prior to the implementation

    d.    Percentage of systems successfully addressed in the testing of the contingency plan

***211. a.*** "Percentage of system users that have received basic awareness training" is an example of implementation metrics. The other three choices are examples of effectiveness metrics.

Implementation metrics measure the results of implementation of security policies, procedures, and controls (i.e., demonstrates progress in implementation efforts). Effectiveness/efficiency metrics measure the results of security services delivery (i.e., monitors the results of security controls implementation).

**212.** **Which of the following IT security metrics focuses on efficiency?**

    a.    Percentage of systems successfully testing the contingency plan at the alternative processing site

    b.    Percentage of systems that use automated tools to validate performance of periodic maintenance

    c.    Percentage of individuals screened before being granted access to organizational information and information systems

    d.    Percentage of system components that undergo maintenance on schedule

***212. d.*** "Percentage of system components that undergo maintenance on schedule" is an example of efficiency metrics. The other three choices are examples of implementation metrics.

Effectiveness/efficiency metrics measure the results of security services delivery (i.e., monitors the results of security controls implementation). Implementation metrics measure the results of implementation of security policies, procedures, and controls (i.e., demonstrates progress in implementation efforts).

**213.** **Which of the following is a prerequisite to IT security training?**

    a.   Security basics

    b.   Awareness

    c.   Security literacy

    d.   Education

***213. b.*** Awareness programs act as a prerequisite to IT security training. Awareness programs set the stage for training by changing organizational attitudes to realize the importance of security and the adverse consequences of its failure.

**214.** **The security objective or principle of integrity does *not* deal with which of the following?**

    a.   Accuracy

    b.   Privacy

    c.   Non-repudiation

    d.   Accountability

***214. b.*** Privacy is a part of a confidentiality objective or principle, whereas the other three choices are part of the integrity objective or principle. Privacy protection is the establishment of controls to ensure the security and confidentiality of data records and restricting access to such records. Confidentiality is preserving authorized restrictions on information access and disclosure, including means for protecting personal privacy and proprietary information. Hence, privacy and confidentiality are related to each other.

Integrity is the property that protected and sensitive data has not been modified or deleted in an unauthorized and undetected manner. Accuracy is a qualitative assessment of correctness of data or freedom from error (i.e., data needs integrity). Non-repudiation is a service that is used to provide assurance of the integrity and origin of data in such a way that the integrity and origin can be verified and validated by a third party. Accountability generates the requirements for actions of an individual to be traced uniquely to that individual (i.e., supports prevention, detection, fault isolation, and non-repudiation). Hence, accuracy, accountability, and non-repudiation all require that data and information must have integrity. If data that an individual is handling is not accurate and if an individual can deny sending or receiving a message, how can that individual be held accountable for his actions? Note that the terms integrity, accuracy, non-repudiation, and accountability have different definitions and meanings depending on the context of use.

**215.** Which of the following verifies that the other three security principles have been adequately met by a specific implementation?

    a.    Assurance

    b.    Integrity

    c.    Confidentiality

    d.    Availability

***215. a.*** Assurance verifies that the security principles such as integrity, availability, confidentiality, and accountability have been adequately met by a specific implementation.

**216.** Regarding information security governance, which of the following should take place for noncompliance?

    a.    Change in policies

    b.    Change in procedures

    c.    Change in practices

    d.    Periodic assessments

***216. d.*** Periodic assessments and reports on activities can be a valuable means of identifying areas of noncompliance. The other three choices can result from the periodic assessments.

**217.** Which of the following must be considered when the system boundaries are drawn and when establishing a control baseline?

    a.    Confidentiality

    b.    Impact levels

    c.    Integrity

    d.    Availability

***217. b.*** The impact levels (i.e., low, moderate, or high) must be considered when the system boundaries are drawn and when selecting the initial set of security controls (i.e., control baseline). Confidentiality, integrity, and availability are security objectives for which potential impact is assessed.

**218.** Which of the following is *not* an element of information quality?

    a.    Reproducibility

    b.    Utility

    c.    Integrity

    d.    Objectivity

***218. a.*** Information quality is an encompassing term composed of utility integrity and objectivity. Reproducibility means that the information can be substantially reproduced, subject to an acceptable degree of imprecision.

**219.** Which of the following information security governance structures provides the creation of interorganizational and intra-organizational communication mechanisms in establishing the appropriate policies, procedures, and processes dealing with risk management and information security strategies?

    a.    Centralized governance

    b.    Decentralized governance

    c.    Hybrid governance

    d.    Virtual governance

***219. a.*** The information security governance model should be aligned with the IT governance model and the corporate governance model. A centralized approach to governance requires strong, well-informed central leadership and provides consistency throughout the organization. Centralized governance structures also provide less autonomy for subordinate (sector) organizations that are part of the parent organization. To achieve the centralized governance, interorganizational and intra-organizational communication mechanisms are created.

Decentralized governance is the opposite of the centralized governance, hybrid governance is a combination of centralized and decentralized governance, and virtual governance does not and should not exist.

**220.** Which of the following outcomes of information security governance, a part of information technology (IT) governance, relates to investments in risk management?

    a.    Strategic alignment

    b.    Risk management processes

    c.    Risk management resources

    d.    Delivered value

***220. d.*** The information security governance model should be aligned with the IT governance model and the corporate governance model. Delivered value means optimizing risk management investments in support of organizational objectives (i.e., demanding value from the investments).

Strategic alignment means risk management decisions made in business functions should be consistent with organizational goals and objectives. Risk management processes frame, assess, respond to, and monitor risk to organizational operations and assets, individuals, and other organizations. Risk management resources deal with effective and efficient allocation of given resources.

**221.** Which of the following information security governance structures establish the appropriate policies, procedures, and processes dealing with risk management and information security strategies at the cost of consistency throughout the organization as a whole?

    a.    Centralized governance

    b.    Decentralized governance

    c.    Hybrid governance

    d.    Virtual governance

***221. b.***    The information security governance model should be aligned with the IT governance model and the corporate governance model. A decentralized approach accommodates subordinate (sector) organizations with divergent business needs and operating unit environments at the cost of consistency throughout the organization as a whole. The effectiveness of this approach is greatly increased by the sharing of risk-related information among subordinate units so that no subordinate sector is able to transfer risk to another without the latter's informed consent. The sector also shares risk-related information with parent organization to determine its impact on the organization as a whole.

Centralized governance is the opposite of the decentralized governance, hybrid governance is a combination of centralized and decentralized governance, and virtual governance does not and should not exist.

**222.** Which of the following is *not* an example of issue-specific policies?

    a.    Use of unauthorized software

    b.    Operational security rules

    c.    Acquisition of software

    d.    Doing computer work at home

***222. b.***    Operational security rules are part of system-specific security policy, whereas the other three choices are part of issue-specific policies.

**223.** Which of the following IT security metrics focuses on effectiveness?

    a.    Average frequency of audit records reviewed and analyzed for inappropriate activity

    b.    Percentage of security incidents caused by improperly configured access controls

    c.    Percentage of audit log findings reported to appropriate officials

    d.    Percentage of systems using automated mechanisms to conduct analysis and reporting of inappropriate activities

***223. b.***    "Percentage of security incidents caused by improperly configured access controls" is an example of effectiveness metrics.

The other three choices deal with efficiency and implementation metrics. Audit records reviewed deals with efficiency metrics, whereas audit log findings and automated mechanisms deal with implementation metrics.

Effectiveness or efficiency metrics measure the results of security services delivery (i.e., monitors the results of security controls implementation).

Implementation metrics measure the results of implementation of security policies, procedures, and controls (i.e., demonstrates progress in implementation efforts).

**224.** **Which of the following IT security metrics focuses on impact?**

    a.    Percentage of information system security personnel that have received security training

    b.    Percentage of systems compliant with the baseline configuration

    c.    Sum of costs of each incident within the reporting period

    d.    Percentage of configuration changes documented in the latest baseline configuration

*224. c.* "Sum of costs of each incident within the reporting period" is an example of impact metrics. The other three choices are examples of implementation metrics.

Impact metrics measure the results of business or mission impact of security activities and events (i.e., provides the most direct insight into the value of security to the firm). Implementation metrics measure the results of implementation of security policies, procedures, and controls (i.e., demonstrates progress in implementation efforts).

**225.** **IT security training provides which of the following levels?**

    a.    Data

    b.    Information

    c.    Knowledge

    d.    Insight

*225. c.* IT security training provides knowledge levels, awareness provides data and information levels, and education provides insight levels.

# SCENARIO-BASED QUESTIONS, ANSWERS, AND EXPLANATIONS

Use the following information to answer questions 1 through 9.

Risk management is a major priority of the SPK Company. The following data has been collected for one asset in the company: Natural threats are realized once every five years. The total asset value is $1,000,000. Every time a threat causes damage, it cost the company an average of $100,000. The company has the choice of getting insurance for $10,000 per year or moving to a new location that will be a onetime cost of $35,000. The SPK priorities in the risk management strategy are accuracy and long-term repeatability of process.

**1.** **What can be done with the residual risk?**

    a.    It can be either assigned or accepted.

    b.    It can be either identified or evaluated.

    c.    It can be either reduced or calculated.

    d.    It can be either exposed or assessed.

*1. a.*    Residual risk is the remaining risk after countermeasures (controls) cover the risk population. The residual risk is either assigned to a third party (e.g., insurance company) or accepted by management as part of doing business. It may not be cost-effective to further reduce residual risk.

**2.** **Which of the following is *not* part of risk analysis?**

    a.    Assets

    b.    Threats

    c.    Vulnerabilities

    d.    Countermeasures

*2. d.*    Countermeasures and safeguards come after performing risk analysis. Risk analysis identifies the risks to system security and determines the probability of occurrence, the resulting impact, and the additional safeguards that mitigate this impact. Assets, threats, and vulnerabilities are part of risk analysis exercise.

**3.** **Security safeguards and controls cannot do which of the following?**

    a.    Risk reduction

    b.    Risk avoidance

    c.    Risk transfer

    d.    Risk analysis

*3. d.*    Risk analysis identifies the risks to system security and determines the probability of occurrence, the resulting impact, and the additional safeguards that mitigate this impact. Risk analysis is a management exercise performed before deciding on specific safeguards and controls. Risk reduction, risk avoidance, and risk transfer are part of risk mitigation, which results from applying the selected safeguards and controls.

**4.** **Selection and implementation of security controls refer to which of the following?**

    a.    Risks analysis

    b.    Risk mitigation

    c.    Risk assessment

    d.    Risk management

**4. b.** Risk mitigation involves the selection and implementation of security controls to reduce risks to an acceptable level. Risk analysis is the same as risk assessment. Risk management includes both risk analysis and risk mitigation.

5. **Which of the following is closely linked to risk acceptance?**

    a.    Risk detection

    b.    Risk prevention

    c.    Risk tolerance

    d.    Risk correction

**5. c.** Risk tolerance is the level of risk that an entity or a manager is willing to assume or accept to achieve a potential desired result. Some managers accept more risk than others do due to their personal affinity toward risk.

6. **The amount of risk an organization can handle should be based on which of the following?**

    a.    Technological level

    b.    Acceptable level

    c.    Affordable level

    d.    Measurable level

**6. b.** Often, losses cannot be measured in monetary terms alone. Risk should be handled at an acceptable level for an organization. Both affordable and technological levels vary with the type of organization (e.g., small, medium, or large size and technology-dependent or not).

7. **Which of the following methods for handling a risk involves a third party?**

    a.    Accept risk

    b.    Share risk

    c.    Reduce risk

    d.    Transfer risk

**7. d.** An insurance company or a third party is involved in transferring risk. The other three choices do not involve a third party because they are handled within an organization. One division's risk can be shared by other divisions of an organization.

8. **Which of the following security risk assessment techniques uses a group of experts as the basis for making decisions or judgments?**

    a.    Risk assessment audits

    b.    Delphi method

    c.    Expert systems

    d.    Scenario-based threats

**8. b.** The Delphi method uses a group decision-making technique. The rationale for using this technique is that it is sometimes difficult to get a consensus on the cost or loss value and the probabilities of loss occurrence. Group members do not meet face-to-face. Rather, each group member independently and anonymously writes down suggestions and submits comments that are then centrally compiled. This process of centrally compiling the results and comments is repeated until full consensus is obtained.

Risk assessment audits are incorrect because these audits do not provide the same consensus as the one reached by a group of experts available in the Delphi method. Usually, one or two individuals perform audits, not groups. Expert system is incorrect because it is a computer-based systems developed with the knowledge of human experts. These systems do not reach a consensus as a group of people. Scenario-based threats are incorrect because possible threats are identified based on scenarios by a group of people. However, this system does not have the same consensus reached as in the Delphi method. The process of submitting results and comments make the Delphi method more useful than the other methods.

9. **The costs and benefits of security techniques should be measured in monetary terms where possible. Which of the following is the most effective means to measure the cost of addressing relatively frequent threats?**

    a.    Single-occurrence losses

    b.    Annual loss expectancy

    c.    Fatal losses

    d.    Catastrophic losses

**9. b.** Annualized loss expectancy (ALE) is the estimated loss expressed in monetary terms at an annual rate, for example, dollars per year. The ALE for a given threat with respect to a given function or asset is equal to the product of the estimates of occurrence rate, loss potential, and vulnerability factor.

A single-occurrence loss (SOL) is incorrect because it is the loss expected to result from a single occurrence of a threat. It is determined for a given threat by first calculating the product of the loss potential and vulnerability factor for each function and asset for the threat analyzed. Then the products are summed to generate the SOL for the threat. Because the SOL does not depend on an estimate of the threat's occurrence rate, it is particularly useful for evaluating rare but damaging threats. If a threat's SOL estimate is unacceptably high, it is prudent risk management to take security actions to reduce the SOL to an acceptable level.

Both fatal losses and catastrophic losses are big and rare. Fatal losses involve loss of human life and catastrophic loss incurs great financial loss. In short, ALE is useful for addressing relatively frequent threats whereas SOL and fatal or catastrophic losses address rare threats.

# SOURCES AND REFERENCES

"Directions in Security Metrics Research (NISTIR 7564)," National Institute of Standards and Technology (NIST), U.S. Department of Commerce, Gaithersburg, Maryland, April 2009.

"Guide for Developing Performance Metrics for Information Security (NIST SP800-80 Draft)," National Institute of Standards and Technology (NIST), U.S. Department of Commerce, Gaithersburg, Maryland, May 2006.

"Information Security Handbook: A Guide for Managers (NIST SP 800-100 Draft)," Chapter 2, Information Security Governance, National Institute of Standards and Technology (NIST), U.S. Department of Commerce, Gaithersburg, Maryland, June 2006.

"Information Security Handbook: A Guide for Managers (NIST SP 800-100 Draft)," Chapter 4, Awareness and Training, National Institute of Standards and Technology (NIST), U.S. Department of Commerce, Gaithersburg, Maryland, June 2006.

"An Introduction to Computer Security: The NIST Handbook (NIST SP 800-12)," Chapter 5, Computer Security Policy, National Institute of Standards and Technology (NIST), U.S. Department of Commerce, Gaithersburg, Maryland, October 1995.

"An Introduction to Computer Security: The NIST Handbook (NIST SP 800-12)," Chapter 6, Computer Security Program Management, National Institute of Standards and Technology (NIST), U.S. Department of Commerce, Gaithersburg, Maryland, October 1995.

"IT Examination Handbook, Outsourcing Technology Services," Federal Financial Institutions Examination Council (FFIEC), Washington, DC, June 2004 (www.ffiec.gov).

"Managing Information Security Risk (NIST SP800-39)," National Institute of Standards and Technology (NIST), U.S. Department of Commerce, Gaithersburg, Maryland, March 2011.

"Minimum Security Requirements for Federal Information and Information Systems (NIST FIPS PUB 200)," National Institute of Standards and Technology (NIST), U.S. Department of Commerce, Gaithersburg, Maryland, March 2006.

"Piloting Supply Chain Risk Management Practices for Federal Information Systems (NISTIR 7622 Draft)," National Institute of Standards and Technology (NIST), U.S. Department of Commerce, Gaithersburg, Maryland, June 2010.

"Recommended Security Controls for Federal Information Systems and Organizations (NIST SP800-53 R3)," National Institute of Standards and Technology (NIST), U.S. Department of Commerce, Gaithersburg, Maryland, August 2009.

"Risk Management Guide for Information Technology Systems (NIST SP 800-30 Revision A Draft)," National Institute of Standards and Technology (NIST), U.S. Department of Commerce, Gaithersburg, Maryland, January 2004.

"Underlying Technical Models for Information Technology Security (NIST SP 800-33)," National Institute of Standards and Technology (NIST), U.S. Department of Commerce, Gaithersburg, Maryland, December 2001.

# DOMAIN 4

# Software Development Security

## TRADITIONAL QUESTIONS, ANSWERS, AND EXPLANATIONS

1. **Which of the following is the correct sequence of steps to be followed in an application-software change control process?**

    1. Test the changes.
    2. Plan for changes.
    3. Initiate change request.
    4. Release software changes.
        a. 1, 2, 3, and 4
        b. 2, 1, 3, and 4
        c. 3, 2, 1, and 4
        d. 4, 3, 1, and 2

    *1. c.* Any application software change must start with a change request from a functional user. An information technology (IT) person can plan, test, and release the change after approved by the functional user.

2. **To overcome resistance to a change, which of the following approaches provides the best solution?**
        a. The change is well planned.
        b. The change is fully communicated.
        c. The change is implemented in a timely way.
        d. The change is fully institutionalized.

**2. d.** Managing change is a difficult process. People resist change due to a certain amount of discomfort that a change may bring. It does not matter how well the change is planned, communicated, or implemented if it is not spread throughout the organization evenly. Institutionalizing the change means changing the climate of the company. This needs to be done in a consistent and orderly manner. Any major change should be done using a pilot approach. After a number of pilots have been successfully completed, it is time to use these success stories as leverage to change the entire company.

3. During the system design of data input control procedures, the least consideration should be given to which of the following items?

   a. Authorization
   b. Validation
   c. Configuration
   d. Error notification

**3. c.** Configuration management is a procedure for applying technical and administrative direction and monitoring to (i) identify and document the functional and physical characteristics of an item or system, (ii) control any changes made to such characteristics, and (iii) record and report the change, process, and implementation status. The authorization process may be manual or automated. All authorized transactions should be recorded and entered into the system for processing. Validation ensures that the data entered meets predefined criteria in terms of its attributes. Error notification is as important as error correction.

4. Software configuration management (SCM) should primarily address which of the following questions?

   a. How does software evolve during system development?
   b. How does software evolve during system maintenance?
   c. What constitutes a software product at any point in time?
   d. How is a software product planned?

**4. c.** Software configuration management (SCM) is a discipline for managing the evolution of computer products, both during the initial stages of development and through to maintenance and final product termination. Visibility into the status of the evolving software product is provided through the adoption of SCM on a software project. Software developers, testers, project managers, quality assurance staff, and the customer benefit from SCM information. SCM answers questions such as (i) what constitutes the software product at any point in time? (ii) What changes have been made to the software product?

How a software product is planned, developed, or maintained does not matter because it describes the history of a software product's evolution, as described in the other choices.

**5.** **What is the main feature of software configuration management (SCM)?**

    a.    Tracing of all software changes

    b.    Identifying individual components

    c.    Using computer-assisted software engineering tools

    d.    Using compilers and assemblers

*5. a.* Software configuration management (SCM) is practiced and integrated into the software development process throughout the entire life cycle of the product. One of the main features of SCM is the tracing of all software changes.

Identifying individual components is incorrect because it is a part of configuration identification function. The goals of configuration identification are to create the ability to identify the components of the system throughout its life cycle and to provide traceability between the software and related configuration identification items.

Computer-assisted software engineering (CASE) tools, compilers, and assemblers are incorrect because they are examples of technical factors. SCM is essentially a discipline applying technical and administrative direction and surveillance for managing the evolution of computer program products during all stages of development and maintenance. Some examples of technical factors include use of CASE tools, compilers, and assemblers.

**6.** **Which of the following areas of software configuration management (SCM) is executed last?**

    a.    Identification

    b.    Change control

    c.    Status accounting

    d.    Audit

*6. d.* There are four elements of configuration management. The first element is configuration identification, consisting of selecting the configuration items for a system and recording their functional and physical characteristics in technical documentation.

The second element is configuration change control, consisting of evaluation, coordination, approval or disapproval, and implementation of changes to configuration items after formal establishment of their configuration identification.

The third element is configuration status accounting, consisting of recording and reporting of information that is needed to manage a configuration effectively.

The fourth element is software configuration audit, consisting of periodically performing a review to ensure that the SCM practices and procedures are rigorously followed. Auditing is performed last after all the elements are in place to determine whether they are properly working.

**7.** **Which of the following is an example of input validation error?**

    a.    Access validation error

    b.    Configuration error

    c.    Buffer overflow error

    d.    Race condition error

*7. c.* In an input validation error, the input received by a system is not properly checked, resulting in a vulnerability that can be exploited by sending a certain input sequence. In a buffer overflow, the input received by a system is longer than the expected input length, but the system does not check for this condition.

In an access validation error, the system is vulnerable because the access control mechanism is faulty. A configuration error occurs when user controllable settings in a system are set so that the system is vulnerable. Race condition error occurs when there is a delay between the time when a system checks to see if an operation is allowed by the security model and the time when the system actually performs the operation.

**8.** **From a risk management viewpoint, new system interfaces are addressed in which of the following system development life cycle (SDLC) phases?**

    a.    Initiation

    b.    Development/acquisition

    c.    Implementation

    d.    Operation/maintenance

*8. d.* In the operation/maintenance phase of the SDLC, risk management activities are performed whenever major changes are made to an IT system in its operational (production) environment (for example, new system interfaces).

**9.** **System assurance requires which of the following?**

    1.    Proof-of-origin

    2.    Proof-of-delivery

    3.    Techniques

    4.    Metrics

        a.    1 and 2

        b.    1 and 3

        c.    2 and 4

        d.    3 and 4

**9. d.** System assurance is the grounds for confidence that the set of intended security controls in an information system are effective in their application. System assurance requires (i) techniques to achieve integrity, confidentiality, availability, and accountability and (ii) metrics to measure them. Proof-of-origin and proof-of-delivery are required in nonrepudiation.

**10.** The initiation phase of the security certification and accreditation process does *not* contain which of the following?

    a. Preparation

    b. Resource identification

    c. Action plan and milestones

    d. Security plan acceptance

**10. c.** The action plan and milestones document is a latter part of security certification and accreditation phases, which describe the measures that have been implemented or planned to correct any deficiencies noted during the assessment of the security controls and to reduce or eliminate known system vulnerabilities.

The other three choices are part of the initiation phase, which is the first phase, where it is too early to develop the action plan and milestones.

**11.** Which of the following comes first in the security certification and accreditation process of an information system?

    a. Security certification

    b. Security recertification

    c. Security accreditation

    d. Security reaccreditation

**11. a.** The security certification work comes first as it determines the extent to which the security controls in the information system are implemented correctly, operating as intended, and producing the desired system security posture. This assurance is achieved through system security assessments. The security accreditation package documents the results of the security certification.

Recertification and reaccreditation occur periodically and sequentially whenever there is a significant change to the system or its operational environment as part of ongoing monitoring of security controls.

**12.** Which of the following security accreditation authority's decision scenarios require justification for the decision?

    1. Full accreditation of the system

    2. Accredit the system with conditions

    3. Deny the system accreditation

    4. Defer the system accreditation

    a.    1 only

    b.    2 only

    c.    1, 2, or 3

    d.    1, 2, 3, or 4

*12. c.*   The security accreditation authority has three major scenarios to work with: (i) accredit the system fully, (ii) accredit the system with conditions, or (iii) deny the system accreditation. In any case, supporting rationale (justification) for the decision is needed. In some cases, the system accreditation can be deferred based on sudden changes in regulatory requirements or unexpected merger and acquisition activities in the company. Management can come back to the deferred decision later.

**13.**   **In the continuous monitoring phase of the security certification and accreditation process, ongoing assessment of security controls is based on which of the following?**

    a.    Configuration management documents

    b.    Action plan and milestone documents

    c.    Configuration control documents

    d.    Security impact analyses documents

*13. b.*   To determine what security controls to select for ongoing review, organizations should first prioritize testing on "action plan and milestones" items that become closed. These newly implemented controls should be validated first.

The other three documents are part of the continuous monitoring phase and come into play when there are major changes or modifications to the operational system.

**14.**   **What is the major purpose of configuration management?**

    a.    To reduce risks from system insertions

    b.    To reduce risks from system installations

    c.    To reduce risks from modifications

    d.    To minimize the effects of negative changes

*14. d.*   The purpose of configuration management is to minimize the effects of negative changes or differences in configurations on an information system or network. The other three choices are examples of minor purposes, all leading to the major purpose. Note that modifications could be proper or improper where the latter leads to a negative effect and the former leads to a positive effect.

**15.**   **The primary implementation of the configuration management process is performed in which of the following system development life cycle (SDLC) phases?**

    a.    Initiation

    b.    Acquisition/development

      c.     Implementation

      d.     Operation/maintenance

*15. d.*   The primary implementation of the configuration management process is performed during the operation/maintenance phase of the SDLC, the operation/maintenance phase. The other phases are too early for this process to take place.

**16.**   **Which of the following phases of the security certification and accreditation process primarily deals with configuration management?**

      a.     Initiation

      b.     Security certification

      c.     Security accreditation

      d.     Continuous monitoring

*16. d.*   The fourth phase of the security certification and accreditation process, continuous-monitoring, primarily deals with configuration management. Documenting information system changes and assessing the potential impact those changes may have on the security of the system is an essential part of continuous monitoring and maintaining the security accreditation.

**17.**   **Constant monitoring of an information system is performed with which of the following?**

      1.     Risk management

      2.     Security certification

      3.     Security accreditation

      4.     Configuration management processes

      a.     1 and 2

      b.     2 and 3

      c.     1, 2, and 3

      d.     1, 2, 3, and 4

*17. d.*   Constant monitoring of a system is performed to identify possible risks to the system so that these can be addressed through the risk management, security certification and accreditation, and configuration management processes.

**18.**   **Which of the following are not the responsibilities of the configuration control review board?**

      1.     Discussing change requests

      2.     Conducting impact analysis of changes

      3.     Requesting funding to implement changes

      4.     Notifying users of system changes

a. 1 and 2

b. 1 and 3

c. 2 and 4

d. 3 and 4

**18. c.** Conducting impact analysis of changes and notifying users of system changes are the responsibilities of the configuration manager, whereas discussing change requests and requesting funding to implement changes are the responsibilities of the configuration control review board.

19. An impact analysis of changes is conducted in which of the following configuration management process steps?

a. Identify changes.

b. Evaluate change request.

c. Implement decisions.

d. Implement approved change requests.

**19. b.** After initiating a change request, the effects that the change may have on a specific system or other interrelated systems must be evaluated. An impact analysis of the change is conducted in the "evaluate change request" step. Evaluation is the end result of identifying changes, deciding what changes to approve and how to implement them, and actually implementing the approved changes.

20. Additional testing or analysis may be needed in which of the following operational decision choices of the configuration management process?

a. Approve

b. Implement

c. Deny

d. Defer

**20. d.** In the "defer" choice, immediate decision is postponed until further notice. In this situation, additional testing or analysis may be needed before a final decision can be made later.

On the other hand, approve, implement, and deny choices do not require additional testing and analysis because management is already satisfied with the testing and analysis.

21. During the initiation phase of a system development life cycle (SDLC) process, which of the following tasks is not typically performed?

a. Preliminary risk assessment

b. Preliminary system security plans

c. High-level security test plans

d. High-level security system architecture

***21. c.*** A security-test-plan, whether high level or low level, is developed in the development/acquisition phase. The other three choices are performed in the initiation phase.

**22.** Security controls are designed and implemented in which of the following system development life cycle (SDLC) phases?

   a.   Initiation

   b.   Development/acquisition

   c.   Implementation

   d.   Disposal

***22. b.*** Security controls are developed, designed, and implemented in the development/acquisition phase. Additional controls may be developed to support the controls already in place or planned.

**23.** Product acquisition and integration costs are determined in which of the following system development life cycle (SDLC) phases?

   a.   Initiation

   b.   Development/acquisition

   c.   Implementation

   d.   Disposal

***23. b.*** Product acquisition and integration costs that can be attributed to information security over the life cycle of the system are determined in the development/acquisition phase. These costs include hardware, software, personnel, and training.

**24.** A formal authorization to operate an information system is obtained in which of the following system development life cycle (SDLC) phases?

   a.   Initiation

   b.   Development/acquisition

   c.   Implementation

   d.   Disposal

***24. c.*** In the implementation phase, the organization configures and enables system security features, tests the functionality of these features, installs or implements the system, and finally, obtains a formal authorization to operate the system.

**25.** Which of the following gives assurance as part of system's security and functional requirements defined for an information system?

   a.   Access controls

   b.   Background checks for system developers

   c.   Awareness

   d.   Training

**25. b.** Security and functional requirements can be expressed as technical (for example, access controls), assurances (for example, background checks for system developers), or operational practices (for example, awareness and training).

26. **System users must perform which of the following when new security controls are added to an existing application system?**

    a.    Unit testing

    b.    Subsystem testing

    c.    Full system testing

    d.    Acceptance testing

**26. d.** If new security controls are added to an existing application system or to a support system, system users must perform additional acceptance tests of these new controls. This approach ensures that new controls meet security specifications and do not conflict with or invalidate existing controls.

27. **Periodic reaccreditation of a system is done in which of the following system development life cycle (SDLC) phases?**

    a.    Initiation

    b.    Development/acquisition

    c.    Implementation

    d.    Operation/maintenance

**27. d.** Documenting information system changes and assessing the potential impact of these changes on the security of a system is an essential part of continuous monitoring and key to avoiding a lapse in the system security reaccreditation. Periodic reaccreditation is done in the operation phase.

28. **Which of the following tests is driven by system requirements?**

    a.    Black-box testing

    b.    White-box testing

    c.    Gray-box testing

    d.    Integration testing

**28. a.** Black-box testing, also known as functional testing, executes part or all the system to validate that the user requirement is satisfied.

White-box testing, also known as structural testing, examines the logic of the units and may be used to support software requirements for test coverage, i.e., how much of the program has been executed.

Gray-box testing can be looked at as anything that is not tested in white-box or black-box. An integration testing is performed to examine how units interface and interact with each other with the assumption that the units and the objects (for example, data) they manipulate have all passed their unit tests.

**29.** **System integration is performed in which of the following system development life cycle (SDLC) phases?**

    a.   Initiation

    b.   Development/acquisition

    c.   Implementation

    d.   Operation/maintenance

*29. c.* The new system is integrated at the operational site where it is to be deployed for operation. Security control settings and switches are enabled.

**30.** **Formal risk assessment is conducted in which of the following system development life cycle (SDLC) phases?**

    a.   Initiation

    b.   Development/acquisition

    c.   Implementation

    d.   Operation/maintenance

*30. b.* Formal risk assessment is conducted in the development/acquisition phase to identify system protection requirements. This analysis builds on the initial (preliminary or informal) risk assessment performed during the initiation phase, but will be more in-depth and specific.

**31.** **Which of the following system development life cycle (SDLC) phases establishes an initial baseline of hardware, software, and firmware components for the information system?**

    a.   Initiation

    b.   Development/acquisition

    c.   Implementation

    d.   Operation/maintenance

*31. d.* Configuration management and control procedures are critical to establishing an initial baseline of hardware, software, and firmware components for the information system. This task is performed in the operation/maintenance phase so that changes can be tracked and monitored. Prior to this phase, the system is in a fluid state, meaning that initial baselines cannot be established.

**32.** **Controlling and maintaining an accurate inventory of any changes to an information system is possible due to which of the following?**

    a.   Configuration management and controls

    b.   Continuous monitoring

    c.   Security certification

    d.   Security accreditation

*32. a.* Configuration management and controls, which is a part of system operation and maintenance phase, deals with controlling and maintaining an accurate inventory of any changes to the system. Security certification and security accreditation are part of system implementation phase, whereas continuous monitoring is a part of operation and maintenance phase.

**33.** **Which of the following does *not* facilitate self-assessments or independent security audits of an information system?**

    a.    Internal control reviews

    b.    Penetration testing

    c.    Developing security controls

    d.    Security checklists

*33. c.* System assessors or auditors do not develop security controls due to loss of objectivity in thinking and loss of independence in appearance. Security controls should be built by system designers and developers prior to performing internal control reviews, conducting penetration testing, or using security checklists by system assessors or auditors. Internal control reviews, penetration testing, and security checklists simply facilitate self-assessments or independent audits of an information system later.

**34.** **In the needs-determination task of the system development life cycle (SDLC) initiation phase, which of the following optimizes the organization's system needs within budget constraints?**

    a.    Fit-gap analysis

    b.    Risk analysis

    c.    Investment analysis

    d.    Sensitivity analysis

*34. c.* Investment analysis is defined as the process of managing the enterprise information system portfolio and determining an appropriate investment strategy. The investment analysis optimizes the organization's system needs within budget constraints.

Fit-gap analysis identifies the differences between what is required and what is available; or how two things fit or how much gap there is between them. Risk analysis is determining the amount of risk and sensitivity analysis can determine the boundaries of the risk in terms of changing input values and the accompanying changes in output values.

**35.** **In the preliminary risk assessment task of the system development life cycle (SDLC) initiation phase, integrity needs from a user's or owner's perspective are defined in terms of which of the following?**

    a.    Place of data

    b.    Timeliness of data

    c.    Form of data

    d.    Quality of data

**35. d.**   Integrity can be examined from several perspectives. From a user's or application owner's perspective, integrity is the quality of data that is based on attributes such as accuracy and completeness. The other three choices do not reflect the attributes of integrity.

**36.**    **An in-depth study of the needs-determination for a new system under development is conducted in which of the following system development life cycle (SDLC) phases?**

    a.    Initiation

    b.    Development/acquisition

    c.    Implementation

    d.    Operation/maintenance

**36. b.**   The requirements analysis task of the SDLC phase of development is an in-depth study of the need for a new system. The requirements analysis draws on and further develops the work performed during the initiation phase. The needs-determination activity is performed at a high-level x of functionality in the initiation phase.

**37.**    **Which of the following should be conducted before the approval of system design specifications of a new system under development?**

    a.    Enterprise security architecture

    b.    Interconnected systems

    c.    Formal risk assessment

    d.    System security specifications

**37. c.**   A formal security risk assessment should be conducted before the approval of system design specifications. The other three choices are considered during a formal security risk assessment process.

**38.**    **Which of the following is often overlooked when determining the cost of a new system's acquisition or development?**

    a.    Hardware

    b.    Software

    c.    Training

    d.    Security

**38. d.**   The capital planning process determines how much the acquisition or development of a new system will cost over its life cycle. These costs include hardware, software, personnel, and training. Another critical area often overlooked is security.

39.  Which of the following is required when an organization uncovers deficiencies in the security controls employed to protect an information system?

   a.   Develop preventive security controls.

   b.   Develop a plan of action and milestones.

   c.   Develop detective security controls.

   d.   Modify ineffective security controls.

**39. b.**   Detailed plans of action and milestones (POA&M) schedules are required to document the corrective measures needed to increase the effectiveness of the security controls and to provide the requisite security for the information system prior to security authorization. The other three choices are not corrective steps requiring action plans and milestone schedules.

40.  The security-planning document developed in the development/acquisition phase of a system development life cycle (SDLC) does *not* contain which of the following?

   a.   Statement of work development

   b.   Configuration management plan

   c.   Contingency plan

   d.   Incident response plan

**40. a.**   The statement of work development is a part of other planning components in the development/acquisition phase of a system development life cycle (SDLC). The other three choices are part of the security-planning document.

41.  In establishing a secure network, which of the following reflects the greatest need for restricting access via secure location?

   a.   Transaction files

   b.   Configuration files

   c.   Work files

   d.   Temporary files

**41. b.**   Configuration files, system files, or files with sensitive information must not be migrated to different storage media and must be retained in a secure location due to their access restrictions. The files listed in the other three choices are not sensitive; they are temporary and don't need to be retained after their use is completed.

42.  Which of the following occurs after delivery and installation of a new information system under acquisition?

   a.   Unit testing

   b.   Subsystem testing

   c.   Full system testing

   d.   Integration and acceptance testing

**42. d.** Integration and acceptance testing occurs after delivery and installation of the new information system. The unit, subsystem and full system testing are not conducted for an acquired system but conducted for the in-house developed system. The integration and acceptance testing is conducted for an acquired system.

**43.** Which of the following should be done prior to final system deployment for operation?

    a.    Conduct a security certification process.

    b.    Describe the known vulnerabilities in the system.

    c.    Establish control verification techniques to provide confidence.

    d.    Document the safeguards that are in place to protect the system.

**43. a.** Prior to final system deployment, a security certification should be conducted to ensure that security controls established in response to security requirements are included as part of the system development process. The other three choices are part of the scope of the security certification process.

**44.** The security accreditation decision reflects which of the following?

    a.    Test-based decision

    b.    Risk-based decision

    c.    Evaluation-based decision

    d.    Results-based decision

**44. b.** The security accreditation decision is a risk-based decision that depends heavily, but not exclusively, on the security testing and evaluation results produced during the security control verification process. The security accreditation focuses on risk, whereas system accreditation focuses on an evaluation based on tests and their results.

**45.** Which of the following are the two key information security steps of the operation phase within the system development life cycle (SDLC)?

    1.    Information preservation

    2.    Security accreditation

    3.    Configuration management and control

    4.    Continuous monitoring

    a.    1 and 2

    b.    2 and 3

    c.    1 and 4

    d.    3 and 4

**45. d.** Managing and controlling the configuration of the system and providing for a process of continuous monitoring are the two key information security steps of the operation/maintenance phase of an SDLC. Information preservation is an activity of the disposal phase, whereas security accreditation is an activity of the implementation phase of an SDLC.

**46.** Which of the following are ways to accomplish ongoing monitoring of security control effectiveness?

1. Security reviews

2. Self-assessments

3. Security test and evaluation

4. Independent security audits

    a. 1 and 2

    b. 2 and 3

    c. 1 and 4

    d. 1, 2, 3, and 4

**46. d.** The ongoing monitoring of security control effectiveness can be accomplished in a variety of ways including security reviews, self-assessments, security test and evaluation, and independent security audits.

**47.** Which of the following is a good definition of security control monitoring?

    a. Verifying the continued effectiveness of security controls over time

    b. Verifying the continued efficiency of security controls over time

    c. Verifying the development effectiveness of security controls over time

    d. Verifying the planning effectiveness of security controls over time

**47. a.** Organizations need periodic and continuous testing and evaluation of the security controls in an information system to ensure that the controls are effective in their application. Security-control monitoring means verifying the continued effectiveness of those controls over time.

**48.** Which of the following statements is not true about a system development life cycle (SDLC) process?

    a. Systems undergo improvements in technology.

    b. Security plans evolve with the follow-on system.

    c. There is a definitive end to an SDLC.

    d. Much of previous operational controls are relevant to the follow-on system.

**48. c.** Usually, there is no definitive end to an SDLC process because the system can become a legacy system for a long-time or it can eventually be replaced with a new system. Systems evolve or transition to the next generation as follow-on systems with changing requirements and technology. Security plans evolve with the system. Much of management and operational controls in the old, legacy system are still relevant and useful in developing the security plan for the follow-on system.

**49.** **If there is a doubt as to whether sensitive information remains on a system, which of the following should be consulted before disposing of the system?**

    a.    Information system owner

    b.    Information system security officer

    c.    Information owner

    d.    Certification and accreditation officer

*49. b.* Some systems may contain sensitive information after the storage media is removed. If there is a doubt whether sensitive information remains on a system, the information system security officer should be consulted before disposing of the system because the officer deals with technical aspects of a system. The other parties mentioned do not have a technical focus but instead have a business focus.

**50.** **Which of the following is similar to security certification and accreditation?**

    a.    Quality assurance

    b.    Quality control

    c.    Operational control

    d.    Management control

*50. b.* Quality control is similar to security certification and accreditation in terms of scope of work and goals. Quality control is a technical control. Quality assurance is included in security planning, which is a management control. Operational control deals with day-to-day procedures.

**51.** **Which of the following are essential components of the security certification and accreditation process?**

    1.    Risk assessment

    2.    Security requirements

    3.    Security plans

    4.    Security controls

        a.    1 and 2

        b.    1 and 3

        c.    2 and 4

        d.    3 and 4

*51. b.* Both risk assessment and security plans are essential components of the security certification and accreditation process. These two components accurately reflect the security requirements and security controls through the system development life cycle (SDLC) methodology. Security requirements and security controls (planned or designed) drive the risk assessment process and security plans.

52. **By accrediting an information system, an organization's management official does which of the following?**

    a.    Avoids the risks

    b.    Limits the risks

    c.    Accepts the risks

    d.    Transfers the risks

*52. c.* By accrediting an information system, an organization's management official accepts the risks associated with operating the system and the associated security implications to the organization's operations, assets, or individuals.

53. **Information system assurance is achieved through which of the following?**

    1.    Understanding of the threat environment

    2.    Evaluation of system requirements sets

    3.    Knowledge of hardware and software engineering principles

    4.    Availability of product and system evaluation results

    a.    1 and 2

    b.    2 and 3

    c.    3 and 4

    d.    1, 2, 3, and 4

*53. d.* System assurance is the grounds for confidence that a system meets its security expectations. Good understanding of the threat environment, evaluation of system requirements sets, knowledge of hardware and software engineering principles, and the availability of product and system evaluation results are required for system assurance.

54. **What should be in place prior to the security certification and accreditation process?**

    a.    The security plan is analyzed.

    b.    The security plan is updated.

    c.    The security plan is accepted.

    d.    The security plan is developed.

*54. d.* During the security certification and accreditation process, the system security plan is analyzed, updated, and accepted. For this to happen, the system security plan must have been developed and in place.

55. **Which of the following should occur prior to a significant change in the processing of an information system?**

    a.    System recertification

    b.    System reaccreditation

    c.    System reauthorization

    d.    System reassessment

**55. c.**    Reauthorization should occur prior to a significant change in processing of an information system. A periodic review of controls should also contribute to future authorizations.

**56.**    **Effective control is achieved when configuration management control is established prior to the start of which of the following?**

    a.    Requirements analysis

    b.    Design

    c.    Coding

    d.    Testing

**56. b.**    The design phase translates requirements into a representation of the software. The design is placed under configuration management control before coding begins.

Requirements analysis is incorrect because it focuses on gathering requirements to understand the nature of the programs to be built. The design must be translated into code-readable form. The coding step performs this task. Code is verified, for example, through the inspection process and put under configuration management control prior to the start of formal testing. After code is generated, program testing begins. The testing focuses on the logical internals of the software, ensuring that all statements have been tested, and on the functional externals; that is, conducting tests to uncover errors to ensure that the defined input can produce actual results that agree with required results.

**57.**    **The security-planning document developed in the development/acquisition phase of a system development life cycle (SDLC) does *not* contain which of the following?**

    a.    System interconnection agreements

    b.    Security tests and evaluation results

    c.    Request for proposal

    d.    Plan of actions and milestones

**57. c.**    The request for proposal development, evaluation, and acceptance are a part of other planning components in the development/acquisition phase of an SDLC. It is a part of project management activities. The other three choices are part of the security-planning document.

**58.**    **A worm has infected a system. What should be the first step in handling the worm incident?**

    a.    Analyze the host computer.

    b.    Disconnect the infected system.

    c.    Analyze the server.

    d.    Identify the worm's behavior.

**58. b.** Worm incidents often necessitate as rapid a response as possible, because an infected system may be attacking other systems both inside and outside the organization. Organizations may choose to disconnect infected systems from networks immediately, instead of performing an analysis of the host first. Next, the analyst can examine fixed (nonvolatile) characteristics of the server's operating system, such as looking for administrative-level user accounts and groups that may have been added by the worm. Ultimately, the analyst should gather enough information to identify the worm's behavior in sufficient detail so that the incident response team can act effectively to contain, eradicate, and recover from the incident.

**59.** **A worm has infected a system. From a network traffic perspective, which of the following contains more detailed information?**

    a.   Network-based IDS and firewalls

    b.   Routers

    c.   Host-based IDS and firewalls

    d.   Remote access servers

**59. c.** Host-based intrusion detection system (IDS) and firewall products running on the infected system may contain more detailed information than network-based IDS and firewall products. For example, host-based IDS can identify changes to files or configuration settings on the host that were performed by a worm. This information is helpful not only in planning containment, eradication, and recovery activities by determining how the worm has affected the host, but also in identifying which worm infected the system. However, because many worms disable host-based security controls and destroy log entries, data from host-based IDS and firewall software may be limited or missing. If the software was configured to forward copies of its logs to centralized log servers, then queries to those servers may provide some useful information (assuming the host logs' integrity is not in doubt).

Network-based IDS is incorrect because it indicates which server was attacked and on what port number, which indicates which network service was targeted. Network-based firewalls are typically configured to log blocked connection attempts, which include the intended destination IP address and port number. Other perimeter devices that the worm traffic may have passed through, such as routers, virtual private network (VPN) gateways, and remote access servers may record information similar to that logged by network-based firewalls.

**60.** **Media sanitization activity is usually most intense during which of the following phases of the system development life cycle (SDLC)?**

    a.   Development/acquisition

    b.   Implementation

    c.   Operation/maintenance

    d.   Disposal

**60. d.** Media sanitization ensures that data is deleted, erased, and written over as necessary. Media sanitization and information disposition activity is usually most intense during the disposal phase of the system life cycle. However, throughout the life of an information system, many types of data storage media will be transferred outside positive control, and some will be reused during all phases of the SDLC. This media sanitization activity may be for maintenance reasons, system upgrades, or during a configuration update.

**61.** The security certification assessor is involved with which of the following activities?

    a.    System development

    b.    System controls

    c.    System implementation

    d.    System operations

**61. b.** The security certification assessor is involved in assessing security controls in an information system to provide an unbiased opinion. The assessor's independence implies that he is not involved in the information system development, implementation, or operation.

**62.** Which of the following threats rely entirely on social engineering techniques?

    1.    Trojan horse

    2.    Mobile code

    3.    Phishing

    4.    Virus hoaxes

        a.    1 and 2

        b.    2 and 3

        c.    1 and 3

        d.    3 and 4

**62. d.** Both phishing and virus hoaxes rely entirely on social engineering, which is a general term for attackers trying to trick people into revealing sensitive information or performing certain actions, such as downloading and executing files that appear to be benign but are actually malicious. Phishing refers to using deceptive computer-based means to trick individuals into disclosing sensitive personal information. Virus hoaxes are false virus warnings. The majority of virus alerts that are sent via e-mail among users are actually hoaxes.

Trojan horse is incorrect because it is a nonreplicating program that appears to be benign but actually has a hidden malicious purpose.

Mobile code is incorrect because it is software that is transmitted from a remote system to be executed on a local system, typically without the user's explicit instruction. Trojan horse and mobile code do not rely on social engineering.

**63.** Defining roles and responsibilities is important in identifying infected hosts with malware incidents before security incidents occur. Which of the following groups can primarily assist in analyzing routers?

    a.   Security administrators

    b.   System administrators

    c.   Network administrators

    d.   Desktop administrators

**63. c.** Organizations should identify which individuals or groups can assist in infection identification efforts. Network administrators are good at analyzing routers along with analyzing network traffic using packet sniffers and misconfigurations. The roles of administrators defined in the other three choices are different due to separation of duties, independence, and objectivity viewpoints.

**64.** Which of the following is *not* a part of software and information integrity for commercial off-the-shelf application security?

    a.   Parity checks

    b.   Cyclical redundancy checks

    c.   Failed security tests

    d.   Cryptographic hashes

**64. c.** An organization employs automated mechanisms to provide notification of failed security tests, which is a control used in the verification of security functionality. The organization employs integrity verification applications on the information system to look for evidence of information tampering, errors, and omissions.

The organization employs good software engineering practices for commercial off-the-shelf integrity mechanisms (for example, parity checks, cyclical redundancy checks, and cryptographic hashes) and uses tools to automatically monitor the integrity of the information system and the applications it hosts.

**65.** Attackers can exploit which of the following flaws to access user accounts, view sensitive files, or use unauthorized functions?

    a.   Broken access control

    b.   Invalidated input

    c.   Broken authentication

    d.   Cross-site scripting flaws

**65. a.** When restrictions on what authenticated users are allowed to do are not properly enforced, it leads to broken access control vulnerability in Web applications. The other three choices do not deal with accessing user accounts, viewing sensitive files, or using unauthorized functions.

66. **What do you call an attacker who can embed malicious commands in application parameters resulting in an external system executing those commands on behalf of the Web application?**

    a. Buffer overflows

    b. Injection flaws

    c. Denial-of-service

    d. Improper error handling

**66. b.** Web applications pass parameters when they access external systems or the local operating system. Injection flaws occur when an attacker can embed malicious commands in these parameters; the external system may execute those commands on behalf of the Web application. The other three choices do not apply here because they do not embed malicious commands.

67. **Both black-box and white-box testing are performed during which of the following?**

    a. Unit testing

    b. Integration testing

    c. System testing

    d. Acceptance testing

**67. a.** A unit test is a test of software elements at the lowest level of development. Black-box testing, also known as functional testing, executes part or all the system to validate that the user requirement is satisfied. White-box testing, also known as structural testing, examines the logic of the units and may be used to support software requirements for test coverage, i.e., how much of the program has been executed. Because the unit test is the first test conducted, its scope should be comprehensive enough to include both types of testing, that is, black box and white box.

Integration testing is incorrect because it comes after completion of unit tests. An integration test is performed to examine how units interface and interact with each other with the assumption that the units and the objects (for example, data) they manipulate have all passed their unit tests. Software integration tests check how the units interact with other software libraries and hardware.

System testing is incorrect because it comes after completion of the integration tests. It tests the completely integrated system and validates that the software meets its requirements.

Acceptance testing is incorrect because it comes after completion of integration tests. It is testing of user requirements in an operational mode conducted by end users and computer operations staff.

**68.** **If manual controls over program changes were weak, which of the following would be effective?**

  a. Automated controls

  b. Written policies

  c. Written procedures

  d. Written standards

***68. a.*** In general, automated controls compensate for the weaknesses in or lack of manual controls or vice versa (i.e., a compensating control). For example, an automated software management system can help in strengthening controls by moving programs from production to test libraries and back. It minimizes human errors in moving wrong programs or forgetting to move the right ones. Written policies, procedures, and standards are equally necessary in manual and automated environments.

**69.** **Which of the following defines a management's formal acceptance of the adequacy of an application system's security?**

  a. System certification

  b. Security certification

  c. System accreditation

  d. Security accreditation

***69. c.*** System accreditation is a management's formal acceptance of the adequacy of an application system's security. The accreditors are responsible for evaluating the certification evidence, deciding on the acceptability of application security safeguards, approving corrective actions, ensuring that corrective actions are accomplished, and issuing the accreditation statement.

System certification is the technical evaluation of compliance with security requirements for the purpose of accreditation. The technical evaluation uses a combination of security evaluation techniques (for example, risk analysis, security plans, validation, verification, testing, security safeguard evaluation, and audit) and culminates in a technical judgment of the extent to which safeguards meet security requirements.

Security certification is a formal testing of the security controls (safeguards) implemented in the computer system to determine whether they meet applicable requirements and specifications.

Security accreditation is the formal authorization by the accrediting (management) official for system operation and an explicit acceptance of risk. It is usually supported by a review of the system, including its management, operational, and technical controls.

A system certification is conducted first and system accreditation is next because the former supports the latter. Security certification and security accreditation processes follow the system certification and system accreditation processes.

**70.** **Which of the following is a nonresident virus?**

    a.    Master boot sector virus

    b.    File infector virus

    c.    Macro virus

    d.    Boot-sector infector

**70. c.** Macro viruses are nonresident viruses. A resident virus is one that loads into memory, hooks one or more interrupts, and remains inactive in memory until some trigger event. All boot viruses and most common file viruses are resident viruses. Macro viruses are found in documents, not in disks.

**71.** **Backdoors are which of the following?**

    a.    They are entry points into a computer program.

    b.    They are choke points into a computer program.

    c.    They are halt points into a computer program.

    d.    They are exit points into a computer program.

**71. a.** Programmers frequently create entry points (backdoors) into a program for debugging purposes and/or insertion of new program codes at a later date. The other three choices do not apply here because they do not deal with entry points.

**72.** **Most Trojan horses can be prevented and detected by which of the following?**

    a.    Removing the damage

    b.    Assessing the damage

    c.    Installing program change controls

    d.    Correcting the damage

**72. c.** Most Trojan horses can be prevented and detected by a strong program change control in which every change is independently examined before being put into use. After a Trojan horse is detected, the cure is to remove it. Next, try to find all the damage it has done and correct that damage.

**73.** **From a risk analysis viewpoint, what does the major vulnerable area in a computer application system include?**

    a.    Internal computer processing

    b.    System inputs and outputs

    c.    Telecommunications and networks

    d.    External computer processing

**73. b.** The biggest vulnerable area is in the manual handling of data before it is entered into an application system or after it has been retrieved from the system in hard copy form. Because human intervention is significant here, the risk is higher. Controls over internal and external computer processing and telecommunications and the network can be made stronger with automated controls.

**74.** Which of the following is *most likely* to be tampered or manipulated with?

    a.    Configuration file

    b.    Password file

    c.    Log file

    d.    System file

**74. c.** A log file is most likely to be tampered (manipulated) with either by insiders or outsiders because it contains unsuccessful login attempts or system usage. A configuration file contains system parameters. A password file contains passwords and user IDs, whereas a system file contains general information about computer system hardware and software.

**75.** Which of the following software assurance processes is responsible for ensuring that any changes to software outputs during the system development process are made in a controlled and complete manner?

    a.    Software configuration management processes

    b.    Software project management processes

    c.    Software quality assurance processes

    d.    Software verification and validation processes

**75. a.** The objectives of the software configuration management (SCM) process are to track the different versions of the software and ensure that each version of the software contains the exact software outputs generated and approved for that version. SCM is responsible for ensuring that any changes to any software outputs during the development processes are made in a controlled and complete manner.

The objective of the project management process is to establish the organizational structure of the project and assign responsibilities. This process uses the system requirements documentation and information about the purpose of the software, criticality of the software, required deliverables, and available time and resources to plan and manage the software development and software assurance processes. It establishes or approves standards, monitoring and reporting practices, and high-level policy for quality, and it cites policies and regulations.

The objectives of the software quality assurance process are to ensure that the software development and software assurance processes comply with software assurance plans and standards, and to recommend process improvement. This process uses the system requirements and information about the purpose and criticality of the software to evaluate the outputs of the software development and software assurance processes.

The objective of the software verification and validation (SV&V) process is to comprehensively analyze and test the software concurrently with processes of software development and software maintenance. The process determines that the software performs its intended functions correctly, ensures that it performs no unintended functions, and measures its quality and reliability. SV&V is a detailed engineering assessment for evaluating how well the software is meeting its technical requirements, in particular its safety, security, and reliability objectives, and for ensuring that software requirements are not in conflict with any standards or requirements applicable to other system components.

**76.** **The Reference Monitor concept is which of the following?**

    a.    It is dependent on mandatory access control policy.

    b.    It is independent of any access control policy.

    c.    It is independent of role-based access control policy.

    d.    It is dependent on discretionary access control policy.

*76. b.* The Reference Monitor concept is independent of any particular access control policy because it mediates all types of access to objects by subjects. Mandatory access control policy is a means of restricting access to objects based on the sensitivity of the information contained in the objects and the formal authorization of subjects to access information of such sensitivity. With role-based access control policy, access decisions are based on the roles (for example, teller, analyst, and manager) that individual users have as part of an organization. Discretionary access control policy is a means of restricting access to objects based on the identity of subjects.

**77.** **Which of the following are essential activities of a comprehensive information security program for an organization on an ongoing basis?**

    1.    Information preservation

    2.    Security test and evaluation

    3.    Security control monitoring

    4.    Security status reporting

        a.    1 and 2

        b.    2 and 3

        c.    1 and 4

        d.    3 and 4

*77. d.* Security-control monitoring and reporting the status of the information system to appropriate management authorities are essential activities of a comprehensive information security program. Information preservation is a part of the disposal phase, whereas security test and evaluation is a part of the implementation phase of a system development life cycle (SDLC). Security-control monitoring and security status reporting are a part of the operation and maintenance phase of an SDLC, which facilitate ongoing work.

**78.** Security certification is made in support of which of the following?

    a.    Security accreditation

    b.    Management controls

    c.    Operational controls

    d.    Technical controls

**78. a.** Security certification is a comprehensive assessment of the management, operational, and technical controls in an information system, made in support of security accreditation, to determine the extent to which the controls are implemented correctly, operating as intended, and producing the desired outcomes.

**79.** Which of the following is *not* one of the primary goals of certification and accreditation of information systems?

    a.    To enable consistent assessment of security controls

    b.    To promote a better understanding of organization-wide risks

    c.    To deliver reliable information to management

    d.    To conduct reaccreditation reviews periodically

**79. d.** Conducting reaccreditation reviews periodically is a mechanical step (a byproduct of the goal) and a secondary goal. The primary goals of certification and accreditation of information systems are to (i) enable more consistent, comparable, and repeatable assessments of security controls in information systems, (ii) promote a better understanding of organization-related risks resulting from the operation of information systems, and (iii) create more complete, reliable, and trustworthy information for authorizing officials (management) to facilitate more informed security accreditation decisions.

**80.** The security accreditation phase does *not* contain which of the following?

    a.    System security plan

    b.    System security assessment report

    c.    Plan of actions and milestones

    d.    Security impact analyses

**80. d.** Security impact analyses are conducted in the continuous monitoring phase whenever there are changes to the information system. The other three choices are part of the security accreditation phase, which comes before the continuous monitoring phase.

**81.** Which of the following is *not* a usual common error or vulnerability in information systems?

    a.    Encryption failures

    b.    Buffer overflows

    c.    Format string errors

    d.    Failing to check input for validity

**81. a.** Usually, encryption algorithms do not fail due to their extensive testing, and the encryption key is getting longer making it more difficult to break into. Many errors reoccur, including buffer overflows, race conditions, format string errors, failing to check input for validity, and computer programs being given excessive access privileges.

**82.** Which of the following is *not* the responsibility of the configuration manager?

   a.   Documenting the configuration management plan

   b.   Approving, denying, or deferring changes

   c.   Evaluating configuration management metric information

   d.   Ensuring that an audit trail of changes is documented

**82. c.** Evaluating configuration management metric information is the responsibility of the configuration control review board, whereas the other three choices are responsibilities of the configuration manager.

**83.** Which of the following tasks are performed during continuous monitoring step of the configuration management (CM) process?

   1.   Configuration verification tests

   2.   System audits

   3.   Patch management

   4.   Risk management

   a.   1 and 2

   b.   2 and 3

   c.   1, 2, and 3

   d.   1, 2, 3, and 4

**83. d.** The configuration management (CM) process calls for continuous system monitoring to ensure that it is operating as intended and that implemented changes do not adversely impact either the performance or security posture of the system. Configuration verification tests, system audits, patch management, and risk management activities are performed to achieve the CM goal.

**84.** Which of the following levels of the software capability maturity model (CMM) is the most basic in establishing discipline and control in the software development process?

   a.   Initial level

   b.   Defined level

   c.   Repeatable level

   d.   Managed level

**84. c.** The Software Engineering Institute (SEI) is a nationally recognized, federally funded research and development center established in the United States to address software development issues. It developed a process maturity framework that would help organizations improve their software development process. In general, the CMM serves as an indicator of the likely range of cost, schedule, and quality results to be achieved by system development projects within an organization. In the repeatable level, basic project management processes are established to track cost, schedule, and functionality. The necessary process discipline is in place to repeat earlier successes on projects with similar applications. The other three choices are not applicable because the correct answer is based on the definition of CMM levels.

**85.** An unauthorized user has successfully accessed a computer-based application system. Which of the preventive controls has failed to work?

      a.    Compatibility tests

      b.    Validity checks

      c.    Security label checks

      d.    Confidentiality tests

*85. a.* As a part of preventive controls, compatibility tests are used to determine whether an acceptable user is allowed to proceed in the system. This test focuses on passwords, access rules, and system privileges.

A validity check is incorrect because it tests for the accuracy of codes such as state, tax rates, and vendor number. A security label check is incorrect because it tests for the specific designation assigned to a system resource such as a file, which cannot be changed except in emergency situations. A confidentiality test is incorrect because it ensures that data is disclosed only to authorized individuals.

**86.** In a distributed computing environment, replicated servers could have negative impact on which of the following?

      a.    Fault-tolerant mechanisms

      b.    Availability

      c.    Scalability

      d.    Recoverability

*86. c.* Just as replication complicates concurrency control, it can affect scalability. The major concern in scalability is determining the effect of increased scale on client performance. Additional storage sites increase the amount of work servers must do to maintain a consistent state of the file system. Similarly, clients in a replicated file system may have more work to do when they make file updates. For this reason, both clients and servers share portions of system management work.

Fault-tolerant mechanisms, availability, and recoverability are incorrect. Replicated servers have a positive impact on system availability and recoverability. If the primary server fails, the replicated server takes over, thus making the system available to system users. Recovery protocols help both servers and clients recover from system failures. Fault-tolerant mechanisms such as disk mirroring and disk duplexing help in recovering from a system failure. They all have a positive effect.

**87.** **Which of the following statements about expert systems is *not* true?**

    a.    Expert systems are aimed at solving problems using an algorithmic approach.

    b.    Expert systems are aimed at solving problems that are characterized by irregular structure.

    c.    Expert systems are aimed at solving problems characterized by incomplete information.

    d.    Expert systems are aimed at solving problems characterized by considerable complexity.

***87. a.*** Expert systems are aimed at problems that cannot always be solved using a purely algorithmic approach. These problems are often characterized by irregular structure, incomplete or uncertain information, and considerable complexity.

**88.** **In the context of expert systems, a heuristic is *not* a:**

    a.    Rule of thumb

    b.    Known fact

    c.    Known procedure

    d.    Guaranteed procedure

***88. d.*** A heuristic is a rule of thumb, a known fact, or even a known procedure that can be used to solve some problems, but it is not guaranteed to do so. It may fail. Heuristics can be conveniently regarded as simplifications of comprehensive formal descriptions of real-world systems. These heuristics are acquired through learning and experience.

**89.** **The architecture of an expert system does *not* include which one of the following?**

    a.    Knowledge base

    b.    Computing environment

    c.    Inference engine

    d.    End user interface

***89. b.*** The computing environment consists of hardware, programming languages, editors and compilers, file management facilities, browsing program code, debugging and tracing program execution, and graphic programming. This computing environment is outside the expert systems architecture because it can change from one organization to another.

On the other hand, knowledge base, inference engine, and end user interface are integral parts of expert systems architecture. Knowledge is stored in the knowledge base using symbols and data structures to stand for important concepts. The symbols and data structures are said to represent knowledge. A software module called the inference engine executes inference procedures. If the user of the expert system is a person, communications with the end user are handled via an end user interface.

**90.** **Expert systems differ from conventional systems in all the following except:**

    a.    Expert system knowledge is represented declaratively.

    b.    Expert system computations are performed through symbolic reasoning.

    c.    Expert system knowledge is combined into program control.

    d.    Expert systems can explain their own actions.

*90. c.* Expert system programs differ from conventional systems in four important ways. First, knowledge is separated from program control; the knowledge base and inference engine are separate. Second, knowledge is represented declaratively. Third, expert systems perform computation through symbolic reasoning. And finally, expert systems can explain their own actions.

**91.** **Which of the following categories of problem-solving activity is best suited to expert systems?**

    a.    Tasks based on a limited domain

    b.    Tasks based on common sense knowledge

    c.    Tasks requiring perceptual knowledge

    d.    Tasks based on creativity

*91. a.* The size of completed expert systems is often large, consisting of hundreds or thousands of rules. If the task is too broad, the development effort may take an inordinate amount of time, or even be impossible. Two important guidelines on evaluating the scope and size of the problem include the task must be narrowly focused and the task should be decomposable. In other words, expert system tasks should be based on a limited domain.

The other three choices are areas to avoid for expert system methods. These include (i) tasks based on common sense, (ii) tasks requiring perceptual (seeing or touching) knowledge, and (iii) tasks requiring creativity. People, not expert systems, are creative.

**92.** **Which of the following statements is *not* true about artificial neural networks (ANNs)?**

    a.    The intention of ANNs is to replicate the workings of the human brain.

    b.    The goal of ANNs is to develop computers that can learn from experience.

    c.    ANNs have a capacity to generalize.

    d.    ANNs complement the existing design of computers.

*92. a.* The intention is not to replicate the workings of the human brain but to use a simple model to see if some of the strengths of the human brain can be shown by computers based on that model. An important goal is to develop computers that can learn from experience. In the process of learning from experience, ANNs show a capacity to generalize. That is, recognizing a new problem as being "close" to the one they know and offering the same solution. ANNs are not meant to replace or supersede the existing design of computers. They are meant to complement them.

**93.** Defining roles and responsibilities is important in identifying infected hosts with malware incidents. Which of the following groups can assist with host scans?

    a.    Security administrators

    b.    System administrators

    c.    Network administrators

    d.    Desktop administrators

**93. a.** Organizations should identify which individuals or groups can assist in infection identification efforts. Security administrators are good at analyzing host scans along with antivirus software, intrusion prevention system (IPS) software, firewalls, and vulnerability assessment results.

**94.** Which of the following tasks must be performed before placing an information system into production operation?

    1.    Analyze functional requirements.

    2.    Analyze assurance requirements.

    3.    Conduct system design reviews.

    4.    Perform system tests.

        a.    1 and 2

        b.    2 and 3

        c.    2 and 4

        d.    3 and 4

**94. d.** System design reviews and system tests should be performed in the implementation phase before placing the system into production operation to ensure that it meets all required security specifications. The results of the design reviews or system tests should be fully documented, updating as new reviews or tests are performed. Analysis of functional requirements and assurance requirements is done in the development/acquisition phase, which is prior to the implementation phase.

**95.** System performance is monitored in which of the following system development life cycle (SDLC) phases?

    a.    Initiation

    b.    Development/acquisition

    c.    Implementation

    d.    Operation/maintenance

**95. d.** During the operation/maintenance phase, the organization should continuously monitor performance of the system to ensure that it is consistent with pre-established user and security requirements and that all needed system modifications are incorporated into the system. Monitoring is done in the operation/maintenance phase of the SDLC because all the development work is completed, and the system should start delivering results. During implementation phase, the system is tested, employees are trained, and the system is not yet ready to put into production operation/maintenance phase to monitor system performance.

**96.** In the needs-determination task of the system development life cycle (SDLC) initiation phase, which of the following is a significant cost driver?

    a.    Performance requirements

    b.    Assurance requirements

    c.    Supportability requirements

    d.    Functional requirements

**96. b.** System assurance is the grounds for confidence that the set of intended security controls in an information system are effective in their application. Information security needs should address the appropriate level of assurance because this is a significant cost driver. The higher the assurance level required, the higher the cost and vice versa. Usually, investment analysis is structured to translate system needs and mission into high-level performance, assurance, functional, and supportability requirements. However, the assurance requirements are the significant cost driver because it integrates all the other requirements at the highest level.

**97.** The security-planning document created in the development/acquisition phase of a system development life cycle (SDLC) does *not* contain which of the following?

    a.    Security awareness and training plan

    b.    Contracting plans and processes

    c.    Rules of behavior

    d.    Risk assessment

**97. b.** The development and execution of necessary contracting plans and processes are a part of other planning components in the development/acquisition phase of an SDLC. The other three choices are part of the security-planning document.

**98.** The security accreditation decision does *not* exclusively depend on which of the following?

    a.    Verified effectiveness of security controls

    b.    Completed security plan

    c.    Security test and evaluation results

    d.    Plan of actions and milestones

**98. c.** The authorizing official in charge of the security accreditation process relies primarily on the other three choices, but not exclusively on the security test and evaluation results produced during the security control verification process. The authorizing official pays more attention to the other three choices because of their significance.

**99.** Which of the following must be done when there is a significant change addressed in the configuration management process?

1. System certification

2. System accreditation

3. System recertification

4. System reaccreditation

    a. 1 and 2

    b. 2 and 3

    c. 3 and 4

    d. 1, 2, 3, and 4

*99. c.* If there were a significant change addressed in the configuration management process, then the system must be recertified and reaccredited. System certification and system accreditation are done when a new system is installed and implemented, prior to any changes.

**100.** Configuration management change control and auditing takes place in which of the following system development life cycle (SDLC) phases?

    a. Initiation

    b. Acquisition/development

    c. Implementation

    d. Operation/maintenance

*100. d.* Configuration management change control and auditing takes place in the operation/maintenance phase of the SDLC. The phases in the other three choices are too early for this activity to take place.

**101.** Security impact analyses are performed in which of the following configuration management processes?

    a. Baseline configuration

    b. Configuration change control

    c. Monitoring configuration changes

    d. Configuration settings

*101. c.* An organization monitors changes to the information system and conducts security impact analyses to determine the effects of the changes. The other three choices are incorrect because they occur prior to the monitoring.

**102.** Application partitioning is achieved through which of the following?

1. User functionality is separated from information storage services.

2. User functionality is separated from information management services.

3. Both physical and logical separation techniques are employed.

4. Different computers and operating systems are used to accomplish separation.

    a. 1 and 2

    b. 3 only

    c. 1, 2, and 3

    d. 1, 2, 3, and 4

**102. d.** The information system physically or logically separates the user functionality (including user interface services) from information storage and management services (for example, database management). Separation may be accomplished through the use of different computers, different CPUs, different instances of the operating system, different network addresses, or a combination of these methods.

**103.** Reconciliation routines in application systems are a part of which of the following?

    a. Authorization controls

    b. Integrity or validation controls

    c. Access controls

    d. Audit trail mechanisms

**103. b.** Integrity or validation controls, which are a part of technical control, include reconciliation routines in application systems. Authorization and access controls, which are a part of technical control, enable authorized individuals to access system resources. Audit trail mechanisms include transaction monitoring.

**104.** Which of the following is the most effective approach in identifying infected hosts with malware incidents and in striking a balance between speed, accuracy, and timeliness?

    a. Forensic identification

    b. Active identification

    c. Manual identification

    d. Multiple identifications

**104. d.** Malware is malicious software and malicious code. In many cases, it is most effective to use multiple identification approaches simultaneously or in sequence to provide the best results for striking a balance between speed, accuracy, and timeliness. Multiple identifications include where a malicious code infection leads to unauthorized access to a host, which is then used to gain unauthorized access to additional hosts (for example, DoS and DDoS attacks).

Forensic identification is effective when data is recent; although, the data might not be comprehensive. Active identification produces the most accurate results; although, it is often not the fastest way of identifying infections due to scanning every host in an organization. Manual identification is not feasible for comprehensive enterprise-wide identification, but it is a necessary part of identification when other methods are not available and can fill in gaps when other methods are insufficient.

**105.** Traditionally, which of the following malware attacker tools is the hardest to detect?

    a.    Backdoors

    b.    Rootkits

    c.    Keystroke loggers

    d.    Tracking cookies

*105. b.* Malware categories include viruses, worms, Trojan horses, and malicious mobile code, as well as combinations of these, known as blended attacks. Malware also includes attacker tools such as backdoors, rootkits, keystroke loggers, and tracking cookies used as spyware. Of all the types of malware attacker tools, rootkits are traditionally the hardest to detect because they often change the operating system at the kernel level, which allows them to be concealed from antivirus software. Newer versions of rootkits can hide in the master boot record, as do some viruses.

**106.** Which of the following virus obfuscation techniques is difficult for antivirus software to overcome?

    a.    Self-encryption

    b.    Polymorphism

    c.    Metamorphism

    d.    Stealth

*106. c.* Older obfuscation techniques, including self-encryption, polymorphism, and stealth, are generally handled effectively by antivirus software. However, newer, more complex obfuscation techniques, such as metamorphism, are still emerging and can be considerably more difficult for antivirus software to overcome. The idea behind metamorphism is to alter the content of the virus itself, rather than hiding the content with encryption.

Self-encryption is incorrect because some viruses can encrypt and decrypt their virus code bodies, concealing them from direct examination. Polymorphism is incorrect because it is a particularly robust form of self-encryption where the content of the underlying virus code body does not change; encryption alters its appearance only. Stealth virus is incorrect because it uses various techniques to conceal the characteristics of an infection, such as interfering with file sizes.

**107.** The goal of which of the following virus obfuscation techniques is to prevent analyzing the virus's functions through disassembly?

    a.    Armoring

    b.    Tunneling

    c.    Self-decryption

    d.    Metamorphism

***107. a.*** The intent of armoring is to write a virus so that it attempts to prevent antivirus software or human experts from analyzing the virus's functions through disassembly (i.e., reverse engineering technique), traces, and other means.

Tunneling is incorrect because it deals with the operating system. A virus that employs tunneling inserts itself into a low level of the operating system so that it can intercept low-level operating system calls. By placing itself below the antivirus software, the virus attempts to manipulate the operating system to prevent detection by antivirus software.

Self-decryption is incorrect because some viruses can encrypt and decrypt their virus code bodies, concealing them from direct examination.

Metamorphism is incorrect because the idea behind it is to alter the content of the virus itself, rather than hiding the content with encryption.

**108.** **Worms do which of the following?**

1. Waste system resources

2. Waste network resources

3. Install backdoors

4. Perform distributed denial-of-service attacks

   a. 1 and 2

   b. 1 and 3

   c. 2 and 4

   d. 1, 2, 3, and 4

***108. d.*** Although some worms are intended mainly to waste system and network resources, many worms damage systems by installing backdoors, perform distributed denial-of-service (DDoS) attacks against other hosts, or perform other malicious acts.

**109.** **Which of the following statements are true about malicious mobile code?**

1. It does not infect files.

2. It does not attempt to propagate itself.

3. It takes advantage of the default privileges.

4. It uses languages such as Java and ActiveX.

   a. 1 and 2

   b. 2 and 3

   c. 3 and 4

   d. 1, 2, 3, and 4

**109. d.** Malicious mobile code differs significantly from viruses and worms in that it does not infect files or does not attempt to propagate itself. Instead of exploiting particular vulnerabilities, it often affects systems by taking advantage of the default privileges granted to mobile code. It uses popular languages such as Java, ActiveX, JavaScript, and VBScript. Although mobile code is typically benign, attackers have learned that malicious code can be an effective way of attacking systems, as well as a good mechanism for transmitting viruses, worms, and Trojan horses to users' workstations.

**110.** **Blended attacks use which of the following?**

1. Multiple infection methods

2. Multiple transmission methods

3. Multiple transmission methods simultaneously

4. Multiple infection methods in sequence

   a. 1 only

   b. 2 only

   c. 3 only

   d. 1, 2, 3, and 4

**110. d.** A blended attack is an instance of malware that uses multiple infection or transmission methods. Blended attacks can spread through such services as instant messaging and peer-to-peer (P2P) file sharing. Blended attacks do not have to use multiple methods simultaneously to spread; they can also perform multiple infections in sequence.

**111.** **Backdoors listen for commands on which of the following?**

1. Source port

2. Destination port

3. TCP port

4. UDP port

   a. 1 only

   b. 2 only

   c. 1 or 2

   d. 3 or 4

**111. d.** Backdoor is a general term for a malicious program that listens for commands on a certain TCP or UDP port. Most backdoors consist of a client component and a server component. The client resides on the intruder's remote computer, and the server resides on the infected system. When a connection between client and server is established, the remote intruder has some degree of control over the infected computer. Both source port and destination port are incorrect because they are too generic to be of any use here.

**112.** **A proactive role to protect an organization from computer-related failures, malfunctions, or disasters is to:**

    a.    Train every employee in the emergency procedures.

    b.    Conduct fire drills regularly every month.

    c.    Train all IT staff in file rotation procedures.

    d.    Incorporate recovery requirements into system design.

*112. d.*   Incorporation of recovery requirements into system design can provide automatic backup and recovery procedures. This helps to prepare for disasters in a timely manner. Training every employee in emergency procedures is incorrect because it does not guarantee that they can respond to a disaster in an optimal manner when needed. Conducting fire drills regularly every month is incorrect because the scope of fire drill may not address all possible scenarios. Disaster recovery goes beyond fire drills; although, the fire drill is a good practice. Training all IT staff in file rotation procedures is incorrect because only key people need to be trained.

**113.** **Rootkits are often used to install which of the following attacker tools?**

    1.    Web browser plug-ins

    2.    E-mail generators

    3.    Backdoors

    4.    Keystroke loggers

        a.    1 only

        b.    2 only

        c.    3 only

        d.    3 and 4

*113. d.*   A rootkit is a collection of files installed on a system to alter the standard functionality of the system in a malicious and stealthy way. Rootkits are often used to install attacker tools such as backdoors and keystroke loggers on a system.

A Web browser plug-in provides a way for certain types of content to be displayed or executed through a Web browser. Attackers sometimes create malicious plug-ins that act as spyware. An example is the spyware dialer, which uses modem lines to dial phone numbers without the user's permission or knowledge. Some dialers are in forms other than Web browser plug-ins, such as Trojan horses.

Malware can deliver an e-mail-generating program to a system, which can be used to create and send large quantities of e-mail to other systems without the user's permission or knowledge. Attackers often configure e-mail generators to send malware, spyware, spam, or other unwanted content to e-mail addresses on a predetermined list.

**114.**   **Which of the following are nonmalware threats?**

1.   Viruses

2.   Worms

3.   Phishing

4.   Virus hoaxes

    a.   1 and 2

    b.   2 and 3

    c.   1 and 3

    d.   3 and 4

*114. d.*   There are two forms of nonmalware threats that are often associated with malware. The first is phishing attacks, which frequently place malware or other attacker tools onto systems. The second is virus hoaxes, which are false warnings of new malware threats. Viruses and worms are true forms of malware threats.

**115.**   **Which of the following is *not* an example of a vulnerability mitigation technique for malware?**

    a.   Patch management

    b.   Antivirus software

    c.   Least privilege

    d.   Host hardening measures

*115. b.*   Antivirus software is an example of a threat mitigation technique for malware. Antivirus software, spyware detection and removal utility software, intrusion prevention systems, firewalls and routers, and application settings are security tools that can mitigate malware threats. Malware often attacks systems by exploiting vulnerabilities in operating systems, services, and applications. Vulnerability can usually be mitigated by patch management, least privilege, and host hardening measures.

**116.**   **Which of the following application settings used to prevent malware incidents will *not* stop phishing and spyware delivery?**

    a.   Filtering spam

    b.   Filtering website content

    c.   Restricting macro use

    d.   Blocking Web browser pop-up windows

*116. c.*   Applications such as word processors and spreadsheets often contain macro languages; macro viruses take advantage of this. Most common applications with macro capabilities offer macro security features that permit macros only from trusted locations or prompt the user to approve or reject each attempt to run a macro. Restricting macro use cannot stop phishing and spyware delivery.

Filtering spam is incorrect because spam is often used for phishing and spyware delivery (for example, Web bugs often are contained within spam), and it sometimes contains other types of malware. Using spam-filtering software on e-mail servers or clients or on network-based appliances can significantly reduce the amount of spam that reaches users, leading to a corresponding decline in spam-triggered malware incidents.

Filtering website content is incorrect because website content-filtering software contains lists of phishing websites and other sites that are known as hostile (i.e., attempting to distribute malware to visitors). The software can also block undesired file types, such as by file extension.

Blocking Web browser pop-up windows is incorrect because some pop-up windows are crafted to look like legitimate system message boxes or websites and can trick users into going to phony websites, including sites used for phishing, or authorizing changes to their systems, among other malicious actions. Most Web browsers can block pop-up windows; other can do so by adding a third-party pop-up blocker to the Web browser.

**117.** **Which of the following is *not* a secondary source for malware incident detection?**

    a.   Antivirus software

    b.   Firewall log files

    c.   Network-based IPS sensors

    d.   Capture files from packet sniffers

***117. a.***   Antivirus software is the primary source of data for malware incident detection. Examples of secondary sources include (i) firewall and router log files, which might show blocked connection attempts, (ii) log files from e-mail servers and network-based IPS sensors, which might record e-mail headers or attachment names, (iii) packet capture files from packet sniffers, network-based IPS sensors, and network forensic analysis tools, which might contain a recording of malware-related network traffic. Host-based IPS is also a secondary source.

**118.** **In the application security environment, system or network transparency is achieved through which of the following security principles?**

    a.   Process isolation and hardware segmentation

    b.   Abstraction and accountability

    c.   Security kernel and reference monitor

    d.   Complete mediation and open design

***118. a.***   Transparency is the ability to simplify the task of developing management applications, hiding distribution details. There are different aspects of transparency such as access failure, location, migration replication, and transaction. Transparency means the network components or segments cannot be seen by insiders and outsiders, and that actions of one user group cannot be observed by other user groups. Transparency is achieved through process isolation and hardware segmentation principles.

The principle of process isolation or separation is employed to preserve the object's wholeness and subject's adherence to a code of behavior. It is necessary to prevent objects from colliding or interfering with one another and to prevent actions of active agents (subjects) from interfering or colluding with one another.

The principle of hardware segmentation provides hardware transparency when hardware is designed in a modular fashion and yet interconnected. A failure in one module should not affect the operation of other modules. Similarly, a module attacked by an intruder should not compromise the entire system. System architecture should be arranged so that vulnerable networks or network segments can be quickly isolated or taken offline in the event of an attack. Examples of hardware that need to be segmented include network switches, physical circuits, and power supply equipment.

The abstraction principle is related to stepwise refinement and modularity of programs. As the software design evolves, each level of module in a program structure represents a refinement in the level of software abstraction. Abstraction is presented in levels, where a problem is defined and a solution is stated in broad terms at the highest level of abstraction (during requirements and analysis phases) and where source code is generated at the lowest levels of abstraction (during programming phase).

The accountability principle holds an individual responsible for his actions. From this principle, requirements are derived to uniquely identity and authenticate the individual, to authorize his actions within the system, to establish a historical track record or account of these actions and their effects, and to monitor or audit this historical account for deviations from the specified code of action.

The security kernel principle is the central part of a computer system (software and hardware) that implements the fundamental security procedures for controlling access to system resources. The principle of a reference monitor is the primary abstraction enabling an orderly evaluation of a standalone computer system with respect to its abilities to enforce both mandatory and discretionary access controls.

The principle of complete mediation stresses that every access request to every object must be checked for authority. This requirement forces a global perspective for access control, during all functional phases (for example, normal operation and maintenance). Also stressed are reliable identification access request sources and reliable maintenance of changes in authority. The principle of open design stresses that design secrecy or the reliance on the user ignorance is not a sound basis for secure systems. Open design enables open debate and inspection of the strengths, or origins of a lack of strength, of that particular design. Secrecy can be implemented through the use of passwords and cryptographic keys, instead of secrecy in design.

**119.** **Which of the following is a reactive countermeasure in defending against worms?**

    a.    Packet filtering firewalls

    b.    Stackguarding

    c.    Virus scanning tool

    d.    Virtual machine

**119. c.** Virus scanners, being one of reactive (detective) countermeasures, search for "signature strings" or use algorithmic detection methods to identify known viruses. These reactive methods have no hope of preventing fast spreading worms or worms that use zero-day exploits to carry out their attacks.

The other three choices are examples of proactive (preventive) countermeasures. Packet-filtering firewalls block all incoming traffic except what is needed for the functioning of the network. Stackguarding prevents worms from gaining increased privileges on a system. A virtual machine prevents potentially malicious software from using the operating system for illicit actions.

**120.** Which of the following is better for training IT staff in malware incident handling?

    a.    Use an isolated test system.

    b.    Use an infected production system.

    c.    Keep the test system and the production system physically separate.

    d.    Keep the test system and the production system logically separate.

**120. a.** Malware test systems and environments are helpful not only for analyzing current malware threats without the risk of inadvertently causing additional damage to the organization, but also for training staff in malware incident handling. An infected production system or a disk image of an infected production system could also be placed into an isolated test environment. Physical separation may not be possible at all times; although, logical separation might be possible. Both physical and logical separation are important but not as important as using an isolated test system.

**121.** Which of the following is *not* part of malware incident detection and analysis phase?

    a.    Understanding signs of malware incidents

    b.    Acquiring tools and resources

    c.    Identifying malware incident characteristics

    d.    Prioritizing incident response

**121. b.** Acquiring tools and resources is a part of the preparation phase. These tools and resources may include packet sniffers and protocol analyzers. The other three choices are incorrect because they are a part of the detection phase. The malware incident response life cycle has four phases, including (i) preparation, (ii) detection and analysis, (iii) containment, eradication, and recovery, and (iv) post-incident activity.

**122.** Which of the following statements is true about application software testing?

    a.    Basic testing equals black-box testing.

    b.    Comprehensive testing equals black-box testing.

    c.    Basic testing equals gray-box testing.

    d.    Comprehensive testing equals focused testing.

**122. *a.*** Basic testing is a test methodology that assumes no knowledge of the internal structure and implementation details of the assessment object. Basic testing is also known as black-box testing.

Comprehensive testing is a test methodology that assumes explicit and substantial knowledge of the internal structure and implementation detail of the assessment object. Comprehensive testing is also known as white- box testing.

Focused testing is a test methodology that assumes some knowledge of the internal structure and implementation detail of the assessment object. Focused testing is also known as gray-box testing.

**123.** Which of the following *cannot* handle the complete workload of a malware incident and *cannot* ensure a defense-in-depth strategy?

    a.    Antivirus software

    b.    E-mail filtering

    c.    Network-based intrusion prevention system software

    d.    Host-based IPS software

**123. *a.*** In a widespread incident, if malware cannot be identified by updated antivirus software, or updated signatures are not yet fully deployed, organizations should be prepared to use other security tools to contain the malware until the antivirus signatures can perform the containment effectively. Expecting antivirus software to handle the complete workload of a malware incident is unrealistic during high-volume infections. By using a defense-in-depth strategy for detecting and blocking malware, an organization can spread the workload across multiple components. Antivirus software alone cannot ensure defense-in-depth strategy. Automated detection methods other than antivirus software are needed to ensure defense-in-depth strategy. These detection methods include e-mail filtering, network-based intrusion prevention system (IPS) software, and host-based IPS software.

**124.** Defining roles and responsibilities is important in identifying infected hosts with malware incidents before security incidents occur. Which of the following groups can primarily assist with identifying infected servers?

    a.    Security administrators

    b.    System administrators

    c.    Network administrators

    d.    Desktop administrators

**124. *b.*** Organizations should identify which individuals or groups can assist in infection identification efforts. System administrators are good at identifying infected servers such as domain name system (DNS), e-mail, and Web servers. The roles of the other three administrators are different from separation of duties, independence, and objectivity viewpoints.

**125.** Which of the following is *true* about a stealth virus?

    a. It is easy to detect.

    b. It is a resident virus.

    c. It can reveal file size increases.

    d. It doesn't need to be active to show stealth qualities.

**125. b.** A stealth virus is a resident virus that attempts to evade detection by concealing its presence in infected files. An active stealth file virus can typically not reveal any size increase in infected files, and it must be active to exhibit its stealth qualities.

**126.** Which of the following is *not* a common tool for eradication of malware from an infected host?

    a. Antivirus software

    b. Spam-filtering software

    c. Spyware detection and removal utility software

    d. Patch management software

**126. b.** Spam-filtering software, whether host-based or network-based, is effective at stopping known email-based malware that uses the organization's e-mail services and is effective at stopping some unknown malware. The most common tools for eradication are antivirus software, spyware detection and removal utility software, patch management software, and dedicated malware removal tool.

**127.** Organizations should strongly consider rebuilding a system that has which of the following malware incident characteristics?

    1. Unauthorized administrator-level access.

    2. Changes to system files.

    3. The system is unstable.

    4. The extent of damage is unclear.

        a. 1 only

        b. 2 and 3

        c. 3 and 4

        d. 1, 2, 3, and 4

**127. d.** If an incident has resulted in unauthorized administrator-level access, changes to system files, unstable system, and the extent of damage is unclear, organizations should be prepared to rebuild each affected system.

**128.** **Which of the following ways should be used to rebuild an infected host with malware incident?**

1. Reinstalling the operating system

2. Reinstalling the application systems

3. Securing the operating and application systems

4. Restoring the data from known good backups

    a. 1 and 2

    b. 3 only

    c. 1, 2, and 3

    d. 1, 2, 3, and 4

*128. d.* Rebuild each affected system by reinstalling and reconfiguring its operating system and applications, securing the operating system and applications, and restoring the data from known good backups.

**129.** **Lessons learned from major malware incidents improve which of the following?**

1. Security policy

2. Software configurations

3. Malware prevention software deployments

4. Malware detection software deployments

    a. 1 only

    b. 1 and 2

    c. 3 and 4

    d. 1, 2, 3, and 4

*129. d.* Capturing the lessons following the handling of a malware incident should help an organization improve its incident handling capability and malware defenses, including needed changes to security policy, software configurations, and malware detection and prevention software deployments.

**130.** **Which of the following is the correct tool and technology deployment sequence for containing malware incidents, especially when a worm attacks the network service?**

1. Internet border and internal routers

2. Network-based firewalls

3. Network- and host-based antivirus software

4. Host-based firewalls

a.   1, 2, 4, and 3

b.   2, 3, 1, and 4

c.   3, 4, 2, and 1

d.   4, 2, 1, and 3

**130. c.**   When organizations develop strategies for malware incident containment, they should consider developing tools to assist incident handlers in selecting and implementing containment strategies quickly when a serious incident occurs.

Network- and host-based antivirus software does detect and stop the worm, and identify and clean the infected systems.

Host-based firewalls do block worm activity from entering or exiting hosts, reconfigure the host-based firewall itself to prevent exploitation by the worm, and update the host-based firewall software so that it is no longer exploitable.

Network-based firewalls do detect and stop the worm from entering or exiting networks and subnets.

Internet border and internal routers do detect and stop the worm from entering or exiting networks and subnets if the volume of traffic is too high for network firewalls to handle or if certain subnets need greater protection.

The incorrect sequences listed in the other three choices does not contain malware incidents because their combined effect is not as strong and effective as the correct sequence.

**131.**   **All the following are characteristics of a managed environment dealing with malware prevention and handling *except*:**

a.   Installing antivirus software

b.   Requiring administrator-level privileges to end users

c.   Using deny-by-default policies

d.   Applying software patches

**131. b.**   Requiring administrator-level privileges is a characteristic of a nonmanaged environment, where system owners and users have substantial control over their own system. Owners and users can alter system configurations, making security weak. In a managed environment, one or more centralized groups have substantial control over the server and workstation operating system and application configurations across the enterprise. Recommended security practices include installing antivirus software on all hosts and keeping it up-to-date, using deny-by-default policies on firewalls, and applying patches to operating systems and applications. These practices enable a consistent security posture to be maintained across the enterprise.

**132.** **Which of the following is required to control the actions of mobile code, stationary code, or downloaded code?**

    a.   Technical controls

    b.   Administrative controls

    c.   Behavioral controls

    d.   Physical controls

*132. c.*   Conceptually, behavioral controls can be viewed as a software cage or quarantine mechanism that dynamically intercepts and thwarts attempts by the subject code to take unacceptable actions that violate policy. As with firewalls and antivirus products, methods that dynamically restrain mobile code were born out of necessity to supplement existing mechanisms, and represent an emerging class of security product. Such products are intended to complement firewall and antivirus products that respectively block network transactions or mobile code based on predefined signatures (i.e., content inspection), and may refer to methods such as dynamic sandbox, dynamic monitors, and behavior monitors, used for controlling the behavior of mobile code. In addition to mobile code, this class of product may also be applicable to stationary code or downloaded code whose trust-worthiness is in doubt.

Technical controls, administrative controls, and physical controls are incorrect because they are not strong enough as the behavioral controls to combat mobile code.

**133.** **Which of the following is basic, low-privilege access to a computer?**

    a.   Application access

    b.   Administrative access

    c.   Privileged access

    d.   Root access

*133. a.*   Application access is basic, low-privilege access. It may include access to data entry, data update, data query, data output, or report programs. Administrative access, privileged access, and root access are advanced levels of access to a computer system that include the ability to perform significant configuration changes to the computer's operating system.

**134.** **Assume that a new computer worm is released that can spread rapidly and damage any computer in an organization unless it is stopped. The organization has 1,000 computers, the budget for in-house technical support is $500,000 per year, and the budget for outsourced technical support is $600,000. It takes an average of 4 hours for one technical support worker to rebuild a computer at a rate of $70 per hour for wages and benefits. What is the total cost for *not* mitigating the worm release?**

    a.   $280,000

    b.   $500,000

    c.   $560,000

    d.   $600,000

*134. c.* The cost not to mitigate = W × T × R, where W is the number of computers or workstations, T is the time spent fixing systems plus lost user productivity, and R is the hourly rate of time spent or lost. During downtime, the computer owner or user is without a computer to do his work, which should be added to the time required to rebuild a computer. This is translated into $560,000 (i.e., 1,000 computers × 8 hours × $70 per hour). $280,000 is incorrect because it fails to take into account the lost user productivity time. This is translated into $280,000 (i.e., 1,000 computers × 4 hours × $70 per hour). $500,000 is incorrect because it assumes the budget for in-house technical support. $600,000 is incorrect because it assumes the budget for outsourced technical support.

**135.** **What is the major principle of configuration management?**

    a.    To reduce risks to data confidentiality

    b.    To reduce risks to data integrity

    c.    To reduce risks to data availability

    d.    To provide repeatable mechanism for effecting system changes

*135. d.* The major principle of configuration management is to provide a repeatable mechanism for effecting system modifications in a controlled environment. Achieving repeatable mechanism can automatically achieve the other three choices.

**136.** **Which of the following refers to the Reference Monitor concept?**

    a.    It is a system access control concept.

    b.    It is a system penetration concept.

    c.    It is a system security concept.

    d.    It is a system-monitoring concept.

*136. a.* The Reference Monitor concept is an access control concept that refers to an abstract computer mediating all accesses to objects by subjects. It is useful to any system providing multilevel secure computing facilities and controls.

**137.** **Which of the following is a malicious code that replicates using a host program?**

    a.    Boot sector virus

    b.    Worm

    c.    Multi-partite virus

    d.    Common virus

*137. d.* A common virus is a code that plants a version of itself in any program it can modify. It is a self-replicating code segment attached to a host executable.

The boot-sector virus works during computer booting, where the master boot sector and boot sector code are read and executed. A worm is a self-replicating program that is self-contained and does not require a host program. A multi-partite virus combines both sector and file-infector viruses.

**138.** **Which of the following is *not* an example of built-in security features?**

    a.    Authentication controls were designed during a system development process.

    b.    Fail-soft security features were installed.

    c.    Least-privilege principles were installed during the post-implementation period.

    d.    Fail-safe security features were implemented.

*138. c.* Built-in security means that security features are designed into the system during its development, not after. Any feature that is installed during post-implementation of a system is an example of built-on security, not built-in. Security and control features must be built in from a cost-benefit perspective.

**139.** **An effective defense against new computer viruses does *not* include which of the following?**

    a.    Program change controls

    b.    Virus scanning programs

    c.    Integrity checking

    d.    System isolation

*139. b.* Computer virus defenses are expensive to use, ineffective over time, and ineffective against serious attackers. Virus scanning programs are effective against viruses that have been reported and ineffective against new viruses or viruses written to attack a specific organization. Program change controls limit the introduction of unauthorized changes such as viruses. Redundancy can often be used to facilitate integrity. Integrity checking with cryptographic checksums in integrity shells is important to defend against viruses. System or equipment isolation to limit the spread of viruses is good, too.

**140.** **Which of the following fully characterizes an information system's security?**

    a.    Confidentiality

    b.    Integrity

    c.    Assurance

    d.    Availability

*140. c.* System assurance is the basis for confidence that the security measures, both technical and operational, work as intended to protect the system and the data and information it processes. For example, software assurance achieves trustworthiness and predictable execution.

The three well-accepted and basic-level security objectives are confidentiality, integrity, and availability, and assurance can be considered an advanced-level security objective because the former culminates into the latter. What good is an information system that cannot provide full assurance with regards to its security?

**141.** Which of the following is an example of both preventive and detective control?

    a.    Audit trails

    b.    Antivirus software

    c.    Policies and procedures

    d.    Contingency plans

*141. b.*   Antivirus software is a preventive control in that it stops a known virus from getting into a computer system. It is also a detective control because it notifies upon detecting a known virus. Audit trails are detective controls; policies and procedures are directive controls, whereas contingency plans are an example of recovery controls.

**142.** Which of the following statements dealing with security principles is *not* true when securing an application environment?

    a.    Information security functions should be isolated from nonsecurity functions.

    b.    Design for protection mechanisms should be simple and small in size.

    c.    Similar security controls should be placed in series and in sequence to achieve defense-of-depth strategy.

    d.    Data-hiding techniques should be practiced during program testing and software maintenance.

*142. c.*   Defending an information system requires safeguards to be applied throughout the system, as well as at points of entry. The selection and placement of security controls should be done in a way that progressively weakens or defeats all attacks. Having a series of similar controls in succession tends to only lengthen the duration of the attack, which is not good. Applying different types of controls that complement each other and are mutually supportive is a much more effective approach in achieving defense-in-depth strategy. Although the capabilities of available safeguards may overlap to some extent, the combined effect should exceed the effects of each control used individually.

The other three choices are true statements in achieving security in an application environment. The information system isolates security functions from nonsecurity functions implemented via partitions and domains that control access to and protects the integrity of the hardware, software, and firmware that perform those security functions. Safety functions should be kept separate from one another. The design of information systems and the design of protection mechanisms in those systems should be as simple as possible. Complexity is at the root of many security issues. The principle of data hiding should be useful during program testing and software maintenance.

**143.** Security controls and audit trails should be built into computer systems in which of the following system development life cycle (SDLC) phases?

    a.    System initiation phase

    b.    System development phase

    c.     System implementation phase

    d.     System operation phase

***143. b.***   During the system development phase, the system is designed, purchased, programmed, developed, or otherwise constructed. During this phase, functional users and system/security administrators develop system controls and audit trails used during the operational phase.

**144.**   **Which of the following levels of the software capability maturity model deal with security requirements?**

    a.     Initial level

    b.     Repeatable level

    c.     Defined level

    d.     Optimizing level

***144. b.***   In the repeatability level of the software capability maturity model, system requirements are defined; these include security, performance, quality, and delivery dates. The purpose is to establish a common understanding between the customer and the software development project team. The other three choices are not correct because each level deals with specific requirements.

**145.**   **Which of the following is *not* a direct method to conduct data leakage attacks?**

    a.     Trojan horse

    b.     Asynchronous attacks

    c.     Logic bombs

    d.     Scavenging methods

***145. b.***   Data leakage is removal of data from a system by covert means, and it might be conducted directly through the use of Trojan horse, logic bomb, or scavenging methods. Asynchronous attacks are indirect attacks on a computer program that act by altering legitimate data or codes at a time when the program is idle and then causing the changes to be added to the target program at later execution.

**146.**   **Which of the following infects both boot-sectors and file-infectors?**

    a.     Worm

    b.     Link virus

    c.     Multi-partite

    d.     Macro

***146. c.***   Multi-partite viruses are a combination of both sector- and file-infector viruses, which can be spread by both methods. A worm is a self-replicating, self-contained program and does not require a host program. Link viruses manipulate the directory structure of the media on which they are stored, pointing the operating system to virus code instead of legitimate code. Macro viruses are stored in a spreadsheet or word processing document.

**147.** **Countermeasures against hidden code attacks include which of the following?**

1. Use war dialing software.

2. Use firewalls.

3. Use layered protections.

4. Disable active-content code.

    a.    1 and 2

    b.    2 and 3

    c.    3 and 4

    d.    1 and 4

***147. c.*** Hidden code attacks are based on data and information. Using layered protections and disabling active-content code (for example, ActiveX and JavaScript) from the Web browser are effective controls against such attacks. War dialing software is good at detecting trapdoors (backdoor modems) and not good against trapdoor attacks. Firewalls are effective against spoofing attacks.

**148.** **The scope of a functional configuration audit does *not* include which of the following?**

    a.    Evaluation of change control

    b.    Testing of software product

    c.    Tracing of system requirements

    d.    Evaluation of test approach and results

***148. a.*** Evaluation of change control is a part of the physical configuration audit, whereas the other choices are part of the functional configuration audit. The physical configuration audit provides an independent evaluation of whether components in the as-built version of the software map to the specifications of the software. Specifically, this audit is held to verify that the software and its documentation are internally consistent and ready for delivery. Activities typically planned and executed as part of the physical configuration audit include evaluation of product composition and structure, product functionality, and change control.

The functional configuration audit provides an independent evaluation of configuration items to determine whether actual functionality and performance are consistent with the requirements specifications. Specifically, this audit is conducted prior to the software delivery to verify that all requirements specified in the requirements document have been met. Activities typically planned and executed as part of a functional configuration audit include testing of software products, tracing of system requirements from their initial specification through system testing, evaluation of the test approach and results attained, and evaluating the consistency between the baselined product elements.

**149.** **Which of the following statements is *not* true about applets?**

    a.    Applets are large application programs.

    b.    Applets are written mostly in Java language.

    c.    Applets are automatically downloaded.

    d.    Applets are small application programs.

*149. a.* Applets are small application programs mostly written in Java programming language that are automatically downloaded and executed by applet-enabled Web browsers.

**150.** **The contingency processes should be tested in which of the following phases of system development life cycle (SDLC)?**

    a.    Initiation

    b.    Development/acquisition

    c.    Implementation

    d.    Operation/maintenance

*150. c.* The contingency processes should be tested and maintained during the implementation phase of the SDLC. The capability to recover and reconstitute data should be considered during the initiation phase. Recovery strategies should be considered during the development phase. The contingency plan should be exercised and maintained during the operation/maintenance phase.

**151.** **Programmers frequently create entry points into a program for debugging purposes and/or insertion of new program codes at a later date. What are these entry points called?**

    a.    Logic bombs

    b.    Worms

    c.    Backdoors

    d.    Trojan horses

*151. c.* Backdoors are also called hooks and trapdoors. Logic bomb is incorrect because it is a program that triggers an unauthorized, malicious act when some predefined condition occurs. Worms are incorrect because they search the network for idle computing resources and use them to execute the program in small segments. Trojan horses are incorrect because a Trojan horse is a production program that has access to otherwise unavailable files and is changed by adding extra, unauthorized instructions. It disguises computer viruses.

**152.** **Software vendors and contractors can install a backdoor entry into their own products or client's computer systems. Which of the following are major risks arising from such installation?**

    a.    Software disconnection and hacker entry

    b.    Remote monitoring and remote maintenance

   c.   Software disconnection and remote monitoring

   d.   Remote maintenance and hacker entry

**152. *a.*** Some vendors can install a backdoor or a trapdoor entry for remote monitoring and maintenance purposes. The good news is that the backdoor is a convenient approach to solve operational problems. The bad news is that the backdoor is wide open for hackers. Also, the vendor can modify the software at will without the user's knowledge or permission. An unhappy vendor can disconnect a user from accessing the software as a penalty for nonpayment or disputes in payment. Access codes should be required for remote monitoring and maintenance.

**153.   A macro virus is *most* difficult to:**

   a.   Prevent

   b.   Detect

   c.   Correct

   d.   Attach

**153. *b.*** A macro virus is associated with a word processing file, which can damage the computer system. Macro viruses pass through the firewall with ease because they are usually passed on as either an e-mail message or simply downloaded as a text document. The macro virus represents a significant threat because it is difficult to detect. A macro virus consists of instructions in Word Basic, Visual Basic for applications, or some other macro languages, and resides in documents. Any application that supports macros that automatically execute is a potential platform for macro viruses. Now, documents are more widely shared through networks and the Internet than via disks.

**154.   Which of the following is *most* vulnerable to Trojan horse attacks?**

   a.   Discretionary access control

   b.   Mandatory access control

   c.   Access control list

   d.   Logical access control

**154. *a.*** Because the discretionary access control system restricts access based on identity, it carries with it an inherent flaw that makes it vulnerable to Trojan horse attacks. Most programs that run on behalf of a user inherit the discretionary access control rights of that user.

**155.   Which of the following is the best place to check for computer viruses?**

   a.   Each computer

   b.   Each workstation

   c.   The e-mail server

   d.   Each network

**155. c.** Virus checkers monitor computers and look for malicious code. A problem is that virus-checking programs need to be installed at each computer, workstation, or network, thus duplicating the software at extra cost. The best place to use the virus-checking programs is to scan e-mail attachments at the e-mail server. This way, the majority of viruses are stopped before ever reaching the users.

**156.** What do you call attacks that can disclose the end users' session token and attack the local machine?

      a.    Broken access control

      b.    Invalidated input

      c.    Broken authentication

      d.    Cross-site scripting flaws

**156. d.** In cross-site scripting (XSS) flaws, the Web application can be used as a mechanism to transport an attack to an end user's browser. A successful attack can disclose the end user's session token, attack the local machine, or spoof content to fool the user.

**157.** A polymorphic virus uses which of the following?

      a.    Inference engine

      b.    Heuristic engine

      c.    Mutation engine

      d.    Search engine

**157. c.** Virus writers use a mutation engine to transform simple viruses into polymorphic ones for proliferation purposes and to evade detection. The other three choices do not deal with the transformation process.

**158.** All the following techniques can help in achieving process isolation security principle *except*:

      a.    Encapsulation

      b.    Naming distinctions

      c.    Virtual mapping

      d.    Security kernel

**158. d.** A security kernel is defined as hardware, firmware, and software elements of a Trusted Computing Base (TCB) that implements the reference monitor concept. A security kernel cannot achieve process isolation.

Techniques such as encapsulation, time multiplexing of shared resources, naming distinctions, and virtual mapping are used to employ the process isolation or separation principle. These separation principles are supported by incorporating the principle of least privilege.

**159.** **Defining roles and responsibilities is important in identifying infected hosts with malware incidents before security incidents occur. Which of the following groups can primarily assist with changes in login scripts?**

    a.    Security administrators

    b.    System administrators

    c.    Network administrators

    d.    Desktop administrators

***159. d.*** Organizations should identify which individuals or groups can assist in infection identification efforts. Desktop administrators are good at identifying changes in login scripts along with Windows Registry or file scans, and good at implementing changes in login scripts. The roles of the other three administrators are different from separation of duties, independence, and objectivity viewpoints.

**160.** **Which of the following is a reactive countermeasure in defending against worms?**

    a.    Integrity checkers

    b.    Software patching

    c.    Host firewalls

    d.    Stateful firewalls

***160. b.*** Software patching, being one of reactive (detective) countermeasures, is mostly done after vulnerability or programming/design error is discovered. These reactive methods have no hope of preventing fast-spreading worms or worms that use zero-day exploits to carry out their attacks.

The other three choices are examples of proactive (preventive) countermeasures. Integrity checkers keep cryptographic hashes of known good instances of files so that integrity comparisons can be made at any time. Host firewalls enforce rules that define the manner in which specific applications may use the network. Stateful firewalls keep track of network connections and monitor their state.

**161.** **Which of the following is an effective means of preventing and detecting computer viruses coming from outside into a network?**

    a.    Install an antivirus program on the network.

    b.    Install an antivirus program on each personal computer.

    c.    Certify all removable media disks prior to their use.

    d.    Train all employees about potential risks.

***161. c.*** It is a common practice for some organizations to certify all removable media disks coming into the organization from outside prior to their use. This is done by a centralized group for the entire location and requires testing the disk for possible inclusion of viruses. The other three choices are effective as internal protection mechanisms against viruses.

**162.** **All the following are examples of measures to defend against computer viruses** *except*:

a. Access controls

b. Audit trails

c. Passwords

d. Least privilege principle

*162. c.* Passwords are administrative controls; although, access controls are technical controls. Access controls include discretionary access controls and mandatory access controls. An audit trail is the collection of data that provides a trace of user actions, so security events can be traced to the actions of a specific individual. To fully implement an audit trails program, audit reduction and analysis tools are also required. Least privilege is a concept that deals with limiting damage through the enforcement of separation of duties. It refers to the principle that users and processes should operate with no more privileges than those needed to perform the duties of the role they are currently assuming.

**163.** **Which of the following security principle balances various variables such as cost, benefit, effort, value, time, tools, techniques, gain, loss, risks, and opportunities involved in a successful compromise of security features?**

a. Compromise recording

b. Work factor

c. Psychological acceptability

d. Least common mechanism

*163. b.* The goal of work factor principle is to increase an attacker's work factor in breaking an information system or a network's security features. The amount of work required for an attacker to break the system or network (work factor) should exceed the value that the attacker would gain from a successful compromise. Various variables such as cost and benefit; effort; value (negative and positive); time; tools and techniques; gains and losses; knowledge, skills, and abilities (KSAs); and risks and opportunities involved in a successful compromise of security features must be balanced.

The principle of compromise recording means computer or manual records and logs should be maintained so that if a compromise does occur, evidence of the attack is available. The recorded information can be used to better secure the host or network in the future and can assist in identifying and prosecuting attackers.

The principle of psychological acceptability encourages the routine and correct use of protection mechanisms by making them easy to use, thus giving users no reason to attempt to circumvent them. The security mechanisms must match the user's own image of protection goals.

The principle of least common mechanism requires the minimal sharing of mechanisms either common to multiple users or depended upon by all users. Sharing represents possible communications paths between subjects used to circumvent security policy.

**164.** Certification and accreditation needs must be considered in all the following phases of system development life cycle *except*:

    a. Initiation

    b. Development/acquisition

    c. Implementation

    d. Operation/maintenance

*164. d.* Certifications performed on applications under development are interleaved with the system development process. Certification and accreditation needs must be considered in the validation, verification, and testing phases employed throughout the system development process (i.e., development and implementation). It does not address the operation/maintenance phase.

**165.** A security evaluation report and an accreditation statement are produced in which of the following phases of the system development life cycle (SDLC)?

    a. Initiation

    b. Development/acquisition

    c. Operation/maintenance

    d. Implementation

*165. d.* The major outputs from the implementation (testing) phase include the security evaluation report and accreditation statement. The purpose of the testing phase is to perform various tests (unit, integration, system, and acceptance). Security features are tested to see if they work and are then certified.

**166.** Which of the following phases of a system development life cycle (SDLC) should *not* be compressed so much for the proper development of a prototype?

    a. Initiation

    b. Development/acquisition

    c. Implementation

    d. Operation/maintenance

*166. c.* System testing, which is a part of implementation, is important to determine whether internal controls and security controls are operating as designed and are in accordance with established policies and procedures.

In the prototyping environment, there is a tendency to compress system initiation, definition, design, programming, and training phases. However, the testing phase should not be compressed so much for quality reasons. By definition, prototyping requires some compression of activities and time due to the speedy nature of the prototyping development methodology without loss of the main features, functions, and quality.

**167.** The activity that would be different between a prototype development approach and the traditional system development approach is:

    a.    How are activities to be accomplished?

    b.    What do users need from the system?

    c.    What should a project plan contain?

    d.    How are individual responsibilities defined?

*167. a.*    Managers still need to define what they want from the system, some assessment of costs/benefits is still needed, and a plan to proceed with individual responsibilities is still required. The difference may be in the way activities are accomplished. The tools, techniques, methods, and approaches used in the prototype development project and traditional system development project are different.

**168.** A general testing strategy for conducting an application software regression testing includes which of the following sequence of tasks?

    a.    Read, insert, and delete

    b.    Precompile, link, and compile

    c.    Prepare, execute, and delete

    d.    Test, debug, and log

*168. c.*    Each test program involves preparing the executable program, executing it, and deleting it. This saves space on mass storage and generates a complete log. This approach is recommended for debugging and validating purposes. Read, insert, and delete include the transfer of all rows from Table A to Table B in that a table is read, inserted, and deleted. A source program is precompiled, linked, and compiled to become an object or executable program. A source program is tested (errors discovered), debugged (errors removed), and logged for review and further action.

**169.** Which of the following tests would be conducted when an application system in an organization exchanges data with external application systems?

    a.    Unit test

    b.    Integration test

    c.    End-to-end test

    d.    System acceptance test

*169. c.*    The purpose of end-to-end testing is to verify that a defined set of interrelated systems, which collectively support an organizational core business area or function, interoperate as intended in an operational environment. These interrelated systems include not only those owned and managed by the organization, but also the external systems with which they interface.

Unit test is incorrect because its purpose is to verify that the smallest defined module of software (i.e., individual subprograms, subroutines, or procedures) works as intended. These modules are internal to an organization. Integration test is incorrect because its purpose is to verify that units of software, when combined, work together as intended. Typically, a number of software units are integrated or linked together to form an application. Again, this test is performed internally in an organization. System acceptance test is incorrect because its purpose is to verify that the complete system satisfies specified requirements and is acceptable to end users.

**170.** **Which of the following can give a false sense of security?**

    a.    A test tool that requires planning.

    b.    A test tool that produces error-free software.

    c.    A test tool that requires time and effort.

    d.    A test tool that requires experience to use

*170. b.* A test tool cannot guarantee error-free software; it is neither a cure-all nor a silver bullet. For some, it may give a false sense of security. The test tool still requires careful planning, time, effort, and experience from which it can use and benefit.

**171.** **Which of the following software configuration-management capabilities available for client/server systems can help to detect and correct errors?**

    a.    Install check-in/check-out modules.

    b.    Archive source code.

    c.    Allow backtracking.

    d.    Assemble new builds.

*171. c.* Errors are made in several places and times: (i) when source code is developed, (ii) when modules are initially written, (iii) when an enhancement is being added to a module, (iv) when another error is fixed, and (v) when code is being moved from one module to another. Software configuration management products have a backtracking feature to correct these types of errors. The product should list the exact source code changes that make up each build. Then, these changes are examined to identify which one can create the new error. The concept of check-in/check-out software enables multiple developers to work on a project without overwriting one another's work. It is a fundamental method of preventing errors from being included or reintroduced into software modules.

**172.** **Which of the following requires a higher level of security protection in terms of security controls?**

    a.    Test procedures

    b.    Test cases

    c.    Test repository

    d.    Test plans

**172. c.**   The test repository consists of test plans, test cases, test procedures, test requirements, and test objectives maintained by the software test manager. Because of the concentrated work products, the test repository needs a higher level of security protection from unauthorized changes. Test procedures, test cases, and test plans are part of test repository.

**173.**  **From a security viewpoint, which of the following pose a severe security problem?**

    a.    Unattended computer operations

    b.    Unattended computer terminal

    c.    Unattended software testing

    d.    Unattended facsimile machine

**173. b.**   An unattended computer terminal represents a severe security violation. An unauthorized user could seize the opportunity to access sensitive data. The data could be copied, deleted, added to, or modified. An intruder can also use this occasion to modify executable files. A virus, Trojan horse, or a password-sniffing program could easily be slipped onto the system in no time. Security logic that detects an idle terminal is needed.

Unattended computer operations are incorrect because they represent a situation where most of computer operational tasks are performed by machines (robots) and less with people.

Unattended software testing is incorrect because testing is conducted by automated test tools without a person watching the testing process. The test tool continues running the test sessions by replaying one or more test scripts. It handles unforeseen circumstances gracefully.

Unattended facsimile machine is incorrect because it can lead to social engineering attacks. The unattended computer operations, software testing, and facsimile machine pose less risk than the unattended computer terminal.

**174.**  **What does the most commonly used application program design structure metrics include?**

    a.    Check-in and check-out indicators

    b.    Fan-in and check-out indicators

    c.    Fan-in and fan-out metrics

    d.    Fan-out metrics and check-in indicators

**174. c.**   Fan-in and fan-out are based on program coupling. Fan-in is a count of the number of modules that call a given module, and fan-out is a count of the number of modules that are called by a given module. Both fan-in and fan-out measure program complexity. Check-in and check-out are program change controls where documents or data/program files will have a check-in or check-out indicator in system libraries to prevent their concurrent use by programmers and computer programs.

**175.** Which of the following application software libraries can raise questions about data ownership rights?

    a.    Test library

    b.    Quality assurance library

    c.    Reusable library

    d.    Production library

*175. c.*   A reusable library can improve software productivity and quality by increasing the efficient reuse of error-free code for both new and modified application software. "Who owns the reusable code?" is a legal question that requires a careful answer due to difficulty in tracing to the original author of the software.

A test library is incorrect because it is where the new software is developed or the existing software is modified. A quality assurance library is incorrect because it is a staging area where final quality reviews and production setup procedures take place. A production library is incorrect because it is the official place where operational programs reside and execute to process data. Data ownership rights in these three libraries (test, quality assurance, and production) are clear and traceable to the author(s).

**176.** Which of the following application software testing approaches does *not* require stubs or drivers?

    a.    Top-down approach

    b.    Bottom-up approach

    c.    Sandwich approach

    d.    Big-bang approach

*176. d.*   The big-bang approach puts all the units or modules together at once, with no stubs or drivers. In it, all the program units are compiled and tested at once.

Top-down approach is incorrect because it uses stubs. The actual code for lower level units is replaced by a stub, which is a throwaway code that takes the place of the actual code. Bottom-up approach is incorrect because it uses drivers. Units at higher levels are replaced by drivers that emulate the procedure calls. Drivers are also a form of throwaway code. Sandwich approach is incorrect because it uses a combination of top-down (stubs) and bottom-up (drivers) approaches.

**177.** Which of the following is a less-formal review technique?

    a.    Inspections

    b.    Traceability analysis

    c.    Reviews

    d.    Walkthroughs

***177. d.*** A walkthrough is an evaluation technique in which a designer or programmer leads one or more other members of the development team through a segment of design or code, whereas the other members ask questions and make comments about technique, style, and identify possible errors, violations of development standards, and other problems. Walkthroughs are similar to reviews but are less formal.

Inspections are incorrect because they are an evaluation technique in which application software requirements, design, code, or other products are examined by a person or group other than the author to detect faults, violations of development standards, and other problems. Inspections are more formal than walkthroughs.

Traceability analysis is incorrect because it is the process of verifying that each specified requirement has been implemented in the design/code, that all aspects of the design/code have their basis in the specified requirements, and that testing produces results compatible with the specified requirements. Traceability analysis is more formal than walkthroughs.

Reviews are incorrect because a review is a meeting at which the requirements, design, code, or other products of software development project are presented to the user, sponsor, or other interested parties for comment and approval, often as a prerequisite for concluding a given phase of the software development process. Reviews are more formal than walkthroughs.

**178.** Inspections *cannot* detect which of the following errors in application software?

    a.    Incomplete requirements errors

    b.    Infeasible requirements errors

    c.    Conflicting requirements errors

    d.    Input/output description errors

***178. d.*** An inspection is an evaluation technique in which software requirements, design, code, or other products are examined by a person or group, other than the author, to detect faults, violations of development standards, and other problems. Input/output description errors are detected in the interface testing phase. The type of errors detected in inspections includes incomplete requirements errors, infeasible requirements errors, and conflicting requirements errors.

**179.** Which of the following is an example of a dynamic analysis to detect application software errors?

    a.    Inspections

    b.    Code reading

    c.    Testing

    d.    Tracing

***179. c.*** Dynamic analysis techniques involve the execution of a product and analysis of its response to sets of input data to determine its validity and to detect errors. The behavioral properties of the program are also observed. The most common type of dynamic analysis technique is testing. Testing of software is usually conducted on individual components (for example, subroutines and modules) as they are developed, on software subsystems when they are integrated with one another or with other system components, and on the complete system. Another type of testing is acceptance testing performed before the user accepts the product.

Inspections, code reading, and tracing are examples of static analysis. Static analysis is the analysis of requirements, design, code, or other items either manually or automatically, without executing the subject of the analysis to determine its lexical and syntactic properties as opposed to its behavioral properties.

**180.** Decision tables are used in which of the following phases of a system development life cycle (SDLC)?

     a.   Initiation

     b.   Development/acquisition

     c.   Implementation

     d.   Operation/maintenance

***180. a.*** The purpose of decision tables is to provide a clear and coherent analysis of complex logical combinations and relationships. This method uses two-dimensional tables to concisely describe logical relationships between Boolean program variables (for example, AND and OR). Advantages of decision tables include (i) their conciseness and tabular nature enables the analysis of complex logical combinations expressed in code and (ii) they are potentially executable if used as specifications. Disadvantages include that they require tedious effort. The requirements analysis, which is a part of initiation phase, is the best place to use the decision table.

**181.** Data-flow diagrams are used in which of the following phases of a system development life cycle (SDLC)?

     a.   Initiation

     b.   Development/acquisition

     c.   Implementation

     d.   Operation/maintenance

***181. a.*** Data-flow diagrams are used to describe the data flow through a program in a diagrammatic form. They show how data input is transformed to output, with each stage representing a distinct transformation. The diagrams use three types of components:

1. Annotated bubbles represent transformation centers, and the annotation specifies the transformation.

2. Annotated arrows represent the data flow in and out of the transformation centers; annotations specify what the data is.

3. Operators (AND and OR) link the annotated arrows.

Data-flow diagrams describe only data and should not include control or sequencing information. Each bubble can be considered a black box that, as soon as its inputs are available, transforms them to outputs. Each bubble should represent a distinct transformation, whose output is somehow different from its input.

**182.** **Desk-checking is practiced in which of the following phases of a system development life cycle (SDLC)?**

    a.    Initiation

    b.    Development/acquisition

    c.    Implementation

    d.    Operation/maintenance

***182. c.*** In desk-checking, programming code is read by an expert, other than the author of the code, who performs any of the following: (i) looking over the code for obvious defects, (ii) checking for correct procedure interfaces, (iii) reading the comments to develop a sense of what the code does and then comparing it to its external specifications, (iv) comparing comments to design documentation, (v) stepping through with input conditions contrived to exercise all paths including those not directly related to the external specifications, (vi) checking for compliance with programming standards and conventions, or (vii) any combination of these. As can be seen, desk-checking is a technical exercise performed by programmers.

**183.** **Finite state machines (FSMs) are used in which of the following phases of a system development life cycle (SDLC)?**

    a.    Initiation

    b.    Development/acquisition

    c.    Implementation

    d.    Operation/maintenance

***183. a.*** The purpose of a finite state machine (FSM) is to define or implement the control structure of a system. Many systems can be defined in terms of their states, inputs, and actions. By defining a system's actions for each input in every state, you can completely define a system. The resulting model of the system is an FSM, which can detect incomplete or inconsistent requirements specifications.

**184.** **Mutation analysis is performed in which of the following phases of a system development life cycle (SDLC)?**

    a.    Initiation

    b.    Development/acquisition

    c.    Implementation

    d.    Operation/maintenance

**184. c.**   The purpose of mutation analysis is to determine the thoroughness with which a program has been tested and, in the process, detect errors. This procedure involves producing a large set of version or mutation of the original program, each derived by altering a single element of the program (for example, changing an operator, variable, or constant). Each mutant is then tested with a given collection of test data sets. Because each mutant is essentially different from the original, the testing should demonstrate that each is different. If each of the outputs produced by the mutants differs from the output produced by the original program and from each other, then the program is considered adequately tested and correct. Mutation analysis requires good automated tools to be effective.

**185.**   **Sensitivity analysis is conducted in which of the following phases of a system development life cycle (SDLC)?**

   a.   Initiation

   b.   Development/acquisition

   c.   Implementation

   d.   Operation/maintenance

**185. c.**   Sensitivity analysis is a new method of quantifying ultra-reliable software during the implementation phase. It is based on a fault-failure model of software and is based on the premise that software testability can predict the probability that failure occurs when a fault exists given a particular input distribution. A sensitive location is one in which faults cannot hide during testing. The internal states are disturbed to determine sensitivity. This technique requires instrumentation of the code and produces a count of the total executions through an operation, an infection rate estimate, and a propagation analysis.

**186.**   **Boundary-value analysis is conducted in which of the following phases of a system development life cycle (SDLC)?**

   a.   Requirements

   b.   Design

   c.   Implementation

   d.   Maintenance

**186. c.**   The purpose of boundary-value analysis is to detect and remove errors occurring at parameter limits or boundaries. The input domain of the program is divided into a number of input classes. The tests should cover the boundaries and extremes of the classes. The tests check that the boundaries of the input domain of the specification coincide with those in the program. Test cases should also be designed to force the output to its extreme values. If possible, a test case that causes output to exceed the specification boundary values should be specified. If output is a sequence of data, special attention should be given to the first and last elements and to lists containing zero, one, and two elements.

**187.** **Error-seeding is planted in which of the following phases of a system development life cycle (SDLC)?**

    a.    Initiation

    b.    Development/acquisition

    c.    Implementation

    d.    Operation/maintenance

*187. c.*    The purpose of error-seeding is to determine whether a set of test cases is adequate. Some known error types are inserted into the program, and the program is executed with the test cases under test conditions. If only some of the seeded errors are found, the test case set is not adequate. One can estimate the number of errors remaining by subtracting the number of real errors found from the total number of real errors. The remaining test effort can then be estimated. If all the seeded errors are found, this indicates that either the test case set is adequate or that the seeded errors were too easy to find.

**188.** **Formal methods or verification of application software is performed in which of the following phases of system development life cycle (SDLC)?**

    a.    Initiation and development

    b.    Development and implementation

    c.    Implementation and operation

    d.    Operation and disposal

*188. a.*    The purpose of formal methods is to check whether software fulfills its intended function. It involves the use of theoretical and mathematical models to prove the correctness of a program without executing it. The requirements should be written in a formal specification language (for example, VDM and Z) so that these requirements can then be verified using a proof of correctness. Using this method, the program is represented by a theorem and is proved with first-order predicate calculus. A number of assertions are stated at various locations in the program and are used as pre- and post-conditions to various paths in the program. The proof consists of showing that the program transfers the pre-conditions into the post-conditions according to a set of logical rules, and that the program terminates.

**189.** **Which of the following techniques *cannot* be used in all phases of a system development life cycle (SDLC)?**

    a.    Prototyping

    b.    Reviews

    c.    Simulation

    d.    Walkthroughs

**189. a.** The purpose of prototyping is to check the feasibility of implementing a system against the given constraints and to communicate the specifier's interpretation of the system to the customer to locate misunderstandings. A subset of system functions, constraints, and performance requirements are selected. A prototype is built using high-level tools and is evaluated against the customer's criteria; the system requirements may be modified as a result of this evaluation. Usually, prototyping is used to define user requirements of the system.

A review is a meeting at which the requirements, design, code, or other products of a software development project are presented to the user, sponsor, or other interested parties for comment and approval, often as a prerequisite for concluding a given phase of the software development process. A review is usually held at the end of a phase, but it may be called when problems arise.

Simulation is used to test the functions of a software system, together with its interface to the real environment, without modifying the environment in any way. The simulation may be software only or a combination of hardware and software.

A walkthrough is an evaluation technique in which a designer or programmer leads one or more other members of the development team through a segment of design or code, whereas the other members ask questions and make comments about technique and style, and identify possible errors, violations of development standards, and other problems. Walkthroughs are similar to reviews but are less formal.

**190.** Techniques such as prototyping and simulation *cannot* be used in which of the following phases of a system development life cycle (SDLC)?

    a.    Initiation

    b.    Development/acquisition

    c.    Implementation

    d.    Operation/maintenance

**190. d.** The purpose of prototyping is to check the feasibility of implementing a system against the given constraints and to communicate the specifier's interpretation of the system to the customer to locate misunderstandings. A subset of system functions, constraints, and performance requirements are selected. A prototype is built using high-level tools and is evaluated against the customer's criteria; the system requirements may be modified as a result of this evaluation. Usually, prototyping is used to define user requirements and design of the system. Simulation or modeling is used to test the functions of a software system, together with its interface to the real environment, without modifying the environment in any way. The simulation may be software only or a combination of hardware and software. A model of the system to be controlled by the actual system under test is created. This model mimics the behavior of the controlled system and is for testing purposes only. Although prototyping and simulation can be used in the system maintenance phase, the payback would be less than the development phase. Usually, the scope of system maintenance can be small and minor, making it cost-prohibitive to the use of prototyping and simulation techniques.

**191.** Which of the following require an extensive testing effort in an application system integration project?

    a.    Regression testing

    b.    Interoperability testing

    c.    Load testing

    d.    Security testing

*191. b.* Adherence to a common standard ensures the interoperability of software components. Extensive testing is required to ensure that software components can communicate effectively in both single-processor and distributed processing environments.

In a networked environment, it must be remembered that, when any component is added or replaced/upgraded, a large number of tests have to be run to ensure that the integrity and performance of the network has been retained. Therefore, tests must be repeatable and well documented. Hence, regression tests are necessary.

In load testing, many combinations and permutations of workload patterns can be imposed on the components of a networked configuration. Although it would be difficult, if not impossible, to test them all, a thorough analysis of the expected workload is required to identify the most likely traffic patterns for this testing procedure. By their nature, networked systems provide a great number of opportunities for violating system security. This is especially true when security levels are not uniformly imposed throughout a configuration made of multiple, interconnected local-area networks. Systemwide security testing is required to identify any security fault that may have been overlooked in the integrated system design.

**192.** The capability of an application system to survive misuse by naive users is examined in which of the following testing approaches?

    a.    Functional testing

    b.    Performance testing

    c.    Resiliency testing

    d.    Recovery testing

*192. c.* Resiliency testing measures durability of the system. In functional testing, correctness of system operation under normal operating conditions is demonstrated. In performance testing, system throughput and response times under varying load conditions are demonstrated. In recovery testing, the ability of the system to resume operating after partial or total system failure is determined. Both the system and individual components are tested to determine the ability to operate within the fallback and recovery structure established for the system.

**193.** From a testing viewpoint, when does a formal change control mechanism start?

    a.    After completion of integration testing

    b.    After completion of unit testing

    c.    After completion of systems testing

    d.    After completion of acceptance testing

**193. a.** Integration testing is the cutoff point for the development project, and, after integration, it is labeled the back end. Integration is the development phase in which various parts and components are integrated to form the entire software product, and, usually after integration, the product is under formal change control. Specifically, after integration testing, every change of the software must have a specific reason and must be documented and tracked. It is too early to have a formal change control mechanism during unit testing because of constant changes to program code. It is too late to have a formal change control mechanism after completing system and acceptance testing.

**194.** **What is the correct sequence of application software testing?**

    a.    Integration test, unit test, systems test, acceptance test

    b.    Unit test, systems test, integration test, acceptance test

    c.    Acceptance test, unit test, integration test, systems test

    d.    Unit test, integration test, systems test, acceptance test

**194. d.** A system development life cycle moves through the unit test, integration test, system test, and acceptance test in that sequence. Programmers perform both the unit test and integration tests, whereas system testing is conducted jointly between users and programmers. End users and production operations staff, from their own viewpoint, perform acceptance testing. The quality of a computer system is enhanced if this sequence is followed during software testing.

**195.** **Effective controls during the application software-testing phase include which of the following?**

    a.    Test cases and test documentation

    b.    Test summaries and test execution reports

    c.    Activity logs, incident reports, and software versioning

    d.    Test cases rejected and test cases accepted

**195. c.** Activity logs contain a record of all the test cases executed. Incident reports show a priority assigned to test problems during test execution. All incidents logged should be resolved within a reasonable time. Software versioning controls the program source versions to ensure that there is no duplication or confusion between multiple versions.

Test cases and test documentation are incorrect because test cases contain a listing of all possible tests to be executed with their associated data and test documentation includes test plans, test objectives, and approaches.

Test summaries and test execution reports are incorrect because test summary is a brief description of what is changing. Key words are used so that project personnel reading the log can scan for items that may affect their work. Test execution reports show a status of software testing execution to management with summary information.

Test cases rejected and test cases accepted are incorrect because they simply list what test cases were rejected or accepted. The documents such as test cases, test documentation, test summaries, test execution reports, and test cases rejected and accepted do not have the same monitoring and controlling effect as do the documents such as activity logs, incident reports, and software versioning.

**196.** Which of the following software testing levels is *least* understood by software developers and end users?

    a.    Integration testing

    b.    Unit testing

    c.    System testing

    d.    Module testing

*196. a.* Integration testing is conducted when software units are integrated with other software units or with system components. Its objective is to test the interfaces among separately tested program units. Software integration tests check how the units interact with other software (for example, libraries) and hardware. Integration testing is in the middle; it is neither unit testing nor system testing. The approach to integration testing varies such as top-down, bottom-up, a combination of top-down and bottom-up (sandwich), or all-at-once (big-bang) approaches. Due to a variety of ways, integration testing can be conducted and because there is no base document such as specifications to rely upon for testing creates difficulty in understanding the objectives of integration testing clearly.

Unit testing and module testing are incorrect because they are best understood of all. Unit testing is the same as module testing. Unit/module test cases are derived from the detailed design documentation of the unit. Each unit or module has a defined beginning and ending and deals with specific inputs and outputs. Boundaries are also well defined.

System testing is incorrect because it is better understood than integration testing. End users know what they expect from the system because it is based on functional instead of structural knowledge. System test cases are derived from the requirements specification document.

**197.** Which of the following system development approaches is *best* when system requirements are fully understood by either the end user or the software developer?

    a.    Waterfall model

    b.    Incremental development model

    c.    Evolutionary development model

    d.    Rapid prototyping model

*197. a.* Functional decomposition works best when the system requirements are completely understood by the software developer or the end user. The waterfall model works with the functional decomposition principle. It assumes that system requirements can be defined thoroughly, and that end users know exactly what they wanted from the system.

Incremental and evolutionary development models are incorrect because successive versions of the system are developed reflecting constrained technology or resources. Requirements are added in a layered manner.

Rapid prototyping model is incorrect because it is quite opposite to the waterfall model. That is, it is good when requirements are not fully understood by both parties. Due to the iterative process, the specification-to-customer feedback cycle time is reduced, thus producing early versions of the system.

**198.** Which of the following is the *least* beneficial of an application software test log?

    a. Recording actions for problem resolution

    b. Tracing events on post-test basis

    c. Reporting problems for compliance to a policy

    d. Promoting tester accountability

*198. c.* An application software test log has several benefits. Reporting problems for the sake of reporting/compliance to a policy or a procedure is the least beneficial. What is done with the report is more important than just reporting. The other three choices are incorrect because they are the most important benefits. The log shows a record of all problems encountered during testing so events can be traced for verification. The log can also be used as a training tool for new testers because the log shows what happened in the past. Most of all, the log indicates what the tester did or did not do during testing. It forces testers to document the actions or decisions taken place during testing.

**199.** The application software test objective of verifying boundary conditions of a program is achieved in which of the following types of software testing approaches?

    a. Stress testing

    b. Conversion testing

    c. Performance testing

    d. Regression testing

*199. a.* Stress testing involves the response of the system to extreme conditions (for example, with an exceptionally high workload over a short span of time) to identify vulnerable points within the software and to show that the system can withstand normal workloads. Examples of testing conditions that can be applied during stress testing include the following: (i) if the size of the database plays an important role, then increase it beyond normal conditions, (ii) increase the input changes or demands per time unit beyond normal conditions, (iii) tune influential factors to their maximum or minimal speed, and (iv) for the most extreme cases, put all influential factors to the boundary conditions at the same time.

Stress testing can detect design errors related to full-service requirements of system and errors in planning defaults when system is overstressed.

Conversion testing is incorrect because it determines whether old data files and record balances are carried forward accurately, completely, and properly to the new system.

Performance testing is incorrect because it measures resources required such as memory and disk and determines system response time. Regression testing is incorrect because it verifies that changes do not introduce new errors.

**200.** **In which of the following system development life cycle (SDLC) models has the concept of application software reuse been incorporated?**

    a.    Waterfall model

    b.    Object-oriented model

    c.    Prototype model

    d.    Spiral model

***200. b.*** The notion of software component reuse has been developed with the invention of object-oriented development approach. After the design model has been created, the software developer browses a library, or repository, that contains existing program components to determine if any of the components can be used in the design at hand. If reusable components are found, they are used as building blocks to construct a prototype of the software.

The waterfall model is incorrect because it takes a linear, sequential view of the software engineering process. The waterfall method is another name for the classic software development life cycle.

The prototype model is incorrect because it is a process that enables the developer to create a model of the software built in an evolutionary manner.

The spiral model is incorrect because it is another type of evolutionary model. It has been developed to provide the best feature of both the classic life cycle approach and prototyping. None of these three choices provide for software reuse.

**201.** **Security categorization is performed in which of the following phases of an application system development life cycle (SDLC)?**

    a.    Initiation

    b.    Development/acquisition

    c.    Implementation

    d.    Operations/maintenance

***201. a.*** Security categorization standards provide a common framework for expressing security needs. Categorization is based on an assessment of the potential impact (i.e., low, moderate, or high) that a loss of confidentiality, integrity, or availability of information systems would have on organizational operations, organizational assets, or individuals. It is a task performed in the initiation phase.

**202.** **Configuration management and control is performed in which of the following phases of a system development life cycle (SDLC)?**

    a.    Initiation

    b.    Development/acquisition

c. Implementation

d. Operations/maintenance

***202. d.*** Configuration management and control ensures adequate consideration of the potential security impacts due to specific changes to an information system or its surrounding environment. It is a task performed in the operation/maintenance phase.

**203.** **Continuous monitoring is performed in which of the following phases of a system development life cycle (SDLC)?**

a. Initiation

b. Development/acquisition

c. Implementation

d. Operations/maintenance

***203. d.*** Continuous monitoring ensures that controls continue to be effective in their application through periodic testing and evaluation. It is a task performed in the operation/maintenance phase.

**204.** **Which of the following are examples of local threats in Windows Extreme Programming (XP) systems?**

a. Unauthorized local access and malicious payloads

b. Boot process and privilege escalation

c. Network services and data disclosure

d. Boot process and data disclosure

***204. b.*** Local threats in Windows XP systems include boot process, unauthorized local access, and privilege escalation. A boot process threat results when an unauthorized individual boots a computer from third-party media (for example, removable drives and universal serial bus [USB] token storage devices), which permits the attacker to circumvent operating system security measures. An unauthorized local-access threat results when an individual who is not permitted to access a computer system gains local access. A privilege escalation threat results when an authorized user with normal user-level rights escalates the account's privileges to gain administrator-level access.

Remote threats in Windows XP systems include network services, data disclosure, and malicious payloads. A network service threat results when remote attackers exploit vulnerable network services on a computer system. This includes gaining unauthorized access to services and data, and causing a denial-of-service (DoS) condition. A data disclosure threat results when a third party intercepts confidential data sent over a network. A malicious payload threat results when malicious payloads (for example, viruses, worms, Trojan horses, and active content) attack computer systems through many vectors. System end users may accidentally trigger malicious payloads.

**205.** **Attackers can use which of the following flaws to attack back-end components through a Web application?**

      a.    Broken access control

      b.    Invalidated input

      c.    Broken authentication

      d.    Cross-site scripting flaws

*205. b.*   According to the open Web application security project, information from Web requests is not validated before being used by a Web application leading to vulnerability from invalidated input.

**206.** **What do you call it when attacks consume Web application resources to a point where other legitimate users can no longer access or use the application?**

      a.    Buffer overflows

      b.    Injection flaws

      c.    Denial-of-service

      d.    Improper error handling

*206. c.*   In denial-of-service attacks, attackers can consume Web application resources to a point where other legitimate users can no longer access or use the application. Attackers can also lock users out of their accounts or even cause the entire application to fail.

**207.** **What do you call it when an attack can cause errors to occur, which the Web application does *not* handle?**

      a.    Buffer overflows

      b.    Injection flaws

      c.    Denial-of-service

      d.    Improper error handling

*207. d.*   Improper error handling means error conditions that occur during normal operation are not handled properly. If an attacker can cause errors to occur that the Web application does not handle, they can gain detailed system information, deny service, cause security mechanisms to fail, or crash the server.

**208.** **The information systems security analyst's participation in which of the following system development life cycle (SDLC) phases provides maximum benefit to the organization?**

      a.    System requirements definition

      b.    System design

      c.    Program development

      d.    Program testing

**208. a.**   It is during the system requirements definition phase that the project team identifies the required controls needed for the system. The identified controls are then incorporated into the system during the design phase. When there is a choice between the system requirements definition phase and the design phase, the auditor would benefit most by participating in the former phase. The analyst does not need to participate in the program development or testing phase.

**209.**   What is a malicious unauthorized act that is triggered upon initiation of a predefined event or condition and resides within a computer program known as?

      a.   Logic bomb

      b.   Computer virus

      c.   Worm

      d.   NAK attack

**209. a.**   A time bomb is a part of a logic bomb. A time bomb is a Trojan horse set to trigger at a particular time, whereas the logic bomb is set to trigger at a particular condition, event, or command. The logic bomb could be a computer program or a code fragment.

Computer virus is incorrect because it "reproduces" by making copies of it and inserting them into other programs. Worm is incorrect because it searches the network for idle computing resources and uses them to execute the program in small segments. NAK (negative acknowledgment character) attack is incorrect because it is a penetration technique capitalizing on a potential weakness in an operating system that does not handle asynchronous interrupts properly, thus leaving the system in an unprotected state during such interrupts. NAK uses binary synchronous communications where a transmission control character is sent as a negative response to data received. Here, negative response means data was not received correctly or that a command was incorrect or unacceptable.

**210.**   What is the name of the malicious act of a computer program looking normal but containing harmful code?

      a.   Trapdoor

      b.   Trojan horse

      c.   Worm

      d.   Time bomb

**210. b.**   A Trojan horse fits the description. It is a program that performs a useful function and an unexpected action as well as a form of virus.

Trapdoor is incorrect because it is an entry point built into a program created by programmers for debugging purposes. Worm is incorrect because it searches the network for idle computing resources and uses them to execute a program in small segments. Time bomb is incorrect because it is a part of a logic bomb, where a damaging act triggers at some period of time after the bomb is set.

**211.** **In the software capability maturity model, continuous process improvement takes place in which of the following levels?**

    a.    Managed level

    b.    Optimizing level

    c.    Defined level

    d.    Repeatable level

*211. b.* Continuous process improvements are expected in the optimizing level of the software capability maturity model. It is enabled by quantitative feedback from the process and from piloting innovative ideas and technologies.

**212.** **Which of the following tests identify vulnerabilities in application systems?**

    a.    Functional test

    b.    Performance test

    c.    Stress test

    d.    Security test

*212. d.* The purpose of security testing is to assess the robustness of the system's security capabilities (for example, physical facilities, procedures, hardware, software, and communications) and to identify security vulnerabilities. All the tests listed in the question are part of system acceptance tests where the purpose is to verify that the complete system satisfies specified requirements and is acceptable to end users.

Functional test is incorrect because the purpose of functional or black-box testing is to verify that the system correctly performs specified functions. Performance test is incorrect because the purpose of performance testing is to assess how well a system meets specified performance requirements. Examples include specified system response times under normal workloads (for example, defined transaction volumes) and specified levels of system availability and mean-times-to-repair. Stress test is incorrect because the purpose of stress testing is to analyze system behavior under increasingly heavy workloads (for example, higher transaction rates), severe operating conditions (for example, higher error rates, lower component availability rates), and, in particular, to identify points of system failure.

**213.** **When does a *major* risk in application software prototyping occur?**

    a.    The prototype becomes the finished system.

    b.    User's expectations are inflated.

    c.    Too much attention is paid to cosmetic details.

    d.    The model is iterated too many times.

*213. a.* The application software prototype becoming the finished system is a major risk in prototyping unless this is a conscious decision, as in evolutionary prototyping where a pilot system is built, thrown away, another system is built, and so on. Inflated user expectations is a risk that can be managed with proper education and training. Paying attention to cosmetic details is not bad except that it wastes valuable time. The prototype model is supposed to be iterated many times because that is the best way to define and redefine user requirements and security features until satisfied.

214. **Security planning is performed in which of the following phases of a system development life cycle (SDLC)?**

    a.   Initiation

    b.   Development/acquisition

    c.   Implementation

    d.   Operations/maintenance

*214. b.* Security planning ensures that agreed-upon security controls, whether planned or in place, are fully documented. It is a task performed in the development/acquisition phase.

215. **Security certification and accreditation is performed in which of the following phases of a system development life cycle (SDLC)?**

    a.   Initiation

    b.   Development/acquisition

    c.   Implementation

    d.   Operations/maintenance

*215. c.* Security certification ensures that the controls are effectively implemented through established verification techniques and procedures and gives an organization confidence that the appropriate safeguards and countermeasures are in place to protect the organization's information systems. Security accreditation provides the necessary security authorization of an information system to process, store, or transmit information that is required. Both security certification and accreditation tasks are performed in the implementation phase.

216. **Which of the following actions is performed in the detailed design phase of a system development life cycle (SDLC) project?**

    a.   Defining control, security, and audit requirements

    b.   Developing screen flows with specifications

    c.   Identifying major purpose(s) of the system

    d.   Developing system justification

*216. b.* A detailed design occurs after the general design is completed where known tasks are described and identified in a much more detailed fashion and are ready for program design and coding. This includes developing screen/program flows with specifications, input and output file specifications, and report specifications.

The other three choices are incorrect because, by definition, they are examples of activities taking place in the general design phase. System requirements are the input to the general design where the system is viewed from top-down and where higher-level design issues are addressed. This includes (i) identifying the purpose and major functions of the system and its subsystems, (ii) defining control, security, and audit requirements, and (iii) developing system justification for the approval of analysis of alternative design choices.

**217.** **When attackers compromise passwords, keys, and session cookies, it can lead to which of the following flaws?**

    a.    Broken access control

    b.    Invalidated input

    c.    Broken authentication

    d.    Cross-site scripting flaws

*217. c.* Broken authentication means account credentials and session tokens are not properly protected. Attackers that can compromise passwords, keys, session cookies, or other tokens can defeat authentication restrictions and assume other user's identities.

**218.** **Attackers use which of the following to corrupt a Web application execution stack?**

    a.    Buffer overflows

    b.    Injection flaws

    c.    Denial-of-service

    d.    Improper error handling

*218. a.* Buffer overflows occur when web application components (for example, common gateway interface, libraries, drivers, and Web application servers) that do not properly validate input can be crashed and, in some cases, used to take control of a process.

**219.** **When Web applications use cryptographic factors that were proven difficult to code properly, it can lead to which of the following?**

    a.    Insecure storage

    b.    Improper error handling

    c.    Injection flaws

    d.    Insecure configuration management

*219. a.* Web applications frequently use cryptographic functions to protect information and credentials in storage. These functions and the code to integrate them have proven difficult to code properly, frequently resulting in weak protection.

**220.** **Protection mechanisms defined in security design architecture include which of the following?**

    a.    Layering, abstraction, and data hiding

    b.    Isolation, segmentation, and separation

    c.    Security kernel, reference monitor, and system high

    d.    Accountability, integrity, and confidentiality

**220. a.** Layering, abstraction, and data hiding are part of security design architecture. The other three choices deal with security control architecture. Layering uses multiple, overlapping protection mechanisms to address the people, technology, and operational aspects of IT. Abstraction is related to stepwise refinement and modularity of computer programs. Data hiding is closely related to modularity and abstraction and, subsequently, to program maintainability.

**221.** **Which of the following *best* defines adequate information security?**

    1.    Security commensurate with risk and harm.

    2.    Operating systems and applications operate effectively.

    3.    Operating systems and applications meet security objectives.

    4.    Operating systems and applications use cost-effective security controls.

        a.    1 and 2

        b.    2 and 3

        c.    3 and 4

        d.    1, 2, 3, and 4

**221. d.** Adequate information security means (i) security commensurate with the risk and the magnitude of harm resulting from the loss, misuse, or unauthorized access to or modification of information, (ii) operating systems and applications operate effectively, (iii) operating systems and applications provide appropriate confidentiality (C), integrity (I), and availability (A), known as CIA security objectives, and (iv) security objectives use cost-effective management, operational, and technical controls (security controls).

**222.** **Computer viruses continue to pose a threat to the following computer services *except*:**

        a.    Integrity

        b.    Availability

        c.    Confidentiality

        d.    Usability

**222. c.** Confidentiality is not affected by the presence of computer viruses in computer systems because confidentiality is ensuring that data is disclosed only to authorized subjects. However, computer viruses affect integrity, availability, and usability. Computer programs can be deleted or modified, thus losing their integrity, the computer system may not be available due to disruption or denial of computer services, and end users may not use the system due to loss of files or disruption of services.

**223.** **Which of the following should have extremely limited access in a client/server environment?**

    a. Source code

    b. Object code

    c. Executable code

    d. Machine code

***223. a.*** Access to source code can provide tremendous assistance to any criminal wishing to penetrate a system's security. Without the source code, an intruder has to probe through a system to find its flaws. Access to the source code helps the intruder to identify gaps or flaws in security. It is important to ensure that adequate security is provided for the system's source code. It is not good to allow source code to reside on client machines or on the server. It should be located only on a workstation belonging to the configuration management group. The workstation should have extremely limited access. If the workstation can be disconnected from the network most of the time, that would provide additional security for the source code. Moreover, the source code is in human-readable format while the other three types of codes listed are not.

**224.** **In the context of a reference monitor concept, a reference validation mechanism doesn't need to meet which one of the following design requirements?**

    a. The reference validation mechanism must be tamperproof.

    b. The reference validation mechanism must be large.

    c. The reference validation mechanism must not be bypassed.

    d. The reference validation mechanism must always be invoked.

***224. b.*** A reference monitor concept is an access control concept that refers to an abstract machine (computer) that mediates all accesses to objects by subjects. The five design requirements that must be met by a reference validation mechanism include (i) it must be tamperproof, (ii) it must not be bypassed, (iii) it must always be invoked, (iv) it must be small enough to be subject to analysis and tests, and (v) it must provide confidence that the other four items are assured. The reference monitor concept is useful to any system providing multilevel secure computing facilities and controls.

**225.** **Which of the following application system development approaches *best* brings the operational viewpoint to the requirements specification phase?**

    a. Waterfall model

    b. Incremental development model

    c. Evolutionary development model

    d. Rapid prototyping model

**225. d.** Due to its iterative process and end-user involvement, the rapid prototype model brings the operational viewpoint to the requirements specification phase. Requirements are defined, refined, tested, and changed until the end user cannot change it any more. Later, these requirements will become input to the design work.

Waterfall model is incorrect because it will not bring the operational viewpoint to the requirements phase until the system is completely implemented. Although the incremental development model and the evolutionary development models are better than the waterfall model, they are not as good as rapid prototyping in terms of bringing the operational viewpoint to the requirements specification.

# SCENARIO-BASED QUESTIONS, ANSWERS, AND EXPLANATIONS

Use the following information to answer questions 1 through 11.

The RGO Company is undertaking a new business process that represents a 15 percent increase in volume and a 10 percent increase in the number of employees. The business is dependent on software to run remote processing. The new process needs to be tested fully before implementation. To maintain the stability of the current business and create a smooth transition to the new business process, the company is going to employ a system development life cycle (SDLC) methodology. RGO cannot afford to fail.

1. **Security categorization is performed in which of the following phases of an SDLC methodology?**

   a.   Initiation

   b.   Development/acquisition

   c.   Implementation

   d.   Operations/maintenance

   *1. a.* Security categorization standards provide a common framework for expressing security needs. Categorization is based on an assessment of the potential impact (i.e., low, moderate, or high) that a loss of confidentiality, integrity, or availability of information systems would have on organizational operations, organizational assets, or individuals. It is a task performed in the initiation phase.

2. **Security planning is performed in which of the following phases of an SDLC?**

   a.   Initiation

   b.   Development/acquisition

   c.   Implementation

   d.   Operations/maintenance

   *2. b.* Security planning ensures that agreed-upon security controls, whether planned or in place, are fully documented. It is a task performed in the development/acquisition phase.

**3.** **Security certification and accreditation is performed in which of the following phases of an SDLC?**

    a.    Initiation

    b.    Development/acquisition

    c.    Implementation

    d.    Operations/maintenance

**3. c.**   Security certification ensures that the controls are effectively implemented through established verification techniques and procedures and gives an organization confidence that the appropriate safeguards and countermeasures are in place to protect the organization's information systems. Security accreditation provides the necessary security authorization of an information system to process, store, or transmit information that is required. Both security certification and accreditation tasks are performed in the implementation phase.

**4.** **Configuration management and control is performed in which of the following phases of an SDLC?**

    a.    Initiation

    b.    Development/acquisition

    c.    Implementation

    d.    Operations/maintenance

**4. d.**   Configuration management and control ensures adequate consideration of the potential security impacts due to specific changes to an information system or its surrounding environment. It is a task performed in the operation/maintenance phase.

**5.** **Continuous monitoring is performed in which of the following phases of an SDLC?**

    a.    Initiation

    b.    Development/acquisition

    c.    Implementation

    d.    Operations/maintenance

**5. d.**   Continuous monitoring ensures that controls continue to be effective in their application through periodic testing and evaluation. It is a task performed in the operation/maintenance phase.

**6.** **Media sanitization is performed in which of the following phases of an SDLC?**

    a.    Development/acquisition

    b.    Implementation

    c.    Operations/maintenance

    d.    Disposition

*6. d.* Media sanitization ensures that data is deleted, erased, and written over as necessary. It is a task performed in the disposition phase.

7. **Security controls and audit trails should be built into computer systems in which of the following SDLC phases?**

    a.   System initiation phase

    b.   System development phase

    c.   System implementation phase

    d.   System operation phase

*7. b.* During the system development phase, the system is designed, purchased, programmed, developed, or otherwise constructed. During this phase, functional users with system/security administrators develop system controls and audit trails used during the operational phase.

8. **A security evaluation report and an accreditation statement are produced in which of the following phases of the SDLC?**

    a.   Requirements definition phase

    b.   Design phase

    c.   Development phase

    d.   Testing phase

*8. d.* Major outputs from the testing phase include the security evaluation report and accreditation statement. The purpose of the testing phase is to perform various tests (unit, integration, system, and acceptance). Security is tested to see if it works and is then certified.

9. **Which of the following phases of a system development life cycle (SDLC) should not be compressed so much for the proper development of a prototype?**

    a.   Initiation

    b.   Development/acquisition

    c.   Implementation

    d.   Operation/maintenance

*9. c.* System testing, which is a part of implementation, is important to determine whether internal controls and security controls are operating as designed and are in accordance with established policies and procedures.

In the prototyping environment, there is a tendency to compress system initiation, definition, design, programming, and training phases. However, the testing phase should not be compressed so much for quality reasons. By definition, prototyping requires some compression of activities and time due to the speedy nature of the prototyping development methodology without loss of the main features, functions, and quality.

**10.** **The activity that would be different between a prototype development approach and the traditional system development approach is:**

    a.    How activities are to be accomplished

    b.    What users need from the system

    c.    What a project plan should contain

    d.    How individual responsibilities are defined

*10. a.*    Managers still need to define what they want from the system, some assessment of costs/benefits is still needed, and a plan to proceed with individual responsibilities is still required. The difference may be in the way activities are accomplished. The tools, techniques, methods, and approaches used in the prototype development project and traditional system development project are different.

**11.** **A general testing strategy for conducting an application software regression testing includes which of the following sequence of tasks?**

    a.    Read, insert, and delete

    b.    Precompile, link, and compile

    c.    Prepare, execute, and delete

    d.    Test, debug, and log

*11. c.*    Each test program involves preparing the executable program, executing it, and deleting it. This saves space on mass storage and generates a complete log. This approach is recommended for debugging and validating purposes. Read, insert, and delete include the transfer of all rows from Table A to Table B in that a table is read, inserted, and deleted. A source program is precompiled, linked, and compiled to become an object or executable program.

# SOURCES AND REFERENCES

"Capability Maturity Model for Software, Version 1.1, Technical Report," CMU/SEI-93-TR-024, Software Engineering Institute (SEI), Carnegie Mellon University (CMU), Pittsburg, Pennsylvania, February 1993. (www.sei.cum.edu/publications/documents/93.reports/93.tr.024.html).

"The Case for Using Layered Defenses to Stop Worms (NSA Report# C43-002R-2004)," National Security Agency (NSA), Fort Meade, Maryland, June 2004.

"Guide for the Security Certification and Accreditation of Federal Information Systems (NIST SP800-37)," National Institute of Standards and Technology (NIST), U.S. Department of Commerce, Gaithersburg, Maryland, May 2004.

"Guide to Securing Microsoft Windows XP Systems for IT Professionals (NIST SP800-68R1)," National Institute of Standards and Technology (NIST), U.S. Department of Commerce, Gaithersburg, Maryland, October 2008.

"Guidelines on Active Content and Mobile Code (NIST SP800-28 V2 Draft)," National Institute of Standards and Technology (NIST), U.S. Department of Commerce, Gaithersburg, Maryland, August 2007.

"Information Security Handbook: A Guide for Managers (NIST SP800-100 Draft)," Chapter 3, System Development Life Cycle, National Institute of Standards and Technology (NIST), U.S. Department of Commerce, Gaithersburg, Maryland, June 2006.

"Information Security Handbook: A Guide for Managers (NIST SP800-100 Draft)," Chapter 11, Certification, Accreditation, and Security Assessments, National Institute of Standards and Technology (NIST), U.S. Department of Commerce, Gaithersburg, Maryland, June 2006.

"Information Security Handbook: A Guide for Managers (NIST SP800-100 Draft)," Chapter 14, Configuration Management, National Institute of Standards and Technology (NIST), U.S. Department of Commerce, Gaithersburg, Maryland, June 2006.

"An Introduction to Computer Security: The NIST Handbook (NIST SP800-12)," National Institute of Standards and Technology (NIST), U.S. Department of Commerce, Gaithersburg, Maryland, October 1995.

"The Open Web Application Security Project," (www.owasp.org), January 2004.

"Security Considerations in the Information Systems Development Lifecycle (NIST SP800-64R1)," National Institute of Standards and Technology (NIST), U.S. Department of Commerce, Gaithersburg, Maryland, October 2003.

"Security Requirements for Cryptographic Modules (NIST FIPS PUB 140-3 Draft)," National Institute of Standards and Technology (NIST), U.S. Department of Commerce, Gaithersburg, Maryland, July 2007.

"Source Code Security Analysis Tool Functional Specification (NIST SP500-268 V1)," National Institute of Standards and Technology (NIST), U.S. Department of Commerce, Gaithersburg, Maryland, May 2007.

# DOMAIN 5

## Cryptography

## TRADITIONAL QUESTIONS, ANSWERS, AND EXPLANATIONS

1. **For security protection mechanisms for cryptographic data in storage, backup, and archives, the storage of keying material is a part of which of the following cryptographic services?**

    a.  Confidentiality

    b.  Availability

    c.  Integrity

    d.  Labels

    *1. b.*   The availability service for data in storage deals with backup and archive storages. During a key's crypto-period, keying material (i.e., keys and initialization vectors) should be stored in both normal operational storage and in backup storage. After the end of a key's crypto-period, keying material should be placed in archive storage. The other three choices do not deal with backup and archive storages.

2. **Which of the following is referred to when two cryptographic key component holders manage the process of handling the two components of a cryptographic key?**

    a.  Key list

    b.  Key escrow

    c.  Key loader

    d.  Key exchange

    *2. b.*   In general, escrow is something (for example, a document or an encryption key) that is delivered to a third party to be given to the grantee only upon the fulfillment of a predefined condition (i.e., a grantor and grantee relationship with a third party in the middle). Key escrow is the processes of managing (for example, generating, storing, transferring, and auditing) the two components of a cryptographic key by two component holders. A key component is the two values from which a key can be derived. A key escrow system entrusts the two components comprising a cryptographic key (for example, a device unique key) to two key component holders (also called escrow agents).

The other three choices are incorrect. Key list is a printed series of key settings for a specific cryptonet. Key lists may be produced in list, pad, or printed tape format. Key loader is a self-contained unit that is capable of storing at least one plaintext or encrypted cryptographic key or key component that can be transferred, upon request, into a cryptographic module. Key exchange is the process of exchanging public keys and other information in order to establish secure communications.

**3.** Transaction privacy controls do *not* include which of the following?

    a.    Secure sockets layer (SSL)

    b.    Mandatory access controls (MAC)

    c.    Transmission layer security (TLS)

    d.    Secure shell (SSH)

***3. b.*** Transaction privacy controls include secure sockets layer (SSL), transport layer security (TLS), and secure shell (SSH) to protect against loss of privacy for transactions performed by an individual. Mandatory access controls (MAC) define access control security policy.

**4.** A cryptographic key has been compromised due to usage and age. The next step is to use which of the following?

    a.    DNSSEC-aware resolver

    b.    Key rollover

    c.    Zone signing key

    d.    Key signing key

***4. b.*** Key rollover is the process of generating and using a new key (symmetric or asymmetric key pair) to replace one already in use. Rollover is done because a key has been compromised as a result of usage and age.

The DNSSEC-aware resolver is incorrect because it is an entity that sends DNS queries, receives DNS responses, and understands the DNSSEC specification, even if it is incapable of performing validation. A zone-signing key is incorrect because it is an authentication key that corresponds to a private key used to sign a zone. A key signing key is incorrect because it is an authentication key that corresponds to a private key used to sign one or more other authentication keys for a given zone.

**5.** Which of the following protocols is used to encrypt individual messages?

    a.    Secure sockets layer (SSL)

    b.    Transport layer security (TLS)

c.     Secure hypertext transfer protocol (S-HTTP)

d.     Hypertext transfer protocol (HTTP)

**5. c.**   Secure hypertext transfer protocol (S-HTTP) is used for encrypting data flowing over the Internet, but it is limited to individual messages. Secure sockets layer (SSL) and transport layer security (TLS) are designed to establish a secure connection between two computers. Hypertext transfer protocol (HTTP) cannot do encryption and is not as secure as S-HTTP.

**6.** **For cryptography, which of the following refers to the worst-case measure of uncertainty for a random variable with the greatest lower bound?**

a.     Max-entropy

b.     Min-entropy

c.     Guessing entropy

d.     Min-Max entropy

**6. b.**   Entropy is the uncertainty of a random variable, which is stated in bits. Min-entropy is the worst-case measure of uncertainty for a random variable with the greatest lower bound. Min-entropy is a measure of the difficulty that an attacker has to guess the most commonly chosen password used in a system. Guessing entropy is a measure of the difficulty that an attacker has to guess the value of a secret (e.g., a password). Guessing entropy refers to an attacker that knows the actual password frequency distribution. Max-entropy and min-max entropy are not usually used in the context of entropy.

**7.** **Countermeasures against brute force attacks on cryptographic keys include which of the following?**

1.     Change keys

2.     Increase key length

3.     Change protocol

4.     Change algorithm

a.     1 and 2

b.     2 and 3

c.     3 and 4

d.     1 and 3

**7. a.**   Changing cryptographic keys frequently and increasing the key length can fight against the brute force attacks on keys. Changing protocols and algorithms cannot fight against the brute force attacks because the changed protocols and algorithms could be subjected to the same attacks or different attacks.

**8.** **For cryptography, what is nonce?**

a.     Timestamp plus sequence number

b.     Checksum plus check digit

    c.    Payload plus protocol

    d.    Public key plus private key

**8. a.**   Nonce is a time-varying and nonrepeating cryptographic value with the use of a timestamp, a sequence number, or combination, which are freshly generated random values. Checksums and check digits are used to ensure data accuracy during data entry and data transmission. Payload is a part of the data stream representing the user information in a communication. Protocol is a set of rules used by two or more entities that describe the message order and data structures for information exchange between the entities. A public key is a cryptographic key, used with a public key cryptographic algorithm, that is uniquely associated with an entity and that may be made public. A private key is a cryptographic key, used with a public key cryptographic algorithm that is uniquely associated with an entity and that is not made public.

**9.**    **For cryptography, which of the following protects the integrity of the data but does not guarantee authenticity of the information?**

    a.    X.509 public key certificate

    b.    Public key certificate

    c.    Private key certificate

    d.    Self-signed certificate

**9. d.**   A self-signed certificate is a public key certificate whose digital signature may be verified by the public key contained within the certificate. The signature on a self-signed certificate protects the integrity of the data but does not guarantee authenticity of the information. The trust of a self-signed certificate is based on the secure procedures used to distribute it.

The X.509 certificate comes in two types: X.509 public key certificate (most common) and the X.509 attribute certificate (less common). A public key certificate is a set of data that uniquely identifies an entity and binds the public key to the entity. The private key is mathematically linked with a corresponding public key.

**10.**    **Which of the following is an example of optional-to-implement cryptographic algorithms that provide greater security?**

    a.    DES

    b.    RSA-512 bit key

    c.    AES-128 bit key

    d.    RC2

**10. c.**   The AES-128 bit key is an example of optional-to-implement encryption algorithm that provides a greater security. Other variants of AES include AES-192 bit keys and AES-256 bit keys. The DES algorithm, RC2, and the RSA-512 bit key do not provide adequate security. The DES and RC2 are examples of mandatory-to-implement encryption algorithms that do not provide adequate security. Mandatory-to-implement algorithms will be in any product that meets the public standards, enabling interoperability between products. Optional-to-implement algorithms are next-generation algorithms with improved security that could increase the longevity of a system.

**11.** Which of the following enables one to locate organizations, individuals, files, and devices in a network whether on the Internet or on a corporate intranet?

    a. Online certificate status protocol (OCSP)

    b. Certificate management protocol (CMP)

    c. Lightweight directory access protocol (LDAP)

    d. Over-the-air rekeying protocol (OTAR)

***11. c.*** A lightweight directory access protocol (LDAP) is a centralized directory that becomes a major focal point as a tool for access control. It uses names, addresses, groups, roles, devices, files, and profiles to enable a modular, expandable access control and single sign-on solution to be deployed rapidly for all application systems.

The other three choices do not have such capabilities as the LDAP does. An online certificate status protocol (OCSP) responder is a trusted system and provides signed status information, on a per certificate basis, in response to a request from a relying party. Both certification authority (CA) and registration authority (RA) software support the use of a certificate management protocol (CMP). An over-the-air rekeying (OTAR) protocol is used in digital radios to handle cryptographic security. LDAP, CRLs, and OCSP are used to provide a path validation in a public-key certificate.

**12.** Most commonly, what are certificate revocation lists (CRLs) distributed through?

    1. Certificate management protocol

    2. LDAP directories protocol

    3. Web servers

    4. HTTP URLs

        a. 1 or 2

        b. 2 or 3

        c. 1 or 3

        d. 3 or 4

***12. b.*** Most commonly, the certificate revocation lists (CRLs) are distributed via lightweight directory access protocol (LDAP) directories or Web servers. The certificate management protocol (CMP) and HTTP uniform resource locators (HTTP URLs) are not used to distribute CRLs. Both the LDAP and HTTP URLs are used to specify the location of CRLs. Both certification authority (CA) and registration authority (RA) software support the use of a certificate management protocol (CMP). An LDAP is a centralized directory that becomes a major focal point as a tool for access control.

**13.** **Which of the following is generally the most difficult method of attacking a computer system?**

    a.    Password cracking

    b.    Packet sniffing

    c.    Encryption key breaking

    d.    Sendmail

**13. c.** Encryption key breaking is not a common method because it is difficult to do and may take years to do. It requires an extensive knowledge of algorithms, hardware, and software that is not possessed by too many people. Password cracking involves guessing a password, which can then be used to gain access to a system. Packet sniffing involves placing a rogue program in a host computer or in a network switch. The program will then monitor all information packets as they go through the network. A malicious code can be sent along with Internet-based e-mail. When the message is received, the attacker's code will be executed.

**14.** **Which of the following does *not* need to be destroyed after the corresponding certificate expires?**

    a.    Old key pairs

    b.    Private key establishment key

    c.    Private signature keys

    d.    Public keys

**14. b.** The user should not destroy the private key establishment key until all symmetric keys established using this key have been recovered or protected by encryption under a different key. Premature destruction of private key establishment keys may prevent recovery of the subscriber's plaintext data. The keys in the other three choices can be destroyed safely.

**15.** **Which of the following provides end-to-end security to protect information on the Internet?**

    a.    DES and RC2

    b.    TLS and SSL

    c.    HTTP and HTTPS

    d.    TDEA and AES

**15. b.** The transport layer security (TLS) and secure socket layer (SSL) protocols are the primary end-to-end security protocols used to protect information on the Internet. TLS is an enhanced version of SSL; these protocols are similar but not identical. TLS is a robust protocol that is used to protect various links, such as authentication server to a wireless access point, the electronic mail link between client and server, or dedicated network infrastructure applications primarily involving machines with no human user involvement.

**16.** **Which of the following are examples of mandatory-to-implement cryptographic algorithms that do *not* provide adequate security over computer networks?**

    a.    AES or 3-TDEA

    b.    RSA or ECDSA

    c.    DES or RC2

    d.    DH or ECDH

*16. c.*   Mandatory-to-implement cryptographic algorithms will be in any cryptographic product that meets the public standards (for example, IETF's RFCs and ANSI) enabling interoperability between products. AES is an optional-to-implement algorithm now that could become mandatory-to-implement in the future. DES and RC2 are mandatory and do not provide adequate security. DH is the Diffie-Hellman algorithm, which is used to provide key agreement. ECDH is the elliptic curve Diffie-Hellman algorithm, which is used to support key establishment; 3-TDEA is three key TDEA; RSA is a public-key algorithm, whereas ECDSA is a digital signature algorithm.

**17.** **Which of the following should *not* be used during a transport layer security (TLS) session between a client and a server?**

    a.    DH key agreement

    b.    RSA key transport

    c.    Ephemeral DH key

    d.    Static-to-static DH key agreement

*17. d.*   A transport layer security (TLS) session requires server authentication and requests certificates from the client and the server. The RSA key transport method implicitly authenticates the server to the client. In a Diffie-Hellman (DH) key agreement, the server authenticates itself by supplying a signed static DH key in a certificate or by signing an ephemeral key and sending a certificate with its public signing key. Thus, the server will always send a certificate, with either a signing key or a key-establishment key. In a static-to-static DH key agreement, client certificates will not contain a signing key thus are not recommended to use in a TLS session. This is because the server may request a certificate from the client.

**18.** **What is encrypting a symmetric key using another symmetric key called?**

    a.    Key transport

    b.    Key update

    c.    Key wrapping

    d.    Key bundle

*18. c.*   A key used for key wrapping is known as a key encrypting key, which is used to encrypt a symmetric key using another symmetric key. Key wrapping provides both confidentiality and integrity protection using a symmetric key.

The other three choices are not used in key wrapping. Key transport is a key establishment procedure whereby one party (sender) selects and encrypts the keying material and then distributes the material to another party (the receiver). Key update is a function performed on a cryptographic key to compute a new but related key. Key bundle is a set of keys used during one operation, typically a TDEA operation.

19. **Which of the following represents the correct order of nodes (from highest to lowest) in a cryptographic key management infrastructure?**

    1.   Client node

    2.   User entities

    3.   Key processing facility

    4.   Service agent

        a.   4, 2, 3, and 1

        b.   3, 4, 1, and 2

        c.   3, 4, 2, and 1

        d.   2, 4, 1, and 3

*19. b.* A key management infrastructure provides a unified and seamless structure for the generation, distribution, and management of cryptographic keys. It starts at the central oversight authority (the highest node, which is not used in the question) and moves down to key processing facility (the next highest node), service agent, client node, and user entities (the lowest node).

20. **In a cryptographic key management infrastructure, which of the following supports single point-of-access for other nodes?**

        a.   Key processing facility

        b.   User entities

        c.   Client nodes

        d.   Service agents

*20. d.* Service agents support an organization's key management infrastructure as single point-of-access for other nodes, including key processing facility, client nodes, and user entities.

21. **A digital signature is implemented using which of the following cryptographic techniques?**

        a.   Public key cryptography

        b.   Key escrow cryptography

        c.   Secret key cryptography

        d.   Hybrid cryptographic systems

**21. a.**   Recent advances in cryptographic technology have lead to the development of public key cryptographic algorithms. These algorithms are referred to as "asymmetric" because they rely on two different keys to perform cryptographic processing of data. These keys are generated and used in pairs consisting of private and public key components.

Public key crypto-systems make possible authentication schemes in which a secret can be verified without the need to share that secret. In public key cryptography, each user independently generates two mathematically related keys. One is typically made public, so it is referred to as the public key. The other is kept private, so it is referred to as the user's private key. The public key becomes in effect part of the user's identity and should be made well known as necessary, like a phone number. Conversely, the private key should be known only to the user because it can be used to prove ownership of the public key and thus the user's identity. It is computationally infeasible to derive a user's private key from the corresponding public key, so free distribution of the public key poses no threat to the secrecy of the private key.

The private key component of the public key cryptography is used to create the digital signatures. Similar to a written signature, a digital signature is unique to the signer except that it can be verified electronically. This is made possible by the fact that in public key crypto-systems, digital signatures are generated with the private key component of the public/private key pair. The corresponding public key is used to verify the signature. Because a given user's private key does not need to be shared with other parties, there is a strong association between the user's identity and possession of the private key.

Key escrow cryptographic techniques are used in electronic surveillance of telecommunications by law enforcement officials. A definition of a key escrow system is that an encryption key or a document is delivered to a third person to be given to the grantee only upon the fulfillment of a condition. A key escrow system is one that entrusts the two components comprising a cryptographic key (for example, a device unique key) to two key component holders (also called "escrow agents").

The key component holders provide the components of a key to a "grantee" (for example, a law enforcement official) only upon fulfillment of the condition that the grantee has properly demonstrated legal authorization to conduct electronic surveillance of telecommunications encrypted using the specific device whose device unique key is being requested. The key components obtained through this process are then used by the grantee to reconstruct the device unique key and obtain the session key that is then used to decrypt the telecommunications that are encrypted with that session key. The digital signature does not use the key escrow cryptography.

The primary feature distinguishing secret key algorithms is the use of a single secret key for cryptographic processing. The use of advanced encryption standard (AES) is an example of secret key cryptography. The AES algorithm can be implemented with reasonable efficiency in the firmware of a smart token. Electronic signatures can use either secret key or public key cryptography. The digital signature is not using the secret key cryptography due to sharing of a secret key by two parties. Hybrid approaches are possible, where public key cryptography is used to distribute keys for use by secret key algorithms. However, the digital signature is not using the hybrid approaches.

**22.** **Effective controls to detect attempts to replay an earlier successful authentication exchange do *not* include:**

    a.   A timestamp

    b.   A sequence number

    c.   An unpredictable value

    d.   A statistical random value

***22. d.*** The emphasis should be to use nonrepeating values in message authentication to ensure that an attempt to replay an earlier successful authentication exchange will be detected. Timestamps, sequence numbers, and unpredictable values can detect replay attempts.

Timestamps assume there is a common reference that logically links a claimant and verifier. On receipt of an authentication message, the verifier calculates the difference between the timestamp in the message and the time of receipt. If this difference is within the expected time window, the message is accepted.

A message with a particular sequence number is accepted only once as agreed by the claimant and verifier in advance. Messages received by a verifier are checked for acceptability within the range of agreed-upon values. An unpredictable value, or challenge, is sent by the verifier, and he will ensure that the same challenge is not reused within the time frame of concern. The values used do not require true statistical randomness. The only requirement is that the values should be unpredictable with a high probability of nonrepeating.

The problem with the statistical random value is that it deals with probabilities of occurrence and sampling methods, which will not meet the requirements of the other three choices.

**23.** **Procedural security controls for recognizing trusted certificate authority (CA) and registration authority (RA) roles should include:**

    1.   Least privilege concept must be practiced.

    2.   Separation of duties concept must be practiced.

    3.   A single person should not generate a new CA key pair.

    4.   A person authorizing certificates to a subject should not be verifying the subject's identity.

        a.   1 and 2

        b.   1 and 4

        c.   3 and 4

        d.   1, 2, 3, and 4

***23. d.*** All four items are examples of procedural security controls for recognizing trusted CA and RA roles. The CA is a trusted third party that generates, issues, signs, and revokes public key certificates. The CA can delegate responsibility for the verification of the subject's identity to an RA. The RA is a trusted entity that establishes and vouches for the identity of a subscriber to a credentials service provider (CSP).

**24.** **Which of the following need *not* be subject to maintenance of special accounting records for cryptographic keying materials?**

    a.    Ephemeral keys

    b.    Encrypted keys

    c.    Decrypted keys

    d.    Key encrypting keys

*24. a.* Ephemeral keys are cryptographic keys that are generated for each execution of a key establishment process and that meet other requirements of the key (for example, unique to each message or session and short-lived). It may not be practical or necessary to maintain accounting records for relatively short-lived keys such as ephemeral keys. This is because user devices (for example, user entities at client nodes) generate ephemeral keys, and they are intended for use within the client node.

The other three choices need accounting records. Encrypted keys are encrypted with a key encrypting key to disguise the value of the underlying plaintext key. The key encrypting key is used for the encryption or decryption of other keys.

**25.** **For the willful or negligent mishandling of cryptographic keying materials, the consequences of policy violation should be commensurate with which of the following?**

    a.    Actual harm

    b.    Known harm

    c.    Potential harm

    d.    Guaranteed harm

*25. c.* The consequences of willful or negligent mishandling of cryptographic keying materials (for example, keys and initialization vectors) should be commensurate with the potential harm that the policy violation can result in for the organization and other affected parties. The actual harm cannot be known in advance, and there is no guarantee that harm will occur for certain.

**26.** **A cryptographic keying material is compromised during the course of regular or normal work. Which of the following actions may not be necessary during the compromise recovery process?**

    a.    Key destruction

    b.    Notification of users of compromised keys

    c.    Emergency key revocation

    d.    Replacement of the compromised keys

*26. a.* Notification of users of compromised keys, emergency key revocation, and secure replacement of the compromised keys are a part of normal recovery procedures. Key destruction must take place only when an external attacker is involved, not when user errors and system problems are involved during the course of regular work. The other three choices are normally used during the compromise recovery process.

**27.** For the encapsulating security protocol (ESP) header of the Internet Protocol security (IPsec), which of the following cryptographic algorithms or modes provides both encryption and integrity services to the ESP-protected traffic?

    a.    AES-128 bit in cipher block chaining (CBC) mode

    b.    AES-128 bit in counter mode

    c.    HMAC SHA1-96 bit

    d.    AES-128 bit in counter mode with CBC-MAC

**27. d.** The AES-128 bit key in counter mode with CBC-MAC provides both encryption and integrity protection. The AES-128 bit in CBC mode and the AES-128 bit in counter mode provide only encryption whereas the HMAC SHA1-96 bit provides only integrity protection. The encrypted ESP should not be used without integrity protection because the ESP needs both encryption and integrity protection.

**28.** Within the Internet Protocol security (IPsec) protocol suite, which of the following should *not* be used because it introduces unnecessary complexity in processing?

    a.    Authentication header (AH)

    b.    Encapsulating security protocol (ESP)

    c.    Security association (SA)

    d.    Internet key exchange (IKE)

**28. a.** The authentication header (AH) protects the Internet Protocol (IP) header and the data following the IP header. However, the AH processing introduces unnecessary complexity. Because the encapsulating security protocol (ESP) can provide equivalent functionality as the AH, the use of AH is not recommended due to its complexity in processing. Moreover, the ESP protects the source and destination addresses in the IP header in both transport and tunnel modes. Hence, the ESP is better than the AH.

**29.** The security of which of the following cryptographic algorithm's confidentiality mechanism is *not* compromised?

    a.    AES-GCM (Galois counter mode)

    b.    AES-GMAC (Galois message authentication code)

    c.    The Internet key exchange (IKE)

    d.    Data encryption standard-cipher block chaining (DES-CBC) mode

**29. c.** The counter value in the AES-GCM or AES-GMAC is used for more than one packet with the same key. Therefore, the security of these algorithms' confidentiality mechanism is compromised. The DES-CBC mode is susceptible to compromise. Also, the AES-GCM and AES-GMAC should not be used with manually distributed keys. Automated keying using the Internet key exchange (IKE) establishes secret keys for the two peers within each security association (SA) with low probability of duplicate keys.

**30.** The transport layer security (TLS) protocol does *not* provide which of the following cryptographic services?

    a.    Authentication

    b.    Integrity

    c.    Nonrepudiation

    d.    Encryption

***30. c.*** After completion of the handshake sequence, the transport layer security (TLS) protocol provides a secure communication channel between the server and client for the duration of a communication session. All cipher suites provide authentication and integrity protection for transferred data, and most TLS cipher suites also provide encryption. If encryption is provided, data is encrypted when sent and decrypted when received. TLS does not, however, provide a cryptographic nonrepudiation service to allow a validation of the session data or authentication after the communication session has been ended by a third party.

**31.** In secure/multipurpose Internet mail extension (S/MIME), TDEA in CBC mode or AES-128 bit in CBC mode is used to provide which of the following?

    a.    Digital signatures

    b.    Hash values

    c.    Key transport

    d.    Encryption

***31. d.*** The secure/multipurpose Internet mail extension (S/MIME) provides a consistent way to send and receive secure Internet mail. However, S/MIME is not restricted to e-mail; it can be used with any transport mechanism that employs MIME protocols, such as HTTP. The TDEA in CBC mode or AES-128-bit key in CBC mode is used to provide encryption only.

**32.** Using the security features within a secure/multipurpose Internet mail extension (S/MIME) implementation, end users should *not* do which of the following?

    a.    Operate their systems according to instructions.

    b.    Use unique digital certificates for each security function.

    c.    Protect their private key from unauthorized disclosure.

    d.    Send the same message both encrypted and in plaintext.

***32. d.*** An end user is the individual using a client to access the system. Even within a centrally managed environment, end users may find that they have a significant amount of control over some of the security features within an S/MIME implementation. End users should not send the same message both encrypted and in plaintext. The end users can do the other three choices.

**33.** **The RSA-1024-bit key or the DSA-1024 bit key is used to provide which of the following?**

    a.    Digital signatures

    b.    Hash values

    c.    Key agreement

    d.    Encryption

***33. a.***   Either the Rivest, Shamir, and Adelman (RSA) or digital signature algorithm (DSA) with key sizes greater than or equal to 1024 bits is used to provide digital signatures. They are not used for hash values and key agreement, although less than 1024-bit keys are used for encryption.

**34.** **The Diffie-Hellman (DH) algorithm is used to provide which of the following?**

    a.    Digital signatures

    b.    Hash values

    c.    Key agreement

    d.    Encryption

***34. c.***   The Diffie-Hellman (DH) algorithm is used to provide key agreement. The DH algorithm cannot provide digital signatures, hash values, and encryption.

**35.** **The owner of a cryptographic key pair demonstrates proof-of-possession by using:**

    a.    Private key

    b.    Public key

    c.    Ephemeral key

    d.    Encrypted key

***35. a.***   The proof-of-possession is a verification process whereby it is proven that the owner of a key pair actually has the private key associated with the public key. The owner demonstrates the possession by using the private key in its intended manner. Without the assurance of possession, it would be possible for the certificate authority to bind the public key to the wrong entity. The other three choices do not demonstrate proof-of-possession.

**36.** **Which of the following can be specified in bits?**

    1.    Security strength of a cryptographic algorithm

    2.    Entropy

    3.    Hash function

    4.    Internet Protocol (IP) address identifier

        a.    1 and 4

        b.    2 and 3

    c.    1, 3, and 4

    d.    1, 2, 3, and 4

**36. d.**    The security strength of a cryptographic algorithm as well as entropy, hash function, and the Internet Protocol (IP) address identifier are specified in bits.

**37.**    **Which of the following is often distributed as a self-signed certificate?**

    a.    Trust anchors

    b.    Root certificate store

    c.    Trust list

    d.    Trust keys

**37. a.**    Certificate authorities (CAs) generally issue a self-signed certificate (called root certificate), which is also called a trust anchor. CAs that a relying party trusts directly are called trust anchors. When multiple trust anchors are recognized, the set of trust anchors is referred to as the trust list. CA certificates play a key role in many protocols and applications and are generally kept in what is often called a root certificate store. Trust keys are used in trust anchors. Root certificate store is used in validating certificate path.

**38.**    **Which of the following does *not* require cryptographic keys?**

    a.    Symmetric key algorithms

    b.    Asymmetric key algorithms

    c.    Cryptographic hash algorithms

    d.    Secret key algorithms

**38. c.**    Cryptographic hash algorithms (hash functions) do not require keys. The hash functions generate a relatively small digest (hash value) from a large input that is difficult to reverse. However, in some instances such as in the generation of hashed message authentication codes (HMAC), keyed hash functions are used.

Symmetric key algorithms (known as secret/private) transform data that is difficult to undo without knowledge of a secret key. Asymmetric key algorithms (known as public) use two related keys to perform their functions (i.e., a public key and a private key forming a key pair).

**39.**    **Which of the following is a noncryptographic technique that provides message integrity and creates insecurity?**

    a.    Message authentication code

    b.    Error detection codes

    c.    Cryptographic checksum

    d.    Block cipher algorithms

**39. b.**    Although message integrity is often provided using noncryptographic techniques known as error detection codes, these codes can be altered by an attacker for his benefit and hence create insecurity. Use of message authentication code (MAC) can alleviate this problem as it is based on block cipher algorithm. The cryptographic checksum is an algorithm that uses the bits in the transmission to create a checksum value and hence is secure. A non-cryptographic technique does not use a cryptographic key.

**40.** **Key wrapping provides which of the following services to the wrapped material?**

    a.    Confidentiality and integrity

    b.    Authentication and integrity

    c.    Accountability and availability

    d.    Assurance and reliability

**40. a.** Key wrapping is the encryption of a key by a key encrypting key using a symmetric algorithm. Key wrapping provides both confidentiality and integrity services to the wrapped material and does not provide services listed in the other three choices.

**41.** **Countermeasures against man-in-the-middle attacks include which of the following?**

1. Implement digital signatures

2. Use split knowledge procedures

3. Use faster hardware

4. Use packet filters

    a.    1 and 2

    b.    2 and 3

    c.    3 and 4

    d.    1 and 4

**41. a.** The man-in-the-middle (MitM) attack takes advantage of the store-and-forward mechanism used by insecure networks such as the Internet. Digital signatures and split knowledge procedures are effective against such attacks. Faster hardware and packet filters are effective against denial-of-service (DoS) attacks.

**42.** **Digital signatures *cannot* provide which of the following security services?**

    a.    Confidentiality

    b.    Authentication

    c.    Integrity

    d.    Nonrepudiation

**42. a.** Digital signatures cannot by themselves provide confidentiality service; instead, they provide authentication, integrity, and non-repudiation services. Specific algorithms used for digital signatures include DSA, RSA, PKCS, and ECDSA.

**43.** **The transport layer security (TLS) protocol does *not* provide which of the following?**

    a.    Integrity

    b.    Error recovery

    c.    Authentication

    d.    Encrypted payload

*43. b.* The transport layer security (TLS) protocol is protected by strong cryptographic integrity, an authentication mechanism, and encrypted payload. The TLS can detect any attack or noise event but cannot recover from errors. If an error is detected, the protocol run is simply terminated. Hence, the TLS needs to work with the TCP (transport control protocol) to recover from errors.

**44.** **Which of the following statements is true about digital signatures using the digital signature algorithm?**

    a.    The length of the digital signature is one-time the length of the key size.

    b.    The length of the digital signature is two-times the length of the key size.

    c.    The length of the digital signature is three-times the length of the key size.

    d.    The length of the digital signature is four-times the length of the key size.

*44. b.* The digital signature algorithm (DSA) produces digital signatures of 320, 448, or 512 bits using the key size of 160, 224, or 256 respectively. Hence, the length of the digital signature is two-times the length of the key size.

**45.** **Cryptographic key establishment schemes use which of the following?**

    a.    Key transport and key agreement

    b.    Key wrapping and key confirmation

    c.    Key usage and key distribution

    d.    Key splits and key bundles

*45. a.* Cryptographic key establishment schemes are used to set up keys to be used between communicating entities. The scheme uses key transport and key agreement. The key transport is the distribution of a key from one entity to another entity. The key agreement is the participation by both entities in the creation of shared keying material (for example, keys and initialization vectors). The key establishment scheme does not deal with the other three choices.

**46.** **Network communication channels contain unintentional errors due to transmission media and create network congestion, leading to lost packets. Which of the following statements is *incorrect* about forward error-correcting codes?**

    a.    Forward error-correcting codes are a subset of non-cryptographic checksums.

    b.    Forward error-correction mechanism should be applied before encryption.

    c.    Forward error-correcting codes can correct a limited number of errors without retransmission.

    d.    Forward error-correction mechanism should be applied after encryption.

**46. b.**   Forward error-correcting codes are a subset of noncryptographic checksums (i.e., they use an algorithm without secret information in terms of a cryptographic key) that can be used to correct a limited number of errors without retransmission. If forward error-correction is applied before encryption and errors are inserted in the ciphertext during transmission, it is difficult to decrypt, thus making the errors uncorrectable. Therefore, it is preferable to apply the forward error-correction mechanism after the encryption process. This will allow the error correction by the receiving entity's system before the ciphertext is decrypted, resulting in correct plaintext.

**47.**    **Which of the following should *not* exist outside the cryptographic boundary of the crypto-module?**

    a.    Shared secrets and intermediate results

    b.    Domain parameters and initialization vectors

    c.    Random number generator seeds and nonce

    d.    Nonce and salt

**47. a.**   Shared secrets are generated during a key establishment process. Intermediate results of cryptographic operations are generated using secret information. Therefore, both shared secrets and intermediate results should not exist outside the cryptographic boundary of the crypto-module due to their sensitivity and criticality. The other three choices either do not exist outside the cryptographic boundary or they are less sensitive and critical.

**48.**    **What describes the crypto-period of a symmetric key?**

    a.    Originator usage period plus retention period

    b.    Retention period minus recipient usage period

    c.    Originator usage period plus recipient usage period

    d.    Recipient usage period minus originator usage period

**48. c.**   The crypto-period of a symmetric key is the period of time from the beginning of the originator usage period to the end of the recipient usage period.

**49.**    **Which of the following should be destroyed immediately after use?**

    a.    Random number generator seeds and intermediate results

    b.    Nonce and shared secrets

    c.    Domain parameters and initialization vectors

    d.    Shared secrets and intermediate results

**49. a.** Both random number generator (RNG) seeds and intermediate results should be destroyed after use due to their sensitivity. Domain parameters remain in effect until changed. Shared secrets and initialization vectors should be destroyed as soon as they are no longer needed. A nonce should not be retained longer than needed for cryptographic processing.

**50.** **Which of the following provides the weakest cryptographic algorithms?**

1. A 160-bit ECDSA key is used to establish a 128-bit AES key.

2. A 256-bit ECDSA key is used to establish a 128-bit AES key.

3. A 256-bit SHA key is used with a 1024-bit RSA key.

4. A 256-bit SHA key is used with a 2048-bit RSA key.

 a. 1 only

 b. 1 and 3

 c. 2 and 3

 d. 2 and 4

**50. b.** The strength of cryptographic protection is determined by the weakest algorithm and the key size used. This is explained as follows:

A 160-bit ECDSA and 128-bit AES provide 80 bits of security.

A 256-bit ECDSA and 128-bit AES provide 128 bits of security.

A 256-bit SHA and 1024-bit RSA provide 80 bits of security.

A 256-bit SHA and 2048-bit RSA provide 112 bits of security.

Therefore, 80 bits of security is weaker than 112 bits and 128 bits of security.

**51.** **How is a cryptographic algorithm's security life defined?**

 a. Security life of data plus retention data life

 b. Originator usage period plus the security life of the data

 c. Recipient usage period plus the retention period

 d. Crypto-period plus security life of the data

**51. b.** A cryptographic algorithm's originator usage period is the period of time that a cryptographic algorithm and the key size are used to apply cryptographic protection. When the security life of the data is taken into account, cryptographic protection should not be applied to data using a given algorithm and key size if the security life of the data extends beyond the end of the algorithm security lifetime. Hence, the algorithm security life is the algorithm originator usage period plus the security life of the data.

**52.** **Which of the following should *not* be distributed?**

    a.    Shared secrets

    b.    Domain parameters

    c.    Initialization vectors

    d.    Random number generator seeds

*52. a.* A shared secret is a secret value that has been computed using a key agreement scheme and is used as input to a key derivation function. Hence, shared secrets should not be distributed while the other three choices can be safely distributed most of the time. Because the initialization vectors are often stored with the data that they protect, a determined attacker (not a normal attacker) could take advantage of them for hacking.

**53.** **Which of the following need *not* be backed up?**

    a.    Private key transport key

    b.    Public key transport key

    c.    Public authentication

    d.    Private signature key

*53. d.* The private signature key need not be backed up because nonrepudiation would be in question. This is because proof-of-origin and proof-of-delivery are needed for a successful nonrepudiation using private signature key by the originator (i.e., the signatory). Therefore, the private signature key should be protected in a safe and secure location. The other three choices can be backed up without any question.

**54.** **What is the *major* advantage of a checksum program?**

    a.    Adds more bytes to programs

    b.    Verifies integrity of files

    c.    Increases boot-up time

    d.    Misleads a program recompilation

*54. b.* A checksum is a program that forms a cryptographic checksum of files in a computer system to allow their integrity to be checked at will. However, the checksum program adds overhead to the system in terms of adding more bytes to each program and increases boot-up time by several minutes. Any attempt to recompile a program will be flagged as a "virus type" activity (when it is not) and will be stopped. It misleads a program recompilation process.

**55.** **Which of the following need *not* be archived?**

    a.    Private signature key

    b.    Symmetric authentication key

    c.    Public authentication key

    d.    Symmetric master key

**55. a.** An archive for keying material (i.e., keys and initialization vectors) should provide both integrity and access control. When archived, keying material should be archived prior to the end of the crypto-period of the key. When no longer required, the keying material should be destroyed. Private signature key need not be archived because it is private but should be protected in a safe and secure location.

Both symmetric and public authentication keys should be archived until no longer required to authenticate the data. A symmetric master key should be archived until no longer needed to derive other keys.

**56.** **What is a simpler alternative to a digital signature?**

    a.    Hash function

    b.    Digital certificate

    c.    Handwritten signature

    d.    Certificate authority

**56. a.** A digital signature provides for nonrepudiation of origin. A simpler alternative to a digital signature is a hash function, where the message is indexed to a digest for integrity checking. It requires that both parties trust one another. However, it is of limited use because it does not provide for repudiation of origin.

A digital certificate contains identification information about its holder. It includes a public key and a unique private key. Exchanging keys and certificates allows two parties to verify each other's identities before communicating. A handwritten signature is similar to a digital signature in that it places a unique mark on a document that verifies the identity of the sender. A major problem with the handwritten signature is that it can be forged. A certificate authority is a third party that distributes public and private key pairs.

**57.** **Which of the following need to be archived?**

    a.    Domain parameters

    b.    Shared secrets

    c.    Random number generator seeds

    d.    Intermediate results

**57. a.** Domain parameters should be archived until all keying material, signatures, and signed data using the domain parameters are removed from the archive. The other three choices should not be archived due to their secrecy and because they are temporary in nature. One exception is that a shared secret is sometimes permanent as in a preshared key (PSK) for a site-to-site IPsec VPN.

**58.** **If cryptographic key materials are compromised, the compromise recovery process can be relatively simple and inexpensive for which of the following?**

    a.    Symmetric keys used by a single user

    b.    A certification authority's private key

c. A key used to protect a large number of stored keys

d. Keys used by many users of large distributed databases

**58. a.** Where symmetric keys or private asymmetric keys are used to protect only a single user's local information in communications between a single pair of users, the compromise recovery process can be relatively simple and inexpensive. The damage assessment and mitigation measures are often local matters. On the other hand, damage assessment can be complex and expensive where (i) a key is shared by or affects a large number of users, (ii) certification authority's (CA's) private key is replaced, (iii) transport keys are widely used, (iv) keys are used by many users of large distributed databases, and (v) a key is used to protect a large number of stored keys.

**59.** **The strength of all cryptographically based mechanisms lies in large part in which of the following?**

a. The strength of the cryptographic algorithm

b. The protection provided to secret key material

c. The strength of the key size

d. The security of communication protocol

**59. b.** For all cryptographically based mechanisms, the strength of the mechanism lies partly in the strength of the cryptographic algorithm (including key size), partly in the security of any communication protocol, and in large part, in the protection provided to secret key material (i.e., keys and initialization vectors). A secret key is a symmetric key that is not made public and requires protection from disclosure.

**60.** **Which of the following is *not* the recommended combination of authentication type key, digital signature key, and key establishment key respectively?**

a. RSA 1024, RSA 2048, and DH 2048

b. ECDSA P-256, ECDSA P-256, and RSA 2048

c. RSA 1024, RSA 2048, and RSA 2048

d. ECDSA P-384, ECDSA P-384, and ECDH P-384

**60. b.** In general, protocols and applications are designed to use cryptographic algorithms from one mathematical family. For most uses, digital signature keys and key establishment keys should provide consistent cryptographic strength. For example, applications that encounter certificates with elliptic curve digital signature algorithm (ECDSA) digital signatures would expect to use elliptic curve Diffie-Hellman (ECDH) for the key establishment key. Rivest, Shamir, and Adelman (RSA) is not compatible with ECDSA, whereas it is compatible with DH. It is advisable that users obtain an authentication type key, a digital signature key, and a key establishment key that are complementary in nature to ensure that the keys can be used together in protocols and applications. Complementary algorithms for public keys enhance interoperability.

**61.** **Which of the following is the major reason for the transport layer security (TLS) protocol to provide end-to-end reliable delivery of data and messages?**

    a.    Cyclical redundancy checks

    b.    Message reassembly

    c.    Forward error correction technique

    d.    Message fragmentation

*61. b.*   Reliable delivery of data implies that all messages presented to the sending TCP/IP stack are delivered in proper sequence by the receiving TCP/IP stack. These messages may be broken up into packets and fragmented or segmented as they are sent and routed through any arrangement of local-area, wide-area, or metropolitan-area networks. During routing through networks, data are augmented with cyclical redundancy checks or forward error correction techniques to help ensure that the delivered messages are identical to the transmitted messages. Reliable delivery means that the messages are properly reassembled and presented in proper sequence to the peer protocol TLS entity. Here, the TLS relies on the communications functionality of the OSI/ISO lower layer protocols.

**62.** **The transport layer security (TLS) protocol version 1.1 mandates the use of which of the following cipher suites?**

    a.    TLS and DES with RC4-40, RC2-CBC-40, and DES-40

    b.    TLS and DHE-DSA with 3DES-EDE-CBC and SHA-1

    c.    TLS and DHE-DSS with 3DES-EDE-CBC and SHA-1

    d.    TLS and RSA with 3DES-EDE-CBC and SHA-1

*62. d.*   The TLS version 1.1 mandates the use of the TLS and RSA with 3DES-EDE-CBC and SHA-1 cipher suite, and is more commonly used. The DES with RC4-40, RC2-CBC-40, and DES-40 cannot be combined with TLS because the algorithm is deprecated. The TLS and DHE-DSA with 3DES-EDE-CBCand SHA-1 is not often used. The TLS version 1.0 uses the TLS and DHE-DSS with 3DES-EDE-CBC and SHA-1.

**63.** **The transport layer security (TLS) protocol's security specification for ensuring confidentiality goal is:**

    a.    Rivest, Shamir, and Adelman (RSA)

    b.    Digital signature algorithm (DSA)

    c.    Triple-data encryption standard (3DES) using encryption-decryption-encryption (EDE) and cipher block chaining (CBC)

    d.    Message digest 5 (MD5)

*63. c.*   The transport layer security (TLS) protocol's security specification for ensuring the confidentiality goal is 3DES-EDE-CBC. RSA is used for key establishment, a DSA is used for digital signatures, and MD5 is used for hash function purposes.

**64.** **What is a digital certificate?**

    a.    A password-protected file

    b.    An encrypted file

    c.    A password-protected and encrypted file

    d.    A password-protected and modem-protected file

**64.c.** A digital certificate is a password-protected and encrypted file that contains identification information about its holder. It is not a modem-protected file.

**65.** **Most commonly used X.509 certificates do *not* refer to which of the following?**

    a.    Tamper-evident envelope

    b.    Attribute certificate

    c.    Public key certificate

    d.    Basic certificate content

**65. b.** The ISO/ITU-T X.509 standard defines two types of certificates: the X.509 public key certificate and the X.509 attribute certificate. Most commonly, an X.509 certificate refers to the X.509 public key certificate. The public key certificate contains three nested elements: (i) the tamper-evident envelope (digitally signed by the source), (ii) the basic certificate content (for example, identifying information and public key), and (iii) extensions that contain optional certificate information. The X.509 attribute certificate is less commonly used.

**66.** **Which of the following features of Secure Hypertext Transfer Protocol (S-HTTP) achieves higher levels of protection?**

    a.    Freshness feature

    b.    Algorithm independence feature

    c.    Syntax compatibility feature

    d.    Recursive feature

**66. d.** In the recursive feature, the message is parsed one protection at a time until it yields a standard HTTP content type. Here, protections are applied in layers, one layer after another to achieve higher levels of protection. S-HTTP uses a simple challenge-response to ensure that data being returned to the server is "fresh." Algorithm independence means new cryptographic methods can be easily implemented. Syntax compatibility means that the standard HTTP messages are syntactically the same as secure HTTP messages.

**67.** **The Secure Sockets Layer (SSL) transport protocol provides all the following services *except*:**

    a.    Mutual authentication

    b.    Message privacy

    c.    Message integrity

    d.    Mutual handshake

***67. d.***    The Secure Sockets Layer (SSL) is an open and nonproprietary protocol that provides services such as mutual authentication, message privacy, and message integrity. Mutual handshake is not done by SSL.

**68.**    **Which of the following can be used with traffic padding security mechanisms?**

    a.    Passwords

    b.    Smart tokens

    c.    Encryption

    d.    Memory tokens

***68. c.***    Traffic padding is a function that generates a continuous stream of random data or ciphertext. True data is mixed with extraneous data thus making it difficult to deduce the amount of traffic, that is, traffic analysis. Encryption is good with traffic padding because it can disguise the true data very well and requires a key to decipher the encrypted data.

Passwords are incorrect because they are most often associated with user authentication, not with traffic padding. Smart tokens and memory tokens are incorrect because they are also used to authenticate users. Memory tokens store, but do not process, information, whereas smart tokens both store and process information.

**69.**    **Effective controls to ensure data integrity of messages does *not* include:**

    a.    Encryption algorithms

    b.    Hashing algorithms

    c.    File seals

    d.    File labels

***69. d.***    File labels are used in computer job runs to process application systems data to ensure that the right file is used. Encryption algorithms, due to their encryption and decryption mechanisms and by keeping the encryption keys secure, provide integrity to the message transmitted or stored. Hashing algorithms are a form of authentication that provides data integrity. File seal is adding a separate signature to software and partly works with virus checking software. When the file seal and virus checking software signatures do not match, it is an indication that data integrity has been compromised.

**70.**    **During the design of data communication networks, a functional capability of providing link encryption and end-to-end encryption is addressed by which of the following?**

    a.    Administrative control

    b.    Access control

    c.    Cost control

    d.    Technical control

**70. b.** Functional capabilities can be placed inside network components to control access and protect information from misuse. Automated access control systems can require users and systems to log on to a network by identifying themselves and providing an automated password or similar control. Link and end-to-end encryption devices can protect information from misuse during transmission over a circuit or through a network. Link encryption is the application of online crypto-operation to a link of a communications system so that all information passing over the link is encrypted in its entirety. End-to-end encryption is the encryption of information at its origin and decryption at its intended destination without any intermediate decryption.

Administrative control is incorrect because it deals with handling the paperwork associated with operating a network. The scope includes receiving requests for service from prospective users, notifying operations personnel of dates that devices should be connected and disconnected, maintaining a directory of network users and services, authorizing users to access the network and, issuing passwords.

Cost control is incorrect because it deals with cost recovery and avoidance. It includes price setting for network services and billing the users. The price of network services is often a function of the volume of information exchanged, the duration of usage, the distance between parties, and the time of day of usage.

Technical control is incorrect because it includes activities such as failure detection, problem diagnosis, and service restoration of network components. The scope includes alarms, status indicators, test-equipment interfaces, remote controls, and automatic monitoring.

**71.** **Which of the following is an example of passive wiretapping?**

    a. Traffic analysis

    b. Message modification

    c. Message delay

    d. Message deletion

**71. a.** Passive wiretapping includes not only information release but also traffic analysis (using addresses, other header data, message length, and message frequency). Security measures such as traffic padding can be used to prevent traffic analysis attacks. Active wiretapping includes message stream modifications, including delay, duplication, deletion, or counterfeiting.

**72.** **What is a hash-based message authentication code (HMAC) based on?**

    a. Asymmetric key

    b. Public key

    c. Symmetric key

    d. Private key

**72. c.**  A hash-based message authentication code (HMAC) is based on a symmetric key authentication method using hash functions. A symmetric key is a cryptographic key that is used to perform both the cryptographic operation and its inverse, for example to encrypt and decrypt, or create a message authentication code (MAC), and to verify the code.

Asymmetric key is incorrect because there are two related keys in asymmetric keys; a public key and a private key that are used to perform complementary operations, such as encryption and decryption, or signature generation and signature verification. Public key is incorrect because it is the public part of an asymmetric key pair that is typically used to verify signatures or encrypt data. Private key is incorrect because it is the secret part of an asymmetric key pair that is typically used to digitally sign or decrypt data.

**73.**   What is the main purpose of a message authentication code (MAC)?

    a.    Recovery

    b.    Prevention

    c.    Detection

    d.    Correction

**73. c.**  A message authentication code (MAC) is a cryptographic checksum on data that uses a symmetric key to detect both accidental and intentional modifications of data.

**74.**   The major functions of a public key used in cryptography include which of the following?

    1.    Encrypt data

    2.    Decrypt data

    3.    Generate signatures

    4.    Verify signatures

        a.    1 only

        b.    2 only

        c.    1 or 4

        d.    2 or 3

**74. c.**  The public key is the public part of an asymmetric key pair that is typically used to encrypt data or verify signatures. The private key is the secret part of an asymmetric key pair that is typically used to decrypt data and to digitally sign (i.e., generate signatures).

**75.**   Approved hash functions must satisfy which of the following properties?

    1.    One-way

    2.    Collision resistant

    3.    Resistant to offline attacks

    4.    Resistant to online attacks

a. 1 only

b. 3 only

c. 4 only

d. 1 and 2

**75. d.** A hash function maps a bit string of arbitrary length to a fixed length bit string. Approved hash functions must satisfy the following two properties: one-way and collision resistant. It is computationally infeasible to find any input that map to any prespecified output or two distinct inputs that map to the same output.

Offline attack is an attack where the attacker obtains some data through eavesdropping that he can analyze in a system of his own choosing. Online attack is an attack against an authentication protocol where the attacker either assumes the role of a claimant with a genuine verifier or actively alters the authentication channel. The goal of the attack may be to gain authenticated access or learn authentication secrets.

**76.** Which of the following is a measure of the amount of uncertainty that an attacker faces to determine the value of a secret?

a. Entropy

b. Random number

c. Nonce

d. Pseudonym

**76. a.** Entropy is a measure of the amount of uncertainty that an attacker faces to determine the value of a secret. Entropy is usually stated in bits as it relates to information theory. It is a statistical parameter.

Random number is incorrect because it can be used to generate passwords or keys. Nonce is incorrect because it is a value used in security protocols that is never repeated with the same key. Pseudonym is incorrect because it is a subscriber name that has been chosen by the subscriber that is not verified as meaningful by identity proofing.

**77.** Which of the following is a nonsecret value that is used in a cryptographic process?

a. Salt

b. Shared secret

c. Min-entropy

d. Guessing entropy

**77. a.** Salt is a nonsecret value that is used in a cryptographic process, usually to ensure that an attacker cannot reuse the results of computations for one instance.

Shared secret is incorrect because it is a secret used in authentication that is known to the claimant and the verifier. Min-entropy is incorrect because it is a measure of the difficulty that an attacker has to guess the most commonly chosen password used in a system.

Guessing entropy is incorrect because it is a measure of the difficulty that an attacker has to guess the average password used in a system.

**78.** **A technique to protect software from potential forgeries is to use:**

    a.    Digital libraries

    b.    Digital signals

    c.    Digital watermarks

    d.    Digital signatures

**78. c.** Digital watermarks are used to prove proprietary rights. It is the process of irreversibly embedding information into a digital signal. An example is embedding copyright information about the copyright owner.

Digital libraries are storage places for data and programs. Digital signals are electronic switches in computers and are represented as binary digits called bits. Digital signatures are a security authorization method to prove that a message was not modified.

**79.** **Which of the following specifically deals with hiding messages and obscuring senders and receivers?**

    a.    Quantum cryptography

    b.    Steganography

    c.    Cryptology

    d.    Cryptography

**79. b.** Steganography is a part of cryptology that deals with hiding messages and obscuring who is sending or receiving them. Message traffic is padded to reduce the signals that otherwise would come from the sudden beginning of messages. Quantum cryptography is based on quantum-mechanics principles where eavesdroppers alter the quantum state of the system.

Cryptology is the science and study of writing, sending, receiving, and deciphering secret messages. It includes authentication, digital signatures, steganography, and cryptanalysis. Cryptology includes both cryptography and cryptanalysis. Cryptology is the science that deals with hidden communications. Cryptography involves the principles, means, and methods used to render information unintelligible and for restoring encrypted information to intelligible form.

**80.** **What is an encryption algorithm that encrypts and decrypts arbitrarily sized messages called?**

    a.    Link encryption

    b.    Bulk encryption

    c.    End-to-end encryption

    d.    Stream encryption

**80. d.**   The cipher block chaining method is used to convert a block encryption scheme with a variable length key into a stream encryption of arbitrarily sized messages.

In link encryption, all information passing over the link is encrypted in its entirety. Link encryption is also called an online encryption. Simultaneous encryption of all channels of a multichannel telecommunications trunk is called a bulk encryption.

In end-to-end encryption, the information is encrypted at its origin and decrypted at its intended destination without any intermediate decryption. End-to-end encryption is also called an offline encryption. In link encryption, bulk encryption, and end-to-end encryption, the algorithm takes a fixed-length block of message (for example, 64 bits in the case of both DES and IDEA).

**81.**    **What is a message authentication code?**

   a.    Data checksum

   b.    Cryptographic checksum

   c.    Digital signature

   d.    Cyclic redundancy check

**81. b.**   A checksum is digits or bits summed according to arbitrary rules and used to verify the integrity of data. All forms of checksums have the same objective, that is, to ensure that the conveyed information has not been changed in transit from sender to recipient. The difference between these checksums is how strong the protective mechanism is for changing the information, that is, how hard it will be to attack for a knowledgeable attacker, not for a natural source. A message authentication code is a cryptographic checksum with the highest form of security against attacks. The public key is used to encrypt the message prior to transmission, and knowledge of a private (secret) key is needed to decode or decrypt the received message.

A data checksum is incorrect because it catches errors that are the result of noise or other more natural or nonintentional sources. For example, most of these errors are due to human errors.

A digital signature is incorrect because it is a form of authenticator. It is decrypted using the secret decryption key and sent to the receiver. The receiver may encrypt, using the public key, and may verify the signature, but the signature cannot be forged because only the sender knows the secret decryption key. Nonpublic key algorithms can also be used for digital signatures. The basic difference between the message authentication code and the digital signature is that although message authentication codes require a secret (private) key to verify, digital signatures are verifiable with a public key, that is, a published value. Message authentication codes are used to exchange information between two parties, where both have knowledge of the secret key. A digital signature does not require any secret key to be verified.

A cyclic redundancy check (CRC) is incorrect because it uses an algorithm for generating error detection bits, and the receiving station performs the same calculation as the transmitting station. If the results differ, then one or more bits are in error. Both message authentication codes and digital signatures operate with keys (whether public or private), are based on cryptography, and are hard to attack by intruders. On the other hand, data checksums and cyclic redundancy checks operate on algorithms, are not based on cryptography, and are easily attacked by intruders.

82.    **For security protection mechanisms for cryptographic data in storage, the encryption mechanism should *not* be easier to recover the key encrypting key than it is to recover the key being encrypted is a part of which of the following cryptographic service?**

    a.    Confidentiality

    b.    Availability

    c.    Integrity

    d.    Labels

*82. a.*    For confidentiality service, encryption with an approved algorithm is needed for the cryptographic module. Moreover, the encryption mechanism should not be an easier way to recover the key encrypting key than it is to recover the key being encrypted. In other words, recovering the key being encrypted should be relatively easier and recovering the key encrypting key should be difficult.

83.    **Which of the following is *least* effective in verifying against malicious tampering?**

    a.    Message authentication code

    b.    Digital signatures

    c.    Message digests

    d.    Cyclic redundancy code

*83. d.*    Checksums are of two types: a cryptographic checksum and a noncryptographic checksum. A cyclic redundancy code is a noncryptographic checksum, which is designed to detect random bit changes, not purposeful alterations or malicious tampering. These checksums are good at finding a few bits changed at random.

The other three incorrect choices are based on cryptographic checksum techniques. Message authentication code is a message digest with a password attached to it. The intent is that someone cannot re-create the code with the same input unless that person also knows the secret key (password). A digital signature is a message digest encrypted with someone's private key to certify the contents. Digital signatures perform three important functions: integrity, authentication, and nonrepudiation. A message digest is a hash code produced by a mathematical function. It takes variable length input and reduces it to a small value, and a small change in the input results in a significant change in the output.

Secure hash algorithms create a short message digest. The message digest is then used, with the sender's private key and the algorithm specified in digital signature standard, to produce a message-specific signature. Verifying the digital signature standard involves a mathematical operation on the signature and message digest, using the sender's public key and the hash standard.

**84.** **What is password hashing?**

    a.    Storing a hash of the password

    b.    Storing the password in a clear text and encrypting it as needed

    c.    Guessing a password

    d.    Cracking a password

**84. a.** Password hashing requires storing a password in its hash form, which is better than storing an unencrypted password. When a password is supplied, it computes the password's hash and compares it with the stored value. If they match, the password is correct. An attacker cannot derive the password from the hashes. It is good to hide the hashed password list.

The other three incorrect choices are weak forms of handling a password. Encrypting passwords leads to judgmental errors. A password can be easily guessed if the user selects the password from a word dictionary. An exhaustive search may then "crack" the password.

**85.** **Which of the following statements is *true* about message padding?**

    a.    It is the same as traffic padding.

    b.    It is similar to a data checksum.

    c.    It is adding additional bits to a message.

    d.    It is the same as one-time pad.

**85. c.** Message padding adds bits to a message to make it a desired length—for instance, an integral number of bytes. Traffic padding involves adding bogus traffic into the channel to prevent traffic analysis, which is a passive attack. Data checksums are digits or bits summed according to arbitrary rules and used to verify the integrity of data. The one-time pad contains a random number for each character in the original message. The pad is destroyed after its initial use.

**86.** **What is a public key cryptographic algorithm that does both encryption and digital signature?**

    a.    Rivest, Shamir, and Adelman (RSA)

    b.    Data encryption standard (DES)

    c.    International data encryption algorithm (IDEA)

    d.    Digital signature standard (DSS)

**86. a.** RSA's technique can be used for document encryption as well as creating digital signatures. DSS is a public key cryptographic system for computing digital signatures only, but not for encryption. Both RSA and DSS appear to be similar. DES is a secret key cryptographic scheme. IDEA is also a secret key cryptographic scheme gaining popularity. Both DES and IDEA use secret (private) key algorithms, whereas DSS and RSA use public key algorithms.

**87.**   **What is a digital signature?**

   a.   A form of authenticator

   b.   An actual signature written on the computer

   c.   The same as the checksum

   d.   Different from analog signature

***87. a.***   A digital signature authorizes and legitimizes the transaction by using a secret decryption key to send it to the receiver. An actual signature written on the computer is incorrect because it is not an actual signature. Instead, a digital signature is decrypted using the secret decryption key and sent to the receiver. Checksum is incorrect because it is a technique to ensure the accuracy of transmission, and it ensures the integrity of files. There is no such thing as an analog signature because a digital signature is needed.

**88.**   **What is a *major* drawback of digital certificates?**

   a.   Certificate authority

   b.   Internet addresses

   c.   Message digest

   d.   Digital signature

***88. b.***   A major drawback of digital certificates is that they do not identify individuals, only Internet addresses. A different person could use the same computer with bad intent and be seen as the legitimate owner of the digital certificate. The certificate authority, the message digest, and the digital signatures are the strengths of digital certificates.

**89.**   **Which of the following methods can prevent eavesdropping?**

   a.   Authentication

   b.   Access controls

   c.   Encryption

   d.   Intrusion detection

***89. c.***   Encryption can be used to prevent eavesdroppers from obtaining data traveling over unsecured networks. The items mentioned in the other three choices do not have the same features as encryption.

Authentication is the act of verifying the identity of a user and the user's eligibility to access computerized information. Access controls determine what users can do in a computer system. Intrusion detection systems are software or hardware systems that detect unauthorized use of, or attack upon, a computer or network.

**90.**   **Which of the following is *more* secure?**

   a.   Private key system

   b.   Public key system

  c. Authentication key system

  d. Encryption key system

***90. b.***  The public key system is more secure because transmission involves the public key only; the private key is never transmitted and is kept secret by its holder. On the other hand, in a private key system, both the sender and the recipient know the secret key and thus it can be less secure. Authentication and encryption key systems are incorrect because they can be either public (more secure) or private (less secure) key systems.

**91.** **For security protection mechanisms for cryptographic data in transit, side channel attacks are possible in which of the following cryptographic services?**

  a. Confidentiality

  b. Availability

  c. Integrity

  d. Labels

***91. c.***  Improper error handling during a transmission between a sender and a receiver can result in side channel attacks, which can result in integrity failures. A security policy should define the response to such a failure. Remedies for integrity failures can include retransmission limited to a predetermined number of times and storing the error data in an audit log for later identification of the source of the error.

The other three choices do not allow side channel attacks because they do not deal with transmission errors. Confidentiality deals with privacy and nondisclosure of information, and more. Availability deals with making data and systems within the reach of users. Labels are used to identify attributes, parameters, or the intended use of a key.

**92.** **Public key authentication systems:**

  a. Are faster than private key systems

  b. Do not use digital signatures

  c. Are slower than private key systems

  d. Do not use alpha characters in the key

***92. c.***  Public key methods are much slower than private methods and cause overhead, which are their main disadvantages. The public key contains alphanumeric characters. The public key systems use digital signatures for authentication.

**93.** **Which of the following is *not* a common route to data interception?**

  a. Direct observation

  b. Data encryption

  c. Interception of data transmission

  d. Electromagnetic interception

**93. b.** There are three routes of data interception: direct observation, interception of data transmission, and electromagnetic interception. Data encryption can be a solution to data interception.

94. The combination of XEX tweakable block cipher with ciphertext stealing and advanced encryption standard (XTS-AES) algorithm was designed to provide which of the following?

1.   Encryption of data on storage devices

2    Encryption of data in transit

3.   Confidentiality for the protected data

4.   Authentication of data

    a.   1 and 2

    b.   1 and 3

    c.   2 and 4

    d.   3 and 4

**94. c.** The XTS-AES mode was designed for the cryptographic protection of data on storage devices that use fixed length data units, and it was not designed for encryption of data in transit. This mode also provides confidentiality for the protected data but not authentication of data or access control.

95. Which of the following is *not* used for public key infrastructure-based (PKI-based) authentication of system users?

    a.   Validates certificates by constructing a certification path to an accepted trust anchor

    b.   Establishes user control of the corresponding private key

    c.   Maps the authenticated identity to the user account

    d.   Uses a radius server with extensible authentication protocol and transport layer security authentication

**95. d.** A radius server with extensible authentication protocol (EAP) and transport layer security (TLS) authentication is used to identify and authenticate devices on LANs and/or WANs. It is not used for authenticating system users. The other three choices are used for PKI-based authentication of system users.

96. Message authentication code (MAC) provides which of the following security services?

    a.   Confidentiality and integrity

    b.   Authentication and integrity

    c.   Accountability and availability

    d.   Assurance and reliability

**96. b.** The message authentication code (MAC) provides data authentication and integrity. A MAC is a cryptographic checksum on the data that is used to provide assurance that the data has not changed and that the MAC was computed by the expected entity. It cannot provide other security services.

**97.** Which of the following are countermeasures against traffic analysis attacks?

1. Traffic flow signal control
2. Traffic encryption key
3. Traffic flow security
4. Traffic padding

   a. 1 and 2
   b. 1 and 3
   c. 2 and 4
   d. 3 and 4

**97. d.** Traffic flow security is a technique to counter traffic analysis attacks, which is the protection resulting from encrypting the source and destination addresses of valid messages transmitted over a communications circuit. Security is assured due to use of link encryption and because no part of the data is known to an attacker. Traffic padding, which generates mock communications or data units to disguise the amount of real data units being sent, also protects traffic analysis attacks.

The other two items cannot control traffic analysis attacks. Traffic flow signal control is used to conduct traffic flow analysis. Traffic encryption key is used to encrypt plaintext or to super-encrypt previously encrypted text and/or to decrypt ciphertext.

**98.** Which of the following refers to a communications network architecture in which user data traversing a global Internet Protocol (IP) network is end-to-end encrypted at the IP layer?

   a. RED
   b. BLACK
   c. Black core
   d. Striped core

**98. c.** Black core refers to a communications network architecture in which user data traversing a core (global) Internet Protocol (IP) network is end-to-end encrypted at the IP layer.

RED refers to data/information or messages that contain sensitive or classified information that is not encrypted whereas BLACK refers to information that is encrypted. Striped core is a communications network architecture in which user data traversing a core (global) IP network is decrypted, filtered, and re-encrypted one or more times. The process of decryption filtering, and re-encryption is performed within a "red gateway"; consequently, the core is "striped" because the data path is alternatively black, red, and black.

**99.** **Digital signature generation should provide security strength of which of the following?**

    a.    Less than 80 bits

    b.    Equal to or greater than 80 bits

    c.    Equal to or greater than 112 bits

    d.    Between 80 and 112 bits

***99. c.*** Digital signature generation should provide security strength of 112 bits or more. Digital signature verification should provide security strength of 80 bits or more. Less than 80 bits or a range between 80 and 112 bits are not acceptable for the digital signature generation.

**100.** **Which of the following is *not* true about a digital signature?**

    a.    It is an encrypted digest of the text that is sent along with a message.

    b.    It authenticates the identity of the sender of a message.

    c.    It guarantees that no one has altered the sent document.

    d.    Electronic signatures and digital signatures are the same.

***100. d.*** A digital signature is an electronic analogue of a handwritten signature in that it can be used to prove to the recipient, or a third party, that the originator in fact signed the message. It is an encrypted digest of the text that is sent along with a message, usually a text message, but possibly one that contains other types of information, such as pictures. A digital signature authenticates the identity of the sender of the message and also guarantees that no one has altered the document.

On the other hand, an electronic signature is a cryptographic mechanism that performs a similar function to a handwritten signature. It is used to verify the origin and contents of a message (for example, an e-mail message). It is a method of signing an electronic message that (i) identifies and authenticates a particular person as the source of the electronic message and (ii) indicates such person's approval of the information contained in the electronic message. Electronic signatures can use either secret key or public key cryptography. Hence, electronic signatures and digital signatures are not the same.

**101.** **Traffic flow confidentiality uses which of the following security controls?**

    a.    Traffic padding and address hiding

    b.    Testwords and traffic padding

    c.    Traffic padding and seals/signatures

    d.    Address hiding and seals/signatures

***101. a.*** Traffic flow confidentiality protects against sensitive information being disclosed by observing network traffic flows. It uses traffic (message) padding and address hiding controls. In traffic padding, "dummy" traffic is generated to confuse the intruder. Address hiding requires that protocol header information be protected from unauthorized attack via cryptographic means.

Testword is incorrect because a string of characters is appended to a transaction by the sending party and verified by the receiving party. A testword is an early technology realization of a seal or signature used in financial transactions. A seal or signature involves cryptographically generating a value that is appended to a plain text data item. Both testwords and seals are used to increase the data integrity of financial transactions.

**102.** **Cryptographic methods work effectively as a security measure for information and communication systems. To achieve that goal, cryptographic methods must meet all the following *except*:**

    a.   Interoperable

    b.   Scalable

    c.   Mobile

    d.   Portable

*102. b.* Scalability means the system can be made to have more or less computational power by configuring it with a larger or smaller number of processors, amount of memory, interconnection bandwidth, number of total connections, input/output bandwidth, and amount of mass storage. Scalability is a technology or organizational issue, not a cryptography issue.

Interoperability is incorrect because it is needed in cryptography where two or more systems can interact with one another and exchange data according to a prescribed method to achieve predictable results. Mobility is incorrect because it is needed in cryptography to authenticate between local and remote systems. Portability is incorrect because it is needed in cryptography between operating systems and application systems. The other three choices are cryptography issues to deal with.

**103.** **Which of the following provides less security?**

    a.   SHA-1

    b.   SHA-224

    c.   SHA-256

    d.   SHA-384

*103. a.* Secure hash algorithm -1 (SHA-1), which is 160 bits, provides less security than SHA-224, SHA-256, and SHA-384. Cryptographic hash functions that compute a fixed size message digest (MD) from arbitrary size messages are widely used for many purposes in cryptography, including digital signatures. A hash function produces a short representation of a longer message. A good hash function is a one-way function: It is easy to compute the hash value from a particular input; however, backing up the process from the hash value back to the input is extremely difficult. With a good hash function, it is also extremely difficult to find two specific inputs that produce the same hash value. Because of these characteristics, hash functions are often used to determine whether data has changed.

Researchers discovered a way to "break" a number of hash algorithms, including MD4, MD5, HAVAL-128, RIPEMD, and SHA-0. New attacks on SHA-1 have indicated that

SHA-1 provides less security than originally thought. Therefore, the use of SHA-1 is not recommended for generating digital signatures in new systems. New systems should use one of the larger and better hash functions, such as SHA-224, SHA-256, SHA-384, and SHA-512.

**104.** In symmetric cryptography, if there are four entities using encryption, how many keys are required for each relationship?

    a.   4

    b.   6

    c.   8

    d.   12

*104. b.* In symmetric cryptography, the same key is used for both encryption and decryption. If there are four entities such as A, B, C, and D, there are six possible relationships such as A-B, A-C, A-D, B-C, B-D, and C-D. Therefore, six keys are required. It uses the formula $(n)(n-1)/2$ where "n" equals the number of entities.

**105.** Which of the following key combinations is highly recommended to use in the triple data encryption algorithm (TDEA)?

    a.   Independent key 1, Independent key 2, Independent key 3

    b.   Independent key 1, Independent key 2, Independent key 1

    c.   Independent key 1, Independent key 2, Independent key 2

    d.   Independent key 2, Independent key 3, Independent key 3

*105. a.* Triple data encryption algorithm (TDEA) encrypts data in blocks of 64 bits, using three keys that define a key bundle. The use of three distinctly different (i.e., mathematically independent) keys is highly recommended because this provides the most security from TDEA; this is commonly known as three-key TDEA (3TDEA or 3TDES). The use of two-key TDEA (2TDEA or 2TDES), in which the first and third keys are identical and the second key is distinctly different, is highly discouraged. Other configurations of keys in the key bundle shall not be used.

**106.** For a cryptographic module, which of the following presents the correct relationships for sensitive security parameters?

    a.   Port security parameters plus private security parameters

    b.   Critical security parameters plus public security parameters

    c.   Data security parameters plus critical security parameters

    d.   Public security parameters plus program security parameters

*106. b.* Critical security parameters (CSP) contain security-related information (for example, secret and private cryptographic keys, and authentication data such as passwords and PINs) whose disclosure or modification can compromise the security of a cryptographic module or the security of the information protected by the module. Public security parameters (PSP) deal with security-related public information (for example, public keys) whose modification can compromise the security of a cryptographic module. Sensitive security parameters (SSP) contain both CSP and PSP. In other words, SSP = CSP + PSP. A trusted channel is generally established to transport the SSPs, data, and other critical information shared by the cryptographic module and the module's operator.

The other three choices are incorrect. A port is a physical entry or exit point of a cryptographic module that provides access to the module for physical signals represented by logical information flows. The port security parameters along with data/program security parameters are not that important to the cryptographic module. The private security parameters do not exist.

**107.** The U.S. government imposes export controls on strong cryptography. Which of the following is the acceptable encryption key for use behind the firewall for use in foreign countries or in networks that include nodes in a foreign country?

    a.    40 bits

    b.    56 bits

    c.    75 bits

    d.    90 bits

***107. a.*** Encryption using keys of 40 or fewer bits is only acceptable for use behind the firewall. Leading cryptographers recommend businesses use key lengths of at least 75 bits, with 90 bits being preferable. The Data Encryption Standard (DES) uses 56 keys, which is still acceptable for near term use.

**108.** Which of the following should be considered during configuration of cryptographic controls in the implementation phase of a system development life cycle (SDLC) as it applies to selecting cryptographic mechanisms?

    1.    Mathematical soundness of the algorithm

    2.    Length of the cryptographic keys

    3.    Key management

    4.    Mode of operation

        a.    2 only

        b.    3 only

        c.    1, 2, and 3

        d.    1, 2, 3, and 4

***108. d.*** In the implementation phase, the focus is on configuring the system for use in the operational environment. This includes configuring the cryptographic controls. After the system has been configured, certification testing is performed to ensure that the system functions as specified and that the security controls are operating effectively. The security provided by a cryptographic control depends on the mathematical soundness of the algorithm, the length of the cryptographic keys, key management, and mode of operation. A weakness in any one of these components may result in a weakness or compromise to the security of the cryptographic control. A weakness may be introduced at any phase of the system life cycle.

**109.** Audit trails should be considered as part of which of the following security controls during the security design, implementation, and use of a cryptographic module?

a. Physical access controls

b. Logical access controls

c. Integrity controls

d. User authentication

**109. c.** Cryptography may provide methods that protect security-relevant software, including audit trails, from undetected modification. This is addressed as part of the integrity controls. Physical access controls are incorrect because they deal with prevention, detection, physical replacement or modification of the cryptographic system, and the keys within the system. Logical access controls are incorrect because they may provide a means of isolating the cryptographic software from attacks and modifications. The cryptographic module boundary may consist of the hardware, operating system, and cryptographic software. User authentication is incorrect because it includes use of cryptographic authentication to provide stronger authentication of users.

**110.** Which of the following is *not* a rule that guides the cryptography implementation in a system development life cycle (SDLC) as it applies to selecting cryptographic mechanisms?

a. Determine what information must be provided using a cryptographic function.

b. Change the cryptographic keys when employees leave the organization.

c. Protect data prior to signature generation/verification or encryption/decryption.

d. Provide the capability for local users to view all data that is being signed or encrypted.

**110. b.** It is a rule to follow in the operation and maintenance phase, not in the implementation phase. For example, cryptographic keys that are never changed, even when disgruntled employees leave the organization, are not secure. The other three choices are incorrect because they are the rules that guide the implementation of cryptography.

**111.** During the operation and maintenance phase of a system development life cycle (SDLC) as it relates to cryptography, which of the following requires configuration management *most*?

1. Hardware and firmware

2. System software maintenance and update

3. Application software maintenance

4. Cryptographic key maintenance

a.  1 and 2

b.  2 and 3

c.  3 and 4

d.  1, 2, 3, and 4

***111. a.*** Configuration management (CM) is needed most for high-risk areas such as hardware and firmware and system software maintenance and update. CM ensures the integrity of managing system and security features through controlling changes made to a system's hardware, firmware, software, and documentation. The documentation may include user guidance, test scripts, test data, and test results. The hardware and firmware maintenance scope covers adding new capabilities, expanding the system to accommodate more users, replacing nonfunctional equipment, changing platforms, and upgrading hardware components. The system software maintenance and update scope includes adding new capabilities, fixing errors, improving performance, and replacing keys.

The application software maintenance scope covers updating passwords, deleting users from access lists, updating remote access, and changing roles and responsibilities of users and maintenance personnel, which are mostly routine in nature. The cryptographic key maintenance scope includes key archiving, key destruction, and key change, as it is mostly done in the disposal phase.

**112.** **During the operational phase of cryptography, key recovery means which of the following?**

1.  Acquiring keying material from backup

2.  Acquiring keying material by reconstruction

3.  Binding keying material to information

4.  Binding keying material to attributes

a.  1 and 2

b.  2 and 3

c.  3 and 4

d.  1, 2, 3, and 4

***112. a.*** Acquiring the keying material from backup or by reconstruction is commonly known as key recovery. The other items deal with key registration, which results in the binding of keying material to information or attributes associated with a particular entity. A trusted third party (for example, Kerberos realm server or a PKI certification authority) performs the binding.

**113.** **During the operational phase of cryptography, which of the following keying material does *not* require backup storage?**

a.  Domain parameters

b.  Passwords

    c.    Audit information

    d.    Random number generator seed

***113. d.***   The keying material backup on an independent, secure storage medium provides a source for key recovery. Keying material maintained in backup should remain in storage for at least as long as the same keying material is maintained in storage for normal operational use. Not all keys need be backed up. For example, random number generator (RNG) seed need not be backed up because it is a secret value that is used to initialize a deterministic random bit generator. In addition, storing the RNG seed would actually decrease the security of the keys by increasing the risk of the material being used to reverse-engineer the keys.

Domain parameters are incorrect because they can be backed up. It is a parameter used with some public key algorithm to generate key pairs, to create digital signatures, or to establish keying material. Passwords are incorrect because they can be backed up. A password is a string of characters (for example, letters, numbers, and other symbols) that are used to authenticate an identity or to verify access authorization. Audit information is incorrect because it can be backed up and can be used to trace events and actions.

**114.**     **During the post-operational phase of cryptography, which of the following keying material does *not* require archive storage?**

    a.    Initialization vector

    b.    Audit information

    c.    Passwords

    d.    Domain parameters

***114. c.***   During the post-operational phase, keying material is no longer in operational use, but access to the keying material may still be possible. A key management archive is a repository containing keying material and other related information of historical interest. Not all keying material needs to be archived. For example, passwords which often change need not be archived because storing passwords for the keys can increase the risk of disclosure.

Initialization vector is incorrect because it can be archived. It can be retained until it's no longer needed to process the protected data. An initialization vector is a vector used in defining the starting point of a cryptographic process. Audit information can be archived and can be retained until no longer needed. Domain parameters are incorrect because they can be archived. These parameters can be retained until all keying material, signatures, and signed data using the domain parameters are removed from the archive.

**115.**     **Regarding cryptographic key management systems, which of the following require frequent audits?**

    a.    Security plans

    b.    Security procedures

    c.    Human actions

    d.    Protective mechanisms

**115. c.**   On a more frequent basis, the actions of the humans who use, operate, and maintain the system should be reviewed to verify that they continue to follow established security procedures. Strong cryptographic systems can be compromised by lax and inappropriate human actions. Highly unusual events should be noted and reviewed as possible indicators of attempted attacks on the system.

Security plans, security procedures, and protective mechanisms are incorrect because they are considered as part of the human actions audit and they continue to support the cryptographic key management policy.

**116.**   **Regarding cryptographic key management system survivability, which of the following keys need to be backed up to decrypt stored enciphered information?**

1.   Master keys

2.   Key encrypting key

3.   Public signature verification keys

4.   Authorization keys

    a.   1 only

    b.   3 only

    c.   4 only

    d.   1, 2, 3, and 4

**116. d.**   Without access to the cryptographic keys that are needed to decrypt information, organizations risk losing their access to that information. Consequently, it is prudent to retain backup copies of the keys necessary to decrypt stored enciphered information, including master keys, key encrypting keys, public signature verification keys, and authorization keys. These items should be stored until there is no longer any requirement for access to the underlying plain text information.

**117.**   **Which of the following is *not* a critical component of cryptographic key management system?**

    a.   Point-to-point environment

    b.   Key distribution center environment

    c.   Key translation center environment

    d.   Key disclosure center environment

**117. d.**   A cryptographic key management system must have three components to operate: a point-to-point environment, a key distribution center environment, and a key translation center environment. A key disclosure center environment is not relevant here.

**118.**   **Which of the following is *not* used to obtain nonrepudiation service?**

    a.   Digital signatures

    b.   Digital message receipts

    c.     Integrity checks

    d.     Timestamps

*118. c.* Nonrepudiation services are obtained by employing various techniques or mechanisms such as digital signatures, digital message receipts, and timestamps, not integrity checks. Integrity checks are used with operating systems.

**119.**    **In cryptographic key management, key zeroization means which of the following?**

    a.     Key recovery

    b.     Key regeneration

    c.     Key destruction

    d.     Key correction

*119. c.* Key zeroization means key destruction. It is a method of erasing electronically stored keys by altering the contents of key storage so as to prevent the recovery of keys. The other three choices do not need key zeroization. Key recovery is a function in the life cycle of keying material in that it allows authorized entities to retrieve keying material from the key backup or archive. Key regeneration and key correction are needed when a key is compromised.

**120.**    **Which of the following binds the identity of a user to his public key?**

    a.     Private key technology and digital certificates

    b.     Symmetric key technology and digital signatures

    c.     Public key technology and digital certificates

    d.     Cryptographic key technology and electronic signatures

*120. c.* Binding an individual's identity to the public key corresponds to the protection afforded to the individual's private signature key. Digital certificates are used in this process.

**121.**    **Public key technology and digital certificates do *not* provide which of the following security services?**

    a.     Authentication

    b.     Nonrepudiation

    c.     Availability

    d.     Data integrity

*121. c.* Public key technology and digital certificates can be used to support authentication, encryption, nonrepudiation, and data integrity, but not availability.

**122.**    **Quantum cryptography could be a possible replacement for public key algorithms used in which of the following computing environments?**

    a.     Utility computing

    b.     On-demand computing

c. Quantum computing

d. Virtual computing

**122. c.** Quantum cryptography is related to quantum computing technology, but viewed from a different perspective. Quantum cryptography is a possible replacement for public key algorithms that hopefully will not be susceptible to the attacks enabled by quantum computing.

Quantum computing deals with large word size quantum computers in which the security of integer factorization and discrete log-based public-key cryptographic algorithms would be threatened. This would be a major negative result for many cryptographic key management systems that rely on these algorithms for the establishment of cryptographic keys. Lattice-based public-key cryptography would be resistant to quantum computing threats.

Utility computing means allowing users to access technology-based services without much technical knowledge. On-demand computing deals with providing network access for self-services. Virtual computing uses virtual machine with software that allows a single host to run one or more guest operating systems. Utility computing, on-demand computing, and virtual computing are part of cloud computing.

**123.** **Which of the following is good practice for organizations issuing digital certificates?**

a. Develop a consulting agreement.

b. Develop an employment agreement.

c. Develop a subscriber agreement.

d. Develop a security agreement.

**123. c.** Prior to issuance of digital certificates, organizations should require a "subscriber agreement" in place that the subscriber manually signs. This agreement describes his obligations to protect the private signature key, and to notify appropriate authorities if it is stolen, lost, compromised, unaccounted for, or destroyed. Often the provisions of a subscriber agreement can be placed into other documents such as an employment contract or security agreement.

**124.** **Which of the following is required to accept digital certificates from multiple vendor certification authorities?**

a. The application must be PKI-enabled.

b. The application must be PKI-aware.

c. The application must use X.509 Version 3.

d. The application must use PKI-vendor plug-ins.

**124. c.** Using the X.509 Version 3 standard helps application programs in accepting digital certificates from multiple vendor CAs, assuming that the certificates conform to consistent Certificate Profiles. Application programs either have to be PKI-enabled, PKI-aware, or use PKI vendor plug-ins prior to the use of X.509 Version 3 standard. Version 3 is more interoperable so that an application program can accept digital certificates from multiple vendor certification authorities. Version 3 standard for digital certificates provides specific bits that can be set in a certificate to ensure that the certificate is used only for specific services such as digital signature, authentication, and encryption.

**125.** Which of the following is primarily required for continued functioning of a public key infrastructure (PKI)?

    a. Disaster recovery plans

    b. Service level plans

    c. Fraud prevention plans

    d. Legal liability plans

**125. a.** At a minimum, organizations should consider establishing backup and recovery sites for their key PKI components (RA, CA, and Directories) that supply the services necessary for application programs to use certificates. A PKI is an infrastructure, like a highway. By itself, it does little. It is useful when application programs employ the certificates and services that it supports. The PKI is a combination of products, services, software, hardware, facilities, policies, procedures, agreements, and people that provide for and sustain secure interactions on open networks such as the Internet. The other three choices are the side effects of using a PKI, which also needs to be developed.

**126.** Which of the following can mitigate threats to integrity when public key cryptography is used?

    a. Data checksums and secure hashes

    b. Public key signatures and secure hashes

    c. Cyclic redundancy checks and secure hashes

    d. Simple checksums and secure hashes

**126. b.** Public key cryptography verifies integrity by using public key signatures and secure hashes. A secure hash algorithm (SHA) is used to create a message digest (hash). The hash can change if the message is modified. The hash is then signed with a private key. The hash may be stored or transmitted with the data. When the integrity of the data is to be verified, the hash is recalculated, and the corresponding public key is used to verify the integrity of the message.

**127.** Which of the following mitigate threats to nonrepudiation?

    a. Secure hashes

    b. Message digest 4

    c. Message digest 5

    d. Digital signatures and certificates

**127. d.** Data is electronically signed by applying the originator's private key to the data. The resulting digital signature can be stored or transmitted with the data. Any party using the public key of the signer can verify the signature. If the signature is verified, then the verifier has confidence that the data was not modified after being signed and that the owner of the public key was the signer. A digital certificate binds the public key to the identity of the signer.

**128.** Regarding data sanitization practices in a cloud computing environment, which of the following is affected *most* when data from one subscriber is physically commingled with the data of other subscribers?

    a.    Data at rest

    b.    Data in transit

    c.    Data in use

    d.    Data to recover

*128. d.* The data sanitization practices have serious implications for security and data recovery in the cloud computing environment and are most affected. Sanitization is the removal of sensitive data from a storage device such as (i) when a storage device is removed from service or moved elsewhere to be stored, (ii) when residual data remains upon termination of service, and (iii) when backup copies are made for recovery and restoration of service. Data sanitization matters can get complicated when data from one subscriber is physically commingled with the data of other subscribers. It is also possible to recover data from failed drives (for example, hard drives and flash drives) that are not disposed of properly by cloud providers.

Procedures for protecting data at rest are not as well standardized in a cloud computing environment. Cryptography can be used to protect data in transit. Trust mechanisms such as requiring service contracts and performing risk assessments can protect data in use because this is an emerging area of cryptography.

**129.** Which of the following provides a unique user ID for a digital certificate?

    a.    User name

    b.    User organization

    c.    User e-mail

    d.    User message digest

*129. d.* The digital certificate contains information about the user's identity (for example, name, organization, and e-mail), but this information may not necessarily be unique. A one-way (hash) function can be used to construct a fingerprint (message digest) unique to a given certificate using the user's public key.

**130.** Which of the following is *not* included in the digital signature standard (DSS)?

    a.    Digital signature algorithm (DSA)

    b.    Data encryption standard (DES)

    c.    Rivest, Shamir, and Adelman algorithm (RSA)

    d.    Elliptic curve digital signature algorithm (ECDSA)

*130. b.* DSA, RSA, and ECDSA are included in the DSS that specifies a digital signature used in computing and verifying digital signatures. DES is a symmetric algorithm and is not included in the DSS. DES is a block cipher and uses a 56-bit key.

DES has been replaced by advanced encryption standard (AES) where the latter is preferred as an encryption algorithm for new products. The AES is a symmetric key encryption algorithm to protect electronic data as it is fast and strong due to its Key-Block-Round combination. The strength of DES is no longer sufficient.

**131.** **What keys are used to create digital signatures?**

    a.    Public-key cryptography

    b.    Private-key cryptography

    c.    Hybrid-key cryptography

    d.    Primary-key cryptography

***131. a.*** Public-key cryptography has been recommended for distribution of secret keys and in support of digital signatures. Private-key cryptography has been recommended for encryption of messages and can be used for message integrity check computations. Hybrid keys combine the best of both public and private keys. Primary keys are used in database design and are not relevant here.

**132.** **Elliptic curve systems are which of the following?**

    1.    Asymmetric algorithms

    2.    Symmetric algorithms

    3.    Public-key systems

    4.    Private-key systems

        a.    2 and 3

        b.    1 and 3

        c.    2 and 4

        d.    1 and 4

***132. b.*** Elliptic curve systems are public-key (asymmetric) cryptographic algorithms. DES is private-key (symmetric) cryptographic algorithms.

**133.** **Data encryption standard (DES) *cannot* provide which of the following security services?**

    a.    Encryption

    b.    Access control

    c.    Integrity

    d.    Authentication

***133. d.*** Data encryption standard (DES) provides encryption, access control, integrity, and key management standards. It cannot provide authentication services. The DES is a cryptographic algorithm designed for access to and protection of unclassified data. Because the original "single" DES is insecure, the Triple DES should be used instead.

**134.** **The elliptic curve system uses which of the following to create digital signatures?**

    a.   Hash algorithm

    b.   Prime algorithm

    c.   Inversion algorithm

    d.   Linear algorithm

*134. a.* The elliptic curve systems are used to create digital signatures with a hash algorithm such as SHA-1 (160-bit key). The SHA-1 is used to generate a condensed representation of a message called a message digest. SHA-1 is a technical revision of SHA. A secure hash algorithm (SHA) is used to generate a condensed message representation called a message digest. SHA is used by PGP or GNU PGP to generate digital signatures.

**135.** **Which of the following clearly defines end-to-end encryption?**

    1.   Encryption at origin

    2.   Decryption at destination

    3.   Visible routing information

    4.   No intermediate decryption

        a.   1 and 2

        b.   3 and 4

        c.   1, 2, and 3

        d.   1, 2, 3, and 4

*135. d.* End-to-end encryption refers to communications encryption in which data is encrypted when being passed through a network (i.e., encryption at origin and decryption at destination) but routing information remains visible without intermediate decryption. End-to-end encryption is safe as end-to-end security in that information is safeguarded from point of origin to point of destination.

**136.** **Which one of the following provides data integrity?**

    a.   Cyclic redundancy checks

    b.   Digitized signatures

    c.   Passwords and PINs

    d.   Biometrics

*136. a.* A cyclic redundancy check (CRC) can be used to verify the integrity of data transmitted over a communications line. Passwords, PINs, and biometrics can be used to authenticate user identity. Digitized signatures do not provide data integrity because they are simply created by scanning a handwritten signature.

**137.** **Symmetric key algorithms are ideally suited for which of the following?**

      a.    Authentication

      b.    Integrity

      c.    Confidentiality

      d.    Nonrepudiation

*137. c.* Symmetric key cryptography is a class of algorithms where parties share a secret key. These algorithms are primarily used to achieve confidentiality but may also be used for authentication, integrity, and limited nonrepudiation services.

**138.** **Which of the following is the *most efficient* way of handling the redundancy built into the encrypted messages in detecting transmission errors?**

      a.    Using cyclic redundancy check (CRC) polynomial code

      b.    Using CRC code

      c.    Using Hamming code

      d.    Using parity bit code

*138. c.* As part of controls, all encrypted messages must contain some redundancy as part of the message but have no meaning to the message, such as cryptographic hash or a Hamming code, to do error detection or correction to make the attacker work harder. The redundancy should not be in the form of "n" zeros at the start or end of a message because they yield predictable results to the attacker. Hamming code is based on Hamming distance, which is the number of bit positions in which two codewords differ. The codeword contains both data and check bits. The goal is to keep the Hamming distance shorter.

The cyclic redundancy code (CRC) is also known as the polynomial code, which is based on treating bit strings as representations of polynomials with coefficients of 0 and 1 only. Checksums based on CRC are not effective in detecting errors because it yields undetected errors due to the lack of random bits in the checksums. The CRC uses an algorithm for generating error detection bits in a data link protocol. The receiving station performs the same calculation as done by the transmitting station. If the results differ, then one or more bits are in error. CRC is not a cryptographically secure mechanism unlike a cryptographic hash or message authentication code (MAC). Hence, CRC is least effective in verifying against malicious tampering of data.

The parity bit code is not as effective as the Hamming code because the former is used to detect single errors whereas the latter is used to detect both single and burst errors. Hence, the Hamming code is the most efficient way of detecting transmission errors.

**139.** **For large volumes of data, asymmetric-key cryptography is *not* efficient to support which of the following?**

      a.    Authentication

      b.    Confidentiality

    c.    Integrity

    d.    Nonrepudiation

**139. b.** Asymmetric key algorithms are used to achieve authentication, integrity, and nonrepudiation, and not to support confidentiality for handling large volumes of data efficiently. These algorithms are used to perform three operations such as digital signatures, key transport, and key agreement. Although the asymmetric key is not efficient to handle large volumes of data, it can be used to encrypt short messages, thus providing for confidentiality for short messages. The asymmetric key (public key) is an encryption system that uses a public-private key pair for encrypting/decrypting data and for generating/verifying digital signature.

**140.** **The secure hash algorithm (SHA) and hash-based message authentication code (HMAC) provide the basis for which of the following?**

    a.    Data integrity

    b.    Confidentiality

    c.    Authentication

    d.    Nonrepudiation

**140. a.** The secure hash algorithm (SHA) and hash-based message authentication code (HMAC) provide the basis for data integrity in electronic communications. They do not provide confidentiality and are a weak tool for authentication or nonrepudiation.

**141.** **Which of the following is *not* part of public key infrastructure (PKI) data structures?**

    a.    Public key certificate

    b.    Certificate revocation lists

    c.    Attribute certificate

    d.    Subject certificate

**141. d.** Two basic data structures are used in PKIs. These are the public key certificates and the certificate revocation lists (CRLs). A third data structure, the attribute certificate, may be used as an addendum. The certificate authority (CA) issues a public key certificate for each identity confirming that the identity has the appropriate credentials. CAs must also issue and process CRLs, which are lists of certificates that have been revoked. The X.509 attribute certificate binds attributes to an attribute certificate holder. This definition is being profiled for use in Internet applications. Subject certificate is meaningless here.

**142.** **Which of the following is an example of asymmetric encryption algorithm?**

    a.    DH

    b.    DES

    c.    3DES

    d.    IDEA

**142. a.**  The concept of public-key cryptography (asymmetric encryption algorithm) was introduced by Diffie-Hellman (DH) to solve the key management problem with symmetric algorithms. The other three choices are incorrect because they are examples of symmetric encryption algorithms.

**143.**  **Which of the following are examples of cryptographic hash functions?**

    a.    SHA and 3DES

    b.    DES and CBC

    c.    MD5 and SHA-1

    d.    DAC and MAC

**143. c.**  Both message digests 4 and 5 (MD4 and MD5) are examples of hashing algorithms. They are effective when they work with SHA-1 algorithms. Cryptographic hash functions such as MD5 and SHA-1 execute much faster and use less system resources than typical encryption algorithms. The other three choices are not relevant here.

**144.**  **Which of the following statement is true about hash functions?**

    a.    They produce a larger message digest than the original message.

    b.    They produce a much smaller message digest than the original message.

    c.    They produce the same size message digest as the original message.

    d.    They produce a much larger message digest than the original message.

**144. b.**  Hash functions produce a much smaller message digest than the original message. Encrypting them saves time and effort and improves performance.

**145.**  **Which of the following is the *best* technique to detect duplicate transactions?**

    a.    ECDSA and SHA

    b.    ECDSA and SHA-1

    c.    ECDSA and MID

    d.    ECDSA and MD5

**145. c.**  When the elliptic curve digital signature algorithm (ECDSA) is used with a message identifier (MID), it provides the capability of detecting duplicate transactions. The MID operates on checking the sequence number of transactions.

**146.**  **Countermeasures against replay attacks do *not* include which of the following?**

    a.    Time-stamps

    b.    Protocols

    c.    Nonces

    d.    Kerberos

**146. b.** The term "protocols" is too generic to be of any use. A replay attack refers to the recording and retransmission of message packets in the network. Nonces are random numbers that are unique and fresh each time of use. Kerberos and timestamps go hand-in-hand.

**147.** A cryptographic module is undergoing testing. Which of the following provides the highest level of testing?

    a.    Algorithm level

    b.    Module level

    c.    Application level

    d.    Product level

**147. c.** The highest level of testing occurs at the application or system level. This level is also called certification testing. Algorithm level and module level are incorrect because they provide low-level testing. Product level is incorrect because it is the next higher level above algorithm and module level testing.

**148.** For message digests to be effectively used in digital certificates, what must they be?

    a.    Access-resistant

    b.    Authorization-resistant

    c.    Collision-resistant

    d.    Attack-resistant

**148. c.** Message digests are used in cryptography to verify digital signatures and to ensure data integrity. A unique user ID is determined by constructing the hash of the client's certificate using a trusted algorithm. For the user ID to be unique, you must have reasonable certainty that another client's certificate will not hash to the same value. This requirement is satisfied as long as the hash function is sufficiently collision-resistant.

**149.** A hash function is which of the following?

    a.    One-to-one function

    b.    One-to-many function

    c.    Many-to-one function

    d.    Many-to-many function

**149. c.** A hash function is a many-to-one function that takes an arbitrary-length-input message and constructs a fixed-length output digest.

**150.** Which of the following is implemented in the Version 3 of X.509 protocol?

    a.    SSL

    b.    Regular MIME

    c.    SHA

    d.    S/MIME

**150. d.**   Secure Multipurpose Internet Mail Extensions (S/MIME) is an open standard where e-mail messages can be digitally signed. Validating the signature on the e-mail can help the recipient know with confidence who sent it and that it was not altered during transmission (i.e., nonrepudiation). Previous versions are implemented in the regular MIME. Both SSL and SHA are not relevant here.

**151.**   **Which of the following is used to encrypt the Internet Protocol (IP) packets?**

    a.    PPTP

    b.    HTTP

    c.    IPsec

    d.    PPP

**151. c.**   Internet Protocol security (IPsec) is a protocol that operates within the Internet protocol (IP). The IP transmits and routes messages, breaks large messages into smaller sizes on one end, and reassembles them into the original message on the other end. IP accomplishes these tasks using the IP header, which is inserted at the beginning of each packet. Point-to-point tunneling protocol (PPTP) hides information in IP packets. Hypertext transfer protocol (HTTP) is a connection-oriented protocol that uses transmission control protocol (TCP) to carry Web traffic between a computer's Web browser and the Web server being accessed. Point-to-point protocol (PPP) is used in router-to-router traffic and home user-to-ISP traffic.

**152.**   **Which one of the following encryption keys is slow?**

    a.    Symmetric

    b.    Asymmetric

    c.    Semi-symmetric

    d.    Semi-asymmetric

**152. b.**   Asymmetric keys (public keys) by definition are slow and suitable for encrypting and distributing keys and for providing authentication. On the other hand, symmetric (private keys) are faster and suitable for encrypting files and communication channels.

**153.**   **Most cryptographic attacks focus on which of the following?**

    a.    Cryptographic keys

    b.    Cryptographic passwords

    c.    Cryptographic parameters

    d.    Cryptographic PINs

**153. c.** A cryptographic module's critical security parameters (CSPs) contain keys, passwords, personal identification numbers (PINs), and other information. CSPs are vulnerable to attacks.

**154.** Which of the following symmetric key block cipher algorithms provide authentication services?

  a. ECB

  b. CBC

  c. CBC-MAC

  d. CFB

**154. c.** In the Advanced Encryption Standard (AES), there are five modes that can provide data confidentiality and one mode that can provide data authentication. The confidentiality modes are the Electronic Codebook (ECB), Cipher Block Chaining (CBC), Cipher Feedback (CFB), Output Feedback (OFB), and Counter (CTR) modes. The authentication mode is the Cipher Block Chaining-Message Authentication Code (CBC-MAC) mode.

**155.** Hash-based message authentication code (HMAC) is heavily used in which of the following?

  a. PPP operations

  b. SET operations

  c. IPsec operations

  d. PPTP operations

**155. c.** Hash-based message authentication code (HMAC) provides message integrity and is fast and therefore heavily used in IPsec operations because of little or no overhead. It requires limited system resources to operate. HMAC uses a key in combination with the hash function to produce a message digest. It can be used with a hash function in combination with a secret key. The other three choices are not relevant here.

**156.** Which of the following statements is *true* about truncation of a message digest in cryptographic applications?

  a. Smaller message digest length is applied to the data to be hashed, and the resulting digest is truncated at the rightmost bits.

  b. Larger message digest length is applied to the data to be hashed, and the resulting digest is truncated at the leftmost bits.

  c. Smaller message digest length is applied to the data to be hashed, and the resulting digest is truncated at the leftmost bits.

  d. Larger message digest length is applied to the data to be hashed, and the resulting digest is truncated at the rightmost bits.

**156. b.** Some cryptographic applications may require a hash function with a message digest length different than those allowed in standards. In such cases, a truncated message digest may be used, whereby a hash function with a larger message digest length is applied to the data to be hashed, and the resulting message digest is truncated by selecting an appropriate number of the leftmost bits. The least significant bit is the rightmost bit of a bit string. The leftmost bit is the most significant bit.

**157.** Secure hash algorithms enable the determination of which of the following?

    a.    Message confidentiality

    b.    Message integrity

    c.    Message availability

    d.    Message identity

**157. b.** Secure hash algorithms (for example, SHA-224, 256,384, and 512) are used to hash a message. These algorithms enable the determination of a message's integrity; meaning any change to the message results in a different message digest. SHA and SHA-1 should not be used because they are not secure. Message identity is a field (for example a sequence number) that may be used to identify a message.

**158.** Which of the following is *not* usually seen on a digital certificate?

    a.    Owner name

    b.    Public key

    c.    Effective dates for keys

    d.    Insurance company name

**158. d.** The information on the digital certificate includes the owner name, public key, and start and end dates of its validity. The certificate should not contain any owner information that changes frequently (for example, the insurance company name).

**159.** What is the *major* requirement for a public key certification authority?

    a.    It must be independent.

    b.    It must have a proper contract.

    c.    It must be trusted.

    d.    It must have a good reputation.

**159. c.** A public key certificate is a credential that binds a key pair and the identity of the owner of the key (i.e., to a legal person). The necessary trust may come from several sources such as the role and independence of the certification authority, reputation, contract, management integrity, and other legal obligations.

**160.** Which of the following statements is true about elliptic curve cryptography?

    a.    It uses an asymmetric-key algorithm.

    b.    It competes with the Whitfield-Diffie algorithm.

    c.    It competes with the digital signature algorithm.

    d.    It uses a symmetric-key algorithm.

**160. *a.*** The elliptic curve is well suited for low bandwidth systems and uses an asymmetric-key algorithm for encryption. The Rivest, Shamir, and Adelman (RSA) and elliptic curve algorithms are used for encryption, where the latter is a new one with shorter key lengths and is less computationally intensive. The Whitfield-Diffie algorithm is used for secure key exchange. The digital signature algorithm is used only for digital signatures. Both Whitfield and digital signatures do not compete with elliptic curve.

**161.** What is the *best* way to encrypt data?

    a.    Bulk encryption

    b.    Link encryption

    c.    Transaction encryption

    d.    End-to-end encryption

**161. *b.*** There are two modes of implementation of encryption in a network, namely link (online) and end-to-end. Link encryption encrypts all the data along a communications path (for example, a satellite link, telephone circuit, or T1 line) and encrypts both headers and trailer of the packet, which is the best thing to do. It provides good protection against external threats such as traffic analysis because all data flowing on links can be encrypted, including addresses and routing information. Although a major advantage of link encryption is that it is easy to incorporate into network protocols at the lower levels of the OSI model, a major disadvantage is that it encrypts and decrypts a message several times at each link or node in the clear text, thus leading to node compromise.

Bulk encryption is simultaneous encryption of all channels of a multichannel telecommunications trunk. Transaction encryption is used in the payment card industry, perhaps using secure electronic transaction (SET) protocol for secure transactions over the Internet.

In end-to-end encryption, a message is encrypted and decrypted only at endpoints, does not encrypt headers and trailers, and operates at the higher levels of the OSI model, thereby largely circumventing problems that compromise intermediate nodes. In this type of encryption, routing information remains visible and is a potential risk.

**162.** What is the correct sequence of keys in a triple data encryption standard (3DES) algorithm operating with three keys?

    a.    Encrypt-decrypt-encrypt

    b.    Decrypt-encrypt-decrypt

c.  Encrypt-encrypt-encrypt

d.  Decrypt-decrypt-decrypt

**162. c.**  With three keys operating, the sequence is encrypt-encrypt-encrypt, that is, one key is used for each mode of operation. Encrypt-decrypt-encrypt is incorrect because it is an example of operating with two keys where the first key is used to encrypt, the second key is to decrypt, and the first key again to encrypt. The other two choices are not meaningful here.

**163.**  **Which of the following is *best* qualified to evaluate the security of Public Key Infrastructure (PKI) systems and procedures?**

a.  Certification authorities

b.  Registration authorities

c.  Trusted third parties

d.  Subscribers

**163. c.**  Trusted third parties, who are independent of the certification and registration authorities and subscribers and who are employed by independent audit or consulting organizations are good candidates to conduct security evaluations (for example, reviews and audits) of the PKI systems and procedures. A written report is published after the security evaluation. A certification authority is a person or institution that is trusted and can vouch for the authenticity of a public key. The authority can be a principal or a government agency that is authorized to issue a certificate. A registration authority manages the certificate life cycle in terms of maintenance and revocation. Subscribers include both individuals and business organizations that use the certificate in their businesses.

**164.**  **Which of the following statements is *not* true about Secure Sockets Layer (SSL)?**

a.  It uses both symmetric and asymmetric key cryptography.

b.  It is used to perform authentication.

c.  It is a point-to-point protocol.

d.  It is a session-oriented protocol.

**164. c.**  Secure sockets layer (SSL) uses a combination of symmetric and asymmetric key cryptography to perform authentication and encryption services. It is a session-oriented protocol used to establish a secure connection between the client and the server for a particular session. SSL is not a point-to-point protocol.

**165.**  **The two protocol algorithms used in cryptographic applications for compressing data are which of the following?**

a.  SHA1 and MD5

b.  3DES and IDEA

c.  DSA and DSS

d.  RSA and SKIPJACK

**165. a.**   The secure hash algorithm (SHA1) produces a 160-bit hash of the message contents. Message digest 5 (MD5) produces a 128-bit hash of the message contents. Many cryptographic applications generate and process both SHA1 and MD5. These are faster and take less space to store data. The algorithms mentioned in the other three choices do not have the ability to compress data. 3DES uses a 168-bit key.

**166.**   Which of the following statements is *not* true about asymmetric-key cryptography?

    a.   It is used to provide an authentication service.

    b.   It is used to provide a digital signature service.

    c.   It can be used to encrypt large amounts of data.

    d.   It can be used to provide nonrepudiation service.

**166. c.**   A disadvantage of asymmetric-key cryptography is that it is much slower than symmetric-key cryptography and is therefore impractical or efficient for use in encrypting large amounts of data. The other three choices are examples of advantages of using the asymmetric-key cryptography.

**167.**   What is the *major* purpose of a digital certificate?

    a.   To achieve the availability goal

    b.   To maintain more information on the certificate

    c.   To verify the certificate authority

    d.   To establish user and device authentication

**167. d.**   Digital certificates are used as a means of user and device authentication. Entities can prove their possession of the private key by digitally signing known data or by demonstrating knowledge of a secret exchanged using public-key cryptographic methods.

**168.**   For integrity protection, most Internet Protocol security (IPsec) implementations use which of the following algorithms?

    1.   SHA-1

    2.   MD5

    3.   HMAC-SHA-1

    4.   HMAC-MD5

        a.   1 only

        b.   2 only

        c.   1 and 2

        d.   3 and 4

**168. d.**   Both HMAC-SHA-1 and HMAC-MD5 algorithms are stronger than SHA-1 or MD5, either alone or together, because they use hash-based message authentication codes (HMACs). Both the SHA-1 and MD5 algorithms are weaker by themselves.

**169.**   **Which of the following methods provide the highest level of security to protect data access from unauthorized people?**

    a.    Encryption

    b.    Callback or dial-back systems

    c.    Magnetic cards with personal identification number

    d.    User ID and password

**169. a.**   Encryption provides the highest level of security to protect data access from unauthorized people. It is the process of transforming data to an unintelligible form in such a way that the original data either cannot be obtained (one-way encryption) or cannot be obtained without using the inverse decryption process (two-way encryption). It is difficult to break the encryption algorithm and the keys used in that process.

Callback or dial-back systems and magnetic cards with personal identification numbers provide medium protection, whereas user identification numbers and passwords provide minimum protection. Callback systems can be negated through the use of call forwarding features in a telephone system. Magnetic cards can be lost, stolen, or counterfeited. User IDs and passwords can be shared with others or guessed by others, a control weakness.

**170.**   **To achieve effective security over transmission, what is the best area where stronger encryption can be applied the most?**

    a.    Packet level

    b.    Record level

    c.    File level

    d.    Field level

**170. d.**   Encryption can protect anything from one message field to an entire message packet in the transmission over network lines. Because the message field is the lowest level element and an important element in terms of message content and value, security is effective and enhanced. Here, encryption is focused on where it matters the most. Note that the field-level encryption is stronger than file-, record-, and packet-level encryption although encryption can be applied at each of these levels.

**171.**   **What is the *least* powerful method of protecting confidential data or program files?**

    a.    Scrambling the data

    b.    Encoding the data before transmission

    c.    Decoding the data after transmission

    d.    Using passwords and other identification codes

***171. d.*** Use of passwords and other identification codes is not powerful due to their sharing and guessable nature. Scrambling, encoding, and decoding are cryptographic methods used in data transmission. Encryption is used in scrambling, encoding (encrypting), and decoding (decrypting) of data. Encryption is the process of transforming data to an unintelligible form in such a way that the original data either cannot be obtained (one way encryption) or cannot be obtained without using the inverse decryption process (two-way encryption). Authorized users of encrypted computer data must have the key that was used to encrypt the data to decrypt it. The unique key chosen for use in a particular application makes the results of encrypting data using the algorithm unique. Using a different key causes different results. The cryptographic security of the data depends on the security provided for the keys used to encrypt and decrypt the data.

**172.** **What is the *best* technique to thwart network masquerading?**

    a.   Dial-back technique

    b.   Dial-forward technique

    c.   File encryption only

    d.   Dial-back combined with data encryption

***172. d.*** Personal computers (PCs) are in increasing use as computer terminal devices are connected to larger host systems and when two or more PCs are connected to networks. Information transmitted over unprotected telecommunications lines can be intercepted by someone masquerading as an authorized user, thereby actively receiving sensitive information.

Encryption can be adapted as a means of remote user authorization. A user key, entered at the keyboard, authenticates the user. A second encryption key can be stored in encrypted form in the calling system firmware that authenticates the calling system as an approved communications endpoint. When dial-back is used with two-key encryption, data access can be restricted to authorized users (with the user key) with authorized systems (those whose modems have the correct second key), located at authorized locations (those with phone numbers listed in the answering system's phone directory).

Dial-back technique alone cannot guarantee protection against masquerading because hackers can use the dial-forward technique to reroute calls and spoof the connection. File encryption only may not be adequate because an intruder may have an opportunity to intercept the key while it is in transit. Managing the encryption key is critical.

**173.** **Which of the following describes message authentication correctly?**

    a.   A process of guaranteeing that the message was sent as received by the party identified in the header of the message.

    b.   A process of guaranteeing that the message was sent as received by the party identified in the footer of the message.

    c.   A process of guaranteeing that the message sent was received at the same time regardless of the location.

    d.   A process of guaranteeing that all delivered and undelivered messages are reconciled immediately.

**173. a.** Message authentication is a process for detecting unauthorized changes made to data transmitted between users or machines or to data retrieved from storage. Message authentication keys should receive greater protection. It is the message header not the footer that identifies the receiving party of the message. There will be some delay for the messages to be transmitted and received, especially to remote, foreign destinations. Undelivered message reports may be produced at specific time intervals, not immediately.

**174.** **What is the control technique that *best* achieves confidentiality of data in transfer?**

    a.    Line encryption

    b.    One-time password

    c.    File encryption

    d.    End-to-end encryption

**174. a.** Here, the communication link from a user site to a CPU computer is encrypted to provide confidentiality. Line encryption protects data in a transfer.

One-time password is incorrect because it ensures that a particular password is used only once, in connection with a specific transaction. It is similar to the one-time key used in the encryption process. The one-time password protects data in process.

File encryption is incorrect because it protects only the file in storage, not the entire communication line where the data transfer is taking place. File encryption protects data in storage.

The end-to-end encryption is incorrect because it is applied to messages on the communication line twice, once by hardware and once by software techniques.

**175.** **Which of the following provides both integrity and confidentiality services for data and messages?**

    a.    Digital signatures

    b.    Encryption

    c.    Cryptographic checksums

    d.    Granular access control

**175. b.** An encryption security mechanism provides security services such as integrity, confidentiality, and authentication. The data and message integrity service helps to protect data and software on workstations, file servers, and other local-area network (LAN) components from unauthorized modification, which can be intentional or accidental.

The use of cryptographic checksums and granular access control and privilege mechanisms can provide this service. The more granular the access control or privilege mechanism, the less likely an unauthorized or accidental modification can occur.

The data and message integrity service also helps to ensure that a message is not altered, deleted, or added to in any manner during transmission. A message authentication code, which is a type of cryptographic checksum, can protect against both accidental and intentional but not against unauthorized data modification. The use of digital signatures can also be used to detect the modification of data or messages. It uses either public key or private key cryptography. A digital signature provides two distinct services: nonrepudiation and message integrity. The message authentication code can also be used to provide a digital signature capability. Nonrepudiation helps ensure that the parties or entities in a communication cannot deny having participated in all or part of the communication.

**176.** Which of the following independent statements is *not* true about security?

    a.    The security of the cryptography can never be greater than the security of the people using it.

    b.    The security of any electronic-mail program cannot be greater than the security of the machine where the encryption is performed.

    c.    The security of an encryption algorithm is no more or less than the security of the key.

    d.    The security of each electronic-mail message is encrypted with a standard, non-random key.

*176. d.*    Each electronic-mail message is encrypted with its own unique key. The security program generates a random key and uses it to encrypt the message. It is true that the (i) security of the cryptography can never be greater than the security of the people using it because it is the people who make the security a success, (ii) security of any electronic-mail program cannot be greater than the security of the machine where the encryption is performed because security is an extension of the machine, and (iii) security of an encryption algorithm is no more or less than the security of the key because it assumes that the algorithm used is a good one.

**177.** Which of the following statements about encryption is *not* true?

    a.    Software encryption degrades system performance.

    b.    Hardware encryption is faster.

    c.    Encryption is a desirable option in a local-area network.

    d.    Key management is an administrative burden.

*177. c.*    Encryption is a desirable option in mainframe but not in a local-area network (LAN) environment due to performance problems. Although hardware-based encryption is faster, it degrades system performance as found in software-based encryption. In addition, keys used in the encryption require management's attention in terms of key distribution and disposition. Therefore, encryption is not a desirable option for LANs. As the capacity of CPU processors increase, it could become a desirable option for LANs for mitigating insider risks.

**178.** Which of the following encryption schemes is *more* secure?

    a.    Encrypting once with the same key

    b.    Encrypting twice with the same key

    c.     Encrypting twice with two keys

    d.     Multiple encryptions with different keys

***178. d.***    Any encryption scheme can be made more secure through multiple encryptions with different keys. Similarly, a triple encryption is stronger than a double or single encryption. However, costs and overhead increase as the number of encryptions increase. Also, system performance degrades as the number of encryptions increase.

For example, 2DES encryption with two keys is no more secure than a 1DES encryption due to the possibility of the meet-in-the middle attack. Therefore, 3DES (triple DES) should be considered.

**179.**    **Which of the following technologies are required to ensure reliable and secure telecommunications networks?**

    a.     Cryptography and trusted encryption keys

    b.     Advanced identification and authentication techniques and cryptography

    c.     Firewalls, cryptography, and trusted encryption keys

    d.     Cryptography, advanced identification and authentication techniques, firewalls, and trusted encryption keys

***179. d.***    Secure and reliable telecommunications networks must have effective ways for authenticating information and assuring the confidentiality of information. There is no single technology or technique that can produce the needed security and reliability of networks. A range of technologies, including cryptography, improved identification and authentication technologies, and firewalls will be required, along with trusted encryption keys and security management infrastructures.

**180.**    **Which of the following should *not* be subject to review during a periodic review of a cryptographic system?**

    a.     Parameters

    b.     Operations

    c.     Keys

    d.     Controls

***180. c.***    A cryptographic system should be monitored and periodically reviewed to ensure that it is satisfying its security objectives. All parameters associated with correct operation of the cryptographic system should be reviewed, and operation of the system itself should be periodically tested and the results evaluated. Certain information, such as secret keys or private keys in public key systems, should not be subject to review. However, nonsecret or nonprivate keys could be used in a simulated review procedure. Physical protection of a cryptographic module is required to prevent physical replacement or modification of the cryptographic system.

**181.** Which of the following threats is *not* addressed by digital signatures and random number challenges?

  a.   Masquerade

  b.   Replay attacks

  c.   Password compromise

  d.   Denial-of-service

**181. d.**   Denial-of-service (DoS) is any action or series of actions that prevent any part of a system from functioning in accordance with its intended purpose. This includes any action that causes the unauthorized destruction, modification, or delay of service.

By using a private key to generate digital signatures for authentication, it becomes computationally infeasible for an attacker to masquerade as another entity. Using random number challenges (tokens) and digital signatures eliminates the need for transmitting passwords for authentication, thus reducing the threat of their compromise. The use of random number challenges also prevents an intruder from copying an authentication token signed by another user and replaying it successfully at a later time. However, a new random number challenge should be generated for each authentication exchange.

**182.** Electronic signatures and handwritten signatures are useful in their own ways. Which of the following statements is *not true* about these two types of signatures?

  a.   Both signatures have the same legal status.

  b.   Both signatures are subject to forgery with equal difficulty.

  c.   Both signatures link a document with a particular person.

  d.   Both signatures are subject to trickery or coercion.

**182. b.**   An electronic signature is a cryptographic mechanism that performs a similar function to a handwritten signature. It is used to verify the origin and contents of a message. For example, a recipient of data (such as an e-mail message) can verify who signed the data and that the data was not modified after being signed. This also means that the originator (for example, sender of an e-mail message) cannot falsely deny having signed the data. Electronic signatures are difficult to forge; although, written signatures are easily forged. Electronic signatures can use either secret (private) key or public key cryptography; however, public key methods are generally easier to use.

The other three choices are incorrect because they are true statements. In general, electronic signatures have received the same legal status as that of written signatures. Cryptography can provide a means of linking a document with a particular person, as is done with a written signature. Electronic signatures rely on the secrecy of the keys, the link or binding between the owner of the key, and the key itself. If a key is compromised due to social engineering by theft, coercion, or trickery, then the electronic originator of a message may not be the same as the owner of the key. Although the binding of cryptographic keys to actual people is a significant problem, it does not necessarily make electronic signatures less secure than written signatures. Trickery and coercion are problems for written signatures as well.

**183.** **Which of the following security services or statements is *not* true about the U.S. digital signature standard (DSS)?**

      a.    It generates a digital signature.

      b.    It does not require a third-party certificate.

      c.    It assures nonrepudiation of a message.

      d.    It verifies a digital signature.

***183. b.***    A digital signature provides two distinct services: nonrepudiation and message integrity. The digital signature standard (DSS) specifies a digital signature algorithm (DSA) that should be used when message and data integrity is required. The DSA digital signature is a pair of large numbers represented in a computer as strings of binary digits. The digital signature is computed using a set of rules (i.e., the DSA) and a set of parameters such that the identity of the signatory and the integrity of the data can be verified.

The DSA provides the capability to generate and verify digital signatures. Signature verification makes use of a public key that corresponds to, but is not the same as, the private key. Each user possesses a private and public key pair. It is assumed that the public knows about public keys. Private keys are never shared. Anyone can verify the signature of a user by employing that user's public key. Only the possessor of the user's private key can perform signature generation. Because of this, nonrepudiation of a message is achieved. This means that the parties to an electronic communication could not dispute having participated in the communication, or it can prove to a third party that data was actually signed by the generator of the signature.

The DSS can be implemented in hardware, software, and/or firmware and is subject to U.S. Commerce Department export controls. The DSS technique is intended for use in electronic mail, electronic funds transfer, electronic data interchange, software distribution, data storage, and other applications that require data integrity assurance and origin authentication.

A digital signature system requires a means for associating pairs of public and private keys with the corresponding users. A mutually trusted third party such as a certifying authority can bind a user's identity and his public key. The certifying authority could issue a "certificate" by signing credentials containing a user's identity and public key. Hence, a third-party certificate is needed.

**184.** **Pretty good privacy (PGP) and privacy enhanced mail (PEM) are electronic-mail security programs. Which of the following statements is *not* true about PGP and PEM?**

      a.    They both encrypt messages.

      b.    They both sign messages.

      c.    They both have the same uses.

      d.    They are both based on public-key cryptography.

***184. c.***    Both pretty good privacy (PGP) and privacy enhanced mail (PEM) encrypt messages and sign messages based on public-key cryptography. However, they operate on different philosophies. PGP is based on a distributed network of individuals. PEM is based on the concept of a hierarchical organization. PGP is suited for individuals communicating on the Internet, whereas PEM might be more suited for application systems in all organizations. PGP is a product, not a standard. It does not interoperate with any other security product, either PEM or non-PEM. PGP is portable to a wide variety of hardware platforms.

**185.** It is particularly important to protect audit trail data against modification during communication between parties. Which of the following security control techniques would protect against such modifications?

 a. Strong access controls, such as passwords

 b. Digital signatures

 c. Logging before and after image records of modifications

 d. Review of audit trail data

***185. b.*** A digital signature is a cryptographic checksum computed as a function of a message and a user's private key. A user's digital signature varies with the data and protects against modification. This does not prevent deletion or modification of the audit trail, but it provides an alert that the audit trail has been altered. Access to online audit logs should be strictly controlled

Passwords are not strong access controls due to their weaknesses, such as sharing or writing them down. Logging before and after image records of modification is incorrect because it is a passive activity and does not protect against modification. Audit trail data can be used to review what occurred after an event, for periodic reviews, and for real-time analysis.

**186.** Cryptography is a branch of mathematics based on the transformation of data. Which of the following is *not* a true statement about cryptography used in computer security?

 a. Cryptography ensures data confidentiality.

 b. Cryptography ensures data integrity.

 c. Cryptography ensures data availability.

 d. Cryptography ensures electronic signatures.

***186. c.*** Cryptography, a hidden writing, is an important tool for protecting information and is used in many aspects of computer security. It can help provide data confidentiality, data integrity, electronic signatures, and advanced user authentication. It has nothing to do with data availability, which is a property that a given resource will use during a given time period.

**187.** In cryptography, the Rivest, Shamir, and Adelman (RSA) scheme has which of the following pairs of characteristics?

 1. Secret key encryption algorithm system

 2. Asymmetric cipher system

 3. Public key encryption algorithm system

 4. Symmetric cipher system

a.  1 and 4

b.  2 and 3

c.  1 and 2

d.  3 and 4

**187. b.** The Rivest, Shamir, and Adelman (RSA) scheme uses a public key encryption algorithm and is an asymmetric cipher system. The data encryption standard (DES) uses a secret key encryption algorithm and is a symmetric cipher system. RSA uses two keys (private and public), whereas DES uses one key (private).

**188.** **What is the *most* common attack against cryptographic algorithms?**

a.  Ciphertext-only attack

b.  Birthday attack

c.  Chosen plain text attack

d.  Adaptive chosen plain text attack

**188. a.** Exploiting a weakness is called an attack. In a ciphertext-only attack, an attacker has some ciphertext encrypted with an algorithm. He does not know the plain text or the key, but he knows the algorithm. His goal is to find the corresponding plain text. This is the most common attack.

A birthday attack is an attack against message digest 5 (MD5), a hash function. The attack is based on probabilities where it finds two messages that hash to the same value (collision) and then exploits it to attack. The attacker is looking for "birthday" pairs of two messages with the same hash values. This attack is not feasible given today's computer technology.

In a chosen plain text attack, the attacker knows the plain text and the corresponding ciphertext and algorithm but does not know the key. This type of attack is harder but still possible. The adaptive chosen plain text attack is a variation of the chosen plain text attack where the selection of the plain text is changed based on the previous attack results.

**189.** **A message authentication code can protect against which of the following combinations of actions?**

1.  Authorized, accidental data modification

2.  Authorized, intentional data modification

3.  Unauthorized, accidental data modification

4.  Unauthorized, intentional data modification

a.  2 and 4

b.  2 and 3

c.  3 and 4

d.  1 and 4

**189. c.**   A message authentication code, a type of cryptographic checksum, can protect against both accidental and intentional, but unauthorized, data modification. Ordinary error detecting codes such as cyclic redundancy codes are not adequate because they cannot detect intentional modification. A message authentication code is initially calculated by applying a cryptographic algorithm and a secret value, called the key, to the data. The initial code is retained. The data is later verified by applying the cryptographic algorithm and the same secret key to the data to produce another, second code; this second code is then compared to the initial code. If the two codes are equal, then the data is considered authentic. Otherwise, an unauthorized modification is assumed. Any party trying to modify the data without knowing the key would not know how to calculate the appropriate code corresponding to the altered data.

**190.**   Which of the following encryption algorithms or schemes is absolutely unbreakable?

    a.   Data encryption standard

    b.   One-time pad

    c.   International data encryption algorithm

    d.   Rivest cipher 2 and 4

**190. b.**   One-time pad is unbreakable given infinite resources. Each random key in the one-time pad is used exactly once, for only one message, and for only a limited time period. The algorithm for a one-time pad requires the generation of many sets of matching encryption keypads. Each pad consists of a number of random key characters, not generated by a cryptographic key generator. Each key character in the pad is used to encrypt one and only one plain text character; then the key character is never used again. The number of random keypads that need to be generated must be at least equal to the volume of plain text messages to be encrypted. Due to the number of random keypads to be generated, this approach is not practical for high-speed communication systems. This is the reason the one-time pad is absolutely unbreakable.

Brute force attack is possible with the data encryption standard (DES) and international data encryption algorithm (IDEA). The key length in Rivest cipher 2 and 4 (RC2 and RC4) is variable, and details of their algorithms are unknown because they are new proprietary algorithms. IDEA is a new algorithm and works as a double-DES (2DES). DES is in the public domain so that anyone can use it. IDEA is patented and requires a license for commercial use. RC2 and RC4 are unpatented but are trade secrets.

**191.**   Which of the following statements is true about one-way hash function and encryption algorithm?

    a.   They both convert a plain text into an unintelligent text.

    b.   They both can reverse from output to input.

    c.   They both do not destroy information.

    d.   They both operate on a key.

**191. *a.*** A hash function can detect modification of a message, independent of any connection with signatures. That is, it can serve as a cryptographic checksum. It is a solution to the problem of signing long messages. A one-way hash function converts an arbitrary-length message into a fixed-length hash. Like an encryption algorithm, a one-way hash function converts a plain text message into an unintelligent text. This is where the similarity stops. However, unlike an encryption algorithm, there is no way to go backward with a one-way hash function. It is impossible to reverse a one-way hash function to get the original input from the output value. An encryption algorithm does not destroy any information. A one-way hash function destroys information and does not have a key. No secrecy is involved in the one-way hash function; the security is in the lack of ability to reverse itself. This property makes it a useful way to identify a message.

**192.** **What do controls to protect against malicious changes to a message include?**

    a.    Data checksums and cyclic redundancy code

    b.    Message integrity code and message authentication code

    c.    Message integrity code and cyclic redundancy code

    d.    Data checksums and message authentication code

**192. *b.*** A message integrity code uses a secret key to produce a fixed length hash code that is sent with the message. Integrity codes are used to protect the integrity of large interbank electronic funds transfers. A message authentication code is a hashed representation of a message and is computed by the message originator as a function of the message being transmitted and the secret key. If the message authentication code computed by the recipient matches the authentication code appended to the message, the recipient is assured that the message was not modified. Both integrity codes and authentication codes are cryptographic checksums, which are stronger than non-cryptographic checksums.

Cryptography can effectively detect both intentional and unintentional modification; however, cryptography does not protect files from being modified. Both secret key and public key cryptography can be used to ensure integrity. When secret key cryptography is used, a message authentication code is calculated and appended to the data. To verify that the data has not been modified at a later time, any party with access to the correct secret key can recalculate the authentication code. The new authentication code is compared with the original authentication code. If they are identical, the verifier has confidence that an unauthorized party has not modified the data.

Data checksums are digits or bits summed according to arbitrary rules and used to verify the integrity of data. A cyclic redundancy code (CRC) uses an algorithm for generating error detection bits in a data link protocol. The receiving station performs the same calculation as done by the transmitting station. If the results differ, then one or more bits are in error. Both data checksums and CRC are not based on cryptographic checksums. Instead, they are based on algorithms.

**193.** Which of the following statements about secret key and message digest algorithms are *not* true?

1. The drive for message digest algorithms starts with public key cryptography.

2. Message digest algorithms make the RSA much more useful.

3. Secret key algorithm is designed to be irreversible.

4. Message digest algorithm is designed to be reversible.

   a. 1 and 2

   b. 3 and 4

   c. 1 and 3

   d. 2 and 4

*193. b.* The significant difference between a secret key algorithm and a message digest algorithm is that a secret key algorithm is designed to be reversible and a message digest algorithm is designed to be impossible to reverse. It is true that the drive for a message digest algorithm started with public key cryptography. Rivest, Shamir, and Adelman (RSA) is used to perform digital signatures on messages. A cryptographically secure message digest function with high performance would make RSA much more useful. This is because a long message is compressed into a small size by first performing a message digest and then computing an RSA signature on the digest.

**194.** When compared to the Rivest, Shamir, and Adelman (RSA) algorithm, the Digital Signature Standard (DSS) does *not* provide:

   a. Digital signature

   b. Authentication

   c. Encryption

   d. Data integrity

*194. c.* Both RSA and DSS provide digital signature, authentication, and data integrity capabilities. RSA provides encryption; DSS does not. The digital signature algorithm (DSA) is specified in the DSS. The DSS contains the DSA to create signatures as well as the secure hash algorithm (SHA) to provide data integrity. SHA is used in electronic mail and electronic funds transfer applications.

**195.** Which of the following attacks are made on block ciphers?

   a. Meet-in-the-middle attacks

   b. Codebook attacks

   c. Man-in-the-middle attacks

   d. Bucket brigade attacks

**195. a.** Meet-in-the-middle (MIM) attacks occur when one end is encrypted and the other end is decrypted, and the results are matched in the middle. MIM attacks are made on block ciphers. A block cipher algorithm is a (i) symmetric key cryptographic algorithm that transforms a block of information at a time using a cryptographic key and (ii) a family of functions and their inverse functions that is parameterized by a cryptographic key; the functions map bit strings of a fixed length to bit strings of the same length. This means, the length of the input block is the same as the length of the output block.

The other three choices are incorrect because they do not use block ciphers. Codebook attacks are a type of attack where the intruder attempts to create a codebook of all possible transformations between plaintext and ciphertext under a single key. Man-in-the-middle (MitM) attacks are a type of attack that takes advantage of the store-and-forward mechanism used by insecure networks, such as the Internet. MitM attacks are also called bucket brigade attacks.

**196.** **Which of the following statements about digital signatures is *not* true?**

    a.    It enhances authentication.

    b.    It makes repudiation by the sender possible.

    c.    It prevents nonrepudiation by the receiver.

    d.    It makes repudiation by the sender impossible.

**196. b.** Digital signatures use Rivest, Shamir, and Adelman (RSA), a public-key (two-key) cryptographic algorithm. RSA enhances authentication and confidentiality due to the use of a two-key system; one key is public and the other one is private. The use of RSA in digital signatures prevents repudiation by the sender as well as by the receiver. Nonrepudiation means the sender cannot say that he never sent the message, and the receiver cannot say that he never received the message. Nonrepudiation is possible due to the use of a two-key system where the private key of the sender and the receiver is kept secret while their public key is known only to each party. Both the sender and the receiver cannot deny having participated in the message transmission.

**197.** **Which of the following statements is true? Rivest, Shamir, and Adelman (RSA) algorithm has a:**

    a.    Slower signature generation and slower verification than DSA

    b.    Slower signature generation and faster verification than DSA

    c.    Faster signature generation and faster verification than DSA

    d.    Faster signature generation and slower verification than DSA

**197. b.** It has been tested and proven that the RSA algorithm has a slower signature generation capability and faster verification than the digital signature algorithm (DSA). On the other hand, the DSA has faster signature generation and slower verification than the RSA.

RSA is much slower to compute than popular secret key algorithms like data encryption standard (DES) and international data encryption algorithm (IDEA). RSA algorithm uses a variable length public key—a long key for enhanced security or a short key for efficiency.

RSA encryption algorithm requires greater computing power (i.e., memory or disk storage space) necessary to generate keys. The keys for RSA algorithm are large numbers generated mathematically by combining prime numbers. The algorithm is powerful and has resisted all attempts to break it to date, except for 40-bit RSA.

**198.** **Cryptography provides all the following services *except*:**

      a.    Authentication

      b.    Confidentiality

      c.    Integrity

      d.    Availability

*198. d.* Availability is the property of a given resource that is usable during a given time period; it is not provided by cryptography. Data communications channels are often insecure, subjecting messages transmitted over the channels to various passive and active attacks (threats). Cryptography is the solution to counteract such threats. Cryptography is the science of mapping readable text, called plain text, into an unreadable format, called ciphertext, and vice versa. The mapping process is a sequence of mathematical computations. The computations affect the appearance of the data, without changing its meaning.

To protect a message, an originator transforms a plain text message into ciphertext. This process is called encryption or encipherment. The ciphertext is transmitted over the data communications channel. If the message is intercepted, the intruder has access to only the unintelligible ciphertext. Upon receipt, the message recipient transforms the ciphertext into its original plain text format. This process is called decryption or decipherment.

The mathematical operations used to map between plain text and ciphertext are identified by cryptographic algorithms. Cryptographic algorithms require the text to be mapped and, at a minimum, require some value that controls the mapping process. This value is called a key. Given the same text and the same algorithm, different keys produce different mappings.

Cryptographic algorithms need not be kept secret. The success of cryptography is attributed to the difficulty of inverting an algorithm. In other words, the number of mappings from which plaintext can be transformed into ciphertext is so great that it is impractical to find the correct mapping without the key. For example, the Data Encryption Standard (DES) uses a 56-bit key. A user with the correct key can easily decrypt a message, whereas a user without the key needs to attempt random keys from a set of more than 72 quadrillion possible values.

Authentication is incorrect because it is one of the services provided by cryptography. Authentication allows the recipient of a message to validate its origin. It prevents an imposter from masquerading as the sender of the message. Confidentiality is incorrect because it is one of the services provided by cryptography. Confidentiality prevents disclosure of the message to unauthorized users. Integrity is incorrect because it is one of the services provided by cryptography. Integrity assures the recipient that the message was not modified en route. Note that the integrity service allows the recipient to detect message modification but not prevent it.

**199.** **Which one of the following items is unrelated to the other three items?**

    a.    S-box

    b.    P-box

    c.    Product ciphers

    d.    Sandbox

*199. d.*   Sandbox is not related to S-box, P-box, and product ciphers. Sandbox is a system that allows an untrusted application to run in a highly controlled environment where the application's permissions are restricted to an essential set of computer permissions. In particular, an application in a sandbox (for example, JavaApplet) is usually restricted from accessing the file system or the network.

The other three choices are related to each other. S-box is a nonlinear substitution table box used in several byte substitution transformations and in the key expansion routine to perform a one-for-one substitution of a byte value. This substitution, which is implemented with simple electrical circuits, is done so fast in that it does not require any computation, just signal propagation.

P-box is a permutation box used to effect a transposition on an 8-bit input in a product cipher. This transposition, which is implemented with simple electrical circuits, is done so fast in that it does not require any computation, just signal propagation.

Product ciphers are a whole series of combination of S-boxes and P-boxes cascaded. In each iteration or round, first there is an S-box followed by a P-box. In addition, there is one P-box at the beginning and one P-box at the end of each round. Common product ciphers operate on k-bit inputs to product k-bit outputs.

**200.** **Which of the following key algorithms decrypt data with the same key used for encryption?**

    a.    Symmetric key algorithm

    b.    Asymmetric key algorithm

    c.    Symmetric and public key algorithms

    d.    Asymmetric and secret key algorithms

*200. a.*   Cryptography is the process of scrambling information in such a manner that it becomes unintelligible and can be unscrambled only by the intended recipient(s). In cryptographic terms, this process involves the encryption of plain text data to produce ciphertext, and the subsequent decryption of ciphertext to recover the original plain text. Encryption and decryption are therefore inverse processes.

Cryptographic processing depends on the use of keys, which are of primary importance in the security of a cryptographic system. Cryptographic keys are conceptually similar to the keys used with padlocks, in the sense that data can be locked, or encrypted, through the use of a key with a cryptographic algorithm. Symmetric key algorithms decrypt data with the same key used for encryption. Asymmetric key algorithms use a pair of keys, consisting of a public key component and a private key component, both having a specific mathematical relationship. Symmetric and asymmetric key algorithms are commonly referred to as secret key and public key algorithms, respectively. Cryptography plays a major role in information security and is a critical component of authentication technology.

**201.** **Common encryption algorithms that implement symmetric cryptography do *not* include which of the following?**

    a.    Digital encryption standard (DES)

    b.    Tripe DES (3DES)

    c.    Rivest, Shamir, and Adelman (RSA)

    d.    Advanced encryption standard (AES)

*201. c.* Symmetric cryptography uses the same key for both encryption and decryption, whereas asymmetric cryptography uses separate keys for encryption and decryption, or to digitally sign and verify a signature. RSA is an example of asymmetric cryptography. DES, 3DES, and AES are examples of symmetric cryptography.

**202.** **Which of the following are examples of block cipher algorithms for encryption and decryption?**

    a.    AES and RAS

    b.    TDEA and DES

    c.    AES and TDEA

    d.    MAC and HMAC

*202. c.* Encryption is used to provide data confidentiality. The data to be protected is called plain-text. Encryption transforms the plain-text data into ciphertext data. Ciphertext can be transformed back into plain-text using decryption. The approved algorithms for encryption and decryption include the advanced encryption standard (AES) and the triple data encryption algorithms (TDEA). Each of these algorithms operates on blocks (chunks) of data during an encryption or decryption operation. For this reason, these algorithms are commonly referred to as block cipher algorithms.

RAS is remote access server, which is not a block cipher, and DES is data encryption standard, which is a block cipher.

Message authentication code (MAC) is incorrect because it is not a block cipher because it provides an assurance of authenticity and integrity. HMAC is a MAC that uses a cryptographic hash function in combination with a secret key. Both MAC and HMAC are based on hash functions, which are used by (i) keyed hash message authentication coded algorithms, (ii) digital signature algorithms, (iii) key derivation functions for key agreement, and (iv) random number generators. Typically, MACs are used to detect data modifications that occur between the initial generation of the MAC and the verification of the received MAC. They do not detect errors that occur before the MAC is originally generated.

**203.** **Cross-certification is *not* allowed in which of the following public key infrastructure (PKI) architectures?**

    a.    Hierarchical PKI model

    b.    Mesh PKI model

    c.    Bridge PKI model

    d.    Complex PKI model

***203. a.*** There are four architectures used to link certificate authorities (CAs), including hierarchical, mesh, bridge, and complex. In a hierarchical PKI model, authorities are arranged hierarchically under a "root CA" that issues certificates to subordinate CAs. A CA delegates when it certifies a subordinate CA. Trust delegation starts at a root CA that is trusted by every node in the infrastructure. Therefore, cross-certification is not allowed in the hierarchical PKI model.

Mesh (network) PKI model is incorrect because trust is established between any two CAs in peer relationships (cross-certification), thus allowing the possibility of multiple trust paths between any two CAs. Independent CAs cross-certify each other resulting in a general mesh of trust relationships between peer CAs. The bridge PKI model was designed to connect enterprise PKIs regardless of the architecture; enterprises can link their own PKIs to those of their business partners. The complex PKI model is a combination of hierarchical PKI model and mesh PKI model because they are not mutually exclusive.

**204.** **Which of the following should *not* be archived during the disposition phase of a system development life cycle (SDLC) because it applies to selecting cryptographic mechanisms?**

    a.    Long-term symmetric key

    b.    Signing keys used by traditional certification authorities (CAs)

    c.    An individual's signing keys

    d.    Signing keys used by non-traditional CAs

***204. c.*** When a system is shut down or transitioned to a new system, one of the primary responsibilities is ensuring that cryptographic keys are properly destroyed or archived. Long-term symmetric keys may need to be archived to ensure that they are available in the future to decrypt data. Signing keys used by traditional and non-traditional CAs may also need to be maintained for signature verification.

An individual's signing keys should not be archived due to constant changes and employee turnover.

**205.** **Which of the following provides the level of "trust" required for the digital certificates to reliably complete a transaction?**

    a.    Certificate policy

    b.    Certification practices statement

c.   Identity proofing

d.   Outsourcing

***205. c.***   A level of "trust" is required for an organization to complete the digital certificate transaction reliably. This includes determining the level of identity proofing required for a subscriber to get a certificate, the strength of the key lengths and algorithms employed, and how the corresponding private key is protected. The Certificate Authority (CA) operates under a Certificate Policy (CP) and Certification Practices Statement (CPS) that collectively describe the CA's responsibilities and duties to its customers and trading partners. Organizations can operate their own certification authority duties or outsource that function.

**206.**   **A birthday attack is targeted at which of the following?**

a.   MD5

b.   SSL

c.   SLIP

d.   SET

***206. a.***   A birthday attack is against message digest 5 (MD5), a hash algorithm. The attack is based on probabilities where it finds two messages that hash to the same value and then exploits it to attack. MD5 is a message authentication method based on producing a 128-bit hash code (signature or fingerprint) from a message. The other three choices are not subjected to birthday attacks. SSL is secure sockets layer, SLIP is serial line interface protocol, and SET is secure electronic transaction.

**207.**   **A fundamental principle for protecting cryptographic keys includes which of the following?**

a.   Zeroization and total knowledge

b.   Split knowledge and dual control

c.   Single control and formal proof

d.   Zero-knowledge proof and triple control

***207. b.***   One of the fundamental principles for protecting keys is the practice of split knowledge and dual control. These are used to protect the centrally stored secret keys and root private keys and secure the distribution of user tokens. Zeroization is a method of erasing electronically stored data by altering the contents of the data storage so as to prevent the recovery of data. Zero-knowledge proof is where one party proving something to another without revealing any additional information. Total knowledge, single control, triple control, and formal proof are not relevant here.

**208.**   **The primary goal of a public key infrastructure (PKI) is to create which of the following?**

a.   Closed environment

b.   Trusted environment

    c.    Open environment

    d.    Bounded environment

***208. b.*** Use of electronic processes provides benefits such as time savings, enhanced services, cost-savings, and improved data quality and integrity. Public key technology can create a trusted environment that promotes the use and growth of all electronic processes, not just digital signatures.

**209.** **In a public key infrastructure (PKI), which one of the following certificate authorities (CA) is subordinate to another CA and has a CA subordinate to it?**

    a.    Root CA

    b.    Superior CA

    c.    Intermediate CA

    d.    Subordinate CA

***209. c.*** This is the definition of an intermediate CA in that he has a superior CA and a subordinate CA. In a hierarchical PKI, the root CA's public key serves as the most trusted datum (i.e., the beginning of trusted paths) for a security domain. The superior CA has certified the certificate signature key of another CA and who constrains the activities of that CA. Another CA certifies the subordinate CA's certificate signature key.

**210.** **Digital signatures are *not* used for which of the following?**

    a.    Authentication

    b.    Availability

    c.    Nonrepudiation

    d.    Integrity

***210. b.*** Digital signatures provide authentication, nonrepudiation, and integrity services. Availability is a system requirement intended to ensure that systems work promptly and that service is not denied to authorized users.

**211.** **What are public-key cryptographic systems known as?**

    a.    Two-keys or asymmetric systems

    b.    Two-keys or symmetric systems

    c.    One-key or symmetric systems

    d.    One-key or asymmetric systems

***211. a.*** Public-key cryptographic systems are known as two-key or asymmetric systems. Private-key cryptographic systems are known as one-key or symmetric systems.

**212.** **Cryptographic key management is a difficult problem for which of the following?**

    a.   Symmetric-key algorithms

    b.   Asymmetric-key algorithms

    c.   Hybrid-key algorithms

    d.   Hash-key algorithms

***212. a.*** In symmetric key algorithms, parties share a single, secret key. Establishing that shared key is called key management, and it is a difficult problem. In asymmetric key algorithms, there are two keys (public and private) for each party. The public and private keys are generated at the same time, and data encrypted with one key can be decrypted with the other key. Hybrid key algorithms combine the best features of public and private key systems. Hash key algorithms is meaningless here.

**213.** **Which of the following should be used to prevent an eavesdropping attack from remote access to firewalls?**

    a.   File encryption

    b.   Bulk encryption

    c.   Session encryption

    d.   Stream encryption

***213. c.*** Session encryption is used to encrypt data between application and end users. This provides strong authentication. File encryption protects data in storage. Bulk encryption is simultaneous encryption of all channels of a multichannel telecommunications trunk. Stream encryption encrypts and decrypts arbitrarily sized messages—not a strong authentication.

**214.** **Common encryption algorithms that implement symmetric cryptography do *not* include which of the following?**

    a.   Elliptic curve DSA (ECDSA)

    b.   Hash message authentication code (HMAC)

    c.   Message digest 5 (MD5)

    d.   Secure hash algorithm (SHA-1)

***214. a.*** Symmetric cryptography uses the same key for both encryption and decryption, whereas asymmetric cryptography uses separate keys for encryption and decryption, or to digitally sign and verify a signature. ECDSA is an example of asymmetric cryptography. HMAC, MD5, and SHA-1 are examples of symmetric cryptography.

**215.** During the operational phase of cryptography, a new key is needed to replace the old key. Which of the following is *not* a method to accomplish this goal?

    a.    Rekeying

    b.    Key update

    c.    Entity deregistration

    d.    Key derivation

**215. c.** The entity deregistration function removes the authorization of an entity to participate in a security domain. Deregistration is intended to prevent other entities from relying on or using the deregistered entity's keying material. At the end of a key's crypto-period, a new key needs to be available to replace the old key if operations are to be continued. This can be accomplished by rekeying, key update, or key derivation.

**216.** Asymmetric authentication is susceptible to known attacks due to which of the following?

    a.    Client authenticates the gateway and then uses that channel to authenticate the client.

    b.    Authenticating the server to the client.

    c.    Authenticating the client to the server.

    d.    Authenticating each endpoint to other.

**216. a.** Asymmetric authentication is susceptible to attacks because of the way the authentication is performed. The client authenticates the gateway and then uses that channel to authenticate the client. It is a weak form of authentication. The other three choices provide strong forms of authentication because they are a function of either transport layer security (TLS) or Internet Protocol security (IPsec).

**217.** Zero-knowledge proof is used in which of the following applications?

    a.    Public-key encryption process

    b.    Zeriozation process

    c.    Degaussing operation

    d.    Data remanence operation

**217. a.** Zero-knowledge proof requires that one party proves something to another without revealing any additional information. This proof has applications in public-key encryption process.

Zeroization process is a method of erasing electronically stored data by altering the contents of the data storage so as to prevent the recovery of data. Degaussing operation is a process whereby the magnetic media is erased, that is, returned to its original state. Data remanence operation is the residual physical representation of data that has been in some way erased.

**218.** Which of the following is *not* part of cryptographic key management process?

    a.    Key layering

    b.    Key distribution

    c.    Key storage

    d.    Key generation

*218. a.* Key management provides the foundation for the secure generation, storage, distribution, and translation of cryptographic keys. Key layering is a meaningless term here.

**219.** An original cryptographic key is split into "n" multiple key components using split knowledge procedure. If knowledge of "k" components is required to construct the original key, knowledge of which of the following provides no information about the original key?

    a.    n − 1 key components

    b.    k − 1 key components

    c.    k − n key components

    d.    n − k key components

*219. b.* This is an application of split knowledge procedure. An original cryptographic key is split into "n" multiple key components, individually providing no knowledge of the original key, which can be subsequently combined to recreate the original cryptographic key. If knowledge of "k" components is required to construct the original key, then knowledge of any k−1 key components provides no information about the original key. However, it may provide information about the length of the original key. Here, "k" is less than or equal to "n."

**220.** Which of the following can mitigate threats to integrity when private key cryptography is used?

    a.    Message authentication code

    b.    Message identifier

    c.    Message header

    d.    Message trailer

*220. a.* When private (secret) key cryptography is used, a data (message) authentication code is generated. Typically, a code is stored or transmitted with data. When data integrity is to be verified, the code is generated on the current data and compared with the previously generated code. If the two values are equal, the integrity (i.e., authenticity) of the data is verified. Message identifier is a field that may be used to identify a message, usually a sequence number. Message header and trailer contain information about the message. The other three choices do not have the code generation and verification capabilities.

**221.** In a public key infrastructure (PKI) environment, finding which of the following is a major challenge in the public-key certificate's path discovery?

    a.    Root certificate

    b.    Trust anchor

    c.    Cross certificate

    d.    Intermediate certificate

***221. d.*** All certification paths begin with a trust anchor, include zero or more intermediate certificates, and end with the certificate that contains the user's public key. This can be an iterative process, and finding the appropriate intermediate certificates is one of PKI's challenges in path discovery, especially when there is more than one intermediary involved. A certificate authority (CA) generally issues a self-signed certificate called a root certificate or trust anchor; this is used by applications and protocols to validate the certificates issued by a CA. Note that CAs issue cross certificates that bind another issuer's name to that issuer's public key.

**222.** Public-key cryptographic systems are *not* suitable for which of the following?

    a.    Link encryption

    b.    End-to-end encryption

    c.    Bulk encryption

    d.    Session encryption

***222. c.*** Public-key cryptographic systems have low bandwidth and hence are not suitable for bulk encryption, where the latter requires a lot of bandwidth. The other three choices are applicable for specific needs.

**223.** Which of the following is an example of public-key cryptographic systems?

    a.    MAC and DAC

    b.    DES and 3DES

    c.    RSA and IDEA

    d.    RSA and DSS

***223. d.*** Public-key cryptography is particularly useful when the parties wanting to communicate cannot rely upon each other or do not share a common key (for example, Rivest-Shamir-Adelman [RSA] and digital signature standard [DSS]). Mandatory access control (MAC) and discretionary access control (DAC) are examples of access control mechanisms. Data encryption standard, DES, (56-bit key), three key triple data encryption standard, 3DES, (168-bit key), and international data encryption algorithm, IDEA, (128-bit key) are examples of private-key cryptographic systems. IDEA is another block cipher, similar to DES, and is a replacement for or an improvement over DES. IDEA is used in pretty good privacy (PGP) for data encryption.

**224.** **Which one of the following is unlike the others?**

    a.    Social engineering attack

    b.    Side-channel attack

    c.    Phishing attack

    d.    Shoulder surfing attack

*224. b.* Side channel attacks result from the physical implementation of a cryptosystem through the leakage of information by monitoring sound from computations to reveal cryptographic key-related information. Side-channel attacks are based on stealing valuable information whereas the other three choices deal with deceiving people.

Social engineering attacks focus on coercing people to divulge passwords and other valuable information. Phishing attack involves tricking individuals into disclosing sensitive personal information through deceptive computer-based means. Phishing is a digital form of social engineering that uses authentic-lookingbut boguse-mails to request information from users or direct them to a fake website that requests valuable personal information. Shoulder surfing attack is similar to social engineering where the attacker uses direct observation techniques such as looking over someone's shoulder to obtain passwords, PINs, and other valuable codes.

**225.** **A cryptographic key may pass through several states between its generation and its distribution. A cryptographic key may *not* enter the compromised state from which of the following states?**

    a.    Pre-activation state

    b.    Destroyed state

    c.    Active state

    d.    Deactivated state

*225. b.* A cryptographic key may pass through several states between its generation and its destruction. Six key-states include pre-activation state, active state, deactivated state, destroyed state, compromised state, and destroyed compromised state. In general, keys are compromised when they are released to or determined by an unauthorized entity. If the integrity or secrecy of the key is suspect, the compromised key is revoked. A cryptographic key may enter the compromised state from all states except the destroyed state and destroyed compromised states. A compromised key is not used to apply cryptographic protection to information. Even though the key no longer exists in the destroyed state, certain key attributes such as key name, key type, and crypto-period may be retained, which is risky.

The other three choices are not risky. In the pre-activation state, the key has been generated but is not yet authorized for use. In this state the key may be used only to perform proof-of-possession or key confirmation. In the active state, a key may be used to cryptographically protect information or to cryptographically process previously protected information (for example, decrypt ciphertext or verify a digital signature) or both. When a key is active, it may be designated to protect only, process only, or both protect and process. In the deactivated state, a key's crypto-period has expired, but it is still needed to perform cryptographic processing until it is destroyed.

# SCENARIO-BASED QUESTIONS, ANSWERS, AND EXPLANATIONS

Use the following information to answer questions 1 through 7.

The ARK Company just discovered that its mail server was used for phishing by an outside attacker. To protect its reputation and reduce future impersonation attacks, the company wants to implement reasonable, cost-effective, public key infrastructure (PKI) tools.

1. **Which of the following is required to accept digital certificates from multiple vendor certification authorities?**

   a. The application must be PKI-enabled.

   b. The application must be PKI-aware.

   c. The application must use X.509 Version 3.

   d. The application must use PKI-vendor plug-ins.

   ***1.c.*** Using the X.509 Version 3 standard helps application programs in accepting digital certificates from multiple vendor CAs, assuming that the certificates conform to a consistent Certificate Profiles. Application programs either have to be PKI-enabled, PKI-aware, or use PKI vendor plug-ins prior to the use of X.509 Version 3 standard. Version 3 is more interoperable so that an application program can accept digital certificates from multiple vendor certification authorities. Version 3 standard for digital certificates provides specific bits that can be set in a certificate to ensure that the certificate is used only for specific services such as digital signature, authentication, and encryption.

2. **Which of the following provides a unique user ID for a digital certificate?**

   a. Username

   b. User organization

   c. User e-mail

   d. User message digest

   ***2. d.*** The digital certificate contains information about the user's identity (for example, name, organization, and e-mail), but this information may not necessarily be unique. A one-way (hash) function can be used to construct a fingerprint (message digest) unique to a given certificate using the user's public key.

3. **Which of the following is *not* included in the digital signature standard (DSS)?**

   a. Digital signature algorithm (DSA)

   b. Data encryption standard (DES)

   c. Rivest, Shamir, Adleman algorithm (RSA)

   d. Elliptic curve digital signature algorithm (ECDSA)

*3. b.* DSA, RSA, and ECDSA are included in the DSS that specifies a digital signature used in computing and verifying digital signatures. DES is a symmetric algorithm and is not relevant here. DES is a block cipher and uses a 56-bit key.

**4.** **Digital signatures are *not* used for which of the following?**

    a.    Authentication

    b.    Availability

    c.    Nonrepudiation

    d.    Integrity

*4. b.* Digital signatures provide authentication, nonrepudiation, and integrity services. Availability is a system requirement intended to ensure that systems work promptly and that service is not denied to authorized users.

**5.** **What keys are used to create digital signatures?**

    a.    Public-key cryptography

    b.    Private-key cryptography

    c.    Hybrid-key cryptography

    d.    Primary-key cryptography

*5. a.* Public-key cryptography has been recommended for distribution of secret keys and in support of digital signatures. Private-key cryptography has been recommended for encryption of messages and can be used for message integrity check computations. Hybrid keys combine the best of both public and private keys. Primary keys are used in database design and are not relevant here.

**6.** **Which of the following is *not* usually seen on a digital certificate?**

    a.    Owner name

    b.    Public key

    c.    Effective dates for keys

    d.    Insurance company name

*6. d.* The information on the digital certificate includes the owner name, the public key, and start and end dates of its validity. The certificate should not contain any owner information that changes frequently (for example, the insurance company name).

**7.** **What is the *major* purpose of a digital certificate?**

    a.    To achieve availability goal

    b.    To maintain more information on the certificate

    c.    To verify the certificate authority

    d.    To establish user authentication

**7. d.** Digital certificates are used as a means of user authentication. Entities can prove their possession of the private key by digitally signing known data or by demonstrating knowledge of a secret exchanged using public-key cryptographic methods.

## SOURCES AND REFERENCES

"Guide to Storage Encryption Technologies for End User Devices (NIST SP800-111)," National Institute of Standards and Technology (NIST), U.S. Department of Commerce, Gaithersburg, Maryland, November 2007.

"Guidelines on Electronic Mail Security (NIST SP800-45V2)," National Institute of Standards and Technology (NIST), U.S. Department of Commerce, Gaithersburg, Maryland, February 2007.

"Guidelines for the Selection and Use of Transport Layer Security (TLS) Implementations (NIST SP800-52)," National Institute of Standards and Technology (NIST), U.S. Department of Commerce, Gaithersburg, Maryland, June 2005.

"Introduction to Public Key Technology and the Federal PKI Infrastructure (NIST SP800-32)," National Institute of Standards and Technology (NIST), U.S. Department of Commerce, Gaithersburg, Maryland, February 2001.

"Recommendation for Key Management (NIST SP800-57)," National Institute of Standards and Technology (NIST), U.S. Department of Commerce, Gaithersburg, Maryland, August 2005.

# DOMAIN 6

## Security Architecture and Design

### TRADITIONAL QUESTIONS, ANSWERS, AND EXPLANATIONS

1. **A trusted channel will *not* allow which of the following attacks?**

    1. Man-in-the-middle attack
    2. Eavesdropping
    3. Replay attack
    4. Physical and logical tampering

        a. 1 and 2
        b. 1 and 3
        c. 1, 2, and 3
        d. 1, 2, 3, and 4

    *1. d.* A trusted channel is a mechanism through which a cryptographic module provides a trusted, safe, and discrete communication pathway for sensitive security parameters (SSPs) and communication endpoints. A trusted channel protects against man-in-the-middle (MitM) attacks, eavesdropping, replay attacks, and physical and logical tampering by unwanted operators, entities, processes, devices, both within the module and along the module's communication link.

2. **Which of the following IT platforms most often face a single point-of-failure situation?**

        a. Desktop computers
        b. Local-area networks

   c.    Servers

   d.    Websites

**2. b.**   A local-area network (LAN) is owned by a single organization; it can be as small as two PCs attached to a single hub, or it may support hundreds of users and multiple servers. LANs are subject to single point-of-failures due to threats to cabling system, such as cable cuts, electromagnetic and radio frequency interferences, and damage resulting from fire, water, and other hazards. As a result, redundant cables may be installed when appropriate. Desktop computers, servers, and websites do not face single point-of-failure problems as LANs do, but they have problems in backing up data and storing the data at an offsite location. The other three choices need data backup policies, load balancing procedures, and incident response procedures.

**3.**   **Which of the following security principles does *not* work effectively?**

   a.    Security-by-rules

   b.    Security-by-obscurity

   c.    Deny-by-default

   d.    Data-by-hiding

**3. b.**   Security-by-obscurity is a countermeasure principle that does not work effectively in practice because attackers can compromise the security of any system at any time. This means trying to keep something secret when it is not does more harm than good.

The other three choices work effectively. Security-by-rules and data-by-hiding are commonly accepted security principles. Deny-by-default is blocking all inbound and outbound traffic that has not been expressly permitted by firewall policy.

**4.**   **Which of the following provides key cache management to protect keys used in encrypted file system (EFS)?**

   a.    Trusted computer system

   b.    Trusted platform module chip

   c.    Trusted computing base

   d.    Trusted operating system

**4. b.**   The trusted platform module (TPM) chip, through its key cache management, offers a format for protecting keys used in encrypted file system (EFS). The TPM chip, which is a specification, provides secure storage of keys on computers. The other three choices do not provide key cache management.

**5.**   **In the encrypted file system (EFS) environment, which of the following is used to secure the storage of key encryption keys on the hard drive?**

   a.    Trusted computer system

   b.    Trusted platform module chip

       c.     Trusted computing base

       d.     Trusted operating system

**5. b.**   Using the trusted platform module (TPM) chip, the key encryption keys are securely stored on the TPM chip. This key is also used to decrypt each file encryption key. The other three choices do not provide secure storage of the key encryption key.

**6.**   **Which of the following provides additional security for storing symmetric keys used in file encryption to prevent offline exhaustion attacks?**

       a.     Encrypt the split keys using a strong password.

       b.     Store the random keys on the computer itself or on the hardware token.

       c.     After a key split, store one key component on the computer itself.

       d.     After a key split, store the other key component on the hardware token.

**6. a.**   When a key is split between the hardware token and the computer, an attacker needs to recover both pieces of hardware to recover (decrypt) the key. Additional security is provided by encrypting the key splits using a strong password to prevent offline exhaustion attacks.

**7.**   **Which of the following storage methods for file encryption system (FES) is the least expensive solution?**

       a.     Public key cryptography standard

       b.     Key encryption key

       c.     Hardware token

       d.     Asymmetric user owned private key

**7. a.**   The file encryption system (FES) uses a single symmetric key to encrypt every file on the system. This single key is generated using the public key cryptography standard (PKCS) from a user's password; hence it is the least expensive solution. Key encryption key is relatively a new technology where keys are stored on the same computer as the file. It utilizes per-file encryption keys, which are stored on the hard disk, encrypted by a key encryption key. The asymmetric user owned private key utilizes per-file encryption keys, which are encrypted under the file owner's asymmetric private key. It requires either a user password or a user token.

**8.**   **Which of the following storage methods for file encryption system (FES) is *less* secure?**

       a.     Public key cryptography standard

       b.     Key encryption key

       c.     Hardware token

       d.     Asymmetric user owned private key

**8. a.** The public key cryptography standard (PKCS) is less secure because the security is dependent only on the strength of the password used. Key encryption key is relatively a new technology where keys are stored on the same computer as the file. It utilizes per-file encryption keys, which are stored on the hard disk, encrypted by a key encryption key. The asymmetric user owned private key utilizes per-file encryption keys, which are encrypted under the file owner's asymmetric private key. It requires either a user password or a user token.

9. Which of the following storage methods for file encryption system (FES) is more expensive?

    a.    Public key cryptography standard

    b.    Key encryption key

    c.    Hardware token

    d.    Asymmetric user owned private key

**9. c.** The file encryption system (FES) uses per-file encryption keys that are split into two components that will be an Exclusive-Or operation (XORed) to re-create the key, with one key component stored on hardware token and the other key component derived from a password using the public key cryptography standard (PKCS) to derive the key. Because of the key split, hardware tokens are more expensive.

The public key cryptography standard (PKCS) generates a single key from a user's password. Key encryption key is relatively a new technology where keys are stored on the same computer as the file. It utilizes per-file encryption keys, which are stored on the hard disk, encrypted by a key encryption key. The asymmetric user owned private key utilizes per-file encryption keys, which are encrypted under the file owner's asymmetric private key. It requires either a user password or a user token.

10. Which of the following storage methods for file encryption system (FES) is highly secure?

    a.    Public key cryptography standard

    b.    Key encryption key

    c.    Hardware token

    d.    Asymmetric user owned private key

**10. c.** Because of the key split, hardware tokens are highly secure if implemented correctly. The other three choices are not highly secure. The public key cryptography standard (PKCS) generates a single key from a user's password. Key encryption key is relatively a new technology where keys are stored on the same computer as the file. It utilizes per-file encryption keys, which are stored on the hard disk, encrypted by a key encryption key. The asymmetric user owned private key utilizes per-file encryption keys, which are encrypted under the file owner's asymmetric private key. It requires either a user password or a user token.

11. Which of the following can limit the number of network access points to an information system that enables monitoring of inbound and outbound network traffic?

    a.    Trusted path

    b.    Trusted computer system

      c.     Trusted computing base

      d.     Trusted Internet connection

**11. d.**   The trusted Internet connection (TIC) initiative is an example of limiting the number of managed network access points. The other three choices do not limit the number of network access points.

**12.**   **The IT architecture and system security design should focus first on which of the following?**

      a.     Information availability

      b.     Hardware availability

      c.     Software availability

      d.     System availability

**12. d.**   System availability, which includes hardware availability and software availability, should be the first focus, and information availability should be the next focus because a system contains information, not the other way around.

**13.**   **Regarding cryptographic modules, which of the following refers to verifying the design between a formal model and functional specifications?**

      a.     Proof-of-wholeness

      b.     Proof-of-origin

      c.     Proof-of-correspondence

      d.     Proof-of-correctness

**13. c.**   The proof-of-correspondence deals with verifying the design between a formal model and the functional specifications. A proof-of-wholeness is having all of an object's parts or components include both the sense of unimpaired condition (i.e., soundness) and being complete and undivided (i.e., completeness). It applies to preserving the integrity of objects in that different layers of abstraction for objects cannot be penetrated, and their internal mechanisms cannot be modified or destroyed. A proof-of-origin is the basis to prove an assertion. For example, a private signature key is used to generate digital signatures as a proof-of-origin. A proof-of-correctness applies mathematical proofs-of-correctness to demonstrate that a computer program conforms exactly to its specifications and to prove that the functions of the computer programs are correct.

**14.**   **Regarding cryptographic modules, the implementation of a trusted channel protects which of the following?**

      1.     Plaintext critical security parameters

      2.     Cryptographic module software

      3.     Use of untrusted software

      4.     Spoofing by a remote system

a. 1 and 2

b. 1 and 3

c. 3 and 4

d. 1, 2, 3, and 4

**14. d.** The implementation of a trusted channel protects plaintext critical security parameters (CSPs) and the software of the cryptographic module from other untrusted software that may be executing on the system. The trusted channel also protects from spoofing by a remote system.

**15.** **For cryptographic modules, additional life-cycle assurance is provided through which of the following?**

1. Automated configuration management

2. Detailed design

3. Low-level testing

4. Operator authentication

a. 1 and 2

b. 2 and 3

c. 3 and 4

d. 1, 2, 3, and 4

**15. d.** For cryptographic modules, additional life-cycle assurance is provided through automated configuration management, detailed design, low-level testing, and operator authentication using vendor-provided authentication information.

**16.** **From a security risk viewpoint, which of the following situations is *not* acceptable?**

a. Fail in a known state

b. Return to an operational state

c. Fail in a safe but unknown state

d. Restore to a secure state

**16. c.** It is not good to assume that an unknown state is safe until proven because it is risky. The other three choices are examples of acceptable situations because of little or no risk.

**17.** **Memory protection is achieved through which of the following?**

1. System partitioning

2. Nonmodifiable executable programs

3. Resource isolation

4. Domain separation

a. 1 and 2

b. 1 and 4

c. 3 and 4

d. 1, 2, 3, and 4

*17. d.* Memory protection is achieved through the use of system partitioning, nonmodifiable executable programs, resource isolation, and domain separation. Inadequate protection of memory leads to many security breaches through the operating system and applications.

**18. Organizations should *not* design which of the following?**

a. Operating system-independent application systems

b. Virtualization techniques

c. Operating system-dependent applications

d. Virtualized networking

*18. c.* Organizations should design operating system-independent application systems because they can run on multiple operating system platforms. Such applications provide portability and reconstitution on different platform architectures, increasing the availability or critical functionality while operating system-dependent application systems are under attack. Virtualization techniques provide the ability to disguise information systems, potentially reducing the likelihood of successful attacks without the cost of having multiple platforms. Virtualized networking is a part of virtualization techniques.

**19. Typically, computer architecture does *not* cover which of the following?**

a. Operating systems

b. Business application systems

c. Computer memory chips

d. Hardware circuits

*19. b.* Computer architecture covers operating systems, computer memory chips, and hardware circuits to make the computer run. However, it does not cover business application systems because they are required to perform a business task or function. Business application systems by themselves do not make the computer run.

**20. A trusted channel can be realized in which of the following ways?**

1. A communication pathway between the cryptographic module and the local endpoints

2. A cryptographic mechanism that does not allow misuse of transitory sensitive security parameters (SSPs)

3. A cryptographic mechanism to protect SSPs during input

4. A cryptographic mechanism to protect SSPs during output

    a.    1 only

    b.    2 only

    c.    1 and 2

    d.    1, 2, 3, and 4

**20. d.** A trusted channel can be realized as follows: It is a communication pathway between the cryptographic module and endpoints that is entirely local, directly attached to the cryptographic module, and has no intervening systems. It is a mechanism that cryptographically protects SSPs during entry and output. It does not allow misuse of any transitory SSPs.

**21.** **Usually, a trusted path is *not* employed for which of the following?**

    a.    To provide authentication

    b.    To provide reauthentication

    c.    To protect cryptographic keys

    d.    To protect user login

**21. c.** A trusted path is employed for high confidence connections between the security functions of the information system (i.e., authentication and reauthentication) and the user (e.g., for login). A trusted path cannot protect cryptographic keys. On the other hand, a trusted platform module (TPM) chip is used to protect small amounts of sensitive information (e.g., passwords and cryptographic keys).

**22.** **Distributed system security services can be no stronger than the underlying:**

    a.    Hardware components

    b.    Firmware components

    c.    Operating system

    d.    Application system

**22. c.** The operating system security services underlie all distributed services. Therefore, distributed system security can be no stronger than the underlying operating system.

**23.** **Which of the following statement is *not* true about operating system security services as a part of multilayer distributed system security services?**

    a.    Security services do not exist at any one level of the OSI model.

    b.    Security services are logically distributed across layers.

    c.    Each layer is supported by higher layers.

    d.    Security services are physically distributed across network.

**23. c.** In multilayer distributed system security services, cooperating service elements are distributed physically across network and logically across layers. Operating system security services (lower layer) underlie all distributed services, and above it are the logical levels of middleware, user-application, and client-server security services (higher layers). System security can be no stronger than the underlying operating system. Each layer depends on capabilities supplied by lower layers, directly on operating system mechanisms. Hence, it is not true that each layer in a multilayer distributed system is supported by higher layers. The other choices are true statements.

**24.** Security domains do *not* contain which of the following key elements?

    a.    Flexibility

    b.    Domain parameters

    c.    Tailored protections

    d.    Domain inter-relationships

**24. b.** Domain parameters are used with cryptographic algorithms that are usually common to a domain of users (e.g., DSA or ECDSA). Security domains can be physical or logical and hence domain parameters are not applicable. Security domain is a system or subsystem that is under the authority of a single trusted authority. These domains may be organized (e.g., hierarchically) to form larger domains. The key elements of security domains include flexibility, tailored protections, domain inter-relationships, and the use of multiple perspectives to determine what is important in IT security.

**25.** Which of the following exists external to the trusted computing base (TCB)?

    a.    Memory channel

    b.    Exploitable channel

    c.    Communications channel

    d.    Security-compliant channel

**25. b.** An exploitable channel is a covert channel usable or detectable by subjects external to the trusted computing base (TCB). The other three choices are incorrect because they do not exist external to the TCB. A memory channel is based on CPU capacity. A communication channel is the physical media and devices that provide the means for transmitting information from one component of a network to other components. A security-compliant channel enforces the network policy.

**26.** Which of the following is *not* an example of a first line-of-defense?

    a.    Physical security

    b.    Network monitors

    c.    Software testing

    d.    Quality assurance

**26. c.** Software testing is a last line-of-defense because it is the last step to ensure proper functioning of security controls. After testing, the system is implemented and ready to operate in the real world.

The other three choices provide first lines-of-defense. Physical security with security guards and keys and locks can prevent threats.

Network monitors can protect against spoofing. Quality assurance programs can improve quality in products and processes through upfront planning.

**27.** **From a security viewpoint, which of the following acts like a first line-of-defense?**

    a.   Remote server

    b.   Web server

    c.   Firewall

    d.   Secure shell program

**27. c.**  A firewall can serve as a first line-of-defense but by no means can it offer a complete security solution. A combination of controls is needed to supplement the firewall's protection mechanism.

The other three choices cannot act like a first line-of-defense. Both remote server and Web server are often the targets for an attacker. A secure shell program replaces the unsecure programs such as `rlogin`, `rsh`, `rcp`, `Telnet`, and `rdist` commands with a more secure version that adds authentication and encryption mechanisms to provide for greater security.

**28.** **Normal information can be reliably sent through all the following ways *except*:**

    a.   Increasing the bandwidth for a covert channel

    b.   Using error correcting code

    c.   Using a hamming code

    d.   Introducing page faults at random

**28. a.**  Increasing the bandwidth can make a covert channel noisy as one of the goals is to reduce its bandwidth. Covert channels are not only difficult to find, but also difficult to block. Normal information cannot be reliably sent through covert channels.

The other three choices can send normal information reliably because they use an error correcting code (e.g., hamming code) or introducing page faults at random (i.e., modulating paging rates between 0 and 1).

**29.** **Covert channel analysis is *not* meaningful for which of the following?**

    a.   Cross-domain systems

    b.   Multilevel secure systems

    c.   Multilayer systems

    d.   Multiple security level systems

**29. c.**  Multilayer systems are distributed systems requiring cooperating elements distributed physically and logically across the network layers. Covert channel analysis is not meaningful for distributed systems because they are not the usual targets for covert storage and timing channels.

The other three choices are good candidates for covert channel analysis and should be tested on all vendor-identified covert channel targets.

30. **All the following are factors favoring acceptability of a covert channel *except*:**

    a.    Floating label

    b.    Low bandwidth

    c.    Fixed label

    d.    Absence of application software

*30. c.* A fixed label contains a subject's maximum security label, which dominates that of the floating label. Hence, a fixed label does not favor acceptability of a covert channel. The other three choices favor a covert channel.

31. **From an information security viewpoint, a Security-in-Depth strategy means which of the following?**

    a.    User training and awareness

    b.    Policies and procedures

    c.    Layered protections

    d.    Redundant equipment

*31. c.* By using multiple, overlapping protection approaches, the failure or circumvention of any individual protection approach does not leave the system unprotected. Through user training and awareness, well-crafted policies and procedures, and redundancy of protection mechanisms, layered protections enable effective security of IT assets to achieve an organization's security objectives. The other three choices are part of the layered protections.

32. **Time-to-exploitation metric can be used to determine the presence of which of the following?**

    a.    Memory channel

    b.    Communications channel

    c.    Covert channel

    d.    Exploitable channel

*32. c.* Time-to-exploitation metric is measured as the elapsed time between when the vulnerability is discovered and the time it is exploited. Covert channels are usually exploitable. The other three choices are a part of the covert channel.

33. **All the following are outside the scope of the Common Criteria (CC) *except*:**

    a.    Evaluation scheme

    b.    Evaluation methodology

    c.    Evaluation base

    d.    Certification processes

***33. c.*** The evaluation base, consisting of an assessment of a protection profile (PP), a security target (ST), or a target of evaluation (TOE) against defined criteria, is within the scope of the Common Criteria (CC).

The evaluation scheme, evaluation methodology, and certification processes are the responsibility of the evaluation authorities that run evaluation schemes and are outside the scope of the CC. The CC for IT security evaluation is the new standard for specifying and evaluating the security features of computer products and systems globally. The CC is intended to replace previous security criteria used in North America and Europe with a standard that can be used everywhere in the world effectively since early 1999.

**34.** **Which of the following cannot be initiated by untrusted software?**

    a.    Trusted channel

    b.    Overt channel

    c.    Security-compliant channel

    d.    Exploitable channel

***34. a.*** A trusted channel cannot be initiated by untrusted software due to its design. The other three choices are not as trustworthy as the trusted channel due to their design.

An overt channel is a path within a computer system or network designed for the authorized data transfer. A security-compliant channel enforces the network policy. An exploitable channel is a covert channel intended to violate the security policy.

**35.** **Countermeasures against emanation attacks include which of the following?**

    1.    High watermark policy

    2.    Information label

    3.    Control zones

    4.    White noise

        a.    1 and 2

        b.    1 and 3

        c.    2 and 3

        d.    3 and 4

***35. d.*** Control zones and white noise are countermeasures against emanation attacks. A control zone is the space surrounding equipment processing sensitive information that is under sufficient physical and technical control to prevent an unauthorized entry or compromise. White noise is a distribution of uniform spectrum of random electrical signals so that an intruder cannot decipher real data from random (noise) data due to use of constant bandwidth.

A high watermark policy is used to maintain an upper bound on fused data. An information label results from a floating label. The high watermark policy, information label, and floating label are part of a covert channel.

**36.** **Which of the following can increase emanation attacks?**

      a.    Greater separation between the system and the receiver

      b.    Higher signal-to-noise ratio

      c.    Wireless local-area network connections

      d.    More workstations of the same type in the same location

***36. c.*** The trend toward wireless local-area network (WLAN) connections can increase the likelihood of successful interception leading to emanation attack. The other three choices decrease the emanation attacks.

**37.** **In the trust hierarchy of a computer system, which of the following is *least* trusted?**

      a.    Operating system

      b.    System user

      c.    Hardware/firmware

      d.    Application system

***37. c.*** In a computer system, trust is built from the bottom layer up, with each layer trusting all its underlying layers to perform the expected services in a reliable and trustworthy manner. The hardware/firmware layer is at the bottom of the trust hierarchy and is the least trusted. The system user layer is at the top of the trust hierarchy and is the most trusted. For example, the users trust the application system to behave in the manner they expect of it. The layers from the top to the bottom include system user, application system, operating system, and hardware/firmware.

**38.** **In organizations, isolating the information system security functions from nonsecurity functions is achieved through:**

      1.    Hardware separation

      2.    Independent modules

      3.    Layered structure

      4.    Minimal interactions

          a.    1 and 2

          b.    2 and 3

          c.    3 and 4

          d.    1, 2, 3, and 4

***38. d.*** An information system isolates security functions from nonsecurity functions by means of partitions and domains, including control of access to and integrity of the hardware, software, and firmware that perform those security functions. The system maintains a separate execution domain (e.g., address space) for each executing process. It employs hardware separation techniques, divides the access control and information flow functions, maintains security functions in largely independent modules that avoid unnecessary interactions between modules, and maintains security functions in a layered structure minimizing interactions between layers of the design.

39. **In the trusted computing base (TCB) environment, the compromise resulting from the execution of a Trojan horse can be examined from which of the following perspectives?**

    a.   Compromise from above

    b.   Compromise from within

    c.   Compromise from below

    d.   Compromise from cross domains

*39. a.* The compromise resulting from the execution of a Trojan horse that misuses the discretionary access control (DAC) mechanism is an example of compromise from above.

The other three choices do not allow such an examination. Compromise from within occurs when a privileged user or process misuses the allocated privileges. Compromise from below occurs as a result of accidental failure of an underlying trusted component. Compromise from cross domains is not relevant here.

40. **All of the following are the most simplest and practical approaches to controlling active content documents and mobile code** *except*:

    a.   Isolation at the system level

    b.   Isolation at the physical level

    c.   Isolation at the program level

    d.   Isolation at the logical level

*40. b.* Isolation can be applied at various levels to minimize harm or damage resulting from inserting malicious hidden code. The simplest one is complete isolation at the system level (high level) and the hardest one is at the physical level (low level) when controlling the active content documents and mobile code. Physical level means being close to the PC/workstation's hardware, circuits, and motherboards, which is not practical with remote computing. This means physical isolation is not always possible due to location variables.

Regarding system level isolation, a production computer system that is unable to receive active content documents cannot be affected by malicious hidden code insertions. Logical level isolation consists of using router settings or firewall rulesets. Program level isolation means isolating tightly bounded, proprietary program components. By integrating products from different manufacturers, you can effectively isolate program components from not using the standard documented interfaces.

41. **Which of the following assumes that control over all or most resources is possible?**

    a.   Security and quality

    b.   Reliability and availability

  c.    Security and survivability

  d.    Integrity and durability

***41. c.***   Security and survivability requirements are based on the bounded system concept, which assumes that control over all resources is possible. Security and survivability must be part of the initial design to achieve the greatest level of effectiveness. Security should not be something added on later to improve quality, reliability, availability, integrity, or durability or when budget permits or after an attack has already occurred.

**42.**   **Which of the following eliminates single point-of-failure?**

  a.    SCSI

  b.    PATA

  c.    RAID

  d.    SATA

***42. c.***   Redundant arrays of independent disks (RAID) protect from single points-of-failure. RAID technology provides greater data reliability through redundancy—data can be stored on multiple hard drives across an array, thus eliminating single points-of-failure and decreasing the risk of data loss significantly. RAID systems often dramatically increase throughput of both reading and writing as well as overall capacity by distributing information across multiple drives. Initially, RAID controllers were based on using small computer systems interface (SCSI), but currently all common forms of drives are supported, including parallel-ATA (PATA), serial-ATA (SATA), and SCSI.

**43.**   **In an end user computing environment, what is the *least* important concern for the information security analyst?**

  a.    Data mining

  b.    Data integrity

  c.    Data availability

  d.    Data usefulness

***43. a.***   Data mining is a concept where the data is warehoused for future retrieval and use. Data mining takes on an important role in the mainframe environment as opposed to the personal computer (end user) environment. Management at all levels relies on the information generated by end user computer systems. Therefore, data security, integrity, availability, and usefulness should be considered within the overall business plans, requirements, and objectives. Data security protects confidentiality to ensure that data is disclosed to authorized individuals only.

Data integrity addresses properties such as accuracy, authorization, consistency, timeliness, and completeness. Data availability ensures that data is available anywhere and anytime to authorized parties. Data usefulness ensures that data is used in making decisions or running business operations.

44. **In the trusted computing base (TCB) environment, which of the following is *not* a sufficient design consideration for implementing domain separation?**

    a.    Memory mapping

    b.    Multistate hardware

    c.    Multistate software

    d.    Multistate compiler

*44. a.* Memory mapping, which is manipulating memory-mapping registers, alone is not sufficient to meet the domain separation requirement but may be used to enhance hardware isolation. The other three choices are examples of good design considerations.

45. **Enforcement of a system's security policy does *not* imply which of the following?**

    a.    Consistency

    b.    Efficiency

    c.    Reliability

    d.    Effectiveness

*45. b.* Assurance of trust requires enforcement of the system's security policy. Enforcement implies consistency, reliability, and effectiveness. It does not imply efficiency because effectiveness is better than efficiency.

46. **For a trusted computing base (TCB) to enforce the security policy, it must contain which of the following?**

    a.    Single-layer and separate domain

    b.    Privileged user and privileged process

    c.    Tamperproof and uncompromisable

    d.    Trusted rule-base and trusted program

*46. c.* For a trusted computing base (TCB) to enforce the security policy, the TCB must be both tamperproof and uncompromisable. The other three choices are not strong.

47. **In the trusted computing base (TCB) environment, resource isolation does *not* mean which of the following?**

    a.    Containment of subjects and objects

    b.    Protection controls of the operating system

    c.    Imposition of mandatory access control

    d.    Auditing of subjects and objects

*47. c.* The trusted computing base (TCB) imposes discretionary access controls (DACs) and not mandatory access controls (MACs). The other three choices, along with discretionary access controls, provide resource isolation.

**48.** **Which of the following can lead to a single point-of-failure?**

   a.   Decentralized identity management

   b.   Universal description, discovery, and integration registry

   c.   Application programming interface

   d.   Web services description language

**48. b.** The universal description, discovery, and integration (UDDI) registry in Web services supports listing of multiple uniform resource identifiers (URIs) for each Web service. When one instance of a Web service has failed, requesters can use an alternative URI. Using UDDI to support failover causes the UDDI registry to become a single point-of-failure.

Centralized identity management, not decentralized identity management, is vulnerable to a single point-of-failure. Application programming interface (API) and Web services description language (WSDL) are not vulnerable to a single point-of-failure because API is defined as a subroutine library, and WSDL complements the UDDI standard.

**49.** **Which of the following is most susceptible to a single point-of-failure?**

   a.   Quarantine server

   b.   Proxy server

   c.   Centralized authentication server

   d.   Database server

**49. c.** A single sign-on (SSO) solution usually includes one or more centralized authentication servers containing authentication credentials for many users. Such a server becomes a single point-of-failure for authentication to many resources, so the availability of the server affects the availability of all the resources that they rely on the server for authentication services. Also, any compromise of the server can compromise authentication credentials for many resources. The servers in the other three choices do not contain authentication credentials.

**50.** **Which of the following provides a centralized approach to enforcing identity and security management aspects of service-oriented architecture (SOA) implementation using Web services?**

   a.   Unified modeling language (UML)

   b.   Extensible markup language (XML) gateways

   c.   Extended hypertext markup language (XHTML)

   d.   Extensible access control markup language (XACML)

**50. b.** Extensible markup language (XML) gateways are hardware- or software-based solutions for enforcing identity and security for SOA. An XML gateway is a dedicated application that enables a more centralized approach at the network perimeter.

The other three choices do not provide identity and security management features. UML simplifies the complex process of software design. XHTML is a unifying standard that brings the benefits of XML to those of HTML. XACML is a general-purpose language for specifying access control policies.

**51.** **An extensible markup language (XML) gateway-based service-oriented architecture's (SOA's) security features do *not* contain which of the following?**

    a.    Firewall

    b.    Public key infrastructure

    c.    Digital signature

    d.    Encryption

*51. a.* An XML gateway-based SOA's security features include public key infrastructure (PKI), digital signatures, encryption, XML schema validation, antivirus, and pattern recognition. It does not contain a firewall feature; although, it operates like a firewall at the network perimeter.

**52.** **The accountability security objective does *not* need which of the following security services?**

    a.    Audit

    b.    Nonrepudiation

    c.    Access control enforcement

    d.    Transaction privacy

*52. d.* Transaction privacy is a security service that fulfills the confidentiality security objective. The other three choices fulfill the accountability security objective.

**53.** **Which of the following security services is *not* common between the availability security objective and the assurance security objective?**

    a.    Audit

    b.    Authorization

    c.    Access control enforcement

    d.    Proof-of-wholeness

*53. a.* Audit security service is needed for the assurance security objective but not to the availability security objective. The other three choices are common to availability and the assurance security objective.

**54.** **Restricting the use of dynamic port allocation routines is a part of which of the following to secure multi-user and multiplatform environments?**

    a.    Management controls

    b.    Technical controls

c.   Physical controls

d.   Procedural controls

**54. *b.*** Controlling the multi-user and multiplatforms requires technical controls such as restricting the use of dynamic port allocation routines. Technical controls are implemented through security mechanisms contained in the hardware, software, or firmware components of a system. Management controls deal with risk management, policies, directives, rules of behavior, accountability, and personnel security decisions. Physical controls and procedural controls are part of operational controls, which are day-to-day procedures, where they are implemented and executed by people, not by systems.

**55.**   **Which of the following refers to logical system isolation solutions to prevent security breaches?**

1.   Demilitarized zones

2.   Screened subnet firewalls

3.   Electronic mail gateways

4.   Proxy servers

a.   1 and 2

b.   1 and 3

c.   3 and 4

d.   1, 2, 3, and 4

**55. *a.*** System isolation means separating system modules or components from each other so that damage is eliminated or reduced. Layers of security services and mechanisms include demilitarized zones (DMZs) and screened subnet firewalls. E-mail gateways and proxy servers are examples of logical access perimeter security controls.

**56.**   **In which of the following security operating models is the minimum user clearance *not* cleared and the maximum data sensitivity not classified?**

a.   Dedicated security mode

b.   Limited access mode

c.   System high-security mode

d.   Partitioned mode

**56. *b.*** Security policies define security modes. A security mode is a mode of operation in which management accredits a computer system to operate. One such mode is the limited access mode, in which the minimum user clearance is not cleared and the maximum data sensitivity is not classified but sensitive.

Dedicated security mode is incorrect. It is the mode of operation in which the system is specifically and exclusively dedicated to and controlled for the processing of one particular type or classification of information, either for full-time operation or for a specified period of time.

System high-security mode is incorrect. It is the mode of operation in which system hardware or software is trusted to provide only need-to-know protection between users. In this mode, the entire system, to include all components electrically and/or physically connected, must operate with security measures commensurate with the highest classification and sensitivity of the information being processed and/or stored. All system users in this environment must possess clearances and authorizations for all information contained in the system, and all system output must be clearly marked with the highest classification and all system caveats, until the information has been reviewed manually by an authorized individual to ensure appropriate classifications and caveats have been affixed.

Partitioned mode is incorrect. It is a mode of operation in which all persons have the clearance, but not necessarily the need-to-know and formal access approval, for all data handled by a computer system.

**57.** **Which of the following is *not* like active content?**

    a.    Character documents

    b.    Trigger actions automatically

    c.    Portable instructions

    d.    Interpretable content

**57. a.** Broadly speaking, active content refers to electronic documents that, unlike past character documents based on ASCII, can carry out or trigger actions automatically without an individual directly or knowingly invoking the actions.

Active content technologies allow code, in the form of a script, macro, or other kind of portable instruction representation, to execute when the document is rendered. Examples of active content include PostScript documents, Web pages containing Java applets and JavaScript instructions, proprietary desktop-application formatted files containing macros, spreadsheet formulas, or other interpretable content, and interpreted electronic mail formats having embedded code or bearing executable attachments. Electronic mail and Web pages accessed through the Internet provide efficient means for conveying active content, but they are not the only ones. Active content technologies span a broad range of products and services, and involve various computational environments including those of the desktop, workstations, servers, and gateway devices.

**58.** **Which of the following creates a covert channel?**

    a.    Use of fixed labels

    b.    Use of variable labels

    c.    Use of floating labels

    d.    Use of nonfloating labels

**58. c.** The covert channel problem resulting from the use of floating labels can lead to erroneous information labels but cannot be used to violate the access control policy enforced by the fixed labels. A fixed label contains a "sensitivity" level and is the only label used for access control. The floating label contains an "information" level that consists of a second sensitivity level and additional security markings.

59. **Attackers installing spyware and connecting the computing platform to a botnet are examples of which of the following?**

    a.   Browser-oriented attacks

    b.   Server-oriented attacks

    c.   Network-oriented attacks

    d.   User-oriented attacks

**59. *a.*** Attackers may take advantage of browser vulnerabilities in mobile code execution environments. Attackers may install spyware, connect the computing platform to a botnet, or modify the platform's configuration, which are examples of browser-oriented attacks.

60. **Which of the following is applied to all aspects of a system design or security solution?**

    a.   Policy

    b.   Procedure

    c.   Standard

    d.   Control

**60. *a.*** A security policy is applied to all aspects of the system design or security solution. The policy identifies security goals (i.e., confidentiality, integrity, and availability) the system should support and theses goals guide the procedures, standards, and controls used in the IT security architecture design.

61. **A system employs sufficient hardware and software integrity measures to allow its use for processing simultaneously a range of sensitive or classified information. Which of the following fits this description?**

    a.   Boundary system

    b.   Trusted system

    c.   Open system

    d.   Closed system

**61. *b.*** A trusted system employs sufficient hardware and software integrity measures to allow its use for processing simultaneously a range of sensitive or classified information.

A boundary system can establish external boundaries and internal boundaries to monitor and control communications between systems. A boundary system employs boundary protection devices (e.g., proxies, gateways, routers, firewalls, hardware/software guards, and encrypted tunnels) at managed interfaces. An open system is a vendor-independent system designed to readily connect with other vendors' products. A closed system is the opposite of an open system in that it uses a vendor-dependent system.

**62.** A flaw in a computer system is exploitable. Which of the following provides the *best* remedy?

  a. Hire more IT security analysts.

  b. Hire more IT system auditors.

  c. Install more IT layered protections.

  d. Hire more IT security contractors.

*62. c.* Layered security protections (defense-in-depth) can be installed to prevent exploitability. Architectural system design can also help prevent exploitability. Layered security protections include least privilege, object reuse, process separation, modularity, and trusted systems. The other three choices do not provide best remedy.

**63.** For the payment card industry data security standard (PCI-DSS), which of the following security controls *cannot* meet the control objectives of building and maintaining a secure network?

  a. Install firewall configurations.

  b. Do not use defaults for system passwords.

  c. Encrypt transmission of cardholder data.

  d. Do not use defaults for security parameters.

*63. c.* The encryption of transmission of cardholder data across open, public networks meets a different control objective of protecting cardholder data, not the control objective of building and maintaining a secure network. The other three choices meet the objective of building and maintaining a secure network.

**64.** For the payment card industry data security standard (PCI-DSS), which of the following security controls *cannot* meet the control objective of maintaining a vulnerability management program?

  a. Regularly update antivirus software.

  b. Protect stored cardholder data.

  c. Maintain secure operating systems.

  d. Maintain secure application systems.

*64. b.* Protecting stored cardholder data meets a different control objective than protecting cardholder data, not the one in the question. The other three choices meet the control objective of maintaining a vulnerability management program.

**65.** Use of cookies on the Web raises which of the following?

  a. Integrity issue

  b. Privacy issue

      c.     Connectivity issue

      d.     Accountability issue

**65. b.** Cookies were invented to enable websites to remember its users from visit to visit. Because cookies collect personal information about the Web user, it raises privacy issues such as what information is collected and how it is used. Cookies do not raise integrity, connectivity, or accountability issues.

**66.** **Which of the following is _not_ a risk by itself for a Structured Query Language (SQL) server?**

      a.     Concurrent transactions

      b.     Deadlock

      c.     Denial-of-service

      d.     Loss of data integrity

**66. a.** The concurrent transaction is not a risk by itself. The SQL server must ensure orderly access to data when concurrent transactions attempt to access and modify the same data. The SQL server must provide appropriate transaction management features to ensure that tables and elements within the tables are synchronized. The other three choices are risks resulting from handling concurrent transactions.

**67.** **System assurance cannot be increased by which of the following?**

      a.     Applying more complex technical solutions

      b.     Using more trustworthy components

      c.     Limiting the extent of a vulnerability

      d.     Installing nontechnical countermeasures

**67. a.** System assurance is grounds for confidence that an entity meets its security objectives as well as system characteristics that enable confidence that the system fulfills its intended purpose. Applying more complex technical solutions can create more complexity in implementing security controls. Simple solutions are better. The other three choices can increase system assurance.

**68.** **Which of the following security services are applicable to the confidentiality security objective?**

      a.     Prevention services

      b.     Detection services

      c.     Correction services

      d.     Recovery services

**68. a.** Only the prevention services are needed to maintain the confidentiality security objective. When lost, confidentiality cannot be restored. The other three choices do not apply to the confidentiality security objective.

**69.** The security services that provide for availability security objectives also provide for which of the following security objectives?

    a.    Integrity

    b.    Confidentiality

    c.    Accountability

    d.    Assurance

*69. a.* Examples of common security services between availability and integrity objectives include access authorization and access control enforcement.

The primary availability services are those that directly impact the ability of the system to maintain operational effectiveness. One aspect of maintaining operational effectiveness is protection from unauthorized changes or deletions by defining authorized access and enforcing access controls. Operational effectiveness is also maintained by detecting intrusions, detecting loss of wholeness, and providing the means of returning to a secure state.

The services that provide for availability also provide for integrity. This is because maintaining or restoring system integrity is an essential part of maintaining system availability.

By definition, integrity is the property that protected and sensitive data has not been modified or deleted in an unauthorized and undetected manner. By definition, availability means ensuring timely and reliable access to and use of data and information by authorized users. How is the data available to authorized users if it was deleted or destroyed?

The security services provided to fulfill the security objectives of availability, confidentiality, accountability, and assurance together have nothing in common.

**70.** Web spoofing using the man-in-the-middle attack is an example of which of the following?

    a.    Browser-oriented attacks

    b.    Server-oriented attacks

    c.    Network-oriented attacks

    d.    User-oriented attacks

*70. c.* An attacker can gain information by masquerading as a Web server using a man-in-the-middle (MitM) attack, whereby requests and responses are conveyed via the imposter as a watchful intermediary. Such a Web spoofing attack enables the imposter to shadow not only a single targeted server, but also every subsequent server accessed on the network.

**71.** To mitigate the risks of using active content, which of the following is an example of a technical safeguard?

    a.    Filters

    b.    Incident response handling

    c.    Security policy

    d.    Risk analysis

***71. a.***   Filters can examine program code at points of entry and block or disable it if deemed harmful. Examples of filters include ingress filtering, egress filtering, and intrusion detection systems. The other three choices are examples of management and operational safeguards (controls).

**72.**    **To mitigate the risks of using active content, which of the following is an example of a technical safeguard?**

    a.    Security audit

    b.    Evaluated technology

    c.    Application settings

    d.    Software cages

***72. d.***   Software cages or quarantine mechanisms (technical safeguards) can constrain a program's code behavior during its execution by dynamically intercepting and thwarting attempts by the subject code to take unacceptable actions that violate security policy. The other three choices are examples of management and operational safeguards.

**73.**    **To mitigate the risks of using active content, which of the following is an example of a technical safeguard?**

    a.    Version control

    b.    Digital signatures

    c.    Patch management

    d.    System isolation

***73. b.***   Digital signatures can prevent a program code execution unless it is digitally signed by a trusted source (a technical safeguard). The other three choices are examples of management and operational safeguards.

**74.**    **To mitigate the risks of using active content, which of the following is an example of a technical safeguard?**

    a.    Virtualization

    b.    Isolate proprietary program components

    c.    Proof carrying code

    d.    Isolate tightly bounded programs

***74. c.***   Proof carrying code (a technical safeguard) contains the safety properties of the program code. The code and the proof are sent together to the code consumer (user) where the safety properties can be verified before the code is executed. The other three choices are examples of management and operational safeguards.

**75.** Which of the following statements are true about the operation of a trusted platform module (TPM) chip?

1.  TPM chip is circumvented when it is shut off with physical access.
2.  TPM chip has an owner password to protect data confidentiality.
3.  TPM data is not cleared when the TPM chip is reset after the password is lost.
4.  TPM data or owner password should be backed up to an alternative secure location.

    a. 1 and 3
    b. 2 and 4
    c. 3 and 4
    d. 1, 2, 3, and 4

*75. b.* Each trusted platform module (TPM) chip requires an owner password to protect data confidentiality. Hence, the selected passwords should be strong. Either the owner password or the data on the TPM should be backed up to an alternative secure location. The TPM chip cannot be circumvented even after it is shut off by someone with physical access to the system because the chip is residing on the computer motherboard. If the owner password is lost, stolen, or forgotten, the chip can be reset by clearing the TPM, but this action also clears all data stored on the TPM.

**76.** A trusted platform module (TPM) chip can protect which of the following?

1.  Digital signatures
2.  Digital certificates
3.  Passwords
4.  Cryptographic keys

    a. 1 and 2
    b. 2 and 4
    c. 3 and 4
    d. 1, 2, 3, and 4

*76. c.* A trusted platform module (TPM) chip is a tamper-resistant integrated circuit built into some computer motherboards that can perform cryptographic operations (including key generation) and protect small amounts of sensitive information, such as passwords and cryptographic keys.

The TPM chip cannot protect the digital signatures and certificates because they require complex cryptographic algorithms for digital signature generation and verification and for validating the digital certificates.

**77.** **Which of the following security controls are needed to protect digital and nondigital media at rest on selected secondary storage devices?**

1. Cryptography

2. Physical security controls

3. Locked storage container

4. Procedural security controls

    a. 1 and 2

    b. 2 and 3

    c. 3 and 4

    d. 1, 2, 3, and 4

*77. a.* Both digital and nondigital media should be protected with cryptography (encryption) and physical security controls when they are at rest on selected secondary storage devices. Locked storage containers and procedural security controls are not appropriate for media at rest.

**78.** **Polyinstantiation approaches are designed to solve which of the following problems in databases?**

    a. Lack of tranquility

    b. Lack of reflexivity

    c. Lack of transitivity

    d. Lack of duality

*78. a.* Lack of tranquility exposes what has been called the "multiple update conflict" problem. Polyinstantiation approaches are the best solution to this problem. Tranquility is a property applied to a set of controlled entities saying that their security level may not change. The principle behind tranquility is that changes to an object's access control attributes are prohibited as long as any subject has access to the object. Reflexivity and transitivity are two basic information flow properties. Duality is a relationship between nondisclosure and integrity.

**79.** **Which of the following strategies is used to protect against risks and vulnerabilities at every stage of system, network, and product life cycles?**

    a. Defense-in-breadth

    b. Defense-in-depth

    c. Defense-in-technology

    d. Defense-in-time

**79. a.**   A defense-in-breadth strategy is used to identify, manage, and reduce risk of exploitable vulnerabilities at every stage of the system, network, or product life cycle. This is accomplished through the use of complementary, mutually reinforcing security strategies to mitigate threats, vulnerabilities, and risks.

Defense-in-depth uses layers of security, defense-in technology uses compatible technology platforms, and defense-in-time considers different time zones in the world to operate global information systems.

**80.**   **Which of the following is a true statement about Active-X content?**

1.   It is language-dependent.

2.   It is platform-specific.

3.   It is language-independent.

4.   It is not platform-specific.

    a.   1 and 2

    b.   2 and 3

    c.   3 and 4

    d.   1 and 4

**80. b.**   Because Active-X is a framework for Microsoft's software component technology, it is platform-specific in that Active-X contents can be executed on a 32-bit or 64-bit Windows platform. It is language-independent because Active-X contents can be written in several different languages, including C, C++, Visual Basic, and Java. Note that Java, Active-X, and plug-ins can be malicious or hostile.

**81.**   **What does implementing security functions in an information system using a layered structure mean?**

1.   Using multilevel secure systems

2.   Using multiple security level systems

3.   Avoiding any dependence by lower layers on the functionality of higher layers

4.   Minimizing interactions between layers of the design

    a.   1 and 3

    b.   2 and 4

    c.   3 and 4

    d.   1, 2, 3, and 4

**81. c.**   Security functions in an information system should be implemented by using a layered structure that minimizes interactions between layers of the design and that avoids any dependence by lower layers on the functionality or correctness of higher layers.

Multilevel or multiple levels do not have interactions or dependencies as the layers do because they deal with security clearances and access authorizations.

82. **To mitigate the risks of using active content, which of the following is an example of hybrid technical safeguards?**

    a.    Risk analysis and security management

    b.    Layered defenses and security policy

    c.    Software cages and digital signatures

    d.    Minimal functionality and least privilege

*82. c.* Hybrid safeguards combine more than one control. Combining software cages and digital signatures is an example of hybrid technical safeguard. The other three choices are examples of management and operational safeguards.

83. **To mitigate the risks of using active content, which of the following is an example of hybrid technical safeguards?**

    a.    Proof carrying code and filters

    b.    Security policy and security audit

    c.    Version control and patch management

    d.    System isolation and application settings

*83. a.* Hybrid technical safeguards combine more than one control. Blending the proof carrying code and filters is an example of hybrid technical safeguard. The blending of proof carrying code and software cage is known as model-carrying code. The other three choices are examples of management and operational safeguards.

84. **Which of the following IT platforms face a single point-of-failure situation?**

    a.    Wide-area networks

    b.    Distributed systems

    c.    Mainframe systems

    d.    Websites

*84. a.* A wide-area network (WAN) is a data communication network that consists of two or more local-area networks (LANs) that are dispersed over a wide geographical area. Communications links, usually provided by a public carrier, enable one LAN to interact with other LANs. If redundant communication links are used, it is important to ensure that the links have physical separation and do not follow the same path; otherwise, a single incident, such as a cable cut, could disrupt both links. Similarly, if redundant communication links are provided through multiple network service providers (NSPs), it is important to ensure that the NSPs do not share common facilities at any point. Hence, the communication links and the network service providers can become a single point-of-failure for WANs.

Distributed systems, mainframe systems, and websites do not have the single point-of-failure problems because WANs are more complicated.

**85.** Which one of the following is *not* related to the others?

    a. Sandbox

    b. S-box

    c. Dynamic sandbox

    d. Behavioral sandbox

*85. b.* S-box is a nonlinear substitution table box used in several byte substitution transformations in the cryptographic key expansion routine to perform a one-for-one substitution of a byte value. S-box is not related to the three choices. An application in a sandbox is usually restricted from accessing the file system or the network (e.g., JavaApplet). Extended technologies of a sandbox include dynamic sandbox or runtime monitor (i.e., behavioral sandbox), which are used in software cages and proof carrying code to protect against active content and for controlling the behavior of mobile code.

**86.** For information assurance vulnerabilities, what is independent validation of an information system conducted through?:

    a. Penetration testing

    b. Conformance testing

    c. Red team testing

    d. Blue team testing

*86. b.* Conformance testing is a type of compliance testing conducted by independent parties to ensure management that system specifications are followed through validation, which may include testing. For example, conformance testing is conducted on a cryptographic module against its cryptographic algorithm standards. Penetration testing is conducted either by a red team or blue team.

**87.** Which of the following statements is *not* true? A data warehouse is:

    a. Distributed

    b. Subject-oriented

    c. Time-variant

    d. Static in nature

*87. a.* Databases can be distributed, but not the data warehouse. A distributed data warehouse can have all the security problems faced by a distributed database. From a security viewpoint, data warehousing provides the ability to centrally manage access to an organization's data regardless of a specific location. A data warehouse is subject-oriented, time-variant, and static in nature.

**88.** Database application systems have similarities and differences from traditional flat file application systems. Database systems differ *most* in which of the following control areas?

    a. Referential integrity

b. Access controls

c. Data editing and validation routines

d. Data recovery

***88. a.*** Referential integrity means that no record may contain a reference to the primary key of a nonexisting record. Cascading of deletes, one of the features of referential integrity checking, occurs when a record is deleted and all other referenced records are automatically deleted. This is a special feature of database applications.

The other three choices are incorrect because they are the same for flat file and database systems. They both need access controls to prevent unauthorized users accessing the system, they both need data editing and validation controls to ensure data integrity, and they both need data recovery techniques to recover from a damaged or lost file.

**89.** **Software re-engineering is where:**

a. Software engineering techniques are applied to fix the old software.

b. The existing system is analyzed and new functionality is added.

c. The existing programming code is manually converted to a database.

d. Software engineering techniques are applied to design a new system.

***89. b.*** Software re-engineering is an approach for adding new functionality to an existing system. Unlike reverse software engineering, which aims to recycle existing specifications into an entirely new system, software re-engineering extends the functionality of a system without re-creating it. Software engineering is the use of a systematic, disciplined, quantifiable approach to the development, operation, and maintenance of software; that is, the use of engineering principles in the development of software. It uses a combination of automated and manual tools, techniques, and procedures.

**90.** **Transaction management mechanisms are applied to ensure that a structured query language (SQL) database remains in a consistent state at all times. Which of the following SQL statements is *not* part of the transaction management functions?**

a. Rollback

b. Roll-forward

c. Commit

d. Savepoint

***90. b.*** A database may be in a consistent or inconsistent state. A consistent state implies that all tables (or rows) reflect some real-world change. An inconsistent state implies that some tables (or rows) have been updated but others still reflect the old world. A transaction management mechanism enables the database to return to the previous consistent state if an error occurs. Roll-forward restores the database from a point in time when it is known to be correct to a later time.

Rollback is incorrect because the rollback statement terminates a transaction and cancels all changes to the database, including data or schema changes. This returns the database to the previous consistent state.

Commit is incorrect because the commit statement terminates a transaction and commits all changes to the database, including both data and schema changes. This makes the changes available to other applications. If a commit statement cannot complete a transaction successfully, for example, a constraint is not met, an exception is raised, and an implicit rollback is performed.

Savepoint is incorrect because the savepoint feature enables a user to mark points in a transaction, creating subtransactions. With this feature, a user can roll back portions of a transaction without affecting other subtransactions.

**91.** The structured query language (SQL) server enables many users to access the same database simultaneously. Which of the following locks is held until the end of the transaction?

    a. Exclusive lock

    b. Page lock

    c. Table lock

    d. Read lock

***91. a.*** It is critical to isolate transactions being done by various users to ensure that one user does not read another user's uncommitted transactions. Exclusive locks are held until the end of the transaction and used only for data modification operations.

The SQL server locks either pages or entire tables, depending on the query plan for the transactions. Read locks are usually held only long enough to read the page and then are released. These are ways to prevent deadlocks when several users simultaneously request the same resource.

**92.** Which of the following is an example of the last line-of-defense?

    a. Perimeter barriers

    b. Property insurance

    c. Separation of duties

    d. Integrity verification software

***92. b.*** Property insurance against natural or manmade disasters is an example of the last line-of-defense, whereas the other three choices are examples of the first line-of-defense mechanisms. The line-of-defenses are security mechanisms for limiting and controlling access to and use of computer system resources. They exercise a directing or restraining influence over the behavior of individuals and the content of computer systems. The line-of-defenses form a core part of defense-in-depth strategy or security-in-depth strategy.

**93.** **Which of the following is an example of second line-of-defense?**

    a.    System isolation techniques

    b.    Minimum security controls

    c.    Penetration testing

    d.    Split knowledge procedures

*93. c.* Penetration testing (e.g., blue team or red team testing) against circumventing the security features of a computer system is an example of the second line-of-defense.

The other three choices are examples of the first line-of-defense mechanisms. Penetration testing follows vulnerability scanning and network scanning, where the latter are first line-of-defenses. Penetration testing either proves or disproves the vulnerabilities identified in vulnerability/network scanning.

The line-of-defenses are security mechanisms for limiting and controlling access to and use of computer system resources. They exercise a directing or restraining influence over the behavior of individuals and the content of computer systems. The line-of-defenses form a core part of defense-in-depth strategy or security-in-depth strategy.

**94.** **Which of the following is an example of last line-of-defense?**

    a.    Quality assurance

    b.    System administrators

    c.    Physical security controls

    d.    Employee bond coverage

*94. d.* Employee bond coverage is a form of insurance against dishonest behavior and actions and is an example of the last line-of-defense. The other three choices are examples of the first line-of-defense mechanisms. The line-of-defenses are security mechanisms for limiting and controlling access to and use of computer system resources. They exercise a directing or restraining influence over the behavior of individuals and the content of computer systems.

**95.** **In a public cloud computing environment, which of the following provides server-side protection?**

    a.    Encrypted network exchanges

    b.    Plug-ins and add-ons

    c.    Keystroke loggers

    d.    Virtual firewalls

*95. d.* Virtual firewalls can be used to isolate groups of virtual machines from other hosted groups, such as the production system from the development system or the development system from other cloud-resident systems. Hardening of the operating system and applications should occur to produce virtual machine images for deployment. Carefully managing virtual machine images is also important to avoid accidentally deploying images under development or containing vulnerabilities.

Plug-ins, add-ons, backdoor Trojan viruses, and keystroke loggers are examples of client-side risks or threats to be protected from. Encrypted network exchanges provide client-side protection.

**96.** **Which of the following is not a core part of defense-in-depth strategy?**

    a.   Least functionality

    b.   Layered protections

    c.   System partitioning

    d.   Line-of-defenses

*96. a.* Least functionality or minimal functionality means configuring an information system to provide only essential capabilities and specifically prohibiting or restricting the use of risky (by default) and unnecessary functions, ports, protocols, and/or services. However, it is sometimes convenient to provide multiple services from a single component of an information system, but doing so increases risk over limiting the services provided by any one component. Where feasible, IT organizations limit component functionality to a single function per device (e.g., e-mail server or Web server, not both). Because least functionality deals with system usability, it cannot support the defense-in-depth strategy (i.e., protecting from security breaches).

The concepts of layered protections, system partitioning, and line-of-defenses form a core part of security-in-depth or defense-in-depth strategy. By using multiple, overlapping protection mechanisms, the failure or circumvention of any individual protection approach will not leave the system unprotected. Through user training and awareness, well-crafted policies and procedures, and redundancy of protection mechanisms, layered protections enable effective protection of IT assets for the purpose of achieving its objectives. System partitioning means system components reside in separate physical domains. Managed interfaces restrict network access and information flow among partitioned system components. The line-of-defenses are security mechanisms for limiting and controlling access to and use of computer system resources. They exercise a directing or restraining influence over the behavior of individuals and the content of computer systems.

**97.** **Most spyware detection and removal utility software specifically looks for which of the following?**

    a.   Encrypted cookies

    b.   Session cookies

    c.   Persistent cookies

    d.   Tracking cookies

*97. d.* Information collected by tracking cookies is often sold to other parties and used to target advertisements and other directed content at the user. Most spyware detection and removal utility software specifically looks for tracking cookies on systems.

Encrypted cookies are incorrect because they protect the data from unauthorized access. Session cookies are incorrect because they are temporary cookies that are valid only for a single website session. Persistent cookies are incorrect because they are stored on a computer indefinitely so that a website can identify the user during subsequent visits.

**98.** **A system is in a failure state when it is *not* in a:**

1. Protection-state

2. Reachable-state

3. System-state

4. Initial-state

    a.    1 or 2

    b.    1 and 3

    c.    3 and 4

    d.    1, 2, 3, and 4

*98. d.* A system must be either in a protection-state or reachable-state. If not, the system is in a failure state. The protection state is a part of system-state, whereas the reachable-state is obtained from an initial-state.

**99.** **A buffer overflow attack is an example of which of the following threat category that applies to systems on the Internet?**

    a.    Browser-oriented

    b.    User-oriented

    c.    Server-oriented

    d.    Network-oriented

*99. c.* A buffer overflow attack is a (i) method of overloading a predefined amount of space in a buffer, which can potentially overwrite and corrupt data in memory, and (ii) condition at an interface under which more input can be placed into a buffer or data holding area than the capacity allocated, overwriting other information. Attackers exploit these methods and conditions through servers to crash a system or to insert specially crafted code that allows them to gain control of the system. Subtle changes introduced into the Web server can radically change the server's behavior (for example, turning a trusted entity into a malicious one), the accuracy of the computation (for example, changing computational algorithms to yield incorrect results), or the confidentiality of the information (for example, disclosing collected information).

The other three choices are incorrect because they do not involve buffer overflow attacks. Web browser-oriented threats can launch attacks against Web browser components and technologies. Web-based applications often use tricks, such as hidden fields within a form, to provide continuity between transactions, which may provide an avenue of attack. Examples of user-oriented threats include social engineering. Examples of network-oriented threats include spoofing, masquerading, and eavesdropping attacks.

**100.** In general, which of the following is legal under reverse-engineering practices?

    a.    Reverse-engineer computer software with intent to launch commercially with similar design.

    b.    Reverse-engineer the design of computer chips for duplication.

    c.    Reverse-engineer a computer program to see how it works and what it does.

    d.    Reverse-engineer the basic input/output system of a personal computer for duplication.

**100. c.** Reverse engineering is the process of analyzing a subject system to identify the system's components and their interrelationships and create representations of the system in another form or at a higher level of abstraction. Some shrink-wrap agreements contain an express prohibition on reverse engineering, decompilation, or disassembly. The correct answer does not hurt the software copyright owner, and it is legal. The other three choices are based on bad intentions on the part of the user and hence can be illegal.

**101.** When the requirements of the ISO's Information Security Management Systems (ISO/IEC 27001) framework are applied to any computing environment, "measure and improve controls" belong to which of the following PDCA cycle steps?

    a.    Plan

    b.    Do

    c.    Check

    d.    Act

**101. c.** According to the International Organization or Standardization (ISO), the Plan-Do-Check-Act (PDCA) cycle is the operating principle of ISO's management system standards. The step "check" measures the results. Specifically, it measures and monitors how far the actual achievements meet the planned objectives.

The step "plan" establishes objectives and develops plans. Specifically, it analyzes an organization's situation, establishes the overall objectives, sets interim targets, and develops plans to achieve them. The step "do" implements the plans. The step "act" corrects and improves the plans by putting them into practice. Specifically, it makes one learn from mistakes in order to improve and achieve better results next time.

**102.** Regarding Common Criteria (CC), which of the following alone is *not* sufficient for use in common evaluation methodology?

    1.    Repeatability

    2.    Objectivity

    3.    Judgment

    4.    Knowledge

a. 1 only

b. 2 only

c. 1 and 2

d. 3 and 4

***102. c.*** Use of a common evaluation methodology contributes to the repeatability and objectivity of the results but it is not by itself sufficient. Many of the evaluation criteria require the application of expert judgment and background knowledge for which consistency is more difficult to achieve.

**103.** **Regarding Common Criteria (CC), precise and universal rating for IT security products is infeasible due to which of the following?**

1. Reducing risks

2. Protecting assets

3. Objective elements

4. Subjective elements

    a. 1 only

    b. 2 only

    c. 1 and 2

    d. 3 and 4

***103. d.*** Evaluation should lead to objective and repeatable results that can be cited as evidence, even if there is no totally objective scale for representing the results of a security evaluation. As the application of criteria contains objective and subjective elements, precise and universal ratings for IT security are infeasible. Reducing risks and protecting assets are the outcomes of a target of evaluation (TOE).

**104.** **Regarding Common Criteria (CC), how should a Security Target (ST) be used?**

1. Before evaluation

2. After evaluation

3. Detailed specification

4. Complete specification

    a. 1 only

    b. 2 only

    c. 1 and 2

    d. 3 and 4

***104. c.*** A typical security target (ST) fulfills two roles such as before and during the evaluation and after the evaluation. Two roles that an ST should not fulfill include a detailed specification and a complete specification.

**105.** **For Common Criteria (CC), how should a Protection Profile (PP) be used?**

1. Specification of a single product

2. Complete specification

3. Requirements specification

4. Baseline

   a. 1 only

   b. 2 only

   c. 1 and 2

   d. 3 and 4

***105. d.*** A protection profile (PP) is typically used as part of a requirement specification, part of a regulation from a specific regulatory entity, or a baseline defined by a group of IT developers. Three roles that a PP should not fulfill include a detailed specification, a complete specification and a specification of a single product.

**106.** **Regarding Common Criteria (CC), the outcome of a target of evaluation (TOE) leads to which of the following?**

1. Objective results

2. Repeatable results

3. Defensible results

4. Evidential results

   a. 1 and 2

   b. 2 and 3

   c. 3 and 4

   d. 1, 2, 3, and 4

***106. d.*** The target of evaluation (TOE) in the Common Criteria (CC) leads to objective and repeatable results that are defensible and can be cited as evidence.

**107.** **Regarding Common Criteria (CC), reference monitor concept is applied to enforce which of the following?**

   a. Security Target (ST)

   b. Target of Evaluations (TOE)

   c. Protection Profile (PP)

   d. System Specifications

***107. b.*** Reference monitor concept is an access control concept referring to an abstract machine that mediates all accesses to objects by subjects. It is applied to enforce target of evaluations (TOE) access control policies during the design of TOE. The Common Criteria (CC) contains criteria to be used by evaluators when forming judgments about the conformance of TOEs to their security requirements. The CC describes the set of general actions the evaluator is to carry out but does not specify procedures to be followed in carrying out those actions.

A protection profile (PP) is a template for a security target (ST). Whereas a ST always describes a specific TOE (e.g., firewall v18.5), a PP is intended to describe a TOE type (e.g., firewall). A PP is an implementation-independent statement of security needs for a product type and a ST is an implementation-dependent construct. The ST may be based on one or more PPs. System specifications refer to the roles that a ST or PP should or should not fulfill.

**108.** **What is a communication channel that enables a process to transfer information in a manner that violates the system's security policy called?**

    a.    Communication channel

    b.    Covert channel

    c.    Exploitable channel

    d.    Overt channel

***108. b.*** This is the definition of a covert channel. A communication channel is the physical media and device that provides the means for transmitting information from one component of a network to other components. An exploitable channel is usable or detectable by subjects external to the Trusted Computing Base (TCB). An overt channel is a path within a network designed for the authorized transfer of data. This is in contrast to a covert channel.

**109.** **Perimeter-based network security technologies such as firewalls are inadequate to protect service-oriented architectures (SOAs) providing Web services due to which of the following reasons?**

    1.    Transport layer security (TLS)

    2.    Hypertext transfer protocol (HTTP)

    3.    Simple object access protocol (SOAP)

    4.    Reverse SOAP

        a.    1 and 2

        b.    1 and 3

        c.    2 and 4

        d.    1, 2, 3, and 4

***109. d.*** Perimeter-based network security technologies (e.g., firewalls) are inadequate to protect SOAs for the following reasons:

➤    The Transport Layer Security (TLS), which is used to authenticate and encrypt Web-based messages, is inadequate for protecting SOAP messages because it is designed to operate between two endpoints. TLS cannot accommodate Web services' inherent capability to forward messages to multiple other Web services simultaneously.

➤ SOAP is transmitted over Hypertext Transfer Protocol (HTTP), which is allowed to flow without restriction through most firewalls. Application-aware firewalls in the form of HTTP proxies for HTTP-based traffic allow organizations to limit what an application-layer protocol can and cannot do.

➤ Because SOAP travels over HTTP, it is traditionally left open for Web traffic at perimeter firewalls. Additionally, with the Reverse SOAP (PAOS) specification, SOAP messages can pass through firewalls that limit incoming HTTP traffic but allow outgoing HTTP traffic. Some firewalls have begun to support blocking or allowing SOAP requests based on the source or destination of the request, but more robust and intelligent firewalls are needed to defend networks against malicious SOAP attacks.

➤ SOAs are dynamic and can seldom be fully constrained to the physical boundaries of a single network.

110. **Which of the following *cannot* protect simple object access protocol (SOAP) messages in a service-oriented architecture (SOA) providing Web services?**

    a. XML encryption

    b. XML gateway

    c. XML signature

    d. XML parser

*110. d.* Ensuring the security of Web services involves augmenting traditional security mechanisms with security frameworks based on use of authentication, authorization, confidentiality, and integrity mechanisms. This augmentation includes the use of XML encryption, XML gateways, and XML signature, which are countermeasures. It is always beneficial to implement defense-in-depth using XML gateways at the perimeter along with WS-Security or HTTPS for all internal Web services.

XML parsers are often the target attacks because they are the first portion of a Web service that processes input from other Web services. Poorly designed or configured XML parsers can be used to compromise the parser regardless of how secure the Web service is.

111. **Which of the following are used to perform data inferences?**

    a. Memory and CPU channels

    b. Exploitable and detectable channels

    c. Storage and timing channels

    d. Buffer and overt channels

*111. c.* Sensitive information can be inferred by correlating data on storage media or observing timing effects of certain operations. Storage and timing channels are part of covert channels, where an unauthorized communications path is used to transfer information in a manner that violates a security policy. An exploitable channel is usable or detectable by subjects external to the Trusted Computing Base (TCB). An overt channel is a path within a network designed for the authorized transfer of data. Memory, CPU, and buffer channels are distracters.

**112.** **The Web service processing model securing simple object access control protocol (SOAP) messages and extensible markup language (XML) documents does *not* deal with which of the following?**

      a.    Chain of auctioneers

      b.    Chain of providers

      c.    Chain of intermediaries

      d.    Chain of consumers

***112. a.*** An electronic auction (e-auction) market taking place on the Internet deals with a chain of auctioneers, not in Web services.

The other three choices deal with the Web services. The Web service processing model requires the ability to secure simple object access protocol (SOAP) messages and extensible markup language (XML) documents as they are forwarded along potentially long and complex chains of consumer, provider, and intermediary services. The nature of Web services processing makes those services subject to unique attacks, as well as variations on familiar attacks targeting Web servers.

**113.** **Which of the following is not a single point-of-failure?**

      a.    Mesh topology

      b.    Star topology

      c.    Bus topology

      d.    Tree topology

***113. a.*** A mesh topology is a network in which there are at least two nodes with two or more paths between them. If one path fails, the network reroutes traffic over an alternative path thus providing a high degree of fault tolerance mechanism. Thus, mesh topology is not vulnerable to a single point-of-failure.

The other three choices are subjected to a single point-of-failure. The single central hub in star and tree topology and the single cable in bus topology are vulnerable to a single point-of-failure.

**114.** **Which of the following describes one process signaling information to another by modulating its own use of system resources in such a way that this manipulation affects the real response time observed by the second process?**

      a.    A communication channel

      b.    A covert storage channel

c.    A covert timing channel

d.    An exploitable channel

***114. c.***    The statement fits the description of a covert timing channel. A communication channel is the physical media and device that provides the means for transmitting information from one component of a network to other components. An exploitable channel is any channel usable or detectable by subjects external to the Trusted Computing Base (TCB).

**115.**    **Which of the following is *not* vulnerable to a single point-of-failure?**

a.    Internet

b.    Converged network

c.    Password synchronization

d.    Domain name system server

***115. a.***    Despite its security weaknesses, the Internet is not vulnerable to a single point-of-failure because it uses a point-to-point protocol (PPP) as the primary data link layer protocol over point-to-point lines. PPP handles error detection, supports multiple framing mechanisms, performs data compression and reliable transmission, enables IP addresses to be negotiated at connection time, and permits authentication. If one path or point fails, the Internet switches to another path or point therefore providing a solid connection.

The other three choices are vulnerable to a single point-of-failure. A converged network combines both data and voice, and as such it is vulnerable. Password synchronization can be a single point-of-failure because it uses the same password for many resources. The domain name system (DNS) server can become a single point-of-failure if there are no fault-tolerant and redundant mechanisms.

**116.**    **It is best to assume that external computer systems are:**

a.    Simple

b.    Secure

c.    Insecure

d.    Complex

***116. c.***    In general, external computer systems should be considered insecure. Until an external system has been deemed trusted, it is safe to assume that it is insecure. Systems can be simple or complex in design, which may or may not affect security.

**117.**    **Which of the following memory protection mechanisms deal with security impact levels?**

a.    System partitioning

b.    Nonmodifiable executable programs

c.    Resource isolation

d.    Domain separation

***117. a.*** An organization partitions the information system into components residing in separate physical domains or environments as deemed necessary. Information system partitioning is a part of a defense-in-depth protection strategy. The system partitioning is based on the system impact levels (i.e., low, medium, or high). Managed interfaces restrict network access and information flow among partitioned system components.

The other three choices are incorrect because they do not deal with security impact levels. A nonmodifiable executable program is the one that loads and executes the operating environment and application system from hardware-enforced and read-only media (e.g., CD-R/DVD-R disk drives). Resource isolation is the containment of subjects and objects in a system in such a way that they are separated from one another. Domain separation relates to the mechanisms that protect objects in the system.

**118.** **Which of the following maintains the integrity of information that is sent over a channel?**

    a.    Communication channel

    b.    Security-compliant channel

    c.    Trusted channel

    d.    Memory channel

***118. c.*** A trusted channel maintains the integrity of information that is sent over it. The other three choices cannot maintain the integrity because they are not trusted.

**119.** **Which of the following enforces the network policy?**

    a.    Exploitable channel

    b.    Communications channel

    c.    Security-compliant channel

    d.    Memory channel

***119. c.*** A security-compliant channel enforces the network policy and depends only upon characteristics of the channel either included in the evaluation or assumed as an installation constraint.

**120.** **The use of which of the following can lead to the existence of a covert channel?**

    a.    Data label

    b.    Dual label

    c.    Floating label

    d.    Fixed label

***120. c.*** The covert channel problem resulting from the use of floating labels can lead to erroneous information labels. A fixed label is a part of a dual label.

**121.** **Which of the following is needed for the correct operation of other security mechanisms?**

    a.    Covert storage channel

    b.    Trusted channel

    c.    Covert timing channel

    d.    Overt channel

*121. b.* A trusted channel is needed for the correct operation of other security mechanisms. An overt channel may not be trusted. A covert storage and timing channel is a part of covert channel.

**122.** **Which of the following determines the extent to which changes to an information system have affected the security state of the system?**

    a.    Information system boundary

    b.    Information system resilience

    c.    Security impact analysis

    d.    Security control assessment

*122. c.* Security impact analysis is conducted to determine the extent to which changes to the information system have affected the security state of the system.

The other three choices do not deal with security states. Information system boundary means all components of a system to be authorized for operation have a defined boundary, and it excludes separately authorized systems to which the system is connected. Information system resilience is the capability of a system to continue to operate while under attack, even if in a degraded or debilitated state, and to rapidly recover operational capabilities for essential functions after a successful attack. Security control assessment is the testing and/or evaluation of the security controls (i.e., management, operational, and technical controls) to determine the extent to which the controls are implemented correctly, operating as intended, and producing the desired outcome with respect to meeting the security requirements of an information system.

**123.** **In the trusted computing base (TCB) environment, which of the following is referred to when a trusted component is accidentally failed?**

    a.    Compromise from above

    b.    Compromise from within

    c.    Compromise from below

    d.    Compromise from cross domains

*123. c.* Compromise from below occurs as a result of malicious or accidental failure of an underlying trusted component. Compromise from above occurs when an unprivileged user can write untrusted code that exploits vulnerability. Compromise from within occurs when a privileged user or process misuses the allocated privileges. Compromise from cross domains is not relevant here.

**124.** When building or acquiring new applications systems, which of the following specifically deal with data security requirements?

    a.    Sequencing plan

    b.    System lifecycle

    c.    Technical architecture

    d.    Logical architecture

*124. d.* A logical (functional) architecture defines in business terms the activities or sub-functions that support the core areas of the business, the relationships among these activities or subfunctions, and the data required to supporting these activities or subfunctions.

A technical (physical) architecture defines subsystems, configuration items, data allocations, interfaces, and commons services that collectively provide a physical view of the target systems environment. The combination of logical and technical architecture can make up the organization's total architecture.

A sequencing plan defines the actions that must be taken and their schedules, along with costs to cost-effectively evolve from the current to the future systems operating environment. A system life cycle defines the policies, processes, and products for managing information technology investments from conception, development, and deployment through maintenance, support, and operation.

**125.** Information architecture does *not* govern which of the following?

    a.    Collection of data

    b.    Management of data

    c.    Use of data

    d.    Archiving of data

*125. d.* Information architecture, which is a part of functional architecture, defines the information that is needed to achieve mission objectives and how the information systems can work together to satisfy those objectives. The architecture provides a standard framework to govern the collection, development, deployment, management, and use of data and resources to accomplish missions and objectives. Archiving of data is an operational issue, not an architecture issue.

**126.** Useful information architecture links better with which of the following?

    a.    Business planning to information technology planning

    b.    Information engineering to information systems

    c.    Applications security to logical security

    d.    Network security to encryption methods

*126. a.* Useful information architecture cannot be developed until an organization establishes a business planning process and links it to strategic information technology planning. This is a high-level planning effort, whereas the items in the other three choices are low-level planning efforts. Information engineering is a systematic process in which information systems are developed to precisely support the business of an organization.

**127.** Which of the following action items is not a part of security principle of "reduce vulnerabilities"?

    a.    Strive for simplicity

    b.    Implement least privilege

    c.    Base security on open standards for portability and interoperability

    d.    Minimize the system elements to be trusted

*127. c.* The action item "Base security on open standards for portability and interoperability" is a part of the ease-of-use security principle. The other three choices are part of the reduce vulnerabilities security principle.

**128.** Which of the following security controls are needed to protect digital and nondigital media during their transport?

    1.    Cryptography

    2.    Physical security controls

    3.    Locked storage container

    4.    Procedural security controls

        a.    1 and 2

        b.    2 and 3

        c.    3 and 4

        d.    1, 2, 3, and 4

*128. d.* Both digital and nondigital media during transport should be protected with cryptography (encryption), physical security controls, locked storage containers, and procedural security controls.

**129.** Information system partitioning is a part of which of the following protection strategies?

    a.    Defense-in-breadth

    b.    Defense-in-depth

    c.    Defense-in-technology

    d.    Defense-in-time

*129. b.* Using a defense-in-depth protection strategy, an information system can be partitioned into components residing in separate physical domains or environments to ensure safe and secure operations. It integrates people, technology, and operations to establish variable barriers across multiple layers and multiple functions.

A defense-in-breadth strategy is used to identify, manage, and reduce risk of exploitable vulnerabilities at every stage of the system, network, or product life cycle. A defense-in technology uses compatible technology platforms, and a defense-in-time considers different time zones in the world to operate global information systems.

**130.** **Which of the following creates several independent demilitarized zones (DMZs) on a network?**

    a.    Multiple encryption methods

    b.    Multihomed firewalls

    c.    Multiple-chip cryptographic modules

    d.    Multilayered switches

*130. b.* Multihomed firewalls providing multiple lines-of-defense are allowed to create several independent demilitarized zones (DMZs)—one interfacing the Internet (public network), one interfacing the DMZ segments, and another one interfacing the internal company network (i.e., intranet). These firewalls have more than one network interface card (NIC) to work with. The other three choices do not have the capability to create several independent DMZs on a network.

**131.** **Entrapment techniques against attacks by outsiders act as which of the following?**

    a.    First line-of-defense

    b.    Second line-of-defense

    c.    Last line-of-defense

    d.    Multiple lines-of-defense

*131. a.* Entrapment techniques provide a first line-of-defense against attacks by outsiders using fake data and systems (decoys, honeypots, and honeynet systems). The line-of-defenses are security mechanisms for limiting and controlling access to and use of computer system resources. They exercise a directing or restraining influence over the behavior of individuals and the content of computer systems.

**132.** **Which of the following is *not* a component of a system's architecture?**

    a.    Functional

    b.    Technical

    c.    Physical

    d.    Mechanical

*132. d.* A system's architecture defines the critical attributes of an organization's collection of information systems in both business/functional and technical/physical terms. Mechanical is not included.

**133.** **Which of the following can represent a single point-of-failure for host applications?**

    a.    Cloud computing

    b.    Smart grid computing

    c.    Utility computing

    d.    Quantum computing

***133. a.***   Cloud computing, which is a form of distributed computing, can become a single point-of-failure due to failure of cloud storage services, network devices, database clusters, and network upgrades for the applications hosted there. In such situations, the services of a second cloud provider could be used to back up data processed by the primary (first) provider to ensure that during a prolonged disruption or serious disaster at the primary site, the data remains available for immediate resumption of critical operations. Note that both the user's data and essential security services may reside in and be managed within the network cloud.

Smart grid computing consists of interoperable standards and protocols that facilitate in providing centralized electric power generation, including distributed renewable energy resources and energy storage. Ensuring cyber security of the smart grid is essential because it improves power reliability, quality, and resilience. The goal is to build a safe and secure smart grid that is interoperable, end-to-end. Smart grid computing needs cyber security measures because it uses cyber computing.

Utility computing means allowing functional users (end-users) to access technology-based services to perform specific and simple tasks (for example, to run a storage backup program and a disk/file recovery program) without requiring much of the technical knowledge. Quantum computing deals with computers with large word sizes.

**134.**   **In a public cloud computing environment, which of the following provides client-side protection?**

    a.    Encrypted network exchanges

    b.    Plug-ins and add-ins

    c.    Keystroke loggers

    d.    Virtual firewalls

***134. a.***   Cloud clients can be browser-based or applications-based. Some organizations deploy hardened browser environments that encrypt network exchanges and protect against keystroke logging.

Plug-ins, add-ins, backdoor Trojan viruses, and keystroke loggers are examples of client-side risks or threats to be protected from. An add-in is a hardware device, such as an expansion board or chip, which can be added to a computer to expand its capabilities. An add-in can also be a supplemental program that can extend the capabilities of an application program. A plug-in is a small software program that plugs into a larger application to provide added functionality (such as graphic, video, and audio files). A keystroke logger is a program designed to record which keys are pressed on a computer keyboard and is used to obtain passwords or encryption keys and thus bypass other security measures.

**135.**   **If website owners want to protect data from unauthorized access, what should they do?**

    a.    Create encrypted cookies

    b.    Create session cookies

    c.    Create persistent cookies

    d.    Create tracking cookies

**135. *a*.**    A cookie is a small data file that holds information about the use of a particular website. Cookies often store data in plain text, which could allow an unauthorized party that accesses a cookie to use or alter the data stored in it. Some websites create encrypted cookies, which protect the data from unauthorized access during a user's Web browsing session.

Session cookies are incorrect because they are temporary cookies that are valid only for a single website session. Persistent cookies are incorrect because they are stored on a computer indefinitely so that a website can identify the user during subsequent visits. These cookies can help websites serve their users more effectively. Unfortunately, persistent cookies also can be misused as spyware to track a user's Web browsing activities for questionable reasons without the user's knowledge or consent. Tracking cookies are incorrect because they are placed on a user's computer to track the user's activity on different websites, creating a detailed profile of the user's behavior.

**136.**    **The detect-and-respond infrastructure for information assurance requires which of the following?**

    1.    Intrusion detection

    2.    Cryptographic key management infrastructure

    3.    Monitoring software

    4.    Public key infrastructure

        a.    1 and 2

        b.    1 and 3

        c.    2 and 3

        d.    3 and 4

**136. *b*.**    The detect-and-respond infrastructure enables rapid detection of, and reaction to, intrusions. The infrastructure required includes technical solutions such as intrusion detection, monitoring software, and skilled specialists often referred to as a computer emergency response team (CERT). The cryptographic key management infrastructure (KMI), which includes public key infrastructure (PKI), provides a common unified process for the secure creation, distribution, and management of the public key certificates and traditional symmetric keys. KMI and PKI are not directly related to detect and respond; although, they are all part of supporting infrastructure addressing information assurance.

**137.**    **Which of the following are the main approaches to mitigate risks in using active content?**

    1.    Principles

    2.    Practices

    3.    Avoidance

    4.    Harm reduction

a. 1 only

b. 2 only

c. 1 and 2

d. 3 and 4

**137. d.** Two main approaches to mitigate the risks in using active content include avoidance, which is staying completely clear of known and potential vulnerabilities and harm reduction, which is applying measures to limit the potential loss due to exposure. The other three choices are incorrect because principles and practices are a part of security policy, which is a part of safeguards or controls.

**138.** **Implementing layered and diverse defenses to an information system means:**

1. Attacks are progressively weakened.

2. Attacks are eventually defeated.

3. Placing identical controls in succession.

4. Placing different controls that complement each other.

   a. 1 and 2

   b. 1 and 3

   c. 2 and 4

   d. 1, 2, 3, and 4

**138. d.** Defending an information system requires safeguards applied not only at points of entry, but also throughout the system. Ideally, selecting and placing security controls are done in such a way that all attacks are progressively weakened and eventually defeated. Having an identical control in succession tends to lengthen the duration of the attack. Applying different types of controls that complement each other and are mutually supportive is a much more effective approach (i.e., defense-in-depth strategy).

**139.** **Structured Query Language (SQL) security threats include which of the following?**

   a. Data retrieval and manipulation

   b. Aggregation and inference

   c. Schema definition and manipulation

   d. Transaction and diagnostic management

**139. b.** Aggregation is the result of assembling or combining distinct units of data when handling sensitive information. Aggregation of data at one sensitivity level may result in all the data being designated at a higher sensitivity level. Inference is derivation of new information from known information. The inference problem refers to the fact that the derived information may be classified at a level for which the user is not cleared. Items included in the other three choices are functions and features of a SQL.

**140.** **A data dictionary is which of the following?**

    a.    It is a central catalog of programs.

    b.    It is a central catalog of processes.

    c.    It is a central catalog of data.

    d.    It is a central catalog of objects.

*140. c.*   A data dictionary is a tool to help organizations control their data assets by providing a central catalog of data. The data dictionary requires security protection.

**141.** **What is a database relation containing multiple rows with the same primary key called?**

    a.    Polyinstantiation

    b.    Polymorphism

    c.    Inference

    d.    Aggregation

*141. a.*   Polyinstantiation enables a relation to contain multiple rows with the same primary key. The multiple instances are distinguished by their security levels. In polymorphism, a name may denote objects of many different classes that are related by some common superclass. Inference is derivation of new information from known information. Aggregation is the result of assembling distinct units of data when handling sensitive information.

**142.** **A data warehouse contains which of the following?**

    a.    Raw data

    b.    Massaged data

    c.    Source data

    d.    Transaction data

*142. b.*   A database contains raw data whereas a data warehouse contains massaged data (i.e., summarized data or correlated data). Source data and transaction data are the same as raw data.

**143.** **Which of the following tools is *most* useful in detecting security intrusions?**

    a.    Data mining tools

    b.    Data optimization tools

    c.    Data reorganization tools

    d.    Data access tools

*143. a.*   Data mining is a set of automated tools that convert the data in the data warehouse to some useful information. It selects and reports information deemed significant from a data warehouse or database. Data mining techniques can also be used for intrusion detection, fraud detection, and auditing the databases. You can apply data mining tools to detect abnormal patterns in data, which can provide clues to fraud.

Data optimization tools improve database performance. Data reorganization tools help relocate the data to facilitate faster access. Data access tools help in reaching the desired data.

**144.** Which of the following can be *most* easily exploited when executing behind firewalls?

    a.    Electronic mail

    b.    Web requests

    c.    Active-X controls

    d.    File transfer protocol

**144. c.** Firewalls are good at preventing vulnerabilities in software inside the firewall from being exposed to the Internet at large. However, firewalls permit Internet requests to access certain software running on machines inside the firewall. This includes e-mail, Web requests, file transfer protocol (FTP), and telnet sessions. The problem with trusted Active-X controls is that an Active-X control can easily exploit vulnerabilities in the firewall that allows the control to make a connection back to a Web server. This means that the Active-X control can behave maliciously by design or through manipulation by a malicious server. The ability for Active-X controls to accept scripting commands makes them vulnerable to manipulation from malicious servers.

**145.** Which of the following has a sound security model to prevent malicious code behavior?

    a.    Active-X controls

    b.    Java Applets

    c.    JavaScripts

    d.    E-mail attachments

**145. b.** Java Applets have a sound security model to prevent malicious code behavior when compared to Active-X controls, JavaScripts, and e-mail attachments. Java applets use a technology-oriented policy called the sandbox concept. The Java Sandbox prevents Java applets from using sensitive system services. With all other forms of active content, the security policy is trust-based. That is, the user must trust the source of the active content and assume the risk in case the active content causes harm, whether through malicious intention or through inadvertent flaws in the code.

Although most malicious file attachments have suspicious file extensions, such as .bat, .cmd, .exe, .pif, .vbs, and .scr, the use of once-benign file extensions, such as .zip, has become more prevalent for malicious file attachments.

**146.** Which one of the following security features and mechanisms is specified by the structured query language (SQL) standards?

    a.    Identification and authentication

    b.    Transaction management

      c.     Auditing

      d.     Fault tolerance

**146. b.** The database language SQL is a standard interface for accessing and manipulating relational databases. Many critical security features are not specified by SQL; others are specified in one version of SQL but omitted from earlier versions. A database may be in a consistent or inconsistent state. A consistent state implies that all tables (or rows) reflect some real-world change. An inconsistent state implies that some tables (or rows) have been updated but others still reflect the old world. Transaction management mechanisms are applied to ensure that a database remains in a consistent state at all times. These mechanisms enable the database to return to the previous consistent state if an error occurs.

Identification and authentication mechanisms are not specified in SQL. However, they are required implicitly. In the simplest case, the user authenticates his identity to the system at logon. That information is maintained throughout the session. The information is passed to the DBMS when the DBMS is accessed. The strength of authentication varies with the type, implementation, and management of the authentication mechanisms. The SQL specification does not include auditing requirements, but SQL products may include some auditing functionality. Warning mechanisms are closely related to auditing requirements. If the SQL processor includes auditing, the operating system must have sufficient access controls to prevent modification of, or access to, the audit trail. Fault tolerance is not required by any SQL specification but is a feature of certain SQL implementations. Fault-tolerant systems address system failure; disk array technology can be used to address storage media failure.

**147.** **Which of the following characterizes the relational database technology?**

      a.     Rows and columns

      b.     Nodes and branches

      c.     Blocks and arrows

      d.     Parents and children

**147. a.** Relational database technology deals with tables, rows, and columns. A hierarchical data model (tree structure) consists of nodes and branches and parents and children. The highest node is called a root. The node types are called segment-types. The root node type is called the root-segment-type. Blocks and arrows can be found in the network data model.

**148.** **In a relational database management system, which one of the following types of security locking mechanisms best achieves the concept of fine-grain locking?**

      a.     Row-level locking

      b.     Table-level locking

      c.     Block-level locking

      d.     File-level locking

**148. a.** A security locking mechanism prevents one transaction from reading or updating a record before another transaction has released its locks on those records. Row-level locks are used for data tables and indexes, which can prevent performance degradation when the database is modified by many users at the same time. The other three choices are incorrect because they offer coarse-grain security locking mechanisms. This is because a row is the smallest level in the database.

**149.** **Which of the following is a disadvantage of distributed database management systems when compared to centralized database management systems?**

    a.    Autonomy

    b.    Reliability

    c.    Flexibility

    d.    Data backup

*149. d.* Distributed database management systems are complex to develop and maintain and mission critical data may need to be placed centrally to use backup facilities typically available at a central location. These are some disadvantages of being distributed.

The other three choices are incorrect. Autonomy and better control are provided to local management. Reliability is increased; that is, if one server goes down, most of the data remains accessible. Flexibility is provided; that is, users tend to request locally created and maintained data more frequently than data from other locations. These are advantages of being distributed.

**150.** **Which one of the following data models is suitable for predetermined data relationships?**

    a.    Hierarchical data model

    b.    Network data model

    c.    Relational data model

    d.    Distributed data model

*150. a.* The hierarchical data structures are suitable for predetermined data relationships, so frequently found, that have a superior/inferior connotation, as parents to child, manager to subordinate, whole to parts, and so on. Despite this naturalism, this model requires the user to understand fairly complex arrangements when a large, diverse database is assembled with it. Depending on the DBMS implementation, this model can be efficient in saving storage and in processing high volume, routine transactions while accessing records one at a time. It has proven also to be an effective model for query techniques that operate on sets of records.

The network model provides somewhat more general structures than the hierarchical, for relating diversified data with concern for saving storage. The resulting database may be complex, and the user, normally a programmer, must carefully track the current reference position among the data occurrences. For this reason, the network structure is said to induce a navigational approach in processing transactions. The network model is capable of high efficiency in performance and storage use. Query facilities, although available, are less developed for this model than for the other models.

The relational model is widely accepted as the most suitable for end users because its basic formulation is easily understood, and its tabular data structure is obvious and appealing to laymen. Query language innovations are most pronounced for this model over others.

The distributed model can be thought of as having many network nodes and access paths between the central and local computers and within the local computer sites. Database security becomes a major issue in a truly distributed environment, where data itself is distributed and there are many access paths to the data from far-flung locations.

**151.** **A restart and recovery mechanism for a database management system (DBMS) would *not* include which of the following?**

    a.    Rollback approach

    b.    Reorganization

    c.    Shadowing approach

    d.    Versioning facility

*151. b.* Reorganization of a database occurs at initial loading and any subsequent reloading. Reorganization eliminates unused space between the valid records as a result of a deletion of some records. Besides reclaiming unused space, reorganization can arrange the records in such a way that their physical sequence is the same or nearly the same as their logical sequence. Reorganization has nothing to do with restart and recovery.

The DBMS must have a comprehensive and reliable recovery system that uses either the rollback approach in which invalid or incomplete transactions and database images are backed up; or the shadowing approach with journaling (or transaction recording) and recovery by reapplying transactions against a previous version of the database. These facilities should also accommodate selected recovery for specific files, records, or logical records.

In addition, the DBMS should also have a versioning facility to track and record changes made to data over time through the history of design changes. The version management system should track version successors and predecessors. Although the rollback approach uses before images, the roll-forward approach uses after images. Both of these images are stored on a log tape. If a database is damaged, the after image copies can be added to a backup copy of the database. The database is rolled forward from a point in time when it is known to be correct to a later time.

**152.** **Which of the following statements is true with respect to data dictionaries?**

    a.    A data dictionary must always be active to be useful.

    b.    An active data dictionary must be dependent on database management systems.

    c.    A passive data dictionary is an important feature of database management systems.

    d.    A data dictionary can exist only with a database system.

*152. b.* In the case of an active data dictionary, there is no option, meaning that the data dictionary and the database management system go together; they need each other to function effectively.

The other three choices are not correct because (i) both active and passive data dictionaries are useful, (ii) a passive data dictionary may or may not require a check for currency of data descriptions before a program is executed, and (iii) nondatabase systems can have data dictionaries.

**153.** **Deadly embraces or deadlock situations in a database can best be handled through which of the following?**

    a.   Prevention

    b.   Detection

    c.   Correction

    d.   Ignoring

*153. a.*   There are two general methods of handling deadlocks. The preferred method involves detecting the probability of deadlock and preventing its occurrence. The other method involves detecting the deadlock when it occurs and doing something to correct it. Deadlocks can be prevented through good database design, especially with physical design efforts. Deadlock situations are too common to ignore. Consistent use of the database can minimize the chances of deadlock.

**154.** **Which of the following is *not* an example of a first line-of-defense?**

    a.   Policies and procedures

    b.   Internal controls

    c.   Audit trails and logs

    d.   Training, awareness, and education

*154. c.*   Audit trails and logs provide after-the-fact information to detect anomalies and therefore cannot provide the first line-of-defenses in terms of preventing an anomaly. Audit trails and logs provide second line-of-defenses, whereas all the other three choices provide first line-of-defense mechanisms.

**155.** **Which of the following is an example of last line-of-defense?**

    a.   Employee vigilance

    b.   Program change controls

    c.   Fault-tolerant techniques

    d.   Exterior protection

*155. a.*   People can detect abnormalities that machines cannot through their common sense; therefore, employee vigilance is the last line-of-defense against anything that has escaped the first and/or second line-of-defense mechanisms. Exterior protection, such as walls and ceilings designed to prevent unauthorized entry, are examples of second line-of-defense, whereas the other three choices are examples of the first line-of-defense mechanisms.

The line-of-defenses are security mechanisms for limiting and controlling access to and use of computer system resources. They exercise a directing or restraining influence over the behavior of individuals and the content of computer systems. The line-of-defenses form a core part of defense-in-depth strategy or security-in-depth strategy.

**156.** **The principal aspects of the defense-in-depth strategy to achieve an effective information-assurance posture do *not* include which of the following?**

    a.   People

    b.   Processes

    c.   Technology

    d.   Operations

*156. b.*   The defense-in-depth strategy achieves an effective information assurance posture and includes people, technology, and operations, but not processes. Organizations address information assurance needs with people executing operations supported by technology.

**157.** **Operations, one of the principal aspects of the defense-in-depth strategy does *not* include which of the following?**

    a.   Certification and accreditation

    b.   Attack sensing and warning

    c.   System risk assessment

    d.   Recovery and reconstitution

*157. c.*   System risk assessment is a part of the technology principal, whereas the other choices are part of the operations principal. Defense-in depth strategy focuses on people, technology, and operations.

**158.** **Technology, one of the principal aspects of the defense-in-depth strategy does *not* include which of the following?**

    a.   Information assurance architecture

    b.   Facilities countermeasures

    c.   Information assurance criteria

    d.   Acquisition integration of evaluated products

*158. b.*   Facilities countermeasures are a part of the people principal, whereas all the other choices are part of the technology principal. Defense-in depth strategy focuses on people, technology, and operations.

**159.** **A strategy of layered protections is needed for which of the following?**

    1.   Multiple points of vulnerability

    2.   Single points-of-failure

    3.   Network boundaries

    4.   Legacy information systems

        a.   1 and 2

        b.   2 and 3

    c.    1, 2, and 3

    d.    1, 2, 3, and 4

**159. c.** Information infrastructures are composed of complicated systems with multiple points of vulnerability, single points-of-failure, and critical areas such as network boundaries. Layers of technology solutions are needed to establish an adequate information assurance posture. Organizations have spent considerable amounts of money on developing large legacy information systems to satisfy unique mission or business needs. These legacy systems will remain in place for some time to come, and slowly will be replaced by commercial off-the-shelf software products. Layered protection is not needed for legacy systems that will be expired soon.

**160.** **Access to all the following should be denied** *except*:

    a.    HTTP cookies

    b.    CGI scripts

    c.    PGP cookie cutter program

    d.    Applets

**160. c.** The full name of a cookie is a Persistent Client State HTTP Cookie, which can be an intrusion into the privacy of a Web user. A cookie is a basic text file, transferred between the Web server and the Web client (browser) that tracks where a user went on the website, how long the user stayed in each area, and so on. The collection of this information behind the scenes can be seen as an intrusion into privacy. Access to hypertext transfer protocol (HTTP) cookies can be denied. The pretty good privacy (PGP) cookie cutter program can prevent information about a user from being captured.

A common gateway interface (CGI) script is a small program to execute a single task on a Web server. These scripts are useful for filling out and submitting Web forms and hold information about the server on which they run. This information is also useful to an attacker, which makes its risky. The script can be attacked while running. Applets enable a small computer program to be downloaded along with a Web page.

Applets have both good and bad features. Making a Web page look richer in features is a good aspect. Siphoning off files and erasing a hard drive are some examples of bad aspects.

**161.** **What is the** *least* **effective way to handle the Common Gateway Interface (CGI) scripts?**

    a.    Avoid them.

    b.    Delete them.

    c.    Execute them.

    d.    Move them away.

**161. c.** Some hypertext transfer protocol (HTTP) servers come with a default directory of CGI scripts. The best thing is to delete or avoid these programs, or move them away to another location. The CGI scripts are dangerous because they are vulnerable to attack while executing.

**162.** Which of the following action items is *not* a part of the security principle of "increase resilience"?

    a.    Implement layered security to ensure no single point of vulnerability.

    b.    Use common languages in developing security requirements.

    c.    Limit or contain vulnerabilities.

    d.    Use boundary mechanisms to separate computing systems and networks.

*162. b.* The action item "Use common languages in developing security requirements" is a part of ease-of-use security principle. The other three choices are part of the increase resilience security principle.

**163.** Which of the following is *not* the common security approach taken by Java and Active-X?

    a.    Hardware

    b.    Software

    c.    Human judgment

    d.    Digital signature

*163. a.* Active-X technology relies on human judgment and the use of digital signatures. Java relies more on software. They are not dependent on hardware.

**164.** What is the *most* effective control against Active-X programs?

    a.    Use digital signatures.

    b.    Issue a policy statement.

    c.    Accept only approved Active-X programs.

    d.    Prohibit all Active-X programs.

*164. d.* The problem with Active-X programs is that users may download a program signed by someone with whom the user is unfamiliar. A policy statement about who can be trusted is difficult to implement. The most effective control is to prohibit all Active-X programs.

**165.** Which of the following represents a single point-of-failure?

    a.    Network server

    b.    Database server

    c.    Firewall

    d.    Router

*165. c.* A firewall tends to concentrate security in a single point, which can lead to the potential of compromising the entire network through a single point. If the firewall fails, the entire network could be attacked. The other three choices are not examples of single point-of-failure.

**166.** **Which of the following is an example of second line-of-defense?**

    a.   Monitoring of systems and employees

    b.   Decoy systems

    c.   Honeypot systems

    d.   Network monitoring

**166. a.**   Monitoring of systems and employees against unauthorized actions is an example of second line-of-defense. An example is keyboard monitoring of an employee's work. The other three choices are examples of the first line-of-defense mechanisms.

The line-of-defenses are security mechanisms for limiting and controlling access to and use of computer system resources. They exercise a directing or restraining influence over the behavior of individuals and the content of computer systems. The line-of-defenses form a core part of defense-in-depth strategy or security-in-depth strategy.

**167.** **Which of the following statements is *not* true about a system's protection profile (PP) format of the Common Criteria (CC)?**

    a.   It records the threats that are being considered.

    b.   It is the result of the initial security analysis.

    c.   It documents the security objectives that are being pursued.

    d.   It records the actual security specifications as they are created.

**167. b.**   The system protection profile (PP) format of Common Criteria (CC) can be used for presenting the results of the needs determination and requirements analysis. Further, a system PP acts as a record of the security analysis performed during this specification generation process. The PP provides all the things mentioned in the other three choices. Therefore, a system PP should be viewed as an evolving document that is not simply the "result" of the initial security analysis, but is also the full record of the security analysis performed during the course of the specification generation process.

**168.** **Which of the following actions is *not* a part of the increase resilience security principle?**

    a.   Operate an IT system to limit damage and to be resilient in response.

    b.   Do not implement unnecessary security mechanisms.

    c.   Isolate public access systems from mission-critical resources.

    d.   Implement audit mechanisms to detect unauthorized use and to support incident investigations.

**168. b.**   The action item "Do not implement unnecessary security mechanisms" is a part of the reduce vulnerabilities. security principle. The other three choices are part of the increase resilience security principle.

**169.** Which of the following is required for a distributed information system to support migration to new technology or upgrade of new features?

1. Modular design

2. Common language

3. Interoperability

4. Portability

    a. 1 and 2

    b. 2 and 3

    c. 1 and 4

    d. 1, 2, 3, and 4

*169. d.* The security design should be modular so that individual parts of the security design can be upgraded without the requirement to modify the entire system. The use of a common language (e.g., the Common Criteria) during the development of security requirements permits organizations to evaluate and compare security products and features. This evaluation can be made in a common test environment. For distributed information systems to be effective, security program designers should make every effort to incorporate interoperability and portability into all security measures, including hardware and software, and implementation practices.

**170.** From a relative risk viewpoint, the need for layered security protection is most important for which of the following systems in order to protect against sophisticated attacks?

    a. Major information systems

    b. Commercial off-the-shelf systems

    c. General support systems

    d. Custom designed application systems

*170. b.* The need for layered security protection is most important when commercial off-the-shelf products are used from software vendors. Practical experience has shown that the current state-of-the-art for security quality in vendor's commercial system products does not provide a high degree of protection against sophisticated attacks. Additional security controls are needed to provide a layered security protection because the vendor product is a generic product with minimal security controls for all customers' use.

The systems in the other three choices are internal systems to an organization that are developed with a specific business purpose and with adequate security controls. General support system is an interconnected set of information resources under the same direct management control that share common functionality, including hardware, software, data/information, applications, communications, and people. An information system is classified as a major system when its development, maintenance, and operating cost are high and when it has a significant role in the overall operations of an organization.

**171.** **Which of the following are required for an information system to become resilient?**

1. Detect and respond capabilities

2. Manage single points-of-failure

3. Implement a response strategy

4. Develop a reporting system

    a. 1 and 2

    b. 2 and 3

    c. 1 and 3

    d. 1, 2, 3, and 4

*171. d.* For information systems to become resilient, organizations should establish detect and respond capabilities, manage single points-of-failure in their systems, implement a response strategy, and develop a reporting system for management.

**172.** **Which of the following does *not* act as the first line-of-defense for protecting the data?**

    a. Passwords

    b. Disk mirroring

    c. Audit trails

    d. Redundant array of independent disk

*172. c.* Audit trails provide information on an after-the-fact basis. They do not prevent bad things from happening.

Disk mirroring, redundant array of independent disk (RAID), and passwords are the first line-of-defenses. Disk mirroring and RAID act as the first line-of-defense for protecting against data loss. Incorrect entry of a password will be rejected thus disallowing an unauthorized person to enter into a computer system. Both disk mirroring and RAID provide redundant services.

The line-of-defenses are security mechanisms for limiting and controlling access to and use of computer system resources. They exercise a directing or restraining influence over the behavior of individuals and the content of computer systems. The line-of-defenses form a core part of defense-in-depth strategy or security-in-depth strategy.

**173.** **Which of the following is the last (final) line-of-defense for the defense-in-depth strategy?**

    a. Perimeter-based security

    b. Network-based computing environment

    c. Host-based computing environment

    d. Host-based security

**173. c.** Detect and respond actions effectively mitigate the effects of attacks that penetrate and compromise the network. The host-based computing environment is the last (final) line-of-defense for the defense-in-depth strategy. The protection approach must take into account some facts such as workstations and servers can be vulnerable to attacks through poor security postures, misconfigurations, software flaws, or end-user misuse.

Perimeter-based security is incorrect because it is a technique of securing a network by controlling accesses to all entry and exit points of the network. Network-based computing environment is incorrect because it focuses on effective control and monitoring of data flow into and out of the enclave, which consists of multiple LANs, ISDNs, and WANs connected to the Internet. It provides a first line-of-defense. Host-based security is incorrect because it is a technique of securing an individual system from attacks.

The line-of-defenses are security mechanisms for limiting and controlling access to and use of computer system resources. They exercise a directing or restraining influence over the behavior of individuals and the content of computer systems. The line-of-defenses form a core part of defense-in-depth strategy or security-in-depth strategy.

**174.** **What do fundamental goals of the defense-in-depth include?**

    a.    Sneak and peek

    b.    Trap and trace

    c.    Detect and respond

    d.    Protect and detect

**174. c.** A fundamental tenet of the defense-in-depth strategy is to prevent a cyber attack from penetrating networks and to detect and to respond effectively to mitigate the effects of attacks that do. Detect and respond capabilities are complex structures that run the gamut of intrusion and attack detection, characterization, and response.

Sneak and peek are incorrect because they are an element of the U.S. Patriot Act of 2001, which was developed to provide convenience to law enforcement authorities in the event of terrorism. Trap and trace are incorrect because they are a part of a criminal investigation. Protect and detect are incorrect because they are a part of physical security function.

**175.** **Which of the following controls provide a first line-of-defense against potential security threats, risks, or losses to the network?**

    a.    Passwords and user IDs

    b.    Software testing

    c.    Dial-back modem

    d.    Transaction logs

**175. a.** Passwords and user identification are the first line-of-defense against a breach to a network's security. Several restrictions can be placed on passwords to improve their effectiveness. These restrictions may include minimum length and format and forced periodic password changes.

Software testing is the last line-of-defense to ensure data integrity and security. Therefore, the software must be tested thoroughly by end users, information systems staff, and computer operations staff.

Switched ports (not Cisco switches) are among the most vulnerable security points on a network. These allow dial in and dial out access. They are security risks because they allow users with telephone terminals to access systems. Although callback or dial-back is a potential control as a first line-of-defense, it is not necessarily the most effective because of the call forwarding capability of telephone circuits.

For online applications, the logging of all transactions processed or reflected by input programs provides a complete audit trail of actual and attempted entries, thus providing a last line-of-defense. The log can be stored on tape or disk files for subsequent analysis. The logging control should include the date, time, user ID and password used, the location, and number of unsuccessful attempts made.

The line-of-defenses are security mechanisms for limiting and controlling access to and use of computer system resources. They exercise a directing or restraining influence over the behavior of individuals and the content of computer systems. The line-of-defenses form a core part of defense-in-depth strategy or security-in-depth strategy.

**176.** Which of the following enables adequate user authentication of mobile hand-held devices?

    a.   First line-of-defense

    b.   Second line-of-defense

    c.   Third line-of-defense

    d.   Last line-of-defense

*176. a.* Enabling adequate user authentication is the first line-of-defense against unauthorized use of an unattended, lost, or stolen mobile hand-held device such as personal digital assistant (PDA) and smartphones. Authentication is the first-line-of-defense.

**177.** Which of the following supports the security-in-depth strategy?

    a.   Abstraction

    b.   Data hiding

    c.   Layering

    d.   Encryption

*177. c.* By using multiple, overlapping protection mechanisms, the failure or circumvention of any individual protection approach will not leave the system unprotected. The concept of layered protections is called security-in-depth or defense-in-depth strategy. Abstraction, data hiding, and encryption are some examples of protection mechanisms, which are part of security-in-depth strategy.

**178.** **If Control A misses 30 percent of attacks and Control B also misses 30 percent of attacks, in combination, what percentage of attacks will be caught?**

    a.    40 percent

    b.    60 percent

    c.    70 percent

    d.    91 percent

*178. d.* Controls work in an additive way, meaning that their combined effect is far greater than the sum of each individual effect. In combination, both controls should miss only 9 percent (i.e., 0.3 x 0.3) of attacks. This means 91 percent (i.e., 100 percent – 9 percent) of attacks should be caught. Forty percent is incorrect because it adds 30 percent and 30 percent and subtracts the result from 100%. Sixty percent is incorrect because it simply adds 30 percent for Control A and B. Seventy percent is incorrect because it subtracts 30 percent from 100 percent, resulting in 70 percent.

**179.** **Pharming attacks are an example of which of the following?**

    a.    Browser-oriented attacks

    b.    Server-oriented attacks

    c.    Network-oriented attacks

    d.    User-oriented attacks

*179. c.* An attacker may modify the domain name system (DNS) mechanism to direct it to a false website. These techniques are often used to perform pharming attacks, where users may divulge sensitive information. Note that pharming attacks can also be initiated by subverting the victim's host computer files.

**180.** **Which of the following is an example of a single point-of-failure?**

    a.    Security administration

    b.    Single sign-on

    c.    Multiple passwords

    d.    Network changes

*180. b.* The single sign-on (SSO) system is an example of a single point-of-failure, where the risk is concentrated rather than diffused. If the sign-on system is compromised, the entire system is vulnerable.

The other three choices are examples of multiple points-of-failure, where many things can go wrong in many places by many individuals. Every time an employee is terminated or parts of the network changed, the security administrator must deactivate all the employee's passwords and reconfigure the network. Here, the risk is spread out, not concentrated.

**181.** Which of the following is an example of a second line-of-defense in attack recognition?

    a.    Firewall

    b.    Attack detection software

    c.    Password

    d.    Internal controls

*181. b.* A firewall, a password, and internal controls are first lines-of-defenses against attacks and fraud. The firewall can be bypassed by a clever attacker using an Internet protocol (IP) spoof attack or by bypassing it completely and gaining access to the network directly through a modem. Because of the difficulty in configuring a firewall, a second line-of-defense is needed, and it is the attack detection software installed either on host or network. If an attack cannot be prevented, it must at least be detected.

The line-of-defenses are security mechanisms for limiting and controlling access to and use of computer system resources. They exercise a directing or restraining influence over the behavior of individuals and the content of computer systems. The line-of-defenses form a core part of defense-in-depth strategy or security-in-depth strategy.

**182.** Which of the following physical security mechanisms provides a first line-of-defense for a data center?

    a.    Interior areas within a building

    b.    Exterior walls of a building

    c.    Perimeter barriers outside a building

    d.    Ceilings of a building

*182. c.* The perimeter barriers such as gates and guards, which are located at an outer edge of a property, provide a first line-of-defense. Exterior walls, ceilings, roofs, and floors of a building themselves provide a second line-of-defense. Interior areas within a building such as doors and windows provide a third line-of-defense. All these examples are physical security mechanisms. The first line-of-defense is always better than the other lines-of-defenses due to cost, time, and effectiveness factors.

The line-of-defenses are security mechanisms for limiting and controlling access to and use of computer system resources. They exercise a directing or restraining influence over the behavior of individuals and the content of computer systems. The line-of-defenses form a core part of defense-in-depth strategy or security-in-depth strategy.

**183.** Which of the following is the correct approach for an information system to separate user functionality from management functionality?

    a.    Application partitioning

    b.    Boundary protection

    c.    Security parameters

    d.    Controlled interfaces

**183. a.** Application partitioning means the information system physically or logically separates user interface services (e.g., public Web pages) from information system storage and management services (e.g., database management). Separation may be accomplished through the use of different computers, different CPUs, different instances of the operating system, different network addresses, or combinations of these or other methods.

Boundary protection is incorrect because it means controlling communications at the external boundary of an information system and at key internal boundaries within the system. The organization physically allocates publicly accessible information system components (e.g., public Web servers) to separate sub-networks with separate, physical network interfaces.

Security parameters are incorrect because they include security labels and markings, which are associated with information exchanged between information systems.

Controlled interfaces are incorrect because they include devices such as proxies, gateways, routers, firewalls, and encrypted tunnels provide controlled interfaces to the Internet or external networks.

**184.** **From a security policy viewpoint, a survivable system should be built based on a specific:**

    a.    Hardware

    b.    Software

    c.    Architecture

    d.    Vendor

**184. c.** An architecture-based approach should be taken to achieve survivability. That is, one should take an approach where design issues, rather than specific hardware or software products or vendors, are key to creating such a system.

**185.** **Which of the following memory protection mechanisms can eliminate the possibility of malicious code insertion?**

    a.    System partitioning

    b.    Nonmodifiable executable programs

    c.    Resource isolation

    d.    Domain separation

**185. b.** A nonmodifiable executable program is the one that loads and executes the operating environment and application system from hardware-enforced and read-only media (e.g., CD-R/DVD-R disk drives). The term operating environment is defined as the code upon which application systems are hosted (e.g., a monitor, executive, operating system, or application system running directly on the hardware platform). Use of nonmodifiable storage ensures the integrity of the software program from the point of creation of the read-only image. It can eliminate the possibility of malicious code insertion via persistent, writeable storage.

System partitioning means breaking the system into components to reside in separate physical domains or environments as deemed necessary. Resource isolation is the containment of subjects and objects in a system in such a way that they are separated from one another. Domain separation relates to the mechanisms that protect objects in the system.

186. **Which of the following provides organizations with the ability to disguise information systems and to reduce the likelihood of successful attacks without the cost of having multiple platforms?**

    a.   Virtual computing

    b.   Virtual machine software

    c.   Virtualization technologies

    d.   Virtualized networking

*186. c.* Virtualization technologies provide organizations with the ability to disguise information systems, potentially reducing the likelihood of successful attacks without the cost of having multiple platforms. Although frequent changes to operating systems and application systems pose configuration management challenges, the changes result in an increased work factor for adversaries to carry out successful attacks. Changing the apparent operating system or application system, as opposed to the actual operating system or application system, results in virtual changes that still impede attacker success while helping to reduce the configuration management effort. To achieve this goal, organizations should employ randomness in the implementation of the virtualization technologies.

Many virtualization solutions allow more than one operating system to run on a single computer simultaneously, each appearing as if it were a real computer. This has become popular recently because it allows organizations to make more effective use of computer hardware. Most of these types virtualization systems include virtualized networking, which allows the multiple operating systems to communicate as if they were on standard Ethernet, even though there is no actual networking hardware.

Virtual machine (VM) is software that allows a single host computer to run one or more guest operating systems. Because each VM is identical to the true hardware, each one can run any operating system that will run directly on the hardware. In fact, different VMs can run different operating systems.

VMs can be used to prevent potentially malicious software from using the operating system for illicit actions. They typically lie between the operating system and the physical hardware. This mediation layer between the software and hardware is a powerful feature that prevents potentially malicious software from interfacing directly with real hardware.

VMs normally provide virtual resources to the operating system. Worms that attempt to run in such an environment can damage only the virtual resources and not the true operating system or hardware. VMs can also help a user recover their system, after an attack has been detected. They often have the capability to restore the system to a previous, uninfected state. Virtual computing and virtualized networking are a part of virtualization techniques or technologies.

**187.** Which of the following is an example of risk on the client side of a network?

    a.    Software development tools

    b.    Scripts

    c.    Document formats

    d.    Active-X controls

*187. d.*   On the browser (client) side, unnecessary plug-ins, add-ons, or Active-X controls should be removed. It is also recommended to substitute programs with lesser functionality in lieu of fully capable helper applications or plug-ins.

The other three choices are risks from the server side. On the server side, any unnecessary software not needed in providing Web services should be removed as well, particularly any software development tools that could be used to further an attack if an intruder should gain an initial foothold. Ideally, server-side scripts should constrain users to a small set of well-defined functionality and validate the size and values of input parameters so that an attacker cannot overrun memory boundaries or piggyback arbitrary commands for execution. Scripts should be run only with minimal privileges (i.e., nonadministrator) to avoid compromising the entire website in case the scripts have security flaws. Potential security weaknesses can be exploited even when Web applications run with low privilege settings. For example, a subverted script could have enough privileges to mail out the system password file, examine the network information maps, or launch a login to a high numbered port.

Whenever possible, content providers and site operators should provide material encoded in less harmful document formats. For example, if document distillers are not available to convert textual documents into portable document format (PDF), an alternative is to make available a version in .rtf (rich text format), rather than a proprietary word processing format.

**188.** Which of the following is an issue when dealing with information cross-domains?

    a.    Authentication policy

    b.    Level of trust

    c.    Common infrastructure

    d.    Shared infrastructure

*188. b.*   An information domain is a set of active entities (e.g., person, process, or devices) and their data objects. The level of trust is always an issue when dealing with cross-domain interactions due to untrusted sources.

Authentication policy and the use of a common and shared infrastructure with appropriate protections at the operating system, application system, and workstation levels are some of solutions for ensuring effective cross-domain interactions.

**189.** Which of the following approaches isolates public-access systems from mission-critical resources?

    1.    Physical isolation

    2.    Demilitarized zones

3. Screened subnets

4. Security policies and procedures

    a. 1 and 2

    b. 2 and 3

    c. 1 and 4

    d. 1, 2, 3, and 4

**189. d.** Mission-critical resources include data, systems, and processes, which should be protected from public-access systems either physically or logically. Physical isolation may include ensuring that no physical connection exists between an organization's public information resources and an organization's critical information. When implementing a logical isolation solution, layers of security services and mechanisms should be established between public systems and secure private systems responsible for protecting mission-critical resources. Security layers may include using network architecture designs such as demilitarized zones (DMZ) and screened subnets. Finally, system designers and administrators should enforce organizational security policies and procedures regarding use of public-access systems.

190. **Enclave boundary for information assurance is defined as which of the following?**

1. The point at which information enters an organization

2. The point at which information leaves an enclave

3. The physical location is relevant to an organization

4. The logical location is relevant to an enclave

    a. 1 and 3

    b. 2 and 4

    c. 3 and 4

    d. 1, 2, 3, and 4

**190. d.** The enclave boundary is the point at which information enters or leaves the enclave or organization. Due to multiple entry and exit points, a layer of protection is needed to ensure that the information entering does not affect the organization's operation or resources, and that the information leaving is authorized. Information assets exist in physical and logical locations and boundaries exist between these locations.

191. **Operations, one of the principal aspects of the defense-in-depth strategy does *not* include which of the following?**

    a. Readiness assessments

    b. Security management

    c. Cryptographic key management

    d. Physical security

***191. d.*** Physical security is a part of the people principal, whereas all the other three choices are part of the operations principal.

**192.** **Border routers, firewalls, and software/hardware guards provide which of the following?**

    a.    First line-of-defense

    b.    Second line-of-defense

    c.    Last-of-defense

    d.    Multiple lines-of-defense

***192. a.*** Border routers, firewalls, and software/hardware guards provide a first line-of-defense against network compromises (e.g., attacks by outsiders). The line-of-defenses are security mechanisms for limiting and controlling access to and use of computer system resources. They exercise a directing or restraining influence over the behavior of individuals and the content of computer systems.

**193.** **How is a Common Gateway Interface (CGI) script vulnerable?**

    a.    Because it is interpreted.

    b.    Because it gives root access.

    c.    Because it accepts checked input.

    d.    Because it can be precompiled.

***193. a.*** The common gateway interface (CGI) scripts are interpreted, not precompiled. As such, there is a risk that a script can be modified in transit and not perform its original actions. CGI scripts should not accept unchecked input.

**194.** **Which of the following form the basic component technology of the Active-X framework?**

    a.    Active-X controls

    b.    Active-X containers

    c.    Active-X documents

    d.    Active-X scripts

***194. a.*** Active-X is a framework for Microsoft's software component technology that allows programs encapsulated in units called "controls" to be embedded in Web pages. A programmer can develop a program, wrap it in an Active-X interface, compile it, and place it on a Web page. When end users point their Web browsers (that support Active-X) at the Web page, the Active-X control downloads and attempts to execute on their computer. Because Active-X controls are simply programs, they can do anything that they are programmed to do, including causing damage by removing critical files.

Other Active-X technologies include Active-X containers, documents, and scripts. An Active-X container is an Active-X application, and an Active-X document is one kind of container. Documents allow the functionality of controls to be extended. Thus, Active-X controls form the basic component technology of the Active-X framework. Active-X containers and scripts pose security risks to the end user.

**195.** What is the first place to focus on security improvements in a client/server system?

    a.   Application software level

    b.   Database server level

    c.   Database level

    d.   Application server level

*195. c.* The first place to focus on security improvements is at the database level. One advantage is that security imposed at the database level will be consistent across all applications in a client/server system.

**196.** Poorly implemented session-tracking may provide an avenue for which of the following?

    a.   Browser-oriented attacks

    b.   Server-oriented attacks

    c.   Network-oriented attacks

    d.   User-oriented attacks

*196. b.* Web-based applications often use tracks, such as session identifiers, to provide continuity between transactions. Poorly implemented session-tracking may provide an avenue for server-oriented attacks.

**197.** Which of the following allows a layered security strategy for information systems?

    1.   Implementing lower assurance solutions with lower costs to protect less critical systems

    2.   Implementing all management, operational, and technical controls for all systems

    3.   Implementing all compensating and common controls for all systems

    4.   Implementing higher assurance solutions only at the most critical areas of a system

        a.   1 and 2

        b.   1 and 4

        c.   2 and 3

        d.   1, 2, 3, and 4

*197. b.* Management should recognize the uniqueness of each system to allow for a layered security strategy. This is achieved by implementing lower assurance solutions with lower costs to protect less critical systems and higher assurance solutions only at the most critical areas of a system. It is not practical or cost-effective to implement all management, operational, technical, compensating, and common controls for all systems.

**198.** Which of the following consists of a layered security approach to protect against a specific threat or to reduce vulnerability?

    1.   Use of packet-filtering routers

    2.   Use of an application gateway

3.   Use of strong password controls

4.   Adequate user training

    a.   1 and 2

    b.   1 and 3

    c.   2 and 3

    d.   1, 2, 3, and 4

***198. d.***   Security designs should consider a layered approach to address or protect against a specific threat or to reduce vulnerability. For example, the use of a packet-filtering router with an application gateway and an intrusion detection system combine to increase the work-factor an attacker must expend to successfully attack the system. Adding good password controls and adequate user training improves the system's security posture even more.

**199.**   **In the trusted computing base (TCB) environment, which of the following is referred to when a failure results from the modifications to the hardware?**

    a.   Compromise from above

    b.   Compromise from within

    c.   Compromise from below

    d.   Compromise from cross domains

***199. c.***   Compromise from below results when a failure occurs due to modification to the hardware. This is because the hardware is located at the bottom of the hierarchy. Compromise from above occurs when an unprivileged user can write untrusted code that exploits vulnerability. Compromise from within occurs when a privileged user or process misuses the allocated privileges. Compromise from cross domains is not relevant here.

**200.**   **Which of the following is the *most* important property of well-designed distributed systems?**

    a.   Fault tolerance through redundancy

    b.   Security protection through isolation

    c.   Extendibility through adaptability

    d.   Distribution transparency through separation of components

***200. d.***   Distribution transparency provides a unified interface to a collection of computing resources using the same names and operations regardless of their location. This means that services are delivered wherever the user is located. New components can be added to the system without interrupting system operations. The other three choices are benefits of well-designed distributed systems.

**201.** Regarding Common Criteria (CC), which of the following provides an implementation-independent statement of security needs?

    a.   Target of evaluation (TOE)

    b.   Security target (ST)

    c.   Protection profile (PP)

    d.   Evaluation of assurance level (EAL)

***201. c.*** Protection profile (PP) is an implementation-independent statement of security needs for a product type.

TOE is incorrect because it is a product that has been installed and is being operated according to its guidance. ST is incorrect because it is an implementation-dependent statement of security needs for a specific identified TOE. EAL is incorrect because it is an assurance package, consisting of assurance requirements, representing a point on the CC predefined assurance scale.

**202.** Which of the following contains a security kernel, some trusted-code facilities, hardware, and some communication channels?

    a.   Security domain

    b.   Security model

    c.   Security perimeter

    d.   Security parameters

***202. c.*** A security perimeter is a boundary within which security controls are applied to protect information assets.

The security domain is a set of elements, a security policy, an authority, and a set of relevant activities. The security model is a formal presentation of the security policy enforced by the system. Examples of security parameters include passwords and encryption keys.

**203.** Phishing attacks are *mostly* an example of which of the following?

    a.   Browser-oriented attacks

    b.   Server-oriented attacks

    c.   Network-oriented attacks

    d.   User-oriented attacks

***203. d.*** In a phishing attack, attackers try to trick users into accessing a fake website and divulging personal information. Social engineering methods are employed in phishing attacks. Note that some phishing attacks can be a blended attack targeting the browser.

**204.** In which of the following security operating modes is the system access secured to at least the top level?

    a.   Multilevel security mode

    b.   Dedicated security mode

c. Compartmented security mode

d. Controlled mode

**204. c.** Compartmented security mode is the mode of operation that allows the system to process two or more types of compartmented information (information requiring a special authorization) or any one type of compartmented information with other than compartmented information. In this mode, system access is secured to at least the top-secret level, but all system users do not necessarily need to be formally authorized to access all types of compartmented information being processed and/or stored in the system.

Multilevel security mode is incorrect. It is the mode of operation that allows two or more classification levels of information to be processed simultaneously within the same system when some users are not cleared for all levels of information present.

Dedicated security mode is incorrect. It is the mode of operation in which the system is specifically and exclusively dedicated to and controlled for the processing of one particular type or classification of information, either for full-time operation or for a specified period of time.

Controlled mode is incorrect. It is a type of multilevel security in which a more limited amount of trust is placed in the hardware/software base of the system, with resultant restrictions on the classification levels and clearance levels that may be supported.

**205.** According to the Common Criteria (CC), security functional requirements do *not* include which of the following?

a. User data protection

b. Security management

c. Configuration management

d. Resource utilization

**205. c.** According to the Common Criteria (CC), configuration management is part of security assurance requirements, not a functional requirement. The other three choices are part of the security functional requirements.

**206.** According to the Common Criteria (CC), security assurance requirements do *not* include which of the following?

a. Privacy

b. Development

c. Tests

d. Vulnerability assessment

**206. a.** According to the Common Criteria (CC), privacy is part of security functional requirements, not a security assurance requirement. The other three choices are part of the security assurance requirements.

**207.** A factor favoring acceptability of a covert channel is which of the following?

    a.    High bandwidth

    b.    Low bandwidth

    c.    Narrow bandwidth

    d.    Broad bandwidth

***207. b.*** Factors favoring acceptability of a covert channel include low bandwidth and the absence of application software that can exploit covert channels.

**208.** An information technology security principle should ensure which of the following?

    a.    No single point of access

    b.    No single point of use

    c.    No single point of responsibility

    d.    No single point of vulnerability

***208. d.*** Good IT principles provide a foundation for better IT security. For example, a sound security policy provides a strong foundation for system design. Similarly, implementing a layered security approach ensures no single point of vulnerability in a computer system. The concern here is that if the single point-of-failure occurs because vulnerability is exploited, then the entire system can be compromised, which is risky.

**209.** What is the *best* time to implement a data dictionary system?

    a.    During the development of a new application system

    b.    During the redesign of an application system

    c.    During the reengineering of an application system

    d.    During the modification of an application system

***209. a.*** Although it is best to implement a data dictionary during development of a new application system, it can also be implemented during a major redesign, reengineering, or maintenance of an existing application system.

**210.** Mapping information security needs to business data is a part of which of the following to secure multi-user and multiplatform environments?

    a.    Management controls

    b.    Technical controls

    c.    Physical controls

    d.    Procedural controls

***210. a.*** Management controls deal with policies and directives. Mapping information security needs to business data is a management policy. Technical controls deal with technology and systems. Physical controls and procedural controls are part of operational controls, which are day-to-day procedures.

**211.** Which of the following is *not* an example of the basic components of a generic Web browser?

    a.    Java

    b.    Active-X

    c.    CGI

    d.    Plug-ins

***211. c.*** The common gateway interface (CGI) is an industry standard for communicating between a Web server and another program. It is a part of a generic Web server. Java, Active X, and plug-ins are incorrect because they are a part of a generic Web browser.

**212.** Masquerading is an example of which of the following threat categories that apply to systems on the Internet?

    a.    Browser-oriented

    b.    Software-oriented

    c.    Server-oriented

    d.    Network-oriented

***212. a.*** Internet-related threats are broken down into three categories: browser-oriented, server-oriented, and network-oriented. Software-oriented is a generic category useful to the other categories. Software-oriented threats may result from software complexity, configuration, and quality. Web servers can launch attacks against Web browser components and technologies. Because browsers can support multiple associations with different Web servers as separate windowed contexts, the mobile code of one context can also target another context. Unauthorized access may occur simply through a lack of adequate access control mechanisms or weak identification and authentication controls, which allow untrusted code to act or masquerade as a trusted component. After access is gained, information residing at the platform can be disclosed or altered.

**213.** Which of the following is required to ensure a foolproof security over a mobile code?

    a.    Firewalls

    b.    Antivirus software

    c.    Intrusion detection and prevention systems

    d.    Cascaded defense-in-depth measures

***213. d.*** Cascaded defense-in-depth measures come close to providing foolproof security over a mobile code with examples such as firewalls, antivirus software, intrusion detection and prevention systems, and behavior blocking technologies. Although firewalls, antivirus software, and intrusion detection and prevention systems provide useful safeguards, they do not provide strong security due to the existence of a variety of techniques for deception such as mutation, segmentation, and disguise via extended character set encoding.

**214.** The Common Criteria (CC) permits which of the following between the results of independent security evaluations?

 a. Usability

 b. Comparability

 c. Scalability

 d. Reliability

***214. b.*** The Common Criteria (CC) permits comparability between the results of independent security evaluations. The evaluation process establishes a level of confidence that the security functionality of IT products and the assurance measures applied to these IT products meet a common set of requirements. The CC is applicable to IT security functionality implemented in hardware, firmware, or software.

Usability is incorrect because it means such things as easy to learn and remember, productivity enhancing, error resistant, and friendly features.

Scalability is incorrect because it means the system can be made to have more or less computational power by configuring it with a larger or smaller number of processors, amount of memory, interconnection bandwidth, input/output bandwidth, and amount of mass storage. Reliability is incorrect because it means the system can be counted upon to perform as expected.

**215.** The Common Criteria (CC) is *not* useful as a guide for which of the following when evaluating the security functionality of IT products?

 a. Development

 b. Evaluation

 c. Procurement

 d. Implementation

***215. d.*** The CC is useful as a guide for the development, evaluation, and/or procurement of products with IT security functionality. The CC is not useful in implementation because implementation scenarios can vary from organization to organization.

**216.** The Common Criteria (CC) addresses which of the following in an uncommon way?

 a. Confidentiality

 b. Risks

 c. Integrity

 d. Availability

***216. b.*** The Common Criteria (CC) addresses information protection from unauthorized disclosure (confidentiality), modification (integrity), or loss of use (availability), which is a common way. The CC is also applicable to risks arising from human activities (malicious or otherwise) and to risks arising from nonhuman activities, which is an uncommon way.

**217.** **The scope of Common Criteria (CC) covers which of the following?**

    a.   Physical protection

    b.   Administrative security

    c.   Electromagnetic emanation control

    d.   Quality of cryptographic algorithm

*217. a.* In particular, the Common Criteria (CC) addresses some aspects of physical protection. CC does not contain security evaluation criteria pertaining to administrative security measures not related directly to the IT security functionality. CC does not cover the evaluation of technical physical aspects of IT security such as electromagnetic emanation control. CC does not cover the inherent qualities of cryptographic algorithms.

**218.** **Which of the following requires that all users must have formal access approval?**

    a.   Compartmented security mode

    b.   System-high security mode

    c.   Controlled mode

    d.   Limited access mode

*218. b.* The system-high security mode requires that if the system processes special access information, all users must have formal access approval.

**219.** **Protecting interconnectivity communication devices is a part of which of the following to secure multi-user and multiplatform environments?**

    a.   Management controls

    b.   Technical controls

    c.   Physical controls

    d.   Procedural controls

*219. c.* Physical controls and procedural controls are part of operational controls, which are day-to-day procedures. Physical security controls (e.g., locked rooms and closets) are used to protect interconnectivity communication devices. Management controls deal with policies and directives. Technical controls deal with technology and systems.

**220.** **Which of the following is *not* a broad-based security objective for ensuring information systems protection?**

    a.   Prepare and prevent

    b.   Breach and damage

    c.   Detect and respond

    d.   Build and grow

*220. b.* Breach and damage are narrow-based security objectives because they signify the occurrence of a security incident and recovery from its damage. The scope of prepare and prevent includes minimizing the possibility of a significant attack on critical information assets and networks. Detect and respond includes identifying and assessing an attack in a timely manner. Build and grow is building organizations and facilities, hiring and training people, and establishing policies and procedures.

**221.** **The totality of protection mechanisms used for enforcing a security policy is which of the following?**

    a.    Trusted computing base

    b.    Trusted path

    c.    Trusted software

    d.    Trusted subject

*221. a.* The trusted computing base (TCB) is the totality of protection mechanisms within a computer system, including hardware, firmware, and software, the combination of which is responsible for enforcing a security policy. The other three choices are part of the TCB.

**222.** **Requiring signed conflict-of-interest and nondisclosure statements are a part of which of the following to secure multi-user and multiplatform environments?**

    a.    Management controls

    b.    Technical controls

    c.    Physical controls

    d.    Procedural controls

*222. d.* Physical controls and procedural controls are part of operational controls, which are day-to-day procedures. Requiring signed conflict of interest and nondisclosure statements are a part of procedural controls. Management controls deal with policies and directives. Technical controls deal with technology and systems.

**223.** **Taken to its extreme, what does active content become?**

    a.    Built-in macro processing

    b.    Delivery mechanism for mobile code

    c.    Scripting language

    d.    Virtual machine

*223. b.* Taken to its extreme, active content becomes, in effect, a delivery mechanism for mobile code. Active content involves a host of new technologies such as built-in macro processing, scripting language, and virtual machine.

**224.** **A denial-of-service attack is an example of which of the following threat categories that apply to systems on the Internet?**

    a.    Browser-oriented

    b.    User-oriented

c. Server-oriented

d. Network-oriented

**224. d.** Attacks can be launched against the network infrastructure used to communicate between the browser and server. An attacker can gain information by masquerading as a Web server using a man-in-the middle attack, whereby requests and responses are conveyed via the impostor as a watchful intermediary. Such a Web spoofing attack allows the impostor to shadow not only a single targeted server, but also every subsequent server accessed. Other obvious attack methods lie outside the browser-server framework and involve targeting either the communications or the supporting platforms. Denial-of-service (DoS) attacks through available network interfaces are another possibility, as are exploits involving any existing platform vulnerability.

225. In the trusted computing base (TCB) environment, which of the following is referred to when a security administrator accidentally or intentionally configures the access tables incorrectly?

a. Compromise from above

b. Compromise from within

c. Compromise from below

d. Compromise from cross domains

**225. b.** Compromise from within results when a security administrator accidentally or intentionally configures the access tables incorrectly. Compromise from above occurs when an unprivileged user can write untrusted code that exploits vulnerability. Compromise from below occurs as a result of accidental failure of an underlying trusted component. Compromise from cross domains is not relevant here.

# SCENARIO-BASED QUESTIONS, ANSWERS, AND EXPLANATIONS

Use the following information to answer questions 1 through 12.

The SRC Company is a software development firm serving major military markets. It builds off-the-shelf software, which eventually is bought by the public. For certification and accreditation purposes, it is applying for evaluation of assurance level (EAL)–4 for two of its new products. The company has a repeatable software development process in place. It semi-formally designs and tests each product. It methodically reviews the development process.

1. Regarding Common Criteria (CC), which of the following provides an implementation-independent statement of security needs?

a. Target of evaluation (TOE)

b. Security target (ST)

    c.    Protection profile (PP)

    d.    Evaluation of assurance level (EAL)

*1. c.*    Protection profile (PP) is an implementation-independent statement of security needs for a product type. TOE is incorrect because it is a product that has been installed and is being operated according to its guidance. ST is incorrect because it is an implementation-dependent statement of security needs for a specific identified TOE. EAL is incorrect because it is an assurance package, consisting of assurance requirements, representing a point on the CC predefined assurance scale.

2.    **The Common Criteria (CC) permits which of the following between the results of independent security evaluations?**

    a.    Usability

    b.    Comparability

    c.    Scalability

    d.    Reliability

*2. b.*    The Common Criteria (CC) permits comparability between the results of independent security evaluations. The evaluation process establishes a level of confidence that the security functionality of IT products and the assurance measures applied to these IT products meet a common set of requirements. The CC is applicable to IT security functionality implemented in hardware, firmware, or software. Usability is incorrect because it means easy to learn and remember, productivity enhancing, error resistant, and friendly. Scalability is incorrect because it means the system can be made to have more or less computational power by configuring it with a larger or smaller number of processors, amount of memory, interconnection bandwidth, input/output bandwidth, and amount of mass storage. Reliability is incorrect because it means the system can be counted upon to perform as expected.

3.    **The Common Criteria (CC) is *not* useful as a guide for which of the following when evaluating the security functionality of IT products?**

    a.    Development

    b.    Evaluation

    c.    Procurement

    d.    Implementation

*3. d.*    The Common Criteria (CC) is useful as a guide for the development, evaluation, and/ or procurement of products with IT security functionality. Implementation scenarios can vary from organization to organization.

4.    **The Common Criteria (CC) addresses which of the following in an uncommon way?**

    a.    Confidentiality

    b.    Risks

    c.    Integrity

    d.    Availability

**4. b.**    The Common Criteria (CC) addresses information protection from unauthorized disclosure (confidentiality), modification (integrity), or loss of use (availability). These are the most common ways. The CC is also applicable to risks arising from human activities (malicious or otherwise) and to risks arising from nonhuman activities, which is an uncommon way.

**5.**    **The scope of Common Criteria (CC) covers which of the following?**

    a.    Physical protection

    d.    Administrative security

    c.    Electromagnetic emanation control

    d.    Quality of cryptographic algorithm

**5. a.**    In particular, the Common Criteria (CC) addresses some aspects of physical protection. Administrative security is incorrect because the CC does not contain security evaluation criteria pertaining to administrative security measures not related directly to the IT security functionality. Electromagnetic emanation control is incorrect because the CC does not cover the evaluation of technical physical aspects of IT security such as electromagnetic emanation control. Quality of cryptographic algorithm is incorrect because the CC does not cover the inherent qualities of cryptographic algorithms.

**6.**    **Which of the following is *not* one of the target audiences of the Common Criteria (CC) from a general interest viewpoint?**

    a.    Security designers

    b.    Consumers

    c.    Developers

    d.    Evaluators

**6. a.**    There are three groups with a general interest in evaluating the security properties of target of evaluations (TOEs): consumers, developers, and evaluators. Additional interest groups that can benefit from information contained in the Common Criteria (CC) are system custodians, system security officers, auditors, security architects, and security designers.

**7.**    **Regarding the Common Criteria (CC), which of the following alone is not sufficient for use in common evaluation methodology?**

1.    Repeatability

2.    Objectivity

3.    Judgment

4.    Knowledge

    a.    1 only

    b.    2 only

    c.    1 and 2

    d.    3 and 4

**7. c.**   Use of a common evaluation methodology contributes to the repeatability and objectivity of the results but it is not by itself sufficient. Many of the evaluation criteria require the application of expert judgment and background knowledge for which consistency is more difficult to achieve.

**8.**    **Regarding the Common Criteria (CC), precise and universal rating for IT security products is infeasible due to:**

1.    Reducing risks

2.    Protecting assets

3.    Objective elements

4.    Subjective elements

    a.    1 only

    b.    2 only

    c.    1 and 2

    d.    3 and 4

**8. d.**   Evaluation should lead to objective and repeatable results that can be cited as evidence, even if there is no totally objective scale for representing the results of a security evaluation. As the application of criteria contains objective and subjective elements, precise and universal ratings for IT security are infeasible. Reducing risks and protecting assets are the outcomes of a target of evaluation (TOE).

**9.**    **Regarding the Common Criteria (CC), how should a Security Target (ST) be used?**

1.    Before evaluation

2.    After evaluation

3.    Detailed specification

4.    Complete specification

    a.    1 only

    b.    2 only

    c.    1 and 2

    d.    3 and 4

**9. c.**   A typical ST fulfills two roles, such as before and during the evaluation and after the evaluation. Two roles that a security target (ST) should not fulfill include a detailed specification and a complete specification.

**10.** **Regarding the Common Criteria (CC), how should a Protection Profile (PP) be used?**

1. Specification of a single product

2. Complete specification

3. Requirements specification

4. Baseline

    a.    1 only

    b.    2 only

    c.    1 and 2

    d.    3 and 4

*10. d.* A protection profile (PP) is typically used as part of a requirement specification, part of a regulation from a specific regulatory entity, or a baseline defined by a group of IT developers. Three roles that a PP should not fulfill include a detailed specification, a complete specification, and a specification of a single product.

**11.** **Regarding the Common Criteria (CC), the outcome of a target of evaluation (TOE) leads to:**

1. Objective results

2. Repeatable results

3. Defensible results

4. Evidential results

    a.    1 and 2

    b.    2 and 3

    c.    3 and 4

    d.    1, 2, 3, and 4

*11. d.* The TOE leads to objective and repeatable results that are defensible and can be cited as evidence.

**12.** **Regarding the Common Criteria (CC), which of the following is not an example of mitigating the effects of a threat?**

    a.    Restricting the ability of a threat agent in accessing IT assets to perform adverse actions

    b.    Making frequent backup copies of IT assets

    c.    Obtaining extra copies or spare parts of IT assets

    d.    Insuring IT assets

**12. a.** Examples of threats include (i) a hacker remotely copying confidential files from a company network, (ii) a worm seriously degrading the performance of a wide-area network, (iii) a virus sending out stored confidential e-mail to random recipients, (iv) a system administrator violating user privacy, and (v) a malicious TOE developer-employee modifying the source code. Restricting the ability of a threat agent to perform adverse actions is an example of diminishing a threat, not mitigating the effects of a threat with security controls.

The other three choices are incorrect because they are examples of mitigating the effects of a threat with security controls (e.g., backup, spare parts, and insurance). Threat agents are entities that can adversely act on assets. Examples of threat agents are hackers, users, computer processes, TOE development personnel, and accidents.

## SOURCES AND REFERENCES

"Common Criteria for Information Technology Security Evaluation Part 1: Introduction and General Model, Version 3.1 and Revision 1," Common Criteria Portal, September 2006. (www.commoncriteriaportal.org/files/ccfiles).

"Engineering Principles for Information Technology Security (NIST SP800-27Revision A)," National Institute of Standards and Technology (NIST), U.S. Department of Commerce, Gaithersburg, Maryland, June 2004.

"Guidelines on Active Content and Mobile Code (NIST SP800-28V2 Draft)," National Institute of Standards and Technology (NIST), U.S. Department of Commerce, Gaithersburg, Maryland, August 2007.

"Guidelines to Federal Organizations on Security Assurance and Acquisition, Use of Tested, Evaluated Products (NIST SP 800-23)," National Institute of Standards and Technology (NIST), U.S. Department of Commerce, Gaithersburg, Maryland, August 2000.

"Information Assurance Technical Framework (IATF), Release 3.1," National Security Agency (NSA), Fort Meade, Maryland, September 2002.

"Information Technology Security Evaluation Criteria (ITSEC), Harmonized Criteria of France – Germany, the Netherlands, the United Kingdom," Commission of the European Communities Directorate XIII/F SOG-IS, June 1991. (www.iwar.org.uk/comsec/resources/standards/itsec.htm).

"Service Component-Based Architectures, Version 2.0," CIO Council, June 2004 (www.cio.gov).

"Underlying Technical Models for Information Technology Security (NIST SP800-33)," National Institute of Standards and Technology (NIST), U.S. Department of Commerce, Gaithersburg, Maryland, December 2001.

# DOMAIN 7

## Security Operations

### TRADITIONAL QUESTIONS, ANSWERS, AND EXPLANATIONS

1. **Regarding media sanitization, which of the following is the correct order for fully and physically destroying hand-held devices, such as cell phones?**

    1. Incinerate
    2. Disintegrate
    3. Pulverize
    4. Shred

        a. 3, 2, 1, and 4
        b. 4, 2, 3, and 1
        c. 1, 4, 3, and 2
        d. 1, 2, 4, and 3

*1. b.* The correct order for fully and physically destroying hand-held devices such as cell phones is shred, disintegrate, pulverize, and incinerate. This is the best recommended practice for both public and private sector organizations.

Shredding is a method of sanitizing media and is the act of cutting or tearing into small particles. Here, the shredding step comes first to make the cell phone inoperable quickly. Disintegration is a method of sanitizing media and is the act of separating the equipment into component parts. Disintegration cannot be the first step because some determined attacker can assemble these parts and can make the cell phone work. Pulverization is a method of sanitizing media and is the act of grinding to a powder or dust. Incineration is a method of sanitizing media and is the act of burning completely to ashes done in a licensed incinerator. Note that one does not need to complete all these methods, but can stop after any specific method and after reaching the final goal based on the sensitivity and criticality of data on the device.

**2.** **Which of the following detects unauthorized changes to software and information for commercial off-the-shelf integrity mechanisms?**

1. Tamper-evident system components

2. Parity checks

3. Cyclical redundancy checks

4. Cryptographic hashes

    a. 2 only

    b. 2 and 3

    c. 3 and 4

    d. 1, 2, 3, and 4

*2. d.* Organizations employ integrity verification mechanisms to look for evidence of tampering, errors, and omissions. Software engineering techniques such as parity checks, cyclical redundancy checks, and cryptographic hashes are applied to the information system. In addition, tamper-evident system components are required to ship from software vendors to operational sites, and during their operation.

**3.** **Effective configuration change controls for hardware, software, and firmware include:**

1. Auditing the enforcement actions

2. Preventing the installation of software without a signed certificate

3. Enforcing the two-person rule for changes to systems

4. Limiting the system developer/integrator privileges

    a. 1 only

    b. 3 only

    c. 2 and 4

    d. 1, 2, 3, and 4

*3. d.* All four items are effective in managing configuration changes to hardware, software, and firmware components of a system.

**4.** **An information system can be protected against denial-of-service (DoS) attacks through:**

1. Network perimeter devices

2. Increased capacity

3. Increased bandwidth

4. Service redundancy

    a. 2 only

    b. 3 only

      c.    4 only

      d.    1, 2, 3, and 4

***4. d.*** Network perimeter devices can filter certain types of packets to protect devices on an organization's internal network from being directly affected by denial-of-service (DoS) attacks. Employing increased capacity and increased bandwidth combined with service redundancy may reduce the susceptibility to some type of DoS attacks. A side-benefit of this is enabling availability of data, which is a good thing.

**5.** **What is the *major* purpose of conducting a post-incident analysis for a computer security incident?**

      a.    To determine how security threats and vulnerabilities were addressed

      b.    To learn how the attack was done

      c.    To re-create the original attack

      d.    To execute the response to an attack

***5. a.*** The major reason for conducting a post-incident analysis is to determine whether security weaknesses were properly and effectively addressed. Security holes must be plugged to prevent recurrence. The other three choices are minor reasons.

**6.** **Which of the following is an example of a reactive approach to software security?**

      a.    Patch-and-patch

      b.    Penetrate-and-patch

      c.    Patch-and-penetrate

      d.    Penetrate-and-penetrate

***6. b.*** Crackers and hackers attempt to break into computer systems by finding flaws in software, and then system administrators apply patches sent by vendors to fix the flaws. In this scenario of penetrate-and-patch, patches are applied after penetration has occurred, which is an example of a reactive approach. The scenario of patch-and patch is good because one is always patching, which is a proactive approach. The scenario of patch-and-penetrate is a proactive approach in which organizations apply vendor patches in a timely manner. There is not much damage done when crackers and hackers penetrate (break) into the computer system because all known flaws are fixed. In this scenario, patches are applied before penetration occurs. The scenario of penetrate-and-penetrate is bad because patches are not applied at all or are not effective.

**7.** **Regarding a patch management program, which of the following is an example of vulnerability?**

      a.    Misconfigurations

      b.    Rootkits

      c.    Trojan horses

      d.    Exploits

**7. a.** Misconfiguration vulnerabilities cause a weakness in the security of a system. Vulnerabilities can be exploited by a malicious entity to violate policies such as gaining greater access or permission than is authorized on a computer. Threats are capabilities or methods of attack developed by malicious entities to exploit vulnerabilities and potentially cause harm to a computer system or network. Threats usually take the form of exploit scripts, worms, viruses, rootkits, Trojan horses, and other exploits.

8. An information system initiates session auditing work at system:

    a.    Restart

    b.    Shutdown

    c.    Startup

    d.    Abort

**8. c.** Information system transitional states include startup, restart, shutdown, and abort. It is critical to initiate session audit work at system startup time so that the system captures and logs all the content related to a user system. These audit logs can be locally or remotely reviewed for later evidence.

9. The *major* reason for retaining older versions of baseline configuration is to support:

    a.    Roll forward

    b.    Rollback

    c.    Restart

    d.    Restore

**9. b.** A rollback is restoring a database from one point in time to an earlier point. A roll forward is restoring the database from a point in time when it is known to be correct to a later time. A restart is the resumption of the execution of a computer system using the data recorded at a checkpoint. A restore is the process of retrieving a dataset migrated to offline storage and restoring it to online storage.

10. Which of the following updates the applications software and the systems software with patches and new versions?

    a.    Preventive maintenance

    b.    Component maintenance

    c.    Hardware maintenance

    d.    Periodic maintenance

**10. a.** The scope of preventive maintenance includes updating applications software and systems software with patches and new versions, replacing failed hardware components, and more.

The other three choices are incorrect because they can be a part of corrective maintenance (fixing errors) or remedial maintenance (fixing faults).

**11.** Regarding incident handling, dynamic reconfiguration does *not* include changes to which of the following?

    a.    Router rules

    b.    Access control lists

    c.    Filter rules

    d.    Software libraries

*11. d.* Software libraries are part of access restrictions for change so changes are controlled. Dynamic reconfiguration (i.e., changes on-the-fly) can include changes to router rules, access control lists, intrusion detection and prevention systems (IDPS) parameters, and filter rules for firewalls and gateways.

**12.** Prior to initiating maintenance work by maintenance vendor personnel who do not have the needed security clearances and access authorization to classified information, adequate controls include:

    1.    Sanitize all volatile information storage components

    2.    Remove all nonvolatile storage media

    3.    Physically disconnect the storage media from the system

    4.    Properly secure the storage media with physical or logical access controls

        a.    1 only

        b.    2 only

        c.    2, 3, and 4

        d.    1, 2, 3, and 4

*12. d.* All four items are adequate controls to reduce the risk resulting from maintenance vendor personnel's access to classified information. For handling classified information, maintenance personnel should possess security clearance levels equal to the highest level of security required for an information system.

**13.** A security configuration checklist is referred to as which of the following?

    1.    Lockdown guide

    2.    Hardening guide

    3.    Security guide

    4.    Benchmark guide

        a.    1 and 2

        b.    1 and 3

        c.    2 and 3

        d.    1, 2, 3, and 4

**13. d.** A security configuration checklist is referred to as several names, such as a lock-down guide, hardening guide, security technical implementation guide, or benchmark guide. These guides provide a series of instructions or procedures for configuring an information system's components to meet operational needs and regulatory requirements.

**14.** Regarding the verification of correct operation of security functions, which of the following is the correct order of alternative actions when anomalies are discovered?

1.  Report the results.

2.  Notify the system administrator.

3.  Shut down the system.

4.  Restart the system.

    a.   1, 2, 3, and 4

    b.   3, 4, 2, and 1

    c.   2, 1, 3, and 4

    d.   2, 3, 4, and 1

**14. d.** The correct order of alternative actions is notify the system administrator, shut down the system, restart the system, and report the results of security function verification.

**15.** The audit log does *not* include which of the following?

    a.   Timestamp

    b.   User's identity

    c.   Object's identity

    d.   The results of action taken

**15. d.** The audit log includes a timestamp, user's identity, object's identity, and type of action taken, but not the results from the action taken. The person reviewing the audit log needs to verify that the results of the action taken were appropriate.

**16.** Which of the following fault tolerance metrics are most applicable to the proper functioning of redundant array of disks (RAID) systems?

1.  Mean time between failures (MTBF)

2.  Mean time to data loss (MTTDL)

3.  Mean time to recovery (MTTR)

4.  Mean time between outages (MTBO)

    a.   1 and 2

    b.   1 and 3

    c.   2 and 3

    d.   3 and 4

*16. c.* Rapid replacement of RAID's failed drives or disks and rebuilding them quickly is important, which is facilitated specifically and mostly through applying MTTDL and MTTR metrics. The MTTDL metric measures the average time before a loss of data occurred in a given disk array. The MTTR metric measures the amount of time it takes to resume normal operation, and includes the time to replace a failed disk and the time to rebuild the disk array. Thus, MTTDL and MTTR metrics prevent data loss and ensure data recovery.

MTBF and MTBO metrics are incorrect because they are broad measures of providing system reliability and availability respectively, and are not specifically applicable to RAID systems. The MTBF metric measures the average time interval between system failures and the MTBO metric measures the mean time between equipment failures.

**17.** **All the following have redundancy built in *except*:**

    a.    Fast Ethernet

    b.    Fiber distributed data interface

    c.    Normal Ethernet

    d.    Synchronous optical network

*17. c.* Normal Ethernet does not have a built-in redundancy. Fast Ethernet has built-in redundancy with redundant cabling for file servers and network switches. Fiber distributed data interface (FDDI) offers an optional bypass switch at each node for addressing failures. Synchronous optical network (SONET) is inherently redundant and fault tolerant by design.

**18.** **Which of the following go hand-in-hand?**

    a.    Zero-day warez and content delivery networks

    b.    Zero-day warez and ad-hoc networks

    c.    Zero-day warez and wireless sensor networks

    d.    Zero-day warez and converged networks

*18. a.* Zero-day warez (negative day or zero-day) refers to software, games, music, or movies (media) unlawfully released or obtained on the day of public release. An internal employee of a content delivery company or an external hacker obtains illegal copies on the day of the official release. Content delivery networks distribute such media from the content owner. The other three networks do not distribute such media.

Bluetooth mobile devices use ad-hoc networks, wireless sensor networks monitor security of a building perimeter and environmental status in a building (temperature and humidity), and converged networks combine two different networks such as voice and data.

**19.** **Which of the following provides total independence?**

    a.    Single-person control

    b.    Dual-person control

    c.    Two physical keys

    d.    Two hardware tokens

**19. a.** Single-person control means total independence because there is only one person performing a task or activity. In the other three choices, two individuals or two devices (for example, keys and tokens) work together, which is difficult to bypass unless collusion is involved.

**20.** The use of a no-trespassing warning banner at a computer system's initial logon screen is an example of which of the following?

    a. Correction tactic

    b. Detection tactic

    c. Compensating tactic

    d. Deterrence tactic

**20. d.** The use of no-trespassing warning banners on initial logon screens is a deterrent tactic to scare system intruders and to provide legal evidence. The other three choices come after the deterrence tactic.

**21.** Countermeasures applied when inappropriate and/or unauthorized modifications have occurred to security functions include:

    1. Reversing the change

    2. Halting the system

    3. Triggering an audit alert

    4. Reviewing the records of change

        a. 1 only

        b. 2 only

        c. 3 only

        d. 1, 2, 3, and 4

**21. d.** Safeguards and countermeasures (controls) applied when inappropriate and/or unauthorized modifications have occurred to security functions and mechanisms include reversing the change, halting the system, triggering an audit alert, and reviewing the records of change. These countermeasures would reduce the risk to an information system.

**22.** Which of the following situations provides no security protection?

    a. Controls that are designed and implemented

    b. Controls that are developed and implemented

    c. Controls that are planned and implemented

    d. Controls that are available, but not implemented

**22. d.** Controls that are available in a computer system, but not implemented, provide no protection.

**23.** **A computer system is clogged in which of the following attacks?**

    a.    Brute force attack

    b.    Denial-of-service attack

    c.    IP spoofing attack

    d.    Web spoofing attack

***23. b.*** The denial-of-service (DoS) type of attack denies services to users by either clogging the system with a series of irrelevant messages or sending disruptive commands to the system. It does not damage the data. A brute force attack is trying every possible decryption key combination to break into a computer system. An Internet Protocol (IP) spoofing attack means intruders creating packets with spoofed source IP addresses. The intruder then takes over an open-terminal and login-connections. In a Web spoofing attack, the intruder sits between the victim user and the Web, thereby making it a man-in-the-middle attack. The user is duped into supplying the intruder with passwords, credit card information, and other sensitive and useful data.

**24.** **Which of the following is *not* an effective, active, and preventive technique to protect the integrity of audit information and audit tools?**

    a.    Backing up the audit records

    b.    Using a cryptographic-signed hash

    c.    Protecting the key used to generate the hash

    d.    Using the public key to verify the hash

***24. a.*** Backing up the audit records is a passive and detective action, and hence not effective in protecting integrity. In general, backups provide availability of data, not integrity of data, and they are there when needed. The other three choices, which are active and preventive, use cryptographic mechanisms (for example, keys and hashes), and therefore are effective in protecting the integrity of audit-related information.

**25.** **Regarding a patch management program, which of the following should *not* be done to a compromised system?**

    a.    Reformatting

    b.    Reinstalling

    c.    Restoring

    d.    Remigrating

***25. d.*** In most cases a compromised system should be reformatted and reinstalled or restored from a known safe and trusted backup. Remigrating deals with switching between using automated and manual patching tools and methods should not be performed on a compromised system.

**26.** Which of the following is the *most* malicious Internet-based attack?

  a.   Spoofing attack

  b.   Denial-of-service attack

  c.   Spamming attack

  d.   Locking attack

**26. b.**   Denial-of-service (DoS) attack is the most malicious Internet-based attack because it floods the target computer with hundreds of incomplete Internet connections per second, effectively preventing any other network connections from being made to the victim network server. The result is a denial-of-service to users, consumption of system resources, or a crash in the target computer. Spoofing attacks use various techniques to subvert IP-based access control by masquerading as another system by using its IP address. Spamming attacks post identical messages to multiple unrelated newsgroups. They are often used in cheap advertising to promote pyramid schemes or simply to annoy people. Locking attack prevents users from accessing and running shared programs such as those found in Microsoft Office product.

**27.** Denial-of-service attacks can be prevented by which of the following?

  a.   Redundancy

  b.   Isolation

  c.   Policies

  d.   Procedures

**27. a.**   Redundancy in data and/or equipment can be designed so that service cannot be removed or denied. Isolation is just the opposite of redundancy. Policies and procedures are not effective against denial-of-service (DoS) attacks because they are examples of management controls. DoS requires technical controls such as redundancy.

**28.** Which of the following denial-of-service attacks in networks is *least* common in occurrence?

  a.   Service overloading

  b.   Message flooding

  c.   Connection clogging

  d.   Signal grounding

**28. d.**   In denial-of-service (DoS) attacks, some users prevent other legitimate users from using the network. Signal grounding, which is located in wiring closets, can be used to disable a network. This can prevent users from transmitting or receiving messages until the problem is fixed. Signal grounding is the least common in occurrence as compared to other choices because it requires physical access.

Service overloading occurs when floods of network requests are made to a server daemon on a single computer. It cannot process regular tasks in a timely manner.

Message flooding occurs when a user slows down the processing of a system on the network, to prevent the system from processing its normal workload, by "flooding" the machine with network messages addressed to it. The system spends most of its time responding to these messages.

Connection clogging occurs when users make connection requests with forged source addresses that specify nonexistent or unreachable hosts that cannot be contacted. Thus, there is no way to trace the connection back; they remain until they time out or reset. The goal is to use up the limit of partially open connections.

**29.** **Smurf is an example of which of the following?**

    a.    IP address spoofing attack

    b.    Denial-of-service attack

    c.    Redirect attack

    d.    TCP sequence number attack

*29. b.* Smurf attacks use a network that accepts broadcast ping packets to flood the target computer with ping reply packets. The goal of a smurf attack is to deny service.

Internet Protocol (IP) address spoofing attack and transmission control protocol (TCP) sequence number attack are examples of session hijacking attacks. The IP address spoofing is falsifying the identity of a computer system. In a redirect attack, a hacker redirects the TCP stream through the hacker's computer. The TCP sequence number attack is a prediction of the sequence number needed to carry out an unauthorized handshake.

**30.** **The demand for reliable computing is increasing. Reliable computing has which of the following desired elements in computer systems?**

    a.    Data integrity and availability

    b.    Data security and privacy

    c.    Confidentiality and modularity

    d.    Portability and feasibility

*30. a.* Data integrity and availability are two important elements of reliable computing. Data integrity is the concept of ensuring that data can be maintained in an unimpaired condition and is not subject to unauthorized modification, whether intentional or inadvertent. Products such as backup software, antivirus software, and disk repair utility programs help protect data integrity in personal computers (PCs) and workstations. Availability is the property that a given resource will be usable during a given time period. PCs and servers are becoming an integral part of complex networks with thousands of hardware and software components (for example, hubs, routers, bridges, databases, and directory services) and the complex nature of client/server networks drives the demand for availability. System availability is increased when system downtime or outages are decreased and when fault tolerance hardware and software are used.

Data security, privacy, and confidentiality are incorrect because they deal with ensuring that data is disclosed only to authorized individuals and have nothing to do with reliable computing. Modularity deals with the breaking down of a large system into small modules. Portability deals with the ability of application software source code and data to be transported without significant modification to more than one type of computer platform or more than one type of operating system. Portability has nothing to do with reliable computing. Feasibility deals with the degree to which the requirements can be implemented under existing constraints.

31. **Which of the following is *not* a part of implementation of incident response support resources in an organization?**

    a.    Help desk

    b.    Assistance group

    c.    Forensics services

    d.    Simulated events

*31. d.* An organization incorporates simulated events into incident response training to facilitate effective response by individuals in crisis situations. The other three choices are possible implementations of incident response support resources in an organization.

32. **Software flaw remediation is *best* when it is incorporated into which of the following?**

    a.    Configuration management process

    b.    Security assessments

    c.    Continuous monitoring

    d.    Incident response activities

*32. a.* Software flaws result in potential vulnerabilities. The configuration management process can track and verify the required or anticipated flaw remediation actions.

Flaws discovered during security assessments, continuous monitoring, incident-response activities, or system error handling activities become inputs to the configuration management process. Automated patch management tools should facilitate flaw remediation by promptly installing security-relevant software updates (for example, patches, service packs, and hot fixes).

33. **Audit trails establish which of the following information security objectives?**

    a.    Confidentiality

    b.    Integrity

    c.    Accountability

    d.    Availability

*33. c.* Accountability is the existence of a record that permits the identification of an individual who performed some specific activity so that responsibility for that activity can be established through audit trails. Audit trails do not establish the other three choices.

**34.** Audit trails are *least* useful to which of the following?

    a.    Training

    b.    Deterrence

    c.    Detection

    d.    Prosecution

*34. a.* Audit trails are useful in detecting unauthorized and illegal activities. They also act as a deterrent and aid in prosecution of transgressors. They are least useful in training because audit trails are recorded after the fact. They show what was done, when, and by whom.

**35.** In terms of audit records, which of the following information is *most* useful?

    1.    Timestamps

    2.    Source and destination address

    3.    Privileged commands

    4.    Group account users

        a.    1 only

        b.    1 and 2

        c.    3 and 4

        d.    1, 2, 3, and 4

*35. c.* Audit records contain minimum information such as timestamps, source and destination addresses, and outcome of the event (i.e., success or failure). But the most useful information is recording of privileged commands and the individual identities of group account users.

**36.** Which of the following is an example of improper separation of duties?

    a.    Computer security is embedded into computer operations.

    b.    Security administrators are separate from security auditors.

    c.    Mission-critical functions and support functions are separate from each other.

    d.    Quality assurance is separate from network security.

*36. a.* A natural tension often exists between computer security and computer operations functions. Some organizations embed a computer security program in computer operations to resolve this tension. The typical result of this organizational strategy is a computer security program that lacks independence, has minimal authority, receives little management attention, and has few resources to work with. The other three choices are examples of proper separation of duties.

**37.** What are labels used on internal data structures called?

    a.    Automated marking

    b.    Automated labeling

    c.    Hard-copy labeling

    d.    Output labeling

***37. b.*** Automated labeling refers to labels used on internal data structures such as records and files within the information system. Automated marking refers to labels used on external media such as hard-copy documents and output from the information system (for example, reports).

**38.** **Which of the following is *not* allowed when an information system cannot be sanitized due to a system failure?**

    a.    Periodic maintenance

    b.    Remote maintenance

    c.    Preventive maintenance

    d.    Detective maintenance

***38. b.*** Media sanitization (scrubbing) means removing information from media such that information recovery is not possible. Specifically, it removes all labels, markings, and activity logs. An organization approves, controls, and monitors remotely executed maintenance and diagnostic activities. If the information system cannot be sanitized due to a system failure, remote maintenance is not allowed because it is a high-risk situation. The other three types of maintenance are low risk situations.

**39.** **Regarding configuration change management, organizations should analyze new software in which of the following libraries before installation?**

    a.    Development library

    b.    Test library

    c.    Quarantine library

    d.    Operational library

***39. b.*** Organizations should analyze new software in a separate test library before installation in an operational environment. They should look for security impacts due to software flaws, security weaknesses, data incompatibility, or intentional malice in the test library. The development library is used solely for new development work or maintenance work. Some organizations use a quarantine library, as an intermediate library, before moving the software into operational library. The operational library is where the new software resides for day-to-day use.

**40.** **Current operating systems are far more resistant to which of the following types of denial-of-service attacks and have become less of a threat?**

    a.    Reflector attack

    b.    Amplified attack

    c.    Distributed attack

    d.    SYNflood attack

***40. d.*** Synchronized flood (SYNflood) attacks often target an application and daemon, like a Web server, and not the operating system (OS) itself; although the OS may get impacted due to resources used by the attack. It is good to know that current operating systems are far more resistant to SYNflood attacks, and many firewalls now offer protections against such attacks, so they have become less of a threat. Still, SYNfloods can occur if attackers initiate many thousands of transmission control protocol (TCP) connections in a short time.

The other three types of attacks are more of a threat. In a reflector attack, a host sends many requests with a spoofed source address to a service on an intermediate host. Like a reflector attack, an amplified attack involves sending requests with a spoofed source address to an intermediate host. However, an amplified attack does not use a single intermediate host; instead, its goal is to use a whole network of intermediate hosts. Distributed attacks coordinate attacks among many computers (i.e., zombies).

**41.** **Which of the following is the correct sequence of solutions for containing a denial-of-service incident?**

1. Relocate the target computer.

2. Have the Internet service provider implement filtering.

3. Implement filtering based on the characteristics of the attack.

4. Correct the vulnerability that is being exploited.

    a. 2, 3, 1, and 4

    b. 2, 4, 3, and 1

    c. 3, 4, 2, and 1

    d. 4, 3, 1, and 2

***41. c.*** The decision-making process for containing a denial-of-service (DoS) incident should be easier if recommended actions are predetermined. The containment strategy should include several solutions in sequence as shown in the correct answer.

**42.** **Computer security incident handling can be considered that portion of contingency planning that responds to malicious technical threats (for example, a virus). Which of the following best describes a secondary benefit of an incident handling capability?**

    a. Containing and repairing damage from incidents

    b. Preventing future damage

    c. Using the incident data in enhancing the risk assessment process

    d. Enhancing the training and awareness program

***42. c.*** An incident capability may be viewed as a component of contingency planning because it provides the ability to react quickly and efficiently to disruptions in normal processing. Incidents can be logged and analyzed to determine whether there is a recurring problem, which would not be noticed if each incident were viewed only in isolation. Statistics on the numbers and types of incidents in the organization can be used in the risk assessment process as an indication of vulnerabilities and threats.

Containing and repairing damage from incidents and preventing future damages are incorrect because they are examples of primary benefits of an incident handling capability. An incident handling capability can provide enormous benefits by responding quickly to suspicious activity and coordinating incident handling with responsible offices and individuals as necessary. Incidents can be studied internally to gain a better understanding of the organization's threats and vulnerabilities. Enhancing the training and awareness program is an example of a secondary benefit. Based on incidents reported, training personnel will have a better understanding of users' knowledge of security issues. Training that is based on current threats and controls recommended by incident handling staff provides users with information more specifically directed to their current needs. Using the incident data in enhancing the risk assessment process is the best answer when compared to enhancing the training and awareness program.

43. **Automatic file restoration requires which of the following?**

   a.   Log file and checkpoint information

   b.   Access file and check digit information

   c.   Transaction file and parity bit information

   d.   Backup file and checkpoint information

**43. a.** Automatic file restoration requires log file and checkpoint information to recover from a system crash. A backup file is different from a log file in that it can be a simple copy of the original file whereas a log file contains specific and limited information. The other three choices do not have the log file capabilities.

44. **Which of the following is the *most* common type of redundancy?**

   a.   Cable backup

   b.   Server backup

   c.   Router backup

   d.   Data backup

**44. d.** In general, redundancy means having extra, duplicate elements to compensate for any malfunctions or emergencies that could occur during normal, day-to-day operations. The most common type of redundancy is the data backup, although the concept is often applied to cabling, server hardware, and network connectivity devices such as routers and switches.

45. **Increasing which one of the following items increases the other three items?**

   a.   Reliability

   b.   Availability

   c.   Redundancy

   d.   Serviceability

**45. c.** Reliability minimizes the possibility of failure and availability is a measurement of uptime while serviceability is a measure of the amount of time it takes to repair a problem or to restore a system following a failure. Increasing redundancy increases reliability, availability, and serviceability.

**46.** **Which of the following is often *overlooked* in building redundancy?**

    a.   Disks

    b.   Processors

    c.   Electrical power

    d.   Controllers

*46. c.*   Redundant electric power and cooling is an important but often overlooked part of a contingency plan. Network administrators usually plan for backup disks, processors, controllers, and system boards.

**47.** **Network availability is increased with which of the following?**

    a.   Data redundancy

    b.   Link redundancy

    c.   Software redundancy

    d.   Power redundancy

*47. b.*   Link redundancy, due to redundant cabling, increases network availability because it provides a parallel path that runs next to the main data path and a routing methodology that can establish an alternative path in case the main path fails. The other three redundancies are good in their own way, but they do not increase network availability. In other words, there are two paths: a main path and an alternative path.

**48.** **What does an effective backup method for handling large volumes of data in a local-area-network environment include?**

    a.   Backing up at the workstation

    b.   Backing up at the file server

    c.   Using faster network connection

    d.   Using RAID technology

*48. b.*   Backing up at the file server is effective for a local-area network due to its greater storage capacity. Backing up at the workstation lacks storage capacity, and redundant array of independent disks (RAID) technology is mostly used for the mainframe. Using faster network connection increases the speed but not backup.

**49.** **Network reliability is increased *most* with which of the following?**

    a.   Alternative cable

    b.   Alternative network carrier

    c.   Alternative supplies

    d.   Alternative controllers

**49. b.** An alternative network carrier as a backup provides the highest reliability. If the primary carrier goes down, the backup can still work. The other three choices do provide some reliability, but not the ultimate reliability as with the alternative network carrier.

**50.** In a local-area network environment, which of the following requires the *least* redundancy planning?

    a.    Cables

    b.    Servers

    c.    Power supplies

    d.    Hubs

**50. d.** Many physical problems in local-area networks (LANs) are related to cables because they can be broken or twisted. Servers can be physically damaged due to disk head crash or power irregularities such as over or under voltage conditions. An uninterruptible power supply provides power redundancy and protection to servers and workstations. Servers can be disk duplexed for redundancy. Redundant topologies such as star, mesh, or ring can provide a duplicate path should a main cable link fail. Hubs require physical controls such as lock and key because they are stored in wiring closets; although, they can also benefit from redundancy, which can be expensive. Given the choices, it is preferable to have redundant facilities for cables, servers, and power supplies.

**51.** System reliability controls for hardware include which of the following?

    a.    Mechanisms to decrease mean time to repair and to increase mean time between failures

    b.    Redundant computer hardware

    c.    Backup computer facilities

    d.    Contingency plans

**51. a.** Mean time to repair (MTTR) is the amount of time it takes to resume normal operation. It is expressed in minutes or hours taken to repair computer equipment. The smaller the MTTR for hardware, the more reliable it is. Mean time between failures (MTBF) is the average length of time the hardware is functional. MTBF is expressed as the average number of hours or days between failures. The larger the MTBF for hardware, the more reliable it is.

Redundant computer hardware and backup computer facilities are incorrect because they are examples of system availability controls. They also address contingencies in case of a computer disaster.

**52.** Fail-soft control is an example of which of the following?

    a.    Continuity controls

    b.    Accuracy controls

    c.    Completeness controls

    d.    Consistency controls

**52. a.** As a part of the preventive control category, fail-soft is a continuity control. It is the selective termination of affected nonessential processing when a hardware or software failure is detected in a computer system. A computer system continues to function because of its resilience.

Accuracy controls are incorrect because they include data editing and validation routines. Completeness controls are incorrect because they look for the presence of all the required values or elements. Consistency controls are incorrect because they ensure repeatability of certain transactions with the same attributes.

**53.** **Information availability controls do *not* include which of the following?**

    a.    Backup and recovery

    b.    Storage media

    c.    Physical and logical security

    d.    Alternative computer equipment and facilities

**53. b.** Storage media has nothing to do with information availability. Data will be stored somewhere on some media. It is not a decision criterion. Management's goal is to gather useful information and to make it available to authorized users. System backup and recovery procedures and alternative computer equipment and facilities help ensure that the recovery is as timely as possible. Both physical and logical access controls become important. System failures and other interruptions are common.

**54.** **From an operations viewpoint, the *first* step in contingency planning is to perform a(n):**

    a.    Operating systems software backup

    b.    Applications software backup

    c.    Documentation backup

    d.    Hardware backup

**54. d.** Hardware backup is the first step in contingency planning. All computer installations must include formal arrangements for alternative processing capability in the event their data center or any portion of the work environment becomes disabled. These plans can take several forms and involve the use of another data center. In addition, hardware manufacturers and software vendors can be helpful in locating an alternative processing site and in some cases provide backup equipment under emergency conditions. The more common plans are service bureaus, reciprocal arrangements, and hot sites.

After hardware is backed up, operating systems software is backed up next, followed by applications software backup and documentation.

**55.** **The primary contingency strategy for application systems and data is regular backup and secure offsite storage. From an operations viewpoint, which of the following decisions is *least* important to address?**

    a.    How often is the backup performed?

    b.    How often is the backup stored offsite?

    c.    How often is the backup used?

    d.    How often is the backup transported?

**55. c.**   Normally, the primary contingency strategy for applications and data is regular backup and secure offsite storage. Important decisions to be addressed include how often the backup is performed, how often it is stored offsite, and how it is transported to storage, to an alternative processing site, or to support the resumption of normal operations. How often the backup is used is not relevant because it is hoped that it may never have to be used.

**56.**    **Which of the following is *not* totally possible from a security control viewpoint?**

    a.    Detection

    b.    Prevention

    c.    Correction

    d.    Recovery

**56. b.**   Prevention is totally impossible because of its high cost and technical limitations. Under these conditions, detection becomes more important, which could be cheaper than prevention; although, not all attacks can be detected in time. Both correction and recovery come after prevention or detection.

**57.**    **The return on investment on quality is highest in which of the following software defect prevention activities?**

    a.    Code inspection

    b.    Reviews with users

    c.    Design reviews

    d.    Unit test

**57. b.**   It is possible to quantify the return on investment (ROI) for various quality improvement activities. Studies have shown that quality ROI is highest when software products are reviewed with user customers. This is followed by code inspection by programmers, design reviews with the project team, and unit testing by programmers.

**58.**    **The IT operations management of KPT Corporation is concerned about the reliability and availability data for its four major, mission-critical information systems that are used by business end-users. The KPT corporate management's goal is to improve the reliability and availability of these four systems in order to increase customer satisfaction both internally and externally. The IT operations management collected the following data on percent reliability. Assume 365 operating days per year and 24 hours per day for all these systems. The IT operations management thinks that system reliability is important in providing quality of service to end-users.**

| SYSTEM | RELIABILITY |
|--------|-------------|
| 1 | 99.50 |
| 2 | 97.50 |
| 3 | 98.25 |
| 4 | 95.25 |

**Which of the following systems has the highest downtime in a year expressed in hours and rounded up?**

    a.     System 1

    b.     System 2

    c.     System 3

    d.     System 4

**58. d.** The system 4 has the highest downtime in hours. Theoretically speaking, the higher the reliability of a system, the lower its downtime (including scheduled maintenance), and higher the availability of that system, and vice versa. In fact, this question does not require any calculations to perform because one can find out the correct answer just by looking at the reliability data given in that the lower the reliability, the higher the downtime, and vice versa.

| SYSTEM | RELIABILITY, PERCENT | DOWNTIME, HOURS | AVAILABILITY, PERCENT |
|--------|----------------------|-----------------|-----------------------|
| 1 | 99.50 | 44 | 99.50 |
| 2 | 97.50 | 219 | 97.50 |
| 3 | 98.25 | 153 | 98.25 |
| 4 | 95.25 | 416 | 95.25 |

Calculations for System 1 are shown below and calculations for other systems follow the System 1 calculations.

Downtime = (Total hours) × [(100 – Reliability%)/100] = 8,760 × 0.005 = 44 hours

   Availability for System 1 = [(Total time – Downtime)/Total time] × 100 = [(8,760 – 44)/8,760] × 100 = 99.50%

   Check: Availability for System 1 = [Uptime/(Uptime + Downtime)] × 100 = (8,716/8,760) × 100 = 99.50%

**59.** Which of the following is the *most* important requirement for a software quality program to work effectively?

    a.    Quality metrics

    b.    Process improvement

    c.    Software reengineering

    d.    Commitment from all parties

**59. d.** A software quality program should reduce defects, cut service costs, increase customer satisfaction, and increase productivity and revenues. To achieve these goals, commitment by all parties involved is the most important factor. The other three factors such as quality metrics, process improvement, and software reengineering have some merit, but none is sufficient on its own.

**60.** As the information system changes over time, which of the following is required to maintain the baseline configuration?

    a.    Enterprise architecture

    b.    New baselines

    c.    Operating system

    d.    Network topology

**60. b.** Maintaining the baseline configuration involves creating new baselines as the information system changes over time. The other three choices deal with information provided by the baseline configuration as a part of standard operating procedure.

**61.** Software quality is *not* measured by:

    a.    Defect levels

    b.    Customer satisfaction

    c.    Time-to-design

    d.    Continuous process improvement

**61. c.** Quality is more than just defect levels. It should include customer satisfaction, time-to-market, and a culture committed to continuous process improvement. Time-to-design is not a complete answer because it is a part of time-to-market, where the latter is defined as the total time required for planning, designing, developing, and delivering a product. It is the total time from concept to delivery. These software quality values lead to quality education, process assessments, and customer satisfaction.

**62.** Which of the following responds to security incidents on an emergency basis?

    a.    Tiger team

    b.    White team

  c. Red team

  d. Blue team

***62. b.*** A white team is an internal team that initiates actions to respond to security incidents on an emergency basis. Both the red team and blue team perform penetration testing of a system, and the tiger team is an old name for the red team.

**63.** **Which of the following is the *most* important function of software inventory tools in maintaining a consistent baseline configuration?**

  a. Track operating system version numbers.

  b. Track installed application systems.

  c. Scan for unauthorized software.

  d. Maintain current patch levels.

***63. c.*** Software inventory tools scan information for unauthorized software to validate against the official list of authorized and unauthorized software programs. The other three choices are standard functions of software inventory tools.

**64.** **A user's session auditing activities are performed in consultation with which of the following?**

  a. Internal legal counsel and internal audit

  b. Consultants and contractors

  c. Public affairs or media relations

  d. External law enforcement authorities and previous court cases

***64. a.*** An information system should provide the capability to capture/record, log, and view all the content related to a user's session in real time. Session auditing activities are developed, integrated, and used with internal legal counsel and internal audit departments. This is because these auditing activities can have legal and audit implications.

Consultants and contractors should not be contacted at all. It is too early to talk to the public affairs or media relations within the organization. External law enforcement authorities should be contacted only after the session auditing work is completed and only after there is a discovery of high-risk incidents.

**65.** **Regarding access restrictions associated with changes to information systems, which of the following makes it easy to discover unauthorized changes?**

  a. Physical access controls

  b. Logical access controls

  c. Change windows

  d. Software libraries

**65. c.** Change windows mean changes occur only during specified times, and making unauthorized changes outside the window are easy to discover. The other three choices are also examples of access restrictions, but changes are not easy to discover in them.

**66.** Which of the following is an example of software reliability metrics?

   a.  Number of defects per million lines of source code with comments

   b.  Number of defects per function point

   c.  Number of defects per million lines of source code without comments

   d.  The probability of failure-free operation in a specified time

**66. d.** Software quality can be expressed in two ways: defect rate and reliability. Software quality means conformance to requirements. If the software contains too many functional defects, the basic requirement of providing the desired function is not met. Defect rate is the number of defects per million lines of source code or per function point. Reliability is expressed as number of failures per "n" hours of operation, mean-time-to failure, or the probability of failure-free operation in a specified time. Reliability metrics deal with probabilities and timeframes.

**67.** From a CleanRoom software engineering viewpoint, software quality is certified in terms of:

   a.  Mean-time between failures (MTBF)

   b.  Mean-time-to-failure (MTTF)

   c.  Mean-time-to-repair (MTTR)

   d.  Mean-time between outages (MTBO)

**67. b.** CleanRoom operations are carried out by small independent development and certification (test) teams. In CleanRoom, all testing is based on anticipated customer usage. Test cases are designed to practice the more frequently used functions. Therefore, errors that are likely to cause frequent failures to the users are found first. For measurement, software quality is certified in terms of mean-time-to failure (MTTF). MTTF is most often used with safety-critical systems such as airline traffic control systems because it measures the time taken for a system to fail for the first time.

Mean-time between failures (MTBF) is incorrect because it is the average length of time a system is functional. Mean-time-to-repair (MTTR) is incorrect because it is the total corrective maintenance time divided by the total number of corrective maintenance actions during a given period of time. Mean-time-between outages (MTBO) is incorrect because it is the mean time between equipment failures that result in loss of system continuity or unacceptable degradation.

**68.** In redundant array of independent disks (RAID) technology, which of the following RAID level does *not* require a hot spare drive or disk?

   a.  RAID3

   b.  RAID4

c. RAID5

d. RAID6

**68. d.**   A hot spare drive is a physical drive resident on the disk array which is active and connected but inactive until an active drive fails. Then the system automatically replaces the failed drive with the spare drive and rebuilds the disk array. A hot spare is a hot standby providing a failover mechanism.

The RAID levels from 3 to 5 have only one disk of redundancy and because of this a second failure would cause complete failure of the disk array. On the other hand, the RAID6 level has two disks of redundancy, providing a greater protection against simultaneous failures. Hence, RAID6 level does not need a hot spare drive whereas the RAID 3 to 5 levels need a shot spare drive.

The RAID6 level without a spare uses the same number of drives (i.e., 4 + 0 spare) as RAID3 to RAID 5 levels with a hot spare (i.e., 3 + 1 spare) thus protecting data against simultaneous failures. Note that a hot spare can be shared by multiple RAID sets. On the other hand, a cold spare drive or disk is not resident on the disk array and not connected with the system. A cold spare requires a hot swap, which is a physical (manual) replacement of the failed disk with a new disk done by the computer operator.

**69.**   **An example of ill-defined software metrics is which of the following?**

a. Number of defects per thousand lines of code

b. Number of defects over the life of a software product

c. Number of customer problems reported to the size of the product

d. Number of customer problems reported per user month

**69. c.**   Software defects relate to source code instructions, and problems encountered by users relate to usage of the product. If the numerator and denominator are mixed up, poor metrics result. An example of an ill-defined metric is the metric relating total customer problems to the size of the product, where size is measured in millions of shipped source instructions. This metric has no meaningful relation. On the other hand, the other three choices are examples of meaningful metrics. To improve customer satisfaction, you need to reduce defects and overall problems.

**70.**   **Which of the following information system component inventory is difficult to monitor?**

a. Hardware specifications

b. Software license information

c. Virtual machines

d. Network devices

**70. c.**   Virtual machines can be difficult to monitor because they are not visible to the network when not in use. The other three choices are easy to monitor.

**71.** Regarding incident handling, which of the following deceptive measures is used during incidents to represent a honeypot?

    a.   False data flows

    b.   False status measures

    c.   False state indicators

    d.   False production systems

**71. d.**   Honeypot is a fake (false) production system and acts as a decoy to study how attackers do their work. The other three choices are also acceptable deceptive measures, but they do not use honeypots. False data flows include made up (fake) data, not real data. System-status measures include active or inactive parameters. System-state indicators include startup, restart, shutdown, and abort.

**72.** For large software development projects, which of the following models provides greater satisfactory results on software reliability?

    a.   Fault count model

    b.   Mean-time-between-failures model

    c.   Simple ratio model

    d.   Simple regression model

**72. a.**   A fault (defect) is an incorrect step, process, or data definition in a computer program, and it is an indication of reliability. Fault count models give more satisfactory results than the mean-time-between-failures (MTBF) model because the latter is used for hardware reliability. Simple ratio and simple regression models handle few variables and are used for small projects.

**73.** The objective "To provide management with appropriate visibility into the process being used by the software development project and of the products being built" is addressed by which of the following?

    a.   Software quality assurance management

    b.   Software configuration management

    c.   Software requirements management

    d.   Software project management

**73. a.**   The goals of software quality assurance management include (i) software quality assurance activities are planned, (ii) adherence of software products and activities to the applicable standards, procedures, and requirements is verified objectively, and (iii) noncompliance issues that cannot be resolved are addressed by higher levels of management.

The objectives of software configuration management are to establish and maintain the integrity of products of the software project throughout the project's software life cycle. The objectives of software requirements management are to establish a common understanding between the customer and the software project requirements that will be addressed by the software project. The objectives of software project management are to establish reasonable plans for performing the software engineering activities and for managing the software development project.

**74.** Which of the following identifies required functionality to protect against or mitigate failure of the application software?

    a.    Software safety analysis

    b.    Software hazard analysis

    c.    Software fault tree analysis

    d.    Software sneak circuit analysis

**74. a.** Software needs to be developed using specific software development and software assurance processes to protect against or mitigate failure of the software. A complete software safety standard references other standards that address these mechanisms and includes a software safety policy identifying required functionality to protect against or mitigate failure.

Software hazard analysis is incorrect because it is a part of software safety. Hazard analysis is the process of identifying and evaluating the hazards of a system, and then making change recommendations that either eliminate the hazard or reduce its risk to an acceptable level. Software hazard analysis makes recommendations to eliminate or control software hazards and hazards related to interfaces between the software and the system (includes hardware and human components). It includes analyzing the requirements, design, code, user interfaces, and changes. Software hazards may occur if the software is improperly developed (designed), the software dispatches incorrect information, or the software fails to transmit information when it should.

Software fault tree analysis is incorrect because its purpose is to demonstrate that the software will not cause a system to reach an unsafe state, and to discover what environmental conditions will allow the system to reach an unsafe state. Software fault tree analysis is often conducted on the program code but can also be applied at other stages of the life cycle process (for example, requirements and design). This analysis is not always applied to all the program code, only to the portion that is safety critical.

Software sneak analysis is incorrect because it is based on sneak circuit analysis, which is used to evaluate electrical circuitry—hence the name software sneak circuit analysis. Sneaks are the latest design conditions or design flaws that have inadvertently been incorporated into electrical, software, and integrated systems designs. They are not caused by component failure.

**75.** Which of the following provides an assessment of software design quality?

    a.    Trace system requirements specifications to system requirements in requirements definition documentation.

    b.    Trace design specifications to system requirements and system requirements specifications to design.

    c.    Trace source code to design specifications and design specifications to source code.

    d.    Trace system test cases and test data designs to system requirements.

**75. b.** The goal is to identify requirements with no design elements (under-design) and design elements with no requirements (over-design). It is too early to assess software design quality during system requirements definition. It is too late to assess software design quality during coding. The goal is to identify design elements with no source code and source codes with no design elements. It is too late to assess software design quality during testing.

**76.** When executed incorrectly, which of the following nonlocal maintenance and diagnostic activities can expose an organization to potential risks?

    a.    Using strong authenticators

    b.    Separating the maintenance sessions from other network sessions

    c.    Performing remote disconnect verification feature

    d.    Using physically separated communications paths

**76. c.** An organization should employ remote disconnect verification feature at the termination of nonlocal maintenance and diagnostic sessions. If this feature is unchecked or performed incorrectly, this can increase the potential risk of introducing malicious software or intrusions due to open ports and protocols. The other three choices do not increase risk exposure. Nonlocal maintenance work is conducted through either an external network (mostly through the Internet) or an internal network.

**77.** Which of the following factors is an important consideration during application system design and development project?

    a.    Software safety

    b.    Completing the project on schedule

    c.    Spending less than budgeted

    d.    Documenting all critical work

**77. a.** Software safety is important compared to the other three choices because lack of safety considerations in a computer-based application system can cause danger or injury to people and damage to equipment and property.

**78.** A software product has the *least* impact on:

    a.    Loss of life

    b.    Loss of property

    c.    Loss of physical attributes

    d.    Loss of quality

**78. c.** Software is an intangible item with no physical attributes such as color and size. Although software is not a physical product, software products have a major impact on life, health, property, safety, and quality of life. Failure of software can have a serious economic impact such as loss of sales, revenues, and profits.

**79.** **A dangerous misconception about software quality is that:**

    a.    It can be inspected after the system is developed.

    b.    It can be improved by establishing a formal quality assurance function.

    c.    It can be improved by establishing a quality assurance library in the system.

    d.    It is tantamount to testing the software.

*79. a.* Quality should be designed at the beginning of the software development and maintenance process. Quality cannot be inspected or tested after the system is developed. Most seem to view final testing as quality testing. At best, this is quality control instead of quality assurance, hopefully preventing shipment of a defective product. Quality in the process needs to be improved, and quality assurance is a positive function.

A software product displays quality to the extent that all aspects of the customer's requirements are satisfied. This means that quality is built into the product during its development process rather than inspected at the end. It is too late to inspect the quality when the product is already built. Most assurance is provided when the needs are fully understood, captured, and transformed (designed) into a software product.

**80.** **From a security risk viewpoint, the job duties of which one of the following should be fully separated from the others?**

    a.    System administrator

    b.    Security administrator

    c.    Computer operator

    d.    System programmer

*80. c.* Separation of duties is a security principle that divides critical functions among different employees in an attempt to ensure that no one employee has enough information or access privileges to perpetrate damaging fraud or conduct other irregularities such as damaging data and/or programs.

The computer operator's job duties should be fully and clearly separated from the others. Due to concentration of risks in one job and if the computer operator's job duties are not fully separated from other conflicting job duties (for example, system administrator, security administrator, or system programmer), there is a potential risk that the operator can issue unprivileged commands from his console to the operating system, thus causing damage to the integrity of the system and its data. In other words, the operator has full access to the computer in terms of running the operating system, application systems, special program, and utility programs where the others do not have such full access. It is good to limit the computer operator's access to systems and their documentation, which will help him in understanding the inner working of the systems running on the computer. At the same time it is good to limit the others' access to the computer systems just enough to do their limited job duties.

**81.** In maintenance, which of the following is *most* risky?

    a.    Local maintenance

    b.    Scheduled maintenance

    c.    Nonlocal maintenance

    d.    Unscheduled maintenance

*81. c.* Nonlocal maintenance work is conducted through either an external network (mostly through the Internet) or an internal network. Because of communicating across a network connection, nonlocal maintenance work is most risky. Local maintenance work is performed without communicating across a network connection. For local maintenance, the vendor brings the hardware and software into the IT facility for diagnostic and repair work, which is less risky. Local or nonlocal maintenance work can be either scheduled or unscheduled.

**82.** The IT operations management of RDS Corporation is concerned about how to increase its data storage capacity to meet its increased growth in business systems. Based on a storage management consultant's report, the RDS management is planning to install redundant array of independent disks 6 (RAID6), which is a block-level striping with double distributed parity system to meet this growth. If four disks are arranged in RAID6 where each disk has a storage capacity of 250GB, and if space efficiency is computed as [1-(2/n)] where "n" is the number of disks, how much of this capacity is available for data storage purposes?

    a.    125GB

    b.    250GB

    c.    375GB

    d.    500GB

*82. d.* The RAID6 storage system can provide a total of 500GB of usable space for data storage purposes. Space efficiency represents the fraction of the sum of the disks' capacities that is available for use.

Space efficiency = $[1-(2/n)] = [1-(2/4)] = 1-0.5 = 0.5$

Total available space for data storage = $0.5 \times 4 \times 250 = 500GB$

**83.** In redundant array of independent disks (RAID) technology, when two drives or disks have a logical joining, it is called:

    a.    Disk concatenation

    b.    Disk striping

    c.    Disk mirroring

    d.    Disk replication

**83. a.** Disk concatenation is a logical joining of two series of data or disks. In data concatenation, two or more data elements or data files are often concatenated to provide a unique name or reference. In disk concatenation, several disk address spaces are concatenated to present a single larger address spaces.

The other three choices are incorrect. Disk striping has more than one disk and more than one partition, and is same as disk arrays. Disk mirroring occurs when a file server contains two physical disks and one channel, and all information is written to both disks simultaneously. Disk replication occurs when data is written to two different disks to ensure that two valid copies of the data are always available.

**84.** All the following are needed for a timely and emergency maintenance work to reduce the risk to an organization *except:*

    a.    Maintenance vendor service-level agreement

    b.    Spare parts inventory

    c.    Help-desk staff

    d.    Commercial courier delivery service agreement

**84. c.** Information system components, when not operational, can result in increased risk to organizations because the security functionality intended by that component is not being provided. Examples of security-critical components include firewalls, hardware/software guards, gateways, intrusion detection and prevention systems, audit repositories, and authentication servers. The organizations need to have a maintenance vendor service-level agreement, stock spare parts inventory, and a delivery service agreement with a commercial transportation courier to deliver the required parts on time to reduce the risk of running out of components and parts.

Help-desk staff, whether they are internal or external, are not needed for all types of maintenance work, whether it is scheduled or unscheduled, or whether it is normal or emergency. Their job is to help system users on routine matters (problems and issues) and escalate them to the right party when they cannot resolve these matters.

**85.** Which of the following is the basis for ensuring software reliability?

    a.    Testing

    b.    Debugging

    c.    Design

    d.    Programming

**85. c.** The basis for software reliability is design, not testing, debugging, or programming. For example, using the top-down design and development techniques and employing modular design principles, software can be made more reliable than otherwise. Reliability is the degree of confidence that a system will successfully function in a certain environment during a specified time period.

Testing is incorrect because its purpose is to validate that the software meets its stated requirements. Debugging is incorrect because its purpose is to detect, locate, and correct faults in a computer program. Programming is incorrect because its purpose is to convert the design specifications into program instructions that the computer can understand.

**86.** **In software configuration management, changes to software should be subjected to which of the following types of testing prior to software release and distribution?**

    a. Black-box testing

    b. Regression testing

    c. White-box testing

    d. Gray-box testing

**86. b.** Regression testing is a method to ensure that changes to one part of the software system do not adversely impact other parts. The other three choices do not have such capabilities. Black-box testing is a functional analysis of a system, and known as generalized testing. White-box testing is a structural analysis of a system, and known as detailed testing or logic testing. Gray-box testing assumes some knowledge of the internal structures and implementation details of the assessment object, and known as focused testing.

**87.** **Which of the following software quality characteristics is difficult to define and test?**

    a. Functionality

    b. Reliability

    c. Usability

    d. Efficiency

**87. c.** Usability is a set of attributes that bear on the effort needed for use, and on the individual assessment of such use, by a stated or implied set of users. In a way, usability means understandability and ease of use. Because of its subjective nature, varying from person to person, it is hard to define and test.

Functionality is incorrect because it can easily be defined and tested. It is a set of attributes that bear on the existence of a set of functions and their specified properties. The functions are those that satisfy stated or implied needs. Reliability is incorrect because it can easily be defined and tested. It is the ability of a component to perform its required functions under stated conditions for a specified period of time. Efficiency is incorrect because it can easily be defined and tested. It is the degree to which a component performs its designated functions with minimum consumption of resources.

**88.** **Portable and removable storage devices should be sanitized to prevent the entry of malicious code to launch:**

    a. Man-in-the-middle attack

    b. Meet-in-the-middle attack

    c.    Zero-day attack

    d.    Spoofing attack

***88. c.*** Malicious code is capable of initiating zero-day attacks when portable and removable storage devices are not sanitized. The other three attacks are network-based, not storage device-based. A man-in-the-middle (MitM) attack occurs to take advantage of the store-and-forward mechanism used by insecure networks such as the Internet. A meet-in-the-middle attack occurs when one end of the network is encrypted and the other end is decrypted, and the results are matched in the middle. A spoofing attack is an attempt to gain access to a computer system by posing as an authorized user.

**89.** **Verification is an essential activity in ensuring quality software, and it includes tracing. Which of the following tracing techniques is *not* often used?**

    a.    Forward tracing

    b.    Backward tracing

    c.    Cross tracing

    d.    Ad hoc tracing

***89. c.*** Traceability is the ease in retracing the complete history of a software component from its current status to its requirements specification. Cross tracing should be used more often because it cuts through the functional boundaries, but it is not performed due to its difficulty in execution. The other three choices are often used due to their ease-of-use.

Forward tracing is incorrect because it focuses on matching inputs to outputs to demonstrate their completeness. Similarly, backward tracing is incorrect because it focuses on matching outputs to inputs to demonstrate their completeness. Ad hoc tracing is incorrect because it involves spot-checking of reconcilement procedures to ensure output totals agree with input totals, less any rejects or spot checking of accuracy of computer calculations such as interest on deposits, late charges, service charges, and past-due loans.

During system development, it is important to verify the backward and forward traceability of the following: (i) user requirements to software requirements, (ii) software requirements to design specifications, (iii) system tests to software requirements, and (iv) acceptance tests to user requirements. Requirements or constraints can also be traced downward and upward due to master-subordinate and predecessor-successor relationships to one another.

**90.** **Which of the following redundant array of independent disks (RAID) data storage systems is used for high-availability systems?**

    a.    RAID3

    b.    RAID4

    c.    RAID5

    d.    RAID6

**90. d.** RAID6 is used for high-availability systems due to its high tolerance for failure. Each RAID level (i.e., RAID0 to RAID6) provides a different balance between increased data reliability through redundancy and increased input/output performance. For example, in levels from RAID3 to RAID5, a minimum of three disks is required and only one disk provides a fault tolerance mechanism. In the RAID6 level, a minimum of four disks is required and two disks provide fault tolerance mechanisms.

In the single disk fault tolerance mechanism, the failure of that single disk will result in reduced performance of the entire system until the failed disk has been replaced and rebuilt. On the other hand, the double parity (two disks) fault tolerance mechanism gives time to rebuild the array without the data being at risk if a single disk fails before the rebuild is complete. Hence, RAID6 is suitable for high-availability systems due to high fault tolerance mechanisms.

**91.** Which of the following makes a computer system *more* reliable?

    a.   N-version programming

    b.   Structured programming

    c.   Defensive programming

    d.   GOTO-less programming

**91. c.** Defensive or robust programming has several attributes that makes a computer system more reliable. The major attribute is expected exception domain (i.e., errors and failures); when discovered, it makes the system reliable.

N-version programming is based on design or version diversity, meaning different versions of the software are developed independently with the thinking that these versions are independent in their failure behavior. Structured programming and GOTO-less programming are part of robust programming techniques to make programs more readable and executable.

**92.** Which of the following is an example of a static quality attribute of a software product?

    a.   Mean-time-between-failure

    b.   Simplicity in functions

    c.   Mean-time-to-repair

    d.   Resource utilization statistics

**92. b.** Software quality attributes can be classified as either dynamic or static. Dynamic quality attributes are validated by examining the dynamic behavior of software during its execution. Examples include mean time between failures (MTBF), mean-time-to-repair (MTTR), failure recovery time, and percent of available resources used (i.e., resource utilization statistics).

Static quality attributes are validated by inspecting nonexecuting software products and include modularity, simplicity, and completeness. Simplicity looks for straightforward implementation of functions. It is the characteristic of software that ensures definition and implementation of functions in the most direct and understandable manner.

Reliability models can be used to predict software reliability (for example, MTBF and MTTR) based on the rate of occurrence of defects and errors. There is a trade-off between complexity and security, meaning that complex systems are difficult to secure whereas simple systems are easy to secure.

**93.** **Auditing an information system is *not* reliable under which of the following situations?**

    a.    When audit records are stored on hardware-enforced, write-once media

    b.    When the user being audited has privileged access

    c.    When the audit activity is performed on a separate system

    d.    When the audit-related privileges are separated from nonaudit privileges

*93. b.* Auditing an information system is not reliable when performed by the system to which the user being audited has privileged access. This is because the privileged user can inhibit the auditing activity or modify the audit records. The other three choices are control enhancements that reduce the risk of audit compromises by the privileged user.

**94.** **Software quality is based on user needs. Which of the following software quality factors address the user's need for performance?**

    a.    Integrity and survivability

    b.    Verifiability and manageability

    c.    Correctness and interoperability

    d.    Expandability and flexibility

*94. c.* Correctness asks, "Does it comply with requirements?" whereas interoperability asks, "Does it interface easily?" Quality factors such as efficiency, correctness, safety, and interoperability are part of the performance need.

Integrity and survivability are incorrect because they are a part of functional need. Integrity asks, "How secure is it?" whereas survivability asks, "Can it survive during a failure?" Quality factors such as integrity, reliability, survivability, and usability are part of the functional need. Verifiability and manageability are incorrect because they are a part of the management need. Verifiability asks, "Is performance verification easy?" whereas manageability asks, "Is the software easily managed?" Expandability and flexibility are incorrect because they are a part of the changes needed. Expandability asks, "How easy is it to expand?" whereas flexibility asks, "How easy is it to change?"

**95.** **Developing safe software is crucial to prevent loss of life, property damage, or liability. Which of the following practices is *least* useful to ensuring a safe software product?**

    a.    Use high coupling between critical functions and data from noncritical ones.

    b.    Use low data coupling between critical units.

    c.    Implement a fail-safe recovery system.

    d.    Specify and test for unsafe conditions.

**95. a.** "Critical" may be defined as pertaining to safety, efficiency, and reliability. Each application system needs a clear definition of what "critical" means to it. Software hazards analysis and fault tree analysis can be performed to trace system-level hazards (for example, unsafe conditions) through design or coding structures back to software requirements that could cause the hazards. Functions and features of software that participate in avoiding unsafe conditions are termed critical. Critical functions and data should be separated from noncritical ones with low coupling, not with high coupling.

Avoiding unsafe conditions or ensuring safe conditions is achieved by separating the critical units from noncritical units, by low data coupling between critical units, and by fail-safe recovery from unsafe conditions when they occur, and by testing for unsafe conditions. Data coupling is the sharing or passing of simple data between system modules via parameter lists. A low data coupling is preferred at interfaces as it is less error prone, ensuring a safety product.

**96.** Developing a superior quality or safe software product requires special attention. Which of the following techniques to achieve superior quality are based on mathematical theory?

    a.    Multiversion software

    b.    Proof-of-correctness

    c.    Software fault tree analysis

    d.    Software reliability models

**96. b.** The proof-of-correctness (formal verification) involves the use of theoretical and mathematical models to prove the correctness of a program without executing it. Using this method, the program is represented by a theorem and is proved with first-order predicate calculus.

The other three choices do not use mathematical theory. Multiversion software is incorrect because its goal is to provide high reliability, especially useful in applications dealing with loss of life, property, and damage. The approach is to develop more than one version of the same program to minimize the detrimental effect on reliability of latent defects.

Software fault tree analysis is incorrect because it identifies and analyzes software safety requirements. It is used to determine possible causes of known hazards. This is done by creating a fault tree, whose root is the hazard. The system fault tree is expanded until it contains at its lowest level basic events that cannot be further analyzed.

Software reliability models are incorrect because they can predict the future behavior of a software product, based on its past behavior, usually in terms of failure rates.

**97.** Predictable failure prevention means protecting an information system from harm by considering which of the following?

    a.    Mean-time-to-repair (MTTR)

    b.    Mean-time-to-failure (MTTF)

    c.    Mean-time between failures (MTBF)

    d.    Mean-time between outages (MTBO)

**97. b.**   MTTF focuses on the potential failure of specific components of the information system that provide security capability. MTTF is the amount of mean-time to the next failure. MTTR is the amount of time it takes to resume normal operation. MTBF is the average length of time the system is functional. MTBO is the mean time between equipment failures that result in a loss of system continuity or unacceptable degradation.

**98.**   **Regarding software installation, "All software is checked against a list approved by the organization" refers to which of the following?**

    a.    Blacklisting

    b.    Black-box testing

    c.    White-box testing

    d.    Whitelisting

**98. d.**   Whitelisting is a method to control the installation of software to ensure that all software is checked against a list approved by the organization. It is a quality control check and is a part of software configuration activity. An example of blacklisting is creating a list of electronic-mail senders who have previously sent spam to a user. Black-box testing is a functional analysis of a system, whereas white-box testing is a structural analysis of a system.

**99.**   **Which of the following is *not* an example of the defect prevention method in software development and maintenance processes?**

    a.    Documented standards

    b.    CleanRoom processes

    c.    Formal technical reviews

    d.    Documentation standards

**99. c.**   Formal technical reviews (for example, inspections and walkthroughs) are used for defect detection, not prevention. If properly conducted, formal technical reviews are the most effective way to uncover and correct errors, especially early in the life cycle, where they are relatively easy and inexpensive to correct.

Documented standards are incorrect because they are just one example of defect prevention methods. Documented standards should be succinct and possibly placed into a checklist format as a ready application reference. A documented standard also permits audits for adherence and compliance with the approved method.

CleanRoom processes are incorrect because they are just one example of defect prevention methods. The CleanRoom process consists of (i) defining a set of software increments that combine to form the required system, (ii) using rigorous methods for specification, development, and certification of each increment, (iii) applying strict statistical quality control during the testing process, and (iv) enforcing a strict separation of the specification and design tasks from testing activities.

Documentation standards are incorrect because they are just one example of defect prevention methods. Standard methods can be applied to the development of requirements and design documents.

**100.** **The scope of formal technical reviews conducted for software defect removal would *not* include:**

    a.   Configuration management specification

    b.   Requirements specification

    c.   Design specification

    d.   Test specification

***100. a.*** The formal technical review is a software quality assurance activity that is performed by software developers. The objectives of these reviews are to (i) uncover errors in function and logic, (ii) verify that software under review meets its requirements, (iii) ensure that software represents the predefined standards. Configuration management specifications are a part of project planning documents, not technical documents. The purpose is to establish the processes that the project uses to manage the configuration items and changes to them. Program development, quality, and configuration management plans are subject to review but are not directly germane to the subject of defect removal.

The other three choices are incorrect because they are part of technical documents. The subject matter for formal technical reviews includes requirements specifications, detailed design, and code and test specifications. The objectives of reviewing the technical documents are to verify that (i) the work reviewed is traceable to the requirements set forth by the predecessor's tasks, (ii) the work is complete, (iii) the work has been completed to standards, and (iv) the work is correct.

**101.** **Patch management is a part of which of the following?**

    a.   Directive controls

    b.   Preventive controls

    c.   Detective controls

    d.   Corrective controls

***101. d.*** Patch management is a part of corrective controls, as it fixes software problems and errors. Corrective controls are procedures to react to security incidents and to take remedial actions on a timely basis. Corrective controls require proper planning and preparation as they rely more on human judgment.

Directive controls are broad-based controls to handle security incidents, and they include management's policies, procedures, and directives. Preventive controls deter security incidents from happening in the first place. Detective controls enhance security by monitoring the effectiveness of preventive controls and by detecting security incidents where preventive controls were circumvented.

**102.** **Locking-based attacks result in which of the following?**

1. Denial-of-service

2. Degradation-of-service

3. Destruction-of-service

4. Distribution-of-service

    a. 1 and 2

    b. 1 and 3

    c. 2 and 3

    d. 3 and 4

*102. a.* Locking-based attack is used to hold a critical system locked most of the time, releasing it only briefly and occasionally. The result would be a slow running browser without stopping it: degradation-of-service. The degradation-of-service is a mild form of denial-of-service. Destruction of service and distribution of service are not relevant here.

**103.** **Which of the following protects the information confidentiality against a robust keyboard attack?**

    a. Disposal

    b. Clearing

    c. Purging

    d. Destroying

*103. b.* A keyboard attack is a data scavenging method using resources available to normal system users with the help of advanced software diagnostic tools. Clearing information is the level of media sanitization that protects the confidentiality of information against a robust keyboard attack. Clearing must be resistant to keystroke recovery attempts executed from standard input devices and from data scavenging tools.

The other three choices are incorrect. Disposal is the act of discarding media by giving up control in a manner short of destruction. Purging is removing obsolete data by erasure, by overwriting of storage, or by resetting registers. Destroying is ensuring that media cannot be reused as originally intended.

**104.** **Which of the following is the correct sequence of activities involved in media sanitization?**

1. Assess the risk to confidentiality.

2. Determine the future plans for the media.

3. Categorize the information to be disposed of.

4. Assess the nature of the medium on which it is recorded.

    a. 1, 2, 3, and 4

    b. 2, 3, 4, and 1

    c. 3, 4, 1, and 2

    d. 4, 3, 2, and 1

**104. c.** An information system user must first categorize the information to be disposed of, assess the nature of the medium on which it is recorded, assess the risk to confidentiality, and determine the future plans for the media.

**105.** All the following are examples of normal backup strategies *except*:

    a. Ad hoc backup

    b. Full backup

    c. Incremental backup

    d. Differential backup

**105. a.** Ad hoc means when needed and irregular. Ad hoc backup is not a well-thought-out strategy because there is no systematic way of backing up required data and programs. Full (normal) backup archives all selected files and marks each as having been backed up. Incremental backup archives only those files created or changed since the last normal backup and marks each file. Differential backup archives only those files that have been created or changed since the last normal backup. It does not mark the files as backed up. The backups mentioned in other three choices have a systematic procedure.

**106.** Regarding a patch management program, which of the following is *not* a method of patch remediation?

    a. Developing a remediation plan

    b. Installing software patches

    c. Adjusting configuration settings

    d. Removing affected software

**106. a.** Remediation is the act of correcting vulnerability or eliminating a threat. A remediation plan includes remediation of one or more threats or vulnerabilities facing an organization's systems. The plan typically covers options to remove threats and vulnerabilities and priorities for performing the remediation.

Three types of remediation methods include installing a software patch, adjusting a configuration setting, and removing affected software. Removing affected software requires uninstalling a software application. The fact that a remediation plan is developed does not itself provide actual remediation work because actions provide remediation work not just plans on a paper.

**107.** **For media sanitization, overwriting *cannot* be used for which of the following?**

1. Damaged media

2. Nondamaged media

3. Rewriteable media

4. Nonrewriteable media

    a. 1 only

    b. 4 only

    c. 1 or 4

    d. 2 or 3

***107. c.*** Overwriting cannot be used for media that are damaged or not rewriteable. The media type and size may also influence whether overwriting is a suitable sanitization method.

**108.** **Regarding media sanitization, which of the following is the correct sequence of fully and physically destroying magnetic disks, such as hard drives?**

1. Incinerate

2. Disintegrate

3. Pulverize

4. Shred

    a. 4, 1, 2, and 3

    b. 3, 4, 2, and 1

    c. 1, 4, 3, and 2

    d. 2, 4, 3, and 1

***108. d.*** The correct sequence of fully and physically destroying magnetic disks such as hard drives (for example, advanced technology attachment (ATA) and serial ATA (SATA) hard drives), is disintegrate, shred, pulverize, and incinerate. This is the best recommended practice for both public and private sector organizations.

Disintegration is a method of sanitizing media and is the act of separating the equipment into component parts. Here, the disintegration step comes first to make the hard drive inoperable quickly. Shredding is a method of sanitizing media and is the act of cutting or tearing into small particles. Shredding cannot be the first step because it is not practical to do for many companies. Pulverization is a method of sanitizing media and is the act of grinding to a powder or dust. Incineration is a method of sanitizing media and is the act of burning completely to ashes done in a licensed incinerator.

Note that one does not need to complete all these methods, but can stop after any specific method and after reaching the final goal based on the sensitivity and criticality of data on the disk.

**109.** Who initiates audit trails in computer systems?

    a.   Functional users

    b.   System auditors

    c.   System administrators

    d.   Security administrators

*109. a.*   Functional users have the utmost responsibility in initiating audit trails in their computer systems for tracing and accountability purposes. Systems and security administrators help in designing and developing these audit trails. System auditors review the adequacy and completeness of audit trails and issue an opinion whether they are effectively working. Auditors do not initiate, design, or develop audit trails due to their independence in attitude and appearance as dictated by their Professional Standards.

**110.** The automatic termination and protection of programs when a failure is detected in a computer system are called a:

    a.   Fail-safe

    b.   Fail-soft

    c.   Fail-over

    d.   Fail-open

*110. a.*   The automatic termination and protection of programs when a failure is detected in a computer system is called fail-safe. The selective termination of affected nonessential processing when a failure is detected in a computer system is called a fail-soft. Fail-over means switching to a backup mechanism. Fail-open means that a program has failed to open due to errors or failures.

**111.** An inexpensive security measure is which of the following?

    a.   Firewalls

    b.   Intrusion detection

    c.   Audit trails

    d.   Access controls

*111. c.*   Audit trails provide one of the best and most inexpensive means for tracking possible hacker attacks, not only after attack, but also during the attack. You can learn what the attacker did to enter a computer system, and what he did after entering the system. Audit trails also detect unauthorized but abusive user activity. Firewalls, intrusion detection systems, and access controls are expensive when compared to audit trails.

**112.** What is the residual physical representation of data that has been in some way erased called?

    a.   Clearing

    b.   Purging

    c.    Data remanence

    d.    Destruction

***112. c.*** Data remanence is the residual physical representation of data that has been in some way erased. After storage media is erased, there may be some physical characteristics that allow the data to be reconstructed, which represents a security threat. Clearing, purging, and destruction are all risks involved in storage media. In clearing and purging, data is removed, but the media can be reused. The need for destruction arises when the media reaches the end of its useful life.

**113.** **Which of the following methods used to safeguard against disclosure of sensitive information is effective?**

    a.    Degaussing

    b.    Overwriting

    c.    Encryption

    d.    Destruction

***113. c.*** Encryption makes the data unreadable without the proper decryption key. Degaussing is a process whereby the magnetic media is erased, i.e., returned to its initial virgin state. Overwriting is a process whereby unclassified data are written to storage locations that previously held sensitive data. The need for destruction arises when the media reaches the end of its useful life.

**114.** **Magnetic storage media sanitization is important to protect sensitive information. Which of the following is *not* a general method of purging magnetic storage media?**

    a.    Overwriting

    b.    Clearing

    c.    Degaussing

    d.    Destruction

***114. b.*** The removal of information from a storage medium such as a hard disk or tape is called sanitization. Different kinds of sanitization provide different levels of protection. Clearing information means rendering it unrecoverable by keyboard attack, with the data remaining on the storage media. There are three general methods of purging magnetic storage media: overwriting, degaussing, and destruction. Overwriting means obliterating recorded data by writing different data on the same storage surface. Degaussing means applying a variable, alternating current fields for the purpose of demagnetizing magnetic recording media, usually tapes. Destruction means damaging the contents of magnetic media through shredding, burning, or applying chemicals.

**115.** **Which of the following redundant array of independent disks (RAID) technology classifications increases disk overhead?**

    a.    RAID-1

    b.    RAID-2

c. RAID-3

d. RAID-4

***115. a.*** Disk array technology uses several disks in a single logical subsystem. To reduce or eliminate downtime from disk failure, database servers may employ disk shadowing or data mirroring. A disk shadowing, or RAID-1, subsystem includes two physical disks. User data is written to both disks at once. If one disk fails, all the data is immediately available from the other disk. Disk shadowing incurs some performance overhead (during write operations) and increases the cost of the disk subsystem because two disks are required. RAID levels 2 through 4 are more complicated than RAID-1. Each involves storage of data and error correction code information, rather than a shadow copy. Because the error correction data requires less space than the data, the subsystems have lower disk overhead.

**116.** **Indicate the correct sequence of degaussing procedures for magnetic disk files.**

1. Write zeros

2. Write a special character

3. Write ones

4. Write nines

   a. 1, 3, and 2

   b. 3, 1, 4, and 2

   c. 2, 1, 4, and 3

   d. 1, 2, 3, and 4

***116. a.*** Disk files can be demagnetized by overwriting three times with zeros, ones, and a special character, in that order, so that sensitive information is completely deleted.

**117.** **Which of the following is the *best* control to prevent a new user from accessing unauthorized file contents when a newly recorded file is shorter than those previously written to a computer tape?**

   a. Degaussing

   b. Cleaning

   c. Certifying

   d. Overflowing

***117. a.*** If the new file is shorter than the old file, the new user could have open access to the existing file. Degaussing is best used under these conditions and is considered a sound and safe practice. Tape cleaning functions are to clean and then to properly wind and create tension in the computer magnetic tape. Recorded tapes are normally not erased during the cleaning process. Tape certification is performed to detect, count, and locate tape errors and then, if possible, repair the underlying defects so that the tape can be placed back into active status. Overflowing has nothing to do with computer tape contents. Overflowing is a memory or file size issue where contents could be lost due to size limitations.

**118.** **Which of the following data integrity problems can be caused by multiple sources?**

    a.    Disk failure

    b.    File corruption

    c.    Power failure

    d.    Memory failure

*118. b.*   Hardware malfunction, network failures, human error, logical errors, and other disasters are possible threats to ensuring data integrity. Files can be corrupted as a result of some physical (hardware) or network problems. Files can also become corrupted by some flaw in an application program's logic. Users can contribute to this problem due to inexperience, accidents, or missed communications. Therefore, most data integrity problems are caused by file corruption.

Disk failure is a hardware malfunction caused by physical wear and tear. Power failure is a hardware malfunction that can be minimized by installing power conditioning equipment and battery backup systems. Memory failure is an example of hardware malfunction due to exposure to strong electromagnetic fields. File corruption has many problem sources to consider.

**119.** **Which of the following provides network redundancy in a local-area-network (LAN) environment?**

    a.    Mirroring

    b.    Shadowing

    c.    Dual backbones

    d.    Journaling

*119. c.*   A backbone is the high traffic density connectivity portion of any communications network. Backbones are used to connect servers and other service providing machines on the network. The use of dual backbones means that if the primary network goes down, the secondary network will carry the traffic.

In packet switched networks, a backbone consists of switches and interswitch trunks. Switched networks can be managed with a network management console. Network component failures can be identified on the console and responded to quickly. Many switching devices are built modularly with hot swappable circuit boards. If a chip fails on a board in the device, it can be replaced relatively quickly just by removing the failed card and sliding in a new one. If switching devices have dual power supplies and battery backups, network uptime can be increased as well.

Mirroring, shadowing, and duplexing provide application system redundancy, not network redundancy. Mirroring refers to copying data as it is written from one device or machine to another. Shadowing is where information is written in two places, one shadowing the other, for extra protection. Any changes made will be reflected in both places. Journaling is a chronological description of transactions that have taken place, either locally, centrally, or remotely.

**120.** Which of the following controls prevents a loss of data integrity in a local-area-network (LAN) environment?

    a.    Data mirroring and archiving

    b.    Data correction

    c.    Data vaulting

    d.    Data backup

***120. a.*** Data mirroring refers to copying data as it is written from one device or machine to another. It prevents data loss. Data archiving is where files are removed from network online storage by copying them to long-term storage media such as optical disks, tapes, or cartridges. It prevents accidental deletion of files.

Data correction is incorrect because it is an example of a corrective control where bad data is fixed. Data vaulting is incorrect because it is an example of corrective control. It is a way of storing critical data offsite either electronically or manually. Data backup is incorrect because it is an example of corrective control where a compromised system can be restored.

**121.** In general, a fail-over mechanism is an example of which of the following?

    a.    Corrective control

    b.    Preventive control

    c.    Recovery control

    d.    Detective control

***121. c.*** Fail-over mechanism is a backup concept in that when the primary system fails, the backup system is activated. This helps in recovering the system from a failure or disaster.

**122.** Which of the following does *not* trigger zero-day attacks?

    a.    Malware

    b.    Web browsers

    c.    Zombie programs

    d.    E-mail attachments

***122. c.*** A zombie is a computer program that is installed on a personal computer to cause it to attack other computers. Attackers organize zombies as botnets to launch denial-of-server (DoS) attacks and distributed DoS attacks, not zero-day attacks. The other three choices trigger zero-day attacks.

With zero-day (zero-hour) attacks, attackers try to exploit computer application vulnerabilities that are unknown to system owners and system administrators, undisclosed to software vendors, or for which no security fix is available. Malware writers can exploit zero-day vulnerabilities through several different attack vectors to compromise attacked systems or steal confidential data. Web browsers are a major target because of their widespread distribution and usage. Hackers send e-mail attachments to exploit vulnerabilities in the application opening the attachment and send other exploits to take advantage of weaknesses in common file types.

**123.** **TEMPEST is used for which of the following?**

    a.    To detect electromagnetic disclosures

    b.    To detect electronic dependencies

    c.    To detect electronic destructions

    d.    To detect electromagnetic emanations

***123. d.*** TEMPEST is a short name, and not an acronym. It is the study and control of spurious electronic signals emitted by electrical equipment. It is the unclassified name for the studies and investigations of compromising electromagnetic emanations from equipment. It is suggested that TEMPEST shielded equipment is used to prevent compromising emanations.

**124.** **Which of the following is an example of directive controls?**

    a.    Passwords and firewalls

    b.    Key escrow and software escrow

    c.    Intrusion detection systems and antivirus software

    d.    Policies and standards

***124. d.*** Policies and standards are an example of directive controls. Passwords and firewalls are an example of preventive controls. Key escrow and software escrow are an example of recovery controls. Intrusion detection systems and antivirus software are an example of detective controls.

**125.** **Which of the following control terms can be used in a broad sense?**

    a.    Administrative controls

    b.    Operational controls

    c.    Technical controls

    d.    Management controls

***125. d.*** Management controls are actions taken to manage the development, maintenance, and use of the system, including system-specific policies, procedures, and rules of behavior, individual roles and responsibilities, individual accountability, and personnel security decisions.

Administrative controls include personnel practices, assignment of responsibilities, and supervision and are part of management controls. Operational controls are the day-to-day procedures and mechanisms used to protect operational systems and applications. Operational controls affect the system and application environment. Technical controls are hardware and software controls used to provide automated protection for the IT system or application. Technical controls operate within the technical system and applications.

**126.** **A successful incident handling capability should serve which of the following?**

    a.   Internal users only

    b.   All computer platforms

    c.   All business units

    d.   Both internal and external users

*126. d.* The focus of a computer security incident handling capability may be external as well as internal. An incident that affects an organization may also affect its trading partners, contractors, or clients. In addition, an organization's computer security incident handling capability may help other organizations and, therefore, help protect the industry as a whole.

**127.** **Which of the following encourages compliance with IT security policies?**

    a.   Use

    b.   Results

    c.   Monitoring

    d.   Reporting

*127. c.* Monitoring encourages compliance with IT security policies. Results can be used to hold managers accountable for their information security responsibilities. Use for its own sake does not help here. Reporting comes after monitoring.

**128.** **Who should measure the effectiveness of security-related controls in an organization?**

    a.   Local security specialist

    b.   Business manager

    c.   Systems auditor

    d.   Central security manager

*128. c.* The effectiveness of security-related controls should be measured by a person fully independent of the information systems department. The systems auditor located within an internal audit department of an organization is the right party to perform such measurement.

**129.** **Which of the following corrects faults and returns a system to operation in the event a system component fails?**

    a.   Preventive maintenance

    b.   Remedial maintenance

    c.   Hardware maintenance

    d.   Software maintenance

*129. b.* Remedial maintenance corrects faults and returns the system to operation in the event of hardware or software component fails. Preventive maintenance is incorrect because it is done to keep hardware in good operating condition. Both hardware and software maintenance are included in the remedial maintenance.

**130.** Which of the following statements is *not* true about audit trails from a computer security viewpoint?

    a.    There is interdependency between audit trails and security policy.

    b.    If a user is impersonated, the audit trail establishes events and the identity of the user.

    c.    Audit trails can assist in contingency planning.

    d.    Audit trails can be used to identify breakdowns in logical access controls.

*130. b.*   Audit trails have several benefits. They are tools often used to help hold users accountable for their actions. To be held accountable, the users must be known to the system (usually accomplished through the identification and authentication process). However, audit trails collect events and associate them with the perceived user (i.e., the user ID provided). If a user is impersonated, the audit trail establishes events but not the identity of the user.

It is true that there is interdependency between audit trails and security policy. Policy dictates who has authorized access to particular system resources. Therefore it specifies, directly or indirectly, what violations of policy should be identified through audit trails.

It is true that audit trails can assist in contingency planning by leaving a record of activities performed on the system or within a specific application. In the event of a technical malfunction, this log can be used to help reconstruct the state of the system (or specific files).

It is true that audit trails can be used to identify breakdowns in logical access controls. Logical access controls restrict the use of system resources to authorized users. Audit trails complement this activity by identifying breakdowns in logical access controls or verifying that access control restrictions are behaving as expected.

**131.** Which of the following is a policy-driven storage media?

    a.    Hierarchical storage management

    b.    Tape management

    c.    Direct access storage device

    d.    Optical disk platters

*131. a.*   Hierarchical storage management follows a policy-driven strategy in that the data is migrated from one storage medium to another, based on a set of rules, including how frequently the file is accessed. On the other hand, the management of tapes, direct access storage devices, and optical disks is based on schedules, which is an operational strategy.

**132.** In which of the following types of denial-of-service attacks does a host send many requests with a spoofed source address to a service on an intermediate host?

    a.    Reflector attack

    b.    Amplifier attack

    c.    Distributed attack

    d.    SYNflood attack

*132. a.* Because the intermediate host unwittingly performs the attack, that host is known as reflector. During a reflector attack, a denial-of-service (DoS) could occur to the host at the spoofed address, the reflector itself, or both hosts. The amplifier attack does not use a single intermediate host, like the reflector attack, but uses a whole network of intermediate hosts. The distributed attack coordinates attacks among several computers. A synchronous (SYN) flood attack is a stealth attack because the attacker spoofs the source address of the SYN packet, thus making it difficult to identify the perpetrator.

**133.** Sometimes a combination of controls works better than a single category of control, such as preventive, detective, or corrective. Which of the following is an example of a combination of controls?

    a.   Edit and limit checks, digital signatures, and access controls

    b.   Error reversals, automated error correction, and file recovery

    c.   Edit and limit checks, file recovery, and access controls

    d.   Edit and limit checks, reconciliation, and exception reports

*133. c.* Edit and limit checks are an example of preventive or detective control, file recovery is an example of corrective control, and access controls are an example of preventive control. A combination of controls is stronger than a single type of control.

Edit and limit checks, digital signatures, and access controls are incorrect because they are an example of a preventive control. Preventive controls keep undesirable events from occurring. In a computing environment, preventive controls are accomplished by implementing automated procedures to prohibit unauthorized system access and to force appropriate and consistent action by users.

Error reversals, automated error correction, and file recovery are incorrect because they are an example of a corrective control. Corrective controls cause or encourage a desirable event or corrective action to occur after an undesirable event has been detected. This type of control takes effect after the undesirable event has occurred and attempts to reverse the error or correct the mistake.

Edit and limit checks, reconciliation, and exception reports are incorrect because they are an example of a detective control. Detective controls identify errors or events that were not prevented and identify undesirable events after they have occurred. Detective controls should identify expected error types, as well as those that are not expected to occur.

**134.** What is an attack in which someone compels system users or administrators into revealing information that can be used to gain access to the system for personal gain called?

    a.   Social engineering

    b.   Electronic trashing

    c.   Electronic piggybacking

    d.   Electronic harassment

***134. a.*** Social engineering involves getting system users or administrators to divulge information about computer systems, including passwords, or to reveal weaknesses in systems. Personal gain involves stealing data and subverting computer systems. Social engineering involves trickery or coercion.

Electronic trashing is incorrect because it involves accessing residual data after a file has been deleted. When a file is deleted, it does not actually delete the data but simply rewrites a header record. The data is still there for a skilled person to retrieve and benefit from.

Electronic piggybacking is incorrect because it involves gaining unauthorized access to a computer system via another user's legitimate connection. Electronic harassment is incorrect because it involves sending threatening electronic-mail messages and slandering people on bulletin boards, news groups, and on the Internet. The other three choices do not involve trickery or coercion.

**135.** Indicate the correct sequence in which primary questions must be addressed when an organization is determined to do a security review for fraud.

1. How vulnerable is the organization?

2. How can the organization detect fraud?

3. How would someone go about defrauding the organization?

4. What does the organization have that someone would want to defraud?

    a.    1, 2, 3, and 4

    b.    3, 4, 2, and 1

    c.    2, 4, 1, and 3

    d.    4, 3, 1, and 2

***135. d.*** The question is asking for the correct sequence of activities that should take place when reviewing for fraud. The organization should have something of value to others. Detection of fraud is least important; prevention is most important.

**136.** Which of the following zero-day attack protection mechanisms is *not* suitable to computing environments with a large number of users?

    a.    Port knocking

    b.    Access control lists

    c.    Local server-based firewalls

    d.    Hardware-based firewalls

***136. a.*** The use of port knocking or single packet authorization daemons can provide effective protection against zero-day attacks for a small number of users. However, these techniques are not suitable for computing environments with a large number of users. The other three choices are effective protection mechanisms because they are a part of multiple layer security, providing the first line-of-defense. These include implementing access control lists (one layer), restricting network access via local server firewalling (i.e., IP tables) as another layer, and protecting the entire network with a hardware-based firewall (another layer). All three of these layers provide redundant protection in case a compromise in any one of them is discovered.

137. **A computer fraud occurred using an online accounts receivable database application system. Which of the following logs is *most* useful in detecting which data files were accessed from which terminals?**

    a.    Database log

    b.    Access control security log

    c.    Telecommunications log

    d.    Application transaction log

*137. b.* Access control security logs are detective controls. Access logs show who accessed what data files, when, and from what terminal, including the nature of the security violation. The other three choices are incorrect because database logs, telecommunication logs, and application transaction logs do not show who accessed what data files, when, and from what terminal, including the nature of the security violation.

138. **Audit trails should be reviewed. Which of the following methods is *not* the best way to perform a query to generate reports of selected information?**

    a.    By a known damage or occurrence

    b.    By a known user identification

    c.    By a known terminal identification

    d.    By a known application system name

*138. a.* Damage or the occurrence of an undesirable event cannot be anticipated or predicted in advance, thus making it difficult to make a query. The system design cannot handle unknown events. Audit trails can be used to review what occurred after an event, for periodic reviews, and for real-time analysis. Reviewers need to understand what normal activity looks like. An audit trail review is easier if the audit trail function can be queried by user ID, terminal ID, application system name, date and time, or some other set of parameters to run reports of selected information.

139. **Which of the following can prevent dumpster diving?**

    a.    Installing surveillance equipment

    b.    Using a data destruction process

    c.    Hiring additional staff to watch data destruction

    d.    Sending an e-mail message to all employees

*139. b.* Dumpster diving can be avoided by using a high-quality data destruction process on a regular basis. This should include paper shredding and electrical disruption of data on magnetic media such as tape, cartridge, or disk.

**140.** Identify the computer-related crime and fraud method that involves obtaining information that may be left in or around a computer system after the execution of a job.

    a.    Data diddling

    b.    Salami technique

    c.    Scavenging

    d.    Piggybacking

*140. c.* Scavenging is obtaining information that may be left in or around a computer system after the execution of a job. Data diddling involves changing data before or during input to computers or during output from a computer system. The salami technique is theft of small amounts of assets (primarily money) from a number of sources. Piggybacking can be done physically or electronically. Both methods involve gaining access to a controlled area without authorization.

**141.** An exception-based security report is an example of which of the following?

    a.    Preventive control

    b.    Detective control

    c.    Corrective control

    d.    Directive control

*141. c.* Detecting an exception in a transaction or process is detective in nature, but reporting it is an example of corrective control. Both preventive and directive controls do not either detect or correct an error; they simply stop it if possible.

**142.** There is a possibility that incompatible functions may be performed by the same individual either in the IT department or in the user department. One compensating control for this situation is the use of:

    a.    Log

    b.    Hash totals

    c.    Batch totals

    d.    Check-digit control

*142. a.* A log, preferably a computer log, records the actions or inactions of an individual during his access to a computer system or a data file. If any abnormal activities occur, the log can be used to trace them. The purpose of a compensating control is balancing weak controls with strong controls. The other three choices are examples of application system-based specific controls not tied to an individual action, as a log is.

**143.** When an IT auditor becomes reasonably certain about a case of fraud, what should the auditor do *next*?

    a.    Say nothing now because it should be kept secret.

    b.    Discuss it with the employee suspected of fraud.

    c.    Report it to law enforcement officials.

    d.    Report it to company management.

*143. d.* In fraud situations, the auditor should proceed with caution. When certain about a fraud, he should report it to company management, not to external organizations. The auditor should not talk to the employee suspected of fraud. When the auditor is not certain about fraud, he should talk to the audit management.

**144.** **An effective relationship between risk level and internal control level is which of the following?**

    a.    Low risk and strong controls

    b.    High risk and weak controls

    c.    Medium risk and weak controls

    d.    High risk and strong controls

*144. d.* There is a direct relationship between the risk level and the control level. That is, high-risk situations require stronger controls, low-risk situations require weaker controls, and medium-risk situations require medium controls. A control is defined as the policies, practices, and organizational structure designed to provide reasonable assurance that business objectives will be achieved and that undesired events would be prevented or detected and corrected. Controls should facilitate accomplishment of an organization's objectives.

**145.** **Incident handling is *not* closely related to which of the following?**

    a.    Contingency planning

    b.    System support

    c.    System operations

    d.    Strategic planning

*145. d.* Strategic planning involves long-term and major issues such as management of the computer security program and the management of risks within the organization and is not closely related to the incident handling, which is a minor issue.

Incident handling is closely related to contingency planning, system support, and system operations. An incident handling capability may be viewed as a component of contingency planning because it provides the ability to react quickly and efficiently to disruptions in normal processing. Broadly speaking, contingency planning addresses events with the potential to interrupt system operations. Incident handling can be considered that portion of contingency planning that responds to malicious technical threats.

**146.** **In which of the following areas do the objectives of systems auditors and information systems security officers overlap the *most*?**

    a.    Determining the effectiveness of security-related controls

    b.    Evaluating the effectiveness of communicating security policies

c.    Determining the usefulness of raising security awareness levels

d.    Assessing the effectiveness of reducing security incidents

***146. a.***    The auditor's objective is to determine the effectiveness of security-related controls. The auditor reviews documentation and tests security controls. The other three choices are the sole responsibilities of information systems security officers.

**147.**    **Which of the following security control techniques assists system administrators in protecting physical access of computer systems by intruders?**

a.    Access control lists

b.    Host-based authentication

c.    Centralized security administration

d.    Keystroke monitoring

***147. d.***    Keystroke monitoring is the process used to view or record both the keystrokes entered by a computer user and the computer's response during an interactive session. It is usually considered a special case of audit trails. Keystroke monitoring is conducted in an effort to protect systems and data from intruders who access the systems without authority or in excess of their assigned authority. Monitoring keystrokes typed by intruders can help administrators assess and repair any damage they may cause.

Access control lists refer to a register of users who have been given permission to use a particular system resource and the types of access they have been permitted. Host-based authentication grants access based upon the identity of the host originating the request, instead of the identity of the user making the request. Centralized security administration allows control over information because the ability to make changes resides with few individuals, as opposed to many in a decentralized environment. The other three choices do not protect computer systems from intruders, as does the keystroke monitoring.

**148.**    **Which of the following is *not* essential to ensure operational assurance of a computer system?**

a.    System audits

b.    System changes

c.    Policies and procedures

d.    System monitoring

***148. b.***    Security is not perfect when a system is implemented. Changes in the system or the environment can create new vulnerabilities. Strict adherence to procedures is rare over time, and procedures become outdated. Thinking risk is minimal, users may tend to bypass security measures and procedures. Operational assurance is the process of reviewing an operational system to see that security controls, both automated and manual, are functioning correctly and effectively.

To maintain operational assurance, organizations use three basic methods: system audits, policies and procedures, and system monitoring. A system audit is a one-time or periodic event to evaluate security. Monitoring refers to an ongoing activity that examines either the system or the users. In general, the more real time an activity is, the more it falls into the category of monitoring. Policies and procedures are the backbone for both auditing and monitoring.

System changes drive new requirements for changes. In response to various events such as user complaints, availability of new features and services, or the discovery of new threats and vulnerabilities, system managers and users modify the system and incorporate new features, new procedures, and software updates. System changes by themselves do not assure that controls are working properly.

**149.** **What is an example of a security policy that can be legally monitored?**

    a.    Keystroke monitoring

    b.    Electronic mail monitoring

    c.    Web browser monitoring

    d.    Password monitoring

*149. d.* Keystroke monitoring, e-mail monitoring, and Web browser monitoring are controversial and intrusive. These kinds of efforts could waste time and other resources due to their legal problems. On the other hand, examples of effective security policy statements include (i) passwords shall not be shared under any circumstances and (ii) password usage and composition will be monitored.

**150.** **What is a common security problem?**

    a.    Discarded storage media

    b.    Telephone wiretapping

    c.    Intelligence consultants

    d.    Electronic bugs

*150. a.* Here, the keyword is common, and it is relative. Discarded storage media, such as CDs/DVDs, paper documents, and reports, is a major and common problem in every organization. Telephone wiretapping and electronic bugs require expertise. Intelligent consultants gather a company's proprietary data and business information and government trade strategies.

**151.** **When controlling access to information, an audit log provides which of the following?**

    a.    Review of security policy

    b.    Marking files for reporting

    c.    Identification of jobs run

    d.    Accountability for actions

*151. d.* An audit log must be kept and protected so that any actions impacting security can be traced. Accountability can be established with the audit log. The audit log also helps in verifying the other three choices indirectly.

**152.** **What is a detective control in a computer operations area?**

    a.    Policy

    b.    Log

    c.    Procedure

    d.    Standard

*152. b.* Logs, whether manual or automated, capture relevant data for further analysis and tracing. Policy, procedure, and standard are directive controls and are part of management controls because they regulate human behavior.

**153.** **In terms of security functionality verification, which of the following is the correct order of information system's transitional states?**

    1.    Startup

    2.    Restart

    3.    Shutdown

    4.    Abort

        a.    1, 2, 3, and 4

        b.    1, 3, 2, and 4

        c.    3, 2, 1, and 4

        d.    4, 3, 2, and 1

*153. b.* The correct order of information system's transitional states is startup, shutdown, restart, and abort. Because the system is in transitional states, which is an unstable condition, if the restart procedures are not performed correctly or facing technical recovery problems, then the system has no choice except to abort.

**154.** **Which of the following items is *not* related to the other items?**

    a.    Keystroke monitoring

    b.    Penetration testing

    c.    Audit trails

    d.    Telephone wiretap

*154. b.* Penetration testing is a test in which the evaluators attempt to circumvent the security features of a computer system. It is unrelated to the other three choices. Keystroke monitoring is the process used to view or record both the keystrokes entered by a computer user and the computer's response during an interactive session. It is considered as a special case of audit trails. Some consider the keystroke monitoring as a special case of unauthorized telephone wiretap and others are not.

**155.** All the following are tools that help both system intruders and systems administrators *except:*

    a.    Network discovery tools

    b.    Intrusion detection tools

    c.    Port scanners

    d.    Denial-of-service test tools

*155. b.* Intrusion detection tools detect computer attacks in several ways: (i) outside of a network's firewall, (ii) behind a network's firewall, or (iii) within a network to monitor insider attacks. Network discovery tools and port scanners can be used both by intruders and system administrators to find vulnerable hosts and network services. Similarly, denial-of-service test tools can be used to determine how much damage can be done to a computing site.

**156.** Audit trail records contain vast amounts of data. Which of the following review methods is *best* to review all records associated with a particular user or application system?

    a.    Batch-mode analysis

    b.    Real-time audit analysis

    c.    Audit trail review after an event

    d.    Periodic review of audit trail data

*156. b.* Audit trail data can be used to review what occurred after an event, for periodic reviews, and for real-time analysis. Audit analysis tools can be used in a real-time, or near real-time, fashion. Manual review of audit records in real time is not feasible on large multi-user systems due to the large volume of records generated. However, it might be possible to view all records associated with a particular user or application and view them in real time.

Batch-mode analysis is incorrect because it is a traditional method of analyzing audit trails. The audit trail data are reviewed periodically. Audit records are archived during that interval for later analysis. The three incorrect choices do not provide the convenience of displaying or reporting all records associated with a user or application, as do the real-time audit analysis.

**157.** Many errors were discovered during application system file-maintenance work. What is the *best* control?

    a.    File labels

    b.    Journaling

    c.    Run-to-run control

    d.    Before and after image reporting

*157. d.* Before and after image reporting ensures data integrity by reporting data field values both before and after the changes so that functional users can detect data entry and update errors.

File labels are incorrect because they verify internal file labels for tapes to ensure that the correct data file is used in the processing. Journaling is incorrect because it captures system transactions on a journal file so that recovery can be made should a system failure occur. Run-to-run control is incorrect because it verifies control totals resulting from one process or cycle to the subsequent process or cycle to ensure their accuracy.

**158.** **Which of the following is *not* an example of denial-of-service attacks?**

    a.    Flaw-based attacks

    b.    Information attacks

    c.    Flooding attacks

    d.    Distributed attacks

**158. *b.*** An information attack is not relevant here because it is too general. Flaw-based attacks take advantage of a flaw in the target system's software to cause a processing failure, escalate privileges, or to cause it to exhaust system resources. Flooding attacks simply send a system more information than it can handle. A distributed attack is a subset of denial-of-service (DoS) attacks, where the attacker uses multiple computers to launch the attack and flood the system.

**159.** **All the following are examples of technical controls for ensuring information systems security *except:***

    a.    User identification and authentication

    b.    Assignment of security responsibility

    c.    Access controls

    d.    Data validation controls

**159. *b.*** Assignment of security responsibility is a part of management controls. Screening of personnel is another example of management controls. The other three choices are part of technical controls.

**160.** **Which of the following individuals or items cause the highest economic loss to organizations using computer-based information systems?**

    a.    Dishonest employees

    b.    Disgruntled employees

    c.    Errors and omissions

    d.    Outsiders

**160. *c.*** Users, data entry clerks, system operators, and programmers frequently make errors that contribute directly or indirectly to security problems. In some cases, the error is the threat, such as a data entry error or a programming error that crashes a system. In other cases, the errors create vulnerabilities. Errors can occur during all phases of the system life cycle. Many studies indicate that 65 percent of losses to organizations are the result of errors and omissions followed by dishonest employees (13%), disgruntled employees (6%), and outsiders/hackers (3%).

**161.** **Which one of the following situations renders backing up program and data files ineffective?**

    a.    When catastrophic accidents happen

    b.    When disruption to the network occurs

    c.    When viruses are timed to activate at a later date

    d.    When backups are performed automatically

*161. c.* Computer viruses that are timed to activate at a later date can be copied onto the backup media thereby infecting backup copies as well. This makes the backup copy ineffective, unusable, or risky. Backups are useful and effective (i) in the event of a catastrophic accident, (ii) in case of disruption to the network, and (iii) when they are performed automatically. Human error is eliminated.

**162.** **What does an ineffective local-area-network backup strategy include?**

    a.    Backing up servers daily

    b.    Securing the backup workstations

    c.    Scheduling backups during regular work hours

    d.    Using file recovery utility programs

*162. c.* It is not a good operating practice to schedule backups during regular work hours because it interrupts the business functions. It is advised to schedule backups during off hours to avoid file contention (when files are open and the backup program is scheduled to run). As the size and complexity of local-area networks (LANs) increase, backups have assumed greater importance with many options available. It is a common practice to back up servers daily, taking additional backups when extensive database changes occur. It is good to secure the backup workstations to prevent interruption of backup processes that can result in the loss of backup data. It is a better practice to use the network operating system's file recovery utility for immediate restoration of accidentally deleted files before resorting to the time consuming process of file recovery from backup tapes.

**163.** **Which one of the following types of restores is used when performing system upgrades and reorganizations?**

    a.    Full restores

    b.    Individual file restores

    c.    Redirected restores

    d.    Group file restores

**163. a.** Full restores are used to recover from catastrophic events or when performing system upgrades and system reorganizations and consolidations. All the data on media is fully restored.

Individual file restores, by their name, restore the last version of a file that was written to media because it was deleted by accident or ruined. Redirected restores store files on a different location or system than the one they were copied from during the backup operations. Group file restores handle two or more files at a time.

164. Which of the following file backup strategies is preferred when a full snapshot of a server is required prior to upgrading it?

    a. Full backups

    b. Incremental backups

    c. Differential backups

    d. On-demand backups

**164. d.** On-demand backups refer to the operations that are done outside of the regular backup schedule. This backup method is most useful when backing up a few files/directories or when taking a full snapshot of a server prior to upgrading it. On-demand backups can act as a backup for regular backup schedules.

Full backups are incorrect because they copy all data files and programs. It is a brute force method providing a peace of mind at the expense of valuable time. Incremental backups are incorrect because they are an inefficient method and copy only those files that have changed since the last backup. Differential backups are incorrect because they copy all data files that have changed since the last full backup. Only two files are needed to restore the entire system: the last full backup and the last differential backup.

165. Which one of the following database backup strategies is executed when a database is running in a local-area-network environment?

    a. Cold backup

    b. Hot backup

    c. Logical backup

    d. Offline backup

**165. b.** Hot backups are taken when the database is running and updates are being written to it. They depend heavily on the ability of log files to stack up transaction instructions without actually writing any data values into database records. While these transactions are stacking up, the database tables are not being updated, and therefore can be backed up with integrity. One major problem is that if the system crashes in the middle of the backup, all the transactions stacking up in the log file are lost.

The idea of cold backup is to shut down the database and back it up while no end users are working on the system. This is the best approach where data integrity is concerned, but it does not service the customer (end user) well.

Logical backups use software techniques to extract data from the database and write the results to an export file, which is an image file. The logical backup approach is good for incremental backups. Offline backup is another term for cold backup.

166. **Contrary to best practices, information systems' security training is usually *not* given to which of the following parties?**

    a.    Information systems security staff

    b.    Functional users

    c.    Computer operations staff

    d.    Corporate internal audit staff

*166. c.* The information systems' security training program should be specifically tailored to meet the needs of computer operations staff so that they can deal with problems that have security implications. However, the computer operations staff is usually either taken for granted or completely forgotten from training plans.

The information systems' security staff is provided with periodic training to keep its knowledge current. Functional users will definitely be given training so that they know how to practice security. Corporate internal audit staff is given training because it needs to review the IT security goals, policies, procedures, standards, and practices.

167. **Which one of the following is a direct example of social engineering from a computer security viewpoint?**

    a.    Computer fraud

    b.    Trickery or coercion techniques

    c.    Computer theft

    d.    Computer sabotage

*167. b.* Social engineering is a process of tricking or coercing people into divulging their passwords. Computer fraud involves deliberate misrepresentation, alteration, or disclosure of data to obtain something of value. Computer theft involves stealing of information, equipment, or software for personal gain. Computer sabotage includes planting a Trojan horse, trapdoor, time bomb, virus, or worm to perform intentional harm or damage. The difference in the other three choices is that there is no trickery or coercion involved.

168. **A fault-tolerant design feature for large distributed systems considers all the following *except*:**

    a.    Using multiple components to duplicate functionality

    b.    Using duplicated systems in separate locations

    c.    Using modular components

    d.    Providing backup power supplies

**168. d.** A fault tolerant design should make a system resistant to failure and able to operate continuously. Many ways exist to develop fault tolerance in a system, including using two or more components to duplicate functionality, duplicating systems in separate locations, or using modular components in which failed components can be replaced with new ones. It does not include providing backup power supplies because it is a part of preventive maintenance, which should be used with fault tolerant design. Preventive maintenance measures reduce the likelihood of significant impairment to components.

**169.** **The process of degaussing involves which of the following?**

    a.    Retrieving all stored information

    b.    Storing all recorded information

    c.    Removing all recorded information

    d.    Archiving all recorded information

**169. c.** The purpose of degaussing is to remove all recorded information from a computer-recorded magnetic tape. It does this by demagnetizing (removing) the recording media, the tape, or the hard drive. After degaussing is done, the magnetic media is in a fully demagnetized state. However, degaussing cannot retrieve, store, or archive information.

**170.** **An audit trail record should include sufficient information to trace a user's actions and events. Which of the following information in the audit trail record helps the most to determine if the user was a masquerader or the actual person specified?**

    a.    The user identification associated with the event

    b.    The date and time associated with the event

    c.    The program used to initiate the event

    d.    The command used to initiate the event

**170. b.** An audit trail should include sufficient information to establish what events occurred and who (or what) caused them. Date and timestamps can help determine if the user was a masquerader or the actual person specified. With date and time, one can determine whether a specific user worked on that day and at that time.

The other three choices are incorrect because the masquerader could be using a fake user identification (ID) number or calling for invalid and inappropriate programs and commands.

In general, an event record should specify when the event occurred, the user ID associated with the event, the program or command used to initiate the event, and the result.

**171.** **Automated tools help in analyzing audit trail data. Which one of the following tools looks for anomalies in user or system behavior?**

    a.    Trend analysis tools

    b.    Audit data reduction tools

    c.     Attack signature detection tools

    d.     Audit data-collection tools

**171. a.**   Many types of tools have been developed to help reduce the amount of information contained in audit records, as well as to distill useful information from the raw data. Especially on larger systems, audit trail software can create large files, which can be extremely difficult to analyze manually. The use of automated tools is likely to be the difference between unused audit trail data and a robust program. Trend analysis and variance detection tools look for anomalies in user or system behavior.

Audit data reduction tools are preprocessors designed to reduce the volume of audit records to facilitate manual review. These tools generally remove records generated by specified classes of events, such as records generated by nightly backups.

Attack signature detection tools look for an attack signature, which is a specific sequence of events indicative of an unauthorized access attempt. A simple example is repeated failed log-in attempts. Audit data-collection tools simply gather data for analysis later.

**172.**    **Regarding a patch management program, which of the following helps system administrators *most* in terms of monitoring and remediating IT resources?**

    1.     Supported equipment

    2.     Supported applications software

    3.     Unsupported hardware

    4.     Unsupported operating systems

        a.     1 only

        b.     2 only

        c.     1 and 2

        d.     3 and 4

**172. d.**   Here, supported and unsupported means whether a company management has approved the acquisition, installation, and operation of hardware and software; approved in the former case and not approved in the latter case. System administrators should be taught how to independently monitor and remediate unsupported hardware, operating systems, and applications software because unsupported resources are vulnerable to exploitation. This is because non-compliant employees could have purchased and installed the unsupported hardware and software on their personal computers, which is riskier than the supported ones. A potential risk is that the unsupported systems could be incompatible with the supported systems and may not have the required security controls.

A list of supported resources is needed to analyze the inventory and identify those resources that are used within the organization. This allows the system administrators to know which hardware, operating systems, and applications will be checking for new patches, vulnerabilities, and threats. Note that not patching the unsupported systems can negatively impact the patching of the supported systems as they both coexist and operate on the same computer or network.

**173.** Which of the following is the *best* action to take when an information system media cannot be sanitized?

    a.    Clearing

    b.    Purging

    c.    Destroying

    d.    Disposal

*173. c.* An information system media that cannot be sanitized should be destroyed. Destroying is ensuring that media cannot be reused as originally intended and that information is virtually impossible to recover or prohibitively expensive to do.

Sanitization techniques include disposal, clearing, purging, and destruction. Disposal is the act of discarding media by giving up control in a manner short of destruction and is not a strong protection. Clearing is the overwriting of classified information such that that the media may be reused. Purging is the removal of obsolete data by erasure, by overwriting of storage, or by resetting registers. Clearing media would not suffice for purging.

**174.** Regarding a patch management program, which of the following benefits confirm that the remediations have been conducted appropriately?

    1.    Avoiding an unstable website

    2.    Avoiding an unusable website

    3.    Avoiding a security incident

    4.    Avoiding unplanned downtime

    a.    1 only

    b.    2 only

    c.    1 and 2

    d.    3 and 4

*174. d.* There are understandable benefits in confirming that the remediations have been conducted appropriately, possibly avoiding a security incident or unplanned downtime. Central system administrators can send remediation information on a disk to local administrators as a safe alternative to an e-mail list if the network or the website is unstable or unusable.

**175.** Regarding a patch management program, which of the following should be used when comparing the effectiveness of the security programs of multiple systems?

    1.    Number of patches needed

    2.    Number of vulnerabilities found

    3.    Number of vulnerabilities per computer

    4.    Number of unapplied patches per computer

a.  1 only

b.  2 only

c.  1 and 2

d.  3 and 4

***175. d.***  Ratios, not absolute numbers, should be used when comparing the effectiveness of the security programs of multiple systems. Ratios reveal better information than absolute numbers. In addition, ratios allow effective comparison between systems. Number of patches needed and number of vulnerabilities found are incorrect because they deal with absolute numbers.

**176.**  **All the following are examples of denial-of-service attacks *except*:**

a.  IP address spoofing

b.  Smurf attack

c.  SYNflood attack

d.  Sendmail attack

***176. a.***  IP address spoofing is falsifying the identity of a computer system on a network. It capitalizes on the packet address the Internet Protocol (IP) uses for transmission. It is not an example of a denial-of-service attack because it does not flood the host computer.

Smurf, synchronized flood (SYNflood), and sendmail attacks are examples of denial-of-service attacks. Smurf attacks use a network that accepts broadcast ping packets to flood the target computer with ping reply packets. SYN flood attack is a method of overwhelming a host computer on the Internet by sending the host a high volume of SYN packets requesting a connection, but never responding to the acknowledgment packets returned by the host. Recent attacks against sendmail include remote penetration, local penetration, and remote denial of service.

**177.**  **Ping-of-death is an example of which of the following?**

a.  Keyboard attack

b.  Stream attack

c.  Piggyback attack

d.  Buffer overflow attack

***177. d.***  The ping-of-death is an example of buffer overflow attack, a part of a denial-of-service attack, where large packets are sent to overfill the system buffers, causing the system to reboot or crash.

A keyboard attack is a resource starvation attack in that it consumes system resources (for example, CPU utilization and memory), depriving legitimate users. A stream attack sends TCP packets to a series of ports with random sequence numbers and random source IP addresses, resulting in high CPU usage. In a piggybacking attack, an intruder can gain unauthorized access to a system by using a valid user's connection.

**178.** **Denial-of-service attacks compromise which one of the following properties of information systems?**

    a.    Integrity

    b.    Availability

    c.    Confidentiality

    d.    Reliability

***178. b.***   A denial-of-service (DoS) is an attack in which one user takes up so much of the shared resource that none of the resource is left for other users. It compromises the availability of system resources (for example, disk space, CPU, print paper, and modems), resulting in degradation or loss of service.

A DoS attack does not affect integrity because the latter is a property that an object is changed only in a specified and authorized manner. A DoS attack does not affect confidentiality because the latter is a property ensuring that data is disclosed only to authorized subjects or users. A DoS attack does not affect reliability because the latter is a property defined as the probability that a given system is performing its mission adequately for a specified period of time under the expected operating conditions.

**179.** **Which of the following is the *most* complex phase of incident response process for malware incidents?**

    a.    Preparation

    b.    Detection

    c.    Recovery

    d.    Remediation

***179. c.***   Of all the malware incident-response life-cycle phases, recovery phase is the most complex. Recovery involves containment, restore, and eradication. Containment addresses how to control an incident before it spreads to avoid consuming excessive resources and increasing damage caused by the incident. Restore addresses bringing systems to normal operations and hardening systems to prevent similar incidents. Eradication addresses eliminating the affected components of the incident from the overall system to minimize further damage to it.

More tools and technologies are relevant to the recovery phase than to any other phase; more technologies mean more complexity. The technologies involved and the speed of malware spreading make it more difficult to recover.

The other three phases such as preparation, detection, and remediation are less complex. The scope of preparation and prevention phase covers establishing plans, policies, and procedures. The scope of detection phase covers identifying classes of incidents and defining appropriate actions to take. The scope of remediation phase covers tracking and documenting security incidents on an ongoing basis to help in forensics analysis and in establishing trends.

**180.** Which of the following determines the system availability rate for a computer-based application system?

    a.   (Available time / scheduled time) x 100

    b.   [(1 + available time) / (scheduled time)] x 100

    c.   [(Available time)/(1 – scheduled time)] x 100

    d.   [(Available time – scheduled time) / (scheduled time)] x 100

*180. a.* System availability is expressed as a rate between the number of hours the system is available to the users during a given period and the scheduled hours of operation. Overall hours of operation also include sufficient time for scheduled maintenance activities. Scheduled time is the hours of operation, and available time is the time during which the computer system is available to the users.

**181.** A computer security incident was detected. Which of the following is the *best* reaction strategy for management to adopt?

    a.   Protect and preserve

    b.   Protect and recover

    c.   Trap and prosecute

    d.   Pursue and proceed

*181. b.* If a computer site is vulnerable, management may favor the protect-and-recover reaction strategy because it increases defenses available to the victim organization. Also, this strategy brings normalcy to the network's users as quickly as possible. Management can interfere with the intruder's activities, prevent further access, and begin damage assessment. This interference process may include shutting down the computer center, closing of access to the network, and initiating recovery efforts.

Protect-and-preserve strategy is a part of a protect-and-recover strategy. Law enforcement authorities and prosecutors favor the trap-and-prosecute strategy. It lets intruders continue their activities until the security administrator can identify the intruder. In the mean time, there could be system damage or data loss. Pursue-and-proceed strategy is not relevant here.

**182.** A computer security incident handling capability should meet which of the following?

    a.   Users' requirements

    b.   Auditors' requirements

    c.   Security requirements

    d.   Safety requirements

*182. a.* There are a number of start-up costs and funding issues to consider when planning an incident handling capability. Because the success of an incident handling capability relies so heavily on the users' perceptions of its worth and whether they use it, it is important that the capability meets users' requirements. Two important funding issues are personnel and education and training.

**183.** Which of the following is *not* a primary benefit of an incident handling capability?

    a.    Containing the damage

    b.    Repairing the damage

    c.    Preventing the damage

    d.    Preparing for the damage

*183. d.*   The primary benefits of an incident handling capability are containing and repairing damage from incidents and preventing future damage. Preparing for the damage is a secondary and side benefit.

**184.** All the following can co-exist with computer security incident handling *except*:

    a.    Help-desk function

    b.    System backup schedules

    c.    System development activity

    d.    Risk management process

*184. c.*   System development activity is engaged in designing and constructing a new computer application system, whereas incident handling is needed during operation of the same application system. For example, for purposes of efficiency and cost-savings, incident-handling capability is co-operated with a user help desk. Also, backups of system resources need to be used when recovering from an incident. Similarly, the risk analysis process benefits from statistics and logs showing the numbers and types of incidents that have occurred and the types of controls that are effective in preventing such incidents. This information can be used to help select appropriate security controls and practices.

**185.** Which of the following decreases the response time for computer security incidents?

    a.    Electronic mail

    b.    Physical bulletin board

    c.    Terminal and modem

    d.    Electronic bulletin board

*185. a.*   With computer security incidents, rapid communications is important. The incident team may need to send out security advisories or collect information quickly; thus some convenient form of communication, such as electronic mail (e-mail), is generally highly desirable. With e-mail, the team can easily direct information to various subgroups within the constituency, such as system managers or network managers, and broadcast general alerts to the entire constituency as needed. When connectivity already exists, e-mail has low overhead and is easy to use.

Although there are substitutes for e-mail, they tend to increase response time. An electronic bulletin board system (BBS) can work well for distributing information, especially if it provides a convenient user interface that encourages its use. A BBS connected to a network is more convenient to access than one requiring a terminal and modem; however, the latter may be the only alternative for organizations without sufficient network connectivity. In addition, telephones, physical bulletin boards, and flyers can be used, but they increase response time.

**186.** Which of the following incident response life-cycle phases is *most* challenging for many organizations?

    a.   Preparation

    b.   Detection

    c.   Recovery

    d.   Reporting

*186. b.* Detection, for many organizations, is the most challenging aspect of the incident response process. Actually detecting and assessing possible incidents is difficult. Determining whether an incident has occurred and, if so, the type, extent, and magnitude of the problem is not an easy task.

The other three phases such as preparation, recovery, and reporting are not that challenging. The scope of preparation and prevention phase covers establishing plans, policies, and procedures. The scope of recovery phase includes containment, restore, and eradication. The scope of reporting phase involves understanding the internal and external reporting requirements in terms of the content and timeliness of the reports.

**187.** Regarding incident response data, nonperformance of which one of the following items makes the other items less important?

    a.   Quality of data

    b.   Review of data

    c.   Standard format for data

    d.   Actionable data

*187. b.* If the incident response data is not reviewed regularly, the effectiveness of detection and analysis of incidents is questionable. It does not matter whether the data is of high quality with standard format for data, or actionable data. Proper and efficient reviews of incident-related data require people with extensive specialized technical knowledge and experience.

**188.** Which of the following statements about incident management and response is *not* true?

    a.   Most incidents require containment.

    b.   Containment strategies vary based on the type of incident.

    c.   All incidents need eradication.

    d.   Eradication is performed during recovery for some incidents.

**188. c.** For some incidents, eradication is either unnecessary or is performed during recovery. Most incidents require containment, so it is important to consider it early in the course of handling each incident. Also, it is true that containment strategies vary based on the type of incident.

**189.** Which of the following is the correct sequence of events taking place in the incident response life cycle process?

  a. Prevention, detection, preparation, eradication, and recovery

  b. Detection, response, reporting, recovery, and remediation

  c. Preparation, containment, analysis, prevention, and detection

  d. Containment, eradication, recovery, detection, and reporting

**189. b.** The correct sequence of events taking place in the incident response life cycle is detection, response, reporting, recovery, and remediation. Although the correct sequence is started with detection, there are some underlying activities that should be in place prior to detection. These prior activities include preparation and prevention, addressing the plans, policies, procedures, resources, support, metrics, patch management processes, host hardening measures, and properly configuring the network perimeter.

Detection involves the use of automated detection capabilities (for example, log analyzers) and manual detection capabilities (for example, user reports) to identify incidents. Response involves security staff offering advice and assistance to system users for the handling and reporting of security incidents (for example, held desk or forensic services). Reporting involves understanding the internal and external reporting requirements in terms of the content and timeliness of the reports. Recovery involves containment, restore, and eradication. Containment addresses how to control an incident before it spreads to avoid consuming excessive resources and increasing damage caused by the incident. Restore addresses bringing systems to normal operations and hardening systems to prevent similar incidents. Eradication addresses eliminating the affected components of the incident from the overall system to minimize further damage to the overall system. Remediation involves tracking and documenting security incidents on an ongoing basis.

**190.** Which of the following is *not* a recovery action after a computer security incident was contained?

  a. Rebuilding systems from scratch

  b. Changing passwords

  c. Preserving the evidence

  d. Installing patches

**190. c.** Preserving the evidence is a containment strategy, whereas all the other choices are part of recovery actions. Preserving the evidence is a legal matter, not a recovery action, and is a part of the containment strategy. In recovery action, administrators restore systems to normal operation and harden systems to prevent similar incidents, including the actions taken in the other three choices.

191. **Contrary to best practices, which of the following parties is usually *not* notified at all or is notified last when a computer security incident occurs?**

    a.  System administrator

    b.  Legal counsel

    c.  Disaster recovery coordinator

    d.  Hardware and software vendors

    ***191. b.*** The first part of a response mechanism is notification, whether automatic or manual. Besides technical staff, several others must be notified, depending on the nature and scope of the incident. Unfortunately, legal counsel is not always notified or is notified thinking that involvement is not required.

192. **Which of the following is *not* a viable option in the event of an audit processing failure or audit storage capacity being reached?**

    a.  Shut down the information system.

    b.  Overwrite the oldest-audit records.

    c.  Stop generating the audit records.

    d.  Continue processing after notification.

    ***192. d.*** In the event of an audit processing failure or audit storage capacity being reached, the information system alerts appropriate management officials and takes additional actions such as shutting down the system, overwriting the oldest-audit records, and stopping the generation of audit records. It should not continue processing, either with or without notification because the audit-related data would be lost.

193. **Which of the following surveillance techniques is passive in nature?**

    a.  Audit logs

    b.  Keyboard monitoring

    c.  Network sniffing

    d.  Online monitoring

    ***193. a.*** Audit logs collect data passively on computer journals or files for later review and analysis followed by action. The other three choices are examples of active surveillance techniques where electronic (online) monitoring is done for immediate review and analysis followed by action.

194. **A good computer security incident handling capability is closely linked to which of the following?**

    a.  Systems software

    b.  Applications software

    c.    Training and awareness program

    d.    Help desk

***194. c.*** A good incident handling capability is closely linked to an organization's training and awareness program. It will have educated users about such incidents so users know what to do when they occur. This can increase the likelihood that incidents will be reported early, thus helping to minimize damage. The help desk is a tool to handle incidents. Intruders can use both systems software and applications software to create security incidents.

**195.** **System users seldom consider which of the following?**

    a.    Internet security

    b.    Residual data security

    c.    Network security

    d.    Application system security

***195. b.*** System users seldom consider residual data security as part of their job duties because they think it is the job of computer operations or information security staff. Residual data security means data remanence where corporate spies can scavenge discarded magnetic or paper media to gain access to valuable data. Both system users and system managers usually consider the measures mentioned in the other three choices.

**196.** **Which of the following is not a special privileged user?**

    a.    System administrator

    b.    Business end-user

    c.    Security administrator

    d.    Computer operator

***196. b.*** A special privileged user is defined as an individual who has access to system control, monitoring, or administration functions. A business end-user is a normal system user performing day-to-day and routine tasks required by his job duties, and should not have special privileges as does with the system administrator, security administrator, computer operator, system programmer, system maintainer, network administrator, or desktop administrator. Privileged users have access to a set of access rights on a given system. Privileged access to privileged function should be limited to only few individuals in the IT department and should not be given to or shared with business end-users who are so many.

**197.** **Which of the following is the major consideration when an organization gives its incident response work to an outsourcer?**

    a.    Division of responsibilities

    b.    Handling incidents at multiple locations

    c.    Current and future quality of work

    d.    Lack of organization-specific knowledge

***197. c.*** The quality of the outsourcer's work remains an important consideration. Organizations should consider not only the current quality of work, but also the outsourcer's efforts to ensure the quality of future work, which are the major considerations. Organizations should think about how they could audit or otherwise objectively assess the quality of the outsourcer's work. Lack of organization-specific knowledge will reflect in the current and future quality of work. The other three choices are minor considerations and are a part of the major considerations.

**198.** The incident response team should work with which of the following when attempting to contain, eradicate, and recover from large-scale incidents?

     a.    Advisory distribution team

     b.    Vulnerability assessment team

     c.    Technology watch team

     d.    Patch management team

***198. d.*** Patch management staff work is separate from that of the incident response staff. Effective communication channels between the patch management team and the incident response team are likely to improve the success of a patch management program when containing, eradicating, and recovering from large-scale incidents. The activities listed in the other choices are the responsibility of the incident response team.

**199.** Which of the following is the foundation of the incident response program?

     a.    Incident response policies

     b.    Incident response procedures

     c.    Incident response standards

     d.    Incident response guidelines

***199. a.*** The incident response policies are the foundation of the incident response program. They define which events are considered as incidents, establish the organizational structure for the incident response program, define roles and responsibilities, and list the requirements for reporting incidents.

**200.** All the following can increase an information system's resilience *except*:

     a.    A system achieves a secure initial state.

     b.    A system reaches a secure failure state after failure.

     c.    A system's recovery procedures take the system to a known secure state after failure.

     d.    All of a system's identified vulnerabilities are fixed.

***200. d.*** There are vulnerabilities in a system that cannot be fixed, those that have not yet been fixed, those that are not known, and those that are not practical to fix due to operational constraints. Therefore, a statement that "all of a system's identified vulnerabilities are fixed" is not correct. The other three choices can increase a system's resilience.

**201.** **Media sanitization ensures which of the following?**

    a.    Data integrity

    b.    Data confidentiality

    c.    Data availability

    d.    Data accountability

***201. b.*** Media sanitization refers to the general process of removing data from storage media, such that there is reasonable assurance, in proportion to the confidentiality of the data, that the data may not be retrieved and reconstructed. The other three choices are not relevant here.

**202.** **Regarding media sanitization, degaussing is the same as:**

    a.    Incinerating

    b.    Melting

    c.    Demagnetizing

    d.    Smelting

***202. c.*** Degaussing reduces the magnetic flux to virtual zero by applying a reverse magnetizing field. It is also called demagnetizing.

**203.** **Regarding media sanitization, what is residual information remaining on storage media after clearing called?**

    a.    Residue

    b.    Remanence

    c.    Leftover data

    d.    Leftover information

***203. b.*** Remanence is residual information remaining on storage media after clearing. Choice (a) is incorrect because residue is data left in storage after information-processing operations are complete but before degaussing or overwriting (clearing) has taken place. Leftover data and leftover information are too general as terms to be of any use here.

**204.** **What is the security goal of the media sanitization requiring an overwriting process?**

    a.    To replace random data with written data.

    b.    To replace test data with written data.

    c.    To replace written data with random data.

    d.    To replace written data with statistical data.

***204. c.*** The security goal of the overwriting process is to replace written data with random data. The process may include overwriting not only the logical storage of a file (for example, file allocation table) but also may include all addressable locations.

**205.** Which of the following protects the confidentiality of information against a laboratory attack?

    a.   Disposal

    b.   Clearing

    c.   Purging

    d.   Disinfecting

**205. c.** A laboratory attack is a data scavenging method through the aid of what could be precise or elaborate and powerful equipment. This attack involves using signal-processing equipment and specially trained personnel. Purging information is a media sanitization process that protects the confidentiality of information against a laboratory attack and renders the sanitized data unrecoverable. This is accomplished through the removal of obsolete data by erasure, by overwriting of storage, or by resetting registers.

The other three choices are incorrect. Disposal is the act of discarding media by giving up control in a manner short of destruction, and is not a strong protection. Clearing is the overwriting of classified information such that the media may be reused. Clearing media would not suffice for purging. Disinfecting is a process of removing malware within a file.

**206.** Computer fraud is increased when:

    a.   Employees are not trained.

    b.   Documentation is not available.

    c.   Audit trails are not available.

    d.   Employee performance appraisals are not given.

**206. c.** Audit trails indicate what actions are taken by the system. Because the system has adequate and clear audit trails deters fraud perpetrators due to fear of getting caught. For example, the fact that employees are trained, documentation is available, and employee performance appraisals are given (preventive measures) does not necessarily mean that employees act with due diligence at all times. Hence, the need for the availability of audit trails (detection measures) is very important because they provide a concrete evidence of actions and inactions.

**207.** Which of the following is *not* a prerequisite for system monitoring?

    a.   System logs and audit trails

    b.   Software patches and fixes

    c.   Exception reports

    d.   Security policies and procedures

**207. c.** Exception reports are the result of a system monitoring activity. Deviations from standards or policies will be shown in exception reports. The other three choices are needed before the monitoring process starts.

**208.** **What is the selective termination of affected nonessential processing when a failure is detected in a computer system called?**

    a.    Fail-safe

    b.    Fail-soft

    c.    Fail-over

    d.    Fail-under

***208. b.*** The selective termination of affected nonessential processing when a failure is detected in a computer system is called fail-soft. The automatic termination and protection of programs when a failure is detected in a computer system is called a fail-safe. Fail-over means switching to a backup mechanism. Fail-under is a meaningless phrase.

**209.** **What is an audit trail is an example of?**

    a.    Recovery control

    b.    Corrective control

    c.    Preventive control

    d.    Detective control

***209. d.*** Audit trails show an attacker's actions after detection; hence they are an example of detective controls. Recovery controls facilitate the recovery of lost or damaged files. Corrective controls fix a problem or an error. Preventive controls do not detect or correct an error; they simply stop it if possible.

**210.** **From a best security practices viewpoint, which of the following falls under the ounce-of-prevention category?**

    a.    Patch and vulnerability management

    b.    Incident response

    c.    Symmetric cryptography

    d.    Key rollover

***210. a.*** It has been said that "An ounce of prevention equals a pound of cure." Patch and vulnerability management is the "ounce of prevention" compared to the "pound of cure" in the incident response, in that timely patches to software reduce the chances of computer incidents.

Symmetric cryptography uses the same key for both encryption and decryption, whereas asymmetric cryptography uses separate keys for encryption and decryption, or to digitally sign and verify a signature. Key rollover is the process of generating and using a new key (symmetric or asymmetric key pair) to replace one already in use.

**211.** **Which of the following must be manually keyed into an automated IT resources inventory tool used in patch management to respond quickly and effectively?**

    a.    Connected network port

    b.    Physical location

    c.    Software configuration

    d.    Hardware configuration

***211. b.***   Although most information can be taken automatically from the system data, the physical location of an IT resource must be manually entered. Connected network port numbers can be taken automatically from the system data. Software and hardware configuration information can be taken automatically from the system data.

**212.**   **Regarding a patch management program, which of the following is *not* an example of a threat?**

    a.    Exploit scripts

    b.    Worms

    c.    Software flaws

    d.    Viruses

***212. c.***   Software flaw vulnerabilities cause a weakness in the security of a system. Threats are capabilities or methods of attack developed by malicious entities to exploit vulnerabilities and potentially cause harm to a computer system or network. Threats usually take the form of exploit scripts, worms, viruses, rootkits, exploits, and Trojan horses.

**213.**   **Regarding a patch management program, which of the following does *not* always return the system to its previous state?**

    a.    Disable

    b.    Uninstall

    c.    Enable

    d.    Install

***213. b.***   There are many options available to a system administrator in remediation testing. The ability to "undo" or uninstall a patch should be considered; however, even when this option is provided, the uninstall process does not always return the system to its previous state. Disable temporarily disconnects a service. Enable or install is not relevant here.

**214.**   **Regarding media sanitization, degaussing is *not* effective for which of the following?**

    a.    Nonmagnetic media

    b.    Damaged media

    c.    Media with large storage capacity

    d.    Quickly purging diskettes

***214. a.***   Degaussing is exposing the magnetic media to a strong magnetic field in order to disrupt the recorded magnetic domains. It is not effective for purging nonmagnetic media (i.e., optical media), such as compact discs (CD) and digital versatile discs (DVD). However, degaussing can be an effective method for purging damaged media, for purging media with exceptionally large storage capacities, or for quickly purging diskettes.

**215.** **Which of the following is the ultimate form of media sanitization?**

    a.    Disposal

    b.    Clearing

    c.    Purging

    d.    Destroying

*215. d.* Media destruction is the ultimate form of sanitization. After media are destroyed, they cannot be reused as originally intended, and that information is virtually impossible to recover or prohibitively expensive from that media. Physical destruction can be accomplished using a variety of methods, including disintegration, incineration, pulverization, shredding, melting, sanding, and chemical treatment.

**216.** **Organizations that outsource media sanitization work should exercise:**

    a.    Due process

    b.    Due law

    c.    Due care

    d.    Due diligence

*216. d.* Organizations can outsource media sanitization and destruction if business and security management decide this would be the most reasonable option for maintaining confidentiality while optimizing available resources. When choosing this option, organizations exercise due diligence when entering into a contract with another party engaged in media sanitization. Due diligence requires organizations to develop and implement an effective security program to prevent and detect violation of policies and laws.

Due process means each person is given an equal and a fair chance of being represented or heard and that everybody goes through the same process for consideration and approval. It means all are equal in the eyes of the law. Due law covers due process and due care. Due care means reasonable care in promoting the common good and maintaining the minimal and customary practices.

**217.** **Redundant arrays of independent disks (RAID) provide which of the following security services *most*?**

    a.    Data confidentiality

    b.    Data reliability

    c.    Data availability

    d.    Data integrity

*217. b.* Forensic investigators are encountering redundant arrays of independent disks (RAID) systems with increasing frequency as businesses elect to utilize systems that provide greater data reliability. RAID provides data confidentiality, data availability, and data integrity security services to a lesser degree than data reliability.

**218.** The *fraud triangle* includes which of the following elements?

    a.    Pressure, opportunity, and rationalization

    b.    Technique, target, and time

    c.    Intent, means, and environment

    d.    Place, ability, and need

*218. a.* Pressure includes financial and nonfinancial types, and it could be real or perceived. Opportunity includes real or perceived categories in terms of time and place. Rationalization means the illegal actions are consistent with the perpetrator's personal code of conduct or state of mind.

**219.** When a system preserves a secure state, during and after a failure is called a:

    a.    System failure

    b.    Fail-secure

    c.    Fail-access

    d.    System fault

*219. b.* In fail-secure, the system preserves a secure condition during and after an identified failure. System failure and fault are generic and do not preserve a secure condition like fail-secure. Fail-access is a meaningless term here.

**220.** Fault-tolerance systems provide which of the following security services?

    a.    Confidentiality and integrity

    b.    Integrity and availability

    c.    Availability and accountability

    d.    Accountability and confidentiality

*220. b.* The goal of fault-tolerance systems is to detect and correct a fault and to maintain the availability of a computer system. Fault-tolerance systems play an important role in maintaining high data and system integrity and in ensuring high-availability of systems. Examples include disk mirroring and server mirroring techniques.

**221.** What do fault-tolerant hardware control devices include?

    a.    Disk duplexing and mirroring

    b.    Server consolidation

    c.    LAN consolidation

    d.    Disk distribution

*221. a.* Disk duplexing means that the disk controller is duplicated. When one disk controller fails, the other one is ready to operate. Disk mirroring means the file server contains duplicate disks, and that all information is written to both disks simultaneously. Server consolidation, local-area network (LAN) consolidation, and disk distribution are meaningless to fault tolerance; although, they may have their own uses.

**222.** **Performing automated deployment of patches is difficult for which of the following?**

    a.    Homogeneous computing platforms

    b.    Legacy systems

    c.    Standardized desktop systems

    d.    Similarly configured servers

***222. b.*** Manual patching is useful and necessary for many legacy and specialized systems due to their nature. Automated patching tools allow an administrator to update hundreds or even thousands of systems from a single console. Deployment is fairly simple when there are homogeneous computing platforms, with standardized desktop systems, and similarly configured servers.

**223.** **Regarding media sanitization, degaussing is an acceptable method for which of the following?**

    a.    Disposal

    b.    Clearing

    c.    Purging

    d.    Disinfecting

***223. c.*** Degaussing is demagnetizing magnetic media to remove magnetic memory and to erase the contents of media. Purging is the removal of obsolete data by erasure, by overwriting of storage, or by resetting registers. Thus, degaussing and executing the firmware Secure Purge command (for serial advanced technology attachment (SATA) drives only) are acceptable methods for purging.

The other three choices are incorrect. Disposal is the act of discarding media by giving up control in a manner short of destruction and is not a strong protection. Clearing is the overwriting of classified information such that that the media may be reused. Clearing media would not suffice for purging. Disinfecting is a process of removing malware within a file.

**224.** **Regarding a patch management program, which of the following should be done before performing the patch remediation?**

    a.    Test on a nonproduction system.

    b.    Check software for proper operation.

    c.    Conduct a full backup of the system.

    d.    Consider all implementation differences.

*224. c.* Before performing the remediation, the system administrator may want to conduct a full backup of the system to be patched. This allows for a timely system restoration to its previous state if the patch has an unintended or unexpected impact on the host. The other three choices are part of the patch remediation testing procedures.

**225.** Regarding a patch management program, an experienced administrator or security officer should perform which of the following?

    a.    Test file settings.

    b.    Test configuration settings.

    c.    Review patch logs.

    d.    Conduct exploit tests.

*225. d.* Conducting an exploit test means performing a penetration test to exploit the vulnerability. Only an experienced administrator or security officer should perform exploit tests because this involves launching actual attacks within a network or on a host. Generally, this type of testing should be performed only on nonproduction equipment and only for certain vulnerabilities. Only qualified staff who are thoroughly aware of the risk and who are fully trained should conduct the tests.

Testing file settings, testing configuration settings, and reviewing patch logs are routine tasks a less experienced administrator or security officer can perform.

# SCENARIO-BASED QUESTIONS, ANSWERS, AND EXPLANATIONS

Use the following information to answer questions 1 through 8.

The GRO Company will face an audit by a federal regulatory body in 30 days. The last update for its policies and procedures was made one year ago after the last audit. It has 50% of the controls in place described in the last audit, and 45% will be turned on before the auditors arrive. The remaining 5% of controls (audit trail software for computer operating systems) will break the financial systems if turned on for more than one hour.

**1.** Who initiates audit trails in computer systems?

    a.    Functional users

    b.    System auditors

    c.    System administrators

    d.    Security administrators

*1. a.* Functional users have the utmost responsibility in initiating audit trails in their computer systems for tracing and accountability purposes. Systems and security administrators help in designing and developing these audit trails. System auditors review the adequacy and completeness of audit trails and issue an opinion whether they are effectively working. Auditors do not initiate, design, or develop audit trails due to their independence in attitude and appearance as dictated by their Professional Standards.

**2.** **An inexpensive security measure is which of the following?**

    a.    Firewalls

    b.    Intrusion detection

    c.    Audit trails

    d.    Access controls

**2. c.** Audit trails provide one of the best and most inexpensive means for tracking possible hacker attacks, not only after attack, but also during the attack. One can learn what the attacker did to enter a computer system, and what he did after entering the system. Audit trails also detect unauthorized but abusive user activity. Firewalls, intrusion detection systems, and access controls are expensive when compared to audit trails.

**3.** **What is an audit trail an example of?**

    a.    Recovery control

    b.    Corrective control

    c.    Preventive control

    d.    Detective control

**3. d.** Audit trails show an attacker's actions after detection; hence they are an example of detective controls. Recovery controls facilitate the recovery of lost or damaged files. Corrective controls fix a problem or an error. Preventive controls do not detect or correct an error; they simply stop it if possible.

**4.** **Which of the following statements is *not* true about audit trails from a computer security viewpoint?**

    a.    There is interdependency between audit trails and security policy.

    b.    If a user is impersonated, the audit trail will establish events and the identity of the user.

    c.    Audit trails can assist in contingency planning.

    d.    Audit trails can be used to identify breakdowns in logical access controls.

**4. b.** Audit trails have several benefits. They are tools often used to help hold users accountable for their actions. To be held accountable, the users must be known to the system (usually accomplished through the identification and authentication process). However, audit trails collect events and associate them with the perceived user (i.e., the user ID provided). If a user is impersonated, the audit trail establishes events but not the identity of the user.

It is true that there is interdependency between audit trails and security policy. Policy dictates who has authorized access to particular system resources. Therefore it specifies, directly or indirectly, what violations of policy should be identified through audit trails.

It is true that audit trails can assist in contingency planning by leaving a record of activities performed on the system or within a specific application. In the event of a technical malfunction, this log can be used to help reconstruct the state of the system (or specific files).

It is true that audit trails can be used to identify breakdowns in logical access controls. Logical access controls restrict the use of system resources to authorized users. Audit trails complement this activity by identifying breakdowns in logical access controls or verifying that access control restrictions are behaving as expected.

**5.** **Audit trails should be reviewed. Which of the following methods is *not* the best way to perform a query to generate reports of selected information?**

    a.    By a known damage or occurrence

    b.    By a known user identification

    c.    By a known terminal identification

    d.    By a known application system name

**5. *a.*** Damage or the occurrence of an undesirable event cannot be anticipated or predicted in advance, thus making it difficult to make a query. The system design cannot handle unknown events. Audit trails can be used to review what occurred after an event, for periodic reviews, and for real-time analysis. Reviewers need to understand what normal activity looks like. Audit trail review is easier if the audit trail function can be queried by user ID, terminal ID, application system name, date and time, or some other set of parameters to run reports of selected information.

**6.** **Audit trail records contain vast amounts of data. Which of the following review methods is *best* to review all records associated with a particular user or application system?**

    a.    Batch-mode analysis

    b.    Real-time audit analysis

    c.    Audit trail review after an event

    d.    Periodic review of audit trail data

**6. *b.*** Audit trail data can be used to review what occurred after an event, for periodic reviews, and for real-time analysis. Audit analysis tools can be used in a real-time, or near real-time, fashion. A manual review of audit records in real time is not feasible on large multi-user systems due to the large volume of records generated. However, it might be possible to view all records associated with a particular user or application and view them in real time.

Batch-mode analysis is incorrect because it is a traditional method of analyzing audit trails. The audit trail data are reviewed periodically. Audit records are archived during that interval for later analysis. All these choices do not provide the convenience of displaying or reporting all records associated with a user or application.

7. **An audit trail record should include sufficient information to trace a user's actions and events. Which of the following information in the audit trail record can help determine if the user was a masquerader or the actual person specified?**

    a.    The user identification associated with the event

    b.    The date and time associated with the event

    c.    The program used to initiate the event

    d.    The command used to initiate the event

*7. b.* An audit trail should include sufficient information to establish what events occurred and who (or what) caused them. In general, an event record should specify when the event occurred, the user ID associated with the event, the program or command used to initiate the event, and the result. Date and timestamps can help determine if the user were a masquerader or the actual person specified.

8. **Automated tools help in analyzing audit trail data. Which one of the following tools looks for anomalies in user or system behavior?**

    a.    Trend analysis tools

    b.    Audit data-reduction tools

    c.    Attack signature-detection tools

    d.    Audit data-collection tools

*8. a.* Many types of tools have been developed to help reduce the amount of information contained in audit records, as well as to distill useful information from the raw data. Especially on larger systems, audit trail software can create large files, which can be extremely difficult to analyze manually. The use of automated tools is likely to be the difference between unused audit trail data and a robust program. Trend analysis and variance detection tools look for anomalies in user or system behavior.

Audit data-reduction tools are preprocessors designed to reduce the volume of audit records to facilitate manual review. These tools generally remove records generated by specified classes of events, such as records generated by nightly backups. Attack signature-detection tools look for an attack signature, which is a specific sequence of events indicative of an unauthorized access attempt. A simple example is repeated failed log-in attempts. Audit data-collection tools simply gather data for analysis later.

## SOURCES AND REFERENCES

"Creating a Patch and Vulnerability Management Program (NIST SP800-40V2)," National Institute of Standards and Technology (NIST), U.S. Department of Commerce, Gaithersburg, Maryland, November 2005.

"Engineering Principles for IT Security (NIST SP800-27 Revision A)," National Institute of Standards and Technology (NIST), U.S. Department of Commerce, Gaithersburg, Maryland, June 2004.

"Guide to Malware Incident Prevention and Handling (NIST SP800-83)," National Institute of Standards and Technology (NIST), U.S. Department of Commerce, Gaithersburg, Maryland, November 2005.

"Guide to Storage Encryption Technologies for End User Devices (NIST SP800-111Draft)," National Institute of Standards and Technology (NIST), U.S. Department of Commerce, Gaithersburg, Maryland, August 2007.

"Guidelines for Media Sanitization (NIST SP800-88 Revision 1)," National Institute of Standards and Technology (NIST), U.S. Department of Commerce, Gaithersburg, Maryland, September 2006.

Walden, Bob. "Data Storage Management." An NSS Group's White Paper, 1991–2001.

# DOMAIN 8

## Business Continuity and Disaster Recovery Planning

### TRADITIONAL QUESTIONS, ANSWERS, AND EXPLANATIONS

1. **Which of the following information technology (IT) contingency solution for servers minimizes the recovery time window?**

    a. Electronic vaulting

    b. Remote journaling

    c. Load balancing

    d. Disk replication

    **1. d.**   With disk replication, recovery windows are minimized because data is written to two different disks to ensure that two valid copies of the data are always available. The two disks are called the protected server (the main server) and the replicating server (the backup server). Electronic vaulting and remote journaling are similar technologies that provide additional data backup capabilities, with backups made to remote tape or disk drives over communication links. Load balancing increases server and application system availability.

2. **Which of the following IT contingency solutions for servers provides high availability?**

    a. Network-attached storage

    b. System backups

    c. Redundant array of independent disks

    d. Electronic vaulting

***2. a.*** Virtualization network-attached storage (NAS) or storage-area network (SAN) provide high availability because it combines multiple physical storage devices into a logical, virtual storage device that can be centrally managed. System backups provide low availability. A redundant array of independent disks and electronic vaulting provide availability levels between high and low.

**3.** **Regarding contingency planning, which of the following IT platforms requires vendor service-level agreements?**

    a.   Desktop computers

    b.   Servers

    c.   Distributed systems

    d.   Wide-area networks

***3. d.*** A wide-area network (WAN) is a data communications network that consists of two or more local-area networks (LANs) that are dispersed over a wide geographical area. WAN communication links, usually provided by a public carrier, enable one LAN to interact with other LANs. Service-level agreements (SLAs) can facilitate prompt recovery following software or hardware problems associated with the network. An SLA also may be developed with the network service provider (NSP) or the Internet service provider (ISP) to guarantee the desired network availability and establish tariffs if the vendor's network is unavailable. Desktop computers, servers, and distributed system are not as complicated as WANs requiring SLAs.

**4.** **Regarding business continuity planning (BCP) and disaster recovery planning (DRP), which of the following contingency solutions for wide-area networks (WANs) increases vulnerability to hackers?**

    a.   Redundant communication links

    b.   Multiple network service providers

    c.   Multiple Internet connections

    d.   Redundant network connecting devices

***4. c.*** It is true that multiple Internet connections increase a network's vulnerability to hackers. But at the same time, multiple Internet connections provide redundancy, meaning that if one connection were to fail, Internet traffic could be routed through the remaining connection. So, there is a trade-off between security and availability.

The other three choices are not vulnerable to hackers. Redundant communication links can include two T-1 connections or the backup link. Multiple network service providers (NSPs) and the Internet service providers (ISPs) providing a robust and reliable service from their core networks. Redundant network connecting devices such as routers, switches, and firewalls can create high availability.

**5.** Regarding BCP and DRP, which of the following IT platforms typically provide some inherent level of redundancy?

    a.    Mainframe systems

    b.    Distributed systems

    c.    Desktop computers

    d.    Websites

*5. b.* Distributed systems use the client-server relationship model to make the application more accessible to users in different locations, and they rely extensively on LAN and WAN connectivity. Because all data resides at a company's headquarters location and is replicated to the local sites, the distributed system provides some inherent level of redundancy. The other three choices cannot provide that kind of redundancy.

**6.** Which of the following IT contingency solutions provides recovery time objectives (RTOs) ranging from minutes to several hours?

    a.    Synchronous mirroring

    b.    Asynchronous shadowing

    c.    Single location disk replication

    d.    Multiple location disk replication

*6. a.* Disk replication can be implemented locally or between different locations. Disk replication techniques are classified as synchronous or asynchronous. With synchronous mirroring, the recovery time objectives (RTOs) can be minutes to several hours (for shorter time periods), and hence should be used for applications that can accept little or no data loss. With asynchronous shadowing, the RTO can range from several hours to a day (for longer time periods), depending on the time that is required to implement the changes in the unapplied logs. Disk replication involves two different disks to ensure that two valid copies of the data are always available.

**7.** The IT operations management of KPQ Corporation is concerned about the reliability and availability data for its four major, mission-critical information systems that are used by business end-users. The KPQ corporate management's goal is to improve the reliability and availability of these four systems in order to increase customer satisfaction both internally and externally. The IT operations management collected the following data on downtime hours that include scheduled maintenance hours and uptime hours for all these systems. Assume 365 operating days per year and 24 hours per day for all these systems. The KPQ functional management thinks that the security goal of availability is more important in ensuring the continuity of business operations than the confidentiality and integrity goals. This is because the availability goal will ensure timely and reliable access to and use of system-related data and information, as it is an indicator of quantity of service.

| SYSTEM | DOWNTIME, HOURS | UPTIME, HOURS |
|--------|-----------------|---------------|
| 1 | 200 | 8,560 |
| 2 | 150 | 8,610 |
| 3 | 250 | 8,510 |
| 4 | 100 | 8,660 |

**Which of the following systems has the highest availability in a year expressed in percentages and rounded up?**

    a.    System 1

    b.    System 2

    c.    System 3

    d.    System 4

**7. d.**   System 4 has the highest availability percentage. Theoretically speaking, the lower the downtime for a system, the higher the availability of that system, and higher the reliability of that system, and vice versa. In fact, this question does not require any calculations to perform because one can find out the correct answer just by looking at the downtime and uptime data given in that the lower the downtime hours, the higher the uptime hours, and the higher the availability of the system, and vice versa.

| SYSTEM | AVAILABILITY, PERCENT | RELIABILITY, PERCENT |
|--------|-----------------------|----------------------|
| 1 | 97.7 | 97.7 |
| 2 | 98.3 | 98.3 |
| 3 | 97.1 | 97.1 |
| 4 | 98.9 | 98.9 |

Calculations for System 1 are shown below and calculations for other systems follow the System 1 calculations.

Availability for System 1 =
    [Uptime/(Uptime + Downtime)] × 100 = [(8,560/8,760)] × 100 = 97.7%

Reliability for System 1 =
    [1 − (Downtime/Downtime + Uptime)] × 100 = [1 − (200/8,760)] × 100 = 97.7%

Check: Reliability for System 1 =
    100 − (100 − Availability percent) = 100 − (100 − 97.7) = 97.7%

This goes to say that the availability and reliability goals are intrinsically related to each other, where the former is a component of the latter.

8. **Regarding BCP and DRP, redundant array of independent disk (RAID) does *not* do which of the following?**

 a. Provide disk redundancy

 b. Provide power redundancy

 c. Decrease mean-time-between-failures

 d. Provide fault tolerance for data storage

*8. b.* Redundant array of independent disk (RAID) does not provide power redundancy and should be acquired through an uninterruptible power supply system. However, RAID provides the other three choices.

9. **Redundant array of independent disk (RAID) technology does *not* use which of the following?**

 a. Electronic vaulting

 b. Mirroring

 c. Parity

 d. Striping

*9. a.* Redundant array of independent disk (RAID) technology uses three data redundancy techniques such as mirroring, parity, and striping, not electronic vaulting. Electronic vaulting is located offsite, whereas RAID is placed at local servers where the former may use the latter.

10. **Regarding BCP and DRP, the board of directors of an organization is *not* required to follow which of the following?**

 a. Duty of due care

 b. Duty of absolute care

 c. Duty of loyalty

 d. Duty of obedience

*10. b.* Duty of absolute care is not needed because reasonable and normal care is expected of the board of directors because no one can anticipate or protect from all disasters. However, the directors need to follow the other three duties of due care, loyalty, and obedience.

11. **Which of the following tasks is *not* a part of business continuity plan (BCP)?**

 a. Project scoping

 b. Impact assessment

 c. Disaster recovery procedures

 d. Disaster recovery strategies

***11. c.*** Tasks are different between a business continuity plan (BCP) and disaster recovery planning (DRP) because of timing of those tasks. For example, disaster recovery procedures come into play only during disaster, which is a part of DRP.

**12.** Which of the following tasks is *not* a part of disaster recovery planning (DRP)?

   a.  Restoration procedures

   b.  Procuring the needed equipment

   c.  Relocating to a primary processing site

   d.  Selecting an alternate processing site

***12. d.*** Tasks are different between business continuity plan (BCP) and disaster recovery planning (DRP) because of timing of those tasks. For example, selecting an alternative processing site should be planned out prior to a disaster, which is a part of a BCP. The other three choices are a part of DRP. Note that DRP is associated with data processing and BCP refers to actions that keep the business running in the event of a disruption, even if it is with pencil and paper.

**13.** Regarding BCP and DRP, critical measurements in business impact analysis (BIA) include which of the following?

   a.  General support system objectives

   b.  Major application system objectives

   c.  Recovery time objectives and recovery point objectives

   d.  Uninterruptible power supply system objectives

***13. c.*** Two critical measurements in business impact analysis (BIA) include recovery time objectives (RTOs) and recovery point objectives (RPOs). Usually, systems are classified as general support systems (for example, networks, servers, computers, gateways, and programs) and major application systems (for example, billing, payroll, inventory, and personnel system). Uninterruptible power supply (UPS) system is an auxiliary system supporting general systems and application systems. Regardless of the nature and type of a system, they all need to fulfill the RTOs and RPOs to determine their impact on business operations.

**14.** Regarding BCP and DRP, which of the following establishes an information system's recovery time objective (RTO)?

   a.  Cost of system inoperability and the cost of resources

   b.  Maximum allowable outage time and the cost to recover

   c.  Cost of disruption and the cost to recover

   d.  Cost of impact and the cost of resources

***14. b.*** The balancing point between the maximum allowable outage (MAO) and the cost to recover establishes an information system's recovery time objective (RTO). Recovery strategies must be created to meet the RTO. The maximum allowable outage is also called maximum tolerable downtime (MTD). The other three choices are incorrect because they do not deal with time and cost dimensions together.

**15.** **Regarding BCP and DRP, which of the following determines the recovery cost balancing?**

    a.    Cost of system inoperability and the cost of resources to recover

    b.    Maximum allowable outage and the cost to recover

    c.    Cost of disruption and the cost to recover

    d.    Cost of impact and the cost of resources

*15. a.* It is important to determine the optimum point to recover an IT system by balancing the cost of system inoperability against the cost of resources required for restoring the system. This is called recovery cost balancing, which indicates how long an organization can afford to allow the system to be disrupted or unavailable. The other three choices are incorrect because they do not deal with the recovery cost balancing principle.

**16.** **Regarding contingency planning, which of the following actions are performed when malicious attacks compromise the confidentiality or integrity of an information system?**

    1.    Graceful degradation

    2.    System shutdown

    3.    Fallback to manual mode

    4.    Alternate information flows

        a.    1 and 2

        b.    2 and 3

        c.    3 and 4

        d.    1, 2, 3, and 4

*16. d.* The actions to perform during malicious attacks compromise the confidentiality or integrity of the information system include graceful degradation, information system shutdown, fallback to a manual mode, alternative information flows, or operating in a mode that is reserved solely for when the system is under attack.

**17.** **In transaction-based systems, which of the following are mechanisms supporting transaction recovery?**

    1.    Transaction rollback

    2.    Transaction journaling

    3.    Router tables

    4.    Compilers

        a.    1 only

        b.    1 and 2

        c.    3 and 4

        d.    1, 2, 3, and 4

*17. b.* Transaction rollback and transaction journaling are examples of mechanisms supporting transaction recovery. Routers use router tables for routing messages and packets. A compiler is software used to translate a computer program written in a high-level programming language (source code) into a machine language for execution. Both router tables and compilers do not support transaction recovery.

18. Regarding contingency planning, which of the following is susceptible to potential accessibility problems in the event of an area-wide disaster?

1. Alternative storage site
2. Alternative processing site
3. Alternative telecommunications services
4. Remote redundant secondary systems

   a. 1 and 2
   b. 2 and 3
   c. 3 only
   d. 1 and 4

*18. a.* Both alternative storage site and alternative processing site are susceptible to potential accessibility problems in the event of an area-wide disruption or disaster. Explicit mitigation actions are needed to handle this problem. Telecommunication services (ISPs and network service providers) and remote redundant secondary systems are located far away from the local area, hence not susceptible to potential accessibility problems.

19. Which of the following ensures the successful completion of tasks in the development of business continuity and disaster recovery plans?

   a. Defining individual roles
   b. Defining operational activities
   c. Assigning individual responsibility
   d. Exacting individual accountability

*19. d.* It is important to ensure that individuals responsible for the various business continuity and contingency planning activities are held accountable for the successful completion of individual tasks and that the core business process owners are responsible and accountable for meeting the milestones for the development and testing of contingency plans for their core business processes.

20. Regarding contingency planning, strategic reasons for separating the alternative storage site from the primary storage site include ensuring:

1. Both sites are not susceptible to the same hazards.
2. Both sites are not colocated in the same area.

3.    Both sites do not have the same recovery time objectives.

4.    Both sites do not have the same recovery point objectives.

    a.    1 and 2

    b.    1, 2, and 3

    c.    1, 2, and 4

    d.    1, 2, 3, and 4

**20. a.**    It is important to ensure that both sites (i.e., alternative storage site and primary storage site) are not susceptible to the same hazards, are not colocated in the same area, have the same recovery time objectives (RTOs), and have the same recovery point objectives (RPOs).

**21.**    **Regarding BCP and DRP, if MAO is maximum allowable outage, BIA is business impact analysis, RTO is recovery time objective, MTBF is mean-time-between-failures, RPO is recovery point objective, MTTR is mean-time-to-repair, and UPS is uninterruptible power supply, which one of the following is related to and compatible with each other within the same choice?**

    a.    MAO, BIA, RTO, and MTBF

    b.    BIA, RTO, RPO, and MAO

    c.    MAO, MTTR, RPO, and UPS

    d.    MAO, MTBF, MTTR, and UPS

**21. b.**    A business impact analysis (BIA) is conducted by identifying a system's critical resources. Two critical resource measures in BIA include recovery time objective (RTO) and recovery point objective (RPO). The impact in BIA is expressed in terms of maximum allowable outage (MAO). Hence, BIA, RTO, RPO, and MAO are related to and compatible with each other. MTBF is mean-time-between-failures, MTTR is mean-time-to-repair, and UPS is uninterruptible power supply, and they have no relation to BIA, RTO, RPO, and MAO because MAO deals with maximum time, whereas MTTF and MTTR deals with mean time (i.e., average time).

**22.**    **Regarding contingency planning, system-level information backups do *not* require which of the following to protect their integrity while in storage?**

    a.    Passwords

    b.    Digital signatures

    c.    Encryption

    d.    Cryptographic hashes

**22. a.**    Backups are performed at the user-level and system-level where the latter contains an operating system, application software, and software licenses. Only user-level information backups require passwords. System-level information backups require controls such as digital signatures, encryption, and cryptographic hashes to protect their integrity.

**23.** Which of the following is an operational control and is a prerequisite to developing a disaster recovery plan?

    a.    System backups

    b.    Business impact analysis

    c.    Cost-benefit analysis

    d.    Risk analysis

***23. a.*** System backups provide the necessary data files and programs to recover from a disaster and to reconstruct a database from the point of failure. System backups are operational controls, whereas the items mentioned in the other choices come under management controls and analytical in nature.

**24.** Which of the following is a critical benefit of implementing an electronic vaulting program?

    a.    It supports unattended computer center operations or automation.

    b.    During a crisis situation, an electronic vault can make the difference between an organization's survival and failure.

    c.    It reduces required backup storage space.

    d.    It provides faster storage data retrieval.

***24. b.*** For some organizations, time becomes money. Increased system reliability improves the likelihood that all the information required is available at the electronic vault. If data can be retrieved immediately from the off-site storage, less is required in the computer center. It reduces retrieval time from hours to minutes. Because electronic vaulting eliminates tapes, which are a hindrance to automated operations, electronic vaulting supports automation.

**25.** Regarding contingency planning, information system backups require which of the following?

    1.    Both the primary storage site and alternative storage site do not need to be susceptible to the same hazards.

    2.    Both operational system and redundant secondary system do not need to be colocated in the same area.

    3.    Both primary storage site and alternative storage site do not need to have the same recovery time objectives.

    4.    Both operational system and redundant secondary system do not need to have the same recovery point objectives.

        a.    1 and 2

        b.    1, 2, and 3

        c.    1, 2, and 4

        d.    1, 2, 3, and 4

**25. a.** System backup information can be transferred to the alternative storage site, and the same backup can be maintained at a redundant secondary system, not colocated with the operational system. Both sites and both systems must have the same recovery time objectives (RTOs) and same recovery point objectives (RPOs). This arrangement can be activated without loss of information or disruption to the operation.

**26.** **Disaster recovery strategies must consider or address which of the following?**

1. Recovery time objective
2. Disruption impacts
3. Allowable outage times
4. Interdependent systems

    a. I only

    b. 1 and 2

    c. 1, 2, and 3

    d. 1, 2, 3, and 4

**26. d.** A disaster recovery strategy must be in place to recover and restore data and system operations within the recovery time objective (RTO) period. The strategies should address disruption impacts and allowable outage times identified in the business impact analysis (BIA). The chosen strategy must also be coordinated with the IT contingency plans of interdependent systems. Several alternatives should be considered when developing the strategy, including cost, allowable outage times, security, and integration into organization-level contingency plans.

**27.** **The final consideration in the disaster recovery strategy must be which of the following?**

    a. Criticality of data and systems

    b. Availability of data and systems

    c. Final costs and benefits

    d. Recovery time objective requirements

**27. c.** The final consideration in the disaster recovery strategy must be final costs and benefits; although, cost and benefit data is considered initially. No prudent manager or executive would want to spend ten dollars to obtain a one dollar benefit. When costs exceed benefits, some managers accept the risk and some do not. Note that it is a human tendency to understate costs and overstate benefits. Some examples of costs include loss of income from loss of sales, cost of not meeting legal and regulatory requirements, cost of not meeting contractual and financial obligations, and cost of loss of reputation. Some examples of benefits include assurance of continuity of business operations, ability to make sales and profits, providing gainful employment, and satisfying internal and external customers and other stakeholders.

The recovery strategy must meet criticality and availability of data and systems and recovery time objective (RTO) requirements while remaining within the cost and benefit guidelines.

**28.** Regarding BCP and DRP, which of the following does *not* prevent potential data loss?

    a.   Disk mirroring

    b.   Offsite storage of backup media

    c.   Redundant array of independent disk

    d.   Load balancing

**28. b.** Although offsite storage of backup media enables a computer system to be recovered, data added to or modified on the server since the previous backup could be lost during a disruption or disaster. To avoid this potential data loss, a backup strategy may need to be complemented by redundancy solutions, such as disk mirroring, redundant array of independent disk (RAID), and load balancing.

**29.** Which of the following is an example of a recovery time objective (RTO) for a payroll system identified in a business impact analysis (BIA) document?

    a.   Time and attendance reporting may require the use of a LAN server and other resources.

    b.   LAN disruption for 8 hours may create a delay in time sheet processing.

    c.   The LAN server must be recovered within 8 hours to avoid a delay in time sheet processing.

    d.   The LAN server must be recovered fully to distribute payroll checks on Friday to all employees.

**29. c.** "The LAN server must be recovered within 8 hours to avoid a delay in time sheet processing" is an example of BIA's recovery time objective (RTO). "Time and attendance reporting may require the use of a LAN server and other resources" is an example of BIA's critical resource. "LAN disruption for 8 hours may create a delay in time sheet processing" is an example of BIA's resource impact. "The LAN server must be recovered fully to distribute payroll checks on Friday to all employees" is an example of BIA's recovery point objective (RPO).

**30.** Which of the following are closely connected to each other when conducting business impact analysis (BIA) as a part of the IT contingency planning process?

    1.   System's components

    2.   System's interdependencies

    3.   System's critical resources

    4.   System's downtime impacts

        a.   1 and 2

        b.   2 and 3

        c.   3 and 4

        d.   1, 2, 3, and 4

**30. c.** A business impact analysis (BIA) is a critical step to understanding the information system components, interdependencies, and potential downtime impact. Contingency plan strategy and procedures should be designed in consideration of the results of the BIA. A BIA is conducted by identifying the system's critical resources. Each critical resource is then further examined to determine how long functionality of the resource could be withheld from the information system before an unacceptable impact is experienced. Therefore, system's critical resources and system's downtime impacts are closely related to each other than the other items.

**31.** Business continuity plans (BCP) need periodic audits to ensure the accuracy, currency, completeness, applicability, and usefulness of such plans in order to properly run business operations. Which one of the following items is a prerequisite to the other three items?

    a.    Internal audits

    b.    Self-assessments

    c.    External audits

    d.    Third-party audits

**31. b.** Self-assessments are proactive exercises and are a prerequisite to other types of audits. Self-assessments are in the form of questionnaires and usually a company's employees (for example, supervisors or mangers) conduct these self-assessments to collect answers from functional management and IT management on various business operations. If these self-assessments are conducted with honesty and integrity, they can be eye-opening exercises because their results may not be the same as expected by the company management. The purpose of self-assessments is to identify strengths and weaknesses so weaknesses can be corrected and strengths can be improved.

In addition, self-assessments make an organization ready and prepared for the other audits such as internal audits by corporate internal auditors, external audits by public accounting firms, and third-party audits by regulatory compliance auditors, insurance industry auditors, and others. In fact, overall audit costs can be reduced if these auditors can rely on the results of self-assessments, and it can happen only when these assessments are done in an objective and unbiased manner. This is because auditors do not need to repeat these assessments with functional and IT management, thus saving their audit time, resulting in reduction in audit costs. However, auditors will conduct their own independent tests to validate the answers given in the assessments. The audit process validates compliance with disaster recovery standards, reviews recovery problems and solutions, verifies the appropriateness of recovery test exercises, and reviews the criteria for updating and maintaining a BCP.

Here, the major point is that self-assessments should be performed in an independent and objective manner without the company management's undue influence on the results. Another proactive thinking is sharing these self-assessments with auditors earlier to get their approval prior to actually using them in the company to ensure that right questions are asked and right areas are addressed.

**32.** A company's vital records program *must* meet which of the following?

    1.    Legal, audit, and regulatory requirements

    2.    Accounting requirements

3. Marketing requirements

4. Human resources requirements

    a. 1 only

    b. 1 and 2

    c. 1, 3, and 4

    d. 1, 2, 3, and 4

**32. d.** Vital records support the continuity of business operations and present the necessary legal evidence in a court of law. Vital records should be retained to meet the requirements of functional departments of a company (for example, accounting, marketing, production, and human resources) to run day-to-day business operations (current and future). In addition, companies that are heavily regulated (for example, banking and insurance) require certain vital records to be retained for a specified amount of time. Also, internal auditors, external auditors, and third-party auditors (for example, regulatory auditors and banking/insurance industry auditors) require certain vital records to be retained to support their audit work. Periodically, these auditors review compliance with the record retention requirements either as a separate audit or as a part of their scheduled audit. Moreover, vital records are needed during recovery from a disaster. In other words, vital records are so vital for the long-run success of a company.

First, a company management with the coordination of corporate legal counsel must take an inventory of all records used in a company, classify what records are vital, and identify what vital records support the continuity of business operations, legal evidence, disaster recovery work, and audit work; knowing that not all records and documents that a company handles everyday are vital records.

Some records are on paper media while other records are on electronic media. An outcome of inventorying and classifying records is developing a list of "record retention" showing each document with its retention requirements in terms of years. Then, a systematic method is needed to preserve and store these vital records onsite and offsite with rotation procedures between the onsite and offsite locations.

Corporate legal counsel plays an important role in defining retention requirements for both business (common) records and legal records. IT management plays a similar role in backing up, archiving, and restoring the electronic records for future retrieval and use. The goal is to ensure that the current version of the vital records is available and that outdated backup copies are deleted or destroyed in a timely manner.

Examples of vital records follow:

➤ **Legal records:** General contracts; executive employment contracts; bank loan documents; business agreements with third parties, partners, and joint ventures; and regulatory compliance forms and reports.

➤ **Accounting/finance records:** Payroll, accounts payable, and accounts receivable records; customer invoices; tax records; and yearly financial statements.

> ➤ **Marketing records:** Marketing plans; sales contracts with customers and distributors; customer sales orders; and product shipment documents.

> ➤ **Human resources records:** Employment application and test scores, and employee performance appraisal forms.

**33.** **IT resource criticality for recovery and restoration is determined through which of the following ways?**

1. Standard operating procedures

2. Events and incidents

3. Business continuity planning

4. Service-level agreements

    a. 1 and 2

    b. 2 and 3

    c. 3 and 4

    d. 1, 2, 3, and 4

*33. c.* Organizations determine IT resource criticality (for example, firewalls and Web servers) through their business continuity planning efforts or their service-level agreements (SLAs), which document actions and maximum response times and state the maximum time for restoring each key resource. Standard operating procedures (SOPs) are a delineation of the specific processes, techniques, checklists, and forms used by employees to do their work. An event is any observable occurrence in a system or network. An incident can be thought of as a violation or imminent threat of violation of computer security policies, acceptable use policies, or standard security practices.

**34.** **An information system's recovery time objective (RTO) considers which of the following?**

1. Memorandum of agreement

2. Maximum allowable outage

3. Service-level agreement

4. Cost to recover

    a. 1 and 3

    b. 2 and 4

    c. 3 and 4

    d. 1, 2, 3, and 4

*34. b.* The balancing point between the maximum allowable outage (MAO) for a resource and the cost to recover that resource establishes the information system's recovery time objective (RTO). Memorandum of agreement is another name for developing a service-level agreement (SLA).

**35.** Contingency planning integrates the results of which of the following?

    a.   Business continuity plan

    b.   Business impact analysis

    c.   Core business processes

    d.   Infrastructural services

**35. b.** Contingency planning integrates and acts on the results of the business impact analysis. The output of this process is a business continuity plan consisting of a set of contingency plans—with a single plan for each core business process and infrastructure component. Each contingency plan should provide a description of the resources, staff roles, procedures, and timetables needed for its implementation.

**36.** Which of the following must be defined to implement each contingency plan?

    a.   Triggers

    b.   Risks

    c.   Costs

    d.   Benefits

**36. a.** It is important to document triggers for activating contingency plans. The information needed to define the implementation triggers for contingency plans is the deployment schedule for each contingency plan and the implementation schedule for the replaced mission-critical systems. Triggers are more important than risks, costs, and benefits because the former drives the latter.

**37.** The *least* costly test approach for contingency plans is which of the following?

    a.   Full-scale testing

    b.   Pilot testing

    c.   Parallel testing

    d.   End-to-end testing

**37. d.** The purpose of end-to-end testing is to verify that a defined set of interrelated systems, which collectively support an organizational core business area or function, interoperate as intended in an operational environment. Generally, end-to-end testing is conducted when one major system in the end-to-end chain is modified or replaced, and attention is rightfully focused on the changed or new system. The boundaries on end-to-end tests are not fixed or predetermined but rather vary depending on a given business area's system dependencies (internal and external) and the criticality to the mission of the organization.

Full-scale testing is costly and disruptive, whereas end-to-end testing is least costly. Pilot testing is testing one system or one department before testing other systems or departments. Parallel testing is testing two systems or two departments at the same time.

**38.** Organizations practice contingency plans because it makes good business sense. Which of the following is the correct sequence of steps involved in the contingency planning process?

1. Anticipating potential disasters

2. Identifying the critical functions

3. Selecting contingency plan strategies

4. Identifying the resources that support the critical functions

    a. 1, 2, 3, and 4

    b. 1, 3, 2, and 4

    c. 2, 1, 4, and 3

    d. 2, 4, 1, and 3

*38. d.* Contingency planning involves more than planning for a move offsite after a disaster destroys a data center. It also addresses how to keep an organization's critical functions operating in the event of disruptions, both large and small. This broader perspective on contingency planning is based on the distribution of computer support throughout an organization. The correct sequence of steps is as follows:

➤ Identify the mission or business or critical functions.

➤ Identify the resources that support the critical functions.

➤ Anticipate potential contingencies or disasters.

➤ Select contingency planning strategies.

**39.** A contingency planning strategy consists of the following four parts. Which of the following parts are closely related to each other?

    a. Emergency response and recovery

    b. Recovery and resumption

    c. Resumption and implementation

    d. Recovery and implementation

*39. b.* The selection of a contingency planning strategy should be based on practical considerations, including feasibility and cost. Risk assessment can be used to help estimate the cost of options to decide an optimal strategy. Whether the strategy is onsite or offsite, a contingency planning strategy normally consists of emergency response, recovery, resumption, and implementation.

In emergency response, it is important to document the initial actions taken to protect lives and limit damage. In recovery, the steps that will be taken to continue support for critical functions should be planned. In resumption, what is required to return to normal operations should be determined. The relationship between recovery and resumption is important. The longer it takes to resume normal operations, the longer the organization will have to operate in the recovery mode. In implementation, it is necessary to make appropriate preparations, document the procedures, and train employees. Emergency response and implementation do not have the same relationship as recovery and resumption does.

**40.** **Contingency planning for local-area networks should consider all the following *except*:**

    a. Incident response

    b. Remote computing

    c. Backup operations

    d. Recovery plans

*40. b.* Remote computing is not applicable to a local-area network (LAN) because the scope of a LAN is limited to local area only such as a building or group of buildings. Wide-area networks or metropolitan-area networks are good for remote computing. A contingency plan should consider three things: incident response, backup operations, and recovery.

The purpose of incident response is to mitigate the potentially serious effects of a severe LAN security-related problem. It requires not only the capability to react to incidents but also the resources to alert and inform the users if necessary.

Backup operation plans are prepared to ensure that essential tasks can be completed subsequent to disruption of the LAN environment and can continue until the LAN is sufficiently restored. Recovery plans are made to permit smooth, rapid restoration of the LAN environment following interruption of LAN usage. Supporting documents should be developed and maintained that minimize the time required for recovery. Priority should be given to those applications and services that are deemed critical to the functioning of the organization. Backup operation procedures should ensure that these critical services and applications are available to users.

**41.** **Rank the following objectives of a disaster recovery plan (DRP) from *most to least* important:**

    1. Minimize the disaster's financial impact on the organization.

    2. Reduce physical damage to the organization's property, equipment, and data.

    3. Limit the extent of the damage and thus prevent the escalation of the disaster.

    4. Protect the organization's employees and the general public.

        a. 1, 2, 3, and 4

        b. 3, 2, 1, and 4

        c. 4, 1, 3, and 2

        d. 4, 2, 1, and 3

*41. c.* The health and safety of employees and general public should be the first concern during a disaster situation. The second concern should be to minimize the disaster's economic impact on the organization in terms of revenues and sales. The third concern should be to limit or contain the disaster. The fourth concern should be to reduce physical damage to property, equipment, and data.

**42.** Rank the following benefits to be realized from a comprehensive disaster recovery plan (DRP) from *most to least* important:

1. Reduce insurance costs.

2. Enhance physical and data security.

3. Provide continuity of organization's operations.

4. Improve protection of the organization's assets.

    a. 1, 2, 3, and 4

    b. 3, 2, 1, and 4

    c. 3, 4, 2, and 1

    d. 4, 2, 3, and 1

*42. c.* The most important benefit of a comprehensive disaster recovery plan is to provide continuity of operations followed by protection of assets, increased security, and reduced insurance costs. Assets can be acquired if the business is operating and profitable. There is no such thing as 100 percent security. A company can assume self-insurance.

**43.** What is the inherent limitation of a disaster recovery planning exercise?

    a. Inability to include all possible types of disasters

    b. Assembling disaster management and recovery teams

    c. Developing early warning monitors that trigger alerts and responses

    d. Conducting periodic drills

*43. a.* Because there are many types of disasters that can occur, it is not practical to consider all such disasters. Doing so is cost-prohibitive. Hence, disaster recovery planning exercises should focus on major types of disasters that occur frequently. One approach is to perform risk analysis to determine the annual loss expectancy (ALE), which is calculated from the frequency of occurrence of a possible loss multiplied by the expected dollar loss per occurrence.

**44.** Which of the following items is usually *not* considered when a new application system is brought into the production environment?

    a. Assigning a contingency processing priority code

    b. Training computer operators

    c. Developing computer operations documentation

    d. Training functional users

*44. a.* An application system priority analysis should be performed to determine the business criticality for each computer application. A priority code or time sensitivity code should be assigned to each production application system that is critical to the survival of the organization. The priority code tells people how soon the application should be processed when the backup computer facility is ready. This can help in restoring the computer system following a disaster and facilitate in developing a recovery schedule.

**45.** Which of the following disaster scenarios is commonly *not* considered during the development of disaster recovery and contingency planning?

    a. Network failure

    b. Hardware failure

    c. Software failure

    d. Failure of the local telephone company

*45. d.* Usually, telephone service is taken for granted by the recovery team members that could negatively affect Voice over Internet Protocol (VoIP) services. Consequently, it is not addressed in the planning stage. However, alternative phone services should be explored. The other three choices are usually considered due to familiarity and vendor presence.

**46.** Which of the following phases in the contingency planning and emergency program is *most* difficult to sell to an organization's management?

    a. Mitigation

    b. Preparedness

    c. Response

    d. Recovery

*46. a.* Mitigation is a long-term activity aimed at eliminating or reducing the probability of an emergency or a disaster occurring. It requires "up-front" money and commitment from management. Preparedness is incorrect because it is a readiness to respond to undesirable events. It ensures effective response and minimizes damage. Response is incorrect because it is the first phase after the onset of an emergency. It enhances recovery operations. Recovery is incorrect because it involves both short- and long-term restoration of vital systems to normal operations.

**47.** Which of the following is the best form of a covered loss insurance policy?

    a. A basic policy

    b. A broad policy

    c. A special all-risk policy

    d. A policy commensurate with risks

*47. d.* Because insurance reduces or eliminates risk, the best insurance is the one commensurate with the most common types of risks to which a company is exposed.

The other three choices are incorrect. A basic policy covers specific named perils including fire, lightning, and windstorm. A broad policy covers additional perils such as roof collapse and volcanic action. A special all-risk policy covers everything except specific exclusions named in the policy.

**48.** **Which of the following IT contingency solutions increases a server's performance and availability?**

    a.    Electronic vaulting

    b.    Remote journaling

    c.    Load balancing

    d.    Disk replication

*48. c.* Load balancing systems monitor each server to determine the best path to route traffic to increase performance and availability so that one server is not overwhelmed with traffic. Electronic vaulting and remote journaling are similar technologies that provide additional data backup capabilities, with backups made to remote tape or disk drives over communication links. Disk replication can be implemented locally or between different locations.

**49.** **Which of the following can be called the disaster recovery plan of last resort?**

    a.    Contract with a recovery center

    b.    Demonstration of the recovery center's capabilities

    c.    Tour of the recovery center

    d.    Insurance policy

*49. d.* According to insurance industry estimates, every dollar of insured loss is accompanied by three dollars of uninsured economic loss. This suggests that companies are insured only for one-third of the potential consequences of a disaster and that insurance truly is a disaster recovery plan of last resort.

**50.** **What should be the *last* step in a risk assessment process performed as a part of business continuity plan?**

    a.    Consider possible threats.

    b.    Establish recovery priorities.

    c.    Assess potential impacts.

    d.    Evaluate critical needs.

*50. b.* The last step is establishing priorities for recovery based on critical needs. The following describes the sequence of steps in a risk assessment process:

1.    Possible threats include natural (for example, fires, floods, and earthquakes), technical (for example, hardware/software failure, power disruption, and communications interference), and human (for example, riots, strikes, disgruntled employees, and sabotage).

2.    Assess impacts from loss of information and services from both internal and external sources. This includes financial condition, competitive position, customer confidence, legal/regulatory requirements, and cost analysis to minimize exposure.

3. Evaluate critical needs. This evaluation also should consider timeframes in which a specific function becomes critical. This includes functional operations, key personnel, information, processing systems, documentation, vital records, and policies and procedures.

4. Establish priorities for recovery based on critical needs.

**51.** **For business continuity planning/disaster recovery planning (BCP/DRP), business impact analysis (BIA) primarily identifies which of the following?**

    a. Threats and risks

    b. Costs and impacts

    c. Exposures and functions

    d. Events and operations

*51. a.* Business impact analysis (BIA) is the process of identifying an organization's exposure to the sudden loss of selected business functions and/or the supporting resources (threats) and analyzing the potential disruptive impact of those exposures (risks) on key business functions and critical business operations. Threats and risks are primary and costs and impacts are secondary, where the latter is derived from the former.

The BIA usually establishes a cost (impact) associated with the disruption lasting varying lengths of time, which is secondary.

**52.** **Which of the following is the best course of action to take for retrieving the electronic records stored at an offsite location?**

    a. Installing physical security controls offsite

    a. Installing environmental security controls offsite

    c. Ensuring that software version stored offsite matches with the vital records version

    d. Rotating vital records between onsite and offsite

*52. c.* The IT management must ensure that electronic records are retrievable in the future, requiring the correct version of software that created the original records is tested and stored offsite, and that the current software version is matched with the current version of vital records.

The other three choices are incorrect because, although they are important in their own way, they do not directly address the retrieval of electronic records. Examples of physical security controls include keys and locks, sensors, alarms, sprinklers, and surveillance cameras. Examples of environmental controls include humidity, air conditioning, and heat levels. Rotating vital records between onsite and offsite is needed to purge the obsolete records and keep the current records only.

**53.** **What is the purpose of a business continuity plan (BCP)?**

    a. To sustain business operations

    b. To recover from a disaster

    c.     To test the business continuity plan

    d.     To develop the business continuity plan

*53. a.* Continuity planning involves more than planning for a move offsite after a disaster destroys a data center. It also addresses how to keep an organization's critical functions operating in the event of disruptions, both large and small. This broader perspective on continuity planning is based on the distribution of computer use and support throughout an organization. The goal is to sustain business operations.

**54.**     **The main body of a contingency or disaster recovery plan document should *not* address which of the following?**

    a.     What?

    b.     When?

    c.     How?

    d.     Who?

*54. c.* The plan document contains only the why, what, when, where, and who, not how. The *how* deals with detailed procedures and information required to carry out the actions identified and assigned to a specific recovery team. This information should not be in the formal plan because it is too detailed and should be included in the detail reference materials as an appendix to the plan. The *why* describes the need for recovery, the *what* describes the critical processes and resource requirements, the *when* deals with critical time frames, the *where* describes recovery strategy, and the *who* indicates the recovery team members and support organizations. Keeping the *how* information in the plan document confuses people, making it hard to understand and creating a maintenance nightmare.

**55.**     **Which of the following contingency plan test results is *most* meaningful?**

    a.     Tests met all planned objectives in restoring all database files.

    b.     Tests met all planned objectives in using the latest version of the operating systems software.

    c.     Tests met all planned objectives using files recovered from backups.

    d.     Tests met all planned objectives using the correct version of access control systems software.

*55. c.* The purpose of frequent disaster recovery tests is to ensure recoverability. Review of test results should show that the tests conducted met all planned objectives using files recovered from the backup copies only. This is because of the *no backup, no recovery* principle. Recovery from backup also shows that the backup schedule has been followed regularly. Storing files at a secondary location (offsite) is preferable to the primary location (onsite) because it ensures continuity of business operations if the primary location is destroyed or inaccessible.

**56.** If the disaster recovery plan is being tested for the first time, which of the following testing options can be combined?

    a.    Checklist testing and simulation testing

    b.    Simulation testing and full-interruption testing

    c.    Checklist testing and structured walk-through testing

    d.    Checklist testing and full-interruption testing

*56. c.* The checklist testing can ensure that all the items on the checklists have been reviewed and considered. During structured walk-through testing, the team members meet and walk through the specific steps of each component of the disaster recovery process and find gaps and overlaps.

Simulation testing simulates a disaster during nonbusiness hours, so normal operations will not be interrupted. Full-interruption testing is not recommended because it activates the total disaster recovery plan. This test is costly and disruptive to normal operations and requires senior management's special approval.

**57.** Which of the following should be consistent with the frequency of information system backups and the transfer rate of backup information to alternative storage sites?

    1.    Recovery time objective

    2.    Mean-time-to-failure

    3.    Recovery point objective

    4.    Mean-time-between-outages

        a.    1 and 2

        b.    1 and 3

        c.    2 and 3

        d.    2 and 4

*57. b.* The frequency of information system backups and the transfer rate of backup information to alternative storage sites should be consistent with the organization's recovery time objective (RTO) and recovery point objective (RPO). Recovery strategies must be created to meet the RTO and RPO. Mean-time-to-failure (MTTF) is most often used with safety-critical systems such as airline traffic control systems (radar control services) to measure time between failures. Mean-time-between-outages (MTBO) is the mean time between equipment failures that result in loss of system continuity or unacceptable degradation. MTTF deals with software issues, whereas MTBO measures hardware problems.

**58.** All the following are misconceptions about a disaster recovery plan *except:*

    a.    It is an organization's assurance to survive.

    b.    It is a key insurance policy.

c.   It manages the impact of LAN failures.

d.   It manages the impact of natural disasters.

**58. *a.*** A well-documented, well-rehearsed, well-coordinated disaster recovery plan allows businesses to focus on surprises and survival. In today's environment, a local-area network (LAN) failure can be as catastrophic as a natural disaster, such as a tornado. Insurance does not cover every loss.

The other three choices are misconceptions. What is important is to focus on the major unexpected events and implement modifications to the plan so that it is necessary to reclaim control over the business. The key is to ensure survival in the long run.

**59.**   Which of the following disaster recovery plan test results would be *most* useful to management?

a.   Elapsed time to perform various activities

b.   Amount of work completed

c.   List of successful and unsuccessful activities

d.   Description of each activity

**59. *c.*** Management is interested to find out what worked (successful) and what did not (unsuccessful) after a recovery from a disaster. The idea is to learn from experience.

**60.**   Which of the following is *not* an example of procedure-oriented disaster prevention activity?

a.   Backing up current data and program files

b.   Performing preventive maintenance on computer equipment

c.   Testing the disaster recovery plan

d.   Housing computers in a fire-resistant area

**60. *d.*** Housing computers in a fire-resistant area is an example of a physically oriented disaster prevention category, whereas the other three choices are examples of procedure-oriented activities. Procedure-oriented actions relate to tasks performed on a day-to-day, month-to-month, or annual basis or otherwise performed regularly. Housing computers in a fire-resistant area with a noncombustible or charged sprinkler area is not regular work. It is part of a major computer-center building construction plan.

**61.**   Which of the following is the *most* important outcome from contingency planning tests?

a.   The results of a test should be viewed as either pass or fail.

b.   The results of a test should be viewed as practice for a real emergency.

c.   The results of a test should be used to assess whether the plan worked or did not work.

d.   The results of a test should be used to improve the plan.

***61. d.*** In the case of contingency planning, a test should be used to improve the plan. If organizations do not use this approach, flaws in the plan may remain hidden or uncorrected. Although the other three choices are important in their own way, the most important outcome is to learn from the test results in order to improve the plan next time, which is the real benefit.

**62.** **A major risk in the use of cellular radio and telephone networks during a disaster include:**

    a.   Security and switching office issues

    b.   Security and redundancy

    c.   Redundancy and backup power systems

    d.   Backup power systems and switching office

***62. a.*** The airwaves are not secure and a mobile telephone switching office can be lost during a disaster. The cellular company may need to divert a route from the cell site to another mobile switching office. User organizations can take care of the other three choices because they are mostly applicable to them, and not to the telephone company.

**63.** **Regarding BCP and DRP, which of the following is *not* an element of risk?**

    a.   Threats

    b.   Assets

    c.   Costs

    d.   Mitigating factors

***63. c.*** Whether it is BCP/DRP or not, the three elements of risk include threats, assets, and mitigating factors.

Risks result from events and their surroundings with or without prior warnings, and include facilities risk, physical and logical security risk, reputation risk, network risk, supply-chain risk, compliance risk, and technology risk.

Threat sources include natural (for example, fires and floods), man-made attacks (for example, social engineering), technology-based attacks (DoS and DDoS), and intentional attacks (for example, sabotage).

Assets include people, facilities, equipment (hardware), software, and technologies.

Controls in the form of physical protection, logical protection, and asset protection are needed to avoid or mitigate the effects of risks. Some examples of preventive controls include passwords, smoke detectors, and firewalls and some examples of reactive/recovery controls include hot sites and cold sites.

Costs are the outcomes or byproducts of and derived from threats, assets, and mitigating factors, which should be analyzed and justified along with benefits prior to the investment in controls.

**64.** **Physical disaster prevention and preparedness begins when a:**

    a.    Data center site is constructed

    b.    New equipment is added

    c.    New operating system is installed

    d.    New room is added to existing computer center facilities

**64. *a.*** The data center should be constructed in such a way as to minimize exposure to fire, water damage, heat, or smoke from adjoining areas. Other considerations include raised floors, sprinklers, or fire detection and extinguishing systems and furniture made of noncombustible materials. All these considerations should be taken into account in a cost-effective manner at the time the data (computer) center is originally built. Add-ons will not only be disruptive but also costly.

**65.** **Disaster notification fees are part of which of the following cost categories associated with alternative computer processing support?**

    a.    Initial costs

    b.    Recurring operating costs

    c.    Activation costs

    d.    Development costs

**65. *c.*** There are three basic cost elements associated with alternate processing-support: initial costs, recurring operating costs, and activation costs. The first two components are incurred whether the backup facility is put into operation; the last cost component is incurred only when the facility is activated.

The initial costs include the cost of initial setup, including membership, construction or other fees. Recurring operating costs include costs for maintaining and operating the facility, including rent, utilities, repair, and ongoing backup operations. Activation costs include costs involved in the actual use of the backup capability. This includes disaster notification fees, facility usage charges, overtime, transportation, and other costs.

**66.** **When comparing alternative computer processing facilities, the *major* objective is to select the alternative with the:**

    a.    Largest annualized profit

    b.    Largest annualized revenues

    c.    Largest incremental expenses

    d.    Smallest annualized cost

**66. *d.*** The major objective is to select the best alternative facility that meets the organization's recovery needs. An annualized cost is obtained by multiplying the annual frequency with the expected dollar amount of cost. The product should be a small figure.

**67.** Which of the following statements is *not* true about contracts and agreements associated with computer backup facilities?

    a.    Small vendors do not need contracts due to their size.

    b.    Governmental organizations are not exempted from contract requirements.

    c.    Nothing should be taken for granted during contract negotiations.

    d.    All agreements should be in writing.

*67. a.* All vendors, regardless of their size, need written contracts for all customers, whether commercial or governmental. Nothing should be taken for granted, and all agreements should be in writing to avoid misunderstandings and performance problems.

**68.** All of the following are key stakeholders in the disaster recovery process *except*:

    a.    Employees

    b.    Customers

    c.    Suppliers

    d.    Public relations officers

*68. d.* A public relations (PR) officer is a company's spokesperson and uses the media as a vehicle to consistently communicate and report to the public, including all stakeholders, during pre-crisis, interim, and post-crisis periods. Hence, the PR officer is a reporter, not a stakeholder. Examples of various media used for crisis notification include print, radio, television, telephone (voice mail and text messages), post office (regular mail), the Internet (for example, electronic mail and blogs), and press releases or conferences.

The other stakeholders (for example, employees, customers, suppliers, vendors, labor unions, investors, creditors, and regulators) have a vested interest in the positive and negative effects and outcomes, and are affected by a crisis situation, resulting from the disaster recovery process.

**69.** Which of the following is the *most* important consideration in locating an alternative computing facility during the development of a disaster recovery plan?

    a.    Close enough to become operational quickly

    b.    Unlikely to be affected by the same contingency issues as the primary facility

    c.    Close enough to serve its users

    d.    Convenient to airports and hotels

*69. b.* There are several considerations that should be reflected in the backup site location. The optimum facility location is (i) close enough to allow the backup function to become operational quickly, (ii) unlikely to be affected by the same contingency, (iii) close enough to serve its users, and (iv) convenient to airports, major highways, or train stations when located out of town.

**70.** Which of the following alternative computing backup facilities is intended to serve an organization that has sustained total destruction from a disaster?

    a.    Service bureaus

    b.    Hot sites

    c.    Cold sites

    d.    Reciprocal agreements

***70. b.*** Hot sites are fully equipped computer centers. Some have fire protection and warning devices, telecommunications lines, intrusion detection systems, and physical security. These centers are equipped with computer hardware that is compatible with that of a large number of subscribing organizations. This type of facility is intended to serve an organization that has sustained total destruction and cannot defer computer services. The other three choices do not have this kind of support.

**71.** A full-scale testing of application systems *cannot* be accomplished in which of the following alternative computing backup facilities?

    a.    Shared contingency centers and hot sites

    b.    Dedicated contingency centers and cold sites

    c.    Hot sites and reciprocal agreements

    d.    Cold sites and reciprocal agreements

***71. d.*** The question is asking about the two alternative computing facilities that can perform full-scale testing. Cold sites do not have equipment, so full-scale testing cannot be done until the equipment is installed. Adequate time may not be allowed in reciprocal agreements due to time pressures and scheduling conflicts between the two parties.

Full-scale testing is possible with shared contingency centers and hot sites because they have the needed equipment to conduct tests. Shared contingency centers are essentially the same as dedicated contingency centers. The difference lies in the fact that membership is formed by a group of similar organizations which use, or could use, identical hardware.

**72.** Which of the following computing backup facilities has a cost advantage?

    a.    Shared contingency centers

    b.    Hot sites

    c.    Cold sites

    d.    Reciprocal agreements

***72. d.*** Reciprocal agreements do not require nearly as much advanced funding as do commercial facilities. They are inexpensive compared to other three choices where the latter are commercial facilities. However, cost alone should not be the overriding factor when making backup facility decisions.

**73.** **Which of the following organization's functions are often ignored in planning for recovery from a disaster?**

    a.    Computer operations

    b.    Safety

    c.    Human resources

    d.    Accounting

*73. c.*   Human resource policies and procedures impact employees involved in the response to a disaster. Specifically, it includes extended work hours, overtime pay, compensatory time, living costs, employee evacuation, medical treatment, notifying families of injured or missing employees, emergency food, and cash during recovery. The scope covers the pre-disaster plan, emergency response during recovery, and post-recovery issues. The major reason for ignoring the human resource issues is that they encompass many items requiring extensive planning and coordination, which take a significant amount of time and effort.

**74.** **Which of the following is the *best* organizational structure and management style during a disaster?**

    a.    People-oriented

    b.    Production-oriented

    c.    Democratic-oriented

    d.    Participative-oriented

*74. b.*   During the creation of a disaster recovery and restoration plan, the management styles indicated in the other three choices are acceptable due to the involvement and input required of all people affected by a disaster. However, the situation during a disaster is entirely different requiring execution, not planning. The command-and-control structure, which is a production-oriented management style, is the best approach to orchestrate the recovery, unify all resources, and provide solid direction with a single voice to recover from the disaster. This is not the time to plan and discuss various approaches and their merits. The other three choices are not suitable during a disaster.

**75.** **The primary objective of emergency planning is to:**

    a.    Minimize loss of assets.

    b.    Ensure human security and safety.

    c.    Minimize business interruption.

    d.    Provide backup facilities and services.

*75. b.*   Emergency planning provides the policies and procedures to cope with disasters and to ensure the continuity of vital data center services. The primary objective of emergency planning is personnel safety, security, and welfare; secondary objectives include (i) minimizing loss of assets, (ii) minimizing business interruption, (iii) providing backup facilities and services, and (iv) providing trained personnel to conduct emergency and recovery operations.

**76.** Which of the following is *most* important in developing contingency plans for information systems and their facilities?

    a.    Criteria for content

    b.    Criteria for format

    c.    Criteria for usefulness

    d.    Criteria for procedures

***76. c.*** The only reason for creating a contingency plan is to provide a document and procedure that will be useful in time of emergency. If the plan is not designed to be useful, it is not satisfactory. Suggestions for the plan content and format can be described, but no two contingency plans will or should be the same.

**77.** All the following are objectives of emergency response procedures *except:*

    a.    Protect life

    b.    Control losses

    c.    Protect property

    d.    Maximize profits

***77. d.*** Emergency response procedures are those procedures initiated immediately after an emergency occurs to protect life, protect property, and minimize the impact of the emergency (loss control). Maximizing profits can be practiced during nonemergency times but not during an emergency.

**78.** The post-incident review report after a disaster should *not* focus on:

    a.    What happened?

    b.    What should have happened?

    c.    What should happen next?

    d.    Who caused it?

***78. d.*** The post-incident review after a disaster has occurred should focus on what happened, what should have happened, and what should happen next, but not on who caused it. Blaming people will not solve the problem.

**79.** An effective element of damage control after a disaster occurs is to:

    a.    Maintain silence.

    b.    Hold press conferences.

    c.    Consult lawyers.

    d.    Maintain secrecy.

**79. b.**  Silence is guilt, especially during a disaster. How a company appears to respond to a disaster can be as important as the response itself. If the response is kept in secrecy, the press will assume there is some reason for secrecy. The company should take time to explain to the press what happened and what the response is. A corporate communications professional should be consulted instead of a lawyer due to the specialized knowledge of the former. A spokesperson should be selected to contact media, issue an initial statement, provide background information, and describe action plans, which are essential to minimize the damage. The company lawyers may add restrictions to ensure that everything is done accordingly, which may not work well in an emergency.

**80.**  **Which of the following statements is *not* true? Having a disaster recovery plan and testing it regularly:**

    a.    Reduces risks

    b.    Affects the availability of insurance

    c.    Lowers insurance rates

    d.    Affects the total cost of insurance

**80. c.**  Both underwriters and management are concerned about risk reduction, availability of specific insurance coverage, and its total cost. A good disaster recovery plan addresses these concerns. However, a good plan is not a guarantee for lower insurance rates in all circumstances. Insurance rates are determined based on averages obtained from loss experience, geography, management judgment, the health of the economy, and a host of other factors. Total cost of insurance depends on the specific type of coverage obtained. It could be difficult or expensive to obtain insurance in the absence of a disaster recovery plan. Insurance provides a certain level of comfort in reducing risks but it does not provide the means to ensure continuity of business operations.

**81.**  **When an organization is interrupted by a catastrophe, which of the following cost categories requires management's greatest attention?**

    a.    Direct costs

    b.    Opportunity costs

    c.    Hidden costs

    d.    Variable costs

**81. c.**  Hidden costs are not insurable expenses and include (i) unemployment compensation premiums resulting from layoffs in the work force, (ii) increases in advertising expenditures necessary to rebuild the volume of business, (iii) cost of training new and old employees, and (iv) increased cost of production due to decline in overall operational efficiency. Generally, traditional accounting systems are not set up to accumulate and report the hidden costs. Opportunity costs are not insurable expenses. They are costs of foregone choices, and accounting systems do not capture these types of costs. Both direct and variable costs are insurable expenses and are captured by accounting systems.

**82.** **Which of the following disaster-recovery alternative facilities eliminates the possibility of competition for time and space with other businesses?**

    a.    Hot sites

    b.    Cold sites

    c.    Mirrored sites

    d.    Warm sites

*82. c.*   A dedicated second site eliminates the threat of competition for time and space with other businesses. These benefits coupled with the ever-growing demands of today's data and telecommunications networks have paved the way for a new breed of mirrored sites (intelligent sites) that can serve as both primary and contingency site locations. These mirrored sites employ triple disaster avoidance systems covering power, telecommunications, life support (water and sanitation), and 24-hour security systems. Mirrored sites are fully redundant facilities with automated real-time information mirroring. A mirrored site (redundant site) is equipped and configured exactly like the primary site in all technical respects. Some organizations plan on having partial redundancy for a disaster recovery purpose and partial processing for normal operations. The stocking of spare personal computers and their parts or LAN servers also provide some redundancy. Hot, cold, and warm sites are operated and managed by commercial organizations, whereas the mirrored site is operated by the user organization.

**83.** **The greatest cost in data management comes from which of the following?**

    a.    Backing up files

    b.    Restoring files

    c.    Archiving files

    d.    Journaling files

*83. b.*   Manual tape processing has the tendency to cause problems at restore time. Multiple copies of files exist on different tapes. Finding the right tape to restore can become a nightmare, unless the software product has automated indexing and labeling features. Restoring files is costly due to the considerable human intervention required, causing delays. Until the software is available to automate the file restoration process, costs continue to be higher than the other choices. Backing up refers to a duplicate copy of a data set that is held in storage in case the original data are lost or damaged. Archiving refers to the process of moving infrequently accessed data to less accessible and lower cost storage media. Journaling applications post a copy of each transaction to both the local and remote storage sites when applicable.

**84.** **All the following need to be established prior to a crisis situation *except:***

    a.    Public relationships

    b.    Credibility

    c.    Reputation

    d.    Goodwill

**84. a.** The other three choices (i.e., credibility, reputation, and goodwill) need to exist in advance of a crisis situation. These qualities cannot be generated quickly during a crisis. They take a long time to develop and maintain, way before a disaster occurs. On the other hand, public (media) relationships require a proactive approach during a disaster. This includes distributing an information kit to the media at a moment's notice. The background information about the company in the kit must be regularly reviewed and updated. When disaster strikes, it is important to get the company information out early. By presenting relevant information to the media, more time is available to manage the actual day-to-day aspects of crisis communications during the disaster.

**85.** Which of the following disaster recovery plan testing options should *not* be scheduled at critical points in the normal processing cycle?

    a.    Checklist testing

    b.    Parallel testing

    c.    Full-interruption testing

    d.    Structured walk-through testing

**85. c.** Full-interruption testing, as the name implies, disrupts normal operations and should be approached with caution.

**86.** The *first* step in successfully protecting and backing up information in distributed computing environments is to determine data:

    a.    Availability requirements

    b.    Accessibility requirements

    c.    Inventory requirements

    d.    Retention requirements

**86. c.** The first step toward protecting data is a comprehensive inventory of all servers, workstations, applications, and user data throughout the organization. When a comprehensive study of this type is completed, various backup, access, storage, availability, and retention strategies can be evaluated to determine which strategy best fits the needs of an organization.

**87.** Which of the following natural disasters come with an advanced warning sign?

    a.    Earthquakes and tornadoes

    b.    Tornadoes and hurricanes

    c.    Hurricanes and floods

    d.    Floods only

**87. c.** The main hazards caused by hurricanes most often involve the loss of power, flooding, and the inability to access facilities. Businesses may also be impacted by structural damage as well. Hurricanes are the only events that give advanced warnings before the disaster strikes. Excessive rains lead to floods. Earthquakes do not give advanced warnings. Tornado warnings exist but provide little advance warning, and they are often inaccurate.

**88.** The *most* effective action to be taken when a hurricane advance warning is provided is to:

    a.    Declare the disaster early.

    b.    Install an uninterruptible power supply system.

    c.    Provide a backup water source.

    d.    Acquire gasoline-powered pumps.

***88. a.*** The first thing is to declare the disaster as soon as the warning sign is known. Protecting the business site is instrumental in continuing or restoring operations in the event of a hurricane. Ways to do this include an uninterruptible power supply (batteries and generators), a backup water source, and a supply of gasoline-powered pumps to keep the lower levels of the facility clear of floodwaters. Boarding up windows and doors is good to protect buildings from high-speed flying debris and to prevent looting.

**89.** Which of the following requires advance planning to handle a real flood-driven disaster?

    a.    Call tree list, power requirements, and air-conditioning requirements

    b.    Power requirements and air-conditioning requirements

    c.    Air-conditioning requirements and media communications

    d.    Call tree list and media communications

***89. b.*** Power and air-conditioning requirements need to be determined in advance to reduce the installation time frames. This includes diesel power generators, fuel, and other associated equipment. Media communications include keeping in touch with radio, television, and newspaper firms. The call tree list should be kept current all the time so that the employee and vendor-notification process can begin as soon as the disaster strikes. This list includes primary and secondary employee names and phone numbers as well as escalation levels.

**90.** Which of the following is of *least* concern in a local-area network contingency plan?

    a.    Application systems are scheduled for recovery based on their priorities.

    b.    Application systems are scheduled for recovery based on the urgency of the information.

    c.    Application systems are scheduled for recovery based on a period of downtime acceptable to the application users.

    d.    Application systems are scheduled for recovery based on a period of downtime tolerable to the application programmers.

***90. d.*** An alternative location is needed to ensure that critical applications can continue to be processed when the local-area network (LAN) is unavailable for an extended period of time. Application systems should be scheduled for recovery and operation at the alternative site, based on their priority, the urgency of the information, and the period of downtime considered acceptable by the application users. It does not matter what the application programmers consider acceptable because they are not the direct users of the system.

**91.** After a disaster, at what stage should application systems be recovered?

    a.    To the last online transaction completed

    b.    To the last batch processing prior to interruption

    c.    To the actual point of interruption

    d.    To the last master file update prior to interruption

*91. c.* The goal is to capture all data points necessary to restart a system without loss of any data in the work-in-progress status. The recovery team should recover all application systems to the actual point of the interruption. The other three choices are incorrect because there could be a delay in processing or posting data into master files or databases depending on their schedules.

**92.** Which of the following may *not* reduce the recovery time after a disaster strikes?

    a.    Writing recovery scripts

    b.    Performing rigorous testing

    c.    Refining the recovery plans

    d.    Documenting the recovery plans

*92. d.* Documenting the recovery plan should be done first and be available to use during a recovery as a guidance. The amount of time and effort in developing the plan has no bearing on the real recovery from a disaster. On the other hand, the amount of time and effort spent on the other three choices and the degree of perfection attained in those three choices will definitely help in reducing the recovery time after a disaster strikes. The more time spent on these three choices, the better the quality of the plan. The key point is that documenting the recovery plan alone is not enough because it is a paper exercise, showing guidance. The real benefit comes from careful implementation of that plan in actions.

**93.** An organization's effective presentation of disaster scenarios should be based on which of the following?

    a.    Severity and timing levels

    b.    Risk and impact levels

    c.    Cost and timing levels

    d.    Event and incident levels

*93. a.* The disaster scenarios, describing the types of incidents that an organization is likely to experience, should be based on events or situations that are severe in magnitude (high in damages and longer in outages), occurring at the worst possible time (i.e., worst-case scenario with pessimistic time), resulting in severe impairment to the organization's ability to conduct and/or continue its business operations.

The planning horizon for these scenarios include short-term (i.e., less than one month outage) and long-term (i.e., more than three month outage), the severity magnitude levels include low, moderate, and high; and the timing levels include worst possible time, most likely time, and least likely time. The combination of high severity level and the worst possible time is an example of high-risk scenario. The other three choices are incorrect because they are not relevant directly to the disaster scenarios in terms of severity and timing levels except that they support the severity and timing levels indirectly.

**94.** The focus of disaster recovery planning should be on:

    a.    Protecting the organization against the consequences of a disaster

    b.    Probability that a disaster may or may not happen

    c.    Balancing the cost of recovery planning against the probability that a disaster might actually happen

    d.    Selecting the best alternative backup processing facilities

***94. a.*** The focus of disaster recovery planning should be on protecting the organization against the consequences of a disaster, not on the probability that it may or may not happen.

**95.** Which of the following statements is *not* true about the critical application categories established for disaster recovery planning purposes?

    a.    Predefined categories need not be followed during a disaster because time is short.

    b.    Each category has a defined time frame to recover.

    c.    Each category has a priority level assigned to it.

    d.    The highest level category is the last one to recover.

***95. a.*** It is important to define applications into certain categories to establish processing priority. For example, the time for recovery of applications in category I could be less than 8 hours after disaster declaration (high priority). The time frame for recovery of category IV applications could be less than 12 hours after disaster declaration (low priority).

**96.** The decision to fully activate a disaster recovery plan is made immediately:

    a.    After notifying the disaster

    b.    Before damage control

    c.    After damage assessment and evaluation

    d.    Before activating emergency systems

***96. c.*** The decision to activate a disaster recovery plan is made after damage assessment and evaluation is completed. This is because the real damage from a disaster could be minor or major where the latter involves full activation only after damage assessment and evaluation. Minor damages may not require full activation as do the major ones. The decision to activate should be based on cost-benefit analysis.

A list of equipment, software, forms, and supplies needed to operate contingency category I (high priority) applications should be available to use as a damage assessment checklist.

**97.** Which of the following IT contingency solutions requires a higher bandwidth to operate?

    a. Remote journaling

    b. Electronic vaulting

    c. Synchronous mirroring

    d. Asynchronous mirroring

**97. c.** Depending on the volume and frequency of the data transmission, remote journaling or electronic vaulting could be conducted over a connection with limited or low bandwidth. However, synchronous mirroring requires higher bandwidth for data transfers between servers. Asynchronous mirroring requires smaller bandwidth connection.

**98.** The business continuity planning (BCP) process should focus on providing which of the following?

    a. Financially acceptable level of outputs and services

    b. Technically acceptable level of outputs and services

    c. Minimum acceptable level of outputs and services

    d. Maximum acceptable level of outputs and services

**98. c.** The business continuity planning (BCP) process should safeguard an organization's capability to provide a minimum acceptable level of outputs and services in the event of failures of internal and external mission-critical information systems and services. The planning process should link risk management and risk mitigation efforts to operate the organization's core business processes within the constraints such as a disaster time.

**99.** Which of the following IT contingency solutions is useful over larger bandwidth connections and shorter physical distances?

    a. Synchronous mirroring

    b. Asynchronous shadowing

    c. Single location disk replication

    d. Multiple location disk replication

**99. a.** The synchronous mirroring mode can degrade performance on the protected server and should be implemented only over shorter physical distances where bandwidth is larger that will not restrict data transfers between servers. The asynchronous shadowing mode is useful over smaller bandwidth connections and longer physical distances where network latency could occur. Consequently, shadowing helps to preserve the protected server's performance. Both synchronous and asynchronous are techniques and variations of disk replication (i.e., single and multiple location disk replication).

**100.** Regarding contingency planning, an organization obtains which of the following to reduce the likelihood of a single point of failure?

    a. Alternative storage site

    b. Alternative processing site

    c.    Alternative telecommunications services

    d.    Redundant secondary system

***100. c.***    An organization obtains alternative telecommunications services to reduce the likelihood of encountering a single point of failure with primary telecommunications services because of its high risk. The other choices are not high-risk situations.

**101.**    **Which of the following is a prerequisite to developing a disaster recovery plan?**

    a.    Business impact analysis

    b.    Cost-benefit analysis

    c.    Risk analysis

    d.    Management commitment

***101. d.***    Management commitment and involvement are always needed for any major programs, and developing a disaster recovery plan is no exception. Better commitment leads to greater funding and support. The other three choices come after management commitment.

**102.**    **With respect to business continuity planning/disaster recovery planning (BCP/DRP), risk analysis is part of which of the following?**

    a.    Cost-benefit analysis

    b.    Business impact analysis

    c.    Backup analysis

    d.    Recovery analysis

***102. b.***    The risk analysis is usually part of the business impact analysis. It estimates both the functional and financial impact of a risk occurrence to the organization and identifies the costs to reduce the risks to an acceptable level through the establishment of effective controls. The other three choices are part of the correct choice.

**103.**    **Which of the following disaster recovery plan testing approaches is *not* recommended?**

    a.    Desk-checking

    b.    Simulations

    c.    End-to-end testing

    d.    Full-interruption testing

***103. d.***    Management will not allow stopping of normal production operations for testing a disaster recovery plan. Some businesses operate on a 24x7 schedule and losing several hours of production time is tantamount to another disaster, financially or otherwise.

**104.**    **The business impact analysis (BIA) should critically examine the business processes *and* which of the following?**

    a.    Composition

    b.    Priorities

    c.    Dependencies

    d.    Service levels

***104. c.*** The business impact analysis (BIA) examines business processes composition and priorities, business or operating cycles, service levels, and, most important, the business process dependency on mission-critical information systems.

**105.** The *major* threats that a disaster recovery contingency plan should address include:

    a.    Physical threats, software threats, and environmental threats

    b.    Physical threats and environmental threats

    c.    Software threats and environmental threats

    d.    Hardware threats and logical threats

***105. c.*** Physical and environmental controls help prevent contingencies. Although many of the other controls, such as logical access controls, also prevent contingencies, the major threats that a contingency plan addresses are physical and environmental threats, such as fires, loss of power, plumbing breaks, or natural disasters. Logical access controls can address both the software and hardware threats.

**106.** Which of the following is often a missing link in developing a local-area network methodology for contingency planning?

    a.    Deciding which applications can be handled manually

    b.    Deciding which users must secure and back up their own-data

    c.    Deciding which applications are to be supported offsite

    d.    Deciding which applications can be handled as standalone personal computer tasks

***106. b.*** It is true that during a disaster, not all application systems have to be supported while the local-area network (LAN) is out of service. Some LAN applications may be handled manually, some as standalone PC tasks, whereas others need to be supported offsite. Although these duties are clearly defined, it is not so clear which users must secure and back up their own data. It is important to communicate to users that they must secure and back up their own data until normal LAN operations are resumed. This is often a missing link in developing a LAN methodology for contingency planning.

**107.** Which of the following uses both qualitative and quantitative tools?

    a.    Anecdotal analysis

    b.    Business impact analysis

    c.    Descriptive analysis

    d.    Narrative analysis

***107. b.*** The purpose of business impact analysis (BIA) is to identify critical functions, resources, and vital records necessary for an organization to continue its critical functions. In this process, the BIA uses both quantitative and qualitative tools. The other three choices are examples that use qualitative tools. Anecdotal records constitute a description or narrative of a specific situation or condition.

**108.** **With respect to BCP/DRP, single point of failure means which of the following?**

    a.    No production exists

    b.    No vendor exists

    c.    No redundancy exists

    d.    No maintenance exists

*108. c.* A single point of failure occurs when there is no redundancy in data, equipment, facilities, systems, and programs. A failure of a component or element may disable the entire system. Use of redundant array of independent disks (RAID) technology provides greater data reliability through redundancy because the data can be stored on multiple hard drives across an array, thus eliminating single points of failure and decreasing the risk of data loss significantly.

**109.** **What is an alternative processing site that is equipped with telecommunications but *not* computers?**

    a.    Cold site

    b.    Hot site

    c.    Warm site

    d.    Redundant site

*109. c.* A warm site has telecommunications ready to be utilized but does not have computers. A cold site is an empty building for housing computer processors later but equipped with environmental controls (for example, heat and air conditioning) in place. A hot site is a fully equipped building ready to operate quickly. A redundant site is configured exactly like the primary site.

**110.** **Which of the following computer backup alternative sites is the *least* expensive method and the *most* difficult to test?**

    a.    Nonmobile hot site

    b.    Mobile hot site

    c.    Warm site

    d.    Cold site

*110. d.* A cold site is an environmentally protected computer room equipped with air conditioning, wiring, and humidity control for continued processing when the equipment is shipped to the location. The cold site is the least expensive method of a backup site, but the most difficult and expensive to test.

**111.** **Which of the following is the correct sequence of events when surviving a disaster?**

    a.    Respond, recover, plan, continue, and test

    b.    Plan, respond, recover, test, and continue

    c.    Respond, plan, test, recover, and continue

    d.    Plan, test, respond, recover, and continue

***111. d.***    The correct sequence of events to take place when surviving a disaster is plan, test, respond, recover, and continue.

**112.**    **Which of the following tools provide information for reaching people during a disaster?**

    a.    Decision tree diagram

    b.    Call tree diagram

    c.    Event tree diagram

    d.    Parse tree diagram

***112. b.***    A call tree diagram shows who to contact when a required person is not available or not responding. The call tree shows the successive levels of people to contact if no response is received from the lower level of the tree. It shows the backup people when the primary person is not available. A decision tree diagram shows all the choices available with their outcomes to make a decision. An event tree diagram can be used in project management, and a parse tree diagram can be used in estimating probabilities and the nature of states in software engineering.

# SCENARIO-BASED QUESTIONS, ANSWERS, AND EXPLANATIONS

Use the following information to answer questions 1 through 7.

The GKM Company has just completed the business impact analysis (BIA) for its data processing facilities. The continuity planning team found in the risk analysis that there is a single point of failure in that backup tapes from offsite locations are controlled by an individual who works for the vendor. The contract for the vendor does not expire for 3 years.

**1.**    **Which of the following uses both qualitative and quantitative tools?**

    a.    Anecdotal analysis

    b.    Business impact analysis

    c.    Descriptive analysis

    d.    Narrative analysis

***1. b.***    The purpose of BIA is to identify critical functions, resources, and vital records necessary for an organization to continue its critical functions. In this process, the BIA uses both quantitative and qualitative tools. The other three choices are incorrect because they are examples that use qualitative tools. Anecdotal records constitute a description or narrative of a specific situation or condition.

**2.** With respect to business continuity planning/disaster recovery planning (BCP/DRP), risk analysis is part of which of the following?

    a.    Cost-benefit analysis

    b.    Business impact analysis

    c.    Backup analysis

    d.    Recovery analysis

*2. b.* The risk analysis is usually part of the business impact analysis (BIA). It estimates both the functional and financial impact of a risk occurrence to the organization and identifies the costs to reduce the risks to an acceptable level through the establishment of effective controls. Cost-benefit analysis, backup analysis, and recovery analysis are part of the BIA.

**3.** With respect to BCP/DRP, the BIA identifies which of the following?

    a.    Threats and risks

    b.    Costs and impacts

    c.    Exposures and functions

    d.    Events and operations

*3. a.* BIA is the process of identifying an organization's exposure to the sudden loss of selected business functions and/or the supporting resources (threats) and analyzing the potential disruptive impact of those exposures (risks) on key business functions and critical business operations. The BIA usually establishes a cost (impact) associated with the disruption lasting varying lengths of time.

**4.** The business impact analysis (BIA) should critically examine the business processes *and* which of the following?

    a.    Composition

    b.    Priorities

    c.    Dependencies

    d.    Service levels

*4. c.* The business impact analysis (BIA) examines business processes composition and priorities, business or operating cycles, service levels, and, most important, the business process dependency on mission-critical information systems.

**5.** The *major* threats that a disaster recovery and contingency plan should address include which of the following?

    a.    Physical threats, software threats, and environmental threats

    b.    Physical threats and environmental threats

    c.    Software threats and environmental threats

    d.    Hardware threats and logical threats

**5. b.**  Physical and environmental controls help prevent contingencies. Although many of the other controls, such as logical access controls, also prevent contingencies, the major threats that a contingency plan addresses are physical and environmental threats, such as fires, loss of power, plumbing breaks, or natural disasters. Logical access controls can address both the software and hardware threats.

6.  **Risks in the use of cellular radio and telephone networks during a disaster include which of the following?**

   a.  Security and switching office

   b.  Security and redundancy

   c.  Redundancy and backup power systems

   d.  Backup power systems and switching office

**6. a.**  The airwaves are not secure, and a mobile telephone switching office can be lost during a disaster. The cellular company may need a diverse route from the cell site to another mobile switching office.

7.  **Contingency planning integrates the results of which of the following?**

   a.  Business continuity plan

   b.  Business impact analysis

   c.  Core business processes

   d.  Infrastructural services

**7. b.**  Contingency planning integrates and acts on the results of the business impact analysis. The output of this process is a business continuity plan consisting of a set of contingency plans—with a single plan for each core business process and infrastructure component. Each contingency plan should provide a description of the resources, staff roles, procedures, and timetables needed for its implementation.

## SOURCES AND REFERENCES

"Contingency Planning Guide for Federal Information Systems (NIST SP 800-34R1)," National Institute of Standards and Technology (NIST), U.S. Department of Commerce, Gaithersburg, Maryland, May 2010.

"Contingency Planning Guide for Information Technology Systems (NIST SP 800-34)," National Institute of Standards and Technology (NIST), U.S. Department of Commerce, Gaithersburg, Maryland, June 2002.

"An Introduction to Computer Security: The NIST Handbook (NIST SP 800-12)," National Institute of Standards and Technology (NIST), U.S. Department of Commerce, Gaithersburg, Maryland, October 1995.

# DOMAIN 9

## Legal, Regulations, Investigations, and Compliance

### TRADITIONAL QUESTIONS, ANSWERS, AND EXPLANATIONS

1. **Computer fraud is discouraged by:**

    a. Willingness to prosecute

    b. Ostracizing whistle blowers

    c. Overlooking inefficiencies in the judicial system

    d. Accepting the lack of integrity in the system

    *1. a.* Willingness to prosecute sends a strong message to potential perpetrators, which could discourage computer fraud. Situational pressures (e.g., gambling and drugs), opportunities to commit fraud (e.g., weak system of controls), and personal characteristics (e.g., lack of integrity and honesty) are major causes of fraud, whether or not computer related. There is nothing new about the act of committing fraud. There is perhaps no new way to commit fraud because someone somewhere has already tried it. The other three choices encourage computer fraud.

2. **When computers and peripheral equipment are seized in relation to a computer crime, what is it is an example of?**

    a. Duplicate evidence

    b. Physical evidence

    c. Best evidence

    d. Collateral evidence

**2. d.**   Collateral evidence is evidence relevant only to some evidential fact, and that is not by itself relevant to a consequential fact. Here, computers and peripheral equipment are examples of collateral evidence because they are a part of the crime scene, not a crime by themselves.

Duplicate evidence is a document that is produced by some mechanical process that makes it more reliable evidence of the contents of the original than other forms of secondary evidence (for example, a photocopy of the original). Modern statutes make duplicates easily substitutable for an original. Duplicate evidence is a part of the best evidence rule.

Direct inspection or observation of people, property, or events obtains physical evidence. Best evidence is primary evidence that is the most natural, reliable, and in writing (for example, a written instrument such as a letter, statement, contract, or deed). It is the most satisfactory proof of the fact based on documentary evidence because the best evidence rule prevents a party from proving or disproving the content of writing by oral testimony. However, oral testimony can be used to explain the meaning of the written instrument where the instrument is subject to more than one interpretation.

**3.**   **In general, which of the following evidence is *not* admissible in a court?**

    a.   Hearsay evidence

    b.   Primary evidence

    c.   Material evidence

    d.   Substantive evidence

**3. a.**   Hearsay evidence, whether oral or written, by itself is not admissible in a court because it is second-hand evidence. It refers to any oral or written evidence brought into court and offered as proof of things said out of court. However, hearsay evidence is admissible when the witness is put under oath in a court's stand and cross examined to state what he saw or heard. This is an example of a court's procedural checks and balances.

The other three choices are admissible in a court of law. Primary evidence is original and best evidence. It is confined to documentary evidence and applies to proof of a writing' content. Material evidence is evidence that was relevant to prove a disputed consequential fact and is also used to say evidence having some weight. Substantive evidence is evidence that is admitted to prove the significance of the party's case rather than to attack the credibility of an opposing witness.

Similarly, business documents (for example, sales orders and purchase orders) created during regular business transactions are considered admissible in a court of law. Another example is photographs represent hearsay evidence but are considered admissible if they are properly authenticated by witnesses who are familiar with the subject.

**4.**   **All of the following are the primary elements of a security incident triad *except:***

    a.   Detect

    b.   Respond

    c.    Report

    d.    Recover

**4. c.**   The primary elements of a security incident triad include detect, respond, and recover. An organization should have the ability to detect an attack, respond to an attack, and recover from an attack by limiting consequences of or impacts from an attack.

The "report" is a secondary element and is a byproduct of the primary elements. Reporting can be done internally to management, which is required, and externally to public (for example, media/press, law enforcement authorities, and incident reporting organizations), which is optional. How much external reporting is done depends on the organization's management openness to report due to adverse publicity and reputation risk involved from bad security breaches.

**5.**   **Which of the following makes the security incident event correlation work much easier and faster?**

    a.    Distributed logging

    b.    Local logging

    c.    Centralized logging

    d.    Centralized monitoring

**5. c.**   Using centralized logging makes security incident event correlation work much easier and faster because it pulls together data from various sources such as networks, hosts, services, applications, and security devices.

**6.**   **Networks and systems profiling is a technical measure for aiding in incident analysis and is achieved through which of the following means?**

    1.    Running file integrity checking software on hosts

    2.    Monitoring network bandwidth usage

    3.    Monitoring host resource usage

    4.    Determining the average and peak usage levels

        a.    2 only

        b.    3 only

        c.    4 only

        d.    1, 2, 3, and 4

**6. d.**   Networks and systems profiling measures the characteristics of expected activity so that changes to it can be more easily identified. Examples of profiling include running integrity checking software on hosts to derive checksums for critical files, monitoring network bandwidth usage, and monitoring host resource usage to determine what the average and peak usage volumes are on various days and times.

7. **The incident response team should discuss which of the following containment strategies with its legal department to determine if it is feasible?**

    a.   Full containment

    b.   Phase containment

    c.   Partial containment

    d.   Delayed containment

**7. d.** When an incident has been detected and analyzed, it is important to contain it before the spread of the incident overwhelms resources or the damage increases. In certain cases, some organizations delay the containment of an incident so that they can monitor the attacker's activity, usually to gather additional evidence. The incident response team should discuss delayed containment strategy with its legal department to determine if it is feasible. The delayed containment strategy is dangerous because an attacker could escalate unauthorized access or compromise other systems in a fraction of a second. The value of delayed containment is usually not worth the high risk that it poses.

8. **During incident handling, incident handlers should *not* focus on which of the following?**

    a.   Incident containment

    b.   Incident eradication

    c.   Attacker identification

    d.   Recovery from incident

**8. c.** During incident handling, system owners and IT security staff frequently want to identify the attacker. Although this information can be important, particularly if the organization wants to prosecute the attacker, incident handlers should stay focused on containment, eradication, and recovery. Identifying the attacker can be a time-consuming and futile exercise that can prevent a team from achieving its primary goal of minimizing the business impact.

9. **Which of the following attacker identification activities can violate an organization's policies or break the law?**

    a.   Validating the attacker's IP address

    b.   Scanning the attacker's systems

    c.   Using incident database

    d.   Monitoring attacker communication channels

**9. b.** Some incident handlers may perform pings, trace-routes, and run port and vulnerability scans to gather more information on the attacker. Incident handlers should discuss these activities with the legal department before performing such scans because the scans may violate an organization's privacy policies or even break the law. The other choices are technical in nature.

**10.** Which of the following post-incident activities and benefits can become the basis for subsequent prosecution by legal authorities?

    a.    Learning and improving

    b.    Training material for new team members

    c.    Follow-up report for each incident

    d.    Lessons learned meetings

*10. c.*   The follow-up report provides a reference that can be used to assist in handling similar, future incidents. Creating a formal chronology of events (including time-stamped information such as log data from systems) is important for legal reasons, as is creating a monetary estimate of the amount of damage the incident caused in terms of any loss of software and files, hardware damage, and staffing costs (including restoring services). This estimate may become the basis for subsequent prosecution activity by legal authorities. The other choices deal with issues that are internal to an organization.

**11.** Which of the following security metrics for incident-related data are generally *not* of value in comparing multiple organizations?

    a.    Number of unauthorized access incidents

    b.    Number of denial-of-service attacks

    c.    Number of malicious code spreads

    d.    Total number of incidents handled

*11. d.*   Security metrics such as the total number of incidents handled are generally not of value in comparing multiple organizations because each organization is likely to have defined key-incident terms differently. The "total number of incidents handled" is not specific and is best taken as a measure of the relative amount of work that the incident response team had to perform, not as a measure of the quality of the team. It is more effective to produce separate and specific incident counts for each incident category or subcategory, as shown in the other three choices. Stronger security controls can then be targeted at these specific incidents to minimize damage or loss.

**12.** Which of the following indications is *not* associated with an inappropriate usage action such as internal access to inappropriate materials?

    a.    User reports

    b.    Network intrusion detection alerts

    c.    Inappropriate files on workstations or servers

    d.    Network, host, and application log entries

*12. d.*   Network, host, and application log entries provide indications of attacks against external parties. The other three choices are examples of possible indications of internal access to inappropriate materials.

**13.** Which of the following is *not* generally a part of auditing the incident response program?

    a.   Regulations

    b.   Security policies

    c.   Incident metrics

    d.   Security best practices

*13. c.*   At a minimum, an incident response audit should evaluate compliance with applicable regulations, security policies, and security best practices. Incident metrics is usually used to measure the incident response team's success. Audits identify problems and deficiencies that can then be corrected.

**14.** Effective means to incident prevention do *not* include which of the following?

    a.   Awareness

    b.   Logs and alerts

    c.   Compliance

    d.   Common sense

*14. b.*   Effective means to incident prevention include awareness, compliance, and common sense. Logs and alerts are detective in nature.

**15.** Which of the following is used to distribute illegal content such as copies of copyrighted songs and movies?

    a.   Quarantine server

    b.   Remote access server

    c.   Warez server

    d.   E-mail server

*15. c.*   A Warez server is a file server that is used to distribute illegal content such as copies of copyrighted songs and movies as well as pirated software.

**16.** Log monitoring *cannot* assist efforts in which of the following?

    a.   Incident handling

    b.   Policy violations

    c.   Auditing

    d.   Data sources

*16. d.*   Various forensic tools and techniques can assist in log monitoring, such as analyzing log entries and correlating log entries across multiple systems. This can assist in incident handling, identifying policy violations, auditing, and other efforts. Data sources include desktops, laptops, servers, removable hard drives, and backup media. Data sources cannot assist in log monitoring.

**17.** **Which of the following requires accountability of a data controller?**

    a.    Organization for Economic Co-Operation and Development (OECD)

    b.    International organization for standards (ISO)

    c.    The Common Criteria (CC)

    d.    The Internet Engineering Task Force (IETF)

*17. a.* The Organization for Economic Co-Operation and Development (OECD) guidelines cover data collection limitations, quality of data, limitations on data use, information system security safeguards, and accountability of the data controller. The ISO, CC, and IETF do not require a data controller.

**18.** **Regarding the United States import and export laws about using encryption in products exporting to trading partners in the world, which of the following is required to monitor internal communications or computer systems and to prepare for disaster recovery?**

    a.    Key renewal

    b.    Key escrow

    c.    Key retrieval

    d.    Key transport

*18. b.* A key escrow system entrusts the two components (encryption and decryption) comprising a cryptographic key to two key component holders such as escrow agents. A key component is the two values from which a key can be derived. Key escrow is a recovery control to protect privacy and commerce in a way that preserves the U.S. law enforcement's ability to monitor internal communications using computer systems in order to protect public safety and national security and to prepare for disaster recovery. Data cannot be recovered if either the encryption key or the decryption key is lost, damaged, or destroyed.

The other three choices are incorrect because they cannot help in key recovery. Key renewal is the process used to extend the validity period of a cryptographic key so that it can be used for an additional time period. Key retrieval helps to obtain a cryptographic key from active or archived electronic storage or from a backup facility. Key transport is the secure movement of cryptographic keys from one cryptographic module to another module.

**19.** **Which of the following minimizes the potential for incident encroachment?**

    1.    Firewalls

    2.    Laws

    3.    Separation of duties

    4.    Regulations

        a.    1 and 2

        b.    2 and 4

> c.  1 and 3
>
> d.  3 and 4

**19. c.**  Firewalls and separation of duties minimize the potential for incident encroachment. A firewall is a technical safeguard that provides separation between activities, systems, or system components so that a security failure or weakness in one is contained and has no impact on other activities or systems (e.g., enforcing separation of the Internet from a local-area network).

The objective of separation of duties is to ensure that no single individual (acting alone) can compromise an application. In both cases, procedural and technical safeguards are used to enforce a basic security policy in that high risk activities should be segregated from low-risk activities and that one person should not be able to compromise a system. These two controls when combined provide a strong barrier for incidents to occur, which minimize the potential for incident encroachment.

Laws and regulations guide the security objectives and form the foundation for developing basic security policies and controls.

**20.**  Which of the following Organization for Economic Co-Operation and Development's (OECD's) principles deal with so that the rights and legitimate interests of others are respected?

> a.  Accountability
>
> b.  Ethics
>
> c.  Awareness
>
> d.  Multidisciplinary

**20. b.**  The ethics principle of OECD states that the information systems and the security of information systems should be provided and used in such a manner that the rights and legitimate interests of others are respected.

**21.**  Which of the following establishes security layers to minimize incident impact?

1.  Zoning

2.  Need-to-know

3.  Compartmentalization

4.  Unique identifiers

> a.  1 and 2
>
> b.  2 and 4
>
> c.  1 and 3
>
> d.  3 and 4

**21. c.**  Zoning and compartmentalization establish security layers to minimize incident impact. The need-to-know principle limits access to data and programs. The unique identifiers provide for individual accountability and facilitate access control.

**22.**  Which of the following generally accepted systems' security principles address the major purpose of computer security?

    a.    Computer security is an integral element of sound management.

    b.    Computer security requires a comprehensive and integrated approach.

    c.    Computer security supports the mission of the organization.

    d.    Computer security should be cost-effective.

**22. c.**  The purpose of the computer security is to protect an organization's valuable resources, such as data, information, hardware, people, and software. When valuable resources are protected, the organization's mission is also accomplished.

**23.**  Which of the following are the primary sources of computer security log data for most organizations?

    1.    Network-based security software logs

    2.    Host-based security software logs

    3.    Operating system logs

    4.    Application system logs

    a.    1 and 2

    b.    2 and 3

    c.    3 and 4

    d.    1, 2, 3, and 4

**23. a.**  Most organizations use several types of network-based and host-based security software to detect malicious activity and protect systems and data from damage. Accordingly, security software is the primary source of computer security log data for most organizations.

**24.**  Which of the following logs record significant operational actions?

    a.    Network-based security software logs

    b.    Host-based security software logs

    c.    Operating system logs

    d.    Application system logs

**24. d.**  Many applications record significant operational actions such as application startup and shutdown, application failures, and major configuration changes. The other three logs do not provide significant operational actions.

25.  **Which of the following is not an example of security software logs?**

    a.    Packet filter logs

    b.    Web server logs

    c.    Firewall logs

    d.    Antimalware software logs

*25. b.*   Web server logs are an example of application logs. The other three logs are examples of security software logs.

26.  **Which of the following logs is primarily useful in analyzing attacks against desktops or workstations?**

    a.    Antimalware software logs

    b.    Packet filter logs

    c.    Firewall logs

    d.    Authentication server logs

*26. a.*   The antimalware software logs have higher accuracy of data than operating system logs from desktops or workstations. Accordingly, these logs are primarily useful in analyzing attacks. The other three logs have a secondary usage.

27.  **Which of the following provides a secondary source in analyzing inappropriate usage?**

    a.    Authentication server logs

    b.    E-mail server logs

    c.    Web server logs

    d.    File sharing logs

*27. a.*   Authentication server logs are a part of security software logs, whereas all the other logs are examples of application logs. These application logs generate highly detailed logs that reflect every user request and response, which provide a primary source in analyzing inappropriate usage. Authentication servers typically log each authentication attempt, including its origin, success or failure, and date and time. Application logs capture data prior to authentication server logs, where the former is a primary source, and the latter is a secondary source.

28.  **All the following can make log generation and storage challenging *except*:**

    a.    Distributed nature of logs

    b.    Log management utility software

    c.    Inconsistent log formats

    d.    Volume of logs

**28. b.** The distributed nature of logs, inconsistent log formats, and volume of logs all make the management of log generation and storage challenging. For example, inconsistent log formats present challenges to people reviewing logs. A single standard format is preferred. Log management utility software may fail or mishandle the log data when an attacker provides binary data as input to a program that is expecting text data. The problem with the log management utility software is not as challenging as with the other three choices.

29. Which of the following solutions to overcome log management challenges address both peak and expected volumes of log data?

    a.    Prioritize log management function.

    b.    Establish policies and procedures for log management.

    c.    Maintain a secure log management infrastructure.

    d.    Provide training for all staff with log management responsibilities.

**29. c.** It is critical to create and maintain a secure log management infrastructure robust enough to handle not only expected volumes of log data, but also peak volumes during extreme situations, such as widespread malware incident, penetration testing, and vulnerability scans. The other three choices do not handle peak and expected volumes of log data.

30. Which of the following are the major reasons for reduced volume of logs?

    1.    Log analysis is a low-priority task.

    2.    Logs are analyzed in a batch mode.

    3.    Log analysis is treated as reactive.

    4.    Log analysis is not cost-effective.

    a.    1 and 2

    b.    2 and 3

    c.    1, 2, and 3

    d.    1, 2, 3, and 4

**30. d.** Log analysis has often been treated as a low-priority task by system or security administrators and management alike. Administrators often do not receive training on doing it efficiently and effectively. Administrators consider log analysis work to be boring and providing little benefit for the amount of time required. Log analysis is often treated as reactive rather than proactive. Most logs have been analyzed in a batch mode, not in a real-time or near-real-time manner.

31. Which of the following Organization for Economic Co-Operation and Development's (OECD's) principles state that information systems and the requirements for its security change over time?

    a.    Proportionality

    b.    Integration

    c.    Reassessment

    d.    Timeliness

***31. c.*** The reassessment principle of OECD states that the security of information system should be reassessed periodically, as information systems and the requirements for its security vary over time.

## 32. Routine log analysis is beneficial for which of the following reasons?

1. Identifying security incidents

2. Identifying policy violations

3. Identifying fraudulent activities

4. Identifying operational problems

    a.    1 only

    b.    3 only

    c.    4 only

    d.    1, 2, 3, and 4

***32. d.*** Routine log analysis is beneficial for identifying security incidents, policy violations, fraudulent activities, and operational problems.

## 33. Which of the following is *not* one of the log management infrastructure tiers?

    a.    Log generation

    b.    Decentralized log storage

    c.    Centralized log consolidation and storage

    d.    Centralized log monitoring

***33. b.*** Log management infrastructure typically uses the following three tiers, such as log generation, centralized log consolidation and storage, and centralized log monitoring. Decentralized log storage is not one of the three tiers, but eventually transferred to the centralized log consolidation and storage.

## 34. Regarding log management infrastructure functions, log viewers provide which of the following capabilities?

1. Log filtering

2. Log aggregation

3. Log normalization

4. Log correlation

    a.    1 and 2

    b.    2 and 3

c. 3 and 4

d. 1, 2, 3, and 4

***34. a.*** Log viewing is displaying log entries in a human-readable format. Some log viewers provide filtering and aggregation capabilities, and cannot provide log normalization and log correlation capabilities.

**35.** **Which one of the following log management functions includes other functions?**

a. Log filtering

b. Log aggregation

c. Log correlation

d. Log parsing

***35. d.*** Log parsing is converting log entries into a different format. For example, log parsing can convert an extensible markup language (XML)-format log into a plaintext file. Log parsing sometimes includes actions such as log filtering, log aggregation, log normalization, and log correlation.

**36.** **Major categories of log management infrastructures are based on which of the following?**

1. Syslog-based centralized logging software

2. Security event management software

3. Network forensic analysis tools

4. Host-based intrusion detection systems

a. 1 and 2

b. 2 and 3

c. 3 and 4

d. 1, 2, 3, and 4

***36. a.*** Log management infrastructures are typically based on one of the two major categories of log management software: syslog-based centralized logging software and security event management (SEM) software. Network forensic analysis tools and host-based intrusion detection systems are examples of additional types (secondary sources) of log management software.

**37.** **Regarding log management infrastructure functions, which of the following defines closing a log and opening a new log when the first log is considered to be complete?**

a. Log archival

b. Log rotation

c. Log reduction

d. Log clearing

***37. b.*** Log rotation is closing a log and opening a new log when the first log is considered to be complete. The primary benefits of log rotation are preserving log entries and keeping the size of logs manageable by compressing the log to save space. Logs can also be rotated through simple scripts and utility software. The other three logs do not provide rotation functions.

**38.** **Regarding log management infrastructure functions, which one of the following is often performed with the other?**

1. Log archival

2. Log reduction

3. Log parsing

4. Log viewing

    a. 1 and 2

    b. 2 and 3

    c. 3 and 4

    d. 1, 2, 3, and 4

***38. a.*** Log reduction is removing unneeded entries or data fields from a log to create a new log that is smaller in size. Log reduction is often performed with log archival so that only the log entries of interest are placed into long-term storage. Log parsing and log viewing are two separate activities.

**39.** **Which of the following is used to ensure that changes to archival logs are detected?**

    a. Log file-integrity checking software

    b. Network forensic analysis tools

    c. Visualization tools

    d. Log management utility software

***39. a.*** To ensure that changes to archived logs are detected, log file-integrity checking can be performed with software. This involves calculating a message digest hash for each file and storing that message digest hash securely. The other three choices do not calculate a message digest.

**40.** **Regarding log management infrastructure, which of the following characterizes the syslog-based centralized logging software?**

1. Single standard data format

2. Proprietary data formats

3. High resource-intensive for hosts

4. Low resource-intensive for hosts

    a. 1 and 3

    b. 1 and 4

c.    2 and 3

d.    2 and 4

***40. b.***  Syslog-based centralized logging software provides a single standard data format for log entry generation, storage, and transfer. Because it is simple in operation, it is less resource-intensive for hosts.

**41.**    **Regarding log management infrastructure, which of the following *cannot* take the place of others?**

1.    Network forensic analysis tools

2.    Syslog-based centralized logging software

3.    Host-based intrusion detection software

4.    Security event management software

    a.    1 and 2

    b.    1 and 3

    c.    2 and 3

    d.    2 and 4

***41. b.***  The network forensic analysis tools and host-based intrusion detection software are often part of a log management infrastructure, but they cannot take the place of syslog-based centralized logging software and security event management software. Syslog-based centralized logging software and security event management software are used as primary tools whereas network forensic analysis tools and host-based intrusion detection software are used as additional tools.

**42.**    **Which of the following are major factors to consider when designing the organizational-level log management processes?**

1.    Network bandwidth

2.    Volume of log data to be processed

3.    Configuration log sources

4.    Performing log analysis

    a.    1 and 2

    b.    2 and 3

    c.    1 and 3

    d.    3 and 4

***42. a.***  Major factors to consider in the design of organizational-level log management processes include the network bandwidth, volume of log data to be processed, online and offline data storage, the security needs for the data, and the time and resources needed for staff to analyze the logs. Configuration log sources and performing log analysis deal with system-level log management processes.

**43.** Regarding log management, the use of which of the following is *not* likely to be captured in logs?

    a.   Data concealment tools

    b.   Antivirus software

    c.   Spyware detection and removal utility software

    d.   Host-based intrusion detection software

**43. a.** The use of most data concealment tools is unlikely to be captured in logs because their intention is to hide. The other three choices are incorrect because they are examples of security applications. Along with content filtering software, they are usually logged.

**44.** What is the major reason why computer security incidents go unreported?

    a.   To avoid negative publicity

    b.   To fix system problems

    c.   To learn from system attacks

    d.   To take legal action against the attacker

**44. a.** Avoiding negative publicity is the major reason; although, there are other minor reasons. This is because bad news can cause current clients or potential clients to worry about their own sensitive information contained in computer systems. Taking legal action is not done regularly because it costs significant amounts of time and money. Fixing system problems and learning from system attacks could be byproducts of a security incident. The other three choices are minor reasons but the overriding reason is avoiding negative publicity.

**45.** A standard characteristic for perpetrating a computer crime does *not* include which of the following?

    a.   Motive

    b.   Action

    c.   Opportunity

    d.   Means

**45. b.** A person must have a motive, the opportunity, and the means to commit a crime. Action is the resulting decision.

**46.** Multiple forensic tools (such as forensic, nonforensic, and hybrid) are used to recover digital evidence from a mobile/cell phone. Which of the following can resolve conflicts from using such multiple forensic tools?

    a.   Virtual machine ware (VMware)

    b.   Universal subscriber identity module (USIM)

    c.   Port monitoring

    d.   Infrared and Bluetooth monitoring

**46. *a.*** Conflicts can arise when using multiple forensic tools due to their incompatibility in functional design specifications. One method to resolve such conflicts is to use a product such as virtual machine ware (VMware) to create a virtual machine (VM) environment on each forensic workstation for the tool to execute. Because multiple independent VMs can run simultaneously on a single workstation, several tools or tool collections that otherwise would be incompatible are readily supported.

The other three choices are incorrect because they do not have the ability to handle conflicts from using multiple tools because they are examples of individual tools. Examples of forensic tools include universal subscriber identity module (USIM) tools, handset tools, and integrated toolkits. A forensic hash is used to maintain the integrity of data by computing a cryptographically strong, non-reversible value over the acquired data. Examples of non-forensic tools include port monitoring to capture protocol exchanges, infrared and Bluetooth monitoring, and phone manager to recover data. For non-forensic tools, hash values should be created manually using a tool, such as SHA-1sum or MD5 sum, and retained for integrity verification. Examples of hybrid forensic tools include port monitoring with monitoring of USIM tool exchanges.

**47.** **Which of the following is *not* a part of active identification of infected hosts with a malware incident?**

    a.    Sinkhole router

    b.    Packet sniffers

    c.    Custom network-based IPS or IDS signatures

    d.    Vulnerability assessment software

**47. *a.*** A sinkhole router is a part of forensic identification, which mitigates extraneous traffic from an ongoing attack. Sources of active identification include login script, custom network-based intrusion prevention system (IPS) or intrusion detection system (IDS) signatures, packet sniffers, vulnerability assessment software, host scans, and file scans.

**48.** **Which of the following is *not* a problem associated with bootleg (pirated) software?**

    a.    It allows users to obtain software from unauthorized sources.

    b.    It introduces viruses that may exist within the software.

    c.    It can be downloaded from the Internet.

    d.    It was freeware software but the owner retains the copyright rights.

**48. *d.*** Freeware is software that is made available to the public at no cost. The author retains copyright rights and can place restrictions on how the program is used. The other three choices are examples of risks and actions involved in pirated software that can lead to legal problems. Control measures include (i) not allowing employees to bring software from home or outside, (ii) not permitting program downloads from the Internet, and (iii) testing the downloaded program on a stand-alone system first before it is allowed on the network.

**49.** **Which of the following is a legal activity?**

    a.   Competitive intelligence

    b.   Industrial espionage

    c.   Economic espionage

    d.   Corporate espionage

**49. *a.*** Competitive intelligence is common and legal. It involves gathering public information, going through waste, or even unobtrusive measures. Economic espionage is not legal because it involves unauthorized acquisition of proprietary or other information by a foreign government to advance its country's economic position. Industrial and corporate espionage is illegal because they deal with stealing information about product formulas and other vital information. High technology and defense industries are potential targets of industrial espionage.

**50.** **Which of the following is legally appropriate?**

    a.   Computer welcome screens

    b.   Pre-logging questionnaires

    c.   Computer unwelcome screens

    d.   Post-logging questionnaires

**50. *b.*** Pre-logging questionnaires include ascertaining whether users are authorized to use the computer and making sure that they access only the data and systems to which they are entitled. Post-logging questionnaires are used after the fact and are not of much use. Both welcome and unwelcome screens make the computer installation and the organization name known to the public. Legal issues may arise from these screens.

**51.** **Which of the following software licensing methods would put a user in a queue to await access?**

    a.   Single licensing method

    b.   Concurrent licensing method

    c.   Site licensing method

    d.   Floating licensing method

**51. *d.*** A floating licensing method puts users on a queue until their turn is up. For example, if software is licensed for 10 users and all are using the software, the 11th user will be asked to wait until one user is logged off. In a single licensing method, only one user is allowed to use the system. For small size user groups, a concurrent licensing method may be useful because it allows multiple users to work simultaneously. A site licensing method is used when there is a large group of users due to volume discount for heavy usage. The other licensing method would not put a user on a queue as the floating method does.

**52.** **What is an effective way to prevent software piracy?**

    a. Dongle device

    b. Awareness

    c. Education

    d. Reminders

*52. a.* A dongle is a small hardware device that is shipped with some software packages. The dongle is hard-coded with a unique serial number that corresponds to the software. When the program runs, it checks for the presence of the device. If the device is not plugged in, the program will not run. Despite inconvenience, it is the most effective way to prevent software piracy. The other three choices are useful to prevent software piracy, but they are not that effective.

**53.** **Computer crime is possible when controls are:**

    a. Predictable, unavoidable

    b. Unpredictable, unavoidable

    c. Predictable, avoidable

    d. Unpredictable, avoidable

*53. c.* When controls are predictable and can be bypassed, computer crime is greatly increased. Predictable means the attacker knows how the system works, when, and how to beat it. When controls are unpredictable, it is difficult for criminal attacks to take place.

**54.** **The *major* reason for the inability to calculate the risk resulting from computer crime is due to:**

    a. Known misbehavior of unknown perpetrators

    b. Unknown misbehavior of unknown perpetrators

    c. Unknown misbehavior of known perpetrators

    d. Known misbehavior of known perpetrators

*54. b.* It is difficult to assess or predict the future of unknown misbehavior of unknown perpetrators.

**55.** **The white-collar criminal tends to be:**

    a. System-motivated

    b. Greed-motivated

    c. Technology-motivated

    d. Situation-motivated

*55. d.* The white-collar criminal tends to be situation-motivated, meaning that a change in his personal lifestyle and job status can make him commit crime.

System-motivated and technology-motivated actions are suitable for a career criminal, not for a white-collar criminal. Greed-motivated is the underlying and lower-level need for all criminals whether it is white-collar, blue-collar, or career criminals, but situation-motivated is a higher-level need suitable to the white-collar criminals.

**56.** **Which of the following is a key to a successful computer crime?**

    a.    System complexity

    b.    System users

    c.    Human skills

    d.    System predictability

**56. d.** Predictability is a key to successful crime as hackers know how the system works. System complexity is a deterrent to crime to a certain extent; system users, and people in general, are unpredictable. Human skills vary from person to person. Computers perform functions the same way all the time given the same input. This consistency opens the door to computer crime.

**57.** **Computer crimes can be minimized with which of the following situations?**

    a.    Static controls and variable features

    b.    Dynamic controls and variable features

    c.    Static controls and static features

    d.    Dynamic controls and static features

**57. b.** Both controls and features of a system can be manual and/or automated. The key is to vary both of them to prevent predictability of the nature of their operation. The degree of variation depends on the criticality of the system in that the greater the criticality the higher the variation.

**58.** **Which of the following should be subject to confidentiality controls?**

    a.    Copyrights

    b.    Patents

    c.    Trade secrets

    d.    Trademarks

**58. c.** Because trade secrets are the targets for employees and industrial espionage alike, they should be subject to confidentiality controls, whereas copyrights, patents, and trademarks require integrity, authenticity, and availability controls.

**59.** **A person threatening another person through electronic mail is related to which of the following computer-security incident types?**

    a.    Denial-of-service

    b.    Malicious code

  c. Unauthorized access

  d. Inappropriate usage

**59. d.** An inappropriate usage incident occurs when a user performs actions that violate acceptable computing-use policies. E-mail harassing messages to coworkers and others are an example of inappropriate usage actions.

A denial-of-service (DoS) attack prevents or impairs the authorized use of networks, systems, or applications by exhausting resources. Malicious code includes a virus, worm, Trojan horse, or other code-based malicious entity that infects a host. Unauthorized access is where a person gains logical or physical access without permission to a network, operating system, application system, data, or device.

**60.** **A compliance auditor's working papers should:**

  a. Provide the principal support for the auditor's report

  b. Not contain critical comments about information security management

  c. Not contain IT management's comments and concerns

  d. Be considered a substitute for computer system logs and reports

**60. a.** The purpose of audit working papers is to document the audit work performed and the results thereof. The other three choices are incorrect because the auditor's working papers can contain comments about information security management as well as IT management responses to the recommendations. The audit working papers are not a substitute for computer system logs and reports because it is the auditor's own work product supporting the auditor's report.

**61.** **Which of the following produces the best results when data is recent; although, it is less comprehensive in identifying infected hosts?**

  a. Forensic identification

  b. Active identification

  c. Manual identification

  d. Multiple identification

**61. a.** If forensic identification data is recent, it might be a good source of readily available information; although, the information might not be comprehensive in identifying infected hosts for legal evidence. The other three choices do not produce legal evidence.

**62.** **Which of the following is preferred when other methods are insufficient in identifying infected hosts?**

  a. Forensic identification

  b. Active identification

  c. Manual identification

  d. Multiple identification

**62. c.** Manual identification methods are generally not feasible for comprehensive enterprisewide identification, but they are a necessary part of identification when other methods are not available and can fill in gaps when other methods are insufficient.

**63.** From a log management perspective, logon attempts to an application are recorded in which of the following logs?

1. Audit log

2. Authentication log

3. Event log

4. Error log

    a. 1 only

    b. 2 only

    c. 1 and 2

    d. 3 and 4

**63. c.** Audit log entries, also known as security log entries, contain information pertaining to audited activities, such as successful and failed logon attempts, security policy changes, file access, and process execution. Some applications record logon attempts to a separate authentication log. Applications may use audit capabilities built into the operating system or provide their own auditing capabilities.

Event log entries typically list all actions that were performed, the date and time each action occurred, and the result of each action. Error logs record information regarding application errors, typically with timestamps. Error logs are helpful in troubleshooting both operational issues and attacks. Error messages can be helpful in determining when an event of interest occurred and identifying important characteristics of the event.

**64.** From a log management perspective, which of the following provides more information on the results of each action recorded into an application event log?

    a. Date each action occurred

    b. What status code was returned?

    c. Time each action occurred

    d. What username was used to perform each action?

**64. b.** Event logs list all actions that were performed, the date and time each action occurred, and the result of each action. Event log entries might also include supporting information, such as what username was used to perform each action and what status code was returned. The returned status code provides more information on the result than a simple successful/failed status.

**65.**    **Spyware is often bundled with which of the following?**

      a.    P2P file sharing client programs

      b.    Network service worms

      c.    Mass mailing worms

      d.    E-mail-borne viruses

*65. a.*   Spyware is often bundled with software, such as certain peer-to-peer (P2P) file sharing client programs; when the user installs the supposedly benign P2P software, it then covertly installs spyware programs.

Network service worms are incorrect because they spread by exploiting vulnerability in a network service associated with an operating system or an application. Mass mailing worms and e-mail-borne viruses are incorrect because mass mailing worms are similar to e-mail-borne viruses, with the primary difference being that mass mailing worms are self-contained instead of infecting an existing file as e-mail-borne viruses do. After a mass mailing worm has infected a system, it typically searches the system for e-mail addresses and then sends copies of itself to those addresses, using either the systems e-mail client or a self-contained mailer built into the worm itself.

**66.**    **Which of the following is *not* an example of security software logs?**

      a.    Intrusion prevention system logs

      b.    Vulnerability management software logs

      c.    Network quarantine server logs

      d.    File sharing logs

*66. d.*   File sharing logs are an example of application logs. The other three choices are examples of security software logs.

**67.**    **Which of the following logs are *most* beneficial for identifying suspicious activity involving a particular host?**

      a.    Network-based security software logs

      b.    Host-based security software logs

      c.    Operating system logs

      d.    Application system logs

*67. c.*   Operating systems logs are most beneficial for identifying suspicious activity involving a particular host, or for providing more information on suspicious activity identified by another host. Operating system logs collect information on servers, workstations, and network connectivity devices (e.g., routers and switches) that could be useful in identifying suspicious activity involving a particular host.

The other three logs are not that beneficial when compared to the operating system logs. Both network-based and host-based security software logs contain basic security-related information such as user access profiles and access rights and permissions. Application system logs include e-mail logs, Web server logs, and file-sharing logs.

**68.** **The chain of custody does *not* ask which of the following questions?**

    a.    Who damaged the evidence?

    b.    Who collected the evidence?

    c.    Who stored the evidence?

    d.    Who controlled the evidence?

**68. *a.*** The chain of custody deals with who collected, stored, and controlled the evidence and does not ask who damaged the evidence. It looks at the positive side of the evidence. If the evidence is damaged, there is nothing to show in the court.

**69.** **Software site licenses are *best* suited for:**

    a.    Unique purchases

    b.    Fixed price license

    c.    Single purchase units

    d.    Small lots of software

**69. *b.*** Software site licenses are best suited for moderate to large software requirements where fixed price license or volume discounts can be expected. Discounts provide an obvious advantage. By obtaining discounts, an organization not only acquires more software for its investment but also improves its software management. Factors that expand the requirements past normal distribution/package practices are also prime candidates for site licenses. Examples of such factors are software and documentation copying and distribution, conversion, and training. Site licenses are not appropriate for software deployed in a unique situation, single purchase units, or small lots of software.

**70.** **Which of the following statements about Cyberlaw is *not* true?**

    a.    A person copying hypertext links from one website to another is liable for copyright infringement.

    b.    An act of copying of graphical elements from sites around the Web and copying them into a new page is illegal.

    c.    The icons are protected under copyright law.

    d.    There are no implications in using the Internet as a computer software distribution channel.

**70. *d.*** The Cyberlaw precludes commercial rental or loan of computer software without authorization of the copyright owner. It is true that a person constructing an Internet site needs to obtain permission to include a link to another's home page or site. There may be copyrightable expressions in the structure, sequence, and organization of those links. A person copying those links into another website could well be liable for copyright infringement. Although it is quite easy to copy graphics from sites around the Web and copy them into a new page, it is also clear that in most cases such copying constitutes copyright infringement. Icons are part of graphics and are protected by copyright laws.

**71.** **Which of the following is a primary source for forensic identification of infected hosts?**

    a.   Spyware detection and removal utility software

    b.   Network device logs

    c.   Sinkhole routers

    d.   Network forensic tools

**71. a.**   Spyware detection and removal utility software is a primary source along with antivirus software, content filtering, and host-based IPS software.

Network device logs, sinkhole routers, and network forensic tools are incorrect because they are examples of secondary sources. Network device logs show specific port number combinations and unusual protocols. A sinkhole router is a router within an organization that receives all traffic that has an unknown route (e.g., destination IP addresses on an unused subnet). A sinkhole router is usually configured to send information about received traffic to a log server and an IDS; a packet sniffer is also used sometimes to record the suspicious activity. Network forensic tools include packet sniffers and protocol analyzers.

**72.** **Which of the following is *not* an example of security software logs?**

    a.   Intrusion detection system logs

    b.   Authentication server logs

    c.   E-mail server logs

    d.   Honeypot logs

**72. c.**   E-mail logs are an example of application logs. The other three logs are examples of security software logs.

**73.** **Logs can be useful for which of the following reasons?**

    1.   To establish baselines

    2.   To perform forensic analysis

    3.   To support internal investigations

    4.   To identify operational trends

        a.   1 only

        b.   3 only

        c.   4 only

        d.   1, 2, 3, and 4

**73. d.** Logs can be useful for establishing baselines, performing auditing and forensic analysis, supporting investigations, and identifying operational trends and long-term problems.

74. **Network time protocol (NTP) servers are used to keep log sources' clocks consistent with each other in which of the following log-management infrastructure functions?**

 a. Log filtering

 b. Log aggregation

 c. Log normalization

 d. Log correlation

**74. c.** In normalization, log data values are converted to a standardized format and labeled consistently. One of the most common uses of normalization is storing dates and times in a single format. Organizations should use time synchronization technologies such as network time protocol (NTP) servers to keep log sources' clocks consistent with each other. The other three choices do not deal with NTP servers.

75. **Regarding log management infrastructure functions, which of the following is performed in support of incident handling or investigations?**

 a. Log clearing

 b. Log retention

 c. Log preservation

 d. Log reduction

**75. c.** Log preservation is performed in support of incident handling or investigations because logs contain records of activity of particular interest.

The other three choices do not support incident handling. Log retention and log preservation are part of the log archival. Log clearing is removing all entries from a log that precede a certain date and time. Log reduction is removing unneeded entries or data fields from a log to create a new log that is similar.

76. **Which of the following is *most* recommended to ensure log file integrity?**

 a. Message digest 5 (MD5)

 b. Secure hash algorithm 1 (SHA-1)

 c. User datagram protocol (UDP)

 d. Transmission control protocol (TCP)

**76. b.** Although both MD5 and SHA-1 are commonly used message digest algorithms, SHA-1 is stronger and better than MD5. Hence, SHA-1 is mostly recommended for ensuring log file integrity. UDP is a connectionless and unreliable protocol used to transfer logs between hosts. TCP is a connection-oriented protocol that attempts to ensure reliable delivery of information across networks.

**77.** **Regarding log management infrastructure, which of the following characterizes the security event management software?**

1. Single standard data format

2. Proprietary data formats

3. High resource-intensive for hosts

4. Low resource-intensive for hosts

    a. 1 and 3

    b. 1 and 4

    c. 2 and 3

    d. 2 and 4

*77. c.* Unlike syslog-based centralized logging software, which is based on a single standard, security event management (SEM) software primarily uses proprietary data formats. Although SEM software typically offers more robust and broad log management capabilities than syslog, SEM software is usually much more complicated and expensive to deploy than a centralized syslog implementation. Also, SEM software is often more resource-intensive for individual hosts than syslog because of the processing that agents perform.

**78.** **Which of the following network operational environment is the easiest in which to perform log management functions?**

    a. Standalone

    b. Enterprise

    c. Custom

    d. Legacy

*78. b.* Of all the network operational environments, the enterprise (managed) environment is typically the easiest in which to perform log management functions and usually does not necessitate special consideration in log policy development. This is because system administrators have centralized control over various settings on workstations and servers and have a formal structure.

The other three choices require special considerations and hence difficult to perform log management functions. For example, the standalone (small office/home office) environment has an informal structure, the custom environment deals with specialized security-limited functionality, and the legacy environment deals with older systems, which could be less secure.

**79.** **Which of the following are major factors to consider when designing the system-level log management processes?**

1. Online and offline data storage

2. Security needs for the data

3. Initiating responses to identified events

4. Managing long-term data storage

    a. 1 and 2

    b. 1 and 4

    c. 2 and 3

    d. 3 and 4

**79. d.** The major system-level processes for log management are configuring log sources, providing ongoing operational support, performing log analysis, initiating responses to identified events, and managing long-term data storage. Online and offline data storage and security needs for the data deal with organizational-level log management processes.

**80.** **Which of the following is an example of deploying malicious code protection at the application server level?**

    a. Workstation operating systems

    b. Web proxies

    c. E-mail clients

    d. Instant messaging clients

**80. b.** Malicious code protection should be deployed at the host level (e.g., server and workstation operating systems), the application server level (e.g., e-mail server and Web proxies), and the application client level (e.g., e-mail clients and instant messaging clients).

**81.** **Regarding signs of an incident, which of the following characterizes an indicator?**

1. Future incident

2. Past incident

3. Present incident

4. All incidents

    a. 2 only

    b. 1 and 2

    c. 2 and 3

    d. 1, 2, 3, and 4

**81. c.** Signs of an incident fall into one of two categories: precursors and indications. An indicator is a sign that an incident may have occurred (past incident) or may be occurring now (present incident). A precursor is a sign that an incident may occur in the future (future incident). An indicator is not based on future incidents or not based on all incidents.

**82.** **Regarding signs of an incident, which of the following is *not* an example of indicators?**

    a.    The antivirus software alerts when it detects that a host is infected with a worm.

    b.    The user calls the help desk to report a threatening e-mail message.

    c.    Web server log entries that show the usage of a Web vulnerability scanner.

    d.    The host records an auditing configuration change in its log.

*82. c.*   "Web server log entries that show the usage of a Web vulnerability scanner" is an example of precursor because it deals with a future incident. The other three choices are examples of indications dealing with the past and present incidents.

**83.** **Which of the following statements are correct about signs of an incident?**

    1.    Not every attack can be detected through precursors.

    2.    Some attacks have no precursors.

    3.    Some attacks that generate precursors cannot always be detected.

    4.    There are always indicators with some attacks.

        a.    1 and 2

        b.    1and 3

        c.    2 and 3

        d.    1, 2, 3, and 4

*83. d.*   A precursor is a sign that an incident may occur in the future (future incident). An indicator is a sign that an incident may have occurred (past incident) or may be occurring now (present incident). It is true that not every attack can be detected through precursors. Some attacks have no precursors, whereas other attacks generate precursors that the organization fails to detect. If precursors are detected, the organization may have an opportunity to prevent the incident by altering the security posture through automated or manual means to save a target from attack. It is true that there are always some attacks with indicators.

**84.** **Which of the following is *not* used as primary source of precursors or indications?**

    a.    Operating system logs

    b.    Services logs

    c.    Network device logs

    d.    Application logs

*84. c.*   Logs from network devices such as firewalls and routers are not typically used as a primary source of precursors or indications. Network device logs provide little information about the nature of activity.

Frequently, operating system logs, services logs, and application logs provide great value when an incident occurs. These logs can provide a wealth of information, such as which accounts were accessed and what actions were performed.

**85.** **Which of the following records the username used to attack?**

    a.    Firewall logs

    b.    Network intrusion detection software logs

    c.    Host intrusion detection software logs

    d.    Application logs

*85. d.* Evidence of an incident may be captured in several logs. Each log may contain different types of data regarding the incident. An application log may contain a username used to attack and create a security incident. Logs in the other three choices do not contain a username.

**86.** **Which of the following records information concerning whether an attack that was launched against a particular host was successful?**

    a.    Firewall logs

    b.    Network intrusion detection software logs

    c.    Host intrusion detection software logs

    d.    Application logs

*86. c.* Evidence of an incident may be captured in several logs. Each log may contain different types of data regarding the incident. A host intrusion detection sensor may record information whether an attack that was launched against a particular host was successful. Logs in the other three choices may also record host-related information but may not indicate whether a host is successful.

**87.** **When applying computer forensics to redundant array of independent disks (RAID) disk imaging, acquiring a complete disk image is important proof as evidence in a court of law. This is mostly accomplished through which of the following?**

    a.    Ensuring accuracy

    b.    Ensuring completeness

    c.    Ensuring transparency

    d.    Using a hash algorithm

*87. d.* In the field of computer forensics and during the redundant array of independent disks (RAID) disk imaging process, two of the most critical properties are obtaining a complete disk image and getting an accurate disk image. One of the main methods to ensure either or both of these properties is through using a hash algorithm. A hash is a numerical code generated from a stream of data, considerably smaller than the actual data itself, and is referred to as a message digest. It is created by processing all of the data through a hashing algorithm, which generates a fixed length output. Here, transparency means that the data is widely accessible to non-proprietary tools.

**88.** Computer security incidents should *not* be prioritized according to:

    a.    Current effect of the incident

    b.    Criticality of the affected resources

    c.    First-come, first-served basis

    d.    Future effect of the incident

*88. c.* Computer security incidents should not be handled or prioritized on a first-come, first-served basis due to resource limitations. Incident handlers should consider not only the current negative technical effect of the incident, but also the likely future technical effect of the incident if it is not immediately contained. The criticality of a resource (e.g., firewalls and Web servers) is based on the data it contains or services it provides to users. The other three choices are the factors to consider during incident prioritization.

**89.** Which of the following indications is *not* associated with a malicious action such as a worm that spreads through a vulnerable service infecting a host?

    a.    No links to outside sources

    b.    Increased network usage

    c.    Programs start slowly and run slowly

    d.    System instability and crashes

*89. a.* There should not be any links to outside sources, and it is an example of possible indications of a malicious action, such as a user who receives a virus hoax message. The other three choices are examples of possible indications of a worm that spreads through a vulnerable service infecting a host.

**90.** Which of the following phases of a computer forensic process dealing with computer incidents *most* often uses a combination of automated tools and manual methods?

    a.    Collection

    b.    Examination

    c.    Analysis

    d.    Reporting

*90. b.* A computer forensic process dealing with computer incidents is composed of four phases: collection, examination, analysis, and reporting. The examination phase most often involves forensically processing large amounts of collected data using a combination of automated and manual methods to assess and extract data of particular interest, while preserving the integrity of the data.

The collection phase is mostly automated in identifying, labeling, recording, and acquiring data from the possible sources of relevant data, while following guidelines, policies, and procedures. The analysis phase is manual in analyzing the results of the examination phase, using legally justifiable methods and techniques. The reporting phase is manual in reporting the results of the analysis phase, which may include describing the actions performed and explaining how tools and procedures were selected.

**91.** **Computer software is properly protected by trade secrets in addition to copyright laws in which of the following countries or regions of the world?**

    a.  Brazil

    b.  Mexico

    c.  Western Europe

    d.  Argentina

*91. c.* Computer software is properly protected by trade secrets in addition to copyright in European Community member nations. Brazil has no specific laws, and Argentina may have some specific laws of trade secret protection. Mexico has laws protecting industrial secrets but not for trade secrets in computer software.

**92.** **Which of the following logs have a secondary usage in analyzing logs for fraud?**

    a.  Antimalware software logs

    b.  Intrusion detection system logs

    c.  Intrusion prevention system logs

    d.  File sharing logs

*92. d.* File transfer protocol (FTP) is used for file sharing where the FTP is subjected to attacks and hence is not a primary source for analyzing fraud. File sharing logs have secondary usages. The other three logs are primarily useful in analyzing fraud.

**93.** **Data diddling can be prevented by all the following *except*:**

    a.  Access controls

    b.  Program change controls

    c.  Rapid correction of data

    d.  Integrity checking

*93. c.* Data diddling can be prevented by limiting access to data and programs and limiting the methods used to perform modification to such data and programs. Rapid detection (not rapid correction) is needed—the sooner the better—because correcting data diddling is expensive.

**94.** **From a malicious code protection mechanism viewpoint, which of the following is *most* risky?**

    a.  Electronic mail

    b.  Removable media

    c.  Electronic mail attachments

    d.  Web accesses

**94. b.**   Malicious code includes viruses, Trojan horses, worms, and spyware. Malicious code protection mechanisms are needed at system entry and exit points, workstations, servers, and mobile computing devices on the network. The malicious code can be transported by electronic mail, e-mail attachments, Web accesses, and removable media (e.g., USB devices, flash drives, and compact disks). Due to their flexibility and mobility, removable media can carry the malicious code from one system to another; therefore it is most risky. Note that removable media can be risky or not risky depending on how it is used and by whom it is used. The other three choices are less risky.

**95.**   Regarding signs of an incident, which of the following is *not* an example of indications?

   a.   The Web server crashes.

   b.   A threat from a hacktivist group stating that the group will attack the organization.

   c.   Users complain of slow access to hosts on the Internet.

   d.   The system administrator sees a filename with unusual characters.

**95. b.**   "A threat from a hacktivist group stating that the group will attack the organization" is an example of precursors because it deals with a future incident. The other three choices are examples of indications dealing with past and present indications.

**96.**   Regarding log management data analysis, security event management (SEM) software does *not* do which of the following?

   a.   Generate original event data.

   b.   Identify malicious activity.

   c.   Detect misuse of systems and networks.

   d.   Detect inappropriate usage of systems and networks.

**96. a.**   Security event management (SEM) software is capable of importing security event information from various network traffic-related security event data sources (e.g., IDS logs and firewall logs) and correlating events among the sources. It generally works by receiving copies of logs from various data sources over secure channels, normalizing the logs into a standard format, and then identifying related events by matching IP addresses, timestamps, and other characteristics. SEM products usually do not generate original event data; instead, they generate meta-events based on imported event data. Many SEM products not only can identify malicious activity, such as attacks and virus infections; they can also detect misuse and inappropriate usage of systems and networks. SEM software can be helpful in making many sources of network traffic information accessible through a single interface.

**97.**   As incident handlers become more familiar with the log entries and security alerts, which of the following are more important to investigate?

   1.   Usual entries with minor risk

   2.   Unusual entries

3. Unexplained entries

4. Abnormal entries

    a. 1 and 2

    b. 2 and 3

    c. 2, 3, and 4

    d. 1, 2, 3, and 4

*97. c.* Incident handlers should review log entries and security alerts to gain a solid under-standing of normal behavior or characteristics of networks, systems, and applications so that abnormal behavior can be recognized more easily. Incident handlers should focus more on major risks such as unusual entries, unexplained entries, and abnormal entries, which are generally more important to analyze and investigate than usual entries with minor risk. This follows the principle of management by exception, which focuses on major risks because management time is limited.

**98.** **Information regarding an incident can be recorded in which of the following places?**

1. Firewall log

2. Network IDS logs

3. Host IDS logs

4. Application logs

    a. 1 only

    b. 2 and 3

    c. 4 only

    d. 1, 2, 3, and 4

*98. d.* Information regarding an incident can be recorded in several places such as firewall, router, network intrusion detection system (IDS), host IDS, and application logs. However, they all record different information at different times.

**99.** **Which of the following is *not* an effective way of managing malicious code protection mechanisms?**

    a. Automatic updating of signature definitions

    b. Preventing nonprivileged users from circumventing controls

    c. Managing malicious code protection mechanisms locally or in a decentralized environment

    d. Testing with a known benign, nonspreading test case

*99. c.* An organization must centrally manage the malicious code protection mechanisms, similar to managing the flaw remediation process. This includes centrally managing the content of audit records generated, employing integrity verification tools, managing spam protection mechanisms, and installing software updates automatically. This is because malicious code protection mechanisms are installed at many system entry and exit points, workstations, servers, and mobile computing devices on the network. A decentralized management approach cannot work efficiently and effectively considering the various system entry and exit points. The other three choices are effective.

**100.** Which of the following is effective at stopping malware infections that exploit vulnerabilities or insecure settings?

- a. Host hardening and patching measures
- b. E-mail server settings
- c. Network server settings
- d. Application client settings

***100. a.*** Vulnerabilities can be mitigated in several ways, including practicing patch management, following the principle of least privilege, and implementing host-hardening measures. The latter includes disabling unneeded services, reconfiguring software, eliminating unsecured file shares, changing default usernames and passwords, requiring authentication before allowing access to a network service, and disabling automatic execution of binaries and scripts.

E-mail server settings are incorrect because they are effective at stopping e-mail-based malware that uses the organization's e-mail services through blocking e-mail attachments. Network server settings are incorrect because they are effective at stopping network service worms. Application client settings are incorrect because they are effective at stopping some specific instances of malware.

**101.** Many computer incidents can be handled more effectively and efficiently if data analysis considerations have been incorporated into:

- a. Organizational policies
- b. Departmental procedures
- c. Information system life-cycle phases
- d. Incident response staffing models

***101. c.*** Many computer incidents can be handled more effectively and efficiently if data analysis considerations have been incorporated into the information system's life cycle.

Examples include (i) configuring mission-critical applications to perform auditing, including recording all authentication attempts, (ii) enabling auditing on workstations, servers, and network devices, and (iii) forwarding audit records to secure centralized log servers.

Organizational policies and departmental procedures are incorrect because most of these considerations are extensions of existing provisions in policies and procedures. Incident response staffing models are incorrect because staffing models are usually a function of the human resources department.

**102.** **Acquiring network traffic data can pose some legal issues. Which of the following should be in place *first* to handle the legal issues?**

1. Access policies

2. Warning banners

3. System logs

4. System alerts

    a. 1 only

    b. 2 only

    c. 1 and 2

    d. 3 and 4

*102. c.* Acquiring network traffic data can pose some legal issues, including the capture (intentional or incidental) of information with privacy or security implications, such as passwords or e-mail contents. The term network traffic refers to computer network communications that are carried over wired or wireless networks between hosts. Access policies and warning banners are the first step to be completed. It is important to have policies regarding the monitoring of networks, as well as warning banners on system that indicate that activity may be monitored. System logs and alerts are part of monitoring activities.

**103.** **Regarding network data analysis, which of the following is *not* a data concealment tool?**

    a. File encryption utility software

    b. Content filtering software

    c. Steganographic tool

    d. System cleanup tool

*103. b.* Some people use tools that conceal data from others. This may be done for benign purposes, such as protecting the confidentiality and integrity of data against access by unauthorized parties, or for malicious purposes, such as concealing evidence of improper activities. Content filtering software, whether network-based or host-based, is not a data concealment tool. This software is effective at stopping known Web-based malware.

Examples of data concealment tools include file encryption utility software, steganographic tools, and system cleanup tools. System cleanup tools are special-purpose software that removes data pertaining to particular applications, such as Web browsers, as well as data in general locations, such as temporary directories.

**104.** **Which of the following is strictly based on a precedent?**

    a. Criminal law

    b. Civil law

    c. Common law

    d. Administrative law

**104. c.**  Common law is also called case law and is based on past and present court cases that become a precedent for future cases. Criminal law deals with crimes, and the government on behalf of the people brings criminal cases. A precedent may not be used. Civil laws rely primarily on statutes for the law without the use of a precedent. Administrative law is based on government's rules and regulations to oversee business activity. A precedent may not be used.

**105.**  **What is a data diddling technique?**

    a.    Changing data before input to a computer system

    b.    Changing data during input to a computer system

    c.    Changing data during output from a computer system

    d.    Changing data before input, during input, and during output

**105. d.**  Data diddling involves changing data before or during input to computers or during output from a computer system.

**106.**  **What is a salami technique?**

    a.    Taking small amounts of assets

    b.    Using a rounding-down fraction of money

    c.    Stealing small amounts of money from bank accounts

    d.    Taking assets, rounding-down of money, and stealing money

**106. d.**  A salami technique is a theft of small amounts of assets and money from a number of sources (e.g., bank accounts, inventory accounts, and accounts payable and receivable accounts). It is also using a rounding-down fraction of money from bank accounts.

**107.**  **Trade secret elements do *not* include which of the following?**

    a.    Secrecy

    b.    Value

    c.    Publicity

    d.    Use

**107. c.**  Publicity is not an element of a trade secret. The basic elements of a trade secret are secrecy, value, and use. There must be a continuous effort to maintain the secret.

**108.**  **Regarding monitoring of information systems, which of the following is the *most* important benefit of alerting security personnel about inappropriate or unusual activities with security implications?**

    a.    Analyzes the communications traffic patterns

    b.    Analyzes the communications event patterns

    c.    Develops profiles representing traffic/event patterns

    d.    Uses the traffic/event profiles to reduce the number of false positives and false negatives

**108. d.** After security personnel are notified about inappropriate or unusual activities, the system triggers a series of alerts. The most important benefit of these alerts is to fine-tune the system-monitoring devices to reduce the number of false positives and false negatives to an acceptable number.

**109.** An attacker sending specially crafted packets to a Web server is an example of which of the following computer-security incident type?

     a.    Denial-of-service

     b.    Malicious code

     c.    Unauthorized access

     d.    Inappropriate usage

**109. a.** A denial of service (DoS) attack prevents or impairs the authorized use of networks, systems, or applications by exhausting resources. An attacker can send specially crafted packets to a Web server.

Malicious code includes a virus, worm, Trojan horse, or other code-based malicious entity that infects a host. Unauthorized access is where a person gains logical or physical access without permission to a network, operating system, application system, data, or device. Inappropriate usage occurs when a person violates acceptable computing use policies.

**110.** Initial analysis revealed that an employee is the apparent target of or is suspected of causing a computer security incident in a company. Which of the following should be notified *first*?

     a.    Legal department

     b.    Human resources department

     c.    Public affairs department

     d.    Information security department

**110. b.** When an employee is the apparent target of or is suspected of causing a computer security incident in a company, the human resources department should be notified first because it can assist with disciplinary actions or employee counseling depending on the nature and extent of the incident. Note that incidents can be accidental/intentional, small/large, or minor/major, and each has its own set of disciplinary actions and proceedings based on the due process.

The other three choices are incorrect because these departments are not the ones that should be notified first, even though they are involved later. The role of the legal department is to review incident response plans, policies, and procedures to ensure their compliance with laws and regulations. The legal department comes into play when an incident has legal ramifications, including evidence collection, prosecution of a suspect, or potential for a lawsuit. The role of the public affairs department is to inform the media and the law enforcement authorities depending on the nature and impact of an incident. The role of the information security department is to conduct the initial analysis of incidents and later to contain an incident with altering network security controls (such as firewall rulesets).

**111.** Which of the following solutions to overcome log management challenges address periodic audits and testing and validation?

    a.    Prioritize log management function.

    b.    Establish policies and procedures for log management.

    c.    Maintain a secure log management infrastructure.

    d.    Provide training for all staff with log management responsibilities.

***111. b.*** Periodic audits are one way to confirm that logging standards and guidelines are being followed throughout the organization. Testing and validation can further ensure that the policies and procedures in the log management process are being performed properly. The other three choices do not address the periodic audits, testing, and validation.

**112.** A well-defined incident response capability helps the organization in which of the following ways?

    1.    Detect incidents rapidly.

    2.    Minimize loss and destruction.

    3.    Identify weaknesses.

    4.    Restore IT operations rapidly.

    a.    1 and 2

    b.    2 and 3

    c.    3 and 4

    d.    1, 2, 3, and 4

***112. d.*** A well-defined incident response capability helps the organization to detect incidents rapidly, minimize loss and destruction, identify weaknesses, and restore IT operations rapidly. Proper execution of the incident response plan is important.

**113.** Regarding incident containment, which one of the following items makes the other items much easier to accomplish?

    a.    Strategies and procedures

    b.    Shutting down a system

    c.    Disconnecting a system from the network

    d.    Disabling certain system functions

***113. a.*** An essential part of incident containment is decision making, such as shutting down a system, disconnecting it from the network, or disabling certain system functions. Such decisions are much easier to make if strategies and procedures for containing the incident have been predetermined.

**114.** Which of the following statements is *not* true about computer security incidents?

  a. After a resource is successfully attacked, it is not attacked again.

  b. After a resource is successfully attacked, other resources within an organization are attacked in a similar manner.

  c. After an incident has been contained, it is necessary to delete malicious code.

  d. After an incident has been contained, it is necessary to disable breached user accounts.

*114. a.* After a resource is successfully attacked, it is often attacked again or other resources within the organization are attacked in a similar manner. After an incident has been contained, eradication may be necessary to eliminate components of the incident, such as deleting malicious code and disabling breached user accounts.

**115.** A reliable way to detect superzapping of work is by:

  a. Comparing current data files with previous data files

  b. Examining computer usage logs

  c. Noting discrepancies by those who receive reports

  d. Reviewing undocumented transactions

*115. a.* Superzapping, which is an IBM utility program, leaves no evidence of file changes, and the only reliable way to detect this activity is by comparing current data files with previous generations of the same file. Computer usage logs may not capture superzapping activity. Users may not detect changes in their reports. It is difficult to find, let alone review, the undocumented transactions. Even if these transactions are found, there is no assurance that the task is complete.

**116.** With respect to computer security, a legal liability exists to an organization under which of the following conditions?

  a. When estimated security costs are greater than estimated losses.

  b. When estimated security costs are equal to estimated losses.

  c. When estimated security costs are less than estimated losses.

  d. When actual security costs are equal to actual losses.

*116. c.* Courts do not expect organizations to spend more money than losses resulting from a security flaw, threat, risk, or vulnerability. Implementing countermeasures and safeguards to protect information system assets costs money. Losses can result from risks, that is, exploitation of vulnerabilities. When estimated costs are less than estimated losses, then a legal liability exists. Courts can argue that the organization's management should have installed safeguards but did not, and that management did not exercise due care and due diligence.

When estimated security costs are greater than estimated losses they pose no legal liability because costs are greater than losses. When estimated security costs are equal to estimated losses the situation requires judgment and qualitative considerations because costs are equal to losses. The situation when actual security costs are equal to actual losses is not applicable because actual costs and actual losses are not known at the time of implementing safeguards.

**117.** **Which of the following is used by major software vendors to update software for their customers?**

    a.    Pull technology

    b.    Push technology

    c.    Pull-push technology

    d.    Push-pull technology

*117. b.*    For convenience, major vendors are offering software updates via secure channels using "push" technology. This technology automatically installs the update files at a scheduled time or upon user request. There is a trade-off here between convenience and security. An attacker can "spoof" a customer into accepting a Trojan horse masquerading as an update. Security technical staff should always review update files and patches before installing them. It is safe to download the update files and patches directly from the vendor's website via a secure connection. The pull technology is used by customers to receive information from websites.

**118.** **Changing firewall rulesets is a part of which of the following recovery actions for a computer security incident?**

    a.    Restoring systems from clean backups

    b.    Replacing compromised files with clean versions

    c.    Employing higher levels of network monitoring

    d.    Tightening network perimeter security

*118. d.*    In recovery from incidents, administrators restore systems to normal operation and harden systems to prevent similar incidents. Changing firewall rule sets is done to tighten network perimeter security. The other three choices are part of the recovery process.

**119.** **Which of the following security techniques allow time for response by investigative authorities?**

    a.    Deter

    b.    Detect

    c.    Delay

    d.    Deny

***119. c.*** If a system perpetrator can be delayed longer while he is attacking a computer system, investigative authorities can trace his origins and location. The other three choices would not allow such a trap.

**120.** **What is most of the evidence submitted in a computer crime case?**

    a.    Corroborative evidence

    b.    Documentary evidence

    c.    Secondary evidence

    d.    Admissible evidence

***120. b.*** Documentary evidence is created information such as letters, contracts, accounting records, invoices, and management information reports on performance and production.

The other three choices are incorrect. Corroborative evidence is additional evidence of a different character concerning the same point (e.g., interviews can be corroborated with gathering objective data). Secondary evidence is any evidence offered to prove the writing other than the writing itself (i.e., a copy of a writing or oral evidence of the writing), and is inferior to primary evidence (best evidence) and cannot be relied upon. Admissible evidence is evidence that is revealed to the triers of fact (judges and/or jurors) with express or implied permission to use it in deciding disputed issues of fact.

**121.** **Which of the following is *not* a criminal activity in *most* jurisdictions?**

    a.    Writing a computer virus program

    b.    Using a computer virus program

    c.    Releasing a computer virus program

    d.    Spreading a computer virus program

***121. a.*** It is the intentions of the developer of a computer virus program that matters the most in deciding what constitutes a criminal activity. Simply writing a virus program is not a criminal activity. However, using, releasing, and spreading a virus with bad intentions of destroying computer resources are the basis for criminal activity.

**122.** **After evidence is seized, a law enforcement officer should follow which of the following?**

    a.    Chain of command

    b.    Chain of control

    c.    Chain of custody

    d.    Chain of communications

***122. c.*** The chain of custody or the chain of evidence is a method of authenticating an object by the testimony of witnesses who can trace possession of the object from hand to hand and from the beginning to the end. Chain of custody is required when evidence is collected and handled so that there is no dispute about it.

The chain of command refers to relationships between a superior and a subordinate in a workplace setting. Both the chain of control and the chain of communications refer to all the participants involved in the control and communications hierarchy.

**123.** **The concept of admissibility of evidence does *not* include which of the following?**

    a.    Relevance

    b.    Competence

    c.    Materiality

    d.    Sufficiency

***123. d.***    Laying a proper foundation for evidence is the practice or requirement of introducing evidence of things necessary to make further evidence relevant, material, or competent. Sufficiency in terms of supporting a finding is not part of the concept of admissibility of evidence.

Relevant evidence is evidence that had some logical tendency to prove or disprove a disputed consequential fact. Competent (reliable) evidence is evidence that satisfied all the rules of evidence except those dealing with relevance. Materiality (significant and substantive) evidence is the notion that evidence must be relevant to a fact that is in dispute between the parties.

**124.** **When large volumes of writing are presented in court, which type of evidence is inapplicable?**

    a.    Best evidence

    b.    Flowchart evidence

    c.    Magnetic tapes evidence

    d.    Demonstrative evidence

***124. a.***    Best evidence is primary evidence, which is the most natural evidence. Best evidence gives the most satisfactory proof of the fact under investigation. It is confined to normal, small size (low volume) documents, records, and papers. Hence, the best evidence is inapplicable to large volumes of writing.

The other three choices are applicable to large volumes of writing. A recommendation for court cases with a large volume of evidence is to assemble a single exhibit book containing all documents, send copies to the defense and to the judge, and introduce it as a single exhibit in court. This saves time in court. Also, preparing a record of exhibits, the counts each is connected with, and the names of the witnesses who are to testify as to each item are part of the evidence. For example, submitting a system flowchart and magnetic tapes evidence is proper to the court. Demonstrative evidence or visual aids can be real things (such as charts and tables) or representation of real things (such as a photograph or blueprint).

**125.** **Evidence is needed to do which of the following?**

    a.    Charge a case

    b.    Classify a case

    c.    Make a case

    d.    Prove a case

***125. d.***   Proper elements of proof and correct types of evidence are needed to prove a case. The other three choices come before proving a case.

**126.**   **What determines whether a computer crime has been committed?**

    a.    When the crime is reported.

    b.    When a computer expert has completed his work.

    c.    When the allegation has been substantiated.

    d.    When the investigation is completed.

***126. c.***   A computer crime is committed when the allegation is substantiated with proper evidence that is relevant, competent, and material.

**127.**   **What is the correct sequence of preliminary security investigation?**

    1.    Consult with a computer expert.

    2.    Prepare an investigation plan.

    3.    Consult with a prosecutor.

    4.    Substantiate the allegation.

        a.    4, 1, 2, and 3

        b.    3, 1, 2, and 4

        c.    4, 2, 3, and 1

        d.    1, 4, 2, and 3

***127. a.***   Substantiating the allegation is the first step. Consulting with a computer expert, as appropriate, is the second step. Preparing an investigation plan is the third step, which sets forth the scope of the investigation and serves as a guide in determining how much technical assistance will be needed. Consulting with a prosecutor is the fourth step, depending upon the nature of the allegation and scope of the investigation. Things to discuss with the prosecutor may include the elements of proof, evidence required, and parameters of a prospective search.

**128.**   **Which of the following crime team member's objectives is similar to that of the information systems security officer involved in a computer crime investigation?**

    a.    Investigator

    b.    District attorney

    c.    Computer expert

    d.    Systems auditor

***128. d.*** A team approach is desirable when a computer-related crime case is a complex one. Each person has a definite and different role and brings varied capabilities to the team approach. Both the system auditor's and the security officer's objectives are the same because they work for the same organization. The objectives are to understand system vulnerabilities, to strengthen security controls, and to support the investigation. A district attorney's role is to prove the case, whereas the objective of the investigator is to gather facts. The role of the computer expert is to provide technical support to the team members.

**129.** In a computer-related crime investigation, what is computer evidence?

    a.    Volatile and invisible

    b.    Apparent and magnetic

    c.    Electronic and inadmissible

    d.    Difficult and erasable

***129. a.*** Discovery and recognition is one of the seven considerations involved in the care and handling of evidence. It is the investigator's capability to discover and to recognize the potential source of evidence. When a computer is involved, the evidence is probably not apparent or not visible to the eyes. Nevertheless, the investigator must recognize that computer storage devices are nothing more than electronic or magnetic file cabinets and should be searched if it would normally be reasonable to search an ordinary file cabinet. The evidence is highly volatile, that is, subject to change.

**130.** When can a video camera be used in caring for and handling computer-related crime evidence?

    a.    Discovery

    b.    Protection

    c.    Recording

    d.    Collection

***130. c.*** Recording is one of the seven recognized considerations involved in the care and handling of evidence. The alleged crime scene should be properly recorded. The use of a video camera to videotape computer equipment, workstations, and so on, and related written documentation at the crime scene is highly encouraged. Remember to photograph the rear side of the computer (particularly the cable connections).

**131.** If a computer or peripheral equipment involved in a computer crime is *not* covered by a search warrant, what should the investigator do?

    a.    Seize it before someone takes it away.

    b.    Leave it alone until a warrant can be obtained.

    c.    Analyze the equipment or its contents, and record it.

    d.    Store it in a locked cabinet in a secure warehouse.

***131. b.*** If a computer or peripheral equipment involved in a computer crime is *not* covered by a search warrant, leave it alone until a warrant can be obtained. In general, a warrant is required for anything to be collected by the investigator. However, if the investigator is a law enforcement officer, he is subject to the Rules of Unreasonable Search and Seizure and needs a search warrant. This is not so with a private investigator.

**132.** **All the following are proper ways to handle the computer equipment and magnetic media items involved in a computer crime investigation *except:***

    a.    Seal, store, and tag the items.

    b.    Seal and store items in a cardboard box.

    c.    Seal and store items in a paper bag.

    d.    Seal and store items in a plastic bag.

***132. d.*** After all equipment and magnetic media have been labeled and inventoried, seal and store each item in a paper bag or cardboard box to keep out dust. An additional label should be attached to the bag identifying its contents and noting any identifying numbers, such as the number of the evidence tag. Do not use plastic bags or sandwich bags to store any piece of computer equipment and/or magnetic storage media because plastic material can cause both static electricity and condensation, which can damage electronically stored data and sensitive electronic components.

**133.** **Indicate the *most* objective and relevant evidence in a computer environment involving fraud.**

    a.    Physical examination

    b.    Physical observation

    c.    Inquiries of people

    d.    Computer logs

***133. d.*** Relevant evidence is essential for a successful computer fraud examination. For example, data usage and access control security logs identify (i) who has accessed the computer, (ii) what information was accessed, (iii) where the computer was accessed, and (iv) how long the access lasted. These logs can be manually or computer maintained; the latter method is more timely and reliable than the former method. The integrity of logs must be proved in that they are original and have not been modified. Physical examination and physical observation may not be possible in a computer environment due to automated records. Inquiries of people may not give in-depth answers due to their lack of specific knowledge about how a computer system works.

**134.** **Which of the following practices is *not* subject to negligent liability?**

    a.    Equipment downtime despite preventive maintenance

    b.    System failure for an online computer service provider

  c.  False statements by online news service provider

  d.  Dissemination of misleading information by an online news service provider

**134. a.**   Online systems and services run a risk that subscribers will receive false or misleading information. The case law ruled that situations described in the other three choices are subject to negligent liability. However, an organization may not be liable if it followed a preventive maintenance program despite equipment downtime. This is because of proactive and preventive actions taken by the organization.

**135.**   **Which of the following is needed to produce technical evidence in computer-related crimes?**

  a.  Audit methodology

  b.  System methodology

  c.  Forensic methodology

  d.  Criminal methodology

**135. c.**   A forensic methodology is a process for the analysis of electronically stored data. The process must be completely documented to ensure that the integrity of the evidence is not questioned in court. The forensic methodology deals with technical evidence.

The audit methodology deals with reviewing business transactions and systems and reaching an opinion by an auditor. The phrases system methodology and criminal methodology have many meanings.

**136.**   **Which of the following is *not* a key factor in a crime warrant search?**

  a.  Ownership

  b.  Occupancy

  c.  Possession

  d.  Purchase

**136. d.**   A key fact in any search is ownership or rightful occupancy of the premises to be searched, and ownership or rightful possession of the items to be seized. Different search and seizure rules apply when the properties and premises are government or privately owned or leased. Purchase has nothing to do with search. One may purchase and others can occupy or possess.

**137.**   **Which of the following is *not* an example of evidentiary errors?**

  a.  Harmless errors

  b.  Reversible errors

  c.  Plain errors

  d.  Irreversible errors

**137. d.** A harmless error is an error that does not affect "a substantial right of a party." A reversible error is one that does affect a substantial right of a party. A plain error is a reversible error that is so obviously wrong that the court will reverse it even though the party harmed failed to take the steps necessary to preserve the error. An irreversible error is not defined in the law.

**138.** Which of the following crime team members has a clear role in solving a computer crime?

    a. Manager

    b. Auditor

    c. Investigator

    d. Security officer

**138. a.** A computer crime involves many individuals from different disciplines with varied experiences. The roles of each of these individuals, especially those of auditor, investigator, and security officer need to be spelled out in a detailed manner due to their overlapping duties. This is important to minimize duplication, confusion, and omission. On the other hand, the duties of the manager of the crime team are clear, that is, to conduct a thorough research, analysis, and investigation of the crime and to solve the crisis.

**139.** Prosecuting a computer crime is complex and demanding. Which of the following pose a major challenge to prosecutors?

    a. Doing special technical preparation

    b. Dealing with special evidence problems

    c. Testifying about technical matters before a judge or jury

    d. Dealing with electronic evidence problems

**139. c.** Computer crime is technical in nature and its evidence is mostly electronic and is based on "hearsay." Trying to convey technical information to nontechnical people such as judges and juror—seven trying to convince them that a crime has actually occurred when no physical equipment has been stolen—can be a major challenge. Preparing technical evidence and collecting proper evidence (paper or electronic) are not major challenges.

**140.** Which of the following is *not* a proper criterion for measuring the effectiveness of a computer-security incident response capability?

    a. Dollars saved

    b. Incidents reported

    c. Vulnerabilities fixed

    d. Tools implemented

**140. a.** The payoff from a computer security incident response capability (CSIRC) cannot be quantified in terms of dollars saved and incidents handled. It may not be possible to satisfactorily quantify the benefits a CSIRC provides within its first year of operation. One of the ways in which a CSIRC can rate its success is by collecting and analyzing statistics on its activity. For example, a CSIRC could keep statistics on incidents reported, vulnerabilities reported and fixed, and tools implemented.

**141.** **A computer-security incident-response capability structure can take different forms, depending on organization size, its diversity of technologies, and its geographic locations. Which of the following organization structures is *best* for reporting computer security-related problems?**

    a.    Centralized reporting

    b.    Decentralized reporting

    c.    Distributed reporting

    d.    Centralized, decentralized, and distributed reporting

*141. a.* When determining a structure for the computer-security incident-response capability (CSIRC), we should keep in mind the objectives of centralized response and avoiding duplication of effort. For example, the help desk function can be integrated with the CSIRC. A CSIRC provides computer security efforts with the capability to respond to computer security-related incidents such as computer viruses, unauthorized user activity, and serious software vulnerabilities in an efficient and timely manner. Possible threats include loss of data confidentiality, loss of data or system integrity, or disruption or denial of system or data availability.

Centralized reporting of CSIRC is more cost-effective because duplication of effort is avoided. It is also less complicated. Being a physically separate group within the organization and functionally separate from the computer security function, end users can contact the CSIRC directly. The other three choices are incorrect because of possible duplication of efforts and difficulty in coordinating and communicating many business units.

**142.** **A computer security incident response capability (CSIRC) needs to retain a variety of information for its own operational use and for conducting reviews of effectiveness and accountability. Which of the following logs *best* reflect the course of each day?**

    a.    Contact logs

    b.    Activity logs

    c.    Incident logs

    d.    Audit logs

*142. b.* Activity logs reflect the course of each day. It is not necessary to describe each activity in detail, but it is useful to keep such a log so that the CSIRC can account for its actions. Noting all contacts, telephone conversations, and so forth ultimately saves time by enabling one to retain information that may prove useful later.

Contact logs are incorrect because they contain vendor contacts, legal and investigative contacts, and other contacts. Incident logs are incorrect because they contain information generated during the course of handling an incident, including all actions taken, all conversations, and all events. Audit logs are incorrect because they contain personal identification and activity information and transaction processing information so that actions can be traced back and forth.

143. **Which of the following approaches provides an effective way of reporting computer security-related problems?**

    a.    Help desks

    b.    Self-help information

    c.    Site security offices

    d.    Telephone hotline

**143. d.**   One basic aim of a computer-security incident-response capability (CSIRC) is to mitigate the potentially serious effects of a severe computer security-related problem. It requires not only the capability to react to incidents but also the resources to alert and inform the users. It requires the cooperation of all users to ensure that incidents are reported and resolved and that future incidents are prevented.

An organization can augment existing computer security capabilities, such as help desks, self-help information, or site security offices, with CSIRC capability. A telephone hotline or e-mail address provides a single point of contact for users with centralized reporting. It is then possible to respond to all incidents and to determine whether incidents are related. With centralized reporting, a CSIRC can also develop accurate statistics on the size, nature, and extent of the security problems within the organization.

144. **A computer security incident is any adverse event whereby some aspect of computer security is threatened. Which of the following is the *best* characteristic of security incident response capability?**

    a.    Proactive

    b.    Reactive

    c.    Proactive and reactive

    d.    Detective

**144. c.**   A computer-security incident-response capability (CSIRC) can help organizations resolve computer security problems in a way that is both efficient and cost-effective. Combined with policies for centralized reporting, a CSIRC can reduce waste and duplication while providing a better posture against potentially devastating threats. A CSIRC is a proactive approach to computer security, one that combines reactive capabilities with active steps to prevent future incidents from occurring.

When not responding to incidents, a CSIRC can take proactive steps to educate its users regarding pertinent risks and threats to computer security. These activities can prevent incidents from occurring. They include informing users about vulnerabilities and heightening awareness of other security threats, procedures, and proper maintenance of their systems. A CSIRC is not solely a reactive capability; it is also a proactive approach to reducing an organization's computer security risk. Detective is not correct because prevention is better than detection, and detection works only in some circumstances.

**145.** **Automatic tools exist to test computer system vulnerability and to detect computer security incidents. Vulnerability testing tools analyze which of the following events?**

    a.    Recurring events

    b.    Current state of the system

    c.    Historical events

    d.    Nonrecurring events

***145. b.*** Security is affected by the actions of both the users and the system administrators. Users may leave their files open to attack; the system administrator may leave the system open to attack by insiders or outsiders. The system can be vulnerable due to misuse of the system's features. Automated tools can search for vulnerabilities that arise from common administrator and user errors. Vulnerability testing tools analyze the current state of the system (a snapshot), which is a limitation. These test tools review the objects in a system, searching for anomalies that might indicate vulnerabilities that could allow an attacker to (i) plant Trojan horses, (ii) masquerade as another user, or (iii) circumvent the organizational security policy.

The other three choices are incorrect because they represent a state that is not accessible by the vulnerability testing tools. Generalized audit software or special utility programs can handle such events better.

**146.** **What is oral testimony?**

    a.    Cumulative evidence

    b.    Proffered evidence

    c.    Direct evidence

    d.    Negative evidence

***146. c.*** Evidence means testimony, writings, material objects, or other things presented to the senses that are offered to prove the existence or nonexistence of a fact. Direct evidence proves a fact without having to use presumptions or inferences to establish that proof (e.g., oral testimony of a witness to a fact). It proves a consequential fact.

The other three choices are incorrect because they do not use oral testimony. Cumulative evidence is evidence introduced to prove a fact for which other evidence has already been introduced. Proffered evidence is evidence that a party seeks to introduce as evidence to prove or defeat some crime, claim, or defense. This can be pros or cons. Negative evidence is evidence that something did not happen or does not exist.

**147.** **Which of the following phases of a security incident investigation process determines whether a computer crime has occurred?**

    a.    Initiating the investigation

    b.    Testing and validating the incident hypothesis

    c.    Analyzing the incident

    d.    Presenting the evidence

**147. c.**   There are four phases in the investigation process. Initiating the investigation (phase 1) includes securing the crime scene, collecting evidence, developing incident hypothesis, and investigating alternative explanations. Testing and validating the incident hypothesis (phase 2) deals with proving or disproving prior assumptions, opinions, conditions, and situations; and validating the accuracy of a computer system's prior security parameters such as configuration settings, firewall rulesets, and account access privileges and authorizations. Analyzing the incident (phase 3) covers analysis of the evidence collected in the previous phases to determine whether a computer crime has occurred. Presenting the evidence (phase 4) involves preparing a report with findings and recommendations to management or law enforcement authorities.

The correct order of the investigation process is gather facts (phase 1), interview witnesses (phase 1), develop incident hypothesis (phase 1), test and validate the hypothesis (phase 2), analyze (phase 3), and report the results to management and others (phase 4).

**148.**    **Which of the following investigative tools is *most* effective when large volumes of evidence need to be analyzed?**

    a.    Interviews

    b.    Questionnaires

    c.    Forensic analysis

    d.    Computer analysis

**148. d.**   Computers can be used to collect and compile and analyze large amounts of data and provide statistics, reports, and graphs to assist the investigator in analysis and decision making. Forensic analysis is the art of retrieving computer data in such a way that will make it admissible in court. Interviews and questionnaires are examples of structured approach used in interrogations.

**149.**    **Which of the following methods is acceptable to handle computer equipment seized in a computer crime investigation?**

    a.    Exposing the magnetic media to radio waves

    b.    Laying the magnetic media on top of electronic equipment

    c.    Subjecting the magnetic media to forensic testing

    d.    Leaving the magnetic media in the trunk of a vehicle containing a radio unit

**149. c.**   Forensic analysis is the art of retrieving computer data in such a way that makes it admissible in court. Exposing magnetic media to magnetic fields, such as radio waves, may alter or destroy data. Do not carry magnetic media in the trunk of a vehicle containing a radio unit, and do not lay magnetic media on top of any electronic equipment.

**150.** To preserve the integrity of collected evidence in a criminal prosecution dealing with computer crime, who should *not* be invited to perform data retrieval and analysis of electronically stored information on a computer?

    a.    A law enforcement staff trained in computers

    b.    A computer consultant with requisite technical experience

    c.    A civilian witness with expertise in computers

    d.    A teenage hacker who is a computer expert

*150. d.* Retrieval and analysis of electronically stored data that could be potential evidence in a criminal prosecution must follow a uniform and specific methodology to prove that the evidence could not have been altered while in the possession of law enforcement. Law enforcement personnel who have received the necessary training to perform this analysis or someone else with the requisite expertise who can withstand challenge in court are essential to ensure the integrity of any resulting evidence because consistency in methodology and procedure may become a critical issue in a criminal prosecution. The proper selection and use of a civilian expert witness to aid in the retrieval and analysis of computer-related evidence is critical. However, the use of a teenage hacker as an expert witness would be inadvisable, at best.

**151.** To properly conduct computer crime investigations, the law enforcement community must receive which of the following?

    a.    Training

    b.    Policies

    c.    Procedures

    d.    Guidelines

*151. a.* Law enforcement staff must be provided with specialized training for investigations in the area of technological crime investigation. The learning curve for this type of instruction can be lengthy due to the complexity and sophistication of the technology. In addition, policies and procedures are needed to ensure consistency in the investigation of computer crimes. The seizure, transportation, and storage of computers and related equipment must be completed according to uniform guidelines.

**152.** From a human nature point of view, a good incident-handling capability is closely linked to which of the following?

    a.    Contingency planning

    b.    Training and awareness

    c.    Support and operations

    d.    Risk management

*152. b.* A good incident-handling capability is closely linked to an organization's training and awareness program and educates users about such incidents and what to do when they occur. This can increase the likelihood that incidents will be reported early, thus helping to minimize damage.

An incident handling capability can be viewed as the component of contingency planning that deals with responding to technical threats, such as viruses or hackers. Close coordination is necessary with other contingency planning efforts, particularly when planning or contingency processing in the event of a serious unavailability of system resources.

**153.** Which of the following are the necessary skills for an incident response team manager?

1. Liaison skills
2. Technical skills
3. Communication skills
4. Problem solving skills

    a. 1 and 3
    b. 3 and 4
    c. 1, 3, and 4
    d. 1, 2, 3, and 4

*153. d.* The incident response team manager must have several skills: acting as a liaison with upper management and others, defusing crisis situations (i.e., having problem-solving skills), technically adept, having excellent communications skills, and maintaining positive working relationships, even under times of high pressure.

**154.** Which of the following is *not* a primary impact of a security incident?

    a. Fraud
    b. Waste
    c. Abuse
    d. Notice

*154. d.* Notice is not a primary impact of a security incident. Fraud, waste, and abuse are potential adverse actions that may result from a breakdown in IT security controls and practices. Consequently, these three are primary impacts of a security incident. "Notice" occurs after an incident is known.

**155.** Which of the following software licensing approaches requires the user to pay for the software when used for commercial purposes after downloading it from the Internet?

    a. Demoware
    b. Timeware
    c. Crippleware
    d. Shareware

*155. d.* The Internet has allowed many software companies to use new means of distributing software. Many companies allow the downloading of trial versions of their product (demoware), sometimes-limited versions (crippleware) or versions that only operate for a limited period of time (timeware). However, many companies take a shareware approach, allowing fully functional copies of software to be downloaded for trial use and requiring the user to register and pay for the software when using it for commercial purposes.

**156.** **From a copyright owner point of view, when is electronic information declared as being used?**

    a.    When a reader has made a purchase

    b.    When a reader has downloaded the information for immediate use

    c.    When a reader buys access to the information

    d.    When a reader has downloaded the information for future use

*156. c.* In using an online information service, readers do not purchase any piece of property; rather they buy access to the electronic information. After the access is permitted, the information is out of the control of the copyright owner and the publisher. For the most part, publishers have no way of knowing the final disposition of the material (that is, downloaded now or later or used now). For this reason, publishers consider information as used as soon as it reaches the reader.

**157.** **What is the major downside to publishing information via digital media?**

    a.    A series of contracts in the distribution chain.

    b.    Many layers of end users.

    c.    A series of data storage media employed by end users.

    d.    Any reader is a potential publisher.

*157. d.* Traditionally, copyright law does not give copyright owners rights to control the access that readers have to information. Copyright owners in the electronic world use contracts to impose restrictions to make sure that they are paid for every instance of access or use. Still, as a practical matter, these restrictions do not prevent unauthorized copying. After users have paid for one legitimate copy of something, there is often not much except moral suasion to prevent them making other copies. Digital information is easily copied and easily transmitted to many locations. These characteristics make electronic distribution an attractive publishing medium; but they have a flip side (downside); almost any reader is a potential publisher of unauthorized copies.

**158.** **For libraries, the copyright law applies to which of the following?**

    a.    Computer data

    b.    Mixed media

    c.    Computer programs

    d.    Digital information

*158. c.* Digital information allows libraries new ways to offer services, and completely new services to offer. Libraries have some uncertainties with regard to copyright laws. For example, libraries may not be the owners of the computer programs. Vendors often say that programs are licensed, not sold. The library, as a licensee rather than an owner, does not have the rights described in the copyright law; these are abrogated by the terms of the license. For example, the copyright law gives the owner of a computer program the right to make an archival (backup) copy under certain conditions.

Some provisions in the copyright law also deal with copying and other uses of computer programs, but do not specifically extend to digital information. Digital information includes multimedia or mixed media databases, which may include images, music, text, or other types of work. Digital information is not just words and numbers. Anything that can be seen or heard can be digitized, so databases can include music, motion pictures, or photographs of art works.

Copyright laws currently refer only to computer programs and not to data or digital information. Computer data is stored in the same medium as computer programs, and it would seem logical to treat them in the same way, but the argument remains that digital data does not fit the definitions currently set out in the copyright laws, so owners have no right to make archival copies. The two points raised here become even more complicated for libraries in the case of mixed-media works where printed material, digital data, computer programs, microfiche, and other forms might be packaged and used together.

**159.** **Which of the following is *not* protected by copyright laws?**

    a.    Program structure

    b.    Program sequence

    c.    Program organization

    d.    User interface

**159. d.**   A court (case law) found that computer programs are protected under copyright against "comprehensive non-literal similarity," and held that "copyright protection of computer programs may extend beyond a program's literal code to its structure, sequence, and organization." The court also said that user interface in the form of input and output reports are not copyrightable.

**160.** **Which of the following is *not* copyrightable?**

    a.    Formats

    b.    Databases

    c.    Program functions

    d.    Program code

**160. a.**   A court (case law) held that formats are not copyrightable. Databases are protected under copyright law as compilations. However, copyright protection in a compilation does not provide protection for every element of the compilation. It extends only to the material contributed by the author of such work, not to preexisting material used in the work. Both program functions and program code are copyrightable.

**161.** Which of the following Pacific Rim countries has trade secret protection provided for computer programs?

 a.   Japan

 b.   Korea

 c.   Taiwan

 d.   Thailand

*161. a.* Japan is the only Pacific Rim nation whose law provides for trade secret protection. Computer programs can be a part of the trade secrets. The owner of a trade secret may request that the media on which the computer program is stored be destroyed. The other countries such as Korea, Taiwan, and Thailand do not have such laws or are in the process of developing one.

**162.** Which of the following logs are useful for security monitoring?

 a.   Network-based security software logs

 b.   Host-based security software logs

 c.   Operating system logs

 d.   Application system logs

*162. d.* Some applications, such as Web and e-mail services, can record usage information that might also be useful for security monitoring. (That is, a ten-fold increase in e-mail activity might indicate a new e-mail-borne malware threat.)

Both network-based and host-based security software logs contain basic security-related information such as user access profiles and access rights and permissions, which is not useful for security monitoring. Operating system logs collect information on servers, workstations, and network connectivity devices (e.g., routers and switches) that could be useful in identifying suspicious activity involving a particular host, but not useful for security monitoring.

**163.** From a computer security viewpoint, accountability of a person using a computer system is *most* closely tied to which of the following?

 a.   Responsibility

 b.   Usability

 c.   Traceability

 d.   Accessibility

*163. c.* The issue here is to determine who did what and when. For accountability to function, information about who attempted an action, what action, when, and what the results were must be logged. This log can be used to trace a person's actions. The logs must not be subject to tampering or loss. Logs provide traceability of user actions.

Responsibility is a broader term defining obligations and expected behavior. The term responsibility implies a proactive stance on the part of the responsible party and a casual relationship between the responsible party and a given outcome. The term accountability refers to the ability to hold people responsible for their actions. People could be responsible for their actions but not held accountable. For example, an anonymous user on a system is responsible for not compromising security but cannot be held accountable if a compromise occurs because the action cannot be traced to an individual.

Usability is incorrect because it deals with a set of attributes that bear on the effort needed for use, and on the individual assessment of such use, by a stated or implied set of users.

Accessibility is incorrect because it is the ability to obtain the use of a computer system or a resource or the ability and means necessary to store data, retrieve data, or communicate with a system. Responsibility, usability, and accessibility are not traceable to an individual's actions.

**164.** Detection measures are needed to identify computer-related criminal activities. Which one of the following measures is reactive in nature?

a. Recording all login attempts

b. Checking the system logs

c. Notifying someone about system anomalies

d. Limiting the number of login attempts

*164. b.* Reactive measures are designed to detect ongoing crimes and crimes that have already been committed. Such measures include performing regular audits of the system and checking the system logs generated automatically by the system. Proactive measures detect crimes before or as they are being committed. Examples include recording all login attempts, notifying the user or security officer about system anomalies by sounding an alarm or displaying a message, and limiting the number of login attempts before automatically disconnecting the login process.

**165.** Which one of the following is *not* intrinsically a computer crime or even a misdeed?

a. Wiretapping

b. Eavesdropping

c. Superzapping

d. Masquerading

*165. c.* Superzapping, a utility program in the IBM mainframe environment, can be thought of as the master key to the computer system. It unlocks most of the security safeguards and integrity controls. In the wrong hands, its use can be damaging. Use of supervisor privileges, root privileges, or the running of programs that bypass security controls is needed to troubleshoot certain operating system problems. In other words, superzapping can be used for both good and bad purposes. The problem is that no audit trail exists.

Wiretapping is incorrect because it is a computer crime. An unauthorized device is attached to a telecommunications circuit for the purpose of obtaining active and/or passive access. Eavesdropping is incorrect because it is a computer crime involving an unauthorized interception of information. Masquerading is incorrect because it is a computer crime, and it is an attempt to gain access to a computer system by posing as an authorized user.

**166.** **Site licenses for buying off-the-shelf personal computer software provide many benefits to vendors and users alike. Which one of the following does *not* determine the need for site licenses?**

    a.    The use of similar software for many computers

    b.    The availability of contract

    c.    The availability of *de jure* standards in place

    d.    The availability of *de facto* standards in place

*166. b.* Site licenses should be considered if an organization needs similar software for many computers, can afford procurement or can get a suitable site license, and has or needs standards (formal or informal) in place. Specific requirements and not the availability of a contract determine site licenses. It takes some effort to award a site license, but when used properly, a site license can provide savings in personnel resources and reduced prices. *De jure* standards are formal, whereas *de facto* standards are informal in nature.

**167.** **Software site license contracts do *not*:**

    a.    Increase support expenses

    b.    Improve management of software inventory

    c.    Facilitate centralized ordering

    d.    Streamline software distribution function

*167. a.* Software site licenses decrease support expenses due to economies of scale. For user organizations a site license permits using many copies of a software package at reduced cost and allows better management of the organization's software inventory. For software vendors a site license can reduce marketing and distribution costs and provide predictable payments.

Site license contracts improve management of software inventories, centralize ordering, and streamline software distribution functions. Accurate inventories are important when ordering software upgrades, designing a local area network, and protecting against computer viruses. Centralized ordering and software distribution functions gain acceptance when they are shown to be advantageous to the organization. A benefit of site licensing is a standardized support, which reduces training and other support expenses, and is the easiest way to gain seamless and transparent sharing of information. The benefits of standardization include ease of information exchange, shared application processing, shared application development, and reduced training time and costs.

**168.** Which one of the following refers to striking a balance between an individual's rights and controls over information about themselves?

    a.    Confidentiality

    b.    Privacy

    c.    Security

    d.    Integrity

**168. b.** Privacy is the right of an individual to limit access to information regarding that individual. Privacy refers to the social balance between an individual's right to keep information confidential and the societal benefit derived from sharing information, and how this balance is codified to give individuals the means to control personal information. Safeguards that help ensure confidentiality of information can be used to protect personal privacy.

Confidentiality is incorrect because it refers to disclosure of information only to authorized individuals, entities, and so forth. Security is incorrect because it refers to the protection individual's desire against unauthorized disclosure, modification, or destruction of information they consider private or valuable. Security and safeguards are often used interchangeably. Integrity is incorrect because it refers to the perfect condition that ensures that only authorized individuals changed the information.

**169.** Which of the following incident detection methods does *not* work well for all situations?

    a.    Intrusion detection software

    b.    Antivirus software

    c.    Log analyzers

    d.    User reports

**169. d.** Automated incident detection methods include intrusion detection software, whether network-based or host-based, antivirus software, and log analyzers. Incidents may also be detected through manual means, such as user reports, but they do not work well for all situations due to their being static in nature. Some incidents have overt signs that can be easily detected, whereas others are virtually undetectable without automation.

**170.** The person who *most* frequently reports illegal copying and use of vendor-developed PC-based software in an organization to either government officers or to the software vendor representative is:

    a.    Systems consultants

    b.    Software dealers

    c.    Hard disk loaders

    d.    Disgruntled employees

**170. d.** In a majority of cases (90-95 percent) illegal copying and use of software is reported by disgruntled employees. The other tips tend to come from systems consultants who work at client sites. Software dealers and hard disk loaders would not report because they are usually involved in illegal copying of the software for their customers.

**171.** **Which of the following logs can be helpful in identifying sequences of malicious events?**

a. Network-based security software logs

b. Host-based security software logs

c. Operating system logs

d. Application system logs

***171. d.*** Application system logs generate highly detailed logs that reflect every user request and response, which can be helpful in identifying sequences of malicious events and determining their apparent outcome. For example, many Web, file transfer protocol (FTP), and e-mail servers can perform such application logging.

Both network-based and host-based security software logs contain basic security-related information such as user access profiles and access rights and permissions, which is not helpful in identifying sequences of malicious events. Operating system logs collect information on servers, workstations, and network connectivity devices (for example, routers and switches) that could be useful in identifying suspicious activity involving a particular host, but is not helpful in identifying sequences of malicious events.

**172.** **A single and effective control procedure to detect illegal use of copyrighted software in the organization is to:**

a. Send an electronic-mail questionnaire to all users.

b. Remind all users periodically not to use illegally obtained software.

c. Develop a software inventory management tool and periodically compare the inventory software list to company purchase orders.

d. Develop a software anti-piracy policy immediately and distribute to all users without fail.

***172. c.*** With the use of either a publicly available software inventory management tool or utility program, the software searches hard disks for the presence of popular applications, and a list is prepared when a match is found. The list is then compared to company issued purchase orders. When illegal software is found, it is destroyed, and a new one is purchased. The software inventory management tool is the best means to do software audits, and it can be managed remotely by system administrators, who are independent from users. The actions suggested in the other three choices are superficial and do not achieve the same purpose as the software inventory management system.

**173.** **Which one of the following statements is true about application software source code escrow?**

a. It uses a key escrow system.

b. It is placing computer programs in a bank vault.

    c.    It is meaningless without an object code escrow.

    d.    It is placing computer programs under third-party custody.

**173. d.** Many application software vendors do not release the source code to the purchaser. This is intended to protect their system's integrity and copyright. The application system is installed in object code. An alternative to receiving the source programs is to establish an escrow agreement by a third-party custodian. In this agreement, the purchaser is allowed to access source programs under certain conditions (e.g., vendor bankruptcy and discontinued product support). A third party retains these programs and documents in escrow. Key escrow system is incorrect because it has nothing to do with application software escrow. A key escrow system is a system that entrusts the two components (private and public key) comprising a cryptographic key used in encryption to two key component holders or escrow agents. Computer programs in a bank vault are incorrect because they do not need to be placed in a bank vault. They can be placed with a third party agent regardless of the location. Object code is incorrect because it is not escrowed; only the source code is.

**174.** **Which of the following statements about Cyberlaw (i.e., law dealing with the Internet) is *true*?**

    a.    All materials published on the Internet and computer bulletin boards are subject to copyright protection only when accompanied by a formal copyright notice.

    b.    The bulletin board provider is liable for copyright infringement on its board only when it is aware of it.

    c.    Organizations own the copyright for building Internet sites by freelance writers.

    d.    An employer will always be the owner of an Internet work created by an employee within the scope of employment.

**174. d.** An employer will be the owner of a work created by an employee within the scope of employment. All material published on the Internet and computer bulletin boards are subject to copyright protection, whether or not it is accompanied by a formal copyright notice. It is true that an independent contractor, a freelancer, may hold the copyright in a work made for someone else if there is no express agreement to the contrary.

**175.** **Under which of the following conditions has a copyright infringement *not* occurred?**

    a.    When a work is viewed.

    b.    When a printed work is "scanned" into a digital file.

    c.    When a work is "uploaded" from a user's computer to a bulletin board system.

    d.    When the contents of a downloaded file are modified.

**175. a.** Viewing a work is harmless, as long it is not used in a commercial way. Usually, copyright laws grant owners certain rights, including the right to reproduce a work. The reproduction work is infringed whenever a work is uploaded from a user's computer to a bulletin board system or other server, downloaded from such a system or server, or transferred from one computer network user to another. An infringing copy is made when a printed work is scanned into a digital file and when the contents of a downloaded file are changed to prepare a derivative work.

**176.** **Under which of the following conditions is the use of an Internet domain name (address)** *not* **illegal?**

   a.   When the same name is used that has been in use for years by a competitor or noncompetitor.

   b.   When a new name is used.

   c.   When the company that assigns an Internet address assigns the same name.

   d.   When the company that assigns an Internet address has no change control system.

*176. b.* The Internet domain name contains elements that are in an electronic address directly following the symbol "@," which serves as the key identifier of a computer connected to the Internet. A new name is not illegal. The case law ruled that the other three choices are illegal uses of a domain name. The company that assigns an Internet address is called a gatekeeper.

**177.** **Sources of legal rights and obligations for privacy over electronic mail do** *not* **include:**

   a.   The law of the country

   b.   Employer practices

   c.   Employee practices

   d.   Employer policies

*177. c.* Because e-mail can cross many state and national boundaries and even continents, it is advised to review the principal sources of legal rights and obligations. These sources include the law of the country and employer policies and practices. Employee practices have no effect on the legal rights and obligations.

**178.** **Which of the following represents risk mitigation measures to detect, limit, or eliminate the malicious code attacks in software?**

   1.   Secure coding practices

   2.   Trusted procurement processes

   3.   Configuration management process

   4.   System monitoring practices

      a. 1 and 3

      b. 3 only

      c. 3 and 4

      d. 1, 2, 3, and 4

*178. d.* The goal is to ensure that software does not perform functions other than those intended. Risk mitigation measures to ensure that software does not perform unintended functions (e.g., malicious code attacks) include strong integrity controls, secure coding practices, trusted procurement processes for acquiring network-related hardware and software, configuration management and control, and system monitoring practices.

**179.** A person sets up an electronic bulletin board on which he encourages others to upload computer-based applications' software and games for free. The software and games are copyrighted. He then transfers the uploaded programs to a second bulletin board without any fees to potential users. The users with password access to the second bulletin board can download the programs. Under this scenario, who would be liable under wire fraud statutes?

    a.    The originator of the bulletin boards

    b.    Users who uploaded the programs to the first bulletin board

    c.    Users who downloaded the programs from the second bulletin board

    d.    Users who downloaded the programs from the first bulletin board

*179. a.* The originator of the bulletin board would be fully liable because he made illegal copying and distribution of copyrighted software available without payment of license fees and royalties to software manufacturers and vendors.

**180.** Which one of the following can cause the *least* damage in terms of severe financial losses?

    a.    Online stalkers

    b.    Computer worm designers

    c.    Computer virus designers

    d.    An employee tapping into a former employer's computer

*180. a.* Online stalking is harassment by a computer via sending threatening or obscene electronic-mail messages. Antistalking laws are state government-dependent and hence not enforced uniformly. The victim may be able to seek a restraining order to stop such online conduct.

The other three choices are incorrect because they cause heavy damage in terms of financial losses. A worm and virus designer can destroy valuable computer programs and tie up the network for hours and days. An employee tapping into a former employer's computer can steal valuable information and can sell it to competitors for financial gain or revenge.

**181.** Which one of the following raises significant legal issues in terms of fair use of copyrighted material?

    a.    Published work on paper

    b.    Unpublished work on paper

    c.    Digitized work on computer

    d.    Out-of-print work on paper

*181. c.* Information that is in digital form, and is thus easy to reuse and manipulate, raises a number of legal issues about what constitutes fair use. For example, if computer software is reverse-engineered, the systems analyst might copy the entire work, not just parts of it. This causes a significant loss of market share to the software vendor.

The other choices deal with paper media where "fair use" is clearly defined in terms of percentage of the work copied or used.

**182.** **Which of the following is a *major* risk of *not* tracking personal computer hardware and software assets?**

    a.    Incorrect amortization charges

    b.    Incorrect depreciation charges

    c.    Charges of software piracy

    d.    Lost vendor discounts

*182. c.* Managing PC hardware and software assets alerts management of any new, unauthorized software brought into the organization for the purpose of using it. These alerts not only find the presence of computer viruses but also protect from software piracy charges. Any unauthorized use of software should be discouraged.

The other three choices are incorrect because incorrect depreciation and amortization charges and lost vendor discounts are also risks, but not as big as the computer viruses and charges of software piracy. Amortization is used for software, whereas depreciation is used for hardware. An incorrect depreciation and amortization charge will result when the hardware and software assets are not properly accounted for and valued for. Vendor purchase discounts will be lost when centralized purchasing management is not aware of the potential assets.

**183.** **A United States organization is transmitting its data outside the country. Its management must be alerted to which of the following?**

    a.    The receiving country's transborder laws

    b.    The transmitting country's transborder laws

    c.    The receiving organization's data center policies

    d.    The transmitting organization's data center policies

*183. a.* Many European countries (e.g., Germany) place strong restrictions on the international flow of personal and financial data. This includes personal records, bank statements, and even mailing lists. Therefore, the transmitting country should be aware of the receiving country's transborder data flow laws. A specific data center's policies have nothing to do with the country's transborder data flow laws.

**184.** **Which one of the following logs helps in assessing the final damage from computer security incidents?**

    a.    Contact logs

    b.    Activity logs

    c.    Incident logs

    d.    Audit logs

**184. c.**  An organization needs to retain a variety of information for its own operational use and for conducting reviews of effectiveness and accountability. Incident logs are generated during the course of handling an incident. Incident logs are important for accurate recording of events that may need to be relayed to others. Information in incident logs is helpful for establishing new contacts; piecing together the cause, course, and extent of the incident; and for post-incident analysis and final assessment of damage. An incident should minimally contain (i) all actions taken, with times noted, (ii) all conversations, including the person(s) involved, the date and time, and a summary, and (iii) all system events and other pertinent information such as user IDs. The incident log should be detailed, accurate, and the proper procedures should be followed so that the incident log could be used as evidence in a court of law.

Contact logs are incorrect because they include such items as vendor contacts, legal and investigative contacts, and other individuals with technical expertise. A contact database record might include name, title, address, phone/fax numbers, e-mail address, and comments.

Activity logs are incorrect because they reflect the course of each day. Noting all contacts, telephone conversations, and so forth ultimately saves time by enabling one to retain information that may prove useful later.

Audit logs are incorrect because they contain information that is useful to trace events from origination to destination and vice versa. This information can be used to make users accountable on the system.

**185.** Software is an intellectual property. Which one of the following statements is true about software use and piracy?

    a.    An employee violated the piracy laws when he copied commercial software at work to use at home for 100 percent business reasons.

    b.    An employee violated the piracy laws when he copied commercial software for backup purposes.

    c.    An employee violated the piracy laws when he copied commercial software at work to use on the road for 100 percent business reasons.

    d.    The terms of the software license contract determines whether a crime or violation has taken place.

**185. d.**  Software piracy laws are complex and varied. A software vendor allows users to have two copies (one copy at work and the other one at home or on the road as long as they are using only one copy at a time), and a copy for backup purposes. Because each vendor's contractual agreement is different, it is best to consult with that vendor's contractual terms.

**186.** Regarding presenting evidence in a court of law, which one of the following items is *not* directly related to the other three items?

    a.    Exculpatory evidence

    b.    Inculpatory evidence

c.   Internal body of evidence

d.   Electronic evidence

***186. c.***   Evidence can be internal or external depending on when and where it is presented. The internal body of evidence is not related to the other three items because it is the set of data that documents the information system's adherence to the security controls applied. It is more of an evidence of internal control documents within an organization, and it might be used in a court of law as external evidence when needed.

The other three choices are incorrect because they are examples of external evidence required in a court of law, and are directly related to each other. Exculpatory evidence is the evidence that tends to decrease the likelihood of fault or guilt. Inculpatory evidence is the evidence that tends to increase the likelihood of fault or guilt. Electronic evidence is data and information of investigative value that is stored on or transmitted by an electronic device.

**187.**   **Your organization is using PC-based local-area networks (LANs), and their use is growing. Management is concerned about the number of users using application software at any given time. At present, management does not have an accurate picture of how many users use an application system to help maintain site license agreements. What would you recommend?**

a.   Obtain software metering and monitoring tools to control application software usage.

b.   Remind all users that only authorized people should use the software.

c.   Conduct periodic audits by auditors.

d.   Conduct random audits by the LAN administrator.

***187. a.***   The maximum number of users allowed per application to help maintain site license agreements can be designated. It shows how people use applications and purchasing unnecessary copies of software can be avoided. If additional copies are needed, the software alerts LAN managers with a screen message. Reminding all users that only authorized people should use the software does not achieve the objective because some people may not follow the directions. Conducting periodic audits by auditors or LAN administrators may not be timely and may not cover all areas of the organization due to time and resource factors.

**188.**   **During detection of malware incidents, which of the following can act as precursors?**

1.   Malware advisories

2.   Security tool alerts

3.   System administrators

4.   Security tools

a.   3 only

b.   4 only

    c.    1 or 2

    d.    3 and 4

***188. c.***   Signs of an incident fall into one of two categories: precursors and indications. A precursor is a sign that an incident (e.g., malware attack) may occur in the future (i.e., future incident). Most malware precursors are either malware advisories or security tool alerts. Detecting precursors gives organizations an opportunity to prevent incidents by altering their security posture and to be on the alert to handle incidents that occur shortly after the precursor.

System administrators and security tools are examples of indications of malware incidents. An indication is a sign that an incident (malware attack) may have occurred or may be occurring. The primary indicators include users, IT staff such as system, network, and security administrators and security tools such as antivirus software, intrusion prevention systems, and network monitoring software.

**189.**   **From a legal standpoint, which of the following pre-logon screen banners is sufficient to warn potential system intruders?**

    a.    No tampering

    b.    No trespassing

    c.    No hacking

    d.    No spamming

***189. b.***   A "no trespassing" notice is an all-inclusive warning to confront potential system intruders. All the other three choices come under "no trespassing."

**190.**   **Which of the following practices will *not* prevent computer security incidents?**

    a.    Collecting incident data

    b.    Having a patch management program

    c.    Hardening all hosts

    d.    Configuring the network perimeter

***190. a.***   Collecting incident data by itself does not prevent computer security incidents. A good use of the data is measuring the success of the incident response team. The other three choices prevent computer security incidents.

**191.**   **Which of the following is *not* the preferred characteristic of security incident-related data?**

    a.    Objective data

    b.    Subjective data

    c.    Actionable data

    d.    Available data

**191. d.** Organizations should be prepared to collect a set of objective and subjective data for each incident. They should focus on collecting data that is actionable, rather than collecting data simply because it is available.

**192.** Which of the following *cannot* be of great value in automating the incident analysis process?

    a.    Event correlation software

    b.    Centralized log management software

    c.    Security software

    d.    Patch management software

**192. d.** Usually, a separate team, other than the incident response team provides patch management services, and the patch management work could be a combination of manual and computer processes. Automation is needed to perform an analysis of the incident data and select events of interest for human review. Event correlation software, centralized log management software, and security software can be of great value in automating the analysis process. The other three choices are used in the detection and analysis phase, which is prior to the recovery phase where patches are installed.

**193.** When applying computer forensics to redundant array of independent disks (RAID) disk imaging technology, which of the following are not used as a hash function in verifying the integrity of digital data on RAID arrays as evidence in a court of law?

    1.    Cyclic redundancy check-32 (CRC-32)

    2.    Checksums

    3.    Message digest 5 (MD5)

    4.    Secure hash algorithm1 (SHA1)

    a.    1 only

    b.    3 only

    c.    1 and 2

    d.    3 and 4

**193. c.** Both CRC-32 and checksums are not used as a hash function in verifying the integrity of digital data on RAID arrays as evidence in a court of law. To be complete and accurate in the eyes of the court, data must be verified as bit-bit match. Failure to provide the court assurance of data integrity can result in the evidence being completely dismissed or used in a lesser capacity as an artifact, finding, or as item of note. The court system needs an absolute confidence that the data presented to it is an exact, unaltered replication of the original data in question.

The CRC-32 is not a hash function, is a 32-bit checksum, and is too weak to be heavily relied upon. The main weakness is that the probability of two separate and distinct data-streams generating the same value using CRC-32 is too high. Checksums are digits or bits summed according to some arbitrary rules and are used to verify the integrity of normal data, but they are not hash functions, as required in disk imaging.

Both MD5 and SHA1 are used as a hash function in verifying the integrity of digital data on RAID arrays as evidence in a court of law. The MD5 is a 128-bit hash algorithm, and is not susceptible to the same weakness of CRC-32. The chances of any two distinct data-streams generating the same hash value using MD5 is extremely low. SHA-1 is a 160-bit hash algorithm, which is computationally stronger than the MD5. In relation to disk imaging, the benefit of using a hash algorithm is that if any bit is changed or missing between the source and the destination copy, a hash of the data-stream will show this difference.

**194.** A user providing illegal copies of software to others is an example of which of the following computer-security incident types?

    a.   Denial-of-service

    b.   Malicious code

    c.   Unauthorized access

    d.   Inappropriate usage

*194. d.* Using file-sharing services (e.g., peer-to-peer, P2P) to acquire or distribute pirated software is an example of inappropriate usage actions. Inappropriate usage occurs when a person violates acceptable computing use policies.

A denial-of-service (DoS) attack prevents or impairs the authorized use of networks, systems, or applications by exhausting resources. Malicious code includes a virus, worm, Trojan horse, or other code-based malicious entity that infects a host. Unauthorized access is where a person gains logical or physical access without permission to a network, operating system, application system, data, or device.

**195.** When should the incident response team become acquainted with its various law enforcement representatives?

    a.   After an incident has occurred

    b.   Before an incident occurs

    c.   During an incident is occurring

    d.   After the incident is taken to court

*195. b.* The incident response team should become acquainted with its various law enforcement representatives before an incident occurs to discuss conditions under which incidents should be reported to them, how the reporting should be performed, what evidence should be collected, and how the evidence should be collected.

**196.** Which of the following is the major reason for many security-related incidents *not* resulting in convictions?

    a.   Organizations do not properly contact law enforcement agencies.

    b.   Organizations are confused about the role of various law enforcement agencies.

    c.    Organizations do not know the attacker's physical location.

    d.    Organizations do not know the attacker's logical location.

**196. a.** The major reason that many security-related incidents do not result in convictions is that organizations do not properly contact law enforcement agencies. An organization should not contact multiple law enforcement agencies because of jurisdictional conflicts. Organizations should appoint one incident response team member as the primary point of contact with law enforcement agencies. The team should understand what the potential jurisdictional issues are (i.e., physical location versus logical location of the attacker).

**197.** **Which of the following are used to capture and analyze network traffic that may contain evidence of a computer security incident?**

1. Packet sniffers

2. Forensic software

3. Protocol analyzers

4. Forensic workstations

    a.    1 and 2

    b.    1 and 3

    c.    2 and 3

    d.    2 and 4

**197. b.** Packet sniffers and protocol analyzers capture and analyze network traffic that may contain malware activity and evidence of a security incident. Packet sniffers are designed to monitor network traffic on wired or wireless networks and capture packets. Most packet sniffers are also protocol analyzers, which mean that they can reassemble streams from individual packets and decode communications that use any of hundreds or thousands of different protocols. Because packet sniffers and protocol analyzers perform the same functions, they could be combined into a single tool.

Computer forensic software is used to analyze disk images for evidence of an incident, whereas forensic workstations are used to create disk images, preserve logs files, and save incident data.

**198.** **Which of the following facilitates faster response to computer security incidents?**

    a.    Rootkit

    b.    Tool kit

    c.    Computer kit

    d.    Jump kit

**198. d.** Many incident response teams create a jump kit, which is a portable bag containing materials such as a laptop computer loaded with the required software, blank media, backup devices, network equipment and cables, and operating system and application software patches. This jump kit is taken with the incident handler during an offsite investigation of an incident for faster response. The jump kit is ready to go at all times so that when a serious incident occurs, incident handlers can grab the jump kit and go, giving them a jump start.

A rootkit is a set of tools used by an attacker after gaining root-level access to a host. The rootkit conceals the attacker's activities on the host, permitting the attacker to maintain root-level access to the host through covert means. Rootkits are publicly available, and many are designed to alter logs to remove any evidence of the rootkit's installation or execution. Tool kit and computer kit are generic terms without any specific value here.

**199.** Which of the following statements about security controls, vulnerabilities, risk assessment, and incident response awareness is *not* correct?

    a.   Insufficient security controls lead to slow responses and larger negative business impacts.

    b.   A large percentage of incidents involve exploitation of a small number of vulnerabilities.

    c.   Risk assessment results can be interpreted to ignore security over resources that are less than critical.

    d.   Improving user awareness regarding incidents reduces the frequency of incidents.

**199. c.** Risk assessments usually focus on critical resources. This should not be interpreted as a justification for organizations to ignore the security of resources that are deemed to be less than critical because the organization is only as secure as its weakest link.

If security controls are insufficient, high volumes of incidents may occur, which can lead to slow and incomplete responses which, in turn, are translated to a larger negative business impacts (e.g., more extensive damage, longer delays in providing services, and longer system unavailability). Many security experts agree that a large percentage of incidents involve exploitation of a relatively small number of vulnerabilities in operating systems and application systems (i.e., an example of Pareto's 80/20 principle). Improving user awareness regarding incidents should reduce the frequency of incidents, particularly those involving malicious code and violations of acceptable use policies.

**200.** Some security incidents fit into more than one category for identification and reporting purposes. An incident response team should categorize incidents by the use of:

    a.   Access mechanism

    b.   Target mechanism

    c.   Transmission mechanism

    d.   Incident mechanism

**200. c.** When incidents fit into more than one category, the incident response team should categorize incidents by the transmission mechanism used. For example, a virus that creates a backdoor that has been used to gain unauthorized access should be treated as a multiple component incident because two transmission mechanisms are used: one as a malicious code incident and the other one as an unauthorized access incident.

**201.** **What is incorrectly classifying a malicious activity as a benign activity called?**

    a.    False negative

    b.    False positive

    c.    False warnings

    d.    False alerts

*201. a.* Forensic tools create false negatives and false positives. False negatives incorrectly classify malicious activity as benign activity. False positives incorrectly classify benign activity as malicious activity. False warnings and false alerts are generated from intrusion detection system sensors or vulnerability scanners.

**202.** **Which of the following computer and network data analysis methods dealing with computer-incident purposes helps identify policy violations?**

    a.    Operational troubleshooting

    b.    Log monitoring

    c.    Data recovery

    d.    Data acquisition

*202. b.* Various tools and techniques can assist with log monitoring, such as analyzing log entries and correlating log entries across multiple systems. This can assist with incident handling, identifying policy violations, auditing, and other efforts.

Operational troubleshooting is incorrect because it applies to finding the virtual and physical location of a host with an incorrect network configuration, resolving a functional problem with an application, and recording and reviewing the current operating system and application configuration settings for a host.

Data recovery is incorrect because data recovery tools can recover lost data from systems. This includes data that has been accidentally or purposely deleted, overwritten, or otherwise modified.

Data acquisition is incorrect because it deals with tools to acquire data from hosts that are being redeployed or retired. For example, when a user leaves an organization, the data from the user's workstation can be acquired and stored in case the data is needed in the future. The workstation's media can then be sanitized to remove all the original user's data.

**203.** **Which of the following is *best* for reviewing packet sniffer data?**

    a.    Security event management software

    b.    Protocol analyzer

    c.    Log filtering tool

    d.    Visualization tool

*203. b.* Packet sniffer data is best reviewed with a protocol analyzer, which interprets the data for the analyst based on knowledge of protocol standards and common implementations.

Security event management software is incorrect because it is capable of importing security event information from various network traffic-related security event data sources (e.g., IDS logs and firewall logs) and correlating events among the sources.

Log filtering tool is incorrect because it helps an analyst to examine only the events that are most likely to be of interest. Visualization tool is incorrect because it presents security event data in a graphical format.

**204.** **What is a technique for concealing or destroying data so that others *cannot* access it?**

    a.    Antiforensic

    b.    Steganography

    c.    Digital forensic

    d.    Forensic science

***204. a.*** Antiforensic is a technique for concealing or destroying data so that others cannot access it. Steganography is incorrect because it embeds data within other data to conceal it. Digital forensic is incorrect because it is the application of science to the identification, collection, analysis, and examination of digital evidence while preserving the integrity of the information and maintaining a strict chain of custody for the evidence. Forensic science is incorrect because it is the application of science to the law.

**205.** **A search warrant is required:**

    a.    Before the allegation has been substantiated

    b.    After establishing the probable cause(s)

    c.    Before identifying the number of investigators needed

    d.    After seizing the computer and related equipment

***205. b.*** After the allegation has been substantiated, the prosecutor should be contacted to determine if there is probable cause for a search. Because of the technical orientation of a computer-related crime investigation, presenting a proper technical perspective in establishing probable cause becomes crucial to securing a search warrant.

**206.** **Law enforcement agencies have developed personality profiles of computer criminals. Careful planning prior to an actual crime is an example of which one of the following characteristics?**

    a.    Organizational characteristics

    b.    Operational characteristics

    c.    Behavioral characteristics

    d.    Resource characteristics

***206. b.*** In many cases, computer crimes are carefully planned. Computer criminals spend a great deal of time researching and preparing to commit crimes. These are grouped under operational characteristics.

Organizational characteristics describe the ways in which computer criminals group themselves with national and international connections. Behavioral characteristics deal with motivation and personality profiles. Resource characteristics address training and equipment needs and the overall support structure.

**207.** **When 'n' incident reports are made by an organization, it can lead to a wrong conclusion that:**

    a.    There are '*n*' plus one incident.

    b.    There are '*n*' minus one incident.

    c.    There are '*n*' incidents.

    d.    There are '*n*' plus or minus one incident.

*207.* **c.** It is important *not* to assume that because only '*n*' reports are made, that '*n*' is the total number of incidents; it is *not* likely that all incidents are reported.

**208.** **Which of the following should be established to minimize security incident impact?**

    a.    Learning and training

    b.    Baselining and safeguarding

    c.    Layering and zoning

    d.    Testing and sampling

*208.* **c.** Layering and zoning requires establishing security layers to minimize incident handling. Zoning or compartmentalizing is a concept whereby an application is segmented into independent security environments. A breach of security requires a security failure in two or more zones/compartments before the application is compromised. This minimizes the impact of a security incident. This layered approach to security can be applied within physical or technical environments associated with an IT system.

Learning is knowledge gained by studying either in the classroom or through individual research and investigation. Training is teaching people the knowledge and skills that can enable them to perform their jobs more effectively. Baseline security is incorrect because it is the minimum-security control required for safeguarding an IT system based on its identified needs for confidentiality, integrity, and availability protection. Sampling is used in testing where a representative sample is taken from a defined population.

**209.** **Which of the following will *not* be liable when a libel is posted on a national electronic online service such as the Internet?**

    a.    The person who originated the defamatory remark

    b.    The person who repeated the defamatory remark

    c.    The person who read the defamatory remark

    d.    The person who republished the defamatory remark

**209. c.** Defamation is destroying of a person's reputation and good name, in the form of a false statement, spoken (slander) or written (libel), and harms that person. Online defamation claims are considered under libel law. The essence of libel is the publication of a false, defamatory, and unprivileged statement to a third person. The originator and each person who repeats or republishes the defamation are liable. The person who read the defamatory work is not liable for anything as long as he or she does not use it in a commercial way.

**210.** **Log analysis is a part of which of the following?**

    a. Directive controls

    b. Preventive controls

    c. Detective controls

    d. Corrective controls

**210. c.** Log analysis is a part of detective controls because it detects errors and anomalies. Detective controls enhance security by monitoring the effectiveness of preventive controls and by detecting security incidents where preventive controls were circumvented.

Directive controls are broad-based controls to handle security incidents, and they include management's policies, procedures, and directives. Preventive controls deter security incidents from happening in the first place. Corrective controls are procedures to react to security incidents and to take remedial actions on a timely basis. Corrective controls require proper planning and preparation as they rely more on human judgment.

**211.** **Which of the following facilitates a computer-security incident event correlation?**

    a. File transfer protocol (FTP)

    b. Network time protocol (NTP)

    c. Internet protocol (IP)

    d. Transmission control protocol (TCP)

**211. b.** Protocols such as the network time protocol (NTP) synchronize clocks among hosts. This is important for incident response because event correlation will be more difficult if the devices reporting events have inconsistent clock settings.

**212.** **Which of the following is required when computer security evidence is transferred from person to person?**

    a. Location and serial number of the computer

    b. Time and date of evidence

    c. Chain of custody forms

    d. Locations where the evidence was stored

**212. c.** Computer security incident evidence is needed for legal proceedings. Evidence should be accounted for at all times; whenever evidence is transferred from person to person; chain of custody forms should detail the transfer and include each party's signature. The other choices are part of evidence log.

**213.** **Inappropriate usage incidents are *not* detected through which of the following ways?**

    a.    Precursors

    b.    User reports

    c.    User's screen

    d.    Threatening e-mail

*213. a.* Usually there are no precursors (future incidents) of inappropriate usage. User reports, such as seeing inappropriate materials on a user's screen or receiving a threatening e-mail, are the usual methods to detect inappropriate usage.

**214.** **The outcomes of which of the following phases of a computer forensic process dealing with computer incidents are used to incorporate into future data analysis efforts?**

    a.    Collection

    b.    Examination

    c.    Analysis

    d.    Reporting

*214. d.* A computer forensic process dealing with computer incidents is composed of four phases: collection, examination, analysis, and reporting. Lessons learned during the reporting phase should be incorporated into future data analysis efforts.

The collection phase is incorrect because it deals with acquiring data from the possible sources of relevant data and complying with the guidelines and procedures that preserve the integrity of the data. The examination phase is incorrect because it applies the tools and techniques to the collected data in order to identify and extract the relevant information while protecting its integrity. The analysis phase is incorrect because it analyzes the results of the examination, which may include the actions used in the examination and recommendations for improvement.

**215.** **In terms of functionality, which of the following is *not* a part of network forensic analysis tools?**

    a.    Internet service provider records

    b.    Packet sniffers

    c.    Protocol analyzers

    d.    Security event management software

*215. a.* Internet service providers (ISPs) may collect network traffic-related data as part of their normal operations and when investigating unusual activity, such as extremely high volumes of traffic or an apparent attack. Normal ISP records might be only for days or hours. Forensic data needs to be available until the investigation is completed. ISP records are a secondary source. Network forensic analysis tools typically provide the same functionality as packet sniffers, protocol analyzers, and security event management software. These are primary tools.

**216.** A search of the malware database did not lead to the identification of the worm. In analyzing the current state of the host, the incident handler feels that the worm has created a backdoor. Which of the following aspects of the host's current state will identify that backdoor?

a. Unusual connections

b. Unexpected listening ports

c. Unknown processes

d. Unusual entries

*216. b.* The analyst can look at several different aspects of the host's current state. It is good to start with identifying unusual connections (e.g., large number, unexpected port number usage, and unexpected hosts) and unexpected listening ports (e.g., backdoors created by the worm). Other steps that may be useful include identifying unknown processes in the running process list, and examining the host's logs to reveal any unusual entries that may be related to the infection.

**217.** In a computer-related crime investigation, maintenance of evidence is important for which of the following reasons:

a. To record the crime

b. To collect the evidence

c. To protect the evidence

d. To avoid problems of proof

*217. d.* It is proper to maintain computer-related evidence. Special procedures are needed to avoid problems of proof caused by improper care and handling of such evidence.

**218.** An effective strategy to analyze indications to investigate the most suspicious activity is accomplished through which of the following?

a. Using an Internet search engine

b. Creating a diagnosis matrix

c. Synchronizing the clocks

d. Filtering of the incident data

*218. d.* An incident indication analyst sees a large volume of data daily for analysis, which consumes large amounts of time. An effective strategy is to filter indications so that insignificant indications are not shown or only significant indications are shown to the analyst.

**219.** Which of the following is directly applicable to computer security incident prioritization?

a. Gap-fit analysis

b. Sensitivity analysis

c. Option analysis

d. Business impact analysis

**219. d.**   A fundamental concept of business continuity planning is business impact analysis (BIA), which refers to determining the impact of particular events. BIA information for an organization may be directly applicable to security incident prioritization.

The other three choices are not related to security incident prioritization. Gap-fit analysis deals with comparing actual outcomes with expected outcomes. Sensitive analysis focuses on "what if" conditions. Option analysis deals with choices available or not available.

**220.** **From a computer-forensic viewpoint, which of the following is *most* useful in prosecution?**

a.   Disk image

b.   Standard file system backup

c.   Deleted files

d.   File fragments

**220. a.**   A disk image preserves all data on the disk, including deleted files and file fragments. A standard file system backup can capture information on existing files, which may be sufficient for handling many incidents, particularly those that are not expected to lead to prosecution. Both disk images and file system backups are valuable regardless of whether the attacker will be prosecuted because they permit the target to be restored while the investigation continues using the image or backup.

**221.** **Which of the following indications is *not* associated with a network-based denial-of-service attack against a particular host?**

a.   Unexplained connection losses

b.   Packets with nonexistent destination addresses

c.   Increased network bandwidth utilization

d.   Firewall and router log entries

**221. b.**   Packets with nonexistent destination addresses are an example of possible indications for a network-based denial-of-service (DoS) attack against a network, not a host. The other choices are examples of indications for network-based DoS attacks against a particular host.

**222.** **Which of the following indications is *not* associated with a malicious action such as root compromise of a host?**

a.   User reports of system unavailability

b.   Highly unusual log messages

c.   Unexplained account usage

d.   Increased resource utilization

**222. d.**   "Increased resource utilization" is an example of possible indications of malicious action such as unauthorized data modification. The other choices are examples of possible indications of root compromise of a host.

223. **From a security incident viewpoint, countermeasures and controls *cannot* do which of the following?**

    a.    Prevent

    b.    Detect

    c.    Respond

    d.    Recover

*223. c.*    Countermeasures and controls prevent, detect, and recover from security incidents, not respond to them. Incident response emphasizes interactions with outside parties, such as the media/press, law enforcement authorities, and incident reporting organizations. It is not easy to exercise control over these outside parties.

224. **Which of the following forensic tools and techniques are useful for complying with regulatory requirements?**

    a.    Operational troubleshooting

    b.    Data recovery

    c.    Due diligence

    d.    Data acquisition

*224. c.*    Regulations require many organizations to protect sensitive information and maintain certain records for audit purposes. Organizations can exercise due diligence and comply with regulatory requirements. Due diligence requires developing and implementing an effective security program to prevent and detect violation of policies and laws. The other three choices deal with day-to-day operations work, not with regulatory requirements.

225. **Computer incident response process is a part of which of the following?**

    a.    Directive controls

    b.    Preventive controls

    c.    Detective controls

    d.    Corrective controls

*225. d.*    Computer incident response process is a part of corrective controls because it manages the unexpected security incidents in a systematic manner. Corrective controls are procedures to react to security incidents and to take remedial actions on a timely basis. Corrective controls require proper planning and preparation as they rely more on human judgment.

Directive controls are broad-based controls to handle security incidents, and they include management's policies, procedures, and directives. Preventive controls deter security incidents from happening in the first place. Detective controls enhance security by monitoring the effectiveness of preventive controls and by detecting security incidents where preventive controls were circumvented.

# SCENARIO-BASED QUESTIONS, ANSWERS, AND EXPLANATIONS

Use the following information to answer questions 1 through 5.

The ERD Company has just had a theft of 2.5 million dollars via the Internet. The IT management believes the cause to be malware installed by an attacker. This represents 2 percent of the company's total assets. The senior executives have been notified, but they will not be available for the next 36 hours. The last policy update for incident response was 4 years ago. Since the update, the people in charge of incident handling have left the company. The contact information for the virtual team is not current.

**1.** A search of the malware database did not lead to the identification of the worm. In analyzing the current state of the host, the incident handler feels that the worm has created a backdoor. Which of the following aspects of the host's current state can identify that backdoor?

    a.    Unusual connections

    b.    Unexpected listening ports

    c.    Unknown processes

    d.    Unusual entries

*1. b.*   The analyst can look at several different aspects of the host's current state. It is good to start with identifying unusual connections (e.g., large number, unexpected port number usage, and unexpected hosts) and unexpected listening ports (e.g., backdoors created by the worm). Other steps that may be useful include identifying unknown processes in the running process list, and examining the host's logs to reveal any unusual entries that may be related to the infection.

**2.** A worm has infected a system. From a network data analysis perspective, which of the following contains more detailed information?

    a.    Network-based IDS and firewalls

    b.    Routers

    c.    Host-based IDS and firewalls

    d.    Remote access servers

*2. c.*   Intrusion detection system (IDS) and firewall products running on the infected system may contain more detailed information than network-based IDS and firewall products. For example, a host-based IDS can identify changes to files or configuration settings on the host that were performed by a worm. This information is helpful not only in planning containment, eradication, and recovery activities by determining how the worm has affected the host, but also in identifying which worm infected the system. However, because many worms disable host-based security controls and destroy log entries, data from host-based IDS and firewall software may be limited or missing. If the software were configured to forward copies of its logs to centralized log servers, then queries to those servers may provide some useful information.

Network-based IDS is incorrect because they indicate which server was attacked and on what port number, which indicates which network service was targeted. Network-based firewalls are typically configured to log blocked connection attempts, which include the intended destination IP address and port number. Other perimeter devices that the worm traffic may have passed through, such as routers, VPN gateways, and remote access servers may record information similar to that logged by network-based firewalls.

3. **Which of the following parties is usually *not* notified at all or is notified last when a computer security incident occurs?**

    a.    System administrator

    b.    Legal counsel

    c.    Disaster recovery coordinator

    d.    Hardware and software vendors

*3. b.*    The first part of a response mechanism is notification, whether automatic or manual. Besides technical staff, several others must be notified, depending on the nature and scope of the incident. Unfortunately, legal counsel is not always notified or is notified thinking that involvement is not required.

4. **An organization just had a computer security incident. Who generally reacts *most* negatively?**

    a.    E-Partners

    b.    Suppliers

    c.    Investors

    d.    Trading partners

*4. c.*    Investors will punish the organization that was subject to a computer security incident such as hacking. They have the most to lose, thereby negatively impacting the company's valuation. The other parties do not have the same stake.

5. **A computer security incident was detected. Which of the following is the *best* reaction strategy for management to adopt?**

    a.    Protect and preserve

    b.    Protect and recover

    c.    Trap and prosecute

    d.    Pursue and proceed

*5. b.*    If a computer site is vulnerable, management may favor the protect-and-recover reaction strategy because it increase defenses available to the victim organization. Also, this strategy can bring normalcy to the network's users as quickly as possible. Management can interfere with the intruder's activities, prevent further access, and begin damage assessment. This interference process may include shutting down the computer center, closing of access to the network, and initiating recovery efforts. Law enforcement authorities and prosecutors favor the trap-and-prosecute strategy. It lets intruders continue their activities until the security administrator can identify the intruder. In the mean time, there could be system damage or data loss.

## SOURCES AND REFERENCES

Anti-Spam Laws. (www.oecd-antispam.org).

"Computer Security Incident Handling Guide (NIST SP800-61 Revision 1)," National Institute of Standards and Technology (NIST), U.S. Department of Commerce, Gaithersburg, Maryland, March 2008.

Corley, Lee Reed, and Shedd. 1993. *The Legal and Regulatory Environment of Business* , Ninth Edition. McGraw-Hill, Inc.

European Union (EU) Laws. (http://europa.eu/scadplus/leg/en).

"Guide to Computer Security Log Management (NIST SP800-92)," National Institute of Standards and Technology (NIST), U.S. Department of Commerce, Gaithersburg, Maryland, September 2006.

"Guide to Integrating Forensic Techniques into Incident Response (NIST SP800-86)," National Institute of Standards and Technology (NIST), U.S. Department of Commerce, Gaithersburg, Maryland, August 2006.

"Guidelines on Cell Phone Forensics (NIST SP800-101)," National Institute of Standards and Technology (NIST), U.S. Department of Commerce, Gaithersburg, Maryland, May 2007.

International Safe Harbor Privacy Principles. (www.ita.doc.gov).

OECD Guidelines for the Security of Information Systems. (www.oecd.org).

Privacy Laws - Organization for Economic Co-operation and Development (OECD). (www.oecd.org).

"Sawyers Internal Auditing by The Institute of Internal Auditors," Altamonte Springs, Florida, 1988.

Stephenson, Peter. 2000. *Investigating Computer-Related Crime.* Boca Raton, FL: CRC Press LLC.

# DOMAIN 10

## Physical and Environmental Security

## TRADITIONAL QUESTIONS, ANSWERS, AND EXPLANATIONS

1. **Regarding physical security of cryptography, which modules are used the *most* in the production, implementation, and operation of encrypting routers?**

   a. Single-chip cryptographic modules

   b. Multiple-chip standalone cryptographic modules

   c. Software cryptographic modules

   d. Hardware cryptographic modules

   *1. b.* Multiple-chip standalone cryptographic modules are physical embodiments in which two or more integrated circuits (IC) chips are interconnected and the entire enclosure is physically protected. Examples of such implementations include encrypting routers or secure radios. Note that the security measures provided to these modules vary with the security levels of these modules.

   The other three choices are incorrect because they are not used in the implementation of encrypting routers or secure radios. Single-chip cryptographic modules are physical embodiments in which a single IC chip may be used as a standalone module or may be embedded within an enclosure or a product that may not be physically protected. Cryptographic modules can be implemented in software, hardware, firmware, and hybrid.

2. **Regarding cryptographic modules, which of the following refers to an attack on the operations of the hardware module that does *not* require physical contact with components within the module?**

    a.    Timing analysis attack

    b.    Noninvasive attack

    c.    Differential power analysis attack

    d.    Simple power analysis attack

**2. *b.*** A noninvasive attack can be performed on a cryptographic module without direct physical contact with the module. Non-invasive attacks attempt to compromise a cryptographic module by acquiring knowledge of the module's critical security parameters without physically modifying or invading the module.

The other three choices are incorrect because their actions are different than a non-invasive attack. A timing analysis attack is an attack on a cryptographic module that is based on an analysis of time periods between the time a command is issued and the time the result is obtained. A differential power analysis attack considers the variations of the electrical power consumption of a cryptographic module to correlate to cryptographic keys used in a cryptographic algorithm. A simple power analysis attack considers the patterns of instruction execution to reveal the values of cryptographic keys.

3. **Regarding physical security of cryptography, which of the following modules are used the *most* in production, implementation, and operation of adapters and expansion boards?**

    a.    Single-chip cryptographic modules

    b.    Multiple-chip standalone cryptographic modules

    c.    Multiple-chip embedded cryptographic modules

    d.    Hardware cryptographic modules

**3. *c.*** Multiple-chip embedded cryptographic modules are physical embodiments in which two or more integrated circuits (IC) chips are interconnected and are embedded within an enclosure or a product that may not be physically protected. Examples of such implementations include adapters and expansion boards. Note that the security measures provided to these modules vary with the security levels of these modules.

The other three choices are incorrect because they are not used in the implementation of adapters and expansion boards. Single-chip cryptographic modules are physical embodiments in which a single IC chip may be used as a standalone module or may be embedded within an enclosure or a product that may not be physically protected. Multiple-chip standalone cryptographic modules are physical embodiments in which two or more IC chips are interconnected and the entire enclosure is physically protected. Cryptographic modules can be implemented in software, hardware, firmware, and hybrid.

**4.** **Regarding cryptography, which of the following externally indicates that the physical security of a cryptographic module was compromised?**

    a.    Tamper attempt

    b.    Tamper evidence

    c.    Tamper detection

    d.    Tamper response

*4. b.* Tamper is an unauthorized modification that alters the proper functioning of a cryptographic module or automated information system security equipment in a manner that degrades the security or functionality it provides. Tamper evidence is the external indication that an attempt has been made to compromise the physical security of a cryptographic module. The evidence of the tamper attempt should be observable by the module operator subsequent to the attempt.

The other three choices are incorrect because do not indicate a compromise and their actions are internal. Tamper attempt means that an attacker has made a serious try to defeat the physical security of a cryptographic module. Tamper detection is the automatic determination by a cryptographic module that an attempt has been made to compromise the physical security of the module. Tamper response is the automatic action taken by a cryptographic module when a tamper attempt has been detected.

**5.** **Which of the following are *not* substitutes for tamper evidence of a cryptographic module?**

    a.    Tamper detection and tamper response

    b.    Tamper attempt and tamper prevention

    c.    Tamper prevention and tamper detection

    d.    Tamper prevention and tamper correction

*5. a.* For cryptographic module, tamper detection and tamper response are not substitutes for tamper evidence. Tamper evidence is the external indication that an attempt has been made to compromise the physical security of a cryptographic module. The sequence of events taking place is as follows: Tamper prevention comes first, detection comes next or at the same time as prevention, evidence comes next or at the same time as detection, and response or correction comes last. The evidence of a tamper attempt should be observable by the module operator subsequent to the attempt. Tamper detection is the automatic determination by a cryptographic module that an attempt has been made to compromise the physical security of the module. Tamper response is demonstrated through tamper correction, which is the automatic action taken by a cryptographic module when a tamper attempt has been detected.

**6.** **Which of the following analyzes the variations of the electrical power consumption of a cryptographic module to extract information about cryptographic keys?**

    a.    Timing analysis attack

    b.    Differential power analysis attack

    c.    Simple power analysis attack

    d.    Electromagnetic emanation attack

***6. b.*** Differential power analysis attack (side-channel attack) considers the variations of the electrical power consumption of a cryptographic module to correlate to cryptographic keys used in a cryptographic algorithm.

The other three choices are incorrect because they do not consider the power differential. A timing analysis attack is an attack on a cryptographic module that is based on an analysis of time periods between the time a command is issued and the time the result is obtained. A simple power analysis attack considers the patterns of instruction execution to reveal the values of cryptographic keys. An electromagnetic emanation attack uses signals to disclose information that is transmitted, received, handled, or processed by any equipment.

**7.** **Which of the following physical security devices is authorized for the protection of unclassified and nonsensitive IT assets?**

    a.    Smart cards

    b.    Memory cards

    c.    Hardware tokens

    d.    Physical tokens

***7. d.*** The physical tokens are authorized for the protection of nonmission-critical, unclassified, and nonsensitive IT assets. Physical tokens consist of keys and unique documents, such as hand-carried orders. When the smart card is used as a repository of information without requiring the cardholder to input a PIN or without presenting a biometric reference sample, the smart card is implemented as a memory card. Hardware tokens can be integrated into either a physical access control or logical access control solution.

**8.** **From a cryptographic module's physical security viewpoint, tamper-evident seals or pick-resistant locks are placed on covers or doors to protect against unauthorized physical access to which of the following?**

    a.    Environmental equipment

    b.    Critical security parameters

    c.    Configuration management system

    d.    Data center furniture

***8. b.*** Tamper-evident coatings or seals or pick-resistant locks are placed on removable covers or doors of the cryptographic module so that they must be broken to attain physical access to the critical security parameters (CSPs). The other three choices do not use pick-resistant locks because they are not high risk.

**9.** **The cryptographic modules that contain software must provide for which of the following to prevent and detect the disclosure and modification of critical security parameters?**

1. Encryption
2. Authentication
3. Fluctuations in temperature
4. Fluctuations in voltage

    a. 1 only

    b. 2 only

    c. 1 and 2

    d. 1, 2, 3, and 4

*9. d.* The cryptographic modules that contain software must provide for the encryption and authentication of all retained parameters and integrity test code when the module is not in use. In addition, environmental failure protection mechanisms that protect the module from fluctuations in temperature and voltage are needed.

**10.** **The highest security level of cryptographic modules requires the environmental failure protection from which of the following?**

1. Nonvisual radiation examination
2. Electro-static discharge
3. Radiation fault induced attacks
4. Tamper detection response circuitry

    a. 1 and 2

    b. 1 and 3

    c. 3 and 4

    d. 1, 2, 3, and 4

*10. d.* The highest security level of cryptographic modules requires environmental failure protection from nonvisual radiation examination, protection from electro-static discharge, protection from radiation fault induced attacks for multichip embodiments, and protection of the tamper detection response circuitry from disablement.

**11.** **Regarding cryptographic module security, which of the following must be zeroized to protect against disablement of services?**

1. Critical security parameters
2. Public security parameters
3. Sensitive security parameters
4. Any security parameter

    a.    1 and 2

    b.    2 and 3

    c.    1, 2, and 3

    d.    1, 2, 3, and 4

**11. c.** Both critical security parameters (CSPs) and public security parameters (PSPs) must be zeroized to protect them against disablement of services. Sensitive security parameters (SSPs) contain both CSPs and PSPs. Any security parameter need not be protected, only when it is sensitive or critical.

**12.** Which of the following is the *first* step to be taken during testing procedures of a cryptographic module that were interrupted when the temperature is outside the module's normal operating range?

    a.    The module enters a failure mode.

    b.    All critical security parameters are immediately zeroized.

    c.    The module is shut down to prevent further operation.

    d.    All public security parameters are immediately zeroized.

**12. c.** The first step is to shut down the module to prevent further operation and to contain the damage. The next step is to zeroize all critical security parameters and public security parameters. The module enters a failure mode is the last step.

**13.** Which of the following conditions can result in a failure of a cryptographic module during its environmental failure testing procedures?

    1.    The module's temperature is gradually decreasing to a lower level.

    2.    The module's temperature is gradually increasing to a higher level.

    3.    The module's voltage is gradually decreasing to a lower level.

    4.    The module's voltage is gradually increasing to a higher level.

    a.    1 and 3

    b.    2 and 3

    c.    2 and 4

    d.    1, 2, 3, and 4

**13. d.** During environmental failure testing procedures, a cryptographic module can fail if the operating temperature or voltage falls outside of the normal operating range. Both the temperature and voltage should stay within the defined operating range.

**14.** Which of the following physical security devices do *not* process information but serve as a repository of information?

    a.    Smart cards

    b.    Memory cards

    c.    Hardware tokens

    d.    Physical tokens

*14. b.*   Memory cards are data storage devices, and they do not process information but serve as a repository of information. When the smart card is used as a repository of information without requiring the cardholder to input a PIN or without presenting a biometric reference sample, the smart card is implemented as a memory card. Hardware tokens can be integrated into either a physical access control or logical access control solution. Physical tokens consist of keys and unique documents, such as hand-carried orders, and provide minimal protection and assurance.

**15.**    **Which of the following physical security devices process data like a simple computer?**

    a.    Smart cards

    b.    Memory cards

    c.    Hardware tokens

    d.    Physical tokens

*15. a.*   A smart card has one or more integrated circuit (IC) chips and can store data using memory chips on the card. The smart cards can process data like a simple computer. When the smart card is used as a repository of information without requiring the cardholder to input a PIN or without presenting a biometric reference sample, the smart card is implemented as a memory card. Hardware tokens can be integrated into either a physical access control or logical access control solution. Physical tokens consist of keys and unique documents such as hand-carried orders.

**16.**    **Which of the following physical security devices are equipped with computing capabilities integrated into the device?**

    a.    Smart cards

    b.    Memory cards

    c.    Hardware tokens

    d.    Physical tokens

*16. c.*   Hardware tokens (e-tokens) are devices with computing capabilities integrated into the device. For example, hardware tokens can be integrated into either a physical access control or logical access control solution. When the smart card is used as a repository of information without requiring the cardholder to input a personal identification number (PIN) or without presenting a biometric reference sample, the smart card is implemented as a memory card. Physical tokens consist of keys and unique documents, such as hand-carried orders.

**17.**    **Which of the following physical security devices are suitable for protecting IT assets with a low risk and low confidentiality level?**

    a.    Smart cards

    b.    Memory cards

    c.    Hardware tokens

    d.    Physical tokens

***17. d.*** Physical tokens provide a low level of assurance and are only suitable for use when protecting IT assets with a low risk and low confidentiality level. Physical tokens consist of keys and unique documents, such as hand-carried orders. When the smart card is used as a repository of information without requiring the cardholder to input a personal identification number (PIN) or without presenting a biometric reference sample, the smart card is implemented as a memory card. Hardware tokens can be integrated into either a physical access control or logical access control solution.

**18.** **From a cryptographic module's physical security viewpoint, which of the following refers to timing analysis attack?**

    a.    Elapsed time between when the command is issued and the time the result is obtained

    b.    Elapsed time between when the vulnerability is discovered and the time it is exploited

    c.    Elapsed time between the beginning and ending of a critical activity

    d.    Elapsed time between the beginning and ending of a non-critical activity

***18. a.*** It is the definition of a timing analysis attack, which is an attack on a cryptographic module that is based on an analysis of time periods between the time a command is issued and the time the result is obtained. It measures the elapsed time. The elapsed time between when the vulnerability is discovered and the time it is exploited is the definition of time-to-exploitation metric. The other two choices are examples of general metrics, not security related.

**19.** **Regarding a cryptographic module, the input or output of critical security parameters (CSPs) require that a split knowledge procedure is performed using which of the following:**

    1.    Physically separated ports

    2.    Environmentally separated ports

    3.    Logically separated interfaces

    4.    Environmentally separated interfaces

        a.    1 and 2

        b.    1 and 3

        c.    1 and 4

        d.    2 and 4

***19. b.*** Security for a cryptographic module requires that an entry or output of critical security parameters (CSPs) using a split knowledge procedure is performed using ports that are physically separated from other ports and interfaces that are logically separated from other interfaces using a trusted channel. CSPs may either be entered into or output from the cryptographic module in an encrypted form. A split knowledge is a process by which a cryptographic key is split into multiple key components, individually providing no knowledge of the original key, which can be subsequently input into, or output from, a cryptographic module by separate entities and combined to re-create the original cryptographic key.

20. **Which of the following is more secure and complex and more difficult to counterfeit and compromise?**

    a.   Physical keys

    b.   Three-plane keys

    c.   Conventional keys with locksets

    d.   Pick-resistant locksets

*20. b.*   A three-plane key (3-plane key) is used as a physical access control method, is more secure and complex, is complicated to copy, requires blank key stocks, which are not readily available to adversaries, and is more difficult to counterfeit, and the locks controlled by 3-plane keys are more difficult to compromise. Physical keys are simple keys that are highly susceptible to copying or theft, and locks controlled by simple keys are easy to compromise. Conventional keys with locksets are inexpensive but easy to duplicate (copy). Pick-resistant locksets are more expensive than conventional keys with locksets, and the keys are much more difficult to duplicate. The pick-resistant locksets are not as strong or secure as the 3-plane keys.

21. **Which of the following is *not* an example of fire suppression and detection devices?**

    a.   Master shutoff valves

    b.   Sprinkler systems

    c.   Fire extinguishers

    d.   Smoke detectors

*21. a.*   Master shutoff valves are closed in the event of a significant water leak. The other three choices are part of the fire suppression and detection devices.

22. **What is the *best* action to take when there is no uninterruptible power supply (UPS) in a data center?**

    a.   Install a surge suppressor.

    b.   Install a line conditioner.

    c.   Install a backup generator.

    d.   Install a transformer.

*22. b.*   Under-voltages represent the majority of power problems (sags and brownouts) for computer systems. Instantaneous power from UPS prevents data loss caused by sags and brownouts. UPS is superior to separate surge suppressors. A line conditioner automatically corrects under-voltages and over-voltages to levels that are safe for the computer system. Both generators and transformers are power sources that need to be cleaned for computer use because computers are sensitive.

**23.** **What is the *best* technique to identify an intruder?**

    a.    Place a bright light in the area.

    b.    Activate an alarm system.

    c.    Post a security guard.

    d.    Install a video camera.

**23. d.** A video camera takes pictures of an intruder, which can be used to establish a positive identification of the intruder and a proof of evidence. The other three choices do not provide a positive identification of the intruder.

**24.** **What would you do *first* in case of a fire in your data center?**

    a.    Call the fire department.

    b.    Pull the fire alarm device.

    c.    Evacuate people from the building.

    d.    Call the police department.

**24. c.** The first thing is to save people's lives, and therefore evacuating people from the building on fire is the right thing to do. The actions mentioned in the other choices can be performed later.

**25.** **The *most* frequently used fencing for physical security purposes is which of the following?**

    a.    Barbed wire

    b.    Concertina wire

    c.    Chain-link

    d.    Barbed tape

**25. c.** A chain-link fence must be securely fastened to rigid metal or reinforced concrete posts set in concrete. It is stronger than other fences. A barbed wire is a twisted, double-stranded fence. A concertina wire is a commercially manufactured wire coil of high-strength-steel barbed wire clipped together at intervals to form a cylinder. A barbed tape consists of barbed wire, barbed tape dispenser, and concertina tape.

**26.** **Which of the following is *more* secure?**

    a.    Eight-foot wall

    b.    Eight-foot wall with barbed wire on top

    c.    Electric gate

    d.    Key and locked door

**26. b.** An eight-foot wall with barbed wire is more secure than the other choices mentioned. The requirements for barbed wire include that its height should not be less than 7 feet, excluding top guard. It is a twisted, double-stranded, 12-gauge wire. Intruders will have a problem climbing or standing over because the wire cannot hold any person straight up. Using a long ladder can circumvent an 8-foot wall. An electric gate can be opened by guessing passwords or other codes used to open and close it. A key and locked door is easy to break in by tampering with it.

27. **The *best* location for a data center in a multistoried building is on which of the following:**

    a. First floor

    b. Basement level

    c. Top floor

    d. Any floor other than the above

*27. d.* The first floor is not a good location to prevent undesirable access. The basement is not good because of flooding and volatile storage. The top floor of a high-rise building is not good because it may be beyond reach of fire department equipment.

28. **Which of the following is *not* a complementary control when implementing the given logical access security controls?**

    a. Access profiles

    b. User ID

    c. ID badge card

    d. Password

*28. c.* Identification (ID) badge cards are an example of physical security controls and are not complementary with the given logical security controls. A function or an area need not be weak to use complementary controls. Complementary controls can enhance the effectiveness of two or more controls when applied to a business function, computer program, or operation. These individual controls are effective as a standalone and are maximized when combined or integrated with each other. In other words, complementary controls have a synergistic effect. Access profiles, user IDs, and passwords go together to provide a moderate level of an access control mechanism. Profiles are needed for each system user to define what he can do on the system. User IDs and passwords are needed to identify and authenticate the user to the computer system. These three controls are examples of logical access security controls, where they provide a technical means of controlling what information users can utilize, the computer programs they can run, and the modifications they can make to programs and data files.

29. **Why is it better to use a biometric control along with an access key?**

    a. It provides a preventive control.

    b. It provides a detective control.

    c. It provides a corrective control.

    d. It provides a two-factor control.

**29. d.** Biometrics and access keys are two separate controls, providing a two-factor authentication. When they are combined in a session, they provide a synergistic or combination control. The total effect is greater than the single control alone.

**30.** **Which of the following is *ineffective* in extinguishing Class A and B fires in a building?**

    a.    Carbon dioxide

    b.    Water fog

    c.    Dry powder

    d.    Dry chemical

**30. c.** Dry powder is effective against Class D fires and ineffective against Class A and B fires. The other three choices are effective against Class A and B fires. Water fog is created by a special nozzle on the water hose.

**31.** **Which one of the following power problems is unlike the others?**

    a.    Sags

    b.    Spikes

    c.    Blackouts

    d.    Surges

**31. c.** A blackout is a total loss of power, lasting several minutes to several hours, caused by damage to power lines and equipment, commonly due to weather conditions. Sags create under-voltage conditions. Spikes and surges create over-voltage conditions.

**32.** **In a fire-extinguishing environment, what is a dry pipe?**

    a.    A sprinkler system in which the water does not enter the pipes until the automatic sensor indicates that there is a fire in the area

    b.    A sprinkler system in which the water is in the pipe, but the outside of the pipe is dry

    c.    A Halon gas system that contains a dry pipe

    d.    A carbon dioxide ($CO_2$) gas system that has a dry chemical to extinguish a fire

**32. a.** The sequence of dry-pipe actions is (i) a heat or smoke sensor is activated first, (ii) water fills the previously empty pipes leading to the sprinklers, (iii) the alarm is sounded, and (iv) the electrical power supply is disconnected automatically. The choice "A sprinkler system in which the water is in the pipe, but the outside of the pipe is dry" is incorrect because water is not in the pipe until the heat or smoke sensor is activated. The choice "A Halon gas system that contains a dry pipe" and the choice "A carbon dioxide ($CO_2$) gas system that has a dry chemical to extinguish a fire" are incorrect because the descriptions are meaningless.

**33.** In most cases, what can take the heat off the fire safely?

 a. Water

 b. Carbon dioxide

 c. Soda ash

 d. Halon gas

***33. a.*** Water takes the heat off the fire, and it is safe compared to the other choices. Carbon dioxide, soda ash, and Halon can be injurious.

**34.** What is an under-voltage in electric power called?

 a. Brownout

 b. Blackout

 c. Burnout

 d. Dropout

***34. a.*** A brownout is a condition in which electrical power dips below normal for more than a few seconds and is caused by under-voltage. Brownouts are a result of a load near to or equaling generating capacity. A blackout is a complete loss of electrical power (that is, actual failure). Blackouts can result from windstorms, floods, failures of electronic system equipment, or human error. A dropout is an area on a disk or tape that cannot effectively record data. Persistent brownouts can cause data corruption and loss and can also cause computer power supplies to overheat and burn out.

**35.** Which of the following fire types is *most* common?

 a. Furniture fires

 b. Electrical fires

 c. Paper fires

 d. Gasoline fires

***35. b.*** Statistics indicate that most fires are electrical in origin. Furniture fires and paper fires are Class A fires, whereas gasoline fires are Class B fires.

**36.** Electronic surveillance and wiretapping has increased due to which of the following?

 a. Telephone lines

 b. Bugging techniques

 c. Microchip technology

 d. Surveillance equipment

***36. c.*** Miniaturization has greatly aided spying. With advances in microchip technology, transmitters can be so small as to be enmeshed in wallpaper, inserted under a stamp, or placed on the head of a nail.

**37.** The failure of a sprinkler system *most* often is due to which of the following reasons?

    a.   Equipment error

    b.   Computer error

    c.   Human error

    d.   Design error

*37. c.* The failure of a sprinkler system most often is due to human error—the water supply was turned off at the time of the fire.

**38.** When freezing temperatures and broken pipes are a problem, which of the following should be used?

    a.   Wet-pipe system

    b.   Dry-pipe system

    c.   Carbon-dioxide system

    d.   Halon system

*38. b.* When freezing temperatures and broken pipes are a problem, the dry-pipe system is useful. Air pressure is maintained in the pipes until a sprinkler head ruptures. Then, the air escapes, and water enters the pipes and exits through the opened sprinklers. With the wet-pipe system, water is in the pipes at all times and is released when heat ruptures the seal in the sprinkler head.

**39.** Which of the following *cannot* defend the computing environment?

    a.   Operating systems

    b.   Biometrics

    c.   Cryptographic key recovery

    d.   Hardware tokens

*39. c.* Operating systems, biometrics, and hardware tokens, either alone or together, can defend the computing environment. The cryptographic key recovery is a part of key management infrastructure/public key infrastructure (KMI/PKI), which is a supporting infrastructure for information assurance. The cryptographic key recovery by itself cannot defend the computing environment.

**40.** Information leakage occurs due to which of the following physical and environmental hazards?

    a.   Flooding

    b.   Electromagnetic radiation

    c.   Vandalism

    d.   Electrical interference

**40. b.** An organization should protect the information system from information leakage due to electromagnetic signal emanations. All the other choices are examples of hazards but not related to an information leakage problem.

**41.** **Which of the following is a direct physical measure used to protect the integrity and confidentiality of transmitted information?**

    a.    Protective distribution system

    b.    Transport layer security

    c.    Internet protocol security

    d.    Cryptographic mechanism

**41. a.** The information system should protect the integrity and confidentiality of transmitted information with a protective distribution system in the first place (a physical measure). The other three choices are alternatives to the protective distribution system. Transport layer security (TLS) is an authentication and security protocol widely implemented in Web browsers and servers. Internet protocol security (IPsec) provides security capabilities at the IP layer of communications. An organization employs cryptographic mechanisms to ensure recognition of changes to information (i.e., integrity) and to prevent unauthorized disclosure of information (i.e., confidentiality) during transmission. The other three choices do not directly deal with physical measures.

**42.** **Which of the following information security control families requires a cross-cutting approach?**

    a.    Contingency planning

    b.    Identification and authentication

    c.    Maintenance

    d.    Physical and environmental protection

**42. d.** Physical and environmental protection requires a cross-cutting approach because it is related to physical and environmental protection, access controls, and incident response control families. Cross-cutting approaches cover more than one security control family. The other three choices require a control-specific approach, meaning they cover only one security control family.

**43.** **Which of the following delays water release?**

    a.    Wet pipe

    b.    Pre-action pipe

    c.    Water pipe

    d.    Gas pipe

**43. b.** A wet pipe releases water at a set temperature. The pre-action pipe sounds an alarm and delays water release. A water pipe does not delay water release. A gas pipe is not relevant here.

**44.** What is the *best* location for a data center?

    a.   Near stairways

    b.   Near elevators

    c.   Near restrooms

    d.   Any location other than the above

**44. d.** The objective is to reduce the risk of close physical proximity in terms of vandalism and other disasters (e.g., bombings). The data center should be remote from publicly used areas due to their easy access for both insiders (disgruntled employees) and outsiders (intruders).

**45.** Which of the following security safeguards is ineffective in an online application system serving multiple users at multiple locations?

    a.   Procedural controls

    b.   Physical controls

    c.   Hardware controls

    d.   Software controls

**45. b.** An online application system serving multiple users at multiple locations assumes that a network is in place. With a network there is often no centralized computer room with physical security controls that can be implemented. Therefore, physical controls are ineffective. Examples of physical controls include locked doors, intrusion detection devices, security guards, and magnetic badge readers that restrict physical access. Procedural controls are incorrect because they include instructions to request a user profile, adding and deleting users, and instructions to request database views, and so on. Hardware controls are incorrect because they include fault tolerance devices such as disk mirroring and disk duplexing, smart card processing, encryption, parity checks, and switched ports. Software controls are incorrect because they include user IDs and passwords, smart card processing, encryption, check digits, and message authentication.

**46.** What is the *most* effective control in handling potential terrorist attacks, especially bombing?

    a.   Use simulation software.

    b.   Examine all letters and parcels coming into a building.

    c.   Hire security guards.

    d.   Keep motor vehicles away from the building.

**46. c.** There is no substitute for vigilant and resourceful security guards protecting the buildings. Simulation software is available that can assess the vulnerability of a structure to explosive blasts by simulating the detonation of devices at various design points. Security can be improved by simply keeping vehicles away from a near proximity to the structure. It also makes sense to examine all letters and parcels coming into a building for explosives.

**47.** Which of the following is the *most* commonly used sprinkler system?

    a. Wet-pipe system

    b. Dry-pipe system

    c. Carbon dioxide system

    d. Halon system

**47. *a.*** Wet-pipe systems are the most commonly used and are applicable when freezing is no threat to their operation. The next most popular one is the dry pipe. The carbon dioxide system is dangerous to people's health, and the Halon system cannot be used any more due to a halt in Halon production.

**48.** Which of the following statements about sprinkler systems is *not* always true?

    a. Sprinkler systems cause water damage.

    b. Sprinkler systems reduce fire damage locally.

    c. Sprinkler systems protect human lives of building occupants.

    d. Sprinkler systems limit fire damage to the building itself.

**48. *a.*** When properly installed, maintained, and provided with an adequate supply of water, automatic sprinkler systems are highly effective in protecting buildings and their contents. Nonetheless, you often hear uninformed people speak of the water damage done by sprinkler systems as a disadvantage. Fires that trigger sprinkler systems cause the water damage. In short, sprinkler systems reduce the fire damage, protect the lives of building occupants, and limit the fire damage to the building itself.

**49.** Which of the following is a physical security measure for cryptographic keys such as plaintext secret keys and private keys during their physical maintenance?

    a. Zeroization proof

    b. Zero-knowledge proof

    c. Zero-defects proof

    d. Zero-quantum proof

**49. *a.*** When performing physical maintenance, all plaintext secret and private keys and other unprotected critical security parameters (CSPs) contained in the cryptographic module should be zeroized. Zeroization proof is a method of erasing electronically stored data by altering the contents of the data storage so as to prevent the recovery of data. The cryptographic module can either perform zeroization procedurally by the operator or automatically.

The other three choices do not provide security measures for cryptographic keys. Zero-knowledge proof deals with keeping information secret in that it refers to one party proving something to another without revealing any additional information. Zero-defects proof is a total quality management concept in which products are made with zero defects—one of the goals of quality. Zero-quantum proof is based on principles of quantum-mechanics where eavesdroppers alter the quantum state of the cryptographic system.

**50.** Which of the following is the *best* defense against hardware-based key loggers?

    a.    Logical security controls

    b.    Physical security controls

    c.    Application security controls

    d.    Network security controls

*50. b.* A key logger is software or hardware that collects every keystroke a user makes on his PC. Law enforcement authorities have used key loggers as a form of wiretap against suspected individuals. Now some viruses and worms can install key loggers to search for passwords and account numbers. The hardware-based key logger device plugs in between the user keyboard and his PC, which requires physical access to the PC to install the device. Under these circumstances, physical security controls are the best defense against hardware-based key loggers.

**51.** Which of the following is *not* an explicit design goal of a physical protection system based on sound engineering principles?

    a.    Provide protection-in-depth.

    b.    Provide line-of-sight to assets.

    c.    Minimize the consequences of component failures.

    d.    Exhibit balanced protection.

*51. b.* Defensive security measures provide barriers to movement of assets and obscures line-of-sight to assets. Obscuring, not providing, a line-of-sight is based on sound engineering design principles. Defensive security measures say that assets should not be visible to outsiders. (For example, a data center should not be visible from the street.) The other three choices are incorrect because they are explicit design goals of a physical protection system based on sound engineering principles.

**52.** Regarding a physical protection system, what is primarily the delay before detection?

    a.    Response

    b.    Deterrent

    c.    Detection

    d.    Defeat

*52. b.* Delay is the slowing down of adversary progress. Delay can be accomplished by response-force personnel (security guards), barriers, locks, and activated and automated delays. The measure of a delay's effectiveness is the time required by the adversary after detection to bypass each delay element. Therefore, delay before detection is primarily a deterrent.

Response is incorrect because it consists of the actions taken by the response force to prevent adversary success. Detection is incorrect because it senses an act of aggression, assesses the validity of the detection, and communicates the appropriate information to a response force personnel (e.g., security guard). Defeat is incorrect because most protective systems depend on response personnel to defeat an aggressor.

**53.** A secure and safe room should have which of the following?

    a.    No more than one door

    b.    No more than two doors

    c.    No more than three doors

    d.    No more than four doors

*53. b.* A secure and safe room should have no more than two doors. These doors should be solid, fireproof, lockable, and observable by physical security staff. One door is for entrance and the other one is for exit according to building fire code. Too many doors provide too many escape routes for an intruder that security staff cannot observe.

**54.** Which of the following is *not* one of the four legs of a fire?

    a.    Heat

    b.    Fuel

    c.    Oxygen

    d.    Smoke

*54. d.* Smoke is a byproduct of a fire whereas heat, fuel, oxygen, and chemical reaction are the four legs of a fire.

**55.** Where do you start when considering physical security protection for new computer facilities?

    a.    Front to back

    b.    Back to front

    c.    Outside in

    d.    Inside out

*55. d.* The best strategy is to start with interior security, proceed to the exterior security, and then to the outer perimeter. This path provides a clear picture of all areas needing protection and ensures completeness of analysis.

**56.** Dry powder is used to extinguish which of the following fires?

    a.    Class A fires

    b.    Class B fires

    c.    Class C fires

    d.    Class D fires

*56. d.* Class D fire is extinguished by dry powder. Class A fire is extinguished by water, Class B by carbon dioxide, and Class C by a nonconducting extinguishing agent.

**57.** **Which of the following physical intrusion-detection system components report on the condition of the system?**

    a.   Motion sensors

    b.   Control unit

    c.   Monitor unit

    d.   Transmission lines

**57. c.** The physical intrusion detection system contains four components: motion sensors, control unit, monitor unit, and transmission lines. These components are integrated to operate in a specified manner. A monitor unit is a device that senses and reports on the condition of a system. Motion sensors detect movement inside the area to be protected. A control unit is the terminal box for all sensors. Transmission lines communicate events, signals, and sensors.

**58.** **Which of the following sensors detect the sounds of forced entry into a computer facility?**

    a.   Proximity sensors

    b.   Microwave sensor

    c.   Ultrasonic sensor

    d.   Photoelectric sensor

**58. c.** Ultrasonic sensors operate by sounds. Proximity sensors employ an electrical field such as electromagnetic or electrostatic. Microwave sensors operate by radio or radar frequency transceiver. A photoelectric sensor operates by an interruption of light beam transmitted to the receiver.

**59.** **Which of the following statements is *true* about physical security and life safety?**

    a.   Physical security strives to control entry.

    b.   Life safety focuses on providing easy exit from a facility.

    c.   Life safety measures are expensive.

    d.   It is possible to achieve an effective balance between physical security and life safety.

**59. d.** It is important to understand that the objectives of physical access controls may be in conflict with those of life safety. Simply stated, life safety focuses on providing easy exit from a facility, particularly in an emergency, whereas physical security strives to control entry. In general, life safety must be given first consideration, but it is usually possible to achieve an effective balance between the two goals. Life safety measures do not need to be expensive; sometimes the least expensive measures work best.

**60.** **Which of the following sensors is used to call for assistance?**

    a.   Contact sensor

    b.   Duress sensor

    c.    Vibration sensor

    d.    Infrared sensor

**60. b.** The duress sensor is used to call for assistance in case of danger, and it consists of a hand- or foot-operated switch usually found in bank teller areas. A contact sensor is activated when an electrical circuit is broken. A vibration sensor detects forced entry through metal barriers placed over windows, for example. An infrared sensor detects body heat.

**61.** **An effective physical security control when accessing sensitive facilities and systems includes which of the following?**

    a.    Smart card

    b.    Biometric measure

    c.    Photo ID

    d.    Combination of smart card, biometric, and photo ID

**61. d.** Smart card technology, in combination with biometrics, offers great levels of security when accessing buildings, computers, and large dollar accounts. The smart card can be used in a number of ways to identify the cardholder to the physical access control system. These include (i) carrying a number that can be used to retrieve the cardholder's access privileges from the physical access control system's files, (ii) carrying access control privileges on-board the card, (iii) carrying a photo ID to verify the cardholder's identity, and (iv) carrying a biometric template against which the cardholder's live scan is compared to verify the cardholder's identity.

**62.** **A power brownout condition is which of the following?**

    a.    Long-term lag

    b.    Long-term sag

    c.    Short-term lag

    d.    Short-term sag

**62. b.** A brownout condition is long-term sag. It is a deliberate reduction of voltage output at a power generating station to respond to high demand and thus avoids an outage. Short-term sag is the description of voltage sag. Long-term and short-term lags are incorrect because they are used in describing economic indicators.

**63.** **A voltage spike is which of the following?**

    a.    It is a sharp but brief increase in voltage.

    b.    It is a slow but brief increase in voltage.

    c.    It is a sharp but brief decrease in voltage.

    d.    It is a slow but brief decrease in voltage.

**63. a.** A voltage spike is a sharp but brief increase in voltage, commonly caused by the turning off of heavy electrical loads such as air conditioners or photocopiers. The other three choices are meaningless.

**64.** **Water sprinklers operate at what temperatures?**

    a.    Between 120 and 130 F

    b.    Between 130 and 165 F

    c.    Between 135 and 145 F

    d.    Between 145 and 160 F

***64. b.*** Most water sprinkler systems operate at temperatures between 130 and 165 degrees Fahrenheit.

**65.** **Which one of the following fire sensors is useful in giving an early warning?**

    a.    Ionization detector

    b.    Photoelectric smoke detector

    c.    Infrared flame detector

    d.    Thermal detector

***65. a.*** The ionization detector is useful in giving an early warning so that human lives can be saved. It uses an ion exchange process to achieve the detection. The photoelectric smoke detector alarms when the source of light is interrupted. The infrared flame detector reacts to emissions from flame. The thermal detector operates on a significant change in temperature.

**66.** **Which one of the following fire stages does *not* produce smoke?**

    a.    Incipient stage

    b.    Smoldering stage

    c.    Flame stage

    d.    Heat stage

***66. a.*** A normal fire proceeds through four stages: the incipient, smoldering, flame, and heat stages. In the incipient stage, no smoke is emitted. Smoke begins to appear in the smoldering stage. In the flame stage, actual flame can be seen. The heat is intense and building up in the final, heat stage.

**67.** **Which one of the following water sprinkler system elements consists of fire-activated devices?**

    a.    Water supply

    b.    Water heads

    c.    Water control valves

    d.    Alarm system

***67. b.*** A water sprinkler system consists of the following elements: water supply, fire-activated sprinkler devices (heads), water control valves, and a mechanism to activate the audible alarm system.

**68.** **What is the *first* step to do in case of a fire?**

    a.    Report the fire.

    b.    Extinguish the fire.

    c.    Avoid panic.

    d.    Do not use elevators.

***68. a.***   As part of fire prevention tips, fire should be reported first, and then attempts should be made to extinguish it. Other actions include (i) never open a "hot" door, (ii) pull alarm system, and (iii) try to escape.

**69.** **Which one of the following is filled with water?**

    a.    Wet-pipe sprinkler system

    b.    Dry-pipe sprinkler system

    c.    Halogenated sprinkler system

    d.    Carbon dioxide sprinkler system

***69. a.***   A wet-pipe sprinkler system is made up of sprinkler devices attached to pipes filled with water. A dry-sprinkler system contains air under pressure. When a sprinkler is activated, the released air opens valves allowing water into the pipes. Halogenated and carbon dioxide sprinkler systems are not relevant here.

**70.** **Which of the following combination controls would not be appropriate in extinguishing fires?**

    a.    Smoke/fire detectors

    b.    Water sprinklers

    c.    Uninterruptible power supply equipment

    d.    Fire or evacuation drills

***70. c.***   Uninterruptible power supply (UPS) equipment does not by itself help in extinguishing a fire. UPS can prolong an electrical power supply when there is a power failure. Smoke/fire detectors combined with water sprinklers can help detect or put out an actual fire. Fire or evacuation drills can help in getting ready for an actual fire. A single control would rarely suffice to meet control objectives. Rather, a combination of controls is needed to make up a whole and to provide a synergistic effect. In the example, all three controls are needed to be effective.

**71.** **Modern dry-pipe systems:**

    a.    Are less sophisticated than water-based sprinkler systems

    b.    Maximize chances of accidental discharge of water

    c.    Are a substitute for carbon dioxide fire-suppression systems

    d.    Are a substitute for water-based sprinkler systems

**71. d.** Dry-pipe systems are more sophisticated than water-based sprinkler systems. They minimize the chances of accidental discharge of water because they discharge water only as needed. Therefore, they are a substitute for water-based sprinkler systems, which are used to extinguish fire. Carbon dioxide is a clean gas and does not leave a residue on computer equipment or magnetic media. However, its use is diminishing due to potential health problems. Carbon dioxide and water sprinklers, respectively, are ranked from most to least harmful to people when activated.

**72.** **Which of the following causes *more* fire fatalities?**

  a.  Smoke

  b.  Toxic gases

  c.  Heat

  d.  Flames

**72. b.** Toxic gases cause more fire fatalities than flames, smoke, or heat.

**73.** **Which one of the following replacements for the Halogenated agents (Halon 1211 and 1301) is the safest to humans?**

  a.  FM-200

  b.  Argon

  c.  Water fog

  d.  Inergen

**73. c.** The production of Halogenated agents (Halon 1211 and 1301) was stopped in January 1994 due to their depletion of the ozone layer. Many replacements were found, but the water fog is the safest one to humans.

**74.** **Which of the following prevents tailgating or piggybacking in a computer center?**

  a.  Cameras

  b.  Mantraps

  c.  Sensors

  d.  Alarms

**74. b.** Tailgating (piggybacking) means an unauthorized person is following an authorized person into a facility. It can be prevented by the use of mantraps where they take a measurement of the body weight of a person entering the computer center doors and combine it with a biometric feature such as a fingerprint scan. If the person is not authorized to enter this highly sensitive area, he will not be allowed to proceed further, and security authorities will be notified.

Surveillance cameras are passive and do not take any action. Sensors and alarms do not have the intelligence built in similar to that of mantraps and can give rise to false alarms.

**75.** Which of the following should be the *first* step to be performed prior to installing cable wires in a computer center facility?

    a.    Implement physical security controls.

    b.    Test the cables.

    c.    Check with local building codes.

    d.    Label the cables.

**75. c.** Prior to any wiring installation, it is good to contact the official local building code standard sources and people to ensure that the planned cable plant is consistent with electrical and fire codes. This is to protect the safety and security of the facility. Physical security controls can include acquiring dedicated space with a locked door to serve as a wiring closet. After checking with the local building codes, the next step is to test the cable for bad spots. By labeling both ends of a cable, a built-in map is available that identifies each cable, its termination point and length, and electrical characteristics.

**76.** Which of the following should be considered as delaying devices in physical security?

    a.    Lights

    b.    Safes

    c.    Locks

    d.    Vaults

**76. c.** Locks are considered as delaying devices only and not bars to entry. The longer it takes to open or break a lock, the shorter the patience for an intruder, and the wider the window of opportunity for detection. The idea is that officials will soon be arriving at the place if it takes longer to open a lock.

Lights serve as a deterrent to violators. Safes provide protection against fire, burglary, and robbery. Vaults are enlarged safes and can be supported by alarm systems.

**77.** Which of the following does *not* assess the vulnerability of a facility to damage or an attack?

    a.    Inspection

    b.    History of losses

    c.    Security controls

    d.    Security budget

**77. d.** Examining a security budget cannot reveal much because there is no direct correlation between the budget and the vulnerability. An inspection of the facility by an experienced inspector can reveal the status of the facility and its associated controls. Examination of the facility's record of losses can reveal how bad the situation is. The degree of security controls installed can reveal whether high-value property is properly safeguarded from theft by insiders or attack by outsiders.

**78.** **Which of the following is a safe practice to ensure physical security?**

    a.    Deter

    b.    Detect

    c.    Delay

    d.    Deny

***78. a.*** It is preferred to deter attacks against property, whether criminal or not. If not deterred, access to selected areas or properties should be denied. If not denied, attacks that occur should be detected. If not detected in time, attacks should be delayed to allow time for response by authorities.

**79.** **How are fires that involve energized electrical equipment rated?**

    a.    Class A fires

    b.    Class B fires

    c.    Class C fires

    d.    Class D fires

***79. c.*** A classification of fires is based on the nature of the combustibles, relating directly to the efficacy of extinguishing agents. Four classes are described as follows:

➤ **Class A:** Fires involving ordinary combustible solids (e.g., wood, cloth, paper, rubber, and many plastics)

➤ **Class B:** Fires involving flammable or combustible liquids and flammable gases

➤ **Class C:** Fires involving energized electrical equipment

➤ **Class D:** Fires involving certain combustible materials such as magnesium and sodium

**80.** **A device or devices that sense(s) vibration or motion is (are) called:**

    a.    Proximity detector and vibration detector

    b.    Seismic detector and vibration detector

    c.    Proximity detector and seismic detector

    d.    Intrusion detector and vibration detector

***80. b.*** A seismic detector is a device that senses vibration or motion and thereby senses a physical attack upon an object or structure. A vibration detector is the same as a seismic detector. A proximity detector is a device that initiates a signal (alarm) when a person or object comes near the protected object. An intrusion detector is a device designed to detect an individual crossing a line or entering an area.

**81.** **Which of the following represents the upper end of the protection scale against electrical problems (e.g., sags) in a computer center?**

    a.    Battery backup

    b.    Power filters

    c.    Power conditioners

    d.    Uninterruptible power supply

*81. d.* The order of the protection scale from the lower end to upper end is as follows: battery backup, power filters, power conditioners, and uninterruptible power supply (UPS). Battery backup has a short life (that is, low-end protection) compared to the UPS (which is high-end protection). Power filters filter the sags, spikes, and impulse noises. Power conditioners regulate the voltage into the system. A UPS can clean up most of the power problems such as spikes, surges, sags, brownouts, blackouts, frequency variations, transient noises, and impulse hits.

**82.** **Which of the following pairs of items create a conflicting situation in a computer center?**

    a.    Fire-resistant file cabinets, vital records

    b.    Sprinkler systems, water damage

    c.    Fire detection systems, alarms

    d.    Furniture and equipment, noncombustible materials

*82. b.* Sprinkler systems are desirable if the computer room construction contains combustible materials. Although sprinklers extinguish fire, extensive water can damage some areas and materials in the room due to use of the sprinkler system. Therefore, sprinkler systems and water damage create a conflicting situation.

Fire-resistant file cabinets and vital records have no conflict because vital records should be stored in a fire-resistant cabinet file. Fire detection systems and alarms have no conflict because fire detection and extinguishing systems should have alarms to signal trouble and to communicate problems to a specific location that is always manned. Furniture and equipment and noncombustible materials have no conflict because furniture and equipment in a computer room should be constructed of metal or other noncombustible material.

**83.** **What is the *least* important factor to be considered when selecting an uninterruptible power system (UPS)?**

    a.    Fuel options

    b.    Electrical load

    c.    Battery duration

    d.    Physical space

*83. a.* The selection of an uninterruptible power system (UPS) is governed by three factors: electrical load, battery duration, and physical space. The electrical load represents the capacity for the UPS to supply power to the equipment properly. The battery duration is simply how long the UPS is supposed to support the equipment. Physical space is required for any UPS. Fuel options, whether to use diesel or natural gasoline, can be considered at a later point in the decision-making process.

**84.** **Which of the following is a proper control in a computer room?**

a.   Smoke detection equipment shuts down the wet-pipe equipment.

b.   Smoke detection equipment shuts down the air conditioning equipment.

c.   Smoke detection equipment shuts down the pre-action pipe equipment.

d.   Smoke detection equipment shuts down the water pipe equipment.

**84. b.**   The smoke detection system should shut down the air conditioning equipment. Similarly, an emergency power shutdown should include shutting down the air conditioning system. The reason is that when there is smoke or a power loss, the air conditioning equipment should be turned off so that people do not inhale smoke.

**85.** **What is *not* a proper place for installing smoke detectors?**

a.   In the ceiling of a building

b.   Under the raised floor

c.   In air return ducts of a building

d.   In water drains on the floor

**85. d.**   Putting a smoke detector in water drains on the floor is improper. For maximum use and benefit, smoke detectors should be installed in the ceiling, under the raised floor, and in air return ducts.

**86.** **Which of the following is the *best* place for sounding an alarm coming from a computer room?**

a.   Local station

b.   Security guard station

c.   Central station

d.   Fire or police station

**86. d.**   The best place for sounding an alarm coming from a computer room is at a fire or police station because immediate action can be taken. There can be a delay at the other three choices.

**87.** **Physical access controls are a part of which of the following?**

a.   Directive controls

b.   Preventive controls

c.   Detective controls

d.   Corrective controls

**87. b.** Physical access controls are a part of preventive controls, as they include locks, security guards, and biometric devices. Preventive controls deter security incidents from happening in the first place.

Directive controls are broad-based controls to handle security incidents, and they include management's policies, procedures, and directives. Detective controls enhance security by monitoring the effectiveness of preventive controls and by detecting security incidents where preventive controls were circumvented. Corrective controls are procedures to react to security incidents and to take remedial actions on a timely basis. Corrective controls require proper planning and preparation as they rely more on human judgment.

**88.** The justification process in selecting electronic surveillance and wiretapping detection equipment includes which of the following?

    a.    Low cost of detection equipment, high value of assets to be protected, and a high rate of equipment usage

    b.    Medium cost of detection equipment, high value of assets to be protected, and a low rate of equipment usage

    c.    High cost of detection equipment, high value of assets to be protected, and a high rate of equipment usage

    d.    Low cost of detection equipment, low value of assets to be protected, and a high rate of equipment usage

**88. c.** The high cost of detection equipment is justified when the assets to be protected are highly valued and when a high rate of use can be made of the equipment. This is based on the cost-benefit principle.

**89.** Which of the following parties poses a greater risk to an organization when guarding against electronic surveillance and wiretapping activities?

    a.    Spy stationed in another building

    b.    Janitor in the same building

    c.    Employee in the same building

    d.    Window washer in the same building

**89. c.** A spy stationed on the same floor in another building a few blocks away can use a telescope to obtain secret data; a window washer can take pictures of documents on desks or walls; a janitor is positioned to take documents discarded in the trash. However, these occurrences are rare. The greatest risk is an employee working in the same building because of proximity and the trust placed in the employee. In addition, the employee knows the nature of the data asset, the value of it, the location of the asset, and the security controls (or lack of security controls) around the asset.

**90.** Which of the following statements is true?

  a.  Both mantraps and turnstiles are physical security controls.

  b.  A mantrap is a physical security control whereas a turnstile is a logical access security control.

  c.  A mantrap is an environmental security control whereas a turnstile is a network security control.

  d.  Both mantraps and turnstiles are cryptographic security controls.

**90. a.**  Both stationary and revolving doors are used in mantraps and turnstiles. Unauthorized individuals entering a data center cannot get out of a mantrap because it is so restrictive in terms of movement. Turnstiles also restrict the movement of an unauthorized individual. Both of these controls are part of the physical security controls within a data center requiring high-level security.

**91.** Any security measure must be cost-beneficial. Uninterruptible power supply (UPS) systems address electric power failures. Which one of the following cost factors is of *least* concern to the installation of a UPS system?

  a.  Size of the gas fuel supply

  b.  Size of the electric load it can support

  c.  Number of minutes it can support the load

  d.  Speed with which it assumes the load when the primary source fails

**91. a.**  A number of security measures are available to address electric power failures differing in both cost and performance. For example, the cost of a UPS depends on the size of the electric load it can support, the number of minutes it can support the load, and the speed with which it assumes the load when the primary power source fails. An onsite power generator can also be installed either in lieu of a UPS or to provide long-term backup to a UPS system. The size of the gas fuel supply is a design decision along with the magnitude of the load the generator will support and the facilities to switch the load from the primary source or the UPS to the on-site generator.

**92.** What instrument measures atmospheric humidity in a computer room?

  a.  Hygrometer

  b.  Hydrometer

  c.  Barometer

  d.  Voltmeter

**92. a.**  A hygrometer is an instrument that measures atmospheric humidity. A hydrometer is an instrument used to determine the specific gravity that sinks in a fluid to a depth used as a measure of the fluid's specific gravity. A barometer is an instrument for measuring atmospheric pressure, used in weather forecasting and in determining elevation. A voltmeter is an instrument for measuring electrical voltage.

**93.** Which of the following is *not* appropriate to provide adequate complementary physical access controls?

    a.    ID badge card

    b.    Password

    c.    Magnetic stripe card

    d.    Visitor log

*93. b.*    Passwords provide logical access controls, not physical access controls. The other three choices are examples of complementary physical access controls. Each control enhances the other. A function or an area doesn't need to be weak to use complementary controls. Complementary controls can magnify the effectiveness of two or more controls when applied to a function, program, or operation. Identification (ID) badge cards, magnetic stripe cards, and visitor logs have a synergistic effect in providing a strong physical access control.

**94.** Which of the following is *not* appropriate to ensure continuity of electric power supply?

    a.    Disk mirroring

    b.    Power line conditioners

    c.    Uninterruptible power supply equipment

    d.    Backup generators

*94. a.*    Disk mirroring is not appropriate to ensure the continuity of the electric power supply because it prevents data loss. It is a fault-tolerant mechanism because it copies and stores data in two places (disks). The other three choices are incorrect because they are needed to provide continuity of the electric power supply. Power line conditioners smooth out power fluctuations. Uninterruptible power supply (UPS) equipment provides relief from short power outages. Backup generators support relief from long power outages.

**95.** Which of the following is *not* a benefit of automated environmental controls over manual monitoring?

    a.    System probes to perform diagnosis and analysis

    b.    Orderly shutdown of the host system

    c.    Slow recovery

    d.    Problem recording and notification

*95. c.*    The automation of monitoring and controlling the environmental system can help minimize the damage and speed up the recovery process. The major objective is to reduce the effect of a disaster resulting from malfunctioning of the environmental control system. Manual monitoring can be time consuming, error prone, and unreliable because it requires constant attention.

**96.** Which of the following controls is *not* appropriate to prevent unauthorized people from entering a computer center?

    a.    Double-locked doors

    b.    CCTV monitors

    c.    Terminal IDs

    d.    Picture ID badges

**96. *c.*** Logical access controls verify the terminal identification (ID) number and are not a part of physical security. Logical access controls provide a technical means of controlling what information users can utilize, the programs they can run, and the modifications they can make. The other three choices deal with physical security, which is the right kind of control to prevent unauthorized people from entering a computer center.

**97.** Which one of the following statements is *not* true regarding a water-based fire extinguishing system?

    a.    Water cools the equipment relatively quickly.

    b.    The release of water can be localized to where it is needed.

    c.    Water and Halon gas systems are mutually exclusive.

    d.    Jet sprayers can be an alternative to water sprinklers.

**97. *c.*** Water and Halon gas should be used with heat and smoke detectors and mechanisms for automatically shutting off electrical power and air conditioning devices. (That is, they are not used in a water-based fire extinguishing system.) It is true that water cools the equipment relatively quickly. It is true that the release of water can be localized to where it is needed. It is true that jet sprayers can be an alternative to water sprinklers. Jet sprayers located on the ceiling spray a fine water mist that turns to steam on contact with the fire, smothering it.

**98.** Controls such as locked doors, intrusion detection devices, and security guards address which of the following risks?

    a.    Heat failure

    b.    Fraud or theft

    c.    Power failure

    d.    Equipment failure

**98. *b.*** Locked doors, intrusion detection devices, and security guards that restrict physical access are important preventive measures to control sabotage, riots, fraud, or theft. Sabotage can be caused by a disgruntled employee as well as by outsiders. Personnel policies should require the immediate termination and removal from the premise of any employee considered a threat. Restricting access to information that may be altered reduces fraud or theft exposures.

Heat failure may cause an inconvenience to employees. Power failure can be controlled by uninterruptible power supply. Equipment failure may result in extended processing delays. Performance of preventive maintenance enhances system reliability and should be extended to all supporting equipment, such as temperature and humidity control systems and alarm or detecting devices.

**99.** Which of the following security controls is the simplest safeguard with the least amount of delay?

    a.    Operating system security controls

    b.    Network security controls

    c.    Physical security controls

    d.    Application system security controls

***99. c.*** Physical security is achieved through the use of locks, guards, and administratively controlled procedures such as visitor badges. It also protects the structures housing the computer and related equipment against damage from accident, fire, and environmental hazards, thus ensuring the protection of their contents. Physical security measures are the first line of defense against the risks that stem from the uncertainties in the environment as well as from the unpredictability of human behavior. Frequently, they are the simplest safeguards to implement and can be put into practice with the least delay. The controls listed in the other three choices take a long time to implement and are not simple to install.

**100.** Which of the following is *not* a technical security measure?

    a.    Hardware

    b.    Software

    c.    Firmware

    d.    Physical control

***100. d.*** A major part of the security of an IT system can often be achieved through non-technical measures, such as organizational, personnel, physical, and administrative controls. However, there is a growing tendency and need to employ technical IT security measures implemented in hardware, software, and firmware either separately or converged.

**101.** Which of the following is *not* a protective measure to control physical access to information system distribution and transmission lines?

    a.    Card readers

    b.    Locked wiring closets

    c.    Locked jacks

    d.    Protected cables

*101. a.*   Card readers are physical access devices to control entry to facilities containing information systems. Protective measures to control physical access to information system distribution and transmission lines include locked wiring closets, disconnected or locked spare jacks, and cables protected by conduit or cable trays.

**102.**   **Biometrics-based access controls are implemented using which of the following?**

    a.   Administrative and directive controls

    b.   Physical and logical controls

    c.   Management and preventive controls

    d.   Corrective and recovery controls

*102. b.*   Physical controls (e.g., memory cards, smart cards, or hardware tokens) are used to identify a user, and logical controls (e.g., fingerprint or voice print) are used to authenticate the same user.

**103.**   **Protective lighting does which of the following for computer facilities?**

    a.   Detection and correction

    b.   Deterrent and detection

    c.   Correction and action

    d.   Protection and correction

*103. b.*   Protective lighting should act as a deterrent and make detection likely. The lighting should enable the security staff to observe others without being seen.

**104.**   **The effectiveness of physical security controls is most determined by which of the following?**

    a.   Control device used

    b.   Vulnerabilities in the device

    c.   Implementation of the device

    d.   Planning device used

*104. b.*   Organizations should determine whether intruders could easily defeat the controls (i.e., vulnerabilities) in the access control devices. Until the vulnerabilities are eliminated, implementation and operation of the control device do not matter much.

**105.**   **Which of the following intruder detection systems *cannot* be used as a primary system?**

    a.   Photoelectric detection systems

    b.   Motion detection systems

    c.   Proximity detection systems

    d.   Audio detection systems

**105. c.**   Proximity detection systems identify the approach or presence of an object or an individual. It is designed to be supplemental and cannot be used effectively as a primary system because of the system's vulnerability to nuisance alarms caused by electric supply fluctuations and by the presence of mops, pails, and so on placed near the system. Animals and birds can trigger a system alarm if it is too sensitive. Therefore, proximity systems should be backed up by other security systems. Photoelectric systems operate based on light, motion systems operate based on signal, and audio systems operate based on sound.

**106.**   Which of the following controls the mantraps in a computer center?

   a.   A person's body weight and a smart card

   b.   A person's body weight and a biometric feature

   c.   A person's body weight and a memory card

   d.   A person's body weight and a personal identification number

**106. b.**   Mantraps are used in highly-sensitive areas and have a built-in weighing scale. The mantrap-controlling software looks at a combination of a person's body weight and a biometric feature such as fingerprint scan, hand geometry, facial recognition, iris scan, and voice recognition, and compares it to stored information about that person. Smart cards, memory cards, and personal identification numbers (PINs) can be stolen or lost, and they are a weak form of authentication even when combined with the body weight. A person's body weight and a biometric features authenticate what the user is, which is stronger than the other controls.

**107.**   The primary function of a physical protection system should be performed in which of the following order?

   a.   Detection, response, and delay

   b.   Detection, delay, and response

   c.   Delay, detection, and response

   d.   Response, delay, and detection

**107. b.**   A physical protection system must accomplish its objectives by either deterrence or a combination of detection, delay, and response, in that order.

**108.**   What must begin after a physical intrusion detection alarm is initiated and reported?

   a.   Communication

   b.   Interruption

   c.   Assessment

   d.   Deployment

**108. c.**   When a physical intrusion detection alarm is initiated and reported, situation assessment begins. You need to know whether the alarm is a valid or a nuisance alarm and details about the cause of the alarm.

**109.** Which of the following is the *most* costly countermeasure to reduce physical security risks?

    a.    Procedural controls

    b.    Hardware devices

    c.    Electronic systems

    d.    Personnel

**109. d.**   Personnel such as security guards are the greatest expense due to direct salaries plus fringe benefits paid to them. It is good to use people only in those areas where procedural controls, hardware devices, or electronic systems cannot be utilized at all or cannot be utilized more effectively.

Procedural controls, such as logging visitors and recording temperatures, are generally the least expensive. They can be manual or automated; the latter can be expensive. Hardware devices can include, for example, locks, keys, fences, gates, document shredders, vaults, and barricades. Electronic systems can include, for example, access controls, alarms, CCTV, and detectors.

**110.** Which of the following is the *last* line of defense in a physical security?

    a.    Perimeter barriers

    b.    Exterior protection

    c.    Interior barriers

    d.    People

**110. d.**   The perimeter barriers (e.g., fences) are located at the outer edge of property and usually are the first line of defense. The exterior protection, such as walls, ceilings, roofs, and floors of buildings, is considered the second line of defense. Interior barriers within the building such as doors and locks are considered the third line of defense. After all the preceding defenses fail, the last line of defense is people—employees working in the building. They should question strangers and others unfamiliar to them.

**111.** Which of the following has a bearing on opportunities for electronic surveillance?

    a.    Electrical characteristics of a building

    b.    Physical characteristics of a building

    c.    Mechanical characteristics of a building

    d.    Environmental characteristics of a building

**111. b.**   The physical characteristics of a building have a bearing on opportunities for audio and electronic surveillance. Some of these factors are poor access control designs, inadequate soundproofing, common or shared ducts, and space above false ceilings that enable access for the placement of devices. Physical inspection of these weak areas can hinder penetration.

**112.** What is the *most* common concern regarding a physical security area?

    a.    Fire suppression system

    b.    Piggybacking

  c. Locks and keys

  d. Natural disasters

**112. b.** Piggybacking occurs when unauthorized access is gained to a computer system or facility via a user's legitimate connection. Then both the authorized and the unauthorized person enter the sensitive area. This kind of entry cannot be predicted or anticipated, and its frequency of occurrence can be high.

Fire suppression systems should not be a concern if tested periodically. Locks and keys are the first line of defense against intruders entering into a computer center building or computer room. Natural disasters are not a concern because of their low frequency.

# SCENARIO-BASED QUESTIONS, ANSWERS, AND EXPLANATIONS

**Use the following information to answer questions 1 through 7.**

The DRS Company is designing a new data center that will centrally process more than 100 offices' global transactions. Each office batch transmits more than 10,000 transactions per day. Each batch consists of a maximum of 1,000 transactions or 1 hour of processing, whichever comes first. The plan calls for a fully redundant data center operation with a maximum of one lost batch in the event of a failover.

**1.** **Which of the following is *not* appropriate to provide adequate complementary physical access controls?**

  a. ID badge card

  b. Password

  c. Magnetic stripe card

  d. Visitor log

*1. b.* Passwords provide logical access controls, not physical access controls. The other three are examples of complementary controls. Each control enhances the other. A function or an area doesn't need to be weak to use complementary controls. Complementary controls can magnify the effectiveness of two or more controls when applied to a function, program, or operation. Identification (ID) badge cards, magnetic stripe cards, and visitor logs have a synergistic effect in providing a strong physical access control.

**2.** **Which of the following controls is *not* appropriate to prevent unauthorized people from entering a computer center?**

  a. Double-locked doors

  b. Television monitors

  c. Terminal IDs

  d. Picture ID badges

*2. c.* Logical access controls verify the terminal identification (ID) number and not a part of physical security. Logical access controls provide a technical means of controlling what information users can utilize, the programs they can run, and the modifications they can make. The other three choices deal with physical security, which is the right kind of control to prevent unauthorized people from entering a computer center.

3. Controls such as locked doors, intrusion detection devices, and security guards address which of the following risks?

    a.    Heat failure

    b.    Fraud or theft

    c.    Power failure

    d.    Equipment failure

*3. b.* Locked doors, intrusion detection devices, and security guards that restrict physical access are important preventive measures to control sabotage, riots, fraud, or theft. Sabotage can be caused by a disgruntled employee and by outsiders. Personnel policies should require the immediate termination and removal from the premise of any employee considered a threat. Restricting access to information that may be altered reduces fraud or theft exposures. Power failure can be controlled by an uninterruptible power supply. Heat failure may cause an inconvenience to employees. Equipment failure may result in extended processing delays. Performance of preventive maintenance enhances system reliability and should be extended to all supporting equipment, such as temperature and humidity control systems and alarm or detecting devices.

4. Which of the following security controls is simple to implement with the least amount of delay?

    a.    Operating system security controls

    b.    Network security controls

    c.    Physical security controls

    d.    Application system security controls

*4. c.* Physical security is achieved through the use of locks, guards, and administratively controlled procedures such as visitor badges. It also protects the structures housing the computer and related equipment against damage from accident, fire, and environmental hazards, thus ensuring the protection of their contents. Physical security measures are the first line of defense against the risks that stem from the uncertainties in the environment and from the unpredictability of human behavior. Frequently, they are the simplest safeguards to implement and can be put into practice with the least delay. The controls listed in the other three choices take a long time to implement and are not simple to install.

5. Which of the following is *not* a technical security measure?

    a.    Hardware

    b.    Software

c.   Firmware

d.   Physical control

**5. d.**   A major part of the security of an IT system can often be achieved through nontechnical measures, such as organizational, personnel, physical, and administrative controls. However, there is a growing tendency and need to employ technical IT security measures implemented in hardware, software, and firmware.

**6.**   **Which of the following security safeguards is ineffective in an online application system serving multiple users at multiple locations?**

a.   Procedural controls

b.   Physical controls

c.   Hardware controls

d.   Software controls

**6. b.**   An online application system serving multiple users at multiple locations assumes that a network is in place. With a network there is often no centralized computer room with physical security controls that can be implemented. Therefore, physical controls are ineffective. Examples of physical controls include locked doors, intrusion detection devices, security guards, and magnetic badge readers that restrict physical access. Procedural controls are incorrect because they include instructions to request a user profile, add and delete users, instructions to request database views, and so on. Hardware controls are incorrect because they include fault-tolerance devices such as disk mirroring and disk duplexing, smart card processing, encryption, parity checks, and switched ports. Software controls are incorrect because they include user IDs and passwords, smart card processing, encryption, check digits, and message authentication.

**7.**   **What is the *most* effective control in handling potential terrorist attacks, especially bombing?**

a.   Use simulation software.

b.   Examine all letters and parcels coming into a building.

c.   Hire security guards.

d.   Keep motor vehicles away from the building.

**7. c.**   There is no substitute for vigilant and resourceful security guards protecting the buildings. Simulation software is available that can assess the vulnerability of a structure to explosive blasts by simulating the detonation of devices at various design points. Security can be improved by simply keeping vehicles away from near proximity to the structure. It also makes sense to examine all letters and parcels coming into a building for explosives.

## SOURCES AND REFERENCES

"Access Control in Support of Information Systems, Security Technical Implementation Guide." (DISA-STIG, Version 2 and Release 2). December 2008. Defense Information Systems Agency (DISA), The U.S. Department of Defense (DOD).

Garcia, Mary Lynn. 2001. *The Design and Evaluation of Physical Protection Systems.* Burlington, MA: Butterworth-Heinemann.

National Fire Protection Association (NFPA) 10, 1998. Quincy, MA.

National Fire Protection Association (NFPA) 25, 1998.Quincy, MA.

*CPP Study Guide*, 10th Edition. 1999. Alexandria, VA: The American Society for Industrial Security (ASIS).

Patterson, David G., III. 2004. *Implementing Physical Protection Systems.* Alexandria, VA: ASIS International.

"Security Requirements for Cryptographic Modules" (NIST FIPS PUB 140-3 draft), July 2007. National Institute of Standards and Technology (NIST), U.S. Department of Commerce, Gaithersburg, Maryland.

Tyska, Louis A. and Fennelly, Lawrence J. 2000. *150 Things You Should Know About Physical Security.* Woburn, MA: Butterworth-Heinemann.

# APPENDIX A

## CISSP Glossary 2012

This appendix provides a glossary of key information systems and information technology security terms useful to the CISSP Exam candidates. Reading the glossary terms prior to reading the practice chapters (domains) can help the candidate understand the chapter contents better. More than one definition of a key term is provided to address multiple meanings and contexts in which the term is used or applied.

The glossary is provided for a clear understanding of technical terms used in the ten domains of this book. The CISSP Exam candidates should know these terms for a better comprehension of the subject matter presented. *This glossary is a good source for answering multiple-choice questions on the CISSP Exam.*

### NUMBERS AND LETTERS

**1G** The first generation of analog-based wireless technology.

**2G** The second generation of digital wireless technology that supports voice and text.

**3G** The third generation of digital wireless technology that supports video.

**4G** The fourth generation of digital wireless technology that provides faster display of multimedia.

**802.1Q** The IEEE standard for virtual local-area networks (VLANs).

**802.2** The IEEE standard for logical link control. (IEEE is Institute of Electrical and Electronics Engineers.)

**802.3** The IEEE standard for carrier sense multiple access with collision detection (CSMA/CD) access method and physical layer specifications for Ethernet local-area networks (LANs).

**802.4** The IEEE standard for Token bus access method and physical layer specifications for LANs.

**802.5** The IEEE standard for Token ring access method and physical layer specifications for LANs.

**802.6**   The IEEE standard for Distributed queue dual bus access method and physical layer specifications for wired metropolitan-area networks (MANs).

**802.11**   The IEEE standard for wireless LAN medium access control (MAC) sublayer and physical layer specifications. It uses a path-sharing protocol.

**802.11a**   The IEEE standard for radio band that is faster than 80211b but has a smaller range.

**802.11b**   The IEEE standard that is inexpensive and popular with sufficient speed but with interference problems.

**802.11e**   The IEEE standard for providing quality of service (QoS).

**802.11f**   The IEEE standard for achieving access point interoperability.

**802.11g**   The IEEE standard that is fast but expensive and is mostly used by businesses.

**802.11i**   The IEEE standard for providing improved security over wired equivalent privacy (WEP).

**802.11n**   The IEEE standard for improving throughput rates.

**802.11r**   The IEEE standard for improving the amount of time for data connectivity.

**802.11t**   The IEEE standard for providing performance metrics.

**802.11w**   The IEEE standard for providing data integrity, data origination authenticity, replay protection, and data confidentiality.

**802.15**   The IEEE standard for wireless personal-area networks (e.g., Bluetooth).

**802.16**   The IEEE standard for air interface for fixed broadband wireless access systems such as wireless MANs.

# A

**Abstraction**   (1) It is related to stepwise refinement and modularity of computer programs. (2) It is presented in levels such as high-level dealing with system/program requirements and low-level dealing with programming issues.

**Access**   (1) The ability to make use of any information system (IS) or information technology (IT) resources. (2) The ability to do something with information in a computer. (3) Access refers to the technical ability to do something (e.g., read, create, modify, or delete a file or execute a program).

**Acceptable level of risk**   A judicious and carefully considered assessment that an IT activity or network meets the minimum requirements of applicable security directives. The assessment should take into account the value of IT assets, threats and vulnerabilities, countermeasures and their efficacy in compensating for vulnerabilities, and operational requirements.

**Acceptable risk**   A concern that is acceptable to responsible management, due to the cost and magnitude of implementing controls.

**Access aggregation**   Combines access permissions either in one system or multiple systems for system user or end-user convenience and efficiency and to eliminate duplicate and unnecessary work. Access aggregation can be achieved through single-sign on system (SSO), reduced sign-on system (RSO), or other methods. Note that access aggregation must be compatible with a user's authorized access rights, privileges, and permissions and cannot exceed them because of an "authorization creep" problem, which is a major risk. Access aggregation process must meet the following requirements:

➤ Support for the separation of duty concept to avoid conflict of interest situations (administrative)

➤ Support for the principles of least privilege and elimination of authorization creep through reauthorization

➤ Support for the controlled inheritance of access privileges

➤ Support for safety through access constraint models such as static and dynamic separation of duties (technical)

➤ Support for safety so that no access permissions can be leaked to unauthorized individuals, which can be implemented through access control configurations and models

➤ Support for proper mapping of subject, operation, object, and attributes

➤ Support for preventing or resolving access control policy conflicts resulting in deadlock situation due to cyclic referencing

➤ Support for a horizontal scope of access controls (across platforms, applications, and enterprises)

➤ Support for a vertical scope of access controls (between operating systems, database management systems, networks, and applications)

**Access authority**   An entity responsible for monitoring and granting access privileges for other authorized entities.

**Access category**   One of the classes to which a user, a program, or a process may be assigned on the basis of the resources or groups of resources that each user, program, or process is authorized to use.

**Access control**   (1) What permits or restricts access to applications at a granular level, such as per-user, per-group, and per-resources.   (2) The process of granting or denying specific requests for obtaining and using information and related information processing services and to enter specific physical facilities (e.g., buildings). (3) Procedures and controls that limit or detect access to critical information resources. This can be accomplished through software, biometrics devices, or physical access to a controlled space. (4) Enables authorized use of a computer resource while preventing unauthorized use or use in an unauthorized manner. (5) Access controls determine what the users can do in a computer system. (6) Access controls are designed to protect computer resources from unauthorized modification, loss, or disclosure. (7) Access controls include both physical access controls, which limit access to facilities and associated hardware, and logical access controls, which prevent or detect unauthorized access to sensitive data and programs stored or transmitted electronically.

**Access control list (ACL)**   A register of (1) users (including groups, machines, programs, and processes) who have been given permission to use a particular system resource and (2) the types of access they have been permitted. This is a preventive and technical control.

**Access control matrix**   A table in which each row represents a subject, each column represents an object, and each entry is the set of access rights for that subject to that object.

**Access control measures and mechanisms**   Hardware and software features (technical controls), physical controls, operational controls, management controls, and various combinations of these designed to detect or prevent unauthorized access to an IT system and to enforce access control. This is a preventive, detective, and technical control.

**Access control policy**   The set of rules that define the conditions under which an access may take place.

**Access control software**   (1) Vendor supplied system software, external to the operating system, used to specify who has access to a system, who has access to specific resources, and what capabilities are granted to authorized users. (2) Access control software can generally be implemented in different modes that provide varying degrees of protection, such as (i) denying access for which the user is not expressly authorized, (ii) allowing access which is not expressly authorized but providing a warning, or (iii) allowing access to all resources without warning regardless of authority.

**Access control triple**   A type of access control specification in which a user, program, and data items (a triple) are listed for each allowed operation.

**Access deterrence**   A design principle for security mechanisms based on a user's fear of detection of violations of security policies rather than absolute prevention of violations.

**Access level**   The hierarchical portion of the security level used to identify data sensitivity and user clearance or authorization. Note: The access level and the non-hierarchical categories form the sensitivity label of an object.

**Access list**   Synonymous with access control list (ACL).

**Access logs**   Access logs will capture records of computer events about an operating system, an application system, or user activities. Access logs feed into audit trails.

**Access matrix**   A two-dimensional array consisting of objects and subjects, where the intersections represent permitted access types.

**Access method**   The technique used for selecting records in a file for processing, retrieval, or storage

**Access mode**   A distinct operation recognized by protection mechanisms as possible operations on an object. Read, write, and append are possible modes of access to a file, while whereas "execute" is an additional mode of access to a program.

**Access password**   A password used to authorize access to data and distributed to all those who are authorized similar access to those data. This is a preventive and technical control.

**Access path**   The sequence of hardware and software components significant to access control. Any component capable of enforcing access restrictions, or any component that could be used to bypass an access restriction should be considered part of the access path.   The access path can also be defined as the path through which user requests travel, including the telecommunications software, transaction processing software, and applications software.

**Access period**   A segment of time, generally expressed on a daily or weekly basis, during which access rights prevail.

**Access port**   A logical or physical identifier that a computer uses to distinguish different terminal input/output data streams.

**Access priorities**   Deciding who gets what priority in accessing a system. Access priorities are based on employee job functions and levels rather than data ownership.

**Access privileges**   Precise statements defining the extent to which an individual can access computer systems and use or modify programs and data on the system. Statements also define under what circumstances this access is allowed.

**Access profiles**   There are at least two types of access profiles: user profile and standard profile. (1) A user profile is a set of rules describing the nature and extent of access to each resource that is available to each user. (2) A standard profile is a set of rules describing the nature and extent of access to each resource that is available to a group of users with similar job duties, such as accounts payable clerks.

**Access rules**   Clear action statements describing expected user behavior in a computer system. Access rules reflect security policies and practices, business rules, information ethics, system functions and features, and individual roles and responsibilities, which collectively form access restrictions. Access rules are often described as user security profiles (access profiles). Access control software implements access rules.

**Access time minimization**   A risk reducing principle that attempts to avoid prolonging access time to specific data or to the system beyond what is needed to carry out requisite functionality.

**Access type**   The nature of an access right to a particular device, program, or file (e.g., read, write, execute, append, modify, delete, or create).

**Accessibility**   The ability to obtain the use of a computer system or a resource or the ability and means necessary to store data, retrieve data, or communicate with a system.

**Account management, user**   Involves (1) the process of requesting, establishing, issuing, and closing user accounts, (2) tracking users and their respective access authorizations, and (3) managing these functions.

**Accountability**   (1) The security goal that generates the requirement for actions of an entity to be traced uniquely to that entity. This supports non-repudiation, deterrence, fault isolation, intrusion detection and prevention, and after-action recovery and legal action. (2) The property that enables system activities to be traced to individuals who may then be held responsible for their actions. This is a management and preventive control.

**Accountability principle**   A principle that calls for holding individuals responsible for their actions. In computer systems, this is enabled through identification and authentication, the specifications of authorized actions, and the auditing of the user's activity.

**Accreditation**   The official management decision given by a senior officer to authorize operation of an information system and to explicitly accept the risk to organizations (including mission, functions, image, or reputation), organization assets, or individuals, based on the implementation of an agreed-upon set of security controls.

**Accreditation authority**   Official with the authority to formally assume responsibility for operating an information system at an acceptable level of risk to organization operations, assets, or individuals. Synonymous with authorizing official or accrediting authority.

**Accreditation boundary**   All components of an information system to be accredited by an authorizing official and excludes separately accredited systems, to which the information system is connected.

**Accreditation package**   The evidence provided to the authorizing official to be used in the security accreditation decision process. Evidence includes, but is not limited to (1) the system security plan, (2) the assessment results from the security certification, and (3) the plan of actions and milestones.

**Accuracy**   A qualitative assessment of correctness or freedom from error.

**Acoustic cryptanalysis attack**   An exploitation of sound produced during a computation. It is a general class of a side channel attack (Wikipedia).

**Activation data**   Private data, other than keys, that is required to access cryptographic modules.

**Active attack**   An attack on the authentication protocol where the attacker transmits data to the claimant or verifier. Examples of active attacks include a man-in-the-middle (MitM), impersonation, and session hijacking. Active attacks can result in the disclosure or dissemination of data files, denial-of-service, or modification of data.

**Active content**   Electronic documents that can carry out or trigger actions automatically on a computer platform without the intervention of a user. Active content technologies allow enable mobile code associated with a document to execute as the document is rendered.

**Active security testing**   (1) Hands-on security testing of systems and networks to identity their security vulnerabilities. (2) Security testing that involves direct interaction with a target, such as sending packets to a target.

**Active state**   The cryptographic key lifecycle state in which a cryptographic key is available for use for a set of applications, algorithms, and security entities.

**Active wiretapping**   The attaching of an unauthorized device, such as a computer terminal, to a communications circuit for the purpose of obtaining access to data through the generation of false messages or control signals or by altering the communications of legitimate users.

**Active-X**   Software components downloaded automatically with a Web page and executed by a Web browser. A loosely defined set of technologies developed by Microsoft, Active-X is an outgrowth of two other Microsoft technologies called OLE (Object Linking and Embedding) and COM (Component Object Model). As a monitor, Active-X can be very confusing because it applies to a whole set of COM-based technologies. Most people, however, think only of Active-X controls, which represent a specific way of implementing Active-X technologies.

**Adaptive maintenance**   Any effort initiated as a result of environmental changes (e.g. laws and regulations) in which software must operate.

**Address-based authentication**   Access control is based on the IP address and/or hostname of the host requesting information. It is easy to implement for small groups of users, not practical for large groups of users. It is susceptible to attacks such as IP spoofing and DNS poisoning.

**Address resolution protocol (ARP)**   A protocol used to obtain a node's physical address. A client station broadcasts an ARP request onto the network with the Internet Protocol (IP) address of the target node with which it wants to communicate, and with that address the node responds by sending back its physical address so that packets can be transmitted to it.

**Add-on security**   (1) A retrofitting of protection mechanisms implemented by hardware or software after the computer system becomes operational. (2) An incorporation of new hardware, software, or firmware safeguards in an operational information system.

**Adequate security**   This proposes that security should commensurate with the risk and the magnitude of harm resulting from the loss, misuse, or unauthorized access to or modification of information. This includes assuring that systems and applications used operate effectively and provide appropriate confidentiality, integrity, and availability services through the use of cost-effective controls (i.e., management, operational, and technical controls).

**Adj-routing information base (RIB)-in**   Routes learned from inbound update messages from Border Gateway Protocol (BGP) peers.

**Adj-routing information base (RIB)-out**   Routes that the Border Gateway Protocol (BGP) router will advertise, based on its local policy, to its peers.

**Administrative account**   A user account with full privileges intended to be used only when performing personal computer (PC) management tasks, such as installing updates and application software, managing user accounts, and modifying operating system (OS) and application settings.

**Administrative law**   Law dealing with legal principles that apply to government agencies.

**Administrative safeguards**   Administrative actions, policies, and procedures to manage the selection, development, implementation, and maintenance of security measures to protect electronic health information (e.g., HIPAA) and to manage the conduct of the covered entity's workforce in relation to protecting that information.

**Administrative security**   The management constraints, operational procedures, accountability procedures, and supplemental controls established to provide an acceptable level of protection for sensitive data, programs, equipment, and physical facilities. Synonymous with procedural security.

**Admissible evidence**   Evidence allowed in a court to be considered by the Trier of fact (such as, jury and/or judge) in making a legal opinion, decision, or conclusion. Admissible evidence must be relevant, competent, and material. "Sufficient" is not part of the concept of admissibility of evidence because it merely supports a legal finding.

Best evidence is admissible because it is the primary evidence (such as, written instruments, such as contracts or deeds). Business records are also admissible when they are properly authenticated as to their contents (that is, notarized or stamped with official seal).

For example, (1) business records, such as sales orders and purchase orders, usually come under hearsay evidence and were not admissible before. They are admissible only when a witness testifies the identity and accuracy of the record and describes its mode of preparation. Today, all business records made during the ordinary course of business are admissible if the business is a legitimate entity. (2) Photographs are hearsay evidence, but they will be considered admissible if properly authenticated by a qualified person who is familiar with the subject portrayed and who can testify that the photograph is a good representation of the subject, place, object, or condition.

**Advanced data communications control procedure (ADCCP)**   Advanced data communications control procedure (ADCCP) is an example of sliding window protocol. ADCCP is a modified

Synchronous Data Link Control (SDLC), which became high-level data link control (HDLC), and later became link access procedure B (LAPB) to make it more compatible with HDLC (Tanenbaum).

**Advanced encryption standard (AES)**   The AES specifies a cryptographic algorithm that can be used to protect electronic data. The AES algorithm is a symmetric block cipher that can encrypt (encipher) and decrypt (decipher) information. Encryption converts data to an unintelligible form called cipher text; decrypting the cipher text converts the data back into its original form, called plaintext. The AES algorithm is capable of using cryptographic keys of 128, 192, and 256 bits to encrypt and decrypt data in blocks of 128 bits. AES is an encryption algorithm for securing sensitive but unclassified material. The combination of XEX tweakable block cipher with cipher text stealing (XTS) and AES is called XTS-AES. The XTS-AES algorithm is designed for the cryptographic protection of data on storage devices that use fixed length data units. It is not designed for encryption of data in transit as it is designed to provide confidentiality for the protected data. The XTS-AES does not provide authentication or access control services.

**Advanced persistent threat**   An adversary with sophisticated levels of expertise and significant resources use multiple different attacks vectors repeatedly (e.g., cyber, physical, and deception) to generate attack opportunities to achieve its objective.

**Agent**   (1) A program used in distributed denial denial-of-service (DDoS) attacks that send malicious traffic to hosts based on the instructions of a handler, also known as a bot. (2) A host-based intrusion detection and prevention program that monitors and analyzes activity and may also perform prevention actions.

**Aggregation**   The result of assembling or combining distinct units of data when handling sensitive information. Aggregation of data at lower sensitivity level may result in the total data being designated at a higher sensitivity level.

**Aggressive mode**   Mode used in Internet Protocol security (IPsec) phase 1 to negotiate the establishment of the Internet key exchange security association (IKESA).

**Agile defense**   Agile defense can handle serious cyber attacks and supply chain attacks as it employs the concept of information system resilience. Information system resilience is the ability of systems to operate while under attack, even in a degraded or debilitated state, and to rapidly recover operational capabilities for essential functions after a successful attack.

**Alarm reporting**   An open system interconnection (OSI) term that refers to the communication of information about a possible detected fault. This information generally includes the identification of the network device or network resource in which the fault was detected, the type of the fault, its severity, and its probable cause.

**Alarm surveillance**   The set of functions that enable (1) the monitoring of the communications network to detect faults and fault-related events or conditions, (2) the logging of this information for future use in fault detection and other network management activities, and (3) the analysis and control of alarms, notifications, and other information about faults to ensure that resources of network management are directed toward faults affecting the operation of the communications network. Analysis of alarms consists of alarm filtering, alarm correlation, and fault prediction. This is a management and detective control.

**Alert** (1) A notice of specific attack directed at an organization's IT resources. (2) A notification of an important observed event.

**Amplifier attack** Like a reflector attack, an amplifier attack involves sending requests with a spoofed source address to an intermediate host. However, an amplifier attack does not use a single intermediate host; instead, its goal is to use a whole network of intermediate hosts. It attempts to accomplish this action by sending an ICMP or UDP request to an expected broadcast address, hoping that many hosts will receive the broadcast and respond to it. Because the attacker's request uses a spoofed source address, the responses are all sent to the spoofed address, which may cause a DoS for that host or the host's network. Network administrators block amplifier attacks by configuring border routers to not forward directed-broadcasts, but some still permit them, which is a countermeasure.

**Analog signal** A continuous electrical signal whose amplitude varies in direct correlation with the original input.

**Anomaly** Any condition that departs from the expected. This expectation can come from documentation (e.g., requirements specifications, design documents, and user documents) or from perceptions or experiences. An anomaly is not necessarily a problem in the software but a deviation from the expected so that errors, defects, faults, and failures are considered anomalies.

**Anomaly-based detection** The process of comparing definitions of what activity is considered normal against observed events to identify significant deviations.

**Anti-jam** Countermeasures ensuring that transmitted information can be received despite deliberate jamming attempts.

**Anti-spoof** Countermeasures taken to prevent the unauthorized use of legitimate identification & authentication (I&A) data, however it was obtained, to mimic a subject different from the attacker.

**Anti-virus software** A program that monitors a computer or network to identify all major types of malware and prevent or contain malware incidents.

**Applets** Small applications written in various programming languages automatically downloaded and executed by applet-enabled World Wide Web (WWW) browsers. Examples include Active-X and Java applets, both of which have security concerns.

**Applicant** A party undergoing the processes of registration and identity proofing.

**Application** The use of information resources (information and information technology) to satisfy a specific set of user requirements.

**Application-based intrusion detection and prevention system** A host-based intrusion detection and prevention system (IDPS) that performs monitoring for a specific application service only, such as a Web server program or a database server program.

**Application content filtering** It is performed by a software proxy agent to remove or quarantine viruses that may be contained in e-mail attachments, to block specific multipurpose Internet mail extension (MIME) types, or to filter other active content, such as Java, JavaScript, and Active-X® Controls.

**Application controls** Preventive, detective, and corrective controls designed to ensure the completeness and accuracy of transaction processing, authorization, and data validity.

**Application firewall** (1) A firewall that uses stateful protocol analysis to analyze network traffic for one or more applications. (2) A firewall system in which service is provided by processes that maintain complete Transmission Control Protocol (TCP) connection-state and sequencing. It often re-addresses traffic so that outgoing traffic appears to have originated from the firewall, rather than the internal host. In contrast to packet filtering firewalls, this firewall must have knowledge of the application data transfer protocol and often has rules about what may be transmitted.

**Application layer** (1) That portion of an open system interconnection (OSI) system ultimately responsible for managing communication between application processes. (2) Provides security at the layer responsible for data that is sent and received for particular applications such as DNS, HTTP, and SMTP.

**Application programming interface (API)** An interface between an application and software service module or operating system component. It is defined as a subroutine library.

**Application-proxy gateway** (1) A firewall capability that combines lower-layer access control with upper- layer functionality, and includes a proxy agent that acts as an intermediary between two hosts that wish to communicate with each other. (2) An application system that forwards application traffic through a firewall. It is also called proxy server. Proxies tend to be specific to the protocol they are designed to forward and may provide increased access control or audit.

**Application service provider (ASP)** An external organization provides online business application systems to customers for a fee to ensure continuity of business. ASP operates with a B2B e-commerce model.

**Application software** Programs that perform specific tasks, such as word processing, database management, or payroll. Software that interacts directly with some non-software system (e.g., human or robot). A program or system intended to serve a business or non-business function, which has a specific input, processing, and output activities (e.g., accounts receivable and general ledger systems).

**Application system partitioning** The information system should separate user functionality, including user interface services, from information system management functionality, including databases, network components, workstations, or servers. This separation is achieved through physical or logical methods using different computers, different CPUs, different instances of the operating system, different network addresses, or combination of these methods.

**Application translation** A function that converts information from one protocol to another.

**Architecture** A description of all functional activities performed to achieve the desired mission, the system elements needed to perform the functions, and the designation of performance levels of those system elements. Architecture also includes information on the technologies, interfaces, and location of functions and is considered an evolving description of an approach to achieving a desired mission.

**Archiving** Moving electronic files no longer being used to less accessible and usually less expensive storage media for safekeeping. The practice of moving seldom used data or programs from the active database to secondary storage media such as magnetic tape or cartridge.

**Assertion** A statement from a verifier to a relying party that contains identity information about a subscriber. Assertions may also contain verified attributes. Assertions may be digitally signed objects or they may be obtained from a trusted source by a secure protocol.

**Assessment method**   One of three types of actions (i.e., examine, interview, and test) taken by assessors in obtaining evidence during an assessment.

**Assessment procedure**   (1) A set of assessment objectives and an associated set of assessment methods and assessment objects. (2) A set of activities or actions employed by an assessor to determine the extent to which a security control is implemented correctly, operating as intended, and producing the desired outcome with respect to meeting the security requirements for the system.

**Asset**   A major application, general support system, high impact program, physical plant, mission critical system or a logically related group of systems. Any software, data, hardware, administrative, physical, communications, or personnel resource within an IT system or activity.

**Asset Valuation**   IT assets include computers, business-oriented applications, system-oriented applications, security-oriented applications, operating systems, database systems, telecommunications systems, data center facilities, hardware, computer networks, and data and information residing in these assets. Assets can also be classified as tangible (physical such as equipment) and intangible (non-physical, such as copyrights and patents). Each type of asset has its own valuation methods.

The value of data and information can be measured by using two methods: book value and current value. A relevant question to ask is what is the worth of particular data to an insider (such as an owner, sponsor, management employee, or non-management employee) and an outsider (such as a customer, supplier, intruder, or competitor)? This means, the value of information is measured by its value to others.

Sensitive criteria for computer systems are defined in terms of the value of having, or the cost of not having, an application system or needed information. The concept of information economics (that is, cost and benefit) should be used here. Organizations should modernize inefficient business processes to maximize the value and minimize the risk of IT investments. The value of IT assets is determined by their replacement cost, recovery cost, and penalty cost.

Information and data are collected and analyzed using several methods for determining their value. Examples of data collection techniques include checklists, questionnaires, interviews, and meetings. Examples of data analysis techniques include both quantitative methods (objective methods using net present value and internal rate of return calculations) and qualitative methods (subjective methods using Delphi techniques and focus groups).

**Assurance**   (1) The grounds for confidence that the set of intended security controls in an information system are effective in their application. (2) It is one of the five security goals. (3) It involves support for our confidence that the other four security goals (integrity, availability, confidentiality, and accountability) have been adequately met by a specific implementation. "Adequately met" includes (i) functionality that performs correctly, (ii) sufficient protection against unintentional errors (by users or software), and (iii) sufficient resistance to intentional penetration or bypass. (4) It is the grounds for confidence that an entity meets its security objectives.

**Assurance testing**   A process used to determine that the system's security features are implemented as designed and that they are adequate for the proposed environment. This process may include hands-on functional testing, penetration testing, and/or verification.

**Asymmetric key algorithm**   An encryption algorithm that requires two different keys for encryption and decryption. These keys are commonly referred to as the public and private keys. Asymmetric algorithms are slower than symmetric algorithms. Furthermore, speed of encryption may be different from the speed of decryption. Generally, asymmetric algorithms are either used to exchange symmetric session keys or to digitally sign a message (e.g., RSA). Cryptography that uses separate keys for encryption and decryption; also known as public-key cryptography.

**Asymmetric key cryptography**   Two related keys, a public key and a private key that are used to perform complementary operations, such as encryption and decryption or signature generation and signature verification.

**Asynchronous attack**   (1) An attempt to exploit the interval between a defensive act and the attack in order to render inoperative the effect of the defensive act. For instance, an operating task may be interrupted at once following the checking of a stored parameter. The user regains control and malevolently changes the parameter; the operating system regains control and continues processing using the maliciously altered parameter.   (2) It is an indirect attack on the program by altering legitimate data or codes at a time when the program is idle, then causing the changes to be added to the target program at later execution.

**Asynchronous transfer mode (ATM) network**   Asynchronous transfer mode (ATM) network is a fast packet switching network, which is the foundation for the broadband integrated services digital network (B-ISDN). ATM uses cell technology to transfer data at high speeds using packets of fixed size. The ATM network is a non-IP wide-area network (WAN) because the Internet Protocol (IP) does not fit well with the connection-oriented ATM network. IP is a connectionless protocol.

**Attack**   (1) The realization of some specific threat that impacts the confidentiality, integrity, accountability, or availability of a computational resource. (2) The act of trying to bypass security controls on a system or a method of breaking the integrity of a cipher. (3) An attempt to obtain a subscriber's token or to fool a verifier into believing that an unauthorized individual possesses a claimant's token. (4) An attack may be active, resulting in the alteration of data, or passive, resulting in the release of data. Note: The fact that an attack is made does not necessarily mean it will succeed. The degree of success depends on system vulnerability or activity and the effectiveness of existing countermeasures.

**Attack-in-depth strategy**   Malicious code attackers use an attack-in-depth strategy in order to carry out their goal. Single-point solutions cannot stop all of their attacks. Defense-in-depth strategy can stop these attacks.

**Attack signature**   A specific sequence of events indicative of an unauthorized access attempt.

**Attacker**   (1) A party who is not the claimant or verifier but wishes wants to successfully execute the authentication protocol as a claimant. (2) A party who acts with malicious intent to assault an information system.

**Attacker's work factor**   The amount of work necessary for an attacker to break the system or network should exceed the value that the attacker would gain from a successful compromise.

**Attribute**   A distinct characteristic of real-world objects often specified in terms of their physical traits, such as size, shape, weight, and color. Objects in cyber-world might have attributes describing things such as size, type of encoding, and network address. Attributes are properties of an entity. An entity is described by its attributes. In a database, the attributes of an entity have their analogues in the fields of a record. In an object database, instance variables may be considered attributes of the object.

**Attribute-based access control (ABAC)**   (1) Access control based on attributes associated with and about subjects, objects, targets, initiators, resources, or the environment. It is an access control ruleset that defines the combination of attributes under which an access may take place. (2) An access control approach in which access is mediated based on attributes associated with subjects (requesters) and the objects to be accessed. Each object and subject has a set of associated attributes, such as location, time of creation, and access rights. Access to an object is authorized or denied depending upon whether the required (e.g., policy-defined) correlation can be made between the attributes of that object and of the requesting subject.

**Attribute-based authorization**   A structured process that determines when a user is authorized to access information, systems, or services based on attributes of the user and of the information, system, or service.

**Attribute certificate**   A live scan of a person's biometric measure is translated into a biometric template, which is then placed in an attribute certificate.

**Audit**   The independent examination of records and activities to assess the adequacy of system controls, to ensure compliance with established controls, policies, and operational procedures, and to recommend necessary changes in controls, policies, or procedures.

**Audit reduction tools**   Preprocessors designed to reduce the volume of audit records to facilitate manual review. Before a security review, these tools can remove many audit records known to have little security significance. These tools generally remove records generated by specified classes of events, such as records generated by nightly backups.

**Audit trail**   (1) A chronological record of system activities that is sufficient to enable the reconstruction and examination of the sequence of events and activities surrounding or leading to an operation, procedure, or event in a security-relevant transaction from inception to results. (2) A record showing who has accessed an IT system and what operations the user has performed during a given period. (3) An automated or manual set of records providing documentary evidence of user transactions. (4) It is used to aid in tracing system activities. This is a technical and detective control.

**Auditability**   Features and characteristics that allow verification of the adequacy of procedures and controls and of the accuracy of processing transactions and results in either a manual or automated system.

**Authenticate**   To confirm the identity of an entity when that identity is presented.

**Authentication**   (1) Verifying the identity of a user, process, or device, often as a prerequisite to allowing access to resources in an information system. (2) A process that establishes the origin of information or determines an entity's identity. (3) The process of establishing confidence of authenticity and, therefore, the integrity of data. (4) The process of establishing confidence in the identity of users or information system. (5) It is designed to protect against fraudulent activity, authentication verifies the user's identity and eligibility to access computerized information. It is proving that users are who they claim to be and is normally paired with the term identification. Typically, identification is performed by entering a name or a user ID, and authentication is performed by entering a password, although many organizations are moving to stronger authentication methods such as smart cards and biometrics. Although the ability to sign onto a computer system (enter a correct user ID and password) is often called "accessing the system," this is actually the identification and authentication function. After a user has entered a system, access controls determine which data the user can read or modify and what programs the user can execute. In other words, identification and authentication come first, followed by access control. Continuous authentication is most effective. When two types of identification are used to authenticate a user, it is called a two-factor authentication process.

**Authentication code**  A cryptographic checksum based on an approved security function (also known as a message authentication code, MAC).

**Authentication, electronic**  The process of establishing confidence in user identities electronically presented to an information system.

**Authentication header (AH)**  An Internet Protocol (IP) device used to provide connectionless integrity and data origin authentication for IP datagrams.

**Authentication-header (AH) protocol**  IPsec security protocol that can provide integrity protection for packet headers and data through authentication.

**Authentication key (WMAN/WiMAX)**  An authentication key (AK) is a key exchanged between the BS and SS/MS to authenticate one another prior to the traffic encryption key (TEK) exchange.

**Authentication mechanism**  A hardware- or software-based mechanism that forces users to prove their identity before accessing data on a device.

**Authentication mode**  A block cipher mode of operation that can provide assurance of the authenticity and, therefore, the integrity of data.

**Authentication period**  The maximum acceptable period between any initial authentication process and subsequent re-authentication process during a single terminal session or during the period data are accessed.

**Authentication process**  The actions involving (1) obtaining an identifier and a personal password from a system user; (2) comparing the entered password with the stored, valid password that is issued to, or selected by, the person associated with that identifier; and (3) authenticating the identity if the entered password and the stored password are the same. Note: If the enciphered password is stored, the entered password must be enciphered and compared with the stored ciphertext, or the ciphertext must be deciphered and compared with the entered password. This is a technical and preventive control.

**Authentication protocol**  (1) A defined sequence of messages between a claimant and a verifier that demonstrates that the claimant has control of a valid token to establish his identity, and optionally, demonstrates to the claimant that he is communicating with the intended verifier. (2) A well-specified message exchange process that verifies possession of a token to remotely authenticate a claimant. (3) Some authentication protocols also generate cryptographic keys that are used to protect an entire session so that the data transferred in the session is cryptographically protected.

**Authentication tag**  A pair of bit strings associated to data to provide assurance of its authenticity.

**Authentication token**  Authentication information conveyed during an authentication exchange.

**Authenticator**  The means used to confirm the identity of a user, processor, or device (e.g., user password or token).

**Authenticity**   (1) The property that data originated from its purported source. (2) The property of being genuine and being able to be verified and trusted; confidence in the validity of a transmission, a message, or message originator. See authentication.

**Authorization**   (1) The privilege granted to an individual by management to access information based upon the individual's clearance and need-to-know principle. (2) It determines whether a subject is trusted to act for a given purpose (e.g., allowed to read a particular file). (3) The granting or denying of access rights to a user, program, or process. (4) The official management decision to authorize operation of an information system and to explicitly accept the risk to organization operations, assets, or individuals, based on the implementation of an agreed-upon set of security controls. (5) Authorization is the permission to do something with information in a computer, such as read a file. Authorization comes after authentication. This is a management and preventive control.

**Authorization boundary**   All components of an information system to be authorized for operation. This excludes separately authorized systems, to which the information system is connected. It is same as information system boundary.

**Authorization key pairs**   Authorization key pairs are used to provide privileges to an entity. The private key is used to establish the "right" to the privilege; the public key is used to determine that the entity actually has the right to the privilege.

**Authorization principle**   The principle whereby allowable actions are distinguished from those that are not.

**Authorization process**   The actions involving (1) obtaining an access password from a computer system user (whose identity has already been authenticated, perhaps using a personal password), (2) comparing the access password with the password associated with protected data, and (3) authorizing access to data if the entered password and stored password are the same.

**Authorized**   A system entity or actor that has been granted the right, permission, or capability to access a system resource.

**Automated key transport**   The transport of cryptographic keys, usually in encrypted form, using electronic means such as a computer network (e.g., key transport/agreement protocols).

**Automated password generator**   An algorithm that creates random passwords that have no association with a particular user.

**Automated security monitoring**   The use of automated procedures to ensure that security controls are not circumvented. This is a technical and detective control.

**Availability**   (1) Ensuring timely and reliable access to and use of information by authorized entities. (2) The ability for authorized entities to access systems as needed.

**Avoidance control**   The separation of assets from threats or threats from assets so that risk is minimized. Also, resource allocations are separated from resource management.

**Awareness (information security)**   Activities which seek to focus an individual's attention on an information security issue or set of issues.

# B

**B2B**   Business-to-business (B2B) is an electronic commerce model involving sales of products and services among businesses (e.g., HP to Costco, EDI, ASP, and exchanges and auctions). Both B2B and B2C e-commerce transactions can take place using m-commerce technology. Reverse auction is practiced in B2B or G2B e-commerce.

**B2C**   Business-to-consumer (B2C) is an electronic commerce model involving sales of products and services to individual shoppers (e.g., Amazon.com, Barnesandnoble.com, stock trading, and computer software/hardware sales). Both B2B and B2C e-commerce transactions can take place using m-commerce technology.

**Backbone**   A central network to which other networks connect. It handles network traffic and provides a primary path to or from other networks.

**Backdoor**   A malicious program that listens for commands on a certain transmission control protocol (TCP) or user datagram protocol (UDP) port. Synonymous with trapdoor.

**Backup**   A copy of files and programs made to facilitate recovery if necessary. This is an operational and preventive control and ensures the availability goal.

**Backup computer facilities**   A computer (data) center having hardware and software compatible with the primary computer facility. The backup computer is used only in the case of a major interruption or disaster at the primary computer facility. It provides the ability for continued computer operations, when needed, and should be established by a formal agreement. A duplicate of a hardware system, of software, of data, or of documents intended as replacements in the event of malfunction or disaster.

**Backup operations**   Methods for accomplishing essential business tasks subsequent to disruption of a computer facility and for continuing operations until the facility is sufficiently restored.

**Backup plan**   Synonymous with contingency plan.

**Backup procedures**   The provisions made for the recovery of data files and program libraries, and for restart or replacement of computer equipment after the occurrence of a system failure or of a disaster. Examples include normal (full) backup, incremental backup, differential backup, image backup, file-by-file backup, copy backup, daily backup, record-level backup, and zero-day backup.

**Bandwidth**   Measures the data transfer capacity or speed of transmission in bits per second. Bandwidth is the difference between the highest frequencies and the lowest frequencies measured in a range of Hertz (that is, cycles per second). Bandwidth compression can reduce the time needed to transmit a given amount of data in a given bandwidth without reducing the information content of the signal being transmitted. Bandwidth can negatively affect the performance of networks and devices, if it is inadequate.

**Banner grabbing**   The process of capturing banner information, such as application type and version, that is transmitted by a remote port when a connection is initiated.

**Base station (WMAN/WiMAX)**   A base station (BS) is the node that logically connects fixed and mobile subscriber stations (SSs) to operator networks. A BS consists of the infrastructure elements necessary to enable wireless communications (i.e., antennas, transceivers, and other equipment).

**Baseline (configuration management)**   A baseline indicates a cut-off point in the design and development of a configuration item beyond which configuration does not evolve without undergoing strict configuration control policies and procedures. Note that baselining is first and versioning is next.

**Baseline (software)**   (1) A set of critical observations or data used for comparison or control. (2) A version of software used as a starting point for later versions.

**Baseline architecture**   The initial architecture that is or can be used as a starting point for subsequent architectures or to measure progress.

**Baseline controls**   The minimum-security controls required for safeguarding an IT system based on its identified needs for confidentiality, integrity, and/or availability protection objectives. Three sets of baseline controls (i.e., low-impact, moderate-impact, and high-impact) provide a minimum security control assurance.

**Baselining**   Monitoring resources to determine typical utilization patterns so that significant deviations can be detected.

**Basic authentication**   A technology that uses the Web server content's directory structure. Typically, all files in the same directory are configured with the same access privileges using passwords, thus not secure. The problem is that all password information is transferred in an encoded, rather than an encrypted, form. These problems can be overcome using basic authentication in conjunction with SSL/TLS.

**Basis path testing**   It is a white-box testing technique to measure the logical complexity of a procedural design. The goal is to execute every computer program statement at least once during testing realizing that many programs paths could exist.

**Basic testing**   A test methodology that assumes no knowledge of the internal structure and implementation details of the assessment object. Basic testing is also known as black box testing.

**Bastion host**   A host system that is a "strong point" in the network's security perimeter. Bastion hosts should be configured to be particularly resistant to attack. In a host-based firewall, the bastion host is the platform on which the firewall software is run. Bastion hosts are also referred to as "gateway hosts." A bastion host is typically a firewall implemented on top of an operating system that has been specially configured and hardened to be resistant to attack.

**Bearer assertion**   An assertion that does not provide a mechanism for the subscriber to prove that he is the rightful owner of the assertion. The relying party has to assume that the assertion was issued to the subscriber who presents the assertion or the corresponding assertion reference to the relying party.

**Behavioral outcome**   What an individual who has completed the specific training module is expected to be able to accomplish in terms of IT security-related job performance.

**Benchmark testing**   Uses a small set of data or transactions to check software performance against predetermined parameters to ensure that it meets requirements.

**Benchmarking**   It is the comparison of core process performance with other components of an internal organization or with leading external organizations.

**Best practices**   Business practices that have been shown to improve an organization's IT function as well as other business functions.

**Beta testing**   Use of a product by selected users before formal release.

**Between-the-lines entry**   (1) Access, obtained through the use of active wiretapping by an unauthorized user, to a momentarily inactive terminal of a legitimate user assigned to a communications channel. (2) Unauthorized access obtained by tapping the temporarily inactive terminal of a legitimate use.

**Binding**   (1) Process of associating two related elements of information. (2) An acknowledgment by a trusted third party that associates an entity's identity with its public key. This may take place through (i) certification authority's generation of a public key certificate, (ii) a security officer's verification of an entity's credentials and placement of the entity's public key and identifier in a secure database, or (iii) an analogous method.

**Biometric access controls**   Biometrics-based access controls are implemented using physical and logical controls. They are most expensive and most secure compared to other types of access control mechanisms.

**Biometric information**   The stored electronic information pertaining to a biometric. This information can be in terms of raw or compressed pixels or in terms of some characteristic (e.g., patterns).

**Biometric system**   An automated system capable of the following: (1) capturing a biometric sample from an end user, (21) extracting biometric data from that sample, (3) comparing the extracted biometric data with data contained in one or more references, (4) deciding how well they match, and (5) indicating whether or not an identification or verification of identity has been achieved.

**Biometric template**   A characteristic of biometric information (e.g., minutiae or patterns).

**Biometrics**   (1) Automated recognition of individuals based on their behavioral and biological characteristics. (2) A physical or behavioral characteristic of a human being. (3) A measurable, physical characteristic or personal behavioral trait used to recognize the identity, or verify the claimed identity, of an applicant. Facial patterns, fingerprints, eye retinas and irises, voice patterns, and hand measurements are all examples of biometrics. (4) Biometrics may be used to unlock authentication tokens and prevent repudiation of registration.

**Birthday attack**   An attack against message digest 5 (MD5), a hash function. The attack is based on probabilities of two messages that hash to the same value (collision) and then exploit it to attack. The attacker is looking for "birthday" pairs—that is, two messages with the same hash values. This attack is not feasible given today's computer technology.

**Bit error ratio**   It is the number of erroneous bits divided by the total number of bits transmitted, received, or processed over some stipulated period in a telecommunications system.

**Bit string**   An ordered sequence of 0's and 1's. The leftmost bit is the most significant bit of the string. The rightmost bit is the least significant bit of the string.

**Black bag cryptanalysis**   A euphemism for the acquisition of cryptographic secrets via burglary, or the covert installation of keystroke logging or Trojan horse software on target computers or ancillary devices. Surveillance technicians can install bug concealed equipment to monitor the electromagnetic emissions of computer displays or keyboards from a distance of 20 or more meters and thereby decode what has been typed. It is not a mathematical or technical cryptanalytic attack, and the law enforcement authorities can use a sneak-and-peek search warrant on a keystroke logger (Wikipedia).

**Black box testing**   A test methodology that assumes no knowledge of the internal structure and implementation detail of the assessment object. It examines the software from the user's viewpoint and determines if the data are processed according to the specifications, and it does not consider implementation details. It verifies that software functions are performed correctly. It focuses on the external behavior of a system and uses the system's functional specifications to generate test cases. It ensures that the system does what it is supposed to do and does not do what it is not supposed to do. It is also known as generalized testing or functional testing, and should be combined with white box testing for maximum benefit because neither one by itself does a thorough testing job. Black box testing is functional analysis of a system. Basic testing is also known as black box testing.

**BLACK concept (encryption)**   It is a designation applied to encrypted data/information and the information systems, the associated areas, circuits, components, and equipment processing of that data and information. It is a separation of electrical and electronic circuits, components, equipment, and systems that handle unencrypted information (RED) in electrical form from those that handle encrypted information (BLACK) in the same form.

**Black core**   A communications network architecture in which user data traversing a core Internet Protocol (IP) network is end-to-end encrypted at the IP layer.

**Blackholing**   Blackholing occurs when traffic is sent to routers that drop some or all of the packets. Synonymous with blackhole.

**Blacklisting**   It is the process of the system invalidating a user ID based on the user's inappropriate actions. A blacklisted user ID cannot be used to log on to the system, even with the correct authenticator. Blacklisting also applies to (1) blocks placed against IP addresses to prevent inappropriate or unauthorized use of Internet resources, (2) blocks placed on domain names known to attempt brute force attacks, (3) a list of e-mail senders who have previously sent spam to a user, and (4) a list of discrete entities, such as hosts or applications, that have been previously determined to be associated with malicious activity. Placing blacklisting and lifting blacklisting are both security-relevant events. Web content filtering software uses blacklisting to prevent access to undesirable websites. Synonymous with blacklists.

**Blended attack**   (1) An instance of malware that uses multiple infection or transmission methods. (2) Malicious code that uses multiple methods to spread.

**Blinding**   Generating network traffic that is likely to trigger many alerts in a short period of time, to conceal alerts triggered by a "real" attack performed simultaneously.

**Block**   Sequence of binary bits that comprise the input, output, state, and round key. The length of a sequence is the number of bits it contains. Blocks are also interpreted as arrays of bytes. A block size is the number of bits in an input (or output) block of the block cipher.

**Block cipher algorithm**   (1) A symmetric key cryptographic algorithm that transforms a block of information at a time using a cryptographic key. (2) A family of functions and their inverse functions that is parameterized by a cryptographic key; the functions map bit strings of a fixed length to bit strings of the same length. The length of the input block is the same as the length of the output block. A bit string is an ordered sequence of 0's and 1's and a bit is a binary digit of 0 or 1.

**Block mirroring**   A method to provide backup, redundancy, and failover processes to ensure high-availability systems. Block mirroring is performed on an alternative site preferably separate from the primary site. Whenever a write is made to a block on a primary storage device at the primary site, the same write is made to an alternative storage device at the alternative site, either within the same storage system, or between separate storage systems, at different locations.

**Blue team**   A group of people responsible for defending an enterprise's use of information systems by maintaining its security posture against a group of mock attackers (i.e., the red team). The blue team must defend against real or simulated attacks.

**Bluetooth**   A wireless protocol developed as a cable replacement to allow two equipped devices to communicate with each other (e.g., a fax machine to a mobile telephone) within a short distance such as 30 feet. The Bluetooth system connects desktop computers to peripherals (e.g., printers and fax machines) without wires.

**Body of evidence**   The set of data that documents the information system's adherence to the security controls applied. When needed, this may be used in a court of law as external evidence.

**Bogon addresses**   Bogon (bogus) addresses refer to an IP address that is reserved but not yet allocated by the Internet registry. Attackers use these addresses to attack so bogon address filters must be updated constantly.

**Boot-sector virus**   A virus that plants itself in a system's boot sector and infects the master boot record (MBR) of a hard drive or the boot sector of a removable media. This boot sector is read as part of the system startup, and thus they are loaded into memory when the computer first boots up. When in memory, a boot-sector virus can infect any hard disk or floppy accessed by the user. With the advent of more modern operating systems and a great reduction in users sharing floppies, there has been a major reduction in this type of virus. These viruses are now relatively uncommon.

**Border Gateway Protocol (BGP)**   An Internet routing protocol used to pass routing information between different administrative domains.

**Border Gateway Protocol (BGP) flapping**   A situation in which BGP sessions are repeatedly dropped and restarted, normally as a result of line or router problems.

**Border Gateway Protocol (BGP) peer**   A router running the BGP protocol that has an established BGP session active.

**Border Gateway Protocol (BGP) session**   A Transmission Control Protocol (TCP) session in which both ends are operating BGP and have successfully processed an OPEN message from the other end.

**Border Gateway Protocol (BGP) speaker**   Any router running the BGP protocol.

**Border router**   Border router is placed at the network perimeter. It can act as a basic firewall.

**Botnet**   Botnet is a jargon term for a collection of software robots, or bots, which run autonomously. A botnet's originator can control the group remotely, usually through a means such as Internet relay chat (IRC), and usually for nefarious purposes. A botnet can comprise a collection of cracked machines running programs (usually referred to as worms, Trojan horses, or backdoors) under a common command and control infrastructure. Botnets are often used to send spam e-mails, launch DoS attacks, phishing attacks, and viruses.

**Bound metadata**   Metadata associated with a cryptographic key and protected by the cryptographic key management system against unauthorized modification and disclosure. It uses a binding operation that links two or more data elements such that the data elements cannot be modified or replaced without being detected.

**Boundary**   A physical or logical perimeter of a system.

**Boundary protection**   Monitoring and control of communications (1) at the external boundary between information systems completely under the management and control of the organization and information systems not completely under the management and control of the organization, and (2) at key internal boundaries between information systems completely under the management and control of the organization.

Boundary protection employs managed interfaces and boundary protection devices.

**Boundary protection device**   A device with appropriate mechanisms that (1) facilitates the adjudication of different interconnected system security policies (e.g., controlling the flow of information into or out of an interconnected system); and/or (2) monitors and controls communications at the external boundary of an information system to prevent and detect malicious and other unauthorized communications. Boundary protection devices include such components as proxies, gateways, routers, firewalls, hardware/software guards, and encrypted tunnels.

**Boundary router**   A boundary router is located at the organization's boundary to an external network. A boundary router is configured to be a packet filter firewall.

**Boundary value analysis**   The purpose of boundary value analysis is to detect and remove errors occurring at parameter limits or boundaries. Tests for an application program should cover the boundaries and extremes of the input classes.

**Breach**   The successful and repeatable defeat (circumvention) of security controls with or without detection or an arrest, which if carried to completion, could result in a penetration of the system. Examples of breaches are (1) operation of user code in master mode, (2) unauthorized acquisition of identification password or file access passwords, (3) accessing a file without using prescribed operating system mechanisms, and (4) unauthorized access to data/program library. Attack + Breach = Penetration.

**Bridge**   A device used to link two or more homogeneous local-area networks (LANs). A bridge does not change the contents of the frame being transmitted but acts as a relay. It is a device that connects similar LANs together to form an extended LAN. It is protocol-dependent. Bridges and switches are used to interconnect different LANs. A bridge operates in the data link layer of the ISO/OSI reference model.

**Brokered trust**   Describes the case where two entities do not have direct business agreements with each other, but do have agreements with one or more intermediaries so as to enable a business trust path to be constructed between the entities. The intermediary brokers operate as active entities, and are invoked dynamically via protocol facilities when new paths are to be established.

**Brooke's law**   States that adding more people to a late project makes the project even more delayed.

**Brouters**   Routers that can also bridge, route one or more protocols, and bridge all other network traffic. Brouters = Routers + Bridges.

**Browser**   A client program used to interact on the World Wide Web (WWW).

**Browser-based threats** Examples include (1) masquerading attacks resulting from untrusted code that was accepted and executed code that was developed elsewhere, (2) gaining unauthorized access to computational resources residing at the browser (e.g., security options) or its underlying platform (e.g., system registry), and (3) using authorized access based on the user's identity in an unexpected and disruptive fashion (e.g., to invade privacy or deny service).

**Browsing** The act of searching through storage to locate or acquire information without necessarily knowing the existence or the format of the information being sought.

**Brute force attack** A form of guessing attack in which the attacker uses all possible combinations of characters from a given character set and for passwords up to a given length. A form of brute force attack is username harvesting, where applications differentiate between an invalid password and an invalid username, which allows attackers to construct a list of valid user accounts. Countermeasures against brute force attacks include strong authentication with SSL/TLS, timeouts with delays, lock-outs of user accounts, password policy with certain length and mix of characters, blacklists of IP addresses and domain names, and logging of invalid password attempts.

**Bucket brigade attack** A type of attack that takes advantage of the store-and-forward mechanism used by insecure networks such as the Internet. It is similar to the man-in-the middle attack.

**Buffer** An area of random access memory or CPU used to temporarily store data from a disk, communication port, program, or peripheral device.

**Buffer overflow attack** (1) A method of overloading a predefined amount of space in a buffer, which can potentially overwrite and corrupt data in memory. (2) It is a condition at an interface under which more input can be placed into a buffer or data holding area than the capacity allocated, overwriting other information. Attackers exploit such a condition to crash a system or to insert specially crafted code that allows them to gain control of the system.

**Bus topology** A bus topology is a network topology in which all nodes (i.e., stations) are connected to a central cable (called the bus or backbone) and all stations are attached to a shared transmission medium. Note that linear bus topology is a variation of bus topology.

**Business continuity plan (BCP)** The documentation of a predetermined set of instructions or procedures that describe how an organization's business functions will be sustained during and after a significant disruption.

**Business impact analysis (BIA)** An analysis of an IT system's requirements, processes, and interdependencies used to characterize system contingency requirements and priorities in the event of a significant disruption.

**Business process improvement (BPI)** It focuses on how to improve an existing process or service. BPI is also called continuous process improvement.

**Business process reengineering (BPR)** It focuses on improving efficiency, reducing costs, reducing risks, and improving service to internal and external customers. Radical change is an integral part of BPR.

**Business recovery/resumption plan (BRP)** The documentation of a predetermined set of instructions or procedures that describe how business processes will be restored after a significant disruption has occurred.

**Business rules processor**   The sub-component of a service-oriented architecture (SOA) that manages and executes the set of complex business rules that represent the core business activity supported by the component.

**Bypass capability**   The ability of a service to partially or wholly circumvent encryption or cryptographic authentication.

# C

**C2C**   Consumer-to-consumer (C2C) is an electronic commerce model involving consumers selling directly to consumers (e.g., eBay).

**Cache attack**   Computer processors are equipped with a cache memory, which decreases the memory access latency. First, the processor looks for the data in cache and then in the memory. When the data is not where the processor is expecting, a cache-miss occurs. The cache-miss attacks enable an unprivileged process to attack other processes running in parallel on the same processor, despite partitioning methods used (for example, memory protection, sandboxing, and virtualization techniques). Attackers use the cache-miss situation to attack weak symmetric encryption algorithms (for example, DES). AES is stronger than DES, and the former should be used during the execution of a processor on a known plaintext.

**Callback**   Procedure for identifying and authenticating a remote information system terminal, whereby the host system disconnects the terminal and reestablishes the contact.

**Campus-area network (CAN)**   An interconnected set of local-area networks (LANs) in a limited geographical area such as a college campus or a corporate campus.

**Capability list**   A list attached to a subject ID specifying what accesses are allowed to the subject.

**Capability maturity model (CMM)**   CMM is a five-stage model of how software organizations improve, over time, in their ability to develop software. Knowledge of the CMM provides a basis for assessment, comparison, and process improvement. The Carnegie Mellon Software Engineering Institute (SEI) has developed the CMM.

**Capture**   The method of taking a biometric sample from an end user.

**Capturing (password)**   The act of an attacker acquiring a password from storage, transmission, or user knowledge and behavior.

**Cardholder**   An individual possessing an issued personal identity verification (PIV) card.

**Carrier sense multiple access (CSMA) protocols**   Carrier sense multiple access (CSMA) protocols listen to the channel for a transmitting carrier and act accordingly. If the channel is busy, the station waits until it becomes idle. When the station detects an idle channel, it transmits a frame. If collision occurs, the station waits a random amount of time and starts all over again. The goal is to avoid a collision or detect a collision (CSMA/CA and CSMA/CD). The CSMA/CD is used on LANs in the MAC sublayer, and it is the basis of Ethernet.

**CERT/CC**   See computer emergency response team coordination center (CERT/CC)

**Certificate** (1) A set of data that uniquely identifies a key pair and an owner that is authorized to use the key pair. The certificate contains the owner's public key and possibly other information, and is digitally signed by a Certification Authority (i.e., a trusted party), thereby binding the public key to the owner. Additional information in the certificate could specify how the key is used and its crypto-period. (2) A digital representation of information which at least (i) identifies the certification authority issuing it, (ii) names or identifies its subscriber, (iii) contains the subscriber's public key, (iv) identifies its operational period, and (v) is digitally signed by the certification authority issuing it.

**Certificate management protocol (CMP)** Both certification authority (CA) and registration authority (RA) software supports the use of certificate management protocol (CMP).

**Certificate policy (CP)** A certificate policy is a specialized form of administrative policy tuned to electronic transactions performed during certificate management. A CP addresses all aspects associated with the generation, production, distribution, accounting, compromise recovery, and administration of digital certificates. Indirectly, a CP can also govern the transactions conducted using a communications system protected by a certificate-based security system. By controlling critical certificate extensions, such policies and associated enforcement technology can support provision of the security services required by particular applications.

**Certificate-related information** Information such as a subscriber's postal address that is not included in a certificate. May be used by a certification authority (CA) managing certificates.

**Certificate revocation list (CRL)** A list of revoked but unexpired public key certificates created and digitally signed or issued by a certification authority (CA).

**Certificate status authority** A trusted entity that provides online verification to a relying party of a subject certificate's trustworthiness, and may also provide additional attribute information for the subject certificate.

**Certification** Certification is a comprehensive assessment of the management, operational, and technical security controls in an information system, made in support of security accreditation, to determine the extent to which the controls are implemented correctly, operating as intended, and producing the desired outcome with respect to meeting the security requirements for the system.

**Certification and accreditation (C&A)** *Certification* is a comprehensive assessment of the management, operational, and technical security controls in an information system, made in support of security accreditation, to determine the extent to which the controls are implemented correctly, operating as intended, and producing the desired outcome with respect to meeting the security requirements for the system.

*Accreditation* is the official management decision given by a senior officer to authorize operation of an information system and to explicitly accept the risk to organization operations (including mission, functions, image, or reputation), organization assets, or individuals, based on the implementation of an agreed-upon set of security controls. It is the administrative act of approving a computer system for use in a particular application. It is a statement that specifies the extent to which the security measures meet specifications. It does not imply a guarantee that the described system is impenetrable. It is an input to the security approval process. This is a management and preventive control.

**Certification agent** The individual group or organization responsible for conducting a security certification.

**Certification authority (CA)**   (1) The entity in a public key infrastructure (PKI) that is responsible for issuing certificates and exacting compliance with a PKI policy. (2) A trusted entity that issues and revokes public key certificates to end entities and other CAs. CAs issue certificate revocation lists (CRLs) periodically, and post certificates and CRLs to a repository.

**Certification authority facility**   The collection of equipment, personnel, procedures, and buildings (offices) that are used by a CA to perform certificate issuance and revocation.

**Certification practice statement (CPS)**   A formal statement of the practices that certification authority (CA) employs in issuing, suspending, revoking, and renewing certificates and providing access to them, in accordance with specific requirements (i.e., requirements specified in the certificate policy, or requirements specified in a contract for services).

**Chain-in-depth**   The market analysis in the supply chain strategy to identify alternative integrators/suppliers (level 1), the suppliers of the integrators/suppliers (level 2), or the suppliers of the suppliers of the integrators/suppliers (level 3), and other deep levels, thus providing a supply chain-in-depth analysis.

**Chain of custody**   A process that tracks the movement of evidence through its collection, safeguarding, and analysis life cycle by documenting each person who handled the evidence, the date/time it was collected or transferred, and the purpose for the transfer.

**Chain of evidence**   A process of recording that shows who obtained the evidence, where and when the evidence was obtained, who secured the evidence, where it was stored, and who had control or possession of the evidence. The chain of evidence ties to the rules of evidence and the chain of custody.

**Chain of trust**   A chain of trust requires that the organization establish and retain a level of confidence that each participating external service provider in the potentially complex consumer-provider relationship provides adequate protection for the services rendered to the organization.

**Chained checksum**   A checksum technique in which the hashing function is a function of data content and previous checksum values.

**Challenge handshake authentication protocol (CHAP)**   An authentication mechanism for point-to-point protocol (PPP) connections that encrypt the user's password. It uses a three-way handshake between the client and the server.

**Challenge-response**   An authentication procedure that requires calculating a correct response to an unpredictable challenge.

**Challenge-response protocol**   An authentication protocol where the verifier sends the claimant a challenge (usually a random value or a nonce) that the claimant combines with a shared secret (often by hashing the challenge and secret together) to generate a response that is sent to the verifier. The verifier knows the shared secret and can independently compute the response and compare it with the response generated by the claimant. If the two are the same, the claimant is considered to have successfully authenticated himself. When the shared secret is a cryptographic key, such protocols are generally secure against eavesdroppers. When the shared secret is a password, an eavesdropper does not directly intercept the password itself, but the eavesdropper may be able to find the password with an offline password guessing attack.

**Channel scanning**   Changing the channel being monitored by a wireless intrusion detection and prevention system.

**Chatterbots**   Bots that can talk (chat) using animation characters.

**Check-digit**   A check-digit calculation helps ensure that the primary key or data is entered correctly. This is a technical and detective control.

**Check-point**   Restore procedures are needed before, during, or after completion of certain transactions or events to ensure acceptable fault-recovery.

**Checksum**   A value automatically computed on data to detect error or manipulation during transmission. It is an error-checking technique to ensure the accuracy of data transmission. The number of bits in a data unit is summed and transmitted along with the data. The receiving computer then checks the sum and compares. Digits or bits are summed according to arbitrary rules and used to verify the integrity of data (that is, changes to data). This is a technical and detective control.

**Chief information officer (CIO)**   A senior official responsible for (1) providing advice and other assistance to the head of the organization and other senior management personnel of the organization to ensure that information technology is acquired and information resources are managed in a manner that is consistent with laws, executive orders, directives, policies, regulations, and priorities established by the head of the organization; (2) developing, maintaining, and facilitating the implementation of a sound and integrated information technology architecture for the organization; and (3) promoting the effective and efficient design and operation of all major information resources management processes for the organization, including improvements to work processes of the organization.

**Chokepoint**   A chokepoint creates a bottleneck in a system, whether the system is a social, natural, civil, military, or computer system. For example, the installation of a firewall in a computer system between a local network and the Internet creates a chokepoint and makes it difficult for an attacker to come through that network channel. In graph theory and network analysis, a chokepoint is any node in a network with a high centrality (Wikipedia).

**Cipher**   (1) A series of transformations that converts plaintext to ciphertext using the cipher key. (2) A cipher block chaining-message authentication code (CBC-MAC) algorithm. (3) A secret-key block-cipher algorithm used to encrypt data and to generate a MAC to provide assurance that the payload and the associated data are authentic.

**Cipher key**   Secret, cryptographic key that is used by the Key Expansion Routine to generate a set of Round Keys; can be pictured as a rectangular array of bytes, having four rows and NK columns.

**Cipher suite**   Negotiated algorithm identifiers, which are understandable in human readable form using a pneumonic code.

**Ciphertext**   (1) Data output from the cipher or input to the inverse cipher. (2) The result of transforming plaintext with an encryption algorithm. (3) It is the encrypted form of a plaintext message of data. Also known as crypto-text or enciphered information.

**Circuit-level gateway firewall**   A type of firewall that can be used either as a stand-alone or specialized function performed by an application-level gateway. It does not permit an end-to-end Transmission Control Protocol (TCP) connection. This firewall can be configured to support application-level service on inbound connections and circuit-level functions for outbound connections. It incurs overhead when examining the incoming application data for forbidden functions but does not incur that overhead on outgoing data.

**Civil law**   Law that deals with suits for breach of contract or tort cases, such as suits for personal injuries.

**Claimant**   (1) A party whose identity is to be verified using an authentication protocol. (2) An entity which is or which represents a principal for the purposes of authentication, together with the functions involved in an authentication exchange on behalf of that entity. (3) A claimant acting on behalf of a principal must include the functions necessary for engaging in an authentication exchange (e.g., a smart card (claimant) can act on behalf of a human user (principal)).

**Claimed signatory**   From the verifier's perspective, the claimed signatory is the entity that purportedly generated a digital signature.

**Class**   (1) A set of objects that share a common structure and a common behavior. (2) A generic description of an object type consisting of instance variables and method definitions. Class definitions are templates from which individual objects can be created.

**Class hierarchy**   Classes can naturally be organized into structures (tree or network) called class hierarchies. In a hierarchy, a class may have zero or more superclasses above it in the hierarchy. A class may have zero or more classes below, referred to as its subclasses.

**Class object**   A class definition. Class definitions are objects that are instances of a generic class, or metaclass.

**Classification**   A determination that information requires a specific degree of protection against unauthorized disclosure together with a designation signifying that such a determination has been made.

**Classification level**   It is the security level of an object.

**Classified information**   Information that has been determined to require protection against unauthorized disclosure and is marked to indicate its classified status when in documentary form.

**CleanRoom development approach**   A radical departure from the traditional waterfall software development approach. The entire team of designers, programmers, testers, documenters, and customers is involved throughout the system development lifecycle. The project team reviews the programming code as it develops it, and the code is certified incrementally. There is no need for unit testing due to code certification, but the system testing and integration testing are still needed.

**Clearance level**   It is the security level of a subject.

**Clearing**   The overwriting of classified information on magnetic media such that the media may be reused. This does not lower the classification level of the media. Note: Volatile memory can be cleared by removing power to the unit for a minimum of 1 minute.

**Click fraud**   Deceptions and scams that inflate advertising bills with improper charge per click in an online advertisement on the Web.

**Client (application)**   A system entity, usually a computer process acting on behalf of a human user that makes use of a service provided by a server.

**Client/server architecture**   An architecture consisting of server programs that await and fulfill requests from client programs on the same or another computer.

**Client/server authentication**   The secure sockets layer (SSL) and transport layer security (TLS) provide client and server authentication and encryption of Web communications.

**Client/server model**   The client-server model states that a client (user), whether a person or a computer program, may access authorized services from a server (host) connected anywhere on the distributed computer system. The services provided include database access, data transport, data processing, printing, graphics, electronic mail, word processing, or any other service available on the system. These services may be provided by a remote mainframe using long-haul communications or within the user's workstation in real-time or delayed (batch) transaction mode. Such an open access model is required to permit true horizontal and vertical integration.

**Client-side scripts**   The client-side scripts such as JavaScript, JavaApplets, and Active-X controls are used to generate dynamic Web pages.

**Cloning**   The practice of re-programming a phone with a mobile identification number and an electronic serial number pair from another phone.

**Close-in attacks**   They consist of a regular type of individual attaining close physical proximity to networks, systems, or facilities for the purpose of modifying, gathering, or denying access to information. Close physical proximity is achieved through surreptitious entry, open access, or both.

**Closed-circuit television**   Closed-circuit television (CCTV) can be used to record the movement of people in and out of the data center or other sensitive work areas. The film taken by the CCTV can be used as evidence in legal investigations.

**Closed security environment**   Refers to an environment providing sufficient assurance that applications and equipment are protected against the introduction of malicious logic during an information system life cycle. Closed security is based upon a system's developers, operators, and maintenance personnel having sufficient clearances, authorization, and configuration control.

**Cloud computing**   It is a model for enabling ubiquitous, convenient, on-demand network access to a shared pool of configurable computing resources (e.g., networks, servers, storage, applications, and services) that can be rapidly provisioned and released with minimal management effort or service provider interaction. This cloud model promotes availability and is composed of five essential characteristics (i.e., on-demand self-service, broad network access, resource pooling, rapid elasticity, and measured service), three service models (i.e., cloud software as a service, cloud platform as a service, and cloud infrastructure as a service), and four deployment models (i.e., private cloud, community cloud, public cloud, and hybrid cloud).

**Cluster computing**   The use of failover clusters to provide high availability of computing services. Failover means the system detects hardware/software faults and immediately restarts the application on another system without requiring human intervention. It uses redundant computers or nodes and configures the nodes before starting the application on it. A minimum of two nodes is required to provide redundancy but in reality it uses more than two nodes. Variations in node configurations include active/active (good for software configuration), active/passive (good for hardware configuration), N+1 (good for software configuration), N+M (where M is more than one standby servers), and N-to-N (where clusters redistribute the services from the failed node to the active node, thus eliminating the need for a standby node). Cluster computing is often used for critical databases, file sharing on a network, high-performance systems, and electronic commerce websites. An advantage of cluster computing is that it uses a heartbeat private network connection to monitor the health and status of each node in the cluster. Disadvantages include (1) split-brain situation where all the private links can go down simultaneously, but the cluster nodes are still working, and (2) data corruption on the shared storage due to duplicate services (Wikipedia).

**Coaxial cable**   It is a thin cable similar to the one used in cable television connection. A coaxial cable has a solid copper wire, an inner insulation covering this core, a braided metallic ground shield, and an outer insulation.

**Code division multiple access (CDMA)**   A spread spectrum technology for cellular networks based on the Interim Standard-95 (IS-95) from the Telecommunications Industry Association (TIA).

**Codebook attack**   A type of attack where the intruder attempts to create a codebook of all possible transformations between plaintext and ciphertext under a single key.

**Coder decoder (CODEC)**   Coverts analog voice into digital data and back again. It may also compress and decompress the data for more efficient transmission. It is used in plain old telephone service (POTS).

**Cohesion**   A measure of the strength of association of the elements within a program module; the modularity is greater for higher strength modules. The best level of cohesion is functional (high-strength) and the worst level of cohesion is coincidental (low-strength). In functional cohesion, all components contribute to the one single function of a module. In coincidental cohesion, components are grouped by accident, not by plan. A higher (strong) cohesion value is better. Interfaces exhibiting strong cohesion and weak coupling are less error prone. If various modules exhibit strong internal cohesion, the inter-module coupling tends to be minimal, and vice versa.

**Cold-site**   A backup facility that has the necessary electrical and physical components of a computer facility, but does not have the computer equipment in place. The site is ready to receive the necessary replacement computer equipment in the event that the user has to move from their main computing location to an alternate site.

**Collision**   A condition in which two data packets are transmitted over a medium at the same time from two or more stations. Two or more distinct inputs produce the same output.

**Collision detection**   When a collision is detected, the message is retransmitted after a random interval.

**Commercial software**   Software available through lease or purchase in the commercial market from an organization representing itself to have ownership of marketing rights in the software.

**Common criteria (CC)**   The Common Criteria represents the outcome of a series of efforts to develop criteria for evaluation of IT security that is broadly useful within the international community. It is a catalog of security functionality and assurance requirements.

**Common data security architecture (CDSA)**   It is a set of layered security services that address communications and data security problems in the emerging Internet and Intranet application space. CDSA focuses on security in peer-to-peer (P2P) distributed systems with homogeneous and heterogeneous platform environments, and applies to the components of a client/server application. CDSA supports existing, secure protocols, such as SSL, S/MIME, and SET.

**Common gateway interface (CGI) scripts**   These are insecure programs that allow the Web server to execute an external program when particular URLs are accessed.

**Common law (case law)**   Law based on preceding cases.

**Common security control**   A security control that is inherited by one or more organization's information systems and has the following properties (1) the development, implementation, and assessment of the control can be assigned to a responsible official or organizational element (other than the information system owner); and (2) the results from the assessment of the control can be used to support the security certification and accreditation processes of an organization's information system where that control has been applied.

**Common vulnerabilities and exposures (CVE)**   A dictionary of common names for publicly known IT system vulnerabilities.

**Communications protocol**   A set of rules or standards designed to enable computers to connect with one another and to exchange information with as little error as possible.

**Communications security**   It defines measures that are taken to deny unauthorized persons information derived from telecommunications facilities.

**Comparison**   The process of comparing a biometric with a previously stored reference template or templates.

**Compartmentalization**   The isolation of the operating system, user programs, and data files from one another in main storage in order to provide protection against unauthorized or concurrent access by other users or programs. This term also refers to the division of sensitive data into small, isolated blocks for the purpose of reducing risk to the data.

**Compensating control (general)**   A concept that states that the total environment should be considered when determining whether a specific policy, procedure, or control is violated or a specific risk is present. If controls in one area are weak, they should be compensated or mitigated for in another area. Some examples of compensating controls are: strict personnel hiring procedures, bonding employees, information system risk insurance, increased supervision, rotation of duties, review of computer logs, user sign-off procedures, mandatory vacations, batch controls, user review of input and output, system activity reconciliations, and system access security controls.

**Compensating security controls**   The management, operational, and technical controls (i.e., safeguards or countermeasures) employed by an organization in lieu of the recommended controls in the low, moderate, or high security baseline controls that provide equivalent or comparable protection for an information system. In other words, compensating controls are applied when baseline controls are not available, applicable, or cost-effective.

**Compiled virus**   A virus that has had its source code converted by a compiler program into a format that can be directly executed by an operating system.

**Compiler**   Software used to translate a program written in a high-level programming language (source code) into a machine language for execution and outputs into a complete binary object code. The availability of diagnostic aids, compatibility with the operating system, and the difficulty of implementation are the most important factors to consider when selecting a compiler.

**Complementary control**   A complementary control can enhance the effectiveness of two or more controls when applied to a function, program, or operation. Here, two controls working together can strengthen the overall control environment.

**Complete mediation**   The principle of complete mediation stresses that every access request to every object must be checked for authority. This requirement forces a global perspective for access control, during all functional phases (e.g., normal operation and maintenance). Also stressed are reliable identification access request sources and reliable maintenance of changes in authority.

**Completeness**   The degree to which all of the software's required functions and design constraints are present and fully developed in the software requirements, software design, and code.

**Compliance**   An activity of verifying that both manual and computer processing of transactions or events are in accordance with the organization's policies and procedures, generally accepted security principles, governmental laws, and regulatory agency rules and requirements.

**Compliance review**   A review and examination of records, procedures, and review activities at a site in order to assess the unclassified computer security posture and to ensure compliance with established, explicit criteria.

**Comprehensive testing**   A test methodology that assumes explicit and substantial knowledge of the internal structure and implementation detail of the assessment object. Comprehensive testing is also known as white box testing.

**Compression**   The process of reducing the number of bits required to represent some information, usually to reduce the time or cost of storing or transmitting it.

**Compromise**   The unauthorized disclosure, modification, substitution, or use of sensitive data (including keys, key metadata, and other security-related information) and loss of, or unauthorized intrusion into, an entity containing sensitive data and the conversion of a trusted entity to an adversary.

**Compromise recording**   Records and logs should be maintained so that if a compromise does occur, evidence of the attack is available to the organization in identifying and prosecuting attackers.

**Compromised state**   A cryptographic key life cycle state in which a key is designated as compromised and not used to apply cryptographic protection to data. Under certain circumstances, the key may be used to process already protected data.

**Computer crime**   Fraud, embezzlement, unauthorized access, and other "white collar" crimes committed with the aid of or directly involving a computer system and/or network.

**Computer emergency response team coordination center (CERT/CC)**   CERT/CC focuses on Internet security vulnerabilities, provides incident response services to websites that have been the victims of attack, publish security alerts, research security and survivability in wide-area-networked computing environments, and develops website security information. It issues security advisories, helps start incident response teams for user organizations, coordinates the efforts of teams when responding to large-scale incidents, provides training to incident handling staff, and researches the causes of security vulnerabilities.

**Computer facility**   Physical resources that include structures or parts of structures to house and support capabilities. For small computers, stand-alone systems, and word processing equipment, it is the physical area where the computer is used.

**Computer forensic process life cycle**   A computer forensic process life cycle consisting of four basic phases: collection, examination, analysis, and reporting.

**Computer forensics**   The practice of gathering, retaining, and analyzing computer-related data for investigative purposes in a manner that maintains the integrity of the data.

**Computer fraud**   Computer-related crimes involving deliberate misrepresentation, alteration, or disclosure of data in order to obtain something of value (usually for monetary gain). A computer system must have been involved in the perpetration or cover-up of the act or series of acts. A computer system might have been involved through improper manipulation of input data; output or results; applications programs; data files; computer operations; communications; or computer hardware, systems software, or firmware.

**Computer network**   A complex consisting of two or more interconnected computers.

**Computer security**   Measures and controls that ensure confidentiality, integrity, and availability of IT assets, including hardware, software, firmware, and information being processed, stored, and communicated.

**Computer security incident**   A violation or imminent threat of violation of computer security policies, acceptable use policies, or standard computer security practices.

**Computer security incident response team (CSIRT)**   A capability set up for the purpose of assisting in responding to computer security-related incidents; also called a computer incident response team (CIRT), a computer incident response center (CIRC), or a computer incident response capability (CIRC).

**Computer virus**   A computer virus is similar to a Trojan horse because it is a program that contains hidden code, which usually performs some unwanted function as a side effect. The main difference between a virus and a Trojan horse is that the hidden code in a computer virus can only replicate by attaching a copy of itself to other programs and may also include an additional "payload" that triggers when specific conditions are met.

**Concentrators**   Concentrators gather together several lines in one central location, and are the foundation of a FDDI network and are attached directly to the FDDI dual ring.

**Concept of operations**   It is a computer operations plan consisting of only one document, where it will describes the scope of entire operational activities.

**Confidentiality**   (1) Preserving authorized restrictions on information access and disclosure, including means for protecting personal privacy and proprietary information. (2) It is the property that sensitive information is not disclosed to unauthorized individuals, entities, devices, or processes. (3) The secrecy of data that is transmitted in the clear. (4) Confidentiality covers data in storage, during processing, and in transit.

**Confidentiality mode**   A mode that is used to encipher plaintext and decipher ciphertext. The confidentiality modes include electronic codebook (ECB), cipher block chaining (CBC), cipher feedback (CFB), output feedback (OFB), and counter (CTR) modes.

**Configuration**   The relative or functional arrangement of components in a system.

**Configuration accounting**   The recording and reporting of configuration item descriptions and all departures from the baseline during design and production.

**Configuration auditing**   An independent review of computer software for the purpose of assessing compliance with established requirements, standards, and baseline.

**Configuration control**   The process for controlling modifications to hardware, firmware, software, and documentation to ensure that an information system is protected against improper modifications before, during, and after system implementation.

**Configuration control board**   An established committee that is the final authority on all proposed changes to the computer system.

**Configuration identification**   The identifying of the system configuration throughout the design, development, test, and production tasks.

**Configuration item**   (1) The smallest component of hardware, software, firmware, documentation, or any of its discrete portions, which is tracked by the configuration management system. (2) A collection of hardware or computer programs or any of its discrete portions that satisfies an end-user function.

**Configuration management**   (1) The management of security features and assurances through control of changes made to a system's hardware, software, firmware, documentation, test cases, test fixtures, and test documentation throughout the development and operational life of the system. (2) The process of controlling the software and documentation so they remain consistent as they are developed or changed. (3) A procedure for applying technical and administrative direction and surveillance to (i) identify and document the functional and physical characteristics of an item or system, (ii) control any changes to such characteristics, and (iii) record and report the change, process, and implementation status. The configuration management process must be carefully tailored to the capacity, size, scope, phase of the life cycle, maturity, and complexity of the system involved. Compare with configuration control.

**Conformance testing**   Conformance testing is a testing to determine if a product satisfies the criteria specified in a controlling standard document (e.g., RFC and ISO).

**Congestion**   Occurs when an additional demand for service occurs in a network switch and when more subscribers attempt simultaneously to access the switch more than the switch can handle. Two types of congestion can take place: (1) network congestion, which is an undesirable overload condition caused by traffic in excess of its capacity to handle, and (2) reception congestion, which occurs at a data switching exchange place.

**Connectionless mode**   A service that has a single phase involving control mechanisms, such as addressing in addition to data transfer.

**Connection-oriented mode**   A service that has three distinct phases: establishment, in which two or more users are bound to a connection; data transfer, in which data are exchanged between the users; and release, in which binding is terminated.

**Connectivity tree**   Routers use the connectivity tree to track Internet group management protocol (IGMP) status and activity.

**Connectors**    A connector is an electro-mechanical device on the ends of cables that permit them to be connected with, and disconnected from, other cables.

**Console**    (1) A program that provides user and administrator interfaces to an intrusion detection and prevention system. (2) A terminal used by system and network administrators to issue system commands and to watch the operating system activities.

**Consumer device**    A small, usually mobile computer that does not run a standard PC-OS. Examples of consumer devices are networking-capable personal digital assistants (PDAs), cell phones, and video game systems.

**Contamination**    The intermixing of data at different sensitivity and need-to-know levels. The lower level data are said to be contaminated by the higher level data; thus, the contaminating (higher level) data may not receive the required level of protection.

**Content delivery networks (CDNs)**    Content delivery networks (CDNs) are used to deliver the contents of music, movies, games, and news providers from their websites to end users quickly with the use of tools and techniques such as caching, replication, redirection, and a proxy content server to enhance the Web performance in terms of optimizing the disk size and preload time.

**Content filtering**    The process of monitoring communications such as e-mail and Web pages, analyzing them for suspicious content, and preventing the delivery of suspicious content to users.

**Contingency plan**    Management policy and procedures designed to maintain or restore business operations, including computer operations, possibly at an alternate location, in the event of emergencies, system failures, or disaster. Also called disaster recovery plan, business resumption plan, or business continuity plan. This is a management and recovery control and ensures the availability goal.

**Continuity of operations plan**    A predetermined set of instructions or procedures that describe how an organization's essential functions will be sustained for up to 30 days as a result of a disaster event before returning to normal operations.

**Continuity of support plan**    The documentation of a predetermined set of instructions or procedures that describe how to sustain major applications and general support systems in the event of a significant disruption.

**Contradictory controls**    Two or more controls are in conflict with each other. Installation of one control does not fit well with the other controls due to incompatibility. This means that implementation of one control can affect other, related controls negatively. Examples include (1) installation of a new software patch that can undo or break another related, existing software patch either in the same system or other related systems. This incompatibility can be due to errors in the current patch or previous patch or that the new patches and the previous patches were not fully tested either by the software vendor or by the user organization and (2) telecommuting work and organization's software piracy policies could be in conflict with each other if noncompliant telecommuters implement such policies improperly and in an unauthorized manner when they purchase and load unauthorized software on the home/work PC.

**Control**    Any protective action, device, procedure, technique, or other measure that reduces exposure. Controls can prevent, detect, or correct errors, and can minimize harm or loss. It is any action taken by management to enhance the likelihood that established objectives and goals will be achieved.

**Control frameworks**   These provide overall guidance to user organizations as a frame of reference for security governance and for implementation of security-related controls. Several organizations within the U.S. and outside the U.S. provide such guidance.

Developed and promoted by the IT Governance Institute (ITGI), Control Objectives for Information and related Technology (COBIT) starts from the premise that IT must deliver the information that the enterprise needs to achieve its objectives. In addition to promoting process focus and process ownership, COBIT looks at the fiduciary, quality, and security needs of enterprises and provides seven information criteria that can be used to generally define what the business requires from IT: effectiveness, efficiency, availability, integrity, confidentiality, reliability, and compliance.

The Information Security Forum's (ISF's) Standard of Good Practice for Information Security is based on research and the practical experience of its members. The standard divides security into five component areas: security management, critical business applications, computer installations, networks, and system development.

Other U.S. organizations promoting information security governance include National Institute of Standards and Technology (NIST) and the Committee of Sponsoring Organizations (COSO) of the Treadway Commission.

Organizations outside the U.S. that are promoting information security governance include Organization for Economic Co-Operation and Development (OECD), European Union (EU), and International Organization for Standardization (ISO).

**Control information**   Information that is entered into a cryptographic module for the purposes of directing the operation of the module.

**Control zone**   Three-dimensional space (expressed in feet of radius) surrounding equipment that processes classified and/or sensitive information within which TEMPEST exploitation is considered not practical. It also means legal authorities can identify and remove a potential TEMPEST exploitation. Control zone deals with physical security over sensitive equipment containing sensitive information. It is synonymous with zone of control.

**Controlled access protection**   Consists of a minimum set of security functions that enforces access control on individual users and makes them accountable for their actions through login procedures, auditing of security-relevant events, and resource isolation.

**Controlled interface**   A boundary with a set of mechanisms that enforces the security policies and controls the flow of information between interconnected information systems. It also controls the flow of information into or out of an interconnected system. Controlled interfaces, along with managed interfaces, use boundary protection devices, such as proxies, gateways, routers, firewalls, hardware/software guards, and encrypted tunnels (e.g., routers protecting firewalls and application gateways residing on a protected demilitarized zone). These devices prevent and detect malicious and other unauthorized communications.

**Controllers (hardware)**   A controller is a hardware device that coordinates and manages the operation of one or more input/output devices, such as computer terminals, workstations, disks, and printers.

**Controlled access area**   Part or all of an environment where all types and aspects of an access are checked and controlled.

**Cookies (website)** (1) A small file that stores information for a website on a user's computer. (2) A piece of state information supplied by a Web server to a browser, in a response for a requested resource, for the browser to store temporarily and return to the server on any subsequent visits or requests. Cookies have two mandatory parameters such as name and value, and have four optional parameters such as expiration date, path, domain, and secure. Four types of cookies exist: persistent, session, tracking, and encrypted.

**Corrective controls** Actions taken to correct undesirable events and incidents that have occurred. Corrective controls are procedures to react to security incidents and to take remedial actions on a timely basis. Corrective controls require proper planning and preparation as they rely more on human judgment.

**Corrective maintenance** Changes to software necessitated by actual errors in a system.

**Correctness** The degree to which software or its components are free from faults and/or meet specified requirements and/or user needs. Correctness is not an absolute property of a system; rather it implies the mutual consistency of a specification and its implementation. The property of being consistent with a correctness criterion, such as a program being correct with respect to its system specification or a specification being consistent with its requirements.

**Correctness proof** A mathematical proof of consistency between a specification and its implementation. It may apply at the security model-to-formal specification level, at the formal specification-to-higher order language code level, at the compiler level, or at the hardware level. For example, if a system has a verified design and implementation, then its overall correctness rests with the correctness of the compiler and hardware. When a system is proved correct, it can be expected to perform as specified but not necessarily as anticipated if the specifications are incomplete or inappropriate. It is also known as proof of correctness.

**Cost-benefit** A criterion for comparing programs and alternatives when benefits can be valued in dollars. Also referred to as benefit/cost ratio, which is a function of equivalent benefits and equivalent costs.

**Cost-risk analysis** The assessment of the costs of potential risk of loss or compromise without data protection versus the cost of providing data protection.

**Countermeasures** Actions, devices, procedures, techniques, or other measures that reduce the vulnerability of an information system. Synonymous with security controls and safeguards.

**Coupling** Coupling is the manner and degree of interdependence between software modules. It is a measure of the degree to which modules share data. A high degree of coupling indicates a strong dependence among modules, which is not wanted. Data coupling is the best type of coupling, and content coupling is the worst. Data coupling is the sharing of data via parameter lists. With data coupling, only simple data is passed between modules. Similar to data cohesion, components cover an abstract data type. With content coupling, one module directly affects the working of another module as it occurs when a module changes another module's data or when control is passed from one module to the middle of another module. A lower (weak) coupling value is better. Interfaces exhibiting strong cohesion and weak coupling are less error prone. If various modules exhibit strong internal cohesion, the intermodule coupling tends to be minimal, and vice versa.

**Coverage attribute** An attribute associated with an assessment method that addresses the scope or breadth of the assessment objects included in the assessment (for example, types of objects to be assessed and the number of objects to be assessed by type). The values for the coverage attribute, hierarchically from less coverage to more coverage, are basic, focused, and comprehensive.

**Covert channel** A communications channel that allows two cooperating processes to transfer information in a manner that violates a security policy but without violating the access control.

**Covert storage channel** A covert channel that involves the direct or indirect writing of a storage location by one process and the direct or indirect reading of the storage location by another process. Covert storage channels typically involve a finite resource shared by two subjects at different security levels.

**Covert timing channel** A covert channel in which one process signals information to another by modulating its own use of system resources (e.g., CPU time) in such a way that this manipulation affects the real response time observed by the second process.

**Cracking (password)** The process of an attacker recovering cryptographic password hashes and using various analytical methods to attempt to identify a character string that will produce one of those hashes.

**Credential** An object that authoritatively binds an identity to a token possessed and controlled by a person. It is evidence attesting to one's right to credit or authority.

**Credentials service provider (CSP)** A trusted entity that issues or registers subscriber tokens and issues electronic credentials to subscribers. The CSP may encompass Registration Authorities (RA) and Verifiers that it operates. A CSP may be an independent third party or may issue credentials for its own use.

**Criminal law** Law covering all legal aspects of crime.

**Criteria** Definitions of properties and constraints to be met by system functionality and assurance.

**Critical security parameter** Security-related information (e.g., secret and private cryptographic keys, and authentication data such as passwords and PINs) whose disclosure or modification can compromise the security of a cryptographic module or the security of the information protected by the module.

**Criticality** A measure of how important the correct and uninterrupted functioning of the system is to the mission of a user organization. The degree to which the system performs critical processing. A system is critical if any of its requirements are critical.

**Criticality level** Refers to the (consequences of) incorrect behavior of a system. The more serious the expected direct and indirect effects of incorrect behavior, the higher the criticality level.

**Cross-certificate** A certificate used to establish a trust relationship between two Certification Authorities (CAs). In most cases, a relying party will want to process user certificates that were signed by issuers other than a CA in its trust list. To support this goal, CAs issue cross-certificates that bind another issuer's name to that issuer's public key. Cross-certificates are an assertion that a public key may be used to verify signatures on other certificates.

**Cross-domain solution** A form of controlled interface that provides the ability to manually and/or automatically access and/or transfer information between different security domains.

**Cross-site request forgery (CSRF)**   An attack in which a subscriber who is currently authenticated to a relying party and connected through a secure session, browsers to an attacker's website which causes the subscriber to unknowingly invoke unwanted actions at the relying party.

**Cross-site scripting (XSS)**   An attacker may use XML injection to perform the equivalent of a XSS, in which requesters of a valid Web service have their requests transparently rerouted to an attacker-controlled Web service that performs malicious operations.

**Cryptanalysis**   The operations performed in defeating cryptographic protection without an initial knowledge of the key employed in providing the protection.

**Cryptanalytic attacks**   Several attacks such as COA, KPA, CTA, CPA, ACPA, CCA, and ACCA are possible as follows.

➤ Ciphertext only attack (COA): An attacker has some ciphertext and he does not know the plaintext or the key. His goal is to find the corresponding plaintext. This is the most common attack and the easiest to defend because the attacker has the least amount of information (i.e., ciphertext only) to work with.

➤ Known plaintext attack (KPA): An attacker is able to match the ciphertext with the known plaintext and the encryption algorithm but does not know the key to decode the ciphertext. This attack is harder, but still common because the attacker tries to deduce the key based on the known plaintext. This attack is similar to brute force attack. The KPA works against data encryption standard (DES) in any of its four operating modes (i.e., ECB, CBC, CFB, and OFB) with the same complexity. DES with any number of rounds fewer than 16 could be broken with a known-plaintext attack more efficiently than by brute force attack.

➤ Chosen text attack (CTA): Less common in occurrence and includes four types of attacks such as CPA, ACPA, CCA, and ACCA.

➤ Chosen plaintext attack (CPA): The attacker knows the plaintext and the corresponding ciphertext and algorithm, but does not know the key. He has selected the plaintext together with its corresponding encrypted ciphertext generated with the secret key. This type of attack is harder but still possible. The CPA attack occurs when a private key is used to decrypt a message. The key is deduced to decrypt any new messages encrypted with the same key. A countermeasure is to use a one-way hash function. The CPA attack against DES occurs when bit-wise complement keys are used to encrypt the complement of the plaintext block into the complement of the ciphertext block. A solution is to not use the complement keys.

➤ Adaptive CPA attack (ACPA): A variation of the CPA attack where the selection of the plaintext is changed based on the previous attack results.

➤ Chosen ciphertext attack (CCA): The attacker selected the ciphertext together with its corresponding decrypted plaintext generated with the secret key.

➤ Adaptive CCA attack (ACCA): A variation of the CCA attack where the selection of the ciphertext is changed based on the previous attack results.

**Cryptographic algorithm**   A well-defined computational procedure that takes variable inputs, including a cryptographic key, and produces an output. The cryptographic algorithms can be implemented in either hardware for speed or software for flexibility.

**Cryptographic boundary**  An explicitly defined continuous perimeter that establishes the physical bounds of a cryptographic module and contains all the hardware, software, and/or firmware components of a cryptographic module.

**Cryptographic authentication**  The use of encryption-related techniques to provide authentication.

**Cryptographic checksum**  A checksum computed by an algorithm that provides a unique value for each possible data value of the object.

**Cryptographic function**  A set of mathematical procedures that provide various algorithms for key generation, random number generation, encryption, decryption, and message digesting.

**Cryptographic hash function**  A mathematical function that maps a bit string of arbitrary length to a fixed length bit string. The function satisfies the following properties: (1) it is computationally infeasible to find any input which maps to any pre-specified output (one-way) and (2) it is computationally infeasible to find any two distinct inputs that map to the same output (collision collision-resistant).

**Cryptographic key**  (1) A value used to control cryptographic operations, such as decryption, encryption, signature generation, or signature verification. (2) A parameter used in connection with a cryptographic algorithm that determines its operation in such a way that an entity with knowledge of the key can reproduce or reverse the operation, while an entity without knowledge of the key cannot. Seven examples include (i) the transformation of plaintext data into ciphertext data, (ii) the transformation of ciphertext data into plaintext data, (iii) the computation of a digital signature from data, (iv) the verification of a digital signature, (v) the computation of an authentication code from data, (vi) the verification of an authentication code from data and a received authentication code, and (vii) the computation of a shared secret that is used to derive keying material.

**Cryptographic key management system (CKMS)**  A set of components that is designed to protect, manage, and distribute cryptographic keys and bound metadata.

**Cryptographic module**  The set of hardware, software, firmware, or some combination thereof that implements approved security functions such as cryptographic logic or processes (including cryptographic algorithms and key generation) and is contained within the cryptographic boundary of the module.

**Cryptographic strength**  A measure of the expected number of operations required to defeat a cryptographic mechanism. This term is defined to mean that breaking or reversing an operation is at least as difficult computationally as finding the key of an 80-bit block cipher by key exhaustion that is it requires at least on the order of $2^{79}$ operations.

**Cryptographic token**  A token where the secret is a cryptographic key.

**Cryptography**  (1) The discipline that embodies the principles, means, and methods for the transformation of data in order to hide their semantic content, prevent their unauthorized use, or prevent their undetected modification. (2) The discipline that embodies principles, means, and methods for providing information security, including confidentiality, data integrity, non-repudiation, and authenticity.  (3) It creates a high degree of trust in the electronic world.

**Cryptology**  The field that encompasses both cryptography and cryptanalysis. The science that deals with hidden, disguised, or encrypted communications. It includes communications security and communications intelligence.

**Crypto-operation**   The functional application of cryptographic methods. (1) Off-line encryption or decryption performed as a self-contained operation distinct from the transmission of the encrypted text, as by hand or by machines not electrically connected to a signal line. (2) Online the use of crypto-equipment that is directly connected to a signal line, making continuous processes of encryption and transmission or reception and decryption.

**Crypto-period**   The time span during which a specific key is authorized for use or in which the keys for a given system may remain in effect.

**Cryptophthora**   It is a degradation of secret key material resulting from the side channel leakage where an attacker breaks down the operation of a cryptosystem to reveal the contents of a cryptographic key.

**Crypto-security**   The security or protection resulting from the proper use of technically sound crypto-systems.

**Cyber attack**   An attack, via cyberspace, targeting an organization's use of cyberspace for the purpose of disrupting, disabling, destroying, or maliciously controlling a computing infrastructure. This also includes destroying the integrity of the data or stealing controlled information.

**Cyber infrastructure**   The scope includes computer systems, control systems, networks (e.g., the Internet), and cyber services (e.g., managed security services).

**Cyber security**   The ability to protect or defend the use of cyberspace from cyber attacks.

**Cyberspace**   A global domain within the information environment consisting of the interdependent network of information systems infrastructures including the Internet, telecommunications network, computer systems, and embedded processors and controllers.

**Cyclic redundancy check (CRC)**   (1) A method to ensure data has not been altered after being sent through a communication channel. It uses an algorithm for generating error detection bits in a data link protocol. The receiving station performs the same calculation as done by the transmitting station. If the results differ, then one or more bits are in error. (2) Error checking mechanism that verifies data integrity by computing a polynomial algorithm based checksum. This is a technical and detective control.

**Cyclomatic complexity metrics**   A program module's cohesion can be measured indirectly through McCabe's and Halstead's cyclomatic complexity metrics and Henri and Kafura's information flow complexity metrics.

# D

**Daemon**   A program associated with UNIX systems that perform a housekeeping or maintenance utility function without being called by the user. A daemon sits in the background and is activated only when needed.

**Dashboards**   Dashboards are one type of management metrics in which they consolidate and communicate information relevant to the organizational security status in near-real time to security management stakeholders. These dashboards present information in a meaningful and easily understandable format to management. Some applications of dashboards include implementation of separation of duties, security authorizations, continuous system monitoring, security performance measures, risk management, and risk assessment.

**Data**   Programs, files, or other information stored in, or processed by a computer system.

**Data administrator (DA)**   A person responsible for the planning, acquisition, and maintenance of database management software, including the design, validation, and security of database files. The DA is fully responsible for the data model and the data dictionary software.

**Data architecture**   Data compilation, including who creates and uses it and how. It presents a stable basis for the processes and information used by the organization to accomplish its mission.

**Data at rest**   Data at rest (data on the hard drive) address the confidentiality and integrity of data in nonmobile devices and covers user information and system information. File encryption or whole (full) disk encryption protects data in storage (data at rest).

**Data authentication code**   The code is a mathematical function of both the data and a cryptographic key. Applying the Data Authentication Algorithm (DAA) to data generates a data authentication code. When data integrity is to be verified, the code is generated on the current data and compared with the previously generated code. If the two values are equal, data integrity (i.e., authenticity) is verified. The data authentication code is also known as a message authentication code (MAC).

**Data block**   A sequence of bits whose length is the block size of the block cipher.

**Data classification**   From data security standpoint, all data records and files should be labeled as critical, noncritical, classified, sensitive, secret, top-secret, or identified through some other means so that protective measures are taken according to the criticality of data.

**Data cleansing**   Includes activities for detecting and correcting data in a database or traditional file that are incorrect, incomplete, improperly formatted, or redundant. Also known as data scrubbing.

**Data communications**   Information exchanged between end-systems in machine-readable form.

**Data confidentiality**   The state that exists when data is held in confidence and is protected from unauthorized disclosure.

**Data contamination**   A deliberate or accidental process or act that results in a change in the integrity of the original data.

**Data custodian**   The individual or group that has been entrusted with the possession of, and responsibility for, the security of specified data. Compare with data owner.

**Data declassification**   Data and storage media declassification is an administrative procedure and decision to remove the security classification of the subject media. It includes actual purging of the media and removal of any labels denoting classification, possibly replacing them with labels denoting that the storage media is unclassified. The purging procedures should include the make, model number, and serial number of the degausser used and the date of the last degausser test if degaussing is done; or the accreditation statement of the software if overwriting is done. The reason for the data downgrade, declassification, regrade, or release should be given along with the current media's classification and requested reclassification of the same media.

**Data dictionary**   A central repository of an organization's data elements and its relationships.

**Data diddling**   The entering of false data into a computer system.

**Data downgrade**   The change of a classification label to a lower level without changing the contents of the data. Downgrading occurs only if the content of a file meets the requirements of the sensitivity level of the network for which the data is being delivered.

**Data element**   A basic unit of information that has a unique meaning and sub-categories (data items) of distinct value. Examples of data elements include gender, race, and geographic location.

**Data encrypting key**   A cryptographic key used for encrypting and decrypting data.

**Data encryption algorithm (DEA)**   The symmetric encryption algorithm that serves as the cryptographic engine for the triple data encryption algorithm (TDEA).

**Data encryption standard (DES)**   A U.S. Government-approved, symmetric cipher, encryption algorithm used by business and civilian government agencies that serve as the cryptographic engine for the triple data encryption algorithm (TDEA). The advanced encryption standard (AES) is designed to replace DES. The original "single" DES algorithm is no longer secure because it is now possible to try every possible key with special purpose equipment or a high performance cluster. Triple DES, however, is still considered to be secure.

**Data file organization**   Deals with the way data records are accessed and retrieved from computer files. When designing a file, security factors, access methods, and storage media costs should be considered. Record keys, pointers, or indexes are needed to read and write data to or from a file. *Record key* is part of a logical record used for identification and reference. A *primary key* is the main code used to store and locate records within a file. Records can be sorted and temporary files created using codes other than their primary keys. *Secondary keys* are used for alternative purposes including inverted files. A given data record may have more than one secondary key. *Pointers* show the physical location of records in a data file. *Addresses* are generated using indexing, base registers, segment registers, and other ways.

**Data flow diagram (DFD)**   A graphic model of the logical relationships within a computer-based application system. DFD is an input to the structure chart.

**Data hiding**   Data/information hiding is closely tied to modularity, abstractions, and maintainability. Data hiding means data and procedures in a module are hidden from other parts of the software. Errors from one module are not passed to other modules; instead they are contained in one module. Abstraction helps to define the procedures, while data hiding defines access restrictions to procedures and local data structures. The concept of data hiding is useful during program testing and software maintenance. Note that layering, abstraction, and data hiding are protection mechanisms in security design architecture.

**Data in transit**   Data in transit (data on the wire) deals with protecting the integrity and confidentiality of transmitted information across internal and external networks. Line encryption protects the data in transit and line encryption protects data in transfer.

**Data integrity**   A property whereby data has not been altered in an unauthorized manner since it was created, transmitted, or stored. Data integrity covers data in storage, during data processing, and while in transit.

**Data key**   A cryptographic key used to cryptographically process data (e.g., encrypt, decrypt, and authenticate).

**Data latency**   A measure of the currency of security-related data or information. Data latency refers to the time between when information is collected and when it is used. It allows an organization to respond to "where the threat or vulnerability is and where it is headed," instead of "where it was." When responding to threats and/or vulnerabilities, this is an important data point that shortens a risk decision cycle.

**Data level**   Three levels of data are possible: Level 1 is classified data. Level 2 is unclassified data requiring special protection, for example, Privacy Act, for Official Use Only, Technical Documents Restricted to Limited Distribution. Level 3 is all other unclassified data.

**Data link layer**   Provides security for the layer that handles communications on the physical network components of the ISO/OSI reference model.

**Data link layer protocols**   Data link layer protocols provide (1) error control to retransmit damaged or lost frames and (2) flow control to prevent a fast sender from overpowering a slow receiver. The sliding window mechanism is used to integrate error control and flow control. In data link layer, various framing methods are used including character count, byte stuffing, and bit stuffing. Examples of data link layer protocols and sliding window protocols include bit-oriented protocols such as SDLC, HDLC, ADCCP, or LAPB (Tanenbaum).

**Data management**   Providing or controlling access to data stored in a computer and the use of input/output devices.

**Data mart**   A data mart is a subset of a data warehouse with its goal to make the data available to more decision makers.

**Data minimization**   A generalization of the principle of variable minimization, in which the standardized parts of a message or data are replaced by a much shorter code, thereby reducing the risk of erroneous actions or improper use.

**Data mining**   Data mining is the process of posing a series of queries to extract information from a database, or data warehouse.

**Data origin authentication**   The corroboration that the source of data received is as claimed.

**Data owner**   The authority, individual, or organization who has original responsibility for the data by management directive or other. Compare with data custodian.

**Data path**   The physical or logical route over which data passes. Note that a physical data path may be shared by multiple logical data paths.

**Data privacy**   It refers to restrictions to prevent unauthorized people having access to sensitive data and information stored on paper or magnetic media and to prevent interception of data.

**Data/record retention**   Retention periods for all data records, paper, and electronic files should be defined to facilitate routine backup, periodic purging (deletion), and archiving of records. This practice will protects the organization from failure to comply with external requirements and management guidelines and help it maximize the use of storage space and magnetic media (e.g., tapes, disks, cassettes, and cartridges).

**Data reengineering**   (1) A system-level process that purifies data definitions and values. This process establishes a meaningful and nonredundant data definitions and valid and consistent data values. (2)

It is used to improve the quality of data within a computer system. It examines and alters the data definitions, values, and the use of data. Data definitions and flows are tracked through the system. This process reveals hidden data models. Data names and definitions are examined and made consistent. Hard-coded parameters that are subject to change may be removed. This process is important because data problems are often deeply rooted within computer systems.

**Data regrade**   Data is regraded when information is transferred from high to low network data and users. Automated techniques such as processing, filtering, and blocking are used during data regrading.

**Data release**   It is the process of returning all unused disk space to the system when a data set is closed at the end of processing.

**Data remanence**   The residual data that may be left over on a storage medium after it has been erased.

**Data sanitization**   Process to remove information from media such that information recovery is not possible. It includes removing all labels, markings, and activity logs. It is the changing of content information in order to meet the requirements of the sensitivity level of the network to which the information is being sent. It uses automatic techniques such as processing, filtering, and blocking during data sanitization.

**Data security**   The protection of data from unauthorized (accidental or intentional) modification, destruction, or disclosure.

**Data storage methods**   (1) Primary storage is the main general-purpose storage region directly accessed by the microprocessor. This storage is called random access memory (RAM), which is a semiconductor-based memory that can be read by and written to by the CPU or other hardware devices. The storage locations can be accessed in any random order. The term RAM generally indicates volatile memory that can be written to as well as read. It loses its contents when the power is turned off. (2) Secondary storage is the amount of space available on disks and tapes, sometimes called backup storage. (3) Real storage is the amount of RAM memory in a system, as distinguished from virtual memory. Real storage is also called physical memory or physical storage. (4) An application program sees virtual memory to be larger and more uniform than it is. Virtual memory may be partially simulated by secondary storage such as a hard disk. Application programs access memory through virtual addresses, which are translated by special hardware and software into physical addresses. Virtual memory is also called disk memory.

**Data warehouse**   A data warehouse facilitates information retrieval and data analysis as it stores pre-computed, historical, descriptive, and numerical data.

**Database administrator (DBA)**   A person responsible for the day-to-day control and monitoring of the databases, including data warehouse and data mining activities. The DBA deals with the physical design of the database while the data administrator deals with the logical design.

**Database server**   A repository for event information recorded by sensors, agents, or management servers.

**Deactivated state**   The cryptographic key life cycle state in which a key is not to be used to apply cryptographic protection to data. Under certain circumstances, the key may be used to process already protected data.

**Decision tables**   Tabular representation of the conditions, actions, and rules in making a decision. Decision tables provide a clear and coherent analysis of complex logical combinations and relationships, and detect logic errors. Used in decision-intensive and computational application systems.

**Decision trees**   Graphic representation of the conditions, actions, and rule of decision making. Used in application systems to develop plans in order to reduce risks and exposures. They use probabilities for calculating outcomes.

**Decrypt**   To convert, by use of the appropriate key, encrypted (encoded or enciphered) text into its equivalent plaintext through the use of a cryptographic algorithm. The term "decrypt" covers the meanings of decipher and decode.

**Decryption**   (1) The process of changing ciphertext into plaintext using a cryptographic algorithm and key. (2) The process of a confidentiality mode that transforms encrypted data into the original usable data.

**Dedicated proxy server**   A form of proxy server that has much more limited firewalling capabilities than an application-proxy gateway.

**Defense-in-breadth**   A planned, systematic set of multidisciplinary activities that seek to identify, manage, and reduce risk of exploitable vulnerabilities at every stage of the system, network, or subcomponent life cycle (system, network, or product design and development; manufacturing; packaging; assembly; system integration; distribution; operations; maintenance; and retirement). It is a strategy dealing with scope of protection coverage of a system. It is also called supply chain protection control. It supports agile defense strategy.

**Defense-in-density**   A strategy requiring stronger security controls for high risk and complex systems and vice versa.

**Defense-in-depth**   (1) Information security strategy integrating people, technology, and operations capabilities to establish variable barriers across multiple layers and dimensions of information systems. (2) An approach for establishing an adequate information assurance (IA) posture whereby (i) IA solutions integrate people, technology, and operations, (ii) IA solutions are layered within and among IT assets, and (iii) IA solutions are selected based on their relative level of robustness. Implementation of this approach recognizes that the highly interactive nature of information systems and enclaves creates a shared risk environment; therefore, the adequate assurance of any single asset is dependent upon the adequate assurance of all interconnecting assets. (3) A strategy dealing with controls placed at multiple levels and at multiple places in a given system. It supports agile defense strategy and is the same as security-in-depth.

**Defense-in-intensity**   A strategy dealing with a range of controls and protection mechanisms designed into a system.

**Defense-in-technology**   A strategy dealing with diversity of information technologies used in the implementation of a system. Complex technologies create complex security problems.

**Defense-in-time**   A strategy dealing with applying controls at the right time and at the right geographic location. It considers global systems operating at different time zones.

**Defensive programming**   Defensive programming, also called robust programming, makes a system more reliable with various programming techniques.

**Degauss**  (1) To apply a variable, alternating current (AC) field for the purpose of demagnetizing magnetic recording media, usually tapes and cartridges. The process involves increasing the AC field gradually from zero to some maximum value and back to zero, which leaves a very low residue of magnetic induction on the media. (2) To demagnetize, thereby removing magnetic memory. (3) To erase the contents of media. (4) To reduce the magnetic flux to virtual zero by applying a reverse magnetizing field. Also called demagnetizing.

**Deleted file**  A file that has been logically, but not necessarily physically, erased from the operating system, perhaps to eliminate potentially incriminating evidence. Deleting files does not always necessarily eliminate the possibility of recovering all or part of the original data.

**Demilitarized zone (DMZ)**  (1) An interface on a routing firewall that is similar to the interfaces found on the firewall's protected side. Traffic moving between the DMZ and other interfaces on the protected side of the firewall still goes through the firewall and can have firewall protection policies applied. (2) A host or network segment inserted as a "neutral zone" between an organization's private network and the Internet. (3) A network created by connecting to firewalls. Systems that are externally accessible but need some protections are usually located on DMZ networks.

**Denial-of-quality (DoQ)**  Denial-of-quality (DoQ) results from lack of quality assurance (QA) methods and quality control (QC) techniques used in delivering messages, packets, and services. DoQ affects QoS and QoP, and could result in DoS.

**Denial of service (DoS)**  (1) Preventing or limiting the normal use or management of networks or network devices. (2) The prevention of authorized access to resources or the delaying of time-critical operations. Time-critical may be milliseconds or it may be hours, depending upon the service provided. Synonymous with interdiction.

**Denial-of-service (DoS) attack**  (1) An attack that prevents or impairs the authorized use of networks, operating systems, or application systems by exhausting resources. (2) A type of computer attack that denies service to users by either clogging the system with a deluge of irrelevant messages or sending disruptive commands to the system. (3) A direct attack on availability, it prevents a financial system service provider from receiving or responding to messages from a requester (customer). DoS attacks on the financial system service provider would not be detected by a firewall or an intrusion detection system because these countermeasures are based on either entry-point or per-host specific, but not based on a per-transaction or operation basis. In these situations, two standards (WS-Reliability and WS-ReliableMessaging) are available to guarantee that messages are sent and received in a service-oriented architecture (SOA). XML-gateways can be used to augment the widely accepted techniques because they are capable of preventing and detecting XML-based DoS. Note that DoS is related to QoS and QoP and is resulting from denial-of-quality (DoQ).

**Deny-by-default**  To block all inbound and outbound traffic that has not been expressly permitted by firewall policy (i.e., unnecessary services that could be used to spread malware).

**Depth attribute**  An attribute associated with an assessment method that addresses the rigor and level of detail associated with the application of the method. The values for the depth attribute, hierarchically from less depth to more depth, are basic, focused, and comprehensive.

**Design verification**  The use of verification techniques, usually computer-assisted, to demonstrate a mathematical correspondence between an abstract (security) model and a formal system specification.

**Designated approving/accrediting authority**   The individual selected by an authorizing official to act on their behalf in coordinating and carrying out the necessary activities required during the security certification and accreditation of an information system.

**Desk check reviews**   A review of programs by the program author to control and detect program logic errors and misinterpretation of program requirements.

**Desktop administrators**   These identify changes in login scripts along with Windows Registry or file scans, and implement changes in login scripts.

**Destroyed compromised state**   The cryptographic key life cycle state that zeroizes a key so that it cannot be recovered and it cannot be used and marks it as compromised, or that marks a destroyed key as compromised. For record purposes, the identifier and other selected metadata of a key may be retained.

**Destroyed state**   The cryptographic key life cycle state that zeroizes a key so that it cannot be recovered and it cannot be used. For record purposes, the identifier and other selected metadata of a key may be retained.

**Destruction**   The result of actions taken to ensure that media cannot be reused as originally intended and that information is virtually impossible to recover or prohibitively expensive.

**Detailed design**   A process where technical specifications are translated into more detailed programming specifications, from which computer programs are developed.

**Detailed testing**   A test methodology that assumes explicit and substantial knowledge of the internal structure and implementation detail of the assessment object. Also known as white box testing.

**Detective controls**   These are actions taken to detect undesirable events and incidents that have occurred. Detective controls enhance security by monitoring the effectiveness of preventive controls and by detecting security incidents where preventive controls were circumvented.

**Device communication modes**   Three modes of communication between devices include simplex (one-way communication in one direction), half-duplex (one-way at a time in two directions), and full-duplex (two-way directions at the same time). The half-duplex is used when the computers are connected to a hub rather than a switch. A hub does not buffer incoming frames. Instead, a hub connects all the lines internally and electronically.

**Dial-back**   Synonymous with callback. This is a technical and preventive control.

**Dial-up**   The service whereby a computer terminal can use the telephone to initiate and effect communication with a computer.

**Dictionary attack**   A form of guessing attack in which the attacker attempts to guess a password using a list of possible passwords that is not exhaustive.

**Differential cryptanalysis attacks**   A technique used to attack any block cipher. It works by beginning with a pair of plaintext blocks that differ in only a small number of bits. An attack begins when some patterns are much more common than other patterns. In doing so, it looks at pairs of plaintexts and pairs of ciphertexts.

**Differential power analysis (DPA)**   An analysis of the variations of the electrical power consumption of a cryptographic module, using advanced statistical methods and/or other techniques, for the purpose of extracting information correlated to cryptographic keys used in a cryptographic algorithm.

**Diffie-Hellman (DH) group**   Value that specifies the encryption generator type and key length to be used for generating shared secrets.

**Digest authentication**   Digest authentication uses a challenge-response mechanism for user authentication with a nonce or arbitrary value sent to the user, who is prompted for an ID and password. It is susceptible to offline dictionary attacks and a countermeasure is to use SSL/TLS. Both basic authentication and digest authentication are useful in protecting information from malicious bots.

**Digital certificate**   A password-protected and encrypted file that contains identification information about its holder. It includes a public key and a unique private key.

**Digital evidence**   Electronic information stored or transmitted in a digital or binary form.

**Digital forensics**   The application of science to the identification, collection, examination, and analysis of data while preserving the integrity of the information and maintaining a strict chain of custody for the data.

**Digital signature**   (1) Electronic information stored or transferred in digital form. (2) A nonforgeable transformation of data that allows the proof of the source (with nonrepudiation) and the verification of the integrity of that data. (3) An asymmetric key operation where the private key is used to digitally sign an electronic document and the public key is used to verify the signature. Digital signatures provide authentication and integrity protection. (4) The result of a cryptographic transformation of data that, when properly implemented, provides the services of origin authentication, data integrity, and signer  nonrepudiation.

**Digital signature algorithm (DSA)**   The DSA is used by a signatory to generate a digital signature on data and by a verifier to verify the authenticity of the signature. It is an asymmetric algorithm used for digitally signing data.

**Digital watermarking**   It is the process of irreversibly embedding information into a digital signal. An example of is embedding copyright information about the copyright owner. Steganography is sometimes applied in digital watermarking, where two parties communicate a secret message embedded in the digital signal. Annotation of digital photographs with descriptive information is another application of invisible watermarking. While some file formats for digital media can contain additional information called metadata, digital watermarking is distinct in that the data is carried in the signal itself.

**Directive controls**   Directive controls are broad-based controls to handle security incidents, and they include management's policies, procedures, and directives.

**Disaster recovery**   The process of restoring an information system (IS) to full operation after an interruption in service, including equipment repair or replacement, file recovery or restoration, and resumption of service to users.

**Disaster recovery plan (DRP)**   A written plan for processing critical applications in the event of a major hardware or software failure or destruction of facilities.

**Discretionary access control (DAC)**   The basis of this kind of security is that an individual user or program operating on the user's behalf is allowed to specify explicitly the types of access other users or programs executing on their behalf may have to the information under the user's control. Compare with mandatory access control.

**Discretionary protection**    Access control that identifies individual users and their need-to-know and limits users to the information that they are allowed to see. It is used on systems that process information with the same level of sensitivity.

**Disinfecting**    Removing malware from within a file.

**Disintegration**    A physically destructive method of sanitizing media; the act of separating into component parts.

**Disk arrays**    A technique used to improve the performance of data storage media regardless of the type of computer used. Disk arrays use parity disk schema to keep track of data stored in a domain of the storage subsystem and to regenerate it in case of a hardware/software failure. Disk arrays use multiple disks and if one disk drive fails, the other one becomes available. They also have seven levels from level zero through six (i.e., redundant array of independent disks –RAID0 to RAID6). They use several disks in a single logical subsystem. Disk arrays are also called disk striping. It is a recovery control.

**Disk duplexing**    The purpose is the same as disk arrays. The disk controller is duplicated. It has two or more disk controllers and more than one channel. When one disk controller fails, the other one is ready to operate. This is a technical and recovery control and ensures the availability goal.

**Disk farm**    Data are stored on multiple disks for reliability and performance reasons.

**Disk imaging**    Generating a bit-for-bit copy of the original media, including free space and slack space.

**Disk mirroring**    The purpose is the same as disk arrays. A file server contains two physical disks and one channel, and all information is written to both disks simultaneously (disk-to-disk copy). If one disk fails, all of the data are immediately available from the other disk. Disk mirroring is also called shadowed disk, and incurs some performance overhead during write operations and increases the cost of the disk subsystem since two disks are required. Disk mirroring should be used for critical applications that can accept little or no data loss. This is a technical and recovery control and ensures the availability goal. Synonymous with disk shadowing.

**Disk replication**    Data is written to two different disks to ensure that two valid copies of the data are always available. Disk replication minimizes the time-windows for recovery.

**Disk striping**    Has more than one disk and more than one partition, and is the same as disk arrays. An advantage of disk arrays includes running multiple drives in parallel, and a disadvantage includes the fact that its organization is more complicated than disk farming and highly sensitive to multiple failures.

**Disposal**    The act of discarding media with no other sanitization considerations. This is most often done by paper recycling containing nonconfidential information but may also include other media. It is giving up control, in a manner short of destruction.

**Disruption**    An unplanned event that causes the general system or major application to be inoperable for an unacceptable length of time (e.g., minor or extended power outage, extended unavailable network, or equipment or facility damage or destruction).

**Distributed computing**    Distributed computing, in contrast to supercomputing, is used with many users with small tasks or jobs, each of which is solved by one or more computers. A distributed system consists of multiple autonomous computers or nodes that communicate through a computer network where each computer has its own local memory and these computers communicate with each other by message passing. There is an overlap between distributed computing, parallel computing, grid computing, and concurrent computing (Wikipedia).

**Distributed denial-of-service (DDoS)**   A denial-of-service (DoS) technique that uses numerous hosts to perform the attack.

A DDoS is a denial-of-service (DoS) technique that uses numerous hosts to perform the attack. An attacker takes control of many computers, which then become the sources ("zombies") for the actual attack. If enough hosts are used, the total volume of generated network traffic can exhaust not only the resources of a targeted host but also the available bandwidth for nearly any organization. DDoS attacks have become an increasingly severe threat, and the lack of availability of computing and network services now translates to significant disruption and major financial loss.

**Distribution attacks**   They focus on the malicious modification of hardware or software at the factory or during distribution. These attacks can introduce malicious code into a product such as a backdoor to gain unauthorized access to information or a system function at a later date.

**Document type definition (DTD)**   A document defining the format of the contents present between the tags in an XML and SGML document, and the way they should be interpreted by the application reading the XML or SGML document.

**Domain**   A set of subjects, their information objects, and a common security policy.

**Domain name system (DNS)**   An Internet translation service that resolves domain names to IP addresses and vice versa. Each entity in a network, such as a computer, requires a uniquely identifiable network address for proper delivery of message information. DNS is a protocol used to manage name lookups for converting between decimal and domain name versions of an address. It uses a name-server (DNS server), which contains a universe of names called name-space. Each name-server is identified by one or more IP addresses. One can intercept and forge traffic for arbitrary name-nodes, thus impersonating IP addresses. Secure DNS can be accomplished with cryptographic protocols for message exchanges between name-servers. DNS transactions include DNS query/response, zone transfers, dynamic updates, and DNS NOTIFY.

**Domain parameter seed**   A string of bits that is used as input for a domain parameter generation or validation process.

**Domain parameters**   Parameters used with cryptographic algorithms that are usually common to a domain of users. A DSA or ECDSA cryptographic key pair is associated with a specific set of domain parameters.

**Domain separation**   It relates to the mechanisms that protect objects in a system. Domain consists of a set of objects that a subject can access.

**Downgrade**   The change of a classification label to a lower level without changing the contents of the data. Downgrading occurs only if the content of a file meets the requirements of the sensitivity level of the network for which the data is being delivered.

**Dual backbones**   If the primary network goes down, the secondary network will carry the traffic.

**Dual cable**   Two separate cables are used: one for transmission and one for reception.

**Dual control**   The process of utilizing two or more separate entities (usually persons) operating in concert to protect sensitive functions or information. All entities are equally responsible. This approach generally involves the split-knowledge of the physical or logical protection of security parameters. This is a management and preventive control.

**Dual-homed gateway firewall**   A firewall consisting of a bastion host with two network interfaces, one of which is connected to the protected network, the other of which is connected to the Internet. IP traffic forwarding is usually disabled, restricting all traffic between the two networks to whatever passes through some kind of application proxy.

**Dual-use certificate**   A certificate that is intended for use with both digital signature and data encryption services.

**Due care**   Means reasonable care, which promotes the common good. It is maintaining minimal and customary practices. It is the responsibility that managers and their organizations have a duty to provide for information security to ensure that the type of control, the cost of control, and the deployment of control are appropriate for the system being managed. Both due care and due diligence are similar to the "prudent man" concept.

**Due diligence**   Requires organizations to develop and implement an effective security program to prevent and detect violation of policies and law. It requires that the organization has taken minimum and necessary steps in its power and authority to prevent and detect violation of policies and law. Due diligence is another way of saying "due care." Both due care and due diligence are similar to the "prudent man" concept.

**Due process**   Means following rules and principles so that an individual is treated fairly and uniformly at all times. It also means fair and equitable treatment to all concerned parties.

**Due professional care**   Individuals applying the care and skill expected of a reasonable prudent and competent professional during their work.

**Dumpster diving**   Going through a company's or an individual's waste containers to find some meaningful and useful documents and records (information) and then use that information against that company or individual to steal identity or to conduct espionage work.

**Dynamic binding**   Also known as run-time binding or late binding. Dynamic binding refers to the association of a message with a method during run time, as opposed to compile time. Dynamic binding means that a message can be sent to an object without prior knowledge of the object's class.

**Dynamic host configuration protocol (DHCP)**   The protocol used to assign Internet Protocol (IP) addresses to all nodes on the network. DHCP allows network administrators to automate and control from a central position the assignment of IP address configurations. The DHCP server is required to log host-names or message authentication code addresses for all clients. DHCP cannot handle manual configurations where a portion of the network IP addresses needs to be excluded or reserved for severs, routers, firewalls, and administrator workstations. Therefore, the DHCP server should be timed to prevent unauthorized configurations.

**Dynamic HTML**   A collection of dynamic HTML technologies for generating the Web page contents on-the-fly. It uses the server-side scripts (e.g., CGI, ASP, JSP, PHP, and Perl) as well as the client-side scripts (e.g., JavaScript, JavaApplets, and Active- X controls).

**Dynamic separation of duty (DSOD)**   Separation of duties can be enforced dynamically (i.e., at access time), and the decision to grant access refers to the past access history (e.g., a cashier and an accountant are the same person but play only one role at a time). One type of DSOD is a two-person rule, which states that the first user to execute a two-person operation can be any authorized user, whereas the second user can be any authorized user different from the first. Another type of DSOD is a history-based separation of duty, which states that the same subject (role) cannot access the same object for variable number of times. Popular DSOD policies are the Workflow and Chinese wall policies.

**Dynamic subsystem**   A subsystem that is not continually present during the execution phase of an information system. Service-oriented architectures and cloud computing architectures are examples of architectures that employ dynamic subsystems.

**Dynamic Web documents**   Dynamic Web documents (pages) are written in CGI, PHP, JSP, ASP, JavaScript, and Active-X Controls.


# E

**E2E**   Exchange-to-exchange (E2E) is an e-commerce model in which electronic exchanges formally connect to one another for the purpose of exchanging information (e.g., stockbrokers/dealers with stock markets and vice versa).

**Easter egg**   An Easter egg is hidden functionality within an application program, which becomes activated when an undocumented, and often convoluted, set of commands and keystrokes are entered. Easter eggs are typically used to display the credits given for the application development team and are intended to be nonthreatening.

**Eavesdropping**   (1) Passively monitoring network communications for data and authentication credentials. (2) The unauthorized interception of information-bearing emanations through the use of methods other than wiretapping. (3) A passive attack in which an attacker listens to a private communication. The best way to thwart this attack is by making it very difficult for the attacker to make any sense of the communication by encrypting all messages. Also known as packet snarfing.

**E-business patterns**   Patterns for e-business are a group of proven reusable assets that can be used to increase the speed of developing and deploying net-centric applications, like Web-based applications.

**Education (information security)**   Education integrates all of the security skills and competencies of the various functional specialties into a common body of knowledge and strives to produce IT security specialists and professionals capable of vision and proactive response.

**Egress filtering**   (1) Filtering of outgoing network traffic. (2) Blocking outgoing packets that should not exit a network. (3) The process of blocking outgoing packets that use obviously false Internet Protocol (IP) addresses, such as source addresses from internal networks.

**El Gamal algorithm**   A signature scheme derived from a modification of exponentiation ciphers. Exponentiation is a mathematical process where one number is raised to some power.

**Electromagnetic emanation attack**   An intelligence-bearing signal, which, if intercepted and analyzed, potentially discloses the information that is transmitted, received, handled, or otherwise processed by any information-processing equipment.

**Electromagnetic emanations (EME)**   Signals transmitted as radiation through the air and through conductors.

**Electromagnetic interference**   An electromagnetic disturbance that interrupts, obstructs, or otherwise degrades or limits the effective performance of electronic or electrical equipment.

**Electronic auction (e-auction)**   Auctions conducted online in which (1) a seller invites consecutive bids from multiple buyers and the bidding price either increases or decreases sequentially (forward auction), (2) a buyer invites bids and multiple sellers respond with the price reduced sequentially, and the lowest bid wins (backward or reverse auction), (3) multiple buyers propose biding prices and multiple sellers respond with asking prices simultaneously and both prices are matched based on the quantities of items on both sides (double auction) and (4) sellers and buyers interact in one industry or for one commodity (vertical auction). Prices are determined dynamically through the bidding process. Usually, negotiations and bargaining power can take place between one buyer and one seller due to supply and demand. Reverse auction is practiced in B2B or G2B e-commerce. Limitations of e-auctions include minimal security for C2C auctions (i.e., no encryption), possibility of fraud (i.e., defective products), and limited buyer participation in terms of invitation only or open to dealers only. B2B auctions are secure due to use of private lines.

**Electronic authentication**   The process of establishing confidence in user identities electronically presented to an information system.

**Electronic business XML (ebXML)**   Sponsored by UN/CEFACT and OASIS, a modular suite of specifications that enable enterprises of any size and in any geographical location to perform business-to-business (B2B) transactions using XML.

**Electronic commerce (EC)**   Using information technology to conduct the business functions such as electronic payments and document interchange. It is the process of buying, selling, or exchanging products, services, or information via computer networks. EC models include B2B, B2B2C, B2C, B2E, C2B, C2C, and E2E. EC security risks arising from technical threats include DoS, zombies, phishing, Web server and Web page hijacking, botnets, and malicious code (e.g., viruses, worms, and Trojan horses) and nontechnical threats include pretexting and social engineering.

**Electronic credentials**   Digital documents used in authentication that bind an identity or an attribute to a subscriber's token.

**Electronic data interchange (EDI) system**   The electronic transfer of specially formatted standard business documents (e.g., purchase orders, shipment instructions, invoices, payments, and confirmations) sent between business partners. EDI is a direct computer-to-computer exchange between two organizations, and it can use either a value-added network (VAN-EDI) or the Internet (Web-EDI) with XML standards.

**Electronic evidence**   Information and data of investigative value that is stored on or transmitted by an electronic device.

**Electronic funds transfer (EFT) system**   Customers paying their bills electronically through electronic funds transfers from banks to credit card companies and others.

**Electronic mail header**   The section of an e-mail message that contains vital information about the message, including origination date, sender, recipient(s), delivery path, subject, and format information. The header is generally left in clear text even when the body of the e-mail message is encrypted. The body contains the actual message.

**Electronic serial number (ESN)**   (1) A number encoded in each cellular phone that uniquely identifies each cellular telephone manufactured. (2) A unique 32-bit number programmed into code division multiple access (CDMA) phones when they are manufactured.

**Electronic signature**   A method of signing an electronic message that (1) identifies and authenticates a particular person as the source of the electronic message and (2) indicates such person's approval of the information contained in the electronic message.

**Electronic surveillance**   The acquisition of a non-public communication by electronic means without the consent of a person who is a party to an electronic communication. It does not include the use of radio direction-finding equipment solely to determine the location of a transmitter.

**Electronic vaulting**   A system is connected to an electronic vaulting provider to allow file/program backups to be created automatically at offsite storage. Electronic vaulting and remote journaling require a dedicated off-site location (e.g., hot site or offsite storage site) to receive the transmissions and a connection with limited bandwidth.

**Elliptic curve DH (ECDH)**   Elliptic curve Diffie-Hellman (ECDH) algorithm is used to support key establishment.

**Elliptic curve digital signature algorithm (ECDSA)**   A digital signature algorithm that is an analog of digital signature algorithm (DSA) using elliptic curve mathematics.

**Emanation attack**   An intelligence-bearing signal, which, if intercepted and analyzed, potentially discloses the information that is transmitted, received, handled, or otherwise processed by any information-processing equipment. A low signal-to-noise ratio at the receiver is preferred to prevent emanation attack. Techniques such as control zones and white noise can be used to protect against emanation attacks.

**Emanation hardware**   An electronic signal emitted by a hardware device not explicitly allowed by its specification.

**Emanations security**   Protection resulting from measures taken to deny unauthorized individuals using information derived from intercept and analysis of compromising emissions from crypto-equipment or an information system.

**Embedded system**   An embedded system that performs or controls a function, either in whole or in part, as an integral element of a larger system or subsystem (e.g., flight simulators).

**Emergency response**   Immediate action taken upon occurrence of events such as natural disasters, fire, civil disruption, and bomb threats in order to protect lives, limit the damage to property, and minimize the impact on computer operations.

**Emergency response time (EMRT)**   The time required for any computer resource to be recovered from disruptive events. It is the time required to reestablish an activity from an emergency or degraded mode to a normal mode. EMRT is also called time-to-recover (TTR).

**Emissions security**   The protection resulting from all measures taken to deny unauthorized persons information of value that might be derived from intercept and from an analysis of compromising emanations from crypto-equipment, computer systems, and telecommunications systems.

**Encapsulating security payload (ESP)**   An IPsec message header designed to provide a mix of security services, including confidentiality, data origin authentication, connectionless integrity, anti-replay service, and limited traffic flow confidentiality.

**Encapsulating security payload (ESP) protocol**   IPsec security protocol that can provide encryption and/or integrity protection for packet headers and data.

**Encapsulation**   (1) The principle of structuring hardware and software components such that the interface between components is clean and well-defined and that exposed means of input, output, and control other than those that exist in the interface do not exist. (2) The packaging of data and procedures into a single programmatic structure. In object-oriented programming languages, encapsulation means that an object's data structures are hidden from outside sources and are accessible only through the object's protocol.

**Enclave**   A collection of information systems connected by one or more internal networks under the control of a single authority and security policy. The systems may be structured by physical proximity or by function, independent of location.

**Enclave boundary**   It is a point at which an enclave's internal network service layer connected to an external network's service layer (i.e., to another enclave or to a wide-area network).

**Encrypt**   (1) To convert plaintext into ciphertext, unintelligible forms, through the use of a cryptographic algorithm. (2) A generic term encompassing encipher and encode.

**Encrypted cookies**   Some websites create encrypted cookies to protect the data from unauthorized access.

**Encrypted file system (EFS)**   In an encrypted file system (EFS), keys are used to encrypt a file or group of files. It can either encrypt each file with a distinct symmetric key or encrypt a set of files using the same symmetric key. The symmetric keys can be generated from a password using public key cryptography standard (PKCS) and protected with trusted platform module (TPM) chip through its key cache management. EFS, which is based on public-key encryption, integrates tightly with the public key infrastructure (PKI) features that have been incorporated into Windows XP. The actual logic that performs the encryption is a system service that cannot be shut down. This program feature is designed to prevent unauthorized access, but has an added benefit of rendering the encryption process completely transparent to the user. Each file that a user may encrypt is encrypted using a randomly generated file encryption key (FEK).

**Encrypted key (ciphertext key)**   A cryptographic key that has been encrypted using an approved security function with a key encrypting key, a PIN, or a password to disguise the value of the underlying plaintext key.

**Encrypted network**   A network on which messages are encrypted (e.g., using DES, AES, or other appropriate algorithms) to prevent reading by unauthorized parties.

**Encryption**   (1) Conversion of plaintext to ciphertext though the use of a cryptographic algorithm. (2) The process of changing plaintext into ciphertext for the purpose of security or privacy.

**Encryption algorithm**   A set of mathematically expressed rules for rendering data unintelligible by executing a series of conversions controlled by a key.

**Encryption certificate**   A certificate containing a public key that is used to encrypt electronic messages, files, documents, or data transmissions, or to establish or exchange a session key for these same purposes.

**Encryption process**   (1) The process of changing plaintext into ciphertext for the purpose of security or privacy. (2) Encryption is the conversion of data into a form, called a ciphertext, which cannot be easily understood by unauthorized people. (3) It is the conversion of plaintext to ciphertext through the use of a cryptographic algorithm. (4) The process of a confidentiality mode that transforms usable data into an unreadable form.

**End-point protection platform**   It is safeguards implemented through software to protect end-user computers such as workstations and laptops against attack (e.g., antivirus, antispyware, antiadware, personal firewalls, and hot-based intrusion detection systems).

**End-point security**   End-point protection platforms require end-point security products such as (1) use of anti-malware software; if not available, use of rootkit detectors, (2) use of personal firewalls, (3) use of host-based intrusion detection and prevention systems, (4) use of mobile code restrictively, (5) use of cryptography in file encryption, full disk encryption, and VPN connections, (6) implementation of TLS or XML gateways or firewalls, (7) placing remote access servers in internal DMZ, and (8) use of diskless nodes and thin clients with minimal functionality.

**End-to-end encryption**   (1) Encryption of information at the origin within a communications network and postponing decryption to the final destination point. (2) Communications encryption in which data is encrypted when being passed through a network, but routing, addresses, headers, and trailer information are not encrypted (i.e., remains visible). (3) It is encryption of information at its origin and decryption at its intended destination without intermediate decryption. This is a technical and preventive control.

**End-to-end security**   The safeguarding of information in a secure telecommunication system by cryptographic or protected distribution system means from point of origin to point of destination. This is a technical and preventive control.

**End-to-end testing**   A testing approach to verify that a defined set of interrelated systems that collectively support an organizational core business area or function interoperates as intended in an operational environment. It is conducted when a major system in the end-to-end chain is modified or replaced.

**End-user device**   A personal computer (e.g., desktop and laptop), consumer device (e.g., personal digital assistant [PDA] and smart phone), or removable storage media (e.g., USB flash drive, memory card, external hard drive, and writeable CD or DVD) that can store information.

**Enhanced messaging service (EMS)**   An improved message system for global system for mobile communications (GSM) mobile phone allowing picture, sound, animation, and text elements to be conveyed through one or more concatenated short message service (SMS).

**Enterprise architecture**   The description of an enterprise's entire set of information systems: how they are configured, how they are integrated, how they interface to the external environment at the enterprise's boundary, how they are operated to support the enterprise mission, and how they contribute to the enterprise's overall security posture.

**Entity**   (1) Any participant in an authentication exchange; such a participant may be human or nonhuman, and may take the role of the claimant and/or verifier. (2) It is either a subject (an active element generally in the form of a person, process, or device that causes information to flow among objects or changes the system state) or an object (a passive element that contains or receives information). Note: Access to an object potentially implies access to the information it contains. (3) It is an active element in an open system. (4) It is an individual (person) or organization, device, or process. (5) A collection of information items conceptually grouped together and distinguished from their surroundings. An entity (party) is described by its attributes, and entities can be linked or have relationships to other entities (parties).

**Entity integrity**   A tuple in a relation cannot have a null value for any of the primary key attributes.

**Entity-relationship-attribute (ERA) diagram**   Used for data intensive application systems and shows the relationships between entities and attributes of a system.

**Entrapment**   The deliberate planting of apparent flaws in a system for the purpose of detecting attempted penetrations.

**Entropy**   (1) The uncertainty of a random variable. (2) A measure of the amount of uncertainty that an attacker faces to determine the value of a secret. Entropy is usually stated in bits.

**Environmental failure protection**   The use of features to protect against a compromise of the security of a cryptographic module due to environmental conditions or fluctuations outside of the module's normal operating range.

**Environmental failure testing**   The use of specific test methods to provide reasonable assurance that the security of a cryptographic module will not be compromised by environmental conditions or fluctuations outside of the module's normal operating range.

**Environmental threats**   Examples of environmental threats include equipment failure, software errors, telecommunications network outage, and electric power failure.

**Ephemeral key pairs**   Ephemeral key agreement keys are generated and distributed during a single key agreement process (e.g., at the beginning of a communication session) and are not reused. These key pairs are used to establish a shared secret (often in combination with static key pairs); the shared secret is subsequently used to derive shared keying material. Not all key agreement schemes use ephemeral key pairs, and when used, not all entities have an ephemeral key pair.

**Ephemeral keys**   Short-lived cryptographic keys that are statistically unique to each execution of a key establishment process and meet other requirements of the key type (e.g., unique to each message or session).

**Equipment life cycle**   Four phases of equipment life cycle (asset management) include: Authorization and acquisition (phase 1), Inventory and audit (phase 2), Use and maintenance (phase 3), and Dispose or replace (Phase 4). Inventory and audit includes tagging the assets, maintaining an inventory of electronic records, taking periodic inventory of these assets through physical counting, and reconciling the difference between the physical count and the book count. Maintenance includes preventive and remedial maintenance, which can be performed onsite, offsite, or both. Examples of equipment located in functional user departments and IT department include routers, printers, scanners, CPUs, disk drives, and tape drives.

**Erasable programmable read-only memory (EPROM)**   A subclass of ROM chip that can be erased and reprogrammed many times.

**Erasure**   A process by which a signal recorded on magnetic media is removed (i.e., degaussed). Erasure may be accomplished in two ways, (1) by alternating current (AC) erasure, by which the information is destroyed by applying an alternating high- and low-magnetic field to the media or (2) by direct current (DC) erasure, by which the media are saturated by applying a unidirectional magnetic field. Process intended to render magnetically stored information irretrievable by normal means.

**Error**   (1) The difference between a computed, observed, or measured value and the true, specified, or theoretically correct value or condition. (2) An incorrect step, process, or data definition often called a bug. (3) An incorrect result. (4) A human action that produces an incorrect result. (5) A system deviation that may have been caused by a fault. (6) A bit error is the substitution of a '0' bit for a '1' bit, or vice versa.

**Error analysis**   The use of techniques to detect errors, to estimate/predict the number of errors, and to analyze error data both singly and collectively.

**Error correction**   Techniques that attempt to recover from detected data transmission errors.

**Error-correction code**   A technique in which the information content of the error-control data of a data unit can be used to correct errors in that unit.

**Error-detection code**   A code computed from data and comprised of redundant bits of information designed to detect, but not correct, unintentional changes in the data.

**Escrow**   Something (e.g., a document or an encryption key) that is "delivered to a third person to be given to the grantee upon the fulfillment of a condition."

**Escrow arrangement**   (1) Placing an electronic cryptographic key and rules for its retrieval into a storage medium maintained by a rusted third party. (2) Something (e.g., a document, software source code, or an encryption key) that is delivered to a third person to be given to the grantee only upon the fulfillment of a condition or a contract.

**Ethernet**   Ethernet is the most widely installed protocol for local-area network (LAN) technology. It uses CSMA/CD for channel allocation. Older versions of Ethernet used a thick coaxial original cable (classic Ethernet), which is obsolete now. Newer versions of Ethernet use a thin coaxial cable with no hub needed, twisted-pair wire (low cost), fiber optics (good between buildings), and switches. Because the Internet Protocol (IP) is a connectionless protocol, it fits well with the connectionless Ethernet protocol. Ethernet uses the bus topology. Ethernet is classified as thick, thin, fast, switched, and gigabit Ethernet based on the cable used and the speed of service. Ethernet operates in the data link layer of the ISO/OSI reference model based on the IEEE 802.3 standard and uses the 48-bit addressing scheme. The gigabit Ethernet supports both full-duplex and half-duplex communication modes, and because no connection is possible, the CSMA/CD protocol is not used.

**Evaluation**   The process of examining a computer product or system with respect to certain criteria.

**Evaluation assurance level (EAL)**   One of seven increasingly rigorous packages of assurance requirements from Common Criteria (CC) Part 3. Each numbered package represents a point on the CC's predefined assurance scale. An EAL can be considered a level of confidence in the security functions of an IT product or system.

**Event**   (1) Something that occurs within a system or network. (2) Any observable occurrence in a network or system.

**Event aggregation**   The consolidation of similar log entries into a single entry containing a count of the number of occurrences of the event.

**Event correlation**   Finding relationships between two or more log entries.

**Event normalization**   Covering each log data field to a particular data representation and categorizing it consistently.

**Event reduction**   Removing unneeded data fields from all log entries to create a new log that is smaller in size.

**Evidence life cycle**   The evidence life cycle starts with evidence collection and identification; analysis; storage; preservation and transportation; presentation in court; and ends when the evidence is returned to the victim (owner). The evidence life cycle is connected with the chain of evidence.

**Examine**   A type of assessment method that is characterized by the process of checking, inspecting, reviewing, observing, studying, or analyzing one or more assessment objects to facilitate understanding, achieve clarification, or obtain evidence, the results of which are used to support the determination of security control effectiveness over time.

**Exclusive-OR operation (XOR)**   The bitwise addition, modulo 2, of two bit strings of equal length.

**Exculpatory evidence**   Evidence that tends to decrease the likelihood of fault or guilt.

**Executive steering committee**   Committees that manage the information portfolio of the organization.

**Exhaustive search attack**   Uses computer programs to search for a password for all possible combinations. An exhaustive attack consists of discovering secret data by trying all possibilities and checking for correctness. For a four-digit password, you might start with 0000 and move on to 0001, 0002, and so on until 9999.

**Expert systems**   Expert systems use artificial intelligence programming languages to help human beings make better decisions.

**Exploit code**   A program that enables attackers to automatically break into a system.

**Exploitable channel**   Channel that allows the violation of the security policy governing an information system and is usable or detectable by subjects external to the trusted computing base (TCB).

**Exposure**   Caused by the undesirable events. Exposure = Attack + Vulnerability.

**Extensibility**  (1) A measure of the ease of increasing the capability of a system. (2) The ability to extend or expand the capability of a component so that it handles the additional needs of a particular implementation.

**Extensible Access Control Markup Language (XACML)**  A general-purpose language for specifying access control policies.

**Extensible authentication protocol (EAP)**  A standard means of extending challenge handshake authentication protocol (CHAP) and password authentication protocol (PAP) to include additional authentication data such as biometric data. EAP is used in authenticating remote users. Legacy EAP methods use MD5-Challenge, One-Time Password, and Generic Token Card. Robust EAP methods use EAP-TLS, EAP-TTLS, PEAP, and EAP-FAST.

**Extensible hypertext Markup Language (XHTML)**  A unifying standard that brings the benefits of XML to those of HTML.

**Extensible Markup Language (XML)**  A cross-platform, extensible, and text-based standard markup language for representing structured data. It provides a cross-platform, software- and hardware-independent tool for transmitting information. XML is a meta-language, a coding language for describing programming languages used on the Web. XML uses standard generalized markup language (SGML) on the Web, and it is like Hypertext Markup Language (HTML). The Web browser interprets the XML tags for the right meaning of information in Web documents and pages. It is a flexible text format designed to describe data for electronic publishing.

**Exterior border gateway protocol (EBGP)**  A border gateway protocol (BGP) operation communicating routing information between two or more autonomous systems (ASs).

**External information system**  An information system or component that is outside of the authorization boundary established by the organization and for which the organization has no direct control over the implementation of required security controls or the assessment of security control effectiveness.

**External information system service provider**  A provider of external information system services to an organization through a variety of consumer-producer relationships. Examples include joint venture, business partnerships, outsourcing arrangements, licensing agreements, and supply chain arrangements.

**External network**  A network not controlled by an organization.

**External testing (security)**  External security testing is conducted from outside the organization's security perimeter.

**Extreme programming**  Extreme programming (XP) is the most well known and widely implemented agile development method for software products. XP uses a test-driven and bottom-up software development approach.

**Extranet**  A private network that uses web technology, permitting the sharing of portions of an enterprise's information or operations with suppliers, vendors, partners, customers, or other enterprises.

# F

**Failover**   (1) The capability to switch over automatically without human intervention or warning to a redundant or standby information system upon the failure or abnormal termination of the previously active system. (2) It is a backup concept in that when the primary system fails, the backup system is automatically activated.

**Fail-safe**   An automatic protection of programs and/or processing systems when hardware or software failure is detected in a computer system. It is a condition to avoid compromise in the event of a failure or have no chance of failure. This is a technical and corrective control.

**Fail-safe default**   Asserts that access decisions should be based on permission rather than exclusion. This equates to the condition in which lack of access is the default, and the "protection scheme" recognizes permissible actions rather than prohibited actions. Also, failures due to flaws in exclusion-based systems tend to grant (unauthorized) permissions, whereas permission-based systems tend to fail-safe with permission denied.

**Fail-secure**   The system preserves a secure condition during and after an identified failure.

**Fail-soft**   A selective termination of affected nonessential processing when hardware or software failure is determined to be imminent in a computer system. A computer system continues to function because of its resilience. Examples of its application can be found in distributed data processing systems. This is a technical and corrective control.

**Fail-stop processor**   A processor that can constrain the failure rate and protects the integrity of data. However, it is likely to be more vulnerable to denial-of-service (DoS) attacks.

**Failure**   It is a discrepancy between external results of a program's operation and software product requirements. A software failure is evidence of software faults.

**Failure access**   A type of incident in which unauthorized access to data results from hardware or software failure.

**Failure control**   A methodology used to detect imminent hardware or software failure and provide fail-safe or fail-soft recovery in a computer system (ANSI and IBM).

**Failure rate**   The number of times the hardware ceases to function in a given time period.

**Fallback procedures**   (1) In the event of a failure of transactions or the system, the ability to fallback to the original or alternate method for continuation of processing. (2) The ability to go back to the original or alternate method for continuation of computer processing.

**False acceptance**   When a biometric system incorrectly identifies an individual or incorrectly verifies an impostor against a claimed identity.

**False acceptance rate (FAR)**   The probability that a biometric system will incorrectly identify an individual or will fail to reject an impostor. The rate given normally assumes passive impostor attempts. The FAR is stated as the ratio of the number of false acceptances divided by the number of identification attempts.

**False match rate**   Alternative to false acceptance rate. Used to avoid confusion in applications that reject the claimant if their biometric data matches that of an applicant.

**False negative**   (1) An instance of incorrectly classifying malicious activity or content as benign. (2) An instance in which a security tool intended to detect a particular threat fails to do so. (3) When a tool does not report a security weakness where one is present.

**False non-match rate**   Alternative to false rejection rate. Used to avoid confusion in applications that reject the claimant if their biometric data matches that of an applicant.

**False positive**   (1) An instance in which a security tool incorrectly classifies benign activity or content as malicious. (2) When a tool reports a security weakness where no weakness is present. (3) An alert that incorrectly indicates that malicious activity is occurring.

**False positive rate**   The number of false positives divided by the sum of the number of false positives and the number of true positives.

**False rejection**   When a biometric system fails to identify an applicant or fails to verify the legitimate claimed identity of an applicant.

**False rejection rate (FRR)**   The probability that a biometric system will fail to identify an applicant, or verify the legitimate claimed identity of an applicant. The FRR is stated as the ratio of the number of false rejections divided by the number of identification attempts.

**Fault**   A physical malfunction or abnormal pattern of behavior causing an outage, error, or degradation of communications services on a communications network. Fault detection, error recovery, and failure recovery must be built into a computer system to tolerate faults.

**Fault injection testing**   Unfiltered and invalid data are injected as input into an application program to detect faults in resource operations and execution functions.

**Fault management**   The prevention, detection, reporting, diagnosis, and correction of faults and fault conditions. Fault management includes alarm surveillance, trouble tracking, fault diagnosis, and fault correction.

**Fault-tolerance mechanisms**   The ability of a computer system to continue to perform its tasks after the occurrence of faults and operate correctly even though one or more of its component parts are malfunctioning. Synonymous with resilience.

**Fault tolerant controls**   The ability of a processor to maintain effectiveness after some subsystems have failed. These are hardware devices or software products such as disk mirroring or server mirroring aimed at reducing loss of data due to system failures or human errors. It is the ability of a processor to maintain effectiveness after some subsystems have failed. This is a technical and preventive control and ensures availability control.

**Fault-tolerant programming**   Fault tolerant programming is robust programming plus redundancy features, and is partially similar to N-version programming.

**Feature**   An advantage attributed to a system.

**Federated trust**   Trust established within a federation, enabling each of the mutually trusting realms to share and use trust information (e.g., credentials) obtained from any of the other mutually trusting realms.

**Federation**   A collection of realms (domains) that have established trust among themselves. The level of trust may vary, but typically include authentication and may include authorization.

**Fetch protection**   A system-provided restriction to prevent a program from accessing data in another user's segment of storage. This is a technical and preventive control.

**Fiber-optic cable**   A method of transmitting light beams along optical fibers. A light beam, such as that produced in a laser, can be modulated to carry information. A single fiber-optic channel can carry significantly more information than most other means of information transmission. Optical fibers are thin strands of glass or other transparent material.

**File**   (1) A collection of related records.   (2) A collection of information logically grouped into a single entity and referenced by a unique name, such as a filename.

**File descriptor attacks**   File descriptors are non-negative integers that the system uses to keep track of files rather than using specific filenames. Certain file descriptors have implied uses. When a privileged program assigns an inappropriate file descriptor, it exposes that file to compromise.

**File encryption**   The process of encrypting individual files on a storage medium and permitting access to the encrypted data only after proper authentication is provided.

**File encryption key (FEK)**   Each owner's file is encrypted under a different randomly generated symmetric file encryption key (FEK).

**File infector virus**   A virus that attaches itself to executable program files, such as word processors, spreadsheet applications, and computer games.

**File integrity checker**   Software that generates, stores, and compares message digests for files to detect changes to the files.

**File protection**   The aggregate of all processes and procedures in a system designed to inhibit unauthorized access, contamination, or deletion of a file.

**File security**   The means by which access to computer files is limited to authorized users only.

**File server**   Sends and receives data between workstation and the server.

**File system**   A mechanism for naming, storing, organizing, and accessing files stored on logical volumes.

**File transfer protocol (FTP)**   A means to exchange remote files across a TCP/IP network and requires an account on the remote computer. Different versions of FTP include trivial FTP (not secure), secure FTP, and anonymous FTP using the "username" anonymous (not secure).

**Finger table**   Used for node lookup in peer-to-peer (P2P) networks. Each node maintains a finger table with entries, indexes, and node identifiers. Each node stores the IP addresses of the other nodes.

**Finite state machine (FSM) model**   The finite state machine (FSM) model is used for protocol modeling to demonstrate the correctness of a protocol. Mathematical techniques are used in specifying and verifying the protocol correctness. In FSM, each protocol machine of the sender or receiver is in a specific state, consisting of all the values of its variables and the program counter. From each state, there are zero or more possible transitions to other states. FSM is a mathematical model of a sequential machine that is composed of a finite set of input events, a finite set of output events, a finite set of states, a function that maps states and input to output, a function that maps states and inputs to states (a state transition function), and a specification that describes the initial state. FSMs are used for real-time application systems requiring better user interface mechanisms (menu-driven systems). In other words, FSM defines or implements the control structure of a system.

**Firewall** (1) A process integrated with a computer operating system that detects and prevents undesirable applications and remote users from accessing or performing operations on a secure computer; security domains are established which require authorization to enter. (2) A product that acts as a barrier to prevent unauthorized or unwanted communications between sections of a computer network. (3) A device or program that controls the flow of network traffic between networks or hosts that employ differing security postures. (4) A gateway that limits access between networks in accordance with local security policy. (5) A system designed to prevent unauthorized accesses to or from a private network. (6) Often used to prevent Internet users from accessing private networks connected to the Internet.

**Firewall control proxy** The component that controls a firewall's handling of a call. The firewall control proxy can instruct the firewall to open specific ports that are needed by a call, and direct the firewall to close these ports at call termination.

**Firewall environment** A firewall environment is a collection of systems at a point on a network that together constitute a firewall implementation. The environment could consist of one device or many devices such as several firewalls, intrusion detection systems, and proxy servers.

**Firewall platform** A firewall platform is the system device upon which a firewall is implemented. An example of a firewall platform is a commercial operating system running on a personal computer.

**Firewall rule set** A firewall rule set is a table of instructions that the firewall uses for determining how packets should be routed between its interfaces. In routers, the rule set can be a file that the router examines from top to bottom when making routing decisions.

**Firmware** (1) Software permanently installed inside the computer as part of its main memory to provide protection from erasure or loss if electrical power is interrupted. (2) The programs and data components of a cryptographic module that are stored in hardware within the cryptographic boundary and cannot be dynamically written or modified during execution.

**Fit-gap analysis** This analysis is a common technique, which can be applied to help define the nature of the required service components. It examines the components within the context of requirements and makes a determination as to the suitability of the service component.

**Flash ROM** Flash read only memory (ROM) is nonvolatile memory that is writable.

**Flaw** An error of commission, omission, or oversight in a system that allows protection mechanisms to be bypassed or disabled. Synonymous with loophole or fault.

**Flaw-based DoS attacks** These make use of software errors to consume resources. Patching and upgrading software can prevent the flaw-based DoS attacks.

**Flooding** Sending large numbers of messages to a host or network at a high rate.

**Flooding attacks** Flooding attacks most often involve copying valid service requests and resending them to a service provider. The attacker may issue repetitive SOAP/XML messages in an attempt to overload the Web service. This type of activity may not be detected as an intrusion because the source IP address is valid, the network packer behavior is valid, and the SOAP/XML message is well- formed. But the business behavior is not legitimate resulting in a DoS attack. Techniques for detecting and handling DoS can be applied against flooding attacks.

**Flow**   A particular network communication session occurring between hosts.

**Flow control**   A strategy for protecting the contents of information objects from being transferred to objects at improper security levels. It is more restrictive than access control.

**Flow-sensitive analysis**   Analysis of a computer program that takes into account the flow of control.

**Focused testing**   A test methodology that assumes some knowledge of the internal structure and implementation detail of the assessment object. Focused testing is also known as gray box testing.

**Folder**   An organizational structure used by a file system to group files.

**Folder encryption**   The process of encrypting individual folders on a storage medium and permitting access to the encrypted files within the folders only after proper authentication is provided.

**Forensic computer**   The practice of gathering, retaining, and analyzing computer-related data for investigative purposes in a manner that maintains the integrity of the data.

**Forensic copy**   An accurate bit-for-bit reproduction of the information contained on an electronic device or associated media, whose validity and integrity has been verified using an accepted algorithm.

**Forensic hash**   It is used to maintain the integrity of an acquired data by computing a cryptographically strong, non-reversible hash value over the acquired data. A hash code value is computed using several algorithms.

**Forensic process**   It is the process of collecting, examining, analyzing, and reporting of facts to gain a better understanding of an event of interest.

**Forensic specialist**   A professional who locates, identifies, collects, analyzes, and examines data while preserving the data's integrity and maintaining a strict chain of custody of information discovered.

**Formal verification**   The process of using formal proofs to demonstrate the consistency (design verification) between a formal specification of a system and a formal security policy model or (implementation verification) between the formal specification and its program implementation.

**Forward cipher**   One of the two functions of the block cipher algorithm that is selected by the cryptographic key.

**Forward engineering**   The traditional process of moving from high-level abstractions and logical, implementation-independent designs to the physical implementation of a system.

**Frame relay**   A type of fast packet technology using variable length packets called frames. By contrast, a cell-relay system such as asynchronous transfer mode (ATM) transports user data in fixed-sized cells.

**Freeware**   Software made available to the public at no cost. The author retains the copyright rights and can place restrictions on the program's use.

**Frequency analysis attacks**   A sequence of letters and words used in cryptographic keys, messages, and conversations between people when they are transforming the plaintext into ciphertext. This transformation is of two types: substitution and permutation. Both substitution ciphers (shifts the letters and words used in the plaintext) and transposition ciphers (permutes or scrambles the letters and words used in the plaintext) are subject to frequency analysis attack. These ciphers can be simple or complex, where the former uses a short sequence of letters and words and the latter uses a long sequence of letters and words. The goal of the attacker is to determine the cryptographic key used in the transformation of the plaintext into the ciphertext to complete his attack.

**Front-end processors (FEP)**   A front-end processor (FEP) is a programmed-logic or stored-program device that interfaces data communication equipment with an input/output bus or the memory of a data processing computer.

**Full disk encryption (FDE)**   The process of encrypting all the data on the hard drive used to boot a computer, including the computer's operating system, and permitting access to the data only after successful authentication with the full disk encryption product. FDE is also called whole disk encryption.

**Full-scale testing**   Full-scale testing or full-interruption testing is disruptive and costly to an organization's business processes and operations as computer systems will not be available on a 24×7 schedule.

**Full tunneling**   A method that causes all network traffic to go through the tunnel to the organization.

**Fully connected topology**   Fully connected topology is a network topology in which there is a direct path (branch) between any two nodes. With n nodes, there are n (n–1) / 2 direct paths or branches.

**Functional design**   A process in which the user's needs are translated into a system's technical specifications.

**Functional testing**   The portion of security testing in which the advertised security mechanisms of a system are tested, under operational conditions, for correct operation. This is a management and preventive control.

**Functionality**   Distinct from assurance, the functional behavior of a system. Functionality requirements include confidentiality, integrity, availability, authentication, and safety.

**Fuzz testing**   Similar to fault injection testing in that invalid data is input into the application via the environment, or input by one process into another process. Fuzz testing is implemented by tools called fuzzers, which are programs or script that submit some combination of inputs to the test target to reveal how it responds.

**Fuzzy logic**   It uses set theory, which is a mathematical notion that an element may have partial membership in a set. Fuzzy logic is used in insurance and financial risk assessment application systems.

# G

**G2B**   Government-to-business (G2B) is an electronic government (e-government) model where interactions are taking place between governments and businesses and vice versa. Examples of interactions include procurement and acquisition transactions with business entities and payments to them (e.g., U.S. DoD doing business with Defense Contractors). Reverse auction is practiced in B2B or G2B e-commerce.

**G2C**   Government-to-citizens (G2C) is an electronic government model where interactions are taking place between a government and its citizens. Examples of interactions include entitlement payments (e.g., retirement and Medicare benefits), tax receipts, and refund payments.

**G2E**   Government-to-employees (G2E) is an electronic government model where interactions are taking place between government agencies and their employees.

**G2G**   Government-to-government (G2G) is an electronic government model where interactions are taking place within a government agency and those between other government agencies.

**Galois counter mode (GCM) algorithm**   Provides authenticated encryption and authenticated decryption functions for both confidential data and non- confidential data. Each of these functions is relatively efficient and parallel; consequently, high-throughput implementations are possible in both hardware and software. GCM provides stronger authentication assurance than a non-cryptographic checksum or error detecting code; in particular, GCM can detect both accidental modifications of the data and intentional, unauthorized modifications. The GCM is constructed with a symmetric key block cipher key a block size of 128 bits and a key size of at least 128 bits. The GCM is a mode of operation of the AES algorithm.

**Galois message authentication code (GMAC)**   Provides authenticated encryption and authenticated decryption for non-confidential data only. GMAC is a specialized GCM when the GCM input is restricted to data that is not be encrypted; and GMAC is simply an authentication mode on the input data.

**Gateway**   It is an interface between two networks and a means of communicating between networks. It is designed to reduce the problems of interfacing different networks or devices. The networks involved may be any combination of local networks that employ different level protocols or local and long-haul networks. It facilitates compatibility between networks by converting transmission speeds, protocols, codes, or security measures. Gateways operate in the application layer and transport layer of the ISO/OSI reference model.

**General packet radio service (GPRS)**   A packet switching enhancement to global system for mobile communications (GSM) and time division multiple access (TDMA) wireless networks to increase data transmission speeds.

**General support system (GSS)**   An interconnected information resource under the same direct management controls that share common functionality. It normally includes hardware, software, information, data, applications, communications, facilities, and people and provides support for a variety of users and/or applications. Individual applications support different mission-related functions. Users may be from the same or different organizations.

**Generalized testing**   A test methodology that assumes no knowledge of the internal structure and implementation detail of the assessment object. Also known as black-box testing.

**Global positioning system (GPS)**   (1) A system for determining position by comparing radio signals from several satellites. (2) A network of satellites providing precise location determination to receivers.

**Global supply chain**   A system of organizations, people, activities, information, and resources, international in scope, involved in moving products or services from supplier/producer to consumer/customer.

**Global system for mobile communications (GSM)**   A set of standards for second generation cellular networks currently maintained by the third generation partnership project (3GPP).

**Gopher**   A protocol designed to allow a user to transfer text or binary files among computer hosts across networks.

**Graduated security**   A security system that provides several levels (e.g., low, moderate, or high) of protection based on threats, risks, available technology, support services, time, human concerns, and economics.

**Granularity**   (1) An expression of the relative size of a data object. (2) The degree to which access to objects can be restricted. (3) Granularity can be applied to both the actions allowable on objects, as well as to the users allowed to perform those actions of the object. (4) The relative fineness or coarseness by which a mechanism can be adjusted. For example, protection at the file level is considered to be coarse granularity, whereas protection at the field level is considered to be of finer granularity. (5) The phrase "the granularity of a single user" means the access control mechanism can be adjusted to include or exclude any single user.

**Graphical user interface (GUI)**   A combination of menus, screen design, keyboard commands, command language, and help screens that together create the way a user interacts with a computer. Allows users to move in and out of programs and manipulate their commands by using a pointing device (often a mouse). Synonymous with user interface.

**Gray box testing**   A test methodology that assumes some knowledge of the internal structure and implementation detail of the assessment object. Focused testing is also known as gray box testing.

**Grid computing**   A form of distributed computing whereby a super virtual computer is composed of many networked and loosely coupled computers working together to perform very large tasks. The grid handles non-interactive workloads that involve a large number of files that are heterogeneous and geographically dispersed. Grids are constructed with middleware and software libraries, and the grid computers are connected to a network (that is, private, public, or the Internet) with a conventional network interface, such as Ethernet. There is an overlap between grid computing, distributed computing, parallel computing, and mesh computing (Wikipedia).

**Group**   A set of subjects.

**Groupware**   Software that recognizes the significance of groups by providing system functions to support the collaborative activities of work groups.

**Guard (hardware and software)**   A mechanism limiting the exchange of information between information systems or subsystems. It operates as a gatekeeper in the form of an application layer guard to implement firewall mechanisms, such as performing identification and authentication functions and enforcing security policies. Guard functionality includes such features as cryptographic invocation check on information that is allowed outside the protected enclave and data content filtering to support sensitivity regrade decisions. The guard functionality, although effective for non-real-time applications (e.g., e-mail) on networks with low sensitivity, has been difficult to scale to highly classified networks and real-time applications.

**Guessing entropy**   A measure of the difficulty that an attacker has to guess the average password used in a system. Entropy is stated in bits. The attacker is assumed to know the actual password frequency distribution.

**Guessing (password)**   The act of repeatedly attempting to authenticate using default passwords, dictionary words, and other possible passwords.

# H

**H.225**   A gatekeeper telephony protocol used in the PC-to-gatekeeper channel (the International Telecommunications Union (ITU) standard).

**H.245**   A telephony protocol used to allow terminals to negotiate options (the ITU standard).

**H.248**   A protocol used in large deployment for gateway decomposition (the ITU standard).

**H.323**   A gateway protocol used in the Internet telephony systems operating with packet-switched networks providing voice and video calling and signaling (the ITU standard).

**Hacker**   Any unauthorized user who gains, or attempts to gain, access to an information system, regardless of motivation.

**Handler**   A type of program used in distributed denial-of-service (DDoS) attacks to control agents distributed throughout a network. Also refers to an incident handler, which refers to a person who performs computer-security incident response work.

**Handshake**   Involves passing special characters (XON/XOFF) between two devices or between two computers to control the flow of information. When the receiving computer cannot continue to receive data, it transmits an XOFF that tells the sending computer to stop transmitting. When transmission can resume, the receiving computer signals the sending computer with an XON. Two types of handshake exist: hardware and software. The hardware handshake uses non-data wires for transmission and the software handshake uses data wires as in modem-to-modem communications over telephone lines.

**Handshaking procedure**   A dialogue between two entities (e.g., a user and a computer, a computer and another computer, or a program and another program) for the purpose of identifying and authenticating the entities to one another.

**Hardening**   Configuring a host's operating system and application systems to reduce the host's security weaknesses.

**Hardware and software monitors**   Hardware monitors work by attaching probes to processor circuits and detecting and recording events at those probes. Software monitors are programs that execute in a computer system to observe and report on the behavior of the system.

**Hardware segmentation**   The principle of hardware segmentation provides hardware transparency when hardware is designed in a modular fashion and when it is interconnected. A failure in one module should not affect the operation of other modules. Similarly, a module attacked by an intruder should not compromise the entire system. System architecture should be arranged so that vulnerable networks or network segments can be quickly isolated or taken off-line in the event of an attack. Examples of hardware that need to be segmented includes network switches, physical circuits, and power supply equipment.

**Hardware tokens**   Hardware tokens (also called hard tokens or eTokens) are devices with computing capability integrated into the device.

**Hash algorithm**   Algorithm that creates a hash based on a message.

**Hash-based message authentication code (HMAC)**   (1) A symmetric key authentication method using hash function. (2) A message authentication code (MAC) that uses a cryptographic key in conjunction with a hash function. (3) A MAC that utilizes a keyed hash.

**Hash code**   The string of bits that is the output of a hash function.

**Hash function**   A function that maps a bit string of arbitrary length to a fixed length bit string. Approved hash functions satisfy the following properties: (1) one-way states that it is computationally infeasible to find any input that maps to any pre-specified output, and (2) collision resistant states that it is computationally infeasible to find any two distinct inputs that map to the same output. The hash function may be used to produce a checksum, called a hash value or message digest, for a potentially long string or message.

**Hash total**   The use of specific mathematical formulae to produce a quantity (often appended to and) used as a checksum or validation parameter for the data it protects. This is a technical and detective control.

**Hash value**   (1) The fixed-length bit string produced by a hash function. (2) The result of applying a hash function to information. See message digest.

**Hashing**   The process of using a mathematical algorithm against data to produce a numeric value that is representative of that data.

**Hedging**   Taking a position opposite to the exposure or risk. Because they reduce exposures and risks, risk mitigation techniques are examples of hedging.

**High assurance guard**   An enclave boundary protection device that controls access between a LAN that an enterprise system has a requirement to protect, and an external network that is outside the control of the enterprise system, with a high degree of assurance.

**High availability**   A failover feature to ensure availability during device or component interruptions.

**High-impact system**   An information system in which at least one security objective (i.e., confidentiality, integrity, or availability) is assigned a potential impact value of high.

**High-level data link control (HDLC) protocol**   HDLC is a bit-oriented protocol with frame structure consisting of address, control, data, and checksum (cyclic redundancy code) fields (Tanenbaum).

**Hijacking**   An attack that occurs during an authenticated session with a database or system. The attacker disables a user's desktop system, intercepts responses from the application, and responds in ways that probe the session.

**Holder-of-key assertion**   An assertion that contains a reference to a symmetric key or a public key (corresponding to a private key) possessed by the subscriber. The relying party may require the subscriber to prove their identity.

**Honeynet**   A network of honeypots designed to attract hackers so that their intrusions can be detected and analyzed, and to study the hackers' behavior. Organizations should consult their legal counsel before deploying a honeynet for any legal ramifications of monitoring an attacker's activity.

**Honeypot**   A fake production system designed with firewalls, routers, Web services, and database servers that looks like a real production system, but acts as a decoy and is studied to see how attackers do their work.   It is a host computer that is designed to collect data on suspicious activity and has no authorized users other than security administrators and attackers. Organizations should consult their legal counsel before deploying a honeypot for any legal ramifications of monitoring an attacker's activity.

**Host**   (1) Any node that is not a router. (2) Any computer-based system connected to the network and containing the necessary protocol interpreter software to initiate network access and carry out information exchange across the communications network. (3) The term can refer to almost any kind of computer, including a centralized mainframe that is a host to its terminals, a server that is host to its clients, or a desktop personal computer (PC) that is host to its peripherals. In network architectures, a client station (user's machine) is also considered a host because it is a source of information to the network, in contrast to a device, such as a router or switch that directs traffic. This definition encompasses typical mainframe computers and workstations connected directly to the communications sub-network and executing the inter-computer networking protocols. A terminal is not a host because it does not contain the protocol software needed to perform information exchange. A router or switch is not a host either. A workstation is a host because it does have such capability. Host platforms include operating systems, file systems, and communications stacks.

**Host-based firewall**   A software-based firewall installed on a server to monitor and control its incoming and outgoing network traffic. Security in host-based firewalls is generally at the application level, rather than at a network level.

**Host-based intrusion detection system (IDS)**   IDS operate on information collected from within an individual computer system. This vantage point allows host-based IDSs to determine exactly which processes and user accounts are involved in a particular attack on the operating system. Furthermore, unlike network-based IDSs, host-based IDSs can more readily "see" the intended outcome of an attempted attack, because they can directly access and monitor the data files and system processes usually targeted by attacks. It is a program that monitors the characteristics of a single host and the events occurring within the host to identify and stop suspicious activity.

**Host-based security**   The technique of securing an individual system from attack. It is dependent on an operating system and its version.

**Host-to-front-end protocol**   A set of conventions governing the format and control of data that are passed from a host to a front-end machine.

**Hot failover device**   Computer systems will have at least one backup mechanism in that when the primary device fails or is taken off-line, the hot failover device comes online and maintains all existing communications sessions; no disruption of communications occurs. This concept can be applied to firewalls.

**Hotfix**   Microsoft's term to bundle hotfixes (patches) into service packs for easier and faster installation.

**Hot-site**   (1) An alternate site with a duplicate IT already set up and running, which is maintained by an organization or its contractor to ensure continuity of service for critical systems in the event of a disaster. (2) A fully operational offsite data processing facility equipped with hardware and system software to be used in the event of a disaster.

**Hot spare**   A hot spare drive is a physical hot standby drive installed in the RAID disk array that is active and connected but is inactive until an active drive fails. When a key component fails, the hot spare is switched into operation. A hot spare reduces the mean time to recovery (MTTR), thus supporting redundancy and availability. Hot spare requires hot swapping or hot plugging by a human operator (Wikipedia).

**Hot spots**   Hot spots consist of one or more Wi-Fi access points positioned on a ceiling or wall in a public place to provide maximum wireless coverage for a wireless LAN.

**Hot wash**   Hot wash is a debriefing session conducted immediately after an exercise or test of an information system with the testing team, non-testing staff, and other participants to share problems and experiences.

**Hubs**   A hub can be thought of a central place from which all connections are made between networks and computers. Hubs are simple devices that connect network components, sending a packet of data to all other connected devices. Hubs operate in the physical layer of the ISO/OSI reference model.

**Human threats**   Examples of human threats include intentional/unintentional errors; sabotage of data, systems, and property; implanting of malicious code; and terrorist attacks.

**Hybrid attack (password)**   A form of guessing attack in which the attacker uses a dictionary that contains possible passwords and then uses variations through brute force methods of the original passwords in the dictionary to create new potential passwords. Hybrid Attack = Dictionary Attack + Brute Force Attack.

**Hybrid security control**   A security control that has the properties of both a common security control and a system-specific security control (i.e., one part of the control is deemed to be common, whereas another part of the control is deemed to be system-specific).

**Hybrid topology**   Hybrid topology is a combination of any two different basic network topologies (e.g., combination of star topology and bus topology). The tree topology is an example of a hybrid topology where a linear bus backbone connects star-configured networks.

**Hyperlink**   An electronic link providing direct access from one distinctively marked place in a hypertext or hypermedia document to another in the same or a different document.

**Hypertext markup language (HTML)**   A markup language that is a subset of standard generalized markup language (SGML) and is used to create hypertext and hypermedia documents on the Web incorporating text, graphics, sound, video, and hyperlinks. It is a mechanism used to create Web pages on the Internet.

**Hypertext transfer protocol (HTTP)**   (1) The native protocol of the Web, used to transfer hypertext documents on the Internet. (2) A standard method for communication between clients and Web servers.

**Hypervisor**   The hypervisor or virtual machine (VM) monitor is an additional layer of software between an operating system and hardware platform that is used to operate multitenant VMs in cloud services. Besides virtualized resources, the hypervisor normally supports other application programming interfaces (APIs) to conduct administrative operations, such as launching, migrating, and terminating VM instances. It is the virtualization component that manages the guest operating systems (OSs) on a host and controls the flow of instructions between the guest OSs and the physical hardware. Compared with a traditional non-virtualized implementation, the addition of a hypervisor causes an increase in the attack surface, which is risky.

# I

**Identification**   (1) The process of verifying the identity of a user, process, or device, usually as a prerequisite for granting access to resources in an IT system. (2) The process of discovering the true identity (i.e., origin, initial history) of a person or item from the entire collection of similar persons or items. Identification comes before authentication.

**Identifier**   A unique data string used as a key in the biometric system to name a person's identity and its associated attributes.

**Identity**   (1) A unique name of an individual person. Because the legal names of persons are not necessarily unique, the identity of a person must include sufficient additional information (for example, an address or some unique identifier such as an employee or account number) to make the complete name unique. (2) It is information that is unique within a security domain and which is recognized as denoting a particular entity within that domain. (3) The set of physical and behavioral characteristics by which an individual is uniquely recognizable.

**Identity-based access control (IBAC)**   An access control mechanism based only on the identity of the subject and object. An IBAC decision grants or denies a request based on the presence of an entity on an access control list. IBAC and discretionary access control are considered equivalent.

**Identity-based security policy**   A security policy based on the identities and/or attributes of the object (system resource) being accessed and of the subject (e.g., user, group of users, process, or device) requesting access.

**Identity binding**   Binding of the vetted claimed identity to the individual (through biometrics) according to the issuing authority.

**Identity management**   Identity management system comprised of one or more systems or applications that manages the identity verification, validation, and issuance process.

**Identity proofing**   (1) A process by which a credential service provider (CSP) and a registration authority (RA) validate sufficient information to uniquely identify a person. (2) The process of providing sufficient information (e.g., identity history, credentials, and documents) to a personal identity verification (PIV) registrar when attempting to establish an identity.

**Identity registration**   The process of making a person's identity known to the personal identity verification (PIV) system, associating a unique identifier with that identity, and collecting and recording the person's relevant attributes into the system.

**Identity token**   A smart card, a metal key, or some other physical token carried by a system user that allows user identity validation.

**Identity verification**   The process of confirming or denying that a claimed identity is correct by comparing the credentials (i.e., something you know, something you have, something you are) of a person requesting access with those previously proven and stored in the personal identity verification (PIV) card or system and associated with the identity being claimed.

**Impact**   The magnitude of harm that can be expected to result from the consequences of unauthorized disclosure of information, unauthorized modification of information, unauthorized destruction of information, loss of information, or loss of information system availability.

**Impersonating**   An attempt to gain access to a computer system by posing as an authorized user. Synonymous with masquerading, spoofing, and mimicking.

**Implementation attacks**   Implementation attacks can occur when hardware or software is not implemented properly or is not used correctly. For example, if a secure socket layer (SSL) protocol or transport layer security (TLS) protocol is implemented improperly or used incorrectly, it is subjected to a man-in-the-middle (MitM) attack. This attack occurs when a malicious entity intercepts all communication between the Web client and the Web server with which the client is attempting to establish an SSL/TLS connection.

**Inappropriate usage**   A person who violates acceptable use of any network or computer policies.

**In-band management**   In in-band management, a secure shell (SSH) session is established with the connectivity device (e.g., routers and switches) in a distributed local-area network (LAN).

**Incident**   (1) An occurrence that actually or potentially jeopardizes the confidentiality, integrity, or availability of an information system or the information the system processes, stores, or transmits or that constitutes a violation or imminent threat of violation of computer security policies, acceptable use policies, or standard security practices.

**Incident handling**   The mitigation of violations of security policies and recommended practices.

**Incident indications**   A sign that an incident (e.g., malware) may have occurred or may be currently occurring.

**Incident precursors**   (1) A sign that a malware attack may occur in the future. (2) A sign that an attacker may be preparing to cause an incident.

**Incident response plan**   The documentation of a predetermined set of instructions or procedures to detect, respond to, and limit consequences of a malicious cyber attack against an organization's IT system(s).

**Incident-response team**   A multidisciplined team consisting of technical, legal, audit, and public affairs specialists to address adverse events.

**Incineration**   A physically destructive method of sanitizing media; the act of burning completely to ashes.

**Incomplete parameter checking**   A system design fault that exists when all parameters have not been fully checked for accuracy and consistency by the operating system, thus makes the system vulnerable to penetration.

**Incorrect file and directory permissions**   File and directory permissions control the access users and processes have to files and directories. Appropriate permissions are critical to the security of any system. Poor permissions could allow any number of attacks, including the reading or writing of password files or the addition of hosts to the list of trusted remote hosts.

**Inculpatory evidence**   Evidence that tends to increase the likelihood of fault or guilt.

**Independent validation and verification**   Review, analysis, and testing conducted by an independent party throughout the life cycle of software development to ensure that the new software meets user or contract requirements.

**Indication**   A sign that an incident (e.g., malware) may have occurred or may be currently occurring.

**Individual accountability**   The ability to positively associate the identity of a user with the time, method, and degree of system access.

**Inference**   Derivation of new information from known information. The inference problem refers to the fact that the derived information may be classified at a level for which the user is not cleared. Users may deduce unauthorized information from the legitimate information they acquire. Inference is a problem that derives primarily from poor database design.

**Inference attacks**   An inference attack occurs when a user or intruder is able to deduce information to which he had no privilege from information to which he has privilege. It is a part of traffic analysis attacks.

**Information architecture**   The technologies, interfaces, and geographical locations of functions involved with an organization's information activities.

**Information assurance**   Measures that protect and defend data/information and information systems by ensuring their availability, integrity, authentication, confidentiality, and nonrepudiation. These measures include providing for restoration of information systems by incorporating protection, detection, and reaction capabilities.

**Information density**   The total amount and quality of information available to all market participants, consumers, and merchants.

**Information economics**   Deals with the principle that the costs to obtain information should be equal to or less than the benefits to be derived from the information.

**Information engineering**   An approach to planning, analyzing, designing, and developing an information system with an enterprise-wide perspective and an emphasis on data and architectures.

**Information flow**   The sequence, timing, and direction of how information proceeds through an organization.

**Information flow control**   Access control based on restricting the information flow into an object (e.g., Bell and La Padula model).

**Information owner**   An official with responsibility for establishing controls for information generation, collection, processing, dissemination, and disposal.

**Information portal**   A single point of access through a Web browser to business information inside and/or outside an organization.

**Information quality**   Information quality is composed of three elements such as utility, integrity, and objectivity.

**Information resources**   Information and related resources, such as personnel, equipment, funds, and information technology.

**Information rights**   The rights that individuals and organizations have regarding information that pertains to them.

**Information security**   The protection of information and information systems from unauthorized access, use, disclosure, disruption, modification, or destruction in order to provide confidentiality, integrity, and availability.

**Information security architecture**   An embedded, integral part of the enterprise architecture that describes the structure and behavior for an enterprise's security processes, information security systems, personnel and organizational subunits, showing their alignment with the enterprise's mission and strategic plans.

**Information security policy**   Aggregate of directives, regulations, rules, and practices that prescribe how an organization manages, protects, and distributes information.

**Information security program plan**   A formal document that provides an overview of the security requirements for an organization-wide information security program and describes the program management controls and common controls in place or planned for meeting those requirements.

**Information system (IS)**   A discrete set of information resources organized for the collection, processing, maintenance, use, sharing, dissemination, or disposition of information.

**Information system owner**   An official responsible for the overall procurement, development, integration, modification, or operation and maintenance of an information system.

**Information system resilience**   The ability of an information system to continue to: (1) operate under adverse conditions or stress, even if in a degraded or debilitated state, while maintaining essential operational capabilities; and (2) recover to an effective operational posture in a time frame consistent with mission needs. It supports agile defense strategy and is the same as resilience.

**Information system security officer (ISSO)**   Individual assigned responsibility by the senior agency information security officer, authorizing official, management official, or information system owner for ensuring the appropriate operational security posture is maintained for an information system or program.

**Information-systems (IS) security**   The protection afforded to information systems in order to preserve the availability, integrity, and confidentiality of the systems and information contained within the systems. Such protection is the application of the combination of all security disciplines that will, at a minimum, include communications security, emanation security, emission security, computer security, operational security, information security, personnel security, industrial security, resource protection, and physical security.

**Information systems security engineering**   The art and science of discovering users' information protection needs and then designing and making information systems, with economy and elegance, so they can safely resist the forces to which they may be subjected.

**Information technology (IT)**   (1) Any equipment or interconnected system or sub-system of equipment that is used in the automatic acquisition, storage, manipulation, management, movement, control, display, switching, interchange, transmission, or reception of data or information by an organization or its contractor. (2) The term IT includes computers, ancillary equipment, software, firmware, and similar procedures, services (including support services), and related resources.

**Information-technology (IT) architecture**   An integrated framework for evolving or maintaining existing IT and acquiring new IT to achieve the organization's strategic goals. A complete IT architecture should consist of both logical and technical components. The logical architecture provides the high-level description of the organization's mission, functional requirements, information requirements, system components, and information flows among the components. The technical architecture defines the specific IT standards and rules used to implement the logical architecture.

**Information type**   A specific category of information (e.g., privacy, medical, proprietary, financial, investigative, contractor sensitive, and security management) defined by an organization or in some instances, by a specific law, executive order, directive, policy, or regulation.

**Information value**   (1) The value of information is dependent on who needs the information (i.e., insider or outsider of an organization) and its worth to this person. (2) A qualitative measure of the importance of the information based upon factors such as level of robustness of the information assurance controls allocated to the protection of information based upon mission criticality, the sensitivity (e.g., classification and compartmentalization) of the information, releasability to other entities, perishability/longevity of the information (e.g., short life data versus long life data), and potential impact of loss of confidentiality, integrity, and availability of the information.

**Infrastructure component**   Software unit that provides application functionality not related to business functionality, such as error/message handling, audit trails, or security.

**Ingress filtering**   (1) Filtering of incoming network traffic. (2) Blocking incoming packets that should not enter a network. (3) The process of blocking incoming packets that use obviously false IP addresses, such as reserved source addresses.

**Inheritance**   (1) A situation in which an information system or an application system receives protection from security controls (or portions of security controls) that are implemented by other entities either internal or external to the organization where the system resides. (2) A mechanism that allows objects of a class to acquire part of their definition from another class (called a super class). Inheritance can be regarded as a method for sharing a behavioral description.

**Initial program load (IPL)**   A process of copying the resident operating system into the computer's read memory.

**Initialization vector (IV)**   (1) A non-secret binary vector used in defining the starting point of an encryption process within a cryptographic algorithm. (2) A data block that some modes of operation require as an additional initial input.

**Inline sensor**   A sensor deployed so that the network traffic it is monitoring must pass through it.

**Input block**   A data block that is an input to either the forward cipher function or the inverse cipher function of the block cipher algorithm.

**Insider attack**   An attack originating from inside a protected network, either malicious or nonmalicious.

**Instant messaging (IM)**   A facility for exchanging messages in real-time with other people over the Internet and tracking the progress of the conversation.

**Integrated services digital network (ISDN)**   A worldwide digital communications network evolving from existing telephone services. The goal of ISDN is to replace the current analog telephone system with totally digital switching and transmission facilities capable of carrying data ranging from voice to computer transmission, music, and video. Computers and other devices are connected to ISDN lines through simple, standardized interfaces. When fully implemented, ISDN is expected to provide users with faster, more extensive communications services in data, video, and voice.

**Integration test**   A process to confirm that program units are linked together and that they interface with files or databases correctly. This is a management and preventive control.

**Integrity**   (1) The property that protected and sensitive data has not been modified or deleted in an unauthorized and undetected manner. (2) Preservation of the original quality and accuracy of data in written or electronic form. (3) Guarding against improper information modification or destruction, (4) Ensuring information nonrepudiation and authenticity. (5) The ability to detect even minute changes in the data.

**Integrity level**   A level of trustworthiness associated with a subject or object.

**Intellectual property**   Useful artistic, technical, and/or industrial information, knowledge or ideas that convey ownership and control of tangible or virtual usage and/or representation.

**Intended signatory**   An entity that intends to generate digital signatures in the future.

**Interception**   The process of slipping in between communications and hijacking communications channels.

**Interdiction**   The act of impeding or denying the use of a computer system resource to a user.

**Interface**   The common boundary between independent systems or modules where communication takes place.

**Interface profile**   The sub-component that provides the capability to customize the component for various users. The interface profile can specify the business rules and workflow that are to be executed when the component is initialized or it can be tailored to suit different deployment architectures and business rules. The profile can specify the architectural pattern that complements the service component.

**Inter-file analysis**   Analysis of code residing in different files that have procedural, data, or other interdependencies.

**Internal border gateway protocol (IBGP)**   A border gateway protocol operation communicating routing information within an autonomous system.

**Internal control**   A process within an organization designed to provide reasonable assurance regarding the achievement of the following primary objectives (1) the reliability and integrity of information, (2) compliance with policies, plans, procedures, laws, regulations, and contracts, (3) the safeguarding of assets, (4) the economical and efficient use of resources, and (5) the accomplishment of established objectives and goals for operations and programs.

**Internal network**   A network where (1) the establishment, maintenance, and provisioning of security controls are under the direct control of organizational employees or contractors or (2) cryptographic encapsulation or similar security technology implemented between organization-controlled endpoints provides the same effect. An internal network is typically organization-owned, yet may be organization-controlled, while not being organization-owned.

**Internal security audit**   A security audit conducted by personnel responsible to the management of the organization being audited.

**Internal security controls**   Hardware, firmware, and software features within an information system that restrict access to resources (hardware, software, and data) only to authorized subjects (persons, programs, processes, or devices). Examples of internal security controls are encryption, digital signatures, digital certificates, and split knowledge. The security controls can be classified as (1) supporting, preventive, detective, corrective, and recovery controls, (2) management, technical, operational, and compensating controls, and (3) common controls, system-specific, and hybrid controls.

**Internal testing (security)**   It is similar to external (security) testing except that the testers are on the organization's internal network behind the security perimeter.

**Internet**   The Internet is the single, interconnected, worldwide system of commercial, governmental educational, and other computer networks that share (1) the protocol suites and (2) the name and address spaces. The Internet is a decentralized, global network of computers (Internet hosts), linked by the use of common communications protocols (TCP/IP). The Internet allows users worldwide to exchange messages, data, and images. It is worldwide "network of networks" that uses the TCP/IP protocol suite for communications.

**Internet-based EDI**   Web EDI that operates on the Internet, and is widely accessible to most companies, including small-to-medium enterprises.

**Internet control message protocol (ICMP)**   A message control and error-reporting protocol between a host server and a gateway to the Internet. ICMP is used by a device, often a router, to report and acquire a wide-range of communications-related information.

**Internet key exchange (IKE) protocol**   Protocol used to negotiate, create, and manage security associations (SAs).

**Internet message access protocol (IMAP)**   A mailbox access protocol defined by IETF RFC 3501. IMAP is one of the most commonly used mailbox access protocols, and offers a much wider command set than post office protocol (POP). It is a method of communication used to read electronic messages stored in a remote server.

**Internet protocol (IP)**   The network-layer protocol in the TCP/IP stack used in the Internet. The IP is a connectionless protocol that fits well with the connectionless Ethernet protocol. However, the IP does not fit well with the connection-oriented ATM network.

**Internet protocol (IP) address**   An IP address is a unique number for a computer that is used to determine where messages transmitted on the Internet should be delivered. The IP address is analogous to a house number for ordinary postal mail.

**Internet Protocol security (IPsec)**   An IEEE Standard, RFC 2411, protocol that provides security capabilities at the Internet Protocol (IP) layer of communications. IPsec's key management protocol is used to negotiate the secret keys that protect virtual private network (VPN) communications, and the level and type of security protections that will characterize the VPN. The most widely used key management protocol is the Internet key exchange (IKE) protocol. IPsec is a standard consisting of IPv6 security features ported over to the current version of IPv4. IPsec security features provide confidentiality, data integrity, and nonrepudiation services.

**Internet service provider (ISP)**   ISP is an entity providing a network connection to the global Internet.

**Interoperability**   (1) A measure of the ability of one set of entities to physically connect to and logically communicate with another set of entities. (2) The ability of two or more systems or components to exchange information and to use the information that has been exchanged. (3) The capability of systems, subsystems, or components to communicate with one another, to exchange services, and to use information including content, format, and semantics.

**Interoperability testing**   Testing to ensure that two or more communications products (hosts or routers) can interwork and exchange data.

**Interpreted virus**   A virus that is composed of source code that can be executed only by a particular application or service.

**Interpreter**   (1) A program that processes a script or other program expression and carries out the requested action, in accordance with the language definition. (2) A support program that reads a single source statement, translates that statement to machine language, executes those machine-level instructions, and then moves on to the next source statement. An interpreter operates on a "load and go" method.

**Inter-procedural analysis**   Analysis between calling and called procedures within a computer program.

**Intranet**   A private network that is employed within the confines of a given enterprise (e.g., internal to a business or agency). An organization's intranet is usually protected from external access by a firewall. An intranet is a network internal to an organization but that runs the same protocols as the network external to the organization (i.e., the Internet). Every organizational network that runs the TCP/IP protocol suite is an Intranet.

**Intrusion**   Attacks or attempted attacks from outside the security perimeter of an information system, thus bypassing the security mechanisms.

**Intrusion detection**   (1) Detection of break-ins or break-in attempts either manually or via software expert systems that operate on logs or other information available on the network. (2) The process of monitoring the events occurring in a computer system or network and analyzing them for signs of possible incidents.

**Intrusion detection and prevention system (IDPS)**   Software that automates the process of monitoring the events occurring in a computer system or network, and analyzing them for signs of possible incidents and attempting to stop detected possible incidents.

**Intrusion detection system (IDS)**   Hardware or software product that gathers and analyzes information from various areas within a computer or a network to identify possible security breaches, which include intrusions (attacks from outside the organization) and misuse (attacks from within the organization).

**Intrusion detection system load balancer**   A device that aggregates and directs network traffic to monitoring systems, such as intrusion detection and prevention sensors.

**Intrusion prevention**   The process of monitoring the events occurring in a computer system or network, analyzing them for signs of possible incidents, and attempting to stop detected possible incidents.

**Intrusion prevention systems (IPS)**   (1) Systems that can detect an intrusive activity and can also attempt to stop the activity, ideally before it reaches its targets. (2) Software that has all the capabilities of an intrusion detection system and can also attempt to stop possible incidents.

**Inverse cipher**   (1) A series of transformations that converts ciphertext to plaintext, using the cipher key. (2) The block cipher algorithm function that is the inverse of the forward cipher function when the same cryptographic key is used.

**Investigation process**   Four phases exist in a computer security incident investigation process: initiating the investigation (phase 1), testing and validating the incident hypothesis (phase 2), analyzing the incident (phase 3), and presenting the evidence (phase 4). The correct order of the investigation process is: gather facts (phase 1); interview witnesses (phase 1); develop incident hypothesis (phase 1); test and validate the hypothesis (phase 2); analyze (phase 3); and report the results to management and others (phase 4).

**Inward-facing**   It refers to a system that is connected on the interior of a network behind a firewall.

**IP address**   An Internet Protocol (IP) address is a unique number for a computer that is used to determine where messages transmitted on the Internet should be delivered. The IP address is analogous to a house number for ordinary postal mail.

**IP payload compression (IPComp) protocol**   Protocol used to perform lossless compression for packet payloads.

**IP spoofing**   Refers to sending a network packet that appears to come from a source other than its actual source.

**Isolation**   The containment of subjects and objects in a system in such a way that they are separated from one another, as well as from the protection controls of the operating system.

**ISO (International Organization for Standardization)**   An organization established to develop and define data processing standards to be used throughout participating countries.

**IT-related risk**   The net mission/business impact considering (1) the likelihood that a particular threat source will exploit, or trigger, particular information system vulnerability, and (2) the resulting impact if this should occur. IT-related risks arise from legal liability or mission/business loss due to, but not limited to (i) unauthorized (malicious, nonmalicious, or accidental) disclosure, modification, or destruction of information, (ii) nonmalicious errors and omissions, (iii) IT disruptions due to natural or man-made disasters, (iv) failure to exercise due care and due diligence in the implementation and operation of the IT function.

**IT security awareness and training program** Explains proper rules of behavior for the use of organization's IT systems and information. The program communicates IT security policies and procedures that need to be followed.

**IT security education** IT security education seeks to integrate all of the security skills and competencies of the various functional specialists into a common body of knowledge, adds a multi-discipline study of concepts, issues, and principles (technological and social), and strives to produce IT security specialists and professionals capable of vision and proactive response.

**IT security goal** The five security goals are confidentiality, availability, integrity, accountability, and assurance.

**IT security investment** An IT application or system that is solely devoted to security. For instance, intrusion detection system (IDS) and public key infrastructure (PKI) are examples of IT security investments.

**IT security metrics** Metrics based on IT security performance goals and objectives.

**IT security policy** The documentation of IT security decisions in an organization. Three basic types of policy exist (1) Program policy high-level policy used to create an organization's IT security program, define its scope within the organization, assign implementation responsibilities, establish strategic direction, and assign resources for implementation. (2) Issue-specific policies address specific issues of concern to the organization, such as contingency planning, the use of a particular methodology for systems risk management, and implementation of new regulations or law. These policies are likely to require more frequent revision as changes in technology and related factors take place. (3) System-specific policies address individual systems, such as establishing an access control list or in training users as to what system actions are permitted. These policies may vary from system to system within the same organization. In addition, policy may refer to entirely different matters, such as the specific managerial decisions setting an organization's electronic mail policy or fax security policy.

**IT security training** IT security training strives to produce relevant and needed security skills and competencies by practitioners of functional specialties other than IT security (e.g., management, systems design and development, acquisition, and auditing). The most significant difference between training and awareness is that training seeks to teach skills, which allow a person to perform a specific function, whereas awareness seeks to focus an individual's attention on an issue or set of issues. The skills acquired during training are built upon the awareness foundation, and in particular, upon the security basics and literacy material.

# J

**Jamming** An attack in which a device is used to emit electromagnetic energy on a wireless network's frequency to make it unusable by the network.

**Java** A programming language invented by Sun Microsystems. It can be used as a general-purpose application programming language with built-in networking libraries. It can also be used to write small applications called applets. The execution environment for Java applets is intended to be safe; executing an applet should not modify anything outside the WWW browser. Java is an object-oriented language similar to C++ but simplified to eliminate language features that cause common programming errors.

Java source code files (files with a Java extension) are compiled into a format called bytecode (files with a .class extension), which can then be executed by a Java interpreter. Compiled Java code can run on most computers because Java interpreters and runtime environments, known as Java Virtual Machines (VMs), exist for most operating system, including UNIX, the Macintosh OS, and Windows. Bytecode can also be converted directly into machine language instructions by a just-in-time compiler.

**JavaScript** A scripting language developed by Netscape to enable Web authors to design interactive sites. Although it shares many of the features and structures of the full Java language, it was developed independently. JavaScript can interact with HTML source code, enabling Web authors to spice up their sites with dynamic content. JavaScript is endorsed by a number of software companies and is an open language that anyone can use without purchasing a license. Recent browsers from Netscape and Microsoft support it, though Internet Explorer supports only a subset, which Microsoft calls Jscript.

**Jitter** Non-uniform delays that can cause packets to arrive and be processed out of sequence.

**Job rotation** A method of reducing the risk associated with a subject performing a (sensitive) task by limiting the amount of time the subject is assigned to perform the task before being moved to a different task. Both job rotation and job vacation practices make a person less vulnerable to fraud and abuse.

**Joint photographic experts group (JPEG)** The JPEG is a multimedia standard for compressing continuous-tone still pictures or photographs. It is the result of joint efforts from ITU, ISO, and IEC.

**Journal** It is an audit trail of system activities, which is useful for file/system recovery purposes. This is a technical and detective control.

# K

**Kerberos** Kerberos is an authentication tool used in local logins, remote authentication, and client-server requests. It is a means of verifying the identities of principals on an open network. Kerberos accomplishes this without relying on the authentication, trustworthiness, or physical security of hosts while assuming all packets can be read, modified, and inserted at will. Kerberos uses a trust broker model and symmetric cryptography to provide authentication and authorization of users and systems on the network. In classic Kerberos, users share a secret password with a key distribution center (KDC). The user, Alice, who wants to communicate with another user, Bob, authenticates to the KDC and is furnished a ticket by the KDC to use to authenticate with Bob. When Kerberos authentication is based on passwords, the protocol is known to be vulnerable to off-line dictionary attacks by eavesdroppers who capture the initial user-to-KDC exchange.

**Kernel** The hardware, firmware, and software elements of a trusted computing base (TCB) that implements the reference monitor concept. It must mediate all accesses, be protected from modification, and be verifiable as correct. It is the most trusted portion of a system that enforces a fundamental property and on which the other portions of the system depend.

**Key** (1) A parameter used in conjunction with a cryptographic algorithm that determines its operation. Examples include the computation of a digital signature from data and the verification of a digital signature. (2) A value used to control cryptographic operations, such as decryption, encryption, signature generation or signature verification.

**Key agreement**   A key establishment procedure (either manual or electronic) where the resultant keying material is a function of information contributed by two or more participants, so that no party can predetermine the value of the keying material independent of the other party's contribution.

**Key attack**   (1) An attacker's goal is to prevent a system user's work simply by holding down the ENTER or RETURN key on a terminal that has not been logged on. This action initiates a very high-priority process that takes over the CPU in an attempt to complete the logon process. This is a resource starvation attack in that it consumes systems resources such as CPU utilization and memory. Legitimate users are deprived of their share of resources. (2) A data scavenging method, using resources available to normal system users, which may include advanced software diagnostic tools.

**Key bundle**   The three cryptographic keys (Key 1, Key 2, Key 3) that are used with a triple-data-encryption algorithm (TDEA) mode.

**Key confirmation**   A procedure to provide assurance to one party (the key confirmation recipient) that another party (the key conformation provider) actually possesses the correct secret keying material and/or shared secret.

**Key encrypting key**   A cryptographic key that is used for the encryption or decryption of other keys.

**Key entry**   A process by which a key and its associated metadata is entered into a cryptographic module in preparation for active use.

**Key escrow**   The processes of managing (e.g., generating, storing, transferring, and auditing) the two components of a cryptographic key by two component holders. A key component is the two values from which a key can be derived.

**Key escrow system**   A system that entrusts the two components comprising a cryptographic key (e.g., a device unique key) to two key component holders (also called escrow agents).

**Key establishment**   (1) The process by which a cryptographic key is securely shared between two or more security entities, either by transporting a key from one entity to another (key transport) or deriving a key from information shared by the entities (key agreement). (2) A function in the life cycle of keying material; the process by which cryptographic keys are securely distributed among cryptographic modules using manual transport methods (e.g., key loaders), automated methods (e.g., key transport and/or key agreement protocols), or a combination of automated and manual methods (consists of key transport plus key agreement).

**Key exchange**   The process of exchanging public keys in order to establish secure communications.

**Key expansion**   Routine used to generate a series of Round Keys from the Cipher Key.

**Key generation material**   Random numbers, pseudo-random numbers, and cryptographic parameters used in generating cryptographic keys.

**Key label**   A text string that provides a human-readable and perhaps machine-readable set of descriptors for the key.

**Key lifecycle state**   One of the set of finite states that describes the accepted use of a cryptographic key in its lifetime. These states include pre-activation; active, suspended, deactivated and revoked; compromised; destroyed; and destroyed compromised.

**Key list**   A printed series of key settings for a specific crypto-net. Key lists may be produced in list, pad, or printed tape format.

**Key loader**   A self-contained unit that is capable of storing at least one plaintext or encrypted cryptographic key or key component that can be transferred, upon request, into a cryptographic module.

**Key management**   The activities involving the handling of cryptographic keys and other related security parameters (e.g., initialization vectors, counters, identity verifications and passwords) during the entire life cycle of the keys, including their generation, storage, establishment, entry and output, and destruction (zeroization).

**Key management infrastructure (KMI)**   A framework established to issue, maintain, and revoke keys accommodating a variety of security technologies, including the use of software.

**Key output**   A process by which a cryptographic key and its bound metadata are extracted from a cryptographic module, usually for remote storage.

**Key owner**   An entity (e.g., person, group, organization, device, and module) authorized to use a cryptographic key or key pair and whose identity is associated with a cryptographic key or key pair.

**Key pair**   A public key and its corresponding private key; a key pair is used with a public key algorithm.

**Key recover**   To reconstruct a damaged or destroyed cryptographic key after an accident or abnormal circumstance or to obtain an electronic cryptographic key from a trusted third party after satisfying the rules for retrieval.

**Key renewal**   The process used to extend the validity period of a cryptographic key so that it can be used for an additional time period.

**Key retrieval**   To obtain an electronic cryptography key from active or archival electronic storage, a backup facility, or an archive under normal operational circumstances.

**Key space**   The total number of possible values that a key, such as a password, can have.

**Key transport**   (1) A process used to move a cryptographic key from one protected domain to another domain, including both physical and electronic methods of movement. (2) A key establishment procedure whereby one party (the sender) selects and encrypts the keying material and then distributes the material to another party (the receiver). (3) The secure transport of cryptographic keys from one cryptographic module to another module.

**Key transport key pairs**   A key transport key pair may be used to transport keying material from an originating entity to a receiving entity during communications, or to protect keying material while in storage. The originating entity in a communication (or the entity initiating the storage of the keying material) uses the public key to encrypt the keying material; the receiving entity (or the entity retrieving the stored keying material) uses the private key to decrypt the encrypted keying material.

**Key update**   A process used to replace a previously active key with a new key that is related to the old key.

**Key validate**   A process by which cryptographic parameters (e.g., domain parameters, private keys, public keys, certificates, and symmetric keys) are tested as being appropriate for use by a particular cryptographic algorithm for a specific security service and application and that they can be trusted.

**Key value (key)**   The secret code used to encrypt and decrypt a message.

**Key wrapping**   A method of encrypting keys (along with associated integrity information) that provides both confidentiality and integrity protection using a symmetric key algorithm.

**Keyboard attack**   A data scavenging method, using resources available to normal system users, which may include advanced software diagnostic tools.

**Keyed-hash based message authentication code (HMAC)**   A message authentication code that uses a cryptographic key in conjunction with a hash function. It creates a hash based on both a message and a secret key.

**Keying material**   The data (e.g., keys and initialization vectors) necessary to establish and maintain cryptographic keying relationships.

**Keystroke logger**   A form of malware that monitors a keyboard for action events, such as a key being pressed, and provides the observed keystrokes to an attacker.

**Keystroke monitoring**   The process used to view or record both the keystrokes entered by a computer user and the computer's response during an interactive session. Keystroke monitoring is usually considered a special case of audit trails.

**Killer packets**   A method of disabling a system by sending Ethernet or Internet Protocol (IP) packets that exploit bugs in the networking code to crash the system. A similar action is done by synchronized floods (SYN floods), which is a method of disabling a system by sending more SYN packets than its networking code can handle.

**Knapsack algorithm**   Uses an integer programming technique. In contrast to RSA, the encryption and decryption functions are not inverse. It requires a high bandwidth and generally is insecure due to documented security breaches.

# L

**Label**   (1) An explicit or implicit marking of a data structure or output media associated with an information system representing the FIPS 199 security category, or distribution limitations or handling caveats of the information contained therein. (2) A piece of information that represents the security level of an object and that describes the sensitivity of the information in the object. Similar to security label.

**Labeling**   Process of assigning a representation of the sensitivity of a subject or object.

**Laboratory attack**   A data scavenging method through the aid of what could be precise or elaborate powerful equipment.

**Latency**   Measures the delay from first bit in to first bit out. It is the time delay of data traffic through a network, switch, port, and link. Also, see data latency and packet latency.

**Lattice**   A partially ordered set for which every pair of elements has a greatest lower bound and a least upper bound.

**Layered solution**   The judicious placement of security protection and attack countermeasures that can provide an effective set of safeguards (controls) that are tailored to the unique needs of a customer's situation. It is a part of security-in-depth or defense-in-depth strategy.

**Layering**   It uses multiple, overlapping protection mechanisms so that failure or circumvention of any individual protection approach will not leave the system unprotected. It is a part of security-in-depth or defense-in-depth strategy.

**Least functionality**   The information system security function should configure the information system to provide only essential capabilities and specifically prohibits or restricts the use of risky (by default) and unnecessary functions, ports, protocols, and/or services. This is based on the principle of least functionality or minimal functionality.

**Least privilege**   (1) Offering only the required functionality to each authorized user so that no one can use functions that are not necessary. (2) The security objective of granting users only those accesses they need to perform their official duties.

**Least significant bit(s)**   The right-most bit(s) of a bit string.

**Legacy environment**   It is a typical custom environment usually involving older systems or applications.

**Letter bomb**   A logic bomb, contained in electronic mail, triggered when the mail is read.

**Library**   A collection of related data files or programs.

**License**   An agreement by a contractor to permit the use of copyrighted software under certain terms and conditions.

**Life cycle management**   The process of administering an automated information system throughout its expected life, with emphasis on strengthening early decisions that affect system costs and utility throughout the system's life.

**Lightweight directory access protocol (LDAP)**   LDAP is a software protocol for enabling anyone to locate organizations, individuals, and other resources (e.g., files and devices in a network) whether on the Internet or on a corporate intranet.

**Line of defenses**   A variety of security mechanisms deployed for limiting and controlling access to and use of computer system resources. They exercise a directing or restraining influence over the behavior of individuals and the content of computer systems. The line-of-defenses form a core part of defense-in-depth strategy or security-in-depth strategy. They can be grouped into four categories—first, second, last, and multiple depending on their action priorities and needs. A first line-of-defense is always preferred over the second or the last. If the first line-of-defense is not available for any reason, the second line-of-defense should be applied. If the second line-of-defense is not available or does not work, then the last line-of-defense must be applied. Note that multiple lines-of-defenses are stronger than a single line-of-defense, whether the single defense is first, second, or last.

**Linear cryptanalysis attacks**   Uses pairs of known plaintext and corresponding ciphertext to generate keys.

**Link control protocol (LCP)**   One of the features of the point-to-point protocol (PPP) used for bringing lines up, testing them, and taking them down gracefully when they are not needed. It supports synchronous and asynchronous circuits and byte-oriented and bit-oriented encodings (Tanenbaum).

**Link encryption**   Link encryption (online encryption) encrypts all of the data along a communications path (e.g., a satellite link, telephone circuit, or T3 line). Since link encryption also encrypts routing data (i.e., headers, trailers, and addresses), communications nodes need to decrypt the data to continue routing so that all information passing over the link is encrypted in its entirety. It provides good protection against external threats such as traffic analysis, packet sniffers, and eavesdroppers. This is a technical and preventive control.

**List-oriented protection system**   A computer protection system in which each protected object has a list of all subjects authorized to access it. Compare with ticket-oriented protection system.

**Local access**   Access to an organizational information system by a user (or an information system) communicating through an internal organization-controlled network (e.g., local-area network) or directly to a device without the use of a network.

**Local-area network (LAN)**   A group of computers and other devices dispersed over a relatively limited area and connected by a communications link that enables a device to interact with any other on the network. A user-owned, user-operated, high-volume data transmission facility connecting a number of communicating devices (e.g., computers, terminals, word processors, printers, and mass storage units) within a single building or several buildings within a physical area. A LAN is a computer network that spans a relatively small area. Most LANs are confined to a single building or group of buildings. However, one LAN can be connected to other LANs over any distance via telephone lines and radio waves. A system of LANs connected in this way is called a wide-area network (WAN). Bridges and switches are used to interconnect different LANs. LANs and MANs are non-switched networks, meaning they do not use routers.

**Local delivery agent (LDA)**   A program running on a mail server that delivers messages between a sender and recipient if their mailboxes are both on the same mail server. An LDA may also process the message based on a predefined message filter before delivery.

**Location-based commerce (L-commerce)**   A mobile-commerce (m-commerce) application targeted to a customer whose location, preferences, and needs are known in real time.

**Lock-and-key protection system**   A protection system that involves matching a key or password with a specific access requirement.

**Locking-based attacks**   Attacks that degrade a system performance and service. This attack is used to hold a critical system locked most of the time, releasing it only briefly and occasionally. The result is a slow running browser. This results in a degradation of service, a mild form of DoS. Countermeasures against locking-based attacks include system backups and upgrading/patching software can help in maintaining a system's integrity.

**Locks**   Locks are used to prevent concurrent updates to a record. Various types of locks include page-level, row-level, area-level, and record-level. This is a technical and preventive control.

**Lockstep computing**   Lockstep systems are redundant computing systems that run the same set of operations at the same time in parallel. The output from lockstep operations can be compared to determine if there has been a fault. The lockstep systems are set up to progress from one state to the next state, as they closely work together. When a new set of inputs reaches the system, the system processes them, generates new outputs, and updates its state. Lockstep systems provide redundancy against hardware failures, not against software failures. Other redundant configurations include dual modular redundancy (DMR) systems and triple modular redundancy (TMR) systems. In DMR, computing systems are duplicated. Unlike the lockstep systems, there is a master/slave configuration in DMR where the slave is a hot-standby to the master. When the master fails at some point, the slave is ready to continue from the previous known good state. In TMR, computing systems are triplicated as voting systems. If one unit's output disagrees with the other two, the unit is detected as having failed. The matched output from the other two is treated as correct. Similar to lockstep systems, DMR and TMR systems provide redundancy against hardware failures, not against software failures (Wikipedia).

**Log**   A record of the events occurring within an organization's systems and networks. Log entries are individual records within a log.

**Log analysis**   Studying log entries to identify events of interest or suppress log entries for insignificant events.

**Log archival**   Retaining logs for an extended period of time, preferably on removable media, a storage area network (SAN), or a specialized log archival appliance or server.

**Log clearing**   Removing all entries from a log that precede certain date and time.

**Log compression**   Storing a log file in a way that reduces the amount of storage space needed for the file without altering the meaning of its contents.

**Log conversion**   Parsing a log in one format and storing its entries in a second format.

**Log correlation**   Correlating events by matching multiple log entries from a single source or multiple sources based on logged values, such as timestamps, IP addresses, and event types.

**Log file integrity checking**   Comparing the current message digest for a log file to the original message digest to determine if the log file has been modified.

**Log filtering**   The suppression of log entries from analysis, reporting, or long-term storage because their characteristics indicate that they are unlikely to contain information of interest.

**Log management**   The process for generating, transmitting, storing, analyzing, and disposing of log data.

**Log management infrastructure**   The hardware, software, networks, and media used to generate, transmit, store, analyze, and dispose of log data.

**Log-off**   Procedure used to terminate connections. Synonymous with log-out, sign-out, and sign-off.

**Log-on**   Procedure used to establish the identity of the user and the levels of authorization and access permitted. Synonymous with log-in, sign-in, and sign-on.

**Log parsing**   Extracting data from a log so that the parsed values can be used as input for another logging process.

**Log preservation**   Keeping logs that normally would be discarded, because they contain records of activity of particular interest.

**Log reduction**   Removing unneeded entries from a log to create a new log that is smaller in size.

**Log reporting**   Displaying the results of log analysis.

**Log retention**   Archiving logs on a regular basis as part of standard operating procedure or standard operational activities.

**Log rotation**   Closing a log file and opening a new log file when the first log file is considered to be complete.

**Log viewing**   Displaying log entries in a human-readable format.

**Logic bomb**   (1) A resident computer program that triggers the penetration of an unauthorized act when particular states of the system are realized. (2) A Trojan horse set to trigger upon the occurrence of a particular logical event. (3) It is a small, malicious program activated by a trigger (such as a date or the number of times a file is accessed), usually to destroy data or source code.

**Logical access control**   The use of information-related mechanisms (e.g., passwords) rather than physical mechanisms (e.g., keys and locks) for the provision of access control.

**Logical access perimeter security controls**   Acting as a first-line-of-defense, e-mail gateways, proxy servers, and firewalls provide logical access perimeter security controls.

**Logical link control (LLC) protocol**   The LLC protocol hides the differences between the various kinds of IEEE 802 networks by providing a single format and interface to the network layer. LLC forms the upper half of the data-link layer with the MAC sublayer below it.

**Logical protection**   Protection against unauthorized access (including unauthorized use, modification, substitution, and disclosure in the case of credentials service providers (CSPs) by means of the module software interface (MSI) under operating system control. The MSI is a set of commands used to request the services of the module, including parameters that enter or leave the module's cryptographic boundary as part of the requested service. Logical protection of software sensitive security parameters (SSPs) does not protect against physical tampering. SSP includes critical security parameters and public security parameters.

**Logical record**   Collection of one or more data item values as viewed by the user.

**Logical system definition**   The planning of an automated information system prior to its detailed design. This would include the synthesis of a network of logical elements that perform specific functions.

**Loop testing**   It is an example of white-box testing technique that focuses exclusively on the validity of loop constructs. Unstructured loops should e redesigned to reflect the use of structured programming constructs because they are difficult and time-consuming to test.

**Low-impact system**   An information system in which all three security objectives (i.e., confidentiality, integrity, or availability) are assigned a potential impact value of low.

# M

**Machine types**   (1) A real machine is the physical computer in a virtual machine environment. A real-time system is a computer and/or software that reacts to events before the events become obsolete. For example, airline collision avoidance systems must process radar input, detect a possible collision, and warn air traffic controllers or pilots while they still have time to react. (2) A virtual machine is a functional simulation of a computer and its associated devices, including an operating system. (3) Multi-user machines have at least two execution states or modes of operation: privileged and unprivileged. The execution state must be maintained in such a way that it is protected from the actions of untrusted users. Some common privileged domains are those referred to as: executive, master, system, kernel, or supervisor, modes; unprivileged domains are sometimes called user, application, or problem states. In a two-state machine, processes running in a privileged domain may execute any machine instruction and access any location in memory. Processes running in the unprivileged domain are prevented from executing certain machine instructions and accessing certain areas of memory. Examples of machines include Turing, Mealy, and Moore machines.

**Macro virus** (1) A specific type of computer virus that is encoded as a macro embedded in some document and activated when the document is handled. (2) A virus that attaches itself to application documents, such as word processing files and spreadsheets, and uses the application's macro-programming language to execute and propagate.

**Magnetic remanence** A measure of the magnetic flux density remaining after removal of the applied magnetic force. It refers to any data remaining on magnetic storage media after removal of the electrical power.

**Mail server** A host that provides "electronic post office" facilities. It stores incoming mail for distribution to users and forwards outgoing mail. The term may refer to just the application that performs this service, which can reside on a machine with other services. This term also refers to the entire host including the mail server application, the host operating system, and the supporting hardware. Mail server administrators are system architects responsible for the overall design and implementation of mail servers.

**Mail transfer agent (MTA)** A program running on a mail server that receives messages from mail user agents (MUAs) or other MTAs and either forwards them to another MTA or, if the recipient is on the MTA, delivers the message to the local delivery agent (LDA) for delivery to the recipient (e.g., Microsoft Exchange).

**Mail user agent (MUA)** A mail client application used by an end user to access a mail server to read, compose, and send e-mail messages (e.g., Microsoft Outlook).

**Mailbombing** Flooding a site with enough mail to overwhelm its electronic mail (e-mail) system. Used to hide or prevent receipt of e-mail during an attack, or as retaliation against a website.

**Main mode** Mode used in IPsec phase 1 to negotiate the establishment of an Internet key exchange security association (IKESA) through three pairs of messages.

**Maintainability** The effort required locating and fixing an error in an operational program or the effort required to modify an operational program (flexibility).

**Maintenance hook** Special instructions in software to allow easy maintenance and additional feature development. These are not clearly defined during access for design specification. Hooks frequently allow entry into the code at unusual points or without the usual checks, so they are a serious security risk if they are not removed prior to live implementation. Maintenance hooks are special types of trapdoors.

**Major application** An application that requires special attention to security because of the risk and magnitude of the harm resulting from the loss, misuse, or unauthorized access to, or modification of, the information in the application. A breach in a major application might comprise many individual application programs and hardware, software, and telecommunications components. Major applications can be either a major application system or a combination of hardware and software in which the only purpose of the system is to support a specific mission-related function.

**Malicious code** (1) Software or firmware intended to perform an unauthorized process that will have adverse impact on the confidentiality, integrity, or availability of an information system. (2) A program that is written intentionally to carry out annoying or harmful actions, which includes viruses, worms, Trojan horses, or other code-based entity that successfully infects a host. Same as malware.

**Malicious code attacks** Malicious code attackers use an attack-in-depth strategy to carry out their goal of attacking with programs written intentionally to cause harm or destruction.

**Malicious mobile code** Software that is transmitted from a remote system to be executed on a local system, typically without the user's explicit instruction. It is growing with the increased use of Web browsers. Many websites use mobile code to add legitimate functionality, including Active X, JavaScript, and Java. Unfortunately, although it was initially designed to be secure, mobile code has vulnerabilities that allow entities to create malicious programs. Users can infect their computers with malicious mobile code (e.g., a Trojan horse program that transmits information from the user's PC) just by visiting a website.

**Malware** A computer program that is covertly placed onto a computer with the intent to compromise the privacy, accuracy, confidentiality, integrity, availability, or reliability of the victim's data, applications, or operating system, or otherwise annoying or disrupting the victim. Common types of malware threats include viruses, worms, malicious mobile code, Trojan horses, rootkits, spyware, freeware, shareware, and some forms of adware programs.

**Malware signature** A set of characteristics of known malware instances that can be used to identify known malware and some new variants of known malware.

**Man-in-the-middle (MitM) attack** (1) A type of attack that takes advantage of the store-and-forward mechanism used by insecure networks such as the Internet (also called bucket brigade attack). (2) Actively impersonating multiple legitimate parties, such as appearing as a client to an access point and appearing as an access point to a client. This allows an attacker to intercept communications between an access point and a client, thereby obtaining authentication credentials and data. (3) An attack on the authentication protocol run in which the attacker positions himself in between the claimant and verifier so that he can intercept and alter data traveling between them. (4) An attack against public key algorithms, where an attacker substitutes his public key for the requested public key.

**Managed or enterprise environment** An inward-facing environment that is very structured and centrally managed.

**Managed interfaces** Managed interfaces allow connections to external networks or information systems consisting of boundary protection devices arranged according to an organization's security architecture.

Managed interfaces employing boundary protection devices include proxies, gateways, routers, firewalls, software/hardware guards, or encrypted tunnels (e.g., routers protecting firewalls and application gateways residing on a protected demilitarized zone). Managed interfaces, along with controlled interfaces, use boundary protection devices. These devices prevent and detect malicious and other unauthorized communications.

**Management controls**   The security controls (i.e., safeguards or countermeasures) for an information system that focus on the management of risk and the management of information system security. They include actions taken to manage the development, maintenance, and use of the system, including system-specific policies, procedures, rules of behavior, individual roles and responsibilities, individual accountability, and personnel security decisions.

**Management message (WMAN/WiMAX)**   A management message (MM) is a message used for communications between a BS and SS/MS. These messages (e.g., establishing communication parameters, exchanging privacy settings, and performing system registration events) are not encrypted and thus are susceptible to eavesdropping attacks.

**Management network**   A separate network strictly designed for security software management.

**Management server**   A centralized device that receives information from sensors or agents and manages them.

**Mandatory access control**   Access controls that are driven by the results of a comparison between the user's trust-level/clearance and the sensitivity designation of the information. A means of restricting access to objects (system resources) based on the sensitivity (as represented by a label) of the information contained in the objects and the formal authorization (i.e., clearance) of subjects (users) to access information of such sensitivity.

**Mandatory protection**   The result of a system that preserves the sensitivity labels of major data structures in the system and uses them to enforce mandatory access controls.

**Mantraps**   Mantraps provide additional security at the entrances to high-risk areas. For highly sensitive areas, mantraps require a biometric measure such as fingerprints combined with the weight of the person entering the facility.

**Market analysis**   Useful in the supply chain activities employing the chain-in-depth concept. Market analysis is conducted when the information system owner does not know who the potential suppliers or integrators are or would like to discover alternative suppliers or integrators or the suppliers of the suppliers or integrators. The market analysis should identify which companies can provide the required items or make suggestions for possible options. Some ways to gather information about potential suppliers or integrators include open sources (such as the press), Internet, periodicals, and fee-based services.

**Marking**   The process of placing a sensitivity designator (e.g., confidential) with data such that its sensitivity is communicated. Marking is not restricted to the physical placement of a sensitivity designator, as might be done with a rubber stamp, but can involve the use of headers for network messages, special fields in databases, and so on.

**Markov models**   They are graphical techniques used to model a system with regard to its failure states in order to evaluate the reliability, safety, or availability of the system.

**Markup language**   A system (as HTML or SGML) for marking or tagging a document that indicates its logical structure (as paragraphs) and gives instructions for its layout on the page for electronic transmission and display.

**Masquerading**   (1) Impersonating an authorized user and gaining unauthorized privileges. (2) An unauthorized agent claiming the identity of another agent. (3) An attempt to gain access to a computer system by posing as an authorized user. (4) The pretense by an entity to be a different entity. Synonymous with impersonating, spoofing, or mimicking.

**Mass mailing worm**   A worm that spreads by identifying e-mail addresses, often by searching an infected system, and then sending copies of itself to those addresses, either using the system's e-mail client or a self-contained mailer built into the worm itself.

**Master boot record (MBR)**   A special region on bootable media that determines which software (e.g., operating system and utility) will be run when the computer boots from the media.

**Maximum signaling rate**   The maximum rate, in bits per second, at which binary information can transfer in a given direction between users over telecommunication system facilities dedicated to a particular information transfer transaction. This happens under conditions of continuous transaction and no overhead information.

**Maximum stuffing rate**   The maximum rate at which bits are inserted or deleted.

**Maximum tolerable downtime**   The amount of time business processes can be disrupted without causing significant harm to the organization's mission.

**Mean-time-between-failures (MTBF)**   (1) The average length of time a system is functional or the average time interval between failures. (2) The total functioning life of an item divided by the total number of failures during the measurement interval of minutes, hours, and days. (3) The average length of time a system or a component works without fault between consecutive failures. MTBF assumes that the failed system is immediately repaired as in MTTR (repair). A high MTBF means high system reliability. MTBF = MTTF + MTTR (repair).

**Mean-time-between-outages (MTBO)**   The mean-time between equipment failures that results in a loss of system continuity or unacceptable degradation, as expressed by MTBO = MTBF/(1-FFAS), where MTBF is the nonredundant mean-time between failures, and FFAS is the fraction of failures for which the failed hardware or software is bypassed automatically. A high MTBO means high system availability.

**Mean-time-to-data loss (MTTDL)**   The average time before a loss of data occurs in a given disk array and is applicable to RAID technology. A low MTTDL means high data reliability.

**Mean-time-to-failure (MTTF)**   The average time to the next failure. It is the time taken for a part or system to fail for the first time. MTTF assumes that the failed system is not repaired. A high MTTF means high system reliability.

**Mean-time-to-recovery (MTTR)**   The time following a failure to restore a RAID disk array to its normal failure-tolerant mode of operation. This time includes the replacement of the failed disk and the time to rebuild the disk array. A low MTTR means high system availability.

**Mean-time-to-repair (MTTR)**   (1) The amount of time it takes to resume normal operation. (2) The total corrective maintenance time divided by the total number of corrective maintenance actions during a given period of time. A low MTTR means high system reliability.

**Mean-time-to-restore (MTTR)**   The average time to restore service following system failures that result on service outages. The time to restore includes all time from the occurrence of the failure until the restoral of service. A low MTTR means high system availability.

**Measures**   All the output produced by automated tools (for example, IDS/IPS, vulnerability scanners, audit record management tools, configuration management tools, and asset management tools) and various information security program-related data (for example, training and awareness data, information system authorization data, contingency planning and testing data, and incident response data). Measures also include security assessment evidence from both automated and manual collection methods. A "measure" is the result of gathering data from the known sources.

**Mechanisms**   An assessment object that includes specific protection-related items (for example, hardware, software, or firmware) employed within or at the boundary of an information system.

**Media**   Physical devices or writing surfaces including, but not limited to, magnetic tapes, optical disks, magnetic disks, large-scale integration (LSI) memory chips, flash ROM, and printouts (but not including display media) onto which information is recorded, stored, or printed within an information system.

**Media access control address**   A hardware address that uniquely identifies each component of an IEEE 802-based standard. On networks that do not conform to the IEEE 802 standard but do conform to the ISO/OSI reference model, the node address is called the Data Link Control (DLC) address.

**Media gateway**   It is the interface between circuit switched networks and IP network. Media gateway handles analog/digital conversion, call origination and reception, and quality improvement functions such as compression or echo cancellation.

**Media gateway control protocol (MGCP)**   MGCP is a common protocol used with media gateways to provide network management and control functions.

**Media sanitization**   A general term referring to the actions taken to render data written on media unrecoverable by both ordinary and extraordinary means.

**Medium/media access control protocols**   Protocols for the medium/media access control sublayer, which is the bottom part of the data link layer of the ISO/OSI reference model, include carrier sense multiple access with collision avoidance and collision detection (CSMA/CA and CSMA/CD), wavelength division multiple access (WDMA), Ethernet (thick, thin, fast, switched, and gigabit), logical link control (LLC), the 802.11 protocol stack for wireless LANs, the 802.15 for Bluetooth, the 802.16 for Wireless MANs, and the 802.1Q for virtual LANs. These are examples of broadcast networks with multi-access channels.

**Meet-in-the-middle (MIM) attack**   Occurs when one end is encrypted and the other end is decrypted, and the results are matched in the middle. MIM attack is made on block ciphers.

**Melting**   A physically destructive method of sanitizing media; to be changed from a solid to a liquid state generally by the application of heat. Same as smelting.

**Memorandum of understanding/agreement**   A document established between two or more parties to define their respective roles and responsibilities in accomplishing a particular goal. Regarding IT, it defines the responsibilities of two or more organizations in establishing, operating, and securing a system interconnection.

**Memory cards**   Memory cards are data storage devices used for personal authentication, access authorization, card integrity, and application systems.

**Memory protection**   It is achieved through the use of system partitioning, non-modifiable executable programs, resource isolation, and domain separation.

**Memory resident virus**   A virus that stays in the memory of infected systems for an extended period of time.

**Memory scavenging**   The collection of residual information from data storage.

**Mesh computing**   Provides application processing and load balancing capacity for Web servers using the Internet cache. It pushes applications, data, and computing power away from centralized points to local points of networks. It deploys Web server farms and clustering concepts, and is based on "charge for network services" model. Mesh computing implies non-centralized points and node-less availability.

Advantages include (1) reduced transmission costs, reduced latency, and improved quality-of-service (QoS) due to a decrease in data volume that must be moved across the network, (2) improved security due to data encryption and firewalls, and (3) limited bottlenecks and single point of failure due to replicated information across distributed networks of Web servers and de-emphasized central network points. Other names for mesh computing include peer-to-peer computing

**Mesh topology**   Mesh topology is a network topology in which there are at least two nodes with two or more paths between them.   The mesh topology is made up of multiple, high-speed paths between several end-points, and provides a high degree of fault tolerance due to many redundant interconnections between nodes. In a true mesh topology, every node has a connection to every other node in the network.

**Message authentication code**   (1) A cryptographic checksum on data that uses a symmetric key to detect both accidental and intentional modifications of the data. (2) A cryptographic checksum that results from passing data through a message authentication algorithm.

**Message digest (MD)**   (1) A digital signature that uniquely identifies data and has the property that changing a single bit in the data will cause a completely different message digest to be generated. (2) The result of applying a hash function to a message; also known as hash value. (3) A cryptographic checksum typically generated for a file that can be used to detect changes to the file. Secure Hash Algorithm-1 (SHA-1) is an example of a message digest algorithm. (4) It is the fixed size result of hashing a message.

**Message identifier (MID)**   A field that may be used to identify a message. Typically, this field is a sequence number.

**Message modification**   Altering a legitimate message by deleting, adding to, changing, or reordering it.

**Message passing**   The means by which objects communicate. Individual messages may consist of the name of the message, the name of the target object to which it is being sent, and arguments, if any. When an object receives a message, a method is invoked which performs an operation that exhibits some part of the object's behavior.

**Message passing systems**   Used in object-oriented application systems.

**Message replay**   Passively monitoring transmissions and retransmitting messages, acting as if the attacker were a legitimate user.

**Messaging interface**   The linkage from the service component to various external software modules (e.g., enterprise component, external system, and gateway) through the use of message middleware (i.e., performing message-routing, data-transformation, and directory-services) and other service components.

**Metadata**   (1) Information used to describe specific characteristics, constraints, acceptable uses, and parameters of another data item such as cryptographic key. (2) It is data referring to other data; data (e.g., data structures, indices, and pointers) that are used to instantiate an abstraction (e.g., process, task, segment, file, or pipe). (3) A special database, also referred to as a data dictionary, containing descriptions of the elements (e.g., relations, domains, entities, or relationships) of a database. (4) Information regarding files and folders themselves, such as file and folder names, creation dates and times, and sizes.

**Metrics**   Tools designed to facilitate decision making and improve performance and accountability through collection, analyses, and reporting of relevant performance-related data. A "metric" is designed to organize data into meaningful information to support decision making (for example, dashboards).

**Metropolitan-area network (MAN)**   A network concept aimed at consolidating business operations and computers spread out in a town or city. Wired MANs are mainly used by cable television networks. MANs and LANs are non-switched networks, meaning they do not use routers. The scope of a MAN falls between a LAN and a WAN.

**Middleware**   Software that sits between two or more types of software and translates information between them. For example, it can sit between an application system and an operating system, a network operating system, or a database management system.

**Migration**   A term generally referring to the moving of data from an online storage device to an offline or low-priority storage device, as determined by the system or as requested by the system user.

**Mimicking**   An attempt to gain access to a computer system by posing as an authorized user. Synonymous with impersonating, masquerading, and spoofing.

**Min-entropy**   A measure of the difficulty that an attacker has to guess the most commonly chosen password used in a system. It is the worst-case measure of uncertainty for a random variable with the greatest lower bound. The attacker is assumed to know the most commonly used password(s).

**Minimization**   A risk-reducing principle that supports integrity by containing the exposure of data or limiting opportunities to violate integrity.

**Minimizing target value**   A risk-reducing practice that stresses the reduction of potential losses incurred due to a successful attack and/or the reduction of benefits that an attacker might receive in carrying out such an attack.

**Minimum security controls**   These controls include management, operational, and technical controls to protect the confidentiality, integrity, and availability objectives of an information system. The tailored baseline controls become the minimum set of security controls after adding supplementary controls based on gap analysis to achieve adequate risk mitigation. Three sets of baseline controls (i.e., low-impact, moderate-impact, and high-impact) provide a minimum security control assurance.

**Minor application** An application, other than a major application, that requires attention to security due to the risk and magnitude of harm resulting from the loss, misuse, or unauthorized access to or modification of the information in the application. Minor applications are typically included as part of a general support system.

**Mirroring** Several mirroring methods include data mirroring, disk mirroring, and server mirroring. They all provide backup mechanisms so if one disk fails, the data is available from the other disks.

**Misappropriation** Stealing or making unauthorized use of a service.

**Mistake-proofing** It is a concept to prevent, detect, and correct inadvertent human or machine errors occurring in products and services. It is also called poka-yoke (Japanese term) and idiot-proofing.

**Mobile code** (1) A program (e.g., script, macro, or other portable instruction) that can be shipped unchanged to a heterogeneous collection of platforms and executed with identical semantics. (2) Software programs or parts of programs obtained from remote information systems, transmitted from a remote system or across a network, and executed on a local information system without the user's explicit installation, instruction, or execution. Java, JavaScript, Active-X, and VBScript are examples of mobile code technologies that provide the mechanisms for the production and use of mobile code. Mobile code can be malicious or nonmalicious.

**Mobile commerce (MC)** Mobile commerce (m-commerce) is conducted using mobile devices such as cell phones and personal digital assistants (PDAs) for wireless banking and shopping purposes. M-commerce uses wireless application protocol (WAP). It is any business activity conducted over a wireless telecommunications networks.

**Mobile-site** A self-contained, transportable shell custom-fitted with the specific IT equipment and telecommunications necessary to provide full recovery capabilities upon notice of a significant disruption.

**Mobile software agent** Programs that are goal-directed and capable of suspending their execution on one platform and moving to another platform where they resume execution.

**Mobile subscriber (WMAN/WiMAX)** A mobile subscriber (MS) is a station capable of moving at greater speeds and supports enhanced power of operations (i.e., self-powered) for laptop computers, notebook computers, and cellular phones.

**Mode of operation** (1) A set of rules for operating on data with a cryptographic algorithm and a key; often includes feeding all or part of the output of the algorithm back into the input of the algorithm, either with or without additional data being processed (e.g., cipher feedback, output feedback, and cipher block chaining). (2) An algorithm for the cryptographic transformation of data that features a symmetric key block cipher algorithm.

**Modem** Acronym for modulation and demodulation. During data transmission, the modem converts the computer representation of data into an audio signal for transmission of telephone, teletype, or intercom lines. When receiving data, the modem converts the audio signal to the computer data representation.

**Moderate-impact system** An information system in which at least one security objective (i.e., confidentiality, integrity, or availability) is assigned a potential impact value of moderate and no security objective is assigned a potential impact value of high.

**Modular design**   Information system project design that breaks the development of a project into various pieces (modules), each solving a specific part of the overall problem. These modules should be as narrow in scope and brief in duration as practicable. Such design minimizes the risk to an organization by delivering a net benefit separate from the development of other pieces.

**Modular software**   Software that is self-contained logical sections, or modules, which carry out well-defined processing actions.

**Modularity**   Software attributes that provide a structure of highly independent modules.

**Monitoring**   Recording of relevant information about each operation by a subject on an object maintained in an audit trail for subsequent analysis.

**Moore's law**   States that that the number of transistors per square inch on an integrated circuit (IC) chip used in computers doubles every 18 months, the performance (microprocessor processing speed) of a computer doubles every 18 months, the cost of a CPU power is halved every 18 months, or the size of computer programs is increased in less than 18 months, where the latter is not a Moore's law.

**Most significant bit(s)**   The left-most bit(s) of a bit string.

**Motion picture experts group (MPEG)**   The MPEG is a multimedia standard used to compress videos consisting of images and sound. MPEG-1 is used for storing movies on CD-ROM while MPEG-2 is used to support higher resolution HDTVs. MPEG-2 is a superset of MPEG-1.

**Multi-exit discriminator (MED)**   A Border Gateway Protocol (BGP) attribute used on external links to indicate preferred entry or exit points (among many) for an autonomous system (AS). An AS is one or more routers working under a single administration operating the same routing policy.

**Multi-drop**   Network stations connected to a multipoint channel at one location.

**Multifactor authentication**   Authentication using two or more factors to achieve the authentication goal. Factors include (2) something you know (e.g., password/PIN), (2) something you have (e.g., cryptographic identification device or token), or (3) something you are (e.g., biometric).

**Multi-hop problem**   The security risks resulting from a mobile software agent visiting several platforms.

**Multilevel secure**   A class of system containing information with different sensitivities that simultaneously permits access by users with different security clearances and needs-to-know but prevents users from obtaining access to information for which they lack authorization.

**Multilevel security mode**   A mode of operation that allows two or more classification levels of information to be processed simultaneously within the same system when not all users have a clearance or formal access approval for all data handled by a computer system.

**Multimedia messaging service (MMS)**   An accepted standard for messaging that lets users send and receive messages formatted with text, graphics, photographs, audio, and video clips.

**Multipartite virus**   A virus that uses multiple infection methods, typically infecting both files and boot sectors.

**Multiple component incident**   A single incident that encompasses two or more incidents.

**Multiplexers**   A multiplexer is a device for combining two or more information channels. Multiplexing is the combining of two or more information channels onto a common transmission medium.

**Multipoint**   A network that enables two or more stations to communicate with a single system on one communications line.

**Multi-processing**   A computer consisting of several processors that may execute programs simultaneously.

**Multi-programming**   The concurrent execution of several programs. It is the same as multi-tasking.

**Multipurpose Internet mail extension (MIME)**   (1) A specification for formatting non-ASCII messages so that they can be sent over the Internet. MIME enables graphics, audio, and video files to be sent and received via the Internet mail system, using the SMTP protocol. In addition to e-mail applications, Web browsers also support various MIME types. This enables the browser to display or output various files that are not in HTML format. (2) A protocol that makes use of the headers in an IETF RFC 2822 message to describe the structure of rich message content.

**Multi-tasking**   The concurrent execution of several programs. It is the same as multiprogramming.

**Multi-threading**   Program code that is designed to be available for servicing multiple tasks at once, in particular by overlapping inputs and output.

**Mutation analysis**   The purpose of mutation analysis is to determine the thoroughness with which an application program has been tested and, in the process, detect errors. A large set of version or mutation of the original program is created by altering a single element of the program (e.g., variable, constant, or operator) and each mutant is then tested with a given collection of test datasets.

**Mutual authentication**   Occurs when parties at both sides of a communication activity authenticate each other. Providing mutual assurance regarding the identity of subjects and/or objects. For example, a system needs to authenticate a user, and the user needs to authenticate that the system is genuine.

# N

**NAK attack**   See Negative acknowledgment (NAK) attack

**Name spaces**   Names are given to objects, which are only meaningful to a single subject, and thus cannot be addressed by other subjects.

**Natural threats**   Examples of natural threats include hurricanes, tornados, floods, and fires.

**Need-to-know**   The necessity for access to, knowledge of, or possession of specific information required to perform official tasks or services. The custodian, not the prospective recipient, of the classified or sensitive unclassified information determines the need-to-know.

**Need-to-know violation**   The disclosure of classified or other sensitive information to a person cleared but who has no requirement for such information to carry out assigned job duties.

**Need-to-withhold**   The necessity to limit access to some confidential information when broad access is given to all the information.

**Negative acknowledgement (NAK) attack** (1) In binary synchronous communications, a transmission control character is sent as a negative response to data received by an attacker. A negative response means a reply was received that indicate that data was not received correctly or that a command was incorrect or unacceptable. (2) A penetration technique capitalizing on a potential weakness in an operating system that does not handle asynchronous interrupts properly, thus leaving the system in an unprotected state during such interrupts. An NAK means that a transmission was received with error (negative). An ACK (acknowledgment) means that a transmission was received without error (positive).

**Net-centric architecture** A complex system of systems composed of subsystems and services that are part of a continuously evolving, complex community of people, devices, information, and services interconnected by a network that enhances information sharing and collaboration. Examples of this architecture include service-oriented architectures and cloud computing architectures.

**Net present value (NPV) method** The most straightforward economic comparison is net present value (NPV). NPV is the difference between the present value (PV) of the benefits and the PV of the costs.

This method can be used to assess the financial feasibility of an investment in information security program.

**Network** (1) Two or more systems connected by a communications medium. (2) An open communications medium, typically, the Internet, that is used to transport messages between the claimant and other parties. Unless otherwise stated no assumptions are made about the security of the network; it is assumed to be open and subject to active attacks (e.g., impersonation, man-in-the-middle, and session hijacking) and passive attacks (e.g., eavesdropping) at any point between the parties (e.g., claimant, verifier, CSP, or relying party).

**Network access control (NAC)** A feature provided by some firewalls that allows access based on a user's credentials and the results of health checks performed on the telework client device.

**Network address translation (NAT)** (1) A routing technology used by many firewalls to hide internal system addresses from an external network through use of an addressing schema. (2) A mechanism for mapping addresses on one network to addresses on another network, typically private addresses to public addresses.

**Network address translation (NAT) and port address translation (PAT)** Both NAT and PAT are used to hide internal system addresses from an external network by mapping internal addresses to external addresses, by mapping internal addresses to a single external address or by using port numbers to link external system addresses with internal systems.

**Network administrator** A person responsible for the overall design, implementation, and maintenance of a network. The scope of responsibilities include overseeing network security, installing new applications, distributing software upgrades, monitoring daily activity, enforcing software licensing agreements, developing a storage management program, and providing for routine backups.

**Network architecture** The philosophy and organizational concept for enabling communications among data processing equipment at multiple locations. The network architecture specifies the processors and terminals and defines the protocols and software used to accomplish accurate data communications. The set of layers and protocols (including formats and standards) that define a network.

**Network-based intrusion detection systems (IDSs)**  IDSs which detect attacks by capturing and analyzing network packets. Listening on a network segment or switch, one network-based IDS can monitor the network traffic affecting multiple hosts that are connected to the network segment.

**Network-based intrusion prevention system**  A program that performs packet sniffing and analyzes network traffic to identify and stop suspicious activity.

**Network-based threats**  Examples include (1) Web spoofing attack, which allows an impostor to shadow not only a single targeted server, but also every subsequent server accessed, (2) masquerading as a Web server using a man-in-the-middle (MitM) attack, whereby requests and responses are conveyed via the imposter as a watchful intermediary, (3) eavesdropping on messages in transit between a browser and server to glean information at a level of protocol below HTTP, (4) modifying the DNS mechanisms used by a computer to direct it to a false website to divulge sensitive information (i.e., pharming attack), (5) performing denial-of-service (DoS) attacks through available network interfaces, and (6) intercepting messages in transit and modify their contents, substitute other contents, or simply replaying the transmission dialogue later in an attempt to disrupt the synchronization or integrity of the information.

**Network behavior analysis system**  An intrusion detection and prevention system (IDPS) that examines network traffic to identify and stop threats that generate unusual traffic flows.

**Network configuration**  A specific set of network resources that form a communications network at any given point in time, the operating characteristics of these network resources, and the physical and logical connections that have been defined between them.

**Network congestion**  Occurs when an excess traffic is sent through some part of the network, which is more than its capacity to handle.

**Network connection**  Any logical or physical path from one host to another that makes possible the transmission of information from one host to the other. An example is a TCP connection.  Also, when a host transmits an IP datagram employing only the services of its "connection-less" IP interpreter, there is a connection between the source and the destination hosts for this transaction.

**Network control protocol (NCP)**  Network Control Protocol (NCP) is one of the features of the Point-to-Point Protocol (PPP) used to negotiate network-layer options independent of the network layer protocol used.

**Network device**  A device that is part of and can send or receive electronic transmissions across a communications network. Network devices include end-system devices such as computers, terminals, or printers; intermediary devices such as bridges and routers that connect different parts of the communications network; and link devices or transmission media.

**Network interface card (NIC)**  Network interface cards are circuit boards used to transmit and receive commands and messages between a PC and a LAN. A NIC operates in the Data Link Layer of the ISO/OSI Reference model.

**Network layer**  Portion of an open system interconnection (OSI) system responsible for data transfer across the network, independent of both the media comprising the underlying sub-networks and the topology of those sub-networks.

**Network layer security**   Protects network communications at the layer that is responsible for routing packets across networks.

**Network management**   The discipline that describes how to monitor and control the managed network to ensure its operation and integrity and to ensure that communications services are provided in an efficient manner. Network management consists of fault management, configuration management, performance management, security management, and accounting management.

**Network management architecture**   The distribution of responsibility for management of different parts of the communications network among different managing-software-products. It describes the organization of the management of a network. The three types of network management architectures are the centralized, distributed, and distributed hierarchical network management architectures.

**Network management protocol**   A protocol that conveys information pertaining to the management of the communications network, including management operations from managers as well as responses to polling operations, notifications, and alarms from agents.

**Network management software**   Software that provides the capabilities for network and security monitoring and managing the network infrastructure, allowing systems personnel to administer the network effectively from a central location.

**Network overload**   A network begins carrying an excessive number of border gateway protocol (BGP) messages, overloading the router control processors and reducing the bandwidth available for data traffic.

**Network protection device**   A product such as a firewall or intrusion detection device that selectively blocks packet traffic based on configurable and emergent criteria.

**Network protection testing**   Testing that is applicable to network protection devices.

**Network scanning tool**   It involves using a port scanner to identify all hosts potentially connected to an organization's network, the network services operating on those hosts (e.g., FTP and HTTP), and specific applications. The goal is to identify all active hosts and open ports.

**Network security**   The protection of networks and their services from all natural and human-made hazards. This includes protection against unauthorized access, modification, or destruction of data; denial-of of-service; or theft.

**Network security layer**   Protecting network communications at the layer of the TCP/IP model that is responsible for routing packets across networks.

**Network service worm**   A worm that spreads by taking advantage of vulnerability in a network service associated with an operating system or an application system.

**Network size**   The total number of network devices managed within the network and all its subcomponents.

**Network sniffing**   A passive technique that monitors network communication, decodes protocols, and examines headers and payloads for information of interest. Network sniffing is both a review technique and a target identification and analysis technique.

**Network tap**    A direct connection between a sensor and the physical network media itself, such as a fiber optic cable.

**Network topology**    The architectural layout of a network. The term has two meanings: (1) the structure, interconnectivity, and geographic layout of a group of networks forming a larger network and (2) the structure and layout of an individual network within a confined location or across a geographic area. Common topologies include bus (nodes connected to a single backbone cable), ring (nodes connected serially in a closed loop), star (nodes connected to a central hub), and mesh.

**Network transparency**    Network transparency is the ability to simplify the task of developing management applications, hiding distribution details. There are different aspects of transparency such as access failure, location, migration replication, and transaction. Transparency means the network components or segments cannot be seen by insiders and outsiders and that actions of one user group cannot be observed by other user groups. It is achieved through process isolation and hardware segmentation concepts.

**Network weaving**    It is a penetration technique in which different communication networks are linked to access an information system to avoid detection and traceback.

**Network worm**    A worm that copies itself to another system by using common network facilities and causes execution of the copy program on that system.

**Neural networks**    They are artificial intelligence systems built around concepts similar to the way the human brain's Web of neural connections to identify patterns, learn, and reach conclusions.

**Node**    A computer system connected to a communications network and participates in the routing of messages within that network. Networks are usually described as a collection of nodes connected by communications links. A communication point at which subordinate items of data originate. Examples include cluster controllers, terminals, computers, and networks.

**Nondiscretionary access controls**    A policy statement that access controls cannot be changed by users, but only through administrative actions.

**Noninvasive attack**    An attack that can be performed on a cryptographic module without direct physical contact with the module. Examples include differential power analysis attack, electromagnetic emanation attack, simple power analysis attack, and timing analysis attack.

**Nonlocal maintenance**    Maintenance activities conducted by individuals communicating through a network, either an external network (e.g., the Internet) or an internal network.

**No-lone zone**    It is an area, room, or space that, when staffed, must be occupied by two or more security cleared individuals who remain within sight of each other.

**Nonce**    (1) An identifier, a counter, a value, or a message number that is used only once. These numbers are freshly generated random values. Nonce is a time-varying value with a negligible chance of repeating (almost non-repeating). (2) A nonce could be a random value that is generated anew or each instance of a nonce, a timestamp, a sequence number, or some combination of these. (3) A randomly generated value used to defeat "playback" attacks in communication protocols. One party randomly generates a nonce and sends it to the other party. The receiver encrypts it using the agreed-upon secret key and returns it to the sender. Because the sender randomly generated the nonce, this defeats playback attacks because the replayer cannot know in advance the nonce the sender will generate. The receiver denies connections that do not have the correctly encrypted nonce. (4) Nonce is a value used in security protocols that is never repeated with the same key. For example, challenges used in challenge-response authentication protocols generally must not be repeated until authentication keys are changed, or there is a possibility of a replay attack. Using a nonce as a challenge is a different requirement than a random challenge because a nonce is not necessarily unpredictable.

**Nonrepudiation**   (1) An authentication that with high assurance can be asserted to be genuine and that cannot subsequently be refuted. It is the security service by which the entities involved in a communication cannot deny having participated. Specifically, the sending entity cannot deny having sent a message (nonrepudiation with proof of origin) and the receiving entity cannot deny having received a message (nonrepudiation with proof of delivery). This service provides proof of the integrity and origin of data that can be verified by a third party. (2) Assurance that the sender of information is provided with proof of delivery and the recipient is provided with proof of the sender's identity, so neither can later deny having processed the information. (3) A service that is used to provide assurance of the integrity and origin of data in such a way that the integrity and origin can be verified and validated by a third party as having originated from a specific entity in possession of the private key (i.e., the signatory). (4) Protection against an individual falsely denying having performed a particular action. It provides the capability to determine whether a given individual took a particular action such as creating information, sending a message, approving information, and receiving a message.

**Nonreversible action**   A type of action that supports the principle of accountability by preventing the reversal and/or concealment of activity associated with sensitive objects.

**Nontechnical countermeasure**   A security measure that is not directly part of the network information security processing system, taken to help prevent system vulnerabilities. Nontechnical countermeasures encompass a broad range of personal measures, procedures, and physical facilities that can deter an adversary from exploiting a system (e.g., security guards, visitor escort, visitor badge, locked closets, and locked doors).

**N-person control**   A method of controlling actions of subjects (people) by distributing a task among more than one (N) subject.

**N-version programming**   N-version programming is based on design or version diversity. The different versions are executed in parallel and the results are voted on.

# O

**Obfuscation technique**   A way of constructing a virus to make it more difficult to detect.

**Object**   The basic unit of computation. An object has a set of "operations" and a "state" that remembers the effect of operations. Classes define object types. Typically, objects are defined to represent the behavioral and structural aspects of real-world entities. Object is a state, behavior, and identity; the terms "instance" and "object" are interchangeable. A passive entity that contains or receives information. Access to an object by a subject potentially implies access to the information it contains. Examples of objects include devices, records, blocks, tables, pages, segments, files, directories, directory trees, processes, domain, and programs, as well as bits, bytes, words, fields, processors, video displays, keyboards, clocks, printers, network nodes, and so on.

**Object code or module**   (1) A source code compiled to convert to object code, a machine-level language. (2) Instructions in machine-readable language are produced by a compiler or assembler from source code.

**Object identifier**   A specialized formatted number that is registered with an internationally recognized standards organization. It is the unique alphanumeric or numeric identifier registered under the ISO registration standard to reference a specific object or object class.

**Object reuse**   The reassignment and reuse of a storage medium (e.g., page frame, disk sector, and magnetic tape) that once contained one or more objects. To be securely reused and assigned to a new subject, storage media must contain no residual data (magnetic remanence) from the object(s) previously contained in the media.

**Off-card**   Refers to data that is not stored within the personal identity verification (PIV) card or to a computation that is not performed by the integrated circuit chip of the PIV card.

**Off-line attack**   An attack where the attacker obtains some data (typically by eavesdropping on an authentication protocol run or by penetrating a system and stealing security files) that he can analyze in a system of his own choosing.

**Off-line cracking**   Off-line cracking occurs when a cryptographic token is exposed using analytical methods outside the electronic authentication mechanism (e.g., differential power analysis on stolen hardware cryptographic token and dictionary attacks on software PKI token). Countermeasures include using a token with a high entropy token secret and locking up the token after a number of repeated failed activation attempts. .

**Off-line cryptosystem**   A cryptographic system in which encryption and decryption are performed independently of the transmission and reception functions.

**Off-line storage**   Data storage on media physically removed from the computer system and stored elsewhere (e.g., a magnetic tape or a disk).

**Offsite storage**   A location remote from the primary computer facility where backup programs, data files, forms, and documentation, including a contingency plan, are stored. These are used at backup computer facilities during a disaster or major interruption at the primary computer facility.

**On-access scanning**   Configuring a security tool to perform real-time scans of each file for malware as the file is downloaded, opened, or executed.

**On-card**   Refers to data that is stored within the personal identity verification (PIV) card or to a computation that is performed by the integrated circuit chip of the PIV card.

**On-demand scanning**   Allowing users to launch security tool scans for malware on a computer as desired.

**One-time password generator**   Password is changed after each use and is useful when the password is not adequately protected from compromise during login. (For example, the communication line is suspected of being tapped.) This is a technical and preventive control.

**One-way hash algorithm**   Hash algorithms that map arbitrarily long inputs into a fixed-size output such that it is very difficult (computationally infeasible) to find two different hash inputs that produce the same output. Such algorithms are an essential part of the process of producing fixed-size digital signatures that can both authenticate the signer and provide for data integrity checking (detection of input modification after signature).

**Online attack**   An attack against an authentication protocol where the attacker either assumes the role of a claimant with a genuine verifier or actively alters the authentication channel. The goal of the attack may be to gain authenticated access or learn authentication secrets.

**Online certificate status protocol (OCSP)**   An online protocol used to determine the status of a public key certificate between a certificate authority (CA) and relying parties. OCSP responders should be capable of processing both signed and unsigned requests and should be capable of processing requests that either include or exclude the name of the relying party making the request. OCSP responders should support at least one algorithm such as RSA with padding or ECDSA for digitally signing response messages.

**Online guessing attack**   An attack in which an attacker performs repeated logon trials by guessing possible values of the token authenticator. Examples of attacks include dictionary attacks to guess passwords or guessing of secret tokens. A countermeasure is to use tokens that generate high entropy authenticators.

**Open design**   The principle of open design stresses that design secrecy or the reliance on the user ignorance is not a sound basis for secure systems. Open design allows for open debate and inspection of the strengths, or origins of a lack of strength, of that particular design. Secrecy can be implemented through the use of passwords and cryptographic keys, instead of secrecy in design.

**Open Pretty Good Privacy (OpenPGP)**   A protocol defined in IETF RFC 2440 and 3156 for encrypting messages and creating certificates using public key cryptography. Most mail clients do not support OpenPGP by default; instead, third-party plug-ins can be used in conjunction with the mail clients. OpenPGP uses a "Web of trust" model for key management, which relies on users for management and control, making it unsuitable for medium- to large-scale implementations.

**Open security environment (OSE)**   An environment that includes systems in which one of the following conditions holds true: (1) application developers (including maintainers) do not have sufficient clearance or authorization to provide an acceptable presumption that they have not introduced malicious logic and (2) configuration control does not provide sufficient assurance that applications are protected against the introduction of malicious logic prior to and during the operation of application systems.

**Open system interconnection (OSI)**   A reference model of how messages should be transmitted between any two end-points of a telecommunication network. The process of communication is divided into seven layers, with each layer adding its own set of special, related functions. The seven layers are the application layer, presentation, session, transport, network, data link, and physical layer. Most telecommunication products tend to describe themselves in relation to the OSI reference model. This model is a single reference view of communication that provides a common ground for education and discussion.

**Open systems**   Vendor-independent systems designed to readily connect with other vendors' products. To be an open system, it should conform to a set of standards determined from a consensus of interested participants rather than just one or two vendors. Open systems allow interoperability among products from different vendors. Major benefits include portability, scalability, and interoperability.

**Open Web application security project (OWASP)** A project dedicated to enabling organizations to develop, purchase, and maintain applications that can be secured and trusted. In 2010, OWASP published a list of Top 10 application security risks. These include injection; cross-site scripting; broken authentication and session management; insecure direct object references; cross-site request forgery; security misconfiguration; insecure cryptographic storage; failure to restrict URL access; insufficient transport layer protection; and unvalidated redirects and forwards.

**Operating system (OS)** The software "master control application" that runs the computer. It is the first program loaded when the computer is turned on, and its main component, the kernel, resides in memory at all times. The operating system sets the standards for all application programs (e.g., Web server and mail server) that run in the computer. The applications communicate with the operating system for most user interface and file management operations.

**Operating system fingerprinting** Analyzing characteristics of packets sent by a target, such as packet headers or listening ports, to identity the operating system in use on the target.

**Operating system log** Provides information on who used computer resources, for how long, and for what purpose. Unauthorized actions can be detected by analyzing the operating system log. This is a technical and detective control.

**Operational controls** Day-to-day procedures and mechanisms used to protect operational systems and applications. They include security controls (i.e., safeguards or countermeasures) for an information system that are primarily implemented and executed by people, as opposed to systems.

**Operational environment** It includes standalone, managed or custom environments, where the latter is either a specialized security-limited functionality or a legacy environment.

**Originator usage period (crypto-period)** The period of time in the crypto-period of a symmetric key during which cryptographic protection may be applied to data.

**Outage** The period of time for which a communication service or an operation is unavailable.

**Output block** A data block that is an output of either the forward cipher function or the inverse cipher function of the block cipher algorithm.

**Outward-facing** Refers to a system that is directly connected to the Internet.

**Over-the-air-key distribution** Providing electronic key via over-the-air rekeying, over-the-air key transfer, or cooperative key generation.

**Over-the-air key transfer** Electronically distributing key without changing traffic encryption key used on the secured communications path over which the transfer is accomplished.

**Over-the-air rekeying (OTAR)** Changing traffic encryption key or transmission security key in remote cryptographic equipment by sending new key directly to the remote cryptographic equipment over the communications path it secures. OTAR is a key management protocol specified for digital mobile radios and designed for unclassified, sensitive communications. OTAR performs key distribution and transfer functions. Three types of keys are used in OTAR: a key-wrapping key, a traffic-encryption key, and a message authentication code (MAC).

**Overt channel** A communication path within a computer system or network designed for the authorized transfer of data. Compare with covert channel.

**Overt testing**   Security testing performed with the knowledge and consent of the organization's IT staff.

**Overwrite procedure**   (1) A software process that replaces data previously stored on storage media with a predetermined set of meaningless data or random patterns. (2) The obliteration of recorded data by recording different data on the same storage surface. (3) Writing patterns of data on top of the data stored on a magnetic medium.

**Out-of-band management**   In out-of-band management, the communications device is accessed via a dial-up circuit with a modem, directly connected terminal device, or LANs dedicated to managing traffic.

**Owner of data**   The individual or group that has responsibility for specific data types and that is charged with the communication of the need for certain security-related handling procedures to both the users and custodians of this data.

# P

**P2P**   Free and easily accessible software that poses risks to individuals and organizations.

**P3P**   According to the Platform for Privacy Preferences Project (P3P), users are given more control over personal information gathered on websites they visit.

**P-box**   Permutation box (P-box) is used to effect a transposition on an 8-bit input in a product cipher. This transposition, which is implemented with simple electrical circuits, is done so fast that it does not require any computation, just signal propagation. The P-box design, which is implemented in hardware for cryptographic algorithm, follows Kerckhoff's principle (security-by-obscurity) in that an attacker knows that the general method is permuting the bits, but he does not know which bit goes where. Hence, there is no need to hide the permutation method. P-boxes and S-boxes are combined to form a product cipher, where wiring of the P-box is placed inside the S-box; the correct sequence is S-box first and P-box next (Tanenbaum).

**Packet**   A piece of a message, usually containing the destination address, transmitted over a network by communications software.

**Packet churns**   Rapid changes in packet forwarding disrupt packet delivery, possibly affecting congestion control.

**Packet filter**   (1) A routing device that provides access control functionality for host addresses and communication sessions. (2) A type of firewall that examines each packet and accepts or rejects it based on the security policy programmed into it in the form of traffic rules. (3) A router to block or filter protocols and addresses. Packet filtering specifies which types of traffic should be permitted or denied and how permitted traffic should be protected, if at all.

**Packet latency**   The time delay in processing voice packets as in Voice over Internet Protocol (VoIP).

**Packet looping**   Packets enter a looping path, so that the traffic is never delivered.

**Packet replay**   Refers to the recording and retransmission of message packets in the network. It is frequently undetectable but can be prevented by using packet time-stamping and packet-sequence counting.

**Packet sniffer**   Software that observes and records network traffic. It is a passive wiretapping.

**Packet snarfing**    Also known as eavesdropping.

**Padded cell systems**    An attacker is seamlessly transferred to a special padded cell host.

**Padding**    Meaningless data added to the start or end of messages. They are used to hide the length of the message or to add volume to a data structure that requires a fixed size.

**Pairwise trust**    Establishment of trust by two entities that have direct business agreements with each other.

**Parameters**    Specific variables and their values used with a cryptographic algorithm to compute outputs useful to achieve specific security goals.

**Pareto's law**    It is called the 80/20 rule, which can be applied to IT in that 80 percent of IT-related problems come from 20 percent of IT-related causes or issues.

**Parity**    Bit(s) used to determine whether a block of data has been altered.

**Parity bit**    A bit indicating whether the sum of a previous series of bits is even or odd.

**Parity checking**    A hardware control that detects data errors during transmission. It compares the sum of a previous set of bits with the parity bit to determine if an error in the transmission or receiving of the message has occurred. This is a technical and detective control.

**Parkinson's law**    Parkinson's law states that work expands to fill the time available for its completion. Regarding IT, we can state an analogy that data expands to fill the bandwidth available for data transmission.

**Partitioned security mode**    Information system security mode of operation wherein all personnel have the clearance, but not necessarily formal access approved and need-to-know, for all information handled by an information system.

**Partitioning**    The act of logically dividing a media into portions that function as physically separate units.

**Passive attack**    (1) An attack against an authentication protocol where the attacker intercepts data traveling along the network between the claimant and verifier, but does not alter the data (i.e., eavesdropping). (2) An attack that does not alter systems or data.

**Passive fingerprinting**    Analyzing packet headers for certain unusual characteristics or combinations of characteristics that are exhibited by particular operating systems or applications.

**Passive security testing**    Security testing that does not involve any direct interaction with the targets, such as sending packets to a target.

**Passive sensor**    A sensor that is deployed so that it monitors a copy of the actual network traffic.

**Passive testing**    Nonintrusive security testing primarily involving reviews of documents such as policies, procedures, security requirements, software code, system configurations, and system logs.

**Passive wiretapping**    The monitoring or recording of data while data is transmitted over a communications link, without altering or affecting the data.

**Passphrase**    A relatively long password consisting of a series of words, such as a phrase or full sentence.

**Password** (1) A protected/private string of letters, numbers, and/or special characters used to authenticate an identity or to authorize access to data and system resources. (2) A secret that a claimant memorizes and uses to authenticate his identity. (3) Passwords are typically character strings (e.g., letters, numbers, and other symbols) used to authenticate an identity or to verify access authorizations. This is a technical and preventive control.

**Password authentication protocol (PAP)** A protocol that allows enables peers connected by a Point-to- Point Protocol (PPP) link to authenticate each other using the simple exchange of a username and password. It is not a secure protocol because it transmits data in a plaintext.

**Password cracker** An application testing for passwords that can be easily guessed such as words in the dictionary or simple strings of characters (e.g., "abcdefgh" or "qwertyuiop").

**Password cracking** The process of recovering secret passwords stored in a computer system or transmitted over a network.

**Password protected** (1) The ability to protect a file using a password access control, protecting the data contents from being viewed with the appropriate viewer unless the proper password is entered. (2) The ability to protect the contents of a file or device from being accessed until the correct password is entered.

**Password synchronization** It is a technology that takes a password from the user and changes the passwords on other system resources to be the same as that password so that the user can use the same password when authenticating to each system resource.

**Password system** A system that uses a password or passphrase to authenticate a person's identity or to authorize a person's access to data and that consists of a means for performing one or more of the following password operations: generation, distribution, entry, storage, authentication, replacement, encryption and/or decryption of passwords.

**Patch** (1) An update to an operating system, application, or other software issued specifically to correct particular problems with the software. (2) A section of software code inserted into a program to correct mistakes or to alter the program, generally supplied by the vendor of software. (3) A patch (sometimes called a "fix") is a "repair job" for a piece of programming. A patch is the immediate solution to an identified problem that is provided to users; it can sometimes be downloaded from the software maker's website. The patch is not necessarily the best solution for the problem, and the product developers often find a better solution to provide when they package the product for its next release. A patch is usually developed and distributed as a replacement for or an insertion in compiled code (that is, in a binary file or object module). In many operating systems, a special program is provided to manage and track the installation of patches.

**Patch management** (1) The systematic notification, identification, deployment, installation, and verification of operating system and application software code revisions, which are known as patches, hot fixes, and service packs. (2) The process of acquiring, testing, and distributing patches to the appropriate administrators and users throughout the organization.

**Payback method** The payback period is stated in years and estimates the time it takes to recover the original investment outlay. The payback period is calculated by dividing the net investment by the average annual operating cash inflows. The payback method can be used to assess the financial feasibility of an investment in information security program.

**Payload** (1) The portion of a virus that contains the code for the virus's objective, which may range from the relatively benign (e.g., annoying people and stating personal opinions) to the highly malicious (e.g., forwarding personal information to others and wiping out systems and files). (2) A protection for packet headers and data in the Internet Protocol security (IPsec). (3) Information passed down from the previous layer to the next layer in a TCP/IP network. (4) A life-cycle function of a worm where it is the code that carries to perform a task beyond its standard life-cycle functions. (5) The input data to the counter with cipher-block chaining-message authentication code (CCM) generation-encryption process that is both authenticated and encrypted.

**Peer review** A quality assurance method in which two or more programmers review and critique each other's work for accuracy and consistency with other parts of the system and detect program errors. This is a management and detective control.

**Peer-to-peer computing** See Mesh computing.

**Peer-to-peer (P2P) file sharing program** Free and easily accessible software that poses risks to individuals and organizations. It unknowingly enables users to copy private files, downloads material that is protected by the copyright laws, downloads a virus, or facilitates a security breach.

**Peer-to-peer (P2P) network** Each networked host computer running both the client and server parts of an application system.

**Perfective maintenance** All changes, insertions, deletions, modifications, extensions, and enhancements made to a system to meet the user's evolving or expanding needs.

**Performance metrics** They provide the means for tying information security controls' implementation, efficiency, effectiveness, and impact levels.

**Performance testing** A testing approach to assess how well a system meets its specified performance requirements.

**Persistent cookie** A cookie stored on a computer's hard drive indefinitely so that a website can identify the user during subsequent visits. These cookies are set with expiration dates and are valid until the user deletes them.

**Personal digital assistant (PDA)** A handheld computer that serves as a tool for reading and conveying documents, electronic mail, and other electronic media over a communications link, and for organizing personal information, such as a name-and-address database, a to-do list, and an appointment calendar.

**Personal identification number (PIN)** (1) A password consisting only of decimal digits. (2) A secret that a claimant memorizes and uses to authenticate his identity.

**Personal identity verification (PIV) card** A physical artifact (e.g., identity card and smart card) issued to an individual that contains stored identity credentials (e.g., photograph, cryptographic keys, and digitized fingerprint representation) such that the claimed identity of the cardholder can be verified against the stored credentials by another person (human readable and verifiable) or an automated process (computer readable and verifiable).

**Penetration** The successful act of bypassing the security mechanisms of a system.

**Penetration signature** The characteristics or identifying marks produced by a penetration.

**Penetration study**   A study to determine the feasibility and methods for defeating system controls.

**Penetration testing**   (1) A test methodology in which assessors, using all available documentation (e.g., system design, source code, and manuals) and working under specific constraints, attempt to circumvent or defeat the security features of an information system. (2) Security testing in which evaluators mimic real-world attacks in an attempt to identify ways to circumvent the security features of an application, system, or network. Penetration testing often involves issuing real attacks on real systems and data, using the same tools and techniques used by actual attackers. Most penetration tests involve looking for combinations of vulnerabilities on a single system or multiple systems that can be used to gain more access than could be achieved through a single vulnerability.

**Per-call key**   A unique traffic encryption key is generated automatically by certain secure telecommunications systems to secure single voice or data transmissions.

**Perfect forward secrecy**   An option available during quick mode that causes a new-shared secret to be created through a Diffie-Hellman exchange for each IPsec SA (security association).

**Perimeter**   A boundary within which security controls are applied to protect assets. A security perimeter typically includes a security kernel, some trusted-code facilities, hardware, and possibly some communications channels.

**Perimeter-based security**   The technique of securing a network by controlling access to all entry and exit points of the network.

**Perimeter protection (logical)**   The security controls such as e-mail gateways, proxy servers, and firewalls provide logical access perimeter security controls, and they act as the first line-of-defense.

**Perimeter protection (physical)**   The objective of physical perimeter or boundary protection is to deter trespassing and to funnel employees, visitors, and the public to selected entrances. Gates and security guards provide the perimeter protection.

**Permissions**   A description of the type of authorized interactions (such as read, write, execute, add, modify, and delete) that a subject can have with an object.

**Personal-area network (PAN)**   It is used by an individual or in a home-based business connecting desktop PC, laptop PC, notebook PC, and PDA with a mouse, keyboard, and printer.

**Personal computer (PC)**   A desktop or laptop computer running a standard PC operating system (e.g., Windows Vista, Windows XP, Linux/UNIX, and Mac OS X).

**Personal firewall**   A software-based firewall installed on a desktop or laptop computer to monitor and control its incoming and outgoing network traffic, and which blocks communications that are unwanted.

**Personal firewall appliance**   A device that performs functions similar to a personal firewall for a group of computers on a home network.

**Personnel screening**   A protective measure applied to determine that an individual's access to sensitive, unclassified automated information is admissible. The need for and extent of a screening process are normally based on an assessment of risk, cost, benefit, and feasibility as well as other protective measures in place. Effective screening processes are applied in such a way as to allow a range of implementation, from minimal procedures to more stringent procedures commensurate with the sensitivity of the data to be accessed and the magnitude of harm or loss that could be caused by the individual. This is a management and preventive control.

**Personnel security**   It includes the procedures to ensure that access to classified and sensitive unclassified information is granted only after a determination has been made about a person's trustworthiness and only if a valid need-to-know exists. It is the procedures established to ensure that all personnel who have access to sensitive information have the required authority as well as appropriate clearances.

**Petri net model**   The Petri net model is used for protocol modeling to demonstrate the correctness of a protocol. Mathematical techniques are used in specifying and verifying the protocol correctness. A Petri net model has four basic elements, such as places (states), transitions, arcs (input and output), and tokens. A transition is enabled if there is at least one input token in each of its input places (states). Petri nets are a graphical technique used to model relevant aspects of the system behavior and to assess and improve safety and operational requirements through analysis and redesign. They are used for concurrent application systems that need data synchronization mechanisms and for analyzing thread interactions.

**Pharming attack**   (1) An attack in which an attacker corrupts an infrastructure service such as domain name service (DNS) causing the subscriber to be misdirected to a forged verifier/relying party, and revealing sensitive information, downloading harmful software, or contributing to a fraudulent act. (2) Using technical means (e.g., DNS server software) to redirect users into accessing a fake website masquerading as a legitimate one and divulging personal information.

**Phishing attack**   (1) An attack in which the subscriber is lured (usually through an e-mail) to interact with a counterfeit verifier, and tricked into revealing information that can be used to masquerade as that subscriber to the real verifier. (2) A digital form of social engineering technique that uses authentic-looking but phony (bogus) e-mails to request personal information from users or direct them to a fake website that requests such information. (3) Tricking or deceiving individuals into disclosing sensitive personal information through deceptive computer-based means.

**Physical access controls**   The controls over physical access to the elements of a system can include controlled areas, barriers that isolate each area, entry points in the barriers, and screening measures at each of the entry points.

**Physical protection system**   The primary functions of a physical protection system include detection, delay, and response.

**Physical security**   (1) It includes controlling access to facilities that contain classified and sensitive unclassified information. (2) It also addresses the protection of the structures that contain the computer equipment. (3) It is the application of physical barriers and control procedures as countermeasures against threats to resources and sensitive information. (4) It is the use of locks, guards, badges, and similar administrative measures to control access to the computer and related equipment.

**Piggybacking, data frames**   Electronic piggybacking is a technique of temporarily delaying outgoing acknowledgements of data frames so that they can be attached to the next outgoing data frames.

**Piggybacking entry**   Unauthorized physical access gained to a facility or a computer system via another user's legitimate entry or system connection. It is same as tailgating.

**Pilot testing**   Using a limited version of software in restricted conditions to discover if the programs operate as intended.

**Ping-of-Death attack**   Sends a series of oversized packets via the ping command. The ping server reassembles the packets at the host machine. The result is that the attack could hang, crash, or reboot the system. This is an example of buffer overflow attack.

**PIV issuer**   An authorized identity card creator that procures blank identity cards, initializes them with appropriate software and data elements for the requested identity verification and access control application, personalizes the cards with the identity credentials of the authorized subjects, and delivers the personalized cards to the authorized subjects along with appropriate instructions for protection and use.

**PIV registrar**   An entity that establishes and vouches for the identity of an applicant to a PIV issuer. The PIV registrar authenticates the applicant's identity by checking identity source documents and identity proofing, and ensures a proper background check has been completed, before the credential is issued.

**PIV sponsor**   An individual who can act on behalf of a department or organization to request a PIV card for an applicant.

**Plain old telephone service (POTS)**   A basic and conventional voice telephone system with a wireline (wired) telecommunication connection. POTS contains a POTS coder decoder (CODEC) as a digital audio device and a POTS filter (DSL filter). Three major components of POTS include local loops (analog twisted pairs going into houses and businesses), trunks (digital fiber optics connecting the switching offices), and switching offices (where calls are moved from one trunk to another). A potential risk or disadvantage of POTS is eavesdropping due to physical access to tap a telephone line or penetration of a switch. An advantage of POTS or mobile phone is that they can serve as a backup for PBX and VoIP system during a cable modem outage or DSL line outage.

**Plaintext**   (1) Data input to the cipher or output from the inverse cipher. (2) Intelligible data that has meaning and can be read, understood, or acted upon without the application of decryption (i.e., plain, clear text, unencrypted text, or usable data).   (3) Usable data that is formatted as input to a mode of operation.

**Plaintext key**   An unencrypted cryptographic key.

**Plan of action and milestones (POA&M)**   A document that identifies tasks needing to be accomplished. It details resources required to accomplish the elements of the plan, any milestones in meeting the tasks, and scheduled completion dates for the milestones.

**Plan-do-check-act (PDCA) cycle**   The PDCA cycle is a core management tool for problem solving and quality improvement. The "plan" calls for developing an implementation plan for initial effort followed by organization-wide effort. The "do" part carries out the plan on a small scale using a pilot organization, and later on a large scale. The "check" part evaluates lessons learned by pilot organization. The "act" part uses lessons learned to improve the implementation.

**Platform**   (1) A combination of hardware and the most prevalent operating system for that hardware. (2) It is the hardware and systems software on which applications software is developed and operated. (3) It is the hardware, software, and communications required to provide the processing environments to support one or more application software systems. (4) It is the foundation technology (bottom-most layer) of a computer system. (5) It is also referred to the type of computer (hardware) or operating system (software) being used.

**Point-to-point network**   Adjacent nodes communicating with one another.

**Point-to-Point Protocol (PPP)**   Point-to-Point Protocol (PPP) is a character-oriented protocol. It is a data-link framing protocol used to frame data packets on point-to-point lines. It is used to connect a remote workstation over a phone line and to connect home computers to the Internet.   The Internet needs PPP for router-to-router traffic and for home user-to-ISP traffic. PPP provides features such as link control protocol (LCP) and network control protocol (NCP). PPP is a multiprotocol framing mechanism for use over modems, HDLC bit-serial lines, and SONET networks. PPP supports error detection, option negotiation, header compression, and reliable transmission using an HDLC. PPP uses byte stuffing on dial-up modem lines, so all frames are an integral number of bytes. PPP is a variant of the HDLC data-link framing protocol and includes PAP, CHAP, and others.

**Point-to-Point Tunneling Protocol (PPTP)**   A protocol that provides encryption and authentication services for remote dial-up and LAN-to-LAN connections. It has a control session and a data session.

**Policy**   A document that delineates the security management structure and clearly assigns security responsibilities and lays the foundation necessary to reliably measure progress and compliance.

**Policy- Based Access Control (PBAC)**   A form of access control that uses an authorization policy that is flexible in the types of evaluated parameters (e.g., identity, role, clearance, operational need, risk, and heuristics).

**Policy decision point (PDP)**   Mechanism that examines requests to access resources, and compares them to the policy that applies to all requests for accessing that resource to determine whether specific access should be granted to the particular requester who issued the request under consideration.

**Policy enforcement point (PEP)**   Mechanism (e.g., access control mechanism of a file system or Web server) that actually protects (in terms of controlling access to) the resources exposed by Web services.

**Polyinstantiation**   Polyinstantiation allows a relation to contain multiple rows with the same primary key; the multiple instances are distinguished by their security levels.

**Polymorphism**   Polymorphism refers to being able to apply a generic operation to data of different types. For each type, a different piece of code is defined to execute the operation. In the context of object systems, polymorphism means that an object's response to a message is determined by the class to which it belongs.

**Pop-up window**   A standalone Web browser pane that opens automatically when a Web page is loaded or a user performs an action designed to trigger a pop-up window.

**Port**   (1) A physical entry or exit point of a cryptographic module that provides access to the module for physical signals represented by logical information flows (physically separated ports do not share the same physical pin or wire). (2) An interface mechanism (e.g., a connector, a pin, or a cable) between a peripheral device (e.g., terminal) and the CPU.

**Port protection device (PPD)**   A port protection device is fitted to a communication port of a host computer and authorizes access to the port itself, prior to and independent of the computer's own access control functions.

**Port scanner**   A program that can remotely determine which ports on a system are open (e.g., whether systems allow connections through those ports).

**Portal**   A high-level remote access architecture that is based on a server that offers teleworkers access to one or more application systems through a single centralized interface.

**Portal VPN**   A single standard secure socket layer (SSL) connection to a website to secure access to multiple network services.

**Portfolio management**   It refers to activities related to the management of IT resources, as one would manage investments in a stock portfolio. The IT portfolio facilitates the alignment of technology investments with business needs and focuses on mitigating IT investment risks.

**Ports**   Ports are commonly used to gain information or access to computer systems. Well-known port numbers range from 0 through 1,023, whereas registered port numbers run from 1,024 through 49,151. When a service is requested from unknown callers, a service contact port (well-known port) is defined.

**Possession and control of a token**   The ability to activate and use the token in an authentication protocol.

**Post office protocol (POP)**   A standard protocol used to receive electronic mail from a server. It is a mailbox access protocol defined by IETF RFC 1939 and is one of the most commonly used mailbox access protocols.

**Potential impact**   The loss of confidentiality, integrity, or availability could be expected to have (1) a limited adverse effect (low), (2) a serious adverse effect (moderate), or (3) a severe or catastrophic adverse effect (high) on organizational operations, systems, assets, individuals, or other organizations.

**Power monitoring attack**   Uses varying levels of power consumption by the hardware during computations. It is a general class of side channel attack (Wikipedia).

**Pre-activation state**   A cryptographic key lifecycle state in which a key has not yet been authorized for use.

**Pre-boot authentication (PBA)**   The process of requiring a user to authenticate successfully before decrypting and booting an operating system.

**Precursor**   (1) A sign that a malware attack may occur in the future. (2) A sign that an attacker may be preparing to cause an incident.

**Pre-message secret number**   A secret number that is generated prior to the generation of each digital signature.

**Presentation layer**   Portion of an ISO/OSI reference model responsible for adding structure to data units that are exchanged.

**Pre-shared key**   Single key used by multiple IPsec endpoints to authenticate endpoints to each other.

**Pretexting**   Impersonating others to gain access to information that is restricted. Synonymous with social engineering.

**Pretty Good Privacy (PGP)**   (1) A standard program for securing e-mail and file encryption on the Internet. Its public-key cryptography system allows for the secure transmission of messages and guarantees authenticity by adding digital signatures to messages. (2) A cryptographic software application for the protection of computer files and electronic mail. (3) It combines the convenience of the Rivest-Shamir-Adleman (RSA) public-key algorithm with the speed of the secret-key IDEA algorithm, digital signature, and key management.

**Preventive controls**   Actions taken to deter undesirable events and incidents from occurring in the first place.

**Preventive maintenance**   Computer hardware and related equipment maintained on a planned basis by the manufacturer, vendor, or third party to keep them in a continued operational condition.

**Prime number generation seed**   A string of random bits that is used to determine a prime number with the required characteristics.

**Principal**   An entity whose identity can be authenticated.

**Principle of least privilege**   The granting of the minimum access authorization necessary for the performance of required tasks.

**Privacy**   (1) The right of an individual to self-determination as to the degree to which the individual is willing to share with others information about himself that may be compromised by unauthorized exchange of such information among other individuals or organizations. (2) The right of individuals and organizations to control the collection, storage, and dissemination of their information or information about themselves. (3) Restricting access to subscriber or relying party information.

**Privacy impact assessment (PIA)**   PIA is an analysis of how information is handled (1) to ensure handling conforms to applicable legal, regulatory, and policy requirements regarding privacy, (2) to determine the risks and effects of collecting, maintaining, and disseminating information in identifiable form in an electronic information system, and (3) to examine and evaluate protections and alternative processes for handling information to mitigate potential privacy risks.

**Privacy protection**   The establishment of appropriate administrative, technical, and physical safeguards to ensure the security and confidentiality of data records to protect both security and confidentiality against any anticipated threats or hazards that could result in substantial harm, embarrassment, inconvenience, or unfairness to any individual about whom such information is maintained.

**Private key**   (1) The secret part of an asymmetric key pair that is typically used to digitally sign or decrypt data. (2) A cryptographic key, used with a public key cryptographic algorithm that is uniquely associated with an entity and not made public. It is the undisclosed key in a matched key pair—private key and public key—used in public key cryptographic systems. In a symmetric (private) key crypto-system, the key of an entity's key pair is known only by that entity.   In an asymmetric (public) crypto-system, the private key is associated with a public key. Depending on the algorithm, the private key may be used to (a) compute the corresponding public key, (b) compute a digital signature that may be verified by the corresponding public key, (c) decrypt data that was encrypted by the corresponding public key, or (d) compute a piece of common shared data, together with other information. (3) The private key is used to generate a digital signature. (4) The private key is mathematically linked with a corresponding public key.

**Privilege management**   Privilege management creates, manages, and stores the attributes and policies needed to establish criteria that can be used to decide whether an authenticated entity's request for access to some resource should be granted.

**Privileged accounts**   Individuals who have access to set "access rights" for users on a given system. Sometimes referred to as system or network administrative accounts.

**Privileged data**   Data not subject to usual security rules because of confidentiality imposed by law, such as legal and medical files.

**Privileged function**   A function executed on an information system involving the control, monitoring, or administration of the system.

**Privileged instructions**   A set of instructions (e.g., interrupt handling or special computer instructions) to control features (such as storage protection features) generally executable only when a computer system is operating in the executive state.

**Privileged process**   A process that is afforded (by the kernel) some privileges not afforded normal user processes. A typical privilege is the ability to override the security *.property. Privileged processes are trusted.

**Privileged user**   An individual who has access to system control, monitoring, or administration functions (e.g., system administrator, information system security officer, system maintainer, and system programmer).

**Probative data**   Information that reveals the truth of an allegation.

**Probe**   A device program managed to gather information about an information system or its users.

**Problem**   Often used interchangeably with anomaly, although problem has a more negative connotation, and implies that an error, fault, failure, or defect does exist.

**Problem state**   A state in which a computer is executing an application program with faults.

**Procedural security**   The management constraints; operational, administrative, and accountability procedures; and supplemental controls established to provide protection for sensitive information. Synonymous with administrative security.

**Process**   Any specific combination of machines, tools, methods, materials, and/or people employed to attain specific qualities in a product or service.

**Process isolation**   The principle of process isolation or separation is employed to preserve the object's wholeness and subject's adherence to a code of behavior.

**Process reengineering**   A procedure that analyzes control flow. A program is examined to create overview architecture with the purpose of transforming undesirable programming constructs into more efficient ones. Program restructuring can play a major role in process reengineering.

**Process separation**   See process isolation.

**Profiling**   Measuring the characteristics of expected activity so that changes to it can be more easily identified.

**Proof carrying code**  As a part of technical safeguards for active content, proof carrying code defines properties that are conveyed with the code, which must be successfully verified before the code is executed.

**Proof-by-knowledge**  A claimant authenticates his identity to a verifier by the use of a password or PIN that he has knowledge of. The proof-by-knowledge applies to mobile device authentication and robust authentication.

**Proof-by-possession**  A claimant authenticates his identity to a verifier by the use of a token or smart card and an authentication protocol. The proof-by-possession applies to mobile device authentication and robust authentication.

**Proof-by-property**  A claimant authenticates his identity to a verifier by the use of a biometric such as fingerprints. The proof-by-property applies to mobile device authentication and robust authentication.

**Proof-of-concept**  A new idea or modified idea is put to test by developing a prototype model to prove whether the idea or the concept works.

**Proof-of-correctness**  Applies mathematical proofs-of-correctness to demonstrate that a computer program conforms exactly to its specifications and to prove that the functions of the computer programs are correct.

**Proof-of-correspondence**  The design of a cryptographic module is verified by a formal model and informal proof-of-correspondence between the formal model and the functional specifications.

**Proof-of-origin**  A proof-of-origin is the basis to prove an assertion. For example, a private signature key is used to generate digital signatures as a proof-of-origin.

**Proof-of-possession**  A verification process whereby it is proven that the owner of a key pair actually has the private key associated with the public key. The owner demonstrates the possession by using the private key in its intended manner.

**Proof-of-possession protocol**  A protocol where a claimant proves to a verifier that he possesses and controls a token (e.g., a key or password).

**Proof-of-wholeness**  Having all of an object's parts or components include both the sense of unimpaired condition (i.e., soundness) and being complete and undivided (i.e., completeness). The proof-of-wholeness applies to preserving the integrity of objects in that different layers of abstraction for objects cannot be penetrated and their internal mechanisms cannot be modified or destroyed.

**Promiscuous mode**  A configuration setting for a network interface card that causes it to accept all incoming packets that it sees, regardless of their intended destinations.

**Proprietary protocol**  A protocol, network management protocol, or suite of protocols developed by a private company to manage network resources manufactured by that company.

**Protected channel**  A session wherein messages between two participants are encrypted and integrity is protected using a set of shared secrets; a participant is said to be authenticated if the other participant can link possession of the session keys by the first participant to a long-term cryptographic token and verify the identity associated with that token.

**Protection bits**   A mechanism commonly included in UNIX and UNIX-like systems that controls access based on bits specifying read, write, or execute permissions for a file's (or directory's) owner, group, or other.

**Protection profile (PP)**   A Common Criteria (CC) term for a set of implementation-independent security requirements for a category of Targets of Evaluation (TOEs) that meet specific consumer needs. It is an implementation-independent statement of security needs for a product type.

**Protection ring**   One of a hierarchy of privileged modes of a system that gives certain access rights to user programs and processes authorized to operate in a given mode.

**Protection suite**   It is a set of parameters that are mandatory for IPsec phase 1 negotiations (encryption algorithm, integrity protection algorithm, authentication method, and Diffie-Hellman group).

**Protective distribution system (PDS)**   Wire line or fiber optic system that includes adequate safeguards and/or countermeasures (e.g., acoustic, electric, electromagnetic, and physical) to permit its use for the transmission of unencrypted information.

**Protective measures**   Physical, administrative, personnel, and technical security measures which, when applied separately or in combination, are designed to reduce the probability of harm, loss, or damage to, or compromise of an unclassified computer system or sensitive and/or mission-critical information.

**Protective technologies**   Special tamper-evident features and materials employed for the purpose of detecting tampering and deterring attempts to compromise, modify, penetrate, extract, or substitute information processing equipment and cryptographic keying material. Examples include white noise and zone of control.

**Protocol**   A set of rules (i.e., data formats and semantic and syntactic procedures) for communications that computers use when sending signals between themselves or permit entities to exchange information. It establishes procedures the way in which computers or other functional units transfer data.

**Protocol converter**   A protocol converter is a device that changes one type of coded data to another type of coded data for computer processing.

**Protocol data unit (PDU)**   A unit of data specified in a protocol and consisting of protocol information and, possibly, user data.

**Protocol entity**   Entity that follows a set of rules and formats (semantic and syntactic) that determines the communication behavior of other entities.

**Protocol governance**   A protocol is a set of rules and formats, semantic and syntactic, permitting information systems to exchange data related to security functions. Organizations use several protocols for specific purposes (such as, encryption and authentication mechanisms) in various systems. Some protocols are compatible with each other while others are not, similar to negative interactions from prescription drugs. Protocol governance requires selecting the right protocols for the right purpose and at the right time to minimize their incompatibility and ineffectiveness (that is, not providing privacy and not protecting IT assets). It also requires a constant and ongoing monitoring to determine the best time for a protocol's eventual replacement or substitution with a better one.

In addition to selecting standard protocols that were approved by the standard setting bodies, protocols must be operationally-efficient and security-effective. Examples include (1) DES, which is weak in security and AES, which is strong in security, and (2) WEP, which is weak in security and WPA, which is strong in security.

**Protocol machine**   A finite state machine that implements a particular protocol.

**Protocol run**   An instance of the exchange of messages between a claimant and a verifier in a defined authentication protocol that results in the authentication (or authentication failure) of the claimant.

**Protocol tunneling**   A method used to ensure confidentiality and integrity of data transmitted over the Internet, by encrypting data packets, sending them in packets across the Internet, and decrypting them at the destination address.

**Proxy**   (1) A program that receives a request from a client, and then sends a request on the client's behalf to the desired destination. (2) An agent that acts on behalf of a requester to relay a message between a requester agent and a provider agent. The proxy appears to the provider agent Web service to be the requester. (3) An application or device acting on behalf of another in responding to protocol requests. (4) A proxy is an application that "breaks" the connection between client and server. (5) An intermediary device or program that provides communication and other services between a client and server. The proxy accepts certain types of traffic entering or leaving a network, processes it, and forwards it. This effectively closes the straight path between the internal and external networks, making it more difficult for an attacker to obtain internal addresses and other details of the organization's internal network.

**Proxy agent**   A proxy agent is a software application running on a firewall or on a dedicated proxy server that is capable of filtering a protocol and routing it to between the interfaces of the device.

**Proxy server**   A server that sits between a client application, such as a Web browser, and a real server. It intercepts all requests to the real server to see if it can fulfill the requests itself. If not, it forwards the request to the real server. A device or product that provides network protection at the application level by using custom programs for each protected application. These programs can act as both a client and server and are proxies to the actual application. Proxy servers are available for common Internet services; for example, a hypertext transfer protocol (HTTP) proxy used for Web access and a simple mail transfer protocol (SMTP) proxy used for e-mail. Proxy servers are also called application gateway firewall or proxy gateway.

**Pseudonym**   A subscriber name that has been chosen by the subscriber that is not verified as meaningful by identity proofing.

**Pseudorandom number generator (PRNG)**   An algorithm that produces a sequence of bits that are uniquely determined from an initial value called a "seed." The output of the PRNG "appears" to be random, i.e., the output is statistically indistinguishable from random values. A cryptographic PRNG has the additional property that the output is unpredictable, given that the seed is not known.

**Public key**   (1) The public part of an asymmetric key pair that is typically used to verify signatures or encrypt data. (2) A cryptographic key used with a public key cryptographic algorithm, that is uniquely associated with an entity and that may be made public. It is the key in a matched key pair of private-key and public-key that is made public, for example, posted in a public directory. In an asymmetric (public) key crypto-system, the public key is associated with a private key. The public key may be known by anyone and, depending on the algorithm, may be used to (i) verify a digital signature that is signed by the corresponding private key, (ii) encrypt data that can be decrypted by the corresponding private key, or (iii) compute a piece of common shared data. (3) The public key is used to verify a digital signature. (4) The public key is mathematically linked with a corresponding private key.

**Public key certificate**   A set of data that unambiguously identifies an entity, contains the entity's public key, and is digitally signed by a trusted third party (certification authority, CA). A digital document issued and digitally signed by the private key of a CA that binds the name of a subscriber to a public key. The certificate indicates that the subscriber identified in the certificate has sole control and access to the private key. A subscriber is an individual or business entity that has contracted with a CA to receive a digital certificate verifying an identity for digitally signing electronic messages.

**Public key (asymmetric) cryptographic algorithm**   A cryptographic algorithm that uses two related keys (a public key and a private key). The two keys have the property that deriving the private key from the public key is computationally infeasible. Public key cryptography uses "key pairs," a public key and a mathematically related private key. Given the public key, it is infeasible to find the private key. The private key is kept secret, whereas the public key may be shared with others. A message encrypted with the public key can only be decrypted with the private key. A message can be digitally signed with the private key, and anyone can verify the signature with the public key. Public key cryptography is used to perform (1) digital signatures, (2) secure transmission or exchange of secret keys, and/or (3) encryption and decryption. Cryptography that uses separate keys for encryption and decryption; also known as asymmetric cryptography.

**Public key cryptography (reversible)**   An asymmetric cryptographic algorithm where data encrypted using the public key can only be decrypted using the private key and, conversely, data encrypted using the private key can only be decrypted using the public key.

**Public key cryptography standard (PKCS)**   The PKCS is used to derive a symmetric encryption key from a password, which can be guessed relatively easily.

**Public key infrastructure (PKI)**   (1) A framework that is established to issue, maintain, and revoke public key certificates. (2) A set of policies, processes, server platforms, software and workstations used for the purpose of administering certificates and public-private key pairs, including the ability to issue, maintain, and revoke public key certificates. (3) An architecture that is used to bind public keys to entities, enable other entities to verify public key bindings, revoke such bindings, and provide other services critical to managing public keys. (4) The PKI includes the hierarchy of certificate authorities (CAs) that allow for the deployment of digital certificates that support encryption, digital signatures, and authentication to meet business needs and security requirements.

**Public security parameter (PSP)**   The PSP deals with security-related public information (e.g., public key) whose modification can compromise the security of a cryptographic module.

**Public seed**   A starting value for a pseudorandom number generator. The value produced by the random number generator (RNG) may be made public. The public seed is often called a "salt."

**Public switched telephone network (PSTN)**   The PSTN is used in the traditional telephone lines. It uses high bandwidth and has quality-related problems. However, the physical security of a PSTN is higher. Voice over IP security (VoIP) is an alternative to the PSTN with reduced bandwidth usage and quality superior to the conventional PSTN.

**Pull technology** Products and services are pulled by companies based on customer orders.

**Pulverization** A physically destructive method of sanitizing media; the act of grinding to a powder or dust.

**Purging** (1) The orderly review of storage and removal of inactive or obsolete data files. (2) The removal of obsolete data by erasure, by overwriting of storage, or by resetting registers. (3) To render stored application, files, and other information on a system unrecoverable. (4) Rendering sanitized data unrecoverable by laboratory attack methods.

**Push technology** Technology that allows users to sign up for automatic downloads of online content, such as virus signature file updates, patches, news, and website updates, to their e-mail addresses or other designated directories on their computers. Products and services are pushed by companies to customers regardless of their orders.

# Q

**Q.931** A protocol used for establishing and releasing telephone connections (the ITU standard).

**Quality assurance (QA)** (1) All actions taken to ensure that standards and procedures are adhered to and that delivered products or services meet performance requirements. (2) The planned systematic activities necessary to ensure that a component, module, or system conforms to established technical requirements. (3) The policies, procedures, and systematic actions established in an enterprise for the purpose of providing and maintaining a specified degree of confidence in data integrity and accuracy throughout the lifecycle of the data, which includes input, update, manipulation, and output.

**Quality control (QC)** A management function whereby control of the quality of (1) raw materials, assemblies, finished products, parts, and components, (2) services related to production, and (3) management, production, and inspection processes is exercised for the purpose of preventing undetected production of defective materials or the rendering of faulty services.

**Quality of protection (QoP)** The quality of protection (QoP) requires that overall performance of a system should be improved by prioritizing traffic and considering rate of failure or average latency at the lower layer protocols. For Web services to truly support QoS, existing QoS support must be extended so that the packets corresponding to individual Web service messages can be routed accordingly to achieve predictable performance. Two standards such as WS-Reliability and WS-Reliable Messaging provide some level of QoS because both of these standards support guaranteed message delivery and message ordering. Note that QoP is related to quality of service (QoS) and DoS which, in turn, related to DoQ.

**Quality of service (QoS)** The quality of service (QoS) is the handling capacity of a system or service. (1) It is the time interval between request and delivery of a message, product, or service to the client or customer. (2) It is the guaranteed throughput level expressed in terms of data transfer rate. (3) It is the performance specification of a computer communications channel or system. (4) It is measured quantitatively in terms of performance parameters such as signal-to-noise ratio, bit error ratio, message throughput rate, and call blocking probability. (5) It is measured qualitatively in terms of excellent, good, fair, poor, or unsatisfactory for a subjective rating of telephone communications quality in which listeners judge the transmission quality. (6) It is a network property that specifies a guaranteed throughput level for end-to-end services, which is critical for most composite Web services in delivering enterprise-wide service-oriented distributed systems. (7) It is important in defining the expected level of performance a particular Web service will have. (8) It is the desired or actual characteristics of a service but not always those of the network service. (9) It is the measurable end-to-end performance properties of a network service, which can be guaranteed in advance by a service-level agreement (SLA) between a user and a service provider, so as to satisfy specific customer application requirements. Examples of performance properties include throughput (bandwidth), transit delay (latency), error rates, priority, security, packet loss, and packet jitter. Note that QoS is related to quality of protection (QoP) and DoS which, in turn, is related to DoQ.

**Quick mode**   Mode used in IPsec phase 2 to negotiate the establishment of an IPsec security association (SA).

**Quantum computing**   Performed with a quantum computer using quantum science concepts (for example, superposition and entanglement) to represent data and perform computational operations on these data. Quantum computing is based on a theoretical model such as a Turing machine and is used in military research and information security purposes (for example, cryptanalysis) with faster algorithms. It deals with large word size quantum computers in which the security of integer factorization and discrete log-based public-key cryptographic algorithms would be threatened. This would be a major negative result for many cryptographic key management systems, which rely on these algorithms for the establishment of cryptographic keys. Lattice-based public-key cryptography would be resistant to quantum computing threats.

**Quantum cryptography**   It is related to quantum computing technology, but viewed from a different perspective. Quantum cryptography is a possible replacement for public key algorithms that hopefully will not be susceptible to the attacks enabled by quantum computing.

**Quarantine**   To store files containing malware in isolation for future disinfection or examination.

# R

**Race conditions**   Race conditions can occur when a program or process has entered into a privileged mode but before the program or process has given up its privileged mode. A user can time an attack to take advantage of this program or process while it is still in the privileged mode. If an attacker successfully manages to compromise the program or process during its privileged state, then the attacker has won the "race." Common race conditions occur in signal handling and core-file manipulation, time-of-check to time-of-use (TOC-TOU) attacks, symbolic links, and object-oriented programming errors.

**Radio frequency identification (RFID)**   It is a form of automatic identification and data capture that uses electric or magnetic fields at radio frequencies to transmit information in a supply chain system.

**Rainbow attacks**   Rainbow attacks occur in two ways: using rainbow tables, which are used in password cracking, and using preshared keys (PSKs) in a wireless local-area network (WLAN) configuration. Password cracking threats include discovering a character string that produces the same encrypted hash as the target password. In PSK environments, a secret passphrase is shared between base stations and access points, and the keys are derived from a passphrase that is shorter than 20 characters, which are less secure and subject to dictionary and rainbow attacks.

**Rainbow tables**   Rainbow tables are lookup tables that contain pre-computed password hashes, often used during password cracking. These tables allow an attacker to crack a password with minimal time and effort.

**Random access memory (RAM)**   A place in the central processing unit (CPU) of a computer where data and programs are temporarily stored during computer processing.

**Random number generator (RNG)**   A process used to generate an unpredictable series of numbers. Each individual value is called random if each of the values in the total population of values has an equal probability of being selected.

**Random numbers**   Random numbers are used in the generation of cryptographic keys, nonces, and authentication challenges.

**Reachability analysis**   Reachability analysis is helpful in detecting whether a protocol is correct. An initial state corresponds to a system when it starts running. From the initial state, the other states can be reached by a sequence of transitions. Based on the graph theory, it is possible to determine which states are reachable and which are not.

**Read-only memory (ROM)**   A place where parts of the operating system programs and language translator programs are permanently stored in microcomputer.

**Read/write exploits**   Generally, a device connected by FireWire has full access to read-and-write data on a computer memory. The FireWire is used by audio devices, printers, scanners, cameras, and GPS. Potential security risks in using these devices include grabbing and changing the screen contents; searching the memory for login ID and passwords; searching for cryptographic keys and keying material stored in RAM; injecting malicious code into a process; and introducing new processes into the system.

**Recipient usage period (crypto-period)**   The period of time during the crypto-period of a symmetric key during which the protected information is processed.

**Reciprocal agreement**   An agreement that allows two organizations to back up each other.

**Reciprocity**   A mutual agreement among participating organizations to accept each other's security assessments in order to reuse information system resources and/or to accept each other's assessed security posture in order to share information.

**Record retention**   A management policy and procedure to save originals of business documents, records, and transactions for future retrieval and reference. This is a management and preventive control.

**Records**   The recordings (automated and/or manual) of evidence of activities performed or results achieved (e.g., forms, reports, and test results), which serve as a basis for verifying that the organization and the information system are performing as intended. Also used to refer to units of related data fields (i.e., groups of data fields that can be accessed by a program and that contain the complete set of information on particular items).

**Recovery**   Process of reconstituting a database to its correct and current state following a partial or complete hardware, software, network, operational, or processing error or failure.

**Recovery controls**   The actions necessary to restore a system's computational and processing capability and data files after a system failure or penetration. Recovery controls are related to recovery point objective (RPO) and recovery time objective (RTO).

**Recovery point objective (RPO)** The point in time in to which data must be recovered after an outage in order to resume computer processing.

**Recovery procedures** Actions necessary to restore data files of an information system and computational capability after a system failure.

**Recovery time objective (RTO)** (1) The overall length of time an information system's components can be in the recovery phase before negatively impacting the organization's mission or business functions. (2) The maximum acceptable length of time that elapses before the unavailability of the system severely affects the organization.

**RED/BLACK concept** A separation of electrical and electronic circuits, components, equipment, and systems that handle unencrypted information (RED) in electrical form from those that handle encrypted information (BLACK) in the same form.

**RED concept (encryption)** It is a designation applied to cryptographic systems when data/information or messages that contains sensitive or classified information that is not encrypted.

**Red team** (1) A group of people authorized and organized to emulate a potential adversary's attack or exploitation capabilities against an enterprise's security posture. The red team's objective is to improve enterprise information assurance by demonstrating the impacts of successful attacks and by demonstrating what works for the defenders (i.e., the blue team) in an operational environment). (2) A test team that performs penetration security testing using covert methods and without the knowledge and consent of the organization's IT staff, but with full knowledge and permission of upper management. The old name for the red team is tiger team.

**Red team exercise** An exercise, reflecting real-world conditions, that is conducted as a simulated adversarial attempt to compromise organizational missions and/or business processes to provide a comprehensive assessment of the security capability of the information system and the organization itself.

**Reduced sign-on (RSO)** The RSO is a technology that allows a user to authenticate once and then access many, but not all, of the resources that the user is authorized to use.

**Redundancy** (1) A concept that can constrain the failure rate and protects the integrity of data. Redundancy makes a confidentiality goal harder to achieve. If there are multiple sites with backup data, then confidentiality could be broken if any of the sites gets compromised. Also, purging some of the data on a backup device could be difficult to do. (2) It is the use of duplicate components to prevent failure of an entire system upon failure of a single component and the part of a message that can be eliminated without loss of essential information. (3) It is a duplication of system components (e.g., hard drives), information (e.g., backup and archived files), or personnel intended to increase the reliability of service and/or decrease the risk of information loss.

**Redundant array of independent disk (RAID)** A cluster of disks used to back up data onto multiple disk drives at the same time, providing increased data reliability and increased input/output performance. Seven classifications for RAID are numbered as RAID-0 through RAID-6. RAID storage units offer fault-tolerant hardware with varying degrees. Nested or hybrid RAID levels occur with two deep levels. A simple RAID configuration with six disks includes four data disks, one parity disk, and one hot spare disk. Problems with RAID include correlated failures due to drive mechanical issues, atomic write semantics (meaning that the write of the data either occurred in its entirety or did not occur at all), write cache reliability due to a power outage, hardware incompatibility with software, data recovery in the event of a failed array, untimely drive errors recovery algorithm, increasing recovery times due to increased drive capacity, and operator skills in terms of correct replacement and rebuild of failed disks, and exposure to computer viruses (Wikipedia).

➤ **RAID-0:** A block-level striping without parity or mirroring and has no redundancy, no fault-tolerance, no error checking, and a greater risk of data loss. However, because of its low overhead and parallel write strategy, it is the fastest in performance for both reading and writing. As the data is written to the drive, it is divided up into sequential blocks, and each block is written to the next available drive in the array. RAID-0 parameters include a minimum of two disks. The space efficiency is 1 and it has a zero fault tolerance disk.

➤ **RAID-1:** Mirroring without parity or striping and offers the highest level of redundancy because there are multiple complete copies of the data at all times (supports disk shadowing and disk duplexing). Because it maintains identical copies on separate drives, RAID-1 is slow in write performance and fast read performance, and it can survive multiple (N-1) drive failures. This means, if N is three, two drives could fail without incurring data loss. RAID-1 parameters include a minimum of two disks. The space efficiency is 1/N, and it has a (N-1) fault tolerance disks.

➤ **RAID-2:** Bit-level striping with dedicated hamming-code parity. RAID-2 parameters include a minimum of three disks; space efficiency is (1- 1/N). Log2 (N-1), and recover from one disk failure. A minimum of three disks must be present for parity to be used for fault tolerance because the parity is an error protection scheme.

➤ **RAID-3:** Byte-level striping with dedicated parity. RAID-3 parameters include a minimum of three disks. The space efficiency is (1- 1/N), and it has one fault tolerance disk.

➤ **RAID-4:** A block-level striping with dedicated parity. RAID-4 parameters include a minimum of three disks. The space efficiency is (1- 1/N), and one fault tolerance disk.

➤ **RAID-5:** A block-level striping with distributed parity. It combines the distributed form of redundancy with parallel disk access. It provides high read-and-write performance, including protection against drive failures. The amount of storage space is reduced due to the parity information taking 1/N of the space, giving a total disk space of (N-1) drives where N is the number of drives. A single drive failure in the set can result in reduced performance of the entire set until the failed drive has been replaced and rebuilt. A data loss occurs in the event of a second drive failure. RAID-5 parameters include a minimum of three disks. The space efficiency is (1- 1/N) and it has one fault tolerance disk.

➤ **RAID-6:** A block-level striping with double distributed parity providing fault tolerance from two drive failures and is useful for high-availability systems. Double parity gives time to rebuild the array without the data being at risk if a single additional drive fails before the rebuild is complete. RAID-6 parameters include a minimum of four disks. The space efficiency is (1- 2/N). It has two fault tolerance disks and two parity disks.

**Reference monitor** (1) A security engineering term for IT functionality that (i) controls all access, (ii) is small, (iii) cannot be bypassed, (iv) is tamper-resistant, and (v) provides confidence that the other four items are true. (2) The concept of an abstract machine that enforces Target of Evaluation (TOE) access control policies. (3) Useful to any system providing multilevel secure computing facilities and controls.

**Reference monitor concept**   An access control concept referring to an abstract machine that mediates all access to objects (e.g., a file or program) by subjects (e.g., a user or process). It is a design concept for an operating system to assure secrecy and integrity.

**Reference validation mechanism**   An implementation of the reference monitor concept. A security kernel is a type of reference validation mechanism. To be effective in providing protection, the implementation of a reference monitor must be (1) tamper-proof, (2) always invoked, and (3) simple and small enough to support the analysis and tests leading to a high degree of assurance that it is correct.

**Referential integrity**   A database has referential integrity if all foreign keys reference existing primary keys.

**Reflection attack**   Occurs when authentication is based on a shared secret key and by breaking a challenge-response protocol with multiple sessions opened at the same time. A countermeasure against reflection attacks is to prove the user identity first so that protocol is not subject to the reflection attack.

**Reflector attack**   A host sends many requests with a spoofed source address to a service on an intermediate host. The service used is typically a user datagram protocol (UDP) based, which makes it easier to spoof the source address successfully. Attackers often use spoofed source addresses because they hide the actual source of the attack. The host generates a reply to each request and sends these replies to the spoofed address. Because the intermediate host unwittingly performs the attack, that host is known as a reflector. During a reflector attack, a DoS could occur to the host at the spoofed address, the reflector itself, or both hosts.

**Registration**   The process through which a party applies to become a subscriber of a credential service provider (CSP) and a registration authority (RA) validates the identity of that party on behalf of the CSP.

**Registration authority (RA)**   A trusted entity that establishes and vouches for the identity of a subscriber to a credential service provider (CSP). The RA's organization is responsible for assignment of unique identifiers to registered objects. The RA may be an integral part of a CSP, or it may be independent of a CSP, but is has a relationship to the CSP(s).

**Regrade**   Data is regraded when information is transferred from high to low or from low to high network data and users. Automated techniques such as processing, filtering, and blocking are used during data regrading.

**Regression testing**   A method to ensure that changes to one part of the software system do not adversely impact other parts.

**Rekey**   The process used to replace a previously active cryptographic key with a new key that was created completely and independently of the old key.

**Related-key cryptanalysis attack**   These attacks choose a relation between a pair of keys but do not choose the keys themselves. These attacks are independent of the number of rounds of the cryptographic algorithm.

**Relay station (WMAN/WiMAX)**   A relay station (RS) is a subscriber station (SS) that is configured to forward traffic to other stations in a multi-hop security zone.

**Release**   The process of moving a baseline configuration item between organizations, such as from software vendor to customer. The process of returning all unused disk space to the system when a dataset is closed at the end of processing.

**Reliability**   (1)The extent to which a computer program can be expected to perform its intended function with the required precision on a consistent basis. (2) The probability of a given system performing its mission adequately for a specified period of time under the expected operating conditions.

**Relying party**   An entity that relies upon the subscriber's credentials or verifier's assertion of an identity, typically to process a transaction or grant access to information or a system.

**Remanence**   The residual information that remains on a storage medium after erasure or clearing.

**Remedial maintenance**   Hardware and software maintenance activities conducted by individuals communicating external to an information system security perimeter or through an external, nonorganization-controlled network (for example, the Internet).

**Remediation plan**   A plan to perform the remediation of one or more threats or vulnerabilities facing an organization's systems. The plan typically includes options to remove threats and vulnerabilities and priorities for performing the remediation.

**Remote access**   (1) Access to an organizational information system by a user or an information system  communicating through an external, non-organization-controlled network (e.g., the Internet). (2) The ability for an organization's users to access its non-public computing resources from locations other than the organization's facilities.

**Remote administration tool**   A program installed on a system that allows remote attackers to gain access to the system as needed.

**Remote journaling**   Transaction logs or journals are transmitted to a remote location. If the server needed to be recovered, the logs or journals could be used to recover transactions, applications, or database changes that occurred after the last server backup. Remote journaling can either be conducted though batches or be communicated continuously using buffering software. Remote journaling and electronic vaulting require a dedicated offsite location (that is, hot-site or offsite storage site) to receive the transmissions and a connection with limited bandwidth.

**Remote maintenance**   Maintenance activities conducted by individuals communicating through an external, nonorganization-controlled network (e.g., the Internet).

**Remote maintenance attack**   Some hardware and software vendors who have access to an organization's computer systems for problem diagnosis and remote maintenance work can modify database contents or reconfigure network elements to their advantage.

**Remote system control**   Remotely using a computer at an organization from a telework computer.

**Removable media**   Portable electronic storage media such as magnetic, optical, and solid-state devices, which can be inserted into and removed from a computing device, and are used to store text, video, audio, and image information. Such devices have no independent processing capabilities. Examples of removable media include hard disks, zip drives, compact disks, thumb drives, flash drives, pen drives, and similar universal serial bus (USB) storage devices. Removable media are less risky than the nonremovable media in terms of security breaches.

**Repeater**   A device to amplify the received signals and it operates in the physical layer of the ISO/OSI reference model.

**Replay**   One can eavesdrop upon another's authentication exchange and learn enough to impersonate a user. It is used in conducting an impersonation attack.

**Replay attack**   (1) An attack that involves the capture of transmitted authentication or access control information and its subsequent retransmission with the intent of producing an unauthorized effect or gaining unauthorized access. (2) An attack in which the attacker can replay previously captured messages (between a legitimate claimant and a verifier) to masquerade as that claimant to the verifier or vice versa.

**Repository**   A database containing information and data relating to certificates; may also be referred to as a directory.

**Request for comment (RFC)**   An Internet standard, developed, and published by the Internet Engineering Task Force (IETF).

**Requirement**   A statement of the system behavior needed to enforce a given policy. Requirements are used to derive the technical specification of a system.

**Reserve keying material**   Cryptographic key held to satisfy unplanned needs. It is also called a contingency key where a key is held for use under specific operational conditions or in support of specific contingency plans.

**Residue**   Data left in storage after information-processing operations are complete; but before degaussing or overwriting has taken place.

**Residual data**   Data from deleted files or earlier versions of existing files.

**Residual risk**   The remaining, potential risk after all IT security measures are applied. There is a residual risk associated with each threat.

**Resilience**   (1) The capability to quickly adapt and recover from any known or unknown changes to the environment through holistic implementation of risk management, contingency measures, and continuity planning. (2) The capability of a computer system to continue to function correctly despite the existence of a fault or faults in one or more of its component parts.

**Resource**   Anything used or consumed while performing a function. The categories of resources are time, information, objects (information containers), or processors (the ability to use information). Specific examples are CPU time, terminal connect time, amount of directly addressable memory, disk space, number of input/output requests per minute, and so on.

**Resource encapsulation**   A method by which the reference-monitor mediates accesses to an information system resource. Resource is protected and not directly accessible by a subject. Satisfies requirement for accurate auditing of resource usage.

**Resource isolation**   It is the containment of subjects and objects in a system in such a way that they are separated from one another, as well as from the protection controls of the operating system.

**Responder**   The entity that responds to the initiator of the authentication exchange.

**Restart**   The resumption of the execution of a computer program using the data recorded at a checkpoint. This is a technical and recovery control.

**Restore**   The process of retrieving a data set migrated to off-line storage and restoring it to online storage. This is a technical and recovery control.

**Retention program**   A program to save documents, forms, history logs, master and transaction data files, computer programs (both source and object level), and other documents of the system until no longer needed. Retention periods should satisfy organization and legal requirements.

**Return on investment (ROI)**   A ratio indicating what percentage of the investment the annual benefit in terms of cash flow is. It is calculated as annual operating cash inflows divided by the annual net investment.

The ROI can be used to assess the financial feasibility of an investment in information security program.

**Reverse engineering**   Used to gain a better understanding of the current system's complexity and functionality and to identify "trouble spots." Errors can be detected and corrected, and modifications can be made to improve system performance. The information gained during reverse engineering can be used to restructure the system, thus making the system more maintainable. Maintenance requests can then be accomplished easily and quickly. Software reengineering also enables the reuse of software components from existing systems. The knowledge gained from reverse engineering can be used to identify candidate systems composed of reusable components, which can then be used in other applications. Reverse engineering can also be used to identify functionally redundant parts in existing application systems.

**Reversible data hiding**   A technique that allows images to be authenticated and then restored to their original form by removing the watermark and replacing the image data, which had been overwritten. This makes the images acceptable for legal purposes.

**Review board**   The authority responsible for evaluating and approving or disapproving proposed changes to a system and ensuring implementation of approved changes. This is a management and preventive control.

**Review techniques**   Passive information security testing techniques, generally conducted manually, used to evaluate systems, applications, networks, policies, and procedures to discover vulnerabilities. Review techniques include documentation review, log review, ruleset review, system configuration review, network sniffing, and file-integrity checking.

**Revision**   A change to a baseline configuration item that encompasses error correction, minor enhancements, or adaptations but to which there is no change in the functional capabilities.

**Revoked state**   The cryptographic key lifecycle state in which a currently active cryptographic key is not to be used to encode, encrypt, or sign again within a domain or context.

**Reuse**   Any use of a preexisting software artifact (e.g., component and specification) in a context different from that in which it was created.

**Rijndael algorithm**   Cryptographic algorithm specified in the advanced encryption standard (AES).

**Ring topology**   Ring topology is a network topology in which all nodes are connected to one another in the shape of a closed loop, so that each node is connected directly to two other nodes, one on either side of it. These nodes are attached to repeaters connected in a closed loop. Two kinds of ring topology exist: token ring and token bus.

**Risk**   (1) A measure of the likelihood and the consequence of events or acts that could cause a system compromise, including the unauthorized disclosure, destruction, removal, modification, or interruption of system assets. (2) The level of impact on organizational operations (including mission, functions, image, or reputation), organizational assets, individuals, or other organizations resulting from the operation of an information system given the potential impact of a threat and the likelihood of that threat occurring. (3) It is the chance or likelihood of an undesirable outcome. In general, the greater the likelihood of a threat occurring, the greater the risk. A risk determination requires a sign-off letter from functional users. (4) A risk is a combination of the likelihood that a threat will occur, the likelihood that a threat occurrence will result in an adverse impact, and the severity of the resulting adverse impact. (5) It is the probability that a particular security threat will exploit a system's vulnerability. Reducing either the vulnerability or the threat reduces the risk. Risk = Threat + Vulnerability.

**Risk adaptive or adaptable access control (RAdAC)**   In RAdAC, access privileges are granted based on a combination of a user's identity, mission need, and the level of security risk that exists between the system being accessed and a user. RAdAC uses security metrics, such as the strength of the authentication method, the level of assurance of the session connection between the system and a user, and the physical location of a user, to make its risk determination.

**Risk analysis**   The process of identifying the risks to system security and determining the likelihood of occurrence, the resulting impact, and the additional safeguards (controls) that mitigate this impact. It is a part of risk management and synonymous with risk assessment.

**Risk assessment**   The process of identifying risks to organizational operations (including mission, functions, image, or reputation), organizational assets, individuals, or other organizations by determining the probability of occurrence, the resulting impact, and additional security controls that would mitigate this impact. Part of risk management, synonymous with risk analysis, incorporates threat and vulnerability analyses, and considers mitigations provided by planned or in-place security controls.

**Risk index**   The difference between the minimum clearance/authorization of system users and the maximum sensitivity (e.g., classification and categories of data processed by a system).

**Risk management**   The program and supporting processes to manage information security risk to organizational operations (including mission, functions, image, or reputation), organizational assets, individuals, or other organizations resulting from the operation of an information system. It includes (1) establishing the context for risk-related activities, (2) assessing risk, (3) responding to risk once determined, and (4) monitoring risk over time. The process considers effectiveness, efficiency, and constraints due to laws, directives, policies, or regulations. This is a management and preventive control.

**Risk Management = Risk Assessment + Risk Mitigation + Risk Evaluation.**   Risk mitigation involves prioritizing, evaluating, and implementing the appropriate risk-reducing controls and countermeasures recommended from the risk assessment process.

**Risk monitoring**   Maintaining ongoing awareness of an organization's risk environment, risk management program, and associated activities to support risk decisions.

**Risk profile**   Risk profiling is conducted on each data center or computer system to identify threats and to develop controls and polices in order to manage risks.

**Risk reduction**   The features of reducing one or more of the factors of risk (e.g., value at risk, vulnerability to attack, threat of attack, and protection from risk).

**Risk response**   Accepting, avoiding, mitigating, sharing, or transferring risk to organizational operations and assets, individuals, or other organizations.

**Risk tolerance**   The level of risk an entity is willing to assume in order to achieve a potential desired result.

**Rivest-Shamir-Adelman (RSA) algorithm**   A public-key algorithm used for key establishment and the generation and verification of digital signatures, encrypt messages, and provide key management for the data encryption standard (DES) and other secret key algorithms.

**Robust authentication**   Requires a user to possess a token in addition to a password or PIN (i.e., two-factor authentication). This type of authentication is applied when accessing an internal computer systems and e-mails. Robust authentication can also create one-time passwords.

**Robust programming**   Robust programming, also called defensive programming, makes a system more reliable with various programming techniques.

**Robustness**   A characterization of the strength of a security function, mechanism, service, or solution, and the assurance (or confidence) that it is implemented and functioning correctly.

**Role**   (1) A distinct set of operations required to perform some particular function. (2) A collection of permissions in role-based access control (RBAC), usually associated with a role or position within an organization.

**Role-based access control (RBAC)**   (1) Access control based on user roles (e.g., a collection of access authorizations a user receives based on an explicit or implicit assumption of a given role). Role permissions may be inherited through a role hierarchy and typically reflect the permissions needed to perform defined functions within an organization. A given role may apply to a single individual or to several individuals. (2) A model for controlling access to resources where permitted actions on resources are identified with roles rather than with individual subject identities. It is an access control based on specific job titles, functions, roles, and responsibilities.

**Role-based authentication**   A cryptographic module authenticates the authorization of an operator to assume a specific role and perform a corresponding set of services.

**Role-based security policy**   Access rights are grouped by role names and the use of resources is restricted to individuals authorized to assume the associated roles.

**Rollback**   Restores the database from one point in time to an earlier point.

**Rollforward**   Restores the database from a point in time when it is known to be correct to a later time.

**Root cause analysis**   A problem-solving tool that uses a cause-and-effect (C&E) diagram. This diagram analyzes when a series of events or steps in a process creates a problem and it is not clear which event or step is the major cause of the problems. After examination, significant root causes of the problem are discovered, verified, and corrected. The C&E diagram is also called a fishbone or

Ishikawa diagram and is a good application in managing a computer security incident response as a remediation step.

**Rootkit** (1) A set of tools used by an attacker after gaining root-level access to a host to conceal the attacker's activities on the host and permit the attacker to maintain root-level access to the host through covert means. (2) A collection of files that is installed on a system to alter the standard functionality of the system in a malicious and stealthy way.

**Rotational cryptanalysis** A generic attack against algorithms that rely on three operations: modular addition, rotation, and XOR (exclusive OR). Algorithms relying on these operations are popular because they are relatively inexpensive in both hardware and software and operate in constant time, making them safe from timing attacks in common implementations (Wikipedia).

**Rotation of duties** A method of reducing the risk associated with a subject performing a (sensitive) task by limiting the amount of time the subject is assigned to perform the task before being moved to a different task.

**Round key** Round keys are values derived by the cipher key using the key expansion routine; they are applied to the state in the cipher and inverse cipher.

**Round-robin DNS** A technique of load distribution, load balancing, or fault-tolerance provisions with multiple, redundant Internet Protocol (IP) service hosts (for example, Web servers and FTP servers). It manages the domain name system (DNS) response to address requests from client computers according to a statistical model. It works by responding to DNS requests not only with a single IP address, but also a list of IP addresses of several servers that host identical services. The order in which IP addresses from the list are returned is the basis for the term round robin. With each DNS response, the IP addresses sequence in the list is permuted. This is unlike the usual basic IP address handling methods based on network priority and connection timeout (Wikipedia).

**Route flapping** A situation in which Border Gateway Protocol (BGP) sessions are repeatedly dropped and restarted, normally as a result of router problems or communication line problems. Route flapping causes changes to the BGP routing tables.

**Router** (1) A physical or logical entity that receives and transmits data packets or establishes logical connections among a diverse set of communicating entities (usually supports both hardwired and wireless communication devices simultaneously). (2) A node that interconnects sub-networks by packet forwarding. (3) A device that connects two or more networks or network segments, and may use Internet Protocol (IP) to route messages. (4) A device that keeps a record of network node addresses and current network status, and it extends LANs. (5) A router operates in the network layer of the ISO/OSI reference model.

**Router-based firewall** Security is implemented using screening routers as the primary means of protecting the network.

**Routine variation** A risk-reducing principle that underlies techniques, reducing the ability of potential attackers to anticipate scheduled events in order to minimize associated vulnerabilities.

**Rubber-hose cryptanalysis** The extraction of cryptographic secrets (for example, the password to an encrypted file) from a person by coercion or torture in contrast to a mathematical or technical cryptanalytic attack. The term rubber-hose refers to beating individuals with a rubber hose until they cooperate in revealing cryptographic secrets. Rubber-hose and social engineering attacks are not a general class of side channel attack (Wikipedia).

**Rule-based access control (RuBAC)**   Access control based on specific rules relating to the nature of the subject and object, beyond their identities such as security labels. A RuBAC decision requires authorization information and restriction information to compare before any access is granted. RuBAC and MAC are considered equivalent.

**Rule-based security policy**   A security policy based on global rules imposed for all subjects. These rules usually rely on a comparison of the sensitivity of the objects being assessed and the possession of corresponding attributes by the subjects requesting access.

**Rules of behavior (ROB)**   Rules established and implemented concerning use of, security in, and acceptable level of risk of the system. Rules will clearly delineate responsibilities and expected behavior of all individuals with access to the system. The organization establishes and makes readily available to all information system users a set of rules that describes their responsibilities and expected behavior with regard to information system usage.

**Rules of engagement (ROE)**   Detailed guidelines and constraints regarding the execution of information security testing. The white team establishes the ROE before the start of a security test. It gives the test team authority to conduct the defined activities without the need for additional permissions.

**Rules of evidence**   The general rules of evidence require that the evidence must be sufficient to support a finding, must be competent (reliable), must be relevant based on facts and their applicability, and must be significant (material and substantive) to the issue at hand. The chain of custody should accommodate the rules of evidence and the chain of evidence.

**Ruleset**   (1) A table of instructions used by a controlled (managed) interface to determine what data is allowable and how the data is handled between interconnected systems. Rulesets govern access control functionality of a firewall. The firewall uses these rulesets to determine how packets should be routed between its interfaces. (2) A collection of rules or signatures that network traffic or system activity is compared against to determine an action to take, such as forwarding or rejecting a packet, creating an alert, or allowing a system event.

# S

**S/MIME**   (1) A version of the multipurpose Internet mail extension (MIME) protocol that supports encrypted messages. (2) A set of specifications for securing electronic mail. The basic security services offered by secure/MIME (S/MIME) are authentication, nonrepudiation of origin, message integrity, and message privacy. Optional security services by S/MIME include signed receipts, security labels, secure mailing lists, and an extended method of identifying the signer's certificate(s). S/MIME is based on RSA's public-key encryption technology.

**Safe harbor principle**   Principles that are intended to facilitate trade and commerce between the U.S. and European Union for use solely by U.S. organizations receiving personal data from the European Union. It is based on self-regulating policy and enforcement mechanism where it meets the objectives of government regulations but does not involve government enforcement.

**Safeguards**   Protective measures prescribed to meet the security requirements (i.e., confidentiality, integrity, and availability) specified for an information system and to protect computational resources by eliminating or reducing the vulnerability or risk to a system. Safeguards may include security features, management constraints, personnel security, and security of physical structures, areas, and devices to counter a specific threat or attack. Available safeguards include hardware and software devices and mechanisms, policies, procedures, standards, guidelines, management controls, technical controls, operational controls, personnel controls, and physical controls. Synonymous with security controls and countermeasures.

**Salami technique**   In data security, it pertains to fraud spread over a large number of individual transactions (e.g., a program that does not round off figures but diverts the leftovers to a personal account).

**Salt**   A nonsecret value that is used in a cryptographic process, usually to ensure that the results of computations for one instance cannot be reused by an attacker.

**Salting (password)**   The inclusion of a random value in the password hashing process that greatly decreases the likelihood of identical passwords returning the same hash.

**Sandbox**   A system that allows an untrusted application to run in a highly controlled environment where the application's permissions are restricted to an essential set of computer permissions. In particular, an application in a sandbox is usually restricted from accessing the file system or the network. A widely used example of applications running inside a sandbox is a JavaApplet. A behavioral sandbox uses runtime monitor for ensuring the execution of mobile code, conforming to the enforcement model.

**Sandbox security model**   Java's security model, in which applets can operate, creating a safe sandbox for applet processing.

**Sandboxing**   (1) A method of isolating application modules into distinct fault domains enforced by software. The technique allows untrusted programs written in an unsafe language, such as C, to be executed safely within the single virtual address space of an application. Untrusted machine interpretable code modules are transformed so that all memory accesses are confined to code and data segments within their fault domain. Access to system resources can also be controlled through a unique identifier associated with each domain. (2) New malicious code protection products introduce a "sandbox" technology allowing users the option to run programs such as Java and Active-X in quarantined sub-directories of systems. If malicious code is detected in a quarantined program, the system removes the associated files, protecting the rest of the system. (3) A method of isolating each guest operating system from the others and restricting what resources they can access and what privileges they can have (i.e., restrictions and privileges).

**Sanding**   The application of an abrasive substance to the media's physical recording surface.

**Sanitization**   The changing of content information in order to meet the requirements of the sensitivity level of the network to which the information is being sent. It is a process to remove information from media so that information recovery is not possible. It includes removing all classified labels, markings, and activity logs. Synonymous with scrubbing.

**S-box**   Nonlinear substitution table boxes (S-boxes) used in several byte substitution transformations and in the key expansion routine to perform a one-for-one substitution of a byte value. This substitution, which is implemented with simple electrical circuits, is done so fast in that it does not require any computation, just signal propagation. The S-box design, which is implemented in hardware for cryptographic algorithm, follows Kerckhoff's principle (security-by-obscurity) in that an attacker knows that the general method is substituting the bits, but he does not know which bit goes where. Hence, there is no need to hide the substitution method. S-boxes and P-boxes are combined to form a product cipher, where wiring of the P-box is placed inside the S-box. (that is, S-box is first and P-box is next.) S-boxes are used in the advanced encryption standard (Tanenbaum).

**Scalability** (1) A measure of the ease of changing the capability of a system. (2) The ability to support more users, concurrent sessions, and throughput than a single SSL-VPN device can typically handle. (3) The ability to move application software source code and data into systems and environments that have a variety of performance characteristics and capabilities without significant modification.

**Scanning** (1) Sequentially going through combinations of numbers and letters to look for access to telephone numbers and secret passwords. (2) Sending packets or requests to another system to gain information to be used in a subsequent attack.

**Scavenging** Searching through object residue (file storage space) to acquire unauthorized data.

**Scenario analysis** An information system's vulnerability assessment technique in which various possible attack methods are identified and the existing controls are examined in light of their ability to counter such attack methods.

**Schema** A set of specifications that defines a database. Specifically, it includes entity names, sets, groups, data items, areas, sort sequences, access keys, and security locks.

**Scoping guidance** Specific factors related to technology, infrastructure, public access, scalability, common security controls, and risk that can be considered by organizations in the applicability and implementation of individual security controls in the security control baseline.

**Screen scraper** A computer program that extracts data from websites. The program captures information from a computer display not intended for processing, captures the bitmap data from a computer screen, or queries the graphical controls used in an application to obtain references to the underlying programming objects. Screen scrapers can extract data from mobile devices (such as, PDAs and SmartPhones) and non-mobile devices. Regarding security threats, the screen scraper belongs to the malware family in that its similar to malware threats including keyloggers, spyware, bad adware, rootkits, backdoors, and bots.

**Screened host firewall** It combines a packet-filtering router with an application gateway located on the protected subnet side of the router.

**Screened subnet firewall** Conceptually, it is similar to a dual-homed gateway, except that an entire network, rather than a single host is reachable from the outside. It can be used to locate each component of the firewall on a separate system, thereby increasing throughput and flexibility.

**Screening router** A router is used to implement part of a firewall's security by configuring it to selectively permit or deny traffic at a network level.

**Script** (1) A sequence of instructions, ranging from a simple list of operating system commands to full-blown programming language statements, which can be executed automatically by an interpreter. (2) A sequence of commands, often residing in a text file, which can be interpreted and executed automatically. (3) Unlike compiled programs, which execute directly on a computer processor, a script must be processed by another program that carries out the indicated actions.

**Scripting language**  A definition of the syntax and semantics for writing and interpreting scripts. Typically, scripting languages follow the conventions of a simple programming language, but they can also take on a more basic form such as a macro or a batch file. JavaScript, VBScript, Tcl, PHP, and Perl are examples of scripting languages.

**Secrecy**  Denial of access to information by unauthorized individuals.

**Secret key**  A cryptographic key that is used with a secret key (symmetric) cryptographic algorithm that is uniquely associated with one or more entities and is not being made public. A key used by a symmetric algorithm to encrypt and decrypt data. The use of the term "secret" in this context does not imply a classification level, but rather implies the need to protect the key from disclosure or substitution.

**Secret key (symmetric) cryptographic algorithm**  A cryptographic algorithm that uses a single, secret key for both encryption and decryption. This is the traditional method used for encryption. The same key is used for both encryption and decryption. Only the party or parties that exchange secret messages know the secret key. The biggest problem with symmetric key encryption is securely distributing the keys. Public key techniques are now often used to distribute the symmetric keys. An encryption algorithm that uses only secret keys. Also known as private-key encryption.

**Secure channel**  An information path in which the set of all possible senders can be known to the receivers or the set of all possible receivers can be known to the senders, or both.

**Secure communication protocol**  A communication protocol that provides the appropriate confidentiality, authentication, and content integrity protection.

**Secure configuration management**  The set of procedures appropriate for controlling changes to a system's hardware and software structure for the purpose of ensuring that changes will not lead to violations of the system's security policy.

**Secure erase**  An overwrite technology using a firmware-based process to overwrite a hard drive, such as ATA or SCSI.

**Secure hash**  A hash value that is computationally infeasible to find a message which corresponds to a given message digest, or to find two different messages which produce the same digest.

**Secure hash standard**  This standard specifies four secure hash algorithms (SHAs): SHA-1, SHA-256, SHA-384, and SHA-512 for computing a condensed representation of electronic data (message) called a message digest. SHAs are used with other cryptographic algorithms, such as the digital signature algorithms and keyed-hash message authentication code (HMAC), or in the generation of random numbers (bits).

**Secure hypertext-transfer protocol (S/HTTP)**  A message-oriented communication protocol that extends the HTTP protocol. It coexists with HTTP's messaging model and can be easily integrated with HTTP applications.

**Secure multipurpose Internet mail extension (S/MIME)**  A protocol for encrypting messages and creating certificates using public key cryptography. S/MIME is supported by default installations of many popular mail clients. It uses a classic, hierarchical design based on certificate authorities for its key management, thus making it suitable for medium- to large-scale implementations.

**Secure operating system**   An operating system that effectively controls hardware and software functions in order to provide the level of protection appropriate to the value of the data and resources managed by the operating system.

**Secure sockets layer (SSL)**   (1) A protocol that provides end-to-end encryption of application layer network traffic. It provides privacy and reliability between two communicating applications. It is designed to encapsulate other protocols, such as HTTP. SSL v3.0 has been succeeded by IETF's TLS. (2) An authentication and security protocol widely implemented in browsers and Web servers for protecting private information during transmission via the Internet.

**Secure sockets layer (SSL) and transport layer security (TLS)**   SSL is a protocol developed by Netscape for transmitting private documents via the Internet. SSL is based on public key cryptography, used to generate a cryptographic session that is private to a Web server and a client browser. SSL works by using a public key to encrypt data that is transferred over the SSL connection. Most Web browsers support SSL and many websites use the protocol to obtain confidential user information, such as credit card numbers. By convention, URLs that require an SSL connection start with "https" instead of "http." SSL has been superseded by the newer TLS protocol. There are only minor differences between SSL and TLS.

**Secure state**   A condition in which no subject can access any object in an unauthorized manner.

**Security**   The quality of state-of-being cost-effectively protected from undue losses (e.g., loss of goodwill, monetary loss, and loss of ability to continue operations). Preservation of the authenticity, integrity, confidentiality, and ensured service of any sensitive or nonsensitive system-valued function and/or information element. Security is a system property. Security is much more than a set of functions and mechanisms. IT security is a system characteristic as well as a set of mechanisms that span the system both logically and physically.

**Security administrator**   A person dedicated to performing information security functions for servers and other hosts, as well as networks.

**Security architecture**   A description of security principles and an overall approach for complying with the principles that drive the system design; i.e., guidelines on the placement and implementation of specific security services within various distributed computing environments.

**Security assertions markup language (SAML)**   (1) An XML-based security specification for exchanging authentication and authorization information between trusted entities over the Internet. Security typically involves checking the credentials presented by a party for authentication and authorization. SAML standardizes the representation of these credentials in an XML format called "assertions," enhancing the interoperability between disparate applications. (2) A specification for encoding security assertions in the extensible markup language (XML). (3) A protocol consisting of XML-based request and response message formats for exchanging security information, expressed in the form of assertions about subjects and between online business partners.

**Security association (SA)**   It is a set of values that define the features and protections applied to a connection.

**Security association (WMAN/WiMAX)**   A security association (SA) is the logical set of security parameters containing elements required for authentication, key establishment, and data encryption.

**Security association lifetime**   How often each security association (SA) should be recreated, based on elapsed time or the amount of network traffic.

**Security assurance**   It is the degree of confidence one has that the security controls operate correctly and that they protect the system as intended.

**Security attribute**   (1) An abstraction representing the basic properties or characteristics of an entity with respect to safeguarding information, typically associated with internal data structures (e.g., records, buffers, and files) within the information system and used to enable the implementation of access control and flow control policies, reflect special dissemination, handling or distribution instructions, or support other aspects of the information security policy. (2) A security-related quality of an object and it can be represented as hierarchical levels, bits in a bit map, or numbers. Compartments, caveats, and release markings are examples of security attributes, which are used to implement a security policy.

**Security audit**   An examination of security procedures and measures for the purpose of evaluating their adequacy and compliance with established policy. This is a management and detective control.

**Security authorization**   The official management decision to authorize operation of an information system and to explicitly accept the risk to an organization's operations and assets based on the implementation of an agreed-upon set of security controls.

**Security banner**   It is a banner at the top or bottom of a computer screen that states the overall classification of the system in large, bold type. It can also refer to the opening screen that informs users of the security implications of accessing a computer resource (i.e., conditions and restrictions on system and/or data use).

**Security boundaries**   The process of uniquely assigning information resources to an information system defines the security boundary for that system. Information resources consist of information and related resources, such as personnel, equipment, funds, and information technology. The scope of security boundaries includes (1) both internal and external systems, (2) both logical and physical access security controls, and (3) both interior and exterior perimeter security controls.

**Security breach**   A violation of controls of a particular information system such that information assets or system components are unduly exposed.

**Security categorization**   The process of determining the security category (the restrictive label applied to classified or unclassified information to limit access) for information or an information system.

**Security category**   The characterization of information or an information system based on an assessment of the potential impact that a loss of confidentiality, integrity, or availability of such information or information system would have on organizational operations, organizational assets, employees and other individuals, and other organizations.

**Security clearances**   Formal authorization is required for subjects to access information contained in objects.

**Security control assessment**   The testing and/or evaluation of the management, operational, and technical security controls in an information system to determine the extent to which the controls are implemented correctly, operating as intended, and producing the desired outcome with respect to meeting the security requirements for the system (i.e., confidentiality, integrity, and availability).

**Security control baseline**   The set of minimum security controls defined for a low-impact, moderate-impact, or high-impact information system.

**Security control effectiveness**   The measure of correctness of implementation (i.e., how consistently the control implementation complies with the security plan) and how well the security plan meets organizational needs in accordance with current risk tolerance.

**Security control enhancements**   Statements of security capability to (1) build in additional, but related, functionality to a basic control, and/or (2) increase the strength of a basic control.

**Security control inheritance**   A situation in which an information system or application receives protection from security controls that are developed, implemented, assessed, authorized, and monitored by entities other than those responsible for the system or application. These entities can be either internal or external to the organization where the system or application resides. Common controls are inherited.

**Security controls**   The management, operational, and technical controls (i.e., safeguards or countermeasures) prescribed for an information system to protect the confidentiality, integrity, and availability of the system and its information.

**Security domain**   (1) Implements a security policy and administered by a single authority. (2) A set of subjects, their information objects, and a common security policy.

**Security evaluation**   An evaluation to assess the degree of trust that can be placed in systems for the secure handling of sensitive information. It is a major step in the certification and accreditation process.

**Security event management tools (SEM)**   A type of centralized logging software that can facilitate aggregation and consolidation of logs from multiple information system components. The SEM tools help an organization to integrate the analysis of vulnerability scanning information, performance data, network monitoring, and system audit record information, and provide the ability to identify inappropriate or unusual activity. For example, the SEM tools can facilitate audit record correlation and analysis with vulnerability scanning information to determine the veracity of the vulnerability scans and correlating attack detection events with scanning results. The sources of audit record information include operating systems, application servers (for example, Web servers and e-mail servers), security software, and physical security devices such as badge readers.

**Security failure**   Any event that is a violation of a particular system's explicit or implicit security policy.

**Security fault analysis**   A security analysis, usually performed on hardware at gate level, to determine the security properties of a device when a hardware fault is detected.

**Security fault injection test**   Involves data perturbation (i.e., alteration of the type of data the execution environment components pass to the application, or that the application's components pass to one another). Fault injection can reveal the effects of security defects on the behavior of the components themselves and on the application as a whole.

**Security features**   The security-relevant functions, mechanisms, and characteristics of system hardware and software. Security features are a subset of system security safeguards.

**Security filter**   A set of software routines and techniques employed in a computer system to prevent automatic forwarding of specified data over unprotected links or to unauthorized persons.

**Security flaw**   An error of commission or omission in a computer system that may allow protection mechanisms to be bypassed.

**Security functions**   The hardware, software, and firmware of the information system responsible for supporting and enforcing the system security policy and supporting the isolation of code and data on which the protection is based.

**Security goals**   The five security goals are confidentiality, availability, integrity, accountability, and assurance.

**Security governance**   Information security governance are defined as the process of establishing and maintaining a framework and supporting management structure and processes. They provide assurance that information security strategies are aligned with and are supportive of business objectives, are consistent with applicable laws and regulations through adherence to policies and internal controls, and provide assignment of responsibility, all in an effort to manage risk. Note that information security governance is a part of information technology governance, which, in turn, is a part of corporate governance.

The information security management should integrate its information security governance activities with the overall organization structure and activities by ensuring appropriate participation of management officials in overseeing implementation of information security controls throughout the organization. The key activities that facilitate such integration are information security strategic planning, information security governance structures (that is, centralized, decentralized, and hybrid), establishment of roles and responsibilities, integration with the enterprise architecture, documentation of security objectives (such as, confidentiality, integrity, availability, accountability, and assurance) in policies and guidance, and ongoing monitoring.

In addition, security governance committee should ensure that appropriate security staff represents in the acquisitions and divestitures of new business assets or units, performing due diligence reviews.

Organizations can use a variety of data originating from the ongoing information security program activities to monitor performance of programs under their purview, including plans of action and milestones, performance measurement and metrics, continuous assessment, configuration management and control, network monitoring, and incident and event statistics.

**Security impact analysis (SIA)**   The analysis conducted by an organization official, often during the continuous monitoring phase of the security certification and accreditation process, to determine the extent to which changes to the information system have affected the security state of the system.

**Security incident**   Any incident involving classified information in which there is a deviation from the requirements of governing security regulations. Compromise, inadvertent disclosure, need-to-know violation, planting of malicious code, and administrative deviation are examples of a security incident.

**Security incident triad**   Includes three elements such as detect, respond, and recover. An organization should have the ability to detect an attack, respond to an attack, and recover from an attack by limiting consequences or impacts from an attack.

**Security-in-depth**   See Defense-in-depth.

**Security kernel**   The central part of a computer system (software and hardware) that implements the fundamental security procedures for controlling access to system resources. A most trusted portion of a system that enforces a fundamental property and on which the other portions of the system depend.

**Security label**   (1) The means used to associate a set of security attributes with a specific information object as part of the data structure for that object. Labels could be designated as proprietary data or public data. (2) A marking bound to a resource (which may be a data unit) that names or designates the security attributes of that resource. (3) Explicit or implicit marking of a data structure or output media associated with an information system representing the security category, or distribution limitations or handling caveats of the information contained therein.

**Security level**   A hierarchical indicator of the degree of sensitivity to a certain threat. It implies, according to the security policy being enforced, a specific level of protection. A clearance level associated with a subject or a classification level (or sensitivity label) associated with an object.

**Security life of data**   The time period during which data has security value.

**Security management**   The process of monitoring and controlling access to network resources. This includes monitoring usage of network resources, recording information about usage of resources, detecting attempted or successful violations, and reporting such violations.

**Security management dashboard**   A tool that consolidates and communicates information relevant to the organizational security posture in near-real time to security management stakeholders.

**Security management infrastructure (SMI)**   A set of interrelated activities providing security services needed by other security features and mechanisms. SMI functions include registration, ordering, key generation, certificate generation, distribution, accounting, compromise recovery, re-key, destruction, data recovery, and administration.

**Security marking**   Human-readable information affixed to information system components, removable media, or system outputs indicating the distribution limitations, handling caveats and applicable security markings.

**Security measures**   Elements of software, firmware, hardware, or procedures included in a system for the satisfaction of security specifications.

**Security mechanism**   A device designed to provide one or more security services usually rated in terms of strength of service and assurance of the design.

**Security metrics**   Security metrics strive to offer a quantitative and objective basis for security assurance.

**Security model**   A formal presentation of the security policy enforced by the system. It must identify the set of rules and practices that regulate how a system manages, protects, and distributes sensitive information.

**Security objectives**   The five security objectives are confidentiality, availability, integrity, accountability, and assurance. Some use only three objectives such as confidentiality, integrity, and availability.

**Security-by-obscurity**   A countermeasure principle that does not work in practice because attackers can compromise the security of any system at any time. The meaning of this principle is that trying to keep something secret when it is not does more harm than good.

**Security-oriented code review**   A code review, or audit, investigates the coding practices used in the application. The main objective of such reviews is to discover security defects and potentially identify solutions.

**Security parameters**   The variable secret components that control security processes; examples include passwords, encryption keys, encryption initialization vectors, pseudo-random number generator seeds, and biometrics identity parameters.

**Security parameters index**   Randomly chosen value that acts as an identifier for an IPsec connection.

**Security perimeter**   A physical or logical boundary that is defined for a system, domain, or enclave, within which a particular security policy, security control, or security architecture is applied to protect assets. A security perimeter typically includes a security kernel, some trusted-code facilities, hardware, and possibly some communications channels.

**Security plan**   A formal document providing an overview of the security requirements for an information system or an information security program and describing the security controls in place or planned for meeting those requirements.

**Security policy**   Refers to the conventional security services (e.g., confidentiality, integrity, and availability) and underlying mechanisms and functions. (2) The set of laws, rules, criteria, and practices that regulate how an organization manages, protects, and distributes sensitive information and critical systems. (3) The statement of required protection for the information objects.

**Security policy filter**   A secure subsystem of an information system that enforces security policy on the data passing through it.

**Security posture**   The security status of an enterprise's networks, information, and systems based on information assurance resources (e.g., people, hardware, software, and policies) and capabilities in place to manage the defense of the enterprise and to react as the situation changes.

**Security priorities**   Security priorities need to be developed so that investments on those areas of highest sensitivity or risk can be allocated.

**Security program assessment**   An assessment of an organization's information security program to ensure that information and information system assets are adequately secured.

**Security protections**   Measures against threats that are intended to compensate for a computer's security weaknesses.

**Security requirements**   (1) The types and levels of protection necessary for equipment, data, information, applications, and facilities to meet security policy. (2) Requirements levied on an information system that are derived from laws, executive orders, directives, policies, procedures, standards, instructions, regulations, organizational mission or business case needs to ensure the confidentiality, integrity, and availability of the information being processed, stored, or transmitted.

**Security safeguards**   The protective measures and controls prescribed to meet the security requirements specified for a computer system. Those safeguards may include but are not necessarily limited to hardware and software security features; operating procedures; accountability procedures; access and distribution controls; management constraints; personnel security; and physical security, which cover structures, areas, and devices.

**Security service**   (1) A processing or communication service that is provided by a system to give a specific kind of protection to resources, where said resources reside with said system or reside with other systems, for example, an authentication service or a PKI-based document attribution and authentication service. A security service is a superset of authentication, authorization, and accounting (AAA) services. Security services typically implement portions of security policies and are implemented via security mechanisms. (2) A service, provided by a layer of communicating open systems, that ensures adequate security of the systems or of data transfers. (3) A capability that supports one, or many, of the security goals. Examples of security services are key management, access control, and authentication.

**Security specification**   A detailed description of countermeasures (safeguards) required to protect a computer system or network from unauthorized (accidental or unintentional) disclosure, modification, and destruction of data or denial of service.

**Security strength**   (1) A measure of the computational complexity associated with recovering certain secret and/or security-critical information concerning a given cryptographic algorithm from known data (e.g., plaintext/ciphertext pairs for a given encryption algorithm). (2) A number associated with the amount of work (that is, the number of operations) that is required to break a cryptographic algorithm or module. The average amount of work needed is 2 raised to the power of (security strength minus 1). The security strength, sometimes, is referred to as a security level.

**Security tag**   An information unit containing a representation of certain security-related information (e.g., a restrictive attribute bit map).

**Security target (ST)**   A set of security requirements and specifications drawn from the Common Criteria (CC) for IT security evaluation to be used as the basis for evaluation of an identified target of evaluation (TOE). It is an implementation-dependent statement of security needs for a specific identified TOE.

**Security test & evaluation (ST&E)**   It is an examination and analysis of the safeguards required to protect an information system, as they have been applied in an operational environment, to determine the security posture of that system.

**Security testing**   The major goal is to determine that an information system protects data and maintains functionality as intended. It is a process used to determine that the security features of a computer system are implemented as designed and that they are adequate for a proposed application environment. This process includes hands-on functional testing, penetration testing, and verification. The purpose is to assess the robustness of the system and to identify security vulnerabilities. This is a management and preventive control.

**Security vulnerability**   A property of system requirements, design, implementation, or operation that could be accidentally triggered or intentionally exploited and result in a security failure.

**Security zone (WMAN/WiMAX)**   A security zone (SZ) is a set of trusted relationships between a base station (BS) and a group of relay stations (RSs) in WiMAX architecture. An RS can only forward traffic to RSs or subscriber stations (SSs) within its security zone.

**Seed key**   It is the initial key used to start an updating or key generation process.

**Seed RNG**   Seed is a secret value that is used once to initialize a deterministic random bit generator in order to generate random numbers and then is destroyed.

**Seeding model**   A seeding model can be used as an indication of software reliability (i.e., error detection power) of a set of test cases.

**Seepage**   The accidental flow to unauthorized individuals of data or information, access to which is presumed to be controlled by computer security safeguards.

**Self-signed certificate**   A public key certificate whose digital signature may be verified by the public key contained within the certificate. The signature on a self-signed certificate protects the integrity of the data, but does not guarantee authenticity of the information. The trust of self-signed certificates is based on the secure procedures used to distribute them.

**Sendmail attack**   Involves sending thousands of e-mail messages in a single day to unwitting e-mail receivers. It takes a long time to read through the subject lines to find the desired e-mail, thus wasting the receiver's valuable time. This is a form of spamming attack. Recent sendmail attacks fall into the categories of remote penetration, local penetration, and remote DoS.

**Sensitive data**   Data that require a degree of protection due to the risk and magnitude of loss or harm which could result from inadvertent or deliberate disclosure, alteration, or destruction of the data (e.g., personal or proprietary data). It includes both classified and sensitive unclassified data.

**Sensitive label**   A piece of information that represents the security level of an object. It is the basis for mandatory access control decisions. Compare with security label.

**Sensitive levels**   A graduated system of marking (e.g., low, moderate, and high) information and information processing systems based on threats and risks that result if a threat is successfully conducted.

**Sensitive security parameter (SSP)**   Sensitive security parameter (SSP) contains both critical security parameter (CSP) and public security parameter (PSP). In other words, SSP = CSP + PSP.

**Sensitive system**   A computer system that requires a degree of protection because it processes sensitive data or because of the risk and magnitude of loss or harm that could result from improper operation or deliberate manipulation of the application system.

**Sensitivity analysis**   Sensitivity analysis is based on a fault-failure model of software and is based on the premise that software testability can predict the probability that failure will occur when a fault exists given a particular input distribution. A sensitive location is one in which faults cannot hide during testing. The internal states are perturbed to determine sensitivity. This technique requires instrumentation of the code and produces a count of the total executions through an operation, an infection rate estimate, and a propagation analysis.

**Sensitivity and criticality**   A method developed to describe the value of an information system by its owner by taking into account the cost, capability, and jeopardy to mission accomplishment or human life associated with the system.

**Sensor**   An intrusion detection and prevention system (IDPS) component that monitors and analyzes network activity and may also perform prevention actions.

**Separation**   An intervening space established by the act of setting or keeping apart.

**Separation of duties**   (1) A security principle that divides critical functions among different employees in an attempt to ensure that no one employee has enough information or access privilege to perpetrate damaging fraud. (2) A principle of design that separates functions with differing requirements for security or integrity into separate protection domains. Separation of duty is sometimes implemented as an authorization rule, specifying that two or more subjects are required to authorize an operation. The goal is to ensure that no single individual (acting alone) can compromise an application system's features and its control functions. For example, security function is separated from security operations. This is a management and preventive control.

**Separation of name spaces**   A technique of controlling access by precluding sharing; names given to objects are only meaningful to a single subject and thus cannot be addressed by other subjects.

**Separation of privileges**   The principle of separation of privileges asserts that protection mechanisms where two keys (held by different parties) are required for access are stronger mechanisms than those requiring only one key. The rationale behind this principle is that "no single accident, deception, or breach of trust is sufficient" to circumvent the mechanism. In computer systems the separation is often implemented as a requirement for multiple conditions (access rules) to be met before access is allowed.

**Serial line Internet Protocol (SLIP)**   A protocol for carrying IP over an asynchronous serial communications line. Point-to-Point Protocol (PPP) replaced the SLIP.

**Server**   (1) A host that provides one or more services for other hosts over a network as a primary function. (2) A computer program that provides services to other computer programs in the same or another computer. (3) A computer running a server program is frequently referred to as a server, though it may also be running other client (and server) programs.

**Server administrator**   A system architect responsible for the overall design, implementation, and maintenance of a server.

**Server-based threats**   These threats are due to poorly implemented session-tracking, which may provide an avenue of attack. Similarly, user-provided input might eventually be passed to an application interface that interprets the input as part of a command, such as a Structured Query Language (SQL) command. Attackers may also inject custom code into the website for subsequent browsers to process via cross-site scripting (XSS). Subtle changes introduced into the Web server can radically change the server's behavior (including turning a trusted entity into malicious one), the accuracy of the computation (including changing computational algorithms to yield incorrect results), or the confidentiality of the information (e.g., disclosing collected information).

**Server farm**   A physical security control that uses a network configuration mechanism to monitor theft or damage because all servers are kept in a single, secure location.

**Server load balancing**   Network traffic is distributed dynamically across groups of servers running a common application so that no one server is overwhelmed. Server load balancing increases server availability and application system availability, and could be a viable contingency measure when it is implemented among different sites. In this regard, the application system continues to operate as long as one or more sites remain operational.

**Server mirroring**   The purpose is the same as the disk arrays. A file server is duplicated instead of the disk. All information is written to both servers simultaneously. This is a technical and recovery control, and ensures the availability goal.

**Server-side scripts**   The server-side scripts such as CGI, ASP, JSP, PHP, and Perl are used to generate dynamic Web pages.

**Server software**   Software that is run on a server to provide one or more services.

**Service**   A software component participating in a service-oriented architecture (SOA) that provides functionality or participates in realizing one or more capabilities.

**Service-component**   Modularized service-based applications that package and process together service interfaces with associated business logic into a single cohesive conceptual module. The aim of a service-component in a service-oriented architecture (SOA) is to raise the level of abstraction in software services by modularizing synthesized service functionality and by facilitating service reuse, service extension, specialization, and service inheritance. The desired features of a service component include encapsulation, consumability, extensibility, standards-based (reuse), industry best practices and patterns, well-documented, cohesive set of services, and well-defined and broadly available licensing or service-level agreement (SLA).

**Service interface**   The set of published services that the component supports. These technical interfaces must be aligned with the business services outlined in the service reference model.

**Service-level agreement (SLA)**   A service contract between a network service provider and a subscriber guaranteeing a particular service's quality characteristics. These agreements are concerned about network availability and data-delivery reliability.

**Service-oriented architecture (SOA)**   A collection of services that communicate with each other. The communication can involve either simple data passing or it could involve two or more services coordinating some activity.

**Service set identifier (SSID)**   A name assigned to a wireless access point.

**Session cookie**   A temporary cookie that is valid only for a single website session. It is erased when the user closes the Web browser, and is stored in temporary memory.

**Session hijack attack**   An attack in which the attacker can insert himself between a claimant and a verifier subsequent to a successful authentication exchange between the latter two parties. The attacker can pose as a subscriber to the verifier or vice versa to control session data exchange.

**Session initiation protocol (SIP)**   SIP is a standard for initiating, modifying, and terminating an interactive user session that involves multimedia elements such as video, voice, instant messaging, online games, and virtual reality. It is one of the leading signaling protocols for Voice over IP (VoIP) along with H.323.

**Session key**   The cryptographic key used by a device (module) to encrypt and decrypt data during a session. A temporary symmetric key that is only valid for a short period. Session keys are typically random numbers that can be chosen by either party to a conversation, by both parties in cooperation with one another, or by a trusted third party.

**Session layer**   Portion of an OSI system responsible for adding control mechanisms to the data exchange.

**Session locking**   A feature that permits a user to lock a session upon demand or locks the session after it has been idle for a preset period of time.

**Shared secret**   A secret used in authentication that is known to the claimant and the verifier.

**Shareware**   Software distributed free of charge, often through electronic bulletin boards, may be freely copied, and for which a nominal fee is requested if the program is found useful.

**Shim**   A layer of host-based intrusion detection and prevention code placed between existing layers of code on a host that intercepts data and analyzes it.

**Short message service (SMS)**   A cellular network facility that allows users to send and receive text messages of up to 160 alphanumeric characters on their handset.

**Shoulder surfing attack**   Stealing passwords or personal identification numbers by looking over someone's shoulder. It is also called a keyboard logging attack because a keyboard is used to enter passwords and identification numbers. Shoulder surfing attack can also be done at a distance using binoculars or other vision-enhancing devices, and these attacks are common when using automated teller machines and point-of-sale terminals. A simple and effective practice to avoid this attack is to shield the keypad with one hand while entering the required data with the other hand.

**Shred**   A method of sanitizing media; the act of cutting or tearing into small particles.

**Shrink-wrapped software**   Commercial software used " out-of-the-box" without change (i.e., customization). The term derives from the plastic wrapping used to seal microcomputer software.

**Side channel attacks**   Side channel attacks result from the physical implementation of a cryptosystem. Examples of these attacks include timing attacks, power monitoring attacks, TEMPEST attacks, and thermal imaging attacks. Improper error handling in cryptographic operation can also allow side channel attacks. In all these attacks, side channel leakage of information occurs during the physical operation of a cryptosystem through monitoring of sound from computations, observing from a distance, and introducing faults into computations, thus revealing secrets such as the cryptographic key, system-state information, initialization vectors, and plaintext. Side channel attacks are possible even when transmissions between a Web browser and server are encrypted. Note that side channel attacks are different from social engineering attacks where the latter involves deceiving or coercing people who have the legitimate access to a cryptosystem. In other words, the focus of side channel attacks is on data and information, not on people. Countermeasures against the side channel attacks include implementing physical security over hardware, jamming the emitted channel with noise (white noise), designing isochronous software so it runs in a constant amount of time independent of secret values, designing software so that it is PC-secure, building secure CPUs (asynchronous CPUs) so they have no global timing reference, and retransmitting the failed (error prone) transmission with a predetermined number of times.

**Sign-off**   Functional users are requested and required to approve in writing their acceptance of the system at various stages or phases of the system development life cycle (SDLC).

**Signal-to-noise ratio**   It is the ratio of the amplitude of the desired signal to the amplitude of noise signals at a given point in time in a telecommunications system. Usually, the signal-to-noise ratio is specified in terms of peak-signal-to-peak-noise ratio, to avoid ambiguity. A low ratio at the receiver is preferred to prevent emanation attack.

**Signatory**   The entity that generates a digital signature on data using a private key.

**Signature**   (1) A recognizable, distinguishing pattern associated with an attack, such as a binary string in a virus or a particular set of keystrokes used to gain unauthorized access to a system. (2) A pattern that corresponds to a known threat. (3) The ability to trace the origin of the data.

**Signature-based detection**   The process of comparing signatures against observed events to identify possible incidents.

**Signature certificate**   A public key certificate that contains a public key intended for verifying digital signatures rather than encrypting data or performing any other cryptographic functions.

**Signature (digital)**   A process that operates on a message to assure message source authenticity and integrity, and may be required for source non-repudiation.

**Signature generation**   The process of using a digital signature algorithm and a private key to generate a digital signature on data. Only the possessor of the user' private key can perform signature generation.

**Signature validation**   The mathematical verification of the digital signature and obtaining the appropriate assurances (e.g., public key validity and private key possession).

**Signature verification**   The process of using a digital signature algorithm and a public key to verify a digital signature. Anyone can verify the signature of a user by employing that user's public key.

**Signed data**   The data or message upon which a digital signature has been computed.

**Simple mail transfer protocol (SMTP)**   It is the most commonly used mail transfer agent (MTA) protocol as defined by IETF RFC 2821. It is the primary protocol used to transfer electronic mail messages on the Internet. SMTP is a host-to-host e-mail protocol. An SMTP server accepts e-mail messages from other systems and stores them for the addressees. It does not provide for reliable authentication and does not require the use of encryption, thus allowing e-mail messages to be easily forged.

**Simple Network Management Protocol (SNMP)**   A Network Management Protocol used with a TCP/IP suite of protocols. SNMP specifies a set of management operations for retrieving and altering information in a management information base, authorization procedures for accessing information base tables, and mappings to lower TCP/IP layers. SNMP (1) is used to manage and control IP gateways and the networks to which they are attached, (2) uses IP directly, bypassing the masking effects of TCP error correction, (3) has direct access to IP datagrams on a network that may be operating abnormally, thus requiring careful management, (4) defines a set of variables that the gateway must store, and (5) specifies that all control operations on the gateway are a side-effect of fetching or storing those data variables (i.e., operations that are analogous to writing commands and reading status). SNMP version 3 should be used because the basic SNMP, SNMP version 1, and SNMP version 2 are not secure.

**Simple Object Access Protocol (SOAP)**   The Simple Object Access Protocol (SOAP) is an approach for performing remote procedure calls (RPCs) between application programs in a language-independent and system-independent manner. SOAP uses the extensible markup language (XML) for communicating between application programs on heterogeneous platforms. The client constructs a request as an XML message and sends it to the server, using HTTP. The server sends back a reply as an XML-formatted message. SOAP is an XML-based protocol for exchanging structured information in a decentralized, distributed environment. The SOAP has headers and message paths between nodes.

**Simple power analysis (SPA) attack**   A direct (primarily visual) analysis of patterns of instruction execution (or execution of individual instructions), obtained through monitoring the variations in electrical power consumption of a cryptographic module, for the purpose of revealing the features and implementations of cryptographic algorithms and subsequently the values of cryptographic keys.

**Simplicity in security**   Security mechanisms and information systems in general should be as simple as possible. Complexity is at the root of many security vulnerabilities and breaches.

**Single-hop problem**   The security risks resulting from a mobile software agent moving from its home platform to another platform.

**Single point-of-failure**   A security risk due to concentration of risk in one place, system, process, or with one person. Examples include placement of Web servers and DNS servers, primary telecommunication services, centralized identity management, central certification authority, password synchronization, single sign-on systems, firewalls, Kerberos, converged networks with voice and data, cloud storage services, and system administrators.

**Single sign-on (SSO)**   A SSO technology allows a user to authenticate once and then access all the resources the user is authorized to use.

**Sink tree**   A sink tree shows the set of optimal routes from all sources to a given destination, rooted at the destination. The goal of all routing algorithms is to identify and use the sink trees for all routers. A sink tree does not contain any loops so each packet is delivered within a finite and bounded number of hops. A spanning tree uses the sink tree for the router initiating the broadcast. A spanning tree is a subset of the subnet that includes all the routers but does not contain any loops.

**Six-sigma**   The phrase six-sigma is a statistical term that measures how far a given process deviates from perfection. The central idea behind six-sigma is that if one can measure how many "defects" are in a process, one can systematically figure out how to eliminate them and get as close to *zero defects* as possible.

**Skimming**   The unauthorized use of a reader to read tags without the authorization or knowledge of the tag's owner or the individual in possession of the tag.

**Sliding window protocols**   Sliding window protocols, which are used to integrate error control and flow, are classified in terms of the size of the sender's window and the size of the receiver's window. When the sender's window and the receiver's window are equal to 1, the protocol is said to be in the stop-and-wait condition. When the sender's window is greater than 1, the receiver can either discard all frames or buffer out-of-order frames. Examples of sliding window protocols, which are bit-oriented protocols, include SDLC, HDLC, ADCCP, and LAPB. All these protocols use flag bytes to delimit frames and bit stuffing to prevent flag bytes from occurring in the data. (Tanenbaum)

**Smart card**   A credit card-sized card with embedded integrated circuits that can store, process, and communicate information. It has a built-in microprocessor and memory that is used for identification of individuals or financial transactions. When inserted into a reader, the card transfers data to and from a central computer. A smart card is more secure than a magnetic stripe card and can be programmed to self-destruct if the wrong password is entered too many times. This is a technical and preventive control.

**Smart grid computing**   Consists of interoperable standards and protocols that facilitate in providing centralized electric power generation, including distributed renewable energy resources and energy storage. Ensuring cyber security of the smart grid is essential because it improves power reliability, quality, and resilience. The goal is to build a safe and secure smart grid that is interoperable, end-to-end. Smart grid computing needs cyber security measures as it uses cyber computing.

**Smelting**   A physically destructive method of sanitizing media to be changed from a solid to a liquid state generally by the application of heat. Same as melting.

**Smurf attack**   A hacker sends a request for information to the special broadcast address of a network attached to the Internet. The request sparks a flood of responses from all the nodes on this first network. The answers are then sent to a second network that becomes a victim. If the first network has a larger capacity for sending out responses than the second network is capable of receiving, the second network experiences a DoS problem as its resources become saturated or strained.

**Sniffer attack**   Software that observes and records network traffic. On a TCP/IP network, sniffers audit information packets. It is a network-monitoring tool, usually running on a PC.

**Social engineering**   (1) The act of deceiving an individual into revealing sensitive information by associating with the individual to gain confidence and trust. (2) A person's ability to use personality, knowledge of human nature, and social skills (e.g., theft, trickery, or coercion) to steal passwords, keys, tokens, or telephone toll calls. (3) Subverting information system security by using nontechnical (social) means. (4) The process of attempting to trick someone into revealing information (e.g., a password) that can be used to attack systems or networks. (5) An attack based on deceiving users or administrators at the target site and is typically carried out by an adversary telephoning users or operators and pretending to be an authorized user, to attempt to gain illicit access to systems. (6) A general term for attackers trying to trick people into revealing sensitive information or performing certain actions, such as downloading and executing files that appear to be benign but are actually malicious.

**Social engineering for key discovery attacks**   It is important for functional users to protect their private cryptographic keys from unauthorized disclosure and from social engineering attacks. The latter attack can occur when users die or leave the company without revealing their passwords to the encrypted data. The attacker can get hold of these passwords using tricky means and access the encrypted data. Examples of other-related social engineering attacks include presenting a self-signed certificate unknown to the user, exploiting vulnerabilities in a Web browser, taking advantage of a cross-site scripting (XSS) vulnerability on a legitimate website, and taking advantage of the certificate approval process to receive a valid certificate and apply it to the attacker's own site.

**SOCKS**   (1) An Internet Protocol to allow client applications to form a circuit-level gateway to a network firewall via a proxy service. (2) This protocol supports application-layer firewall traversal. The SOCKS protocol supports both reliable TCP and UDP transport services by creating a shim-layer between the application and the transport layers. The SOCKS protocol includes a negotiation step whereby the server can dictate which authentication mechanism it supports. (3) A networking-proxy protocol that enables full access across the SOCKS server from one host to another without requiring direct IP reachability. (4) The SOCKS server authenticates and authorizes the requests, establishes a proxy connection, and transmits the data. (5) SOCKS are commonly used as a network firewall that enables hosts behind a SOCKS server to gain full access to the Internet, while preventing unauthorized access from the Internet to the internal hosts. SOCKS is an abbreviation for SOCKetServer.

**Softlifting**   Illegal copying of licensed software for personal use.

**Software**   The computer programs and possibly associated data dynamically written and modified.

**Software assurance**   Level of confidence that software is free from vulnerabilities, either intentionally designed into the software or accidentally inserted at anytime during its life cycle, and that the software functions in the intended manner.

**Software-based fault isolation**   A method of isolating application modules into distinct fault domains enforced by software. The technique allows untrusted programs written in an unsafe programming language (e.g., C) to be executed safely within the single virtual address space of an application. Access to system resource can also be controlled through a unique identifier associated with each domain.

**Software cages**   As a part of technical safeguards for active content, software cages constrain the mobile code's behavior (e.g., privileges or functions) during execution. Software cage and quarantine mechanism are part of behavior controls that dynamically intercept and thwart attempts by the subject code to take unacceptable actions that violate a security policy. Mobile code based on predefined signatures (i.e., content inspection) refers to technologies such as dynamic sandbox, dynamic monitors, and behavior monitors, which are used for controlling the behavior of mobile code. Statistics are used to verify the behavioral model.

**Software development methodologies**   Methodologies for specifying and verifying design programs for system development. Each methodology is written for a specific computer language.

**Software enhancement**   Significant functional or performance improvements.

**Software engineering**   The use of a systematic, disciplined, quantifiable approach to the development, operation, and maintenance of software, that is, the use of engineering principles in the development of software.

**Software escrow arrangement**   Something (e.g., a document, software source code, or an encryption key) that is delivered to a third person to be given to the grantee only upon the fulfillment of a condition or a contract.

**Software library**   The controlled collection of configuration items associated with defined baselines: Three libraries can exist: (1) dynamic library used for newly created or modified software elements, (2) controlled library used for managing current baselines and controlling changes to them, and (3) static library used to archive baselines.

**Software life cycle**   The sequence of events in the development or acquisition of software.

**Software maintenance**   Activities that modify software to keep it performing satisfactorily.

**Software operation**   Routine activities that make the software perform without modification.

**Software performance engineering**   A method for constructing software to meet performance objectives.

**Software quality assurance**   The planned systematic pattern of all actions necessary to provide adequate confidence that the product or process by which the product is developed conforms to established requirements.

**Software reengineering**   The examination and alteration of a subject system to reconstitute it in a new form and the subsequent implementation of the new form. Software reengineering consists of reverse engineering followed by some form of forward engineering or modification. One reason to consider reengineering is the possible reduction of software maintenance costs. The goal is to improve the quality of computer systems.

**Software release**   An updated version of commercial software to correct errors, resolve incompatibilities, or improve performance.

**Software reliability**   The probability that given software operates for some time period, without system failure due to a software fault, on the machine for which it was designed, given that it is used within design limits.

**Software repository**   A permanent, archival storage place for software and related documentation.

**Software security**   Those general-purpose (executive, utility, or software development tools) and application programs and routines that protect data handled by a computer system and its resources.

**Source code**   A series of statements written in a human-readable computer programming language.

**Spam**   The abuse of electronic messaging systems to indiscriminately send unsolicited bulk commercial e-mail messages and junk e-mails.

**Spam filtering software**   A computer program that analyzes e-mails to look for characteristics of spam, and typically places messages that appear to be spam in a separate e-mail folder.

**Spamming**   Posting identical messages to multiple unrelated newsgroups on the Internet (e.g., USENET). Often used as cheap advertising to promote pyramid schemes or simply to annoy other people.

**Spanning port**   A switch port that can see all network traffic going through the switch.

**Spanning tree**   Multicast and broadcast routing is performed using spanning trees, which makes excellent use of bandwidth where each router must know which of its lines belong to the tree. The spanning tree is also used in conducting risk analysis, to build plug-and-play bridges, and to build Internet relay chat (IRC) server network so it routes messages according to a shortest-path algorithm.

**Specialized security with limited functionality**   An environment encompassing systems with specialized security requirements, in which higher security needs typically result in more limited functionality.

**Specification**   (1) An assessment object that includes document-based artifacts (e.g., policies, procedures, plans, system security requirements, functional descriptions, and architectural designs) associated with an information system. (2) A technical description of the desired behavior of a system, as derived from its requirements. (3) A specification is used to develop and test an implementation of a system.

**Split domain name system (DNS)**   Implementation of split domain name system (DNS) requires a minimum of two physical files (zone files) or views. One file or view should exclusively provide name resolution for hosts located inside the firewall and for hosts outside the firewall. The other file or view should provide name resolution only for hosts located outside the firewall on in the DMZ and not for any hosts inside the firewall. In other words, split DNS requires one physical file for external clients and one physical file for internal clients.

**Split knowledge**   (1) A process by which a cryptographic key is split into multiple key components, individually sharing no knowledge of the original key, which can be subsequently input into, or output from, a cryptographic module by separate entities and combined to recreate the original cryptographic key. (2) The condition under which two or more parties separately have part of the data, that, when combined, will yield a security parameter or that will allow them to perform some sensitive function. (3) The separation of data into two or more parts, with each part constantly kept under control of separate authorized individuals or teams so that no one individual will be knowledgeable of the total data involved.

**Split tunneling** (1) A virtual private network (VPN) client feature that tunnels all communications involving an organization's internal resources through the VPN, thus protecting them, and excludes all other communications from going through the tunnel. (2) A method that routes organization-specific traffic through the SSL VPN tunnel, but other traffic uses the remote user's default gateway.

**Spoofing attacks** Many spoofing attacks exist. An example is the Internet Protocol (IP) spoofing attack, which refers to sending a network packet that appears to come from a source other than its actual source. It involves (1) the ability to receive a message by masquerading as the legitimate receiving destination or (2) masquerading as the sending machine and sending a message to a destination.

**Spread spectrum** Uses a wide band of frequencies to send radio signals. Instead of transmitting a signal on one channel, spread spectrum systems process the signal and spread it across a wider range of frequencies.

**Spyware** (1) It is malware intended to violate a user's privacy. (2) It is a program embedded within an application that collects information and periodically communicates back to its home site, unbeknownst to the user. Spyware programs have been discovered with many shareware or freeware programs and even some commercial products, without notification of this hidden functionality in the license agreement or elsewhere. Notification of this hidden functionality may not occur in the license agreement. News reports have accused various spyware programs of inventorying software on the user's system, collecting or searching out private information, and periodically shipping the information back to the home site. (3) It is software that is secretly or surreptitiously installed into an information system to gather information on individuals or organizations without their knowledge. It is a type of malicious code and malware.

**Spyware detection and removal utility** A program that monitors a computer to identify spyware and prevent or contain spyware incidents.

**Stackguarding** Stackguarding technology makes it difficult for attackers to exploit buffer overflows and to prevent worms from gaining control of low-privilege accounts.

**Standard** An established basis of performance used to determine quality and acceptability. A published statement on a topic specifying characteristics, usually measurable, that must be satisfied or achieved in order to comply with the standard.

**Standalone system** A small office/home office (SOHO) environment.

**Standard generalized markup language (SGML)** A markup language used to define the structure and to manage documents in electronic form.

**Standard user account** A user account with limited privileges that will be used for general tasks such as reading e-mail and surfing the Web.

**Star topology** Star topology is a network topology in which peripheral nodes are connected to a central node (station) in that all stations are connected to a central switch or hub. An active star network has an active central node that usually has the means to prevent echo-related problems.

**State attacks**   Asynchronous attacks that deal with timing differences and changing states. Examples include time-of-check to time-of-use (TOC-TOU) attack and race conditions.

**Stateful inspection**   Packet filtering that also tracks the state of connections and blocks packets that deviate from the expected state.

**Stateful protocol analysis**   A firewalling capability that improves upon standard stateful inspection by adding basic intrusion detection technology. This technology consists of an inspection engine that analyzes protocols at the application layer to compare vendor-developed profiles of benign protocol activity against observed events to identify deviations, allowing a firewall to allow or deny access based on how an application is running over a network.

**Stateless inspection**   See "Packet filtering."

**State transition diagram (STD)**   It shows how a system moves from one state to another, or as a matrix in which the dimensions are state and input. STDs detects errors such as incomplete requirements specifications and inconsistent requirements. STDs represent a sequential, natural flow of business transactions. STD are used in real-time application systems to express concurrency of tasks. They are also called state charts.

**Static key**   It is a key that is intended for use for a relatively long period of time and is typically intended for use in many instances of a cryptographic key establishment scheme. Static key is in contrast with an ephemeral key, where the latter is used for a short period of time.

**Static key agreement key pairs**   Static key agreement key pairs are used to establish shared secrets between entities, often in conjunction with ephemeral key pairs. Each entity uses their private key agreement key(s), the other entity's public key agreement key(s) and possibly their own public key agreement key(s) to determine the shared secret. The shared secret is subsequently used to derive shared keying material. Note that in some key agreement schemes, one or more of the entities may not have a static key agreement pair.

**Static separation of duty (SSOD)**   As a security mechanism, SSOD addresses two separate but related problems: static exclusivity and assurance principle.

Static exclusivity is the condition for which it is considered dangerous for any user to gain authorization for conflicting sets of capabilities (e.g., a cashier and a cashier supervisor). The motivations for exclusivity relations include, but are not limited to, reducing the likelihood of fraud or preventing the loss of user objectivity.

Assurance principle is the potential for collusion where the greater the number of individuals that are involved in the execution of a sensitive business function, such as purchasing an item or executing a trade, the less likely any one user will commit fraud or that any few users will collude in committing fraud.

Separation of duties constraints may require that two roles be mutually exclusive, because no user should have the privileges from both roles. Popular SSOD policies are the RBAC and RuBAC.

**Static Web documents**   Static Web documents (pages) are written in HTML, XHTML, ASCII, JPEG, XML, and XSL.

**Stealth mode**   Operating an intrusion detection and prevention sensor without IP addresses assigned to its monitoring network interfaces.

**Steering committee**   A group of management representatives from each user area of IT services that establishes plans and priorities and reviews project's progress and problems for the purpose of making management decisions.

**Steganography**   Deals with hiding messages and obscuring who is sending or receiving them. The art and science of communicating in a way that hides the existence of the communication. For example, a child pornography image can be hidden inside another graphic image file, audio file, or other file format.

**Step restart**   A restart that begins at the beginning of a job step. The restart may be automatic or deferred, where deferral involves resubmitting the job.

**Storage security**   The process of allowing only authorized parties to access stored information.

**Stream attack**   The process of ending transmission control protocol (TCP) packets to a series of ports with random sequence numbers and random source Internet Protocol (IP) addresses. The result is high CPU usage leading to resource starvation effect. Once the attack subsided, the system returns to normal conditions.

**Stream cipher algorithm**   An algorithm that converts plaintext into ciphertext one bit at a time and its security depends entirely on the insides of the keystream generator. Stream ciphers are good for continuous streams of communication traffic.

**Stress testing**   Application programs tested with test data chosen for maximum, minimum, and trivial values, or parameters. The purpose is to analyze system behavior under increasingly heavy workloads and severe operating conditions, and, in particular, to identify points of system failure.

**Stretching (password)**   The act of hashing each password and its salt thousands of times, which makes the creation of rainbow tables more time-consuming.

**Striped core**   A communications network architecture in which user data traversing a core IP network is decrypted, filtered, and re-encrypted one or more times in a red gateway. The core is striped because the data path is alternately black, red, and black.

**Strongly bound credentials**   Strongly bound credential mechanisms (e.g., a signed public key certificate) require little or no additional integrity protection.

**Structure charts**   A tool used to portray the logic of an application system on a hierarchical basis, showing the division of the system into modules and the interfaces among modules. Like data flow diagrams (DFDs), structure charts can be drawn at different levels of detail from the system level to a paragraph level within a program. Unlike DFDs, structure charts indicate decision points and explain how the data will be handled in the proposed system. A structure charts is derived directly from the DFD with separate branches for input, transformation, and output.

**Subclass**   A class that inherits from one or more classes.

**Subject**   Technically, subject is a process-domain pair. An active entity (e.g., a person, a process or device acting on behalf of user, or in some cases the actual user) that can make a request to perform an operation on an object (e.g., information to flow among objects or changes a system state). It is the person whose identity is bound in a particular credential.

**Subject security level**   A subject's security level is equal to the security level of the objects to which it has both read and write access. A subject's security level must always be dominated by the clearance of the user with which the subject is associated.

**Subscriber**   (1) An entity that has applied for and received a certificate from a certificate authority. (2) A party who receives a credential or token from a credential service provider (CSP) and becomes a claimant in an authentication protocol.

**Subscriber identity module (SIM)**   A smart card chip specialized for use in global system for mobile communications (GSM) equipment.

**Subscriber station (WMAN/WiMAX)**   A subscriber station (SS) is a fixed wireless node and is available in outdoor and indoor models and communicates only with BSs, except during mesh network operations.

**Substitution table box**   Nonlinear substitution table boxes (S-boxes) used in several byte substitution transformations and in the key expansion routine to perform a one-for-one substitution of a byte value. This substitution, which is implemented with simple electrical circuits, is done so fast in that it does not require any computation, just signal propagation. The S-box design, which is implemented in hardware for cryptographic algorithm, follows Kerckhoff's principle (security-by-obscurity) in that an attacker knows that the general method is substituting the bits, but he does not know which bit goes where. Hence, there is no need to hide the substitution method. S-boxes and P-boxes are combined to form a product cipher, where wiring of the P-box is placed inside the S-box (i.e., S-box is first and P-box is next). S-boxes are used in the advanced encryption standard (AES).

**Subsystem**   A major subdivision or component of an information system consisting of information, information technology, and personnel that perform one or more specific functions.

**Superuser**   A user who is authorized to modify and control IT processes, devices, networks, and file systems.

**Supervisor state**   One of two generally possible states in which a computer system may operate and in which only certain privileged instructions may be executed. The other state in which a computer system may operate is *problem-state* in which privileged instructions may not be executed. The distinction between the supervisor state and the problem state is critical to the integrity of the system.

**Supplementary controls**   The process of adding security controls or control enhancements to a baseline security control in order to adequately meet the organization's risk management needs. These are considered additional controls; after comparing the tailored baseline controls with security requirements definition or gap analysis, these controls are added to make up for the missing or insufficient controls.

**Supply chain**   A system of organizations, people, activities, information, and resources involved in moving a product or service from supplier/producer to consumer/customer. It uses a defense-in-breadth strategy.

**Supply chain attack**   An attack that allows an adversary to utilize implants or other vulnerabilities inserted prior to installation in order to infiltrate data or manipulate IT hardware, software, operating systems, IT peripherals or services at any point during the life cycle of a product or service.

**Support software**    All software that indirectly supports the operation of a computer system and its functional applications such as macroinstructions, call routines, and read and write routines.

**Supporting controls**    Generic controls that underlie most IT security capabilities. These controls must be in place in order to implement other controls, such as prevent, detect, and recover. Examples include identification, cryptographic key management, security administration, an system protection.

**Susceptibility analysis**    Examination of all susceptibility information to identify the full range of mitigation desired or possible that can diminish the impacts from exposure of vulnerabilities or access by threats.

**Suspended state**    The cryptographic key life cycle state used to temporarily remove a previously active key from that status but making provisions for later returning the key to active status, if appropriate.

**Symbolic links**    A symbolic link or symlink is a file that points to another file. Often, there are programs that will change the permissions granted to a file. If these programs run with privileged permissions, a user could strategically create symlinks to trick these programs into modifying or listing critical system files.

**Symmetric key algorithm**    A cryptographic algorithm that uses the same secret key for an operation and its complement (e.g., encryption and decryption, or create a message authentication code and to verify the code).

**Symmetric key cryptography**    (1) A cryptographic key that is used to perform both the cryptographic operation and its inverse (e.g., to encrypt and decrypt a message or create a message authentication code and to verify the code). (2) A single cryptographic key that is used with a secret (symmetric) key algorithm.

**Synchronization (SYN) flood attack**    (1) A stealth attack because the attacker spoofs the source address of the SYN packet, thus making it difficult to identify the perpetrator. (2) A method of overwhelming a host computer on the Internet by sending the host a high volume of SYN packets requesting a connection but never responding to the acknowledgement packets returned by the host. In some cases, the damage can be very serious. (3) A method of disabling a system by sending more SYN packets than its networking code can handle.

**Synchronization protocols**    Protocols that allow users to view, modify, and transfer or update data between a cell phone or personal digital assistant (PDA) and a PC or vice versa. The two most common synchronization protocols are Microsoft's ActiveSync and Palm's HotSync.

**Synchronous communication**    The transmission of data at very high speeds using circuits in which the transfer of data is synchronized by electronic clock signals. Synchronous communication is used within the computer and in high-speed mainframe computer networks.

**Synchronous optical network (SONET)**    A physical layer standard that provides an international specification for high-speed digital transmission via optical fiber. At the source interface, signals are converted from electrical to optical form. They are then converted back to electrical form at the destination interface.

**Synchronous transmission**    The serial transmission of a bit stream in which each bit occurs at a fixed time interval and the entire stream is preceded by a specific combination of bits that initiate the timing.

**Syntax error**   An error resulting from the expression of a command in a way that violates a program's syntax rules. Syntax rules specify precisely how a command, statement, or instruction must be given to the computer so that it can recognize and process the instruction correctly.

**Syslog**   A protocol that specifies a general log entry format and a log entry transport mechanism. Log facility is the message type for a syslog message.

**System**   A discrete set of information resources organized for the collection, processing, maintenance, use, sharing, dissemination, or disposition of information. A generic term used for briefness to mean either a major/minor application (MA) or a general support system (GSS).

**System administrator**   A person who manages a multiuser computer system, including its operating system and applications, and whose responsibilities are similar to that of a network administrator. A system administrator would perform systems programmer activities with regard to the operating system and network control programs.

**System availability**   (1) A timely, reliable access to data, system, and information services for authorized users. (2) A measure of the amount of time that the system is actually capable of accepting and performing a user's work. (3) The availability of communication ports and the amount or quantity of service received in a given period. (4) Can be viewed as a component of system reliability. The availability of a computer system can be expressed as a percentage in several ways, as follows:

Availability = (Uptime)/(Uptime + Downtime) × 100
Availability = (Available time/Scheduled time) × 100
Availability = [(MTTF)/(MTTF + MTTR)] × 100
Availability = (MTTF/MTBF) × 100

**System confidentiality**   Assurance that information is not disclosed to unauthorized individuals, processes, or devices.

**System development life cycle (SDLC)**   A systematic process for planning, analyzing, designing, developing, implementing, operating, and maintaining a computer-based application system. The scope of activities associated with a system, encompassing the system's initiation, development and acquisition, implementation, operation and maintenance, and ultimately its disposal that instigates another system initiation.

**System development methodologies**   Methodologies developed through software engineering to manage the complexity of system development. Development methodologies include software engineering aids and high-level design analysis tools.

**System high**   The highest security level supported by a system at a particular time or in a particular environment (e.g., military/weapon systems, aircraft systems, and nuclear systems).

**System integrity**   (1) Quality of a system or product reflecting the logical correctness and reliability of the operating system; verification that the original contents of information have not been altered or corrupted. (2) The quality that a system has when it performs its intended function in an unimpaired manner, free from unauthorized manipulation of the system, whether intentional or accidental.

**System integrity exposure**   A condition that exists when there is a potential of one or more programs that can bypass the installation's control and (a) circumvent or disable store or fetch protection, (b) access a protected resource, and (c) obtain control in authorized (supervisor) state. This condition can lead to compromise of systems protection mechanisms and data integrity.

**System inventory**   Organizations require a system inventory in place. All systems in the inventory should be categorized as a first step in support of the security planning activity and eventually in the assessment of the security controls implemented on the system.

**System life**   A projection of the time period that begins with the installation of a system resource (e.g., software or hardware) and ends when the organization's need for that resource has terminated.

**System low**   The lowest security level supported by a computer system at a particular time or in a particular environment.

**System manager**   The IT manager who is responsible for the operation of a computer system.

**System parameter**   A factor or property whose value determines a characteristic or behavior of the system.

**System reliability**   The terms system reliability and system availability are closely related and often used (although incorrectly) synonymously. For example, a system that fails frequently but is restarted quickly has high availability even though its reliability is low. To distinguish between the two, reliability can be thought of as the quality of service and availability as the quantity of service. System reliability is measured in terms of downtime hours in a given period of time.

**System resilience**   The ability of a computer system to continue to function correctly despite the existence of a fault or faults in one or more of its component parts.

**System security plan**   Formal document that provides an overview of the security requirements for the information system and describes the security controls in place or planned for meeting those requirements.

**System-specific control**   A security control for an information system that has not been designated as a common security control or the portion of a hybrid control that is to be implemented within an information system.

**Systems engineering**   The systematic application of technical and managerial processes and concepts to transform an operational need into an efficient, cost-effective system using an iterative approach to define, analyze, design, build, test, and evaluate the system.

**Systems software**   (1) A major category of programs used to control the computer and process other programs, such as secure operating systems, communications control programs, and database managers. (2) Contrasts with applications software, which comprises the data entry, update, query, and report programs that process an organization's data. (3) The operating system and accompanying utility programs that enable a user to control, configure, and maintain the computer system, software, and data.

**System transparency**   Transparency is the ability to simplify the task of developing management applications, hiding distribution details. There are different aspects of transparency such as access failure, location, migration replication, and transaction. Transparency means the network components or segments cannot be seen by insiders and outsiders and that actions of one user group cannot be observed by other user groups. It is achieved through process isolation and hardware segmentation concepts.

**Switches** Switches, in the form of routers, interconnect when the systems forming one workgroup are physically separated from the systems forming other workgroups. For example, Ethernet switches establish a data link in which a circuit or a channel is connected to an Ethernet network. Switches and bridges are used to interconnect different LANs. A switch operates in the Data Link Layer of the ISO/OSI reference model.

# T

**T- lines** High-speed data lines leased from communications providers such as T-1 lines.

**Tailgating** Same as piggybacking.

**Tailored security control baseline** A set of security controls resulting from the application of tailoring guidance to the security control baseline. Tailoring is the process by which a security control baseline is modified based on (1) the application of scoping guidance; (2) the specification of compensating security controls, if needed; and (3) the specification of organization-defined parameters in the security controls via explicit assignment and selection statements. In other words, the tailoring process modifies or aligns the baseline controls to fit the system conditions.

**Tainted input** Input data that has not been examined or sanitized prior to use by an application.

**Tamper** Unauthorized modification that alters the proper functioning of cryptographic or automated information system security equipment in a manner that degrades the security or functionality it provides.

**Tamper detection** The automatic determination by a cryptographic module that an attempt has been made to compromise the physical security of the module.

**Tamper evidence** The external indication that an attempt has been made to compromise the physical security of a cryptographic module. The evidence of the tamper attempt should be observable by an operator subsequent to the attempt.

**Tamper response** The automatic action taken by a cryptographic module when a tamper attempt has been detected.

**Tandem computing** Tandem computers use single point tolerance system to create nonstop systems with uptimes measured in years. Single point tolerance means single backup where broken parts can be swapped out with new ones while the system is still operational (that is, hot swapping). The single point tolerant systems should have high mean time between failures (MTBF) and low mean time to repair (MTTR) before the backup fails (Wikipedia).

**Tap** An analog device that permits signals to be inserted or removed from a twisted pair or coax cable.

**Target of evaluation (TOE)** A Common Criteria (CC) term for an IT product or system and its associated administrator and user guidance documentation that is the subject of a security evaluation. A product that has been installed and is being operated according to its guidance.

**Target identification and analysis techniques** Information security testing techniques, mostly active and generally conducted using automated tools, used to identify systems, ports, services, and potential vulnerabilities. These techniques include network discovery, network port and service identification, vulnerability scanning, wireless scanning, and application security testing.

**Target vulnerability validation techniques**   Active information security testing techniques that corroborate the existence of vulnerabilities. These techniques include password cracking, remote access testing, penetration testing, social engineering, and physical security testing.

**TCP wrappers**   Transmission control protocol (TCP) wrapper, a network security tool, allows the administrator to log connections to TCP service. It can also restrict incoming connections to these services from systems. These features are useful when tracking or controlling unwanted network connection attempts.

**Teardrop attack**   This freezes vulnerable hosts by exploiting a bug in the fragmented packet reassembly routines. A countermeasure is to install software patches and upgrades.

**Technical attack**   An attack that can be perpetrated by circumventing or nullifying hardware and software protection mechanisms, rather than by subverting system personnel or other users.

**Technical controls**   (1) An automated security control employed by the system. (2) The security controls (i.e., safeguards or countermeasures) for an information system that are primarily implemented and executed by the information system through mechanisms contained in the hardware, software, or firmware components of the system.

**Technical security**   The set of hardware, firmware, software, and supporting controls that implement security policy, accountability, assurance, and documentation.

**Technical vulnerability**   A hardware, firmware, communication, or software flaw that leaves a computer processing system open for potential exploitation, either externally or internally, thereby resulting in risk for the owner, user, or manager of the system.

**Technology convergence**   It occurs when two or more specific and compatible technologies are combined to work in harmony. For example, in a data center physical facility, physical security controls (keys, locks, and visitor escort), logical security controls (biometrics and access controls), and environmental controls (heat and humidity) can be combined for effective implementation of controls. These controls can be based on

**Technology gap**   A technology that is needed to mitigate a threat at a sufficient level but is not available.

**Telecommuting**   The ability for an organization's employees and contractors to conduct work from locations other than the organization's facilities.

**Telework**   The ability for an organization's employees and contractors to conduct work from locations other than the organization's facilities.

**Telework device**   A consumer device or PC used for performing telework.

**Telnet**   Protocol used for (possibly for remote) login to a computer host.

**TEMPEST**   A short name referring to investigation, study, and control of compromising emanations from telecommunications and automated information systems equipment. (i.e., spurious electronic signals emitted by electrical equipment). A low signal-to-ratio is preferred to control the tempest shielded equipment.

**TEMPEST attack**   Based on leaked electromagnetic radiation, which can directly provide plaintext and other information that an attacker needs to attack. It is a general class of side channel attack (Wikipedia).

**Test**   A type of assessment method that is characterized by the process of exercising one or more assessment objects under specified conditions to compare actual with expected behavior, the results of which are used to support the determination of security control effectiveness over time.

**Test design**   The test approach and associated tests.

**Test harness**   Software that automates the software engineering testing process to test the software as thoroughly as possible before using it on a real application. If appropriate, the component should include the source code (for "white box" components) and a "management application" if the data managed by the component must be entered or updated independent of the consuming application. Finally, a component should be delivered with samples of consumption of the component to indicate how the component operates within an application environment.

**Test plan**   A plan that details the specific tests and procedures to be followed when testing software.

**Test procedure**   Detailed instructions for the setup, execution, and evaluation of results for a given test case.

**Testability**   Effort required for testing a computer program to ensure it performs its intended function.

**Test-word**   A string of characters (a test-word) is appended by a sending institution to a transaction sent over unprotected telex/telegraph networks. The receiving institution repeats the same process using the received transaction data, and was thereby able to verify the integrity of the transaction. A test-word is an early-technology realization of a seal.

**Thick client**   In a client/server system, a thick client is a software application that requires programs other than just the browser on a user's computer, that is, it requires code on both a client and server computers (e.g., Microsoft Outlook). The terms "thin" and "thick" refer to the amount of code that must be run on the client computer. Thick clients are generally less secure than thin clients in the way encryption keys are handled.

**Thin client**   In a client/server system, a thin client is a software application that requires nothing more than a browser and can be run only on the user's computer (e.g., Microsoft Word). The terms "thin" and "thick" refer to the amount of code that must be run on the client computer. Thin clients are generally more secure than thick clients in the way encryption keys are handled.

**Thrashing**   A situation that occurs when paging on a virtual memory system is so frequent that little time is left for useful work.

**Thread testing**   It examines the execution time behavior of computer programs. A thread can be a sequence of programmer statements (source code) or machine instructions (object code). Petri nets can be used to analyze thread interactions. In the finite-state-machine (FSM) model, program paths are converted to threads.

**Threat**   An entity or event with the potential to harm a system. Threats are possible dangers to a computer system, which may result in the interception, alteration, obstruction, or destruction of computing resources, or in some other way disrupt the system. It is any circumstance or event with the potential to adversely impact organization operations (including mission, functions, image or reputation), organizational assets, individuals, and other organizations through an information system via unauthorized access, destruction, disclosure, modification of information, and/or denial of service. Threat is the potential for a threat-source to successfully exploit a particular information system's vulnerability. It is an activity (deliberate or unintentional) with the potential for causing harm to an automated information system and a potential violation of system security. Threats arise from internal system failures, human errors, attacks, and natural catastrophes. Threats can be viewed in terms of categories and classes, as shown in the following table:

| CATEGORIES | CLASSES |
|---|---|
| Human categories | Intentional or unintentional |
| Environmental categories | Natural or man-made (fabricated) |

**Threat agent/source**   The intent and method targeted at the intentional exploitation of vulnerability or a situation and method that may accidentally trigger vulnerability. It is a method used to exploit vulnerability in a system, operation, or facility.

**Threat analysis**   The examination of threat-sources against system vulnerabilities to determine the threats for a particular system in a particular operational environment. Threat is threat-source and vulnerability pair, which can be analyzed in parallel. However, threat analysis cannot be performed until after vulnerability analysis has been conducted because vulnerabilities lead to threats, which, in turn, lead to risks.

**Threat assessment**   A process of formally evaluating the degree of threat to an information system or enterprise and describing the nature of the threat.

**Threat event**   A catastrophic occurrence. Examples include fire, flood, power outage, and hardware/software failures.

**Threat monitoring**   The analysis, assessment, and review of audit trails and other data collected to search out system events that may constitute violations or attempted violations of system security.

**Threat-source/agent**   The intent and method targeted at the intentional exploitation of a vulnerability or a situation and method that may accidentally trigger a vulnerability. It is a method used to exploit vulnerability in a system, operation, or facility.

**Threshold**   A value that sets the limit between normal and abnormal behavior.

**Ticket-oriented protection system**   A computer protection system in which each subject maintains a list of unforgeable bit patterns, called tickets, one for each object the subject is authorized to access (e.g., Kerberos). Compare this with list-oriented protection system.

**Tiger team**   Conducts penetration testing to attempt a system break-in. It is an old name to discover system weaknesses and to recommend security controls. The new name is red team.

**Timebomb**   A variant of the Trojan horse in which malicious code is inserted to be triggered later at a particular time. It is a resident computer program that triggers an unauthorized act as a predefined time.

**Time-dependent password**   A password that is valid only at a certain time of the day or during a specified interval of time.

**Time division multiple access (TDMA)**   Form of multiple access where a single communication channel is shared by segmenting it by time. Each user is assigned a specific time slot. It is a technique to interweave multiple conversations into one transponder so as to appear to get simultaneous conversations.

**Time-outs for inactivity**   The setting of time limits for either specific activities or for nonactivity.

**Time-stamping**   The method of including an unforgeable time stamp with object structures, used for a variety of reasons such as sequence-numbering and expiration of data.

**Time-to-exploitation**   The elapsed time between the vulnerability is discovered and the time it is exploited.

**Time-to-Live (TTL) hack**   The Time-To-Live (TTL) hack or hop count prevents IP packets from circulating endlessly in the Internet.

**Time-to-recover (TTR)**   The time required for any computer resource to be recovered from disruptive events, specifically, the time required to reestablish an activity from an emergency or degraded mode to a normal mode. It is also defined as emergency response time (EMRT).

**Timing attack**   A side channel attack in which the attacker attempts to compromise a cryptosystem by analyzing the time taken to execute cryptographic algorithms. Every logical operation in a computer takes time to execute, and the time can differ based on the input; with precise measurements of the time for each operation, an attacker can work backward to the input. Information can leak from a system through measurement of the time it takes to respond to certain queries. Timing attacks result from poor system/program design and implementation methods. Timing attacks and sidechannel attacks are useful in identifying or reverse-engineering a cryptographic algorithm used by some device. Other examples of timing attacks include (1) a clock drift attack where it can be used to build random number generators, (2) clock skew exploitation based on CPU heating, and (3) attackers who may find fixed Diffie-Hellman exponents and RSA keys to break cryptosystems (Wikipedia).

**TOC-TOU attack**   TOC-TOU stands for Time-of-check to time-of-use. An example of TOC-TOU attack is when one print job under one user's name is exchanged with the print job for another user. It is achieved through bypassing security controls by attacking information after the controls were exercised (that is, when the print job is queued) but before the information is used (that is, prior to printing the job). This attack is based on timing differences and changing states.

**Token**   (1) Something that the claimant possesses and controls (typically a key or password) used to authenticate the claimant's identity. (2) When used in the context of authentication, a physical device necessary for user identification. (3) A token is an object that represents something else, such as another object (either physical or virtual). (4) A security token is a physical device, such as a special smart card, that together with something that a user knows, such as a PIN, can enable authorized access to a computer system or network.

**Token authenticator**   The value that is provided for the protocol stack to prove that the claimant possesses and controls the token. Protocol messages sent to the verifier are dependent upon the token authenticator, but they may or may not explicitly contain it.

**Token device**   A device used for generating passwords based on some information (e.g., time, date, and personal identification number) that is valid for only a brief period (e.g., one minute).

**Top-down approach** An approach that starts with the highest-level component of a hierarchy and proceeds through progressively lower levels.

**Topology** (1) The physical, nonlogical features of a card. A card may have either standard or enhanced topography. (2) The structure, consisting of paths and switches, that provides the communications interconnection among nodes of a network.

**Total risk** The potential for the occurrence of an adverse event if no mitigating action taken (i.e., the potential for any applicable threat to exploit a system vulnerability).

**Tracing** An automated procedure performed by software that shows what program instructions have been executed in a computer program and in which sequence they have been executed. Tracing can also be performed manually by following the path of a transaction or an activity from beginning to the end and vice versa.

**Tracking cookie** A cookie placed on a user's computer to track the user's activity on different websites, creating a detailed profile of the user's behavior.

**Traffic analysis attack** (1) The act of passively monitoring transmissions to identify communication patterns and participants. (2) A form of passive attack in which an intruder observes information about calls (although not necessarily the contents of the messages) and makes inferences from the source and destination numbers or frequency and length of the messages. The goal is to gain intelligence about a system or its users, and may not require the examination of the content of the communications, which may or may not be decipherable. (3) A traffic flow signal from a reader could be used to detect a particular activity occurring in the communications path. (4) An inference attack occurs when a user or intruder is able to deduce information to which he had no privilege from information to which he has privilege. Traffic-flow security protection can be used to counter traffic analysis attacks.

**Traffic encryption key (TEK)** A key is used to encrypt plaintext or to super-encrypt previously encrypted text and/or to decrypt ciphertext.

**Traffic-flow security** The protection resulting from encrypting the source and destination addresses of valid messages transmitted over a communications circuit. Security is assured due to use of link encryption and because no part of the data is known to an attacker.

**Traffic load** The number of messages input to a network during a specific time period.

**Traffic padding or flooding** A protection to conceal the presence of valid messages on a communications circuit by causing the circuit to appear busy at all times. Unnecessary data are sent through the circuit to keep it busy and to confuse the intruder. It is a countermeasure against the threat of traffic analysis.

**Trans-border data flow** Deals with the movement and storage of data by automatic means across national or federal boundaries. It may require data encryption when data is flowing over some borders.

**Transaction** An activity or request to a computer. Purchase orders, changes, additions, and deletions are examples of transactions recorded in a business information environment. A logical unit of work for an end user. Also, used to define a program or a dialog in a computer system.

**Transmission control protocol (TCP)** A reliable connection and byte-oriented transport layer protocol within the TCP/IP suite.

**Transmission control protocol/Internet protocol (TCP/IP)**   TCP/IP is the protocol suite used by the Internet. A protocol suite is the set of message types, their formats, and the rules that control how messages are processed by computers on the network.

**Transmission medium**   The physical path between transmitters and receivers in a communication network. A mechanism that supports propagation of digital signals. Examples of a transmission medium are cables such as leased lines from common commercial carriers, fiber optic cables, and satellite channels.

**Transmittal list**   A list, stored and transmitted with particular data items, which identifies the data in that batch and can be used to verify that no data are missing.

**Transport layer**   Portion of an open system interconnection (OSI) system responsible for reliability and multiplexing of data across network to the level required by the application.

**Transport-layer security (TLS)**   (1) An authentication and security protocol widely implemented in Web browsers and Web servers. (2) Provides security at the layer responsible for end-to-end communications. (3) Provides privacy and data integrity between two communicating applications. (4) It is designed to encapsulate other protocols, such as HTTP. TLS is new and SSL is old.

**Transport mode**   IPsec mode that does not create a new IP header for each protected packet.

**Tranquility**   A property applied to a set of (typically untrusted) controlled entities saying that their security level may not change.

**Tranquility principle**   A request that changes to an object's access control attributes are prohibited as long as any subject has access to the object.

**Trap**   A message indicating that a fault condition may exist or that a fault is likely to occur. In computer crime investigations, trap and trace means the attacker's phone call is trapped and traced.

**Trapdoor**   A hidden software or hardware mechanism that responds to a special input used to circumvent the system's security controls. Synonymous with backdoor.

**Tree topology**   Tree topology is a network topology which resembles an interconnection of start networks in that individual peripheral nodes are required to transmit to and receive from one another node only toward a central node. The tree topology is not required to act as repeaters or regenerators. The tree topology, which is a variation of bus topology, is subject to a single-point of failure of a transmission path to the node. The tree topology is an example of a hybrid topology where a linear bus backbone connects star-configured networks.

**Triangulation**   Identifying the physical location of a detected threat against a wireless network by estimating the threat's approximate distance from multiple wireless sensors by the strength of the threat's signal received by each sensor, and then calculating the physical location at which the threat would be the estimated distance from each sensor.

**Triple DES (3DES)**   An implementation of the data encryption standard (DES) algorithm that uses three passes of the DES algorithm instead of one as used in ordinary DES applications. Triple DES provides much stronger encryption than ordinary DES but it is less secure than AES.

**Tripwire**   Tripwire, a network security tool, monitors the permissions and checksums of important system files to detect if they have been replaced or corrupted. Tripwire can be configured to send an alert to the administrator should any file's recomputed checksum fail to match its baseline, indicating that the file has been altered.

**Trojan horse (aka Trojan)**   (1) A useful or seemingly useful program that contains hidden code of a malicious nature. When the program is invoked, so is the undesired function whose effects may not become immediately obvious. (2) It is a nonself-replicating program that appears to have a useful purpose, but actually has a hidden malicious purpose. The name stems from an ancient exploit of invaders gaining entry to the city of Troy by concealing themselves in the body of a hollow wooden horse, presumed to be left behind by the invaders as a gift to the city. (3) A computer program with an apparent or actual useful function that contains additional (hidden) functions that surreptitiously exploit the legitimate authorizations of the invoking process to the detriment of security or integrity. (4) It usually masquerades as a useful program that a user would wish to execute.

**True negative**   A tool reports a weakness when it is not present.

**True positive**   A tool reports a weakness when it is present.

**Trust**   (1) A characteristic of an entity (e.g., person, process, key, or algorithm) that indicates its ability to perform certain functions or services correctly, fairly, and impartially, and that the entity and its identity are genuine. (2) A relationship between two elements, a set of activities and a security policy in which element X trusts element Y if and only if X has confidence that Y will behave in a well-defined way (with respect to the activities) that does not violate the given security policy. (3) It is a belief that a system meets its specifications. (4) The willingness to take actions expecting beneficial outcomes based on assertions by other parties.

**Trust anchor (public key)**   (1) One or more trusted public keys that exist at the base of a tree of trust or as the strongest link on a chain of trust and upon which a public key infrastructure (PKI) is constructed. (2) A public key and the name of a certification authority (CA) that is used to validate the first certificate in a sequence of certificates. (3) The trust anchor public key is used to verify the signature on a certificate issued by a trust anchor CA. The security of the validation process depends upon the authenticity and integrity of the trust anchor. Trust anchors are often distributed as self-signed certificates.

**Trust anchor (DNS)**   A validating DNSSEC-aware resolver uses a public key or hash as a starting point for building the authentication chain to a signed domain name system (DNS) response. In general, a validating resolver will need to obtain the initial values of its trust anchors via some secure or trusted means outside the DNS protocol. The presence of a trust anchor also implies that the resolver should expect the zone to which the trust anchor points to be signed. This is sometimes referred to as a "secure entry point."

**Trust anchor store**   The location where trust anchors are stored. Here, store refers to placing electronic data into a storage medium, which may be accessed and retrieved under normal operational circumstances by authorized entities.

**Trust list**   It is the collection of trusted certificates used by the relying parties to authenticate other certificates.

**Trusted certificate**   A certificate that is trusted by the relying party on the basis of secure and authenticated delivery. The public keys included in trusted certificates are used to start certification paths. It is also known as a trust anchor.

**Trusted channel**   (1) A mechanism by which two trusted partitions can communicate directly. (2) A trusted channel may be needed for the correct operation of other security mechanisms. (3) A trusted channel cannot be initiated by untrusted software and it maintains the integrity of information that is sent over it. (4) A channel where the endpoints are known and data integrity and/or data privacy is protected in transit using SSL, IPsec, and a secure physical connection. (5) A mechanism through which a cryptographic module provides a trusted, safe, and discrete communication pathway for sensitive security parameters (SSPs) and other critical information between the cryptographic module and the module's intended communications endpoint. A trusted channel exhibits a verification component that the operator or module may use to confirm that the trusted channel exists. A trusted channel protects against eavesdropping, as well as physical or logical tampering by unwanted operators/entities, processes, or other devices, both within the module and along the module's communication link with the intended endpoint (e.g., the trusted channel will not allow man-in-the-middle (MitM) or replay types of attacks). A trusted channel may be realized in one or more of the following ways: (i) A communication pathway between the cryptographic module and endpoints that are entirely local, directly attached to the cryptographic module, and has no intervening systems, and (ii) A mechanism that cryptographically protects SSPs during entry and output and does not allow misuse of any transitory SSPs.

**Trusted computer system**   (1) A system that employs sufficient hardware and software assurance measures to allow its use for processing simultaneously a range of sensitive or classified information. (2) A system believed to enforce a given set of attributes to a stated degree of assurance (confidence).

**Trusted computing**   Trusted computing helps network administrators to keep track of host computers on the network. This tracking and controlling mechanism ensures that all hosts are properly patched up, the software version is current, and that they are protected from malware exploitation. Trusted computing technologies are both hardware-based and software-based techniques to combat the threat of possible attacks. It includes three technologies such as trusted platform module, trusted network connect, and trusted computing software stack.

**Trusted computing base (TCB)**   The totality of protection mechanisms within a computer system, including hardware, firmware, and software, where this combination is responsible for enforcing a security policy. It provides a basic protection environment and provides additional user services required for a trusted computer system. The capability of a TCB to correctly enforce a security policy depends solely on the mechanisms within the TCB and on the correct input by system administrative personnel of parameters (e.g., a user's clearance) related to the security policy.

**Trusted distribution**   A trusted method for distributing the trusted computing base (TCB) hardware, software, and firmware components, both originals and updates, that provides methods for protecting the TCB from modification during distribution and for detection of any changes to the TCB that may occur.

**Trusted functionality**   That which is determined to be correct with respect to some criteria, e.g., as established by a security policy. The functionality shall neither fall short of nor exceed the criteria.

**Trusted operating system (TOS)**   A trusted operating system is part of a trusted computing base (TCB) that has been evaluated at an assurance level necessary to protect the data that will be processed.

**Trusted path**   (1) A means by which an operator and a security function can communicate with the necessary confidence to support the security policy associated with the security function. (2) A mechanism by which a user (through an input device) can communicate directly with the security functions of the information system with the necessary confidence to support the system security policy. This mechanism can only be activated by the user or the security functions of the information system and cannot be imitated by untrusted software.

**Trusted platform module (TPM) chip**   A tamper-resistant integrated circuit built into some computer motherboards that can perform cryptographic operations (including key generation) and protect small amounts of sensitive information, such as passwords and cryptographic keys. TPM chip, through its key cache management feature, protects the generated keys used in encrypted file system (EFS).

**Trusted relationships**   Policies that govern how entities in differing domains honor each other's authorizations. An authority may be completely trusted for example, any statement from the authority will be accepted as a basis for action or there may be limited trust, in which case only statements in a specific range are accepted.

**Trusted software**   It is the software portion of a trusted computing base (TCB).

**Trusted subject**   A subject that is part of the trusted computing base (TCB). It has the ability to violate the security policy but is trusted not to actually do so. For example, in the Bell-LaPadula model, a trusted subject is not constrained by the star-property and thus has the capability to write sensitive information into an object whose level is not dominated by the (maximum) level of the subject, but it is trusted to only write information into objects with a label appropriate for the actual level of the information.

**Trusted system**   Employing sufficient integrity measures to allow its use for processing intelligence information involving sensitive intelligence sources and methods.

**Trusted third party (TTP)**   An entity other than the owner and verifier that is trusted by the owner or the verifier or both. Sometimes shortened to "trusted party."

**Trustworthiness**   (1) The attribute of a person or enterprise that provides confidence to others of the qualifications, capabilities, and reliability of that entity to perform specific tasks and fulfill assigned responsibilities. (2) A characteristic or property of an information system that expresses the degree to which the system can be expected to preserve the confidentiality, integrity, and availability of the information being processed, stored, or transmitted by the system.

**Trustworthy system**   Computer hardware, software, and procedures that (1) are reasonably secure from intrusion and misuse, (2) provide a reasonable level of availability, reliability, and correct operation, (3) are reasonably suited to performing their intended functions, and (4) adhere to generally accepted security principles.

**Truth table**   Computer logic blocks can use combinational logic (without memory) or sequential logic (with memory). The combinational logic can be specified by defining the values of the outputs for each possible set of input values using a truth table. Each entry in the table specifies the value of all the outputs for that particular input combination. Truth tables can grow in size quickly and may be difficult to understand. After a truth table is constructed, it can be optimized by keeping nonzero output values only.

**Tuning**   Altering the configuration of an intrusion detection and prevention system (IDPS) to improve its detection accuracy.

**Tunnel mode**   IPsec mode that creates a new IP header for each protected packet.

**Tunnel virtual private network (VPN)**   A secure socket layer (SSL) connection that allows a wide variety of protocols and applications to be run through it.

**Tunneled password protocol**   A protocol where a password is sent through a protected channel to a cryptographically authenticated verifier. For example, the transport layer security (TLS) protocol is often used with a verifier's public key certificate to (1) authenticate the verifier to the claimant, (2) establish an encrypted session between the verifier and claimant, and (3) transmit the claimant's password to the verifier. The encrypted TLS session protects the claimant's password from eavesdroppers.

**Tunneling**   (1) It is a technology enabling one network to send its data via another network's connections. Tunneling works by encapsulating a network protocol within packets carried by the second network. (2) A high-level remote access architecture that provides a secure tunnel between a telework client device (a personal computer used by a remote worker) and a tunneling server through which application system traffic may pass. (3) A method of circumventing a firewall by hiding a message that would be rejected by the firewall inside a second, acceptable message.

**Tunneling attack**   An attack that attempts to exploit a weakness in a system at a level of abstraction lower than that used by the developer to design and/or test the system.

**Tunneling router**   A router or system capable of routing traffic by encrypting it and encapsulating it for transmission across an untrusted network, for eventual decryption and de-encapsulation.

**Turnstiles**   Turnstiles will decrease the everyday piggybacking or tailgating by forcing people to go through a turnstile one person at a time. Turnstiles are used in data centers and office buildings.

**Twisted-pair wire**   Twisted-pair wire is the most commonly used media, and its application is limited to single building or a few buildings, and used for lower performance systems.

**Two-factor authentication**   A type of authentication that requires two independent methods to establish identity and authorization to perform security services. The three most recognized factors are (1) something you are (e.g., biometrics), (2) something you know (e.g., password), and (3) something you have (e.g., smart card).

**Two-part code**   It is a code consisting of an encoding section (first part) arranged in alphabetical or numeric order and a decoding section (second part) arranged in a separate alphabetical or numeric order.

**Two-person control**   Continuous surveillance and monitoring of positive control material at all times by a minimum of two authorized individuals, each capable of detecting incorrect and unauthorized procedures with respect to the task being performed and each familiar with established security and safety requirements.

**Two-person integrity**   System of storage and handling designed to prohibit individual access by requiring the presence of at least two authorized individuals, each capable of detecting incorrect or unauthorized security procedures with respect to the task being performed.

**Type I and II reports**   The Statement on Auditing Standards 70 (SAS 70) of the American Institute of Certified Public Accountants (AICPA) prescribe Type I and Type II attestation reports for its clients after the auditors' review of the client's information systems. The SAS 70 is applicable to service organizations (software companies) that develop, provide, and maintain software used by user organizations (that is, user clients and customers). The Type I report states that information systems at the service organizations for processing user transactions are suitably designed with internal controls to achieve the related control objectives. The Type II report states that internal controls at the service organizations are properly designed and operating effectively. The Type I and the Type II reports are an essential part of the ISO/IEC 27001 dealing with information technology, security techniques, and information security management systems requirements.

**Types of evidence**   The types of evidence required to be admissible in a court of law to prove the truth or falsity of a given fact include the best evidence rule (primary evidence that is natural and in writing), oral testimony from a witness (secondary and direct evidence), physical evidence (tools and equipment), Change to circumstantial evidence based on logical inference (introduction of a defendant's fingerprint or DNA sample), corroborative evidence (oral evidence consistent with a written document), authentication of records and their contents, demonstrative evidence (charts and models), and documentary evidence such as business records produced in the regular course of business (purchase orders and sales orders).

# U

**UMTS subscriber identity module (USIM)**   A module similar to the SIM in GSM/GPRS networks, but with additional capabilities suited to third-generation networks.

**Unauthorized access**   A person gains logical or physical access without permission to a network, system, application, data, or other IT resource.

**Uncertainty**   The probability of experiencing a loss as a consequence of a threat event. A risk event that is an identifiable uncertainty is termed as known unknown.

**Unclassified information**   Any information that doesn't need to be safeguarded against disclosure but must be safeguarded against tampering, destruction, or loss due to record value, utility, replacement cost, or susceptibility to fraud, waste, or abuse.

**Unified modeling language (UML)**   Activities related to the industry-standard unified modeling language (UML) for specifying, visualizing, constructing, and documenting the artifacts of software systems. It simplifies the complex process of software design, making a "blueprint" for construction.

**Uniform resource locator (URL)**   It is the global address of documents and other resources on the World Wide Web. The first part of the address indicates what protocol to use, and the second part specifies the IP address or the domain name where the resource is located.

**Unit testing**   Focuses on testing individual program modules, and is a part of white-box testing technique. Program modules are collections of program instructions sufficient to accomplish a single, specific logical function.

**Universal description, discovery, and integration (UDDI)**   An XML-based lookup service for locating Web services in an Internet topology. UDDI provides a platform-independent way of describing and discovering Web services and the Web service providers. The UDDI data structures provide a framework for the description of basic service information, and an extensible mechanism to specify detailed service access information using any standard description language. UDDI is a single point-of-failure.

**Universal mobile telecommunications system (UMTS)**   A third-generation mobile phone technology standardized by the 3GPP as the successor to GSM.

**Universal serial bus (USB)**   A hardware interface for low-cost and low-speed peripherals such as the keyboard, mouse, joystick, scanner, printer, and telephony devices.

**Unrecoverable bit error rate (UBE)**   The rate at which a disk drive is unable to recover data after application of cyclic redundancy check (CRC) codes and multiple retries.

**Update (patch)**   An update (sometimes called a "patch") is a "repair" for a piece of software (application or operating system). During a piece of a software's life, problems (called bugs) will almost invariably be found. A patch is the immediate solution that is provided to users; it can sometimes be downloaded from the software vendor's website. The patch is not necessarily the best solution for the problem, and the product developers often find a better solution to provide when they package the product for its next release. A patch is usually developed and distributed as a replacement for or an insertion in compiled code (that is, in a binary file or object module). In larger operating systems, a special program is provided to manage and keep track of the installation of patches.

**Upgrade**   A new version of an operating system, application, or other software.

**Usability**   A set of attributes that bear on the effort needed for use, and on the individual assessment of such use, by a stated or implied set of users.

**User**   An individual, system, or a process authorized to access an information system by directly interacting with a computer system.

**User authentication**   User authentication can be achieved with either secret or public key cryptography. Creating a one-time password is an example of achieving user authentication and increasing security.

**User-based threats**   Examples include attackers using social engineering and phishing attacks, where the attackers try to trick users into accessing a fake website and divulging personal information. In some phishing attacks, users receive a legitimate-looking e-mail asking them to update their information on the company's website. Instead of legitimate links, however, the URLs in the e-mail actually point to a rogue website.

**User datagram protocol (UDP)**   A commonly used transport layer protocol of the TCP/IP suite. It is a connectionless service without error correction or retransmission of misordered or lost packets. It is easier to spoof UDP packets than TCP packets, because there is no initial connection setup (handshake) involved between the two connected systems. Thus, there is a higher risk associated with UDP-based services.

**User-directed access control**   Access control in which users (or subjects generally) may alter the access rights. Such alterations may be restricted to certain individuals approved by the owner of an object.

**User entitlement**   Occurs when a user can access a system's resources that he is authorized to access, no more or no less. It assumes that users have certain rights, obligations, and limitations and that they must adhere to the rules of behavior (ROB) at all times in order to keep their entitlement in honesty and integrity. For example, internal users must not misuse or abuse their access rights because they can modify data and cause damage to computer systems and IT assets similar to hackers.

User entitlement operates based on the principles of access control lists, access profiles, access levels, and access types (read, write, execute, append, modify, delete, or create), and access accountability. Users must understand the user entitlement rules, which are follows:

➤ Users are assigned with specific roles and de-roles based on their job duties and responsibilities

➤ User capabilities are revoked from roles and as such are revoked from users

➤ Objects can be assigned to object groups based on secrecy levels of the objects

➤ Object groups are organized according to the business functions of an organization

**User ID**   A unique symbol or character string used by a system to identify a specific user.

**User interface**   A combination of menus, screen design, keyboard commands, command language, and help screens that together create the way a user interacts with a computer. Hardware, such as a mouse or touch screen, is also included. Synonymous with graphical user interface (GUI).

**User profile**   Patterns of a user's activity used to detect changes in normal routines.

**Utility computing**   Based on the concept of "pay and use" with regards to computing power in the form of computations, storage, and Web-based services, similar to public utilities (such as, gas, water, and electricity). Utility computing is provided through "on demand" computing and supports cloud computing, grid computing, and distributed computing (Wikipedia).

**Utility program**   (1) A computer program that supports the operation of a computer. Utility programs provide file management capabilities, such as sorting, copying, archiving, comparing, listing, and searching, as well as diagnostic routines that check the health of the computer system. It also includes compilers or software that translates a programming language into machine language. (2) A computer program or routine that performs general data and system-related functions required by other application software, the operating system, or users. Examples include copy, sort, or merge files. (3) It is a program that performs a specific task for an information system, such as managing a disk drive or printer.

# V

**Valid password**   A personal password that authenticates the identity of an individual when presented to a password system or an access password that allows the requested access when presented to a password system.

**Validation**   (1) The performance of tests and evaluations in order to determine compliance with security specifications and requirements. (2) The process of evaluating a system or component (including software) during or at the end of the development process to determine whether it satisfies specified requirements. (3) The process of demonstrating that the system under consideration meets all respects the specification of that system.

**Value-added network (VAN)**   A network of computers owned or controlled by a single entity used for data transmission (e.g., EDI and EFT), electronic mail, information retrieval, and other functions by subscribers. EDI can be VAN-based or Web-based.

**Variable minimization**    A method of reducing the number of variables which a subject has access, not exceeding the minimum required, thereby reducing the risk of malicious or erroneous actions by that subject. This concept can be generalized to include data minimization.

**Vendor governance**    Requires a vendor to establish written policies, procedures, standards, and guidelines regarding how to deal with its customers or clients in a professional and business-like manner. It also requires establishing an oversight mechanism and implementing best practices in the industry. Customer (user) organizations should consider the following criteria when selecting potential hardware, software, consulting, or contracting vendors.

➤ Experience in producing or delivering high quality security products and services on-time and all the time

➤ A track-record in responding to security flaws in vendor products, project management skills, and cost and budget controls

➤ Methods to handle software and hardware maintenance, end-user support, and maintenance agreements

➤ The vendor's long-term financial, operational, and strategic viability

➤ Adherence to rules of engagement (ROE) during contractual agreements, procurement processes, and red team testing

**Verification**    (1) The process of comparing two levels of system specification for proper correspondence (e.g., security policy models with top-level specification, top-level specification with source code, or source code with object code). (2) The process of evaluating a system or component (including software) to determine whether the products of a given development process satisfy the requirements imposed at the start of that process. This process may or may not be automated. (3) The process of affirming that a claimed identity is correct by comparing the offered claims of identity with previously proven information stored in the identity card.

**Verified name**    A subscriber name that has been verified by identity proofing.

**Verifier**    (1) An entity that verifies the authenticity of a digital signature using the public key. (2) An entity that verifies the claimant's identity by verifying the claimant's possession of a token using an authentication protocol. To do this, the verifier may also need to validate credentials that link the token and identity and check their status. A verifier includes the functions necessary for engaging in authentication exchanges.

**Verifier impersonation attack**    A scenario where an attacker impersonates the verifier in an authentication protocol, usually to capture information (e.g., password) that can be used to masquerade as that claimant to the real verifier.

**Version (configuration management)**    It is a change to a baseline configuration item that modifies its functional capabilities. As functional capabilities are added to, modified within, or deleted from a baseline configuration item, its version identifier changes. Note that baselining is first and versioning is next.

**Version (software)**    A new release of commercial software reflecting major changes made in functions.

**Version control**    A mechanism that allows distinct versions of an object to be identified and associated with independent attributes in a well-defined manner.

**Version scanning**   The process of identifying the service application and application version in use.

**Victim**   A machine or a person that is attacked.

**Virtual disk encryption**   The process of encrypting a container, which can hold many files and folders, and permitting access to the data within the container only after proper authentication is provided. A container is a file encompassing and protecting other files.

**Virtual local-area network (VLAN)**   A network configuration in which frames are broadcast within the VLAN and routed between VLANs. VLANs separate the logical topology of the LANs from their physical topology.

**Virtual machine (VM)**   Software that allows a single host to run one or more guest operating systems.

**Virtual network perimeter**   A network that appears to be a single protected network behind firewalls, which actually encompasses encrypted virtual links over untrusted networks.

**Virtual password**   A password computed from a passphrase that meets the requirements of password storage.

**Virtual private dial network (VPDN)**   A virtual private network (VPN) tailored specifically for dial-up access.

**Virtual private network (VPN)**   (1) It is used for highly confidential data transmission. (2) It is an Internet Protocol (IP) connection between two sites over a public IP network so that only source and destination nodes can decrypt the traffic packets. (3) A means by which certain authorized individuals (such as remote employees) can gain secure access to an organization's intranet by means of an extranet (a part of the internal network that is accessible via the Internet). (4) A tunnel that connects the teleworker's computer to the organization's network. (5) A virtual network, built on top of an existing physical network that provides a secure communications tunnel for data and other information transmitted between networks. (6) VPN is used to securely connect two networks or a network and a client system, over an insecure network such as the Internet. (7) A VPN typically employs encryption to secure the connection. (8) It is a protected information system link utilizing tunneling, security controls, and endpoint address translation giving the impression of a dedicated (leased) line. (9) A VPN is a logical network that is established, at the application layer of the open systems interconnection (OSI) model, over an existing physical network and typically does not include every node present on the physical network. Authorized users are granted access to the logical network. For example, there are a number of systems that enable one to create networks using the Internet as the medium for transporting data. These systems use encryption and other security mechanisms to ensure that only authorized users can access the network and that the data cannot be intercepted.

**Virtual (pure-play) organizations**   Organizations that conduct their business activities solely online through the Internet.

**Virtualization**   The simulation of the software and/or hardware upon which other software runs using virtual machine. It allows organizations to reduce costs by running multiple Web servers on a single host computer and by providing a mechanism for quickly responding to attacks against a Web server. There are several concepts in virtualization such as application virtualization, bare metal (native) virtualization, full virtualization, hosted virtualization, operating system virtualization, para-virtualization, and tape virtualization.

**Virus**  (1) It is a self-replicating computer program that runs and spreads by modifying other programs or files. (2) It is a malware computer program form that can copy itself and infect a computer without permission or knowledge of the user. A virus might corrupt or delete data on a computer, use e-mail programs to spread itself to other computers, or even erase everything on a hard disk. It is similar to a Trojan horse insofar as it is a program that hides within a program or data file and performs some unwanted function when activated. The main difference is that a virus can replicate by attaching a copy of itself to other programs or files, and may trigger an additional "payload" when specific conditions are met.

**Virus hoax**  An urgent warning message about a nonexistent virus.

**Virus signature**  Alternations to files or applications indicating the presence of a virus, detectable by virus scanning software.

**Virus trigger**  A condition that causes a virus payload to be executed, usually occurring through user interaction (e.g., opening a file, running a program, and clicking on an e-mail file attachment).

**Voice over Internet Protocol (VoIP)**  It is the transmission of voice over packet-switched IP networks used in traditional telephone handsets, conferencing units, and mobile units.

**Volatile memory**  Memory that loses its content when power is turned off or lost.

**Volatile security controls**  Measure how frequently a control is likely to change over time subsequent to its implementation. These controls should be assessed and monitored more frequently, and examples include configuration management family (for example, configuration settings, software patches, and system component inventory). This is because system configurations experience high rates of change, and unauthorized or unanalyzed changes in the system configuration often render the system vulnerable to exploits.

**Volume encryption**  The process of encrypting an entire volume, which is a logical unit of storage composing a file system, and permitting access to the data on the volume only after proper authentication is provided.

**Vulnerability**  Flaws or weaknesses in an information system; system security policies and procedures; hardware, system design, and system implementation procedures; internal controls; technical controls; operational controls; and management controls that could be accidentally triggered or intentionally exploited by a threat-source and result in a violation of the system's security policy. Note that vulnerabilities lead to threats that, in turn, lead to risks. Vulnerabilities ⇨ Threats ⇨ Risks.

**Vulnerability analysis**  The systematic examination of systems in order to determine the adequacy of security measures, to identify security deficiencies, and to provide data from which to predict the effectiveness of proposed security measures. Vulnerability analysis should be performed first followed by threat analysis because vulnerabilities ⇨ threats ⇨ risks.

**Vulnerability assessment**  (1) A formal description and evaluation of the vulnerabilities in an information system. (2) It is a systematic examination of the ability of a system or application, including current security procedures and controls to withstand assault. (3) A vulnerability assessment may be used to (i) identify weaknesses that would be exploited, (ii) predict the effectiveness of proposed security measures in protecting information resources from attack, and (iii) confirm the adequacy of such measures after implementation.

**Vulnerability audit**   The process of identifying and documenting specific vulnerabilities in critical information systems.

**Vulnerability database**   A security exposure in an operating system or other system software or application software component. A variety of organizations maintain publicly accessible databases of vulnerabilities based on the version number of the software. Each vulnerability can potentially compromise the system or network if exploited.

**Vulnerability scanning tool**   A technique used to identify hosts and host attributes, and then to identify the associated vulnerabilities.

# W

**Walk throughs**   A project management technique or procedure where the programmer, project team leader, functional users, system analyst, or manager reviews system requirements, design, and programming and test plans and design specifications and program code. The objectives are to (1) prevent errors in logic and misinterpretation of user requirements, design and program specifications and (2) prevent omissions. It is a management and detective control. In a system walkthrough, for example, functional users and IS staff together can review the design or program specifications, program code, test plans, and test cases to detect omissions or errors and to eliminate misinterpretation of system or user requirements. System walkthroughs can also occur within and among colleagues in the IS and system user departments. It costs less to correct omissions and errors in the early stages of system development than it does later. This technique can be applied to both system development and system maintenance.

**War dialing**   It involves calling a large group of phone numbers to detect active modems or PBXs.

**War driving**   When attackers and other malicious parties drive around office parks and neighborhoods with laptop computers equipped with wireless network cards in an attempt to connect to open network points is called war driving.

**Warez**   A term widely used by hackers to denote illegally copied and distributed commercial software from which all copy protection has been removed. Warez often contains viruses, Trojan horses, and other malicious code, and thus is very risky to download and use (legal issues notwithstanding).

**Warm-site**   An environmentally conditioned workspace that is partially equipped with IT information systems and telecommunications equipment to support relocated IT operations in the event of a significant disruption.

**Warm start**   A restart that allows reuse of previously initialized input and output work queues. It is synonymous with system restart, initial program load, and quick start.

**Waterfall model**   A traditional system development model, which takes a linear and sequential view of developing an application system. This model will not bring the operational viewpoint to the requirements phase until the system is completely implemented.

**Watermarking**   A type of marking that embeds copyright information about the copyright owner.

**Wavelength division multiple access (WDMA) protocol**   The WDMA protocol is an example of medium/media access control (MAC) sublayer protocol that contains two channels for each station.

A narrow channel is provided as a control channel to signal the station, and a wide channel is provided so that the station can output data frames.

**Weakly bound credentials**   Weakly bound credentials (e.g., unencrypted password files) require additional integrity protection or access controls to ensure that unauthorized parties cannot spoof and/or tamper with the binding of the identity to the token representation within the credential.

**Weakness**   A piece of code that may lead to vulnerability.

**Weakness suppression system**   A feature that permits the user to a flag a line of code not to be reported by the tool in subsequent scans.

**Web 2.0**   The second-generation of Internet-based services that let people collaborate and create information online in new ways, such as social networking sites, wikis, and communication tools.

**Web administrator**   The Web equivalent of a system administrator. Web administrators are system architects responsible for the overall design, implementation, and maintenance of a Web server. They may or may not be responsible for Web content, which is traditionally the purview of the Webmaster.

**Web-based threats**   Examples include security assertions markup language (SAML) threats and extensible markup language (XML) threats. Examples of SAML threats include assertion manufacture, modification, disclosure, repudiation, redirect, reuse, and substitution. Examples of XML threats include dictionary attacks, DoS attacks, SQL command injection attacks, confidentiality and integrity attacks, and XML injection attacks.

**Web browser**   Client software used to view Web content, which includes the graphical user interface (GUI), MIME helper applications, language and byte code Java interpreters, and other similar program components.

**Web browser plug-in**   A mechanism for displaying or executing certain types of content through a Web browser.

**Web bug**   (1) A tiny image, invisible to a user, placed on Web pages in such a way to enable third parties to track use of Web servers and collect information about the user, including IP address, host name, browser type and version, operating system name and version, and Web browser cookies. (2) It is a tiny graphic on a website that is referenced within the hypertext markup language (HTML) content of a Web page or e-mail to collect information about the user viewing the HTML content.

**Web content filtering software**   A program that prevents access to undesirable websites, typically by comparing a requested website address to a list of known bad websites with the help of blacklists.

**Web documents**   Forms and interactive Web pages are created using hypertext markup language (HTML). XML can replace HTML.

**Webmaster**   A person responsible for the implementation of a website. Webmasters must be proficient in hypertext markup language (HTML) and one or more scripting and interface languages, such as JavaScript and Perl. They may or may not be responsible for the underlying server, which is traditionally the responsibility of the Web server administrator.

**Web mining**   Data mining techniques for discovering and extracting information from Web documents. Web mining explores both Web content and Web usage.

**Web-oriented architecture (WOA)**    A set of Web protocols (e.g., HTTP and plain XML) to provide dynamic, scalable, and interoperable Web services.

**Web portal**    Provides a single point of entry into the service-oriented architecture (SOA) for requester entities, enabling them to access Web services transparently from any device at virtually any location.

**Web server**    A computer that provides World Wide Web (WWW) services on the Internet. It includes the hardware, operating system, Web server software, transmission control protocol/Internet protocol (TCP/IP), and the website content (Web pages). If the Web server is used internally and not by the public, it may be known as an "intranet server."

**Web server administrator**    The Web server equivalent of a system administrator. Web server administrators are system architects responsible for the overall design, implementation, and maintenance of Web servers. They may or may not be responsible for Web content, which is traditionally the responsibility of the Webmaster.

**Web service**    A software component or system designed to support interoperable machine or application-oriented interaction over a network. A Web service has an interface described in a machine-processable format (specifically services description language WSDL). Other systems interact with the Web service in a manner prescribed by its description using SOAP messages, typically conveyed using HTTP with an XML serialization in conjunction with other Web-related standards.

**Web service interoperability (WS-I) basic profile**    A set of standards and clarifications to standards that vendors must follow for basic interoperability with SOAP products.

**Web services description language (WSDL)**    An XML format for describing network services as a set of endpoints operating on messages containing either document-oriented or procedure-oriented information. WSDL complements the universal description, discovery, and integration (UDDI) standard by providing a uniform way of describing the abstract interface and protocol bindings and deployment details of arbitrary network services.

**Web services security (WS-Security)**    A mechanism for incorporating security information into SOAP messages. WS-Security uses binary tokens for authentication, digital signatures for integrity, and content-level encryption for confidentiality.

**White box testing**    A test methodology that assumes explicit and substantial knowledge of the internal structure and implementation detail of the assessment object. It focuses on the internal behavior of a system (program structure and logic) and uses the code itself to generate test cases. The degree of coverage is used as a measure of the completeness of the test cases and test effort. White box testing is performed at individual components level, such as program or module, but not at the entire system level. It is also known as detailed testing or logic testing, and should be combined with black box testing for maximum benefit because neither one by itself does a thorough testing job. White box testing is structural analysis of a system. Comprehensive testing is also known as white box testing.

**White noise**    A distribution of a uniform spectrum of random electrical signals so that an intruder cannot decipher real data from random (noise) data due to use of constant bandwidth. White noise is a good security control to prevent electromagnetic radiations (emanations).

**White team**    A neutral team of employees acting as observers, referees, and judges between a red team of mock attackers (offenders) and a blue team of actual defenders of their enterprise's use of information systems. The white team establishes rules of engagement (ROE) and performance metrics for security tests. The white team is also responsible for deriving lessons-learned, conducting the post engagement assessment, and communicating results to management. Occasionally, the white team also performs incident response activities and addresses bot attacks on an emergency basis.

**Whitelisting**   (1) Whitelisting is a method for controlling the installation of software by ensuring that all software is checked against a list approved by the organization, (2) Whitelisting technology only allows known good applications and does not allow any new or unknown exploits to access a system, (3) A list of discrete entities, such as hosts or applications that are known to be benign, and (4) A list of e-mail senders known to be benign, such as a user's coworkers, friends, and family. Synonymous with whitelists.

**Whole disk encryption**   The process of encrypting all the data on the hard drive used to boot a computer, including the computer's operating system, and permitting access to the data only after successful authentication with the full disk encryption product. It is also called full disk encryption (FDE).

**Wide-area network (WAN)**   (1) A communications network that connects geographically separated areas. It can cover several sites that are geographically distant. A WAN may span different cities or even different continents. (2) A network concept to link business operations and computers used across geographical locations. (3) A data communications network that spans any distance and is usually provided by a public carrier. Users gain access to the two ends of the network circuit and the carrier handles the transmission and other services in between. WANs are switched networks, meaning they use routers.

**Wi-FI protected access 2 (WPA2)**   WPA2 is an implementation of the IEEE 80211i security standard, and its security is better than that of WEP.

**Wiki**   A collaborative website where visitors can add, delete, or modify content, including the work of previous authors.

**WiMAX**   A wireless standard (IEEE 802.16) for making broadband network connections over a medium-sized area such as a city for wireless MANs. WiMAX stands for Worldwide Interoperability for Microwave Access.

**Wired Equivalent Privacy (WEP)**   A security protocol for wireless local-area networks (WLANs) defined in the 802.11b standard. WEP was intended to provide the same level of security as that of a wired LAN. LANs are inherently more secure than WLANs because LANs have some or the entire network inside a building that can be protected from unauthorized access. WLANs, which are over radio waves, therefore are more vulnerable to tampering. WEP attempted to provide security by encrypting data over radio waves so that it is protected as it is transmitted from one endpoint to another. NOTE: WEP has been broken and does not provide an effective security service against a knowledgeable attacker. Software to break WEP is freely available on the Internet.

**Wireless Access Point (WAP)**   It is a device that acts as a conduit to connect wireless communication devices together to allow them to communicate and create a wireless network.

**Wireless application protocol**   A standard for providing cellular telephones, pagers, and other handheld devices with secure access to e-mail and text-based Web pages. It is a standard that defines the way in which Internet communications and other advanced services are provided on wireless mobile devices. It is a suite of network protocols designed to enable different types of wireless devices to access files on an Internet-connected Web server.

**Wireless fidelity (Wi-Fi)** Wi-Fi is a term describing a wireless local-area network (WLAN) that observes the IEEE 802.11 family of wireless networking standards.

**Wireless intrusion detection and prevention system (WIDPS)** An intrusion detection and prevention system (IDPS) that monitors wireless network traffic and analyzes its wireless networking protocols to identify and stop suspicious activity involving the protocols themselves.

**Wireless local-area network (WLAN)** A type of local-area network that uses high-frequency radio waves rather than wires to communicate between nodes. WLAN uses the IEEE 802.11 standard. Specifically, wireless LANs operate with transmission modes such as infrared, spread spectrum schemes, a multichannel frequency division multiplexing (FDM) system, and CSMA/CA. WLAN is a telecommunications network that enables users to make short-range wireless connections to the Internet or another network such as wireless MAN or wireless WAN.

**Wireless Markup Language (WML)** A scripting language used to create content in the wireless application protocol (WAP) environment. WML is based on XML minus unnecessary content to increase speed.

**Wireless metropolitan-area network (WMAN)** Wireless MANs are broadband systems that use radio to replace the telephone connections. WMAN is a telecommunications network that enables users to make medium-range wireless connections to the Internet or another network such as wireless LAN or wireless WAN. WMAN uses the IEEE 802.16 standard (WiMAX) and quality of service (QoS) is important.

**Wireless personal-area networks (WPANs)** They are small-scale wireless networks that require no infrastructure to operate (e.g., Bluetooth). They are typically used by a few devices in a single room to communicate without the need to physically connect devices with cables. WPAN uses the IEEE 802.15 standard.

**Wireless Robust Security Network (RSN)** A robust security network (RSN) is defined as a wireless security network that allows the creation of RSN associations (RSNA) only. RSNAs are wireless connections that provide moderate to high levels of assurance against WLAN security threats through the use of a variety of cryptographic techniques. Wireless RSN uses the IEEE 802.11i standard.

**Wireless Sensor Network (WSN)** Wireless sensor network (WSN) is a collection of interconnected wireless devices that are embedded into the physical environment to provide measurements of many points over large space. The WSN can be used to establish building security perimeters and to monitor environmental changes (e.g., temperature and power) in a building.

**Wireless wide-area network (WWAN)** A telecommunications network that offers wireless coverage over a large geographical area, typically over a cellular phone network.

**Wiretapping** (1) The collection of transmitted voice or data and the sending of that data to a listening device. (2) Cutting in on a communications line to get information. Two types of wiretapping exist: active and passive. Active wiretapping is the attaching of an unauthorized device, such as a computer terminal, to a communications circuit for the purpose of obtaining access to data through the generation of false messages or control signals or by altering the communications of legitimate users. Passive wiretapping is the monitoring and/or recording of data transmitted over a communication link.

**Work factor** The amount of work necessary for an attacker to break the system or network should exceed the value that the attacker would gain from a successful compromise.

**Workflow Management System (WFMS)** A computerized information system that is responsible for scheduling and synchronizing the various tasks within the workflow, in accordance with specified task dependencies, and for sending each task to the respective processing entity (e.g., Web server or database server). The data resources that a task uses are called work items. WFMS is the basis for work flow policy access control system.

**Workflow manager** The sub-component that enables one component to access services on other components to complete its own processing in a service-oriented architecture (SOA). The workflow manager determines which external component services must be executed and manages the order of service execution.

**Workstation** (1) A piece of computer hardware operated by a user to perform an application. Provides users with access to the distributed information system or other dedicated systems; input/output via a keyboard and video display terminal; or any method that supplies the user with the required input/output capability. Computer power embodied within the workstation may be used to furnish data processing capability at the user level. (2) A high-powered PC with multifunctions and connected to the host computer.

**World Wide Web (WWW)** A system of Internet hosts that support documents formatted in HTML, which contains links to other documents (hyperlinks), and to audio and graphics images. Users can access the Web with special applications called browsers (e.g., Netscape and Internet Explorer).

**Worm** A self-replicating and self-contained program that propagates (spreads) itself through a network into other computer systems without requiring a host program or any user intervention to replicate.

**Write** A fundamental operation that results only in the flow of information from a subject to an object.

**Write access** Permission to write an object.

**Write blocker** A device that allows investigators to examine media while preventing data writes from occurring on the subject media.

**Write protection** Hardware or software methods of preventing data from being written to a disk or other medium.

# X

**X3.93** Used for data encryption algorithm (All standards starting with X belong to International Organization for Standards ISO).

**X9.9** Used for message authentication.

**X9.17** Used for cryptographic key management (Financial Institution Key Management).

**X9.30** Used for digital signature algorithm (DSA) and the secure hash algorithm (SHA-1).

**X9.31** Used for rDSA signature algorithm.

**X9.42** Used for agreement of symmetric keys using discrete logarithm cryptography.

**X9.44** Used for the transport of symmetric algorithm keys using reversible public key cryptography.

**X9.52**   Used for triple data encryption algorithm (TDEA).

**X9.62**   Used for elliptic curve digital signature algorithm.

**X9.63**   Used for key agreement and key transport using elliptic curve-based cryptography.

**X9.66**   Used for cryptography device security.

**X12**   Defines EDI standards for many U.S. industries (e.g., healthcare and insurance).

**X.21**   Defines the interface between terminal equipment and public data networks.

**X.25**   A standard for the network and data link levels of a communications network. It is a WAN protocol.

**X.75**   A standard that defines ways of connecting two X.25 networks.

**X.121**   Network user address used in X.25 communications.

**X.400**   Used in e-mail as a message handling protocol for reformatting and sending e-mails.

**X.500**   A standard protocol used in electronic directory services.

**X.509**   A standard protocol used in digital certificates and defines the format of a public key certificate.

**X.800**   Used as a network security standard.

**X. 509 certificate**   Two types of X.509 certificates exist: The X.509 public key certificate (most commonly used) and The X.509 attribute certificate (less commonly used). The X.509 public key certificate is created with the public key for a user (or device) and a name for the user (or device), together with optional information, is rendered unforgeable by the digital signature of the certification authority (CA) that issued the certificate, and is encoded and formatted according to the X.509 standard. The X.509 public key certificate contains three nested elements: (1) the tamper-evident envelope, which is digitally signed by the source, (2) the basic certificate content (e.g., identifying information about a user or device and public key), and (3) extensions that contain optional certificate information.

**XACML**   Extensible access control markup language (XACML) combined with extensible markup language (XML) access control policy is a framework that provides a general-purpose language for specifying distributed access control policies.

**XDSL**   Digital subscriber line is a group of broadband technology connecting home/business telephone lines to an Internet service provider's (ISP's) central office. Several variations of XDSL exist such as SDSL, ADSL, IDSL, and HDSL.

**XHTML**   Extended hypertext markup language (XHTML) is a unifying standard that brings the benefits of XML to those of HTML. XHTML is the new Web standard and should be used for all new Web pages to achieve maximum portability across platforms and browsers.

**XML**   Extensible markup language, which is a meta-language, is a flexible text format designed to describe data for electronic publishing. The Web browser interprets the XML, and the XML is taking over the HTML for creating dynamic Web documents.

**XML encryption**   A process/mechanism for encrypting and decrypting XML documents or parts of documents.

**XML gateways**   XML gateways provide sophisticated authentication and authorization services, potentially improving the security of the Web service by having all simple object access protocol (SOAP) messages pass through a hardened gateway before reaching any of the custom-developed code. XML gateways can restrict access based on source, destination, or WS-Security authentication tokens.

**XML schema**   A language for describing and defining the structure, content, and semantics of XML documents.

**XML signature**   A mechanism for ensuring the origin and integrity of XML documents. XML signatures provide integrity, message authentication, or signer authentication services for data of any type, whether located within the XML that includes the signature or elsewhere.

**XOR**   Exclusive OR, which is a Boolean operation, dealing with true or false condition (that is, something is either true or false but not both). It is the bitwise addition, modulo2, of two bit strings of equal length. For example, XOR is central to how parity data in RAID levels is created and used within a disk array (that is, yes parity or no parity). It is used for the protection of data and for the recovery of missing data.

**XOT**   X.25 over transmission control protocol (TCP).

**XPath**   Used to define the parts of an XML document, using path expressions.

**XQuery**   Provides functionality to query an XML document.

**XSL**   Extensible style language (XSL) file is used in dynamic content generation where Web pages can be written in XML and then converted to HTML.

# Z

**Zero-day attacks**   A zero-day attack or threat is a computer threat that tries to exploit computer application vulnerabilities that are unknown to others, undisclosed to the software vendor, or for which no security fix is available. Zero-day attacks, exploits, and incidents are the same.

**Zero-day backup**   Similar to normal or full backup where it archives all selected files and marks each as having been backed up. An advantage of this method is the fastest restore operation because it contains the most recent files. A disadvantage is that it takes the longest time to perform the backup.

**Zero-day exploits**   Zero-day exploits (actual code that can use a security vulnerability to carry out an attack) are used or shared by attackers before the software vendor knows about the vulnerability. Zero-day attacks, exploits, and incidents are the same.

**Zero-day incidents**   Zero-day incidents are attacks through previously unknown weaknesses in computer networks. Zero-day attacks, exploits, and incidents are the same.

**Zero day warez**   Zero day warez (negative day) refers to software, games, videos, music, or data unlawfully released or obtained on the day of public release. Either a hacker or an employee of the releasing company is involved in copying on the day of the official release.

**Zero fill**   To fill unused storage locations in an information system with the representation of the character denoting "0."

**Zero-knowledge proof**   One party proving something to another without revealing any additional information. This proof has applications in public-key encryption and smart card implementations.

**Zero-knowledge password protocol**   A password based authentication protocol that allows a claimant to authenticate to a verifier without revealing the password to the verifier. Examples of such protocols include EKE, SPEKE, and SRP.

**Zero quantum theory**   Zero quantum theory is based on the principles of quantum-mechanics where eavesdroppers can alter the quantum state of the cryptographic system.

**Zeroize**   To remove or eliminate the key from a cryptographic equipment or fill device.

**Zeroization**   A method of erasing electronically stored data, cryptographic keys, credentials service providers (CSPs), and initialization vectors by altering or deleting the contents of the data storage to prevent recovery of the data.

**Zipf's law**   Applicable to storage management using video servers, where videos can be stored hierarchically in tape (low capacity) to DVD, magnetic disk, and RAM (high capacity). The Zipf's law states that the most popular movie is seven times as popular as the number seventh movie, which can help in planning the storage space. An alternative to tape is optical storage.

**Zombie**   A computer program that is installed on a system to cause it to attack other computer systems in a chain-like manner.

**Zone drift error**   A zone drift error results in incorrect zone data at the secondary name servers when there is a mismatch of data between the primary and secondary name servers. The zone drift error is a threat due to domain name system (DNS) data contents.

**Zone file**   The primary type of domain name system (DNS) data is zone file, which contains information about various resources in that zone.

**Zone of control**   Three-dimensional space (expressed in feet of radius) surrounding equipment that processes classified and/or sensitive information within which TEMPEST exploitation is not considered practical. It also means legal authorities can identify and remove a potential TEMPEST exploitation.

Control zone deals with physical security over sensitive equipment containing sensitive information. It is synonymous with control zone.

**Zone signing key (ZSK)**   A zone signing key is an authentication key that corresponds to a private key used to sign a zone.

**Zone transfer**   Zone transfer is a part of domain name system (DNS) transactions. Zone transfer refers to the way a secondary (slave) name server refreshes the entire contents of its zone file from the primary (master) name server.

# SOURCES AND REFERENCES

"Assessment of Access Control Systems (NIST IR7316)," National Institute of Standards and Technology (NIST), U.S. Department of Commerce, Gaithersburg, Maryland, September 2006.

"Border Gateway Protocol Security (NIST SP 800-54)," National Institute of Standards and Technology (NIST), U.S. Department of Commerce, Gaithersburg, Maryland, June 2007.

"Computer Security Incident Handling Guide (NIST SP 800-61 Revision 1)," National Institute of Standards and Technology (NIST), U.S. Department of Commerce, Gaithersburg, Maryland, March 2008.

"Contingency Planning Guide for IT Systems (NIST SP 800-34)," National Institute of Standards and Technology (NIST), U.S. Department of Commerce, Gaithersburg, Maryland, June 2002.

"Digital Signature Standard –DSS (NIST FIPS PUB 186-3)," National Institute of Standards and Technology (NIST), U.S. Department of Commerce, Gaithersburg, Maryland, June 2009.

"Electronic Authentication Guidelines (NIST SP800-63-1 Draft)," National Institute of Standards and Technology (NIST), U.S. Department of Commerce, Gaithersburg, Maryland, December 2008.

"A Framework for Designing Cryptographic Key Management Systems (NIST SP800-130 Draft)," National Institute of Standards and Technology (NIST), U.S. Department of Commerce, Gaithersburg, Maryland, June 2010.

"Glossary of Key Information Security Terms" (NIST IR 7298 Revision 1), National Institute of Standards and Technology (NIST), U.S. Department of Commerce, Gaithersburg, Maryland, February 2011.

"Guide for Assessing the Security Controls in Federal Information Systems (NIST SP 800-53A)," National Institute of Standards and Technology (NIST), U.S. Department of Commerce, Gaithersburg, Maryland, July 2008.

"Guide to Enterprise Telework and Remote Access Security (NIST SP800-46 R1)," National Institute of Standards and Technology (NIST), U.S. Department of Commerce, Gaithersburg, Maryland, June 2009.

"Guide to Intrusion Detection and Prevention Systems, IDPS, (NIST SP 800-94)," National Institute of Standards and Technology (NIST), U.S. Department of Commerce, Gaithersburg, Maryland, February 2007.

"Guide to Secure Web Services (NIST SP 800-95)," National Institute of Standards and Technology (NIST), U.S. Department of Commerce, Gaithersburg, Maryland, August 2007.

"Guide to SSL VPNs (NIST SP 800-113 Draft)," National Institute of Standards and Technology (NIST), U.S. Department of Commerce, Gaithersburg, Maryland, August 2007.

"Guide to Storage Encryption Technologies for End User Devices (NIST SP 800-111 Draft)," National Institute of Standards and Technology (NIST), U.S. Department of Commerce, Gaithersburg, Maryland, August 2007.

"Guidelines on Cell Phone Forensics (NIST SP 800-101)," National Institute of Standards and Technology (NIST), U.S. Department of Commerce, Gaithersburg, Maryland, May 2007.

"Guidelines on Cell Phone and PDA Security (NIST SP800-124)," National Institute of Standards and Technology (NIST), U.S. Department of Commerce, Gaithersburg, Maryland, October 2008.

"Guidelines on Electronic Mail Security (NIST SP 800-45, Version 2)," National Institute of Standards and Technology (NIST), U.S. Department of Commerce, Gaithersburg, Maryland, February 2007.

"Guidelines on Firewalls and Firewall Policy (NIST SP 800-41 Revision 1)," National Institute of Standards and Technology (NIST), U.S. Department of Commerce, Gaithersburg, Maryland, September 2009.

"Guidelines on Security and Privacy in Public Cloud Computing (NIST SP 800-144 Draft)," National Institute of Standards and Technology (NIST), U.S. Department of Commerce, Gaithersburg, Maryland, January 2011.

"Information Assurance Technical Framework (IATF)," National Security Agency (NSA), Release 3.1, Fort Meade, Maryland, September 2002.

"Information Security Continuous Monitoring for Federal Information Systems and Organizations (NIST SP800-137 Draft)," National Institute of Standards and Technology (NIST), U.S. Department of Commerce, Gaithersburg, Maryland, December 2010.

"The Institute of Electrical and Electronics Engineers, Inc.," IEEE Standard 802-2001, New York, New York, Copyright 2002.

"Institute of Standards and Technology (NIST)," U.S. Department of Commerce, Gaithersburg, Maryland, June 2010.

"Managing Information Security Risk (NIST SP800-39)," National Institute of Standards and Technology (NIST), U.S. Department of Commerce, Gaithersburg, Maryland, March 2011.

"Managing Risk from Information Systems: An Organizational Perspective (NIST SP800-39)," National Institute of Standards and Technology (NIST), U.S. Department of Commerce, Gaithersburg, Maryland, April 2008.

"Piloting Supply Chain Risk Management Practices for Federal Information Systems (NISTIR7622 Draft)," National Institute of Standards and Technology (NIST), U.S. Department of Commerce, Gaithersburg, Maryland, June 2010.

"Recommended Security Controls for Federal Information Systems and Organizations (NIST SP800-53 R3)," National Institute of Standards and Technology (NIST), U.S. Department of Commerce, Gaithersburg, Maryland, August 2009.

"Service Component-Based Architectures, Version 2.0," CIO Council, June 2004 (www.cio.gov).

Tanenbaum, Andrew S. *Computer Networks* by Chapter 5, Fourth Edition, Prentice Hall PTR, Upper Saddle River, New Jersey, Copyright 2003.

"Technical Guide to Information Security Testing (NIST SP 800-115 Draft)," National Institute of Standards and Technology (NIST), U.S. Department of Commerce, Gaithersburg, Maryland, November 2007.

"Telecommunications: Glossary of Telecommunication Terms, Federal Standard 1037C," U.S. General Services Administration (GSA), Washington, DC, August 1996.

"User's Guide to Securing External Devices for Telework and Remote Access (NIST SP 800-114)," National Institute of Standards and Technology (NIST), U.S. Department of Commerce, Gaithersburg, Maryland, November 2007.

"Wikipedia Encyclopedia," Definitions for certain terms were adapted from Wikipedia (www.wikipedia.org).

# APPENDIX B

## CISSP Acronyms and Abbreviations 2012

This appendix consists of a list of selected information system and network security acronyms and abbreviations, along with their generally accepted definitions. When there are multiple definitions for a single term, the acronym or abbreviation is stacked next to each other.

## NUMERIC

**2TDEA**  Two key triple DEA

**3TDEA**  Three key triple DEA

**3DES**  Three key triple data encryption standard

**1G**  First generation of analog wireless technology

**2G**  Second generation of digital wireless technology

**3G**  Third generation of digital wireless technology

**4G**  Fourth generation of digital wireless technology

## A

**AAA**  Authentication, authorization, accounting

**ABAC**  Attribute-based access control

**ACE**  Access control entry

**ACK**  Acknowledgment

**ACL**  Access control list

**ADCCP**  Advanced data communication control procedure

**ADSL**   Asymmetric digital subscriber line

**AES**   Advanced encryption standard

**AES-CBC**   Advanced encryption standard – Cipher block chaining

**AES-CTR**   Advanced encryption standard – Counter mode

**AH**   Authentication header

**AIN**   Advanced intelligent networks

**AK**   Authorization key

**ALE**   Annual loss expectancy

**ALG**   Application layer gateway

**ANI**   Automatic number identification

**ANN**   Artificial neural network

**AP**   Access point

**APDU**   Application protocol data unit

**API**   Application programming interface

**ARP**   Address resolution protocol

**AS**   Authentication server/authentication service/autonomous system

**ASCII**   American standard code for information interchange

**ASP**   Active server page

**ATA**   Advanced technology attachment

**ATM**   Asynchronous transfer mode/automated teller machine

**AV**   Anti-virus

**AVP**   Attribute-value par

# B

**B2B**   Business-to-business electronic commerce model

**B2B2C**   Business-to-business-to-consumer electronic commerce model

**B2C**   Business-to-consumer electronic commerce model

**B2E**   Business-to-employees electronic commerce model

**BCP**   Business continuity plan

**BGP**   Border gateway protocol

**BIA**   Business impact analysis

**BIOS**   Basic input/output system

**BITS**   Bump-in-the-stack

**BOOTP**   Bootstrap protocol

**BPI**   Business process improvement

**BPR**   Business process reengineering

**BRP**   Business recovery (resumption) plan

**BS**   Base station

**BSS**   Basic service set

# C

**C2B**   Consumer-to-business electronic commerce model

**C2C**   Consumer-to-consumer electronic commerce model

**C&A**   Certification and accreditation

**CA**   Certification authority

**CAC**   Common access card

**CAN**   Campus-area network

**CASE**   Computer-aided software engineering

**CBC**   Cipher block chaining

**CBC-MAC**   Cipher block chaining-message authentication code

**CC**   Common Criteria

**CCE**   Common configuration enumeration

**CCMP**   Cipher block chaining message authentication code protocol

**CCTV**   Closed circuit television

**CDMA**   Code division multiple access

**CDN**   Content delivery network

**CEO**   Chief executive officer

**CER**   Crossover error rate (biometrics)

**CERT**   Computer emergency response team

**CFB**   Cipher feedback

**CGI**   Common gateway interface

**CHAP**   Challenge-handshake authentication protocol

**CHIPS**  Clearing house interbank payment system

**CIDR**  Classless inter-domain routing

**CIO**  Chief information officer

**CIRC**  Computer incident response center

**CIRT**  Computer incident response team

**CISO**  Corporate information security officer

**CKMS**  Cryptographic key management systems

**CM**  Configuration management

**CMAC**  Cipher-based method authentication code

**CMM**  Capability maturity model

**CMS**  Configuration management system

**CMVP**  Cryptographic module validation program

**CONOP**  Concept of operations (i.e., only one document)

**COOP**  Continuity of operations

**COTS**  Commercial off-the-shelf

**CP**  Certificate policy

**CPE**  Common platform enumeration

**CPS**  Certification practice statement

**CPU**  Central processing unit

**CRAM**  Challenge-response authentication mechanism

**CRC**  Cyclic redundancy check

**CRL**  Certificate revocation list

**CRM**  Customer relationship management

**CS**  Client/server

**CSIRC**  Computer security incident response capability

**CSIRT**  Computer security incident response team

**CSMA/CA**  Carrier sense multiple access with collision avoidance

**CSMA/CD**  Carrier sense multiple access with collision detection

**CSRC**  Computer security resource center

**CSO**  Chief security officer

**CSP**  Credentials service provider/critical security parameter

**CTO**  Chief technology officer

**CTR**  Counter mode encryption

**CVE**  Common vulnerabilities and exposures

**CVSS**  Common vulnerability scoring system

# D

**DA**  Data administration/administrator/destination address

**DAA**  Designated approving authority/designated accrediting authority

**DAC**  Discretionary access control

**DAD**  Duplicate address detection

**DASD**  Direct access storage device

**DBA**  Database administrator

**DBMS**  Database management system

**DC**  Domain controller

**DCE**  Distributed computing environment/data circuit terminating equipment

**DCL**  Data control language

**DD**  Data dictionary

**DDL**  Data definition language

**DDP**  Distributed data processing

**DDOS**  Distributed denial-of-service

**DEA**  Data encryption algorithm

**DES**  Data encryption standard

**DESX**  Extended data encryption standard

**DFD**  Data flow diagram

**DH**  Diffie-Hellman

**DHCP**  Dynamic host configuration protocol

**DISA**  Direct inward system access/U.S. Defense Information Systems Agency

**DML**  Data manipulation language

**DMZ**  Demilitarized zone

**DNS**  Domain name system

**DNP**    Distributed network protocol

**DNS**    Domain name system

**DOM**    Document object model

**DoS**    Denial-of-service

**DoQ**    Denial-of-quality

**DPA**    Differential power analysis

**DRP**    Disaster recovery plan

**DSA**    Digital signature algorithm

**DSL**    Digital subscriber line

**DSP**    Digital signal processors

**DSS**    Digital signature standard

**DVMRP**    Distance vector multicast routing protocol

# E

**E2E**    Exchange-to-exchange electronic commerce model

**EAL**    Evaluation assurance level

**EAP**    Extensible authentication protocol

**EBCDIC**    Extended binary coded decimal interchange code

**EBGP**    Exterior border gateway protocol

**EBTS**    Electronic benefit transfer system

**EC**    Electronic commerce

**ECC**    Elliptic curve cryptography

**ECDSA**    Elliptic curve digital signature algorithm

**ECDH**    Elliptic curve Diffie-Hellman

**ECP**    Encryption control protocol

**ECPA**    Electronic communications privacy act

**EDC**    Error detection code

**EDI**    Electronic data interchange

**EDIFACT**    Electronic data interchange for administration, commerce, and transport

**EDMS**    Electronic document management system

**EEPROM**    Electronically erasable, programmable read-only memory

**EES**   Escrowed encryption standard

**EFP**   Environmental failure protection

**EFS**   Encrypted file system

**EFT**   Environmental failure testing

**EFTS**   Electronic funds transfer system

**EGP**   Exterior gateway protocol

**EH**   Extension header

**EIDE**   Enhanced IDE (integrated drive electronics)

**EISA**   Extended industry-standard architecture

**EME**   Electromagnetic emanation

**EMRT**   Emergency response time

**EPICS**   Electronic product code information services

**ERD**   Entity relationship diagram

**ERP**   Enterprise resource planning

**ESN**   Electronic serial number

**ESP**   Encapsulating security payload

**EU**   European Union

# F

**FAT**   File allocation table

**FDDI**   Fiber distributed data interface

**FDE**   Full disk encryption

**FDM**   Frequency division multiplexing

**FEK**   File encryption key

**FFC**   Finite field cryptography

**FMEA**   Failure mode and effect analysis

**FMR**   False match rate

**FRR**   False rejection rate

**FSM**   Finite-state-machine

**FTP**   File transfer protocol

# G

**G2B**  Government-to-business electronic commerce model

**G2C**  Government-to-citizens electronic commerce model

**G2E**  Government-to-employees electronic commerce model

**G2G**  Government-to-government electronic commerce model

**GCM**  Galois counter mode

**GKEK**  Group key encryption key

**GMAC**  Galois message authentication code

**GPS**  Global positioning system

**GSM**  Global system for mobile communications

**GSSP**  Generally accepted system security principles

**GTC**  Generic token card

**GUI**  Graphical user interface

# H

**HA**  High availability

**HAZMAT**  Hazardous materials

**HDL**  Hardware description language

**HDLC**  High-level data-link control

**HDSL**  High data rate DSL

**HERF**  Hazards of electromagnetic radiation to fuel

**HERO**  Hazards of electromagnetic radiation to ordnance

**HERP**  Hazards of electromagnetic radiation to people

**HERM**  Hazards of electromagnetic radiation to materials

**HIP**  Host identity protocol

**HMAC**  Hash-based (keyed-hash) message authentication code

**HSSI**  High-speed serial interface

**HTML**  Hypertext markup language

**HTTP**  Hypertext transfer protocol

**HTTPS**   Hypertext transfer protocol over SSL

**HVAC**   Heating, ventilation, and air conditioning

# I

**IA**   Identification and authentication/Information assurance

**I/O**   Input/output

**IAB**   Internet architecture board

**IAM**   Information Assurance Manager/Infosec Assessment Methodology

**IAO**   Information assurance officer

**IATF**   Information assurance technical framework

**IBAC**   Identity-based access control

**IBC**   Iterated block cipher

**IBE**   Identity-based encryption

**IBGP**   Internal border gateway protocol

**IC**   Integrated circuit

**ICMP**   Internet control message protocol

**ICP**   Internet cache protocol

**ICSA**   International computer security association

**ICV**   Integrity check value

**ID**   Identification

**IDE**   Integrated drive electronics

**IDEA**   International data encryption algorithm

**IDMS**   Identity management system

**IDPS**   Intrusion detection and prevention system

**IDS**   Intrusion detection system

**IE**   Internet Explorer

**IEC**   International electro-technical commission

**IEEE**   Institute of electrical and electronics engineers

**IETF**   Internet engineering task force

**IGMP**   Internet group management protocol

**IGRP**   Interior gateway routing protocol

**IGP**   Interior Gateway Protocol

**IKE**   Internet key exchange

**IM**   Instant messaging

**IMAP**   Internet Message Access Protocol

**IMM**   Information management model

**IOCE**   International organization on computer evidence

**IP**   Internet Protocol

**IPA**   Initial privacy assessment

**IPComp**   Internet Protocol payload compression protocol

**IPS**   Intrusion prevention system

**IPsec**   Internet Protocol security

**IPX**   Internetwork packet exchange

**IRC**   Internet relay chat

**IRTF**   Internet research task force

**IS**   Information system

**ISA**   Industry-standard architecture

**ISAKMP**   Internet security association and key management protocol

**ISATAP**   Intra-site automatic tunnel addressing protocol

**ISC2**   International information systems security certification and consortium institute

**ISDL**   ISDN-based DSL

**ISDN**   Integrated services digital network

**ISF**   Information security forum

**ISID**   Industrial security incident database

**ISLAN**   Integrated services LAN

**ISMAN**   Integrated services MAN

**ISO**   International organization for standardization

**ISP**   Internet service provider

**ISSA**   Information Systems Security Association

**ISSO**   Information systems security officer

**IT**   Information technology

**ITL**   Information technology laboratory

**ITSEC**   Information Technology Security Evaluation Criteria

**ITU**   International Telecommunication Union

**IV**   Initialization vector

# J

**JAD**   Joint application design

**JBOD**   Just a bunch of disks

**JCP**   Java community process

**JIT**   Just-in-time

**JPEG**   Joint photographic experts group

**JRE**   Java runtime environment

**JSM**   Java security manager

**JSP**   Java server page

**JVM**   Java virtual machine

# K

**KDC**   Key distribution center

**KEK**   Key encryption key

**KG**   Key generator

**KGD**   Key generation and distribution

**KMF**   Key management facility

**KMM**   Key management message

**KSG**   Key stream generator

**KSK**   Key signing key

**KWK**   Key wrapping key

# L

**LAN**   Local-area network

**LAPB**   Link access procedure B

**LCD**   Liquid crystal display

**LCP**   Link control protocol

**LDA**   Local delivery agent

**LDAP**   Lightweight directory access protocol

**LM**   LanManager

**LMDS**   Local multipoint distribution service

**LMP**   Link manager protocol

**LOS**   Line-of-sight

**LRA**   Local registration authority

**L2TP**   Layer 2 tunneling protocol

**LTP**   Lightweight transport protocol

# M

**MAC**   Mandatory Access Control/Media Access Control/Medium Access Control/ message authentication code

**MAN**   Metropolitan area network

**MBR**   Master boot record

**MC**   Mobile commerce

**MD**   Message digest

**MGCP**   Media gateway control protocol

**MHS**   Message handling system

**MIC**   Message integrity check/message integrity code/mandatory integrity control

**MIDI**   Musical instrument digital interface

**MIM**   Meet-in-the-middle (attack)

**MIME**   Multipurpose Internet mail extensions

**MIN**   Mobile identification number

**MIP**   Mobile Internet protocol

**MitM**   Man-in-the-middle (attack)

**MIPS**   Million instructions per second

**MMS**   Multimedia messaging service

**MM**   Management message

**MOA**   Memorandum of agreement

**MOU**   Memorandum of understanding

**MPEG**   Moving picture coding experts group

**MS**   Mobile subscriber

**MSI**   Module software interface

**MSISDN**   Mobile subscriber integrated services digital network

**MSP**   Message security protocol

**MTBF**   Mean-time-between-failures

**MTBO**   Mean-time-between-outages

**MTD**   Maximum tolerable downtime

**MTM**   Mobile trusted module

**MTTDL**   Mean-time-to-data loss

**MTTF**   Mean-time-to-failure

**MTTR**   Mean-time-to-recovery

Mean-time-to-repair

Mean-time-to-restore

# N

**NAC**   Network Access Control

**NAK**   Negative acknowledgment

**NAP**   Network Access Protection

**NAPT**   Network address and port translation

**NAS**   Network access server

**NAT**   Network Address Translation

**NBA**   Network behavior analysis

**NCP**   Network Control Protocol

**NDAC**   Nondiscretionary access control

**NetBIOS**   Network Basic Input/Output System

**NFAT**   Network Forensic Analysis Tool

**NFS**   Network file system/network file sharing

**NH**   Next header

**NIAC**   National infrastructure advisory council

**NIAP**   National information assurance partnership

**NIC**   Network interface card

**NID**   Network interface device

**NIPC**   National infrastructure protection center

**NIS**   Network information system

**NIST**   National Institute of Standards and Technology

**NISTIR**   National Institute of Standards and Technology Interagency Report

**NLOS**   Nonline-of-sight (non LOS)

**NNTP**   Network News Transfer Protocol

**NS**   Name server

**NSA**   National Security Agency

**NTFS**   NT file system

**NTLM**   NT LanManager

**NTP**   Network Time Protocol

**NVD**   National Vulnerability Database

**NVLAP**   National Voluntary Laboratory Accreditation Program

# O

**OASIS**   Organization for the Advancement of Structured Information Standards

**OCSP**   Online Certificate Status Protocol

**OECD**   Organization for Economic Co-operation and Development

**OFB**   Output feedback (mode)

**OLE**   Object linking and embedding

**OOD**   Object-oriented design

**OOP**   Object-oriented programming

**ONS**   Object naming service

**OOB**   Out-of-band

**OpenPGP**   Open Specification for Pretty Good Privacy

**OS**   Operating system

**OSE**   Open system environment

**OSI**   Open system interconnection

**OSPF**   Open shortest path first

**OSS**   Open-source software

**OTAR**   Over-the-air rekeying

**OTP**   One-time password

**OVAL**   Open vulnerability and assessment language

# P

**P2P**   Peer-to-peer

**P3P**   Platform for privacy preferences project

**PAC**   Protected access credential/privilege attribute certificate

**PAD**   Packet assembly and disassembly/peer authorization database

**PAN**   Personal-Area Network

**PAP**   Password authentication protocol/policy access point

**PAT**   Port address translation

**PATA**   Parallel ATA (advanced technology attachment)

**PBA**   Pre-boot authentication

**PBAC**   Policy-Based Access Control

**PBE**   Pre-boot environment

**PBX**   Private branch exchange

**PC**   Personal computer

**PCI**   Payment card industry/personal identity verification card issuer

**PCIDSS**   Payment card industry data security standard

**PCMCIA**   Personal computer memory card international association

**PCN**   Process control network

**PCP**   IP payload compression protocol

**PCS**   Process control system

**PDA**   Personal digital assistant

**PDF**   Portable document format

**PDP**   Policy decision point

**PDS**   Protective distribution systems

**PEAP**   Protected Extensible Authentication Protocol

**PEM**   Privacy enhanced mail

**PEP**   Policy enforcement point

**PERT**   Program evaluation and review technique

**PGP**   Pretty Good Privacy

**PHP**   PHP hypertext preprocessor

**PIA**   Privacy impact assessment

**PII**   Personally identifiable information

**PIN**   Personal identification number

**PIP**   Policy information point

**PIV**   Personal identity verification

**PKCS**   Public key cryptography standard

**PKI**   Public key infrastructure

**PKM**   Privacy key management

**POA&M**   Plan of action and milestones

**POC**   Point of contact/proof of concept

**POP**   Post office protocol/proof-of-possession

**POS**   Point-of-sale

**POTS**   Plain old telephone service

**PP**   Protection profile

**PPD**   Port protection device

**PPP**   Point-to-Point Protocol

**PPTP**   Point-to-Point-Tunneling Protocol

**PRNG**   Pseudorandom number generator

**PSK**   Pre-shared key

**PSP**   Public security parameters

**PSTN**   Public switched telephone network

**PTM**   Packet transfer mode

**PVC**   Permanent Virtual Circuit

**PVP**   Patch and vulnerability group

# Q

**QA**   Quality assurance

**QC**   Quality control

**QoP**   Quality of protection

**QoS**   Quality of service

# R

**RA**   Registration authority

**RAD**   Rapid application development

**RAdAC**   Risk adaptive access control

**RAD**   Rapid application development

**RADIUS**   Remote Authentication Dial-In User Service

**RAID**   Redundant array of independent disks

**RAM**   Random access memory

**RAP**   Rapid application prototyping

**RARP**   Reverse Address Resolution Protocol

**RAS**   Remote Access Server/Registration, Admission, Status channel

**RAT**   Remote Administration Tool

**RBAC**   Role-based access control

**RBG**   Random bit generator

**RC**   Rivest cipher

**RCP**   Remote Copy Protocol

**RDBMS**   Relational database management system

**RDP**   Remote Desktop Protocol

**RED**   Random early detection

**REP**   Robots exclusion protocol

**RF**   Radio frequency

**RFC**   Request For Comment

**RFI**   Radio frequency interference/request for information

**RFID**   Radio frequency identification

**RFP**   Request for proposal

**RFQ**   Request for quote

**RIB**   Routing information base

**RIP**   Routing Information Protocol

**RMF**   Risk management framework

**RNG**   Random number generator

**ROE**   Rules of engagement

**ROI**   Return On Investment

**ROM**   Read-only memory

**RPC**   Remote procedure call

**RPO**   Recovery point objective

**RR**   Resource record

**RS**   Relay station

**RSA**   Rivest-Shamir-Adelman (algorithm)

**RSBAC**   Ruleset-based access control

**RSN**   Robust security network

**RSO**   Reduced sign-on

**RSS**   Really simple syndication

**RSTP**   Real-time streaming protocol

**RSVP**   Resource reservation protocol

**RTCP**   Real-time transport control protocol

**RTF**   Rich Text Format

**RTO**   Recovery time objective

**RTP**   Real-Time Transport Protocol

**RuBAC**   Rule-based access control

# S

**S/MIME**   Secure/multipurpose (multipart) Internet mail extensions

**SA**   Security Association/source address

**SACL**   System access control list

**SAD**   Security association database

**SAFER**   Secure and fast encryption routine

**SAML**   Security assertion markup language

**SAN**   Storage area network

**SAS**   Statement on auditing standards

**SATA**   Serial ATA (advanced technology attachment)

**S-BGP**   Secure border gateway protocol

**SC**   Supply chain

**SCAP**   Security Content Automation Protocol

**SCP**   Secure Copy Protocol

**SCM**   Software configuration management

**SCSI**   Small Computer Systems Interface

**SCTP**   Stream Control Transmission Protocol

**SD**   Secure digital

**SDLC**   System development lifecycle/Synchronous DataLink Control

**SDP**   Service Discovery Protocol

**SDSL**   Symmetrical DSL

**SEI**   Software Engineering Institute

**SEM**   Security event management

**SET**   Secure electronic transaction

**SFTP**   Secure file transfer protocol

**SHA**   Secure hash algorithm

**SHS**   Secure hash standard

**SIA**   Security impact analysis

**SID**   Security Identifier

**SIM**   Subscriber identity module

**SIP**   Session Initiation Protocol

**SKEME**   Secure Key Exchange Mechanism

**SKIP**   Simple Key Management for Internet Protocol

**SLA**   Service-level agreement

**SLIP**   Serial Line Interface Protocol

**SFTP**   Secure file transfer protocol

**SHTTP**   Secure Hypertext Transfer Protocol

**SRPC**   Secure remote procedure call

**SMDS**   Switched Multimegabit Data Service

**SME**   Subject matter expert

**SMS**   Short message service/systems management server

**SMTP**   Simple Mail Transfer Protocol

**SNA**   System Network Architecture

**SNMP**   Simple Network Management Protocol

**SNTP**   Simple Network Time Protocol

**SOA**   Service-oriented architecture

**SOAP**   Simple Object Access Protocol/Service-oriented architecture protocol

**SOCKS**   Socket security

**SOHO**   Small office/home office

**SOL**   Single occurrence loss

**SONET**   Synchronous optical network

**SOP**   Standard operating procedure

**SOW**   Statement of work

**SP**   Service pack

**SPA**   Simple power analysis

**SPI**   Security Parameters Index

**SPKI**   Simple public key infrastructure

**SPML**   Service Provisioning Markup Language

**SPX**   Sequenced Packet Exchange

**SQL**   Structured Query Language

**SRTP**   Secure Real-Time Transport Protocol

**SSDP**  Simple Service Discovery Protocol

**SSE-CMM**  Systems Security Engineering Capability Maturity Model

**SPX**  Sequential packet exchange

**SR**  Service release

**SS**  Subscriber station

**SSDP**  Simple Service Discovery Protocol

**SSH**  Secure Shell

**SSID**  Service set identifier

**SSL**  Secure Sockets Layer

**SSO**  Single sign-on

**SSP**  Sensitive security parameter

**ST**  Security target

**STD**  State transition diagram

**ST&E**  Security test and evaluation

**STIG**  Security Technical Implementation Guide (by DISA for U.S. DoD)

**STS**  Security Token Service

**SUID**  Set-user-ID

**SV&V**  Software Verification and Validation

**SVC**  Switched Virtual Network

**SWIFT**  Society for Worldwide Interbank Financial Telecommunication

**SYN**  Synchronized

**SZ**  Security zone

# T

**TA**  Timing analysis

**TACACS**  Terminal Access Controller Access Control System

**TCB**  Trusted computing base

**TCG**  Trusted computing group

**TCP**  Transmission Control Protocol

**T/TCP**  Transactional TCP

**TCP/IP**  Transmission Control Protocol/Internet Protocol

**TCSEC**   Trusted Computer System Evaluation Criteria

**TDEA**   Triple Data Encryption Algorithm (Triple DEA or Triple DES)

**TDM**   Time division multiplexing

**TDMA**   Time division multiple access

**TEK**   Traffic encryption key

**TFTP**   Trivial File Transfer Protocol

**TGS**   Ticket-granting service

**TKIP**   Temporal key integrity protocol

**TLS**   Transport layer security

**TOC-TOU**   Time-of-check to time-of-use

**T&E**   Test & evaluation

**TOE**   Target of evaluation

**TOS**   Trusted operating system

**ToS**   Type of Service

**TPM**   Trusted Platform Module

**TQM**   Total quality management

**TS**   Target server

**TSIG**   Transaction signature

**TSN**   Transition Security Network

**TSP**   Time- stamp Protocol

**TTL**   Time-to-Live

**TTR**   Time-to-recover

**TTLS**   Tunneled transport layer security

**TTP**   Trusted third party

# U

**UAC**   User Account Control

**UDDI**   Universal description, discovery, and integration

**UDF**   Universal Disk Format

**UDP**   User Datagram Protocol

**ULP**   Upper layer protocol

**UML**   Unified modeling language

**UPS**   Uninterruptible power supply

**URI**   Uniform Resource Identifier

**URL**   Uniform Resource Locator

**USB**   Universal Serial Bus

# V

**V&V**   Verification and Validation

**VAN**   Value-added network

**VB**   Visual Basic

**VBA**   Visual Basic for Applications

**VBScript**   Visual Basic Script

**VDSL**   Very high-speed DSL

**VHD**   Virtual hard drive

**VHF**   Very high frequency

**VLAN**   Virtual local-area network

**VM**   Virtual machine

**VoIP**   Voice over Internet Protocol

**VPN**   Virtual private network

**VRRP**   Virtual Router Redundancy Protocol

**VSAT**   Very small aperture terminal

# W

**W3C**   World Wide Web consortium

**WAN**   Wide-area network

**WAP**   Wireless access point/Wireless application protocol

**WBS**   Work breakdown structure

**WCCP**   Web Cache Coordination Protocol

**WCDMA**   Wideband code division multiple access

**WDM**   Wavelength division multiplexing

**WDMA**   Wavelength division multiple access

**WDP**   Wireless Datagram Protocol

**WEP**   Wired Equivalent Privacy

**WfMS**   Workflow management system

**WiFi**   Wireless Fidelity

**WiMax**   Worldwide Interoperability for Microwave Access

**WfMS**   Workflow management system

**WLAN**   Wireless local-area network

**WLL**   Wireless local loop

**WMAN**   Wireless metropolitan-area network

**WML**   Wireless Markup Language

**WMM**   WiFi multimedia

**WOA**   Web-oriented architecture

**WORM**   Write Once, Read Many

**WPA**   Wi-Fi Protected Access

**WPAN**   Wireless personal-area network

**WS**   Web services

**WSDL**   Web services description language

**WS-I**   Web service interoperability organization

**WSP**   Wireless Session Protocol

**WTLS**   Wireless transport layer security

**WTP**   Wireless transaction protocol

**WWAN**   Wireless wide-area network

**WWW**   World Wide Web

## XYZ

**XACL**   XML Access Control Language

**XACML**   Extensible Access Control Markup Language

**XCBC**   XOR cipher block chaining

**XCCDF**   Extensible configuration checklist description format

**XDSL**   Digital Subscriber Line

**XHTML**   Extended hypertext markup language

**XML**   Extensible Markup Language

**XOR**   Exclusive OR

**XP**   Extreme programming

**XrML**   eXtensible Rights Markup Language

**XSD**   XML schema definition

**XSL**   Extensible style language

**XSS**   Cross-site scripting

**ZSK**   Zone Signing Key

## SOURCES AND REFERENCES

"Digital Signature Standard (NIST FIPS PUB 186-3)," National Institute of Standards and Technology (NIST), U.S. Department of Commerce, Gaithersburg, Maryland, June 2009.

"Establishing Wireless Robust Security Networks: A Guide to IEEE 802.11i (NIST SP800-97)," National Institute of Standards and Technology (NIST), U.S. Department of Commerce, Gaithersburg, Maryland, February 2007.

"Guide to Adopting and Using the Security Content Automation Protocol SCAP (NIST SP800-117 Draft)," National Institute of Standards and Technology (NIST), U.S. Department of Commerce, Gaithersburg, Maryland, May 2009.

"Guidelines on Cell Phone Forensics (NIST SP800-101)," National Institute of Standards and Technology (NIST), U.S. Department of Commerce, Gaithersburg, Maryland, May 2007.

"Guidelines on Cell Phone and PDA Security (NIST SP800-124)," National Institute of Standards and Technology (NIST), U.S. Department of Commerce, Gaithersburg, Maryland, October 2008.

"Guidelines on Firewalls and Firewall Policy (NIST SP800-41R1)," National Institute of Standards and Technology (NIST), U.S. Department of Commerce, Gaithersburg, Maryland, September 2009.

"Guidelines for Securing Radio Frequency Identification (RFID) Systems (NIST SP800-98)," National Institute of Standards and Technology (NIST), U.S. Department of Commerce, Gaithersburg, Maryland, August 2007.

"Information Security Continuous Monitoring for Federal Information Systems and Organizations (NIST SP800-137) 1," National Institute of Standards and Technology (NIST), U.S. Department of Commerce, Gaithersburg, Maryland, December 2010.

"Managing Information Security Risk (NIST SP800-39)," National Institute of Standards and Technology (NIST), U.S. Department of Commerce, Gaithersburg, Maryland, March 2011.

"Piloting Supply Chain Risk Management Practices for Federal Information Systems (NISTIR7622 Draft)," National Institute of Standards and Technology (NIST), U.S. Department of Commerce, Gaithersburg, Maryland, June 2010.

"Security Requirements for Cryptographic Modules (NIST FIPS FUB 140-3 Draft)," National Institute of Standards and Technology (NIST), U.S. Department of Commerce, Gaithersburg, Maryland, July 2007.

"System and Network Security Acronyms and Abbreviations (NISTIR7581)," National Institute of Standards and Technology (NIST), U.S. Department of Commerce, Gaithersburg, Maryland, September 2009.

# INDEX

security controls, 1007
threat, 1032
vulnerabilities, 59, 759, 1045
assets, 877
alerts, 807
BCP, 724
DRP, 724
information, 339
physical tokens, 833–834
risk analysis, 309, 347
valuation, 877
assurance, 29, 343, 368, 401, 878. *See also specific assurance types*
access controls, 359–360
audits, 544
conformance testing, 556
enforcement, 542
integrity, 286
layered protections, 598
metrics, 354–355
risk mitigation, 287
security controls, 384
software, 376
testing, 878
trustworthiness, 295
asymmetric keys, 493
advantages, 497–498
algorithms, 453, 490–491, 496, 877–878
authentication, 489–490, 519
confidentiality, 489–490
cryptography, 878
ECDSA, 518
electronic authentication, 4–5
HMAC, 464–465
integrity, 489–490
IPsec, 182–183
nonrepudiation, 489–490
public keys, 465
RSA, 506–507, 514
SSL, 497
VPN, 182–183
asynchronous attacks, 131, 151, 261, 403, 878

asynchronous digital subscriber line (ADSL), 228–229, 264
asynchronous mirroring, 736
asynchronous transfer mode (ATM), 157, 158–159, 235–236, 878
ATA. *See* advanced technology attachment
ATM. *See* asynchronous transfer mode
ATMs. *See* automated teller machines
attacks, 269, 297, 878. *See also specific attack types*
browsers, 547
cryptography, 493–494, 507
detection software, second line-of-defense, 592
logs, 772
NAK, 260
out-of-band, 102–103
username, 772
attack signature, 878
detection tools, 676, 697
attackers
identification, 746, 878
work factor, 878
attack-in-depth strategy, 878
attacks, servers, session-tracking, 598
attended access, 50–51
attributes, 878
certificates, 462, 879
attribute-based access control (ABAC), 7, 9, 879
auctions, 244, 919
audits, 366, 879
access controls, 30
assurance, 544
availability, 544
backup, 481
BCP, 711
cryptography, 481–482
data reduction tools, 675–676, 697
data-collection tools, 676, 697
humans, 481–482

incident response handling, 748
network intrusion attacks, 57
periodic, 780
processing failure, 684
reduction tools, 879
reliability, 647
risk assessment, 314, 348–349
SCM, 353
self-assessment, 362, 711
storage, 684
vulnerabilities, 1046
audit logs, 232, 807–808
accountability, 668
logon attempts, 764
passivity, 684
timestamps, 618
audit records
backup, 621
IDS, 98
privileged user accounts, 647
audit trails, 409, 654, 670, 879
accountability, 624
authentication, 479
automated tools, 675–676, 697
contingency plan, 661
cryptography, 479
detective controls, 285, 402, 624, 689, 695
digital signatures, 506
first line-of-defense, 582, 588
fraud, 687
functional users, 654
ID, 675, 697
logical access controls, 82–83, 661
periodic review, 696
reconstruction of transactions, 104
reviews, 664, 696
security administrators, 693–694
security controls, 506
security policy, 660

## C